JOHN

Interpreted by
Early Christian and Medieval Commentators

THE CHURCH'S BIBLE

General Editor

Robert Louis Wilken

•   •

The Song of Songs
Richard A. Norris Jr.

Isaiah
Robert Louis Wilken

Matthew
D. H. Williams

John
Bryan A. Stewart *&* Michael A. Thomas

Romans
J. Patout Burns Jr.

1 Corinthians
Judith L. Kovacs

JOHN

Interpreted by
Early Christian and Medieval Commentators

Translated and Edited by

Bryan A. Stewart *&* Michael A. Thomas

WILLIAM B. EERDMANS PUBLISHING COMPANY
GRAND RAPIDS, MICHIGAN

Wm. B. Eerdmans Publishing Co.
2140 Oak Industrial Drive NE, Grand Rapids, Michigan 49505
www.eerdmans.com

26 25 24 23 22 21 20 19 18   1 2 3 4 5 6 7 8 9 10

ISBN 978-0-8028-2580-3

Library of Congress Cataloging-in-Publication Data

Names: Stewart, Bryan A., 1973- editor, translator. | Thomas, Michael A.,
    1970- editor, translator.
Title: John / interpreted by early Christian and medieval commentators ;
    translated and edited by Bryan A. Stewart & Michael A. Thomas.
Description: Grand Rapids : Eerdmans Publishing Co., 2017. | Series: The
    church's Bible | Includes bibliographical references and index.
Identifiers: LCCN 2017027730 | ISBN 9780802825803 (hardcover : alk. paper)
Subjects: LCSH: Bible. John—Criticism, interpretation, etc.—History—Early
    church, ca. 30-600. | Bible. John--Criticism, interpretation,
    etc.—History—Middle Ages, 600-1500.
Classification: LCC BS2615.52 .J647 2017 | DDC 226.5/0609—dc23
    LC record available at https://lccn.loc.gov/2017027730

Permissions:

Cyril of Alexandria, Norman Russell. Copyright © 2000 Routledge. Reproduced by permission of Taylor & Francis
    Books UK.
Cyril of Jerusalem, Edward Yarnold, S.J. Copyright © 2000 Routledge. Reproduced by permission of Taylor & Francis
    Books UK.
Demonstrations of Aphrahat, the Persian Sage, translated by Adam Lehto, Gorgias Eastern Christian Studies 27. Copy-
    right © 2010 Gorgias Press. Used with permission.
Ephrem the Syrian: Hymns, translated by Kathleen McVey. Copyright © 1989 Paulist Press. Used with permission.
Gregory the Great: Forty Gospel Homilies, translated by Dom David Hurst. Copyright © 1990 Cistercian Publications.
    Used with permission.
Kontakia of Romanos, Byzantine Melodist vol. 1: On the Person of Christ, edited by Marjorie Carpenter. Copyright ©
    1970 by the Curators of the University of Missouri, University of Missouri Press, Columbia, Missouri 65201. Used
    by permission.
Theodore of Mopsuestia: Commentary on John, translated by George Kalantzis, Early Christian Studies 7. Copyright ©
    2004 St. Paul's Press. Used with permission: www.cecs.acu.edu.au.
Theophylact: The Explanation of the Holy Gospel according to John, translated by Fr. Christopher Stade. Copyright ©
    2007 Chrysostom Press 2007. Used with permission.
Works of Saint Augustine. Copyright © 1992, 1996, 2000, 2005, 2009, and 2012 New City Press. Used with permission.
Works on the Spirit: Athanasius the Great and Didymus the Blind, edited and translated by Mark DelCogliano, Andrew
    Radde-Gallwitz, and Lewis Ayers, Popular Patristics Series 43. Copyright © 2011 St. Vladimir's Seminary Press.
    Used with permission: www.svspress.com.
Venerable Bede: Homilies on the Gospels, translated by Lawrence T. Martin and David Hurst, 2 volumes. Copyright ©
    1991 Cistercian Publications. Used with permission.
Scripture quotations are from Revised Standard Version of the Bible. Copyright © 1946, 1952, and 1971 National Council
    of the Churches of Christ in the United States of America. Used by permission. All rights reserved worldwide.

Dedications

Bryan
To the glory of God and the building up of Christ's Church

Michael
To my brothers and sisters in the faith at Concordia

Contents

CONTENTS

Series Preface

The volumes in The Church's Bible are designed to present the holy Scriptures as understood and interpreted during the first millennium of Christian history. The Christian church has a long tradition of commentary on the Bible. In the early church all discussion of theological topics, of moral issues, and of Christian practice took the biblical text as the starting point. The recitation of the Psalms and meditation on books of the Bible, particularly in the context of the liturgy or of private prayer, nurtured the spiritual life. For most of the Church's history theology and scriptural interpretation were one. Theology was called *sacra pagina* (the sacred page), and the task of interpreting the Bible was a spiritual enterprise.

During the first two centuries interpretation of the Bible took the form of exposition of select passages on particular issues. For example, Irenaeus, bishop of Lyons, discussed many passages from the Old and New Testaments in his defense of the apostolic faith against the gnostics. By the beginning of the third century Christian bishops and scholars had begun to preach regular series of sermons that followed the biblical books verse by verse. Some wrote more scholarly commentaries that examined in greater detail grammatical, literary, and historical questions as well as theological ideas and spiritual teachings found in the texts. From Origen of Alexandria, the first great biblical commentator in the church's history, we have, among others, a large verse-by-verse commentary on the Gospel of John, a series of homilies on Genesis and Exodus, and a large part of his *Commentary on the Epistle to the Romans*. In the course of the first eight hundred years of Christian history Christian teachers produced a library of biblical commentaries and homilies on the Bible.

Today this ancient tradition of biblical interpretation is known only in bits and pieces, and even where it still shapes our understanding of the Bible, for example, in the selection of readings for Christian worship (e.g., Isa 7 and Isa 9 read at Christmas), or the interpretation of the Psalms in daily prayer, the spiritual world that gave it birth remains shadowy and indistinct. It is the purpose of this series to make available the richness of the church's classical tradition of interpretation for clergy, Sunday school and Bible class teachers, men and women living in religious communities, and all serious readers of the Bible.

Anyone who reads the ancient commentaries realizes at once that they are deeply spiritual, insightful, edifying, and, shall we say, "biblical." Early Christian thinkers moved in the world of the Bible, understood its idiom, loved its teaching, and were filled with awe before its mysteries. They believed in the maxim "Scripture interprets Scripture." They knew something that has largely been forgotten by biblical scholars, and their commentaries are an untapped resource for understanding the Bible as a book about Christ.

The distinctive mark of The Church's Bible is that it draws extensively on the ancient commentaries, not only on random comments drawn from theological treatises, sermons, or devotional works. Its volumes will, in the main, offer fairly lengthy excerpts from the ancient commentaries and from series of sermons on specific books. For example, in the first volume on the Song of Songs, there are long passages from Origen of Alexandria's *Commentary on the Song of Songs,* from Gregory of Nyssa's *Homilies on the Song,* and from Bernard of Clairvaux's sermons on the Song. Some passages will be as brief as a paragraph, but many will be several pages in length, and some longer. We believe that only through a deeper immersion in the ancient sources can contemporary readers enter into the inexhaustible spiritual and theological world of the early church and hence of the Bible.

It is also hoped that longer passages will be suitable for private devotional reading and for spiritual reading in religious communities, in Bible study groups, and in prayer circles.

ROBERT LOUIS WILKEN
General Editor

Acknowledgments

This has been a decade-long endeavor, and a project of this magnitude could never have been completed alone. I am grateful to Robert Louis Wilken for his confidence in me from the start (newly minted PhD though I was), and his unfailing support in providing the encouragement, direction, and resources necessary to complete the project. I am also indebted to Michael Thomas for his assistance in bringing the volume to its end. He shared in much of the workload and took responsibility for many of the chapters in this volume. Despite his heavy teaching load over the years, his dedication to the project has been tireless and his quality of work excellent. Without his partnership, this volume would still be incomplete.

There have been several individuals who helped with first-draft translations of many passages. To them I offer sincere thanks: Kevin Clemens, Olivia Hilmer, Ron Bentley, Jen Benedict, Lloyd Pierson, Abram Ring, Adam Bloom, Fr. Gregory Edwards, Fr. Chris Richardson, Dan Grigalanz, Joseph Trigg, and Emme Davis. Jason Scully, Kelli Bryant, Paul Stevenson, and Adam McCollum were especially helpful in translating passages from Syriac texts. Without their efforts, those passages would not be included in the present volume.

I am also grateful for the various institutional supports I received over the years. The interlibrary loan staffs at Valparaiso University and McMurry University regularly (and cheerfully) secured for me numerous critical sources necessary for the project. My two years as a Lilly Fellow postdoctoral candidate at Valparaiso University afforded me the time and resources needed for this volume. The Center for Catholic and Evangelical Theology funded many of the costs associated with this project. Linda Bieze and the editorial staff at Eerdmans have been helpful in preparing the manuscript for publication. Finally, I offer thanks to Bill Eerdmans and the Eerdmans Publishing Company for their commitment to the task of making the ancient Christian interpretive tradition readily available to the modern reader.

Bryan A. Stewart

As I finish my part of this volume, I am reminded of what a great debt I owe to so many people who have supported and encouraged me throughout this endeavor. First, I must thank Robert Louis Wilken, the General Editor of The Church's Bible series. He could have chosen dozens of scholars more seasoned, gifted, and knowledgeable than myself; I'm humbled that he would entrust part of this project to me. Second, I must express my sincere appreciation to Bryan Stewart, my co-editor in this project. He did the yeoman's task of completing the greater part of this work, steering the project, coordinating with Eerdmans, and patiently enduring my various failings. It's been an utter pleasure to work with him on this project, which would not have been possible without his professionalism and expertise.

Numerous people at Concordia University in Portland, OR, supported and enabled the completion of this project. My colleagues in the Department of Religion were unflagging in their encouragement. The College of Arts and Sciences and the Provost's Office awarded me a sabbatical leave and valuable funds. The CU library staff secured obscure volumes for me despite the time and cost. At Concordia University I am privileged to teach some exceptional students. I must thank my students who took REL 325 in Spring 2016; they read an earlier draft of this entire volume and provided invaluable comments and corrections. Hopefully, the experience was as valuable to them as it was to me.

Finally, I need to express thanks to my family—Darien, Delaynie, and Kimberly: While this project has required too much time away from you, I hope that you can take some pride in this volume in the years to come.

Dei memor, gratus amicis
(mindful of God, grateful to friends)

MICHAEL A. THOMAS

Interpreting the New Testament

The traditional greeting on Easter morning is "Christ is risen!" To which the response is: "He is risen indeed. Alleluia!" This ancient phrase echoes the greeting of the angel to Mary Magdalene and Mary the mother of James and Joseph as they arrived at the sepulchre to anoint the body of Jesus: "He is not here; for he has risen, as he said" (Matt 28:6). After the two disciples recognized Christ in the breaking of bread on the road to Emmaus, they immediately rose and returned to the others gathered in Jerusalem, announcing: "The Lord has risen indeed, and has appeared to Simon!" (Luke 24:34).

The resurrection of Christ is the ground of Christian belief and the wellspring from which the books of the New Testament flow. The gospels culminate in the resurrection, at the beginning of the Epistle to the Romans Paul invokes the resurrection as warrant for his apostleship, and he brings 1 Corinthians to a close with a magnificent peroration on the resurrected body. In places 1 Peter reads like an Easter baptismal sermon ("we have been born anew to a living hope through the resurrection of Jesus Christ from the dead" [1 Pet 1:3]), and in the Acts of the Apostles the disciples of Christ are portrayed again and again as "witnesses" to the resurrection (1:22; 2:32; 3:15, et al.).

The New Testament is a collection of books whose authors bore witness in their lives (and some in their deaths) to the living Christ. "It is no longer I who live," writes Saint Paul in Galatians, "but Christ who lives in me" (Gal 2:20). Before there was a book, there were persons who handed on Christ's sayings and told of the marvelous things God had worked in him. First came Christ, then the witnesses, then the books. This ordering of things is at the heart of the early interpretation of the New Testament. The goal was to delve more deeply into the mystery of God revealed in Christ, to whom the writings bear witness. In introducing the volumes on the New Testament in this series, it may be helpful to say a few things about how the early Christians approached this task.

We are inclined to begin with the book, with historical context and social setting, words and idioms, grammar and literary forms, religious and theological vocabulary, and the many other topics that command our attention. But the early Christians began with the risen Christ, and long before there was a book the faith was handed on orally. Although St. Paul said that he had received his commission "through a revelation of Jesus Christ" (Gal 1:12), not from a human intermediary, he associated himself with traditions that he had received from others. "For I *delivered* to you as of first importance what I also *received*, that

Christ died for our sins in accordance with the scriptures, that he was buried, that he was raised on the third day in accordance with the scriptures, and that he appeared to Cephas, then to the Twelve. Then he appeared to more than five hundred brethren at one time, most of whom are still alive, though some have fallen asleep. Then he appeared to James, then to all the apostles. Last of all, as to one untimely born, he appeared to me" (1 Cor 15:3–8).

The memory of Christ centered on his death and resurrection, and the brief narrative of his birth, suffering, death, burial, and resurrection formed the core of early Christian tradition. It was complemented by "sayings" of Jesus, but the sayings were understood in light of the events, as the structure of the gospels makes plain. The setting of the early confessions of faith was almost certainly Christian worship, and they reflect local catechetical instruction. The details varied from place to place, but the central narrative remained constant. Here, for example, is a somewhat freer (and idiosyncratic) form that appears in 1 Peter: "For Christ also *died for sins once for all*, the righteous for the unrighteous, that he might bring us to God, *being put to death in the flesh but made alive in the spirit*; in which he went and preached to the spirits in prison, who formerly did not obey when God's patience waited in the days of Noah, during the building of the ark, in which few, that is, eight persons, were saved through water. Baptism, which corresponds to this, now saves you, not as a removal of dirt from the body but as an appeal to God for a clear conscience, through the *resurrection of Jesus Christ, who has gone into heaven and is at the right hand of God*, with angels, authorities, and powers subject to him" (1 Pet 3:18–22).

The mention of baptism indicates that the early tradition also included how one was to understand Christian practices. In 1 Corinthians Paul's language about the Lord's Supper is similar to what he had used about the resurrection: "For I *received* from the Lord what I also *delivered* to you, that the Lord Jesus on the night when he was betrayed took bread, and when he had given thanks, he broke it, and said, 'This is my body which is for you. Do this in remembrance of me.' In the same way also the cup, after supper, saying, 'This cup is the new covenant in my blood. Do this, as often as you drink it, in remembrance of me.' For as often as you eat this bread and drink this cup, you proclaim the Lord's death until he comes" (1 Cor 11:23–26). Though Paul says that he had received the account about the Last Supper directly from the Lord, the terms "received" and "delivered" are the customary words for handing on tradition. Paul is repeating word for word what he has received from others.

Early in the church's history, then, the living Christ was identified by verbal formulas and practices, notably baptism and the Eucharist. The purpose of the creedlike summaries of faith was primarily catechetical, but they served as guarantors of the truth of what had taken place during Christ's lifetime and unlocked the Jewish Scriptures, what Christians would later call the Old Testament. This is evident in an illuminating testimony from Ignatius, bishop of Antioch, at the end of the first century. The Christians in Philadelphia in western Asia Minor were divided over some aspects of Christian teaching, and Ignatius exhorted them to abandon their contentiousness. Apparently some had argued that the only way the matter could be settled was by appeal to what they called "the archives," that is, the Old Testament. "If I do not find it in the archives, I do not believe it to be in the gospel," they said. Ignatius, however, demurred. "For me," he writes, "the archives are Jesus Christ, the inviolable archives are his cross and death and his resurrection and faith through him."[1] Although most, if not all, of the books of the New Testament had been written by the time he became bishop, Ignatius makes no mention of Christian writings to settle the dispute. He appeals only to the person of Christ and the brief narrative of his saving deeds, not to written documents.

The time was fast approaching, however, when oral tradition would be complemented by written documents. But not replaced! Even after the writings of the apostles formed the "canon" of writings we call the New Testament, the oral witness of the apostles remained alive. Irenaeus, bishop of Lyons, at the end of the second century still conceived of apostolic tradition in terms of persons first, books second. "The Lord of all gave to his apostles the power of the gospel, and through them we have learned the truth, that is, the teaching of the Son of God. . . . We have not learned the plan of our salvation from any others than those through whom the gospel came to us. They first proclaimed it, and then later by the will of God handed it down to us in writings."[2] For Saint Irenaeus the most authentic tradition was oral, what "the elders, the disciples of the apostles, have handed on to us."[3]

At the same time Irenaeus is the first writer to draw on the apostolic writings as part of an authoritative collection. He does not use the term "New Testament" but its basic structure of Gospels, the Acts of the Apostles, and Epistles is clearly visible in his works. In fact, a large part of his work against the gnostics is given over to the exegesis of specific passages from the New Testament that were in dispute. But the books did not stand on their own. They needed to be explained and individual passages fitted into the pattern of God's saving work in Christ. For this task the oral tradition confessed in the rule of faith and explained by teachers whose lineage could be traced back to the apostles was indispensable. Without a grasp of the plot that holds the books together, said Irenaeus, the Bible is as vacuous as a mosaic in which the tiny colored stones have been arbitrarily rearranged without reference to the original design. Even the apostolic writings, the Christian Scriptures, required a framework of interpretation, a canopy of beliefs and practices to envelop the texts.

The oral tradition took form in a tripartite, that is, trinitarian, rule of faith that identified God by narrating key events recorded in the Scriptures, the creation of the world, the inspiration of the prophets, the coming of Christ in the flesh, his death and resurrection, the outpouring of the Holy Spirit. Though drawn from the New Testament, the rule was distinct from the apostolic writings; it was a brief confession handed on at baptism that provided a key to the Scriptures. In other words, the Scriptures were read and interpreted in light of the church's tradition. Or, to put it more precisely, the tradition embodied in the apostolic writings, that is, the New Testament, was complemented by the tradition, equally apostolic, that had been handed on orally (primarily in Christian worship) from one generation to another. The New Testament was the book of the church, and interpretation took place within a context of shared beliefs and practices.

For example, during the great debate over the relation of the Son to the Father in the fourth century, Athanasius, bishop of Alexandria, used Irenaeus's principle of interpretation to marshal scriptural support for the decrees of the Council of Nicea. Arius, whose

---

1. *Philadelphians* 8.
2. *Against Heresies* 3, preface.
3. *Demonstration of the Apostolic Preaching* 3.

teaching had been condemned at the council, had called attention to the word "therefore" in Phil 2:9, "*Therefore* God has highly exalted him [Christ] and bestowed on him the name which is above every name." In his view the "therefore" implied that the Son had "become" God and was not God from eternity. Athanasius showed that this was an idiosyncratic and "private" interpretation contrary to the "church's sense of the Scripture" handed on orally and expressed in other texts in the New Testament, for example, John 1:1, "and the Word was God," or Heb 1:6, "Let all God's angels worship him." For good measure he points out that three verses earlier Saint Paul had said that Christ, who was "in the form of God, did not count equality with God a thing to be grasped" (Phil 2:6).[4]

By the third century the canon of the New Testament was universally recognized, though certain books remained in dispute, for example, the Apocalypse. Writers such as Tertullian in North Africa and Clement and Origen in Alexandria had at their disposal a Christian Bible composed of two parts, Old Testament and New Testament. But the written Scripture never replaced the living tradition, and its interpretation was guided by the rule of faith and Christian practice. The engine that drove interpretation was the church's faith in the triune God confessed in the baptismal creed, made present through Christ in the consecrated bread and wine of the Eucharist, whose power and love were confirmed in the lives of the faithful by the searing flame of the Holy Spirit. Once there was a written Scripture, interpretation inevitably entered a new phase. The church fathers did not doubt that the apostolic writings bore witness to the one God, Creator of all things, to the Son Jesus Christ the Lord, and to the outpouring of the Holy Spirit to call into one fellowship a new people. But interpretation not only has to do with the big picture but is most decidedly an exercise in particularity, how specific words and passages are to be understood and related to the faith delivered to the apostles. This was a demanding assigment that could be accomplished only through study, prayer, and, let it not be forgotten, argument and debate. Even in the early centuries the New Testament required interpretation, and its readers no less than we had to train their minds and tutor their affections to discern its meaning. All this took time and hard labor, and the number and variety of commentaries and homilies on books and passages of the New Testament during the early centuries of the church's history is astonishing. Yet the purpose of commentary was always kept in sight. Interpretation was a spiritual voyage of discovery, a way of exploring the luminous world revealed in the coming of Christ.

A good illustration is Gregory of Nyssa's interpretation of the word "righteousness" or "justice" (either a possible translation of a single Greek word), which occurs twice in the Beatitudes: "Blessed are those who hunger and thirst for righteousness (or justice), for they shall be satisfied." And: "Blessed are those who are persecuted for the sake of justice [or righteousness], for theirs is the kingdom of heaven" (Matt 5:6, 10). The same term occurs in the writings of Saint Paul, and Gregory of Nyssa, a fourth-century Greek commentator, noted in particular its use in 1 Corinthians: "[God] is the source of your life in Christ Jesus, whom God made our wisdom, our *righteousness* [or justice] and sanctification and redemption" (1 Cor 1:30).

In a homily on the fourth beatitude Gregory asks: "What is justice?" to which he gives a traditional philosophical answer: justice is to give to each according to his worth. But then

---

4. *Against the Arians* 1.37–44.

he observes that there is a higher form of justice, not based on merit. This is the justice we are to desire; hence the beatitude speaks of those who "hunger and thirst for justice." Here the homily takes a surprising turn as Gregory offers what he calls a "bolder interpretation": in the beatitude the Lord proposes to his followers that he himself is what they desire, "for he became for us wisdom from God, justice, sanctification, and redemption" (1 Cor 1:30).

By appealing to 1 Corinthians Gregory opens the beatitude to a christological interpretation. In his view it is speaking about hungering and thirsting for the living God, as David said in the psalm, "My soul thirsts for the living God" (Ps 42:2). By interpreting the words of Jesus with the help of Saint Paul, a procedure, one might observe, that would be shunned by a modern interpreter, Gregory is able to transform the beatitude into an invitation to seek not only "justice" but the living God, or, better, to find justice by knowing Christ. The one who tastes the Lord "has received God into himself and is filled with him for whom he has thirsted and hungered. He acknowledges that he has been filled with the one he desires when he says, 'Christ lives in me' (Gal 2:20)."[5]

Some texts posed perplexing theological problems, as, for example, the passage at the beginning of the Gospel of John: "No one has ever seen God" (John 1:18). The text is straightforward enough: God has never been seen. First Tim 6:16 went further: "no one has ever seen or can see [God]."[6] Yet the prophet Isaiah said explicitly that he had seen God: "In the year that King Uzziah died I *saw* the Lord sitting upon a throne, high and lifted up" (Isa 6:1). How was one to reconcile these passages and relate the words of John to other texts, for example, the report in the book of Genesis that Jacob saw God "face to face" (Gen 32:30)?

For many modern interpreters theological questions—for example, what it means to see God—are quite secondary to the task of interpretation and the unity of the Bible; that is, how one book in the Scriptures is to be understood in relation to other parts of the Bible is peripheral to their exegesis. Isaiah is Isaiah, and John is John. But early Christian commentators believed that the Bible spoke with a single (though nuanced) voice, and they took apparent inconsistencies between biblical authors as an invitation to probe beneath the surface of the inspired words, that is, to penetrate the spiritual reality about which the text spoke, in this case to grasp what it means to see God. "Seeing," they explained, was a form of knowledge, and they claimed that when all the relevant passages are considered, the Scriptures teach that God can be known, although the fullness of his divinity, his ineffable nature or essence, is beyond our comprehension. "It is one thing to see," writes Augustine, "it is another to grasp the whole by seeing."[7] One writer said that in the Scriptures "see" means the same as "possess," citing the words of the psalmist: "May you see the good things of Jerusalem" (Ps 128:5), where "see" means "to find." Hence he concludes that one who sees God "possesses all that is good."[8] By drawing on the many uses of the word "see" in the Scriptures (including the beatitude, "Blessed are the pure in heart, for they shall see God" [Matt 5:8]) Christian thinkers were able to explore the place of the vision of God in Christian life and hope.[9]

---

5. *Homily 4 on the Beatitudes* (Gregorii Nysseni Opera VII/II.122–23).

6. 1 John 4:12, "No man has ever seen God," was also cited.

7. *Letter* 147.8.21. This letter, a little treatise "on seeing God," discusses the relevant biblical texts.

8. Gregory of Nyssa, *Homily on the Beatitudes* (Gregorii Nysseni Opera VII/II.138).

9. Jerome, *Commentary on Isaiah* 6:1 (Corpus Christianorum 73:84–85); Gregory the Great, *Moralia* 18.88.

At times a single biblical word could inspire a preacher to lyrical heights. In a memorable sermon on the phrase "that God may be all in all" (1 Cor 15:28), Augustine asked, "What is the meaning of 'all'? [God] will be for you whatever you desired here on earth, whatever you valued. What did you want here, what did you love? To eat and drink? He himself will be food for you, he himself will be drink. What did you want here? A fragile and transient bodily health? He himself will be immortality for you. What did you look for here? Wealth? Greedy man, what is it that will satisfy you if God himself does not? Well, what did you love? Glory, honors? God will be your glory."[10]

When they listened to the Scriptures read in divine worship or pondered its words in prayer, the early Christians heard the Word of God spoken to their communities and to their lives. In his *Commentary on the Gospel of John* Origen of Alexandria, the first and greatest biblical scholar in the early church, explained that "a gospel" is a "discourse containing an account of things that have happened which, because of the good they bring, are a source of joy to the hearer." The gospel is a "word that makes present something good for the believer or a word that the promised good is present." Its subject, continues Origen, is the "presence of Jesus Christ, the first-born of all creation (Col 1:15), among men for their salvation." Accordingly, the gospels are the "firstfruits" of the Scriptures, and the "firstfruits" of the gospels is the Gospel according to John, "whose meaning cannot be understood unless one reclines on Jesus' breast (John 13:23) and accepts Mary from Jesus as his own mother."[11]

Anyone who wrote a commentary on the gospels in this spirit would discover much in the biblical text that a strictly historical approach would miss. And the reader of Origen's *Commentary on John* will not be disappointed. Not only was Origen engaged with the spiritual and theological meaning of the text, but he also assumed that to understand the gospel one must know Christ, in his words "recline on Jesus' breast." But his commentary is also a work of great scholarship and learning. In the first book he devotes many pages to a single word, "beginning," in the opening sentence, "In the beginning was the Word." Because "beginning" is the first significant term to appear in the gospel, it sends him off on a discussion of the many uses of "beginning" in the Scriptures. And this in turn allows him to explain why Christ is identified with "beginning." Christ, writes Origen, is the beginning of those "made in the image of God" because he is the "first-born of all creation" (Col 1:15); he is the beginning of knowledge because he is called "Wisdom" (1 Cor 1:24); he is the beginning of life because he is the "first-born from the dead" (Col 1:18); he is the beginning of creation, that is, the agent of creation, because he is "the beginning of [God's] ways for his work" (Prov 8:22).[12]

Origen is interpreting Scripture by Scripture, an axiom accepted by all early Christian writers. "The entire Scripture is one book and was spoken by the one Holy Spirit," wrote Cyril of Alexandria, another prolific biblical commentator.[13] Accordingly, it was presumed that the interpreter would draw on passages from the entire Bible to illuminate and explain

---

10. *Sermon* 158.9.
11. *Commentary on John* 1.27.
12. *Commentary on John* 1.90–108.
13. *Commentary on Isaiah* 29:11–12 (*Patrologia Graeca* 70:655a).

the text under discussion. The technique most often used was word association, seeking words or images that are the same or similar to what is found in the text, as Origen did when he explained "beginning" in his *Commentary on John*. The term could be "life," or "water," or "rock," or "rain," or "man," or "mountain," or a myriad of other words or images. As the expositors sought appropriate texts, they were led to yet more passages, and the commentaries and homilies often read like a pastiche of biblical verses. Yet there was method in their exegetical artistry. As words and phrases were invested with meanings drawn from elsewhere in the Scriptures, they acquired a theological clarity and sonority that only the Bible could give. In effect the words of the Gospel of John become "biblical" rather than simply Johannine; that is, the context of understanding was formed by the Bible as a whole, not just the Gospel of John.

We are so accustomed to think of context as literary or historical that we forget that the words of the Bible have a life that transcends their original setting. Think how a verse from the New Testament can sound when read in Christian worship. It is traditional to read from the book of Titus on Christmas Eve: "For the grace of God has appeared for the salvation of all men, training us to renounce irreligion and worldly passions, and to live sober, upright, and godly lives in this world" (Tit 2:11–13). When this passage is read in the Liturgy for the Nativity of Christ, the word "appear" rings out clearly like the peal of a single bell announcing the birth of Christ, the incarnation of the divine Word. While this understanding of the verse is certainly implicit within the text, the liturgical setting gives the word "appear" a concreteness and directness that it does not have in the context of the epistle, and the Liturgy, in turn, acquires a word so fitting and right that Tit 2:11 seems composed primarily for the occasion.

Under the tutelage of the church fathers, one learns to read the Bible very closely and to pay particular attention to the subtlety and resonance of its words. As Augustine once remarked: "My heart is exercised by the pounding of the *words* of your holy Scripture."[14] One also learns to see things whole, to interpret individual texts in light of the central biblical narrative and the Christ confessed in the creeds and celebrated in the church's worship.

But there is something else to keep in mind while reading the volumes in this series. For the church fathers biblical interpretation had to do with the bearing of the text on the present. The interpreter is not a disinterested observer, a voyeur; rather, he is a participant in the mystery about which he speaks. This can be illustrated by a story told about Saint Antony, the monk of the Egyptian desert.

> Once some visitors came to Antony and asked him for a good word. He told them that they should heed the Scriptures. When they pressed him for specifics, he said they should follow the word of Jesus in Matthew: "If anyone strikes you on one cheek, turn to him the other also" (Matt 5:39). But they objected, "We can't do that!" So Antony tempered the exhortation: "If you can't do that, at least allow one cheek to be struck." Again they replied, "We cannot do that." So Antony revised the saying another time: "If you are not able to do that, at least do not return evil for evil." But again they protested. Realizing that it was futile to try to teach such folk how to understand the Bible, he

---

14. *Confessions* 12.1.

instructed his disciples to "Take a little porridge" to them because "they are ill." And to the visitors he said, "If you cannot do this, or that, what can I do for you? What you need is prayers."[15]

The Bible is a book about how to live in the knowledge of God and of oneself. God's Word is not something to be looked at but something to be acted on. Saint Bernard said it well: the interpreter must see himself in that which is said. It is not enough, observes Origen, to say, "'Christ was crucified'; one must say with Saint Paul, 'I am crucified with Christ' (Gal 2:20). Likewise it is not enough to say, 'Christ is raised'; one who knows Christ says, 'We shall also live with him' (Rom 6:8)."[16] This is why Saint Augustine said that anyone who "thinks he has understood the divine Scriptures . . . but does not build up the double love of God and neighbor, has not succeeded in understanding them."[17]

The first major commentaries on the New Testament were written by Origen of Alexandria in the early third century. Like many of the biblical commentaries from the early church, they have come down to us in fragmentary condition. Fortunately, we still possess large sections of his massive *Commentary on the Gospel of John*. It is not certain whether he completed it, but it took him six books just to reach John 1:29. In addition, he authored a *Commentary on the Gospel of Matthew* and delivered series of homilies on the Gospel of Luke. Others followed his example—some writing commentaries, others delivering homilies that went through a book chapter by chapter. For the Fourth Gospel we have homilies by John Chrysostom and Augustine as well as commentaries by Theodore of Mopsuestia and Cyril of Alexandria. On Matthew there are commentaries by Jerome and Cyril and homilies by Ambrose and John Chrysostom, to mention some of the more important. The Gospel of Mark did not receive a commentary until the Venerable Bede in the eighth century.

Origen also expounded the Pauline epistles. From his commentary on Romans we have only fragments in Greek, but a Latin translation of it was made in the early church. Homilies on the letters to the Corinthians and commentaries on Paul's minor epistles exist only in fragments. The Latin commentator Ambrosiaster wrote a complete commentary on the Pauline epistles, and Jerome also commented on a number of the letters, including Galatians and Ephesians. Theodore of Mopsuestia wrote a commentary on the minor Pauline epistles, John Chrysostom preached homilies on all of Paul's letters (including Hebrews), and Theodoret of Cyrrhus also commented on the entire corpus. Only fragments of Cyril of Alexandria's commentaries on Saint Paul remain. John Chrysostom is one of the few who have preached an entire series of homilies on the Acts of Apostles. Augustine delivered a series of sermons on 1 John, and Victorinus and Jerome wrote on the Apocalypse.

Even this partial survey gives some idea of the extent to which the church fathers devoted their energies to expounding the New Testament. Commentaries and homilies, however, are only a small part of the exegetical harvest of the early church. There are sermons and lengthy letters on particular texts, for example, Gregory of Nyssa on 1 Cor 15:28 and Augustine on Jas 2:10, and homilies on sections of books, for example, the Beatitudes

15. *Patrologia Graeca* 65:84c.
16. *Against Celsus* 2.69.
17. *On Christian Doctrine* 1.86.

or the Lord's Prayer.[18] In the new English translation of Augustine's sermons, three volumes are devoted to sermons on passages from the New Testament,[19] and Gregory the Great has a series of forty homilies dealing with select texts from the New Testament.[20] There are also works dealing specifically with the infancy narratives of the gospels and essays that attempt to harmonize the gospels. Finally, there are wide-ranging discussions of many texts from the New Testament in theological essays, spiritual tracts, and the like.

Given this vast, diffuse, and often formless body of material, it is often difficult to learn how early Christian thinkers interpreted specific passages in the New Testament. In recent years some of the commentaries from the early church on the New Testament have been translated into English for the first time. For example, Origen's commentaries on the Gospel of John and Romans and his homilies on Luke are now available,[21] as are Ambrose's homilies on Luke,[22] Theodoret of Cyrrhus on the Pauline epistles,[23] and Origen and Jerome on Ephesians.[24] Nevertheless, the great body of commentaries and homilies remain untranslated in English, and may never be translated.

The Church's Bible will provide commentaries on select books of the New Testament drawn from the writings of the church fathers, and in some cases from medieval authors. We have made a selection of passages from the ancient commentaries and homilies that treat books chapter by chapter. In addition, we have included occasional comments on particular verses drawn from theological writings, sermons, and other early Christian writings. Our aim is not a comprehensive survey of early Christian exegesis of the books of the New Testament, but commentaries that we hope will be interesting, theologically significant, and spiritually uplifting to readers of the New Testament today.

In the excerpts the specific text under discussion is printed in bold. When a passage is cited from elsewhere in the Scriptures, it is printed in italics.

The authors and works from which the selections are taken are given in the appendixes.

Robert Louis Wilken

---

18. *St. Gregory of Nyssa: The Lord's Prayer; The Beatitudes,* trans. Hilda C. Graef (New York: Newman, 1954).

19. *The Works of Saint Augustine: A Translation for the 21st Century,* III.3–5, trans. Edmund Hill, O.P. (Brooklyn and New Rochelle, NY: New City Press, 1990–92), 3:3–5.

20. *Gregory the Great: Forty Gospel Homilies,* trans. Dom David Hurst (Kalamazoo, MI: Cistercian, 1990).

21. *Origen: Commentary on the Gospel according to John,* trans. Ronald E. Heine, 2 vols. (Washington, DC: Catholic University of America Press, 1989, 1993); *Origen: Homilies on Luke; Fragments on Luke,* trans. Joseph T. Lienhard, S.J. (Washington, DC: Catholic University of America Press, 1996); *Origen: Commentary on the Epistle to the Romans,* trans. Thomas P. Schreck, 2 vols. (Washington, DC: Catholic University of America Press, 2001, 2002).

22. *Exposition of the Holy Gospel according to Saint Luke: Saint Ambrose of Milan,* trans. Theodosia Tomkinson (Etna, CA: Center for Traditionalist Studies, 2003).

23. *Commentary on the Letters of St. Paul by Theodoret of Cyrus,* trans. Robert C. Hill (Brookline, MA: Holy Cross Orthodox Press, 2002).

24. Robert E. Heine, *The Commentaries of Origen and Jerome on St. Paul's Epistle to the Ephesians* (New York: Oxford University Press, 2002).

An Introduction to John

The Gospel of John held a cherished place in the minds and hearts of early Christian interpreters. It was for them, the "spiritual gospel,"[1] or in the words of Origen of Alexandria, "the firstfruits of the gospels." While scholars today debate its origins and authorship,[2] early Christians were unanimous in attributing it to the apostle John, the "beloved disciple" of the gospel itself. Reclining "close to the breast of Jesus" (John 13:23, 25), John had deeply imbibed the rich wisdom of Christ, and for early Christians, John was the most theologically sublime of all the gospels. Using the fourfold creature of Revelation 4 (lion, ox, human, eagle), early Christians routinely ascribed the image of the eagle to the Gospel of John. As one anonymous fourth-century commentator explained, "the eagle flies higher than any other birds and alone sets its unblinking gaze upon the rays of the sun."

Early Christian thinkers observed that the Synoptic Gospels (Matthew, Mark, and Luke) began with Christ's birth or baptism and focused largely on his earthly ministry of teaching and healing. The opening verses of the Gospel of John, however, immediately transport the reader to soaring theological heights: "In the beginning was the Word and the Word was with God and the Word was God" (1:1). Of these words Augustine remarked: "Not only does John rise above land and every realm of air and sky, but also above the whole host of angels, and every invisible order of powers. . . . John spoke about the Lord's divinity in a way that no else ever did."

Trinitarian and Christological Considerations

The Gospel of John was most significant for understanding the person of Christ and the doctrine of the Holy Trinity. The exalted theology of the prologue was a gold mine for Trin-

---

1. The phrase comes from Clement of Alexandria (as recorded by Eusebius of Caesarea, *Ecclesiastical History* 6.14.7). See also Maurice F. Wiles, *The Spiritual Gospel: The Interpretation of the Fourth Gospel in the Early Church* (Cambridge: Cambridge University Press, 1960); and W. A. Smart, *The Spiritual Gospel* (New York: Abingdon-Cokesbury, 1946), esp. 37–61.

2. Explorations on the origins and authorship of the Gospel of John abound. A classic examination of the topic is Raymond Brown, *The Community of the Beloved Disciple* (New York: Paulist Press, 1979), esp. 13–91. For a fine summary of the history of scholarship on these questions, see John Ashton, *Understanding the Fourth Gospel*, 2nd ed. (Oxford: Oxford University Press, 2009), 15–27, 90–101.

itarian thought. Early Christian commentators saw clearly the significance of the wording of the first verse: "In the beginning was the Word, and the Word was with God and was God." Because Christ, the Word, was explicitly named God, his full divinity was unquestioned. Yet because this same Word was also with God, the church maintained a distinction between the Father and the Son. Tertullian of Carthage, more than a century before the Council of Nicea, explained it this way: "There is one who exists from the beginning and another with whom he existed—one is the Word of God; the other is God. Of course the Word *is* God, but only as the Son of God, not as the Father." Over two hundred years later, Cyril of Alexandria maintained a similar logic: "By being with God he might be known as another person alongside the Father, and the Son might be believed to be separate and distinct. By being God, he is understood both as having the same nature as the Father and as existing from him, as both being God and coming forth from God."

Verse 3 of the prologue was further evidence of Christ's eternal divinity. Because the Word was with God in the beginning and "all things were made through him" (1:3), the Word could not be part of created reality. He must have existed from all eternity with the Father. As Augustine of Hippo concluded, "If he is not made, he is not a creature; and if he is not a creature, he is of the same substance as the Father. For every substance that is not God is a creature, and that which is not a creature is God." The prologue set the stage for further meditation on the mystery of the Trinity.

The prologue, however, was not the only section of the gospel significant for Trinitarian thinking. Jesus's own words, and those of his disciples, became important evidence for Christ's full divinity. In some cases, the very grammar of a biblical verse held theological weight. For example, early Christians paid careful attention to the declaration of Jesus in John 10:30: "I and the Father are one." These were no careless, merely symbolic, words. Jesus's pronouncement indicated both the unity and the plurality of the Godhead. The unity of the Godhead was expressed by the use of the word "one," but plurality was indicated by the use of two subjects. As Tertullian of Carthage explained in a careful, minute examination of the passage: "In the phrase, 'I and the Father are one,' the subjects of the sentence (*I* and *Father*) are masculine nouns, indicating two persons, but the predicate nominative (*one*) is neuter, indicating its reference to a 'unity of being,' not persons."

Other passages, like John 14:9, also pointed early Christians to the doctrine of Christ's full divinity with the Father. When Philip asked Jesus to "show us the Father," Jesus replied with the words, "He who has seen me has seen the Father" (14:9). As the Son of God, Christ so perfectly reflected the image of the Father, that to have seen the Son was to have seen the Father. Yet as Hilary of Poitiers was careful to point out, Christ is not the image of the Father in the same way that a lifeless piece of art reflects an object. The Son is a distinct, living person within the Godhead, sharing full divinity with the Father. He explains that "through the Son, the Father is seen. This is the mystery that the Son reveals: they are one God, but not one person." Like many early Christian thinkers, Hilary's interpretation of the Johannine text was informed by the Nicene Creed's articulation of one God in three persons (Father, Son, and Holy Spirit). Other words and phrases from the Creed ("substance," "essence," "very God of very God," "begotten, not made") also routinely appear in the church father's interpretation of the Gospel of John.

Not only the words of Jesus, but those of his disciples, like Thomas, also accentuated

Christ's divinity. In John 20, Jesus appeared after his resurrection to a group of disciples in an upper room. When Thomas, who was absent, learned of Christ's appearance, he famously pronounced: "Unless I see in his hands the print of the nails, and place my finger in the mark of the nails, and place my hand in his side, I will not believe" (20:25). Yet when Christ presented himself before Thomas, encouraging him to do the very thing he asserted, Thomas answered, "My Lord and my God!" (20:28). For early Christians, these were no empty words of exclamation. They were nothing less than a profound confession of faith, echoing the words of that quotidian Jewish prayer, itself a confession of monotheism: "Hear, O Israel: The LORD our God is one LORD" (Deut 6:4). Thomas, a faithful Jew who would have prayed Deuteronomy 6 every day, was now applying the words of that prayer to Jesus. Hilary of Poitiers captured the mind of the early church when he explained: "In the end Thomas understood the truth of the evangelical mystery and confessed Christ as both his Lord and his God. This was not a name of honor, but a confession of Christ's very nature. He believed that Christ was God in his very substance and power."

Early interpreters also wrestled with understanding the central Christian confession that Christ was both divine *and* human. While the Gospel of John is often described as having a "high Christology" for its exalted prologue and depictions of Jesus's intimate relationship with the Father, John records the human side of Christ as well.[3] Before his encounter with the Samaritan woman at the well in chapter 4 (unique to John's Gospel), we are told that Jesus was "wearied with his journey" (4:6). Likewise, in the account of the raising of Lazarus (also unique to John), Jesus was twice "deeply moved" (11:33, 38) and himself "wept" (11:34) at the sight of the crowds mourning over the death of Lazarus. After predicting his coming passion and betrayal, Jesus twice confessed to being "troubled" in "soul" and "spirit" (12:27; 13:21). The reality of Christ's physical body is also emphasized in the resurrection appearances of John's Gospel. In his appearance to the disciples, Christ could be touched and handled. He instructed Thomas: "Put your finger here, and see my hands; and put out your hand, and place it in my side" (20:27). His humanity is again displayed in the final chapter of the gospel when Jesus joined his disciples in a breakfast of fish and bread. All these episodes were clear indications of Christ's full humanity, and became the basis for further reflection upon Christ's incarnation.

Naturally, the declaration of John 1:14 was an essential Christological passage for early Christian thinkers: "And the Word became flesh and dwelt among us." The divine Word took on human flesh, not by changing his divine essence, but by fully assuming our human nature. The salvific consequences of the incarnation were not lost on ancient commentators. It was only through Christ's full assumption of human flesh that our union with God might be possible. As John Chrysostom observed: "God's own Son became the Son of Man that he might make the children of human beings into children of God." The prologue marked the centrality of the incarnation for understanding the rest of the book, and early interpreters were mindful of that theme in their expositions of later chapters of the gospel.

3. For a thorough consideration of the Christology of the Gospel of John, including a helpful review of modern scholarship on the question, see Paul N. Anderson, *The Christology of the Fourth Gospel: Its Unity and Disunity in the Light of John 6 (With a New Introduction, Outlines, and Epilogue)* (Eugene, OR: Cascade, 2010), esp. 1–47.

Sacramental Theology

Trinitarian and Christological matters were not the only concerns. Early Christians also discovered a rich sacramental theology in the Fourth Gospel. Scholars today are quick to point out that the Gospel of John omits both Christ's baptism in the Jordan and the institution of the Last Supper as found in the other canonical gospels. Yet, for early Christians, the Gospel of John was nevertheless laden with sacramental imagery.[4] As priests and bishops of communities of prayer and worship, these ancient Christian interpreters routinely perceived allusions to the sacraments of Baptism and Eucharist in John's text.

Christ's pronouncement to Nicodemus that, "unless one is born of water and the Spirit, he cannot enter the kingdom of God" (3:5), was an obvious reference to the sacrament of Christian baptism. Just as physical existence required a physical birth, so too Christ's words taught that spiritual life and entrance into God's kingdom required the spiritual rebirth of baptism. Like Augustine, early thinkers recognized that Nicodemus failed to perceive Christ's spiritual referent: "Although there are two births, Nicodemus understood only one. One is of the earth, the other of heaven; one is of the flesh, the other of the Spirit; one is of mortality, the other of eternity; one is of male and female, the other of God and the church." Other references to water, like the "living water" of John 4 and 7, and the flow of "blood and water" from Christ's side in John 19, were also interpreted in light of baptism.

In a more figural way, the washing of the blind man's eyes in the pool of Siloam (John 9), and especially the healing of the lame man at the pool by the Sheep Gate (John 5), also pointed early Christians to baptism. John Chrysostom drew a parallel between the healing powers of the pool waters and the healing waters of baptism. The latter "are portrayed beforehand by the pool as in a figure." Likewise, Ambrose of Milan observed that just as an angel gave healing powers to the pool (John 5:4), so too the Holy Spirit effects spiritual healing at the baptismal waters. As Christians began to construct elaborate baptismal fonts and pools, the healing pools of John 5 and 9 would become a natural reminder of the church's baptismal liturgy.[5]

As mentioned, John's Gospel contains no account of the Last Supper as found in the Synoptic Gospels. Yet, John 13 does record a final meal shared by Jesus and his disciples. In a moving narrative unique to John, Jesus donned the role of a servant and humbly washed the disciples' feet. As one might expect, early Christians perceived a sacramental significance in the scene. The washing of the disciples' feet with water echoed for them the spiritual washing at baptism. The removal of dust and grime from their feet suggested the spiritual removal of the stain of sin. For example, Christ's declaration that "he who has bathed does not need to wash, except for his feet" (13:10) became for the Venerable Bede, and other early interpreters, an illustration of "the cleansing which was given once in baptism but also the

---

4. For a modern scholarly review of Johannine sacramentalism see Raymond Brown, *The Gospel according to John*, vol. 1, Anchor Bible 29 (Garden City, NY: Doubleday, 1966), cxi–cxiv.

5. Because the early church performed baptisms by immersion, biblical references to pools of water would naturally evoke the church's sacramental rite. For a careful analysis of early Christian art and architecture in relation to Christian baptism, see Robin Jensen, *Baptismal Imagery in Early Christianity: Ritual, Visual, and Theological Dimensions* (Grand Rapids: Baker Academic, 2012).

washing away of the daily sins of the faithful." Once again, the church's ritual act with water helped illuminate the meaning behind passages like John 13.

Eucharistic imagery was readily available as well. That sacramental participation with Christ was discovered in the parable of the vine and the vinedresser, with the language of "abiding" in Christ. As Cyril of Alexandria asked, "Can anyone make sense of this and offer an interpretation that fails to mention the power of the blessed mystery [i.e., the Eucharist]?" However, the central passage for Eucharistic interpretation came from Christ's bread from heaven discourse in John 6. The words of Christ clearly evoked the Christian ritual meal. When Christ proclaims that "I am the bread of life; he who comes to me shall not hunger, and he who believes in me shall never thirst" (6:35), the image of eating and drinking invited ancient commentators to think of the Eucharist. Christ's invitation became, as it did for Cyril of Alexandria, a promise of "Eucharistic participation in his holy flesh and blood which restores humans wholly to incorruption." Later, when Augustine read Christ's warning that "your fathers ate manna, and they died" (6:49), he was reminded of the Christian version of heavenly food in the Eucharist, and Paul's warning about eating and drinking judgment upon oneself (1 Cor 11:29).

An even more obvious link to the Eucharist was Christ's pronouncement toward the end of the chapter: "The bread which I shall give for the life of the world is my flesh" (6:51); and his extended discourse a few verses later: "Unless you eat the flesh of the Son of man and drink his blood, you have no life in you; he who eats my flesh and drinks my blood has eternal life. . . . He who eats my flesh and drinks my blood abides in me, and I in him" (6:53–56). For ancient Christians, references to eating flesh and drinking blood could mean only one thing: participation in the Eucharistic meal. Christ's words were taken with utter seriousness. "He who does not take the sacrament, does not have life," said Augustine; and "those who do not receive Jesus through the mystery of the Eucharist will remain wholly bereft of any share in and taste of that holy and blessed life," concluded Cyril of Alexandria. In these and a variety of other ways, early Christians discovered a lush sacramental theology in the Gospel of John.

Figural Readings

In some cases early Christian commentators, following the example of the apostle Paul, used a figural or allegorical interpretation to expound the text. In discussing Abraham's two sons, one by the slave woman Hagar and one by Abraham's wife Sarah, Paul wrote: "This is an allegory: these women are two covenants" (Gal 4:24). Likewise, in his epistle to the Corinthians, Paul understood the Israelite wanderings in the wilderness, and their encounters with spiritual food and miraculous drink, as a figure of Christ and the church: "All ate the same supernatural food and all drank the same supernatural drink. For they drank from the supernatural Rock which followed them, and the Rock was Christ" (1 Cor 10:3–4). Early Christian interpreters followed this biblical and apostolic example of finding Christ and the church throughout Scripture. Although this approach lent itself most naturally to reading Old Testament texts, the Gospel of John could yield figural interpretations as well.

One example is the interpretation of Jesus's discourse with Nicodemus in John 3.

There, Christ alluded to an episode in Israelite history recorded in Num 21. The Israelites, complaining again about their ill-perceived fate, received the punishment of venomous serpents that attacked and killed many of the people. To heal their wounds, Moses constructed a bronze snake and lifted it on a pole; those who looked upon the snake were healed. Drawing upon this account, Jesus declared to Nicodemus: "As Moses lifted up the serpent in the wilderness, so must the Son of man be lifted up, that whoever believes in him may have eternal life" (3:14–15).

Other aspects of the story of the serpent on the pole also held meaning, for they represented, in the words of Cyril of Alexandria, "the entire mystery of the incarnation." The ancient Israelites typified believers in Christ. The venom of the snakes signified the deadly poison of sin. The lifting of the bronze serpent upon a pole evoked the lifting of Christ upon the cross. Taking these figures together, early interpreters like Augustine could proclaim: "Just as the Israelites fixed their eyes on that serpent and did not perish from the bites of the serpents, even so will those who fix their eyes with faith upon the death of Christ be healed from the bites of their sins." A typological reading of the text allowed the early church to discern deeper and richer meanings in the gospel.

Any number of details within the Johannine text could become the basis for further allegorical readings. When Jesus cleansed the temple of oxen, sheep, pigeons, and money-changers in John 2, each element of the narrative became for early Christians symbolic of something else, such as members of the church or the human soul. The Samaritan woman of John 4 evoked the gentile church coming to faith in Christ. The Good Shepherd discourse of John 10 allowed for a variety of figural interpretations of the shepherd, gate, sheep, thieves, and hirelings. Christ's undivided tunic in John 19 became a symbol of the undivided church spread across the world. The final breakfast with the disciples in John 21 intimated the eschatological banquet to come in Christ's kingdom.

Numbers also held hidden meaning for early interpreters. The six water jars of John 2 symbolized the six ages of the world leading to fulfillment in Christ, the new wine. The loaves and fishes of John 6 produced a variety of meanings connected with the numbers five and two. Lazarus's four days in the tomb (John 11) indicated the growing stages of habitual sin. The mention of 153 fish in John 21 invited ancient commentators to discover a hidden meaning in the number. To modern ears, these kinds of figural readings may sound far-fetched and untethered to the authorial intent of the passage, but for the early church, all of Scripture was a divinely inspired and interconnected web. To those with eyes of faith, a deeper, spiritual meaning was there.

John and the Unity of Scripture

Indeed, for early Christians the proper reading of Scripture was not simply a matter of focusing upon one particular book, chapter, or verse. Because the early church understood the Bible as essentially one single book, the interpretation of one passage was almost always considered in light of the totality of Scripture, both in its relation to the broader drama of redemption, and in the way it might echo similar words and phrases elsewhere in the Bible. For example, the chronology of the Gospel of John is seemingly framed around traditional

Jewish feast days (Tabernacles, Dedication [i.e., Hanukkah], and especially Passover).[6] Because Christians believed that Christ was the final and perfect sacrifice, the frequent mention of feasts in John's Gospel gave early interpreters an opportunity to explore the entire sacrificial system of the Old Testament in light of the coming of Christ.

Other connections to the broader scope of redemption were made possible when ancient readers observed details of the passage echoing similar aspects of the biblical story elsewhere. Christ's use of spit and clay to heal the man born blind in chapter 9 evoked for early interpreters God's original creation of humanity from dust (Gen 2:7). Irenaeus explains: "Just as we are formed in the womb by the Word, this very same Word formed the power of sight in the one who had been blind from his birth (9:1). . . . He declares the original formation of Adam, the manner in which he was created, and by whose hand he was formed, demonstrating the whole from a part. The Lord, carrying out the will of the Father and forming the power of sight, is the one who made the whole man."

Irenaeus was not alone in connecting details of the Johannine text with the broader story of the Bible. When early Christians read about Christ's arrest in the "garden" (18:1) and his subsequent burial in a "new tomb" in a "garden" (19:41), the original garden of Eden came readily to mind. Cyril of Alexandria beautifully captured the interpretive mind of the early church: "This garden was a kind of summation of all places, a return to that ancient garden. The beginning of our sad estate occurred in paradise, while Christ's suffering also began in the garden, a suffering which brought the restoration of all that happened to us long ago."

Cyril further explains: "Nothing is placed in the writings of the saints without a reason. Even something which seems minor proves to be worth our effort, since it has value." For this reason, even a small detail in the text was worthy of further examination, especially if the wording echoed another passage in Scripture. Jesus being "wearied from his journey" (4:6) reminded early Christians of similar words in Isa 40:28: "The Lord . . . does not faint or grow weary," and made possible a fuller exploration of the reality of the incarnation. Christ's references to "a spring of water welling up to eternal life" (4:14) and the Spirit being "rivers of living water" (7:38) compelled ancient readers to search for biblical references in the Psalms ("there is a river whose streams make glad the city of God" [Ps 46:4]), Isaiah (the righteous "will spring up like grass amid waters, like willows by flowing streams" [Isa 44:4]), and Jeremiah ("they have forsaken me, the fountain of living waters, and hewed out cisterns for themselves" [Jer 2:13]).

Christ's claim to be "the light of the world" (8:12) came to be connected to passages like Isa 9:1–2: "Galilee of the nations, the people who dwelled in darkness have seen a great light"; and Ps 36:9: "For with thee is the fountain of life; in thy light do we see light." In a similar way, texts like Ezek 18:3, "The fathers have eaten sour grapes, and the children's teeth are set on edge," and Deut 24:16, "The fathers shall not be put to death for the children," became important exegetical background to the disciples' question about the blind man in John 9:2: "Rabbi, who sinned, this man or his parents, that he was born blind?"

The details of Christ's passion, likewise, became important to the early church fathers. Christ's silence before his accusers brought to mind the famous passage from Isa 53:

---

6. See, for example, Aileen Guilding, *The Fourth Gospel and Jewish Worship* (Oxford: Clarendon, 1960).

"Like a lamb that before its shearers is dumb, so he opened not his mouth." The soldiers' treatment of Christ's clothes became the fulfillment of Ps 22:18: "They divide my garments among them, and for my raiment they cast lots." Even a minor detail such as Christ's "purple garment" held significance, for it connected the minds of ancient readers to a Christological reading of Isa 63:1: "Who is this that comes from Edom, in crimsoned garments from Bozrah?" The Bible was an interrelated tapestry of associated words, phrases, and theological meaning, and the Gospel of John was read within the context of the Bible as a whole.

John and the Synoptics

Putting the Gospel of John into conversation with the rest of Scripture was not limited to Old Testament allusions, however. Early interpreters also explored John's relation to the other three canonical gospels, Matthew, Mark, and Luke. Early commentators were aware of the differences between John and the Synoptic Gospels and attempted to explain the dissimilarities.[7] In general, however, the apparent discrepancies between John and the other gospels presented no serious challenge to their understanding of Scripture as God's inspired word.

Harmonization was often their first recourse. Augustine of Hippo wrote an entire treatise called *The Harmony of the Gospels* in which each of the four canonical gospels was brought into agreement with the others. He was not alone. Other interpreters would often do the same in the course of a homily or commentary. To give just one example, John Chrysostom addressed the cleansing of the temple, recorded in all four gospels. In John 2, Jesus's cleansing of the temple presumably occurred near the beginning of his ministry, whereas the other canonical gospels place the event at the end, just prior to Christ's passion. Chrysostom concluded that there were two cleansings, "one at the beginning of his ministry and one near the very coming of his passion." For him, this also helped explain the difference in Jesus's words. In John, Jesus declared, "You shall not make my Father's house a house of trade" (2:16). The Synoptics record a much more strident admonition: "Do not make my Father's house a den of robbers" (Matt 21:13; Mark 11:17; Luke 19:46), a stronger expression more fitting to the end of his ministry.

Despite the variances and apparent discrepancies, early Christians understood the gospels as divinely inspired texts. As Hilary of Poitiers reminded his readers: "Each of the gospels completes what is lacking in the others. We learn some things from one, other things from another, and so on, because all are the proclamation of one Spirit." Origen of Alexandria, likewise, accounted for differences based on the depth of meaning in the person of Jesus, and the various perspectives of each author. Yet, harmonization was not the only approach. Origen also allowed for certain historical differences within the gospels, as for example, when gospel authors changed the order of things "in order to aid the

---

7. For the definitive modern treatment of the relationship between John and the Synoptics, including a summary of the history of scholarship on the question, see D. Moody Smith, *John among the Gospels*, 2nd ed. (Columbia: University of South Carolina Press, 2001).

mystical meaning of those events." Because the biblical authors were divinely inspired, the deeper spiritual truth may be presented in a way that obscures the historical chronology. Never mind, says Origen: "Their aim was to present the truth spiritually and literally at the same time when possible, but when it was not possible to present both, they preferred the spiritual over the literal." The important point was the spiritual message. Occasionally, selections in this volume have been chosen to illustrate the ways early Christians handled differences between John and the Synoptic Gospels.

Moral Application

Whatever the perspective on John's Gospel, whether theological, sacramental, figural, or historical, the primary aim of all early Christian interpreters was to feed the Christian people and aid the soul in its spiritual journey. As a result, much of John's Gospel was employed for pastoral exhortation. The changing of water into wine (John 2) became for John Chrysostom an illustration of the believer's need for Christ to transform our weak and watery wills into the strong state of wine, "the cause of merriment to themselves and to others." The Samaritan woman of John 4 became a model of zealous faith, proclaiming the gospel to others. "Let us hear ourselves in that woman," wrote Augustine, "let us recognize ourselves in her, and in that woman let us give thanks to God." Early Christians also used Jesus's treatment of the Samaritan as an example of the way in which women should be treated in the church and home, with respect and dignity. The man who was "ill for thirty-eight years" (John 5) stood as an illustration of persevering in prayer, even when it seems that God does not hear. In a similar way, the ill man of John 5 and the dead Lazarus of John 11 became an occasion for early Christian preachers to address the way suffering and dying challenge our faith in a loving God.

The events of John 6 held several moral applications. John Chrysostom used the feeding of the five thousand to rail against the sin of gluttony, while Cyril of Alexandria exhorted believers to put away all worries and fears, based on Christ's words: "It is I; do not be afraid" (6:20). The death of Lazarus in John 11 and Jesus's own death predicted in John 13 allowed early interpreters to exhort their audiences about how to grieve the loss of loved ones and how to face one's own impending death. Likewise, Jesus's proclamation, "Greater love has no man than this, that a man lay down his life for his friends" (15:13), became the basis for encouragement toward persecution and martyrdom.

In the end, the Gospel of John, according to the Venerable Bede, encouraged each Christian to pursue one of "two ways of life in the church," the active or contemplative life. The active life, represented by the apostle Peter, was for all. It involved a life of service to God and neighbor through ministering to the poor, visiting the sick, and caring for the dying or dead. The apostle John, however, Christ's "beloved" who reclined upon his breast, represented the contemplative way. Such a life meant first practicing the active way and then learning "to be free of all affairs of the world and directing the eye of the mind toward love alone." Very few would ever ascend to such a life. Yet for the early church, the Gospel of John stood as the supreme exhortation toward such a life, as well as the shining example of it, for John's alone was the "spiritual gospel."

Commentaries and Homilies on John

Because the Gospel of John was a lengthy and theologically rich book, there are many commentaries and homilies from the early church. Most of the selections in this volume are drawn from six writers. Origen of Alexandria, one of the first and greatest commentators on Scripture, wrote a lengthy commentary on John. Of the thirty-two volumes, only nine have survived. From John Chrysostom we have a series of eighty-eight exegetical homilies that cover the entirety of John's Gospel. These are often detailed verse-by-verse expositions interwoven with theological reflection and moral application. Theodore of Mopsuestia wrote a commentary on the Fourth Gospel, originally in Greek, but now preserved in its fullest form only in Syriac. Augustine of Hippo has provided us with 124 tractates (sermons) on the Gospel of John. Augustine was the most prolific and influential Latin commentator on the gospel. From Cyril of Alexandria we have a lengthy and detailed twelve-volume commentary on John's Gospel. Cyril's commentary is especially good at locating the Gospel of John within the grand scope of the drama of redemption from creation to the eschaton. Finally, John Scotus Eriugena wrote a commentary on John's Gospel that combined exegetical study, theological reflection, and neo-Platonic philosophy.

Additionally, the Gospel of John was cited in a variety of sermons, treatises, polemical texts, catechetical works, ascetical writings, and liturgical poetry. Excerpts from thinkers such as Irenaeus of Lyons, Tertullian of Carthage, Hilary of Poitiers, Cyril of Jerusalem, Ambrose of Milan, John Cassian, Peter Chrysologus, Leo the Great, Romanos the Melodist, the Venerable Bede, and many more are included as well. Each provides additional insight into the way the early church read the Fourth Gospel. All told, nearly eighty different works, from forty different authors, are represented in the excerpts included in this volume.

Using This Commentary

This volume follows the traditional format for a commentary. It begins with a chapter on the authorship of the gospel, then proceeds to offer selections on each chapter. A reader will be able to search for ancient commentary on a specific passage or verse, and need not read through chapter by chapter. Note, however, that some portions of John's Gospel received very little attention from the early church and for that reason not every verse receives commentary. Also, this volume is not a comprehensive presentation of every interpretation of the Gospel of John from the early church. The primary source material from which to choose was vast, and judicious selection of excerpts was necessary. Excerpts were chosen on the basis of what the editors deemed most edifying both spiritually and theologically. Oftentimes, when a certain interpretation is repeated by multiple commentators, only one interpretation is presented. The goal is to illustrate the various ways the gospel was read and to invite readers to explore other commentators listed in the appendix.

Some excerpts are quite long in order to provide a fuller context for a specific interpretation. Rarely can ancient Christian interpretation be fully understood from a single line or two. Only by reading a longer excerpt can one see the way the ancient commentators wrestled with understanding the text. Scripture contains a rich tapestry of words, images, phrases, and ideas, and Christian interpretation developed slowly over time. Where appropriate, a brief footnote may be provided to help clarify the point being made. Other times, it may be necessary to read a selection again, allowing for a more meandering exposition than we are accustomed to in our age of sound-bytes and character-limited tweets. The reader is encouraged to take it slowly and ponder the mysterious and fascinating world of early Christian interpretation.

Arrangement of each chapter is as follows. A brief editorial introduction provides a summary of the excerpts to follow, highlighting particularly important themes, passages, or verses. Then there is a pericope from the chapter as a whole followed by excerpts on individual verses or sections. Within these smaller divisions, excerpts are arranged chronologically, earlier church fathers appearing before later ones.

Passages and verses being commented on are in **bold**. Other biblical citations, and passages from elsewhere in John, are provided in *italics*. All references conform to the Revised Standard Version unless indicated otherwise. In some instances, the Latin (Vulgate) or Greek text available to the early Christian interpreter may vary slightly from our contemporary manuscripts. Significant deviations will be noted.

Sources for the Interpretation of the Gospel of John

An appendix at the end of this volume provides a full list of authors used, along with brief biographical information. A second appendix provides the sources from which the excerpts are drawn, arranged in the order in which they appear in this volume.

BRYAN A. STEWART

Preface: The Gospel of John in the Early Church

The excerpts presented here address the authorship and character of the Gospel of John and its relation to the Synoptic Gospels (Matthew, Mark, and Luke) in early Christian commentators. They unanimously believed that the disciple John, son of Zebedee, wrote the Fourth Gospel. The Muratorian Fragment, one of the earliest extant canon lists of the New Testament, suggests that John wrote his gospel with the encouragement and approval of his fellow disciples and other bishops. This tradition is echoed and augmented to include the gospel's purpose in combating early Christian heresies that denied Christ's full divinity and pre-incarnate existence, as seen in excerpts from an anonymous fourth-century writer, Cyril of Alexandria, and Sophronius of Jerusalem. John Chrysostom extols the beauty and eloquence of John's Gospel, calling it a "voice sweeter and more useful than all lutists and musicians." For Chrysostom, the message of John's Gospel is all the more marvelous when one considers the disciple's family background. His heavenly words that draw the reader to sublime contemplation were written by a poor, uneducated fisherman hailing from a backwater region of the Roman Empire. Only the inspiration of the Spirit could produce "the best philosophy and way of life."

Many early Christian writers used the fourfold creature of Revelation 4 (lion, ox, man, eagle) as a pictorial image for each of the four gospels. Irenaeus ascribes the lion to John, "powerful and glorious" in its presentation of Christ's generation from the Father. Augustine and our anonymous fourth-century writer, in what has become the more traditional attribution, compare John to the eagle for his unblinking gaze into the high and exalted divinity of Christ. In a similar vein, John Scotus Eriugena offers a classic presentation of John's Gospel as the work of heightened contemplation, rather than action. As one who lies close to the breast of Jesus (cf. John 13:23, 25), John represents the intellectual contemplation of Christ's eternal divine existence.

Comparison with the other canonical gospels also occupied the attention of early Christian thinkers. Origen of Alexandria appears especially aware of the seeming discrepancies between the four gospels in their literal sense. He eases the tension by noting that in order to convey the necessary spiritual truth, some of the gospel writers have rearranged the narrative historically in order to convey more powerfully the spiritual message. Likewise, because Jesus has many meanings, the gospels each capture different aspects of Christ. Nevertheless, for Origen, John towers above them all as the "firstfruits of the gospels." Augustine notes that Matthew, Mark, and Luke concern themselves with the humanity of Jesus while John addresses

1

Christ's divinity. Cyril of Alexandria employs the idea of four travelers all journeying to the same city, but by different routes. And Theodore of Mopsuestia suggests that John wrote his gospel in order to address what was lacking in the first three. He opines that "the Gospel of the blessed John is the perfection and completion of all that the other evangelists intended."

(1) Muratorian Fragment

The Fourth Gospel is that by John, one of the disciples. To his fellow disciples and bishops who were encouraging him to write he said, "Fast together with me today for three days and let us discuss whatever is revealed to each of us." That night it was revealed to Andrew, one of the apostles, that John should record everything under his own name, and that each of them would review it. And so while different principles are taught by the individual gospels, it makes no difference to the faith of believers, since all essential matters are declared in each of the gospels by one principal Spirit: Christ's birth, passion, resurrection, his life with his disciples, and things concerning his twofold coming, the first in lowliness when he was despised, which has already occurred, the second in manifest royal power, which is yet to come. So why is it any wonder if John constantly sets forth these individual things in his letters as well, saying, *We have written to you those things which we have seen with our eyes and heard with our ears and touched with our hands* (1 John 1:1). Thus he avows that he is not only an eyewitness and hearer but also a writer of all the wonders of the Lord, in their proper order.

(2) Irenaeus of Lyons

It is not possible for the gospels to be either more or less in number than they are. For there are four zones of the world in which we live, and four chief winds. Likewise, the church is scattered throughout the world, and the gospel and Spirit of life are the *pillar and bulwark* of the church (1 Tim 3:15). It is fitting, then, for the church to have four pillars, everywhere breathing forth incorruptibility and bringing life to humanity. From this it is clear that the Word, who is the Creator of all things, who *sits upon the cherubim* (Ps 99:1) and *holds together all things* (cf. Col 1:17), and who was made manifest to humanity, has given us a fourfold gospel held together by one Spirit. . . . For the cherubim were four-faced, and their faces reflected the various activities of the Son of God. As Scripture says, *the first living creature was like a lion* (Rev 4:7), signifying his powerful, authoritative, and kingly aspect. The *second creature was like an ox* (Rev 4:7), signifying his sacrificial and priestly order. The *third, with a face of a man* (Rev 4:7), represents his advent as a man. And the *fourth, like a flying eagle* (Rev 4:7), indicates the gift of the Spirit hovering over the church.

The gospels, among which Christ himself sits, are in agreement with these images. The Gospel according to John recounts his original, powerful, and glorious generation from the Father, saying, **In the beginning was the Word, and the Word was with God, and the Word was God** (John 1:1), and **all things were made through him, and without him was**

not anything made (1:3). This is why that gospel is full of all confidence, for such is Christ's character. Likewise, the Gospel according to Luke takes up his priestly character and begins with Zechariah the priest offering sacrifice to God (Luke 1:8–9). . . . Again, Matthew recounts Christ's birth as a man, saying, *The book of the genealogy of Jesus Christ, the son of David, the son of Abraham* (Matt 1:1), and *the birth of Jesus Christ took place in this way* (Matt 1:18). So Matthew is the gospel of his humanity, and this is why Christ's humble and gentle character is maintained throughout the whole gospel. Finally, Mark begins with the prophetical Spirit descending upon us from on high, saying, *The beginning of the gospel of Jesus Christ, the Son of God, as it is written in Isaiah the prophet* (Mark 1:1–2), indicating the wingéd and soaring aspect of the gospel.

(3) Origen of Alexandria

If someone should examine the disagreements between the gospels in their literal sense . . . he would grow dizzy and would either withdraw from the true validity of the gospels and choose one of them at random so as not to dare to reject the faith about our Lord, or he would admit that there are four gospels but say that their truthfulness does not lie in their literal sense.

In order to gain some understanding of the evangelists' intention in these matters, we should also add the following. The word which God gives to the saints, along with his presence which is with them when he reveals himself at chosen times in their life—all of this, let us assume, comes to people who see (in the Spirit) what lies before them. Such people are numerous and exist in a variety of places, and not everyone is given the same grace. As a result, each person proclaims what he sees in the Spirit concerning God, his words, and his appearance to the saints. One person would proclaim things that were said and done by God to one righteous man in one place, while someone else would proclaim the things prophesied and accomplished for a different man, and yet another person would want to offer instruction about a third man besides the other two previously mentioned. Let us assume that there is also a fourth person who acts in a similar way to the first three. These four people agree with each other in regards to certain things suggested to them by the Spirit, but they differ in small ways with each other concerning other matters.

Their reports are something like this: God appeared to one man at such and such a time and place, has done such and such things to him, appeared to him in such and such a manner, and led him to such and such a place where he did these things. The second person then proclaims that God appeared at a time which is in agreement with the first account, in some city, but to a second man whom he understands to be far removed from the place of the first man. He also recounts that other words were spoken to this man whom we assume (according to our hypothesis) was a second man. Assume similar things for the third and the fourth reports.

As we have said previously, these reports agree with each other about God and the kindness he shows to some. But if someone supposes that these four reports were history which attempted to portray events through historical accounts, and supposes that God is circumscribed in space and unable to present multiple appearances of himself in multiple places or to speak multiple things at the same time, it would seem impossible that the four hypothetical persons could all be telling the truth. . . .

Therefore, in regards to these four reports which I have hypothesized about, each of whom desired to teach us figuratively about the things which they had seen in their minds, a wise person would understand the true meaning of their accounts and would find no discrepancy between them. We ought to understand the four evangelists in the same way. They made much use of the deeds and words of Jesus according to his wonderful and paradoxical power. In other places in Scripture, however, they have interwoven together their spiritual understanding of things with words referring to sensible things.

Indeed I do not condemn the authors for changing, in some ways, what happened historically in order to aid the mystical meaning of those events. As a result, they have reported what happened in one place as if it happened in another, and what happened at one time as if it happened in another, and in this way have created a report with apparent discrepancies. Their aim was to present the truth spiritually and literally at the same time when possible, but when it was not possible to present both, they preferred the spiritual over the literal. . . .

Jesus, too, has many meanings, and it is likely that the various evangelists took their ideas from these meanings and wrote the gospels, even at times being in agreement with each other concerning some things. . . . I have discussed all these things about the apparent discrepancies in the gospels with a desire to present their agreement by means of spiritual interpretation.

(4) Origen of Alexandria

The gospels are fourfold as if they were the primordial elements of the faith of the church, the elements of which the entire world which is being reconciled to God in Christ is composed. As Paul says, *in Christ God was reconciling the world to himself* (2 Cor 5:19), the world whose sin Jesus bore. And concerning the world of the church, it is written: **Behold, the Lamb of God who takes away the sin of the world** (1:29). In my opinion, you have given me the task of interpreting, according to my ability, the firstfruits of the gospels: the Gospel according to John, the gospel which speaks of the one whose genealogy is given and who had his origin from one who is without genealogy.

Matthew, writing to the Hebrews who expected the Messiah to come from the line of Abraham and David, said, *The book of the genealogy of Jesus Christ, the son of David, the son of Abraham* (Matt 1:1). Mark, understanding fully what he was writing about, explained, *the beginning of the gospel* . . . (Mark 1:1).[1] But the greater and more perfect accounts of Jesus are saved for the one who lay upon Jesus's breast (cf. John 13:23). None of the others demonstrated Christ's divinity as purely as John did, who presented him saying, **I am the light of the world** (8:12); **I am the way, and the truth, and the life** (14:6); **I am the resurrection** (11:25); **I am the door** (10:9); **I am the good shepherd** (10:11); and

---

1. There is a lacuna in Origen's text at this point.

in the Apocalypse, *I am the Alpha and Omega, the beginning and the end, the first and the last* (Rev 22:13).

One must dare to say, then, that the gospels are the firstfruits of all the Scriptures and that the firstfruit of the gospels is the Gospel according to John. No one can understand its meaning who does not rest upon the breast of Jesus (cf. John 13:23) or does not receive from Jesus Mary as his own mother (cf. John 19:27). It is necessary for us to become another "John," just as John was shown by Jesus to be another "Jesus." If Mary had no son other than Jesus (which is held by those who have sound beliefs about her), and Jesus said to his mother, **Behold your son** (19:27) and not "Behold, this man is *also* your son," then it was the same thing as saying, "Behold, this man is Jesus whom you bore." Indeed everyone who has been perfected *lives no more but Christ lives in him* (cf. Gal 2:20); and since Christ lives in such a person, it is said about that one to Mary, *Behold*, Christ, *your son*.

(5) John Chrysostom

The son of thunder (cf. Mark 3:17), the beloved of Christ (cf. John 19:26), the pillar of churches throughout the whole world, the one who holds the keys of heaven, the one who drinks the cup of Christ and has been baptized in his baptism, who lies upon the master's breast with great confidence, this one is now presented to us. . . . This one now appears before us without hypocrisy (for in him there is no hypocrisy, forgery, or fiction). With an open face he proclaims the open truth, persuading those who hear him that he is none other than what he is by his appearance, looks, and voice. He needs no musical instruments for his proclamation, such as a lute, lyre, or some other such thing. He accomplishes it all with his tongue, sending forth a voice sweeter and more useful than all lutists and musicians. The entire heavens are his stage, the world his theatre. His audience are all the angels and all people who are angels or who desire to become angels, for they alone are able to hear clearly such harmonious music, and to demonstrate it by their lives. . . . Heavenly powers stand by to aid this apostle, astonished at the beauty of his soul, his understanding, and the maturity of his virtue by which he drew Christ to himself and received that spiritual grace. Like some well-made, bejeweled lyre with strings of gold, John prepared his soul and offered it to the Spirit for some great and exalted speech.

Therefore because it is no longer the fisherman, the son of Zebedee, but the one who knows the *depths of God* (1 Cor 2:10)—I mean the Spirit, who plucks the strings of the lyre—let us pay careful attention. What he says to us, he doesn't speak in a human fashion but from the depths of the Spirit, from those hidden things which not even the angels knew before they came to pass. For what we know, they too with us, and through us, have learned from his voice. . . .

If we saw someone from above suddenly stooping down from the heights of heaven, promising to describe that place with precision, would we not all rush after him? So now also, let us direct our attention, for this man speaks to us from heaven. He is not of this world, as Christ himself says: **You are not of the world** (15:19); he has the Counselor speaking in him, the ever-present one who knows the things of God as precisely as the human soul knows the things belonging to itself (cf. 1 Cor 2:10–11)—the Spirit of holiness, the righteous Spirit, which gently leads us to heaven and gives us other eyes prepared to see the future as if it's happening in the present, and granting us to behold heavenly things, even while in the body. Now then, let us offer to him an entire life of utter tranquility. Let no one sluggish, no one drowsy, no one foul enter here and remain, but let us remove ourselves to heaven. There, he speaks these things to those who are citizens of that place. We will gain nothing great by remaining on earth. The words of John mean nothing to those who do not desire to be delivered from this swinish life, just as the things of this world mean nothing to him. Although thunder amazes our souls by making a sound without being seen, this man's voice disturbs none of the faithful, but rather frees them from confusion and trouble. However, it does amaze the demons alone, and those who serve them. Therefore, in order to see how his voice amazes them, let us maintain silence, both outwardly and in our minds, but especially in our minds. What use is it to silence the mouth if the soul is disturbed with great turmoil? I seek for that tranquility of mind and soul since it's the attentive soul that I need.

Now then, let no desire for wealth, lust for glory, the tyranny of anger, or the remaining throng of other passions trouble us. It is impossible for the ear, without first being cleansed, to behold clearly the sublimity of what is spoken, or to understand properly the awe-inspiring and hidden nature of these mysteries and all other virtue contained in these divine oracles. For if someone is unable to learn well a melody on a flute or lyre without all careful attention, how would someone who sits listening to mystical voices be able to hear with a lazy soul?

(6) John Chrysostom

If John was going to converse with us and speak to us words of his own, we would need to say something about his family, his homeland, and his education. But since it is not he, but God through him, who speaks to humanity, it seems to me superfluous and extraneous to investigate his background. Nevertheless, such an endeavor is not superfluous but exceedingly necessary, for when you have learned who John was, where he came from, whom he came from, and what kind of man he was, and then you hear his voice and all his wisdom, you will certainly understand that his words were not his own but those of the divine power that stirred his soul.

What then was his homeland? He had none but a poor village in a sorry country which produced nothing worthwhile. The scribes disparage Galilee saying, **Search and you will see that no prophet is to rise from Galilee** (7:52). Even the **Israelite indeed**[2] disparages it saying, **Can anything good come out of Nazareth?** (1:46–47). And being from this land, he was not even from a region of some distinction in it. Likewise, he did not come from a distinguished family; his father was a poor fisherman, so poor that he led his own children into the same vocation. You all know that no craftsman wants to make his son inherit the same vocation, unless poverty particularly constrains him, especially if the work is paltry. And nothing can be poorer, more worthless, and more unlearned than a fisherman

---

2. John Chrysostom means Nathanael.

(although even among them some are greater and some lesser). And this apostle of ours held the lower rank, for he didn't catch fish from the sea but made his living on some small harbor. As he was engaged with this task with his father and his brother James, *mending their broken nets* (Matt 4:21)—itself signifying their extreme poverty—when Christ called them.

As for his outward education, we learn from these things that he had none at all. Elsewhere Luke testifies to this, saying not only that he was ignorant, but uneducated as well (cf. Acts 4:13). This is what we would suppose for someone who was so poor and never entered into the marketplaces, nor ran in respectable circles, but was rather tied down to his fishing. Even if he did encounter certain fish merchants or army cooks, why would he come to be in a better state than the irrational beasts? How could he not imitate the speechlessness of the fish?

And so, this fisherman who spends his time in the harbor with nets and fish, who comes from Bethsaida of Galilee, whose father is a poor fisherman (the poorest of the poor), whose ignorance is of the extreme, who never learned his letters either before or after he encountered Christ, let's see what he says and what he speaks about. Is it about things in the countryside, things in the rivers, or the fish market? These are the kinds of things we would expect to hear from a fisherman. But fear not; we'll hear nothing about these things. We'll hear about heavenly things which no one had ever learned before this man. Pay attention, as is fitting, to the one who speaks from the treasures of the Spirit, as one who has just arrived from heaven itself. He comes to us bringing sublime teaching and the best philosophy and way of life. . . .

He speaks everything with assurance. As if he stands upon a rock, he is never overturned. Having been deemed worthy to enter into the very innermost sanctuary, and having the Lord of all speaking in him, he is subject to nothing that is human. . . .

Indeed, from this and from everything else, it's clear that nothing of this man is human. Divine and heavenly are the teachings which come to us through this divine soul. We won't hear clanging words, ringing speech, or a superfluous and useless ordering and arrangement of words and sentences (for these things are far from all wisdom); rather, we will observe irresistible and divine power, invincible force of correct teachings, and an abundance of ten thousand good things.

(7) Augustine of Hippo

In the four gospels, or rather the four books of the one gospel, Saint John the apostle, who is not unjustly compared to the eagle because of his spiritual understanding, raised his preaching much higher than the other three; and in doing so, he also wanted our hearts to be raised up. The other three evangelists, as if walking with the Lord as a man on earth, speak little about his divinity; yet John, as if reluctant to remain on earth, raised himself up, as seen when he thunders in the beginning of his discourse. Not only does he rise above land and every realm of air and sky, but also above the whole host of angels, and every invisible order of powers, coming finally to the one through whom all things were made, saying, **In the beginning was the Word, and the Word was with God, and the Word was**

God. He was in the beginning with God; all things were made through him, and without him was not anything made (1:1–3).

The rest of what he preached also agreed with this great exalted beginning, and he spoke about the Lord's divinity in a way that no else ever did. He uttered that which he had imbibed. Not without reason, in this same gospel, is it related that he was lying on the Lord's breast at dinner (cf. John 13:23). He was drinking from that breast in secret; but what he imbibed secretly, he uttered openly. In this way, all nations might hear not only of Christ's incarnation, his passion, and the resurrection of the Son of God, but also what he was before the incarnation, the only-begotten of the Father, the Word of the Father, co-eternal with the one who begot him, equal to him by whom he was sent. In that mission he was made less, so that the Father might be greater.

(8) Augustine of Hippo

The Gospel of John remains, to which none of the others can be compared. . . . It's clearly agreed that the other three—that is to say, Matthew, Mark, and Luke—are especially concerned with the humanity of our Lord Jesus Christ, in both his kingly and priestly aspects. . . . On the other hand, John presents and recommends to us the divinity of Christ, by which he is equal to the Father, according to which he is **the Word** and God **with God**, and **the Word became flesh in order to dwell among us** (1:14), and according to which he **and the Father are one** (10:30). Like an eagle, John focuses on Christ's more exalted sayings and, in a certain manner, only rarely descends to earth. In short, although John clearly testifies to his knowledge of Christ's mother, he says nothing about Jesus's birth (as do Matthew and Luke), nor does he commemorate Christ's baptism (as do the other three gospels). Instead, he only recalls the lofty and sublime testimony of John the Baptist, and leaving the other gospels behind, he proceeds with Jesus to the wedding in Cana of Galilee. . . .

Keep in mind that this very Gospel of John, which draws us so excellently to the contemplation of truth, also quite excellently teaches us about the sweetness of love. Since that teaching is both the truest and the most salutary, *for great is the might of the Lord; he is glorified by the humble* (Sir 3:20), the evangelist who commends Christ far more highly than the others, is also the one whose writings present Jesus washing his disciples' feet (cf. John 13:5).

(9) Anonymous

The gospels surpass all the pages of divine Scripture, for while the law and the prophets predicted what would come, the gospels speak of their completion. However, among these gospel writers, John stands out for his depth of understanding of divine mysteries. For sixty-five years, from the time of the Lord's ascension to the final days of Domitian,[3] he

---

3. AD 96.

preached the word of God without the aid of writing. But when Domitian was killed, Emperor Nerva[4] permitted John to return from exile to Ephesus. Being urged by the bishops of Asia, he wrote about the co-eternal divinity of Christ with the Father, countering the heretics who had invaded his churches in his absence and who were denying Christ's existence before Mary. Therefore, among the four animals John is compared to the soaring eagle, for the eagle flies higher than any other birds and alone sets its unblinking gaze upon the rays of the sun. Indeed, the other evangelists, although adequately presenting Christ's earthly birth and his temporal deeds performed in his humanity, spoke very little about his divinity. Just like animals that go about on foot, they traveled about with the Lord on earth. John, however, dwells very little on Christ's earthly activities, but instead contemplates the more sublime power of his divinity and soars with the Lord to heaven. For the one who has reclined on the Lord's breast during supper (cf. John 13:23) was able to drink heavenly wisdom more excellently from the very fount of the Lord's breast. If indeed John had read the three gospels of the evangelists and had approved of their faithfulness and veracity, he saw lacking in them other historical facts, especially things the Lord had done at the very beginning of his earthly preaching, that is, before John the Baptist was imprisoned. So acting as if some facts had been left out by the other evangelists, John wrote about the things Jesus did before the Baptist's imprisonment, and was especially careful to highlight the divinity of Christ and the mystery of the Trinity. Indeed the other three evangelists described in abundant detail the earthly words and deeds of the Lord which are especially useful for influencing our morality in this present life. They dwelt upon the active life in which one works to cleanse the heart for seeing God. Truly, John does speak a little about the deeds of the Lord; however, he more diligently commits to recording the words of the Lord which indicate the unity of the Trinity and the blessedness of eternal life.

So, by commending for us the virtue of contemplation, he accomplished his purpose for preaching: in contemplation, one is emptied in order to see God. This indeed is John, whom the Lord called from the wave-tossed storm of marriage and to whom, being a virgin, Christ entrusted his virgin mother.

(10) Cyril of Alexandria

There was no small outrage about the beliefs of the heretics during John's day; and the harm of the scandal was devouring the souls of the simpler folk like a plague. Some of them were being dragged away from the truth by the folly of these men, believing that the Word had scarcely been called into existence when he became man. Therefore, the more sensible believers joined together and approached the Savior's disciple—I mean John, of course—and told him of the disease that was oppressing the brethren, and revealed the folly of those who were teaching these false doctrines. So they earnestly begged John to assist them with the enlightenment of the Spirit and to stretch forth a saving hand to those who were already ensnared within those diabolical nets. Grieving, then, over those who were lost and being corrupted in mind, and likewise considering that it was quite

---

4. AD 96–98.

improper to offer no help for those who would live after them, the disciple set about the task of writing a book. He left some things to the other evangelists to explain more broadly—such as the legal genealogies and Christ's birth according to the flesh. But he himself quite vehemently and vigorously sprang upon the folly of those heretics, by saying: **In the beginning was the Word** (1:1).

(11) Cyril of Alexandria

The holy evangelists have an exceedingly remarkable accuracy in their writings, *For it is not they who speak*, according to the word of the Savior, *but the Spirit of the Father which is in them* (Matt 10:20). Nevertheless, if one looked at the loftiness of the subject matter in John, the keenness of his understanding, and the continuous and well-connected presentation of his ideas, one would be quite reasonable to say that the writings of John marvelously surpass the other gospels. Indeed, they are all racing with one another to explain the divine teachings, and they take off from the starting line to drive their chariots towards a single goal; yet, in a sense, their forms of discourse are quite different. To me, they seem to resemble those who have been called together into one city, but who have decided to travel by different routes. We can find one evangelist composing an incredibly detailed account of our Savior's genealogy according to the flesh by tracing his line from Abraham through Joseph (Matt 1:1–17), while another evangelist does the same by tracing Christ's line from Joseph to Adam (Luke 3:23–38). We discover that the blessed John, however, is not overly concerned about these matters; instead, he employs a zealous and fired-up act of the intellect in order to try to grasp things above the human mind, daring to illuminate the ineffable and unutterable begetting of the Word of God (John 1:1).

(12) Theodore of Mopsuestia

The evangelist John was one of the Twelve; he was the youngest of the group. He was a guileless boy, set apart from the deceit of natural cunning, and for that reason he had acquired great boldness with our Lord. In fact, it was said that John was loved by Christ more than all of the disciples (cf. John 13:23), although in many places we find the blessed Simon to be the first among the disciples. . . .

After our Lord was taken up into heaven, the apostles remained in Jerusalem for a long time, traveling around to the cities in its vicinity. . . . In this way the blessed John also came and dwelled in Ephesus, while he was visiting all of Asia and blessing its inhabitants through his words. At this time, the tradition of the writings of the other evangelists—Matthew, Mark, and Luke—existed, since they had composed the books of the gospels. A bit of "good news" was spread about in every inhabited place, and all of the believers were diligent in their love to acquire through these books a knowledge of the Lord's life while he was on earth.

The believers in Asia all agreed that John's testimony was truer than anyone else's, and that he should write a gospel since he was with the Lord from the beginning and had imbibed excellent grace because of his love. And so they brought the books of the gospels to John, seeking to learn his opinion about the matters written in them. John highly praised the truth of these writings, but he did say that some minor miracles and events that should have been included were lacking, and that there was almost no doctrine in them at all. Again, he said that it was right for these men to have recorded such things about the Lord's coming in the flesh; indeed, the only thing lacking was some reference to Christ's divinity, lest after the passage of time, when people were familiar with these words, they would think only about Christ's identity in terms of these words alone.

For this reason, all the brethren asked him to record diligently all those things which he thought were necessary and which were lacking in the writings of the others. So without delay, he published the matter directly, thinking it would be shameful for many to experience such a great loss because of a little laziness. So this is why he wished to write a gospel, and why he proclaimed the doctrine about Christ's divinity from the beginning, seeing that such a beginning was quite fitting for the teaching of the gospel. Thus he approached the incarnation of the Lord who came in the flesh, while also discussing the baptism of John. He was convinced that there is no truer beginning than this one for these things that happened and were reported at the coming of the Lord in the flesh. . . .

Now he also published those things that were left out by the others. He alone mentions Christ's coming to the wedding feast and clearly says that this was the beginning of the signs. And nearly all of the teachings John mentions are left out by the other evangelists. The same thing is true in regard to Christ's miracles. If he does mention somewhere a sign which those other evangelists had also recollected, it is because he remembers in every way the usefulness of the action. For example, he remembers the sign that the bread from five loaves of bread satisfied five thousand men, *besides women and children* (Matt 14:21). The same sign was also remembered by those other evangelists, but John also had to record the doctrine joined to it, for in doing so he approached the words of the Eucharistic mysteries. The occasion of these words was a miracle Christ performed, and John did not want to remember the teaching about the Eucharist without mentioning the miracle related to Christ's words.

In short, it would not be wrong to call the Gospel of the blessed John the perfection and completion of all that the other evangelists intended, even if lacking in their books. So John wrote what they had intended to say but had left out of their own writings. For this reason John was also very diligent about the order in which things happened, because none of the other evangelists were concerned about it. There is no time to say why they did so, but the other evangelists recorded many things as occurring first, although they happened afterwards. And they recorded other things as happening later, although they were first. Anyone can discover this if you read their books carefully. . . . The blessed John took great pains to record first those events which happened first and after them the events which came later, along with the rest of the matters that occurred. Even so, he left out many things in the middle, so long as it was said by those other evangelists.

(13) Sophronius of Jerusalem

John, **the beloved disciple** (13:23), was the son of Zebedee and the brother of James, who was beheaded by Herod after the passion of the Lord (cf. Acts 12:1–2). John was the last of the evangelists to write a gospel. At the request of the bishops of Asia, he wrote his gospel to combat the teachings of Cerinthus[5] and other heretics, and especially the newly appeared doctrine of the Ebionites,[6] who claimed that Christ did not exist until Mary gave birth to Him. This prompted John to expound on Christ's divine generation.

There is another reason why he wrote. After examining the Gospels of Matthew, Mark, and Luke from the beginning to end, John confirmed that they had recorded the truth (in contrast to authors of the other, so-called gospels then in circulation). Then he composed his own gospel, focusing on the final year of the Lord's earthly ministry and on his passion. John omitted most of the events of the previous two years because these had already been faithfully recorded by Matthew, Mark, and Luke. A careful study of the four gospels will resolve the apparent discrepancies between John's narrative and the narratives of the other three evangelists.

(14) John Scotus Eriugena

O blessed John, it is with good reason that you were called John. The name John is Hebrew, but translated into Greek and Latin it means "to whom it has been given." Who among theologians has been given what has been given to you? Clearly you are able to penetrate the hidden mysteries of the highest good and to recount to the human mind and senses what was revealed and declared to you. Tell me, I pray, who else was given such a great grace as this?

Perhaps someone will say such a grace was given to the head of the apostles, I mean Peter, who, when the Lord asked him whom he thought he was, responded, *You art the Christ, the Son of the living God* (Matt 16:16). However, it would not be rash, I think, to say that Peter spoke this way more as an example of faith and action than of knowledge and contemplation. Obviously Peter is always presented as a model of faith and action, while John resembles an example of contemplation and knowledge. Indeed, John lies **close to the breast** of the Lord (13:23), which is the mystery of contemplation, while Peter often falters, which is the symbol of hasty action.

In fact, carrying out divine commands, before making them a habit, may destroy the pure splendor of virtue and in time be deceived in its judgment, darkened by the fog of earthly thinking. The perceptiveness of inward contemplation, however, after it has perceived the appearance of the truth, is neither repelled, nor does it falter or become hidden in perpetual darkness.

---

5. Cerinthus was an early-second-century gnostic Christian in Asia Minor who attributed the created world to a lesser deity, and held that Christ was not fully divine.

6. The Ebionites were a form of Jewish Christianity that upheld the law of Moses and rejected the divinity of Christ.

Nevertheless, both apostles run to the tomb (cf. John 20). Christ's tomb is holy Scripture in which the profoundest mysteries of his divinity and humanity are secured as if by a stone. But John quickly runs ahead of Peter—for the power of contemplation which has been thoroughly purified penetrates the inner secrets of divine activity more sharply and more quickly than the power of action, which needs further purification.

Nevertheless, although both apostles run to the tomb and enter it, Peter enters first, and then John. If Peter symbolizes faith, then John signifies understanding. Therefore, since it is written, *If you do not believe, neither shall you understand* (Isa 7:9), faith necessarily enters the tomb of holy Scripture first followed by understanding, for which faith has prepared the entrance. . . .

We do not prefer John over Peter, we only compare contemplation to action—the soul perfectly purified compared to the soul still needing purification. We compare a virtue that has already arrived at an immutable state to a virtue still ascending there. We are not considering here the personal merit of each apostle, but only investigating the beautiful distinctions within the divine mysteries.

So Peter (that is, virtue in action) perceives, through the power of faith and action, the Son of God confined in flesh in a marvelous and ineffable manner. But John (that is, the highest contemplation of truth) marvels at the *Word* of God in itself, absolute and infinite in its beginning, that is, in the Father (cf. John 1:1–2).

Peter, led by divine revelation, observes eternity and time made one in Christ; but John alone leads the knowledge of faithful souls to Christ's eternity. Therefore, the spiritual bird, swift-flying, God-beholding—I mean John, the theologian—surpasses all visible and invisible creation, traverses all understanding, and having been deified, enters into God who deifies him.

O Blessed Paul, you were *caught up*, as you yourself claim, *to the third heaven* (2 Cor 12:2); but you were not caught up beyond every heaven. You were caught up *into Paradise* (2 Cor 12:3), but you were not caught up beyond every paradise. John, however, went beyond every heaven formed and every paradise created, that is, beyond every human and angelic nature.

In the *third heaven*, O instrument of election and teacher of the Gentiles, you heard words *that cannot be told, which man may not utter* (2 Cor 12:4). But John, the observer of the inmost truth, who went beyond every heaven into the paradise of paradises, into the very source of all things, heard the one **Word** through whom **all things are made** (1:3). He was allowed to speak this *Word*, and to proclaim it to human beings as far as it may be proclaimed. Therefore he cried out with confidence: **In the beginning was the Word** (1:1).

John 1

Of all the material in the Gospel of John, the first chapter received the most attention from ancient Christian writers. John's prologue offered rich material for discussing Trinitarian and Christological ideas, and the church fathers explored the first verse at length: In the beginning was the Word, and the Word was with God, and the Word was God *(1:1). Hilary of Poitiers and Gregory of Nyssa, for example, use that verse to explain the eternal and divine nature of the Word; and the Venerable Bede sees the opening verses of John's Gospel as an antidote to various heretical views of Christ.*

Several writers discuss the meaning of the word beginning. *After ruling out a variety of possible meanings, Origen of Alexandria cites the personification of Wisdom in Prov 8:22 ("God created me at the beginning of his ways for his work") to show that Wisdom was also in the beginning. John Chrysostom recognizes that the words* in the beginning, *and even the word* was, *have nothing to do with time. The verse is speaking about "eternal and unending existence." The key, says Chrysostom, is to understand the difference between human beings and God, between created things and uncreated things. The former always entails temporality; the latter indicates eternity. Because the opening words of John's Gospel speak about the* Word of God, *they necessarily indicate eternity. Moreover, whereas Gen 1:1 speaks explicitly about heaven and earth being "created," the evangelist in John 1 quite intentionally avoids speaking of the* Word as created *in the beginning.*

Theodore of Mopsuestia also has an extended discussion of the meaning of the word beginning, *arguing that while a beginning can refer to something that came into existence first, the Gospel of John implies something more; something can exist as beginning even when nothing else exists (such as a foundation of a house as a beginning even if there is no house yet). From this line of reasoning, Theodore argues that the phrase* in the beginning was the Word *does not mean "in his own beginning," but refers simply to the Word's eternal existence before all else. Since the* Word was *in the beginning, he was not simply the first of all created things, but rather, existed eternally, with no origin in time.*

Likewise, Cyril of Alexandria takes pains to explain why the term beginning *(1:1), when used in reference to the Word, does not refer to a spatial or temporal beginning. Cyril admits that while we often speak of a temporal* beginning, *the* beginning *in reference to the Word carries a different connotation. Because of the intimate connection between Father and Word, the eternal existence of the Father demands the eternal existence of his Word. To explain the possibility of the generation of one thing without the loss of eternal existence, Cyril uses the examples of the rays of the sun and heat from a fire. Though rays and heat derive their existence from a source, they nevertheless have always existed with their source. The same is true, explains Cyril, with the Father and the Son, his Word.*

*The second half of verse 1 (*and the Word was with God, and the Word was God*) also receives significant comment. For Tertullian, Theodore of Mopsuestia, Cyril of Alexandria, and John Chrysostom, the phrase* with God *(1:1) indicates that there are distinct persons within the unified Godhead. Because the* Word *was with God the Father, the Word must be distinguished from the Father as a separate person. Yet the next clause—*and the Word was God *(1:1)—shows that they equally share the essence of the Godhead. Origen of Alexandria compares the* Word *that was* with God *(1:1) to previous words of God that came to the prophets. The fundamental difference, according to Origen, is that while the prophets experienced God's word coming to be with them, the* Word *in John's Gospel was always* with God. *Moreover, the* Word's *existence* with God *indicates something about its essential nature: his being* with God *also means that he* was God. *With God indicates something about its essential nature: his being* with God *also means that he* was God.

Theodoret of Cyrus, Theodore of Mopsuestia, and Augustine of Hippo all offer a Christological interpretation of verse 3: all things were made through him. *When joined to the language of beginning in verse 1, the creation of all things by the Word indicates his eternal existence and shared essence with the Father. As Augustine says, if the Word was not part of the created order, then he must be God, for "every substance that is not God is a creature, and that which is not a creature is God."*

Verse 4, In him was life, and the life was the light of men *leads John Chrysostom to a consideration of God's undiminished reality, just as light is undiminished by illuminating countless objects. Augustine of Hippo sees this verse as speaking of our need for participation in the Word, who is light. That participation happens, according to Augustine, through the incarnation, so that, in words reminiscent of the Eastern doctrine of theosis, by "becoming a partaker of our mortality Christ made us partakers of his divinity."*

*Against those who reject the prophetic predictions of Christ's coming, Origen of Alexandria uses verse 7 (*He came for testimony, to bear witness to the light*) to explain both the prophetic role of John the Baptist and the countless prophets who came before Christ. As Origen explains, "if you deny the prophets' testimony about Christ, you deprive the prophetic chorus their greatest gift."*

Theodore of Mopsuestia and Augustine of Hippo explore the distinction between John the Baptist as a light and Christ, the true light *(1:9). Theodore sees the work of John as lasting only a time, while Christ's enlightening is eternal. And Augustine recognizes that the Baptist can only be called a light because he was first enlightened by the* true light *(1:9) of Christ.*

The notion of becoming children of God *(1:12) leads Augustine to a moving discussion of adoption, noting that while human couples may rejoice over an only son who will gain their inheritance, God deigned to send his only Son so that he might secure countless adopted children who would share in the inheritance with Christ. Cyril of Alexandria and Leo the Great likewise marvel at the blessing of the incarnation wherein, as Leo says, "Sinfulness returns to innocence and our old nature becomes new; strangers receive adoption and foreigners enter into an inheritance!"*

Verse 14 (And the Word became flesh and dwelt among us) *leads several thinkers to consider the dual nature of Christ and the meaning of the word* became. *Novatian, Theodore of Mopsuestia, John Chrysostom, Augustine of Hippo, and Leo the Great all agree that the incarnation entailed no change to the divine essence; instead the Word assumed, or took on, human flesh without losing his divinity. Chrysostom offers the analogy of a king who converses with a poor beggar. The king's condescension does not diminish the royal glory but instead elevates the poor beggar's dignity. The same is true with Christ who did not change into flesh, but assumed flesh without changing his essence. Augustine makes a comparison to our acts of speech wherein a thought is communicated to physical ears through sensible sounds and yet remains unchanged in its essential nature.*

Several church fathers underscore the salvific consequences of the incarnation for humankind. Hilary of Poitiers, Jerome, Augustine of Hippo, and the Venerable Bede all proclaim that because God the Word descended to take on human flesh, human beings now have salvation by being drawn into the life of God. Jerome, for example, suggests that the Word became flesh "so that we might cross over from the flesh into the Word." And Augustine sees the incarnation as teaching that if the Son of God became a son of man for our sake, how much more will we be made children of God by his grace?

Both John Chrysostom and Augustine explore the meaning of the phrase grace upon grace *(1:16). Chrysostom suggests that the Israelites, too, were saved by grace in forgiveness of sins and in God's giving the law, but now Christians receive even more—grace upon grace—in the gift of the Spirit. Augustine explores that theme of abundant grace with a lengthy discussion of the grace of faith and eternal life given by God without any obligation on his part or any merit on ours.*

Verses 17–18 compel interpreters to explain the meaning of terms such as law *and* grace. *Augustine explains how the law works only to demonstrate and convict us of sin so as to prepare us for the grace that comes in Christ. Likewise, the Venerable Bede contrasts the work of the law with that of grace. Finally, Cyril of Alexandria suggests that grace did come through the law; yet what Christ brings is far superior in its ability to impart the fullness of the truth, leading Cyril to compare the positive aspects of the law with the superiority of the spiritual grace brought by Christ.*

In John 1:19–25, John the Baptist interacts with the messengers from the priests, Levites, and Pharisees. This leads Origen of Alexandria to explore why the Baptist answers the way he does in response to their questions about his identity. In particular, Origen explains why John said he was not the prophet *(1:21) when it seems clear that he was, indeed, a prophet. Origen solves the problem with a discussion of the difference between "a prophet" (which John was) and "the prophet" of Deut 18 (which John was not). Likewise, both Augustine and Gregory the Great explore a similar puzzle in the text: Why does John deny that he is Elijah when elsewhere Jesus says that John was, in fact, Elijah (Matt 11:14)? Using Luke 1:17 as the interpretive key, they conclude that the Baptist came in "the spirit of Elijah" but not in his body. So what John denied about his body, Jesus affirmed about his spirit. In his role as forerunner, John is Elijah metaphorically. But literally, in the body, he was not.*

Gregory the Great sees John's ministry of baptism (1:25–34) as a forerunner to the Christian sacrament of baptism (v. 26). John's comments about Christ's sandal (v. 27) are interpreted as a model of the virtue of humility. Augustine discusses the efficacy and temporary nature of John's baptism, explaining that it was only a preparation for Christ; once Christ has come there is no longer a need for John's baptism to continue (vv. 31–35).

The Baptist's declaration that Jesus was the Lamb of God *in 1:29 and 1:35 becomes rich material for Christian commentary on Christ's role as a sacrificial lamb. Some compare the ancient sacrificial system to Christ (Origen, Chrysostom, Leo, and Bede). Others explore the efficacy of Christ's sacrificial death (Augustine and Cyril). Still others examine the literary and theological connections between Christ, the lamb, and the predicted sacrificial lamb of Isaiah 53 (Origen, Cyril, Mopsuestia, and Leo).*

Near the end of the chapter, the changing of Simon's name to Peter *(rock)—verse 42— prompts Augustine to discuss the need for Christians to build their lives on the "rock" of the church through hearing the word and acting upon it. The renaming of Peter, says Augustine, is intended to get listeners to understand the need for hearing combined with action. Finally, Nathanael's encounter with Christ in verses 43–51 leads Augustine toward an allegorical interpretation: Nathanael represents the church, and the fig tree represents the sins under which we all sat before being brought to Christ.*

John 1:1–18

[1]In the beginning was the Word, and the Word was with God, and the Word was God. [2]He was in the beginning with God; [3]all things were made through him, and without him was not anything made that was made. [4]In him was life, and the life was the light of men. [5]The light shines in the darkness, and the darkness has not overcome it. [6]There was a man sent from God, whose name was John. [7]He came for testimony, to bear witness to the light, that all might believe through him. [8]He was not the light, but came to bear witness to the light. [9]The true light that enlightens every man was coming into the world. [10]He was in the world, and the world was made through him, yet the world knew him not. [11]He came to his own home, and his own people received him not. [12]But to all who received him, who believed in his name, he gave power to become children of God; [13]who were born, not of blood nor of the will of the flesh nor of the will of man, but of God. [14]And the Word became flesh and dwelt among us, full of grace and truth; we have beheld his glory, glory as of the only Son from the Father. [15](John bore witness to him, and cried, "This was he of whom I said, 'He who comes after me ranks before me, for he was before me.'") [16]And from his fulness have we all received, grace upon grace. [17]For the law was given through Moses; grace and truth came through Jesus Christ. [18]No one has ever seen God; the only Son, who is in the bosom of the Father, he has made him known.

1:1–2 In the beginning was the Word, and the Word was with God, and the Word was God. He was in the beginning with God.

---

(1) Tertullian of Carthage

If we understand these words simply as they are written, undoubtedly there is one who exists from **the beginning** and another **with** whom he existed—one is the **Word** of God; the other is **God.** Of course the **Word** *is* **God**, but only as the Son of God, not as the Father. It is **through** one (the Word) that **all things were made**; it is by the other (God) that **all things were made** (1:3). We have often discussed the sense in which we call the **Word** "another." By calling him "another" we must understand that he is not identical with the Father; indeed, he is not identical, yet not separate either. He is "another" by relationship, not by division. Therefore, he who **became flesh** (1:14) is not the same as the one from whom the **Word** came.

(2) Origen of Alexandria

The Greeks are not the only ones who say that the word **beginning** (1:1) has many meanings. If anyone should pay attention to this word—gathering texts from everywhere and examining them carefully—and desires to understand an explanation for it in each place in Scripture, he will find even in the divine writings a multitude of meanings. . . .

Although many meanings occur to us in our present investigation of the word **beginning**, let us see how we ought to understand the phrase **In the beginning was the word** (1:1). It is obvious that we should not understand it as meaning a change, as in speaking of a progression or measurement of time, for example in the passage, *The beginning of a good way is to do justice* (Prov 16:7 LXX). . . . So it cannot mean progression or measurement in that sense. And for that reason **beginning** here does not have to do with the beginning of things at creation.

It is possible that it refers to the means by which God acted, since *he commanded and they were created* (Ps 148:5). Perhaps Christ is the Creator to whom the Father said, *Let there be light* (Gen 1:3) and *Let there be a firmament* (Gen 1:6). For as the **beginning**, Christ is the Creator, by which he is also Wisdom. As Wisdom he is also called **beginning**, for Wisdom says in Solomon: *God created me at the beginning of his ways for his work* (Prov 8:22) so that **the Word** might be **in the beginning** (1:1), that is, in Wisdom. . . .

In general it is proper to say that the Son of God is the **beginning** of things that exist since he says, *I am the beginning and the end, the Alpha and the Omega, the first and the last* (Rev 22:13). Nevertheless, we need to understand that he is not the **beginning** of everything by which he is named. For how can he be the **beginning** if he is the Life which was in the **Word**, and if the **Word** clearly is the **beginning** of life itself? It is even clearer that since as he is *the first-born from the dead* (Col 1:18), he cannot be the **beginning**. If, then, we should examine carefully all the meanings applied to him, he is the **beginning** only in regards to his being Wisdom. He is not even **beginning** in regards to his being the Word since **in the**

beginning was the Word (1:1). As someone might boldly say: Wisdom is older than all the meanings in the names of the *first-born of all creation* (Col 1:15). . . .

Since then it was our intention to see clearly the meaning of the phrase **In the beginning was the word** (1:1), and Proverbs bears witness to *Wisdom* (8:22), and Wisdom is understood as preceding the **Word** which announces it, we understand that the **Word in the beginning** (1:1) is always in Wisdom. Being in Wisdom, which is called *beginning* (Prov 8:22), does not prevent the **Word** from being **with God** (1:1) and being **God** himself. It is not merely that the **Word was with God**, but that he was **with God** in Wisdom, that is, **in the beginning**.

(3) Origen of Alexandria

Let us now examine the meaning of the phrase **the Word was with God** (1:1). It is helpful to compare this **Word** with the "word" which is said to have come to certain individuals, such as: *The word of the Lord which came to Hosea, the son of Beeri* (Hos 1:1), and *The word came to Isaiah the son of Amoz concerning Judah and Jerusalem* (Isa 2:1), and *The word which came to Jeremiah concerning the drought* (Jer 14:1). . . .

On the one hand, the **Word** comes to be **with** those men who previously did not experience the coming of the Son of God, who is the **Word**. On the other hand, that **Word** does not come to be **with God** as if he were not with him previously. Rather, he is said always to exist with the Father: **And the Word was with God**, not "he came to be" **with God**. This verb **was** is applied to the **Word** when he *was* **in the beginning** and **he** *was* **with God**, not being separated from the **beginning**, nor departing from the Father. Likewise, he does not come to be **in the beginning** from non-existence, nor does he come to be **with God** from not being **with God**, for before all ages, **In the beginning was the Word, and the Word was with God**.

So to discover the meaning of the phrase **the Word was with God**, we compared prophetical texts which spoke about the **word** coming to Hosea, Isaiah, and Jeremiah. And we observed the clear difference between "he has come to be" or "he came to be" compared to he **was**. We will now add that in coming to the prophets, the **Word** enlightens them with the light of knowledge, causing them to see things clearly which they were unable to perceive beforehand. In being **with God** (1:1), however, and because he is **with God**, the **Word** *is* **God** (1:1).

Perhaps John sees a similar logic in his argument and did not place **the Word was God** before **the Word was with God**, so that we might not be prevented from seeing the force of each of the propositions in the series as they are asserted. The first was **In the beginning was the Word**, the second was **the Word was with God**, and then **the Word was God**. Obviously the propositions indicate some order: first **In the beginning was the Word**, then **the Word was with God**, and thirdly **the Word was God**. The reason is so that we might understand that the **Word is God** by his being **with God**, as it says: **the Word was with God**, followed by **the Word was God**.

(4) Hilary of Poitiers

The evangelist says: **In the beginning was the Word** (1:1). What does it mean: **in the beginning was**? Time fades, centuries become part of the past, and the ages give way. Imagine any kind of **beginning** in your mind; you cannot place it in time, for the one we are discussing **was**, that is, existed. Look to the world and understand what is written about it: *In the beginning God created the heavens and the earth* (Gen 1:1). Therefore, **in the beginning**, that which is created came into being, and you establish a time for that which came into being **in the beginning**. Yet my illiterate, unschooled fisherman[1] is freed from the centuries, freed from time. He conquers every **beginning**: for there **was** that which *is*! It is not constrained by time; it did not begin; it did not come into being **in the beginning**. It simply **was**. . . .

He also says: **and the Word was God** (1:1). The sound of voice and the eloquence of thought cease. This **Word** is an entity, not a sound; a nature, not speech; God, not emptiness. But I tremble to say it, the insolent speech disturbs me. I hear: **and the Word was God** (1:1)—I, to whom the prophets have proclaimed that God is one (cf. Deut 6:4). But lest my misgivings increase any further, explain this great mystery, my fisherman! Refer all things to the one God without insult, without abrogation, without time. . . . That which he was, he could not have ceased to be: for he **was** implies being beyond time. What does the fisherman say for himself? **all things were made through him** (1:3). Therefore, if nothing exists without the one **through whom all things** began, then he, **through whom all things were made**, is infinite. For time is a demonstrable and measured extension—not in space but in duration. And since **all things** come from him, nothing exists apart from him. Therefore time itself also comes from him.

(5) Gregory of Nyssa

The apostle says that the Son *bears the very stamp of the Father's nature* (Heb 1:3). It is clear that the *stamp of the Father's nature* is just as great as the Father's nature itself, for it is impossible for the *stamp* to be lesser than the *nature* discerned in it. The great John also teaches the same thing when he says **In the beginning was the Word, and the Word was with God** (1:1). By saying that he was *in* the beginning, and not *after* the beginning, John shows us that **the beginning** was never without **the Word**. By demonstrating that the **Word was with God** (1:1), he indicates that the Son lacks nothing that belongs to the Father. The **Word** is contemplated as a whole, along **with** the whole being of **God**. If the **Word** had lacked something in his own magnitude, so that it were not possible for him to be completely **with God**, then we would have to believe that the part of God which extends beyond **the Word** would be without **the Word**. In truth, the entire magnitude of **the Word** is contemplated along with the entire magnitude of God. There is no place for speaking of "greater" or "lesser" things in regards to the doctrine of God.

1. John the evangelist.

(6) John Chrysostom

In the beginning was the Word, and the Word was with God (1:1). All the other evangelists begin their gospels with the unfolding of the divine plan. Matthew says, *The book of the genealogy of Jesus Christ, the son of David* (Matt 1:1); Luke begins his narrative for us with the account of Mary; and in the same way Mark focuses on similar things, recounting the history of the Baptist. John hints at these things briefly, but only later, when he said **the Word became flesh** (John 1:14). He passes by everything else—Christ's conception, his birth, his upbringing, his growth—and immediately describes for us his eternal generation. Why?

Here's why. Because the other evangelists focused chiefly on matters of Christ's humanity, John was concerned that because of these narratives some debased people might dwell on these matters alone. That is what happened with Paul of Samosata.[2] By steering away from such earthly things those who might stumble, and drawing them up to heaven, the evangelist appropriately begins his narrative from above, from the **Word**'s eternal existence. So while Matthew begins his narrative with King Herod, Luke with Tiberius Caesar, and Mark with the baptism of John, this evangelist omits all these events and ascends beyond all time and age. There he propels the minds of his listeners to the words **in the beginning** (1:1) and doesn't allow them to rest there, nor does he set any historical limit, as the others did with Herod, Tiberius, and John the Baptist.

Beyond these things, there is something else worthy of admiration: although John was fully engaged with a more exalted subject matter, he did not neglect the incarnation. And while the others were eager to describe the incarnation, they too weren't silent about his eternal nature. This is very appropriate, for one Spirit moved the souls of each evangelist, and they display much agreement in their narratives. But you, my beloved, when you hear **the Word**, never put up with those who say that he is something created, or with those who think that he is simply a "word." For there are many "words" of God which the angels perform; none of those "words" are God. They are all prophecies or commands, for in Scripture it is customary to call the laws of God—his commands and prophecies—"words" of God. This is why Scripture speaks of angels, saying, *You mighty ones who do his word* (Ps 103:20). This **Word**, however, is a being with substance, proceeding unchanged from the Father himself. As I have said before, he made this clear by the use of the term **Word**.

(7) John Chrysostom

Coming to **the beginning** (1:1) we seek to understand what kind of **beginning**. Then we discover the word **was** (1:1) and it always overwhelms our mind, because it gives us nothing on which to fix our thoughts. Always looking to what lies beyond, it is never able to stop; it becomes exhausted and turns again to things below. **In the beginning was** (1:1) means nothing other than eternal and unending existence. Do you grasp the truth of this philosophy and divine teaching, unlike that of the Greeks who fix times and say that some of the gods

---

2. Paul of Samosata was a third-century bishop of Antioch who reportedly denied the Son's preexistence in favor of emphasizing Jesus's ordinary humanity. His teaching was condemned at synods in 264 and 268.

are older and some younger? Nothing like this comes to us. For if God exists, as indeed he does, there is nothing before him. If he is the Creator of all, he is the first. If he is the Lord and master of all, all things come after him, both creatures and ages. . . .

What am I saying then? That the first **was**, used of **the Word** (1:1), signifies eternal existence alone, for it says **In the beginning was the Word** (1:1). And the second **was** (1:1)[3] signifies a particular existence. Since being eternal and without beginning belongs most to God himself, that is put first; then, so that someone might not hear **In the beginning** (1:1) and say that the **Word** was unbegotten, he immediately remedies this: before he says what he is, he says that he **was with God** (1:1). So that no one would think that **the Word** is simply the same as something spoken and thought, he adds the definite article . . . in addition to introducing the second clause. For he does not say "he was *in* God," but he **was with God** (1:1), revealing to us the eternity of his person. Then, as he proceeds, he reveals it more clearly by adding **and the Word was God** (1:1).

Someone might say that the Word had been created. But what prevented the evangelist from saying, "In the beginning God *created* the Word"? When Moses spoke about the earth he did not say, "In the beginning was the earth," but that *God created* it, and then it **was**. What then prevented John from saying that "In the beginning God *created* the Word"? If Moses was afraid that someone might say that the earth was uncreated, how much more ought John to fear the same thing about the Son, if he was indeed created? . . .

Just as the phrase **In the beginning was the Word** demonstrates his eternity, so also the phrase **He was in the beginning with God** (1:2) has declared to us his co-eternity with the Father. So when you hear **In the beginning was the Word** (1:1), he then adds **He was in the beginning with God** (1:2) so that you won't think that **the Word** is eternal but suspect that the life of the Father is older by some greater interval of time, ascribing a beginning to the only-begotten. The **Word** is eternal just as the Father himself is eternal. The Father was never devoid of his **Word**, but was always God **with God**, yet each in his own person.

"How then," someone might ask, "can the evangelist say that the Word was **in the world** (1:10) if he was **with God**?" (1:2). Because he was both **with God** and also **in the world**. Neither the Father nor the Son are limited in any way. For if *his greatness has no limit* (Ps 145:3 [144:3 LXX]) and *his understanding is beyond measure* (Ps 147:5 [146:5 LXX]), it's obvious that his essence has no beginning in time. You have heard that *In the beginning God created the heavens and the earth* (Gen 1:1). What do you think this *beginning* is? Obviously that the heavens and earth were created before all visible things. So in the same way, when you hear that the only-begotten was **in the beginning** (1:2), understand him to exist before all things intellectual and before all ages.

But if someone should say, "How is it that he can be a Son and yet not younger than the Father, since that which proceeds from something else must necessarily be later than that from which it proceeds?" Remember that these notions are most certainly human ways of thinking. Whoever seeks answers on these matters will seek answers for other questions even more absurd. We shouldn't even give an ear to such queries, for our homily concerns God, not the nature of humanity which is subject to the common sequence and laws of

---

3. Chrysostom is referring to the clause **and the word *was* with God.**

nature concerning these notions. Nevertheless, in order to assure the weaker-minded, let me address these concerns.

Tell me, do the sun's rays shine forth from the substance of the sun or from something else? Anyone in their right mind has to confess that it's from the substance itself. And yet, although the rays of the sun shine forth from the sun itself, we wouldn't say that they come later in time than the substance of the sun, since the sun has never appeared without its rays. So then, if with visible and sensible bodies there are things that proceed from something and yet are not later in time than the thing from which they proceeded, why don't you believe the same for the invisible and ineffable nature? The same thing is true here, in a manner appropriate to its essence. For this reason Paul calls him this as well, presenting him as from the Father and co-eternal with him (cf. Heb 1:3). What else, tell me? Were not all the ages and every interval of time made through him? Anyone in their right mind must confess this. Therefore nothing exists between the Son and the Father, and if nothing, then the Son is not later than the Father, but co-eternal. The words "before" and "after" are obviously notions of time, since without ages or time no one would even be able to contemplate these words. But God is beyond time and ages.

Moreover, if you really say that you have discovered a beginning for the Son, see whether your logic and line of reasoning doesn't require you to reduce the Father to a beginning as well—an older beginning to be sure, but a beginning nonetheless. Tell me, when you have assigned some limit and beginning to the Son, would you not proceed upward from him and say that the Father was "before" him? It's quite clear that you would. Tell me, then, what was the duration of the Father's existence beforehand? Whether you say it was of little or of great duration, you have still reduced the Father to a beginning. Obviously, when you measure the distance between them, whether you say it's a little or a lot, it wouldn't be possible to measure it unless there was a beginning on each side. And so I have come to the conclusion of your argument: you have given the Father a beginning as well; not even the Father is without a beginning! Don't you see that what the Savior said is true, and the force of his saying is found everywhere? What does he say? *He who does not honor the Son does not honor the Father* (5:23).

(8) Theodore of Mopsuestia

In the beginning was the Word (1:1). In my opinion, there is nothing wrong with saying that the blessed evangelist John was unfamiliar with the power of this utterance when Jesus spoke it,[4] but that he taught it later, after he understood its meaning. In fact, in my opinion, the significance of these words is not only beyond anyone's grasp, but also exalted above all human nature. Not only was John able to understand the essence of **the Word**, but he was also able to speak about what he understood. He could speak succinctly about the incomprehensible essence of God **the Word**, whereas another person would be unable, even with ten thousand words, to express what he understood.

So whenever I consider these words, I am always amazed at how the heretics strive against all of this grandeur. To me the one who stubbornly resists these words is taken up

---

4. Theodore seems to think that Jesus spoke these words directly to John during his earthly life.

with the "wisdom" of the Greek philosophers who seek to abolish all of the teachings and religions existing among humans. . . .

Let us consider the word **beginning**. But before doing so let me describe the way human beings ordinarily use the word. We say that **the beginning** refers to something that exists before others; the word **beginning** comes second to nothing, for if it came after something else, it would not be first. And if it is not first, it is certainly not the **beginning**!

However, if you want to investigate more deeply, you will find that this term **beginning** refers to something more than merely that which comes first. A thing can be "first" even if it cannot be called a **beginning** (as in a case where it would not be accurate to describe it as a **beginning**). Yet, the word "first" is connected to the word **beginning** in every way—unless someone inappropriately calls the thing that is first a **beginning**. So by mentioning the word "first," we understand the word **beginning**, and see that the word "first" is connected to the word **beginning** in every way because a **beginning** is "first." . . .

So what am I trying to say by this line of argument? That once we look into it carefully, the word **beginning** entails *more* than the word "first." We understand that the word "first" means that something comes after it. A **beginning**, too, is the **beginning** of something, but we also know that it is not necessarily called a **beginning** because of what follows. Instead, it was the **beginning** even when those things coming after it, which would call it their **beginning**, had not occurred. Again, we accurately call it "first" when something follows after it. And a **beginning** is called "first" as well, but can also exist before those things which came afterward, whose **beginning** it is said to be. . . .

In this way we also call the **beginning** of a house the foundation because the house begins to be built from no other place except its foundation. No house is built if there is no foundation. Now even though the foundation is built because of the house, it nevertheless exists before the house is built. In the same way we also say that Adam is the **beginning** of human beings because there was no one from the human race before him. Adam existed when no one else had been created. Therefore according to the common use of sensible people, the **beginning** refers to what is "first" in itself, not to what is "first" by construction or designation. . . .

Those surprising heretics disregard all of this—both the customary usage of all the sages . . . and what's even more important, the common practice of Scripture. They deceive many with their profane arguments, saying that **in the beginning** means "in *his own* beginning," as one who has an origin. Meanwhile, they do not understand what a great difference there is between "he **was**" and "he **had**," that is, how opposed they are to each other. If he *had* an origin, he was not **in the beginning**. But if he *was* **in the beginning**, he has no origin. It is not hard to see how exceedingly foolish their argument is, because none of the things which came into existence from non-existence can be said to be present at their own **beginning**. . . .

(9) Theodore of Mopsuestia

The evangelist quite accurately said, not **the Word** "of God," but simply **the Word**. He knew well that both God's command and the servant who acts according to God's will are called "word of God," as in the case of the prophets: "The word of God came upon so and so." This word of God is a revelation given to them by God's will so they can proclaim the word. In the same way the apostle says, *The word of God which was preached to you by us* (2 Cor 1:19), referring to his proclamation. And in another place he says, *The word of the cross is folly to those who are perishing* (1 Cor 1:18), referring to the preaching of the cross. . . .

So when divine Scripture speaks about the word of God, it does not speak about it indefinitely. Whether Scripture says the word of God, the word of the Lord, the word of the cross, or the word which was sent, it also qualifies each "word" by adding another phrase. But here the blessed John calls him simply, **the Word**. In short, then, when someone asks, "Why does he call him **the Word**?" we say this: Scripture does not always use the term **Word** in reference to a person; however, here it does use the term **Word** in reference to a person—the Son—without addition or qualification, simply and unambiguously identifying him this way.

But when some try to explain the reason why he was called **Word**, they aver that it is meant figuratively. By God's help we have clearly shown[5] that he was not designated **Word** in the sense they argued. What then should we say? To us, word has a twofold meaning. It includes both what is spoken with the voice by our tongue, and what resides secretly in our mind (what we say is implanted in our rational soul or what is natural to it). However, we are not arguing about the meaning of this term. This word is from the soul and is known to be always with it. An example will clear up the uncertainty for us: we see that this word in the soul is never cut off, divided, or separated from it in time. Rather, the word is always with and in the soul. How much more appropriate is it to believe that it is possible for the Son to come from the Father without being cut off or separated from him. Nor did he receive his existence in time, but rather he is always with him and beside him. Since there is no time between them, the Son is ever with the Father, and the Father is his only source. In his essence the Son is with the Father and united to him. . . .

When the evangelist said **In the beginning was the Word** (1:1a), he sufficiently explained the essence of his nature. Then he called him **Word** by example and dispelled any uncertainty. Finally, in that passage where he said **He was in the beginning** (1:2), he demonstrated that he was not without a source, but that in essence he is eternally with his source.[6] He does this by joining the first statement with another: **and the Word was with God** (1:1); that is, he was with him, beside him, and united to him. This was what he wanted to say by, **the Word was with God**. While he said that he was **in the beginning**, he clearly demonstrated that he was not without a source, but that he was with his source in essence. And to the phrase **was with God**, he adds **and the Word was God** (1:1). He did not say he **was God** before saying he **was with God**. Rather, after saying he **was with God** he then adds that he **was God**, meaning this: he was the same nature as the one whom he **was with**. This statement is quite similar to what the apostle says: after he calls him *the reflection of his glory*, he adds, *and the very stamp of his nature* (Heb 1:3), affirming their perfect similarity while also avoiding the notion that there is no difference.

---

5. In an earlier passage not presented here.

6. Theodore is saying that although the Word was begotten of the Father, and therefore has a "source," the Word nevertheless eternally exists with his "source," the Father.

(10) Augustine of Hippo

I dare say, my brothers and sisters, that perhaps not even John spoke about the full reality of what is, only that which he was able. After all, he spoke as a man about God, and even though inspired by God, he was still a man. Because he was inspired, he spoke; if he had not been inspired he would have remained silent. Since he was a human being, even though inspired, he did not say everything, but only what he could say as a human being. This John, you see, my dearest brothers and sisters, was one of those mountains of which it is written: *May the mountains receive peace for your people and the hills justice* (Ps 72:3). . . .

So then, brothers and sisters, John was one of these *mountains*, and he said, **In the beginning was the Word, and the Word was with God, and the Word was God** (1:1). This mountain had received peace, and he was contemplating the divinity of the Word. What was this mountain like? How high was it? It had soared above all the peaks of the earth, soared beyond all the plains of the air, soared beyond the dizzy heights of the stars, and soared beyond all the choirs and legions of the angels. For, unless he soared above and beyond all these created things, he would never reach the one **through whom all things were made** (1:3). You can only have a sense of all that he surpassed if you notice where he ended up. . . . Are you asking about heaven and earth? They were created. Are you asking about the things in heaven and on earth? Obviously, even more clearly, they were created. Are you asking about spiritual creatures, about angels, archangels, thrones, dominions, powers, and princedoms (cf. Col 1:16)? They too were created. In fact, once the psalm listed all these things, it finished in this way: *He spoke and they were made; he gave the command, and they were created* (Ps 148:5 Vulgate). If *he spoke and they were made*, then they were made through **the Word**; but if they were made through **the Word**, then the only way John's heart could have arrived at what he said—**In the beginning was the Word, and the Word was with God, and the Word was God** (1:1)—was by soaring above all the things that were created through **the Word**. . . .

So then, our hope is to be placed in the one from whom the *mountains* receive. When we lift up our eyes to the Scriptures, because the Scriptures have been provided by human beings, we are lifting up our eyes to the *mountains* from where our help will come (cf. Ps 121:1–2). Even so, because those who wrote the Scriptures were human beings, they were not shining on their own; but Christ **was the true light who enlightens everyone coming into this world** (1:9).

(11) Cyril of Alexandria

It is not possible to understand the word **beginning** altogether as a temporal reference for the **only Son** (1:18), since he is before all time and has his existence before eternity; in these matters the divine nature refuses to be delimited by an end. According to what is sung in the psalms, he will always remain the same: *But thou art the same, and thy years have no end* (Ps 102:27).[7] From what temporal or spatial **beginning** would we understand

---

7. Cyril takes the psalm to refer to Christ, the Word of God.

the Son to proceed? He did not start at a beginning and move toward an end, because he is indeed God by nature, and for this reason cries out, *I am the life* (14:6). **Beginning** itself would never think to exist entirely in itself, failing to look toward its proper end. Just as the **beginning** is named in reference to the end, so also the end is named in reference to the **beginning**. But, again, in these matters we would be talking about a **beginning** which is in fact a quantity relating to time. Therefore, since the Son is more ancient than eternity itself, he will escape being born in time. He was always in the Father as in his source, as he himself said: *I came from the Father and have come* (16:28). Therefore, with the Father being understood as his source, **the Word** was in him, being his wisdom, power, character, reflection, and the image of his being. If there was no time[8] when the Father was without his **Word**, wisdom, character, and reflection, then we ought to confess that the Son, who is these very things to the eternal Father, is also everlasting. For how is he the perfect character and *very stamp* of the Father (cf. Heb 1:3) unless he is formed after that beauty, whose image he is?

There is absolutely nothing wrong with thinking that the Son is in the Father as in a source; for the name "source" here only signifies "out of which." But the Son is in the Father and from the Father. He was not created externally or in time, but exists in the very substance of the Father's being, shining forth from him like the sun's reflection or like natural heat from a fire. In such examples, it is possible to see one thing begotten from another, but at the same time ever co-existent and united with its source. The one is unable to exist in itself and preserve the true principle of its own nature apart from the other. How can the sun ever exist without its reflection? How can the reflection exist without the sun reflecting within itself? How too can there be fire if it does not have heat? And where does the heat come from except from the fire or from something else resembling fire in its essential quality? Therefore, as with these examples, one thing participating in another does not preclude their co-existence; instead, it demonstrates that a generated entity is always united with that which generated it, possessing one nature with its source. The same is true with the Son. Even if he is understood to be in the Father and from the Father, the Son will not come before us as a foreign or strange entity who exists as a secondary being to the Father; rather, he exists in the Father, eternally co-existent, and shining forth from him according to the ineffable manner of divine generation. . . .

Observe the thoughtfulness of John who is filled with the Spirit. He had just taught that **In the beginning was the Word** (that is, "in God the Father," as we have said). In all likelihood, however, his enlightened eye of understanding perceived well that some, out of great ignorance, would say that the Father and the Son are one and the same. They would distinguish the Holy Trinity in name only, but not allow them to exist in their specific persons. As a result, they do not understand that the Father is the Father and not the Son, nor that the Son is the Son alone and not the Father (as the word of truth teaches).[9] It was necessary, then, for the evangelist to be prepared to conquer and destroy this argument,

---

8. Arius, whose teaching was condemned at the Council of Nicea, was known for the slogan: "There was [a time] when he [the Word] was not."

9. Cyril is speaking against modalism, which sees the Father, Son, and Holy Spirit as all the same person, just in different forms.

one that he had heard in his time or was soon to hear. In addition to **In the beginning was the Word** he immediately adds, **and the Word was with God** (1:1), necessarily saying **was** because of his generation before time. Yet by saying **the Word was *with* God**, he shows that the Son is one, having existence by himself, and God the Father is another, whom **the Word was *with***. For how could that which is perfectly one in number be understood to exist **with** itself, or alongside itself? . . .

And the Word was God (1:1). Someone might resist the words of truth and question the holy evangelist, saying: **The Word was with God** (1:1)? So let it be; we agree with you about what has been written. Let the Father and the Son exist separately. What then should we think about the nature of **the Word**? Being **with God** does not fully reveal his essence. Since the divine Scriptures preach only one God, we will attribute the divine essence to the Father alone, whom **the Word was with**.

As if someone was already saying this, what then does the preacher of truth say in response? Not only that the **Word was with God** but that he **was God** (1:1). By being **with God** he might be known as another person alongside the Father, and the Son might be believed to be separate and distinct. By being **God**, he is understood both as having the same nature as the Father and as existing from him, as both being **God** and coming forth from **God**. It is inconceivable, with the Godhead being universally confessed as one, that the Holy Trinity should not have the same nature, and so bear the one nature as the one principle of Godhead. Therefore, he **was God** (1:1). He did not become so later on, but again, **he was**, if indeed being eternal necessarily follows from being God, since that which came into existence temporally, or was ever brought into existence from non-existence, would not be God by nature. Therefore, since **God the Word** is eternal by virtue of the word **was**, and of the same essence with the Father by virtue of being **God**, how much ought we to think that those who suppose that the Word is inferior in any way or even unlike the Father who begot him, be found liable of punishment and vengeance? They do not shudder to embark upon this impiety, already daring to speak to others such things *without understanding either what they are saying or the things about which they make assertions* (1 Tim 1:7).

(12) Venerable Bede

Marvelously, in the beginning of his gospel the blessed John both sublimely instructs us toward a proper faith for those who rightly believe in the divinity of the Savior, and also forcefully overpowers the faithlessness of heretics. For there were some heretics who said that if Christ was born, then there was a time when he did not exist.[10] John refutes them in the first verse when he says: **In the beginning was the Word** (1:1). Indeed, he did not say, "In the beginning the Word came to exist," because he intended to reveal clearly that the **Word** was begotten of the Father without any beginning in time; he was not begotten in time, but appeared before the emergence of time, as it says in Proverbs: *The Lord possessed me in the beginning of his ways, before he made anything from the beginning. I was appointed from eternity* (Prov 8:22–23 Vulgate).

---

10. Bede refers to Arius who was famous for the motto: "There was [a time] when he [the Word] was not."

In the same way, there were heretics who denied that there are three persons in the sacred Trinity, and say that the same God is Father when he wants, Son when he wants, and Holy Spirit when he wants, yet he is one.[11] Demolishing their error, John adds: **and the Word was with God** (1:1). For if one was **with** the other, surely the Father and the Son are two, not one. To say that God is in one instance the Father, in another the Son, and again in another the Holy Spirit, is equivalent to saying that the nature of the divine substance is changeable. Yet the apostle James plainly says: *with whom there is no variation or shadow due to change* (Jas 1:17).

Likewise there were some perpetrators of a perverse teaching who confessed that Christ was only a man, and did not believe that he was truly God.[12] John consequently crushes such thinking when he says: **and the Word was God** (1:1). There were others who at least thought that Christ was God, but that he was created at the time of the incarnation, and not eternally begotten from the Father before the ages. Of these, one is recalled to have said: "I don't envy Christ becoming God, because even I, if I wish, can become like him."[13] Again, the evangelist refutes this abominable opinion when he says: **He was in the beginning with God** (1:2). That is to say, this **Word**, which is **God**, did not begin in time, but **in the beginning** he was God, **with God**.

In the same way, there were enemies of the truth who did not deny that Christ already existed before he was born of the virgin; yet they did not believe that he was God, begotten of the Father. Rather, they believed that he was made by the Father, and therefore was less than the Father because he was a creature.[14] Our gospel passage condemns even these people when it says: **All things were made through him, and without him was not anything made that was made** (1:3). For if no creatures were made without him, surely it is obvious that the one through whom every creature was made, is himself not a creature.

1:3 All things were made through him, and without him was not anything made.

---

(13) Theodore of Mopsuestia

He was in the beginning with God and all things were made through him (1:2–3). The evangelist made this statement about him with good reason, distinguishing **him** from **all things made**. While **he was in the beginning with God**, all created things came **through him**. Clearly he makes a distinction by contrasting **he was in the beginning** with **all things**

11. Sabellius taught divine modalism, the idea that God was only one divine person who presented himself in three different modes or masks, as Father or Son or Holy Spirit.

12. Photinus ostensibly denied the divinity of Christ and taught that Christ was merely a man adopted by God.

13. A reference to an Adoptionist view like that of Paul of Samosata, who believed that the man Jesus was adopted as divine because of his perfection in virtue.

14. Bede may have in mind the Eunomians, a later wave of (extreme) Arianism that taught that Christ was not fully God.

were made through him. Therefore he was not **made** because he already existed **in the beginning**, but everything else was **made** because they did not exist beforehand. . . . And because he wants to strengthen the idea even more he says, **and without him was not anything made that was made** (1:3). By these statements he made known that the Son was always with the Father as one who is like the Father in nature and the Father's partner in creation, and that with the Father he **made all things** when it was time for them to be **made**.

(14) Augustine of Hippo

Those who have asserted that our Lord Jesus Christ is not God, or is not true God, or is not with the Father the one and only God, or is not truly immortal because he is subject to change, these all have been refuted by the utterance of the clearest and most consistent divine testimonies. For example: **In the beginning was the Word, and the Word was with God, and the Word was God** (1:1). It's clear that we are to take the **Word of God** for the only Son of God, of whom he goes on to say, **And the Word became flesh** (1:14), referring to his incarnate birth which took place in the time of the virgin. Now in this passage he clearly shows that he is not only God but also of the same substance as the Father, for after saying **and the Word was God**, he adds, **He was in the beginning with God; all things were made through him, and without him was not anything made that was made** (1:2–3). By **all things** he means only what has been made, that is, every creature. So it is crystal clear that he through whom **all things were made** was not made himself. If he is not made he is not a creature; and if he is not a creature he is of the same substance as the Father. For every substance that is not God is a creature, and that which is not a creature is God.

(15) Augustine of Hippo

Take a look at the structure of the world. Observe what has been made through the Word, and then you will have some idea of what the Word is like. Take a look at the two parts of the world, heaven and earth; who can find words to talk about the splendor of the heavens? Who can find words to talk about the fruitfulness of the earth? Who can fittingly praise the changing seasons, fittingly praise the energy stored in seeds? You will notice how much I am leaving out, because if I went on listing things for a long time I would still in all probability be saying less than you can think up for yourselves. From the structure of the world, then, think about what the Word must be like **through** which the world was made—and this structure is not the only thing that was **made**. **All** these **things**, after all, can be seen, because they strike the senses of the body. But **through** that Word, angels too were made; **through** that Word archangels were also made; powers, thrones, dominions, princedoms—**through** that Word **all things were made** (1:3). Let that give you some idea of what the Word is like.

1:4-5 In him was life, and the life was the light of men. The light shines in the darkness, and the darkness has not overcome it.

---

(16) John Chrysostom

Let's give our attention to what follows. After John speaks about the Creator, saying **all things were made through him and without him was not anything made that was made** (1:3), he adds a word about his providence, saying **in him was life** (1:4). So that no one would doubt the multitude and magnitude of the things he made, John added, **in him was life** (1:4). Just as you can't diminish the great abyss of the mother of all water springs, no matter how much you take away, so also with the activity of the only-begotten, no matter how much you believe he has produced and made, he doesn't become diminished. Or, to use a more familiar example, I'll speak of light—something the evangelist also quickly added saying, **and the life was the light** (1:4). However many thousands of things a light illuminates, its own brightness is not diminished. It's the same with God. Before beginning his work and after completing it, he remains unfailingly the same. He is undiminished and unwearied by the greatness of his creation.

(17) Augustine of Hippo

The light shines in the darkness and the darkness has not overcome it (1:5). The **darkness** signifies the foolish minds of people blinded by depraved desires and unbelief. To cure these and make them well, the Word, **through** whom **all things were made, became flesh and dwelt among us** (1:3, 14). Our enlightenment is to participate in the Word, that is, in that **life which is the light of men** (1:4). Yet we were absolutely incapable of such participation, and quite unfit for it—so unclean were we through sin—that we had to be cleansed. Furthermore, the only thing to cleanse the wicked and the proud is the blood of the just man and the humility of God; to contemplate God, which by nature we are not, we would have to be cleansed by him who became what by nature we are and what by sin we are not. By nature we are not God, by nature we are human; by sin we are not just. So God became a just man to intercede with God for sinful humanity. The sinner did not match the just, but human did match human. So he applied to us the similarity of his humanity in order to take away the dissimilarity of our iniquity. And becoming a partaker of our mortality he made us partakers of his divinity.

1:6–9 There was a man sent from God, whose name was John. He came for testimony, to bear witness to the light, that all might believe through him. He was not the light, but came to bear witness to the light. The true light that enlightens every man was coming into the world.

---

(18) Origen of Alexandria

He came for testimony, to bear witness to the light, that all might believe through him (1:7).

There are some heretics who claim to believe in Christ but deny that his coming was predicted by the prophets, because their beliefs lead them to imagine another god besides the Creator. They attempt to overthrow the **testimony** of the prophets. They say that the Son of God has no need of **testimony** because he has what is worthy of belief both in his saving words which he announced with power, and in his marvelous works which can immediately amaze anyone at all. . . .

We must say to them that there are many ways to be called to faith. Some who are not struck by a certain demonstration are struck by another. And God has many means to present himself to us so that we might accept that the God who reigns over all created things became incarnate. It is possible, therefore, to see some amazed at Christ through the predictions of the prophets. They are struck with amazement at the voice of so many prophets who came before him, establishing the place of Christ's birth, the country of his upbringing, the power of his teaching, the performance of marvelous deeds, and the destruction of human suffering by the resurrection. . . .

Why should we be amazed if, just as many of Christ's genuine disciples were ascribed as witnesses of Christ, so the prophets who perceived him were given the gift of God to preach Christ beforehand, teaching not only those who came after the coming of Christ what is necessary to think about the Son of God, but also those in previous generations? For just as the one who does not know the Son does not have the Father (cf. 1 John 2:23), so we should think the same for the previous era: *Abraham rejoiced that he was to see the day* of Christ; *he saw it and was glad* (8:56). So if you deny the prophets' testimony about Christ, you deprive the prophetic chorus of their greatest gift. What excellence would the prophecy inspired by the Holy Spirit have, if we exclude from it the things concerning the incarnation of our Lord? . . .

But even before the prophetic testimonies, the Baptist's *leaping* for joy *in the womb* of Elizabeth at the greeting of Mary (Luke 1:41) was a **testimony** about Christ. His action testified to Christ's divine conception and birth. For what is John except a **testimony** and forerunner of Jesus everywhere? He precedes his birth and then dies a little before the death of the Son of God, so that, by appearing before Christ's coming not only to those in birth but also to those anticipating freedom from death through Christ, he might *make ready for the Lord a people prepared* (Luke 1:17). The testimony of John anticipates even the second, more divine, coming of Christ. For *if you are willing to accept it*, Christ says, *he is Elijah who is to come. He who has ears to hear, let him hear* (Matt 11:14–15).

Since there was **the beginning in** which **the Word was** (1:1)—which we have shown from Proverbs to be Wisdom (cf. Prov 8:22)—and since the Word existed, and **in him was life, and the life was the light of men** (1:4)—I want to know why **the man sent from God, whose name was John, came for testimony, to bear witness to the light** (1:6–7). Why did he not come **to bear witness to the** life, or **to bear witness to the** Word, or the beginning, or any other aspect of Christ at all? Consider whether it's not perhaps *because the people who sat in darkness have seen a great light* (Matt 4:16; cf. Isa 9:2) or because **The light shines in the darkness** and is not **overcome** by it (1:5). Those who are in **darkness**, that is humans, need **light**.

(19) John Chrysostom

The true light that enlightens every man was coming into the world (1:9). If he who **enlightens every man was coming into the world** (1:9), how have so many remained unenlightened? Indeed, not all have recognized the majesty of Christ. So how does he **enlighten** *every* man? By doing so at least as far as is fitting for him. If some willfully shut their eyes of understanding and are unwilling to receive the rays of his **light**, then their darkness is due not to the nature of the **light** but to the wickedness of those who willingly deprive themselves of the gift. His grace has been shed upon all; he does not turn away Jew, Greek, barbarian, Scythian, free, slave, man, woman, old, or young (cf. Col 3:11). Rather, he accepts all alike and calls them all with the same honor. But those who are unwilling to enjoy this gift should rightly consider their blindness to be their own. For when the way is open to all and there is nothing preventing them, those who are willingly evil remain outside, and perish for no other reason than their own wickedness.

(20) Theodore of Mopsuestia

After he said that John the Baptist **was not the light** (1:8) he added a contrast with Christ: **The true light that enlightens every man was coming into the world** (1:9). He did this in order to show that John had a purpose for a short while because he was only preaching to the Jews. That is the work of a lamp; it shines for a little while and afterward is extinguished. But Christ, as the eternal **light**, never grows dark. He indicates this by speaking of **the true light** that endures until the end of the world, giving its help to everyone.

(21) Augustine of Hippo

Why did he add the word **true** (1:9)? Because a person who has been **enlightened** is also called **light**, but the **true light** is the one who **enlightens**. For even our eyes are called lights, and yet unless a lamp is lit during the night, or the sun comes out in the day, these lights open to no avail. In this way, then, John too was a **light**, but not the **true light** because, while yet unenlightened, he was darkness; yet by being enlightened, he became **light**.

1:10–13 The world was made through him, yet the world knew him not. He came to his own home, and his own people received him not. But to all who received him, who believed in his name, he gave power to become children of God; who were born, not of blood nor of the will of the flesh nor of the will of man, but of God.

---

(22) Augustine of Hippo

He came to his own home and his own people received him not (1:11). Did they fail to receive him without exception? Were none of them saved? After all, nobody will be saved except those who have received Christ at his coming. But he added, **But to all who received him** (1:13). What did he bestow on them? Great kindness; great mercy! His birth was unique as the son of God, but he did not wish to remain the only son of God. Many couples who have had no children adopt when they are older and so come to have by choice what nature was unable to provide; that is what human beings do. But someone who has an only son rejoices in him all the more, because he alone will take possession of the whole inheritance and not have anyone else to divide it with and thus turn out the poorer. Not so God; he sent the very same one and only Son he had begotten, through whom he had created everything, into this world so that he should not be alone but should have adopted brothers and sisters. You see, we were not born of God in the same way as that only-begotten Son of his; we were adopted through the Son's grace. For the only-begotten Son came to forgive sins—those sins which had us so tied up that they were an impediment to his adopting us. He forgave those he wished to make his brothers and sisters and made them co-heirs. That, after all, is what the apostle says: *If a son then an heir* (Gal 4:7); and again: *heirs of God and fellow heirs with Christ* (Rom 8:17). No, he was not afraid of having *fellow heirs*, because his inheritance is not whittled down if many possess it. They themselves, in fact, become the inheritance which he possesses, and he in turn becomes their inheritance.

(23) Cyril of Alexandria

The Son came and indeed became man, enveloping our life in his. He was the first holy, wondrous, and truly novel birth and life. He was the firstborn of the Holy Spirit (I mean according to the flesh). When that grace is transferred directly to us, **not of blood nor of the will of the flesh nor of the will of man, but of God** (1:13), and we have been spiritually reborn through the Spirit and have a spiritual likeness to the one who is truly the Son by nature, we might call God "Father." And so we will also remain incorruptible, no longer having the first man, that is Adam, as our father, in whom we perished. Christ says at some point, *Call no man your father on earth, for you have one Father, who is in heaven* (Matt 23:9). Elsewhere he indicates why he came into our estate, that he might lead us to his own God-befitting estate: *I am ascending to my Father and your Father, to my God and your God* (20:17). His Father by nature is he who is in heaven, our God. But since he who is truly the Son by nature became like us, he calls him God according to the logic befitting his incarnation, and he gave his own Father to us as well. For it is written, **But to all who received him, who believed in his name, he gave power to become children of God** (1:12).

(24) Leo the Great

The Lord Jesus Christ, being born true man yet never ceasing to be true God, made in himself the beginning of a *new creation* (2 Cor 5:17). In the form of his birth he gave the human race a spiritual beginning, so that by destroying the stain of our birth according to the flesh, there might be a regenerative birth without the seed of sin, about whom it is said: **who were born, not of blood nor of the will of the flesh nor of the will of man, but of God** (1:13). What mind can comprehend this mystery? What tongue can speak of this grace? Sinfulness returns to innocence and our old nature becomes new; strangers receive adoption and foreigners enter into an inheritance!

1:14 And the Word became flesh and dwelt among us, full of grace and truth; we have beheld his glory, glory as of the only Son from the Father.

---

(25) Novatian

Who can doubt that Christ is human when Scripture speaks of his nativity and his becoming flesh, saying **the Word became flesh and dwelt among us** (1:14)? Since he is **the Word of God** (1:1), who could hesitate to proclaim that he is God, especially when one considers how the gospels have presented both the human and divine natures in one union at Christ's birth? . . .

This **Word** descended from heaven as a bridegroom joined to flesh, so to speak, so that by the assumption of flesh the Son of Man might be able to ascend to the place from which the Son of God—the **Word**—had descended. Through that union, the flesh bears **the Word** of God while the Son of God assumes the fragility of flesh. Joined in marriage to the flesh, he ascends to that place from which he had descended without flesh, and now recovers that glory which he is shown to have possessed before the creation of the world. If all this is so, he is most unmistakably proven to be God.

(26) Hilary of Poitiers

Each one has the power to be the child of God. This fact itself might somehow ensnare the weakness of our frightened faith because it is incredibly painful to hope for something which is difficult to believe (even if it is what we desire). Therefore, God **the Word became flesh** (1:14), and through God **the Word** becoming **flesh**, the **flesh** is set on a course toward God **the Word**.

The **Word** made **flesh** was none other than God **the Word**, and the **flesh** was our own. Lest we deny these truths, he **dwelt among us** (1:14); and as he **dwelt** among us he remained God. While he **dwelt among us**, the **flesh** that God used to **become flesh** was none other than our own. By honoring this **flesh** which he took up, he was not deprived of his own qualities because he was nevertheless the **only Son from the Father, full of grace and truth** (1:14). He was perfect both in his divinity and in our humanity.

(27) Jerome

We already said before, and now it must be asserted more fully, that we are not one in the Father and the Son by nature, but by grace. The human soul is not of the same substance as God, which the Manicheans are accustomed to say. But *thou . . . hast loved them even as thou hast loved me* (17:23). So, you see, we are taken up into participation with his substance not by nature, but by grace. The reason why the Father loves us is because the Father loved the Son and his members, namely those in his body. **But to all who received Christ, who believed in his name, he gave power to become children of God; who were born, not of blood nor of the will of the flesh nor of the will of man, but of God** (1:12–13). **And the Word became flesh** (1:14) so that we might cross over from the flesh into the Word.

(28) John Chrysostom

Having already said that those who received him were **born of God** and made **children of God** (1:13), he now indicates the cause and reason for this ineffable honor: because **the Word became flesh** (1:14) and the Master took *the form of a servant* (Phil 2:7). God's own Son became the Son of Man that he might make the children of human beings into children of God. For when that which is exalted associates with that which is lowly, its own glory is diminished in no way. Instead, it elevates the other from its great lowliness, and this is what happened with Christ. His condescension in no way lessens his own nature. Instead he raised us—who had always sat in disgrace and darkness—to an ineffable glory. In the same way, a king who kindly and genuinely converses with a poor beggar in no way dishonors himself. Instead he makes the beggar famous and admired by all. In the case of extraneous human dignity, keeping company with a lesser person in no way diminishes the more honorable person. How much more will it be true for that pure and blessed essence, which has nothing extraneous to it, nor does its existence come and go, but possesses all good things unalterably and permanently? So when you hear, **the Word became flesh** (1:14), don't be shocked or dismayed. His essence wasn't changed into flesh (this would be truly impious to imagine); instead he remained what he was and took upon himself the *form of a servant* (Phil 2:7).

Why then does the evangelist use the word **became**? To stop the mouths of the heretics. Since some say that the whole business of the incarnation was merely an appearance, play acting, and a myth, the evangelist wanted to remove their blasphemy ahead of time, writing: **became**. He wanted to indicate not a change of essence (perish the thought!), but the assumption of **flesh** itself. For example, when Scripture says that *Christ redeemed us from the curse of the law, having become a curse for us* (Gal 3:13) he does not mean his essence relinquished its own glory and became a curse in his essence. . . . That's not what he means. Rather, taking upon himself the curse intended for us, Christ no longer leaves us under the curse. It's the same thing here: the evangelist says that he **became flesh**, not by changing his essence into **flesh**, but by assuming **flesh** and allowing his essence to remain unharmed. . . .

So the evangelist only uses the word **became** so that you wouldn't think the incarnation was a mere appearance. We can demonstrate this further by looking at what follows and seeing how he clarifies his argument and demolishes wicked suggestions. For he adds: **and dwelt among us** (1:14). . . .

What then was the tent in which he **dwelt**?[15] Hear the prophet saying: *In that day I will raise up the tent of David that is fallen* (Amos 9:11). That tent was indeed fallen; our nature had fallen beyond cure and only needed that powerful hand. For there was no way to raise it again unless the one who had formed it in the first place would stretch forth his hand and impress his image upon it afresh by the rebirth of **water and the Spirit** (cf. 3:5). And behold the awesome and inexpressible mystery: he dwells in this tent forever! He didn't enclose himself in our flesh only to leave it again later. He intends to possess it forever. If this wasn't the case, he wouldn't have considered it worthy of the royal throne, nor would he have allowed it to be worshiped by all the host of heaven, the angels, archangels, thrones, principalities, rulers, and powers. What word, what thought can express such a marvelous and awesome honor bestowed upon our race? What angel or archangel? None at all, either in heaven or on earth! Such is the excellence of God. So great and marvelous is his kindness that an accurate description of it transcends not only the human tongue but even the power of angels.

(29) John Chrysostom

Once the evangelist said that we became **children of God** (1:12), and then indicated that **the Word** becoming **flesh** (1:14) was the cause, he again mentions another advantage we enjoy from his becoming **flesh**. What is it? **We have beheld his glory, glory as of the only Son from the Father** (1:14). We couldn't have **beheld** this **glory** if it hadn't been shown to us through a body like our own. Those in ancient times couldn't even bear to look at the glorified face of Moses, who shared in the same nature with us. That righteous man needed a veil to cover his pure glory and to show them a kind and gentle face of the prophet (Exod 34:29–35). If that were so, how could we creatures of clay and dust have endured the uncovered Godhead, who is inaccessible even to the heavenly powers? Therefore he **dwelt among us** (1:14) so that we might safely be able to approach him, speak to him, and converse with him.

---

15. Chrysostom is playing with the verb in verse 14: "dwelt" (*eskēnōsen*), which shares the derivative word: "tent" (*skēnē*). A more literal rendering might be: **What then was the tent in which he tented?**

(30) Theodore of Mopsuestia

And the Word became flesh (1:14). He employed this term **Word** very clearly. "Behold," John says, "he took it upon himself to become flesh." This was the supposition of those who saw Christ—because in his human existence many thought he was only a man because of his outward appearance. Therefore, in order to explain what happened John says, he **dwelt among us** (1:14); that is, he **became flesh** because he resided in our nature. . . . Likewise, instead of saying "he became human," John says, he **became flesh**. He did not use the word **became** to indicate change; it only seemed this way because of his human appearance.

(31) Augustine of Hippo

How did Wisdom come if not by the **Word becoming flesh** and **dwelling among us** (1:14)? It's similar to when we speak. In order for our thoughts to reach the minds of our hearers through their physical ears, the word in our minds becomes a sound; we call this speech. Yet this does not mean that our thought is turned into that sound. While remaining undiminished in itself, it takes on the form of a spoken utterance by which it inserts itself into their ears, without bearing the stigma of any change in itself. That is how the **Word** of God was not changed in the least, and yet **became flesh**, in order to **dwell among us**.

(32) Augustine of Hippo

So that human beings might be born of God, God was first of all born of them. Christ, after all, is God, and Christ was born of a human being. He was only looking for a mother on earth, because he already had a Father in heaven; he was born of God that we might be fashioned, *born of a woman* (Gal 4:4) that we might be refashioned. Don't be astonished, then, at being made a child by grace because you were born of God according to his Word. First, that Word wanted to be born of a human being so that you might be assured of being born of God and might say to yourself, "Not without reason did God choose to be born of a human being; for thus did he regard me of some value, such that he would make me immortal and he would be born mortal for my sake." It would seem incredible to us that human beings were actually born of God. That's why, after saying they were born of God, as though to save us from being overwhelmed and flabbergasted at such grace, he says, to set your mind at ease, **And the Word became flesh and dwelt among us** (1:14). So why be astonished that human beings are born of God? Observe God himself being born of human beings: **And the Word became flesh and dwelt among us.**

Now, because **the Word became flesh and dwelt among us**, by his very birth he made an ointment with which the eyes of our hearts could be cleaned, that we might see his majesty through his humility. That is why **the Word became flesh and dwelt among us**—he healed our eyes. And what follows? **And we have beheld his glory** (1:14). No one could see **his glory** without being healed by the lowliness of his flesh. Why would we not have been able to behold it? Would you, my beloved, please pay close attention and see what I am saying! It's as if dust had got into someone's eye, earth got into it, injured the eye, and the eye could not see the light. The injured eye was anointed; it had been injured by earth, and yet earth is put into it for healing. After all, all ointments and medicines have earth as their source. You were blinded by dust, you are healed by dust; so flesh blinded you; flesh heals you. The soul, you see, had become fleshly-minded by giving its consent to fleshly-minded inclinations, and that is how the eye of the heart had been blinded. **The Word became flesh**; this doctor made you an ointment for the eyes. And since he came in the **flesh** to extinguish the vices of the **flesh** and to slay death with death, that's why it came to be that you, because **the Word became flesh**, would be able to say, **We have beheld his glory**. What sort of **glory**? That of becoming the Son of man? That is his humility, not **his glory**. But, once healed by flesh, where is the heart's gaze drawn to? It says, **we have beheld his glory, glory as of the only Son from the Father, full of grace and truth** (1:14).

(33) Augustine of Hippo

This faith of ours promises—on the strength of divine authority, not of human argument—that the whole person (who consists, of course, of soul and body alike) is going to be immortal, and therefore truly happy. That's why the gospel didn't just stop when it had said that Jesus **gave all who received him the power to become children of God** (1:12). It briefly explained what receiving him meant, saying, those **who believed in his name** (1:12), and then showed how they would become children of God by adding, that they **are born, not of blood nor of the will of the flesh nor of the will of man, but of God** (1:13). But in case this feebleness that is humanity, which we see and carry around with us, should despair of attaining such eminence, it went on to say **And the Word became flesh and dwelt among us** (1:14). This was to convince us of what might seem incredible by showing us its opposite. The Son of God by nature became the Son of man by mercy for the sake of human children (that's the meaning of **the Word became flesh and dwelt among us**). Surely, then, how much easier is it to believe that human children by nature can become **children of God** by grace, and dwell in God? For it is in him alone and thanks to him alone that they can be happy, by sharing in his immortality; it was to persuade us of this: that the Son of God came to share in our mortality.

(34) Leo the Great

Christ who is true God is also true man. In this unity there is no falsehood as long as the humility of man and the height of the Godhead exist simultaneously. Just as God is not changed by showing compassion, so man is not consumed by divine excellence. Each nature, with the help of the other, does what is proper to itself. Indeed, **the Word** accomplishes what is proper to **the Word**, and the **flesh** what is proper to the **flesh**. One nature flashes with miracles, the other yields to injuries. Just as **the Word** does not shrink back from the equality of the Father's glory, so the **flesh** does not abandon the nature of our race. He is one and the same—and let us say it again—truly Son of God, and truly

Son of Man. He is God because **In the beginning was the Word, and the Word was with God, and the Word was God** (1:1); he is man because **the Word became flesh and dwelt among us** (1:14). He is God in that **all things were made through him, and without him was not anything made that was made** (1:3), man in that he was *born of woman, born under the law* (Gal 4:4).

(35) Venerable Bede

Hence it is proper, dear friends, that we who, in this yearly devotion, recall to mind again the human nativity of our redeemer,[16] must always, not just annually, embrace in constant love both his divine and human nature equally. Through his divine nature we were created when we did not exist; and by his human nature we were re-created when we were lost. Certainly the divine power of our Creator was able to re-create us without his assumption of humanity; yet the human weakness of our same redeemer was unable to re-create us without divinity assuming it, dwelling within it, and working through it. For that reason **the Word became flesh** (1:14); that is to say, God became man and **dwelt among us** (1:14) so that by having dwelt among us in the form of a human being, he might be able to unite with us; by speaking to us he might instruct us and offer to us a way of living; by dying he might fight against our enemy for us; and by rising he might destroy death. Moreover, by his co-eternal divinity with the Father, he might truly and inwardly raise us to the divine life, grant us the forgiveness of sins and the gifts of the Holy Spirit, and after the perfection of good works, he might not only lead us to see the glory of his illustrious humanity, but also show us the immutable essence of his divine majesty, in which he lives and reigns with the Father in the unity of the Holy Spirit, forever and ever. Amen.

1:16 And from his fullness have we all received, grace upon grace.

---

(36) John Chrysostom

Our passage—**And from his fullness have we all received, grace upon grace** (1:16)—demonstrates that the Jews were saved by grace. *It was not because you were more numerous,* God says, *but because of your fathers that I chose you* (Deut 7:7). Now if they were not chosen by God for their own virtue, then it's obvious that they received this honor by **grace**. We too are all saved by grace, though not in the same manner. Our salvation does not have the same results, but greater and more exalted ones; the **grace** we receive is not like the **grace** they received. For not only were we granted forgiveness of sins (since this is something we share in common with them—*for all have sinned* [Rom 3:23]), but we also received righteousness, sanctification, adoption, and a far more glorious and abundant **grace**: the

---

16. Bede is delivering a Christmas sermon.

Spirit. By this **grace** we have become the beloved of God, no longer just his servants, but his children and friends. This is why it says, **grace upon grace** (1:16).

Even the law came from **grace**, as well as our being created from nothing. We didn't receive our existence as a reward for past virtue—how could we? we didn't even exist!—but from God who is always the initiator of blessings. Not only were we created from nothing, but once God created us, he immediately taught us what to do and what not to do, implanting this law in our very nature and entrusting us with an impartial conscience. All of this was a great **grace** and an unspeakable kindness. And after this natural law had become corrupted, God restored it by giving his written law; this too was **grace**. We might have expected God to have corrected and punished those who corrupted the commandment once given to them, but this isn't what happened. He restored them again and pardoned them, not out of obligation to them, but as a gift of his mercy and **grace**. . . . And so even God's sending of the law was an act of mercy, pity, and **grace**, and this is why our passage says, **grace upon grace** (1:16).

(37) Augustine of Hippo

What was the **grace** we first **received**? Faith! Walking in faith, we are walking in **grace**. How, after all, did we deserve to have faith? What previous merits did we have to show? Let no one pat himself on the back; let each one return to his conscience, probe into the hiding places of his thoughts, go back to the sequence of his actions; let each one not look at what he now is, if already something, but look at what he was, in order to be something; each one will find that he only deserved punishment. So if what you deserved was punishment, and the one who came would not punish sins, but would pardon them, you have been given a **grace**—not paid back as per invoice. . . .

So what then is **grace upon grace**? By faith we gain God. Seeing that we did not deserve to be forgiven our sins, by the very fact of receiving such an undeserved gift, that is called **grace**. What does **grace** mean? Given *gratis*. What does *gratis* mean? Bestowed, not paid back. If you were owed it, then it was a payment as per invoice, not a **grace** bestowed on you. If it was really owed to you, that means you were good; if however, and this is the truth, you were bad, but believed in the one *who justifies the ungodly* (Rom 4:5)—for what does *justifies the ungodly* mean if not "makes godly people out of ungodly ones"?—then think about what you had coming to you through the law and about what you actually obtained through **grace**. But having obtained this **grace** of faith, you will be just as a result of your faith, since *he who through faith is righteous shall live* (Rom 1:17), and you will gain God, by living from faith. When you have gained God by living from faith, you will receive immortality and eternal life as your reward. That too is **grace**. For what merit do you receive eternal life? For **grace**. If faith were a **grace**, in fact, and eternal life a kind of payment as per invoice for faith, it does indeed look like God is paying you back eternal life as something owed—but owed to whom? To one who believes, because you have earned it by faith. But because faith itself is **grace**, eternal life too is **grace upon grace**.

1:17–18 For the law was given through Moses; grace and truth came through Jesus Christ. No one has ever seen God; the only Son, who is in the bosom of the Father, he has made him known.

(38) Augustine of Hippo

For the law was given through Moses; grace and truth came through Jesus Christ (1:17). We turn to the apostle and he tells us that we are not under **the law** but under **grace** (cf. Rom 6:14). *He sent forth his Son*, therefore, *born of woman, born under the law, to redeem those who were under the law, so that we might receive adoption as sons* (Gal 4:4–5). See, that's what Christ came for, *to redeem those who were under the law*, so that we might no longer be under **the law** but under **grace**. Who then gave **the law**? The one who gave **grace** also gave **the law**; but he sent **the law** through a servant, while he came down himself with **grace**. And how was it that human beings came to be under **the law**? By not fulfilling **the law**. The one who fulfills **the law**, you see, is not under **the law** but with **the law**; while the one who is under **the law** is not lifted up but pressed down by **the law**. Thus, **the law** finds guilty all human beings under **the law**; and, therefore, it is held over their head so as to manifest their sins, rather than to take them away. So then, **the law** issues orders; the lawgiver shows mercy in what **the law** commands. Human beings who have tried to fulfill, by their own strength of character, what was commanded by **the law**, have been tumbled head over heels by their self-assurance and have fallen. They are not with **the law**, but have been found guilty under **the law**; and since they could not fulfill **the law** on their own and were guilty under **the law**, they implored the help of a liberator. The guilt of **the law** made the proud sick and the sickness of the proud became the confession of the humble. Now that the sick confess that they are ill, let the doctor come and heal the sick. . . .

This **grace** was not in the Old Testament, because **the law** threatened but brought no relief. It gave orders; it did not heal. It pointed out frailty; it did not get rid of it. But it was preparing the ground for that doctor who was going to come with **grace and truth**; as a doctor who wants to cure someone first sends along his slave, that the doctor might find the patient bandaged up. The patient was not in good health, did not want to be healed, and, to avoid treatment, was boasting about his health. The **law** was sent and bound him; he found himself guilty, and he then cried out from the bandages. . . .

For the law was given through Moses; grace and truth came through Jesus Christ (1:17). **The law was given through** a slave; it made people guilty. An indulgence was given by the emperor; it delivered the guilty. **The law was given through Moses**. The slave must not claim credit for any more than what was done by him. Chosen for a great ministry as *one faithful in God's house as servant* (Heb 3:5), he can act according to **the law**; he cannot absolve from the guilt of **the law**. So then, **the law was given through Moses; grace and truth came through Jesus Christ.**

And in case anyone should say, "Did not both **grace and truth** come about through Moses, who saw God?" the evangelist immediately added, **No one has ever seen God** (1:18). How was God made known to Moses? By the Lord revealing him to his servant. Which

Lord? Christ himself, who sent the **law** ahead through a slave, in order to come himself with **grace and truth**, for **no one has ever seen God**.

How did he appear to that servant, to the extent that he was able to grasp what he saw? He says, **the only Son, who is in the bosom of the Father, he has made him known** (1:18). What is **in the bosom of the Father**? In the Father's inner counsels. God, of course, does not have a **bosom** as we have in our clothes, nor is he to be thought of as sitting as we do, or perhaps as having wrapped himself in something in order to have a **bosom**. But because our **bosom** is intimately close to us, the Father's inner counsels are called the Father's **bosom**. The one in the Father's inner counsels who knows the Father, he it is that has interpreted him; for **no one has ever seen God**. So then, he came and told what he had seen. But what had Moses seen? Moses saw a cloud (Exod 19:19), an angel (Exod 33), a fire (Exod 3:2)—all parts of creation. These things bore the image of the Lord, but did not manifest his very presence. You have it plainly in the law: *Thus the Lord used to speak to Moses face to face, as a man speaks to his friend* (Exod 33:11). Continue on and you find Moses saying, *If I have found favor in thy sight, show me now thy ways, that I may see thee* (Exod 33:13). Not only did Moses say it, he got his answer: *You cannot see my face* (Exod 33:20). So then, my brothers and sisters, an angel representing the Lord was talking to Moses; and everything that was done there through the angel promised this **grace** and this **truth** yet to come.

(39) Cyril of Alexandria

The apostle says: let the lover of learning examine the evangelical **grace** given to us through the Savior, as opposed to the **grace** of the **law** which is given through Moses. Then you will see that the Son is greatly superior in this respect; he decreed better laws than the administrators of the old law, and introduced things superior to everything which came through Moses. **For the law**, he says, **was given through Moses, and grace and truth came through Jesus Christ** (1:17). Therefore, the lover of inquiry and the companion of hard work will see again what the distinction is between the **law** and the **grace** which **came through** the Savior. . . . The **law** condemned the world, as Paul says: through it, God *constrained all things under sin* (Gal 3:22). It showed that we are subject to punishment, but even more so, the Savior himself sets us free. For he did not come *to judge the world, but to save the world* (12:47).

Even **the law** gave **grace** to humanity, calling all to the knowledge of God and drawing the wayward away from the worship of idols. In addition to this, it pointed out evil and taught the good, if not perfectly, then at least pedagogically and usefully. But the **truth and grace which came through** the only-begotten introduced the good to us not in types, nor by engraving beneficial things in shadows, but with shining and most pure commandments, leading us by the hand to the perfect knowledge of faith. On the one hand, **the law** gave *the spirit of slavery which leads to fear*, but on the other hand Christ gave *spirit of sonship* which leads to freedom (Rom 8:15). Likewise, **the law** introduces the circumcision of the flesh, which is *nothing*: *for circumcision is nothing*, as Paul writes in one place (1 Cor 7:19). But our Lord Jesus Christ introduces the circumcision of the spirit and heart through faith. **The law** baptizes with mere water those who are tainted, but the Savior baptizes *with the Holy Spirit and with fire* (Matt 3:11). **The law** introduces the tabernacle as the antitype of true things, but the Savior draws up to heaven itself and enters the true tabernacle which *the Lord set up and not man* (Heb 8:2).

It is not difficult to pile up other examples in verbal proofs; nevertheless, we must honor our limits, except that we will say only this, for your profit and out of necessity: the blessed Paul in a few words gives the answer being sought. He speaks about the **grace** of **the law** and the Savior: *For if there was splendor in the dispensation of condemnation, the dispensation of righteousness must far exceed it in splendor* (2 Cor 3:9). The commandment which came **through Moses**, he says, is *the ministration of condemnation*, but **the grace which came through** the Savior is called *the ministration of righteousness* which is also freely given to acquire the greatest glory. Therefore, since **the law** which condemns **was given through Moses**, but the **grace** which justifies **came through** the only-begotten, how then is he not superior in glory, says the apostle, through whom superior things were decreed?

(40) Venerable Bede

For the law was given through Moses; grace and truth came through Jesus Christ (1:17). Indeed the law was given through Moses, and in that law it was determined by a heavenly judgment what must be done and what must be avoided. What the law anticipated, however, was fulfilled only in the grace of Christ. The law is able to show transgressors their sin, to teach them justice, and to make known to them their guilt. However, the grace of Christ, *poured into the hearts* of the faithful *through the Spirit of love* (Rom 5:5), fulfills what the law taught. . . .

The law was given through Moses when the people were instructed to be cleansed by the sprinkling of the blood of a lamb (cf. Exod 24:8); **grace and truth**, which were symbolized in the law, **came through Jesus Christ** when he suffered on the cross and washed us *from our sins by his blood* (Rev 1:5). **The law was given through Moses** because when he instructed the people with saving commands, he warned that if they observed these laws they would enter into the land of promise and live in it forever, but if they observed other laws, they would be scattered by the enemy. **Grace and truth came through Jesus Christ** because when the gift of his Spirit was given, he granted the ability to understand and keep the law spiritually, and led those who kept it into the true blessedness of heavenly life which the land of promise symbolized.

John 1:19–28

[19] And this is the testimony of John, when the Jews sent priests and Levites from Jerusalem to ask him, "Who are you?" [20] He confessed, he did not deny, but confessed, "I am not the Christ." [21] And they asked him, "What then? Are you Elijah?" He said, "I am not." "Are you the prophet?" And he answered, "No." [22] They said to him then, "Who are

you? Let us have an answer for those who sent us. What do you say about yourself?" [23]He said, "I am the voice of one crying in the wilderness, 'Make straight the way of the Lord,' as the prophet Isaiah said." [24]Now they had been sent from the Pharisees. [25]They asked him, "Then why are you baptizing, if you are neither the Christ, nor Elijah, nor the prophet?" [26]John answered them, "I baptize with water; but among you stands one whom you do not know, [27]even he who comes after me, the thong of whose sandal I am not worthy to untie." [28]This took place in Bethany beyond the Jordan, where John was baptizing.

1:21 "Are you Elijah? . . . Are you the prophet?"

---

(41) Origen of Alexandria

"Are you the prophet?" He answered, "No" (1:21). If the *law and the prophets* were *until John* (cf. Matt 11:13), then what else could we call John except a **prophet**? As his father Zechariah prophesied when filled with the Holy Spirit: *And you, child, will be called the prophet of the Most High; for you will go before the Lord to prepare his ways* (Luke 1:76). Unless someone thinks that "called" is not the same thing as "being," then John was a **prophet**. Moreover, to those who thought John was a **prophet**, Jesus said: *Why then did you go out? To see a prophet? Yes, I tell you, and more than a prophet* (Matt 11:9). We need to observe that in saying, *Yes, I tell you*, Jesus establishes John as a **prophet** and does not dismiss that notion. The Savior says that John is a *prophet and more than a prophet*. So how can John, being a **prophet**, say, **No**, to the priests and Levites who ask, **Are you the prophet?** (1:21)?

We should reply to this that it is not the same thing to ask, **Are you *the* prophet?** as it is to ask, **Are you *a* prophet?** We made the same observation (earlier) when we investigated the difference between "the God" and "a god," and between "the Word" and "a word." Since it is written in Deuteronomy, *The Lord your God will raise up for you a prophet like me from among you, from your brethren—him you shall heed; it shall be that every soul that does not listen to that prophet shall be destroyed from the people* (Acts 3:22–23; Deut 18:15), it was anticipated that a prophet would be raised up who was like Moses in some way who would mediate between God and humanity, and who would receive the covenant from God and give a new covenant to his disciples. The people of Israel knew that none of the (previous) prophets were the one predicted by Moses.

Just as they wondered whether John was the Christ, so too they wondered whether he was *the* **prophet**. It is not remarkable that those who wondered whether John was the Christ should also not really understand that the one who was the Christ was also *the* **prophet**. Therefore, uncertainty about John's identity leads to ignorance about Christ and **the prophet** being the same person.

(42) Augustine of Hippo

First of all, John—*among those born of women there has risen no one greater* (Matt 11:11)—said, "**I am not the Christ." And they asked him, "Are you Elijah?" He said, "I am not"** (1:20–21). Christ sends Elijah ahead of him, but John said, **I am not**, and therefore gives us a problem. For it is to be feared that, failing to understand, some will assume that John was contradicting what Christ said. You see, there is a place in the gospel where the Lord Jesus Christ was saying things about himself, and his disciples answered, *Why do the scribes* (that is, those learned in the law) *say that first Elijah must come?* Jesus replied, *Elijah has already come, and they did to him whatever they pleased* (Matt 17:10–12); and *if you want to know, it is John the Baptist* (Matt 11:14).[17] The Lord Jesus Christ said, *Elijah has already come, and he is John the Baptist*; yet when John was questioned, he admitted that he was not Elijah, any more than he was the Christ. Of course, just as he was telling the truth when he admitted he was not the Christ, so too it was true when he admitted he was not Elijah. So how then are we to reconcile the words of the herald with the words of the judge? It's impossible that the herald should be lying; for he was only saying what he was hearing from the judge. Why then does he say, **I am not Elijah**, while the Lord says that he is Elijah? Because the Lord Jesus Christ wished to prefigure in John his own second coming in the future, and he wanted to say that John was in the spirit of Elijah, and thus, what John was at his first coming, Elijah would be at the second coming. Just as there are two comings, two advents, so there are two heralds. The judge is the same both times, of course, but while there are not two judges, there are two heralds. The judge had to come first, that he might be judged. He sent the first herald ahead of him and called him Elijah, because at his second coming Elijah will be what John was at the first.

Would you, my brothers and sisters, please notice that what I am saying is true? When John was conceived, or rather once he was born, the Holy Spirit prophesied what would be fulfilled with regard to this man: *And he will go before* the Most High *in the spirit and power of Elijah* (Luke 1:17). Not Elijah himself, but *in the spirit and power of Elijah*. What does that mean, *in the spirit and power of Elijah*? With the same Holy Spirit, he will have the role of Elijah. Why the role of Elijah? Because what Elijah must be for the second coming, John was for the first coming. Rightly then did John respond with the literal truth, because the Lord was speaking in a figurative way when he said, "He is Elijah," while this man, as I said, meant it literally when he said, **I am not Elijah**. If you concentrate on the role of the forerunner, John himself is Elijah, for what he was at the first coming, the other will be at the second. If you are asking who he was literally, then John was John and Elijah was Elijah. So the Lord rightly pointed out how John prefigured Elijah by saying, "He is Elijah," while John rightly stated the literal truth, **I am not Elijah**. Neither John nor the Lord speaks falsely; nothing false from the herald, nor from the judge—as long as you really understand. Who though, will understand? Anyone who has imitated the humility of the herald, and recognized the high dignity of the judge. Nothing, you see, is more humble than this herald. My brothers and sisters, John had no greater merit than his humility, such that when he was in a position to deceive people, and to be taken for the Christ, and to be regarded as the Christ (so great

---

17. Augustine's Latin text is different and does not agree with the Greek at this point.

was his grace and so excellent his renown), he still admitted openly and said, **I am not the Christ**. Can it be that you are not Elijah? If he now said, "I am Elijah," it would mean that Christ was already arriving at his second coming to judge, not still at his first coming to be judged. So, as if to say, "Elijah is still to come," he said, **I am not Elijah**. But notice the humble Christ before whom John came, so as not to experience the high and mighty Christ before whom Elijah is going to come. That, after all, is how the Lord finished his statement: *He himself is John the Baptist, who is going to come* (Matt 11:14). John came as a figure of how Elijah will be in his coming. Then, Elijah will actually be Elijah; now, he was John by comparison. Now, John was actually John; by comparison, he is Elijah. Each herald was compared to the other, each retained his own identity; but there is one Lord and judge, whether this herald or that one precedes him.

1:26-27 John answered them, "I baptize with water; but among you stands one whom you do not know, even he who comes after me, the thong of whose sandal I am not worthy to untie."

---

(43) Gregory the Great

A saint is not diverted from his devotion to goodness, even when questioned by a perverse mind. So John responds to words of hatred with words of life, immediately saying: **I baptize with water; but among you stands one whom you do not know** (1:26). John baptizes not with the Spirit but with water, because he was unable to remit sins. The bodies which he baptized, he washed with water, but he did not wash their minds with forgiveness. Why then does John baptize if his baptism does not forgive sins, except that he is preserving his call as forerunner? Just as his birth anticipated the Lord's birth, so his baptizing anticipated the Lord's baptizing; and just as John's preaching made him the forerunner of Christ, so his baptizing made him a forerunner in imitation of the sacrament. By these actions, he announces the mystery of our Redeemer, declaring that Christ stood among us and yet remained unknown (cf. 1:26). The Lord appeared in the flesh—visible in body, invisible in majesty. . . .

The human eye is unable to penetrate the mystery of Christ's incarnation. It's impossible to ascertain how the Word came to have a body, how the highest and life-giving Spirit gives life within a mother's womb, and how he who has no beginning both comes to be and is conceived. Therefore the **thong of the sandal** represents the bonds of mystery, and John is not strong enough to **untie the thong of his sandal**, because even the one who acknowledges the mystery of the incarnation through the spirit of prophecy, is unable to understand it. Then what does it mean to say: **the thong of whose sandal I am not worthy to untie** (1:27), unless it's an open and humble profession of his own ignorance? It's as if he was saying: "Why is it surprising that Jesus comes before me? I understand that he was born after me, but the mystery of his nativity I do not grasp." Pay attention to John! Filled with the spirit of prophecy, he shines with a wonderful knowledge, and yet implies that there is something about which he does not understand.

John 1:29–34

[29]The next day he saw Jesus coming toward him, and said, "Behold, the Lamb of God, who takes away the sin of the world! [30]This is he of whom I said, 'After me comes a man who ranks before me, for he was before me.' [31]I myself did not know him; but for this I came baptizing with water, that he might be revealed to Israel." [32]And John bore witness, "I saw the Spirit descend as a dove from heaven, and it remained on him. [33]I myself did not know him; but he who sent me to baptize with water said to me, 'He on whom you see the Spirit descend and remain, this is he who baptizes with the Holy Spirit.' [34]And I have seen and have borne witness that this is the Son of God."

1:29 "Behold, the Lamb of God, who takes away the sin of the world!"

---

(44) Origen of Alexandria

There are five living creatures which are offered as sacrifices on the altar, three of which live on the land and two of which fly. It seems worthwhile to me to investigate why John calls the Savior a **lamb** but none of the rest. . . . Therefore, for those who desire to understand accurately the spiritual meaning of the sacrifices, we must investigate the ways in which these animals serve as an example and shadow of heavenly things, and why Scripture commands each of the living creatures to be sacrificed. In particular, we must collect references to the **lamb**. . . .

We find that the **lamb** is offered among the perpetual sacrifices. As it is written:

> And these are the things that you shall do on the altar: two yearling lambs without blemish each day upon the altar perpetually, an offering in perpetuity. The one lamb you shall do in the morning, and the second lamb you shall do in the evening. And a tenth of fine flour mixed with beaten oil, the fourth of a hin, and a libation, the fourth of a hin of wine, with the one lamb. And the second lamb you shall do in the evening. In accordance with the morning sacrifice, and in accordance with its libation you shall do, an odor of fragrance, an offering to the Lord, a sacrifice in perpetuity throughout your generations, at the doors of the tent of witness before the Lord, by which I will be known to you there so as to speak to you. And I will there prescribe for the sons of Israel, and I will be regarded as holy by my glory. And I will consecrate the tent of witness. (Exod 29:38–44 LXX)

What other perpetual sacrifice can be spiritual to a spiritual person, than the Word at its height, the Word symbolically called **lamb** which descends even while the soul is being illuminated—for this would be the perpetual morning sacrifice—and then ascends again at the end of the mind's contemplation of more heavenly matters? The mind cannot always remain among higher things since the soul has been ordered to be joined to an earthly, burdened body.

If someone should ask what the saint should do between dawn and evening, let us apply the principle from the details of the sacrifices and then follow it in these matters as well. For there, too, the priests offer the perpetual offerings as the beginning of the sacrifices, and then, before the perpetual evening sacrifice, they offer the sacrifices prescribed by the law such as those relating to transgressions, unintentional sins (Num 15:25), deliverance (Lev 3:1–2), vows (Lev 27), jealousy (Num 5:15), the Sabbath (Num 28:9–10), the new moon (Num 28:11–15), and the rest which would be too long to discuss right now. Likewise, after we have begun to make our offering relating to the image, that is Christ, we will be able to understand numerous beneficial things. . . .

Consider John's word about Jesus when he says, This is the **Lamb of God who takes away the sin of the world** (1:29). From the standpoint of the very economy of the bodily coming of the Son of God in human life, we will understand that the **lamb** refers to nothing other than his humanity. For *like a sheep he was led to the slaughter and as a lamb is silent before the one shearing it* (Isa 53:7 LXX), saying, *I was like an innocent lamb led to the slaughter* (Jer 11:19 LXX). So also in the book of Revelation a **lamb** is seen *standing as though it had been slain* (Rev 5:6). For mysterious reasons, this slain **lamb** became the expiation for the whole world. In agreement with the Father's love for humanity, the Son accepted his own slaughter on behalf of the world, purchasing us with his own blood from the one who had bought us when we sold ourselves to sins.

The one who led this **lamb** to the slaughter was God-in-man, our *great high priest* (Heb 8:1), who reveals this reality when he says, *No one takes my soul from me, but I lay it down of my own accord. I have power to lay it down, and I have power to take it again* (10:18).

(45) John Chrysostom

John the Baptist says **Behold** (1:29), because for a long time many people had been seeking the one whom John was talking about. This is why John indicates his presence, saying **Behold**, this is the one you have sought for so long; this is **the Lamb** (1:29). He calls Jesus **the Lamb** to remind the Jews of Isaiah's prophecy and the shadow of the Mosaic law, and to lead them from the type to the truth. The ancient **lambs** didn't entirely take away sin from anyone. This **Lamb** took away **the sin of the** whole **world** (1:29).

(46) Augustine of Hippo

Jesus comes, and what does John say? **Behold, the Lamb of God** (1:29). If a **lamb** is innocent, then John too is a **lamb**. Was he not innocent as well? But then who is innocent? How innocent? All of us come from that transplant and that cutting about which David sighs as he chants, *I was brought forth in iniquity, and in sin did my mother conceive me* (Ps 51:5). Only that **Lamb**, however, did not come in such a way. For he was not *brought forth in iniquity*, because he was not conceived from mortality. Nor *in sin did* his *mother conceive* him. He whom a virgin conceived was born by a virgin, because she conceived by faith and accepted him by faith. So then, **Behold, the Lamb of God**. This one does not have Adam's heritage: he took Adam's flesh, but he did not carry Adam's sin. The one who did not take on sin from our lump (cf. 1 Cor 5:7) is the one **who takes away** our **sin. Behold, the Lamb of God, who takes away the sin of the world**.

(47) Augustine of Hippo

Christ is **the Lamb** in a unique sense, of course, because the disciples were also called lambs: *Behold, I send you out as sheep in the midst of wolves* (Matt 10:16). They were also called light: *You are the light of the world* (Matt 5:14); but in a different way was it said of him: *The true light that enlightens every man was coming into the world* (1:9). Likewise, he is **the Lamb** in a unique sense because he alone is without stain, without sin—not one whose stains had been wiped away, but one who had no stain to begin with. What, after all, was the significance of John saying about the Lord, **Behold, the Lamb of God**? Was not John himself a **lamb**? Was not John a holy man? Was he not the friend of the bridegroom? So then, Christ is **Lamb** in a unique sense: This is **the Lamb of God** because, in a unique sense, only by the blood of this **Lamb** could human beings be redeemed.

(48) Theodore of Mopsuestia

Let us observe how typical it is for the divine Scriptures to apply terms appropriately, according to the facts. After the evangelist called Christ the one who **takes away the sin of the world**, he did not say "the only Son" or "the Son of God" or "he is in the bosom of the Father," as he did earlier. We might think that now would be the appropriate time to speak about the majesty of Christ's nature, so as to confirm the coming of the blessings he promised. But he did not talk about this; instead, he spoke of Christ in reference to his passion: **the Lamb of God**. He was called **lamb** and *sheep* (cf. Isa 53:7) because of his death, and by his passion he put an end to **sin** and the reign of mortality. Because death pressed in upon us, our Lord and Savior Jesus Christ came and released us from all these things. And when he put an end to death by his own death, he destroyed the **sin** which was firmly planted in our nature because of mortality. While he has already made us immortal by a promise, he will at last make us immortal in reality when he defeats **sin** by the gift of immortality. . . .

Obviously John said, **Behold, the Lamb of God** because he was showing them that the one they were expecting had already come. It is appropriate to say this, for according to the word of Isaiah, it says, *like a lamb that is led to the slaughter, and like a sheep that before its shearers is dumb* (Isa 53:7). They were expecting one to come who would die for the sake of all, and absolve the sins of all. So it was right for John to say **Behold, the Lamb of God**, that is, "This is the one whom Isaiah predicted." . . .

(49) Leo the Great

O Lord, you drew all things to yourself so that what was celebrated in the one temple of Judea in shadowy signs, is now celebrated everywhere by the piety of all nations in full and unhidden rite. Now, when the various fleshly sacrifices have ceased, the offering of your body and blood together fulfill all those different victims, since you are the true **Lamb of God, who takes away the sin of the world** (1:29). Thus you make perfect in yourself all mysteries, so that just as there is one sacrifice for every victim, so there may be one kingdom for every race.

(50) Cyril of Alexandria

The words, *Prepare the way* (Matt 3:3), are no longer appropriate since the one for whom the preparation was made has appeared before our eyes. The facts of the matter needed another expression. It was necessary to explain who it is who comes forth, and to whom he comes, having descended to us from heaven. **Behold**, he says, **the Lamb of God who takes away the sin of the world**, whom the prophet Isaiah signified to us, saying, *As a sheep was led to the slaughter, and as a lamb before his shearer, he was dumb* (Isa 53:7). He is the one of old, John says, whom the law typified through Moses. Previously, God saved in part, not stretching out his mercy to all, for it came in a type and a shadow. But now, the ancient one who was pictured through mysteries—the true **lamb**, the blameless sacrifice—is led to the slaughter for all. This happens so that he might **take away the sin of the world**; so that he might conquer the destroyer of the whole world; so that he might abolish death, dying for all; so that he might break the curse over us; so that hereafter the words *You are dust and to dust you shall return* (Gen 3:19) might cease; so that there might be a second Adam, not from dust but from heaven (cf. 1 Cor 15:47); and so that there might be the beginning of all good things for humanity's nature—deliverance from alien corruption, the gift of eternal life, the foundation of our renewal in God, the beginning of godliness and righteousness, and the way to the kingdom of heaven. *For one lamb died for all* (cf. 2 Cor 5:15), restoring to God the Father the entire company on earth, *one for all*, so that he might gain all, and that from here on, all *might no longer live for themselves but for the one who died for them and rose again* (2 Cor 5:15).

Since we were burdened by many sins, and therefore in debt to death and corruption, the Father gave his Son as a ransom for us, *one for all*, since all are in him and he is above all. One died for all that all might live in him. Death, having swallowed up the **lamb** once for all, vomited all in him and with him. For all were in Christ who died and rose again on our account and on our behalf. But when sin was abolished, why did he allow death not to be abolished entirely—death which was from sin and on account of sin? When the root was killed, why would the sprout which came from it be preserved any further? Why will we still die when sin has been destroyed?

Therefore, when we celebrate the sacrifice of the **Lamb of God** we say: *Where is your sting, oh death? Where is your victory, oh grave?* (cf. Hos 13:14; 1 Cor 15:55). As the psalmist sings, *all iniquity will stop her mouth* (Ps 107:42 [106:42 LXX]), no longer being able to accuse those who have sinned out of weakness. *For God is the one who justifies, who will condemn?* (Rom 8:33–34). *Christ has redeemed us from the curse of the law, being made a curse for us* (Gal 3:13) so that we might escape the ruin which comes from iniquity.

(51) Venerable Bede

The paschal **lamb**, which once freed the people from their Egyptian slavery, properly prefigures Christ. This **lamb** was offered in memory of the very liberation it had brought about, thereby sanctifying the same people year after year until the one for whom the paschal **lamb** served as a great witness should come. And so he, who was to be offered to the Father on our behalf as sacrifice and pleasing odor, and who had been made *a priest forever after the order of Melchizedek* (Heb 7:17), transferred the mystery of his passion into the bread and wine once the **lamb** had been offered.

1:31 "For this I came baptizing with water, that he might be revealed to Israel."

---

(52) Augustine of Hippo

What was the value of John's baptism? My brothers and sisters, if it had any value, it would have continued to this day, and people would still be baptized with the baptism of John, and, in that way, would come to the baptism of Christ. But what did he say? **That he might be revealed to Israel** (1:31), that is, John came to baptize in water so that Christ might be manifested to Israel, to the people of Israel. John received the ministry of baptism in the water of repentance to prepare a way for the Lord, although the Lord was not yet present; but once the Lord had become known it was superfluous to prepare a way for him, because he himself had become the way for those who knew him. That is why John's baptism did not last.

1:32 "I saw the Spirit descend as a dove from heaven, and it remained on him."

---

(53) Theodore of Mopsuestia

And John testified and said, "I saw the Spirit descend as a dove from heaven, and it remained on him (1:32). It is evident from this that the **descent** of the **Spirit** at our Lord's baptism came upon him in the form of a **dove** which was not visible to everyone nearby. Instead, John alone saw it in a spiritual vision, like the prophets used to see things that were not visible to everyone while they were among the multitude. Would it not have been superfluous to say, **John testified and said, "I saw the Spirit"** if everyone nearby saw the same thing?

Therefore, it is foolish for people to say that because a **dove** is inferior to a man, the Holy Spirit is inferior to Christ our Lord. For John beheld a vision of the Spirit, not its nature. And not a single person standing there saw it, for John received his vision by a revelation of the Spirit, just as Peter saw the sheet full of all kinds of animals descending from heaven while he was praying on the roof (Acts 10:9–16).

John 1:35-42

³⁵The next day again John was standing with two of his disciples; ³⁶and he looked at Jesus as he walked, and said, "Behold, the Lamb of God!" ³⁷The two disciples heard him say this, and they followed Jesus. ³⁸Jesus turned, and saw them following, and said to them, "What do you seek?" And they said to him, "Rabbi" (which means Teacher), "where are you staying?" ³⁹He said to them, "Come and see." They came and saw where he was staying; and they stayed with him that day, for it was about the tenth hour. ⁴⁰One of the two who heard John speak, and followed him, was Andrew, Simon Peter's brother. ⁴¹He first found his brother Simon, and said to him, "We have found the Messiah" (which means Christ). ⁴²He brought him to Jesus. Jesus looked at him, and said, "So you are Simon the son of John? You shall be called Cephas" (which means Peter).

1:38 Jesus turned, and saw them following, and said to them, "What do you seek?" And they said to him, "Rabbi" (which means Teacher), "where are you staying?"

---

(54) John Chrysostom

Jesus turned, and saw them following, and said to them, "What do you seek?" (1:38). We are taught by this that God does not overcome our wills with gifts, but when we begin, when we supply the willingness, then he also gives us many opportunities for salvation. **What do you seek?** What does this mean? The one who knows the hearts of men, the one who enters into our thoughts—this one asks a question! But he does this not in order to learn something (for how could that be), but rather to give them direction through the questions, and embolden them, showing them that they are worthy to hear him. It was likely that they would blush and be anxious, as if they were unknown to him, even when their teacher, John the Baptist, testified about him. Therefore, removing all these things—the shame and the fear—he questions them and does not allow them to go as far as the house in silence.

Yet the same thing would have happened if he had not questioned them. Following him, they would have remained with him, and walking by foot, they would have approached the house. Why then does he question them? For this reason, as I said: to calm their minds, still blushing and distressed, and to give them an opportunity to be bold. And not only by following him, but also through their questions, they made their desire clear. Before they had even learned from him or heard him, they call him **Teacher** (1:38), enrolling themselves as his disciples and demonstrating why they were following: to hear something profitable.

Notice their good sense. They did not say, "Teach us your doctrine" or some other requirement. What did they say? **Where are you staying?** (1:38). They came, as I said before, to say something to him in quietness, to hear something from him, and to learn. They don't hesitate or say, "Surely, we will come tomorrow and hear you speaking in public." Instead, they showed their great zeal for listening, and did not turn aside even for an hour. The sun was nearly setting, for he says, **It was about the tenth hour** (1:39). This is why Christ doesn't give them directions or tell them the place, but persuades them all the more to follow, showing them that he accepts them. This is also why Christ does not say, "Now is not a good time for you to enter my house; hear me tomorrow if you want, and go home for now." Instead he converses with them as friends and long-time acquaintances.

1:42 "You are Simon the son of John? You shall be called Cephas" (which means Peter).

---

(55) Augustine of Hippo

He brought him to Jesus. Jesus looked at him, and said, "So you are Simon the son of John? You shall be called Cephas" (which means Peter) (1:42). It's not a big deal that the Lord said whose son this man was. What was so great that the Lord knew this? He knew the names of all his saints, whom he predestined *before the foundation of the world* (Eph 1:4); are you astonished when he says to one man, "You are the son of so-and-so, and you shall be called such-and-such"? It's great, instead, that he changed his name and transformed Simon into Peter; the name Peter comes from rock (*petra*); the rock, however, is the church. Therefore, the church is signified in the name of Peter. And who is safe but the one who builds upon the rock?

And what does the Lord say? *Every one then who hears these words of mine and does them will be like a wise man who built his house upon the rock* (he does not yield to temptations); *and the rain fell, and the floods came, and the winds blew and beat upon that house, but it did not fall, because it had been founded on the rock. And every one who hears these words of mine and does not do them* (now let every one of us, please, be afraid and be put upon our guard) *will be like a foolish man who built his house upon the sand; and the rain fell, and the floods came, and the winds blew and beat against that house, and it fell; and great was the fall of it* (Matt 7:24–27). What good does it do to enter the church if someone wants to build upon sand? Listening without acting is indeed building, but building upon sand. If one never listens, after all, one does not build anything either; but whoever hears, builds. We want to know what is built upon. For, if someone hears and acts, they build upon rock; if someone hears and does not act, they build upon sand. There are two kinds of builders; those who build on rock and those who build on sand. . . .

So then, this is what you, my beloved, should know; that unless you are both hearing and acting, you are not building upon rock, and you do not belong to that great name, which the Lord recommended to us. He was catching your attention, you see; because if the man had been called **Peter** before, you would not have seen the mystery of the rock in this way. You would have thought his being called **Peter** was just a matter of chance, not part of God's providence. That's why he wanted him called something else first, so that by the change of name the vital power of the mystery might be impressed upon us.

John 1:43–51

⁴³The next day Jesus decided to go to Galilee. And he found Philip and said to him, "Follow me." ⁴⁴Now Philip was from Bethsaida, the city of Andrew and Peter. ⁴⁵Philip found Nathanael, and said to him, "We have found him of whom Moses in the law and also the prophets wrote, Jesus of Nazareth, the son of Joseph." ⁴⁶Nathanael said to him, "Can anything good come out of Nazareth?" Philip said to him, "Come and see." ⁴⁷Jesus saw Nathanael coming to him, and said of him, "Behold, an Israelite indeed, in whom is no guile!" ⁴⁸Nathanael said to him, "How do you know me?" Jesus answered him, "Before Philip called you, when you were under the fig tree, I saw you." ⁴⁹Nathanael answered him, "Rabbi, you are the Son of God! You are the King of Israel!" ⁵⁰Jesus answered him, "Because I said to you, I saw you under the fig tree, do you believe? You shall see greater things than these." ⁵¹And he said to him, "Truly, truly, I say to you, you will see heaven opened, and the angels of God ascending and descending upon the Son of man."

1:48 "When you were under the fig tree, I saw you."

---

(56) Augustine of Hippo

It should be asked whether this **fig tree** has any significance. Listen to him, my brothers and sisters: *We found the fig tree cursed, because it only had leaves and had no fruit* (cf. Matt 21:19).[18] At the origins of the human race, when Adam and Eve had sinned they made themselves aprons out of fig leaves (cf. Gen 3:7 Vulgate); thus, fig leaves are understood to mean sins. Now Nathanael was under the **fig tree** as if under the shadow of death. The Lord saw him, and of him it was said, *Those who sat under the shadow of death, on them has light shined* (Isa 9:2). So then, what was said to Nathanael? "You ask me, Nathanael, **How did you know me?** (1:48). You are talking to me now because Philip called you." The Lord had already seen that anyone called by an apostle belonged to his church.

O church, O Israel, **in whom** there **is no guile** (1:47), if you are the people of Israel **in whom** there **is no guile**, you have now already come to know Christ through the apostles, as Nathanael knew Christ through Philip. But his mercy saw you before you came to know him, while you were lying flat on your back under sin. Did we, in fact, first go looking for Christ or was he the one who came looking for us? Did we, the sick, first go to the doctor or was it the doctor who came to the sick? Wasn't the sheep lost, and didn't the shepherd leave the ninety-nine and go looking for it and find it, bringing it back joyfully on his shoulders (Luke 15:4–5)? Wasn't that coin lost when that woman lit a lamp and searched for it everywhere in the house until she found it? And when she found it, she said to her neighbors, *Rejoice with me, because I have found the coin which I had lost* (Luke 15:4–10). In the same way we too were lost like sheep and lost like the coin. Our shepherd found the

---

18. Augustine's text does not match Matthew exactly.

sheep, but he first went looking for the sheep; the woman found the coin, but first she was looking for the coin. . . .

And so when Nathanael said, **How did you know me?** (1:48) the Lord said to him, **Before Philip called you, when you were under the fig tree, I saw you** (1:48). O Israel without **guile**, whoever you are, O people living by faith, before I called you through my apostles, while you were *under the shadow of death*, and you did not see me, I saw you.

John 2

The story of the marriage at Cana afforded ancient Christians the opportunity to address the blessing of marriage. Augustine of Hippo, Cyril of Alexandria, Romanos the Melodist, and the Venerable Bede, for example, all suggest that Jesus came to the wedding to sanctify marriage and the act of procreation. Of particular interest are the words of Jesus to Mary: O woman, what have you to do with me? (2:4). Irenaeus, John Chrysostom, and Theodore of Mopsuestia see in these words a rebuke of Mary's misunderstanding, haste, or selfish desire for personal glory, while Augustine of Hippo and Bede contrast Jesus's harsh words here with his tender compassion and love for his mother at the cross. Irenaeus and Romanos the Melodist address the meaning of Jesus's comment in verse 4 (My hour has not yet come) through a discussion of the divinely ordered plan of salvation.

In discussing the filling of the water jars by the servants (2:6-11), both Irenaeus of Lyons and John Chrysostom see Christ's miracle of turning water into wine as an affirmation that the God of creation is also the God who sent his Son Jesus. Augustine sees in the six water jars (2:6) a typology referring to the six ages of the world, the sixth being the age of the gospel of Christ.

Moving to the temple-cleansing passage, several commentators offer figural interpretations. Origen of Alexandria compares the Israelite Passover and its regulations with the Christian Passover celebrated in a spiritual manner. Noting Jesus's action of driving out of the temple those who were selling oxen and sheep and pigeons (2:14), Origen of Alexandria sees these as referring to the dispositions of the soul, and both Augustine and Cyril of Alexandria offer a charming illustration of our need to beware the disciplinary cords of sin. Yet Augustine, the Venerable Bede, and Cyril of Alexandria also understand the merchants in the temple as hypocritical leaders in the church who need to be driven out with discipline.

Jesus's words you shall not make my Father's house a house of trade (2:16) lent themselves to a discussion of the uniqueness of Jesus's relationship to God the Father, as seen in the selection from Cyril of Alexandria. Interestingly, John Chrysostom, recognizing that the other gospels record Jesus clearing the Temple at the end of his ministry, concludes that Jesus performed this action on two separate occasions.

Verse 19 (Destroy this temple, and in three days I will raise it up) and verse 21 (But he spoke of the temple of his body) were routinely drawn upon in discussions of the importance of the body in the resurrected state. Irenaeus of Lyons, Tertullian of Carthage, Augustine of

Hippo, and John of Damascus all argue that because, according to Christ's words, the body is in fact a temple of God, it too will participate in our salvation.

Likewise, Augustine of Hippo, Theodoret of Cyrus, and Leo the Great use this same verse to explain that Christ is both human and divine. Theodoret, for example, argues that Christ said Destroy this temple *(2:19), rather than "Destroy me" to show that "it was not God who was being* destroyed, *but the* temple*" of his body. In a related way, verse 19 was employed by Augustine of Hippo and John Cassian in defense of the deity of Christ in being able to raise himself from the dead.*

John 2:1–11

¹On the third day there was a marriage at Cana in Galilee, and the mother of Jesus was there; ²Jesus also was invited to the marriage, with his disciples. ³When the wine gave out, the mother of Jesus said to him, "They have no wine." ⁴And Jesus said to her, "O woman, what have you to do with me? My hour has not yet come." ⁵His mother said to the servants, "Do whatever he tells you." ⁶Now six stone jars were standing there, for the Jewish rites of purification, each holding twenty or thirty gallons. ⁷Jesus said to them, "Fill the jars with water." And they filled them up to the brim. ⁸He said to them, "Now draw some out, and take it to the steward of the feast." So they took it. ⁹When the steward of the feast tasted the water now become wine, and did not know where it came from (though the servants who had drawn the water knew), the steward of the feast called the bridegroom ¹⁰and said to him, "Every man serves the good wine first; and when men have drunk freely, then the poor wine; but you have kept the good wine until now." ¹¹This, the first of his signs, Jesus did at Cana in Galilee, and manifested his glory; and his disciples believed in him.

(1) Romanos the Melodist

Strophe 2: The one who had no mortal **marriage**, he who alone is holy and awesome,
    Was present in the bridal chamber, as the divine John taught.
He who experienced childbirth without wedding came to the **marriage**
    He who alone is borne upon the wings of the Cherubim,
    He who exists in the *bosom of the Father* (1:18), inseparable from him,
    Reclined in a mortal home;
He who knew no sin dined with sinners,
    In order that he might by his presence show that marriage is to be honored.
    He who has in wisdom made all things.

Strophe 5: When Christ was present at the **marriage** feast, and the crowd of guests were
    faring sumptuously,

The supply of **wine failed** them, and their joy was turned to distress.
The bridegroom was upset; the cupbearers muttered unceasingly;
There was this one sad display of penury,
And there was no small clamor in the room.
Recognizing it, the all-holy Mary
Came at once and said to her son: "**They have no wine** (2:3),
But I beg you, my son, show that you can do all things,
Thou who hast in wisdom made all things."

Strophe 6:   We beg you, holy virgin, from what sort of miracle did you know
How your son would be able to offer **wine**
when he had not harvested the grapes
And had never before worked wonders, as John, inspired of God wrote?[1]
Teach us, how, when you had never gazed upon
And never made trial of his miracles,
How did you summon him to this miracle?
For the question now posed to us in this matter is not simple,
As to how you said to your son: "Give them **wine**,"
He who has in wisdom made all things.

Strophe 7:   Let us learn the word which the mother of the God of all said to us:
"Listen," she said, "my friends, instruct yourselves and know the mystery;
I have seen my son working miracles even before this miracle;
John was not yet his disciple,
John was not yet discipled to Christ
At the time when he did those miracles.
The first, the very beginning of his miracles, is this one
Which John beheld in Cana, as my son knew,
He who has in wisdom made all things.

Strophe 8:   "Seeing that no one among men clearly has faith
In things written in books by those
who were not eyewitnesses of his grace,
I shall omit these things; but I shall touch
on more important matters of which I have knowledge.
For I know that I did not know a husband,
And I bore a son—beyond natural law and reason,
And I know that I remained a virgin as I had been.
Do you, O man, ask for a miracle greater than this birth?
Gabriel came to me saying how this one would be born,
He who has in wisdom made all things."

---

1. Romanos refers to this being **the first of his signs** (2:11).

Strophe 10: But Christ, seeing his mother saying, "Grant me this request,"
        At once said to her:
            "What do you wish, **O woman? My hour has not yet come"** (2:4).
    Certain men made use of this saying as a pretext for impiety;
        They said that Christ submitted to necessity,
        They said that he was a slave to periods of time;
        But they do not understand the meaning of his phrase.
    However, the mouth of the impious who practice evil has been stopped,
        Since straightaway he performed the miracle,
            He who has in wisdom made all things.

Strophe 11: "Now answer, my child," said the all-holy mother of Christ,
        "Thou who dost control with measurement the periods of time,
            How, my son and Lord, dost thou await a time?
    Thou who hast regulated the division of the seasons,
            how dost thou await a season?
    Thou who art the Creator of the visible and invisible,
    Thou who, as master, dost day and night regulate
    The ceaseless revolutions, as thou dost will them—
    Thou who hast defined the years in beautifully ordered cycles—
        How, then, dost thou await a time for the miracle which I ask of thee
            Who hast in wisdom made all things?"

Strophe 12: "I knew before you told me, revered virgin, that the **wine** was just
            Beginning to **fail** for them,"
    The ineffable and merciful one straightaway answered his holy mother.
    "I know all the concerns of your heart which you set in motion in this matter;
        For within yourself you reasoned as follows:
        'Necessity now summons my son to a miracle,
        And he puts it off under the pretext of "time."'
    Holy mother, learn now the meaning of the delay,
        For when you know it, I shall grant you this favor,
            I, who have in wisdom made all things.

Strophe 14: "Listen carefully, Holy One, how I was able in another way
        To ransom the fallen and not take on the form of a poor slave;
    However, I did allow being conceived and born as a man,
        And taking milk at your breasts, O virgin,
        And everything in me progressed in order;
        For as far as I am concerned nothing is without order.
    And so now I am willing to accomplish the miracle in a well-regulated order,
        A thing which I consent to do for the salvation of man,
            I, who have in wisdom made all things.

Strophe 15: "Mark what I say, holy one, for at this time I was willing first
      To announce to the Israelites and to teach them the hope of faith,
      In order that in the presence of miracles they might learn thoroughly
         who has sent me
      And that they might know with certainty the glory of my Father,
      And his will, for he desires that in every way
      I be glorified along with him by all men.
   For what he who has begotten me has done, these things I also do,
      Since I am consubstantial with him and his Spirit,
        I, who have in wisdom made all things.

Strophe 16: "For if they had understood all these things at the time
      When they saw the awesome miracles,
      They would understand that I am God before time,
        even though I have become man.
   But now, contrary to order, before the teaching, you have asked for miracles;
      And it is for this reason that I delayed a short time in answer to you:
      If I was waiting for the time to perform miracles,
      It was for this reason alone.
   But since it is necessary that parents be honored by their children,
      I shall pay observance to you, Mother, for I am able to do all things,
        I, who have in wisdom made all things."

Strophe 20: When Christ, as a sign of his power, clearly changed the **water** into **wine**,
      All the crowd rejoiced, for they considered the taste marvelous.
   Now we all partake at the banquet in the church
      For the **wine** is changed into Christ's blood
      And we drink it with a holy joy,
      Praising the great bridegroom,
   For he is the true **bridegroom**, the Son of Mary,
      The Word before all time who took the form of a servant (cf. Phil 2),
      He who hast in wisdom made all things.

2:1 On the third day there was a marriage.

---

(2) Ammonius of Alexandria

The Lord came to the **marriage** in order to sanctify not only the living, but also those who were about to be born. He demonstrated that he himself ordained **marriage** from the beginning when he gave Eve to Adam. Likewise he shamed those heretics who disparage **marriage**.

(3) Augustine of Hippo

Because the Lord had been invited to the **marriage**, he came. He wanted to show, even apart from its mystical significance, that marriage had been instituted by him. For there would be those about whom the apostle spoke who *forbid marriage* (1 Tim 4:3) and say that marriage is an evil made by the devil. In the gospel, the same Lord, when asked whether it is permissible for a man to divorce his wife for any cause, says that it is not allowed except for fornication. In his response, if you remember, he said: *What therefore God has joined together, let not man put asunder* (Matt 19:6).

Those who are well instructed in the catholic faith know that God instituted **marriage**, and because this union is from God, divorce is from the devil. The reason it is permissible to divorce one's wife in the case of fornication is this: if she does not remain faithful to her vows she shows that she did not really want to be a wife. Nor should one think that women who make a vow to remain chaste, and are even ranked higher in honor and holiness in the church, have nothing to do with marriage. For they, with the whole church, take part in a **marriage** in which Christ is the bridegroom (Eph 5:32). For this reason Christ, who had been **invited**, came to the **marriage** to affirm marital purity and to show forth the mystery of **marriage**. Even the bridegroom in that marriage represented the person of the Lord, for about him it was said: **You have kept the good wine until now** (2:10). For the **good wine**, that is the gospel, Christ **kept until now**.

(4) Cyril of Alexandria

The evangelist comes next to the beginning of his miracles; even Christ seems called to it involuntarily. When a **marriage** celebration is being performed (and it is certainly clear that this was an honorable occasion), **the mother** of the Savior **was there**; and **Jesus** himself, **having been invited**, arrives together **with his** own **disciples**, working miracles rather than feasting with them. Yet, he also comes to the **marriage** to sanctify the very beginning of human birth (insofar as he came in the flesh). It was necessary that he, who was renewing the very nature of humanity and restoring it entirely for the better, should not only give his blessing to those who have already been called into existence, but also make his grace ready for those who are yet to be born, and render holy their coming into existence.

There is also a third reason that he came to the wedding: God had said to the woman, *In pain you shall bring forth children* (Gen 3:16). How necessary was it, then, that this curse be driven away? How else could we escape **marriage** being under a curse? And the Savior, being a lover of humanity, removed this curse. He, who is the cheerfulness and joy of all, had honored **marriage** by his presence in order that he might drive out the ancient grief of childbearing. For *if anyone is in Christ, he is a new creation. The old has passed away*, as Paul says, *and the new has come* (2 Cor 5:17). Therefore, he comes **with his** own **disciples** to the **marriage**. In order for those who wished to see wonders to be present, they needed to be with the worker of miracles. In that way, they received the miracle as a nourishment for their faith. And when the **wine failed** the guests, **the mother** called the

Lord, relying on his customary goodness and his customary love for humanity, saying **They have no wine** (2:3). Since everything he desires is in his power to do, she urges him toward the miracle. . . .

This first miracle accomplished many excellent things. Honorable **marriage** was sanctified and the curse against women was banished. No longer will they bear children *in pain* (Gen 3:15), and Christ blesses the very beginning of our birth. The glory of our Savior shone forth like the rays of the sun. And what is more, the disciples were confirmed in their faith by the working of this miracle.

So much for the historical sense. But I think it is necessary to consider also the spiritual sense of what has been said, and to discern what is being signified. The Word of God came down from heaven, as Scripture says, in order that, having taken on human nature as a bridegroom, he might woo us to bring forth spiritual seeds of wisdom. And for this reason, humankind is fittingly called a bride and the Savior a bridegroom (Eph 5:23–33), since the divine Scripture lifts up ordinary language to express things that are above. But the marriage is consummated on the **third day** (2:1), that is, in the last times of the present age. The number three introduces the beginning, middle, and end, for all of time is measured out this way. This also seems to agree with one of the holy prophets who said, *He will strike us and he will bind us up. After two days, he will heal us; and on the third day we shall arise and live before him and we shall know him. Let us follow on to know the Lord; we shall find him sure as the dawn* (Hos 6:1–3). He strikes us on account of the transgression of Adam, saying, *You are dust, and to dust you shall return* (Gen 3:19). That which had been wounded with corruption and death he himself bound up on the **third day**, that is, not on the first, or in the middle, but in the last days when, having become man on our account, he made our entire nature sound, raising it from the dead in himself. Indeed, for this reason, he is called *the first-fruits of those who have fallen asleep* (1 Cor 15:20).

Therefore in saying that it was the **third day** when the **marriage** was consummated, he signifies the end times. He also mentions the place, for he says **in Cana of Galilee** (2:11). Let the lover of learning again take note, for the celebration is not in Jerusalem, but the feast is outside of Judea, performed in the region of the gentiles: *Galilee of the Gentiles* as the prophet says (Isa 9:1). And I suppose it is entirely clear that the synagogue of the Jews rejected the bridegroom from heaven, but the church of the gentiles received him quite gladly. But the Savior does not come to the **marriage** of his own account; he was being called by the many voices of the saints.

(5) Venerable Bede

When he was **invited to a marriage**, our Lord and Savior not only deigned to come, but even to work miracles there to gladden the guests. Even if we leave aside the figural meanings regarding heavenly sacraments, still according to the literal sense this miracle confirms the faith of devout believers. . . . For if there were fault in an immaculate **marriage** bed and in a **marriage** celebrated with due chastity, the Lord would by no means have wished to come to this **marriage**, and by no means would he have wished to consecrate it with the

first of his signs. Conjugal chastity is good, the continence of a widow is better, and the perfection of a virgin is best. Therefore, in order to demonstrate his approval of the choice of all these ranks while still affirming the merit of each, he deigned to be born from the inviolate womb of the virgin Mary. Soon after being born he was blessed by the prophetic voice of the widow Anna (Luke 2:36–38). Then as a young man he was **invited** by those celebrating a **marriage**, and he honored them by the presence of his power.

But there is a more profound gladness in the heavenly figural meanings. . . . In a certain place he said concerning himself and his faithful ones, *Can the children of the bridegroom mourn as long as the bridegroom is with them? The days will come, when the bridegroom is taken away from them, and then they will fast* (Matt 9:15 Vulgate). From the time that the incarnation of our Savior was first promised to the patriarchs, it was always awaited by many of the saints with tears and mourning until he came. Similarly, from that time when, after his resurrection, he ascended to heaven, all the hope of the saints hangs upon his return. Only while he was in the company of human beings were they unable to weep and mourn. They had in the body the one whom they loved spiritually. Therefore the bridegroom is Christ, the bride is the church, and *the children of the bridegroom*, or *of the marriage* (Mark 2:19) are each and every one of his faithful. The time of the **marriage** is that time when, through the mystery of the incarnation, he joined the holy church to himself. Thus it was not by chance, but for the sake of a certain mystical meaning, that he came to a **marriage** celebrated on earth in the customary fleshly way, since he descended from heaven to earth in order to connect the church to himself in spiritual love. . . .

But we are also told that this **marriage** was performed in **Cana of Galilee** (which means "in the zeal of emigration"). Typologically speaking, this denotes that those who are aflame with the zeal of pious devotion, and who know how to emulate the greater charismatic gifts, and to emigrate from vices to virtues by doing good works, and from earthly to eternal things by hoping and loving—these are especially worthy of Christ's grace.

While the Lord was reclining at the **marriage**, the **wine failed**, so that, when in a marvelous fashion he made better **wine**, the glory of God lying hidden in a human being might be manifested, and the faith of those who believed in him might increase. If we seek the mystical meaning in this, when the Lord appeared in the flesh the undiluted sweetness of meaning according to the law had gradually begun to **fail** of its former virtue because of its fleshly interpretation by the Pharisees. Christ soon turned those seemingly fleshly mandates into spiritual teaching. He changed the whole exterior appearance of the letter of the law into the gospel virtue of heavenly grace—which is the meaning of his having made **wine** from **water**. . . .

But as different as **water** is from **wine**, so is the difference between the way the Scriptures were understood before the Savior's coming and what he himself revealed to the apostles when he came, and which he left to be perpetually followed by their disciples. Of course, the Lord could have filled empty **jars** with **wine**, since in the elementary stages of the world's creation he created all things out of nothing. But he preferred to make **wine** from **water** in order to teach that he had not come to cancel and repudiate the law and the prophets, but to fulfill them, nor to do and to teach other things through the grace of the gospel than what the law and the prophets of Scripture had indicated that he would do and teach.

2:3–4 "They have no wine." And Jesus said to her, "O woman, what have you to do with me?"

---

(6) Irenaeus of Lyons

In Christ, nothing is out of place and untimely, just as there is nothing out of accord in the Father. While all things are foreknown by the Father, they are accomplished by the Son, arranging things well in their proper time. This is why, when Mary rushes to the remarkable sign of the **wine** and desires to participate in the profitable cup (cf. 1 Cor 10:16–17) before its time, the Lord denounces her untimely haste and says: **O woman, what have you to do with me? My hour has not yet come** (2:4). He was awaiting that hour which was foreknown by the Father. This is why, when men often desired to seize him, **No one**, it says, **laid hands on him, because his hour** of being seized **had not yet come** (7:30), nor the time of his passion which had been foreknown by the Father, just as the prophet Habakkuk also says, *In this, thou shalt be acknowledged when the years draw nigh, thou shalt be manifested when the time is come; when my soul is troubled, thou wilt in wrath remember mercy* (Hab 3:2 Vulgate). Paul also says: *But when the time had fully come, God sent forth his son* (Gal 4:4).

By this we know that all things which were foreknown by the Father, our Lord accomplishes in the right order and time—at the hour known in advance—for he is one and the same, rich and great. He serves the rich and great will of the Father. He himself is the Savior of those who are saved, the Lord of those things which he rules, the God of all created things, the only-begotten of the Father, the Christ who was proclaimed, the Word of God who became incarnate when *the time had fully come* (Gal 4:4) and the Son of God became the Son of Man.

(7) John Chrysostom

"How then," someone says, "did his mother come to imagine something great concerning her son?" Because at that time, he was beginning to be made known by the witness of John and from what John had said to his disciples. And before all this, the conception itself and all that happened after his birth[2] had inspired in her this great notion concerning her son. For Scripture says she heard these things concerning the child, and *she kept all these things in her heart* (Luke 2:51). "Therefore," someone says, "why didn't she speak these things beforehand?" Because, just as I have said, he was only then beginning to be revealed. Indeed, before this, he lived as one of the multitude and his mother was not bold enough to speak such things to him. But when she heard that John came on his account and heard what John testified about him, and that he had disciples, only then, being bold, does she summon him and (because they lacked wine) say, **They have no wine** (2:3). For she desired both to do

---

2. Chrysostom probably has in mind the birth narrative accounts of the visit of the shepherds and the magi (cf. Luke 2:8–20 and Matt 2:1–12)

them a favor and to make herself more illustrious through her child. Perhaps she suffered some human disposition, just like his brothers who said *Show yourself to the world* (7:4), desiring to gain glory from his miracles. For this reason, Jesus answered more vehemently, saying **O woman, what have you to do with me? My hour has not yet come** (2:4). Yet he greatly respected his mother; listen to Luke who explains how he *was obedient* to his parents (Luke 2:51). John the evangelist himself demonstrates how he provided for her beforehand even at the very moment of the cross (cf. John 19:26–27).

Where parents do not impede or stop godly activity, it is absolutely necessary to obey—and not to do so is a great danger! But when they demand obedience at the wrong time and impede spiritual activity, it is not safe to obey. Therefore, he answered here and elsewhere again: *Who is my mother and who are my brothers?* (Matt 12:48) since they did not yet know who he was. But since she gave birth to him, following the custom of other mothers, she commands him in all things, though she ought to have feared and worshiped him as Lord. . . . This is why he said, *Who are my mother and my brothers?* He said this, not to insult the one who had given birth to him (banish the thought!), but to bring her the greatest benefit and not allow her to think lowly things about him. If he cared for other people, and used every means to instill in them an opinion befitting him, how much more for his mother? Since it was likely that if she also heard these words from her son, she would not want to be convinced but would altogether claim herself worthy of the chief rank, being his mother. This is why he answered those who addressed him. In no other way could he lead her up from that lowly idea to that exalted one, if she always expected to be honored by him as her son, but did not expect that he should come as her Lord.

It was then for this reason that he said, **O woman, what have you to do with me?** (2:4), and also for another reason no less important. What was that? So that the miracles performed would not be under suspicion. The request ought to have come from those who needed it, not from his mother. Why so? Because things done at the request of family members, even if they are great, often offend the onlookers. When those who have the need make the request, however, the miracle is without suspicion, the praise is pure, and the benefit is great.

If some excellent physician comes into the house of those who are sick, and listens not to those who are ill or their relatives, but is exhorted only by his own mother, he would be under suspicion and become an offense to those who are ill. None of those present or lying there would think that he was able to perform anything great and noble. Therefore, he rebuked her here, saying, **O woman, what have you to do with me?** (2:4), teaching her not to do such things in the future. While he was concerned with honoring his mother, he was much more concerned for the salvation of her soul and for doing good for the multitude, for whom he took on flesh. . . .

"And why," someone says, "after saying **My hour has not yet come** (2:4), and having rejected her, did he do what his mother said?" Mostly so that those who opposed him and thought that he was subject to the **hour** would have sufficient proof that he was not subject to the **hour**. If he was subject to it, how could he have done what he did before the proper **hour** had come? He also did it to honor his mother, so that he might not completely oppose her suggestion, take it as weak, or dishonor the one who bore him, being in the presence of so many (for she brought the servants to him).

(8) Theodore of Mopsuestia

When the wine failed, the mother of Jesus said to him, "They have no wine" (2:3). Like any mother, the Lord's mother was enticing him to perform a sign because she wanted her son's greatness to be revealed. She thought that the lack of wine was an opportune occasion for the deed. But our Lord says to her, **O woman, what have you to do with me? My hour has not yet come** (2:4). We can read this in another way: **my hour has not yet come** means, "What are you seeking to entice me to do? Do not think that there are two distinct times for me, one for knowing and one for doing . . . Power is always at hand for me to act whenever and however I want. And I am not incapable of demonstrating my power unless the need of those who receive it demands it. So the pretext you present (namely, the lack of wine) is an insult to me, as if I only gained my power because of the need of others, and not because it was my will for their need to exist in the first place."

(9) Augustine of Hippo

He did nothing by force, but everything by persuading and teaching. As you see, with the old slavery having been completed, the time of freedom had dawned and now humans are suitably and profitably persuaded that they have been created with free will. By his miracles, he who was God produced confidence in God, and by his passion, he produced confidence in the human nature which he bore. Thus, speaking to the crowds as God, he denied his own mother when she was announced, and yet, as the gospel says, he was a child submissive to his parents (cf. Luke 2:51). For in our doctrine, God and man appeared in different ways in the life of Jesus. Likewise, when changing water into wine, he speaks as God: "Depart from me, **O woman, what have you to do with me? My hour has not yet come**" (2:4). However, when the hour had come when as man he should die, he recognized his mother from the cross and commended her to the disciple whom he loved more than the others (John 19:26–27).

(10) Augustine of Hippo

Those who deny that our Lord Jesus Christ had Mary as his mother on earth ought to be detested. Rather, his incarnation honored both sexes, male and female, and revealed that both are included in God's care, not only what he assumed, but that also through which he assumed it, being a man born from a woman. Nor are we compelled to deny the mother of Christ because he said, **What have you to do with me? My hour has not yet come** (2:4). Rather, he admonishes us to understand that as God he has no mother, and was preparing to demonstrate his majestic character by turning water into wine. However, when he was crucified, he was crucified as a man. That was the hour which had not yet come when he said, **What have you to do with me? My hour has not yet come** (2:4), that is, "the hour in which I will recognize you." For at that time, being crucified as a man, he recognized his mother, a human, and commended her to his most beloved human disciple.

(11) Cyril of Alexandria

But the **wine failed** the feasters (2:3); the law perfected nothing and the Mosaic writing was not enough for perfect joy. Neither was the very measure of innate sobriety presented as something that could save us. Therefore it would be true to say about us, **They have no wine** (2:3). However, our richly endowed God does not disregard our nature worn away with the lack of good things. He promised a **wine** better than the first: *For the letter kills, but the Spirit gives life* (2 Cor 3:6). The law does not have perfection in good things, but the divine instructions of the evangelical teaching introduce the fullest blessing. The **steward of the feast** (2:9) marveled at the new **wine**. I suppose each of those appointed to the divine priesthood and entrusted with the house of our Savior Christ is amazed at the doctrine which is above the law. But Christ commands it to be given to himself first, because, according to the voice of Paul, *it is the hard-working farmer who ought to have the first share of the crops* (2 Tim 3:6). Let the hearer think again about what I am saying.

(12) Venerable Bede

Let us seek the meaning of what Jesus's mother said to him when the wine ran short: **They have no wine** (2:3), and his answer: **O woman, what is that to me and you? My hour has not yet come** (2:4).[3] He would not dishonor his mother, since he orders us to honor our father and mother; and he would not deny that she was his mother, since he did not disdain to adopt flesh from her virginal flesh, as the apostle also bears witness when he says, *who was descended from* the seed of *David according to the flesh* (Rom 1:3). How could he be of David's seed according to the flesh if he were not from the body of Mary according to the flesh, since she descended from the seed of David? But when he was to work a miracle he said, **O woman, what is that to me and you?** By this he signified that he had received no beginning from his mother in time, but had always possessed eternity from his Father. **O woman**, he says, **what is that to me and you? My hour has not yet come.** It is as if he had said, "There is nothing in common between the divinity which I always possessed from the Father, and your flesh, from which I adopted flesh. My **hour has not yet come** when, by dying, I may demonstrate the weakness of the humanity taken from you. First I must disclose the power of my eternal deity by exercising my powers."

The **hour came**, however, to show what was in common between him and his mother when, as he was about to die on the cross, he took care to commend her, a virgin, to the virgin disciple (John 19:26–27). When he was enduring the weakness of the flesh, he dutifully acknowledged his mother, from whom he had received his flesh. And commended her to the disciple whom he especially loved. But when he was about to do divine things he pretended not to acknowledge her because he recognized that she was not the source of his divine birth.

---

3. Bede is citing the Vulgate, which differs slightly from the RSV translation: **What do you have to do with me?**

2:6, 9 Six stone jars were there . . . and the steward of the feast tasted the
water now become wine.

---

(13) Irenaeus of Lyons

The **wine** which God made naturally in the vineyard, and which was drunk first, was good.
For none of those who drank it thought it was cheap, and even the Lord partook of it. But
the **wine** which was made by the Word immediately and simply from water, for the use of
those invited to the **marriage**, was better. For although the Lord was able, without anything
from creation, to supply **wine** to those being entertained and to fill those who were hungry
with food, he did not do so. Rather, taking bread from the earth and giving thanks (cf. Luke
22:19), and again, making **water** into **wine**, he fed those reclining at the table and he gave
drink to those invited to the **marriage**, thereby demonstrating that the God who made the
earth and commanded it to bear fruit (Gen 1:1, 11), who established the waters and brought
forth the springs (Gen 1:9), is the one who in these last times through his Son gave to humanity the blessing of food and the favor of drink. The one who is beyond understanding
acts through that which is understood, the one who is invisible acts through that which
is visible, since there is nothing outside of him, existing in the *bosom of the Father* (1:18).

(14) John Chrysostom

Why did Christ not perform the miracle before **filling the jars**, which would have been
much more marvelous? It's one thing to change existing matter into something else, and
another to make something exist out of nothing. Because, the latter indeed would have been
more marvelous but it would not have seemed believable to the people. This is why he often
purposely scales back the greatness of his miracles so that they may be more acceptable.

Why then, someone says, did he not bring the **water** himself, which he then showed
to be **wine**, instead of commanding the **servants**? Again, for the same reason, and so that
he might have those who drew the water as witnesses that what happened was no illusion.
If some were inclined to act shamelessly, the **servants** would be able to tell them, "We
drew the water." But he also refutes those who speak against the church. Since there are
some who say that the Creator of the world is another god, and the visible things are not
God's, but someone else's opposed to God, he bridles their madness and does most of his
miracles from existing matter. If the Creator were opposed to God, Jesus would not have
used matter belonging to another as a proof of his own power. Now, indeed, in order to
demonstrate that he is the one who changes the **water** in the grape vine and turns the rain
into **wine** through the roots, he produced in the **marriage** feast all at once what in nature
happens over a long time. . . .

Such miracles of Jesus are much more beautiful and grander than those things that
happen naturally. Likewise, on other occasions, when he corrected a crippled part of the
body, he presented it better than a healthy one. Therefore, not only the **servants**, but the
bridegroom and the **steward of the feast** would testify that is was **wine** that had been

made—and the best **wine**! Those who drew the **water** would testify that it had been made by Christ, so that if the miracle was not revealed then, in the end it would not be silenced. So, he provided many forcible testimonies for the future. Indeed, he had the **servants** as witnesses that he made the **water** into **wine**, and the bridegroom and **steward of the feast** as witnesses that the **wine** was good. It was likely that the bridegroom answered and said something about these things, but the evangelist, being driven on to more pressing matters, only touched on this point and hurried on to the rest. It was necessary to learn that he made the **wine**, and that the **wine** was good, but what the bridegroom said to the **steward of the feast**, the evangelist did not think it necessary to relate.

Many of the **signs** first done were more obscure, but over time have become clearer when reported more accurately by those who knew them from the beginning. Therefore, Jesus made **wine** from **water** then, and both then and now he does not stop changing our frivolous wills which wash away like water. For there are—yes there are!—people who do not differ from **water** in any way—cold, frivolous, and never stable! Let us bring such people to the Lord that he might transform their wills into the state of **wine**, that they might no longer be washed away like **water**, but have stability and be the cause of merriment to themselves and to others.

(15) Augustine of Hippo

Being enabled by the one in whose name we promised to treat these matters, let us begin to uncover the deeper meaning of the mysteries. There was prophecy in ancient times; at no time was that gift of prophecy absent. But when Christ is not discerned in the prophecy it is like **water**. In **water**, **wine** is in some way latent. The apostle explains how we should understand **water**: *To this day*, he says, *when Moses is read, that very same veil is placed upon their heart; and it is not lifted because in Christ it is made void. And when you go over to the Lord, the veil will be removed* (2 Cor 3:14–16).[4] By *veil* he means the covering of prophecy that makes it difficult to understand. The *veil* is *lifted* when you have *gone over to the Lord*; therefore lack of understanding is *lifted* when you have *gone over to the Lord*, and what was **water** becomes **wine** to you. Read all the prophetic books and if Christ is not understood in them, what will you find that is not insipid and fatuous? If, however, you understand Christ to be present in them, what you read not only tastes good, it even inebriates, transporting the mind outside the body so that, *forgetting* what is past you *strain forward to what lies ahead* (Phil 3:13). . . .

When this passage (which is certainly clear) is understood, all the mysteries latent in this miracle of the Lord will be revealed. Take note of what he says, namely that it was necessary that the things written about Christ were fulfilled. Where were they written? *In the law*, he says, *and the prophets, and the psalms* (Luke 24:44). He left out none of the ancient Scriptures. The disciples were **water**, and for that reason they are said to be *foolish* (Luke 24:25) because at that point they still tasted **water**, not **wine**. But how did he make **wine** from **water**? When he opened their understanding and explained the Scriptures to

---

4. Augustine does not quote the passage exactly.

them, beginning with Moses through all the prophets. So, now inebriated they said: *Was our heart not burning on the road, when he opened the scriptures to us?* (Luke 24:32). They discerned Christ in the books in which they previously had not seen him. Therefore our Lord Jesus Christ changed **water** into **wine** and what was tasteless now has taste; what before had no effect now inebriates.

He could have had the **water** poured out and then himself put in **wine** from the hidden hollows of creation. Did he not provide bread when he fed many thousands—for five loaves would not satisfy five thousand men, nor fill twelve baskets? The omnipotence of the Lord was, as it were, a font of bread. If he could do these things he would have been able, after the **water** had been poured out, to have **wine** poured in. But if he had done this, he would have seemed to reject the ancient Scriptures. When, however, he changed that **water** into **wine**, he showed us that the ancient Scripture was also from him; for the jars were filled at his command. Indeed, although the ancient Scripture is also from the Lord, it has no taste if Christ is not discerned in it.

(16) Augustine of Hippo

God created humankind according to his own image on the sixth day for a reason; for in that sixth age, the renewal of our mind is manifested through the gospel, according to the image of the one who created us. **Water** is changed into **wine**, so that now we may taste Christ manifested in the law and the prophets. Therefore, **there were six water jars** (2:6) which he ordered to be filled with water. Those **six water jars** signify the six ages in which prophecy was not lacking. These six eras, separated and distinct by turning points, would be like empty vessels if they were not filled by Christ. Why have I said that the eras would run together senselessly unless the Lord Jesus were preached in them? The prophecies were fulfilled, the jars are full; but so that the **water** may be turned into **wine**, let Christ be understood in all that prophecy. . . .

Even the first **jar** held a prophecy about Christ. But since those things which I am saying were not prophesied among the people, it was still **water**; it was not yet changed into **wine**. Because the Lord illuminated us through the apostle, so that he may show us what we should seek in that one sentence—*the two shall become one flesh; this mystery is a profound one in Christ and the church* (Eph 5:31–32)—now it is permissible for us to seek Christ everywhere and to drink **wine** from all the **jars**. Adam sleeps so that Eve may be made (cf. Gen 2:21–22); Christ dies so that the church may be made. Eve came from the side of sleeping Adam; the side of the dead Christ is pierced with a lance (cf. John 19:33–34) so that the mysteries may flow forth, by which the church may be formed. To whom would it not be clear that future things were prefigured in those former deeds, seeing that the apostle says that Adam himself is a figure of *the one who was to come*? As he says: *who was a type of the one who was to come* (Rom 5:14). All things were prefigured mystically. . . .

Christ was also figured in Noah; and in that ark, the whole world. Why then were all the living animals enclosed in that ark (cf. Gen 7:7–9) unless they signify all the nations? God did not lack the ability to create all kinds of animals. When there were no animals yet in existence, did he not say: *Let the earth bring forth* (Gen 1:24) and the earth brought forth?

. . . He made them by a word and could remake them by a word; unless he was revealing a mystery, and was filling another **jar** of prophetic dispensation so that the figure of the world might be freed through the wood because the Life of the world would be fixed onto wood?

In the third **jar**, it was said to Abraham himself, as I have already recalled: *by your descendants shall all the nations be blessed* (Gen 22:18). Who would not see whose figure his only son represented, who carried wood for himself to the sacrifice, where he himself was led to be sacrificed? The Lord carried his own cross just as the gospel says (cf. John 19:17). It should suffice to have mentioned this about the third **jar**.

About David, however, why will I say that his prophecy pertained to all the nations, when we heard the psalm a little while ago? (It is difficult to find a psalm where this does not resound.) But certainly, as I said, we sang: *Arise, O God, judge the earth; for to thee belong all the nations* (Ps 82:8). . . . To what God is it said: *Arise*, unless to him who slept? *Arise, O God, judge the earth*, as if it were said: You slept and have been judged by the earth; *arise*, so that you may *judge the earth*. To what fulfillment does that prophecy extend? *For to thee belong all the nations.*

Now in the fifth age, as in the fifth **jar**, Daniel saw a stone cut without hands from a mountain. That stone smashed all the kingdoms of the earth and had grown and become a huge mountain so that it fills the entire face of the earth. What is clearer, my brothers and sisters? A stone is cut from a mountain; that is, a stone which the builders rejected and it became the cornerstone (cf. Ps 118:22). From which mountain is it cut, except from the kingdom of the Jews, from whom our Lord Jesus Christ was born according to the flesh? It is cut without hands, without human work, since he sprang from a virgin without the marital embrace. That mountain from which it was cut had not filled the entire face of the earth; for the kingdom of the Jews had not reigned over all the nations. But truly we see that the kingdom of Christ occupies all the nations.

The sixth age pertains to John the Baptist, the one whom *among those born of women there has risen no one greater* (Matt 11:11); about whom it is said: *He is more than a prophet* (Matt 11:9). How does he himself show that Christ was sent to all the nations? When the Jews came to him in order to be baptized, so that they may not be prideful of the name of Abraham, he says, *You brood of vipers! Who warned you to flee from the wrath to come? Bear fruit that befits repentance* (Matt 3:7–8), that is, be humble; for he was speaking to the proud. . . . Let us ask ourselves and we will see that it has been done. We have come from the nations, and we would not come from the nations unless God had raised children of Abraham from stones. We were made children of Abraham by imitating faith, not by being born through his flesh. Just as they were disinherited by degeneracy, so we were adopted by imitating. Therefore, brothers and sisters, that prophecy of the sixth **jar** signifies all the nations.

John 2:12–17

¹²After this he went down to Capernaum, with his mother and his brothers and his disciples; and there they stayed for a few days. ¹³The Passover of the Jews was at hand, and Jesus went up to Jerusalem. ¹⁴In the temple he found those who were selling oxen

and sheep and pigeons, and the money-changers at their business. ¹⁵ And making a whip of cords, he drove them all, with the sheep and oxen, out of the temple; and he poured out the coins of the money-changers and overturned their tables. ¹⁶ And he told those who sold the pigeons, "Take these things away; you shall not make my Father's house a house of trade." ¹⁷ His disciples remembered that it was written, "Zeal for thy house will consume me."

2:13 The Passover of the Jews was at hand.

---

(17) Origen of Alexandria

We need to provide a few words regarding the difficulties in these teachings, for they need their own special and voluminous study. We need to see every spiritual teaching in the law, especially what relates to the feasts, and most especially, to the **Passover**. The **Passover of the Jews** consists of a lamb which is sacrificed, being taken by each man *according to their fathers' houses* (Exod 12:3). It is a rite performed by the slaughter of tens of thousands of lambs and goat-kids in proportion to the number of houses of the people. But *Christ our Passover is sacrificed* (1 Cor 5:7).

Again, unleavened bread is part of the **Passover**, since all *leaven shall* be *put away out of your houses* (Exod 12:15). But we feast *not with the old leaven*, or *the leaven of malice and evil, but with the unleavened bread of sincerity and truth* (1 Cor 5:8). If there is some third name beyond the two we have spoken of, namely, "the Lord's **Passover**" and "the Feast of Unleavened Bread," we must investigate carefully, because such realities offer an example and shadow of heavenly things. Not only *food and drink, new moons and Sabbaths* (Col 2:16), but also the feasts are a shadow of the things to come. . . .

Now the **Word became flesh** (1:14) and the Lord says, *unless you eat the flesh of the Son of man and drink his blood, you have no life in you; he who eats my flesh and drinks my blood has eternal life, and I will raise him up at the last day. For my flesh is food indeed, and my blood is drink indeed. He who eats my flesh and drinks my blood abides in me, and I in him* (6:53–56). If so, then perhaps this is the flesh which *takes away the sin of the world* (1:29), and this is the blood which needs to be *put on the two doorposts and the lintel of the houses in which* we *eat* the **Passover** (Exod 12:7). We must eat from the flesh of that lamb at the time of the world which is *night* (Exod 12:8); and we must eat the meat *roasted* with fire *with unleavened bread* (Exod 12:8). For the word of God is not only flesh. He also says, *I am the bread of life* (6:35) and *this is the bread which comes down from heaven, that a man may eat of it and not die. I am the living bread which came down from heaven; if any one eats of this bread, he will live for ever* (6:50–51). . . .

We eat the flesh of the lamb and the *unleavened bread with bitter herbs* (Exod 12:8) either by grieving with a divine and penitent grief over our sins—a grief which creates in us a repentance for salvation that is not to be regretted—or, we seek and are nourished from the visions of the truth discovered because of our trials. One must not eat the flesh of the lamb *raw* (Exod 12:9), as the slaves of the law do like the irrational and savage beasts. In comparison to those who are truly rational through their desire to understand the spiritual realities of the Word, the first group shares the way of savage animals.

We must also attempt to change the rawness of Scripture into *boiled* (Exod 12:9) food, and not to change what is written into something weak, watery, and lifeless. This is the sort of thing those who have *itching ears and turn away from truth* (2 Tim 4:3) do. They change the anagogical meaning to correspond with their own manner of life so that it has an inconsistent and watery meaning. But we, with a boiling spirit and fiery words given by God, such as Jeremiah received from the one saying to him, *Behold, I have given my words in your mouth as fire* (Jer 5:14 LXX), let us roast the meat of the lamb so that those eating of it might say, as Christ speaks in us, *Did not our hearts burn within us while he opened to us the scriptures?* (Luke 24:32). For this reason, we must seek this end by roasting the meat of the lamb. . . .

With the night gone and the next day come, we will eat *unleavened bread*, having none of that older bread leavened from below. We will eat this *unleavened bread* and it will be useful to us, until the manna coming after the *unleavened bread* is given. This is the angelic food and not food of humans. Let the sheep be sacrificed for each of us in every house of our fathers. If one man transgresses by not sacrificing the sheep, let another observe all the commandments by sacrificing, and by boiling it completely without breaking any of its bones.

In short, let *Christ our Passover*, having been *sacrificed* (1 Cor 5:7), be rendered in harmony with the interpretation of the apostle and the lamb in the gospel. One must not suppose that historical things are types of historical things and corporeal of corporeal. Rather, corporeal things are types of spiritual things and historical of things that cannot be seen.

2:14–16 In the temple he found those who were selling oxen and sheep and pigeons, and the money-changers at their business. And making a whip of cords, he drove them all, with the sheep and oxen, out of the temple. . . . "You shall not make my Father's house a house of trade."

---

(18) Origen of Alexandria

I think that our passage may indicate a deeper meaning, so that we might understand these things to symbolize the coming discontinuation of the **temple** services with its priests and physical sacrifices, that the law would no longer be observed even if the Jews wanted to. . . .

But it is also possible that the natural **temple** represents the soul well trained in reason, which is higher than the body because of its innate reason. Jesus ascends to it from Capernaum, the low-lying region below, and before Jesus applies his disciplinary action, we find in it earthly, foolish, and dangerous impulses, and things which appear beautiful but are not. Jesus **drives** these **out** (2:15) with his word twisted out of doctrines of demonstration and rebuke. He does this so that his **Father's house** might not be **a house of trade** (2:16), but also so that it might receive for its own salvation that of others, a worship of God which is performed by heavenly and spiritual laws.

The **oxen** symbolize earthly realities, for **oxen** plow the ground. The **sheep** symbolize foolish and brutish things since they are enslaved more than all irrational creatures. The **pigeons** represent empty and unstable thoughts, and the **coins**, the things which merely appear beautiful. . . .

Do not Jesus's actions of **pouring out the coins of the money-changers** and **overturning their tables** (2:15) accuse him of violence? Who, being beaten with a **whip of cords** by someone they did not care for, and being driven out, would not cry out and take justice into their own hands, especially when there was such a great crowd present who were insulted by Jesus and had similar feelings about him? Consider also the Son of God taking the **cords** and twisting a **whip** for himself to **drive them out of the temple**. Does this not seem arrogant and impudent and uncivilized? Only one refuge of defense remains if we want to salvage the historical narrative: the divine power of Jesus means that he alone is able, when he wanted, to extinguish the enkindled anger of his enemies, to overcome the multitudes by divine grace, and to bring their tumultuous plans to naught. For *the Lord brings the counsel of the nations to naught; he frustrates the plans of the peoples. The counsel of the Lord stands for ever* (Ps 33:10–11). So none of the exceedingly amazing things he did, or his divine calling to faith those who beheld him, weaken this narrative, if it truly happened. This seems to be an even greater work than the one done in Cana of Galilee when he changed water into wine. In that miracle, lifeless matter was transformed, but in this one the will of thousands was enslaved.

(19) Cyril of Jerusalem

We worship the Father of Christ, who made heaven and earth, the God of Abraham, Isaac, and Jacob, to whose honor the former **temple** was built, opposite us here.[5] For we will not assent to the heretics who divide the Old Testament from the New, but will believe Christ who said about the **temple**: *Did you not know that I must be in my Father's house?* (Luke 2:49). And again: **Take these things away; you shall not make my Father's house a house of trade** (2:16), by which he most clearly confessed that the **temple** in Jerusalem was the house of his own Father.

(20) John Chrysostom

Another evangelist says that while casting them out, Jesus said, *Do not make my Father's house a den of robbers* (Matt 21:13; Mark 11:17; Luke 19:46). This evangelist, however, says **a house of trade** (2:16), not in opposition to the others, but showing that Jesus did this a second time, and that both occasions did not occur at the same time. He did it once at the beginning of his ministry and once near the very coming of his passion. Therefore, at the latter occasion, using much stronger words, he called it a *den* (*of robbers*), but at the beginning of his miracles, he does not do so, but has used a much softer rebuke. From this observation, it is likely that this event took place a second time.

---

5. That is, in Jerusalem, where Cyril is bishop.

"And why," someone says, "has Christ done this same thing and used such strong words against them, which he does nowhere else, even when insulted and reviled and called a **Samaritan** and **demoniac** by them (8:48)? Not being content with words alone, he even took a **whip of cords** (2:15) and cast them out!" When others were receiving benefit, the Jews accused him and were inflamed, but when it was likely that those who were rebuked[6] would become wild, the Jews do not use such a manner with him. They did not rebuke or insult him. What did they say? **What sign have you to show us for doing this?** (2:18). Do you see the excess of malignity and how the benefits done to others provoked them even more? On one occasion he said that the **temple** had been made a *den of robbers* by them, showing that what was sold was by theft, robbery, and greed, and that they were rich from the misfortune of others. But here, he calls it a **house of trade** (2:16), indicating their shameless business. Since he was about to heal on the Sabbath and do many such things which they thought were transgressions of the law, in order that someone might not think that he did these things as a rival god and being contrary to the Father, he corrected such opinions of theirs. The one who demonstrated such zeal for the **house** would not be opposed to the Lord of the **house** and to worshiping in it. Therefore, it was fitting even in the first years, in which he lived according to the law, to show his reverence for the lawgiver and that he did not come as a rival lawgiver. Since it was likely that those years would be forgotten in the passing of time (years which were not known to everyone because of his being raised in a poor and unimpressive home), he does this in the presence of all (for many were present since the feast was near), even at great risk.

He did not simply **drive them out**, but also **overturned their tables** and **poured out** the money, and by this helped them to understand that the one who threw himself into danger for the good order of the **house** would not despise the Lord of the **house**. If he did these things as a hypocrite, he needed only to exhort them publicly. But placing himself in danger was extremely daring. It was no ordinary thing to surrender himself to the rage of such market goers, and to provoke against himself the businessmen full of great disorderliness by upbraiding them and causing them financial loss. This was not the action of a hypocrite but of one choosing all suffering for the sake of the good order of the **house**.

In this way, he shows his agreement with the Father not only by what he does but by what he says. For he does not say "the holy house," but **my Father's house** (2:16). See, he even calls him **Father** and they are not angered, for they think that he spoke in a general way. Later, when he spoke more clearly so as to establish that idea of his equality, they become enraged.

(21) Augustine of Hippo

What have we heard, brothers and sisters? Behold, the **temple** was still a figure, and the Lord **drove out** from there all those who were seeking their own things, who had come for the purpose of business. And what were those men **selling** there? What people needed for the sacrifices of that time. For you know, my beloved, that such sacrifices were given to

---

6. That is, the money-changers.

that people because of their carnality and stony heart still in them, sacrifices which held them from falling into idolatry; and they were offering sacrifices there, **oxen**, **sheep**, and **pigeons**; you know, because you have read it. It was not, therefore, a great sin if they were **selling** in the **temple** what was being purchased so that it may be offered in the **temple**; and nevertheless, he **drove** them **out** of there. . . .

He showed us a certain sign because he made a **whip of** little **cords** and then scourged the undisciplined, those conducting business from the **temple** of the Lord. For truly, each one twists a **cord** for himself with his own sins. The prophet says: *Woe to those who draw iniquity as a long cord!* (Isa 5:18 Latin). Who makes a long **cord**? Who adds sin to sin? How are sins added to sins? When sins committed are covered with other sins. Someone committed a theft, and so that it not be discovered what he did, he seeks an astrologer. It would be enough that he committed the theft; why do you wish to add sin to sin? Behold, two sins! When you are prohibited from approaching the astrologer, you blaspheme the bishop. When you hear: Send that man outside the church; you say: I am leading myself to the sect of the Donatists;[7] behold you add a fourth sin. The **cord** grows; fear the **cord**! It is good for you that you are corrected here when you are scourged; lest it be said in the end: *Bind him hand and foot and cast him into the outer darkness* (Matt 22:13). For *Each man is bound with the cords of his own sins* (Prov 5:22 Vulgate). The Lord says the former, Scripture says the latter; but the Lord says both. People are bound by their own sins and are *cast* into the *outer darkness*.

Who, nevertheless, are they who **sell** the **oxen**, so that in the figure, we may seek the mystery of the activity? Who are they who **sell sheep** and **pigeons**? They are those who seek their own interests in the church rather than the interests of Jesus Christ. They have everything for sale who do not wish to be redeemed; they do not wish to be bought, they wish to **sell**. Yet it is good for them that they be redeemed by the blood of Christ so that they may come to the peace of Christ. . . .

Who therefore **sells** the **oxen**? The **oxen** are understood as those who have dispensed sacred Scripture to us. The **oxen** were the apostles, the **oxen** were the prophets. Therefore the apostle says, *You shall not muzzle an ox when it is treading out the grain. Is it for oxen that God is concerned? Does he not speak entirely for our sake? Indeed, it was written for our sake, because the plowman should plow in hope and the thresher thresh in hope of a share in the crop* (1 Cor 9:9–10). Therefore, those **oxen** have left us the memory of Scripture. For they have not dispensed from their own selves because they sought the glory of the Lord.

(22) Cyril of Alexandria

Take these things away; you shall not make my Father's house a house of trade (2:16). Christ commands as a lord, but as a teacher he leads by the hand to that which is fitting, juxtaposing both his correction and an explanation of their failure. He has no embarrassment that in this correction the one being reproved might be angry about these things. But it must be noted that he again calls God his own **Father** in a unique way, as he alone exists

---

7. A schismatic community in North Africa.

from him by nature and is truly begotten. If he does not exist in this way, and the Word is merely a son like us, as one of us, meaning by **adoption** and the **will** of the Father alone (cf. John 1:13), by what grace does he seize for himself alone the boast supposedly common to all, proclaiming: **you shall not make *my* Father's house**, rather than "*our* Father's house"? This was probably more suitable to say if he understood himself as one who was not a son by nature. But since he is not among the sons by grace, but, being the Word, knows that he exists from the essence of God the Father, he sets himself apart from the others, calling God his own **Father**. It is appropriate for those who have been called to sonship and have that honor added to them from outside, to say, when praying, *Our Father who art in heaven* (Matt 6:9). But the Only Begotten, alone being One from One, reasonably calls God his own **Father**.

(23) Venerable Bede

Oxen and sheep and doves were being purchased so that they might be offered in the **temple**. **The money-changers** were sitting at their tables so that between the buyers and sellers of the sacrificial offerings there might be a ready exchange of money. It seems, then, that since these things were being bought for the purpose of offering them to the Lord in the **temple**, they were being lawfully sold in the **temple**. But our Lord was unwilling that anything having to do with earthly trade be practiced in his house, not even what might be considered acceptable. He scattered the fraudulent traders, and **drove them out**, together with the things that had to do with the business of trade.

When he saw persons in the **temple** buying the sacrificial offerings which were to be made to him, he promptly got rid of them. What then, my brothers and sisters, do you suppose our Lord would do if he should discover people involved in disputes, wasting time gossiping, indulging in unrestrained laughter, or engaged in any other sort of wicked actions? I say this about those who enter a church, and not only disregard their intention to pray, but also act so as to increase their need for prayer. Moreover, they convict themselves of this kind of foolish behavior by wrangling, hatred, and even disparaging others. They pile sins upon sins, weaving, as it were, a very long **cord** by their heedless addition. They are not afraid of being condemned for this at the examination of the strict judge. . . .

Oxen represent teaching about the heavenly life, **sheep** the works of undefiled piety, and **doves** the gifts of the Holy Spirit. It is with the help of **oxen** that we usually plow a field. The field is the human heart, carefully cultivated by the Lord's heavenly teaching and properly prepared to receive the seeds of the word of God. Innocent **sheep** furnish their fleece to clothe human beings. The Spirit descended upon our Lord in the appearance of a **dove** (cf. Luke 3:22). But those other persons sell **oxen** who impart the word of the gospels to their hearers, not out of divine love, but with a view to earthly gain. The apostle censures such as these: *they proclaim Christ not sincerely* (Phil 1:17). They sell **sheep** who carry out the works of piety for the sake of human praise. Of them our Lord says, *they have received their reward* (Matt 6:5). They sell **doves** who give the grace of the Spirit they have received not without recompense, as has been commanded (cf. Matt

10:8), but for pay. They bestow the imposition of hands by which the Spirit is received, albeit not for monetary gain but to gain the favor of the public. They confer sacred orders, not on the merit of the ordinand's life but as a personal favor. They are **money-changers** in the **temple** who perform their service in the church and do not pretend that they are doing it for heavenly reasons but clearly for earthly purposes, seeking their own advantage and not that of Jesus Christ.

Our Lord shows that reward awaits hypocritical workers of this sort when he made a **whip of cords** and **drove them all** out of the **temple**. They are cast out as sharers of *the inheritance of the saints* (Col 1:12) if, after they are chosen to be among the saints, they either perform good acts deceitfully or evil acts openly. He also **drives out the sheep** and **oxen** when he shows that both the life and teaching of such persons deserve condemnation. The **cords** with which he expelled the wicked persons from the **temple** by **whipping** them are the progressive development of their evil actions. They provide material to the strict judge for condemning those who are to be rejected. So it is that Isaiah says, *Woe to those who draw iniquity with cords of vanity* (Isa 5:18 Vulgate); and Solomon says in the book of Proverbs, *The iniquities of the wicked ensnare him, and he is caught in the cords of his sin* (Prov 5:22 Vulgate). The person who heaps sins upon sins, for which he will be condemned more severely, is like one lengthening the cords with which he can be bound and **whipped**, adding to them little by little. Jesus also scattered the **coins** of the **money-changers** whom he had expelled and whose **tables** he had **overturned**. When the damned are condemned in the end, he will even take away the form of those things they have loved, according to what is written, *And the world passes away, and the lust of it* (1 John 2:17). . . .

There follows: **His disciples remembered that it was written, "Zeal for thy house will consume me"** (2:17). Our Savior **drove out** the wicked from the **temple** because of **zeal for** his Father's **house**. Let us also be **zealous**, dearly beloved, for the **house** of God. As much as we can, let us devote ourselves to seeing that nothing evil be done there. If we see a brother or sister who belongs to the **house** of God swollen up with pride, given to slander, a slave to drunkenness, enfeebled because of self-indulgence, wild with fury, or enslaved by any other vice, let us strive, as much as we are able, to reprimand them and correct their perversity and corruption.

John 2:18–22

[18]The Jews then said to him, "What sign have you to show us for doing this?" [19]Jesus answered them, "Destroy this temple, and in three days I will raise it up." [20]The Jews then said, "It has taken forty-six years to build this temple, and will you raise it up in three days?" [21]But he spoke of the temple of his body. [22]When therefore he was raised from the dead, his disciples remembered that he had said this; and they believed the scripture and the word which Jesus had spoken.

2:19, 21 "Destroy this temple, and in three days I will raise it up. . . ." But he spoke of the temple of his body.

---

(24) Irenaeus of Lyons

Paul says that the temple of God is created matter: *Do you not know that you are God's temple and that God's Spirit dwells in you? If anyone destroys God's temple, God will destroy him. For God's temple is holy, and that temple you are* (1 Cor 3:16–17). Here he clearly declares that the body is the temple in which the Spirit dwells, just as the Lord says about himself: **Destroy this temple, and in three days I will raise it up. But**, it says, **he spoke of the temple of his body** (2:19, 21). Paul too understands our bodies to be not only a **temple**, but also members of Christ, as he says to the Corinthians: *Do you not know that your bodies are members of Christ? Shall I therefore take the members of Christ and make them members of a prostitute?* (1 Cor 6:15). He does not say this about some other "spiritual" man, for such a one cannot be united with a prostitute. But he says that our *body*, that is the flesh, when it perseveres in holiness and cleanliness, is said to be a *member of Christ*. But when it is involved with a prostitute, it is made a *member of the prostitute*. For this reason, he says, *If anyone destroys God's temple, God will destroy him* (1 Cor 3:17). Therefore, how is it not the greatest blasphemy to say that the **temple** of God, in which the Spirit of the Father dwells, and which is a member of Christ, does not participate in salvation, but is fit for destruction? Is that not the height of blasphemy? Since our bodies, however, are raised up not by their own nature but by God, he says to the Corinthians: *The body is not meant for immorality, but for the Lord, and the Lord for the body. And God raised the Lord and will also raise us up by his power* (1 Cor 6:13–14).

(25) Tertullian of Carthage

There is, I suppose, one proclamation of God held before all people: the resurrection of the dead—a decisive, settled, and clear phrase. I will take this very phrase, examine it in detail, and determine what it refers to. When I hear that a rising again hangs over someone, I must ask what part of him was appointed to fall, since nothing is expected to rise again unless it has first fallen. Whoever is ignorant that the flesh fell through death is unable to know that it rises through life. Nature pronounces God's thought: *You are dust, and to dust you shall return* (Gen 3:19). Even the one who does not hear it, sees it: all death ends in the ruin of our limbs. This fate of the body, the Lord also pronounced, when, clothed in that very substance, he said: **Destroy this temple, and in three days I will raise it up** (2:19). For he made clear what part of him was to be divided, destroyed, cast down, raised, and reawakened—although he carried around a *soul trembling even to death* (Matt 26:38), but a soul not dying through death—for Scripture also says, **he spoke of his body** (2:21).

It is precisely the flesh which is destroyed in death, and for that reason the word "cadaver" comes from *cadendo* ("falling"). . . . Now, from the meaning of the word, we must say what destiny is indicated. Indeed, because the word "resurrection" refers to that which has fallen, that is the flesh, so the same meaning will hold for the word "dead," since the phrase "resurrection of the dead" refers to that which has fallen down. . . . If it is the body that is dead, then there will be a resurrection of the body when we speak of the "resurrection of the dead."

(26) Origen of Alexandria

Now both of these things—the **temple** and the **body of Jesus**—seem to me, at least according to one interpretation, to be a figure of the church which is *built from living stones, a spiritual house for a holy priesthood* (1 Pet 2:5), *built upon the foundation of the apostles and prophets, Christ Jesus being the cornerstone* (Eph 2:20). The church is called a **temple** (cf. 1 Cor 3:16–17), . . . so the resurrection of Christ from the passion of the cross contains the mystery of the resurrection of the whole body of Christ.

(27) Theodore of Mopsuestia

Jesus answered them, "Destroy this temple, and in three days I will raise it up" (2:19). He seems to be putting an end not only to the **temple** commerce, but also to the custom of sacrifices. It was because of the sacrifices that the sellers of bulls and doves were conducting their business—so that those who came from a distance would be able to buy something to offer in sacrifice. This is why the Lord introduced the subject of the resurrection, saying something like: "If you want to understand my actions, wait a little while. When you have killed me, after my resurrection, I will reveal who I am to each and every person. These ancient rites will come to an end, and a new custom, a new way, and a new era will be inaugurated and proclaimed after my resurrection."

Yet our Lord was saying these things cryptically and mystically by way of symbols signifying his intentions. He did nothing openly, for he knew that those who heard him were unable to receive what he was saying. Not even the disciples understood him, as the evangelist said (cf. John 2:22). So while his activity of driving away those who were selling bulls and sheep seemed to put an end to commerce in the **temple**, in truth he was indicating that the sacrifices of dumb animals were about to cease.

(28) Augustine of Hippo

Raise me up that I may requite them (Ps 41:10). You certainly must not think, brothers and sisters, that because he says, *Raise me up*, the Son is less powerful than the Father, and was unable to raise himself. What he raised up was what was prone to die; flesh died, and flesh was raised up. So that you do not think that God, the Father of Christ, had the power to raise up Christ—that is, to raise the flesh of his Son—but that Christ himself, who is the Word of God and equal to the Father, had no power to raise his own flesh, listen to the evangelist, **Destroy this temple, and in three days I will raise it up** (2:19). To make sure that we would not be in doubt about what he meant, the evangelist added, **he spoke of the temple of his body** (2:21). *Raise me up that I may requite them* (Ps 41:10).

(29) Augustine of Hippo

Now turn your attention to the lies of false witnesses as recorded in the gospel, and see how they relate to the resurrection. They demanded of the Lord, **What sign have you to show us for doing this?** (2:18). Over and above the sign he had already given them, the sign of Jonah (Matt 12:40), he made the same point again through a new parable, to make sure that this, his greatest sign, was abundantly clear. **Destroy this temple, and in three days I will raise it up. The Jews then said, "It has taken forty-six years to build this temple, and will you raise it up in three days?"** Then the evangelist adds an explanation: **But he spoke of the temple of his body** (2:19–21). By this simile he declared that he would manifest his power to men and women. He used the **temple** as a figure of his flesh, for his **body** was the **temple** of the Godhead hidden within. The Jews were accustomed to see this material **temple**, but they did not see its indwelling divinity.

From these words of the Lord, in which he foretold his future resurrection under the image of a rebuilt **temple**, perjured witnesses concocted a lying charge to bring against him. When asked what they had heard him say, they alleged, *We heard him say, "I will destroy this temple and in three days I will build another"* (Mark 14:58). They had certainly heard him say **in three days I will raise it up** (2:19). But they had not heard him say, *I will destroy it*; what they heard was **Destroy it** (2:19). They altered one word, or a few letters, to support their false evidence against him. But against whom are you changing a word, O human futility, human feebleness? You change a word against the unchangeable Word! You may well change your own word, but can you change the Word of God? . . .

Assuredly Christ did **destroy** that **temple**; he himself **destroyed** it, he who said, **I have power to lay down my life, and I have power to take it up again. No one takes it away from me; but I lay it down of my own accord, and I take it up again** (10:17–18). He **destroyed** the **temple** by his own gracious will, but it was **destroyed** also by your ill-will.

(30) Augustine of Hippo

He sent from heaven and saved me (Ps 57:3). It is quite obvious that the man Jesus, this very flesh, this very Son of God, has been saved already insofar as he partakes of our nature. The Father did send from heaven and save him; the Father sent from heaven and raised him from the dead. But you need to keep in mind that the Lord also raised himself. Both truths are stated in Scripture—that the Father raised him and that he raised himself. Affirming that the Father raised Christ, the apostle says, *he became obedient to the point of death, even death on a cross. Therefore God has highly exalted him and bestowed on him the name which is above every name* (Phil 2:8–9). You have there a statement that the Father raised and exalted his Son. Now listen to another, showing that the Son also raised up his own flesh. Using the imagery of the temple he said to the Jews, **Destroy this temple, and in three days *I* will raise it up** (2:19); and the evangelist explained to us what he meant: **he spoke of the temple of his body** (2:21).

(31) John Cassian

Let us consider that statement of the blessed evangelist John, by which the ambiguity of the question [about prayer] is clearly solved:[8] *And this is the confidence which we have in him, that if we ask anything according to his will he hears us* (1 John 5:14). Therefore he commands us to have a full and indubitable *confidence* of a favorable answer only in those things which are not for our convenience or temporary comfort but are in agreement with the will of the Lord. We are also taught to include this sentiment in the Lord's Prayer, saying *Thy will be done* (Matt 6:10)—*thy will*, certainly, not ours. . . .

Even our Lord uses this thought when praying in the character of the man which he had assumed. He did this so that he might provide us with a form of prayer, just as his example did in other matters, saying: *My Father, if it be possible, let this cup pass from me; nevertheless, not as I will but as thou wilt* (Matt 26:39), even though his will was not at variance with his Father's will. . . . Even if we read of the Father: *For God so loved the world that he gave his only Son* (3:16), we likewise discover of the Son: *who gave himself for our sins* (Gal 1:4). Just as it is said of the one: *He who did not spare his own Son but gave him up for us all* (Rom 8:32), so also it is said of the other: *He was offered because he himself willed it* (Isa 53:7 Vulgate). In this way, the Father and the will of the Son are shown to be one in all things. Even in the mystery of the resurrection of the Lord himself, there is no difference of activity. Just as the blessed apostle proclaimed that the Father performed the resurrection of his body, saying: *God the Father who raised him from the dead* (Gal 1:1), so also the Son testifies that he himself will raise the temple of his body, saying **Destroy this temple and in three days I will raise it up** (2:19). Therefore, having been instructed by these examples of the Lord which we have mentioned, we ought also to conclude all our supplications similarly and always add this phrase to all our petitions: *nevertheless, not as I will but as thou wilt* (Matt 26:39).

(32) Theodoret of Cyrus

And we confess our Lord Jesus Christ, perfect God and perfect man, of a rational soul and body, begotten of the Father before all ages, according to his divinity. But in these last days, for us and for our salvation, he was born of the Virgin Mary. He is the same substance with the Father according to his divinity, the same substance with us according to his humanity. For there was a union of the two natures. Therefore, we confess one Christ, one Son, one Lord. We do not destroy the union, but believe that it was made without confusion, believing the Lord when he says to the Jews: **Destroy this temple, and in three days I will**

---

8. John Cassian is addressing the question of whether we can be confident that God hears our prayers.

raise it up (2:19). If there had been a mixture and confusion of the two, and a single nature resulted from the two, he should have said, "Destroy *me*, and in three days I shall be raised." But showing that as God by nature he is one thing and as a **temple**, he is another, but that there is one Christ, he says, **Destroy this temple, and in three days I will raise it up** (2:19), clearly teaching that it was not God who was being **destroyed**, but the **temple**. And the nature of his **temple** could undergo destruction, but the power of his divinity raised what was being **destroyed**.

(33) Leo the Great

About what you wrote at the end of your intimate letter, I am utterly amazed that any intelligent person of the catholic faith should be troubled with uncertainty about whether Christ's flesh remained in the tomb when Christ descended to hell. For just as the flesh truly died and was buried, so also it truly was raised again on the third day. For the Lord himself declared this when he said to the Jews: **Destroy this temple, and in three days I will raise it up** (2:19), and the evangelist added: **But he spoke of the temple of his body** (2:21). David the prophet also predicted such truth and speaks in the person of the Lord and Savior, saying, *Moreover, my flesh will dwell in hope. For thou wilt not abandon my soul to Hades, nor let thy Holy One see corruption* (Ps 16:9–10). By these words, it is quite clear that the Lord's flesh indeed lay buried and was not subject to corruption since it was quickly revived by the return of the soul and was resurrected.

(34) John of Damascus

Not by word alone, but by deed did the Lord manifest the resurrection of the body. First, he raised up Lazarus who had been dead four days and was stinking (John 11:39–44). He did not raise the soul of the body, but the body also with the soul; and he did not raise another body, but the same one that had died. How could the resurrection of the dead man be known and believed if the characteristic features of his identity did not endure? In order to demonstrate his own divinity and confirm both his and our resurrection, he raised up Lazarus who would again return to death. And the Lord himself became the firstfruits of the resurrection no longer subject to death. Therefore, the divine apostle Paul said, *If the dead are not raised, then Christ has not been raised. Therefore our faith is futile and we are still in our sins* (1 Cor 15:16–17), and *Christ has been raised, the first-fruits of those who have fallen asleep* (1 Cor 15:20) and *the first-born from the dead* (Col 1:18). And again: *For since we believe that Jesus died and rose again, even so, through Jesus, God will bring with him those who have fallen asleep* (1 Thess 4:14). Even so, he said, as the Lord rose again.

It is clear that the resurrection of the Lord was the union of the immortalized body and the soul (for these had been divided), for he said: **Destroy this temple, and in three days I will build it up** (2:19).[9] The holy gospel is a trustworthy witness that he spoke about

---

9. John of Damascus quotes John 2:19 slightly differently than the New Testament: **I will *raise* it up.**

his own body: *Handle me and see*, the Lord said to his own disciples who thought that they saw a spirit, *that it is I myself and I am not changed, for a spirit has not flesh and bones as you see that I have* (Luke 24:37, 39). When he had said this, he showed them his hands and his side, and held them forth for Thomas to touch (John 20:27). Indeed are these not sufficient reasons to believe in the resurrection of bodies?

John 2:23-25

²³**Now when he was in Jerusalem at the Passover feast, many believed in his name when they saw the signs which he did;** ²⁴**but Jesus did not trust himself to them,** ²⁵**because he knew all men and needed no one to bear witness of man; for he himself knew what was in man.**

(35) John Chrysostom

That these men were not among the genuine disciples, the following demonstrates, for it says, **Jesus did not trust himself to them** (2:24). Why? Because **he knew all men and needed no one to bear witness of man; for he himself knew what was in man** (2:25). What it means is this: he who possesses the heart and enters into the mind gave no heed to outward words. Clearly knowing their temporary passion, he did not have confidence in them as with perfected disciples, nor did he entrust all his doctrines to them as to those who had already been made steadfast believers. To know the things which are in the human hearts belongs only to God *who fashions the heart* (Ps 33:15). *For you alone*, it says, *established the heart* (cf. 1 Kgs 8:39). Therefore, he had no need of witnesses in order to learn the thoughts of his own creatures. He had no confidence in them because of their temporary belief. Men, who know neither the present nor the future, often, without holding anything back, speak and entrust everything to those who draw near deceitfully but who withdraw a little later. Christ, however, does not do so, for he clearly knew all their secrets.

(36) Cyril of Alexandria

Now when he was in Jerusalem at the Passover feast, many believed in his name when they saw the signs which he did (2:23). Christ does not stop saving and helping. For he leads them to himself with wise words, but also, astounding them with divine power, he sweeps them toward faith. And from the things which they saw being performed, they are persuaded to agree that the worker of these admirable things is truly God.

But Jesus did not trust himself to them (2:24). The understanding of those who have recently believed is not firm, nor is the mind made solid by new wonders. How would those who have just recently been instructed, already be made strong in piety? In this way[10] does

---

10. I.e., with reserve and caution.

Christ **trust himself** (2:24) to the newcomers, demonstrating that genuineness toward God is a great thing and most worthy of love, and that it is not immediately available to those who want to seize it, but comes by being fixed with desire for the good through practice over time.

Let the stewards of the Savior's mysteries learn from these things not to allow someone to enter into the sacred veil[11] too quickly, nor to trust new converts, baptized too early and not believing in Christ as Lord of all in due time, to approach the divine tables. In order that he might be a pattern for us and teach us for whom initiation into the mysteries is more suitable, he indeed receives those who believe, but is seen not yet trusting them, as it says: **he did not trust** (2:24). So it is clear here that newcomers should not spend merely a brief time in instruction, for even so they will scarcely become faithful.

Because he knew all men and needed no one to bear witness of man; for he himself knew what was in man (2:25). This honor, along with the other qualities in Christ, is divine, and is in none of the created things. For the psalmist attributes it to him alone who is truly God, saying, *He fashions their hearts as one, he understands all their deeds* (Ps 33:15). But if God alone understands the things in us, and Christ also understands them, how will he not be God by nature, who knows the *secret things* (Sus 42) and knows the *deep and hidden things* (Dan 2:22), just as it is written? *For what person knows a man's thoughts except the spirit of the man which is in him?* (1 Cor 2:11). Although no one knows, God will not be ignorant since he is not counted among the "all," of whom the "no one" would naturally be meant. But since he is outside of all things and all things are under his feet, he will know (all things). And Paul also will testify to this, saying, *For the word of God is living and active, sharper than any two-edged sword, piercing to the division of soul and spirit, of joints and marrow, and discerning the thoughts and intentions of the heart. And before him no creature is hidden, but all are open and laid bare to his eyes* (Heb 4:12–13).[12] For since he *planted the ear*, he hears all things, and since he *formed the eye* (Ps 94:9), he perceives. Indeed, he is introduced in Job, saying, *Who is this who hides counsel from me, holding words in his heart, and thinks to conceal them from me?* (Job 38:2 LXX). Therefore, in order that we might understand the Son as being God by nature, the evangelist necessarily says that he **needed no one to bear witness of man; for he himself knew what was in man** (2:25).

---

11. That is, the screen that separated the sanctuary from the nave of the church, commonly used in Eastern Orthodox churches and later called the iconostasis.

12. The early church regularly understood Paul to be the author of the book of Hebrews.

John 3

Jesus's nighttime encounter with Nicodemus in John 3 elicits extended discussions of the meaning of the sacrament of baptism. The words unless one is born anew, he cannot see the kingdom of God *(3:3) are understood by Justin Martyr to mean that one must be baptized for salvation and spiritual birth. That line of interpretation is carried forth by others like Theodore of Mopsuestia, the Venerable Bede, and John Scotus Eriugena.*

The reference to being born of water and the Spirit *(3:5) evokes further discussions of Christian baptism. John Chrysostom contrasts physical birth with spiritual birth, offering a delightful comparison between the original creation in Genesis 1–2 with the new creation afforded at baptism. Theodore of Mopsuestia makes the Trinitarian point that the Spirit is rightfully included with the Father and the Son in baptism, because the Spirit is the agent that accomplishes the rebirth through water. John Scotus Eriugena provides a helpful discussion about why physical water was ordained for a spiritual reality. And the Venerable Bede, commenting on verse 6, observes that the spiritual birth of baptism may appear devoid of meaning, but those who know what is happening understand that a real change takes place at the font, "that a child of death descends, and a child of the resurrection comes up."*

*John 3:13—*No one has ascended into heaven but he who descended from heaven, the Son of man—*receives attention from Augustine of Hippo and John Scotus Eriugena. Christ* descended *by taking on our humanity in the flesh so his* ascension *will draw up all humanity with him to the heavenly realm. As Scotus affirms, "all whom he saved* ascend *in him, now by faith and in hope, but in the end by vision and in reality."*

Although John 3:16, so popular among Christians today, receives little commentary in the early church, the preceding verses draw more attention. John Chrysostom, Theodore of Mopsuestia, Augustine of Hippo, Cyril of Alexandria, and the Venerable Bede all explore the spiritual connection between the events of Num 21 and the words of John 3:14–15: as Moses lifted up the serpent in the wilderness, so must the Son of man be lifted up. *For these thinkers, the events in the wilderness allow a comparison between the "ancient types" and the work of Christ on the cross. Just as the Israelites beheld the uplifted bronze serpent and temporarily escaped death, so too those who believe on the crucified Christ will enjoy life eternal. Augustine and Bede further the comparison with an analogy between the healing from the fiery bites of the serpents in the wilderness and the present healing from the venom of sin.*

*The words of John 3:17–18—*For God sent the Son into the world, not to condemn the world . . . he who does not believe is condemned already—*raise questions about the matter of condemnation. Irenaeus of Lyons argues that condemnation arises as the result of our free will that rejects God, while John Chrysostom uses this text to explain the two advents of Christ—the first to offer forgiveness, the second to bring judgment. In the delay of God's judgment, Chrysostom sees an "unspeakable abundance of benevolence." Theodore of Mopsuestia emphasizes that disbelief is its own punishment, while reminding us that God's ultimate purpose is to save, not condemn. Considering verse 21, Augustine wonders what it means to* do what is true *and* come to the light, *concluding that the only good work one can do is to confess one's sin and thereby be united to God.*

The latter half of chapter 3 moves to John the Baptist's testimony about Jesus. Although Jesus's baptism is not recorded in the Gospel of John, chapter 3 nevertheless raises questions about both the efficacy of John's baptism and the purpose of Christ's own baptism by John. John Scotus Eriugena says that John's baptism did not secure forgiveness of sin but instead worked as a catechetical preparation for baptism in Christ. Scotus also explains Christ's baptism as honoring Christ's forerunner, authenticating John's baptism, and even providing sanctification for Christ's humanity.

Augustine of Hippo puzzles over verse 30: He must increase, but I must decrease. *How can Jesus be said to* increase *(3:30) since he is God? Moreover, noticing that John the Baptist is said to* decrease, *Augustine rejects an interpretation that sees* increase *merely as Christ's human growth. Instead, Augustine concludes that the* increase *spoken of here refers to the increase of God's glory in us. Like light, which seems to* increase *in someone cured of blindness, so God's glory, even while remaining perfect, should* increase *in us. John Scotus offers a similar interpretation but emphasizes the* increase *of our understanding of God over time.*

Considering the words He who comes from above is above all *(3:31), Cyril of Alexandria offers an extended Christological discussion of the phrase* from above. *Arguing against those who say that it refers to Christ's exalted status as a creature, Cyril offers an exegetical argument for why* from above *must refer to his eternal generation from the Father. Combining this phrase with the later expression* from heaven *in the same verse (3:31), John Scotus wonders whether* from above *and* from heaven *are intended to mean different things or the same.*

John Chrysostom takes up the words in John 3:36—he who believes *in the Son has eternal life; he who does not* obey *the Son shall not see life. Chrysostom explores whether "faith alone" is sufficient for eternal life, or whether a life of obedience is also required. Both Augustine of Hippo and John Scotus Eriugena explore the meaning of the phrase* the wrath of God rests upon him. *The implication, they argue, is that all are born under God's wrath through Adam's curse. Those who refuse Christ simply remain in that state.*

John 3:1–13

[1]Now there was a man of the Pharisees, named Nicodemus, a ruler of the Jews. [2]This man came to Jesus by night and said to him, "Rabbi, we know that you are a teacher come from God; for no one can do these signs that you do, unless God is with him." [3]Jesus answered him, "Truly, truly, I say to you, unless one is born anew, he cannot see the kingdom of God." [4]Nicodemus said to him, "How can a man be born when

he is old? Can he enter a second time into his mother's womb and be born?" ⁵Jesus answered, "Truly, truly, I say to you, unless one is born of water and the Spirit, he cannot enter the kingdom of God. ⁶That which is born of the flesh is flesh, and that which is born of the Spirit is spirit. ⁷Do not marvel that I said to you, 'You must be born anew.' ⁸The wind blows where it wills, and you hear the sound of it, but you do not know whence it comes or whither it goes; so it is with every one who is born of the Spirit." ⁹Nicodemus said to him, "How can this be?" ¹⁰Jesus answered him, "Are you a teacher of Israel, and yet you do not understand this? ¹¹Truly, truly, I say to you, we speak of what we know, and bear witness to what we have seen; but you do not receive our testimony. ¹²If I have told you earthly things and you do not believe, how can you believe if I tell you heavenly things? ¹³No one has ascended into heaven but he who descended from heaven, the Son of man."

3:3 "unless one is born anew"

---

(1) Justin Martyr

I will explain the way in which we dedicated ourselves to God, having been made new through Christ, lest if the matter is ignored, my explanation might appear to mislead. As many as are persuaded and believe that what we teach and say is true, and who promise to be able to live this way, are taught to pray and ask God through fasting for the forgiveness of their former sins as we pray and fast with them. Then they are led by us to a place where there is water, and are **born anew** in the same way that we ourselves were **born anew**. They are washed in water in the name of God, the Lord and Father of all, and of Jesus Christ our Savior, and of the Holy Spirit. For Christ also said, **unless one is born anew, he cannot enter the kingdom of** heaven (3:3). . . .

We learn the reason for this practice from the apostles. At our first birth we were born without our knowledge and choice—out of the usual tender union which produces children—and have been brought up in bad habits and wicked behaviors. But so that we might not remain children of necessity or ignorance, but children of choice and knowledge, and so that we might obtain forgiveness of former sins, there is pronounced in the water over the one who has chosen to be **born anew** and has repented of one's sins, the name of God the Father and Lord of all . . . and the name of Jesus Christ who was crucified by Pontius Pilate, and the name of the Holy Spirit.

(2) Theodore of Mopsuestia

Rabbi, we know that you are a teacher sent from God; for no one can do these signs that you do, unless God is with him (3:2). Nicodemus begins his words with praises, for people are accustomed to begin with words like these, especially when they address an illustrious person. For this reason, Nicodemus says, "We are convinced that you are a true teacher and that you come from God, for the miracles that you performed make this known to us." But our Lord did not give heed to his praises. Jesus knew (as the evangelist tells us) that one's innermost thoughts did not always agree with one's words. Therefore, Jesus began to speak to Nicodemus with words suitable for someone who wants to teach, especially when speaking to one like Nicodemus who had confessed his conviction that the teacher had come from God. . . .

So Jesus said to Nicodemus, **Truly, truly, I say to you, unless one is born anew, he cannot see the kingdom of God** (3:3). What he meant was this: "If you believe that I came as a teacher from God, and the miracles I did persuaded you of this, as you say, then our teaching requires that one lives differently and expects the beginning of new birth. Indeed we expect to see **the kingdom of God**; but since we are mortal, we cannot receive it unless we die, rise, and become incorruptible. We believe that this happens through a form of baptism. We are **born anew** in a form of the resurrection, as we move from one state of being to another."

(3) Venerable Bede

Jesus answered him, "Truly, truly, I say to you, unless one is born anew, he cannot see the kingdom of God" (3:3). This statement shines forth all the more clearly in the sight of all the faithful, for it is obvious that without the light of rebirth they cannot be faithful. Who indeed is capable of securing the forgiveness of sins, and of entering the **kingdom** of heaven, without the bath of regeneration? Nicodemus, who **came to Jesus by night** (3:2), did not yet know how to grasp the mysteries of the light. Even the **night** during which he **came** indicates the ignorance by which he was oppressed. He did not yet belong to the number of that fellowship to whom the apostle says, *Once you were darkness, but now you are light in the Lord* (Eph 5:8). Rather, he remained in the company of those to whom Isaiah speaks: *Arise, shine,* O Jerusalem; *for your light has come, and the glory of the LORD has risen upon you* (Isa 60:1).

(4) John Scotus Eriugena

Jesus answered him, "Truly, truly, I say to you, unless one is born anew, he cannot see the kingdom of God" (3:3). It may be asked why Jesus answers Nicodemus by talking about the second birth, which is according to the Spirit, when Nicodemus does not seem to have asked about it. Here is the answer: because the Lord saw that Nicodemus believed as others believed who had seen his signs, supposing that faith alone would be enough for them without the benefit of spiritual birth and the sacraments. He immediately began to teach him about the birth that is according to the Spirit. This is as much as to say openly: "It is not enough for you just to believe in me unless you receive the sacrament of baptism and understand the power of spiritual birth." . . .

Nicodemus said to him, "How can a man be born when he is old? Can he enter a second time into his mother's womb and be born?" (3:4). He who has so far been born only according to the flesh, understood in a fleshly way, and accordingly answered in a fleshly way, because he had not been born by the sacrament of baptism and by the Spirit. Nonetheless, he had spoken truly, because no one can be born twice according to the flesh, just as no one can be born twice according to the Spirit. Just as one is born once in the flesh from the flesh, so one is born once in the Spirit from the Spirit. Once one has received the sacrament of baptism, no one can repeat it.

3:5 "Unless one is born of water and the Spirit, he cannot enter the kingdom of God."

---

(5) John Chrysostom

Unless, he says, **one is born of water and the Spirit, he cannot enter the kingdom of** heaven (3:5).[1] Nicodemus didn't understand this either. For nothing is worse than transforming spiritual things into arguments. This failure did not allow Nicodemus to imagine anything lofty and great. This is why we are called "faithful," so that leaving the weakness of earthly arguments we might ascend to the height of faith and conform most of our blessings to this teaching. If Nicodemus had done this, he wouldn't have thought it was impossible. What then does Christ do? Leading Nicodemus away from this notion of being attached to earthly things, and showing that he doesn't speak of a physical birth, he says, **Unless one is born of water and the Spirit, he cannot enter the kingdom of** heaven (3:5).

He spoke these things, willing to draw him to faith by fear of threats, and to persuade him not to think it was impossible, eagerly turning him away from the notion of a physical birth. "I mean," he says, "another birth, O Nicodemus. Why do you drag the expression to earth? Why do you subject the matter to the laws of nature? This birth is higher than labors such as these; it has nothing in common with you. It's called a birth and shares its name, but it differs in reality. Give up such common notions; I introduce to the world another kind of birth. I want people to be born in a different manner; I came bringing a means of creation unheard of. I formed earth and water (Gen 1–2), but that which was formed was not beneficial and the vessel was perverted. Therefore, I no longer want to form life from earth and water but **from water and Spirit**" (3:5). . . .

Christ begins first with **water**, which is lighter than earth but thicker than air. For just as in the beginning the earth was presented as the primary element, but the whole person came from the One who formed it, so also now **water** is presented as the primary element, but the whole person comes from the grace of the **Spirit**. Formerly, *man became a living being* (Gen 2:7), but now he becomes a *life-giving spirit* (1 Cor 15:45). There is a great difference between the two. While the soul does not produce life in another, the **Spirit** not only lives in himself but also produces life in others. This is how the apostles raised the dead (cf. Acts 9:39–42; 20:8–12).

---

1. The Greek here is **kingdom of God,** but Chrysostom uses "kingdom of heaven," perhaps thinking of the phrase more common in the Gospel of Matthew.

Again, human beings were formed last, after the created world. But now, it's just the opposite, for before the new creation, a new humanity is created. Christ is born first and then the world is changed. Just as *in the beginning* (Gen 1:1) God formed humanity complete, so now he fashions humanity complete. Formerly, he said *Let us make a helper for him* (Gen 2:18), but here there is nothing like this. Does the one who receives the grace of the Spirit need some other help? What need of helpers is there for the one perfected in the body of Christ? Formerly, he *made man in the image of God* (Gen 1:26), but now, God has united us to himself. Formerly, he commanded humanity to rule over the fish and beasts, but now he has exalted our firstfruits above the heavens. Formerly, he gave human beings a garden as a dwelling place, but now he has opened heaven to us. Formerly, human beings were fashioned on the sixth day, when the world was about to be completed, but now it was on the first day, in the beginning, when light was made. From all of this it's clear that the things accomplished in baptism are of another, better life and of a state having no end.

(6) Theodore of Mopsuestia

Truly, truly, I say to you, unless one is born of water and the Spirit, he cannot enter the kingdom of God (3:5). Since Nicodemus had asked, **Can he enter a second time into his mother's womb and be born?** (3:4), our Lord explained to him how this happens through **water and the Spirit**. He speaks of **water** because the action is accomplished in **water**, and **Spirit** because this is what accomplishes the operation through **water**. . . .

For this reason, in baptism we name the **Spirit** together with the Father and the Son, but we do not mention the **water**, in order to make it clear that **water** is something used only as a sign. We invoke the **Spirit** as the one who acts together with the Father and the Son, because when Nicodemus asked, **Can one enter into his mother's womb and be born?** our Lord responded by saying, through **water and the Spirit**. . . .

Now, baptism is also said to be a sign of death and resurrection and for this reason it is also called regeneration. Just as the one who is resurrected after he dies is considered to be created again, so also the one who is born in baptism is said to be born again—as one who dies in the **water** and then is resurrected through the power of **the Spirit**. While the immersion represents burial, the lifting of the head at each invocation represents the resurrection that takes place through the power of **the Spirit**.

(7) Augustine of Hippo

Nicodemus, who came to Jesus during the **night**, did not perceive the Spirit and the life. Jesus says to him, **unless one is born of water and the Spirit, he cannot enter the kingdom of God** (3:5). Nicodemus, perceiving only his own flesh, and not yet tasting the flesh of Christ in his mouth, asks, **How can a man be born when he is old? Can he enter a second time into his mother's womb and be born?** (3:4). He was acquainted only with one kind of birth—that which is from Adam and Eve. He did not yet recognize that birth which is from God and the church. He knew only those parents who beget death, and was not yet aware of those parents who beget life. He was acquainted only with those parents who beget successors, but did not yet recognize those parents who, always alive, beget children who will remain.

Therefore, although there are two births, Nicodemus understood only one. One is of the earth, the other of heaven; one is of the flesh, the other of the Spirit; one is of mortality, the other of eternity; one is of male and female, the other of God and the church. But these same two births are each singular, neither one nor the other can be repeated. Nicodemus understood the birth of the flesh rightly, and so must you understand the birth of the Spirit in the way Nicodemus understood the birth of the flesh. What did Nicodemus understand? **Can a man enter a second time into his mother's womb and be born?** (3:4). Likewise, if someone says to you that you should be spiritually born again, you must respond with Nicodemus's words: **Can a man enter a second time into his mother's womb and be born?** (3:4). Already I am born of Adam; Adam is unable to beget me again. Already I am born of Christ; Christ is unable to beget me again. Just as it's impossible to reenter the womb, so likewise one cannot repeat baptism.

*　　*　　*

The Lord says to Nicodemus, and explains to him, **Truly, truly, I say to you, unless one is born of water and the Spirit, he cannot enter the kingdom of God** (3:5). "You," he says, "understand only a fleshly birth, when you say, **Can a man enter a second time into his mother's womb and be born?** (3:4). It's necessary for a person to be born **of water and the Spirit** on account of the **kingdom of God**. If he is born on account of the temporal inheritance of a human father, he is born of the innermost part of his fleshly mother. If he is born on account of the everlasting inheritance of God the Father, he is born of the innermost part of the church. A father, who will eventually die, begets by his wife a child who will succeed him. Likewise, God begets children by the church who are not successors, but who endure with him." And so it follows: **That which is born of the flesh is flesh, and that which is born of the Spirit is spirit** (3:6).

Therefore we are born spiritually, and in the Spirit we are born through word and sacrament. The Spirit is near so that we might be born; the Spirit is invisibly near *whence* you are born, because you are born invisibly. Thus it is said, **Do not marvel that I said to you, You must be born anew. The wind blows where it wills, and you hear the sound of it, but you do not know whence it comes or whither it goes** (3:7–8). No one sees the Spirit, so how do we hear the voice of the Spirit? A psalm is uttered; that is the voice of the Spirit. The gospel is spoken; that is the voice of the Spirit. The divine word sounds forth; that is the voice of the Spirit. **You hear the sound of it, but you do not know whence it comes or whither it goes** (3:8). But if you are born of the Spirit, you also will be this way, so that one who is not yet born of the Spirit will not know *whence* you come or *whither* you go. For this reason it is said, **so it is with every one who is born of the Spirit** (3:8).

(8) John Scotus Eriugena

Jesus answered, "Truly, truly, I say to you, unless one is born of water and the Spirit, he cannot enter the kingdom of God" (3:5). Earlier he said, **He cannot see the kingdom of God** (3:3), but now, changing the verb, he says, **He cannot *enter* the kingdom of God** (3:5). From this we can infer that it is not one thing to **see the kingdom of God** and another to **enter the kingdom of God**. They mean the same thing. Thus he who **sees the kingdom of God, enters** it, and he who **enters** it, **sees** it. To **see** is to **enter** and to **enter** is to **see**, that is, to know the truth.

Unless one has been born of water and of the Spirit (3:5), that is, by a visible sacrament and by an invisible understanding. This means as much as to say: if someone visibly receives the symbol of baptism and does not perceive the Spirit which is the understanding of the symbolwhe cannot **enter the kingdom of God**. This can also be understood to mean: **of water**, that is, the visible symbol, and **of the** Holy **Spirit**.

It may be asked why the Lord established the visible sacrament of baptism in water, when it would seem that spiritual teaching alone suffices by faith for one's birth from the Spirit. To this it should be said: because man is constituted of a visible body and an invisible soul, it was necessary for there to be a visible sacrament for the cleansing of the visible body, just as the invisible teaching of the faith is necessary for the sanctification of the invisible soul. For even though the visible sacrament of baptism does not yet seem to provide the body anything in this life, nonetheless, in the future resurrection it will make the mortal immortal, and the corruptible incorruptible, along with the other benefits that belong to the glory of the future resurrection. At the same time, even in the present life the power of baptism sanctifies the bodies of the faithful, when they are made a temple of the Holy Spirit, as the apostle said: *Do you not know that your bodies are a temple of the Holy Spirit?* (1 Cor 6:19).

3:6 "That which is born of the flesh is flesh."

---

(9) Venerable Bede

That which is born of the flesh is flesh, and that which is born of the Spirit is spirit (3:6). By its nature **spirit** is invisible; **flesh** is visible, and so fleshly generation is carried out in visible stages—one who is **born of the flesh** develops through moments in time. Spiritual generation is carried out entirely invisibly. We see the one being baptized descend into the font, we see him being immersed, we see him come up out of the water; but what is done in that *washing of regeneration* (Tit 3:5) cannot be seen. Only the piety of the faithful knows that a sinner descends into the font, and a purified person comes up; that a child of death descends, and a child of the resurrection comes up; that a child of original sin descends, and a child of reconciliation comes up; that a child of wrath descends, and a child of mercy comes up; that a child of the devil descends, and a child of God comes up. Only the church, a mother who gives birth,[2]

2. Early Christians considered the church their spiritual "mother."

knows these things; otherwise, to the eyes of the foolish, the person seems to come forth from the font just as he went in, and the entire action seems to be a game.

In the end, those groaning in torment will say as they see the glory of the saints, *These are the ones whom we once held in derision and made a byword of reproach; why are they numbered among the sons of God?* (Wis 5:4–5). And the apostle John says, *Beloved, we are God's children now; it does not yet appear what we shall be* (1 John 3:2). **That which is born of the Spirit is spirit**, because the person who is regenerated invisibly **of water and the Spirit** (3:5) is changed into a new human being, and from being fleshly one becomes spiritual.

Rightly then is one called not only spiritual but even **spirit**, because just as the substance of a **spirit** is invisible to our sight, so the one who is invisibly renewed by the grace of God becomes spiritual and a child of God, although appearing visibly to all as flesh and the child of a human being.

3:13 "No one has ascended into heaven but he who descended from heaven."

---

(10) Augustine of Hippo

Notice that Christ was both here and in heaven. He was here in the flesh, and he was in heaven in his divinity—or rather, he was everywhere in his divinity. He was born of his mother without leaving his Father. Two births of Christ are understood, one divine, the other human. By one we were created, by the other we were re-created. Both are marvels, the first without a mother, the second without a father. Because he received his body from Adam (since Mary was from Adam) and because that body was also to be resurrected, he spoke of something earthly when he said, **Destroy this temple, and in three days I will raise it up** (2:19). However, he spoke of something heavenly when he said, **Unless someone is born of water and the Spirit, he will not see the kingdom of God** (3:5).

See, brothers and sisters, God himself willed to be a son of man, and he willed us to be children of God. He himself **descended** for us; let us **ascend** to him. Indeed he alone has **descended** and **ascended** who said this: **No one has ascended into heaven but the one who descended from heaven** (3:13). Will those, then, whom he made children of God not **ascend** into heaven? Clearly they will **ascend**. We are promised this: *They will be like angels of God* (Matt 22:30). But how, then, has **no one ascended but he who descended**? Since one has **descended**, one has **ascended**. What of the rest? What are we to understand except that they will be members of him so that one may **ascend**?

For this reason he continues, **No one has ascended into heaven except the one who descended from heaven, the Son of man who is in heaven** (3:13). Are you surprised that he was both here and in heaven? He made his disciples like that. Hear the apostle Paul, who says, *Our dwelling, however, is in heaven* (Phil 3:20). If the man, Paul the apostle, was walking in the flesh on earth and was also dwelling in heaven, is it not possible for the God of heaven and earth to be both in heaven and on earth?

If, then, **no one except he** has **descended** and **ascended**, what hope is there for the rest? There is this hope for the rest. He himself **descended** for this reason: that they might be one in him and with him through whom they are to **ascend**. The apostle said, *It does not say, "And to offsprings," referring to many; but referring to one, "And to your offspring," which is Christ* (Gal 3:16). And, to the faithful he said, *You, however, are Christ's; but if you are Christ's, then you are Abraham's offspring* (Gal 3:29). What he says the one is, this he says we all are.

(11) John Scotus Eriugena

As concerns his **descent** and **ascent**, he explained this clearly elsewhere, saying *I came from the Father and have come into the world; again, I am leaving the world and going to the Father* (16:28). His leaving the Father is becoming a man, and his return to the Father is the deification, the assumption to the very summit of divinity, of the human being he took on. He **descended** alone, because only he became incarnate. But if he **ascended** alone, what hope is there for those for whom he **descended**? It is actually great and beyond explanation. All whom he saved **ascend** in him: now by faith and in hope, in the end by vision and in reality. John said this in his epistle: *We are God's children now; it does not yet appear what we shall be, but we know that when he appears we shall be like him, for we shall see him as he is* (1 John 3:2). Thus he **descended** alone and he **ascended** alone, because with all the members of his body he is one God, the unique Son of God. Therefore all who believe in him are one in him. So one Christ, the body with all its members, **ascended** to the Father.

John 3:14–16

[14]**"And as Moses lifted up the serpent in the wilderness, so must the Son of man be lifted up,** [15]**that whoever believes in him may have eternal life.** [16]**For God so loved the world that he gave his only Son, that whoever believes in him should not perish but have eternal life."**

(12) John Chrysostom

This passage seems to be dependent upon what came earlier and has a strong connection to it. Having spoken of the great benefit brought to people through baptism, he proceeds to discuss the cause of it—and one not inferior to it—namely, the benefit of the cross. This is similar to what Paul says when, arguing with the Corinthians, he presents these benefits together: *Was Paul crucified for you, or were you baptized into the name of Paul?* (1 Cor 1:13). These two things demonstrate his unspeakable love most fully—that Christ suffered and died for his enemies, and that he offered complete forgiveness of sins through baptism.

Why did Christ not say plainly, "I am about to be crucified," but instead directed his listeners to the ancient type? First, so that you might learn that the ancient realities relate to the new, and that the former are not alien to the latter. Second, so that you might know that he did not come to his passion unwillingly. In addition to these reasons, so that you might learn that while no harm comes to him from the event of the passion, salvation flows from it to many.

He leads us to the ancient narrative so that no one might ask, "How can someone who believes on the Crucified One be saved when he himself is held back by death?" Well if the Jews, beholding the bronze image of a serpent, escaped death (Num 21:9), how much more will those who believe on the one who was crucified, also fittingly enjoy a much greater benefit. The passion occurs not because of the weakness of the one crucified or because the Jews were superior in strength, but because **God loved the world** (3:16). For this reason his living temple is crucified so that **whoever believes in him should not perish but have eternal life** (3:16). Do you see the cause of the crucifixion and the salvation which results from it? Do you see the similarity between the type and the truth? There, the Jews escaped death, but only a temporal one; here those who believe escape an eternal death. There, the hanging serpent heals the bite of the serpent; here the crucified Jesus heals the wounds of the spiritual dragon. There, the one who sees with natural eyes was healed; here the one who sees with the eyes of understanding casts away all sins. There, that which hung was bronze, shaped into the form of a serpent; here it was the Lord's *body prepared* by the Spirit (cf. Heb 10:5). There, the serpent bit and a serpent healed; so also here death destroyed and a death saved. But while the serpent which destroyed had venom, the one which saved was free from venom. Here again it is the same, for while death which destroyed had sin, just as the serpent had venom, so the death of the Lord was free from all sin, just as the bronze serpent was free from venom. *For*, it says, *he committed no sin, and no guile was found on his lips* (1 Pet 2:22). And this is what Paul says: *He disarmed the principalities and powers and made a public example of them, triumphing over them in him* (Col 2:15). Just as some noble athlete, by lifting up his opponent and throwing him, displays a clearer victory, so also Christ. With all the world watching, he cast down the adversarial powers, healed those who were filled with sin in the wilderness, and having been hung on the cross, delivered them from all venomous beasts. Yet he did not say "must hang" but **must be lifted up** (3:14). Therefore he put forth what seemed to be a milder expression because of his audience and because it was similar to the type.

For God so loved the world that he gave his only Son, that whoever believes in him should not perish but have eternal life (3:16). What he says is something like this: "Do not marvel that I am about to **be lifted up** so that you might be saved. For this seems good to the Father and **he so loved you** as to give the Son for the slaves—even arrogant slaves. In fact, no one would do this for a friend, nor so quickly for a righteous man, as Paul declared: *One will hardly die for a righteous man* (Rom 5:7). Paul spoke at more length since he was conversing with believers. Here, Christ speaks simply, but with more significance, since his speech was toward Nicodemus. Each word had a great significance. By saying **God loved** and **the world** he indicated the great intensity of God's love, for the difference between the two was great and infinite. God is the Immortal One, without beginning, the Infinite Majesty; those in the world come from dust and ashes, are full of immeasurable sins, arrogant, and always giving offense. These **he loved**.

Again, the words he introduces next are likewise significant, saying, **he gave his only Son** (3:16)—not a slave, not an angel, not an archangel. In fact, no one would demonstrate such zeal for a child as God did for his arrogant servants. Therefore he doesn't display his passion very openly, but instead obscurely. However, the profit of his passion he displays clearly and openly, saying **that whoever believes in him should not perish but have eternal life** (3:16). He said that he **must be lifted up** (3:14), hinting at his death. But so that his hearer might not become sorrowful at these words, supposing something human concerning him and thinking that his death meant a non-existence, observe how Christ corrects this, saying that the "Son of God" was the one given and the cause of life—even eternal life.

The one who offers life to others through death was not about to remain in death forever. For if those who believe in the Crucified One don't perish, how much more will he who was crucified not perish? The one who takes away the destruction of others, how much more is he free from it? The one who presents life to others, how much more does he bring forth life for himself? Do you see the need for faith everywhere? He says that the cross is a spring of life which reason cannot easily accept, as the mocking Greeks testify. But the faith which surpasses the weakness of arguments may easily receive it and retain it. Where did **God so love the world**? From no other place than from his goodness alone.

(13) Theodore of Mopsuestia

After speaking about his ascension . . . Jesus added the following remark: **And as Moses lifted up the serpent in the wilderness, so must the Son of man be lifted up, that whoever believes in him may have eternal life** (3:14–15). What he means is this: "Let no cross terrify you in any way and let nothing distract you from my words." In the wilderness, **Moses lifted up the serpent**, which is bronze in nature, and the power of the one who commanded the snake to be lifted up redeemed those who looked upon it. So too when Jesus bore our human condition and suffered the crucifixion, because of the power dwelling in him, he made those who believe in him worthy of eternal life. Likewise, the bronze serpent, lifeless on its own, delivered, through another power, those who were perishing from serpent bites (so long as they looked at it). So too Jesus, even though he seems mortal and suffers, gives life to those who believe in him, through the power dwelling in him.

(14) Augustine of Hippo

Christ took up death and hung it on a cross, and from death itself mortals are set free. The Lord calls to mind what was done symbolically with the ancients: **And as Moses**, he said, **lifted up the serpent in the wilderness, so must the Son of man be lifted up, that whoever believes in him** may not die, but **may have eternal life** (3:14–15). This is a great mystery, and those who read it know it. So let those now hear who either have not read it, or who have perhaps forgotten what was read or heard. The people of Israel were being overcome in the wilderness by the bites of serpents, and there was a great carnage of the dead; it was the blow of God rebuking and scourging them so that he might instruct them (Num 21). That a great mystery of something to come was demonstrated there, the Lord himself testifies in this reading, so that no one may be able to interpret it in another way than that which the truth itself indicates. Moses was commanded by the Lord to make a bronze serpent and to lift it up on a piece of wood in the desert. He was commanded to admonish the people of Israel, so that if anyone was bitten by a serpent, he would look to the serpent lifted up on the wood. It was done: the people were bitten, they gazed upon it, and they were healed.

What are the biting serpents? The sins of the mortality of the flesh. Who is the uplifted serpent? The death of the Lord on the cross. For since there was death from the serpent, by the likeness of the serpent death is symbolized. The bite of the serpent was deadly; the death of the Lord was life-giving. The serpent is looked upon, so that the serpent may have no power. What is this? Death is looked upon so that death may have no power. But whose death? The death of life, if we can say so, the death of life. Indeed, since we can say it, it is said marvelously. But is there anything which was to be accomplished which should be left unsaid? Do I hesitate to say what the Lord has considered worthy for me to do? Is not Christ life? Yet Christ was on the cross. Is not Christ life? Yet Christ died. In the death of Christ death died; since life, having died, killed death, the fullness of life swallowed up death; death was swallowed up in the body of Christ. Even this we shall say in the resurrection, when now triumphant we shall sing: *O death, where is thy strife? O death, where is thy sting?* (1 Cor 15:55).[3]

Meanwhile, brothers and sisters, so that we may be healed of sin, let us only fix our eyes upon Christ crucified; since he said, **As Moses lifted up the serpent in the wilderness, so must the Son of man be lifted up, that whoever believes in him** may not die, but **may have eternal life** (3:14–15). Just as the Israelites fixed their eyes on that serpent and did not perish from the bites of the serpents, even so will those who fix their eyes with faith upon the death of Christ be healed from the bites of their sins. The Israelites were healed from death to a temporary life, but this says: **so that they may have eternal life**. This is the difference between the symbolized likeness and the thing itself; the symbol offered temporary life; the thing itself of which it was the symbol, offers eternal life.

(15) Severian of Gabala

How did the image of the accursed one bring life to our ancestors?[4] Or again, how did the image of the accursed one bring salvation to the people in distress? Would it not have been more believable to say, "If any of you has been bitten, look to God in heaven above, or to the tabernacle of God, and you will be saved?" But Moses disregarded these things and firmly established the image of the cross alone. Why then did Moses do this? For he is also the one who said to the people, *Do not make for yourself a graven image or any likeness of anything that is in heaven above, or that is in the earth beneath, or that is in the water under the earth* (Exod 20:4). But why should I myself speak these things to the ignorant? Speak, O most faithful servant of God.[5] Will you do what you forbid? Will you affirm what you refute? The one who says, *Do not make a graven image*, who cries out in condemnation of the golden

---

3. Augustine's text reads *strife* for *victory* in his reference to the Corinthian text.

4. Severian means that the serpent being used to heal in Num 21:8–9 is the same image (a serpent) of the enemy who caused Eve to disobey in the garden (Gen 3:1–6).

5. Severian means Moses.

calf (Exod 32:19–20), will you cast a bronze serpent, and do it not secretly, but openly and known to all? "But," Moses says, "I prescribed these things as law to extirpate impiety and to lead the people from all apostasy and idolatry. But now I cast a bronze serpent for the good, to prefigure the truth. Just as I established the tabernacle and everything in it—even the cherubim, in the likeness of invisible things, hovering over the holy place—as a type and shadow of the things to come, so also I set up a serpent for the people's salvation, so that these tests might prepare them beforehand for the image of the sign of the cross, the Savior, and the redemption found in it." And for this most trustworthy word, beloved, hear what the Lord cries out and says: **As Moses lifted up the serpent in the wilderness, so must the Son of man be lifted up, that whoever believes in him may not perish, but have eternal life** (3:14–15).

(16) Cyril of Alexandria

Jesus explained things sufficiently and presented to Nicodemus the reason why his teaching did not rush on to infinite and immeasurable realities, but rather returns to those symbolic actions of Moses. He also knows well that only by leading Nicodemus by the hand—through figurative expressions rather than spiritual propositions—would Nicodemus be able to arrive at the knowledge of the truth. For this reason, Jesus says that he certainly **must be lifted up as the serpent which was lifted by Moses** (3:14). By this he shows that the study of history is absolutely necessary. He speaks simply to one with no understanding: *Search the scriptures because they are the ones that bear witness to me* (5:39). While serpents were springing up among the Israelites in the wilderness, the Israelites were dropping like ears of corn. Greatly distressed by the danger so unexpectedly imposed on them, they uttered most piteous cries and called for salvation from God above. Since he was both a good and compassionate God, he commanded Moses to set up for them a bronze serpent (Num 21:8–9), and indeed commanded them to practice beforehand salvation by faith. The remedy for one bitten was to behold the serpent placed before one's face, and faith along with sight produced complete deliverance for those who beheld it. On the one hand, these events record history. On the other hand, as typological acts, they represent the entire mystery of the incarnation.

The serpent signifies the bitter and murderous sin which altogether consumes the race on earth (cf. Gen 3), in various ways biting the human soul and spreading the varied poison of wickedness. There was no other way to escape it from conquering us except through the aid of heaven alone. Therefore, God the Word came *in the likeness of sinful flesh in order to condemn sin in the flesh*, as it is written (Rom 8:3). To those who gaze upon him through a more earnest faith, or through a search of divine doctrines, he might be shown a patron of indissoluble salvation. The serpent, however, was lifted up on an exalted base, and this clearly and completely represented Christ in his unique manifestation so that he, **being lifted up from the earth**, as he himself says somewhere (12:32), would be known to all by the passion of the cross.

(17) Venerable Bede

Since ascension and entry into the kingdom cannot happen without faith and the sacraments of the Lord's passion, he added: **And as Moses lifted up the serpent in the wilderness, so must the Son of man be lifted up, that whoever believes in him may have eternal life** (3:14–15). With the wonderful skill of heavenly teaching, the Lord directs our attention to the teacher of the Mosaic law, and to the spiritual meaning of this law, by recalling some of the ancient history and explaining that it happened as a figure of his own passion and of human salvation. The book of Numbers records that the people of Israel were wearied in the desert from their long journeying and exertion, and murmured against the Lord and Moses. So the Lord sent fiery **serpents** in among them. When they cried out to Moses because of their wounds and the death of many of them, and Moses prayed for them, the Lord ordered him to make a bronze serpent and set it up as a sign (cf. Num 21:5–8). He said, *every one who is bitten, when he sees it, shall live* (Num 21:8), and so it happened.

The wounds caused by the fiery **serpent** are the poisonous enticements of the vices, which afflict the soul and bring about its spiritual death. The people murmuring against the Lord and stricken by the **serpents'** bites provide an excellent instance of how one may recognize from the results of an external scourge what a great calamity a person might suffer inwardly by murmuring. The lifting up of the bronze **serpent** (when those who were stricken beheld it, they were cured) is our Redeemer's suffering on the cross. Only by faith in him is the kingdom of death and sin overcome. The sins which drag down soul and body to destruction at the same time are appropriately represented by **serpents**, not only because they were fiery and poisonous and artful at bringing about death, but also because our first parents were led into sin by a **serpent** (cf. Gen 3:1–13), and from being immortal they became mortal by sinning.

The Lord is aptly made known by the bronze **serpent**, since he came *in the likeness of sinful flesh* (Rom 8:3). Just as the bronze **serpent** had the likeness of a fiery **serpent**, but had absolutely none of the strength of harmful poison in its members—rather by being lifted up it cured those who had been stricken by the live **serpents**—so the Redeemer of the human race did not clothe himself in *sinful flesh*, but in the *likeness of sinful flesh*, in order that by suffering death on the cross in this *likeness* he might free those who believed in him from all sin and even from death itself.

And as Moses lifted up the serpent in the wilderness, so must the Son of man be lifted up (3:14). Just as those who looked at the bronze **serpent** which had been **lifted up** as a sign were cured at that time from temporal death and the wounds which the **serpents'** bites had caused, so too those who look at the mystery of the Lord's passion by believing, confessing, and sincerely imitating it are saved forever from every death they have incurred by sinning in mind and body.

Hence he added: **that whoever believes in him may have eternal life** (3:15). The meaning of this sentence is evident: **whoever believes** in Christ not only escapes the perdition incurred as a penalty, but also attains **eternal life**. But there is this difference between the figure and the truth—through the former, temporal life was only prolonged, but through the latter, a life is granted which will continue without end. But we must zealously take care that worthy works complete what our understanding comprehends so well, so that the confession of our right faith may deservedly bring us, by a pious and sober way of life, to the perfection of the life that has been promised us.

But these things were said about the Son of Man, who would be **lifted up** on the cross and suffer death. So that Nicodemus would not suppose it was solely from the Son of Man that **eternal life** was to be looked for, our Lord took care to disclose to him as well the mystery of his divinity, and to show that the Son of God and the Son of Man were one and the same Savior of the world. For there follows: **For God so loved the world that he gave his only Son, that whoever believes in him should not perish but have eternal life** (3:16).

At this point we must note that John repeats about the Son of God what he had mentioned earlier about the Son of Man **lifted up** on the cross: **that whoever believes in him should not perish but have eternal life** (3:15, 16). Our Redeemer and Maker, who was Son of God before the ages, became Son of Man at the end of the ages. Thus the one who, through the power of his divinity, had created us to enjoy the happiness of everlasting life, might himself restore us, through the weakness of our humanity, to recover the life we had lost.

John 3:17–21

[17]"For God sent the Son into the world, not to condemn the world, but that the world might be saved through him. [18]He who believes in him is not condemned; he who does not believe is condemned already, because he has not believed in the name of the only Son of God. [19]And this is the judgment, that the light has come into the world, and men loved darkness rather than light, because their deeds were evil. [20]For every one who does evil hates the light, and does not come to the light, lest his deeds should be exposed. [21]But he who does what is true comes to the light, that it may be clearly seen that his deeds have been wrought in God."

3:17–18 "God sent the Son into the world, not to condemn the world. . . . He who believes in him is not condemned."

---

(18) Irenaeus of Lyons

As many as preserve their love for him, to these God offers his own fellowship; and the fellowship of God is life and light and the enjoyment of all good things which come from him. And as many as willingly depart from God, to these he brings the separation they have chosen; and separation from God is death, separation from light is darkness, and separation from God is the loss of all good things which come from him. Those therefore who through their apostasy discard the things just mentioned, are deprived of all good things and abide in full **condemn**ation, not that God **condemns** them beforehand, but that **condemn**ation comes to them by being deprived of all good things.

The good things that come from God are eternal and without end. Because of this, the loss of them is eternal and without end, just as when there is continuous light, those who have blinded themselves or are blinded by others, are continuously deprived of the enjoyment of light. Light has not brought upon them the **condemn**ation of blindness; blindness itself brings on their sorrowful state. This is why the Lord said, **He who believes in me is not condemned**, that is, he is not separated from God, for he is united to God through faith; **but he who does not believe**, he says, **is condemned already, because he has not believed in the name of the only Son of God** (3:18), that is, he has separated himself from God by his free will.

(19) John Chrysostom

There are two advents of Christ: one which has occurred already and one which is to come. But the two have different purposes. The first occurred not so that he might examine our deeds, but that he might forgive. The second will occur not so that he might forgive, but that he might examine. For this reason, concerning the first he says, **I did not come to condemn the world, but that I might save the world** (3:17). Concerning the second he says: *When the Son comes in the glory* of the Father, *he will place the sheep at his right and the goats at his left* (Matt 25:31, 33). Some will enter into life and some into eternal punishment. Indeed, even the first advent was for judgment with respect to the principle of justice. Why? Because before his coming, there was a natural law, prophets, a written law and instruction, immeasurable promises, manifestations of signs, punishments, penalties, and many other things capable of setting people right. It followed that he would demand an account for all these things. But since he is benevolent, he does not make an examination, but for a time forgives. If he had made an examination, all would have been destroyed at once. *For all have sinned and fall short of the glory of God* (Rom 3:23). Do you see the unspeakable abundance of his benevolence?

He who believes in the Son is not condemned. He who does not believe is condemned already (3:18). Yet, if he did not come to **condemn** the world, how is **he who does not believe condemned already** (3:18), if the time of **condemn**ation is not yet present? Either he means that unrepentant disbelief is itself punishment (for being without light also contains in itself a great punishment), or he speaks beforehand of what is to come.

Just as a murderer, even if not **condemn**ed by the decision of the judge, has still been **condemn**ed by the nature of the act, so also the unbeliever. Adam also died on the day in which he ate from the tree, for so the sentence: *For in the day that you eat from the tree* it says *you will die* (Gen 2:17); and yet he lived. How then did he die? By the sentence and by the nature of the act. For the one who has made himself liable to **condemn**ation is under penalty by the sentence, even if not in actuality for a time.

Some might hear, **I came not to condemn the world** (3:17), and become indifferent to sin, thinking that sin will go without punishment. Therefore, Christ prevents this contempt by saying, **he is condemned already** (3:18). Since the **condemn**ation is future and not yet present, he presents the fear of punishment and indicates the **condemn**ation as being **already** (3:18). Even this itself is a sign of great benevolence, not only in giving his Son, but also delaying the time of **condemn**ation so that those who have sinned and not believed might have the ability to wash away their transgressions.

(20) Theodore of Mopsuestia

Christ said that the Son of Man would be raised up, and that this was the reason God gave his only Son. But since those who do not believe in him would be found guilty, he correctly added: **For God sent the Son into the world, not to condemn the world, but that the world might be saved through him** (3:17). He returns again to the purpose of what happened to him: "The purpose established by God was not for a person to be found guilty, but for everyone to be saved."

Then what? **He who believes in him is not condemned; he who does not believe is condemned already, because he has not believed in the name of the only Son of God** (3:18). What he means is this: "The purpose of God is for everyone to believe and be saved; this is why I came to humanity. Those **who do not believe** are the cause of their own damnation, but those who **believe** have the right to be saved. So if some **do not believe**, they are the cause of their own punishment, for his gracious gift is available to all who want it."

And this is the judgment, that the light has come into the world, and men loved darkness rather than light (3:19). "This is why," he says, "they are especially guilty, because the light did come to them. They did not desire happiness; they closed the eyes of their souls and turned toward evil."

3:19-21 "And this is the judgment. . . . He who does what is true comes to the light."

---

(21) Augustine of Hippo

My brothers and sisters, whose deeds does the Lord find good? No one's. He finds everyone's **deeds evil**. Therefore, how have certain people done **what is true** and **come to the light**? For this is what follows in the text: **But he who does what is true comes to the light, that it may be clearly seen that his deeds have been wrought in God** (3:21). How have certain people **wrought** good **deeds**, so that they might come to the **light**, that is, to Christ? How have certain people **loved darkness**? God finds all people sinners, and cures them all of their sins. That serpent (in which was symbolized the death of the Lord) cured those who had been bitten. Because of the serpent's bite a serpent was set up, that is, the death of the Lord is raised up because of mortal humans, whom God finds unjust. If all this is true, then how do we understand: **And this is the judgment, that the light has come into the world, and men loved darkness rather than light, because their deeds were evil** (3:19)? What is this? Whose works are good? Have you not come so that you might justify your impious selves? But the text says, **They loved darkness rather than light**. This is where he placed the force of his words. Many loved their sins, and many confessed their sins. The one who confesses his sins and reproaches them now acts with God. God reproaches your sins; and if you reproach them, you will be united with God.

There are two things then, as it were: the person and the sinner. The one you call the person, God has made; the one you call a sinner, the person himself has made. Destroy the one you have made, so that God may save the one he has made. It's right to hate your own deeds in yourself and love God's works in you. However, when what you have made begins to displease you, that is your good works springing forth, because you have reproached your **evil deeds**. The confession of **evil deeds** is the foundation of good ones.

When you **do what is true**, you **come to the light**. What does it mean, to **do what is true**? You don't stroke your ego, you don't flatter yourself, you don't fawn over yourself. You don't say "I am righteous" when you are wicked. And in this way you begin to **do what is true**. You **come to the light** so that it may be clearly seen that your **deeds** have been done in God. This very sin of yours which displeases you would not have done so unless God had manifested it to you and revealed the truth to you. But the one who has been warned and still loves his sin, hates the guiding **light** and flees it, so that the **evil deeds** which he loves are not exposed. The one who does the truth reproaches the **evil deeds** in himself. He does not forgive himself or pardon himself, in order that God will pardon him. But what he desires God to pardon, he himself admits it. He **comes to the light** and gives thanks for it, since it revealed what he hated in himself. This man says to God *hide thy face from my sins* (Ps 50:11 Vulgate). With what other expression does he speak, unless he should say again, *For I know my transgressions, and my sin is ever before me* (Ps 51:3)? Let that be before yourself what you would not want to be before God. But if you put your sin behind you, God will hurl it back in front of your eyes; and he will hurl it before you when there will be no more fruit of repentance.

John 3:22–36

²²**After this Jesus and his disciples went into the land of Judea; there he remained with them and baptized.** ²³**John also was baptizing at Aenon near Salim, because there was much water there; and people came and were baptized.** ²⁴**For John had not yet been put in prison.** ²⁵**Now a discussion arose between John's disciples and a Jew over purifying.** ²⁶**And they came to John, and said to him, "Rabbi, he who was with you beyond the Jordan, to whom you bore witness, here he is, baptizing, and all are going to him."** ²⁷**John answered, "No one can receive anything except what is given him from heaven.** ²⁸**You yourselves bear me witness, that I said, I am not the Christ, but I have been sent before him.** ²⁹**He who has the bride is the bridegroom; the friend of the bridegroom, who stands and hears him, rejoices greatly at the bridegroom's voice; therefore this joy of mine is now full.** ³⁰**He must increase, but I must decrease."** ³¹**He who comes from above is above all; he who is of the earth belongs to the earth, and of the earth he speaks; he who comes from heaven is above all.** ³²**He bears witness to what he has seen and heard, yet no one receives his testimony;** ³³**he who receives his testimony sets his seal to this, that God is true.** ³⁴**For he whom God has sent utters the words of God, for it is not by measure that he gives the Spirit;** ³⁵**the Father loves the Son, and has given all things into his hand.** ³⁶**He who believes in the Son has eternal life; he who does not obey the Son shall not see life, but the wrath of God rests upon him.**

3:23–24 John also was baptizing at Aenon . . . for John had not yet been put in prison.

---

(22) John Scotus Eriugena

How, one might ask, did John's baptism benefit those who were baptized by him? In no way should it be believed to secure forgiveness of original sin or, for that matter, even the sins any particular person committed. What, then, did it secure? A great benefit, to be sure. Inasmuch as instruction in the faith is useful to catechumens not yet baptized, so John's baptism benefited those baptized in it before they underwent Christ's baptism. John preached repentance, announced in advance Christ's baptism, and drew those he baptized into an awareness of the truth that was coming into the world. Do not the church's ministers do the same thing every day? First he instructs those coming to faith, then he convinces them of their sin, then he promises them forgiveness of all sins in baptism, and thus he draws them into an awareness and enjoyment of the truth.

In order to put a finishing touch of praise on the benefit of John's baptism, the evangelist mentions when John was **baptizing**. Indeed, the forerunner had to fulfill his duty of being a forerunner in all things, so that, just as he preceded Christ in his birth and in his preaching, so he also preceded him in a similar baptism. Just as the dawn precedes the sunrise, so John's sacraments preceded Christ's works, and, just as, to a certain extent, the dawn dissipates darkness, so the teaching and the mystery of the forerunner began to dissipate the whole world's shadows of ignorance. Thus, so that Christ's baptism should not appear suddenly in the world, a figure of baptism preceded it, so that the truth might illuminate more profoundly and more brightly, since the figure of the truth had already satisfied those sitting in darkness.

One might also ask why Christ was baptized by his servant. To this the following can be said: Christ deigned to be baptized by a servant to honor the function of his forerunner and to demonstrate its authenticity to the Jews and to the whole world. But if this was the only reason why the master was baptized by his servant, why was not Christ alone baptized by John? Because the master had so much humility as to praise and testify to his servant's baptism. In addition, if Christ alone had been baptized by John, it would seem as if John's baptism conferred greater benefits than Christ's. Thus one might suppose that the unique baptism, by which the master was baptized, was much better than the baptism by which many were baptized by the master himself and his disciples. But so that we might not think this, many were baptized by John.

If one should ask if there was any benefit to the master himself being baptized by his forerunner, some answer, not incongruously, that Christ sanctified, to some extent, John's baptism. But that baptism brought no benefit to Christ. Nonetheless, we know that Greek authors[6] resolutely assert that the sanctification of Christ's humanity came about by means of John's baptism. They argue this, principally, from the descent of the Holy Spirit in the form of a dove on him when he was baptized. This is not extraordinary, because the

---

6. It is uncertain whom Eriugena means.

evangelist says: *And Jesus increased in wisdom and in stature, and in favor with God and man* (Luke 2:52). Why should it be extraordinary if Christ, by means of his forerunner's sacrament of baptism, received some increment to his humanity, by virtue, for example, of his humility, on account of which he did not disdain his servant's baptism? He received grace so that, by virtue of his baptism, all who believe in him might receive forgiveness of every sin, both original and personal.

3:26–27 "No one can receive anything except what is given."

---

(23) John Chrysostom

No one can receive anything except what is given him from heaven (3:27). Don't be startled if John the Baptist speaks here of Christ in a more humble manner, for it wasn't possible all at once to teach those who from the beginning had been preoccupied by such passions. He wants to astound and frighten them for a while and to show that they're fighting against none other than God when they fight against Christ. As Gamaliel also said: *You will not be able to overthrow* him. *You might even be found opposing God* (Acts 5:39). Here also Christ secretly establishes this same idea by saying, **No one can receive anything except what is given him from heaven** (3:27). He means nothing else except that they were attempting impossibilities and are again found to be opposing God. . . .

He gently encourages them, showing them that it is God, not a man, who surpasses them, and that one shouldn't marvel if the things which he did were glorious and as a result **all are going to him** (3:26). Such are the divine realities, and God is the one who establishes them because no human was able to do such things. So while all human endeavors are easy to detect, unsound, and collapse quickly and are destroyed, the endeavors of God are not like that. They are not human in nature. Observe then how they said, **to whom you bore witness** (3:26). That which they thought they had presented for Christ's destruction, he turned against them. Even earlier, having shown that his glory did not come to him from his own testimony, he silences them here with these words, saying, **No one can receive anything except what is given him from heaven** (3:27).

3:29 "He who has the bride is the bridegroom."

---

(24) Ammonius of Alexandria

Christ is the **bridegroom**, the church is the **bride**, and the place of baptism is the bride-chamber. Here lies that spiritual union, since all things are bright and filled with joy and gladness there. For what is more blessed than to be purified from sins, to be united to God, and to *become partakers of the divine nature* (2 Pet 1:4) through possession of the Holy Spirit? These things are the *guarantee* of more perfect things to come (cf. 2 Cor 5:5; Eph

1:14). When the **bridegroom** returns and brings the pure souls in with him, the door of the bride-chamber is shut. Only those who are inside experience his joy, and no one will enter there any longer.

> 3:30 "He must increase but I must decrease."

---

(25) Augustine of Hippo

He must increase but I must decrease (3:30). What is this? He must be exalted, but I must be humbled. How does Jesus **increase**? How does God **increase**? What is perfect does not **increase**. In fact, God neither **increases** nor **decreases**. If he **increases**, he is not perfect; if he **decreases**, he is not God. But Jesus is God; how does he **increase**? Perhaps in age, since he deigned to become a man, and was a boy? While he is the Word of God, as an infant he lay in a manger, and while he himself created his own mother, he sucked the milk of infancy from his mother. Therefore, since Jesus **increased** in fleshly age, perhaps for that reason it was said **He must increase, but I must decrease**. But how could this be? John and Jesus, in terms of the flesh, were the same age; they had six months between them, and they **increased** equally. If our Lord Jesus Christ wanted to be here for a longer time before his death, and wanted John to be here with him, they would have increased equally, just like they were able to age equally. So why say, **He must increase but I must decrease?** . . .

This is a great mystery! Understand, my dear people, before the Lord Jesus came, people gloried in themselves. Jesus came so that the glory of humanity might **decrease** and the glory of God might **increase**. He came without sin and found all humanity to be with sin. If he came to forgive sins, let God do it abundantly and let humanity confess it. The lowliness of humanity is its confession, and the exaltation of God is his compassion. Therefore, if Jesus came to forgive sins, let us acknowledge our own lowliness and let God carry out his own compassion. **He must increase but I must decrease**; that is, "He must give, but I must receive." "He must be glorified, but I must confess." Let us confess our own position and confess God. Let us hear the apostle speaking to a proud and elated man who wishes to exalt himself: *What have you that you did not receive? If then you received it, why do you boast as if it were not a gift?* (1 Cor 4:7). Therefore, let us understand that since we have *received*—we who wished to call our own what was not ours—let us **decrease**. It is a good thing for us that God be glorified in us. We are **decreased** in ourselves so that we may be **increased** in God. . . .

The apostle says this, the holy Scripture says this: *Let him who boasts, boast of the Lord* (1 Cor 1:31). Do you wish to boast of yourself? You wish to **increase**, but you **increase** wickedly in your own wickedness. Whoever **increases** wickedly is rightly **decreased**. Therefore let God **increase**, who is always perfect; let him **increase** in you. The more you understand God and comprehend him, the more God **increases** in you (even though he does not **increase** himself, being always perfect). Yesterday you understood a little bit; today you understand more; tomorrow you will understand even more. The very light of God grows in you, and so God, who always remains perfect, **increases**. It's like when one's eyes are cured from former blindness, and he begins to see a little light; the next day he sees more and the third day even more light seems to **increase** in him. The light, of course, is perfect, whether one sees it or not. Even so is the inner man. Indeed, he advances in God and God seems to **increase** in him; yet he **decreases** that he may fall from his own glory and rise into the glory of God.

(26) John Scotus Eriugena

He must increase, but I must decrease (3:30). Jesus, who until now you consider only a man and of no power, must **increase** in your minds. He must **increase**, so that you may not only know that he is true man, but also true God and equal to the Father. Thus he must **increase** in your minds, but I, John the Baptist, must **decrease**. You suppose that I am greater than I am, and that he is actually less than he is. Your opinion about me must **decrease** in you, but your opinion about him must **increase** in you. If you knew how, you could arrive at this conclusion from visible signs. I shall be beheaded (cf. Mark 6:27–28); he will be raised on the cross. By this you know that he must always **increase** in the minds of those who believe perfectly in him, but I must **decrease**, so that no one may consider me greater than I am and than what I have received from him. The same thing is signified by his being born when the light begins to **increase** and the darkness to **decrease**, while, by contrast, I was born when the light actually begins to **decrease** and the darkness to **increase**.

This can also be understood another way: John symbolizes the law, but Christ symbolizes himself, that is, the truth. When the truth appeared in the world, the law, that is, the works of the flesh, began to **decrease**. Knowing this, the forerunner, a prophet and more than a prophet (cf. Matt 11:9; Luke 7:26) said, "**He must increase, but I must decrease.** He who is the truth, **increases** in the world, he becomes most gloriously known to those who do believe and will come to believe in him. But the law, which I symbolize, **decreases** as the truth **increases**." . . .

3:31 He who comes from above is above all.

---

(27) Cyril of Alexandria

He who comes from above is above all . . . (3:31). It is no great thing, he says, or exceedingly admirable if Christ surpasses the glory of humanity. He does not set the limits of his own glory at this point but, as God, he is over **all** creation and **above all** created things (3:31). He is not like one numbered among **all** things but as one excluded from **all** created things, divinely set over **all** things. He adds the reason, shaming the one who resists and silencing the one who opposes: he says **he who comes from above** (3:31), that is, the one who has been begotten of the source from above, preserving in himself by nature the fatherly goodness, will admittedly obtain an existence **above all things** (3:31). It was impossible for the Son not to be seen entirely in this way, just as we understand the worth of the one who begot him. How could the Son, excelling in such a nature, who is the *reflection and stamp* of the Father (Heb 1:3), be less than the Father in glory? Would not that which belongs to the Father be dishonored in the Son, and would we not insult the image of the begotten one, by considering him inferior? I suppose this will be obvious to everyone. Indeed, for this reason it is written *that all may honor the Son even as they honor the Father. He who does not honor the Son does not honor the Father* (5:23). The one who exalts him with an honor equal to God the Father because he comes from him by nature—how would he not hereafter be understood as surpassing the nature of created things? This is the meaning of the phrase **he is above all things** (3:31).

I perceive again that the mind of those who fight against Christ is in no way content. Rather it will likely come babbling ceaselessly and saying, "When the blessed Baptist says that the Lord is originated **from above** what argument will convince us that **from above** means 'from the essence of the Father,' and not rather 'from heaven,' or even 'from his inherent superiority over all things,' so that he is considered to be **above all things**?" Therefore, when they attack us with these objections, they will hear in return, "We will not follow your most unsound arguments, O most excellent ones, but rather the divine Scripture and the holy writings alone."

We must find in the Scriptures how the expression **from above** is used. Let them hear one of those clothed in the Spirit crying out, *Every good endowment and every perfect gift is from above, coming down from the Father of lights* (Jas 1:17). See! He explicitly says that **from above** means *from the Father*. Knowing that nothing is superior to created things except the inexpressible nature of God, he rightly describes it with the expression **from above**. . . .

If you suppose that **from above** ought to mean "from heaven," let the word be applied to every angel and rational power. Those who inhabit the city **above** come to us "from heaven" and they *ascend and descend on the Son of man*, as the Savior says somewhere (1:51). What then persuaded the blessed Baptist to ascribe particularly to the Son alone that authority which belongs to many, and to use the expression **he who comes from above** (3:31) for one who simply *descends* from above? Indeed we would then need to make such dignity common with the others, saying "Those who come from above are above all." But the Baptist knew that the expression belonged to the one Son, as one begotten from the highest source.

Therefore, **from above** does not mean "from heaven," but rather is understood piously and truly in the way we have already said above. How will he be in any way **above all** if **from above** does not mean "from the Father" but rather "from heaven"? If this were true, each of the holy angels would be **above all**, having come from there. . . .

Perhaps, however, our opponents[7] will be ashamed of their absurd investigation and will say that **from above** means not "from heaven" but "from his inherent superiority over all things." Come then, examine more precisely the force of their words, and let us see where their argument will lead. First then, it is both foolish and altogether incomprehensible to say that the Son himself comes from his own dignity, or to say that he comes from some place or from someone, and that this same one, proceeding from his own superiority, is **from above**. In addition, I would also ask them with great gladness whether they will grant

---

7. Most likely Arians.

to the Son the "superiority over all" as essential and permanent to himself, or as assumed from outside himself, as an acquired property? They say that his superiority is acquired in nature and that he is honored with dignities from outside himself. If that is true, then it is necessary to confess that the only-begotten can exist devoid of glory, stripped of the "acquired" grace (as they call it), deprived of being **above all**, and appear emptied of the superiority at which they now marvel, since something acquired may be lost when it is not connected to the essence of the subject. In fact, this will mean that there will be some change and alteration in the Son, and the psalmist himself will lie, vainly singing: *The heavens will perish, but thou dost endure; they will all wear out like a garment, and thou changest them like a raiment and they pass away. But thou art the same and thy years have no end* (Ps 102:26–27). How is he the same if he changes with us, even with changes for the worse? It would seem that he vainly glories in himself when he says, *Behold, behold, I am and I do not change* (Mal 3:6) and *besides me there is no God* (Isa 45:5). Would not the passions of the begotten one rise up to the Father himself, since he is his *stamp* and *exact image* (Heb 1:3; Col 1:15)? Therefore, God the Father will be changeable as well, and his superiority over all is something added to him. I will leave the rest aside, for quite obviously the nature of the image holds also for the archetype. But they will not say that his superiority is added to his nature (shuddering at such difficulties and absurdities their argument produces); rather, they will say his superiority is essential and permanent.

Then again, O most excellent ones, how will you not agree with us (even unwillingly) that the Son, being by nature God, is **from above** and for this reason comes from the unique essence of God the Father? . . . He who is set apart in his essence from the things made, and by nature escapes being classified as part of creation—what else could he be except God? . . . If then the Son is God by nature, and is ineffably begotten from God the Father, then **from above** signifies the nature of the begotten-one.

(28) John Scotus Eriugena

He who comes from heaven is above all (3:31). In this saying he repeats what he has said before: **He who comes from above is above all** (3:31). They are the same words except that, instead of **comes from heaven** he says **comes from above**. Why did he repeat himself, and what does it mean? Does **comes from heaven** perhaps mean one thing and **comes from above** mean something else? Christ came **from heaven** and Christ came **from above**. That is why he is **above all** people and **above all** things. Well then, one can understand this difference between **comes from above** and **comes from heaven**. When he said **comes from above**, we understand the loftiness of human nature before the first man's trespass, from which lofty height we cannot doubt but that the man Christ came. If he had come from man after that sin, perhaps he would not have been without sin himself. But since he was actually without sin, we must surely believe that he took on a man without sin. Our Lord Jesus Christ, Maker and Savior of human nature, took something from the first man before and took as well from the second man after sin. What did he receive from the man before sin? Existence without sin, because human nature was completely without sin before it sinned. What did he receive from the man after sin? To die for sin without having any guilt for sin.

Therefore the first phrase, **He who comes from above**, can surely be understood: "Who comes from the loftiness of human nature, made in the image of God, as it was before it sinned." No one came from there, except him alone. Whoever comes into the world, comes from a sinful human; only he who was without sin proceeds from man before sin. As for the second phrase, **He who comes from heaven is above all**, we understand that in the word **heaven** is signified the Father from whom Christ was sent into the world, as he himself said: **I came from the Father and have come into the world** (16:28). So we must believe that the only-begotten Son of God is exalted **above** all things in two ways: first, because he who came from **above**, before humanity sinned, is exalted **above** all humanity; second, because in virtue of the loftiness of divinity, in which he is equal to the Father, he is **above** every created being.

He bears witness to what he has seen and heard (3:32). What is it that the Son of God **has seen**? Nothing but to know that he is in the Father and that he is his equal. **And heard**. What has he **heard**? He **heard** the Father say, *Today I have begotten you* (Ps 2:7). He **has seen** himself, as regards his divinity, in the Father and he has **heard** from his Father that he begot him as his equal. **He bears witness to**. To what does he **bear witness**? That he is the Son of God. Where does he **bear witness**? Look above, where he says about himself: **For God sent the Son into the world, not to condemn the world, but that the world might be saved through him. He who believes in him is not condemned; he who does not believe is condemned already, because he has not believed in the name of the only Son of God** (3:17–18). This then is what the Son of God saw and what he **bore witness** about himself.

3:34 For he whom God has sent utters the words of God.

---

(29) John Scotus Eriugena

For he whom God has sent utters the words of God (3:34). This he says only of God's Son who, being **sent** from the Father, speaks **the words of God**. But the prophets too, were they not **sent** by him? And the apostles too, were they not **sent** by him and did they not speak his **words**? Why is it said only of Christ: **He whom God has sent utters the words of God**? In effect, he seems to say: "**He whom God sent utters the words of God** who sent him." This is what the prophets did, and the apostles as well. Therefore what greater thing was given to Christ, that was not given to the others? Pay attention to the words: **He whom God**, that is, the Father, **has sent utters the words of God**. In this case he who was **sent** is God; therefore, he utters **the words of God**. This means: he whom **God sent** is indisputably God, and, as a result, his **words** are **the words of God**. Therefore the Son's words are **the words of God** because they bear witness to himself, that he is God. The words of the prophets and apostles are **the words of God**, because they spoke **the words of God**—the Holy Spirit spoke in them—nonetheless those words did not belong to them as their own **words**, but were actually **the words of God**. Christ's **words** belong to him, and are called **the words of God** with good cause, because he is God by nature, completely God and completely wisdom, and the fullness of God's gifts is in him (cf. Isa 11:2–3).

3:36 He who believes in the Son has eternal life.

---

(30) John Chrysostom

Knowing how effective punishment is (for many people are led not by the promise of good things as much as by the threat of terrible consequences), Christ finally concludes his discourse here and says: **he who believes in the Son has eternal life; he who does not obey the Son shall not see life, but the wrath of God rests upon him** (3:36). . . . "Is it enough then," someone will say, "to believe in the Son to have eternal life?" Certainly not! Listen even to Christ indicating this when he says, *Not everyone who says to me "Lord, Lord" shall enter the kingdom of heaven* (Matt 7:21). The blasphemy against the Holy Spirit alone is enough to cast someone into hell (cf. Matt 12:31–32).

Why am I speaking about a matter of theology? Because even if someone rightly believes in the Father and the Son and the Holy Spirit, but does not lead a right life, his faith is of no use to him for salvation. Likewise when Christ says, *And this is eternal life, that they know thee the only true God* (17:3), don't let us think that this is sufficient for our salvation. We also need a most exact life and manner of conduct. Even when he spoke here—**He who *believes* in the Son has eternal life** (3:36)—and quite effectively established what follows, his argument proceeds not only from good things but also to their opposites, adding **he who does not *obey* the Son shall not see life, but the wrath of God rests upon him** (3:36). Nevertheless, we do not say that faith alone is sufficient for salvation. Even the numerous things spoken about one's life in the gospels demonstrate this. Indeed, for this reason, he doesn't say, "This alone is eternal life," nor "the one who *just* believes in the Son has eternal life." In each instance it's obvious that believing does contain life, but, in fact, if an exact manner of life does not follow, much punishment will result.

(31) Augustine of Hippo

Listen to what follows: **He who believes in the Son has eternal life; he who does not obey the Son shall not see life, but the wrath of God rests upon him** (3:36). He did not say: **the wrath of God *comes* to him**, but **the wrath of God *rests upon* him**. All who are born mortal have the **wrath of God upon** them. What **wrath of God**, you might ask? The **wrath** first received by Adam. The first man sinned and heard: *You shall die* (Gen 2:17). He was made mortal, and so we began to be born as mortals—born into the **wrath of God**. But then the Son, having no sin, came and clothed himself in human flesh; he donned the garment of mortality. If he shared with us in the **wrath of God**, are we slow to share with him in the grace of God? Therefore, whoever does not want to believe in God, **the wrath of God rests upon him**. What is the **wrath of God**? The apostle speaks of this: *so we were by nature children of wrath, like the rest of mankind* (Eph 2:3). Therefore, everyone is a child of **wrath**, because we come from the curse of death. Believe in Christ, who was made mortal on your behalf, so that you might receive his immortality. Once you receive his immortality, you will no longer be prone to death. He lived while you were dying; he died so that you might live. He brought the grace of God, and removed the **wrath of God**. God conquered death so that death shall not conquer humanity.

(32) John Scotus Eriugena

He who believes in the Son has eternal life (3:36). Why? Because the Son himself is **eternal life**, as he himself said: **I am the truth and the life** (14:6). For good reason therefore **he who believes in the Son has eternal life**. It is as if he had said, "He who believes in the Son, has the Son, and by doing so has eternal life, for the Son is eternal life. **He who does not believe in the Son, will not see eternal life.**[8] By the same token, **he who does not believe in the Son**, will not see the Son, who is life. **But the wrath of God rests upon him** (3:36). He did not say, **The wrath of God** will *come over* him, but he said: **The wrath of God *rests upon* him**. What is that **wrath of God**? Nothing else but that curse, by which God cursed the sin of the first man, when he broke his commandment, saying *The ground is cursed because of you* (Gen 3:17). The result of that sin is death, corruption, and a total ignorance of the truth, all of which remain over him. Of that wrath the apostle says: *Once you were children of wrath, like the rest of mankind* (Eph 2:3). **The wrath of God** can be understood as original sin, because that original sin provoked **the wrath of God** over human nature, and that original sin remains in those who do not wish to believe in him who died for them.

---

8. RSV: **He who does not *obey* the Son shall not see life.**

John 4

John 4 presents the Samaritan woman's remarkable and life-changing encounter with Jesus at the well. Before moving into commentary on specific passages, the current chapter begins with general selections summarizing that meeting. In the poetic excerpts of Romanos the Melodist and Ephrem the Syrian, the Samaritan woman is given an allegorical interpretation. Romanos sees in her a figure of "the espoused church of the nations" who, like the Samaritan woman, forsakes foreign husbands (gods) in preference for Christ. Ephrem, in his poetic description of the woman, likens her to Mary the mother of Jesus: both women willingly received the Savior and in turn presented him to the world for salvation.

Early Christian thinkers also understood the Samaritan woman as a model of genuine faith. John Chrysostom takes her as a paragon of earnestness in learning and progress in faith, admonishing his audience to imitate her piety. Augustine of Hippo, Romanos, and Ephrem see the Samaritan woman as a figure of the church. Exploring the woman's mimetic value as one who genuinely progresses from ignorance to understanding and faith, Augustine exhorts: "Let us recognize ourselves in her." Likewise, Maximus of Turin offers a moving portrait of the transformation of the Samaritan from sinner to purified preacher of Christ who now represents the church, purified from sins by the waters of baptism and proclaiming Christ as Savior to the world.

More specific commentary on this chapter begins with verse 6 and the description of Jesus as being wearied (4:6). Several thinkers wrestle with the question of how Christ, who is God, can be wearied, especially in light of texts like Isa 40:28, which explicitly assert that God does not grow weary or hungry. John Chrysostom, Augustine of Hippo, Cyril of Alexandria, and John Scotus Eriugena all agree that John 4:6 affirms the reality of the incarnation—that Christ's weariness speaks of his true humanity. Moving in a different interpretive direction, Ambrose of Milan suggests that Jesus's weariness points to Christ's weariness over our unbelief and delay in coming to him; and Chrysostom uses the disciples' lack of concern over hunger as a pastoral admonition to have the same attitude, rather than the typical excessive concern for mealtimes.

Ancient commentators unanimously agree that the gift of God (4:10) refers to the Holy Spirit, often using John 7 as a cross-reference in support. Christ's exhortation to the woman in verse 16 (Call your husband) leads commentators like Augustine and Scotus Eriugena to consider the figurative meaning of husband as a call to summon our "understanding" or "intellect" in order to perceive Christ's words in a spiritual, rather than physical, manner.

John 4:21–24 provides an occasion for a variety of discussions on proper worship. Origen *of Alexandria uses Jesus's words in 4:22* (salvation is from the Jews) *as evidence that the God of the Jews is also the God of the whole world; therefore, there is one God to be worshiped by all. John Chrysostom, Ambrose of Milan, and Cyril of Alexandria all discuss what the divine Jesus means when he uses the plural pronoun, saying* we worship *(4:22). These thinkers teach that such language affirms the full expression of Christ's humanity in the incarnation. Because Christ identifies with humanity, whose nature it is to worship, Christ the man worships, even while simultaneously (as the Word) he receives worship alongside the Father. Finally, much attention is paid to the meaning of verse 23* (the true worshipers will worship the Father in spirit and truth). *Origen and Didymus the Blind both see this as a call to worship "spiritually," rather than in types and shadows, now that the truth (Christ) has arrived. John Scotus Eriugena offers a similar interpretation, suggesting that these words call us to the worship of the truth (Christ) in a spiritual manner, that is, with spiritual understanding. Hilary of Poitiers, John Chrysostom, Theodore of Mopsuestia, and Scotus Eriugena all agree that God's invisible and incorporeal nature requires worship not in a specific location, but* in spirit and truth, *that is, with our own invisible nature in the soul and mind. Hilary, Gregory of Nazianzus, and Basil of Caesarea offer profound Trinitarian explanations, arguing that the Spirit is both the one through whom we worship and the one to whom our worship is offered.*

*According to Cyril of Alexandria, Christ's words about himself in 4:26—*I who speak to you am he—*are the climax of his intentionally gradual self-revelation to the woman. She understands him first as a man, then as a prophet, and finally as the Messiah. Cyril also finds in this text a model for how teachers in the church should instruct newcomers to the faith: gradually and carefully. More broadly, Origen and Cyril of Alexandria explore negative Jewish attitudes toward women and Samaritans. Jesus's discussion with a woman, and the disciples marveling over it (4:27), becomes a caution against our pride and disdain for those who seem beneath us. Cyril makes application to teachers in the church, urging them not to neglect their ministry to women in addition to men.*

The leaving of the water jar *(4:28) prompts Origen of Alexandria toward a two-layered interpretation. On the literal level, the woman's action demonstrates her great eagerness for proclaiming the newfound Christ. On a spiritual level, the jar represents her previous beliefs which she now leaves behind in favor of better things found in Christ. John Chrysostom compares the woman's response at the end of the narrative with the apostles' response to their own encounter with Jesus, noting how she exceeds their faith and eagerness in proclaiming Christ.*

Origen of Alexandria understands the food *Jesus speaks of in verse 34 as the salvation of humanity. Interestingly, Origen reads this verse not,* to accomplish *his work, but to* perfect his work, *prompting him to ask what imperfection in God's creation was in need of perfecting. Cyril of Alexandria again finds an application for teachers in the church. Just as Jesus disregarded food offered by his disciples, so too teachers in the church should be more interested in the salvation of others than for their own bodily concerns.*

In John 4:35–36 Origen of Alexandria understands the passage allegorically: the sowers *are Moses and the prophets, and the* reapers *are the apostles who* harvest *the crops by bringing them to full faith in Christ. While Chrysostom's approach is not quite so allegorical, he does offer a discussion of the power and force of the metaphorical language used by Jesus. Cyril of Alexandria picks up on this idea as well and draws out the meaning of the* harvest *metaphor in light of the gathering of believers into the threshing-floor of the church.*

Finally, the healing of the official's son in 4:43–54 garners significant discussion about the state of the official's faith. John Chrysostom observes that while the text says the official believed Jesus (4:50), full belief came only after he received word that his son was healed. This becomes an admonition to believe Christ "not because of his miracles, but because of his teaching." Augustine makes a similar point. John Cassian and Cyril of Alexandria see this narrative as an example of God's abundant grace given even to those who falter in their faith. Both John Chrysostom and Cyril of Alexandria note two healings rather than one—both the ill son who is healed of his disease and the official, whose weak faith is made strong. Gregory the Great wonders why the official, who seemingly came to Jesus in faith, heard the words: Unless you see signs and wonders, you will not believe *(4:48). Gregory sees the weakness of the official's faith in his notion that Christ had to be physically present in order to heal. Jesus's healing by command alone is a corrective to the official's incomplete faith.*

(1) Romanos the Melodist

Prooimion: When the Lord came to the **well,**
> The **woman of Samaria** (4:7) asked the All-merciful One:
> "**Give me** the **water** of faith,
>> And I shall receive the flowing streams of the font:
>>> Exceedingly great joy and redemption."

Strophe 4: What then does the Bible teach? Christ, it says, the source
> Of the breath of life for all, when he was
> **Weary from a journey, sat down** (4:6) near a spring of Samaria.
And it was the season of burning heat. It was **the sixth hour** (4:6),[1] as the Scripture says,
> It was the middle of the day when the Messiah came to illumine those in darkness.
> The Spring came upon the spring, not to drink but to cleanse.
The fountain of immortality was near the stream of the wretched woman as though it were in need.
> He is tired from walking, he who tirelessly walked on the sea,
> He who furnished
>> Exceedingly great joy and redemption.

Strophe 7: Lo, it seems to me that she is the painter of two images, the
> **Woman of Samaria** (4:7) from Sychar: an image of the church and of Mary.
Again, let the woman speak to the Creator: "**How is it that you ask me?** (4:9)
>> If I give you to drink, and you drink, you will transgress the Jewish law,
>> And I shall from the water receive you as espoused husband."

1. 12:00 noon.

How beautiful are the words of the **woman of Samaria**, they roughly sketch for me
> The baptismal font at the spring from which he took her as servant,
He who furnishes
> Exceedingly great joy and redemption.

Strophe 12: O wise enigmas! O wise characteristics!
> In the faith of the holy woman is pictured
> All the features of the church in true colors which do not grow old;
For the way in which the woman denied a **husband** when she had many,
> Is just the way the church denied many gods, like husbands,
> And left them and became betrothed to one Master in coming for the water.
She had **five husbands** and the sixth she did not have; and leaving the **five**
> Husbands of impiety, she now takes thee, as the sixth, as she comes
> From the water,
> > Exceedingly great joy and redemption.

Strophe 14: The espoused church of the nations, then, left these things,
> And she hurries here to the well of the baptismal font
> And denies the things of the past, just as the woman of Samaria did;
For she did not conceal what had formerly been true from him who knows all in advance,
> But she said, "I do not have." She did not say, "I have not had," meaning, I think, this:
> "Even if I formerly had husbands, I do not now wish to have
These husbands which I did have; for I now possess thee who hast now taken me in thy net;
> And I am by faith rescued from the filth of my sins
> That I may receive
> > Exceedingly great joy and redemption."

Strophe 22: Crowds of Samaritans came to the Creator,
> Leaving their houses; and they were shown in their faith to be
> Like the homes of the one who speaks in the inspired Scriptures:
They say: "As is written, I shall swell in and tarry among
> The homes of those who abandon all: fields, parents, and all that is held dear,
> And I shall be their God and Savior from snares;
And they will be my people, sanctified, and making their dwelling
> In the Trinity, eternal, indivisible, which bounteously
> Pours forth
> > Exceedingly great joy and redemption."

(2) Ephrem the Syrian

Blessed are you, drawer of ordinary water,
who turned out to be a drawer of **living water**.
You found the treasure, another source,
from whom a flood of mercies flows.
The spring had dried up, but it broke through to you and gave you a drink.
He was poor, but he asked in order to enrich you.
You left behind your pitcher, but were filled with understanding
and gave your people to drink.
Blessed are you to whom he gave **living water** to drink,
and you did not **thirst** again, as you said.
For he called the truth **living water**,
since all who hear it will not **thirst** again.
Blessed are you who learned the truth and did not **thirst**;
for one is the Messiah and there are no more.

(3) Ephrem the Syrian

Blessed are you, O woman, for not suppressing
your judgment about what you discovered.
The glorious treasury was himself present
for your need because of his love.
Your love was zealous to share your treasure with your city.
Blessed woman, your discovery became
the Discoverer of the lost.
    Refrain: Glory to the Discoverer of all! . . .
O, to you, woman in whom I see
a wonder as great as in Mary!
For she from within her womb
in Bethlehem brought forth his body as a child,
but you by your mouth made him manifest
as an adult in Shechem, the town of His father's household.
Blessed are you, O woman, who brought forth by your mouth
light for those in darkness.
Mary, the thirsty land of Nazareth,
conceived our Lord by her ear.
You too, O woman thirsting for water,
conceived the Son by your hearing.
Blessed are your ears that drank the source
that gave drink to the world.
Mary planted him in the manger,
but you planted him in the ears of his hearers.

Your word, O woman, became a mirror
in which he might see your hidden heart.
The Messiah, you said, **will come,**
And when he comes, he will give us everything (4:25).
Behold the Messiah for whom you waited, modest woman! . . .
Your voice, O woman, first brought forth fruit,
before even the apostles, with the *kerygma*.[2]
The apostles were forbidden to announce him
among the pagans and the Samaritans (cf. Matt 10:5).
Blessed is your mouth that he opened and confirmed.
The storehouse of life took and gave you to sow.
Into a city that was dead as Sheol
you entered and revived your dead.
Blessed are you, O woman!

(4) John Chrysostom

Christ spoke one thing to her, but she understood something else, hearing nothing more than the words. At the time she was unable to understand any lofty idea. Yet, if she had spoken hastily, she would have said, "If you had living water, you would not have asked me, but would have provided for yourself first. But now you are boasting." She says nothing of the sort, but responds with great reasonableness, both now and later. In the beginning she says, **How is it that you, a Jew, ask a drink of me?** (4:9). She doesn't speak as if she's conversing with a stranger or enemy, saying, "Far be it from me to give something to a hostile man who is an enemy of our nation." Afterward, again, when she heard him speaking great words (a thing which enemies are most annoyed at) she neither laughs at him nor ridicules him. What does she say? **Are you greater than our father Jacob, who gave us the well, and drank from it himself, and his sons and his cattle?** (4:12). Do you see how she thrusts herself into the Jewish nobility, saying something like this: "Jacob used this water, and had nothing more to give us"? In saying these things, she shows that from Christ's first response she was thinking great and lofty things. Her words, **He drank from it himself, and his sons and his cattle** (4:12), show nothing less than her understanding that there was better water, but that she hadn't found it or fully understood it. In other words, to put it more clearly, what she means to say is this: "You cannot say that Jacob gave us this well but used another one himself, for he and his sons drank from it, which they would not have done if they had another one better than this. So Jacob isn't able to give a drink from this well, and you're not able to have a well better than this unless you confess that you're greater than Jacob. Where then will you get this water which you have promised to give us?" . . .

If the Samaritan woman shows such zeal to learn something profitable, and remains with Christ without even knowing him, what pardon will we receive who know him and are neither by the well, nor in the desert, nor in the middle of the day, nor under the burning

2. I.e., preaching.

heat, but are under this roof enjoying shade and coolness at dawn? Yet we don't care to hear what's being said, but grow weary. The woman wasn't like this; she was so inspired by what was said that she even called others. . . . Let us then imitate the Samaritan woman. Let us converse with Christ. For even now he stands in our midst, speaking to us through the prophets and the disciples. Let us hear and obey.

(5) John Chrysostom

The woman believed immediately, showing that she was much wiser than Nicodemus (John 3). Not only was she wiser, but more courageous; for Nicodemus heard a myriad of similar teachings and neither summoned anyone else to it nor spoke openly about it. The woman acted like the apostles, preaching to all, calling them to Jesus, and drawing out an entire city to him. When Nicodemus heard Christ, he said, *How can this be?* (3:9); and when Christ provided the clear proof of the wind, Nicodemus did not accept his word. Not so the woman. Indeed, at first she doubted, but later, receiving the word as a declaration, without evidence, she immediately hastened to receive it. When Christ said, **It will become in him a spring of water welling up to eternal life** (4:14), she immediately says, **Give me this water, that I may not thirst, nor come here to draw** (4:15). . . .

When she gained a clearer insight, but without complete understanding (for she said, **Give me this water, that I may not thirst, nor come here to draw**), at first she prefers him to Jacob: "For I do not need this spring if I receive that water from you." Do you see how she gives Christ preference to the patriarch? This comes from a wise soul. She had shown her high regard for Jacob, but she sees one better than he and was not held back by her previous assumption. . . .

For this reason, having fixed her mind by promises, Christ still employs sensory words because she could not yet grasp the exact meaning of spiritual realities. If he had said, "If you believe in me, you will never thirst" she would not have understood him, not knowing who it was who conversed with her or what kind of thirst he was talking about. Why then does he not do this with the Jews as well? They had seen many signs; the woman saw none but heard the words first. This is why he later reveals his power through prophecy and does not immediately present his reproof. What does he say? **Go, call your husband and come here.** And she says, **I have no husband.** Then Jesus says to her, **You are right in saying, "I have no husband," for you have had five husbands, and he whom you now have is not your husband; this you said truly.** And the woman says to him, **Sir, I perceive that you are a prophet** (4:16-19). O how great the spiritual insight of the woman! How humbly she receives his reproof! . . .

"And what should we understand," someone says, "from the saying **Go call your husband**?" (4:16). His words were about the gift and grace which surpasses human nature. The woman urgently sought to receive it, and Christ said, **Call your husband**, as if indicating that he too must share in these things. But she is eager to receive it, and so conceals the shamefulness of her situation, thinking that she converses with a man, and says, **I have no husband.** Upon hearing this, Christ finally and appropriately presents his reproof, speaking with accuracy on both counts. He numbered all those former husbands, and then reproved her for the one she was concealing.

What then did the woman say? She was not annoyed, neither did she leave him and flee, nor think it was an insult. Instead, she marvels at him and persists all the more, saying, **I perceive that you are a prophet** (4:19). Behold her understanding! She did not immediately run away but continues to consider him and marvel at him. **I perceive** means "It seems to me that you are a prophet." Then, when she suspected that he was a prophet, she doesn't ask about his life, or about bodily health, or possessions or riches, but immediately asks about doctrines. What did she say? **Our fathers worshiped on this mountain** (she spoke about the time of Abraham, for they say that this was where his son was taken up [cf. Gen 22:1–2]), and **how do you say that in Jerusalem is the place where men ought to worship?** (4:20). Do you see how much more exalted in understanding she had become? The one who at first was anxious about no longer being bothered with thirst now asks about doctrines.

What, then, did Christ do? He didn't answer the question—he didn't seek simply to give an answer to what was said, for this was beside the point. Instead, he leads the woman again to greater heights. He doesn't converse with her about spiritual matters at first, until she confesses that he is a prophet, so that she might now listen with great conviction to what he says. Being persuaded of this, she would no longer have any doubts about what would be said to her.

Let us then be ashamed and blush! A woman who had five husbands, and is a Samaritan, had such zeal for doctrines that neither the time of day, nor her coming for another purpose, nor anything else diverted her from seeking such things. But as for us, not only do we not seek after doctrines, but we are disposed toward all things with simplicity and carelessness. For this reason everything is neglected. Which of you could tell me that while at home you took a Christian book into your hands and approached the contents and searched the Scripture? No one can tell me they do this! In most houses, we find games and dice but nowhere books, except among a few. Even these have the same attitude as those who don't have books; they bind them up and always put them away in chests, caring only about the delicacy of their things, and the beauty of the letters, not for reading them. . . . But the Scriptures were not given to us so that we could just have them in books, but that we might engrave them upon our hearts.

(6) Augustine of Hippo

And there came a woman (4:7): a figure of the church, not already justified, but about to be justified, for this drives their conversation. The woman arrives ignorant, she approaches him, and he spends time with her. Let's consider both what happens and why: **There came a woman of Samaria to draw water** (4:7). The Samaritans did not belong to the people of Judea; for, although they lived in neighboring lands, they were foreigners. . . .

In the imagery of the matter, it's significant that the woman, who was a figure of the church, comes from foreigners. The church was about to come from the gentiles, foreign to the stock of the Jews. Therefore, let us hear ourselves in that woman, let us recognize ourselves in her, and in that woman let us give thanks to God for ourselves. She was a figure, not the truth; she was set forth as a figure and became the truth. She believed in him who presented that woman as a figure for us. **She came**, therefore, **to draw water** (4:7). She had simply come **to draw water**, as both men and women are accustomed to do.

Jesus said to her, "Give me a drink." For his disciples had gone away into the city to buy food. The Samaritan woman said to him, "How is it that you, a Jew, ask a drink of me, a woman of Samaria?" For Jews have no dealings with Samaritans (4:7–9). . . . And now, hear who asks for a drink: **Jesus answered her, "If you knew the gift of God, and who it is that is saying to you, 'Give me a drink,' you would have asked him, and he would have given you living water"** (4:10). He asks to **drink**, and promises **drink** in return. He desires as one about to receive, and he flows forth as a person about to satisfy. **If you knew the gift of God**, he says. The **gift of God** is the Holy Spirit. But so far he speaks to the woman carefully, and little by little enters into her heart. Perhaps he already teaches. What is more pleasant or kinder than this exhortation?: **If you knew the gift of God, and who it is that is saying to you, "Give me a drink," you would have asked him, and he would have given you living water** (4:10). So far he builds suspense. **Living water** is the name commonly given to that which departs from a spring. . . .

Yet the woman, now in a state of suspense, says: **Sir, you have nothing to draw with, and the well is deep** (4:11). See how she understood the words **living water** as the water which was in that well: "You wish to give **living water** to me, but I carry a vessel for drawing water, and you do not. **Living water** is here, how are you going to give it to me?" Comprehending in a physical manner, that woman understands something else, and thus in a certain way knocks so that the teacher may open what is closed. She was knocking in ignorance, not in eagerness; she was still worthy of compassion and not yet of instruction.

The Lord says something even clearer about the **living water**. The woman had said: "**Are you greater than our father Jacob, who gave us the well, and drank from it himself, and his sons, and his cattle?** (4:12). You're not able to give me this **living water** because you have nothing with which to draw it up; perhaps you are promising us another spring? Can you be better than our father who dug this well, and who used it himself along with his family?" Therefore, the Lord explained what he meant by **living water: Jesus said to her, "Every one who drinks of this water will thirst again, but whoever drinks of the water that I shall give him will never thirst; the water that I shall give him will become in him a spring of water welling up to eternal life"** (4:13). Then more openly the Lord said: **The water that I shall give him will become in him a spring of water welling up to eternal life. Whoever drinks of this water will never thirst** (4:14). How could it be any clearer, that he was promising not visible but invisible water? It could not be clearer, since he spoke not about the flesh but about the spirit. Nevertheless that woman still understands in a physical way; she was delighted not to thirst, and believes that it was physical water the Lord had promised her.

(7) Maximus of Turin

Christ himself is the fount of mercy who, in the gospel we have just heard, asks for water from the Samaritan woman, but then forgives her sins. He rejects the water from the well but bestows an everlasting fountain of life. The text says, **Everyone who drinks of this water will thirst again, but whoever drinks of the water that I shall give him will never thirst** (4:13–14). Therefore the Savior asks the woman for water and pretends to be thirsty so that he might grant eternal grace to those who thirst. The fount was not able to be thirsty, nor was he, in whom there is **living water**, able to draw up water containing earthly dregs. Was Christ then thirsty? Clearly, he was thirsty, not for human drink, but for salvation; he was thirsty not for the water of the earth, but for the redemption of the human race. Therefore, in a remarkable way, the fount, sitting beside the well, produces streams of mercy at that very spot. With **living**, moving **water**, he purifies the woman who is fornicating with a sixth man, not her husband, but an adulterer. By some new kind of marvel the woman, who had come to the well as a Samaritan prostitute, returns from Christ the fount chaste! The one who had come desiring water carried back purity. When the Lord exposes her sins, she immediately recognizes them, confesses Christ, and proclaims him Savior. Abandoning her vessel of water, she brings back to the city not a water jar, but grace. Indeed, she seems to return with an empty load, but she returns with full holiness—full, I say, because she who had come as a sinner returns as a preacher, and she who parted with her vessel of water brought back the fullness of Christ, bearing no detriment to her city. Even if she had not brought back water to her fellow citizens, she nevertheless carried the fount of salvation. Therefore, having been sanctified through faith in Christ, the woman returned home.

Thus, I think that the prophet spoke about this, saying: *This is the way of an adulteress when she has washed herself, she says that she has done nothing wrong* (Prov 30:20 Vulgate). Clearly this is said about her who, after she washed herself at the fount of the Savior, did not remember the fault of her sins, but cleansing her stains with **living water**, she achieves virtue as a preacher and, compelled by the zeal of faith, is drawn toward evangelizing rather than dwelling on her sins. In a certain way, she says that she has *done nothing wrong* while she is a messenger of the truth. Through forgetfulness, she denies her sexual impurity while she proclaims chastity by her devotion. This is the power of Christ the Lord, that however much one is a sinner, whoever is washed in the **water** of Christ is restored afresh to virginity and will not remember what was done before. In this new birth, one displays the innocence of infancy but does not recognize the sins of youth, while the one who was an adulterer through the corruption of sin becomes a virgin through faith in Christ. . . .

Previously, we wanted to show that the **water** of Christ washed away the filth of the Samaritan woman better than the **water** of Samaria, and that his pure mercy cleansed sin better than the well. Clearly, his pure mercy cleanses stains better than the well because **water** from a well washes only the outside of the body while the benevolence of mercy purifies the inner soul. We also demonstrated that the woman from the gospel was compared to that prophetical prostitute who, after she washed herself with **living water**, having undergone a forgetfulness of her sins, exults in the splendor of purity. . . . Who, then, is this prostitute, this Samaritan woman whose stains of adultery the fount of Christ wiped away? Let us eagerly seek the answer! I think that this woman is the church, gathered together from the gentiles, which had completed five thousand years when, in the six thousandth year, it submitted to the fornication of idolatry. But when the fount of Christ came it was cleansed of all its disgrace, and through faith in the Savior, cleansed its stains which were obtained by the adulteries of sacrilege. Abandoning as foolish the first **water**, their ancestral worship, it proclaimed the coming of the Lord to the whole world. This, I say, was the prostitute who, after she was washed, said that she had done *nothing wrong* (Prov 30:20). After the church has been cleansed by the splendor of baptism, it does not remember its diabolical acts of impiety, but exults in the worship of the truth. Having been transformed from a prostitute into a virgin, it does not dwell on its prior sins, but glories in the purity of virtue.

John 4:1-8

¹**Now when the Lord knew that the Pharisees had heard that Jesus was making and baptizing more disciples than John** ²**(although Jesus himself did not baptize, but only his disciples),** ³**he left Judea and departed again to Galilee.** ⁴**He had to pass through Samaria.** ⁵**So he came to a city of Samaria, called Sychar, near the field that Jacob gave to his son Joseph.** ⁶**Jacob's well was there, and so Jesus, wearied as he was with his journey, sat down beside the well. It was about the sixth hour.** ⁷**There came a woman of Samaria to draw water. Jesus said to her, "Give me a drink."** ⁸**For his disciples had gone away into the city to buy food.**

(8) Ambrose of Milan

If you seek Jesus, abandon the *broken cisterns* (cf. Jer 2:13), for Christ was accustomed to **sit** not by a cistern but by a **well**. That Samaritan woman who had faith, who desired to draw up water, found him there. Although you ought to come early in the morning, nevertheless even if you come late, even in the **sixth hour**, you will find Jesus **wearied from the journey** (4:6). He is **wearied**, but **wearied** with you, because he has sought you for so long. Your unbelief all this time has **wearied** him. Yet he is not offended, if only you will come. The one who gives asks to drink. But he drinks not the water of a flowing stream, but your salvation. He drinks your affection. He drinks the cup, that is, that passion which atoned for your sins so that you, drinking his sacred blood, might quench the thirst of this world.

(9) John Chrysostom

Jesus, wearied (4:6). What does Isaiah say? *The great God will not grow hungry, nor will he thirst, nor will he become wearied, and there is no searching of his understanding* (Isa 40:28 LXX). The evangelist Matthew writes about Christ in his gospel that *he fasted forty days and forty nights, and afterward he was hungry* (Matt 4:2). Likewise, the evangelist John says, as you have just heard: **Jesus, wearied as he was with his journey, sat down beside the well. It was about the sixth hour** (4:6). Indeed, one gospel says that he *was hungry* and the other that he was **wearied**. But the prophet Isaiah, clearly speaking by the Holy Spirit, says, *The great God will not grow hungry, nor will he thirst, nor will he become wearied and there is no searching of his understanding* (Isa 40:28 LXX). How can we preserve the harmony between the gospels and the prophets? Clearly the prophet was not lying. May it never be! Nor did the apostles write things opposed to the Holy Spirit and the prophet.

The incarnation of our great God and Savior contains a marvelous, twofold combination—I am speaking here of his divinity and his humanity according to his good pleasure and will. For this reason, the prophet announces the power and majesty of his divinity, but the apostles and evangelists clearly speak about the incarnation in the body.

(10) John Chrysostom

Here we learn of his strength in the **journey**, and his disregard for food as something of little importance. So the disciples themselves were taught this attitude toward such things. They were not fixated on supplies for the road, as is obvious from another evangelist who says that when Jesus spoke to them about the *leaven of the Pharisees* (Matt 16:6), the disciples thought that it was because they had not brought bread. When he introduces the hungry disciples plucking ears of corn and eating them (cf. Matt 12:1), or recording that Jesus came to the fig tree because he was hungry (cf. Matt 21:1–19), there is no other reason for this than to teach us to think lightly of the stomach, and not to think that serving the stomach is something worth pursuing. Observe them in this situation as well. They neither carry anything with them nor, since they didn't bring anything with them, do they care about **food** at the very beginning of the day—they were buying **food** at the time when everyone else was having their meal![3] This isn't like us. As soon as we rise from bed, before anything else, we focus on our meals, calling cooks and attendants, and overseeing them with great earnestness. We focus on daily matters before spiritual matters, and give things which should have been less important the honor of necessity. So everything is topsy-turvy. Instead, we ought first to give our attention to all spiritual matters and then, having accomplished these things, to occupy ourselves with other matters.

(11) Augustine of Hippo

Jesus, wearied as he was with his journey, sat down beside the well. It was about the sixth hour (4:6). Now the mystery begins. Jesus is not **wearied** without reason. The power of God is not **wearied** without reason. The one who restores those who are **weary** is not himself **wearied** without reason. The one without whom we grow **weary** and with whom we are strengthened—this one is not **wearied** without reason. Nevertheless, Jesus is **wearied**, and he is **wearied with his journey**. He **sat down**, and **sat down beside the well**, and being **wearied, he sat down** at **about the sixth hour**.

All these things hint at something. They endeavor to point out something. They make us pay attention, and admonish us to knock. May he who himself thought it fitting to admonish us, saying, *Knock and it will be opened to you* (Matt 7:7)—may he open to me and to you. It was for you that Jesus is **wearied from his journey**.

We find Jesus strong and we find Jesus weak: a Jesus who is both strong and weak. We find him strong because, *In the beginning was the Word and the Word was with God and the Word was God. He was in the beginning with God* (1:1–2). Do you want to see just how strong this Son of God is? *All things were made through him and without him was*

---

3. Chrysostom is referring to the time of day in the passage, "the sixth hour," that is, midday.

not anything made that was made (1:3), and they were made without effort. What then is stronger than him through whom *all things were made* without effort?

Do you want to encounter him weak? *The Word became flesh and dwelt among us* (1:14). By the strength of Christ he created you, and by the weakness of Christ he re-created you. By the strength of Christ he brought into existence that which did not exist; by the weakness of Christ he caused that which did exist not to perish. He formed us by his strength; he sought after us in his weakness.

(12) Cyril of Alexandria

Behold, Jesus was **wearied with his journey** (4:6). Who experienced this? Will you present us with the Almighty Lord lacking strength? Will you ascribe to the only-begotten of the Father toil from the **journey**, so that the one who is known to be without suffering is now understood to suffer? Or will you act rightly and refuse to think this way? These accusations apply to the nature of the body alone. Say instead that toil was fitting for humanity, rather than for the one whom we understand to exist as the Word unveiled[4] in himself. So, containing in his own nature the ability to do all things and to be himself the strength of all, he is said to be **wearied**—for I do not divide the one Christ into a duality of sons, even if he makes the suffering of humanity his own. Yet he remains incapable of suffering since, even though he became a man, it was not in his nature to be **wearied**.

So, if he says something which we think is more fitting for a human, but not at all for God, let us not immediately grope after texts. When we are most in need of the skill which leads to piety, let us not then be caught up in extreme ignorance, completely undoing the truth of the incarnation, and rashly ascending to the very Godhead of the Word. Out of such great ignorance we are grasping at things beyond our comprehension. If he had not really taken the title "human," or the *form of a servant* (Phil 2:7), it would be appropriate to be disturbed when someone attributes to him characteristics befitting a slave. Then we would demand that everything said about him be appropriate to God. However, if we are without a doubt confident and secure in a steadfast faith that according to the voice of John, *The Word became flesh and dwelt among us* (1:14), then when you see him being spoken about in a fleshly way, that is, as a human, accept the declaration befitting a human as the confirmation of our preaching. There was no other way to know clearly that God the Word had become human unless the one who does not suffer, did suffer something, and the exalted one had been recorded as having spoken lowly words.

(13) John Scotus Eriugena

Jesus, wearied as he was with his journey, sat down beside the well (4:6). Jesus's **weariness** is a sign of his incarnation. Of course, it was his purpose to assume our nature of original sin, **wearied** by the labors and distresses of this world. It was his path to descend

---

4. That is, not clothed in human flesh.

from his divinity and take up the likeness of our nature. Without any effort on his part, he created us through his divinity; but through his humanity, he re-created us with great effort. Remaining changeless and eternal in himself and his Father, he moved himself as if on a **journey** of temporary dispensation in the flesh.

John 4:9–26

[9]The Samaritan woman said to him, "How is it that you, a Jew, ask a drink of me, a woman of Samaria?" For Jews have no dealings with Samaritans. [10]Jesus answered her, "If you knew the gift of God, and who it is that is saying to you, 'Give me a drink,' you would have asked him, and he would have given you living water." [11]The woman said to him, "Sir, you have nothing to draw with, and the well is deep; where do you get that living water? [12]Are you greater than our father Jacob, who gave us the well, and drank from it himself, and his sons, and his cattle?" [13]Jesus said to her, "Every one who drinks of this water will thirst again, [14]but whoever drinks of the water that I shall give him will never thirst; the water that I shall give him will become in him a spring of water welling up to eternal life." [15]The woman said to him, "Sir, give me this water, that I may not thirst, nor come here to draw." [16]Jesus said to her, "Go, call your husband, and come here." [17]The woman answered him, "I have no husband." Jesus said to her, "You are right in saying, 'I have no husband'; [18]for you have had five husbands, and he whom you now have is not your husband; this you said truly." [19]The woman said to him, "Sir, I perceive that you are a prophet. [20]Our fathers worshiped on this mountain; and you say that in Jerusalem is the place where men ought to worship." [21]Jesus said to her, "Woman, believe me, the hour is coming when neither on this mountain nor in Jerusalem will you worship the Father. [22]You worship what you do not know; we worship what we know, for salvation is from the Jews. [23]But the hour is coming, and now is, when the true worshipers will worship the Father in spirit and truth, for such the Father seeks to worship him. [24]God is spirit, and those who worship him must worship in spirit and truth." [25]The woman said to him, "I know that Messiah is coming (he who is called Christ); when he comes, he will show us all things." [26]Jesus said to her, "I who speak to you am he."

4:10–14 "living water . . . welling up to eternal life"

---

(14) John Chrysostom

Scripture sometimes calls the grace of the Spirit, fire, and sometimes **water** (4:13), showing that these names point not to its substance, but its activity; for the Spirit, being invisible and simple, is not made up of different substances. So John declares this, saying, *He will baptize you with the Holy Spirit and with fire* (Matt 3:11). And Christ says, *Out of his heart shall flow rivers of living water. Now this he said about the Spirit, which they were about to receive* (7:38–39). In the same way, while conversing with the woman, he calls the Spirit **water**. For

whoever drinks of the water that I shall give him will never thirst (4:13). So he refers to the Spirit by the name of fire (cf. Matt 3:11; Luke 3:16; 1 Thess 5:19) to hint at the rousing and warming aspects of grace, as well as its ability to consume sins. But by calling it **water** he hints at the purification that comes from it, and the great refreshment which it produces for those minds that receive it. This is appropriate, for the Spirit transforms the eager soul into a kind of paradise flowing with every sort of tree, fruitful and ever-blooming, neither feeling despondency nor yielding to the plots of Satan, and it easily *quenches all the flaming darts of the evil one* (Eph 6:16).

(15) Theodore of Mopsuestia

Because the woman did not yet understand what he was saying, nor what **living water** was, she said to him, **Sir, you have nothing to draw with, and the well is deep; where do you get that living water?** (4:11) . . . Because she was compelled to know more, she said to him, "**Are you greater than our father Jacob, who gave us the well, and drank from it himself, and his sons, and his cattle?** (4:12). Do you actually have greater power than the one who dug this well? He and his sons refreshed themselves by it, and he even left us the fruit of his labor so that we might refresh ourselves as well. So it is fitting that we should expect you to do something new since without human labor or activity, and even without a bucket, you can give water suitable for drinking." Then, in order to teach her that his statement was not about these waters, our Lord said to her, **Everyone who drinks of this water will thirst again, but whoever drinks of the water that I shall give him will never thirst; the water that I shall give him will become in him a spring of water welling up to eternal life** (4:13–14). . . . He was right to say this, for the power of the Spirit is like this. We too receive the firstfruits of the Spirit with the hope of the future resurrection. Now this is accomplished typologically for us, but in the future we expect to receive perfect grace when, through our participation in Christ, we will remain incorruptible.

(16) Augustine of Hippo

Let's not brush aside the fact that the Lord was promising something spiritual. What does he mean, saying, **Every one who drinks of this water will thirst again** (4:13)? It's true both for this **water** and for the water's deeper meaning. Because the **water** in the well is worldly pleasures in the shadowy depths; from here people draw water with the jar of desire. You see, they lean in and lower their jar of desire, in order to reach a tempting drink from the depths. They enjoy the worldly pleasures once they have lowered their jar and sent it down. Anyone who doesn't release their desire is unable to reach the tempting pleasures. Therefore, consider the water jar your desire, and the deep waters, your pleasure; when anyone has reached down to worldly pleasures, one finds there food, drink, a bath, entertainment, sexual intercourse. Could it really be that he will not thirst again? So Jesus says, "**Every one who drinks of this water will thirst again** (4:13); but if he accepts water from me, **he will**

never thirst" (4:14). The Scripture says, *We shall be satisfied with the goodness of thy house* (Ps 65:4). Therefore, what kind of water was he going to give, other than the water he just spoke of: *For with thee is the fountain of life* (Ps 36:9)? How will they thirst, who *feast on the abundance of thy house* (Ps 36:8)?

Christ was promising a certain feasting and fullness of the Holy Spirit, but the Samaritan woman didn't yet understand. Not understanding, how did she respond? **The woman said to him, "Sir, give me this water, that I may not thirst, nor come here to draw"** (4:15). Her need was urging her toward the task, but her weakness refused the labor. Would that she had heard: *Come to me, all who labor and are heavy laden, and I will give you rest* (Matt 11:28)! Jesus was saying this to her so that she might not toil; but the woman didn't yet understand.

(17) Cyril of Alexandria

While encouraging her to wonder at the **gift of God**, Christ introduces himself as its supplier. He says: **If you knew the gift of God, and who it is that is saying to you, "Give me a drink," you would have asked him** (4:10). Who would properly grant the things of God? Would it not be one who is God by nature?

The **living water** (4:10) is what he calls the life-giving **gift** of the Spirit. Through this **gift** alone—although parched to its roots in the mountains, as it were, and rendered dry and barren of all virtue by the devil's evil doing—humanity swiftly returns to the pristine beauty of its nature. It drinks in the life-giving grace, blossoms all over with various kinds of good things, and finally, growing into a virtue-loving state of mind, sends up its shoots well nourished in its love for God. God speaks to us a similar word through the prophet Isaiah: *The wild beasts will honor me, the jackals and the ostriches; for I give water in the wilderness, rivers in the desert, to give drink to my chosen people, the people whom I formed for myself that they might declare my praise* (Isa 43:20–21). Another of the saints also says that the soul of the righteous person will be *like a fruitful tree* (Jer 38:12 LXX) and that they *will spring up like grass amid waters, like willows by flowing streams* (Isa 44:4).

Well now, we could pile up other testimonies from the divine Scripture in addition to those quoted above. Through such witnesses it would be very easy to show that the divine Spirit is often called by the name of **water**, but it is not the time for us to linger here. Therefore, we will swim elsewhere, hastening on to the great, wide sea of divine visions.

(18) John Scotus Eriugena

Jesus answered her, "If you knew the gift of God, and who it is that is saying to you, 'Give me a drink,' you would have asked him, and he would have given you water" (4:10). It is as if he said: "If you, woman, had known me and believed in me completely, and if you knew about the **gift of God**, which is the Holy Spirit, you would have asked me for a drink, and because of your faith I would have given you **living water**, namely, the Holy Spirit" (cf. John 7:38–39).

The woman said to him, "Sir, you have no bucket, and the well is deep; how, then, do you have living water?" (4:11). Still thinking of physical things and not yet believing, the woman did not understand what he was saying to her. She thought the Lord was speaking to her about physical water, but he was discussing spiritual matters. . . .

Jesus responded and **said to her, "Everyone who drinks of this water**, which you, O woman, wish to drink, and which you suppose I seek from you, **will thirst again"** (4:13). For clearly such water only temporarily quenches a temporal thirst. "**But whoever drinks of the water that I shall give him will never thirst"** (4:14). He could have said: "To anyone who believes in me, I will give the gift of the Holy Spirit which proceeds through me from the Father. He will not thirst again." For the psalmist said, *I shall be satisfied when thy glory shall appear* (Ps 16:15 Vulgate).

But, **the water that I shall give him will become in him a spring of water welling up to eternal life** (4:14). Spiritual **water**, that is, the gift of the Holy Spirit, **wells up to eternal life**. Worldly **water** flows downward, but spiritual **water wells** upward and carries those who **drink** it to **eternal life** and blessedness.

The woman said to him, "Sir, give me this water, that I may not thirst, nor come here to draw" (4:15). So nature begins to understand its state, for the desires of the rational creature (signified by the Samaritan woman) are concerned with blessedness and true understanding. Likewise, the church begins to understand the faith more deeply. Before, it simply used faith to quench its **thirst**; now it begins to enter into theological understanding.

4:16	"Go, call your husband."

---

(19) Augustine of Hippo

Wanting the woman to understand, **Jesus said to her, "Go, call your husband, and come here"** (4:16). . . . Therefore, my brothers and sisters, let's listen and understand what the Lord says: He tells the woman to **call** her **husband**. Let's investigate the **husband** of the soul. Isn't Jesus himself the true **husband** of the soul? Now, let your understanding be present because what we're about to say will scarcely be understood by anyone but intent listeners; let your understanding be present so that perhaps understanding itself will be the **husband** of the soul.

Therefore Jesus, seeing that the woman didn't understand, but wishing her to understand, said, "**Call your husband** (4:16); you don't understand what I'm saying because your understanding isn't present. I'm speaking about the Spirit, but you hear it as though I were speaking about the flesh. The things I speak about have nothing to do with the pleasures of the ears, the eyes, smelling, tasting, or touching. My discourse is understood by the mind alone, and absorbed by understanding alone. Your understanding isn't present; how can you comprehend what I'm saying? **Call your husband**, send forth your understanding. What does it mean to you, to have a soul? It's no great thing, because cattle have one, too. How then are you better than the cows? You have understanding, which cattle do not have! Therefore, what does it mean to **call your husband**? You don't understand, you don't comprehend me. I speak to you of the gift of God, but you ruminate on the flesh. You don't wish to thirst for earthly things, but I speak to you of the Spirit. Your understanding is gone; **Call your husband!** *Be not like a horse or a mule, without understanding*" (Ps 32:9).

Therefore, my brothers and sisters, to have a soul but no understanding—that is, not relying on it nor living according to it—such is the life of cattle. There is something common between us and the cattle, in that we both live in the flesh; but the flesh must be ruled by understanding. Understanding reigns supreme over the impulses of the soul when it moves itself according to the flesh and desires to rush off, uninhibited, toward earthly delights.

(20) John Scotus Eriugena

Jesus said to her, "Go, call your husband, and come here" (4:16). It is as if he had said: "You seek from me **water welling up to eternal life**, clearly meaning the Holy Spirit, whose **eternal life** I give as a gift. You will not be able to drink such water, unless you **call** forth your **husband**. Hurry, then! If you want to drink, **call your husband**, and **come here** with him." That is, believe in Christ, so that you and **your husband** might drink in the Holy Spirit. Here, at this point, the passage moves from a general meaning to a spiritual one. We have already mentioned that the Samaritan woman is a symbol for the whole church gathered from all the gentiles, and for all human nature. In fact, this same woman presents the figure of each soul that is established in the unity of the church and shares in human nature. So the **woman** represents the rational soul, and **her husband** represents the intellect. This intellect is called a variety of things: sometimes the intellect, sometimes the mind, sometimes the soul, and still more often, the spirit. . . . The rational soul is unable to obtain the gifts of God except through the **husband**, that is, through the intellect which holds an authority over all of nature. Therefore, the woman (or the soul, as we have seen) is rightly ordered to **call her husband**—that is, her intellect—to herself. By doing so, she is able to drink the spiritual gifts. When she is separated from the intellect, there is no way for her to partake of divine grace. Therefore Jesus says, "**Call your husband, and come here**; for without **your husband**, you would not even imagine coming to me." When the intellect is absent, no one knows how to ascend to the heights of theological wisdom or how to partake of spiritual gifts.

4:24 "God is spirit, and those who worship him must worship in spirit and truth."

---

(21) Origen of Alexandria

We understand that the phrase **neither on this mountain** (4:21) clearly refers to the piety expressed among the heterodox in the illusion of their gnostic doctrines and "higher principles." And the phrase **nor in Jerusalem will you worship the Father** (4:21) refers to the church's faith as followed by most people. Those who are perfect and holy, being more perceptive, more perspicacious, and more godly, will surpass such **worship** whenever they **worship the Father**.

Just as the angels do not **worship the Father in Jerusalem** (as even the Jews would agree), because there is a better way to worship than in Jerusalem, so also those who can already be *equal to angels* (Luke 20:36) in their disposition, do not **worship the Father in Jerusalem**. They **worship** in a better way than those **in Jerusalem**, even if, for the sake of those **in Jerusalem**, they accommodate themselves to those **in Jerusalem**, becoming *Jews to the Jews, in order to win Jews* (1 Cor 9:20). . . .

* * *

I do not know how the heterodox deny the God of Abraham, Isaac, and Jacob, the fathers of the Jews, since the Savior clearly contradicts them by saying that **salvation is from the Jews** (4:22). If the Savior fulfills the law, and certain things which occurred during the Lord's earthly visit fulfilled what was written in the prophets, how is it not obvious that **salvation** comes **from the Jews**? The God of the Jews and the gentiles is the same God, *since God is one; and he will justify the circumcised on the ground of their faith and the uncircumcised through their faith* (Rom 3:30). We do not annul the law through our faith, but through it we establish the law.

But the hour is coming, and now is, when the true worshipers will worship the Father in spirit and truth (4:23). Those who do not profess to worship the Father at all ought not to be called **worshipers** of God. But of all those who do profess to worship the Creator, there are some who live no longer in the flesh but in the **Spirit**, because they *walk by the Spirit, and do not gratify the desires of the flesh* (Gal 5:16); and there are some who live not in the **Spirit** but in the flesh, because they wage war according to the flesh. This being the case, we must say that those who worship the Father **in spirit** rather than in flesh, and **in truth** rather than in types, are the true **worshipers**. Those who do not **worship** in this way are not true **worshipers**.

(22) Hilary of Poitiers

We ought to consider carefully how and why it was written in the gospel that **God is spirit** (4:24). Everything is spoken for a reason, and the purpose of the words will be understood from the meaning of what is said. We must keep this in mind lest, from the Lord's response that **God is spirit** (4:24), the use and gift, as well as the name, of the Holy Spirit be denied. The Lord spoke with the Samaritan woman because he came for the redemption of the whole world. After much discussion about **living water**, her **five husbands**, and the current man who was not her husband, the woman responded: **Sir, I perceive that you are a prophet. Our fathers worshiped on this mountain; and you say that in Jerusalem is the place where men ought to worship** (4:19–20). The Lord replied: **Woman, believe me, the hour is coming when neither on this mountain nor in Jerusalem will you worship the Father. You worship what you do not know; we worship what we know, for salvation is from the Jews. But the hour is coming, and now is, when the true worshipers will worship the Father in spirit and truth, for such the Father seeks to worship him. For God is spirit, and those who worship him must worship in spirit and truth** (4:21–24).

Being mindful of her ancestral tradition, the woman thought that God must be worshiped either on a mountain, as in Samaria, or in a temple, as in Jerusalem. Samaria, through their transgression of the law, had chosen a place on the mountain for worshiping God, while the Jews thought that the temple built by Solomon was the true place of worship. Both of these presumptions confined the God in whom all things exist and outside of whom nothing exists either to an elevated mountain ridge or to a constructed hollow building.

Therefore, since God is invisible, incomprehensible, and infinite, the Lord said that the time had come when God would be worshiped neither on a mountain nor in a temple, because **God is spirit** and the Spirit is neither confined nor contained. The power of his nature is everywhere; it is absent nowhere, overflowing into all things. Therefore, those who are **true worshipers** will **worship in spirit and truth**. Those who will worship God the Spirit **in the Spirit** have the Spirit for assistance in worship but also honor the same Spirit; there is a distinction in the way each is involved in worship. Neither the name of the Holy Spirit nor the gift of the Holy Spirit is destroyed just because it was said **God is spirit**. To the woman who confined God to a temple or a mountain, Christ responded that all things are in God, and he is in himself—invisible and incomprehensible. He must be worshiped also by invisible and incomprehensible means. So he indicates both the nature of the gift and the honor due the Spirit when he taught that **God** the **Spirit** must be worshiped **in the Spirit**. He indicated the freedom and knowledge of the worshiper, as well as the infinite extent of the one worshiped, since **God** the **Spirit** is worshiped **in the Spirit**.

(23) Didymus the Blind

Since God is invisible, his incorporeality follows from his invisibility. If God is incorporeal, then he is invisible. If this is true, then the **Spirit** mentioned here cannot be merely moving air. Although with human beings our spirit is revealed through the body, this is not necessary with God.

The **light** mentioned earlier (cf. John 3:19–21) does not illuminate the eyes, but the mind (for it is an intellectual, not a physical, **light**). The one who is called love is not a disposition, but a being who loves and cares for what he has made. In the same way he does not call the **Spirit** a wind, but presents him as an incorporeal and life-giving being.

All who learn that **God is Spirit, worship** him spiritually, that is, **in spirit and truth**. They no longer **worship** the God of all in the ancient types.[5] Christ is speaking here of a distinction between the letter and the **spirit**, between the type and the truth. These types served their purpose until now, but when the **truth** came with the advent of Christ, they have all come to an end.

(24) Gregory of Nazianzus

"But," someone says, "who worshiped the Spirit in the time of the old covenant or in that of the new? Who prayed to him? Where is it written that we ought to worship him or pray to him? Where do you get this idea?" . . . For now, it is enough to say this: the Spirit is

---

5. That is, for example, in a temple where animal sacrifices are offered.

the one in whom we worship, and the one through whom we pray. Scripture says, **God is spirit, and those who worship him must worship in spirit and truth** (4:24). Again, *for we do not know how to pray as we ought, but the Spirit himself intercedes for us with sighs too deep for words* (Rom 8:26). And: *I will pray with the spirit and I will pray with the mind also* (1 Cor 14:15)—that is, in the mind and in the Spirit. Therefore, to worship or pray to the Spirit seems to me nothing other than the Spirit offering prayer or worship to himself.

(25) Basil of Caesarea

The phrase **worship in spirit** (4:24) suggests the activity of our minds which happens in the **light** (cf. 3:21), as we learn from what was said to the Samaritan woman. Because she was deceived by her native custom into thinking that worship occurred at a specific location, our Lord brought her to a new understanding and said that one **must worship in spirit and truth** (4:24). By the word **truth**, he clearly means himself. Therefore, just as we speak of **worship** in the Son as worship in the image of God the Father, so also we speak of **worship in the spirit** as showing in himself the Godhead of the Lord.

Even in **worship** the Holy Spirit is inseparable from the Father and the Son. If you were outside the Spirit, you would not be worshiping at all. But being in him, you will in no way separate him from God any more than you will separate light from the objects seen. It is impossible to see the image of the invisible God, except by the enlightenment of the Spirit, just as, gazing on an image, one is at a loss to separate the light from the image. The source of sight is necessarily observed at the same time as the objects seen. So as an appropriate consequence, we behold the *reflection of the glory of God* through the enlightenment of the Spirit, and through his *very stamp* (Heb 1:3) we are led up to the one of whom he is the *very stamp* and the identical seal.

(26) Ambrose of Milan

If anyone says that the Son also worships God the Father because it is written, **You worship what you do not know; we worship what we know, for salvation is from the Jews** (4:22), let him consider when Christ said this, to whom it was said, and for whose desire it was given. Indeed, in the earlier verses (not without reason), it was declared that *Jesus, wearied as he was with his journey, sat down* (4:6) and requested a drink from a Samaritan woman. He spoke as a man, since as God he could neither be wearied nor thirsty. So when the Samaritan woman addressed him as a Jew, and thought he was a prophet, he answered her as a Jew who spiritually taught the mysteries of the law: **You worship what you do not know; we worship what we know** (4:22). He says **we** because he associates himself with humanity. How then is he associated with humanity if not according to the flesh? And to show that he answered her according to the incarnation, he added: **For salvation is from the Jews** (4:22).

Immediately after this, he distinguished his human disposition, saying: **The hour is coming, and now is, when the true worshipers will worship the Father** (4:23). He did not say "we will worship," which he certainly would have said if he had assumed participation in our obedience. To be sure, when we read that Mary worshiped him (cf. Matt 28:9), we ought to understand that he cannot, in the same nature, worship as a servant and be worshiped as God. Rather, as a human he is said to worship among humans, and as God he is worshiped by his servants.

Therefore, we read and believe many things according to the mystery of the incarnation. And yet in the very disposition of our human nature, we may see the divine majesty. Jesus was **wearied from the journey,** so that he may restore the wearied. He asks for a drink, while giving spiritual drink to the thirsty. He is hungry, while delivering the food of salvation to the hungry. He dies to live again. He is buried to rise again. He hangs upon the trembling cross, strengthening those who tremble. He covers the heavens with darkness that he may bring light. He causes the earth to shake that he may make it firm. He stirs up the sea that he might soothe it. He uncovers the tombs of the dead that he might show that they are homes of the living. He is born of a virgin that we may believe he is born of God. He pretends not to know so that he might make the ignorant knowledgeable. It is said that he worships as a Jew so that he may be worshiped as the true Son of God.

(27) John Chrysostom

Jesus revealed a magnificent teaching to the woman, one which he did not speak even to Nicodemus (John 3) or Nathanael (John 1). The woman was eager to show that her people were more honored than the Jews, and she cleverly suggests this by mentioning their forefathers. But Christ did not address this question . . . ; rather, removing the privileges of both patterns of worship, he kindles her soul by indicating that neither Jews nor the Samaritans have anything great compared to what he was about to give. Then he introduces the difference. Even so, he quite plainly declared that the Jews were more honored, not preferring one place to another, but giving them precedence because of their intention. It was as if he said, "About the 'place' there is no longer a need to argue, but in terms of the 'manner,' certainly the Jews have the advantage over the Samaritans. **For you worship,**" he says, "**what you do not know; we worship what we know**" (4:22). . . . Do not marvel that he counts himself among the Jews. He speaks toward the woman's understanding of him as being a prophet of the Jews. Therefore, he says *we* worship (4:22), for it's clear to all that he is among those things which are worshiped. To worship belongs to the creation; to be worshiped belongs to the Lord of creation. But for now, he converses as a Jew. Thus, the **we** here means "we Jews." . . .

But the hour is coming, and now is, when the true worshipers will worship the Father in spirit and truth (4:23). . . . Who then are the **true worshipers**? Those who do not restrict their **worship** to a place and who serve God **in spirit**. . . . Thus, **worship** must also be incorporeal and offered by that incorporeal nature in us, that is, the purity of soul and mind. Therefore he says, **those who worship him must worship in spirit and truth** (4:24). Since both the Samaritans and the Jews were careless about the soul, they expended great effort on the body, purifying it in all sorts of ways. But Christ says that the incorporeal one is served not by the purity of the body, but by the incorporeal nature in us, that is, the mind. Do not, then, sacrifice sheep and calves, but offer to God your entire self, and make this your burnt offering, for this is the *living sacrifice* to be *presented* (Rom 12:1). We must worship **in truth**, for as the former things were types—circumcision, burnt offerings, sacrifices, and incense—now they no longer exist, but all is **truth**. Now, we must circumcise not our flesh, but our evil thoughts, and we must crucify ourselves, and eradicate and slaughter our unreasonable desires.

(28) Theodore of Mopsuestia

Christ did not say salvation is "in the Jews" but **from the Jews** (4:22); redemption was not "in" them but **from** them because Christ, who was in the flesh, was **from** them. "So then," he says, "truth is with the Jews, but both places of worship are coming to an end." How and in what way does he say, **But the hour is coming, and now is, when the true worshipers will worship the Father in spirit and truth, for such the Father seeks to worship him. God is spirit, and those who worship him must worship in spirit and truth** (4:23–24)? The time will come—and even now has begun—in which God will be worshiped according to what is proper and suitable to his nature. God is incorporeal, that is, not confined by places. He is in every place, and it is fitting to worship him with this understanding in mind. The true worshiper is one who honors God with a right intention and believes with a pure conscience that you can speak with the Infinite One in every place. So let there not be dispute about whether God is only here or there, and whether he can be worshiped in one place alone. That idea gives more insult than honor to God, and is contrary to the proper understanding worshipers should have.

(29) Cyril of Alexandria

He says that the Samaritans **do not know** while the Jews **do know** what they worship. He asserts that salvation will come from the latter people, namely from himself, for Christ is of the line of David in flesh, and David was born of the tribe of Judah. He classifies himself as a man like other worshipers, though he is one with God the Father and is worshiped by us and the holy angels. Since he has taken on the *form of a servant* (Phil 2:7), he fulfills the duties appropriate for a servant without failing to be God and Lord and one who is to be worshiped. Even though born a man, he remains the same and always continues to preserve the purpose of his dispensation in the flesh. . . .

Christ does not offer worship as God the Word, but being born among us, he demonstrated how he rightly experienced this as a man, because of the incarnation. We will not seek assurances from external sources, but again will know it from his own words. For what else does he say to the woman from Samaria? **You worship what you do not know; *we* worship what *we* know** (4:22). Is it not quite evident to all, therefore, that he says such things, using the plural grammatical number (that is, **we**) and counting himself among those who worship out of slavish necessity, because he is born in slavish humanity? Tell me, what was preventing him from assigning this worship to his own person in the singular (that is, "I") if he wanted us to perceive him as a worshiper? Then he should have said, "*I* worship what *I* know" so that, being unassociated with anyone else, he might claim the meaning of what he said for himself alone. In fact, he is both most proper and extremely infallible in saying **we**, because he is now included among *servants* because of his humanity, is numbered among the worshipers, and is a Jew because of his homeland.

(30) John Scotus Eriugena

But the hour is coming, and now is (4:23). He says that **the hour** is his presence in the flesh. He says, "You, O woman, ask about the place of worshiping me. So I say to you, **The hour is coming**; I am present; I am now in the flesh, **when the true worshipers will worship the Father in spirit and truth** (4:23). Before I came, no one was able to **worship the Father in spirit and truth**, except the patriarchs and prophets through whom my incarnation was revealed ahead of time by the Spirit. Therefore, O woman, neither on this mountain nor in Jerusalem will the true worshipers worship my Father and me, but within the innermost temple of their own hearts and minds. First they will be cleansed by faith, then enlightened by knowledge, and finally perfected by becoming like God. On the mountain of theology they will **worship in spirit**, for they will have been enlightened by the Holy Spirit for this task."

    For such the Father seeks to worship him (4:23), that is, those who worship him in their own spirit and in the truth of their own knowledge. By this account, what he predicted he now fulfills, saying: **God is Spirit, and those who worship him must worship in Spirit and truth** (4:24). It is as though he said: "If God was corporeal or had a body, perhaps he would have sought a physical place to be worshiped in. But because he is **Spirit**, he seeks those who will worship him in their **spirit** and understanding through true knowledge."

4:26 "I who speak to you am he."

---

(31) Cyril of Alexandria

Jesus said to her, "I who speak to you am he" (4:26). Christ does not reveal himself to uneducated or completely ignorant souls; instead, he illuminates and appears to those who are already more disposed toward wanting to learn something, who are struggling with the beginning of faith in simple words, and who are compelled toward the knowledge of more perfect things. This is just what the Samaritan woman seems to us, considering divine realities more simplistically than she ought. . . . Then she says: **We know that Messiah is coming (he who is called Christ); when he comes, he will show us all things** (4:25). Do you see how well prepared the woman was for believing? As if being elevated upon some staircase, she leaps up from trivial questions to a more exalted state. So it was right for Christ to expose her now to the clear proclamation of what she longed for, and to offer her long-held hope as now being present before her, saying, **I who speak to you am he** (4:26). Therefore, those who hold a teaching vocation in the churches should offer clear instruction to newcomers. They should make Jesus known to them clearly and raise them up from lesser instruction to a more perfect knowledge of the faith.

John 4:27–42

[27]Just then his disciples came. They marveled that he was talking with a woman, but none said, "What do you wish?" or, "Why are you talking with her?" [28]So the woman left her water jar, and went away into the city, and said to the people, [29]"Come, see a man who told me all that I ever did. Can this be the Christ?" [30]They went out of the city and were coming to him. [31]Meanwhile the disciples besought him, saying, "Rabbi, eat." [32]But he said to them, "I have food to eat of which you do not know." [33]So the disciples said to one another, "Has any one brought him food?" [34]Jesus said to them, "My food is to do the will of him who sent me, and to accomplish his work. [35]Do you not say, 'There are yet four months, then comes the harvest'? I tell you, lift up your eyes, and see how the fields are already white for harvest. [36]He who reaps receives wages, and gathers fruit for eternal life, so that sower and reaper may rejoice together. [37]For here the saying holds true, 'One sows and another reaps.' [38]I sent you to reap that for which you did not labor; others have labored, and you have entered into their labor." [39]Many Samaritans from that city believed in him because of the woman's testimony, "He told me all that I ever did." [40]So when the Samaritans came to him, they asked him to stay with them; and he stayed there two days. [41]And many more believed because of his word. [42]They said to the woman, "It is no longer because of your words that we believe, for we have heard for ourselves, and we know that this is indeed the Savior of the world."

4:28–30 The woman left her water jar. . . . "Can this be the Christ?"

---

(32) Origen of Alexandria

After his disciples arrived, they **marveled** (4:27). Previously they had beheld the majesty of his divinity. Now they **marveled** at the way such a person would speak with a woman. We, on the other hand, are taken in by pride and arrogance, and disdain those beneath us. We forget that the words *Let us make man in our image, after our likeness* (Gen 1:26) apply to everyone. When we do not remember the one who formed us in the womb (cf. Jer 1:5), who individually formed each of our hearts (cf. Ps 33:15), and who understands all of our works, we fail to understand that God is a helper to the humble and lowly, a protector of the weak, a shelter for those who have been given up in despair, and a Savior for those who have been given up as hopeless (cf. Jdt 9:11).

Christ, however, employed this woman as an apostle, so to speak, to those in the city. Since his words excited her so much, she **left her water jar** (4:28), went into the city, and said to the people: **Come, see a man who told me all that I ever did. Can this be the Christ?** (4:28–30). When **they went out of the city and were coming to him** (4:30), Christ did not disappoint this woman. **The Word** (1:1) revealed himself most clearly, for when the disciples came, they **marveled** to find that this woman, so easily deceived, was considered worthy to have a conversation with the **Word**. Yet, being convinced that the **Word** does all things well, the disciples did not rebuke him or question the discussion and conversation he was having with the Samaritan woman (cf. 4:27)....

I think there was a good reason why the evangelist wrote that **the woman left her water jar and went away into the city** (4:28). On the literal level, this shows the Samaritan woman's great eagerness, who **left the water jar** and thought more about benefiting the multitudes than about the humbler task of caring for the body. She was moved with a great love for humanity. Desiring to preach the good news of Christ to her fellow citizens, she testified that he had told her **all that she ever did** (4:29). She invited them to see a man whose speech was greater than man's, even though he looked like a man. Therefore, we too ought to forget the concerns of the body; and leaving them behind, we should be eager to give to others the benefit which we have partaken of. Those who truly know how to read, the evangelist summons us to this task by writing such praise of the woman.

Let us also consider the spiritual sense of the **water jar**, which the Samaritan woman **left** when she received the words of Jesus. Perhaps she **left** the **water jar**, which is exalted for its depth of teaching, because she despises those things she once believed, and has now received something better than the **water jar**, namely, **water** which was already becoming in her **water welling up to eternal life** (4:14). How could she have graciously preached Christ to her fellow citizens unless she had partaken of this **water**, amazed at him who had announced to her **everything she ever did**? How could she have done this if she had not partaken of this **water** of salvation through what she heard?

(33) John Chrysostom

Observe the woman's zeal and understanding! She came to draw water; and when she happened upon the true fount, she despised the physical one. She teaches us, even if through a small example, to overlook all the concerns of life and to make no account of them when we are listening to spiritual matters. What the apostles did, the woman did, by her own ability, even better. When the apostles were called, they left their nets; but the woman, unbidden, being commanded by no one, left her **water jar** (4:28). Excited by joy, she performed the work of the evangelists. She called not one or two people, as Andrew or Philip did (cf. John 1:40–51), but aroused the entire populace of the city, and so brought them to Christ. Observe how wisely she spoke. She did not say, "Come, behold the Christ"; rather, using the same accommodation with which Christ swept her up, she drew them: **Come**, she says, **see a man who told me all that I ever did** (4:29)....

She did not say, "Come, believe," but **Come, see**, which was a softer way of putting it and so drew them to Christ. Do you see the wisdom of this woman? She knew (and knew certainly) that having tasted of that fount, they would be affected in the same way as she herself was. Someone else who was thicker-headed would have hidden Christ's reproof; but the woman puts her life on display and thrusts it into the midst of all so that they might be drawn in to Christ's embrace.

(34) Cyril of Alexandria

The disciples are amazed at the extreme gentleness of the Savior, and they marvel at his relaxed manner. Christ thought there was no value in recoiling from conversation with a woman, like some who are wild with pure piety; instead he extends his benevolence to all and shows through his actions that because he is entirely one Creator, he does not give life through faith to men alone, but sweeps up the female sex as well. Again, let the one who teaches in the churches benefit from this model as well: do not refuse to help women. We should completely follow the requirements of preaching, and not just one's own will.

4:34 "My food is to do the will of him who sent me."

---

(35) Origen of Alexandria

Jesus said to them, "My food is to do the will of him who sent me, and to perfect his work" (4:34).[6] This is appropriate **food** for the Son of God, for he does the Father's **will**. By his act of willing he also does what was in the Father, so that the **will** of God is in the **will** of the Son, and the **will** of the Son is indistinguishable from the **will** of the Father. As a result, there are no longer two wills but one. This single **will** is the reason the Son says: **I and the Father are one** (10:30). Because of this **will**, the one who has seen Jesus has seen the Son and has also seen the one who sent him (cf. John 14:9). . . .

Now the phrase which follows shows that the **will** has to do with a disposition, since after speaking about **doing the will**, he adds: **to perfect the work** of God (4:34). We need to continue our consideration more fully so that we can see what he means by the phrase: I will **perfect his work** (4:34). Some more simple-minded person will say that it was the **work** that was commanded, that is, the **work** belonging to the one who commands. It is as though we said that when builders or farmers did the **work** for which they were employed, they said that they **perfected** the **work** of their employer.

Someone will say that since **the work** of God is **perfected** by Christ, then it is obvious that it was imperfect before it was **perfected**. How then was God's **work** imperfect? How is God's **work perfected** by the one who said: *The Father who sent me is greater than I* (14:28)? But the **perfection** of the **work** was the **perfection** of the rational creature, for this *Word* which *became flesh* (1:14) came to **perfect** that which was imperfect. Now then, are we saying that God's **work** was created imperfect and the Savior was sent to **perfect** this imperfect **work**? Is it not absurd to think that the Father would be a Creator of imperfect things and the Savior would **perfect** the imperfect because it was created imperfectly?

Indeed, I think that some deeper mystery lies in these passages. Perhaps the rational creature was not entirely imperfect when it was placed in paradise. How would God have placed an entirely imperfect creature in paradise to *till it and keep it* (Gen 2:15)? It would

---

6. RSV: *accomplish* **the work of God.** The Greek word can mean either accomplish or perfect, but Origen clearly understands the sense of "perfection" throughout this passage.

not be reasonable to call "imperfect" the one who is able to till the *tree of life* (Gen 2:9) and everything that God planted and brought forth afterward. Perhaps then, although originally **perfect**, the rational creature became imperfect through disobedience and then needed someone who could **perfect** it from its imperfection. This, then, is why the Savior was sent: first, to **do the will of the one who sent** him (4:34), having become his worker on earth; and second, to **perfect the work** of God so that each one who has been **perfected** might be adapted for *solid food* and be joined to wisdom. *Solid food is for the perfect, for those who have their faculties trained by practice to distinguish good from evil* (Heb 5:14). And the one who speaks wisdom says, *among the perfect we do impart wisdom* (1 Cor 2:9). So whenever each of us, a **work** of God, has been **perfected** by Jesus, we will say, *I have fought the good fight, I have finished the race, I have kept the faith. Henceforth there is laid up for me the crown of righteousness* (2 Tim 4:7–8).

(36) Cyril of Alexandria

Meanwhile the disciples besought him, saying, "Rabbi, eat" (4:31). The divine evangelist arranges the compilation of his book quite skillfully, and omits nothing which he believes will be entirely useful to the readers. Hear then how he introduces Jesus to us again as a model of a most remarkable act. I think that nothing is placed in the writings of the saints without a reason. Even something which seems minor proves to be worth our effort, since it has value. Therefore, the conversion of the Samaritans had begun, and even though they were not yet expecting him (although as God he knew they were coming), he whole-heartedly works for the salvation of those who were called, and despises bodily food, even though he is **wearied with his journey,** as it is written (4:6). He performs this action in order to benefit the teachers in the churches and to persuade them to disregard all weariness and apply their efforts toward those being saved rather than toward their own bodily care. The prophet says, *Cursed are those who do the work of the Lord with slackness* (Jer 48:10). Therefore, in order that we might learn that it was not the Lord's custom to eat during such times, the evangelist introduces the disciples **beseeching him** (4:31) and all but falling at his feet, trying to persuade him to take a little of their provisions as inevitable and necessary food. They **had gone away into the city to buy food** (4:8), and having now acquired it, they brought it to him. . . .

    Jesus said to them, "My food is to do the will of him who sent me, and to accomplish his work" (4:34). Being entirely open, he disclosed to his disciples the most transparent truth, and to those who would yet become teachers of the world he introduces himself as a model of an earnest and exceedingly excellent zeal. In this way he becomes a model for how to attend to the needs of the body appropriately, as of secondary importance. In saying that his most delightful **food** was **to do the will of the one who sent** him **and to accomplish his work** (4:34), he refers to the **work** of the apostolic ministry and clearly indicates what kind of habits they should have. It seems that they should be centered on the task of teaching alone; they should cease from caring for the luxuries of the flesh.

4:35 "'There are yet four months, then comes the harvest.'"

---

(37) Origen of Alexandria

Consider whether the **sowers** (4:36) signify Moses and the prophets who wrote things *for our instruction, upon whom the end of the ages has come* (1 Cor 10:11), and who proclaimed the coming of Christ. Consider whether the **reapers** (4:36) signify the apostles who received Christ and *beheld his glory* (1:14), agreeing with the prophetical and spiritual seeds about him. They reaped these seeds through a full investigation and understanding of *the mystery hidden for ages* (Eph 3:9), but was *made manifest at the end of the times* (1 Pet 1:20) and which were *not made known to the sons of men in other generations as it has now been revealed to his holy apostles and prophets* (Eph 3:5). But the complete plan, *according to the revelation of the mystery which was kept secret for long ages but is now disclosed through the prophetic writings* and the appearance of our Lord Jesus Christ (Rom 16:25–26), when the true light shone upon the **fields** and made them **already white for the harvest** (4:35)—this was the "seed."

By this interpretation, the **fields** in which the seeds were scattered signify the writings of the law and the prophets. These fields were not **white** for those who had not comprehended the coming of the Word. They are **white** to those who have become disciples of the Son of God and who have obeyed the one who says: **Lift up your eyes, and see how the fields are already white for harvest** (4:35). As true disciples of Jesus, then, let us **lift up our eyes and see the fields** which were sown by Moses and the prophets, so that we may see their **white**ness and how we may now **reap** (4:36) and gather their fruit to eternal life with the hope also of a reward from the Lord of the **fields** and the supplier of the seeds (cf. 2 Cor 9:10). Therefore, the **sower** and the **reaper** will **rejoice together** when *pain and sorrow and sighing have fled away* in the age to come (Isa 35:10 LXX). Everyone, whoever they are, will agree with what has been read: *many will come from east and west and sit at table with Abraham, Isaac, and Jacob in the kingdom of heaven* (Matt 8:11).

(38) John Chrysostom

Do you not say, "There are yet four months, then comes the harvest"? I tell you, lift up your eyes, and see how the fields are already white for the harvest (4:35). Behold how Christ uses common words to guide them to understand the greatest things. In saying **food** he signified nothing other than the salvation of those who would come. The **field** and the **harvest** signify the same thing: the multitude of souls prepared to receive his preaching. The **eyes** he speaks of here are those of both the mind and the body (for they now saw the multitude of the Samaritans coming). The readiness of their will he called **the fields already white**. Just as when ears of corn have become **white** when they are ready for **harvest**ing, so also, he says, are those now prepared and made ready for salvation.

Why didn't he say clearly that the people who were prepared to receive his word, who had been instructed by the prophets and were now bringing forth fruit, were coming to believe? Why does he speak instead about **fields** and **harvests**? What is his intention with these figures of speech? He does this not just here, but all throughout the gospel. The prophets also use the same figure of speech, saying many things metaphorically. What, then, is the reason for this, for the grace of the Spirit didn't ordain these things thoughtlessly? Why then? What's the reason? There are two reasons. First, so that his speech might paint a more vivid picture before our eyes.

For when the mind is inspired to behold an ordinary object as an image depicted in a painting, the image takes on even greater significance. This is one reason. The second is to sweeten the description so that the memory of what is said might last longer. For a declarative statement doesn't overwhelm and grip the hearer as much as a depiction through popular images and the portrayal of experience. Christ's parable accomplishes this with great wisdom.

(39) Cyril of Alexandria

Do you not say, "There are yet four months, then comes the harvest"? (4:35). Christ makes the present circumstances the occasion for his discourse, and uses more common observations to form his narrative about spiritual ideas. It was **yet** winter at that time, and the fresh buds of new seedlings were barely emerging from the soil. With **four months** gone, they await the **harvest** at the hand of the reaper. Christ says, **Do you not say, "There are yet four months, then comes the harvest"? I tell you, lift up your eyes, and see how the fields are already white for harvest** (4:35). That is, lifting up the eye of understanding a little from earthly matters, behold the spiritual sowing. It has **whitened** and advanced already to the threshing-floor. Already it summons the reaper's sickle.

We can understand the clear meaning here through a comparison with daily life. Understand that the spiritual sowing and the large array of spiritual ears of corn are those who have been cultivated beforehand by the voice of the prophets and have been brought to faith in Christ. They are **white** because they have been made ripe **already**—prepared for faith and molded toward piety. The reaper's sickle is the glimmering, incisive word of the apostles, shearing off the hearers from their worship according to the law, and moving them to the threshing-floor, that is, to the church of God. There, being ground and pressed with good works, they will be presented as pure wheat, worthy of the gatherer's granary.

John 4:43–54

[43] After the two days he departed to Galilee. [44] For Jesus himself testified that a prophet has no honor in his own country. [45] So when he came to Galilee, the Galileans welcomed him, having seen all that he had done in Jerusalem at the feast, for they too had gone to the feast. [46] So he came again to Cana in Galilee, where he had made the water wine. And at Caper'na-um there was an official whose son was ill. [47] When he heard that Jesus had come from Judea to Galilee, he went and begged him to come down and heal his son, for he was at the point of death. [48] Jesus therefore said to him, "Unless you see signs

and wonders you will not believe." ⁴⁹The official said to him, "Sir, come down before my child dies." ⁵⁰Jesus said to him, "Go; your son will live." The man believed the word that Jesus spoke to him and went his way. ⁵¹As he was going down, his servants met him and told him that his son was living. ⁵²So he asked them the hour when he began to mend, and they said to him, "Yesterday at the seventh hour the fever left him." ⁵³The father knew that was the hour when Jesus had said to him, "Your son will live"; and he himself believed, and all his household. ⁵⁴This was now the second sign that Jesus did when he had come from Judea to Galilee.

(40) John Chrysostom

Unless you see signs and wonders you will not believe (4:48). Even when the official approached to summon Christ, it was done in faith. After this, the evangelist testifies to it, saying that when Jesus said **Go; your son will live, the man believed his word and went** (4:50). So what is he saying here? Either he said these things in astonishment at the Samaritans because they believed without any signs, or he addresses Capernaum which was thought to be his own city, and the one where the official was from. Someone else in Luke says, *I believe*; and says again: *help my unbelief* (Mark 9:24).[7] So if this official believed, his belief was not entirely sound. This is clear from his inquiry about when the fever left him (cf. 4:52), for he wanted to learn whether it happened by itself or by the command of Christ. Therefore, when he knew that it was **yesterday at the seventh hour, he believed and all his household** (4:52, 53). Do you see that he believed when his servants spoke, but not when Christ spoke? So Christ spoke these things (4:48) and rebuked the official's lack of understanding when he approached him. In this way Christ drew him toward faith, because before the miracle, he had not believed strongly. . . . Here, Christ healed the father, who was weak in understanding, no less than the son, persuading us to pay attention to Christ not because of his miracles, but because of his teachings. The miracles are not for the believing, but for the unbelieving and those thicker-headed types.

(41) Augustine of Hippo

And behold there was an official, whose son was ill . . . he went to Jesus and begged him to come down, to the city or his house, **and heal his son, for he was at the point of death** (4:46–47). He who **begs**, did he not believe? What do you expect to hear from me? Ask what the Lord perceived in that man. Having been asked such things, he responds: **Unless you see signs and wonders you will not believe** (4:48). He accuses the man of being either feeble or frigid in faith, or of having no faith at all, but nevertheless a man who desires to test, by means of the health of his son, what Christ is like, who he is, and how much he is able to accomplish. Although we hear words of **begging**, we do not see a disbelieving heart; however, the one who both hears the words and gazes upon the heart divulges it to us. In the

---

7. Not in Luke as Chrysostom says.

same way, the evangelist's testimony of the story shows that the man did not yet believe, who desired that the Lord come to his own house to heal his son. After it was announced that his son was healed, and he discovered that his son was healed in that very hour in which the Lord said: **Your son will live** (4:50), then the evangelist says, **And he himself believed, and all his household** (4:53). So if that man and **all his household believed** because the health of his son was announced to him, and he compared the hour of that announcement with the hour of its being foretold when he **begged** Christ, then he was not yet believing.

(42) John Cassian

No one should think that the whole of salvation stands on the strength of our faith, according to the impious opinion of some who assign everything to free will and assert that the grace of God is dispensed according to the merit of each person. We, however, proclaim clearly and absolutely the opinion that the grace of God sometimes overflows and goes beyond even the constraints of human faithlessness. We recall that this was the case with that **official** in the gospel who believed it was easier to **heal** his **ill son** than to raise him when dead. He **begged** the Lord to come quickly, saying: **Sir, come down before my child dies** (4:49). For this faithlessness Christ rebuked him with these words: **Unless you see signs and wonders you will not believe** (4:48). Nevertheless, he did not exercise his divine grace according to the man's weak faith, nor did he rid that deadly **feverish illness** by his bodily presence, as the man supposed was necessary, but by the word of his power, he said, **Go; your son will live** (4:50).

(43) Cyril of Alexandria

The **official** comes as to one with power to heal, but he does not yet understand that he is by nature God. He calls him **Sir** (4:49), but does not at all give him the true dignity of lordship. He should have immediately fallen before him, not simply so that he might visit his home and accompany him to the **ill son**, but so that with authority and God-befitting action, Christ might drive away the sickness that fell on him. Why was it necessary for Jesus to be present with the **ill** boy, whom he was certainly able to **heal** even if absent? . . .

Jesus therefore said to him, "Unless you see signs and wonders you will not believe" (4:48). The official ought to have come to Jesus believing, but here we see that Christ does not contend with our ignorance. As God, he again displays kindness even to those who stumble. Therefore, Jesus teaches the man what he should have been respected for doing, even though he did not do it. He reveals himself at once as the author of the best things and the supplier of good things in prayer. In the command **Go** (4:50), there is faith, and in the phrase **your son will live** (4:50), there is the fulfillment of the official's desires, being carried out with some great and God-befitting authority.

The man believed the word that Jesus spoke to him and went his way. As he was going down, his servants met him and told him that his son was living (4:50–51). The one command of the Savior immediately heals two souls. In the **official** he produces unusual faith, but also rescues the child from bodily death. Which healing occurred first is difficult to say. I suppose both occurred simultaneously, the disease being released at the command of our Savior. When the **servants** met the official and reported the child's healing, it made clear the swiftness of the divine commands (Christ himself very clearly arranging this). And with the fulfillment of his hope, their master's weak faith is quickly and firmly bolstered.

(44) Gregory the Great

From the reading of the holy gospel you have just heard, brothers and sisters . . . I see that this alone requires an explanation: why did the one who came seeking a cure for his son hear the words: **Unless you see signs and wonders, you will not believe** (4:48)? The one who sought a cure for his son certainly **believe**d. He would never have sought a cure from him unless he **believe**d that he could do it. So why did Christ say, **Unless you see signs and wonders, you will not believe** (4:48)? The official **believe**d before he saw a sign!

Remember, however, what he asked for and you will know plainly that he wavered in his faith. He asked for Jesus to come down and heal his son. He sought the physical presence of the Lord, who is nowhere absent in his spirit. So he did not fully **believe** in the one whom he considered unable to heal unless he was physically present. If he had believed completely, he would have known that there is no place where God is not present. Therefore, he was distrustful to a large degree, because he did not honor the greatness of God, but merely his bodily presence. So while he asked for his son to be cured, he doubted in his faith. He had come to someone whom he believed capable of healing, but he thought this man was absent from his dying son. But the Lord, who was asked to come quickly, demonstrated that he was not absent from the place to which he was summoned, and the one who created everything by his own will restored the boy's health by his command alone.

John 5

The Sheep Gate surrounded by the ill and lame drew the attention of many of the early church fathers. Tertullian, Ambrose, Augustine, and John Chrysostom each sought to explain the bizarre account regarding the agitation of the water: For an angel went down at a certain time into the pool and stirred up the water; then whoever stepped in first, after the stirring of the water, was made well of whatever disease he had *(5:4).[1] Some interpreted the pool as a figure of the baptismal font in which the water with the intervention of the angel of God removes sins and provides healing. For Augustine, the water in the pool symbolized the Jewish people who were stirred up by the words and actions of Christ. However, for those who left behind the five porticoes, which signified the five books of the law of Moses, and entered the pool, there was healing. Bede follows Augustine's exegetical lead but slightly changes his own exposition. According to him, the movement of the water symbolizes the Lord's passion caused by the Jews being agitated against him. Those who entered the pool of baptism were healed and freed from the porticoes of the law. John Chrysostom and Bede both find significance in the description of the paralytic:* One man was there, who had been ill for thirty-eight years *(5:5). John Chrysostom marvels at his tenacity and perseverance and exhorts his own congregation to pattern their faith after this example. Bede finds numerical symbolism in this and concludes that this detail hints at his illness. He calculates that there are ten commandments and four gospels, which taken as a whole offer the complete disclosure of God's perfect law, symbolized by the number forty. However, the paralytic lacks the dual command upon which all these hang: to love God and love neighbor. Therefore, he* had been ill for thirty-eight years *(5:5).*

Augustine found Jesus's tripartite command equally puzzling. He comments that Jesus certainly healed the paralytic with the word: Rise *(5:8)! What then is the reason for the two additional commands? He concludes that they reflect the dual command to love God and love neighbor.* Take up your pallet *(5:8)[2] calls to mind Paul's exhortation: Bear one*

---

1. Some ancient manuscripts insert verse 4 into chapter 5. Although the RSV does not include verse 4, it has been inserted in the biblical citation below and marked off with brackets, because many of the church fathers comment on it.

2. While the RSV uses the word *pallet*, other translations have *mat* (NRSV) or *bed* (NKJV) as alternative translations. These all hint at the underlying Greek word, which means "a poor person's bed."

another's burdens, and so fulfill the law of Christ (Gal 6:2). Augustine concludes that this command pertains to the love of one's neighbor. Walk *(5:8) is expounded as the command to love God.*

Several of the church fathers, including Gregory of Nazianzus, John Chrysostom, and Cyril of Jerusalem, comment on Jesus's exhortation to the healed paralytic: Sin no more, that nothing worse befall you *(5:14). For Gregory, this poignantly shows that sin is to be taken seriously; sin is equated with illness and death! Cyril of Jerusalem similarly warns his audience that sin has dire consequences but that Christ's grace, which conquers sin, is free. John Chrysostom notes that illness can be an admonishment in this life for sin. However, he stresses that not all illness is a result of sin.*

As this chapter unfolds, several statements by Christ provide the occasion for lengthy expositions on the relationship of the Father and the Son. This was why the Jews sought all the more to kill him, because he not only broke the Sabbath but also called God his Father, making himself equal with God *(5:18). Hilary of Poitiers states that the Jews knew who he was and what he was claiming, and this is why they sought to kill him. Augustine is more nuanced. He states that they were wrong in their appraisal that he was* making himself equal with God, *because he was begotten as equal with God. They saw the flesh but did not perceive the Word. The following verse drew many clarifying comments:* Jesus said to them, "Truly, truly, I say to you, the Son can do nothing of his own accord, but only what he sees the Father doing" *(5:19). Cyril of Alexandria, Ambrose, Hilary, and Theodore of Mopsuestia argue that the phrase* can do nothing of his own accord *does not connote weakness or inequality. Rather, it indicates an equality of essence. Christ does the same things as the Father, because he carries out the same work though he has taken on human flesh.*

Augustine wrestles with how to interpret Christ's statement about eternal life in light of the doctrine of the final resurrection and judgment: Truly, truly, I say to you, he who hears my word and believes him who sent me, has eternal life; he does not come into judgment, but has passed from death to life *(5:24). Although at first glance this statement might seem to contradict other passages in the New Testament, Augustine contends that Scripture is both complementary and true. He argues that this verse speaks of a resurrection before the resurrection. Those who believe in Christ are raised to the Christian life, and they pass from death to a life of faith.*

Gregory the Great exhorts the faithful to follow Christ's example of humility: I seek not my own will but the will of him who sent me *(5:30). Augustine and Cyril find numerous examples of faithful people who testified to Christ throughout the Scriptures. While John the Baptist is specifically called* a burning and shining lamp *(5:35), they state that all the words and people who testified to Christ were lamps casting light in the darkness. John Chrysostom, however, notes that this testimony is not always clear and the meaning is not always evident. The Jews thought that they understood the Scriptures. Jesus chastises them:* You search the scriptures, because you think that in them you have eternal life; and it is they that bear witness to me; yet you refuse to come to me that you may have life *(5:39–40). For John Chrysostom and Cyril of Alexandria, the Jews failed to find the meaning of the Scriptures, because they failed to see that they point to Christ Jesus. That said, both commentators agree that the meaning is sometimes hidden in passages that are subtle and difficult to understand.*

John 5:1–5

[1]After this there was a feast of the Jews, and Jesus went up to Jerusalem. [2]Now there is in Jerusalem by the Sheep Gate a pool, in Hebrew called Bethzatha, which has five porticoes.[3] [3]In these lay a multitude of invalids, blind, lame, paralyzed. [[4]For an angel went down at a certain time into the pool and stirred up the water; then whoever stepped in first, after the stirring of the water, was made well of whatever disease he had.] [5]One man was there, who had been ill for thirty-eight years.

5:1 After this there was a feast of the Jews, and Jesus went up to Jerusalem.

---

(1) Irenaeus of Lyons

According to the Jewish custom, every year Jews from the whole country assembled at Jerusalem and celebrated the paschal feast there. At the time of the Passover, the Lord also went up to Jerusalem after his baptism. After he had made wine out of water at Cana of Galilee, he went up for the first time to the paschal feast (cf. John 2:1–11). At that time John, the Lord's disciple, wrote that *many believed in his name when they saw the signs which he did* (2:23). From there, Jesus withdrew to Samaria, where he conversed with the Samaritan woman (4:1–42) and cured the centurion's son with a word spoken from a distance, saying, *Go; your son will live* (4:50). After these events, he went up to Jerusalem for the **feast** (5:1) of the Passover a second time. Then he cured the paralytic who was lying by the pool for **thirty-eight years** (5:5). *Jesus said to him, "Rise, take up your pallet, and walk"* (5:8). After departing from there, he crossed over the sea of Tiberius and found a great multitude which had followed him. He satisfied the whole crowd with five loaves (6:12). Afterward, there remained *twelve baskets filled with fragments* (6:13). Finally, after he had raised Lazarus from the dead (11:1–44) and the Pharisees plotted against him (11:54), he withdrew into the city of Ephraim. It is written that *six days before the Passover, Jesus came to Bethany* (12:1). From Bethany, Jesus went up to Jerusalem, ate the Passover meal, and suffered on the following day. Every person will agree that these three celebrations of the Passover are not from a single year.

---

3. Some ancient manuscripts read alternatively Bethesda and Bethsaida.

5:2-5 Now there is in Jerusalem by the Sheep Gate a pool . . . which has five porticoes. In these lay a multitude of invalids, blind, lame, paralyzed. For an angel went down at a certain time into the pool and stirred up the water; then whoever stepped in first, after the stirring of the water, was made well of whatever disease he had.

---

(2) Tertullian of Carthage

If it seems strange for an **angel** (5:4) to enter into the water, it should be understood as an anticipation of what is to come.[4] An **angel**, after entering the water, **stirred up the pool** of Bethsaida (5:4). Those who complained of various illnesses continually watched for the disturbance. For whoever was the first to enter into the water, stopped complaining after he washed in the **pool**. This figure of corporeal healing proclaims a spiritual healing according to the rule that carnal things always prefigure spiritual ones (cf. 1 Cor 15:46). Therefore, when the grace of God advanced among men (1:16-17), more power was granted to the **waters** and to the **angel**. They who previously cured the defects of the body now heal the spirit. They who used to bring temporal health now restore eternal health. They who set an individual free once a year, now save people daily since death is destroyed though the washing away of sins (cf. Rom 6:3-4). When the guilt is removed, then the penalty is also removed. In this way, humans will be restored to *likeness* with God, who previously were made in the *image* of God (Gen 1:26-27).[5] The *image* is thought to be in a man's form and the *likeness* in his eternity. Truly, he receives once again the Spirit of God which he had first received from his divine breath but had subsequently lost through sin.

(3) Ambrose of Milan

Don't believe only what you can see with your eyes. For if you do, you will not be able to proclaim the great mystery *which no eye has seen, nor ear heard, nor the heart of man conceived* (1 Cor 2:9). I see water every day. Is the water in which I bathed without ever being fully cleansed able to cleanse me now? In this way, you may realize that water does not cleanse without the Spirit. Understand that the three elements in baptism—*the water, the blood*, and *the Spirit* (cf. 1 John 5:6)—are one. If you take away one of these, it is no longer the sacrament of baptism. For what is water without the cross of Christ? It is just ordinary water deprived of any sacramental effect. Similarly, there is no sacrament of rebirth without water! Jesus said, *Unless one is born of water and the Spirit, he cannot enter the kingdom of God* (3:5). Even the catechumen believes in the cross of the Lord Jesus with which he is

---

4. Tertullian has in mind the sacrament of baptism.

5. Many of the early church fathers held that humans received the image of God at creation but will receive the likeness to God only when they reach spiritual perfection. Tertullian here is connecting that perfection with baptism, which is considered a spiritual rebirth.

marked. However, unless he is baptized in the name of the Father, Son, and Holy Spirit, he cannot receive remission of sins nor gain this spiritual gift.

A certain Syrian [Naaman] *immersed himself seven times* (cf. 2 Kgs 5:14) under the law, but you were baptized in the name of the Trinity. Remember what you did: you confessed the Father, the Son, and the Holy Spirit. Note well the order of events in this faith: you died to the world and rose again to God. You were buried to the world, so to speak, in the water and died to sin. Then, you rose again to eternal life. Therefore, believe that these waters are not devoid of power. Accordingly, it is written: **For an angel went down at a certain time into the pool and stirred up the water; then whoever stepped in first, after the stirring of the water, was made well of whatever disease he had** (5:4). This pool was in Jerusalem. Every year one person was healed in this pool, but no one was healed before the **angel** descended. The water was **stirred up** as a sign that the angel had descended for those who did not believe. They had this sign, but you have faith. For them an angel descended, but for you the Holy Spirit did; for them a created being **stirred up** the waters, but for you Christ himself, the Lord of all created beings, works.

(4) John Chrysostom

What kind of healing is this? What sort of mystery does it signify to us? These things were not written superficially or without a purpose; they sketch out for us what is to come, as in a figure and type, so that what was unusually strange and unexpected might not destroy the power of faith among the many. What then do they sketch out? First a baptism of great power was given; then, an even greater gift was bestowed, a baptism that cleansed all sins and delivered us from death to life. Therefore, these things are portrayed beforehand by the **pool** (5:4) as in a figure and in many other ways. At first, water was given which purified the stains of our bodies as well as defilements that seem to come from the flesh—from the care of the dead, from leprosy, and from other such things. For this reason in the Old Testament many things are done through **water**. . . . God first healed bodily defilements through water, and then he healed other kinds of illnesses. He desires that we approach the gift of baptism, for he no longer simply heals our defilements, he also heals our spiritual ailments.

And **an angel came down and troubled the water** (5:4) and infused it with healing powers in order that the Jews might learn that the Lord of angels is certainly capable of healing every disease of the soul. But it was not simply the nature of the water that healed; if so it would always happen. Instead, the water was combined with the activity of the **angel**. Similarly with us, it is not the water alone that works. Rather, when the water receives the grace of the Spirit, then it removes every sin. Around this **pool** lay **a multitude of invalids, blind, lame, and paralyzed waiting for the movement of the water** (5:3–4). Those who wanted to be healed were hindered by their weaknesses. But now each person has the power to move forward. It is not an **angel** who **stirs up the water**, but it is the Lord of angels who accomplishes all things. He cannot say, "Now **I have no man** to help me." He cannot say, "*While I am going, another steps down before me*" (5:7). Even if the whole world should come, Christ's grace is not used up. His activity is not exhausted but remains the same, even as much as it was before. Just as the rays of the sun shine forth each day and are not diminished and just as the light is not lessened from its great abundance, the activity of the Spirit is in no way exhausted by the **multitude** of those who use it. This miracle occurred so that those who have known for a long time that water can heal the diseases of the body might easily believe that it can also heal the diseases of the soul.

(5) Augustine of Hippo

I recall that on many occasions we have spoken about this **pool** which was encircled by **five porticoes** (5:2) where a great number of sick were lying. . . . The **pool** and the **water** (5:4) mentioned here seem to me to signify the Jewish people. That groups of people are signified by the term "waters" is clearly indicated by the Apocalypse of John, when many *waters are shown to him* (Rev 17:15). When he inquired as to what they were, John was told that the *waters* signified peoples. The water spoken of here refers to that people who were encircled by **five porticoes**. These are understood to be the five books of Moses. But those books produce sickness in men and not health! For the law convicts sinners; it does not absolve them. For that reason, the *letter* without grace led to guilt, but those who acknowledged grace were set free (cf. 2 Cor 3:6). For the apostle says *if a law had been given which could make alive, then righteousness would indeed be by the law* (Gal 3:21). Why, then, was the law given? He goes on to say: *The scripture consigned all things to sin, that what was promised to faith in Jesus Christ might be given to those who believe* (Gal 3:22). What could be more evident? Do these words not explain to us the five porticoes and the crowds of sick people? The **five porticoes** are the books of the law. Why did the **five porticoes** not heal the sick? Because *if a law had been given which could make alive, then righteousness would indeed be by the law* (Gal 3:21). Why then did the **porticoes** continue to hold those whom they were not healing? Because *the scripture consigned all things to sin, that what was promised to faith in Jesus Christ might be given to those who believe* (Gal 3:22).

How did it happen then that those who were not healed in the **porticoes** (5:2) were healed in the moving **water** (5:4)? For suddenly the **water** seemed to be moved, although the one who moved it was not seen. Of course, you believe that this happened by angelic power. Yet it is not without some deeper significance. After the **water** moved, the one who was able threw himself into the **pool**, and he alone was healed. Anyone who threw himself in after that first one did so in vain. What, therefore, does this mean except that when Christ came to the Jewish people he disturbed sinners by doing great things and teaching useful things? Just as here, he disturbed the water with his own presence and roused it to point toward his suffering. Although he remained concealed, he was the one who agitated the **water** (5:4).

5:5 One man was there, who had been ill for thirty-eight years.

(6) John Chrysostom

Be ashamed! Be ashamed! Deplore our great laziness! **This sick man** spent **thirty-eight years** lying there (5:5). He did not get what he wished for, but he did not give up. Nor did he get any help. This was not due to his own carelessness but because he was pushed aside by others and treated poorly. Even though he was treated this way, he did not lose heart. By contrast, if we pray diligently for ten days seeking some favor and do not receive it, then we are reluctant to try again in the future with the same eagerness. In our human pursuits we have no difficulty persevering for a long time—doing military service, engaging in strenuous labor, and doing menial work—and often we lose that which we hoped to gain in the end. But we are not able to persevere in the service of our Lord with the requisite effort. This is true in spite of the fact that it is possible to receive from him a reward which far outstrips our efforts. As Scripture says, *hope does not disappoint* (Rom 5:5).

(7) Venerable Bede

One man was there, who had been ill for thirty-eight years (5:5). This man, who was imprisoned by his illness for decades, signifies any sinner who is weighed down by the scale and number of his wicked deeds. The length of his illness also signifies the seriousness of his guilt. He had been oppressed by this infirmity for forty years minus two. In Scripture the number forty, which is produced by multiplying ten by four, usually signifies the perfection of a right way of life. Anyone who does the works of a perfect way of life fulfills the ten commandments of the law in accordance with the four books of the holy gospel. However, anyone who lives in such a way as to neglect the love of God and neighbor, which Scripture extols equally both in the law and in the gospel, falls short of perfection by two.

John 5:6–13

[6]When Jesus saw him and knew that he had been lying there a long time, he said to him, "Do you want to be healed?" [7]The sick man answered him, "Sir, I have no man to put me into the pool when the water is troubled, and while I am going another steps down before me." [8]Jesus said to him, "Rise, take up your pallet, and walk." [9]And at once the man was healed, and he took up his pallet and walked. Now that day was the Sabbath. [10]So the Jews said to the man who was cured, "It is the Sabbath, it is not lawful for you to carry your pallet." [11]But he answered them, "The man who healed me said to me, 'Take up your pallet, and walk.'" [12]They asked him, "Who is the man who said to you, 'Take up your pallet, and walk'?" [13]Now the man who had been healed did not know who it was, for Jesus had withdrawn, as there was a crowd in the place.

5:6–8 When Jesus saw him and knew that he had been lying there a long time, he said to him, "Do you want to be healed?" The sick man answered him, "Sir, I have no man to put me into the pool when the water is troubled, and while I am going another steps down before me." Jesus said to him, "Rise, take up your pallet, and walk."

(8) Cyril of Jerusalem

So Jesus approached **the sick man** (5:7); uninvited, the doctor visited the patient. It should not surprise us that he visited the man lying by the pool, since he came down to us uninvited from heaven. **Do you want to be healed?** (5:6), he asked him. By means of this question, he led him on to knowledge and aroused him in turn to question. This was a great and gracious gift. He could not pay the fee, so he has a voluntary healer. "Yes, Lord," he replied. "My protracted sufferings have made me desire to be healthy. I do long for it, but **I have no man**" (5:7). Do not be downcast, my friend, because you **have no man**. You have God standing beside you, who is in one respect man, in another God, for we must profess both truths. To acknowledge his humanity without acknowledging his divinity is useless. Rather, it brings a curse, for *Cursed is the man who trusts in man* (Jer 17:5). . . . You have the fountain, *for with you is the fountain of life* (Ps 36:9), the fountain which is the source of all fountains. If anyone drinks from this water, *rivers of living water shall flow* (7:38), not water that flows downward, but water that *wells up* (4:14)—for Jesus's water does not make us leap down from above but leap up from earthly things to heavenly ones—water that *wells up to eternal life* (4:14). For Jesus is the source of blessings. . . . You have the one who walked on the waters, who rebuked the winds, who controlled the sea, the one beneath whom the sea was spread like a floor, and who gave Peter the same power to walk on it. When there was no glimmer in the night, the Light was there unrecognized. For as he walked on the waters, no one recognized him by glimpsing his face, but the familiar voice revealed his presence. Thinking they saw a ghost, they were terror-struck. But Jesus said to them, *Take heart, it is I; have no fear* (Matt 14:27). Peter replied, *Lord, if it is you*—or rather the one whom the Father has revealed to me—*bid me come to you on the water* (Matt 14:28–29). "*Come*," said Jesus, unstinting in sharing his gifts.

So the one who controlled and created the waters was there beside the water of the pool. **I have no man**, the paralytic said to him, **to put me into the pool when the water is troubled** (5:7). "Why are you waiting for the waters to be disturbed?" the Savior asked him. Do not be disturbed; be healed! Why are you waiting for a visible movement? The word of command is swifter than thought. Simply look at the power of the spring and recognize God appearing in the flesh. Do not judge by his appearance, but by the word which he accomplishes through the appearance. **I have no man to put me into the pool when the water is troubled** (5:7). "Why do you wait for what is trivial?" Jesus asked him. Why do you look to the waters for healing? The Resurrection has told you, "**Rise** up." The Savior is everything for everyone everywhere: bread for the hungry, water for the thirsty, resurrection for the dead, a physician for the sick, redemption for the sinner.

Jesus said to him, **Rise, take up your pallet, and walk** (5:8). The disease had been protracted, but the treatment was instantaneous; for years the sinews had been paralyzed, instantaneously they were restored. For the very creator of the sinews was here, the one who contrived the various cures for the blind and who used a salve of mud to dispense a miraculous remedy. If mud is applied to a man who can see, it impedes his vision; but Jesus used mud to give sight to the blind (John 9:1–7). In other cases Jesus used other means to exercise his healing power: in this case by the words **Rise, take up your pallet, and walk** (5:8). Imagine the onlookers' amazement! Regardless how wonderful the sight, their lack of faith was strange. The years-old disease was cured, but the protracted incredulity was not. The Jews remained ill and had no desire to be cured.

(9) Augustine of Hippo

Jesus said three things: **Rise, take up your pallet, and walk** (5:8). **Rise** was not a command for action, but the working of the cure! But he commanded two other things of the cured man: **Take up your pallet and walk** (5:8). I ask you, why would **walk** not suffice? Or why would **rise** not be enough? When that man **rose**, he was already healed. He would not have remained in that place. Would he not have arisen for the very purpose of leaving there? For this reason, it is curious to me that Jesus, after finding him lying there without two things, ordered him to do two things. It is as if by ordering him to do these two things, he completed what the sick man was lacking.

How might we find those two commandments of love signified in these commands of the Lord? He said, **Take up your pallet and walk** (5:8). Brothers and sisters, call to mind with me what those two commandments are. They should be very well known. They should not be remembered only when they are mentioned to us but should never be absent from your hearts. Remember always that God and neighbor must be loved: *God with all your heart, and with all your soul, and with all your mind* and *your neighbor as yourself* (Matt 22:37–39). These commands must always be considered carefully, pondered, preserved, acted upon, and fulfilled. The love of God is prioritized in respect to the order of the commands, but the love of neighbor takes precedence in the order of action. No one who would teach you these two commands would recommend the love of neighbor first and the love of God second, but God first and the neighbor second. However, because you do not yet see God, you become worthy of seeing him by loving your neighbor; by loving your neighbor, you purify your eyes for seeing God, as John clearly says, *For he who does not love his brother whom he has seen, cannot love God whom he has not seen* (1 John 4:20).

Notice that you are told to *love God* (Matt 22:37). If you say to me, "Show me whom I am to love," what will I say except that which John himself says, *No one has ever seen God* (1:18)? But you must not think that you are wholly unsuited to seeing God, for he says, *God is love, and he who abides in love abides in God* (1 John 4:16). Therefore, love your neighbor and look inside yourself to discover where that love is coming from. As much as you are able, you will see God there. Begin to love your neighbor. *Break your bread with the one who is hungry, and bring the homeless poor into your house, if you see one naked, clothe him, and you shall not neglect any of the relatives of your seed. Then the light shall break forth early in the morning* (Isa 58:7–8). Your God is both your *light* and your *dawn*, because he will come to you after the darkness of this world, for he neither rises nor sets, because he endures forever. . . . Therefore, it seems to me that the phrase **Take up your pallet** (5:8) means *Love your neighbor* (Matt 22:39).

The reason why the *love of neighbor* is represented by **taking up your pallet** is still hidden and requires more explanation. It should not upset us that a *neighbor* is represented by a pallet which is an inert and unthinking object. Let the *neighbor* not be upset if he is represented to us as an object that lacks a soul and sense perception. Our Lord and Savior, Jesus Christ, was called a *cornerstone*, because he was joining together in himself two peoples (Eph 2:20). He was also called a rock from which water gushed forth: *And the Rock was Christ* (1 Cor 10:4). What is so strange about a neighbor being wood if Christ is a rock? Yet the neighbor is not just any ordinary kind of wood, just as Christ is not any ordinary rock, but one from which water gushed forth for the thirsty (Num 20:11; cf. 1 Cor 10:4). Nor was Christ an ordinary stone but a *cornerstone* which joins together two walls coming from different directions. Nor should you understand the neighbor to be ordinary wood, but a **pallet**. *Bear one another's burdens, and so fulfill the law of Christ* (Gal 6:2). Therefore, the *law of Christ* is love, and love is not fulfilled unless we *bear one another's burdens. Bearing with one another in love*, he says, *eager to maintain the unity of the Spirit in the bond of peace* (Eph 4:2–3). When you were sick, your *neighbor* carried you. Since you have been healed, carry your *neighbor. Bear one another's burdens, and so fulfill the law of Christ* (Gal 6:2). In this way you will *fulfill* what was lacking to you.

Take up your pallet (5:8). But when you have taken it up, do not stay. **Walk**! By loving and caring for your neighbor, you are traveling on a journey. Where are you going, except to the Lord God, whom we must love with *all our heart, and with all our soul, and with all our mind* (Matt 22:37)? We have not yet reached the Lord, but our neighbor is with us. So carry your neighbor, who is traveling with you, so that you may reach him with whom you long to dwell. Therefore, **take up your pallet and walk** (5:8).

5:9 And at once the man was healed, and he took up his pallet and walked. Now that day was the Sabbath.

---

(10) Cyril of Jerusalem

If they should have marveled at the event, they would have also worshiped the healer of souls and bodies. But they grumbled, for grumbling ran in their family (Exod 15:24; 16:2). They inverted good and evil, calling bitter sweet and sweet bitter. With full deliberation, Jesus used to work on the Sabbath, doing works that transcended the Sabbath in order to teach a lesson by the very act of working. . . . He offered an object lesson by healing on the Sabbath, not pitting argument against argument, but using the work to persuade the onlookers.

They said, **It is the Sabbath, it is not lawful for you to carry your pallet** (5:10). Although the lawgiver himself was present, he was not the one who said "it is not lawful." The text *Appoint, O Lord, a lawgiver against them* (Ps 9:20 [9:21 LXX]) refers to the Savior. They were at once answered by the man who had just been healed in soul and body. Wisdom lent him wise words; although he was unable to answer them in legal terms, his reply was concise. He said, "You are all aware how long I have been ill, how many years I have been bed-ridden and how helpless my case has been. Not one of you ever did me the service of lifting me up and putting me first into the pool to be cured. So when you have done nothing to help me, why do you now act like lawyers and say: **It is not lawful for you to carry your pallet on the Sabbath** (5:10)? I can answer you very briefly: **the man who cured me told me** to do it. You may think nothing of me, but the event should leave you dumbfounded. He put no ointment on me; he employed no medical techniques or aids. He simply spoke, and the effect followed. He gave me an order, and I am obeying it. I trust his command, because his command healed me. If the man who gave me the order did not have the power to heal me by his orders, it would not be right for me to obey him. But since my illness, which for many years has been plain to see, has ceased at his command, it is right for me to listen to him, seeing that my illness has listened to him and departed. It was the man who healed me who said to me: **Take up your pallet**" (5:11).

(11) John Chrysostom

This healing is certainly wonderful, but the event that took place afterward is much more so! For him to believe at first when no one was harassing him is surely not as marvelous as later when the Jews were raging, encircling, accusing, and besieging him. Although they said, **It is not lawful for you to carry your pallet** (5:10), he not only ignored their rage but even proclaimed with amazing courage his healer in the very midst of them and put an end to their shameless talk. I think that this was very brave. When the Jews were conspiring against him and saying in a disparaging and insolent manner, **It is the Sabbath, it is not lawful for you to carry your pallet** (5:10), listen to what he said: **The man who healed me said to me, "Take up your pallet, and walk"** (5:11). By this reply, it was as though he was saying, "You are insane and out of your minds if you think that I, after being cured of a long and difficult illness, will disparage my healer and not obey his every command! If the cured man wished to be unscrupulous, he could have said something very different: "I did not do this on my own, but someone else told me to do it. If this action is unlawful, blame the one who ordered me to do it, and I will put down my **pallet**." By this, he would have downplayed the cure. In this scenario, he would have done this, because he knew that they were angrier with Jesus because he cured the sick than that he himself violated the Sabbath. But in fact the man who had been cured did not conceal his healing. He did not speak in that way nor did he offer any excuse, but he acknowledged his healer and proclaimed all this in a loud voice.

(12) Cyril of Alexandria

And at once the man was healed, and he took up his pallet and walked. Now that day was the Sabbath (5:8–9). This command illustrates clearly that he is God and that he has power and authority over humanity! Jesus does not pray for the man who is lying there to be freed from his sickness. This would make Christ seem like one of the holy prophets. Instead, as the Lord of Power, he authoritatively commands it to happen. He tells the man to go home joyfully and to take his **pallet** on his shoulders. This was to serve as a reminder of the power of Jesus who healed him. At once the sick man did what was commanded and obtained through his obedience and faith the gift which he had desired for so long. . . . Christ heals the man on the **Sabbath**. Immediately after the man is healed, Jesus orders him to break the law. He convinces him to walk on the **Sabbath**. He is even weighted down by his **pallet**! Yet God clearly cries out through one of his holy prophets: *Do not carry burdens out of your houses on the day of the Sabbath* (Jer 17:22). Certainly no one who is rational would say that this man became completely disdainful of the divine command. Rather, this is a type. Christ was teaching the Jews that they should be healed by obedience and faith in the last days of this age. I think this is what **Sabbath** means. It is the "last" day of the week. After one receives healing through faith and has been changed into a new life, the old letter of the law becomes unnecessary. The worship and customs of the Jews should be rejected as opaque mysteries. For this reason I think the blessed Paul writes with rhetorical flair to those who after experiencing the faith were returning to the law: *I say to you that if you receive circumcision, Christ will be of no advantage to you* (Gal 5:2); and also, *You are severed from Christ, you who would be justified by the law; you have fallen away from grace* (Gal 5:4).

5:13 Now the man who had been healed did not know who it was, for Jesus had withdrawn, as there was a crowd in the place.

---

(13) Cyril of Jerusalem

Now the man who had been healed did not know who [his healer] was (5:13). We can see how far our Savior was from vainglory. Having worked the cure, he slipped away, not wanting to receive credit for the cure. We do just the opposite. If we ever experience dreams or perform works of healing with our hands or drive away demons by an invocation, we are so far from hiding our success that we boast of it even before we are questioned. Jesus teaches us by his own example not to speak about ourselves.

John 5:14–18

[14]Afterward, Jesus found him in the temple, and said to him, "See, you are well! Sin no more, that nothing worse befall you." [15]The man went away and told the Jews that it was Jesus who had healed him. [16]And this was why the Jews persecuted Jesus, because he did this on the Sabbath. [17]But Jesus answered them, "My Father is working still, and I am working." [18]This was why the Jews sought all the more to kill him, because he not only broke the Sabbath but also called God his Father, making himself equal with God.

5:14 Afterward, Jesus found him in the temple, and said to him, "See, you are well! Sin no more, that nothing worse befall you."

---

(14) Cyril of Jerusalem

Once the cure was provided, Jesus slipped away so as not to receive the credit. He withdrew at the right time and came back at the right time. In order to set the healing of the soul alongside the physical cure, he came once the crowd had dispersed, and **said to him, "See, you are well! Sin no more, that nothing worse befall you"** (5:14). What a versatile healer! Sometimes he heals the soul before the body, sometimes vice versa. **Sin no more, that nothing worse befall you.** This one example contains a general lesson, for the words apply not only to that one man but to us all. If ever we suffer illness or grief or hardship, we should not blame God. *God cannot be tempted with evil and he himself tempts no one* (Jas 1:13). Each of us *is bound by the ropes of his own sin* (Prov 5:22 LXX) and scourged. **Sin no more, that nothing worse befall you.** Let everyone attend to these words. Let the fornicator now set aside his lust; let the miser now turn almsgiver; let the thief now heed the words, **Sin no more!** God's forgiveness is great; his grace is generous. But do not let the vastness of his mercy lead you to presumption or make his forbearance a reason for sin. Rather let your carnal passions in the future be healed and make the following words your own since they fit your case so well: *While we were living in the flesh, our sinful passions, aroused by the law, were at work in our members . . .* (Rom 7:5). When the apostle said, *While we were living in the flesh*, he was not speaking of the flesh which clothes us but of our carnal actions . . . for he was still clothed in flesh himself. But just as God said before bringing about the flood, *My spirit shall not abide in these humans forever, because they are flesh . . .* (Gen 6:3)—for the spirit had been transformed into carnal desire—in the same sense the apostle says, *While we were living in the flesh. . . .*

> **Sin no more, that nothing worse befall you.** These words contain a message for us all; I only wish everyone had ears to hear them. When words reach the hearing of the flesh, they are not always admitted to the mind. This is what the Savior implied when he said, *He who has ears to hear, let him hear* (Matt 11:15), for he was speaking to people who had the ears of the flesh. So let everyone listen to Jesus, avoid sin in the future, and run instead to the one who forgives our sins. If we are ill, let us seek refuge with him; if our spirits are afflicted, let us have recourse to the doctor of knowledge; if we are hungry, let us accept his bread; if we are dead, let us share his resurrection; if we have grown old in ignorance, let us ask Wisdom to grant us wisdom.

(15) John Chrysostom

Afterward, Jesus found him in the temple, and said to him, "See, you are well! Sin no more, that nothing worse befall you" (5:14). Sin is a terrible thing. It is horrible and the ruin of the soul! Evil deeds often by their very excesses overflow and attack the body. While it is generally true that when the soul itself is diseased we feel no pain, we use every power at our disposal to free the body of its sickness even when it is subject to even a small amount of pain. This is because we are aware of the illness. For this reason, God often punishes the body for the transgressions of the soul in order that through the punishment of the inferior part (i.e., the body), the better part might receive some healing as well. . . . Christ did this very thing when he said: **See, you are well! Sin no more, that nothing worse befall you.**

What do we learn from this? First, we discover that the disease developed in him as a result of sin. Second, that the doctrine of hell should be believed. Third, that long and unending punishment is a reality. Where then are the people who ask, "Must I suffer an eternal punishment when I committed a murder which took only one hour or committed adultery which lasted only for a moment?" Yes! Notice that the paralytic had not sinned for as many years as he suffered punishment. Truly, sins are judged according to the nature of the offense not according to the time it took to commit them. . . . Someone will ask, "Why are not all punished in this way?" Certainly we see many people who do evil who nonetheless are healthy, vigorous, and enjoying great fortune. Let us not be encouraged in this fact; rather, let us weep especially for them. Since they have not suffered at all here, this is a guarantee of their greater suffering in the world to come. In order to demonstrate this, Paul said: *But when we are judged by the Lord, we are chastened so that we may not be condemned along with the world* (1 Cor 11:32). In this life admonishments are a form of correction, but those in the world to come are a form of punishment.

Someone will then ask, "Are all illnesses punishments for sin?" No! Not all are, but many. Some arise from laziness. I say this because gluttony, drunkenness, and idleness are the cause of some sickness. We must therefore pay attention to one thing: we should receive every punishment with gratitude. At times, the penalty comes to punish the sin. In the book of Kings, we see a man who is afflicted with a foot disease for this very reason (1 Kgs 15:23). Conversely, the punishment may be given to increase one's righteousness; God says to Job, *Do you think I have dealt with you in any other way than that you might appear to be right?* (Job 40:8 LXX [NETS]).

(16) Gregory of Nazianzus

What should I say? What is my point? Yesterday, you were like the Canaanite woman who was *bent over* by sin; today, you have been straightened up by the Word (cf. Luke 13:11).[6] Do not be *bent over* again and condemned to the earth or receive an incurable curvature as if you were weighted down with a wooden collar by the devil. Yesterday, you were like the woman being bled dry by a horrible *hemorrhage*, because you were pouring out your crimson sin (Matt 9:20). Today you have touched the *fringe* of Christ, and your bleeding has stopped and you are healthy once again (Matt 9:20). Be careful that you remain clean so that you will not again have a hemorrhage. For you might

---

6. The woman featured in Luke 13 is not identified by the gospel writer as a Canaanite. It might be that Gregory has conflated this story with the Canaanite woman whose daughter was possessed by a demon (Matt 15:22–28).

not be able to take hold of Christ once again to steal salvation. Even though he is very merciful, Christ does not like to be stolen from frequently. Yesterday, you were like the man who was lying upon a **pallet**, worn out and paralyzed (5:8). You had no one to help you into the **pool** when the water was stirred up (5:4). Today you have the one who is in one person both man and God or better God and man. You were lifted up from your pallet, or rather you took up your pallet, and confessed this gift of healing publicly. Do not be thrown down upon your bed again by sinning. Do not succumb to the evil slothfulness of a body which is paralyzed by pleasures. But remain as you are now. **Walk!** Remember his command: **See, you are well! Sin no more, that nothing worse befall you** (5:14). This will happen if you prove that you are sinful after you have received this blessing! You have heard the loud voice, crying **Lazarus, come out** (11:43) as you yourself lie in the tomb. This did not happen after four days but after many. You were freed from the wrappings of your grave clothes. Do not once again become dead. Do not live with those who *dwell in the tombs* (Mark 5:3). Do not bind yourself with the chains of your own sins, for it is not clear whether you will rise again from the tomb until the final and universal resurrection when *God will bring every deed into judgment* (Eccl 12:14). Every deed will be judged—not healed—and everyone will give an account of every deed accumulated for good or evil.

5:17–18 "My Father is working still, and I am working." . . . he . . . called God his father, making himself equal with God.

---

(17) Hilary of Poitiers

If someone doubts that the Son is equal to the Father, let him learn about Christ's nature accurately from the Jews, or at least let him learn from the gospel that he was actually born. It is written: **This was why the Jews sought all the more to kill him, because he not only broke the Sabbath but also called God his Father, making himself equal with God** (5:18). This passage is different from most others since it does not give us the words spoken by the Jews themselves, but gives us the evangelist's explanation of why they wished to kill the Lord. We see that no excuse of misunderstanding can exonerate the sinfulness of these blasphemers, for we have the evangelist's evidence that the true nature of Christ was fully revealed to them. They spoke of his birth: **[He] also called God his Father, making himself equal with God** (5:18). . . . Certainly, he announced the equality of his nature with God since he called **God his** own **Father**. It is clear that equality is by definition the absence of differences among those who are equal. Is it also not obvious on account of his birth that there is no difference between the Son and Father in respect to his nature? This is the only logical origin of true equality; birth is only capable of producing a nature equal to its very origin.

(18) Theodore of Mopsuestia

When they accused our Lord of breaking the **Sabbath**, he avoided their accusation by genuinely identifying who he was. He did not mention the others who had performed work on the **Sabbath**, even though there were many things he could have said about the invisible angels who fulfilled the divine commandments on the **Sabbath** by moving the waters in accordance with God's command (cf. 5:4). But what did he say? **My Father is working still, and I am working** (5:17). He did not want to mention those invisible beings, because everyone of them moves according to God's command. Instead, he mentioned his **Father**, who acts continually in accordance with his own will and authority. Even on the **Sabbath** he does not refrain from doing things that are for our own benefit, because he knows that any time is fitting for our salvation. Jesus mentions his **Father** in order to make it known that the authority which is in the Father is also in him. His **Father** has the authority to **work** continually, because he is not subject to the law (even though he established the law of **Sabbath** rest for others). In the same way, Jesus has an equal authority, and there is no commandment or law that prevents him from doing his will. . . .

What he means is this: "My Father never ceases from working and neither do I. Just as it is his work to carry out his plan for human beings and there is no law preventing him from this nor any regulation that impedes him from acting, so too I work whenever I want. There is no time limit for my work of saving human beings. Just as he has the authority to work, so do I. Therefore if you accuse me for working on the **Sabbath**, then you should blame the Father for working as well. If no one accuses the Father (since his dominion gives him this authority), then no one should accuse me, for I have an equal authority to work whenever I want." . . .

Breaking the **Sabbath** was a transgression of the commandment, but Christ's claim implied equality with God. If his actions are proven to be merely human, there would be no greater impiety than this. For this reason, the evangelist correctly added: **This was why the Jews sought all the more to kill him, because he not only broke the Sabbath but also called God his Father, making himself equal with God** (5:18). . . . If he had simply called God **his Father**, they would not have grumbled. But he called him **his Father** as if he was from him and equal to him in power and authority. He made this point clear when he responded to the accusation of breaking the **Sabbath** by saying, **My Father is working still, and I am working** (5:17).

However, some people, who easily distort the meaning of texts because they do not consider all the details, argue that Jesus did not **make himself equal with God**, only that the Jews thought he did. And so, according to this argument, our Lord attempted to remove their misunderstanding by responding to them: *Truly, truly, I say to you, the Son can do nothing of his own accord* (5:19). . . . From every angle we look at it, it seems to me that it would have been impossible for the Jews to come to this conclusion about our Lord on their own accord. They persecuted him, as the evangelist said, because he broke the **Sabbath**; they did not accuse him of breaking the **Sabbath** because he had **made himself equal with God**. Instead, they accused him of transgressing the commandment. The evangelist did not say that the Jews initially accused Jesus of **making himself equal** to God; only when Jesus responded, **My Father is working still, and I am working** (5:17), did the evangelist then add that they persecuted him not only for Sabbath breaking, but also because **he called God his Father, making himself equal with God** (5:18). So we are left with this conclusion: the Jews thought Jesus was **making himself equal with God** when he said that God was his Father.

(19) Augustine of Hippo

The very expression employed by the Lord, **My Father is working still** (5:17), points to the ongoing nature of God's work, by which he holds together and manages the whole of creation. It could have been understood differently if he had said, "and is now working." Then, we would not have to take the work as being continuous. But by saying **still**, he forces us to understand it in the other sense. It means from the time when he originally had established all things. Moreover, it is written about his wisdom: *She reaches with might from one end of the world to the other and orders all things well* (Wis 8:1 LXX), and it is also written that her movement is swifter and more nimble than all movements (cf. Wis 7:24). From this it is clear to those who look into the matter carefully that she bestows this incomparable and inexpressible and—if you can grasp it—her motionless movement *orders all things well*, so that undoubtedly if she abstains from this activity or withdraws this movement, they will perish immediately.

Similarly the apostle Paul when he was proclaiming God to the Athenians said that *in him we live and move and are* (Acts 17:28). Interpreted straightforwardly—to the extent of the capacity of the human mind—this will support the conviction which leads us to believe and confess that God is ceaselessly at work in all the things which he has created. We are not *in him* in respect to our substance or in the way as it is said that *he has life in himself* (5:26). But evidently, since we are something different from him, we are only *in him* because he is working at this. This is his work by which he holds all things together and by which his wisdom *reaches with might from one end of the world to the other and orders all things well* (Wis 8:1 LXX), and it is by this arrangement that *in him we live and move and are* (Acts 17:28). From this it follows that if he withdraws his work from all things, *we will neither live* nor *move* nor *be*.

It is certainly clear that God did not cease from the work of controlling the things that he had created for even a single day. If they should be deprived of the natural movements by which they are kept alive and active and so remain what they are or if God's wisdom withdrew that movement from them by which she *orders all things well*, they would indeed stop being anything at all. For this reason, we understand that the phrase God *rested from all his works* means that he did not create the natural world anymore. It does not mean however that he stopped holding together and directing the ones which he had already set in place. Thus both statements are true: that *God rested on the seventh day* (Gen 2:2) and that **he is working still** (5:17).

(20) Augustine of Hippo

For this reason, the Jews sought all the more to kill him, because not only did he break the Sabbath, but he said that God was his own Father, making himself equal to God (5:18). He did not say **that God was his own Father** in the ordinary sense. But in what way? **Making himself equal to God.** For we all say to God, *Our Father who art in heaven* (Matt 6:9). We read also that the Jews said, *For you are our Father* (Isa 63:16). Certainly, it was not because he said that God was his Father that they were angry. Rather, he said it in a very different way than men do. Notice that the Jews understand what the Arians do not, for the Arians state that the Son is not equal with the Father.[7] For this reason, this heresy was driven out of the church. The very slayers of Christ, being utterly blind, still understood the words of Christ. Yet they did not comprehend that he was the Christ nor did they perceive that he was the Son of God. Nevertheless, they did understand that these words implied that the Son of God was equal to God. They did not know who he was, but they did perceive the meaning of what he had declared: **He said that God was his own Father, making himself equal to God** (5:18). But was he not equal with God? He did *not* **make himself equal**, but he was begotten from the Father as equal. If he had made himself equal, he would be cast down on account of thieving. The one who wished to make himself equal with God, although he was not, was cast down. The angel became the devil (Isa 14:12 LXX) and gave to humans that arrogance by which he himself was cast down. The fallen one, envious of their position, said to humans: "*Eat . . . and you would be like gods*" (Gen 3:5). In other words, he said, "Seize for yourselves by force that for which you were not made and for which, through my thieving, I was cast down." He did not reveal this plainly, but he tried to persuade them of this. Christ, however, was begotten equal to the Father. He was not made but was begotten of the substance of the Father. Accordingly, the apostle Paul declares the following about him: *[He] who, though he was in the form of God, did not count equality with God a thing to be grasped* (Phil 2:6). What does the phrase *did not count equality with God a thing to be grasped* mean? He did not steal his equality with God. But he was equal to God when he was begotten. How do we become equal with God? *He emptied himself, taking the form of a servant, being born in the likeness of men* (Phil 2:7). He emptied himself not by losing what he was but by taking to himself what he was not. The Jews, despising the nature of servitude, were not able to understand that the Lord Christ was equal to the Father. They did not doubt in the least that he said this about himself. But for this very reason they were enraged against him! Despite this, he nevertheless endured and even sought to heal their rage. . . .

The Jews were moved to anger and incensed! On the one hand they were right, because a man dared to make himself equal to God. But on the other hand, they were wrong, because they did not perceive that God was in the man. They saw the body but

---

7. The primary doctrine of the Arians, which reached its apogee in the fourth and fifth centuries, posited that the Son was less than the Father in essence (*ousia*). Arians rejected the concept of equality of the Father and the Son—*homoousios*—which was included in the creedal statement at the Council of Constantinople (381) to render Arian theology a heresy.

did not know the God. They observed the residence but did not know the resident. That body was a temple: inside it, God was enshrined. It was not the *flesh* (cf. 1:14) that Jesus equated to the Father. It was not the *form of a servant* (Phil 2:7) that Jesus compared to the Lord. It was not what he became for us that was equal to the Father but what he was when he made us. You know who Christ is—I speak to true Christians—because you have believed correctly: Christ is not Word only, nor just flesh, but *the Word became flesh and dwelt among us* (1:14). I repeat once again what you already know about the Word: *In the beginning was the Word, and the Word was with God, and the Word was God* (1:1). This is equality with the Father. But *the Word became flesh and dwelt among us* (1:14). The Father is superior to this flesh. Therefore, the Father is simultaneously equal and greater. He is equal to the Word and greater than the flesh. He is equal to the Word through whom he made us, and he is greater than the one who was made for us. Let us evaluate the things we know by this central tenet of the faith. Certainly you ought to know this and hold it firmly so that your faith will not weaken and be ripped from your heart by human arguments. . . . We know that the Son of God is equal to the Father, because we know him *in the beginning* as God *the Word* (1:1). Why then did the Jews seek to kill him? **Because he not only broke the Sabbath but also called God his Father, making himself equal with God** (5:18). They saw the flesh, but they did not perceive the Word.

John 5:19-23

[19]Jesus said to them, "Truly, truly, I say to you, the Son can do nothing of his own accord, but only what he sees the Father doing; for whatever he does, that the Son does likewise. [20]For the Father loves the Son, and shows him all that he himself is doing; and greater works than these will he show him, that you may marvel. [21]For as the Father raises the dead and gives them life, so also the Son gives life to whom he will. [22]The Father judges no one, but has given all judgment to the Son, [23]that all may honor the Son, even as they honor the Father. He who does not honor the Son does not honor the Father who sent him."

5:19 "Truly, truly, I say to you, the Son can do nothing of his own accord."

---

(21) Ambrose of Milan

Finally, everyone should believe that work of the Father and Son is in unity and that there is no difference either in time or in the order of operations. Jesus says, "The works which I do, he does" (cf. 5:17). In order that one may not think that there is any difference in the particular works but may know that the will, the operation, and the power of the Father and Son are equal, wisdom says concerning the Father: **For whatever he does, that the Son does likewise** (5:19). The action of either the Father or the Son does not take place before or after the action of the other but is the result of one operation. For this reason, the Son says that he can do nothing by himself, for his work cannot be distinguished from the work of the Father. In a similar manner, the action of the Holy Spirit is not separated from the Father and the Son. Therefore, whatever the Holy Spirit utters, he is understood to have heard it from the Father.

(22) Theodore of Mopsuestia

The Son cannot do anything,[8] **but only what he sees the Father doing; for whatever he does, that the Son does likewise** (5:19). The meaning of the text is this: We use the word **cannot** in two ways, as does the divine Scripture. In one way, Scripture says that *the blood of bulls and goats cannot take away sins* (Heb 10:4), obviously meaning that the blood of goats is so weak that it **cannot** forgive sins. In another way, Scripture says that there are *two unchangeable things, in which God cannot prove false* (Heb 6:18); yet this is not implying that there is weakness in God, but rather that it is improper and impossible for God to *prove false*. This is actually a great example of his strength. It is impossible for God to *prove false*, that is, God **cannot** lie. This is said about God because of his great strength in virtue. Because he is mighty and faithful in truth, he would never succumb to falsehood because of weakness.

From what has been said, it is clear that we should not understand the words, **The Son cannot do anything of his own accord**, as a weakness, because people do many things on their own accord. Instead, we should look for another meaning. Why can the Son not do **anything of his own accord**? Because, his inseparable equality with the Father (since his natural conjunction makes for a great unanimity of will), makes it impossible for the Son to want anything the Father does not want. Divine nature does not learn events over time; rather, from the beginning, his foreknowledge knows all future events and their results. So also the Son equally possesses this knowledge. He participates in everything with the Father, including his will. Neither his will nor thoughts differ from the Father's, because he equally desires to do what the Father does. . . .

After he said, **But only what he sees the Father doing**, he adds, **For whatever** the Father **does, that the Son does likewise** (5:19). He does this in order to teach us clearly about the equality of action between Father and Son, and so that we will not think that the Father creates some things and the Son creates other things—this would produce the idea that there is a division in creation, some things being attributed to the Father and other things attributed to the Son. He did not say that the Son does *similar* things to the Father. The Father does not do some things and then the Son does similar things to the Father. Rather, he says, "Whatever the Father does, I do it too. Because we share a common action, he and I do all things together."

---

8. The RSV reads, **The Son can do nothing of his own accord** (5:19).

(23) John Chrysostom

The Son can do nothing of his own accord (5:19). But he has done the opposite. By saying this, he takes away nothing from himself but secures his equality with the Father. Pay close attention! The phrase being examined is not an error. For the phrase **of his own accord** (5:19) is found in many places throughout Scripture. It is applied both to Christ and the Holy Spirit. It is important to learn the meaning of this expression so that we might not commit the greatest sin! If someone understands this phrase in an isolated manner—as is easy to do—it would result in a great error. Christ did not say that he is not able on his own to do some things and not others. Rather, he says unequivocally: **The Son can do nothing of his own accord** (5:19).

Speaking against my opponent, I will ask the following: "Is the Son not able to do anything by himself?"[9] If he does not reply, I will state that he did not do the greatest things by himself. Even Paul says boldly, *[Christ], though he was in the form of God, did not count equality with God a thing to be grasped, but emptied himself, taking the form of a servant, being born in the likeness of men* (Phil 2:6–7). Christ himself says in another place: *I lay it down of my own accord* (10:18). Do you understand that he has authority over both life and death and worked out by himself the economy of salvation? We, who are entirely worthless, do many things ourselves, choose evil by ourselves and pursue virtue by ourselves. For if we did not do these things by ourselves, and with our own force, then we would not fall into hell when we sin or gain the kingdom when we do what is right. Therefore the phrase **he can do nothing of his own accord** (5:19) must mean that he can do nothing opposed to the Father, nothing different, nothing unusual. This is a great statement which shows his equality and great harmony. . . . This phrase does not suggest weakness but testifies to his great power. Paul speaks similarly about the Father elsewhere: *So that through two unchangeable things, in which it is impossible that God should prove false* (Heb 6:18); and, *If we are faithless, he remains faithful—for he cannot deny himself* (2 Tim 2:13). Certainly the word *impossible* does not indicate powerlessness but power. Even unspeakable power! Therefore, what he means is that the divine essence does not accept every kind of nature. When we say that God is unable to sin, we are not accusing him of weakness. Similarly, when he says, I **can do nothing of** my **own accord** (5:19), he means: "It is utterly impossible for me to do anything contrary to the Father."

(24) Cyril of Alexandria

Jesus said to them, "Truly, truly, I say to you, the Son can do nothing of his own accord, but only what he sees the Father doing; for whatever he does, that the Son does likewise" (5:19). This shows the excellent skill of a teacher. He does not speed up

---

9. The exact name of his "opponent" cannot be recovered. However, John Chrysostom's argument implies that his opponent held an extreme form of Arianism (e.g., Aetians, Anomoeans, or Eunomians), which argued that Christ was unlike the Father in both will and substance.

his discourse and outpace the knowledge of his students. Rather he explains the lesson clearly and in various ways. He uses different words and often simplifies the difficult things being considered. Here also he blends human concepts with divine ones and brings them together into one statement. He downplays slightly the honor due to the only-begotten nature but then elevates the human nature. Since he was at the same time both Lord and also a servant, he says **the Son can do nothing of his own accord, but only what he sees the Father doing; for whatever he does, that the Son does likewise** (5:19). He declares that he is equal in his essence, for he is able to do the works of God the Father without distinction and to accomplish things similarly to the one who brought him into existence. Things which share the same nature will work in concert with each other; in contrast, things which do not share the same nature will differ in their manner of working. Christ, as true God from true God the Father, says that he is able to do the same things as the Father. However, he says that he **can do nothing of his own accord but only what he sees the Father doing** (5:19) so that he may not appear to be equal to the Father only in respect to power but also in sharing the same mind and will with him in every way. . . . Indeed, in the phrase **for whatever he does, that the Son does likewise** (5:19), which is speaking about the Father, Christ clearly teaches that he has seemingly equal power on account of the unchangeable and similar actions in every way. How then is he inferior if he displays equality with God the Father in his deeds? Will something which is produced in a fire work differently than that produced in another fire although no difference is perceived in its function? How could this be? How then could the Son perform similar deeds to the Father, if he is inferior and lacks equal power with him?

5:20-23 "Greater works than these will he show him, that you may marvel. For as the Father raises the dead and gives them life, so also the Son gives life to whom he will."

---

(25) Hilary of Poitiers

For the Father loves the Son, and shows him all that he himself is doing; and greater works than these will he show him, that you may marvel. For as the Father raises the dead and gives them life, so also the Son gives life to whom he will (5:20-21). Is there any other probable rationale for this statement regarding how God works except to teach us about his true birth, namely that the Son was born from God the Father? The only other explanation is that the only-begotten God was so ignorant that he needed God to **show him all**. This explanation is impossible and purports a mindless blasphemy. The Son, who is omniscient, does not need to be taught. For this reason after the statement **for the Father loves the Son, and shows him all that he himself is doing** (5:20), we are told that all of this is for our instruction in the faith and so that the Father and Son are equally confessed by us. We are also kept from concluding erroneously that the Father **shows him all that he himself is doing** because the Son's knowledge is imperfect. With this as his goal, he says, **And greater works than these will he show him, that you may marvel. For as the**

Father raises the dead and gives them life, so also the Son gives life to whom he will (5:20–21). From this we learn that the Son will fully know all that the Father **will show him**. He knows that he will be shown how to give life to the dead from his Father's example. He says that the Father will show the Son things so that they **may marvel**. Then he tells them what these things are: **For as the Father raises the dead and gives them life, so also the Son gives life to whom he will** (5:21). They share the same power, for they share the same nature. The works are shown to help our faith. They are not due to his ignorance. They do not convey to the Son things that he does not already know but bolster our confidence to proclaim his birth by showing us that the Father has revealed all the works which he is able to do. The words used in this divine discourse have been selected with great care so that no ill-chosen words would suggest a difference in nature between the two. Christ says that the Father's works were shown to him. He did not, in contrast, say that he was given a powerful nature so that he could do them. By this he wants to make it clear to us that the Father's **showing** was a key part of the process of his birth. By the Father's love, he imparted to him at the very time of his birth the knowledge of the works which he willed the Son to do. This was to prevent us from supposing that the Son is by nature ignorant and different from the Father's, because it was said that the Father **shows him** (5:20). The Son makes it clear that he already knows the things that are to be shown to him. Indeed, he is very far from needing the authoritative example which would enable him to act, for **the Son gives life to whom he will** (5:21). . . .

In order to prevent the notion that to **give life to whom he will** (5:21) is only the prerogative of the unbegotten Sovereign and not the power of the one who was truly born, he is quick to add, **The Father judges no one, but has given all judgment to the Son** (5:22). The phrase **has given all judgment** teaches us about both his birth and his sonship. Only a nature which is entirely one with the Father's could possess **all** things. A son can possess nothing, except by gift. But he **has given all judgment to the Son** (5:22), for **the Son gives life to whom he will** (5:21). Now we should not think that **judgment** is removed from the Father, even though he does not exercise it. The Son's power of judgment proceeds entirely from the Father's since it is a gift from him. The reason why judgment has been given to the Son is made clear by the words which follow: **The Father judges no one, but has given all judgment to the Son, that all may honor the Son, even as they honor the Father. He who does not honor the Son does not honor the Father who sent him** (5:22–23). What possible excuse remains for doubt or for the impiety of denial? The gift of **judgment** is given so that the Son may receive **honor** equal to that which is offered to the Father. It follows then that he who dishonors the Son is guilty of dishonoring the Father as well. How can we imagine that the nature given to him by birth is different from the Father's? He is the Father's equal in work, in power, in honor, in the punishment meted out to those who do not believe. This entire divine discourse therefore is nothing other than an unfolding of the mystery of his birth. The only distinction between the Father and Son that is justified or even plausible is that the latter was born. Yet he was born in such a sense as to be one with the Father.

(26) Augustine of Hippo

Let us once again remember how this discourse started. It began when a man *who had been ill for thirty-eight years* (5:5) was healed. . . . Suddenly, he was made whole while the Jews were astonished and filled with anger. They desired the darkness from the Sabbath even more than light from the miracle. Speaking to those who were angry, he says, **greater works than these will he show him** (5:20). Greater than what? Greater than what you have seen! A man, **who had been ill for thirty-eight years** (5:5), was made whole. The Father is going to show the Son **greater works than these**? What then are **greater works**? He continues: **For as the Father raises the dead and gives them life, so also the Son gives life to whom he will** (5:21). Certainly, these are **greater works**! . . . But what does this mean? Does it mean that the Father will raise some and the Son others? Surely *all things were made through him* (1:3). What then shall we say, brothers and sisters? Christ raised Lazarus. . . . When Christ raised Lazarus, did not the Father raise him also? Was it the work of the Son alone without the Father? Read the section again and see that he calls on the Father so that Lazarus may live again (cf. 11:41–44). As a man, he calls on the Father; as God, he works with the Father. Lazarus, who was raised from the dead, was raised both by the Father and the Son in accordance with the gift and grace of the Holy Spirit. It was a miraculous work accomplished by the Trinity. Let us not understand the verse, **For as the Father raises the dead and gives them life, so also the Son gives life to whom he will** (5:21), in such a way as to assume that some are raised from the dead and given life by the Father and others by the Son. Rather, the Son raises and gives life to the same ones whom the Father raises and gives life, because *all things were made through him, and without him was not anything made that was made* (1:3). To show that he has been given equal power by the Father, he says **the Son gives life to whom he will** (5:21) so that he might show his own will by that deed. In order that no one will say that the Father, who has divine power, raises the dead by the Son as if the latter does not have his own power but is merely a servant like an angel, he shows the power of the Son clearly when he says **so also the Son gives life to whom he will** (5:21). It is not true that the Father wills something different from the Son. Rather, the Father and Son have one substance and therefore one will.

Who are the dead to whom the Father and Son **give life**? Are they the ones whom we have spoken about—Lazarus (11:43–44), the widow's son (Luke 7:14), or the daughter of the ruler of the synagogue (Luke 8:54)? We know that they were raised by Christ the Lord. Instead, he wants to show us something else, namely the resurrection of the dead, which we all look for. He is not referring to the resurrection which a few have experienced in order that others might believe. Although Lazarus was raised from the dead, he died again. In contrast, we shall rise to live forever. Is it the Father or the Son who carries out final resurrection? Truly, it is the Father in the Son. . . . From where do we prove that he is speaking of the final resurrection? From the place where he said, **As the Father raises the dead and gives them life, so also the Son gives life to whom he will** (5:21). To prevent us from understanding that the resurrection he performs here is merely a miracle and not the final resurrection, he continues by adding, **The Father judges no one, but has given all judgment to the Son** (5:22). . . .

Certainly there is a true and powerful sense, if we are able to grasp it somehow, in which **the Father judges no one, but has given all judgment to the Son** (5:22). This is stated because only the Son will appear to humans at the judgment. The Father will remain hidden; the Son will be visible. How will the Son be visible? He will appear in the form in which he ascended. In the form of God, he was hidden along with the Father; in the form of a servant, he appeared to humans. . . . The Son will appear to them who are to be judged and will judge them. The Scriptures show us even more clearly that it is the Son who will appear. On the fortieth day after his resurrection, he ascended into heaven with his disciples looking into heaven. They heard an angelic voice: *Men of Galilee, why do you stand looking into heaven? This Jesus, who was taken up from you into heaven, will come in the same way as you saw him go into heaven* (Acts 1:11). How did they see him ascend? He was in the flesh which they had touched and felt. It was marked by the wounds which they had touched and confirmed. He was in the body in which he had visited them for forty days. He appeared to them in truth and not in a false manner. He was not a phantom, shadow, or ghost, but he said directly: *See my hands and my feet, that it is I myself; handle me, and see; for a spirit has not flesh and bones as you see that I have* (Luke 24:39). Certainly that body is worthy of its heavenly home, for it is not subject to death nor is it changed by the passage of time. It is not like the body which grows to that age from infancy and which from that age of maturity declines to old age. Instead he remains just as he ascended so that he could come to those to whom his word was proclaimed according to his will. Therefore, he will come in human form. Even the wicked will see this form. Those on his right and those on his left will see him, as it is written: *They look on him whom they have pierced* (Zech 12:10). If *they* will *look on him whom they have pierced*, they will look on that same body which they stabbed with the spear, for a spear does not pierce the Word. The wicked will be able to look upon the body which they wounded, but they will not see God concealed within this body. After the **judgment**, those on his right will be able to see him truly. This is what he means when he says, **The Father judges no one, but has given all judgment to the Son** (5:22). The Son will come to the **judgment** in a visible, human body able to be seen by all. *Then the King will say to those at his right hand, "Come, O blessed of my Father, inherit the kingdom prepared for you from the foundation of the world"* (Matt 25:34). *Then he will say to those at his left hand, "Depart from me, you cursed, into the eternal fire prepared for the devil and his angels"* (Matt 25:41).

Pay attention! The human form of Christ will be seen by the pious and the impious, by the righteous and the wicked, by the believers and the unbelievers, by those who rejoice and those who mourn, by those who trusted and those who were confused. Be assured, they will all see! After the Son has appeared at the **judgment** in that form which he took from us and the **judgment** is concluded . . . what will happen next? When will all the faithful see the form of God which they are thirsting to see? When will they see the *Word* who *was in the beginning*, God with God, by whom *all things were made* (1:1–3)? When will they see that form of God which the apostle Paul references when he says *though he was in the form of God, [he] did not count equality with God a thing to be grasped* (Phil 2:6)? That form in which the equality of Father and Son is recognized is lofty! It is ineffable, incomprehensible, especially to those who are small. When will this form be seen? Pay attention! On his right are the righteous and on his left are the wicked. All of them will see the man Christ, the Son of Man. They will see the one who was pierced, the one who was crucified, the one who was brought low, the one who was born of a virgin, the Lamb of the tribe of Judah. . . . Let those who are on his right hand enter into the eternal inheritance promised long ago. The martyrs believed in this eternal inheritance without seeing it and as a consequence spilled their blood without delay. Let them enter and behold it. When will they go there? Let the Lord himself answer: *And they will go away into eternal punishment, but the righteous into eternal life* (Matt 25:46).

Notice, he has mentioned *eternal life*. But has he told us what we will see there and whether we will know the Father and the Son? What if we should live forever but not see the Father and the Son? Listen to another section of Scripture where he has referenced *eternal life* and described what it is . . . : *He who has my commandments and keeps them, he it is who loves me; and he who loves me will be loved by my Father, and I will love him and manifest myself to him* (14:21). Let us reply to the Lord and ask, "What great thing is this, Lord God? What is so great? Will you show yourself to us? Did you not also show yourself to the Jews? Did they who crucified you not see you? When you appear at the judgment and we stand at your right hand, will not those who are standing on your left also see you? In what way will you show yourself to us? Do we not truly see you now when you are speaking?" He answers: "I will show myself in the form of God, but now you are only seeing the form of a servant. I will not deceive you, O faithful human! Believe that you will see me. You love, even though you do not see. Will love itself not lead you to see? Continue to love and persevere in your love." He who has purified your heart says, "I will not betray your love." Why have I purified your heart? So that you will see God. *Blessed are the pure in heart, for they shall see God* (Matt 5:8).

(27) Cyril of Alexandria

The Father judges no one, but has given all judgment to the Son (5:22). He introduces another incredible and amazing concept and in many ways persuades them that he is truly God by nature. Certainly, it is not right for anyone to judge the world unless he is God over all things. The divine Scriptures call God to do this. One psalm states, *Arise, O God, judge the earth* (Ps 82:8); another says, *Because God is judge, this one he humbles and that one he exalts* (Ps 75:7 [74:8 LXX]). Christ says that the Father has given him the power of **judgment**. He did not lack this authority since he is Word and God and possesses authority over all things. But he teaches that this authority resides in his divine nature and was given over to him as a man in reference to the incarnation. Because he was man, he rightly states that he received this authority, since it was said to him: *What do you have that you did not receive?* (1 Cor 4:7). Regarding this, someone who is opposed to us, might say, "The Son states directly that he received the power of judgment from the Father.[10] If so, he receives it as one who did not already possess it. How then is it not true that the one who gives this authority is not greater and possesses a higher nature than the one who must receive it?" How do we respond to this? Here is our argument which seems reasonable to me. It takes

---

10. Throughout this excerpt, Cyril is presenting an interlocutor to offer possible rejections to his argument, which he in turn refutes.

into account of course the time of the incarnation and is definitely compatible with the economy of the flesh when he was called a *servant* and *humbled himself, being born in* our *likeness* (Phil 2:7–8). But since you wish to act disdainfully against the simpler doctrines and to subject them to punctilious examination, let us then answer your arguments by saying the following. It is not always true or even necessary that the one who gives something to someone else offers it to a person who lacks that object. Nor is it true that the one who gives something is by definition greater than the one who receives it. What will you conclude when you hear the holy psalmist saying in the Spirit: *Give glory to God!* (Ps 68:34 [67:35 LXX]). Will we conclude that the psalmist believes that God is in need of glory or that we are greater than the creator since we are commanded to offer him such praise? Even you who insolently blaspheme would not dare to say this! The Godhead is full of glory. He does not receive it from us. He is not thought to be lesser by receiving glory, which he himself has, from those who offer it to him as a gift. Often it is observed that the one who receives something is not of less worth than the one who gave it. It follows then that the Father is not of a more lofty nature than his only-begotten Son just because he **has given all judgment to the Son** (5:22). . . . Someone might also say: "Since it was stated **that all may honor the Son, even as they honor the Father** (5:23), you think that we should praise the Son with equal **honors** as the Father. However, you do not know that you have moved far from the truth. For the word **as** does not necessarily suggest the complete equality of deeds but often intimates some sort of likeness. This is seen when the Savior teaches: *Be merciful, even* as *your Father is merciful* (Luke 6:36). Are we able to be as merciful as the Father just because of the word **as**? Similarly, Christ speaks to his own Father about his disciples: *You have loved them even* as *you have loved me* (17:23). We will not conclude that the disciples are loved as the Son just because of the word **as**. Why do you confuse the meanings and push these phrases toward blasphemy by arguing that this text does not command the hearers to honor the Son in equal measure as the Father? How can we answer such things? Those who fight against God bark at us with these wicked words. As Paul says, the *dogs* are outside, the *evil-workers* are outside, and *those who mutilate the flesh* (Phil 3:2) are likewise outside of the true faith. For we are the sons of truth and are *children of light* (Eph 5:8). We will glorify the only-begotten along with God the Father with an equal measure of honor and glory as God from God, Light from Light, and Life from Life.

For most people, it is not safe to meddle with the received faith! Nevertheless, we must examine the meaning of the word **as** so that our opponents will not continue to think they are so brilliant. When the word **as** is used to refer to things which are dissimilar in nature, it does not indicate a complete and indistinguishable equality. Rather, it introduces a notion of similarity and likeness, just as our opponents pointed out above. In contrast, if this word is applied to things which are similar in every respect, then it certainly suggests an "equality" and a "similarity" in all things. . . . I might say, "The sun in heaven is bright, and the silver of the earth is also bright." But the nature of these two things is different. Let's imagine that some rich man says to his servants, "Shine up this silver so that it is *as* bright as the sun." According, we would certainly say that the earthly material does not reach an equal brightness as the sun, but it shares a certain similarity and likeness since the word **as** is used. Let's bring Peter and John from the group of holy disciples into this discussion. They shared an exact similarity with each other in regard to their nature and their piety.

The word **as** might be used in reference to them if someone were to say, "Let John be honored by all, just as Peter is." Will the word **as** diminish the necessity of equal honor being brought to both? I do not think that anyone would say this, for there is nothing preventing equal honor being offered to both." According to this analogy, why would we draw back from crowning both the Son and the Father with equal honor when the word **as** is used? . . . Since I have demonstrated earlier that he was God the Creator and true Life (cf. John 1:2–4) and shared the exalted work of God the Father, he adds appropriately **that all may honor the Son, even as they honor the Father** (5:23). What then causes one to hold back? What is there to prevent someone from offering an equal amount of honor to the one in whom there exists the very attributes of the Father? We will honor the very nature of God the Father which shines through the Son. For this reason, he says, **He who does not honor the Son does not honor the Father who sent him** (5:23).

John 5:24–29

[24] "**Truly, truly, I say to you, he who hears my word and believes him who sent me, has eternal life; he does not come into judgment, but has passed from death to life.** [25]**Truly, truly, I say to you, the hour is coming, and now is, when the dead will hear the voice of the Son of God, and those who hear will live.** [26]**For as the Father has life in himself, so he has granted the Son also to have life in himself,** [27]**and has given him authority to execute judgment, because he is the Son of man.** [28]**Do not marvel at this; for the hour is coming when all who are in the tombs will hear his voice** [29]**and come forth, those who have done good, to the resurrection of life, and those who have done evil, to the resurrection of judgment.**"

(28) Augustine of Hippo

He who hears my word and believes him who sent me, has eternal life; he does not come into judgment, but has passed from death to life (5:24). Recall what we presented above, namely that *the Father raises the dead and gives them life, so also the Son gives life to whom he will* (5:21). He is already starting to reveal himself. Look, the dead are rising already! *He who hears my word and believes him who sent me, has eternal life; he does not come into judgment* (5:21). . . . Prove from this that he has risen once again! He says that he **has passed from death to life** (5:24). Anyone who **has passed from death to life** has undoubtedly risen again. For he could not pass **from death to life** unless he were first dead and not alive. But after he has passed, he will no longer be dead but alive! For the one who *was dead is alive; he was lost and is found* (Luke 15:32). It follows then that a resurrection takes place now. Humans pass from death to life. They pass from the death of faithlessness to a life of faith; from a death of lies to the life of truth; from the death of impiousness to a life of righteousness. These are a sort of resurrection of the dead. . . .

    Truly, truly, I say to you, the hour is coming, and now is (5:25). We certainly look for a resurrection of the dead at the end of time, as we have believed. Actually, we have not looked, but are certainly bound to look for it, for it is not a false thing we believe, because the dead will rise in the end. The Lord Jesus willingly revealed to us *a* resurrection of the dead before *the* resurrection of the dead. It is not a resurrection as that of Lazarus (John 12:43), or of the widow's son (Luke 6:14), or of the daughter of the ruler of the synagogue (Matt 5:41). They were raised from the dead only to die again (for in these cases there was *a* resurrection of the dead before *the* resurrection of the dead). But, as he says here, he **has eternal life; he does not come into judgment, but has passed from death to life** (5:24). To what sort of life? To eternal life. It is not a resurrection as of the body of Lazarus. Although he indeed passed from the death of the tomb to the life of man, he did not pass to eternal life since he was bound to die once again. In contrast, when the dead rise again at the end of the world, they will pass to eternal life. When our Lord Jesus Christ, our heavenly Master, the Word of the Father, and the Truth, showed us *a* resurrection of the dead before *the* resurrection of the dead to eternal life, he said **the hour is coming** (5:25). On account of your faith in the resurrection of the flesh, you certainly wait for that hour at the end of the world. However, in order that you would not look here for that hour, he added, **and now is** (5:25). Therefore, he did not say **the hour is coming** (5:25) as if speaking of that last hour when *with the archangel's call, and with the sound of the trumpet of God. And the dead in Christ will rise first; then we who are alive, who are left, shall be caught up together with them in the clouds to meet the Lord in the air; and so we shall always be with the Lord* (1 Thess 4:16–17). That hour will certainly come. However, it is not **now**. But consider what this hour is: **the hour is coming, and now is** (5:25). . . .

What then? How do we understand these two resurrections? Do we understand that they who rise now will not rise at the end? Is the resurrection for some now and for others then? That is not the case! If we have rightly believed, we already have this resurrection. Yet, we, who have already risen, are looking for another resurrection at the end. If we continue steadfastly in the same faith, we have already risen to eternal life and then too will rise to eternal life when we will be made equal to the angels (Luke 20:36). Let Christ clarify and explain what we have boldly stated just now: there is a resurrection before the resurrection, not of different people, but the same. It is not a resurrection like Lazarus experienced, but a resurrection into eternal life. He will unveil it clearly. Listen to the Master . . . **Truly, truly, I say to you, the hour is coming, and now is, when the dead**—notice that a resurrection is asserted—**will hear the voice of the Son of God, and those who hear will live** (5:25). . . . They who **will hear** are those who "will obey." They who obey will then live. Let them be certain of this: **will live**! Christ, the Word of God, is proclaimed to us. He is the Son of God, by whom all things were made, who, in accordance with the divine will, became incarnate. He was born of a virgin, was an infant in the flesh, a young man in the flesh, suffered in the flesh, died in the flesh, rose again in the flesh, and ascended in the flesh. He promised a resurrection to the flesh and promised a resurrection to the mind—to the mind before the flesh, to the flesh after the mind. **Those who hear** and obey, **will live**! **Those who** do not **hear** and do not obey—that is, those who hear and yet despise the message—**will** not **live** (5:25). . . . **For the hour is coming** when the dead will rise. This hour will take place at the end of the world when the dead will rise. They rise now in the mind; at that time they will rise in the flesh. They rise now in the mind by the Word of God, the Son of God; at that time they will rise in the flesh by the Word of God who was made flesh, the Son of Man. . . .

Let the Lord state this even more clearly so that those heretics who deny the resurrection of the body might not find a reason for their sophistic criticism. Certainly, the meaning of these words already shines with clarity! When it was said above that **the hour is coming**, he added **and now is** (5:25). But in this verse, when it says **the hour is coming** (5:28), he did not add **and now is** (5:25). Let him with the clear truth, break off all the handles, loops, and pegs of their sophistic attacks and destroy all the nooses of entangling objections. **Do not marvel at this; for the hour is coming when all who are in the tombs** (5:28). . . . What is clearer? What is more distinct? The bodies of the just and unjust are in the **tombs**; the souls of them, however, are not in the **tombs**. The soul of the righteous man was in the *bosom of Abraham* (Luke 16:22–23); the soul of the wicked man was tormented in hell. Neither of them was in the **tombs**. I beg you to pay careful attention, for he said previously **the hour is coming and now is** (5:25). You certainly know, brothers and sisters, that we get bread of the belly only with work. How much greater is the work required to get bread of the mind! With effort, you stand and listen. With greater exertion, we stand and speak. If we work for your benefit, you certainly should work with us for your own sake. Previously, when he said **the hour is coming** and added **and now is** (5:25), what did he add to this? **When the dead will hear the voice of the Son of God, and those who hear will live** (5:25). He did not say that *all* **the dead will hear . . . and those who hear will live** (5:25), for he had in mind the unrighteous. Certainly it is not the case that all the unrighteous obey the gospel. The apostle says clearly, *But they have not all obeyed the gospel* (Rom 10:16). But **those who hear will live** (5:25), because all who obey the gospel shall pass by faith to eternal life. However, not all obey; and **this is now**. But certainly, in the end, **all who are in the tombs** (5:28)—both the just and the unjust—**will hear his voice and come forth** (5:28–29). Why does he not say **and will live** (5:25)? Surely, all **will come forth**, but not all **will live**. For in the verse that he said above, **and those who hear will live** (5:25), he intended for it to be understood that there is eternal and blessed life in the hearing and obeying. Not all those who come forth from the graves will hear and obey. It follows then that in the reference to the graves and by the expression **come forth** from the **tombs**, we clearly understand these are about the resurrection of bodies.

(29) Cyril of Alexandria

Do not marvel at this; for the hour is coming when all who are in the tombs will hear his voice and come forth, those who have done good, to the resurrection of life, and those who have done evil, to the resurrection of judgment (5:28–29). With these words he intimates the time of the resurrection of all. Concerning this, the divine Paul wrote to us: *The Lord himself will descend from heaven with a cry of command, with the archangel's call, and with the sound of the trumpet of God* (1 Thess 4:16) to *judge the world in righteousness* (Acts 17:31) and to dispense judgment to everyone in accordance with their works. Nevertheless, he guides the ignorant Jews by repeating the same things to understand clearly that Christ will do greater works than those by which he healed the paralytic man and that he will be revealed as the judge of the world. After comparing the healing of one sick person to the resurrection of the dead, he shows that the activity that loosens the bonds of death and destroys the corruption of all is greater and more important. It is understandable that he says about the lesser miracle, **Do not marvel at this** (5:28). Certainly we should not think that by these words he intends to discount his wonderful miracles or that he commands them not to marvel at those events at which one rightly might be amazed. Instead, he wants those who are amazed by these deeds to know and believe that those marvelous events are relatively insignificant. For in both word and deed, he as God raises not only those who are sick from minor diseases but also those who have already been baptized by death and are oppressed by an indestructible corruption. For this reason, he introduces a greater deed; he says, **The hour is coming when all who are in the tombs will hear his voice** (5:28). For how would the one who is able to bring into existence by his word things which did not previously exist not be able to bring back to life that which had already been made?

John 5:30–36

[30]"I can do nothing on my own authority; as I hear, I judge; and my judgment is just, because I seek not my own will but the will of him who sent me. [31]If I bear witness to myself, my testimony is not true; [32]there is another who bears witness to me, and I know that the testimony which he bears to me is true. [33]You sent to John, and he has borne witness to the truth. [34]Not that the testimony which I receive is from man; but I say this that you may be saved. [35]He was a burning and shining lamp, and you were willing to rejoice for a while in his light. [36]But the testimony which I have is greater than that of John; for the works which the Father has granted me to accomplish, these very works which I am doing, bear me witness that the Father has sent me."

5:30 "I can do nothing on my own authority; as I hear, I judge; and my judgment is just."

---

(30) John Chrysostom

He seems to say something strange and contradictory to the prophets, for they assert that God is the one who judges the whole earth (i.e., the human race). David proclaimed this in many places. He said, *He will judge the peoples with equity* (Ps 96:10), and *God is a righteous judge, strong and patient* (Ps 7:11 LXX). The prophets and Moses also declare this as well. But Christ said, *The Father judges no one, but has given all judgment to the Son* (5:22). This phrase is capable of confusing any Jew who heard it and might lead someone to suppose that Jesus was opposed to God. However, when he says this, he adjusts his language to account for their weakness. In order to dispel this dire suspicion just mentioned, he says, *I can do nothing of my own accord* (5:19). In other words, he says you will not see me doing and hear me saying anything strange or in contradiction to what the Father wills.

He said previously that he was the Son of Man and showed that at that time they thought he was a man (cf. John 3:13–14). He repeats this idea once again here. Similarly, when he said before that *We speak of what we have heard and bear witness to what we have seen* (3:11)[11] and when John says, *He bears witness to what he has seen yet no one receives his testimony* (3:32), they spoke about exact knowledge, not simply about what is heard and seen. So also here, when he speaks of **hearing**, he says that it is impossible for him to **will** anything other than what the Father wills (cf. 5:30). However, he did not speak very plainly, for they would not have accepted it immediately upon hearing it. How then did he speak to them? In human terms and with great accommodation: **As I hear, I judge** (5:30). He does not speak about being instructed, for he does not say, "As I am taught," but **as I hear**. Nor does he speak as if he needed to **hear** anything. He did not need to be taught. Nor did he need to **hear** either. By this he displays the same mind and the immutability of his **judgment**. Instead, he intimates the following: "I judge just as if the Father himself were the one judging." Then he adds: I know that **my judgment is just, because I seek not my own will but the will of him who sent me** (5:30). What do you mean? Do you have a **will** that is separate from the Father? In another place, you said, "Just as you and I are one" (cf. John 17:21). And again, speaking of your shared will and purpose, you said, "Grant that they may be one in us, that is, one in faith with us."

Do you perceive that the words which seem most humble are actually the ones which contain a higher meaning hidden within? For what he intimates is this: It is not that the will of the Father is one thing and his will is another, but rather "there is just one divine mind and will of the Father which is also my will." . . . So he means nothing more than this: "I do not possess a will which is separate and apart from the Father. If he wills something, then so do I; if I will something, then so does he. Just as no one should object to the judging of the Father, so no one would object to me, for every judgment proceeds from the same mind."

(31) Cyril of Alexandria

The Father is not imagined as doing anything solely and independently without the Son for he gave to him both power and might, because *all things were made through him, and without him was not anything made that was made* (1:3). Nor does the Son do anything by himself apart from the Father. Accordingly, he says, **I can do nothing on my own authority** (5:30), and *the Father who dwells in me does his works* (14:10). We should not suppose that the Father strengthens the Son or gives him authority over all things because the Son is inherently weak. If this were the case, the Son would no longer be God by nature but rather by the reception of the Godhead's glory. In that case, the Father himself would no longer exist in the state of sublime perfection, for the Word, the symbol of his nature, would require (by deficiency) power and authority from another. An analogy will be sought regarding the disbursal of such attributes and will be applied

---

11. Chrysostom changes the text to say **what we have heard** rather than **what we known**. Likely this change is intended to correspond better with his later point about Jesus "hearing" from the Father.

to the archetype and the image. This will take our argument quickly into unending controversies and lead into the deep sea of blasphemy. But since the Son is of the essence of the Father and receives by nature all the attributes of the Father who generated him and acquires essentially by reason of nature as such, the Son is in the Father and the Father is in the Son. For this reason, he often truly and innocently attributes to the Father the power of his own actions. He does not deny himself the ability to do them, but he credits all actions to the operations of the one Godhead, for there is one Godhead in the Father, Son, and Holy Spirit.

(32) Gregory the Great

Stubborn people should be admonished so that they will acknowledge the haughtiness of their thoughts and learn how to conquer themselves. If not, they will resist the correct advice of others and will remain captive to their pride. They are to be exhorted to examine carefully how the Son of Man, whose will is always one with the Father's, might serve as an example of how to subdue our own will. He says, **I seek not my own will but the will of him who sent me** (5:30). To prove even more clearly the importance of this virtue, he declared that he would subordinate himself willingly at the last judgment, saying, **I can do nothing on my own authority; as I hear, I judge** (5:30). With what justification can a man refuse to submit to the will of another when he sees that the Son of God and of Man on the very day when he returns to reveal the glory of his power demonstrates that he does not **judge** according to his **own authority**?

5:31-32 "If I bear witness to myself, my testimony is not true; there is another who bears witness to me, and I know that the testimony which he bears to me is true."

---

(33) John Chrysostom

If a person who is inexperienced in mining begins to dig a mine, he would not produce any gold. By his haphazard and discombobulated efforts he would work without results and perhaps even cause harm. It is the same with those who do not know the order of holy Scripture and fail to analyze its distinctive forms and laws but merely peruse all of it in the same way. They mix gold with earth and will not be able to discover the treasure lying hidden within it.

I am saying this because the text before us currently contains much gold. It is not readily visible but is covered over and hidden in darkness. Therefore, it is necessary that we discover its true sense by digging and sifting. Who would not be immediately disturbed when hearing Christ say, **If I bear witness to myself, my testimony is not true** (5:31)? I say this partly because he certainly bore witness to himself on many occasions. For example, when talking with the Samaritan woman, he said, **I who speak to**

you am he (4:26). Similarly, he said to the blind man, *It is he who speaks to you* (9:37). In reproaching the Jews, he asked: *Do you say (to me), "You are blaspheming," because I said, "I am the Son of God"?* (10:36). He did this many other times. If all these statements are lies, what hope of salvation do we have in them? Where shall we discover the truth, when the Truth itself says, **My testimony is not true** (5:31)? Not only does this statement seem contradictory, but there is another one which is equally confusing. Further on, he says, *Even if I do bear witness to myself, my testimony is true* (8:14). Which one then should I accept? Which one should I consider a lie? If we take them according to their literal sense, without trying to learn about the person to whom they were spoken or the reason, both will be false. If his **testimony is not true**, then it is not possible that this very statement is true! This is the case not only with regard to the second statement but with the first as well.

What then is the meaning of these statements? We need a great deal of vigilance, or rather God's grace in abundance, in order to venture beyond the mere words. It is in this very way that the heretics go astray. They do not seek to learn the point of view of the speaker or the perspective of his audience. Similarly, if we do not supply this information and other aspects as well—such as the times, places, and opinions of the listeners—many absurd conclusions will follow. What, then, is the meaning of this text? The Jews were going to provoke him as follows: "If you bear witness to yourself, then your testimony is not true." Therefore, he uttered the statement above in anticipation of this, as if to say, "You will surely say, 'We do not believe you. For a man who bears witness to himself is never considered trustworthy.'" It follows then that the phrase **is not true** must not be read in the literal sense, but in the light of the suspicious attitude of the audience. In other words, **my testimony is not true** in your eyes. He did not say these words with his own virtue in mind, but in consideration of their suspicious attitude. So when he said, **My testimony is not true**, he was condemning their attitude and the accusation that they would level against him.

When he says, *Even if I testify concerning myself, my testimony is true* (8:14), here he shows the core of the matter. It is necessary to hold that he is worthy to be believed as God even when he speaks of himself. Since he spoke about the resurrection of the dead and judgment, and that all who believe in him will not be judged but will go to life, and that he will sit and demand an account of all, and that he has the same authority and power as the Father, he necessarily put their objection first so that he could prepare them for these statements. Jesus says, "I said that just *as the Father raises the dead and gives them life, so also the Son gives life to whom he will* (5:21). I said that *the Father judges no one, but has given all judgment to the Son* (5:22). I said that it is necessary to *honor the Son, even as they honor the Father* (5:23). I said that *he who does not honor the Son does not honor the Father* (5:23). I said that *he who hears my word and believes* will not see death but *has passed from death to life* (5:24). I said that my *voice* (5:25) will raise the dead—some now and some after these things are completed. I said that I will demand an account of transgressions from all. I said that I judge justly and will repay those who walk uprightly." It follows then that all these statements—even if they were not the exact words—were answers . . . to their objections. He spoke them first so that he could move on to prove the truth of these words. Perhaps, you will object: "You say these things, but you are not a witness that should be believed, for you testify about yourself." First, he destroyed their obstinacy by stating beforehand what they were about to say and showing that he knows the inner thoughts of their hearts. Moreover, he offers clear and undeniable evidence of his power after their objections, by introducing three witnesses of his words: the works which he did, the testimony of the Father, and the proclamation of John. He placed John, the least of these witnesses, first. He says, **There is another who bears witness to me, and I know that his testimony is true** (5:32). To this, he added, **You sent to John and he testified to the truth** (5:33). If my testimony is not true, how can you say, **I know that his testimony is true** and **he testified to the truth**? Do you perceive how apparent it is that the words, **My testimony is not true** (5:31), are spoken with their hidden thoughts in mind?

5:35 "He was a burning and shining lamp, and you were willing to rejoice for a while in his light."

---

(34) Augustine of Hippo

All humans are **lamps** (5:35), for they can be both lighted and snuffed out. Certainly, when the **lamps** smell good, they give light and burn with the spirit.[12] However, when they are extinguished after burning, they then smell bad. The servants of God have remained good **lamps**, not due to their own strength, but from the oil of his mercy. In fact, the grace of God is free; it is the oil of the **lamps**. "Certainly, I have labored more than all of them," a particular lamp says. However, it adds, "Yet, not I, but the grace of God within me," so that he might not seem to burn by his own strength. So every prophecy preceding the Lord's coming is a **lamp**. Concerning this, the apostle Peter says, *And we have the prophetic word made more sure. You will do well to pay attention to this as to a lamp shining in a dark place, until the day dawns and the morning star rises in your hearts* (2 Pet 1:19). Thus, the prophets are **lamps**, and their prophecy is one great **lamp**.

What about the apostles? Certainly they are also **lamps**. Only Christ is not a lamp, for he is not lighted and snuffed out, because *as the Father has life in himself, so he has granted the Son also to have life in himself* (5:26). It follows then that the apostles are also lamps. They give thanks because they have been kindled by the light of truth and burn with the spirit of love. The oil of God's grace is given to them. If they were not **lamps**, the Lord would not have said to them, *You are the light of the world* (Matt 5:14). After he said, *You are the light of the world*, he shows that they should not think that they are the type of light of which it is said, *The true light that enlightens every man was coming into the world* (1:9). This was said about the Lord to distinguish him from John. It has been said about John the Baptist that *he was not the light, but came to bear witness to the light* (1:8) so that you might not ask, "How was **he not the light**? when Christ says regarding him that **he was a burning and shining lamp** (5:35)." Similarly, when he said to the apostles, *You are*

---

12. Cf. Acts 18:15; Rom 12:11.

the light of the world (Matt 5:14), he immediately added, *A city set on a hill cannot be hid. Nor do men light a lamp and put it under a bushel, but on a stand, and it gives light to all in the house* (Matt 5:15) so that they might not think that something had been attributed to them that was to be understood only about Christ. . . . He said: *Let your light so shine before men, that they may see your good works and give glory*—not to you!—but *to your Father who is in heaven* (Matt 5:16). Moses testified to Christ. John bore **witness** to Christ (5:33). The rest of the prophets and apostles testified to Christ. Before all of these witnesses, he placed the testimony of his own **works** (cf. 5:36). But through them, God alone bore witness to his Son. But God testifies to his Son in another way. God reveals his Son through the Son himself, and he reveals himself through the Son. If someone comes to him, he will not need lamps. And by digging more deeply, he will truly build his house upon the rock (cf. Matt 7:24).

(35) Cyril of Alexandria

He was a burning and shining lamp, and you were willing to rejoice for a while in his light (5:35). He compares the holy Baptist to a **lamp**. He showed forth the **light** before the Lord's coming as he was able. However, he did not shine with his own **light**, for the light in the **lamp** is not generated from itself but is given and added from outside. In this way you will see the radiance from Christ in the Spirit shining in the saints. For this reason, those who think and act wisely confess by their own mouths, **And from his fullness have we all received** (1:16). The Lord himself shined forth from **light**, that is from the essence of the Father, for the only-begotten is by nature **light**. Creation partakes of that **light** and so too does everything which is given the power of reason and thinking. It is a vessel which has the capacity to be filled with divine Light because it was fashioned superbly by God, the most excellent creator of all things. The blessed Baptist then is a **lamp** in accordance with the explanation given above. The Savior saying this succinctly reminds the foolish Pharisees of the utterance of God the Father, who said of John, *I have prepared a lamp for my anointed* (Ps 132:17). . . .

I think that we have followed the well-traveled and commonly used method of interpretation of this passage, and we have set forth its meaning according to our ability. However, since the word of the Savior contains a deeper meaning and signifies that John was not merely **a lamp** but was **burning and shining**, we hold that it is necessary to apply ourselves more earnestly to the impact of the words and trace out the beauty of the truth and to take hold of the more subtle concepts. The sentence will be brought forward once again. The Lord says, **He was a lamp**. This alone would have been sufficient to call attention to the holy Baptist and to remind the audience of the prophecy concerning him which reads, *I have prepared a lamp for my anointed* (Ps 132:17). But since he adds the words **burning and shining** to **a lamp**, it is clear that he leads them back not only to the prophet's voice but to some prefiguring of the law which represents John, as in a figure and shadow, beforehand as the torchbearer. He performed this function well by testifying to Christ the Lord. He convicts the Pharisees, who were constantly immersed in the law of Moses, of being ignorant although they held themselves arrogantly to be wise. In fact, they only seemed to be wise, for they did not really understand the law. This then is the entire aim of this discourse. But I think we should show clearly, by calling upon the divine oracle, that the blessed Baptist is not simply **a lamp**, but **a burning and shining lamp**.

John 5:37–47

[37]"And the Father who sent me has himself borne witness to me. His voice you have never heard, his form you have never seen; [38]and you do not have his word abiding in you, for you do not believe him whom he has sent. [39]You search the scriptures, because you think that in them you have eternal life; and it is they that bear witness to me; [40]yet you refuse to come to me that you may have life. [41]I do not receive glory from men. [42]But I know that you have not the love of God within you. [43]I have come in my Father's name, and you do not receive me; if another comes in his own name, him you will receive. [44]How can you believe, who receive glory from one another and do not seek the glory that comes from the only God? [45]Do not think that I shall accuse you to the Father; it is Moses who accuses you, on whom you set your hope. [46]If you believed Moses, you would believe me, for he wrote of me. [47]But if you do not believe his writings, how will you believe my words?"

5:37–38 "And the Father who sent me has himself borne witness to me."

---

(36) John Chrysostom

And the Father who sent me has himself borne witness to me (5:37). Where did the Father bear witness to him? At the Jordan River. *This is my beloved Son, with whom I am well pleased* (Matt 3:17). Yet, they needed proof beyond this. The witness of John was clear, for the Jews had come to him and could not deny what he said (cf. 3:26). The testimony from the various miracles was similarly clear, for they had seen the miracles performed and had heard from the one who had been healed and believed. Yet it was from these events that they drew up their accusations. Therefore, it was necessary to give evidence proving the testimony of the Father. In order to do this, he added, **His voice you have never heard** (5:37). How then did Moses say, *Moses spoke, and God answered him* (Exod 19:19)? How then did David say, *I hear a voice I had not known* (Ps 81:5)? Again Moses asks, *Did any people ever hear the voice of God* (Deut 4:33)? **His form you have never seen** (5:37). Yet, Isaiah, Jeremiah, Ezekiel, and many others are said to have seen him. What does Christ say next? He guides them step-by-step toward a philosophical doctrine which shows that God does not have either a voice or a physical form. He is much loftier than such forms or sounds. For when the Lord says, **His voice you have never heard** (5:37), he does not mean that God actually utters a **voice**, which is just inaudible. Likewise, when he says, **His form you have never seen** (5:37), he does not mean that God has a **form**, which is just invisible.

Neither of these things belongs to God. In order that they might not say, "You are a brag-gart! God spoke only to Moses!"—but they actually said this very thing: *We know that God has spoken to Moses, but as for this man, we do not know where he comes from* (9:29)—he said these things to demonstrate that God does not have a **voice** or a **form**. Why then have I named these two things? Not only **have you never heard his voice** and **you have never seen his form** (5:37), it is not even possible for you to assert that you have received and kept his commandments—that is, the ordinances, the commandments, the law and the prophets—of which you boast constantly and are so supremely confident. Even though God established them, **you do not have his word abiding in you, for you do not believe** (5:38) in me. Although the Scriptures everywhere say that it is necessary to be mindful of me, **you do not believe**. It is quite clear that **you do not have his word abiding in you** (5:38). For this reason, he adds, **For you do not believe him whom he has sent** (5:38). Accordingly then that they cannot argue the following: How, if we **have never heard his voice**, **has** he **borne witness to** you (5:37)?

5:39-40 "You search the scriptures, because you think that in them you have eternal life; and it is they that bear witness to me; yet you refuse to come to me that you may have life."

---

(37) John Chrysostom

Christ urged the Jews not merely to read the Scriptures but carefully to **search** them and reflect upon them. Therefore, he did not say "read the Scriptures," but **search the scrip-tures** (5:39). Since he was foreshadowed in earlier times in accordance with the needs of the people in those periods, the texts about him required a great deal of careful study. So he now commands them to search out the meaning of the Scriptures carefully so that they will discover what lies hidden in their depths. Their meaning is not stated on the surface or set forth in the literal sense but lies buried deep like a treasure. The one who seeks for hidden objects will not be able to find what he searches for if he does not do so carefully and persistently. For this reason, when he had said **search the scriptures**, he added **because you think that in them you have eternal life** (5:39). He did not say "you have," but **you think**. This is to show that they gained no significant and tangible benefit if they thought that they would obtain salvation by the mere reading of the Scriptures, for in fact they lacked faith. So what he meant is something like this: Do you not marvel at the Scriptures? Do you not think that they are sources of all life? From them even I am currently drawing support. **It is they that bear witness to me yet you refuse to come to me that you may have life** (5:39-40). Reasonably then he said **you think**, because they did not wish to believe but bragged only about the fact that they read it. . . . Jesus declared that the Scriptures **bear witness** to him. However, he did not say where exactly they **bear witness**, for he wanted to encourage them toward a greater reverence and to send them **searching**.

5:45–46 "Do not think that I shall accuse you to the Father; it is Moses who accuses you, on whom you set your hope. If you believed Moses, you would believe me, for he wrote of me."

---

(38) Cyril of Alexandria

Do not think that I shall accuse you to the Father; it is Moses who accuses you, on whom you set your hope (5:45). After he said that the Pharisees wanted to live more arrogantly than piously and after he taught that they had turned aside to complete unbelief due to this attitude, he says that **Moses accuses** them. Ironically, it was their custom to boast very arrogantly about Moses. When the man who was blind from his birth once asked them regarding Christ: **Do you too want to become his disciples?** (9:27), they cried out immediately and said directly, **You are his disciple, but we are disciples of Moses!** (9:28). Therefore, the Lord says that Moses himself **accuses you, on whom you set your hope** (5:45). However, the Lord, reviled by all, will denounce your foolishness before God. In accordance with his saying to the Jews, **Do not think that I shall accuse you to the Father** (5:45), we do not hold that those who reject Christ will be held blameless by him. For what could we say when we hear him say, *So everyone who acknowledges me before men, I also will acknowledge before my Father who is in heaven; but whoever denies me before men, I also will deny before my Father who is in heaven* (Matt 10:32–33)? Should we not reasonably infer that they will be accused to God the Father due to their denial of Christ? I suppose that this is evident to everyone. The Jews are certainly not free from this accusation—in fact, it pertains to them most directly—because they have denied Christ by their unbelief for a long time. They dismissed his admonitions and paid no attention to his divine and heavenly teachings. Instead they devoted themselves entirely to keeping the Mosaic law so that they were seen even from a distance boldly proclaiming, *We know that God has spoken to Moses, but as for this man, we do not know where he comes from* (9:29). For this reason, he necessarily convicts them of transgressing against **Moses on whom** they boast. He says that they need no other accuser, for the law given through **Moses** is completely sufficient to **accuse** them for their unbelief even if the voice of the Judge—that is, Christ—is silent.

    If you believed Moses, you would believe me, for he wrote of me (5:46). After the Lord stated that the Jews would be accused by Moses and would be indicted by him for their unbelief, he rightly adds the following. He teaches that he reasonably finds them guilty . . . , for it is clear that he is speaking truthfully. It is as if he said, you may reject my words, but I will not put up with not being **believed**. Defer to your own Moses and trust him whom you admire, for by this you will truly know the very one whom you dishonor ignorantly. Discard your types which fight against the truth, for in his books I am foreshadowed. For this reason, the Lord says, **Moses** will **accuse you** (5:45) when he sees that you fail to believe his writings about **me**.

John 6

The church fathers expound the feeding of the five thousand against the backdrop of the Old Testament and in light of the Eucharistic practices of the church. For Augustine, the five barley loaves (6:9) symbolize the five books of the law of Moses. The two fish (6:9) signify the figures of the priest and king in the Old Testament. The boy who had the loaves and the fishes serves as a figure of the Jewish people. Augustine and John Scotus Eriugena interpret the distribution of the bread as the spreading of the gospel. Scotus offers both a literal and spiritual interpretation of this miracle, while John Chrysostom seizes on the verb gather up (6:12), which he takes to mean "ponder."

Both Augustine and Cyril of Alexandria see great significance in the fact that the disciples are in a boat that is besieged from every side by a violent storm (6:17–18). The boat is a symbol of the church. Both Augustine and Cyril comment on the words immediately the boat was at the land to which they were going (6:21). With Jesus, they do not have to row back to land. For Augustine the journey progressed from the "fluid to the solid, from the agitated to the firm, and from the way to the goal."

Augustine and John Chrysostom say that the miracle of manna in the desert was a figure of Christ, the true bread from heaven. Some writers draw a contrast between the crowd that seeks to secure this bread always (6:35) to fill their bellies and the Samaritan woman in John 4 who moves beyond the physical to secure the spiritual, living water which the Lord provides. Accordingly, Cyril of Alexandria explains that the bread of life (6:35) is the holy flesh and blood which restores humans wholly to incorruption and drives death away. Augustine exhorts Christians to eat the heavenly bread and come to the altar with a pure heart. Approach the holy meal with forgiveness in your heart, for you will then be forgiven.

Some—even those among his disciples—took great offense at the Lord's statements and said, This is a hard saying; who can listen to it? (6:60). Others, following Peter, responded with a confession: Lord, to whom shall we go? You have the words of eternal life; and we have believed, and have come to know, that you are the Holy One of God (6:68–69). For Augustine and John Chrysostom, the term eternal (6:54) means spiritual. Those who eat ordinary food for the purpose of sustaining temporal life will eventually die of old age, disease, or injury; but those who eat the true food and true drink (6:55), that is, the body and blood of the Lord, will inherit eternal life (6:54).

John 6:1–15

[1]After this Jesus went to the other side of the Sea of Galilee, which is the Sea of Tiberias. [2]And a multitude followed him, because they saw the signs which he did on those who were diseased. [3]Jesus went up on the mountain, and there sat down with his disciples. [4]Now the Passover, the feast of the Jews, was at hand. [5]Lifting up his eyes, then, and seeing that a multitude was coming to him, Jesus said to Philip, "How are we to buy bread, so that these people may eat?" [6]This he said to test him, for he himself knew what he would do. [7]Philip answered him, "Two hundred denarii would not buy enough bread for each of them to get a little." [8]One of his disciples, Andrew, Simon Peter's brother, said to him, [9]"There is a lad here who has five barley loaves and two fish; but what are they among so many?" [10]Jesus said, "Make the people sit down." Now there was much grass in the place; so the men sat down, in number about five thousand. [11]Jesus then took the loaves, and when he had given thanks, he distributed them to those who were seated; so also the fish, as much as they wanted. [12]And when they had eaten their fill, he told his disciples, "Gather up the fragments left over, that nothing may be lost." [13]So they gathered them up and filled twelve baskets with fragments from the five barley loaves, left by those who had eaten. [14]When the people saw the sign which he had done, they said, "This is indeed the prophet who is to come into the world!" [15]Perceiving then that they were about to come and take him by force to make him king, Jesus withdrew again to the mountain by himself.

6:7–13 One of his disciples, Andrew, Simon Peter's brother, said to him, "There is a lad here who has five barley loaves and two fish; but what are they among so many?" . . . So the men sat down, in number about five thousand. . . . So they gathered them up and filled twelve baskets with fragments from the five barley loaves, left by those who had eaten.

---

(1) Theodore of Mopsuestia

So the men sat down, in number about five thousand. Jesus then took the loaves, and when he had given thanks,[1] **he distributed them to those who were seated; so also the fish** (6:10–11). The evangelist added the phrase **as much as they wanted** (6:11) to indicate it was both **as much as they wanted** and **as much as** they were able to eat. Jesus multiplied the bread and the fish that much. This is a very powerful sign. Of necessity, it filled those who were hungry . . . and after they were satisfied, it gave them provisions for the journey and something for them to take home. . . . This is what the statement **as much as they wanted** indicates. . . . **So they gathered them up and filled twelve baskets** (6:13). Therefore, the Lord ordered them to gather the leftovers, so that the impression of the miracle might

---

1. The Syriac verb, in both the *Peshitta* and Theodore's text, means "he had blessed," not **he had given thanks** (6:10). This is likely an allusion to the Eucharistic celebration.

remain in their memory for as long as they enjoyed what remained.[2] Those fragments were left over so that this miracle might become known everywhere according to his will . . . and the number of baskets was equal to the number of disciples. This miracle showed the abundance of his grace through the large amount of what was left. Moreover, it proved that he was doing everything according to his will, for what remained matched the number of those who would carry them.

(2) John Chrysostom

He commanded them to sit down at once, as though the table were prepared and ready. This command also seized the disciples' attention. They obeyed at once and were not confused since they had benefited from his questioning. They did not ask: What is this? Why did you give the order to sit when there is nothing in front of us? In this way, they began to believe even before seeing the miracle. The ones who in the beginning were so faithless as to ask, **How are we to buy bread?** (6:5), then began to command the crowd to sit down.

Why is it that he did not pray when he was about to cure the paralytic, or to raise the dead, or to calm the sea? Why does he pray here when performing the miracle of the loaves (6:11)? It was to show that those who are about to eat should give **thanks** (6:11) to God. In addition, he did it in the case of this lesser miracle so that you might learn that he did not do it out of necessity. If he needed to pray before doing a miracle, he would have done so in the instances of the greater miracles. Since he performed these other miracles without praying, it is certainly clear that he prayed before this miracle as a condescension to our lowliness. In addition, a great number of people were present. It was necessary therefore that they should become convinced that he had come in accordance with the will of God. This is the reason why he does not exhibit this behavior when he performed miracles without witnesses. However, when he does them in the midst of crowds, he removes their suspicion by giving **thanks** (6:11) to God and shows them that he is not an enemy or adversary of the one who has begotten him.

He gave the food to those who were seated, and they were filled (6:11-12). Do you understand how much of a difference there is between a servant and a master? The former, since they only had a little amount of grace, worked small miracles accordingly. In contrast, God, who acts with unlimited power, works all of his miracles with complete freedom. **He told his disciples, "Gather up the fragments left over, that nothing may be lost." So they gathered them up and filled twelve baskets . . .** (6:12-13). This was not an empty display of power but was done purposefully so that the miracle was not thought to be an illusion. In addition, this is why he started with a substantial material when he miraculously produced the loaves. Why did he not give the loaves to the crowds to carry away but gave them only to the disciples? In particular he wished to instruct those who were going to be teachers of the world. Certainly, the people would not derive any great benefit from his miracles; they forgot these almost immediately and would ask for another miracle. In contrast, the

---

2. Theodore emphasizes that the bread remained edible for a long period of time. This aspect of Christ's miracle allowed them to recall this event days later and to tell others about it.

disciples would obtain more than a transitory profit from them. What happened was a re-proach—and not merely a coincidental one—to Judas, since he also carried a basket. That these details were intended for their instruction is plain from what was said later, when he reminded them in the words: *Do you not yet perceive? Do you not remember . . . how many baskets you gathered?* (Matt 16:9). For the same reason the number of the baskets of fragments was equal to the number of the disciples. Later, when they had been instructed, there were not so many basketfuls, only seven (cf. Matt 15:37).[3]

I marvel not only at the large number of loaves that he brought about, but also in addition to the number, at the size of the surplus. He planned it so that there was neither too much nor too little remaining. Foreseeing how much they would consume, he produced just the amount he desired; this was an indication of his ineffable power. The fragments, therefore, confirmed the miracle. They testified to the miracle on both accounts; namely, that what had happened was not an illusion and that they had been fed by these miraculous loaves. The multiplication of the fish was accomplished at the same time by using actual fish. After the resurrection, it was no longer achieved by means of material elements.[4] Why was that? It happened so that you might learn in this instance being discussed that he did not need to use matter nor did he need to use elementary materials as the basis of his miracles; rather, he did it to shut up the mouths of the heretics!

(3) Augustine of Hippo

It is not enough to admire the miracles of Christ. Let us seek in them what they might tell us about Christ. They have a language of their own that needs to be comprehended. Since Christ is the Word of God, even the actions of the Word are a word to us. Since we have heard how great this miracle is, let us also search out how profound it is. Let us not be delighted only with its surface, but let us also seek to know its depth. This miracle, which we admire on the outside, has something within. . . .

To run through it briefly, the **five loaves** (6:9) are understood as the five books of Moses. Rightly, they are not made of wheat but of **barley** (6:9), because they belong to the Old Testament. For you know that barley was created in such a way that one can scarcely get its kernel; for this kernel is clothed with a covering of husk. This husk adheres tena-ciously, so that it is stripped off only with effort. Such is the letter of the Old Testament, clothed with the coverings of carnal mysteries; however, if one gets to its kernel, it feeds and satisfies.

A **lad** was carrying **five loaves and two fish** (6:10). If we should seek to know who this boy was, perhaps he was the people of Israel; for they carried these things with a boyish understanding and were not eating. The things which he was carrying, when kept shut, were a burden, but when they are opened, become food. Moreover, the **two fish** seem to us to signify those two sublime personages in the Old Testament who were anointed to become holy and to rule over the people: the priest and the king. Christ,

3. John Chrysostom has conflated the two different accounts of the feeding of the multitudes.
4. See John 21.

who was signified through these two persons, now at last came in mystery. He who was known only in part in the kernel of the **barley** came now at last. He came as one person carrying both personages in himself, both priest and king. He was the priest who offered to God the victim on our behalf, namely, himself. He was the king, because we are ruled by him. Those things which were being carried in a concealed way are now opened. Thanks be to him!

He fulfilled what was promised in the Old Testament in his very person. He ordered the **loaves** to be broken. By being broken, they were multiplied. Nothing is truer! How many books have those five books of Moses made when they are explained, just as if they are broken when discussed? But because of the ignorance of the first people, [the kernel] in that **barley** was covered. It was said about this first people, *To this day whenever Moses is read a veil lies over their minds* (2 Cor 3:15). The veil had not yet been taken away, because Christ had not yet come. The veil of the temple had not yet been torn into pieces when he was hanging on the cross (Matt 27:51). Because the people's ignorance was in the law, the Lord's test therefore unveiled the ignorance of the disciple. It follows then that nothing lacks meaning. All things give signs, but they require one who understands. Accordingly, the number of the people who were fed signifies the people placed under the law. Why were there **five thousand men** (6:10) except that they were under the law, and this law is set out in the five books of Moses? Similarly, the sick were brought forth from those *five porticoes* (5:2) but were not healed. But there he cured a sick man. Here he fed the masses from **five loaves** (6:9). In addition, they were reclining in the **grass** (6:10); therefore they understood in a carnal manner and rested upon carnal things, *for all flesh is grass* (Isa 40:6).

What are the **fragments** (6:13) except what the people could not eat? They are also understood as matters which contain a more hidden meaning which the multitude cannot grasp. . . . Why were **twelve baskets** (6:13) filled? This was done both marvelously—because a great thing was done—and it was done profitably—because a spiritual thing was done. They who at the time saw it, marveled; but we, hearing of it, do not marvel. For it was done so that they might see it, but it was written so that we might hear it. What the eyes were able to do in their case, faith does the same in ours. We perceive with the mind what we could not with the eyes. We are privileged before them, because it is said regarding us, **Blessed are they who see not, and yet believe** (20:29). I add that we have understood perhaps what that crowd did not understand. We have been fed in reality, in that we have been able to get at the kernel of the **barley** (6:9).

(4) Cyril of Alexandria

One of his disciples, Andrew, Simon Peter's brother, said to him, "There is a lad here who has five barley loaves and two fish; but what are they among so many?" (6:8-9). Andrew thinks and reasons like Philip, and he is guilty of holding similar doubts about Christ, the Savior. Neither of them considered his power, nor were they persuaded that he was able to do all things easily by the greatness of the previous miracles. Andrew points out what the **lad** has but is certainly weak in faith, for he asks, **But what are they among**

so many? But he should return deliberately to his memory of the deeds which have already been done miraculously. He should consider that it is not unusual or exceptional for the Lord who had changed water into wine, healed the paralytic, and drove away a terrible disease with just one word, to create food from an inanimate substance and miraculously multiply the very small amount that was at hand. Should not the authority that enabled one miracle work in the other? Therefore, these two disciples answered more ineptly than they should have. For this reason we must examine this account once again. Sometimes the missteps made by the saints are profitable, for they often contain within something hidden which proves helpful to ease the burden of their apparent weakness.

After pondering the situation, one of the previously mentioned holy disciples said simply, **Two hundred denarii would not buy enough bread for each of them to get a little** (6:7). The other plainly said of the **five loaves and two fish: But what are they among so many?** (6:9). By their own words, they point out the great crowd that was about to be fed and thus elevate the miracle and highlight the power of the Savior. In this way, the force of their doubt is changed into a strong witness for Christ. When they confessed that a large amount of money **would not buy enough** to provide the crowd even a little relief, they crown the divine Master of the Host by this very sentiment. Although there was nothing—as Andrew says, **but what are they among so many?**—Christ richly increased his miracle of love toward the crowd.

Similarly, we find a weakness of faith in the wise Moses while he was in the wilderness. The people of Israel were weeping and lusting bitterly for the tables of Egypt. They remembered the unclean plates of meat and yearned after the strangest delights—onions, garlic, and other stinky things—(cf. Num 11:4–5); they disregarded the good things of God and attacked Moses, their mediator and leader. But God was cognizant of those things the people were yearning for, and he promised to provide them with meat. However, when the promise of generosity was made by God while they were in the wilderness and it seemed difficult according to human reasoning for this to be accomplished, Moses came to God and cried out: *The people among whom I am number six hundred thousand on foot; and thou hast said, "I will give them meat, that they may eat a whole month!" Shall flocks and herds be slaughtered for them, to suffice them? Or shall all the fish of the sea be gathered together for them, to suffice them? And the* LORD *said to Moses, "Is the* LORD'*s hand shortened? Now you shall see whether my word will come true for you or not"* (Num 11:21–23).

One might reasonably respond to the words of Philip and Andrew similarly: *Is the* LORD'*s hand shortened?* Let us also take this as an example and posit that a weakness of faith is the worst illness and surpasses all evil. If God does something or promises to do it, may it be fully accepted with simple faith. Let God not be criticized due to our inability and our own powerlessness to understand how things too lofty for us will happen. . . . These things that are beyond us are received by faith and not by intellectual inquiry. Just as the one who believes is admired, so also the one who falls into unbelief is not free from condemnation. The savior himself testifies to this when he says: *He who believes in him is not condemned; he who does not believe is condemned already, because he has not believed in the name of the only Son of God* (3:18).

6:14–15 "This is indeed the prophet who is to come into the world!" Perceiving then that they were about to come and take him by force to make him king, Jesus withdrew again to the mountain by himself.

---

(5) John Chrysostom

They said, "This is indeed the prophet. . . . Perceiving then that they were about to come and take him by force to make him king, Jesus withdrew again to the mountain by himself (6:14–15). Oh, the overmastering power of gluttony! He had performed innumerable miracles more wondrous than these, but in none of these instances had they offered this acknowledgment except in the one where they had been satiated. Is it not clear from this declaration that they were awaiting a chosen prophet? Formerly some had asked, **Are you the prophet?** (1:21). But these people say, **This is indeed the prophet. Perceiving then that they were about to come and take him by force to make him king, Jesus withdrew again to the mountain by himself** (6:14–15). Unbelievable! How great is the tyranny of gluttony! How great is the fickleness of humans! No longer do they guard the law. No longer do they fret over violations of the Sabbath. No longer are they zealous for God. All such considerations are cast aside when their bellies have been filled! He was a **prophet** in their eyes. They were about to choose him for their **king**. But Christ flees! Why does he do this? To teach us to despise worldly honors and to show us that he needed nothing on earth. For he who chose all lowly things—mother, house, city, upbringing, and clothing—would not afterward be made illustrious by things on earth. The things which he had from heaven were glorious and marvelous: angels, a star, his Father's loud proclamation, the Spirit testifying, and the prophets announcing him long ago. His possessions on earth were all lowly so that his power might be manifest even more. He came to teach us to despise the things of the world. We were not to be amazed or astonished by the splendors of this life, but to laugh scornfully at them and to desire the things which are to come. For the one who admires the things which are here will not admire those in the heavens. For this reason he says to Pilate, *My kingship is not of this world* (18:36). . . . When the prophet Zechariah said, *Behold your king comes to you . . . humble and riding on an ass . . .* (Zech 9:9), he spoke of that kingdom which is in the heavens, but not of this on earth. Similarly, Christ says, *I do not receive glory from men* (5:41).

Let us learn, brothers and sisters, to despise and to resist the honor that humans give. We have been honored with the greatest of honors! Compared with this, the honor of humans is truly an insult, ridicule, and mockery. Just as the riches of this world compared with those riches are like poverty and just as life apart from that is death—as Jesus said, *Leave the dead to bury their own dead* (Matt 8:22)—so compared with that, any honor given by humans is shame and ridicule. Let us not chase after it. If those who confer this honor are considered less than a shadow or a dream, then their honor is even less so. The glory of humans is like the flower of the grass (cf. 1 Pet 1:24). . . . In short, if you desire glory, then seek it, but let it be eternal glory! It is shown on a more glorious stage and gives greater profit. For humans demand that you spend it for their pleasure; in contrast, Christ gives you one hundred times what you give him and then adds eternal life! Which of the two is better then? To be admired on earth or in heaven? By humans or by God? For loss or for gain? To wear a crown for a single day or for eternity?

(6) Augustine of Hippo

Why did he ascend the **mountain** after he perceived that they wished to **take him by force to make him king** (6:15)? He was certainly not the type of king crowned by humans. Rather, he is the sort that would create a kingdom for them. Might it not be the case that Jesus, whose deeds are often words, signifies something to us here too? Regarding "they wished to **take him by force to make him king**" (6:15) and "**Jesus withdrew again to the mountain**" (6:15), is his reaction really silence? Does it say nothing? Mean nothing? Or was this desire to **take him by force to make him king** an intentional anticipation of the time of his kingdom? He had come at this time not to reign immediately but to reign in a different sense, as when we pray: "Your kingdom come!" Certainly, he reigns always with the Father since he is the Son of God, the Word of God, **the Word** by whom **all things were made** (1:1–3). The prophets foretold his kingdom when Christ was made man and when he made his followers Christians. Subsequently, there will be a kingdom of Christians. Presently they are being gathered together, prepared, and redeemed by the blood of Christ. In the future, after the judgment . . . is executed by the Son of Man, his kingdom will be made manifest and the glory of the saints will be revealed. The apostle said of this kingdom, *Then comes the end, when he delivers the kingdom to God the Father* (1 Cor 15:24). Christ also references this himself when he said, *Come, O blessed of my Father, inherit the kingdom prepared for you from the foundation of the world* (Matt 25:34). Both the disciples and the people who believe in him thought that he had come to reign immediately. Therefore, they wished to **take him by force to make him king** (6:15).

(7) John Scotus Eriugena

When the people saw the sign which he had done, they said, "This is indeed the prophet who is to come into the world!" (6:14). In this way the imperfect crowd is proved wrong. They were saying, **This is indeed the prophet who is to come into the world!** (6:14), on account of the visible sign and not on account of the intelligible power of the sign. In this miracle one should inquire about why there are **five barley loaves** (6:13). What does it mean the **twelve baskets** (6:13) are filled only by the **fragments** of the five loaves but not by **fragments of** the **two fish** (6:9) despite the fact that the gospel says that **five thousand** (6:10) people were filled by five loaves and two fish? The depth of this mystery seems so obscure to me that it can hardly be investigated. Indeed, Augustine in his exposition of John does not treat this but passes it by. However, what is read in Mark might seem to suffice for many: *And they took up twelve baskets full of broken pieces and of the fish* (Mark 6:43). . . . Matthew and Luke mention the fragments without discrimination, leaving it ambiguous as to whether they are fragments of the loaves only (as John) or of loaves and fishes together (as Mark) (cf. Matt 14:20 and Luke 9:17).

Let us therefore try, to whatever extent the light of our minds allows, to make an inquiry without prejudging against other senses. We said before that fivefold number of the loaves indicated the five senses of the body or the five Mosaic books and that the two fish were symbols of both Testaments. So first one must ask what the difference is between the mysteries and the symbols of either Testament (one is the testament of the law and the one of grace). Properly understood, the mysteries are those things which are handed down allegorically, both in regard to what was done and what was said. They were both done in accordance with the things that happened and were spoken, because they were narrated. For example, the Mosaic tabernacle was both constructed according to what happened and was spoken and narrated by the text of the holy Scripture. Similarly, the sacraments of legal sacrifices were both done (according to history) and spoken (according to narration). Circumcision likewise was both done in the flesh and narrated in the letter. In the New Testament, too, the mystery of baptism and of the Lord's body and blood and of holy chrismation were accomplished in what happened and are handed down and spoken of in the letters. This form of the sacraments is reasonably called by the Fathers an allegory of what was done and spoken. Another form is that which properly took the name symbol and is called an allegory of what is spoken but not of what was done, because it consists only in things spoken of spiritually but not in sensible things done. Therefore, mysteries are those things in either Testament that were both done according to history and narrated according to the letter, but symbols are those things which were not done but were spoken of by doctrine alone as if they were done. For example, in the old law it was written: *You shall not boil a kid in its mother's milk* (Exod 23:19; 34:26; Deut 14:21). Even if this is read as never having happened in history, as Augustine testifies, it is nevertheless spoken and written and is handed down as if it had happened, since the truth of the divine history is not found only in the narration of what had happened. Again in the psalms: *The mountains skipped like rams, the hills like lambs* (Ps 114:4). For in these places of divine Scripture and in many similar ones, an allegory only of what was said but not of what was both said and done is understood.

In the New Testament many things are narrated which were not done according to history but were only recounted as if they were done. Examples of this are found especially in the allegory of the Lord's parables: for example, in the parable of the rich man and the pauper Lazarus reclining in the bosom of Abraham, about the chasm between them, about the fire, and about the tongue and the finger. All of those things, which no authority hands down as having actually occurred with respect to the deeds, were said entirely in a figure. This form is to be noted in almost all the parables and is properly called "symbolic"; although the tendency of holy Scripture is to put symbols in the place of mysteries and mysteries in the place of symbols by a certain proximity and similarity. Therefore, we propose a certain similarity by which we might suggest what we wish to assert.

A people of carnal beliefs took precedence in both the old law and in the new. For this reason it is now supposed that nothing exists beyond the letter and bodily senses. But one is able to ascend higher, beyond the letter of Scripture and above those things which are received through the senses. Similarly, in the old law and also in the New Testament, there are said to have been those who were perfect and wise in action and knowledge of spiritual meanings who, like the disciples, ascended with Christ to the height of contemplation, as if up a **mountain** (6:15). Those who were carnal were left behind under the letter and the physical sense, reclining upon the *grass* (6:10) of temporal deeds: *All flesh is grass, and all its beauty like the flower of the field* (Isa 40:6). Therefore, let us consider that the **multitude** (6:5) of the simple people of faith spiritually reside on the mountainsides or on the plain, that is, below the height of divine understandings. For we are led to understand from the text of this gospel that the Lord fed the crowd not at the summit of a mountain but in a certain plain, where there was **much grass** (6:10). Therefore, it says, **Jesus withdrew again to the mountain by himself** (6:15).

Accordingly, we should understand that the Lord with his disciples alone had first ascended the mountain and then later descended again to the lower places. Once the miracle had been accomplished, **Jesus withdrew again to the mountain** (6:15). Before this **multitude** that was hungering for the faith of Christ were placed **five loaves** and **two fish** (6:9), that is, sacraments, that were both done and spoken, and symbols, which are only spoken but not done. Taking the **five loaves** and the **two fish** and **giving thanks** (6:11)—obviously to the Father who wanted to feed his faithful on symbols and sacraments—Christ gave these to his disciples, his teachers, his servants; they **distributed** (6:11) them to the crowd. The **barley loaves** (6:9) are broken by the disciples when the mysteries of either law are divided by them into things done and into their spiritual meanings. The simple and carnal feed upon history; **the disciples gather** (6:13) the divine meanings of that very history like spiritual **fragments** (6:13). The **fragments** that the carnal eat and by which they are filled are the deeds done; the **fragments** that the spiritual eat are the divine meanings of the deeds done. For example, in the book of Genesis it is narrated that the fleshly Israel crossed the Red Sea (Exod 14:29).[5] To this point, the simple Christian, as if sitting on the **grass** (6:10) of temporal and fleshly things, feeds upon the history alone. For whatever was done there was known by means of the five corporeal senses. For the Israelites were seen crossing the sea with dry feet and the Egyptians were seen to have been killed. This is also heard by similar people from which the details of the sea are tasted, smelled, and touched. The faithful soul which is still simple considers and ponders all of these details from which it is filled, as if by certain **fragments** of the divine history. But the **fragment** cannot contain the meaning of the letter itself. Therefore it is gathered by those who understand spiritual things so that it will not be lost but might benefit those who are able to understand.

John 6:16–25

[16]**When evening came, his disciples went down to the sea,** [17]**got into a boat, and started across the sea to Capernaum. It was now dark, and Jesus had not yet come to them.** [18]**The sea rose because a strong wind was blowing.** [19]**When they had rowed about three or four miles, they saw Jesus walking on the sea and drawing near to the boat. They were frightened,** [20]**but he said to them, "It is I; do not be afraid."** [21]**Then they were glad to take him into the boat, and immediately the boat was at the land to which they were going.** [22]**On the next day the people who remained on the other side of the sea saw that**

---

5. John Scotus clearly means the Exodus, not Genesis.

there had been only one boat there, and that Jesus had not entered the boat with his disciples, but that his disciples had gone away alone. [23]However, boats from Tiberias came near the place where they ate the bread after the Lord had given thanks. [24]So when the people saw that Jesus was not there, nor his disciples, they themselves got into the boats and went to Capernaum, seeking Jesus. [25]When they found him on the other side of the sea, they said to him, "Rabbi, when did you come here?"

6:16–21 When evening came, his disciples went down to the sea, got into a boat, and started across the sea to Capernaum.... When they had rowed about three or four miles, they saw Jesus walking on the sea and drawing near to the boat. They were frightened, but he said to them, "It is I; do not be afraid."

---

(8) Augustine of Hippo

When he was on the mountain, what were the disciples experiencing in the **boat** (6:17)? From that perspective the boat prefigured the church. If we who are in the church do not in the first instance perceive how that boat was foundering, those events are ephemeral and without deeper significance. But if we see the truth of those signs in the life of the church, it becomes clear that the actions of Christ are a type of communication. **When evening came, his disciples went down to the sea, got into a boat, and** came **across the sea to Capernaum** (6:16–17). It says that they came **across the sea to Capernaum** quickly.[6] The text then goes back and explains how they sailed over the lake. While they were sailing to that place—where it already said that they had arrived—the text explains once again what happened: **It was now dark, and Jesus had not yet come to them** (6:17). Certainly it was dark, for the Light had not yet come! **It was now dark, and Jesus had not yet come to them** (6:17). As the end of the world comes closer, errors grow, terrors become frequent, iniquity spreads, and unbelief increases. Consequently, the light, which is shown clearly and completely by John the Evangelist to be love when he says: *He who hates his brother is in the darkness* (1 John 2:11), is often extinguished. This darkness of brotherly hatred grows daily, and Jesus has not yet come. What makes it clear that it is growing? *Because iniquity will abound, the love of many will grow cold* (Matt 24:12). The darkness grows, and Jesus has not yet come. When darkness grows, when love grows cold, when iniquity abounds, these are the waves assaulting the boat. The storms and the waves are the shouts of slanderers. From these, love grows cold; from these, the waves are enlarged and the ship is battered.

The sea rose because a strong wind was blowing (6:18). Darkness was increasing, comprehension was lessening, and iniquity was growing. **When they had rowed about twenty-five or thirty stadia . . .** (6:19).[7] Meanwhile, they were still pushing on

---

6. Augustine's commentary follows the Latin text of verse 17, which states that the disciples **came across the sea to Capernaum.**

7. The RSV has rendered the original distance measured as stadia into the more familiar mile for modern

and moving forward. Those winds and storms and waves and darkness did not cause the boat to stall or to break up and sink, but it was proceeding forward despite all those troubles. Because *iniquity has abounded* and the *love of many grows cold*, the waves grow, the darkness is increased, the wind rages, but regardless the ship proceeds, for *he who endures to the end will be saved* (Matt 24:13). In addition, the number of stadia should not be ignored, for it signifies something. **When they had rowed about twenty-five or thirty stadia**, Jesus came to them. Since it was an estimate and not a precise number, either **twenty-five** or **thirty** would have been sufficient. Would the truth have been in danger if one were to say **about twenty-five stadia** or **about thirty stadia**, given that it was an estimate? From **twenty-five** he created **thirty**. Let us examine the number **twenty-five**. From where is it derived? From where does it come? From fives. The number five refers to the law. There are the five books of Moses. There are five porticoes containing the sick (5:2–3), and the five loaves feeding five thousand men (6:5–15). It follows then that the number **twenty-five** signifies the law, for five times five equals **twenty-five**, the square of the number five. But before the gospel came to this law, perfection was lacking. Perfection is contained in the number six; accordingly, God "perfected" the world in six days (cf. Gen 1:31–2:2). Five is multiplied by six in order that the law may be fulfilled by the gospel. Five times six equals **thirty**.

To those who fulfill the law, Jesus came. How did he come? He came trampling on the waves, pressing the swells of this world under his feet and smashing all the loftiness of this age. This is done as long as time is added and as long as the life of this age continues. Tribulations are increased in this world, evils are multiplied, afflictions are added, and all these things are piled up. Jesus crosses over and tramples upon the waves. Despite this, the tribulations are so great that even those who believe in Jesus and who try to persevere even to the end fear that they may fail. While Christ treads upon the waves and pushes down the ambitions and heights of this age, Christians fear. These things were foretold to them, were they not? Certainly, when Jesus was walking on the waves, **they were frightened** (6:20), just as other Christians. Although they hope in a future age and they see the loftiness of this age being trampled down, they are very often troubled about the disease of human affairs. They open the gospel, they open the scriptures, and they find all these things predicted, because the Lord does these very things. He tramples down the heights of the world so that he may be glorified by the humble, concerning whose loftiness it is foretold: *The swords of the enemy failed completely, and the cities you destroyed* (Ps 9:6 [9:7 LXX]). Why are you then afraid, Christians? Christ says, **It is I; do not be afraid** (6:20). Why are you alarmed by these things? Why are you afraid? I have foretold these events. I myself do them; they must be done! **It is I; do not be afraid. Then they were glad to take him into the boat** (6:20–21). After recognizing him and rejoicing, they were freed from their fears. **And immediately the boat was at the land to which they were going** (6:21). The journey ended at the land, from the fluid to the solid, from the agitated to the firm, from the way to the goal.

---

readers. In order to follow Augustine's argumentation, the translation of John 6:19 (**When they had rowed about three or four miles**) will read **When they had rowed about twenty-five to thirty stadia.**

(9) Cyril of Alexandria

When evening came, his disciples went down to the sea, got into a boat, and started across the sea to Capernaum (6:16–17). After performing that miracle, someone might ask why Jesus's ability to walk the sea is immediately introduced. Here is a reasonable explanation. When Jesus wanted to feed the crowds of people, Philip and Andrew assumed that he would not be able to do it. One of them said that a large amount of money *would not buy enough bread for each of them to get a little* (6:7). The other remarked that one of the lads was found with *five loaves and two fish* (6:9) but that this was not sufficient for so great a crowd. From what they said, it seems that they thought he could do nothing extraordinary. To break free of so limited a vision and to enlighten the apostles whose minds were still weak, he had to show them that he does whatever he wills in a wondrous way, for he is unrestrained by the laws of nature. The order that seems built into things does not restrict him at all. Even water, which by nature is a liquid and cannot support human bodies, is firm under his feet, because *with God all things are possible* (Matt 19:26).

When **evening** came and the crowd seeking him lost interest as time passed, the group of holy **disciples went down to the sea.** They sailed away at once, for they obeyed without delay their God and Teacher in every way. **It was now dark, and Jesus had not yet come to them. The sea rose because a strong wind was blowing** (6:17–18). Many events all at once are converging in an auspicious way. The circumstances drive the disciples to seek after the Savior more zealously. The deep darkness of the night, which hovers like smoke above the raging waves, makes them worry and strips them of the ability to know where to steer. At the same time the fierceness of the **winds** drives the waves with a rushing sound and lifts the swells to an extraordinary height. This makes them worry even more. While these events are taking place, the text says, **Jesus had not yet come to them** (6:17). This detail shows how serious the danger they were in. That Christ was not with the sailors increased their fear. Therefore, those who are not with Jesus because they are separated or seemingly absent from him through their departure from his holy laws and are cut off due to their sin from the one who is able to save are tossed about as if by a storm. If it is oppressive to be in spiritual darkness and if it is distressing to be swallowed up by the bitter sea of pleasures, let us receive Jesus. This will deliver us from dangers and from death in sin. The meaning of what has been said will be clearly seen in what happens next. He will certainly come to his disciples.

When they had rowed about three or four miles, they saw Jesus walking on the sea and drawing near to the boat. They were frightened, but he said to them, "It is I; do not be afraid" (6:19–20). When they were a long way from land and in the middle of the sea, it seemed that they would not be saved from their danger. After being called three times, Christ appears to them.[8] When fear had severed all hope of life, he delivered those in danger. He appears to them miraculously so that they would gain greater benefit. They are astonished to see Jesus walking through the middle of the sea and on the water itself. In fact, this miracle increases their fear. But Christ removes their anxieties at once when he says, **It is I; do not be afraid.** It is necessary for those to whom Christ is present to put

---

8. It is unclear what Cyril has in mind when he states that Jesus has been called "three times."

away all their worries and to overcome all dangers boldly. On account of this we will see once again that we should have a courageous spirit which is valiant in the face of temptations and manifests enduring fortitude due to our hope in Christ. Even though the fear of temptation which surrounds us is great, stand firmly confident in the fact that we are certainly saved. Notice that Christ does not appear to those in the boat as soon as they set sail or when the dangers begin. Rather, he appears when they are **three or four miles** (6:19) from the land. The grace of the Savior does not come to us when problems first torment us. Instead when fear is at its highest and danger appears greatest and when we are found in the middle of the waves of tribulations—when Christ is least expected—then he appears. He removes our fear and frees us from every danger. By his divine power he changes what we dread into joy, as if calming the storm.

Then they were glad to take him into the boat, and immediately the boat was at the land to which they were going (6:21). The Lord not only frees the sailors from all dangers by shining upon them miraculously but also frees them from both toil and sweat. By his divine powers, he thrusts the ship forward to the opposite shore. While they expected that they would continue to row and only reach the shore with great difficulty, the Lord relieves them of their toil. In a short period of time, the worker of many miracles reveals himself to them and strengthens their faith. When Christ appears and shines upon us, we will succeed against all hope without any toil. When he comes to us, we, who were in danger because we did not have him, will no longer need to labor to accomplish what is profitable for us. Christ is our deliverance from all danger. To those who receive him, he is the fulfillment of achievements beyond all hope.

Since we have discussed every portion of this subject in detail, let us figure out the spiritual interpretation by joining the meaning of this section with the previous portions of the text. We said previously that Jesus ascended into heaven as one ascends a mountain. That is to say, he was taken up after his resurrection from the dead. After this happened, his disciples, who represent typologically the ecclesiastical teachers throughout all time, are alone and by themselves. They swim through the waves of this present life as a type of sea and confront many temptations. While teaching and preaching, they endure awful dangers from those who oppose the faith and war against the gospel. But they will be freed from both their fear and every danger. They will rest from their labor and suffering when Christ appears to them in his divine power and places the whole world under his feet. Since the sea is often understood typologically as the world in the divine Scriptures, as it says in the psalms: *Yonder is the sea, great and wide, which teems with things innumerable, living things both small and great* (Ps 104:25), I think that this is what his walking on the water signifies. When Christ comes, as it is written, *in the glory of his Father* (Matt 16:27), then the ship of the holy apostles (i.e., the church) and those who sail within her (i.e., those who through faith and love are above the things of this world), will gain **the land to which they were going** (6:21) without delay and without toil. For it was their goal to reach the kingdom of heaven, as if reaching a fair harbor.

The Savior corroborates this interpretation when he says to his disciples, *A little while, and you will see me no more; again a little while, and you will see me* (16:16). He also says, *In the world you have tribulation; but be of good cheer, I have overcome the world* (16:33). In the **evening** (6:16), the Lord descended the mountain and came to his disciples who were watchful. When they saw him coming, they were **afraid** (16:20) and trembled. This was made known to us, so that a necessary lesson might be understood. He will descend from heaven—as at **evening**—while the world is still sleeping and slumbering in much sin. Therefore, he also says to us, *Watch therefore, for you do not know on what day your Lord is coming* (Matt 24:42). The parable of the virgins will also teach us this (cf. Matt 25:1–13). He says that there were five wise virgins and five foolish ones: *As the bridegroom was delayed, they all slumbered and slept. But at midnight there was a cry, "Behold, the bridegroom! Come out to meet him!"* (Matt 25:5–6). Do you see how the *bridegroom* is announced to us at midnight? The divine Paul will tell us what the *cry* is and what will happen during that *meeting*. He said previously, *For the Lord himself will descend from heaven with a cry of command, with the archangel's call, and with the sound of the trumpet of God* (1 Thess 4:16). He said to another of the saints who would be raised, *We who are alive, who are left, shall be caught up together with them in the clouds to meet the Lord in the air; and so we shall always be with the Lord* (1 Thess 4:17). However, the disciples were seized with fear despite the fact that they both saw him walking toward them and were found working and watching. This shows that when the judge comes, he will terrify everyone! The righteous man, although he knows beforehand that the judge will come, does not neglect his virtuous labor, and takes care to watch carefully with vigilance, will nevertheless certainly shake within himself, as if tested by fire. But the Lord does not enter the **boat** with his disciples as if he were going to sail with them. Rather he moves it to the **land** (6:21). At that time Christ will not serve to work alongside those who honor him to secure their virtue; rather, he will give them what they have already achieved, their desired end.

John 6:26–35

²⁶Jesus answered them, "Truly, truly, I say to you, you seek me, not because you saw signs, but because you ate your fill of the loaves. ²⁷Do not labor for the food which perishes, but for the food which endures to eternal life, which the Son of man will give to you; for on him has God the Father set his seal." ²⁸Then they said to him, "What must we do, to be doing the works of God?" ²⁹Jesus answered them, "This is the work of God, that you believe in him whom he has sent." ³⁰So they said to him, "Then what sign do you do, that we may see, and believe you? What work do you perform? ³¹Our fathers ate the manna in the wilderness; as it is written, 'He gave them bread from heaven to eat.'" ³²Jesus then said to them, "Truly, truly, I say to you, it was not Moses who gave you the bread from heaven; my Father gives you the true bread from heaven. ³³For the bread of God is that which comes down from heaven, and gives life to the world." ³⁴They said to him, "Lord, give us this bread always." ³⁵Jesus said to them, "I am the bread of life; he who comes to me shall not hunger, and he who believes in me shall never thirst."

6:26–27 Jesus answered them, "Truly, truly, I say to you, you seek me, not because you saw signs, but because you ate your fill of the loaves. Do not labor for the food which perishes, but for the food which endures to eternal life, which the Son of man will give to you; for on him has God the Father set his seal."

(10) Augustine of Hippo

After the miraculous sacrament, he begins a discourse which perhaps will feed them further. He will fill their minds, whose bellies have been filled with the loaves, with words, if they will receive them. But if they do not receive them, let the fragments they did not take be retrieved so they are not lost. So, let him speak and let us hear. **Jesus answered them, "Truly, truly, I say to you, you seek me, not because you saw signs, but because you ate your fill of the loaves"** (6:26). You seek me because of the flesh not because of the spirit. Many seek Jesus only so he will do them some temporal good. One man has a business venture; he seeks the intervention of the clergy. Another is oppressed by someone more powerful; he flees to the church. Another desires intercession between himself and another with whom he has little influence. So another, and another. The church today is filled with such people. Jesus is rarely sought for himself. **Jesus answered them, "Truly, truly, I say to you, you seek me, not because you saw signs, but because you ate your fill of the loaves. Do not labor for the food which perishes, but for the food which endures to eternal life"** (6:26–27). You **seek me** for the sake of something else; **seek me** for my sake. He suggests that he is himself that **food**. This is clear in the following words: **which the Son of man will give to you** (6:27). I think that you expected once again to eat bread, to sit down, and to be filled. But he had said, **Do not labor for the food which perishes, but for the food which endures to eternal life** (6:27). In the same way, he said to the Samaritan woman: *If you knew . . . who it is that is saying to you, "Give me a drink," you would have asked him, and he would have given you living water. The woman said to him, "Sir, you have nothing to draw with, and the well is deep; where do you get that living water?" . . . Jesus said to her, "Everyone who drinks of this water will thirst again, but whoever drinks of the water that I shall give him will never thirst"* (4:10–11, 13–14). She rejoiced and desired to receive this gift so that she would no longer become tired from drawing the water and no longer suffer bodily thirst. Thus, in the middle of this sort of conversation, he turns to discuss a spiritual drink. Here he does the very same thing.

(11) Cyril of Alexandria

Do not labor for the food which perishes, but for the food which endures to eternal life, which the Son of man will give to you; for on him has God the Father set his seal (6:27). As God, he was not ignorant of the charges that would come from Jewish stupidity or the reason why they were often so foolishly enraged. He knew that they, only seeing the flesh and not perceiving that God the Word dwelt within, would ask themselves: "Who is this who uses words that are only proper to God? Who can give humans **food which endures to eternal life**?" (6:27). Such a thing, which is appropriate to God alone who is over all, is wholly foreign to human nature. The Savior accordingly defends himself with reasonable arguments. Preemptively he discredits their insolent chatter. He says that **the Son of man will give** them **food which endures to eternal life** (6:27). Immediately he affirms that he is **sealed** by the **Father**. Sealed either means that he is anointed—for the one who is anointed is sealed—or that he has been formed by the Father in his very nature. It is as if he said, "I am able to **give** you **food which endures** and delivers **eternal life** and joy. Although I seem to be like a man with flesh, I was anointed and sealed by God the Father as an exact likeness with him." He said, "You shall see that the Father is in me and I am in him by nature, even though I was born for your sake according to the divine order of the economy, a man from a woman (John 14:10). I can do all things in harmony with the divine authority and in no way fall short of the power intrinsic to my Father." Although God the Father gives you spiritual **food which endures to eternal life**, it is certain that **the Son will give** it also (6:27). It is made from his flesh since he is the exact image of the Father. His likeness to the Father in every way is understood not according to the image of the flesh or in any bodily form but in respect to his divine glory, equal power, and royal authority. We must note once again that when he says that the **Son of man will give** divine things and that he has been **sealed** with the image of God the Father, he did not experience the division which separated the temple of the virgin from the true, divine nature of the Son; rather, he desires to define himself in such a way as to be thought of as one. Truly Christ is over us as one, since he bears his own royal, purple robe—I mean his human body or his temple, specifically his soul and body. For Christ is one, united from both soul and body.

However, the one who resists Christ will say once again: "Most excellent sir, present the clear truth about your power. Do not deal cleverly with this saying and turn it shamefully however you want." Certainly, in this passage the Son is not shown to be of the essence of the Father but rather is shown to be a copy of his essence. Suppose we say something like the following: A seal or signet ring is pressed into wax or some other substance which can receive it. It leaves an imprint only of its likeness. Once the signet is removed by the one who pressed it, it loses nothing of itself. In the same way, the Father after impressing and imprinting himself wholly upon the Son creates the most accurate likeness of himself and in no way loses any part of his very essence, nor is he thought to be a mere image or accurate likeness.

Let anyone who desires knowledge notice that our opponent like a snake is now striking toward us and rearing up its head which is filled with venom.[9] But the one who *crushed the heads of the dragons* (Ps 74:14 [73:14 LXX]) will shatter him too and give us the power to escape his wicked stubbornness. Let our opponent, who has been blasting us with these dreadful words, answer the following: Does the seal or signet ring, which is made of wood, iron, or gold, seal with an impression the material upon which it is pressed? Is it not understood as a seal distinct from the impression? I suppose that any one of our opponents, even against his will, is held in check by the truth and would claim that it is sealed with an impress. For according to logic, it is not a seal if it is without an impression. The Son *bears the very stamp of the nature* (Heb 1:3) of God the Father as Scripture testifies, for he is by nature in and of the image. . . . The Word of the essence of the Father is not bare Word without flesh. He is sealed by the Father, and through him all things which are brought into

---

9. It is unclear which opponent Cyril is referencing.

the likeness of God as much as possible are sealed. In this way we understand the saying, *The light of your face was stamped upon us, O Lord* (Ps 4:6 [4:7 LXX]). He says that the countenance of God the Father is the Son who is the impress. The light of the countenance is the grace which the Spirit gives to creation. By this we are remolded into likeness with God through faith. We receive from him, as if by a seal, conformity with the Son who is the image of the Father in order that the fact that we were made after the image and the likeness of the creator might be preserved in us. Since the Son is certainly the countenance of God the Father, he is surely also the very impress with which God seals us.

6:30–34 So they said to him, "Then what sign do you do, that we may see, and believe you? What work do you perform? Our fathers ate the manna in the wilderness."

---

(12) John Chrysostom

Our fathers ate the manna in the wilderness (6:31). There are none who are more sense-less, none who are more unreasonable, than these people! While the miracle was still in their hands, they spoke as though nothing had been done. **What sign do you do** (6:30)? After speaking in this way, they do not even permit him to choose the **sign** but desire to make him show only the one that was done in the days of their fathers. Therefore, they say, **Our fathers ate the manna in the wilderness** (6:31). By this, they think that they can provoke him to work a miracle that might give them carnal nourishment. Why else would they mention none of the other miracles from the past—although many took place at that time in Egypt, at the sea, and in the wilderness—except that miracle of the **manna**? Was it not because they really desire that one because of the tyranny of their stomachs? After you saw his miracle and called him a prophet and tried to make him a king (cf. 6:15), how is it that you now have become thankless and thoughtless and ask for a sign as if none had been done? You utter words that are fitting for parasites and hungry dogs! Does the **manna** now seem wonderful to you? Is your soul not already dried up?

Note well their hypocrisy. They did not say, "Moses did this sign, what **do you do?**" For they thought that this would annoy him. In fact, they addressed him with great rever-ence for a while because they expected food. They also did not say, "God did this, what **do you do?**" For they did not want to seem to make him equal with God. Nor did they adduce Moses, so that they might not seem to lower him. They instead chose the intermediate way: **Our fathers ate the manna in the wilderness.** Certainly, he might have replied, "But now I have done greater miracles than **Moses** since I did not need a rod or prayer but did it on my own accord. Even if you recall the **manna**, notice that I have given you bread!" However, it was not the time for such arguments. He desired only one thing: to bring them spiritual food. So pay attention to his infinite wisdom and his way of answering them. **It was not Moses who gave you the bread from heaven; my Father gives you the true bread from heaven** (6:32). Why did he not say, **It was not Moses who gave** it to **you**, but me? Instead, he puts God in the place of **Moses**, and himself in the place of the **manna**. Why? Because, as is seen from what follows, the sickness of his hearers was so great. He did not even seize their attention, even after he said the following: **You seek me, not because you saw signs, but because you ate your fill of the loaves** (6:26). Even though they sought these carnal things, he would have corrected them by these words had they not been so resistant. When he promised the Samaritan woman that he would give her the water, he did not mention the Father. What does he say to her? *If you knew the gift of God, and who it is that is saying to you, "Give me a drink," you would have asked him, and he would have given you living water* (4:10). And again, he says, *The water that I shall give* (4:14). He does not refer her to the Father. However, in this account he mentions the Father so that you might know how great was the faith of the Samaritan woman and how great the sickness of the Jews.

(13) Theodore of Mopsuestia

Our fathers ate the manna in the wilderness; as it is written, "He gave them bread from heaven to eat" (6:31). In comparing the **manna**, they wanted to diminish his gift of bread so that they could show that they considered Moses to be more exceptional than Christ. However, from what is written in the Scriptures, the opposite is made clear. Although God provided the **manna** (6:31) to them in the wilderness, they did not grow weary of saying against God, *Even though he struck the rock and water gushed out, and torrents overflowed, can he not also give bread [to his people]?* (Ps 78:20). While their **fathers** were asking for *bread*—which they considered to be superior—and were testing God by saying that he was not able to provide it, these people preferred the gift of **manna** (6:31), because they considered what was given to their ancestors to be greater than what was given to them. It was only natural, since they called them their **fathers**, that they did not reject their verdict which considered *bread* to be something amazing. Even though they received what seemed better to their **fathers**, they themselves should have acknowledged the greatness of the present gift. But the ungratefulness of both is one and the same; they were always criticizing what was present by comparing it to what was missing.

Jesus then said to them, "Truly, truly, I say to you, it was not Moses who gave you the bread from heaven; my Father gives you the true bread from heaven. For the bread of God is that which comes down from heaven, and gives life to the world" (6:32–33). . . . It is indeed clear, then, that he is speaking about his body, for it is eaten allegorically in the institution of the mystery (i.e., the Eucharist). For the **bread** (6:33), which was given to the disciples by our Lord, is a type of the food which is his body. Down to this very day, we place it on the altar and receive it with our hands as the body of our Lord. For he makes this very clear in the words that come later, when he says, *And the bread which I shall give . . . is my flesh* (6:51).

(14) Augustine of Hippo

So they said to him, "Then what sign do you do, that we may see, and believe you? What work do you perform?" (6:30). Was it a small thing that they were fed with five loaves?

Certainly they knew this, but they preferred manna from heaven to this food. Indeed, the Lord Jesus stated that he was superior to Moses. Indeed, Moses did not daresay that he gives **the food which perishes, but the food which endures to eternal life** (6:27). The Lord promised something more than Moses did. Through Moses, in fact, a kingdom was promised: a land flowing with milk and honey, temporal peace, an abundance of children, health of body, and all the rest. These were indeed temporal things. Yet in a figurative way they were also spiritual, because they were promised to the people in the Old Testament. Therefore, they showed the promises through Moses and the promises through Christ. The one promised a full stomach on earth, but from the food that perishes. Christ promised **not the food which perishes, but the food which endures to eternal life** (6:27). They heard that he promised more, but they had not yet, as it were, seen him doing greater things. As a result they recalled what sort of things Moses had done. They wanted still greater things to be done by him who promised such great things. **So they said to him, "Then what sign do you do, that we may see, and believe you?"** (6:30).

So that you might know that they were comparing those miracles of Moses to this miracle and thus were judging these miracles which Jesus was doing as lesser, they said, **Our fathers ate the manna in the wilderness** (6:31). What is **manna**? . . . **As it is written, "He gave them bread from heaven to eat"** (6:31). Through Moses, our fathers received **bread from heaven**, but he did not say, **Do not labor for the food which perishes** (6:27). In contrast you promise **not the food which perishes, but the food which endures to eternal life** (6:27), yet you do not perform deeds like Moses. He did not give out barley loaves, but he gave **manna from heaven**.

Jesus then said to them, "Truly, truly, I say to you, it was not Moses who gave you the bread from heaven; my Father gives you the true bread from heaven. For the bread of God is that which comes down from heaven, and gives life to the world" (6:32–33). That is the true **bread** which gives life to the world, and this is the **food** about which I spoke before when I said, **Do not labor for the food which perishes, but for the food which endures to eternal life** (6:27). Manna signified this; indeed, all those signs signified me. You loved the signs that pointed to me. Do you now despise the one who was signified? Moses did not give **bread from heaven**. God gives the **bread**! But which bread? **Manna**, perhaps? No, but the bread which **manna** signified: namely, the Lord Jesus himself.

6:35 Jesus said to them, "I am the bread of life; he who comes to me shall not hunger, and he who believes in me shall never thirst."

---

(15) John Chrysostom

I am the bread of life (6:35). Now he takes them into the substance of the mysteries. First he speaks of his Godhead in the words: **I am the bread of life**. He was not saying this of his body. Later, he said in reference to his body: *The bread which I shall give for the life of the world is my flesh* (6:51). But in this case he is speaking about his Godhead. This is so because the Godhead becomes **bread** through God the Word, just as in like manner this **bread** becomes **bread from heaven** (6:32) because the Spirit comes upon it.[10] In this place he does not make use of witnesses to support his statements, as he had done in the previous location, for he had the miracle of the loaves itself as evidence and an audience who pretended for the first time to believe him. At this gathering, they were raising objections and finding fault with him. That is why he revealed himself as God. Now as long as these men had the expectation of enjoying bodily refreshment, they persevered and were not disturbed at his words. Afterward, they gave up this hope. However, not even at that point did Christ keep silence. He uttered many rebuttals. Those who kept saying that he was a **prophet** (6:14) while they were eating now took offense and said that he was only the son of the carpenter. However, while they were eating the loaves, they did not say this, but rather said, **This is indeed the prophet** (6:14). They also desired **to make him king** (6:15). Ostensibly, then, they were provoked because he said that he *came down from heaven* (6:41); but in actuality, this did not cause their annoyance. They were disappointed that their hopes of enjoying food for their bodies were dashed. Besides, if they really were provoked, they should have made inquiry and sought to learn how he was the **bread of life** (6:35) and how he had **come down from heaven** (6:33). But they did not do this. Rather, *the Jews murmured at him* (6:41).

(16) Cyril of Alexandria

I am the Bread of Life; he who comes to me shall not hunger, and he who believes in me shall never thirst (6:35). There is something hidden in these words that needs explanation. It was the custom of Christ the Savior not to deprecate praise of the holy ones of old, but to crown them with worthy honors. When some of the more ignorant people, not knowing how much greater he was than those ancient worthies, offered them greater glory, he persuades them—which was definitely to their benefit—to adopt a more appropriate attitude and to contemplate who the only-begotten is and how he entirely surpasses the holy ones of old in excellence. But he does not make his point openly. He hides it somewhat to put aside their boasting. However, as one looks at what transpired, it is evident that his superiority was recognized. Take for example when he was speaking with the Samaritan woman, to whom he promised to give *living water* (4:10). Since the woman did not understand what he was saying, the woman asked, *Are you greater than our father Jacob, who gave us the well?* (4:12). Since the Savior wished to persuade her that he was both greater than Jacob and more worthy of greater belief, he goes on to explain the difference between the two kinds of water. He says, *Whoever drinks of the water that I shall give him will never thirst; the water that I shall give him will become in him a spring of water welling up to eternal life* (4:14). What does he mean by this? Surely he means that the one who gives greater gifts must necessarily be better than the person with whom he is compared.

He is now using a similar pedagogical method. Jews were acting arrogantly toward him and dared to raise Moses the lawgiver at every turn. They often asserted that they

10. John Chrysostom is likely thinking of the Eucharistic prayer spoken by the priest over the host.

should follow his teaching rather than Christ's, for they thought that the supply of manna and the flowing of water from the rock were absolute proof of his superiority in all things and over our Savior Jesus Christ himself. Christ was compelled to return to his usual method. He does not state directly that he is superior to Moses because his hearers were hard set against him and were vexed with him. Rather, he turns to the very event which caused them to marvel. By comparing it to an event that was greater, he proves that it is of less importance. **He who comes to me**, he says, **shall not hunger, and he who believes in me shall never thirst** (6:35). In other words: "Yes, certainly I agree with you that the manna was given though Moses. But those who ate it grew hungry. I will also concur that water was given to you from the rocks. But those who drank it grew thirsty. These gifts only brought them temporary enjoyment. But **he who comes to me shall not hunger, and he who believes in me shall never thirst**" (6:35).

What does Christ promise? Nothing corruptible. Rather, he promises the Eucharistic participation of his holy flesh and blood which restores humans wholly to incorruption so that they have no further need of the things that drive death away from the flesh, by which I mean, food and drink. In this place, he seems to call water the sanctification brought about by the Spirit or the divine and Holy Spirit himself, as he is often named by the divine Scriptures. The holy body of Christ gives life to those who receive it, and as it is comingled with our bodies, it keeps us incorruptible. It is considered the body of him who is by nature life and not of anyone else, since it contains within itself the full power of the Word that is united with it. Additionally, it is filled with his activity by which all things are enlivened and connected with his being. Since all these things are true, let those who have been baptized and tasted the divine grace know that if they go reluctantly or rarely at all to church and for a long time cease to receive the Eucharistic gift given by Christ yet feign a harmful reverence as a reason for not participating in him sacramentally, they exclude themselves from eternal life. They refuse to be given life. This refusal, although it seems to be the result of reverence, becomes a snare and stumbling block. Instead, they should urgently draw upon their internal power and purpose so that they may eagerly remove their sin and try to live a more spiritual life and thus hasten courageously to participate in life.

John 6:36-40

[36]"But I said to you that you have seen me and yet do not believe. [37]All that the Father gives me will come to me; and him who comes to me I will not cast out. [38]For I have come down from heaven, not to do my own will, but the will of him who sent me; [39]and this is the will of him who sent me, that I should lose nothing of all that he has given me, but raise it up at the last day. [40]For this is the will of my Father, that everyone who sees the Son and believes in him should have eternal life; and I will raise him up at the last day."

6:37–39 "Him who comes to me I will not cast out. For I have come down from heaven, not to do my own will, but the will of him who sent me."

---

(17) Augustine of Hippo

The source of every disease is pride, because the source of all sins is pride. When a physician deals with an illness and heals merely the symptoms and not the cause itself which was the occasion for the symptom, the disease seems to be cured for a time. However, since the cause remains, it strikes again. . . . By removing the cause, no more sores can exist. From what source does wickedness come from? From pride. Heal pride, and there will be no wickedness. In order that the cause of all diseases—that is, pride—might be healed, the Son of God humbled himself and came down. Why, therefore, are you proud, human? God humbled himself for your sake. Perhaps it would be shameful for you to imitate a humble man. At least, imitate a humble God. The Son of God came in the form of a man and humbled himself. You are taught to be humble; you are not told to become a mindless animal instead of a human. Since God became human, know that you are a human. All humility is found in this, that you know yourself. God teaches us what humility is when he said, **For I have come down from heaven, not to do my own will, but the will of him who sent me** (6:38). For this is the mark of humility. Pride does its own will, but humility does the will of God. Therefore, **him who comes to me I will not cast out** (6:37). Why? . . . As a humble man, I have come. I have come to teach humility. I have come, as a master of humility. He who comes to me is connected to me; he who comes to me becomes humble. The one who cleaves to me will be humble, because he does not do his own will, but God's. Accordingly, he will not be **cast out**, because he was **cast out** when he was proud.

(18) Cyril of Alexandria

For I have come down from heaven, not to do my own will but the will of him who sent me; and this is the will of him who sent me, that I should lose nothing of all that he has given me, but raise it up at the last day (6:38–39). To a person who considers this passage superficially, it will seem difficult and perhaps be considered a stumbling block with regard to the faith. For this reason, some expect us to fall into difficulties caused by our opponents that will prove hard to overcome. But there is nothing whatsoever difficult in this passage. As it is written, *They are all straightforward to those who understand, and upright to those who find knowledge* (Prov 8:9), that is to those who piously study to interpret and understand the mysteries contained in the divine Scriptures. In these words, Christ gives us clear proof and assurance that the one who comes to him will not be **cast out** (6:37). For this very reason, he says, **I have come down from heaven** (6:38). For this very reason, "I became a man according to the good pleasure of God the Father and refused to be distracted by anything that was not according to his plan until I should destroy the power of death and secure for those who believe in me eternal life and the resurrection of the dead." What then was willed and not willed by Christ? The treatment that he received from the Jews—the dishonor, castigation, the insults, the disdain, the scourging, the spit, the false charges, and last of all the death of the flesh. For our sake, Christ underwent these things willingly. If he could have accomplished what he desired for us without suffering, he would hardly have wished to suffer. However, because the Jews were undoubtedly going to inflict these things upon him, he accepts the suffering and turns what he did not will into what he wills on account of the benefit that would come from his passion. God the Father agreed with him and concurred that he should undergo all these things willingly for the salvation of all. In this especially we see the unlimited goodness of the divine nature, for it did not refuse to turn that which was despised into what was willed for our sake. You will certainly understand from the following that the suffering on the cross was not desired by our Savior, Christ, but it was willed for our sake and the good pleasure of God the Father. When he was about to ascend to the Father and offered his discourse to God in the form of a prayer, he said, *My Father, if it be possible, let this cup pass from me; nevertheless, not as I will, but as thou wilt* (Matt 26:39). It is very clear to everyone that the Word is God, immortal and incorruptible, and by nature very life itself; therefore, he could not cower before death. However, since he took on flesh, he allows himself to experience all things proper to the flesh. When death is at the door, he allows his flesh to cower in the face of death so that he might be shown to be truly a man.

Consequently, he says, *If it be possible, let this cup pass from me* (Matt 26:39). He means this: *If it be possible*, Father, that I might secure life for those who have fallen under the power of death so that death might die without suffering death myself in the flesh, *let this cup pass from me*. But since this cannot happen in any other way, *not as I will, but as thou wilt*. Do you see how powerless human nature is, even in Christ himself, on its own? But through the Word which is united with it, the flesh is brought back to a courage befitting God and is retrained for a more noble purpose. It does not rely upon what seems good according to its own will but instead follows the direction of the divine will and runs willingly toward whatever the law of our creator calls us. You may learn from the text that follows that we say these things correctly, for *the spirit indeed is willing, but the flesh is weak* (Matt 26:41). Christ certainly was not ignorant that to seem to be defeated by death and to feel the fear on account of this fell far short of the dignity which is appropriate to God. For this reason, he added a very strong defense. He stated that the *flesh was weak* because of what is proper to it and what it is by nature. In contrast, he stated that the *spirit was willing* because it knows that it cannot suffer any harm. Do you see how death was not willed by Christ on account of the flesh and the disgrace of suffering? By contrast, do you see how death was willed by him until he could deliver the desired completion for the sake of the entire world, that is the good pleasure of the Father—which is namely the salvation and life of all? Did he not truly indicate something similar to this when he said that **this is the will** of the Father: so that nothing that has been brought to him will perish, he will **raise it up at the last day** (6:39)? As we have taught previously, God the Father in his love for humanity brings all those who lack life and salvation to Christ, who is life and the Savior.

6:40 "For this is the will of my Father, that everyone who sees the Son and believes in him should have eternal life; and I will raise him up at the last day."

(19) John Chrysostom

For this is the will of my Father, that everyone who sees the Son and believes in him should have eternal life; and I will raise him up at the last day (6:40). Why does he constantly mention the resurrection? Could it be that humans cannot comprehend God's providence by the present circumstances alone? Might it be that those who do not enjoy results in their present life would become despondent for this reason, but would wait for the things that are to come? Might it be that those who are not punished in their present life would not despise him and look for another life? Those kinds of people gain nothing. But let us endeavor to gain something by having the resurrection ring continually in our ears. If we desire to seize, steal, or do wrong, let us immediately contemplate that day! Let us imagine that we are at the *judgment seat* (2 Cor 5:10). Such reflections will correct the evil impulse more effectively than any bit (cf. Ps 32:9). Let us continually say to ourselves and others, "There is a resurrection! A fearful tribunal awaits us!" If we see anyone who is insolent and impertinent with the good things of this world, let us make the same remark and show him that all those things remain here. If we notice that someone is grieving and restless, let us say the same and show him that his sadness will have an end. If we see yet another who is careless and rash, let us say the same utterance over him and reveal that he will have to render an account for his carelessness. This saying, more than any other, is able to offer a cure for our souls.

There is a resurrection! And that resurrection is at hand; it is not far away nor at a distance: *For yet a little while, and the coming one shall come and shall not tarry* (Heb 10:37); and again, *For we must all appear before the judgment seat of Christ* (2 Cor 5:10). Both the good and the bad must appear: the former to be shamed before the eyes of all and the latter to be made more glorious in the presence of all. Just as those who serve as judges here punish the wicked and honor the good in public, so also will it be there. The one group will receive the greater shame and the other will obtain more conspicuous glory. Let us ourselves imagine these things each day. If we are constantly recalling them, no present concerns will be able to harm us. *For the things that are seen are transient, but the things that are unseen are eternal* (2 Cor 4:18). Let us continually tell ourselves and others that there is a resurrection, a judgment, and an examination of our actions. Let anyone who thinks that there is such a thing as fate repeat this, and they will be immediately delivered from the rottenness of their disease. For if there is a resurrection and a judgment, there is no fate, even though they adduce ten thousand arguments and choke themselves to prove it! However, I am ashamed to teach Christians about the resurrection. All those who need to learn that there is a resurrection and who have not completely convinced themselves that the affairs of this world do not happen by fate, happenstance, or chance, cannot be Christians. Therefore, I entreat and implore you so that we will cleanse ourselves from all wickedness and do everything in our power to secure pardon and forgiveness on that day.

John 6:41–51

[41]The Jews then murmured at him, because he said, "I am the bread which came down from heaven." [42]They said, "Is not this Jesus, the son of Joseph, whose father and mother we know? How does he now say, 'I have come down from heaven'?" [43]Jesus answered them, "Do not murmur among yourselves. [44]No one can come to me unless the Father who sent me draws him; and I will raise him up at the last day. [45]It is written in the prophets, 'And they shall all be taught by God.' Everyone who has heard and learned from the Father comes to me. [46]Not that anyone has seen the Father except him who is from God; he has seen the Father. [47]Truly, truly, I say to you, he who believes has eternal life. [48]I am the bread of life. [49]Your fathers ate the manna in the wilderness, and they died. [50]This is the bread which comes down from heaven, that a man may eat of it and not die. [51]I am the living bread which came down from heaven; if any one eats of this bread, he will live forever; and the bread which I shall give for the life of the world is my flesh."

6:47–48 "Truly, truly, I say to you, he who believes has eternal life. I am the bread of life."

---

(20) Theodore of Mopsuestia

Truly, truly, I say to you, he who believes has eternal life (6:47). Therefore, do not doubt what I am saying. I will give **eternal life** to those who belong to me, for **I am the bread of life** (6:48). He was aware that the statement that he would give **eternal life** was not persuasive for those listening to him. Indeed, it was evident that the **bread** which was eaten was not endowed by its very nature with the power that could give **eternal life**. How could they be persuaded that it could give to others what it did not have in its nature? For this reason, he finally stated all this plainly. This time he used a symbolic name, and he solved the difficulty of this statement with an illustration. He called himself **the bread** (6:48).

6:49–50 "Your fathers ate the manna in the wilderness, and they died. This is the bread which comes down from heaven, that a man may eat of it and not die."

---

(21) Theodore of Mopsuestia

Your fathers ate the manna in the wilderness, and they died. This is the bread which comes down from heaven (6:49–50). **Your fathers ate the manna** and were not spared from the sentence of death. All of them perished in the **wilderness**, because they were not deemed worthy to enter the promised land. But whoever partakes of this food will be raised from death. However, the statement "he will **not die**" (6:50) does not mean that he *will not taste death* (cf. Matt 16:28). Instead it means that from the very time when a person believes that death has been destroyed, then there really is not a death that he will **die**. The blessed Paul also says this very thing: *But we would not have you ignorant, brethren, concerning those who are asleep, that you may not grieve as others do who have no hope* (1 Thess 4:13). Here he called those who hope in the resurrection *those who are asleep*.

(22) Augustine of Hippo

Your fathers, he says, **ate manna in the wilderness, and they died** (6:49). What are you proud of? **Your fathers ate manna, and they died**. Why did they eat and die? Because they believed what they saw but did not perceive what they did not see. For that reason they are indeed **your fathers** because you are like them. My brothers and sisters, do we who eat the **bread which comes down from heaven** (6:50) not also die in respect to a visible and corporeal death? So they have died in respect to the visible and fleshly death of this body. As I said, however, we too shall die in that way. But their fathers died in accordance with that death about which the Lord frightens us. In contrast, Moses ate the **manna**, Aaron ate the **manna**, Phineas, too, ate the **manna**, and many others who pleased the Lord were there and ate it. But they have not died that sort of death. Why? Because they understood the visible food spiritually. They hungered spiritually and they tasted spiritually so that they might be filled spiritually.

Today we, too, receive visible food. The substance of the sacrament is one thing; the efficacy of it is another. How many after receiving this food from the altar die? For this reason the apostle says, *He eats and drinks judgment upon himself* (1 Cor 11:29). The morsel of the Lord was not poison to Judas. He took it, and when he received it, the enemy entered into him (cf. John 13:26–27). This was not because he received an evil thing but because an evil man received a good thing in an evil manner. Be watchful, brothers and sisters. Eat the heavenly bread spiritually. Carry innocence to the altar. Even if there are daily sins, at least let them not be mortal.[11] Before you approach the altar, observe what you are to say, *Forgive us our debts, as we also forgive our debtors* (Matt 6:12; cf. Luke 11:4). You forgive; you will be forgiven. Approach without anxiety; it is bread, not poison. But see to it that you forgive; for if you do not forgive, you lie, and you lie to him whom you cannot deceive. You can lie to God; you cannot deceive God. He knows what he does. He sees you within, he examines you within, he inspects you, he judges you, and he either damns or crowns you. . . .

Jesus begins his discourse as follows: **Do not murmur among yourselves** (6:43), O murmurers, offspring of murmurers! **Your fathers ate the manna in the wilderness, and they died** (6:49), not because manna was an evil thing, but because they ate it in an evil manner. **This is the bread which comes down from heaven** (6:50). Manna was a sign of this bread; the altar of God likewise signified this bread. Those were mysteries! As signs, they are different, yet in respect to the thing which is signified, they are alike. Listen to the apostle. He says, *I want you*

---

11. This foreshadows the distinction between venial and mortal sins commonly found in medieval Christianity.

to know, brethren, that our fathers were all under the cloud, and all passed through the sea, and all were baptized into Moses in the cloud and in the sea, and all ate the same supernatural food (1 Cor 10:1–3). Of course, it is the same spiritual food. Although corporeally it was a different thing, for they **ate manna** and we eat something else. But they ate the spiritual food which we eat. Similarly, they are our **fathers** and not the **fathers** (6:49) of those [Jews]. . . .

And he added, *And all drank the same supernatural drink* (1 Cor 10:4). They drank one thing, and we drink something different in how it looks, but this drink signified the same spiritual power. How is it *the same drink*? He says, *They drank from the supernatural Rock which followed them, and the Rock was Christ* (1 Cor 10:4). As with the bread, so with the drink. Symbolically, the rock is Christ; the true Christ is in the Word and in the flesh. How were they able to drink from it? The rock was *struck twice with a rod* (Num 20:11). The double-striking signifies the two pieces of wood of the cross. **This is** therefore **the bread which comes down from heaven, that a man may eat of it and not die** (6:50). This statement refers to the efficacy of the sacrament, not to the visible elements. It refers to the one who eats internally, not externally, to the one who eats with his heart, not the one who chews with his teeth.

6:51 "I am the living bread which came down from heaven; if any one eats of this bread, he will live forever; and the bread which I shall give for the life of the world is my flesh."

---

(23) Cyril of Alexandria

I am the living bread which came down from heaven; if any one eats of this bread, he will live forever; and the bread which I shall give for the life of the world is my flesh (6:51). I die for all so that I may give **life** to all. I made **my flesh** a ransom for the flesh of all. Death itself will die in my death. He says the fallen nature of humanity will rise again along with me. For this reason, I became like you, a human and one from the seed of Abraham, so that I might *be made like* my *brethren in every respect* (Heb 2:17). The blessed Paul, understanding completely what Christ proclaims to us here, says the following: *Since therefore the children share in flesh and blood, he himself likewise partook of the same nature, that through death he might destroy him who has the power of death, that is, the devil* (Heb 2:14). In no other way was it possible that the one who held the power of death—and death itself—could be destroyed unless Christ gave himself for us as a single ransom for all. For this reason, he says in the psalms that he offers himself as an unblemished sacrifice to God the Father: *Sacrifice and offering you did not want, but ears you fashioned for me. Whole burnt offering and one for sin you did not request. Then I said, "Look, I have come; in a scroll of a book it is written of me. To do your will, O my God, I desired"* . . . (Ps 40:6–8 [39:7–9 LXX]). Since *the blood of goats and bulls and with the ashes of a heifer* (Heb 9:13) was not sufficient to purge sins and since the slaughter of animals could never have destroyed the power of death, Christ himself came to undergo punishment for all. As Isaiah the prophet says, *With his stripes we are healed* (Isa 53:5). It is also written: *He himself bore our sins in his body on the tree* (1 Pet 2:24). He was crucified for the sake of all in order that all of us might live in him since *one has died for all* (2 Cor 5:14). It was not possible that he could be *held by death* (Acts 2:24). Corruption could not conquer that which is by nature life itself. Christ gave his own **flesh** for the **life of the world** (6:51). We know this from his very words, for he said, *Holy Father, keep them* (17:11) and *for their sake I consecrate myself* (17:19). He says that he sanctifies himself, yet this sanctification does not aid in purifying his soul or spirit (as it happens with us) nor is it helped by the participation of the Holy Spirit, for the Spirit was in him by nature. He was, is, and always will be holy. He says, **I consecrate myself.** He means that "I offer and present myself as a spotless sacrifice, a sweet-smelling odor." Whatever is brought to the divine altar is sanctified and called holy according to the law. But Christ gave his own body **for the life** of all. Through this, he makes **life** dwell in us. How? I will give an answer as far as I am able. Since the life-giving Word of God entered into flesh, he transformed it into a good thing itself, into **life**. According to the mysterious character of this union, he united wholly with flesh and rendered it capable of giving **life** which he is by nature. Therefore, the body of Christ gives life to all who partake of it. When the body of Christ enters a dying man, it expels death and removes corruption, for it perfectly contains the Word which abolished corruption.

John 6:52–62

[52]The Jews then disputed among themselves, saying, "How can this man give us his flesh to eat?" [53]So Jesus said to them, "Truly, truly, I say to you, unless you eat the flesh of the Son of man and drink his blood, you have no life in you; [54]he who eats my flesh and drinks my blood has eternal life, and I will raise him up at the last day. [55]For my flesh is food indeed, and my blood is drink indeed. [56]He who eats my flesh and drinks my blood abides in me, and I in him. [57]As the living Father sent me, and I live because of the Father, so he who eats me will live because of me. [58]This is the bread which came down from heaven, not such as the fathers ate and died; he who eats this bread will live forever." [59]This he said in the synagogue, as he taught at Capernaum. [60]Many of his disciples, when they heard it, said, "This is a hard saying; who can listen to it?" [61]But Jesus, knowing in himself that his disciples murmured at it, said to them, "Do you take offense at this? [62]Then what if you were to see the Son of man ascending where he was before?"

6:52–56 "How can this man give us his flesh to eat?" So Jesus said to them, "Truly, truly, I say to you, unless you eat the flesh of the Son of man and drink his blood, you have no life in you; . . . he who eats my flesh and drinks my blood abides in me, and I in him."

---

(24) Ambrose of Milan

Truly, truly, I say to you, unless you eat the flesh of the Son of man and drink his blood, you have no life in you (6:53). He begins first by speaking as the Son of Man. You do not think that what he said as the **Son of man** concerning his **flesh** and **blood** pertains to his Godhead, do you? Next he adds, **For my flesh is food indeed, and my blood is drink indeed** (6:55). When you hear him speak of his **flesh** and **blood**, do you perceive the sacrament of the Lord's death (6:52) or do you disregard his Godhead? Listen to his own words: *A spirit has not flesh and bones* (Luke 24:39). As often as we receive the sacramental elements that are transformed into **flesh** and the **blood** by the mysterious work of holy prayer, we *proclaim the Lord's death* (1 Cor 11:26).

(25) Augustine of Hippo

The Jews then disputed among themselves, saying, "How can this man give us his flesh to eat?" (6:52). Of course, they argued with one another because they did not understand the bread of harmony. Nor did they want to take it. For those who eat such bread do not argue with one another, because *we who are many are one body, for we all partake of the one bread* (1 Cor 10:17). And through it, *God settles the solitary ones into a home* (Ps 68:6 [67:7 LXX]).

What they are seeking through arguing with one another—**How can** the Lord **give us his flesh to eat?**—they are not able to hear at that time. Yet it is still said to them, **Truly, truly, I say to you, unless you eat the flesh of the Son of man and drink his blood, you have no life in you** (6:53). Certainly, you are ignorant about how and in what manner this bread is eaten; nevertheless, **unless you eat the flesh of the Son of man and drink his blood, you have no life in you** (6:53). Of course, he was speaking these things to living men and not to corpses. So that they would not understand this as referring to physical life and would not also argue about this matter, he continued and added, **He who eats my flesh and drinks my blood has eternal life** (6:54). It follows then that he who does not **eat** this bread or **drink** this **blood** does not have **eternal life**. While men can live a temporal life without that bread, they cannot in any way possess eternal life. He who **does** not **eat his flesh** or **drink his blood** does not have **life** in him; conversely, he who **eats his flesh and drinks his blood** has life. To both of these he adds the word **eternal.**

This is not so in respect to this food which we take for the purpose of sustaining temporal life. He who does not take it will not live. Indeed, many who take it die possibly of old age, disease, or some accident. But in respect to this **true food** and **true drink**, that is, the body and blood, this is not the case. For he who does not take it, does not have life. Conversely, he who takes it, does have life. That is, of course, **eternal life**. . . .

He says, **For my flesh is food indeed, and my blood is drink indeed** (6:55). Although humans desire **food** and **drink** so that they will not hunger and thirst, only this **food** and **drink** truly provide this. Those who receive it are made immortal and incorruptible and join the community of saints where there will be peace and perfect unity. For this reason, our Lord Jesus Christ revealed in his body and **blood** those things which are reduced from many elements into a single thing: from many grains one thing is made; from many grapes a single thing flows together. Next, he explains how all this happens and what it means to eat his body and drink his **blood: He who eats my flesh and drinks my blood abides in me, and I in him** (6:56). To eat that food and to drink that **drink** is to dwell in Christ and have him dwelling in you. Conversely, he who does not dwell in Christ and in whom Christ does not dwell certainly does not eat his **flesh** or drink his **blood**. Rather when he eats and drinks the sacrament, *he eats and drinks judgment upon himself* (1 Cor 11:29) because he presumed to approach the sacraments of Christ in an impure manner. One is worthy to take the sacraments only if he is pure. About such people it is said, *Blessed are the pure in heart, for they shall see God* (Matt 5:8).

(26) Cyril of Alexandria

Truly, truly, I say to you, unless you eat the flesh of the Son of man and drink his blood, you have no life in you (6:53). Christ is truly patient and full of mercy, as one sees from the words before us now. In no way does he reproach the small-mindedness of unbelievers but freely gives them the life-giving knowledge of the mystery. As God, he overcame the arrogance of those who caused him pain, and he tells them the things by which they will attain eternal life. He does not teach them yet how he will give them his flesh to eat, for he knew that they were in darkness and were not at all capable of understanding the ineffable. But he shows them profitably how many positive benefits would come from their eating. By persuading them to desire to live in a state of greater preparation for unending joy, he might teach them to have faith. When people have come to have faith, the power of learning follows naturally. For this reason, the prophet Isaiah says, *And if you do not believe, neither shall you understand* (Isa 7:9 LXX). Therefore, it was right that the knowledge of those things that they were ignorant of would be introduced once faith had taken root in them instead of the investigation preceding faith.

I think that this is why the Lord rightly refrained from telling them how he would give them his flesh to eat and urges them to believe before inquiring. It was for those who had believed for a long time that he broke the bread and gave it to them saying, *Take, eat; this is my body* (Matt 26:26). Similarly he passed the cup around to them saying, *Drink of it, all of you; for this is my blood of the covenant, which is poured out for many for the forgiveness of sins* (Matt 26:27–28). Do you see how he does not explain the mode of the mystery to those who were still senseless and rejected faith without inquiry but how in contrast he declares it most clearly to those who had already had faith? Let those who have not yet accepted faith in Christ on account of their foolishness listen carefully to the saying: **Unless you eat the flesh of the Son of man and drink his blood, you do not have eternal life in you** (6:53–54).

Those who do not receive Jesus through the mystery of the Eucharist will remain wholly bereft of any share in and taste of that holy and blessed life. Since he was begotten of a living Father, by nature he is **life**. His holy body is no less **life**-giving, since it has been constituted from and ineffably united with the Word that gives **life** to all things. For this reason, his body is construed as his and is thought to be one with him. After the incarnation, he is indivisible except in respect to the knowledge that the Word that came from the Father and the temple that came from the virgin are not of a similar nature. The body is not consubstantial with the Word from God. But they are one since they have come together and are combined in an ineffable manner. Since the **flesh** of the Savior became **life**-giving—

in that it was united to that which is by nature **life**, the Word from God—when we eat it, we then have that **life** within ourselves. We are also united to the **flesh** of the Savior in the same way as the **flesh** is indwelt by the Word of God.

For this reason, when the Savior raised the dead, he is seen to be operating not by the Word alone nor by commands which pertain to God alone, but he deliberately used his holy **flesh** as a type of co-worker. In this way he showed that his **flesh** was capable of giving **life** and that it was united with him, for it was really his own body and not that of another. When he raised the little daughter of the ruler of the synagogue, Scripture says, *Taking her by the hand he called, saying, "Child, arise"* (Luke 8:54). While giving **life** as God to her by his all-powerful command, he also gives **life** through the touch of his holy **flesh** showing that there was one corresponding action through both. At another time when he was going into the city called Nain, *a man who had died was being carried out, the only son of his mother* (Luke 7:12). Again he *touched the bier . . . and he said, "Young man, I say to you, arise"* (Luke 7:14). He touches the dead and by this act gives **life** to those who had already decayed. If he gives **life** to those who have already decayed by merely a touch of his holy **flesh**, how much more shall we benefit when we eat the **life**-giving Eucharist? It will certainly transform those who partake of it into its own good, that is, immortality.

Do not marvel at this! Do not ask yourself in a Jewish manner "how?" Rather, consider that water is cold by nature but when it is poured into a kettle and set on the fire, it forgets its own nature entirely and moves to the energy of that which has mastered it. In the same way, although we are corruptible through the nature of our **flesh**, we also through our mingling with **life** abandon our weakness and are transformed fully into its property, that is, into **life**. For it was necessary that not only should our soul be re-created through the Holy Spirit into newness of **life** but also that our coarse and earthly body should be sanctified and brought into incorruption by a coarser yet similar participation. Do not let the Jews, as slow as they are, suppose that we have discovered some kind of new mystery. They can find it in the older writings of Moses, already foreshadowing and bearing the force of truth although it was accomplished only outwardly. Tell me, what drove out the Destroyer? What made it possible that their ancestors did not die with the Egyptians when Death, the conqueror of all, was arming himself against the firstborn sons? Is it not obvious to all that when in obedience to the divine law they sacrificed the lamb, ate its **flesh**, anointed the doorposts with **blood**, death was compelled to pass them by as a sanctified people (cf. Exod 12:7)? For the Destroyer, that is the death of the body, was drawn up against the whole of humanity on account of the transgression of the first man. At that time, we first heard, *You are dust, and to dust you shall return* (Gen 3:19). However, since Christ was going to overthrow this terrible tyrant by existing in us as **life** itself through his holy **flesh**, this mystery was foreshadowed to those who lived long ago. They tasted the **flesh** of the lamb and were sanctified and preserved by its **blood**. The one who was sent to destroy them passed them by in accordance with the will of God since they had partaken of the lamb. Why do you Jews become angry at being called now from types to the reality, when Christ says, **Unless you eat the flesh of the Son of man and drink his blood, you have no life in you** (6:53)? Certainly, you should have been able to comprehend these mysteries somewhat more easily since you had been instructed in advance by the books of Moses and led unequivocally by the most ancient figures toward the obligations of the faith.

He who eats my flesh and drinks my blood has eternal life, and I will raise him up at the last day (6:54). It is right to admire the holy evangelist who has openly proclaimed at this point: *And the Word became flesh* (1:14). He did not refrain from saying that he *became flesh* (in contrast to saying that he was made *in* the flesh) so that he could reveal the union. We do not say that God the Word who is from the Father was transformed into the nature of **flesh** or that the **flesh** was somehow changed into the Word. For each aspect remains what it is by nature. Christ is one from both natures. In a way that is unfathomable and surpasses all human understanding, the Word was united with his own **flesh** and thereby transformed the **flesh** into his very being by that very energy which lies in his power that enables him to give **life** to that which lacks **life**. By this he drove out the corruption from our nature and removed even death which had long conquered us by means of sin. Therefore, the one who **eats** the holy **flesh** of Christ **has eternal life**, for the **flesh** has in itself the Word which is by nature **life**! For this reason he says, **I will raise him up at the last day** (6:54). Instead of saying, "My body will raise him up" (that is, the person who eats it), he has used the word **I**. He is not different from his own flesh and not wholly different in respect to his nature; after the union, he cannot be divided into two distinct sons. Therefore he says that **I**, who have come to be in him through my **flesh**, **will raise him** who eats my flesh **up at the last day** (6:54). It was certainly impossible that the one who is **life** by nature failed to overcome corruption and conquer death! Although death, which attacked us on account of the transgression,[12] compels the human body toward the punishment of decay, we will certainly be **raised up** since Christ dwells in us through his own **flesh**. It is not believable—indeed, it is not even possible!—that **life** itself should not enliven the ones in whom he dwells. It is as if one took an ember and put it into a bundle of tinder in order that the preserved spark might catch hold. So also in us, our Lord Jesus hides **life** in his own **flesh** and places it in us as a spark of immortality and thereby abolishes the corruption that is in us.

For my flesh is food indeed, and my blood is drink indeed (6:55). Once again he draws a contrast between the mystery of the Eucharist and the manna and the delight of the cup with the water which sprang from the rocks. What he has said before using different words, he says once again shaping the same discourse in a different way. He does not tell them to marvel greatly over the **manna**, but to receive him as the **bread from heaven** (6:50) and the giver of **eternal life** (6:54). *Your fathers ate the manna in the wilderness, and they died. This is the bread which comes down from heaven, that a man may eat of it and not die* (6:49–50). He says that the **manna** for a time held off the needs of the body and drove away the pains of hunger. Afterward, however, the **manna** proved powerless and did not supply those who ate it with **eternal life**. It was therefore not the true food, **the bread from heaven** (6:50). However, the holy body of Christ which gives immortality and **eternal life** (6:54) is certainly the true food. They also drank water from the rock (cf. Num 20:11). He asks, what happened next? What was the benefit to those who drank this water? *They died* (6:49). That water, therefore, was not the true drink. The true drink

---

12. Cyril has in mind the first transgression, i.e., the fall of Adam and Eve.

is the precious **blood** (6:54) of Christ which tears out from the roots all corruption and extracts death which dwells in human flesh. It is not the **blood** of just anyone, but the **blood** of the one who is by nature very **life** itself (6:53). Therefore, we are called both the body and members of Christ since we have received in ourselves through the Eucharist the Son himself (cf. 1 Cor 12:27).

He who eats my flesh and drinks my blood abides in me, and I in him (6:56). By these words Christ explains what he means in a different way. Since his discourse is somewhat difficult to understand for those who are not well schooled—for it requires the insight of faith rather than of inquiry—he makes it easier in many ways by doubling back again and again. From every angle he illumines what is useful. He establishes a desire for it as if preparing the ground and laying a foundation. He says that **he who eats my flesh and drinks my blood abides in me, and I in him** (6:56). If someone were to melt together two pieces of wax, he would certainly see one in the other. In a similar manner, I suppose, anyone who receives the **flesh** of our Savior Christ and **drinks** his precious **blood**, as he himself says, becomes one with him. He is mixed and intermingled with him through this participation, and he comes to be in Christ and Christ is found also in him. Christ taught us this in the Gospel according to Matthew, when he says, *The kingdom of heaven is like leaven which a woman took and hid in three measures of flour, till it was all leavened* (Matt 13:33). Who the *woman* is, what the number *three* means, and what the word *measure* itself indicates, will be discussed at the appropriate place. At this point, we will speak only about the *leaven*. Paul says, *that a little leaven leavens the whole lump* (1 Cor 5:6). In this way the smallest portion of the Eucharist mixes itself with our whole body and fills it with its own mighty energy. Christ then comes to be in us, and we come to be in him. For this reason, one may truly say that the *leaven* is in *the whole lump*, and by like reasoning that *the lump* is in the *whole leaven*. In brief that is the meaning of these words. If we long for **eternal life** (6:54) and if we pray to have the giver of immortality within ourselves, let us not refuse the Eucharist as those who are more impetuous, and let us not provide the devil who is steeped in wickedness to lay a trap and snare for us in a form of a perilous reverence. Someone might say, "Yes, but it is written: *Anyone who eats and drinks without discerning the body eats and drinks judgment upon himself* (1 Cor 11:29). I have examined myself and found that I am not worthy." But when will you be worthy? When will you present yourself to Christ? If you are always going to be scared away due to your failings, you will never stop stumbling! As the psalmist says, *Transgressions—who shall detect them?* (Ps 19:12 [18:13 LXX]). You will be entirely unable to participate in that **life**-giving sanctification. Make up your mind to lead a holier life in harmony with the law. Receive the Eucharist. Believe that it has the power to expel not only death but also the diseases that are in us. When Christ has come to be within us, he calms the law which rages in the members of the flesh (cf. Rom 7:23). He rekindles our piety toward God and at the same time extinguishes our passions. He does not count our transgressions against us. Rather, he heals our sickness. He bandages that which was crushed and raises what was fallen, as *the good shepherd lays down his life for the sheep* (10:11).

6:57 "As the living Father sent me, and I live because of the Father, so he who eats me will live because of me."

---

(27) Basil of Caesarea

Now let us examine, insofar as we are able, the meaning of the words of holy Scripture, that our opponents snatch up and twist to fit their interpretation and push against us to destroy the glory of the only-begotten. First of all, consider the words, **I live because of the Father** (6:57). This is one of the spears that those impious ones hurl toward heaven. I do not think that these words refer to his eternal nature, for whatever lives on account of something else cannot be self-generated. Similarly, whatever is warmed by another cannot be the source of the warmth. But the one who is both our Christ and our God says, *I am the resurrection and the life* (11:25). I perceive that his life in the flesh at this time is given life because of the Father. However, he came to live the life of humanity on account of his own will. He did not say, "I have lived because of the Father," but **I live because of the Father** (6:57). This clearly indicates the present time. Christ, who has the Word of God in his very self, is able to name the life which he lives: "life" itself. We learn from the following statement that this is what he means. He says, **He who eats me will live because of me** (6:57). When we **eat** his **flesh** and **drink** his **blood** (6:56), we are made partakers of his Word and wisdom through his incarnate and visible life. He called his mystic sojourn among us **flesh** and **blood** and taught about practical knowledge, physical nature, and theology by which our soul is fed and simultaneously trained for the contemplation of the actual realities. This is perhaps what he meant when he said, **I live because of the Father** (6:57).

6:60 Many of his disciples, when they heard it, said, "This is a hard saying; who can listen to it?"

---

(28) John Chrysostom

He called himself *living bread* (6:51), because he joins together this life and the life to come for us. Therefore he added, *If any one eats of this bread, he will live forever* (6:51). Surely, *bread* here means either the teachings of salvation or faith in him or his body. Both strengthen the soul. Yet, when he said in another place, *If any one hears my word, he will never taste death* (8:52), they were scandalized. Here, however, they did not have such a reaction. Perhaps, this is because they still were in awe of him on account of the loaves he had miraculously brought into being.

Notice also the distinction he made between the living bread and the manna. He instructed them in the effects that each of these foods produces. To demonstrate that the manna had no unusual effect, he added, *Your fathers ate the manna in the wilderness, and they died* (6:49). Next, he offered them very convincing evidence that they were deemed worthy of much greater blessings than their fathers, for he referred indirectly to those well-known and wonderful men who lived at the time of Moses. After he had said that they who had eaten manna had died, he added, *If anyone eats of this bread, he will live forever* (6:51). He did not use the words *in the wilderness* (6:49) without purpose. Rather, he implies that the manna was not provided for a long period of time and did not accompany them into the promised land.

This bread, however, is not that kind: *And the bread which I shall give for the life of the world is my flesh* (6:51). With good reason someone might ask perplexed whether that was a good time for him to say these words? At this time they were not then constructive or helpful but were rather injurious to what had already been built up. Scripture says, **Many of his disciples, when they heard it, said, "This is a hard saying; who can listen to it?"** (6:60). It seems that these teachings ought to have been given to the disciples alone, as Matthew has said, "He taught them privately" (cf. Mark 4:34).[13]

What reply should we offer to this objection? These teachings were both very profitable and very necessary. They were urgently asking for food, albeit bodily food. They were reminding him of the nourishment provided for their forefathers. They were stressing the greatness of the manna. But in order to prove that all this was type and figure, while the reality which was signified was actually present, he made mention of spiritual nourishment.

But, you will argue, he ought to have said, "*Your fathers ate the manna in the wilderness* (6:49), and I have provided bread for you." However, there is a great difference between these two. Indeed, the latter might seem inferior to the former, because the *manna* was brought from above, while the miracle of the loaves took place on earth. Since they were seeking food brought down from heaven, he kept saying repeatedly for this very reason: *I have come down from heaven* (6:42, 50–51).

If someone now should ask, "Why in the world did he shroud his explanation in mystery?" we should reply that it was the right time for such words. The obscurity of the meaning of what is said always attracts the attention of the listeners and makes them listen more carefully. They should not have been scandalized, but they should have asked questions and made inquiries. Instead, they went away. If, indeed, they thought he was a prophet, they should have believed his words. The scandal was due to their perversity not the puzzling meaning of his words. Note also how he had gradually bound his disciples to himself, for it was they who said, *Lord, to whom shall we go? You have the words of eternal life* (6:68). This was notwithstanding the fact that he represented himself as the giver, not his Father: *The bread which I shall give . . . is my flesh* (6:51). The crowd did not react as his disciples did. Rather, they acted in the opposite way: **This is a hard saying** (6:60). And they went away.

Yet this teaching was not strange, nor was it new. Truly, John the Baptist had implied it when he addressed him as *Lamb* (1:29). You might say, "Regardless, they did not know." I am fully aware they did not know; even the disciples did not completely understand. Since they did not understand clearly about his resurrection, for they were ignorant of the meaning of the words, *Destroy this temple, and in three days I will raise it up* (2:19). How much more would they not understand these words? Certainly, the former statements

---

13. John Chrysostom had in mind the statement from the Gospel of Mark, not Matthew.

were less obscure than these. They certainly knew that prophets had raised people from the dead even if the Scriptures did not say this directly and clearly. But no part of Scripture had ever stated that someone ate flesh! Nevertheless, his disciples believed and followed him and confessed that he had *the words of eternal life* (6:68). It is the role of a disciple not to inquire impertinently into the teachings of his master but to listen and believe and wait for the proper time for explanation.

John 6:63-71

[63]"It is the spirit that gives life, the flesh is of no avail; the words that I have spoken to you are spirit and life. [64]But there are some of you that do not believe." For Jesus knew from the first who those were that did not believe, and who it was that would betray him. [65]And he said, "This is why I told you that no one can come to me unless it is granted him by the Father." [66]After this many of his disciples drew back and no longer went about with him. [67]Jesus said to the twelve, "Do you also wish to go away?" [68]Simon Peter answered him, "Lord, to whom shall we go? You have the words of eternal life; [69]and we have believed, and have come to know, that you are the Holy One of God." [70]Jesus answered them, "Did I not choose you, the twelve, and one of you is a devil?" [71]He spoke of Judas the son of Simon Iscariot, for he, one of the twelve, was to betray him.

6:63 "It is the spirit that gives life, the flesh is of no avail."

---

(29) John Chrysostom

It is the spirit that gives life, the flesh is of no avail; the words that I have spoken to you are spirit and life (6:63). By this he means that you must hear spiritually what is said about Christ. The one who hears only in a carnal way is not helped nor does he gain any advantage. To question how he came **down from heaven** (6:50), to assume that he was the son of Joseph, and to ask, **How can this man give us his flesh to eat?** (6:52) was carnal. This is a fleshly way of thinking. They should have understood these matters in a mystical and spiritual sense. But you will ask, "How could those men understand what was meant by **eating** his **flesh**?" Regardless, they should have waited for a proper time to gain understanding; they should have asked questions without growing weary of doing so. **The words that I have spoken to you are spirit and life** (6:63); that is, they are divine and spiritual, with no carnal or natural application. They are both free from and independent of the laws that govern earthly things. They have a different sense entirely. Just as he said here **spirit** instead of "listening with the spiritual faculties," so when he said **flesh**, he did not mean "earthly things" but instead "listening to him with an earthly viewpoint." At the same time, he was telling them by implication that they always had earthly desires, when they should have been seeking spiritual things. For if a person listens with an earthly view, it **is of no avail** (6:63).

(30) Theodore of Mopsuestia

It is the spirit that gives life, the flesh is of no avail (6:63). For it is not the body by its own nature that **gives** this help, but through the body, the divine nature, which itself is not endued with a body, **gives life**. Here, then, it becomes clear that he is talking about the nature of the only-begotten. For after he said, *ascending where he was before* (6:62), he added, **It is the spirit that gives life, the flesh is of no avail** (6:63). Through the relationship that exists with that nature, he gives *life* to those who *eat* (6:56) him. For indeed, through the mystery of the Eucharist which is done in our presence, we believe that this very thing takes place in the figure of the body of our Lord through the descent of the Holy Spirit.

(31) Augustine of Hippo

Why does Jesus add, **It is the spirit that gives life, the flesh is of no avail; the words that I have spoken to you are spirit and life** (6:63)? . . . O Lord, good teacher, how does **the flesh avail nothing** when you have said, **Unless you eat my flesh and drink my blood, you have no life** in you (6:53)? . . . If Christ helped us through his flesh, how then **is the flesh of no avail** (6:63)? Through his **flesh**, the Spirit accomplished something for our salvation. The **flesh** was a vessel. Note what it had, not what it was. The apostles were sent; did their flesh not help us? If the flesh of the apostles assisted us, could the flesh of the Lord have availed nothing? How does the sound of a word come to us except through the voice of the flesh? Where does the pen come from? Or the writings? All these things are works of the flesh. But the spirit is playing it, as if it is a musical instrument. So then the phrase **the spirit gives life, the flesh is of no avail** (6:63) indicates how they understood **flesh**. But I do not give my flesh to be eaten in that way.

For this reason, he says, **The words that I have spoken to you are spirit and life** (6:63). For we have said, brothers and sisters, that the Lord had shown that we *abide in* him and he in us by eating his *flesh* and drinking his *blood* (6:56). We *abide in* him when we are his members (cf. Eph 5:30); but he abides in us when we are his temple. To be his members we have to be bound together in unity. What made it possible for us to be united except love? Where does the love of God come from? Ask the apostle! He says, *God's love has been poured into our hearts through the Holy Spirit which has been given to us* (Rom 5:5). It follows then that it is **the spirit that gives life** (6:63), for **the spirit** produces living members from the body which **the spirit** itself enlivens. O human, does **the spirit**, which is in you and makes it certain that you are a person, give life to a member that is separated from your flesh? I call your soul your spirit. Your soul gives life only to the members that are in your flesh. If you should remove one of your members, it is no longer given life from your soul since it is not bound in unity to your body.

These words are uttered so that we might love unity and fear separation. For a Christian should dread nothing so much as to be separated from the body of Christ. If he is separated from the body of Christ, he is no longer a member of him; if he is not a member of him, he is not enlivened by **the spirit**. The apostle says, *Anyone who does not have the*

Spirit of Christ does not belong to him (Rom 8:9). Accordingly, **it is the spirit that gives life, the flesh is of no avail; the words that I have spoken to you are spirit and life** (6:63).

6:67 Jesus said to the twelve, "Do you also wish to go away?"

---

(32) Augustine of Hippo

All the things the Lord said about his *flesh* and *blood* and the promise of *eternal life* (6:54), he shares with us out of his goodness. And he wishes that those who *eat* his *flesh* and *drink* his *blood* know that in doing so they *abide in* him and he *abides in* them (6:56); and those who did not believe would not know because they understood spiritual things in a carnal way. Though some were scandalized and perished (cf. 6:60), the Lord remained to console the disciples who stayed. Although he knew that they would remain with him, he asked as if testing them: **Do you also wish to go away?** (6:67). He did this that we could learn that they would remain steadfast.

Dearest brothers and sisters, let all of these lessons help us reach this end: we should not simply eat the flesh and blood of Christ in the sacrament as many wicked men do. Rather, we should eat and drink, filled with the Spirit. We should abide as members of the Lord's body, be enlivened by his Spirit, and not be tripped up even though many who eat and drink the sacrament with us will suffer eternal torments at the end. In the present time, Christ's body is as it were mixed together on the threshing-floor: *But the Lord knows those who are his* (2 Tim 2:19). If you know what it is you are threshing, though it is hidden, the threshing does not destroy what will be gotten rid of by the winnowing process. Brothers and sisters, we also are certain that all of us who are in the Lord's body and abide in him so that he may abide in us must live among wicked men who blaspheme Christ. Although only a few blaspheme with their mouths, many do so with their lives. Of necessity we must live among them until the end.

John 7

John 7 deals with Jesus's continuing engagement with Jewish religious leadership and mounting tension over the interpretation of the Mosaic law, Christ's identity, and his authority. However, for ancient interpreters, the most pressing issues pertain to puzzling questions raised by the text. Augustine of Hippo observes that Jesus says, My time has not yet come (7:6); yet according to Paul, God sent forth his Son "when the time had fully come" (Gal 4:4). What could this mean? Augustine explains that Jesus was being urged by his family to pursue the wrong kind of glory, but that Christ understood the way to glory through the cross. Augustine exhorts his hearers to seek the glory of Christ through the way of humility.

In 7:8–10 there is an apparent difficulty because Jesus said he would not go up to Jerusalem for the festival, but then later he alters course and does in fact go in private (7:10). John Chrysostom explains that Jesus did not mean that he would never go up to Jerusalem, only that the time for his suffering and crucifixion had not yet come. Likewise, Chrysostom sees in Jesus a response of gentleness and patience as he prepares for his coming suffering, a gentleness that should become the model for all who are tempted by the passion of anger. Cyril of Alexandria sees Jesus's brothers (or cousins) as representing the entire nation of Israel, and Jesus's refusal to participate in the festivals becomes a testimony that Jewish worship foreshadows Christian worship. Drawing on texts from the prophets and the declaration that God is spirit (John 4), Cyril says that Christ's action demonstrates that true worship is in "spirit and in truth" rather than according to the requirements of the law. Augustine puzzles over why Christ would go up to the feast in private. He explains that like all the Jewish feast days, the Feast of Tabernacles was a shadow and figure of things to come. Only in the church is that hidden mystery made known, and so while Christ was present at the feast, he was hidden from view. In the same way, Cyril of Alexandria explains what appears to be a deception in Christ, arguing that Christ's purpose was not simply to attend the feast joyfully with everyone else, but also to go to admonish the people.

Augustine connects John 7:16 (My teaching is not my own) with the gospel prologue: as the Word of the Father, Christ himself is the very teaching of the Father. Augustine concludes that Christ's words here speak to his essential equality with the Father.

Jesus's words about the observance of circumcision and Sabbath in 7:23–24 lead Augustine to discuss the spiritual meaning of circumcision, while Theodore of Mopsuestia

226

explains the logic of Jesus's comparison with the Mosaic command to circumcise on the Sabbath.

Hilary of Poitiers uses Jesus's words in verse 29 (I know him, for I come from him, and he sent me) *to discuss the Trinitarian relationship between the Father and the Son. In particular, Hilary wonders whether Christ's coming* from him *indicates his being created or being "naturally begotten." Hilary notes that if Christ is a work of creation, then all of creation is "from" the Father, and likewise all should know the Father equally with Christ. Yet Christ possesses unique knowledge of the Father, indicating Christ's singular birth. As Hilary puts it: "His unique knowledge comes from his unique birth."*

Examining this same passage, Chrysostom explains how it can be that Jesus affirms that the Jews know him (v. 28) and then immediately afterward says that they do not know him (v. 29). There are two kinds of knowledge, he says: the knowledge of the truth about something, and knowledge as a relationship with and acceptance of the truth. Though Christ's opponents knew his identity, they refused to accept it.

Ancient writers provide much discussion about Jesus's promise of the Spirit and its comparison with living waters *in 7:37–39. Cyril of Jerusalem explains this comparison by noting the variety of ways the Spirit works in the life of the church, just as water works upon the earth in a variety of ways. Ambrose of Milan connects this passage to the sevenfold gifts of the spirit of Isa 11, explaining that "there is one river, but many streams of the gifts of the* Spirit." *Just as many rivers have one source and one nature, so too the Holy Spirit, though manifested in a variety of ways, has one divine nature and source.*

Augustine uses verse 38 (Out of his heart shall flow rivers of living water) *to offer a poignant, even humorous, commentary on the kinds of things we tend to long for in this life—wealth, fame, power, health, long life, beauty—noting that Christ promises none of these to those who believe in him. Instead, Christ promises eternal life, the* rivers of living water. *Cyril of Alexandria interprets the reference to the coming Spirit with a sweeping survey of God's plan of salvation. Beginning with humanity's loss of the Spirit at the fall, Cyril explores the way Christ's incarnation, in taking upon himself the totality of human nature, restores the Spirit to humanity once again.*

Verse 39 (for as yet the Spirit had not been given) *leads Augustine to wonder how the Spirit could not be available to the disciples and other saints of old when several figures from the early chapters of Luke seem to be filled with the Spirit (Simeon, Anna, Zechariah, and Mary). The difference, suggests Augustine, is the mode of giving. While the Spirit was operative in individuals prior to Christ's glorification, it was only at Pentecost that a unique, communal giving of the Spirit was bestowed. The Spirit's gift of speaking in tongues is fully realized in the church now spread abroad, speaking the languages of the world.*

John 7:1–13

[1]**After this Jesus went about in Galilee; he would not go about in Judea, because the Jews sought to kill him.** [2]**Now the Jews' feast of Tabernacles was at hand.** [3]**So his brothers said to him, "Leave here and go to Judea, that your disciples may see the works you are doing.** [4]**For no man works in secret if he seeks to be known openly. If you do these things,**

show yourself to the world." ⁵For even his brothers did not believe in him. ⁶Jesus said to them, "My time has not yet come, but your time is always here. ⁷The world cannot hate you, but it hates me because I testify of it that its works are evil. ⁸Go to the feast yourselves; I am not going up to this feast, for my time has not yet fully come." ⁹So saying, he remained in Galilee. ¹⁰But after his brothers had gone up to the feast, then he also went up, not publicly but in private. ¹¹The Jews were looking for him at the feast, and saying, "Where is he?" ¹²And there was much muttering about him among the people. While some said, "He is a good man," others said, "No, he is leading the people astray." ¹³Yet for fear of the Jews no one spoke openly of him.

7:6 "My time has not yet come."

---

(1) Augustine of Hippo

Jesus said to them, "My time has not yet come, but your time is always here" (7:6). What is this? Had the time of Christ **not yet come**? Why had Christ come if his **time had not yet come**? Have we not heard the apostle saying, *When the time had fully come, God sent forth his Son* (Gal 4:4)? If, then, he was sent *when the time had fully come*, he was sent when he was supposed to be sent. He came when the time was right. So what does he mean, **My time has not yet come** (7:6)?

Brothers and sisters, imagine the attitude of those who spoke to Jesus and seemed to be admonishing their brother. Admonishing him in a worldly way, from an earthly perspective, they advised him not to be obscure or to hide himself in the pursuit of glory. This is why the Lord said, **My time has not yet come**. To those who gave him advice about glory, he answered: "The **time** for my glory **has not yet come**."

Notice how profound this is. They admonished him about his glory, but he wanted to lead the way to that height with humility, to pave a way to that lofty state through humility. Certainly, those disciples who wanted to sit down, *one at his right hand and one at his left* (Mark 10:37), were seeking glory. They were focused on where they were going, but didn't see how to get there. The Lord called them back to the path so they could arrive at their native land in the proper way.

The native land is indeed lofty, but the way is lowly. The life of Christ is the native land, but the death of Christ is the way. The dwelling of Christ is the native land, but the suffering of Christ is the way. What native land are you seeking if you reject the way? Ultimately Christ asks those who seek that height: *Can you drink the cup which I shall drink?* (Matt 20:22). Notice how he arrives at the height which you desire, clearly calling to mind the *cup* of humility and suffering. . . .

Let us, then, have a right spirit. The time of our glory has not yet come. Tell the lovers of this age, as though they were the brothers of the Lord, **Your time is always here.** Our **time has not yet come** (7:6). Let us venture to say something else as well. Because we are the body of our Lord Jesus Christ, because we are his members, and because we recognize our head with joy, let us by all means say this: it was proper for him to say this, even for our sake. When the lovers of this age taunt us, let us tell them, **Your time is always here.** Our **time has not yet come.** For the apostle said to us, *You have died, and your life is hid with Christ in God.* When will our time come? *When Christ who is your life appears,* he says, *then you also will appear with him in glory* (Col 3:3–4).

(2) Theodore of Mopsuestia

Jesus said to them, **my time has not yet come, but your time is always here** (7:6). What he means is this: "You think the time for going up and revealing yourselves is whenever you want it to be, for time makes no difference to you. But because of the astonishing and great nature hidden within me, I conceal myself for the time because it is necessary for the plan to unfold. **My time** will arrive when my identity will be made known openly before all." He is referring to his crucifixion and those things which came to pass afterward, as he also said in another passage: *The hour has come for the Son of man to be glorified* (12:23).

7:8 "I am not going up to this feast."

---

(3) John Chrysostom

The world cannot hate you (7:7), for how could it hate those who desire the things it desires and those who strive for the things it strives for? **But it hates me because I testify of it, that its works are evil** (7:7); that is to say, "Because I reprove and convict it, that is why I am hated." Let's learn from these words to master anger and not to be indignant even if those who give us advice are worthless. Christ meekly endured unbelievers giving him advice—even though the advice they gave wasn't right and didn't stem from pure motives. So, what pardon shall we who are dust and ashes obtain if we're annoyed at those who give us advice, and consider them beneath us, even though those who give it are hardly more worthless than we are? Notice at any rate how Christ rejects their accusation with all meekness. When they said, **Show yourself to the world** (7:4), he refutes their accusation and says, **The world cannot hate you, but it hates me** (7:7). "I am so far from seeking glory from others," he says, "that I don't stop convicting them even though I know that it only breeds hatred and plots for my death." . . .

Why on earth does he send them to the **feast,** saying, **Go to the feast, I am not going up** (7:8)? To demonstrate that he didn't say these things to entreat them or because he wanted to be flattered, but out of deference to the performance of Jewish rites. But someone might ask why he did go up when he had said, **I am not going up** (7:8). Because, he didn't say **I am not** ever **going up,** but rather, "now," that is, "with you; **for my time has not yet fully come** (7:8)." Indeed, he was about to be crucified at the coming Passover. So then, "why didn't he **go up** with them as well? If he didn't **go up,** because it was **not yet his time,** he shouldn't have gone up at all." Because, on the contrary, he didn't **go up** to suffer, but to teach them.

"But why **go up** secretly? By going up openly he could have been in their midst and restrained their unruly assault, which he often did." But he didn't want to do that every time. If he had gone up openly and blinded them again, his deity would have been even more conspicuous; for the moment there was no need for that, so instead he concealed it. Yet since they thought it was cowardly to stay behind, he demonstrated the opposite, showing both his courage and discretion. Because he foresees when the time of his suffering would finally be at hand, then he would especially want to **go up** to Jerusalem. It seems to me that just by saying, **Go to the feast yourselves** (7:8), he means, "Don't think that I'm forcing you to stay with me against your will." Yet by adding, **My time has not yet fully come** (7:8), he makes it clear that he had to perform miracles and preach sermons so that greater multitudes might believe and his disciples might be strengthened by seeing the confidence and suffering of their teacher.

Let us then learn of his gentleness and meekness when he said, *Learn from me; for I am gentle and lowly in heart* (Matt 11:29); and let us extirpate all bitterness. If anyone is puffed up against us, let us be lowly. If anyone is insolent, let us be conciliatory. If anyone bites and devours in derision and mockery, let us not give way, lest in avenging ourselves we destroy ourselves. Anger is indeed a beast, passionate and impetuous. So let us sing to ourselves charms from the divine Scriptures; let us say, *You are dust and ashes* (cf. Gen 3:19); and *How can earth and ashes behave arrogantly?* (Sir 10:9); and *A man's anger tips the scale to his ruin* (Sir 1:22); and *An ill-tempered man is not respected* (Prov 11:25 LXX). Nothing is more shameful, nothing uglier, than an angry face. If that's true of the face, how much more of the soul? Just as there's often a foul odor when you stir up mud, so too when the soul is disturbed by anger there is much disgrace and unpleasantness.

. . . Therefore, to deliver ourselves from punishment in the present age and from retribution in the age to come, let us cast out this passion of anger. Let us exhibit all meekness and gentleness that we might *find rest for* our *souls* both here and in the kingdom of heaven (Matt 11:29). May we all reach it through the grace and loving-kindness of our Lord Jesus Christ. Through him and with him be glory to the Father, together with the Holy Spirit, now and always, forever and ever. Amen.

(4) Theodore of Mopsuestia

In order to explain why he declines to go up to Jerusalem, he said, **The world cannot hate you, but it hates me because I testify of it that its works are evil. Go to the feast yourselves; I am not going up** now **to this feast, for my time has not yet fully come** (7:7-8).[1] What he means is this: "It is right for you to go up because there is nothing hindering you; but they hate me because I rebuke their wickedness. So I appease their anger through uncertainty and delay. That is why I avoid **going up** *now*, but will go up at a time that is right for me." He said carefully and correctly, **I am not going up** *now* (7:8), in order to show that he would go up, just not now, at the beginning of the festival.

---

1. Theodore's interpretation rests on his inserted word "now" in the biblical passage.

(5) Cyril of Alexandria

Indeed the Lord now plainly denies that he wants to join with the Jews in keeping the festival, that is to say, to go with them as one who would cheerfully participate in those shadows. What was once spoken to a few (although he uses the terms "brothers" by convention), will effectively apply to the entire race of Israel. Indeed no one will say (properly speaking) that Jesus avoided being with his brothers because of something in them; he was seen with them in Galilee. One suspects that there was a good reason for his dwelling with them, namely, because he shared their ethnicity according to the flesh. So it is obvious that, just as the entire Jewish nation is represented through his brothers, Christ avoids keeping the festival with them in accordance with the proclamation of one of the holy prophets: *I have hated, I have pushed aside your festivals, and I will not smell your offerings in your festival gatherings. Therefore even if you should bring me your whole burnt offerings and sacrifices, I will not accept them; nor will I show regard to your peace offerings. Remove from me the noise of your songs, and I will not hear the psalms of your instruments* (Amos 5:21–23 LXX).

According to the voice of the Savior himself, *God is spirit, and those who worship him must worship in spirit and truth* (4:24). Being **spirit,** he would naturally delight in spiritual honors and offerings, which are also seen typologically in the commands of the law—the sacrifices of both oxen and sheep, and especially the appointed sacrificial offerings of frankincense, fine wheat flour, wine, and olive oil. These more visible forms indicate the variety of moral virtue needed in those who are worshiping in spirit. "You therefore," Christ says, "who still love the shadow, have both a more earthly and more Jewish disposition about these things; **you go** to the festival in shadows and types. It is not pleasant for me to celebrate the feast this way. I will not go up **to this feast** which is clearly a type and figure, for I have no delight in its outward form. Rather I wait for the time of the true festal assembly, which has **not yet been fulfilled** (7:8). For then," he says, "I will be with my followers rejoicing in the brightness of the saints, and in the glory of the Father, flashing with surpassing brilliance."

He does, however, refer to "his" and calls the time his own, for the feast is his, and he is the master of the banquet. The blessed Jeremiah[2] attributes it to him, proclaiming to those who have neglected their piety toward God, and who have made no efforts demonstrating their desire to excel in goodness: *What will you do in the day of the festal assembly, and in the days of the feast of the Lord?* (Hos 9:5 LXX). Speaking to those who completely avoid the effort to be morally virtuous, and who lack the radiant garment of love for God, he says, "*What will you do in the day of the festal assembly?* How will you come to the divine and heavenly feast? Will not the master of the banquet rightly expel you from the joyous choir of those who were invited, saying, *Friend, how did you get in here without a wedding garment?*" (Matt 22:12)? . . . So in saying that they will **go up** to worship, he demonstrates that they are no longer performing the law, but rather worshiping in spirit, fulfilling the Feast of Tabernacles according to the truth, as if they are clearly singing that verse in the psalm: *Blessed be the Lord, for he has heard the voice of my prayer. My heart has hoped in him, and I was helped and my flesh has revived* (Ps 28:6–7 [27:6–7 LXX]).

---

2. Cyril mistakenly attributes a passage from Hosea to Jeremiah.

7:9–10 Then he also went up, not publicly but in private.

---

(6) Augustine of Hippo

So saying, he remained in Galilee. But after his brothers had gone up to the feast, then he also went up, not publicly but in private (7:9–10). Therefore **he went up to this feast,** not because he was desiring to gain fleeting personal fame quickly, but to teach something beneficial, to set the human race aright, to inform them of the eternal **feast** day, and to turn their love away from this worldly generation and redirect it to God. What does this mean: **He went up . . . in private?** The Lord has not made this part clear. It seems to me, brothers and sisters, that his **private** ascent should symbolize something; for it's reasonable to think that he would have gone up at noon on the **feast** day, or in the middle of the **feast** days, so he could teach publicly. But the text says **in private;** he did not offer his wisdom to the masses. It's not without meaning that Christ **went up to the feast in private,** because he was lying low that very **feast** day. Now, my own interpretation is hidden as well. Therefore it will be made clear; the veil will be lifted, and what was **private** will be revealed.

Everything which was said in ancient times to the people of Israel in the many Scriptures of the ancient law, what they were to do with the sacrifices, or the priests, or the **feast** days, or absolutely anything by which they worshiped God—whatever was said or taught to them—these were shadows of future times. What future times? The ones that are fulfilled in Christ. The apostle has something to say about this: *For all the promises of God find their Yes in him* (2 Cor 1:20). That is, they are fulfilled in him. He says in another place: *Now these things happened to them as a figure,*[3] *but they were written down for our instruction, upon whom the end of the ages has come* (1 Cor 10:11). Elsewhere the apostle says: *Christ is the end of the law* (Rom 10:4). Yet again, in another place: *Therefore let no one pass judgment on you in questions of food and drink or with regard to a festival or a new moon or a Sabbath. These are only a shadow of what is to come* (Col 2:16–17).

So if all these things were shadows of the future, then the Jewish **Feast** of Tabernacles was a shadow of the future as well. This was the **feast** day Skenopegia, Feast of Tabernacles (cf. Lev 23:34), the specific shadow of future times which we are looking into. Let me explain this **feast** day. It was a celebration of the tents (tabernacles), since the Jewish people, after they were freed from Egypt, lived in tents while they were crossing the desert to the promised land. Let us consider what this is, and we will become that very thing; we, I say, who are the body of Christ, if indeed we are. But we are because of Christ's worthiness, not by our own merit. Pay attention, brothers and sisters! We were led out of Egypt, where we served the devil as a pharaoh, where we toiled in the dust to satisfy his worldly desires. We labored greatly in these deeds. But then Christ called to us as if we were making bricks, saying: *Come to me, all who labor and are heavy laden, and I will give you rest* (Matt 11:28). From here we were led through baptism as through the Red Sea (red because it was conse-

---

3. RSV says **happened to them as a** *warning*, but Augustine wants to underscore the figurative aspect of the Old Testament.

crated with the blood of Christ), and we put distance between us and our dead enemies who had been pursuing us. Just before we had arrived at the promised land (that is, the eternal kingdom), we stayed in tabernacles in the desert. Those who recognize these things are in the tents for it would happen that some people would recognize such things. The one who understands that he is a foreigner in the world, is in the tent. He understands that he is a wanderer when he catches himself sighing for his homeland. And when the body of Christ is in the tents, Christ himself is in the tents. Even then, he is not present openly, but secretly. For a shadow was still veiling the light; when the light arrived, the shadow withdrew. Christ was **in private**—he was at the Skenopegia, but a hidden Christ.

Only now, when these things are made manifest, do we acknowledge that we are trekking through the wilderness. For if we acknowledge it, then we are in the wilderness. What is the wilderness? It is the desert. Why in the desert? Because in this world a desert is where one thirsts on a waterless path. We thirst so that our thirst might be quenched. For *blessed are those who hunger and thirst for righteousness, for they shall be satisfied* (Matt 5:6). In the desert, our thirst is quenched by stones: for *the Rock was Christ* (1 Cor 10:4) and it was struck with a rod so that water would pour forth (cf. Num 20:11). It had to be struck twice for water to flow out; the two striking rods form the cross. Therefore, all these things which were part of an allegory find their meaning in us. It is not without purpose that the text says of the Lord: **He went up to the feast, not publicly but in private.** The meaning of **in private** is that Christ was hidden on that **feast** day; and that very **feast** day symbolized the body of Christ as it journeys through the wilderness.

(7) Cyril of Alexandria

Once he had said that he would not go up to this **feast**, and allowed his brothers to go if they wished, he went up alone after them (for he had confirmed that his **time had not yet come** [7:6]). In doing this, he did not say one thing and then turn around and do the opposite of what he said. To do that would be to speak falsely, and further, it would be deceitful. It was said that a lie was never found in his mouth (Isa 53:9), and in truth he was willing to do the very thing he promised.

He did not go up with the purpose of celebrating the **feast** with them. Rather, he went up so that he might admonish them. Since he came to save, he went in order to speak about and usher in the things which lead to eternal life. This was his goal, as he would clearly demonstrate. That was why he did not want to go with those who were going to the **feast**; instead he wanted to arrive with sadness and **in private**, rather than openly and cheerfully like those who go to a festival.

Certainly, when he was finally going up to his saving passion, he did not arrive **in private**, but rode on a colt as a figure of the new people. . . . Here, by coming up **in private**, he clearly demonstrates that the Christ came to Jerusalem not in order to feast with them, but rather to reason with them.

John 7:14–24

[14]About the middle of the feast Jesus went up into the temple and taught. [15]The Jews marveled at it, saying, "How is it that this man has learning, when he has never studied?" [16]So Jesus answered them, "My teaching is not mine, but his who sent me; [17]if any man's will is to do his will, he shall know whether the teaching is from God or whether I am speaking on my own authority. [18]He who speaks on his own authority seeks his own glory; but he who seeks the glory of him who sent him is true, and in him there is no falsehood. [19]Did not Moses give you the law? Yet none of you keeps the law. Why do you seek to kill me?" [20]The people answered, "You have a demon! Who is seeking to kill you?" [21]Jesus answered them, "I did one deed, and you all marvel at it. [22]Moses gave you circumcision (not that it is from Moses, but from the fathers), and you circumcise a man upon the sabbath. [23]If on the sabbath a man receives circumcision, so that the law of Moses may not be broken, are you angry with me because on the sabbath I made a man's whole body well? [24]Do not judge by appearances, but judge with right judgment."

7:14 Jesus went up into the temple and taught.

---

(8) Cyril of Alexandria

About the middle of the feast Jesus went up into the temple and taught (7:14). The teaching of our Savior is particularly appropriate for the **temple**. Where else would it be more fitting to hear the divine voice than in the places where the divine is supposed to reside? Indeed, God tends for all places; we should not think that he is limited by space. Rather, according to his own nature, he is completely uncontained by created things. Nevertheless, it is more appropriate for us to think that he resides in holy places, and to suppose that it is most reasonable that, especially in holy places, we would hear whatever the divine nature thinks appropriate. This again has been written symbolically and in shadows by those who came before, and Christ has now refashioned it into truth. God says to Moses the prophet, *You shall put the mercy seat on the top of the ark; and in the ark you shall put the testimony that I shall give you. There I will meet with you, and from above the mercy seat, from between the two cherubim that are upon the ark of the testimony, I will speak with you of all that I will give you in commandment for the people of Israel* (Exod 25:21–22). Our Lord Jesus Christ, **about the middle of the feast,** as it is written, entered as God, into the holy places dedicated to God. There he spoke to the crowds, although he **went up in private** (7:10), just as God descended **in private** upon the mercy seat in the tabernacle and was scarcely perceived whenever it was time for him to speak. Even then God spoke with one person, the blessed Moses, and not to anyone else. So too Christ was teaching one race, the Jews, and was speaking with one people; he had not yet revealed his grace or made it common for all nations.

Quite well then does the blessed evangelist say not simply that Christ went "in" but that he **went *up* into the temple**. It is a lofty thing, and much more elevated than our earthbound baseness, to enter into the place of divine education and to dwell in the holy places. The symbol of this has come to be true among us. Christ is the one who sanctifies the temple, as Moses symbolized this by anointing and sanctifying the tabernacle itself with holy oil, as it is written (Lev 8:10). . . . But none of these things which occurred symbolically were itself the truth, for whose sake these shadowy things were prefigured. We can see this even in the holy prophets. One of them, against his own will, was told to sleep with a prostitute (Hos 1:2), another to walk around naked (Isa 20:2), and yet another to lie on his right side for a very long time (Ezek 4:6). These things happened in order to teach us, not because of their own inherent value. So in this way the blessed Moses was ordered to sanctify the tabernacle (even though it was more fitting for him to be sanctified by it). All this happened so that in him Christ again might be understood as the one who sanctifies his own **temple**, although Christ dwelt in the flesh among the Jews and spoke to the crowds in the **temple**, just as God had long ago done from the mercy seat.

7:16 "My teaching is not mine, but his who sent me."

---

(9) Augustine of Hippo

My teaching, he says, **is not mine, but his who sent me** (7:16). This is the first mystery; for with these few words he seems to have contradicted himself. He does not say "This teaching is not mine," but rather, *My* **teaching is not mine** (7:16). If it is not yours, in what way is it yours? If it is yours, in what way is it not yours? Indeed, you say both—**my teaching** and **not mine**. If he had said, "This teaching is not mine," then there would have been no problem. To be sure, brothers and sisters, first consider the question and then wait for an answer—in that order. For how is one able to understand the explanation if one does not first see the question which is given? Therefore, what the Lord says is in question: **My . . . not mine** (7:16). This seems to be a contradiction; on the one hand he says **my**, and on the other, **not mine**.

We will find an answer to our question if we consider more closely what the holy evangelist says at the beginning of that same gospel: *In the beginning was the Word, and the Word was with God, and the Word was God* (1:1). What is the **teaching** of the Father, if not the **Word** of the Father? Christ himself, then, is the **teaching** of the Father, if indeed he is the **Word** of the Father. Because the **Word** cannot belong to no one, but must belong to someone, he said it was both his own **teaching**, he himself, and **not** his **teaching**, because he is the **Word** of the Father. What is yours as much as yourself? What is not yours as much as you, if what you are belongs to someone else? . . .

Therefore, I say briefly to you my brothers and sisters, it seems to me that the Lord Jesus Christ said, **My teaching is not mine**, as if he had said, "I am not from myself." For we confess and believe that the Son is equal to the Father, and that there is neither any difference in their natures or essence, nor were there any intervals of time between begetter and begotten. Nevertheless, although we say these things, we also maintain that the Father is one and the Son is another. However, the Father does not exist if he does not have the

Son, and the Son does not exist if he does not have the Father. Yet God the Son is from the Father while God the Father is not from the Son. He is the Father of the Son, but not God from the Son, while the other is Son of the Father, and God from the Father. For the Lord Christ is said to be "light from light."[4] Therefore, the light which is not "from light,"[5] and the equal light that is "from light,"[6] are simultaneously one light, not two lights.

(10) Cyril of Alexandria

We must recognize that Christ's saying that he has been **sent** (7:16) does not indicate a secondary place of dignity after the Father. We must not understand his mission as one befitting a servant, even if, *taking the form of a servant* (Phil 2:7), he may rightly say these words about himself. He was, in fact, **sent** out like a word from the mind or like a ray of light from the sun. These examples are, I think, manifestations of the realities in which they exist, since they seem to proceed from within, while yet existing naturally and indistinguishably in those realities from which they come. Indeed, although a word appears to proceed from the mind and a ray from the sun, we should not therefore think that those generating realities[7] would then exist separate from the realities that proceeded from them.[8] Rather, we will see that they both exist one in the other. Not only will the mind never be word-less but neither will there be a word without a mind in which it was formed. Likewise, we should understand the other example of the sun and its rays in the same way.

7:23–24 "If on the sabbath a man receives circumcision. . . . Do not judge by appearances."

---

(11) John Chrysostom

Do not judge by appearances (7:24). What does **by appearances** mean? Christ says: "Since Moses has the greater glory among you, don't cast your vote according to the status of the person, but according to the nature of things, for that is judging **with right judgment** (7:24)."

. . . Let's trust that this has been said not only to the people of that time, but also to us, so that we might never pervert justice, but instead do everything for the sake of justice. Whether someone is rich or poor, let us not be concerned with whom the person is, but rather examine the facts. Scripture says, *You shall not be partial to a poor man in his suit* (Exod 23:3). What does that statement mean? "Do not cave in, do not be moved," it is saying, "if a poor man happens to commit injustice." If it's inappropriate to show favor to a poor

---

4. Alluding to the Nicene Creed.
5. That is, the Father.
6. That is, the Son.
7. The mind and the sun.
8. The word and the rays.

man, then it's much more the case with a rich man. I'm speaking not only to those who are judges, but to everyone, that they might nowhere pervert justice, but instead preserve it inviolate everywhere.

Scripture says, *The Lord loves justice, but he who loves injustice hates his own soul* (Ps 11:7, 5 [10:7, 5 LXX]). Let us, then, neither hate our own souls, nor love injustice. What one gains from injustice in the present is surely little, even nothing, while in the future it will cause great ruin; indeed, not even here will we profit from it. Whenever we live luxuriously with a bad conscience, is that not a punishment and a retribution? So let us love justice, and never impair the law of justice. How will we profit from the present life if we do not take virtue with us when we depart? . . . Of one thing alone do we have need: virtue of the soul. It will be able to bring us safely through, and deliver us from everlasting fire; it will convey us to the kingdom of heaven. May we all reach that kingdom through the grace and loving-kindness of our Lord Jesus Christ. Through him and with him be glory to the Father, together with the Holy Spirit, now and always, and forever and ever. Amen.

(12) Augustine of Hippo

Perhaps this **circumcision** points to the Lord himself, whom the others scorned because he went about curing and healing. By law **circumcision** was to be administered on the eighth day (cf. Lev 12:3). What is **circumcision** except a removal of the flesh? This **circumcision**, then, points to a removal of fleshly desire from the heart.

Circumcision then was given for a reason. The law designated that it be done in that particular part of the body because human beings are procreated through that organ. Death entered the world through one man just as the resurrection of the dead entered through one man: *Sin came into the world through one man, and death through sin* (Rom 5:12). Therefore, whoever is born with a foreskin is born that way because every human being is born with original sin.

God does not cleanse us from either the sin with which we are born or the sin which we add by living badly, except by that stone knife, which is Christ the Lord, for *the rock was Christ* (1 Cor 10:4). The Israelites circumcised with a stone knife, and they represented Christ with the name *Rock*. However, when he came to them, they did not recognize him, but sought to kill him instead.

Why circumcise on the eighth day unless it's because after the seventh day of the week the Lord rose on the Lord's day? Therefore, the resurrection of Christ circumcised us, and although it happened on the third day from the passion, it was on the eighth day of the week. Listen to the apostle exhorting those who are circumcised by the true Rock: *If, then, you have been raised with Christ, seek the things which are above, where Christ is seated at the right hand of God. Set your minds on things that are above, not on things that are on earth* (Col 3:1–2).

He is talking about **circumcision**. When Christ rose from the dead, he took away your carnal longings. He took away your evil desires. He took away all the excess evil with which you were born and, what is much worse, that which you added by living badly. Having been circumcised by the *Rock*, why do you still *set your minds on things that are on earth*?

(13) Theodore of Mopsuestia

Moses gave you circumcision (not that it is from Moses, but from the fathers), and you circumcise a man upon the sabbath. If on the sabbath a man receives circumcision, so that the law of Moses may not be broken, are you angry with me because on the sabbath I made a man's whole body well? (7:22-23). Jesus used a powerful example. What he means is this: "Moses **gave** both **circumcision** and the **sabbath**, even commanding that a man be circumcised on the **sabbath**. It was appropriate for him to establish the **sabbath**, for no one had kept it until then. On the other hand, when Moses **gave circumcision**, it was superfluous, for **circumcision** had already been given by the **fathers**. But he also **gave circumcision** in order to demonstrate that the keeping of the **sabbath** is not compulsory, that sometimes it is right to break the **sabbath**. So if the **sabbath** can be **broken** because of **circumcision**—since this was pleasing to Moses and not considered a transgression of the law—then why do you consider it a transgression of the law when a man is healed on the **sabbath**?"

This is why he continued to put them to shame when he said, **Do not judge by appearances, but judge with right judgment** (7:24). What he means is this: "If someone who does something on the **sabbath** is considered a transgressor of the law, then Moses should be the first one to be accused. But if Moses is not **judged** to be a transgressor of the law, then how much more should I also be exonerated for my actions?" When he had said these words, they were silent because they were struck with a clear rebuke.

John 7:25–31

[25]Some of the people of Jerusalem therefore said, "Is not this the man whom they seek to kill? [26]And here he is, speaking openly, and they say nothing to him! Can it be that the authorities really know that this is the Christ? [27]Yet we know where this man comes from; and when the Christ appears, no one will know where he comes from." [28]So Jesus proclaimed, as he taught in the temple, "You know me, and you know where I come from? But I have not come of my own accord; he who sent me is true, and him you do not know. [29]I know him, for I come from him, and he sent me." [30]So they sought to arrest him; but no one laid hands on him, because his hour had not yet come. [31]Yet many of the people believed in him; they said, "When the Christ appears, will he do more signs than this man has done?"

7:28 "You know me, and you know where I come from?"

---

(14) Hilary of Poitiers

The Son does not claim for himself anything less than that which the Father says of him. Just as the Father said *This is my Son*, which is a demonstration of his nature, in that same passage he adds: *Listen to him* (Matt 17:5), which states the mystery and faith for which he came down from heaven. We are admonished to make the same confession for our salvation. The Son taught in his own words the truth of his birth and when he had come says: **You know me, and you know where I come from? But I have not come of my own accord; he who sent me is true, and him you do not know. I know him, for I come from him, and he sent me** (7:28–29). Nobody knows the Father, as the Son often declares. Therefore he says that he is known to himself alone, because he is **from him**.

I wonder, however, when he says that he is **from him**, does he mean that he was created or that he is one naturally begotten? If he is created, then the whole creation would also be **from** God. Yet the Son says that he **knows** God because he is **from him**; why then does the whole creation not **know** the Father? If he has been created rather than begotten, then it would seem that he was **from** God along with all other things which are **from** God. Why then is he not ignorant of the Father, like the other things, which are also **from** God?

On the other hand, if his being **from** God seems to give him a unique knowledge of God, is not the very fact that he is **from** God unique to him? Of course! It is because he is the true Son of God by nature. Therefore he alone will **know** God because he alone is **from him**.

So you see, his unique knowledge comes from his unique birth. Because he is **from him**, not by the power of creation—for everything **from** God exists through the power of creation—but by a true begetting, therefore the Son alone **knows** the Father, while others, though they are also **from him**, are ignorant of him.

(15) John Chrysostom

How can Christ say that they **know** him and **know where** he is **from**, and then say that they **know** neither him nor the Father? He's not being contradictory—far from it—but is rather quite consistent with himself. He's speaking of a different knowledge when he says **you do not know him**. In a similar way the Scripture says, *The sons of Eli were worthless men; they did not know the Lord* (1 Sam 2:12), and again, *Israel did not know me* (Isa 1:3 LXX). Paul says something similar: *They profess to know God, but they deny him by their deeds* (Tit 1:16). It's possible then for someone who **knows**, not to **know**! This is what he means, "If you know me, then you know that I am the Son of God." For the words **where I am from** don't refer to a place. That's clear from what follows: **I have not come of my own accord, but the one who sent me is true, and him you do not know.** He is speaking here of an ignorance demonstrated through deeds, just as Paul says, *They profess to know God, but they deny him by their deeds* (Tit 1:16). Theirs was not a sin of ignorance, but of wickedness and an evil will; and though they knew the truth, they wanted to seem ignorant. . . .

When they said, **We know where he is from** (7:27), they were indicating nothing other than that he was from the earth and that he was the carpenter's son. Yet Christ led them up to heaven by saying, **You know where I am from**, that is, "not from where you suppose, but from where the one who sent me is." To say, **I have not come of my own accord**, intimates that they knew that he had been sent by the Father, though they did not disclose it.

John 7:32-36

[32]The Pharisees heard the crowd thus muttering about him, and the chief priests and Pharisees sent officers to arrest him. [33]Jesus then said, "I shall be with you a little longer, and then I go to him who sent me; [34]you will seek me and you will not find me; where I am you cannot come." [35]The Jews said to one another, "Where does this man intend to go that we shall not find him? Does he intend to go to the Dispersion among the Greeks and teach the Greeks? [36]What does he mean by saying, 'You will seek me and you will not find me,' and, 'Where I am you cannot come'?"

7:34 "Where I am going you cannot follow."

---

(16) John Chrysostom

In order that no one should think (as the Jewish leaders thought) that the phrase **I shall be with you a little longer** (7:33) referred to a common death, and that no one should think that he would do nothing after his death, he added, **Where I am, you cannot come** (7:34). If he was going to remain dead, they would be able to go there, for we all depart to that place. Therefore his words humbled the simpler in the crowd, frightened the bolder, and made those who were more learned seek eagerly to hear him. Little time now remained, not even a year, and they would not always have the benefit of his teaching. He did not say simply, "Here I am," but, "I am **with you**"; that is, "Even if you persecute me and drive me away, for a little while I will not stop speaking and urging upon you those matters concerning your good order and your salvation." . . .

These things indeed were spoken to the Jews; but there is fear that what was said to them might be true for us as well, that where he is, we **cannot come** (7:34) because of our sinful lives. About the disciples he says, *I desire that they also may be with me where I am* (17:24); but about us I fear that the opposite might be said: **Where I am you cannot come** (7:34). For when we act contrary to his commandments, how will we be able to **come** there? Even in the present life, if some soldier acts unworthily toward the king, he will not be able to see the king, but being discharged from his authority, he will be subjected to the worst punishment.

(17) Augustine of Hippo

He did not say, "Where I will be," but **Where I am** (7:34, 36). Christ was always present in that place to which he was returning; he came in such a way that he never left that place. So he says elsewhere: *No one has ascended into heaven but he who descended from heaven, the Son of man who is in heaven* (3:13); he did not say **who was in heaven**. He was speaking on earth, but was talking about being in heaven at the same time. He came in such a way that he never left that place; and so he has returned, that he might not abandon us.

Why are you all amazed? God has done this. A mere human is physically in one place and moves from one place to another. When he arrives at his destination, he is no longer in the place from which he came. Christ the Lord, however, was on earth in his visible flesh, but his invisible majesty was both on earth and in heaven. Therefore he says, **Where I am you cannot come** (7:34, 36). He does not say, "You *will not* be able," but "you *are not* able," for at that time they were not yet able.

So that you might not despair, he said something like this to his disciples: **Where I am** going **you cannot come**. When he was praying for them, he said: *Father, I desire that they also, whom thou hast given me, may be with me where I am* (17:24). Finally, he explained to Peter: *Where I am going you cannot follow me now; but you shall follow afterward* (13:36).

The Jews said, not to Christ himself, but **to one another, "Where does this man intend to go that we shall not find him? Does he intend to go to the Dispersion among the Greeks and teach the Greeks?"** (7:35). They did not know what they were saying, but because Christ willed it, they prophesied. Christ was about to go to the gentiles, not with his body, but with his feet. What were his feet? His were the feet that Saul desired to trample by persecution, while the head cried to him: *Saul, Saul, why do you persecute me?* (Acts 9:4).

What kind of statement is this, that **You will seek me and you will not find me** (7:34), and **Where I am you cannot come** (7:34, 36)? Why the Lord said this, they did not yet know, and still, without knowing it, they predicted something that was yet to be. The Lord said that they did not know the place (if it must be called a place), which is the *bosom of the Father* (1:18), from which the only-begotten Son never leaves. Nor were they able to conceive of the place where Christ was, from which Christ never left, to which Christ was about to return, and where Christ was staying all along. How can the human heart conceive of this, much less the tongue explain it? They did not understand this at all, and yet in this situation they foretold our salvation. They prophesied that the Lord should go to the **Dispersion among the Greeks** (7:35) and fulfill what they were saying unawares. *A people whom I had not known served me; as soon as they heard of me they obeyed me* (Ps 18:43–44). The ones whose very eyes beheld him did not hear; but those in whose ears he resounded did hear.

John 7:37–52

[37]**On the last day of the feast, the great day, Jesus stood up and proclaimed, "If any one thirst, let him come to me and drink.** [38]**He who believes in me, as the scripture has said, 'Out of his heart shall flow rivers of living water.'"** [39]**Now this he said about the Spirit, which those who believed in him were to receive; for as yet the Spirit had not been given, because Jesus was not yet glorified.**

[40]**When they heard these words, some of the people said, "This is really the prophet."** [41]**Others said, "This is the Christ." But some said, "Is the Christ to come from Galilee?** [42]**Has not the scripture said that the Christ is descended from David, and comes from Bethlehem, the village where David was?"** [43]**So there was a division among the people over him.** [44]**Some of them wanted to arrest him, but no one laid hands on him.**

⁴⁵The officers then went back to the chief priests and Pharisees, who said to them, "Why did you not bring him?" ⁴⁶The officers answered, "No man ever spoke like this man!" ⁴⁷The Pharisees answered them, "Are you led astray, you also? ⁴⁸Have any of the authorities or of the Pharisees believed in him? ⁴⁹But this crowd, who do not know the law, are accursed." ⁵⁰Nicodemus, who had gone to him before, and who was one of them, said to them, ⁵¹"Does our law judge a man without first giving him a hearing and learning what he does?" ⁵²They replied, "Are you from Galilee too? Search and you will see that no prophet is to rise from Galilee."

7:38–39 "'Out of his heart shall flow rivers of living water.'" . . . This he said about the Spirit.

---

(18) Cyril of Jerusalem

Now then, let us return to the divine Scriptures. Indeed, let us *drink water from our own cisterns* (that is, the holy fathers), *and from the springs of our own well* (Prov 5:15). Let us drink from the *living water, welling up to eternal life* (4:10, 14). The Savior **said this about the Spirit, which those who believed in him were to receive** (7:39). Look at what he says: "the one who **believes** in me." But not simply this; he also sends us back to the Old Testament and adds: **As the scripture has said, "Out of his heart shall flow rivers of living water"** (7:38).⁹ He is talking not about **rivers** perceived by the senses which simply **water** the earth to produce thorns and trees, but **rivers** which illuminate souls. In another place he says, *The water that I shall give him will become in him a spring of living water welling up to eternal life* (4:14). This is a new kind of **water**, **living** and **welling up, welling up** for those who are worthy.

Why did he call this spiritual grace **water**? Because **water** nourishes all things, and it produces vitality and life. Because while rain showers come down from heaven in one form, they work in a variety of ways. . . . So also the Holy **Spirit**, being one unique and indivisible reality, *apportions* grace *to each one as he wills* (1 Cor 12:11). Just as the dry tree partakes of **water** and then sends forth its branches, so also the soul in sin, when it has been made worthy of the Holy **Spirit** through repentance, produces the fruit of righteousness. Although one in nature, the **Spirit** works many virtues by the command of God and in the name of Christ. He uses the tongue of one for wisdom and enlightens the soul of another for prophecy. He gives to one the power to cast out demons, but to another he gives the ability to interpret the divine Scriptures. He strengthens the chastity of one and teaches another to be merciful. He instructs one to fast and discipline himself, teaches another to disregard the concerns of the body, and prepares another for martyrdom. Different things for different people, and yet not different from the Spirit himself, as it is written (cf. 1 Cor 12:7–11).

---

9. The Old Testament scriptural reference is unknown. Cf. Jer 2:13.

(19) Ambrose of Milan

Perhaps some might consider the **Spirit** less significant, and think that the **Spirit** is of a lesser majesty because **water** seems like only a small portion of a **spring** (cf. 4:10). Examples taken from the created order seem inappropriate for divinity; nevertheless, so that they do not jump to wrong conclusions from this comparison, let them learn that the Holy **Spirit** is called not only **water**, but also a **river**, according to the passage: **"Out of his heart shall flow rivers of living water." Now this he said about the Spirit, which those who believed in him were to receive** (7:38–39). So the Holy **Spirit** is a **river**—the greatest **river**—which according to the Hebrews flowed from Jesus over their lands. At least this is what we have heard from the mouth of the prophet Isaiah (cf. Isa 66:12). This is the great **river** which always **flows** and never dries up. Not only is it a **river**, but also a *stream of lavish and overflowing majesty*, as David said: *there is a river whose streams make glad the city of God* (Ps 46:4). That city of God, Jerusalem, is not watered by the course of some earthly **river**. Rather, that Holy **Spirit** who proceeds from the **spring of life** (cf. 4:14) and nourishes us with just a small drink, seems to **flow** more abundantly among those heavenly thrones, dominions and powers, with angels and archangels surging in the full course of the seven virtues of the **Spirit** (cf. Isa 11:2). If a **river** rises over its banks and overflows, how much more the **Spirit** who rises over every creature. When he **flows**, as it were, over the remaining lower fields of our minds, he makes glad that heavenly nature of creatures by the extravagant abundance of his holiness.

Do not let it disturb you that the **Spirit** is described here as a **river** and elsewhere *seven spirits* (Rev 1:4; Isa 11:2). In the holiness of these seven gifts of the **Spirit**, as Isaiah said, the fullness of virtue is indicated: *the spirit of wisdom and understanding, the spirit of counsel and might, the spirit of knowledge and of piety, and the fear of the Lord* (Isa 11:2). Thus there is one **river**, but many streams of the gifts of the **Spirit**, and so this **river** rises *from the spring of life* (cf. 4:14; Ps 36:9). Do not let this divert your attention to lesser ideas just because there seems to be a certain difference between a **spring** and a **river**. Holy Scripture has made provision so that the weakness of human nature may not be misled by the lowliness of the language. Look at any **river**: it comes from its **spring**, but has one nature and one magnificence and beauty. You would also be correct to say that the Holy **Spirit** is of one substance with God the Father and the Son of God, of one brightness and glory. I accept by faith this summary of the unity of their power and will not fear questions about differences of majesty. The Son of God said, *Whoever drinks of the water that I shall give him, will have in him a spring of water welling up to eternal life* (4:14). This **spring** is certainly the grace of the Spirit, a **river** proceeding from the living **spring**. Therefore, the Holy **Spirit** is also the **spring of life**.

(20) Augustine of Hippo

Consider: Christ did not promise us earthly and temporal wealth, or fame and power in this age. You see, all these things are given to evil people as well so they will not be highly valued by good people. He didn't promise health in the body—not because he doesn't grant that, but because, as you know, he grants it to sinners, too. He didn't promise long life. After all, what is the value of long life if it must end sometime? He certainly didn't promise us longevity when we believe in him. Everyone longs for a decrepit old age before it arrives, but everyone complains about it when it does.

He didn't promise a beautiful body. That's driven away either by sickness in the body or by that same old age you longed for. You want to be beautiful and you want to be old, but you can't possess both of those desires at the same time. If you grow old, you will not be beautiful; once old age arrives, beauty will flee. The strength of beauty and the sighing of old age cannot abide in one person.

So when he said, **Let the one who believes in me come and drink, and "Out of his heart shall flow rivers of living water"** (7:38), he didn't promise us any of these things. He did promise eternal life, a life where we will fear nothing, a life where we will not be disturbed, a life we will not leave, where we will neither mourn the one who has left nor long for the one who has not arrived. These, then, are the kinds of things he promised us when we love him, when we burn with the love of the Holy **Spirit**. This is why he refused to give us that **Spirit** until he was **glorified** so that he could show in his own body the life that we ourselves do not yet have but hope for in the resurrection.

(21) Cyril of Alexandria

A rational being, that is humanity, existed in the beginning without corruption. The source of humanity's incorruption and constancy in all virtue is evident from the indwelling of the Spirit of God. As it is written, *he breathed into his face the breath of life* (Gen 2:7). Nevertheless, upon that ancient deception when humanity turned aside to sin, progressing little by little over time, humanity endured the loss of the Spirit (among other good things). Finally, we not only became subject to corruption, but also disposed toward all sin. However, when the creator of all resolved, out of his goodness, to *unite all things in Christ* (Eph 1:10), he desired to restore the nature of humanity back to its original state, and promised to return to it (among other things) the Holy Spirit as well. There was no other way to restore us to the stability of good things. Therefore, promising the appointment of the Spirit's return to us, he says: *In those days* (clearly, those of the Savior) *I will pour out my Spirit on all flesh* (Joel 2:28). The time of God's generosity has brought upon the earth the only-begotten in flesh, that is, a man *born from a woman* according to the holy Scriptures (Gal 4:4). Therefore, God the Father bestowed the Spirit again and Christ received the Spirit as a firstfruits of our renewed nature: *John bore witness saying "I saw the Spirit descend from heaven, and it remained on him"* (1:32). . . . So, the only-begotten did not receive the Holy Spirit for himself—for the Spirit is of him and in him and through him, as we already said before. Since he was a man, however, he has our entire nature in himself, so that he might restore all, transforming us into that ancient state of being.

Moreover, we must consider this as well: through the use of wise reasoning and confirmation by the words of divine Scripture, we will see that he received the Holy Spirit not *for* himself, but rather *in* himself. For all good things proceed through him to us as well. Our forefather Adam did not preserve the gift of the Spirit. He was deceitfully turned aside to disobedience and sin, and his nature entirely lost the divinely bestowed benefit. Therefore, it was necessary for God the Word, who knows no changing (cf. Ja 1:17), to become human. As a result, when he received the Spirit as a man, he preserved what was good in our nature. The divine psalmist himself also offers an explanation of these mysteries for us, saying to the Son: *You love righteousness and hate wickedness. Therefore God, your God, has anointed you with the oil of gladness above your fellows* (Ps 45:7). "For since," he says, "you always loved righteousness (for you are a righteous God, unable to be turned away from it) and you always hated wickedness (for hatred of wickedness has been naturally rooted in you as the righteous-loving God), therefore God the Father has anointed you. Because you have in your own nature the advantage of an unchanging righteousness, you could never be dragged over to sin, which you did not know. Therefore, by becoming human you undoubtedly preserved in human nature that holy anointing, that is, the Spirit from God the Father."

So the only-begotten became human like us so that when the good returned first in him, then the grace of the Spirit planted firmly within him may finally be guarded strongly in our nature. It is as if the only-begotten Word of God the Father had imparted to us the unchanging quality of his own nature, since the nature of humanity had been condemned in Adam as entirely unable to possess it, sinking into error all too easily. . . .

If we examine why the outpouring of the Spirit did not come before the resurrection, but after it, know that when Christ unleashed the bonds of death and lived again, he became the firstfruits of our renewed nature; so how could those who came before the firstfruit have been made alive by the Spirit? A plant does not normally shoot up from the earth unless it has emerged from its own root entirely (for that is the beginning of its growth); in the same way, it was impossible for us, who have our Lord Jesus Christ as the root of our incorruption, to be seen shooting up before the root.

7:39 As yet the Spirit had not been given, because Jesus was not yet glorified.

---

(22) Augustine of Hippo

What kind of statement is this: **For as yet the Spirit had not been given, because Jesus was not yet glorified** (7:39)? Its meaning is apparent. It doesn't mean that the **Spirit** of God, which was at rest in God, didn't exist, but that it was not yet in those who believed in Jesus. The Lord Jesus arranged not to give them the **Spirit** just mentioned until after his resurrection. There was a reason for this decision. If by chance we were to ask, he would nod his assent to let us in; and if we were to knock on the door, he would open it so we might enter. Piety knocks, not the hand (though the hand also knocks by never ceasing to perform deeds of mercy). So then, why did the Lord Jesus Christ decide not to give the Holy Spirit until he had been **glorified**?

Before we say whatever we can possibly manage to say on this topic, first we must inquire (so it doesn't trouble anyone) how the **Spirit** was not yet among holy people? In the gospel we read about Simeon who, in the Holy Spirit, recognized the newborn Lord (cf.

Luke 2:25–35). Anna the widowed prophetess recognized him (cf. Luke 2:36–38), and John himself, who baptized the Lord, recognized him as well (cf. John 1:29). Zechariah said many things when he was filled with the Holy Spirit (cf. Luke 1:67–79), and Mary received the Holy Spirit when she conceived the Lord (cf. Luke 1:35). So we have a number of instances which speak of the Holy Spirit before the Lord was **glorified** by the resurrection of his flesh. The prophets, also, who foretold the coming of Christ, did not possess some other spirit.

Nevertheless, there was a certain mode of giving which was not at all apparent beforehand. Never before have we read that a gathering of people received the Holy **Spirit** and spoke in the tongues of all nations (cf. Acts 2:1–4). After his resurrection, however, when he first appeared to his disciples, he said to them: *Receive the Holy Spirit* (20:22). This **Spirit** is the referent of the text **as yet the Spirit had not been given, because Jesus was not yet glorified** (7:39). The same Lord who brought the first human to life, and lifted him from the mire, by whose breath he gave life to his limbs (cf. Gen 2:7)—this is the same one who breathed upon the disciples so they might rise out of the mud and renounce their filthy acts: *And when he had said this, he breathed on them* (20:22). Then, for the first time after his resurrection, the Lord, whom the evangelist called **glorified**, gave the Holy Spirit to his disciples. He stayed with them for forty days, as the book of Acts shows (cf. Acts 1:3), and when they had drawn together and were watching, he ascended into heaven (cf. Acts 1:9). Then after ten days' time, on the day of Pentecost, the Lord sent down his Holy Spirit. The disciples, who as I said were gathered together in one place, were filled with this gift and spoke in the tongues of all nations (cf. Acts 2:1–4).

Brothers and sisters, should we believe that someone has not received the Holy Spirit, because although he was baptized and believes in Christ, he does not speak the tongues of all nations? God forbid that such faithlessness should tempt our hearts. We are sure that everyone receives the Holy Spirit; as often as the water jar of faith is carried to the *wellspring* (cf. John 4), it is filled. Therefore, since the Holy Spirit is even now being received, someone might say: "How is it that no one speaks in the tongues of all nations?" Because: now the church as a whole speaks the tongues of all nations. Earlier, the church existed in a single nation, which then spoke all these tongues. By speaking in foreign tongues, the church signified what would come to pass, that, by thriving among the nations, it would come to speak all tongues. . . .

The church, now that it has spread through the nations, speaks all tongues. The church is the body of Christ, and in this body, you are its *members* (cf. 1 Cor 12:12–27). So then, when you are *members* of a body that speaks all tongues, know that you yourself speak all these tongues. The unity of all the members harmonizes by loving, and the composite whole then speaks as a single person would speak. Therefore we receive the Holy Spirit if we love the church, if we are joined together in love, and if we rejoice in a single name and an all-encompassing love. Brothers and sisters, believe that when anyone loves the church of Christ, he has the Holy Spirit.

John 8

The well-known story of the woman caught in adultery (John 7:53–8:11), does not appear in any of the earliest manuscripts of the Gospel of John. Moreover, of the earliest commentators on the Gospel of John, the Eastern writers Origen of Alexandria, John Chrysostom, Theodore of Mopsuestia, and Cyril of Alexandria make no comment upon this passage, suggesting that their versions of John did not contain this passage. Only Latin writers, for example, Augustine of Hippo and the Venerable Bede (along with a brief passage from the Eastern Apostolic Constitutions*), provide us with early Christian interpretation of these verses. In a moving retelling of the scene, Augustine explains the motives of the scribes. Noting Jesus's reputation for gentleness, and his claims to upholding justice, the scribes hope to catch Jesus in a trap in which he must betray one virtue or the other. Augustine points out the brilliance of Jesus's response, which preserved both his gentleness and his justice. In telling the woman,* Neither do I condemn you; go, and do not sin again *(8:11), Augustine remarks: "The Lord has indeed condemned—but he condemned the sins, not the sinners." The Venerable Bede follows Augustine's focus on the balance between mercy and justice, but adds a typological interpretation. Jesus bending to the ground twice represents the kind of humility we all must display in our lives. Bede: "We should subject ourselves to a suitably humble examination, lest perhaps we be entangled in the same things that we censure our neighbors for." Finally, the fourth-century church order* Apostolic Constitutions *uses the compassion of Jesus toward the adulterous woman as "a model to imitate" in caring for the repentant sinner.*

Following the story of the adulteress is Jesus's discourse on himself as the light of the world (8:12–20). Theodore of Mopsuestia links Jesus's announcement to be the light of the world *(8:12) with the promise of Isa 9 ("Galilee of the nations . . . have seen a great light"), and Augustine combines verse 12 with Ps 36:9 ("For with thee is the fountain of life; in thy light do we see light"), noting that God is both that which we thirst for and that which we look for.*

Regarding Christ's words about knowing whence I have come and whither I am going *(8:14), Novatian sees a clear claim of divinity. Augustine ponders Christ's claim to* judge no one *(8:15) in light of the Christian's creedal profession that Christ will "judge the living and the dead." His solution is to see Christ's judgment eschatologically, at the end. His first coming was "one of healing, not one of judging." For Augustine the order is essential: "mercy first, and then judgment."*

*Christ's words in verse 18 (*I bear witness to myself, and the Father who sent me bears witness to me*) elicit Trinitarian considerations. Tertullian argues against opponents who so emphasized the oneness of God that they could not see that the Son was distinct. He sees here a demonstration of two persons. If the Father and the Son were in fact the same person, Jesus would not have appealed to the command about having two witnesses. Ambrose argues a similar line—the Father and the Son count as two witnesses—but notes also that Jesus "neither mixed together their plurality nor separated the unity of their divine essence." Likewise, verse 19 (*if you knew me, you would know my Father*) prompts Augustine to address the relationship between the Father and the Son. Just as we might point to the similarity between two people, yet not deny that there are two, so also Christ's words here support a relationship of similarity, not a conflation into one person.*

In John 8:21-20, Jesus speaks about his coming death. Novatian recognizes that Christ's claim to be not of this world *(8:23) indicates his divinity, but that in another sense, Christ* is *of this world, since he is also human. Augustine notes that in Jesus's words* unless you believe that I am he *(8:24), there is actually no predicate nominative (*he*) to complete the sentence. Like the divine name given to Moses in Exod 3:14 ("I am who I am"), Jesus declares his divinity with the simple words* I am. *Cyril sees the same connection here between Christ and the God of the Old Testament, marshaling a number of prophetic passages fulfilled in the coming of Christ.*

In verse 28b, Christ claims to speak as the Father taught me, *leading Augustine to ask what that would mean, given the Son's divinity. Instead of being taught through physical hearing which produces understanding, Augustine suggests that the Son's existence by the Father's begetting is itself a knowing: for the Son, "to exist and to know are . . . the same thing." Cyril of Alexandria comments on the first part of this verse, using Jesus's words to emphasize that the crucifixion and resurrection (*when you have lifted up the Son of man*) are the "clearest proof that he is God by nature" (*then you will know that I am he*).*

In the next section of John 8, confrontation with the Jewish leadership mounts. Verses 31-38 address questions of spiritual freedom and slavery. Chrysostom notes the irony in the Jewish leaders' objection to being called slaves *(8:33). By focusing on their freedom from humans, they fail to understand their bondage to sin. Theodore of Mopsuestia observes that the only way we can attain freedom from sin is through Christ, the true Son. Through him alone, we are "made worthy of the rank of sons" and "receive true freedom indeed." Augustine notes that* slavery to sin *is the worst of all because we can never get away from it: "A guilty conscience doesn't flee from itself." Like Mopsuestia, Augustine sees true freedom coming only through participation in the Son. Yet even this freedom is no license to sin; it is, instead, a new form of slavery: "free from sin, but a slave of righteousness."*

Verses 39-40 address arguments over Abraham: If you were Abraham's children, you would do what Abraham did *(8:39). Origen of Alexandria observes that the last phrase is literally "the works which Abraham did." He is keen to understand just what the "works" were which Abraham did (and which we should imitate). Reading the Old Testament figuratively, Origen notes that Abraham left his country and father's house and followed God (Gen 12:1). So too, the Christian imitates Abraham's works by abandoning those aspects of our lives not in accord with God's will. Augustine observes that Jesus condemned his opponents' lifestyle, not their ethnic lineage. Moreover, now in Christ, those who imitate*

Abraham's faith, as Paul commends in Gal 3, will become Abraham's children, even without the ethnic lineage.

Christ's claim that I proceeded and came forth from God *(8:42) leads several interpreters to offer Trinitarian readings. Origen of Alexandria combines Mic 1:3 ("the Lord is coming out of his place") with Phil 2:6–7 ("he emptied himself and took the form of a servant") to see Christ's proceeding from God as a reference to the incarnation. Novatian, on the other hand, understands Christ's words entirely as a reference to his divine, eternal nature. One who proceeded from God must be divine. Hilary of Poitiers combines these two interpretations. Christ's procession refers to his eternal, incorporeal begetting. His coming forth refers to his incarnation.*

John 8:44–47 produces several pastoral insights into the spiritual life. Origen of Alexandria employs the phrase desires of the devil *(8:44) as an exhortation about the Christian life. It is more than just the things we do; we must also consider the things we* desire *to do, for in many cases, sin arises in our lives because of wicked* desires *implanted there by the devil. Origen also observes that Jesus's words in verse 45 about unbelief highlight the various degrees of belief and unbelief. The remedy, says Origen, is to call upon the physician of the soul who will "work to bring us the gift of believing." Gregory the Great says that verse 47 (He who is of God hears the words of God) is a call to examine our own lives to see whether we not only hear God's words with our ears, but also put them into practice.*

Regarding the double accusation against Jesus that he is a Samaritan and has a demon *(8:48–49), early interpreters wonder why Jesus denies the second accusation but not the first. Origen of Alexandria turns to Luke 10 and the parable of the good Samaritan to suggest that Jesus, as the Samaritan of the parable, tacitly accepted the charge in John 8. Augustine of Hippo and Gregory the Great, however, both employ an etymological solution, suggesting that since Samaritan means "watchman," Jesus was implicitly affirming his role as "watchman" over humanity.*

Several writers wrestle with Christ's promise that if anyone keeps my word, he will never see death *(8:51), noting that death is still very much a part of the human experience. Didymus the Blind observes that there is a difference between* tasting death *(8:52) and* seeing *death. All will* taste *earthly death, but those who keep Jesus's words will never* see *death. Cyril of Alexandria and Peter Chrysologus agree. Deliverance from eternal death, not physical death, is what Christ promised. Yet Chrysologus asks the troubling question: If Christ was able to prevent death, why does he allow us to experience it? His answer: "We cannot know how good the good is except by an awareness of evil."*

Christ's claim that Abraham rejoiced that he was to see my day *(8:56) compels many interpreters to ascertain what Abraham saw about Christ. Augustine of Hippo seems to favor a revelation of Christ's eternal glory with the Father, although he makes allowance for a vision of the incarnation as well. Theodore of Mopsuestia and Cyril of Alexandria turn to Abraham's near-sacrifice of Isaac in Gen 22, suggesting that in that moment Abraham envisioned the incarnation and the sacrificial death of Christ. Gregory the Great stands apart as one connecting Abraham's foreseeing Christ with the three angelic visitors in Gen 18.*

Finally, Christ's claim that before Abraham was, I am *(8:58) elicits much comment. Novatian sees it as a clear proclamation of Christ's eternal, preexistent divinity. Augustine and Cyril of Alexandria both make much of the verbal tenses. The past tense* was *is used of*

Abraham—a mere creature—while the present tense am *is used of Christ—the eternal one. John Chrysostom and Gregory the Great draw upon Exod 3:14 and the divine name ("I am who I am") as a proof that Christ's words here in John 8 indicate his divinity and shared essence with the Father.*

John 7:53–8:11

⁷꞉⁵³**They went each to his own house,** ⁸꞉¹**but Jesus went to the Mount of Olives.** ²**Early in the morning he came again to the temple; all the people came to him, and he sat down and taught them.** ³**The scribes and the Pharisees brought a woman who had been caught in adultery, and placing her in the midst** ⁴**they said to him, "Teacher, this woman has been caught in the act of adultery.** ⁵**Now in the law Moses commanded us to stone such. What do you say about her?"** ⁶**This they said to test him, that they might have some charge to bring against him. Jesus bent down and wrote with his finger on the ground.** ⁷**And as they continued to ask him, he stood up and said to them, "Let him who is without sin among you be the first to throw a stone at her."** ⁸**And once more he bent down and wrote with his finger on the ground.** ⁹**But when they heard it, they went away, one by one, beginning with the eldest, and Jesus was left alone with the woman standing before him.** ¹⁰**Jesus looked up and said to her, "Woman, where are they? Has no one condemned you?"** ¹¹**She said, "No one, Lord." And Jesus said, "Neither do I condemn you; go, and do not sin again."**

(1) Augustine of Hippo

Pay attention now! The Lord's gentleness is tested here by his enemies. **The scribes and the Pharisees brought a woman who had been caught in adultery, and placing her in the midst they said to him, "Teacher, this woman has been caught in the act of adultery. Now in the law Moses commanded us to stone such. What do you say about her?" This they said to test him, that they might have some charge to bring against him** (8:3–6). . . .

We know well, brothers and sisters, that a wondrous kindness shone forth from the Lord. They criticized him for exercising too much kindness, too much grace. Naturally, it was foretold of him: *Gird your sword upon your thigh, O mighty one, in your glory and majesty! In your majesty ride forth victoriously for the cause of truth and to defend the right* (Ps 45:3–4). Therefore he imparted truth like a teacher, peace like a liberator, and justice like a prosecutor. Because of these things, the prophet had foretold by the Holy Spirit that he would reign. When he spoke, his truth was acknowledged; when he was unmoved by his enemies, his gentleness was praised. So his enemies were tortured with envy and spite for these two things (his truth and his gentleness) and were downright scandalized by the addition of the third, that is, justice. Why? Because the law had decreed that adulterers should be stoned (cf. Lev 20:10), and the law could not possibly call for an unjust act. If anyone were to speak against what the law commanded, they would have been accused of injustice. . . .

But consider: whom were they plotting against? Perversion plotted against what is right, falseness against what is true, a corrupt heart against a noble heart, idiocy against wisdom. When would these men prepare their traps, and not first thrust their own heads into them? See, the Lord maintained justice in his response, but didn't turn away from gentleness either. The one for whom the trap was set was not captive; those who were laying the traps were the captive ones because they did not believe in the one who was able to pluck them out of their traps.

How did the Lord Jesus respond? How did truth respond? How did wisdom respond? How did justice itself respond, against whom an accusation was being prepared? He did not say, "Do not stone her!" lest he seem to speak against the law. Yet he refrained from saying "Stone her!" because he didn't come to destroy what he had found, but to seek out what had already been lost. How did he respond? See how full of justice he is, how full of gentleness and wisdom! He said, **Let him who is without sin among you be the first to throw a stone at her** (8:7). O wise response! How did he turn them back into themselves? Publicly they were making accusations, but inwardly they were not scrutinizing themselves. They saw an adulteress but did not examine themselves. As transgressors, they wanted to fulfill the law by slander rather than by truth, by condemning adultery with chastity. . . .

This is the voice of justice: Let the sinner be punished, but not by other sinners. Let the law be fulfilled, but not by transgressors of the law. Indeed, this is the voice of justice. When they were struck by this justice as if by a wooden rod, having examined themselves and discovered their guilt, **they went away, one by one** (8:9). Only two remained: the miserable one and the merciful one. . . .

After all the others had left and only the woman remained, he lifted his eyes to the woman. We heard the voice of justice; let us hear the voice of gentleness. I believe that woman was absolutely terrified when she heard the word of the Lord: **Let him who is without sin among you be the first to throw a stone at her** (8:7). Everyone else suddenly focused on themselves, and when they departed to confess their sins, they left behind the woman with the greatest sin to the man who was utterly without sin. Because she had heard him say, **Let him who is without sin among you be the first to throw a stone at her** (8:7), she was expecting to be punished by the one in whom no sin could be found. However, the man who had repelled his adversaries with the tongue of justice lifted his gentle gaze to her and asked: **Has no one condemned you?** (8:10). She responded, **No one, Lord** (8:11). And he replied, **Neither do I condemn you** (8:11)—I, the one who perhaps you feared would condemn you because you have found no sin in me.

Neither do I condemn you (8:11). What is this, Lord? Does this mean you favor sins? Clearly that's not the case. Pay attention to what follows: **Neither do I condemn you; go, and do not sin again** (8:11). The Lord had indeed condemned—but he condemned the sins, not the sinners. If he favored sins, he would have said: "I will not condemn you; carry on, and live as you wish. Be confident in my promise of freedom, and however much you sin, I will free you from the punishments of gehenna and the tortures of hell." He didn't say this. . . .

So people are in danger of two things: presumption and despair, opposite things, opposite feelings. Who is deceived by presumption? The person who says: "The Lord is good, the Lord is gracious, so let me do whatever I want, whatever I feel like. Let me loosen the reins on my passions; let me fulfill the desires of my soul. Why? Because God is merciful, God is good, God is gentle." These kind of people are endangered by presumption.

But those who have fallen into grave sins are caught in despair and think they can never be forgiven, even with repentance. So deciding that they are undoubtedly destined for damnation, they say to themselves: "We are already bound for damnation; why not do as we please in the spirit of gladiators destined for the sword?" Certainly those in despair are troublesome; since they have nothing to fear, they should be greatly feared. . . .

What then does the Lord do with those threatened by either disease? To the ones who are endangered by presumption, he says this: *Delay not to be converted to the Lord, and defer it not from day to day. For his wrath shall come on a sudden, and in the time of vengeance he will destroy thee* (Sir 5:8–9 Vulgate). To those who are endangered by despair, what does he say? "On whatever day the wicked man is converted, I will forget all his sins" (cf. Ezek 18:21–22). That is, to those who are endangered by despair, he shows the refuge of grace; to those who are endangered by presumption and have squandered themselves away in delay, he has made the exact day of death uncertain. You cannot know when you will reach your last hour. Are you ungrateful that you have today in which you may be corrected? So the Lord says to the woman: **Neither do I condemn you**, but while you have been made safe from your past, take care for the future. **Neither do I condemn you**. I have wiped out the sins you have committed; stay true to my instructions, so you might find what I have promised.

(2) *Apostolic Constitutions*

Let the bishop take care, as much as he can, that those who are blameless may not fall into sin, and let him receive and heal those who turn from their sins. If in his lack of mercy he changes his mind and does not receive them, he sins against the Lord his God. He makes himself more just than the justice of God and refuses to receive the one whom he has already received through Christ. . . . When the Jewish elders set before Christ another sinful woman and departed, leaving the judgment to him, the Lord who knows the hearts of all asked the woman whether the elders condemned her. When she said **No**, he said to her: **Go; neither do I condemn you** (8:11).

O bishops, you ought to have this Jesus, our Savior, our King, our Lord and our God as a model to imitate. You should be meek, quiet, compassionate, merciful, peaceful, lacking anger, apt teachers, able to reprove, hospitable, and comforting. You should not be violent, inclined to rage, arrogant, boastful, proud, lovers of wine, drunkards, extravagant, or inclined to luxury and expensive things. You should use the gifts of God not as others, but as your own, acting like those who have been appointed good stewards, and as those who will be asked by God to give an account.

(3) Venerable Bede

We ought to consider the present reading from the holy gospel, dearly beloved, being especially attentive and always call it to mind, since it commends to us our maker's greatest gift. Behold, as we have heard, a sinful woman was presented to him by her wicked accusers. He did not command that they stone her, in accordance with the command of the law, but he commanded her accusers first to consider themselves, and then to pass sentence upon the sinner accordingly. Then, from consideration of their own weakness, they might recognize how they should show mercy to others. . . .

Testing him, the scribes brought a woman who had been apprehended in adultery, asking what he would order to be done since Moses had given a mandate to stone such people. If he also determined that she was to be stoned they would scoff at him inasmuch as he had forgotten the mercy which he was always teaching. If he forbade the stoning, they would gnash their teeth at him, and, as they saw it, rightly condemn him as a promoter of wicked deeds contrary to the law. Far be it from earthly stupidity to find out what he would say, and from heavenly wisdom to fail to know what he would answer. Far be it from blind wickedness to stand in the way of the *sun of righteousness* (Mal 4:2), to keep him from giving light to the world.

Jesus bent down and wrote with his finger on the ground (8:6). Humility is represented by Jesus's **bending down**; subtlety of discernment is represented by **his finger**, which is flexible because of the physical arrangement of its joints. Besides, by the **ground** we are shown the human heart, which customarily produces the fruits of good or bad acts. When the Lord had been implored to make a judgment concerning the sinful woman, he did not immediately give judgment, but first **bending down he wrote with his finger on the ground**. Then at last, he made a judgment on what he was being obstinately asked about. Figuratively, this teaches us that when we look at any of our neighbors' errors, we should not judge by censuring them before we turn humbly back to our own conscience and meticulously clear it of guilt with the **finger** of discretion, and before we discriminate by painstaking examination between what in us is pleasing to our Maker and what is displeasing. . . .

Do you want to hear about his restraint as he shows mercy? **Let him who is without sin among you** (8:7). Do you want to hear about his justice in judging? **Be the first to throw a stone at her** (8:7). He said, "If Moses gave you a mandate to stone such a woman as this, see that he did not command sinners to do this, but the just. First fulfill the justice of the law yourself, and, with this done, being *innocent in hands and clean of heart* (Ps 23:4 Vulgate) come together to stone the guilty woman. First, carry out the spiritual edicts of the law (faith, mercy and love), and with this done turn aside to judge fleshy things."

When the Lord had given judgment, **once more he bent down and wrote on the ground** (8:8). In accordance with our usual human manner, we can understand that the reason why the Lord might wish to **bend** before his unprincipled tempters and to **write on the ground** was that by directing his look elsewhere he might give them the freedom to go away. He foresaw that as they had been astounded by his answer, they would be more inclined to depart quickly than to ask him more questions. Accordingly, **when they heard it, they went away, one by one, beginning with the eldest** (8:9).

Figuratively speaking, the fact that both before and after he gave his opinion he **bent** and **wrote on the ground** admonishes us that both before we rebuke a sinning neighbor and after we have rendered to him the ministry of due correction, we should subject ourselves to a suitably humble examination, lest perhaps we be entangled in the same things that we censure our neighbors for, or in any other sort of misdeeds. It often comes about, for example, that people who publicly judge a murderer to be a sinner may not perceive the worse evil of hatred with which they themselves despoil someone in secret. People who bring an accusation against a fornicator may ignore the plague of pride with which they congratulate themselves for their own chastity. People who condemn a drunkard may not see the venom of envy which eats away at them.

In dangers of this sort, what saving remedy is left except that, when we look at some other sinner, we immediately **bend down**—that is, we humbly observe how we would be cast down by our frail condition if divine benevolence did not keep us from falling? Let us **write with a finger on the ground**—that is, let us meticulously ponder with discrimination whether we can say with blessed Job, *our heart does not reproach us for any of our days* (Job 27:6), and let us painstakingly remember that *if our hearts condemn us, God is greater than our hearts, and he knows everything* (1 John 3:20). . . .

Neither do I condemn you, he said. **Go, and do not sin again** (8:11). Since he is merciful and kind, he released her from her past sins; since *he is righteous and loves righteous deeds* (Ps 11:7), he forbade her to sin anymore. But because some could doubt whether Jesus was able to forgive sins, since they knew that he was a true human being, he deigned to show more clearly what he was capable of in his divinity.

John 8:12–20

[12]Again Jesus spoke to them, saying, "I am the light of the world; he who follows me will not walk in darkness, but will have the light of life." [13]The Pharisees then said to him, "You are bearing witness to yourself; your testimony is not true." [14]Jesus answered, "Even if I do bear witness to myself, my testimony is true, for I know whence I have come and whither I am going, but you do not know whence I come or whither I am going. [15]You judge according to the flesh, I judge no one. [16]Yet even if I do judge, my judgment is true, for it is not I alone that judge, but I and he who sent me. [17]In your law it is written that the testimony of two men is true; [18]I bear witness to myself, and the Father who sent me bears witness to me." [19]They said to him therefore, "Where is your Father?" Jesus answered, "You know neither me nor my Father; if you knew me, you would know my Father also." [20]These words he spoke in the treasury, as he taught in the temple; but no one arrested him, because his hour had not yet come.

8:12 "I am the light of the world."

---

(4) Theodore of Mopsuestia

The region of Galilee was reviled because of its hatred toward those who feared God; nevertheless, it is written by the prophet: *Galilee of the nations, the people who dwelled in darkness have seen a great light* (Isa 9:1–2). This makes it clear that God chose the nation of Galilee, according to this prophecy, to receive the abundance of his great and precious gifts. Jesus said to them, **I am the light of the world** (8:12). What he means is this: "Do you not recall what the prophet said? The Galileans will delight in *a great light*. **I am that light**, and not only am I sufficient for them, but for everyone. Those who follow me will not be harmed by evil. I am sufficient for every person."

(5) Augustine of Hippo

The unfailing light, the light of wisdom, spoke through the veil of flesh and said to human beings, **I am the light of the world. He who follows me will not walk in darkness but will have the light of life** (8:12). How does he take you away from the eyes of the flesh and call you back to the eyes of the heart? It was not enough to say, **He who follows me will not walk in darkness but will have the light**. He added: **of life**.

This is similar to where it is written, *With thee is the fountain of life* (Ps 36:9a). My brothers and sisters, notice how the words of the Lord agree with the truth of that psalm. There in the psalm, *light* is placed beside the *fountain of life*.[1] Here in our passage, the Lord speaks of the **light of life**. In a physical sense, however, **light** is one thing and a *fountain* another. The mouth seeks a *fountain*, the eyes, **light**. When we are thirsty we look for a *fountain*. When we are in the dark, we look for a **light**. If we happen to be thirsty at night we **light** a lamp so we can get to the *fountain*. It is not this way with God. What is **light** is also a *fountain*. The one who provides you **light** so you can see also flows out to you so you can drink.

8:14 "My testimony is true, for I know whence I have come."

---

(6) Novatian

If Christ is only human, why does he say, **Even if I do bear witness to myself, my testimony is true, for I know whence I have come and whither I am going, but you do not know whence I come or whither I am going. You judge according to the flesh** (8:14–15)?

---

1. Augustine is drawing upon the second half of the verse (which he does not quote): *In thy light do we see light* (Ps 36:9b).

Notice: he also says that he will return to that place from which he testified he had come before he was sent from heaven. Therefore, he descended from that place where he came in the same way that he will return to the place from which he descended. We learn from this that if Christ was only human, he would not have come from heaven, and thus he would not depart to that place again since he had not come from there. However, since he comes from that place from which no human is able to come, he made it clear that he came as God. . . . His opponents failed to consider that since a human cannot come from heaven and so rightly return to heaven, the one who did descend from the place where no human can come, must be God.

(7) Augustine of Hippo

Jesus answered and said to them, "Even if I do bear witness to myself, my testimony is true, because I know whence I have come and whither I am going" (8:14). A light reveals both itself and other things. You light a lamp, for instance, to look for your tunic, and the burning lamp is responsible for you finding the tunic. But you never light a lamp to see a burning lamp, do you? Indeed, a burning lamp can make other things visible that are covered in darkness, but it can also reveal itself to your eyes. . . .

Therefore, the light **bears witness** to itself. It opens healthy eyes. It is a **witness** to itself, that it may be recognized as light. But what do we make of the unbeliever? Surely the light isn't hidden from them, is it? It's present to them, as well, but they don't have the eyes of the heart with which to see it.

Hear what the gospel itself said about them at an earlier point: *The light shines in the darkness, and the darkness has not understood it* (1:5). For this reason the Lord said (and he spoke truly), **Even if I do bear witness to myself, my testimony is true because I know whence I have come and whither I am going** (8:14). He wanted us to understand that he was referring to the Father; the Son was glorifying the Father. One who is equal glorifies the one who sent him; how much more should humans glorify the one who created them?

8:15 "You judge according to the flesh, I judge no one."

---

(8) Augustine of Hippo

Jesus says, **I judge no one** (8:15). Are we to understand from this statement that the Lord Jesus Christ does not **judge** anyone? Don't we confess that Jesus rose from the dead on the third day, ascended into heaven, is seated there at the right hand of the Father, and from there will **judge** the living and the dead?[2] Is this not our faith, of which the apostle spoke, *Man believes with his heart and so is justified, and he confesses with his lips and so is saved* (Rom 10:10)? Therefore, when we confess this, do we contradict the Lord? We speak about

---

2. A reference to the Apostles' Creed.

the coming judgment of the living and the dead, and yet Jesus says, **I judge no one** (8:15). This question can be answered in two ways: either as we are currently considering it: **I judge no one.** Or, as he says in another place, *I did not come to judge the world but to save the world* (12:47) where he does not deny the judgment, but makes a distinction about it. Or perhaps because he had already said, **You judge according to the flesh**, he then added, **I judge no one** (8:15), implying the words, "according to the flesh."

Therefore we hold to and declare nothing which is contrary to our faith about Christ the **Judge**; let no scruple of doubt remain in your heart. Christ comes first to save, and only then to **judge**. Those who have refused to be saved are about to be sentenced to punishment; but those who believe and do not reject salvation are about to be brought to life. So the first dispensation of our Lord Jesus Christ is one of healing, not one of **judging**. If he had come first intending to **judge**, he would have discovered no one for whom the reward of justice could be given. Because he saw that all were sinners, and no one was completely free from the death of sin, his mercy had to be requested first, and then his judgment had to be revealed, as the psalm has sung about him: *I will sing of mercy and judgment to thee, O Lord* (Ps 100:1 Vulgate). Indeed, he does not say judgment and then mercy, for if judgment came first, there would be no mercy. Hence mercy first, and then judgment.

8:16–18 "Yet even if I do judge, my judgment is true, for it is not I alone that judge, but I and he who sent me. In your law it is written that the testimony of two men is true; I bear witness to myself, and the Father who sent me bears witness to me."

---

(9) Tertullian of Carthage

When Christ says that he is not alone (saying **but I and he who sent me** [8:16]), does he not indicate two persons, even if inseparable? Indeed, this was the sum of what he was teaching, that there were two inseparable persons. Accordingly, he points out the law which requires the witness of two men, and adds: **I bear witness to myself, and the Father who sent me bears witness to me** (8:18). If there had been only one person, the **Father** being the same person as the Son, he would not have defended himself with the law which imposes confidence in two witnesses, not one. Likewise, having been asked where the **Father** is, he said that neither he nor the **Father** was known by them (cf. 8:19). He said there were two persons they did not know, and that if they had known him, they would have known the **Father**. Of course, he did not mean that he himself was both the **Father** and the Son, only that because of their indivisibility, it was not possible to know or not know the one without the other.

(10) Ambrose of Milan

Among humans, or within humans, there can be a unity of any one thing, such as a unity of love, desire, flesh, devotion, or faith. But a general unity which embraces in itself everything according to the divine glory—this is unique to the Father, Son, and Holy Spirit. When the Lord described the diversity that exists among humans, who have nothing in themselves by which they can arrive at a unity of an indivisible essence, he said: **In your law it is written that the testimony of two men is true** (8:17). When he said that **the testimony of two men is true**, and then comes to his own testimony and that of his **Father**, he did not say, "Our testimony is true since it is the testimony of two gods"; rather, he said, **I bear witness to myself, and the Father who sent me bears witness to me** (8:18). He said something similar a little earlier: **If I do judge, my judgment is true, for it is not I alone that judge, but I and** the Father **who sent me** (8:16). In both places, he indicated the **Father** and the Son, but he neither mixed together their plurality nor separated the unity of their divine essence.

8:19 "Where is your Father?" Jesus answered, "You know neither me nor my Father."

---

(11) Augustine of Hippo

They said, **Where is your Father?** (8:19). Since they judged the words of Christ according to the flesh, they were only able to grasp the **Father** of Christ in the same manner. Christ who spoke was visibly flesh, but secretly the Word; man revealed, God concealed. They saw his clothing, but disregarded what was clothed. They disregarded it because they did not **know**; they did not **know** because they did not see; they did not see because they were blind; they were blind because they did not believe. . . .

Those that understand according to the flesh had asked, **Where is your Father?** Now hear this, Arians: **You know neither me nor my Father; if you knew me, you would know my Father also** (8:19). What can the words *If you knew me, you would know my Father also* mean if not, *I and the Father are one* (10:30)? When you see someone similar to someone else (pay attention my beloved, for it is a common way of speaking; don't let that which is ordinary seem difficult to you). So, when you see someone similar to someone else, and you find out to whom he is similar, you say with amazement: "Oh, how similar that man is to the other!" You wouldn't say this unless there were two people. In this case, someone who doesn't know that person whom you are reminded of by the first man, replies: "Is he truly similar in this way?" And you reply to him: "Indeed, don't you know the one I'm referring to?" He then says: "I don't know him." And so that he might know the one you're referring to, you use the presence of the one he sees in front of him, and say: "If you've seen this man, you've see that other man." Clearly, by saying this, you didn't declare that they are one person, or deny that there are two. Rather, because of the great similarity between the two, you responded that in knowing the one you come to know the other, for there is a strong similarity and no difference at all between them. This is why the Lord says, **If you knew me, you would know my Father also**, not because the Son is the Father, but because the Son shares a similarity with the Father. Let the Arian believer blush in shame at this!

John 8:21–30

²¹Again he said to them, "I go away, and you will seek me and die in your sin; where I am going, you cannot come." ²²Then said the Jews, "Will he kill himself, since he says, 'Where I am going, you cannot come'?" ²³He said to them, "You are from below, I am from above; you are of this world, I am not of this world. ²⁴I told you that you would die in your sins, for you will die in your sins unless you believe that I am he." ²⁵They said to him, "Who are you?" Jesus said to them, "Even what I have told you from the beginning. ²⁶I have much to say about you and much to judge; but he who sent me is true, and I declare to the world what I have heard from him." ²⁷They did not understand that he spoke to them of the Father. ²⁸So Jesus said, "When you have lifted up the Son of man, then you will know that I am he, and that I do nothing on my own authority but speak thus as the Father taught me. ²⁹And he who sent me is with me; he has not left me alone, for I always do what is pleasing to him." ³⁰As he spoke thus, many believed in him.

8:23 He said to them, "You are from below, I am from above; you are of this world, I am not of this world."

---

(12) Novatian

So that his identity not be kept secret, Christ declares from where he came: **I am from above**, that is, from heaven, from the place from which no human can come. Humans were not made in heaven. The one who is **from above** is God, and for this reason, he is not **of this world**.

In a certain sense, however, he is **of this world** since Christ is not only God but also human. It would be correct to say that he is **not of this world** with respect to the divinity of the Word, but he is **of this world** with respect to the frailty of the body he assumed. He is human and divine combined, God and man united together. This is why Christ emphasized one part of his unique divinity since the Jewish blindness saw in Christ only his physical aspect. In our present passage, he passed over in silence the frailty of the body which is **of this world** and spoke of his divinity alone which is **not of this world**. Though they were inclined to believe that he was only human, Christ was able to have them consider his own divinity so that they might believe he was God. Wanting to overcome their unbelief about his divinity, he temporarily omits mentioning his share in the human condition and instead presents his unique divinity.

8:24 "I told you that you would die in your sins, for you will die in your sins unless you believe that I am he."

---

(13) Augustine of Hippo

Pay attention to what the Lord Christ says: **you will die in your sins unless you believe that I am** (8:24).[3] What does it mean, **unless you believe that I am**? **I am** what? He added nothing; and because he added nothing, he evoked much. One would expect him to say just what he was; yet, he didn't say. What would we expect him to say? Perhaps: **unless you believe that I am** the Christ; **unless you believe that I am** the Son of God; **unless you believe that I am** the Word of the Father; **unless you believe that I am** the author of the world; **unless you believe that I am** the former and re-former of humanity, the creator and re-creator, the maker and re-maker. **You will die in your sins unless you believe that I am** this. He evokes much when he says **I am**, because God also said the same thing to Moses: *I am who I am* (Exod 3:14). Who can adequately say what **I am** means?

God sent his messenger, his servant Moses, to liberate God's people from Egypt (you have read this, heard it, and understood it; still I remind you). God sent Moses, trembling, making excuses, but in the end, obedient. When Moses was making excuses, he said to God, whom he understood to be speaking in the angel: "If the people should say to me, 'And who is this God who sent you,' what shall I tell them?" And the Lord said to him: *I am who I am*, and then repeated: *Say to the sons of Israel, 'The one who is has sent me to you'* (cf. Exod 3:13–14). In that passage, he does not say *I am* God, or *I am* the maker of the world, or *I am* the creator of all things, or *I am* the one who brings liberty to these people, but only this: *I am who I am*, and *Say to the sons of Israel, 'The one who is.'* . . .

So, promising that we will not **die in our sins**, it seems to me that the Lord Jesus Christ said in these words: **Unless you believe that I am**, nothing other than **unless you believe that I am** God, **you will die in your sins**. Thank God that he said **unless you believe**, and not "unless you comprehend," for who can comprehend this? . . . Look, the Lord does not say, "Unless you comprehend that I am"; rather, he says something which we are able to do: **Unless you believe that I am, you will die in your sins**.

(14) Cyril of Alexandria

For you will die in your sins unless you believe that I am he (8:24). Not only does he say that it is necessary to **believe**, but he affirms that it is necessary to **believe** in him. We are justified by **believ**ing in him as God from God, as the Savior, Redeemer, and King of the whole world, and truly the Lord. Therefore, he says, you will perish if you do not **believe that I am he** (8:24). But the **I** of which he speaks is written in the prophets: *Shine forth, shine forth O Jerusalem, for your light has come and the glory of the Lord has risen upon you* (Isa

---

3. RSV: **I am he.** Both the Greek and Latin texts of this passage simply say, **I am,** and Augustine uses that ambiguity to press his point.

60:1 LXX). **I am**, he says, **he** who long ago commanded a departure from the vices of the soul, and promising loving treatment, saying, *Return, O faithless sons, and I will heal your faithlessness* (Jer 3:22). I am **he** who said that the God-fitting, most ancient goodness and incomparable patience be poured out on you, and for this reason cried out, *I, I am he who blots out your sins and I will not remember them* (Isa 43:25). **I am**, he says, **he** who speaks through Isaiah the prophet: *Wash yourselves, make yourselves clean, remove the evil of your hearts from before my eyes; cease from your wickedness and come, let us reason together, says the Lord; though your sins are like scarlet, I will make them white as snow; though they are red like crimson, I will make them white as wool* (Isa 1:16, 18). . . .

I am, he says, even he whom the law preached through Moses, saying thus: *The Lord your God will raise up for you a prophet like me from your brethren; him you shall heed just as you desired of the Lord your God at Mt. Horeb on the day of assembly* (Deut 18:15–16). . . .

Truly, no argument will provide escape from the necessity of punishment for those who do not believe in him. The divinely inspired Scriptures are filled with testimonial words concerning him, and Christ's works themselves produced a brilliant harmony with what was prophesied about him long ago.

8:28 So Jesus said, "When you have lifted up the Son of man, then you will know that I am he, and that I do nothing on my own authority but speak thus as the Father taught me."

---

(15) Augustine of Hippo

What, then, do we say, brothers and sisters? How did the **Father** speak to the Son, since the Son said, **I speak thus as the Father taught me** (8:28)? . . . I say something, and if you understood what I said, I really did speak. My words made a sound, and the sound struck your ears; through your sense of hearing, the sounds carried a meaning to your mind, that is, if you understood it. . . .

Without a doubt, if what I said is true, and you not only heard this truth but understood it as well, then two different things happened here: hearing and understanding. The hearing occurred because of something I did, but who made you understand? I spoke to your ears so that you heard, but who spoke to your mind so that you understood? Without a doubt, someone also spoke something to your mind so that not only did the sounds of these words strike your ears, but something of the truth also penetrated into your mind. Someone also spoke to your mind, but you did not see him. If you understood it, brothers and sisters, someone also spoke to your mind, and understanding is the work of God. Who spoke this to your mind if you understood? The one to whom the psalm says, *Give me understanding that I may learn thy commandments* (Ps 119:73). . . .

If then, as I was about to say, God speaks to your minds without sound, how does he speak to his Son? Think about it this way, brothers and sisters, as much as you can. As I said, think about it this way if it's acceptable in some way to compare small things to large. The **Father** spoke to the Son incorporeally because the **Father** begot the Son incorporeally.

Nor did he teach him as if he had begotten him ignorant. Rather, to have **taught** him is the same as having begotten him already knowing. This is what **the Father taught me** means; "the Father begot me as one knowing." If the nature of truth is simple (and few people understand this), then it's the same thing for the Son to exist and to know.

The Son obtains the ability to know from the same one who gives him the ability to exist. And the Son does not first exist by him and later learn from him. Rather, just as in begetting the Son, the **Father** gave him the ability to exist, so also in begetting him, the **Father** gave him the ability to know. As I said, in the simple nature of truth, to exist and to know are not two different things but the same thing.

(16) Cyril of Alexandria

When you have lifted up the Son of man, then you will know that I am he (8:28). Christ says, You look only on the flesh and think that I am a mere man after your fashion. My claim to godhead and the glory derived from it do not so much as enter your thoughts. Therefore, you will be given a clear sign that I am "God from God," and "light from light"[4]— your dreadful and most lawless deed of effrontery, namely, the cross and the death of my flesh upon it.

You will see the final result of your rebellion and the snare of death crumbling (for I will rise from the dead). Then, compelled against your own will, you will assent to the words which I spoke to you and confess that I am God by nature. I will be victorious over death and corruption. Having life by my own nature, I will raise my temple (cf. John 2:21). Ruling over death and diminishing the snares of corruption are fitting for God by nature alone. How then will I not be revealed as one conquering all things powerfully and without difficulty (with every objection and every doubt removed)?" Therefore, the Savior said that the cross will be a fitting sign to the Jews, and the clearest proof that he is God by nature.

John 8:31–38

[31]Jesus then said to the Jews who had believed in him, "If you continue in my word, you are truly my disciples, [32]and you will know the truth, and the truth will make you free." [33]They answered him, "We are descendants of Abraham, and have never been in bondage to any one. How is it that you say, 'You will be made free'?" [34]Jesus answered them, "Truly, truly, I say to you, every one who commits sin is a slave to sin. [35]The slave does not continue in the house for ever; the son continues for ever. [36]So if the Son makes you free, you will be free indeed. [37]I know that you are descendants of Abraham; yet you seek to kill me, because my word finds no place in you. [38]I speak of what I have seen with my Father, and you do what you have heard from your father."

---

4. Phrases from the Nicene Creed.

8:33 "We are descendants of Abraham, and have never been in bondage to any one."

(17) John Chrysostom

Someone asks, "Be made **free** from what?" From sins! What then do those boasters say? **We are the descendants of Abraham and have never been in bondage to any one** (8:33). . . . There are many even now who feel ashamed about insignificant matters and this kind of bondage, but no longer feel ashamed about the bondage of sin. They would prefer to be called slaves to that bondage of sin ten thousand times over, rather than be called a slave to physical bondage just once. . . .

Why did Christ not rebuke them? Indeed, they were in bondage many times, in Egypt and Babylonia and many other places. This is the reason: his words were not for love of honor but for salvation. Out of kindness he was urging them toward this goal. He might have spoken of the four hundred years of bondage;[5] he might have spoken of the seventy.[6] He might have spoken of the years under the judges, at one time twenty, at another two, and at another seven. He might have spoken about how they never stopped being in bondage. But he was not interested in showing their slavery to humans, but to sin. This is the most dangerous bondage from which God alone can deliver us, for forgiveness of sins belongs to no other.

8:34-36 "Everyone who commits sin is a slave to sin. . . . If the Son makes you free, you will be free indeed."

(18) Theodore of Mopsuestia

Among human beings, the will of their master determines whether or not **slaves** remain in the house, for their masters cast them out whenever they want. The **son**, however, is the heir and master of the house. This is what he means to say: "The subject of my speech is not about **slave**ry according to the flesh; I am speaking with you about true **free**dom." . . .

"So," he says, "the one who is a **slave to sin** (because he is far from every good thing that is from God) is continually given over to punishment. The one who has been made worthy of **free**dom and has received the status of a **son** will continually delight in the good things that are from God, and can never be driven away from them. Therefore, if you are **free**d through me and are made worthy of the rank of **sons** (cf. Gal 4:7), then you will receive true **free**dom **indeed**."

5. While in slavery to the Egyptians.
6. During the Babylonian exile.

(19) Augustine of Hippo

Truly, truly, I say to you, every one who commits sin is a slave to sin (8:34). O wretched **slave**ry! When people suffer under evil masters, they commonly desire to be sold, not seeking to be free of a master but at the very least to change masters. What can the **slave to sin** do? To whom can he object? Before whom can he object? Whom can he ask to be sold? Sometimes, when the **slave** of a man is worn out by the cruel commands of his master, he finds rest by fleeing. But where does the **slave to sin** flee? He drags himself along wherever he flees. A guilty conscience doesn't flee from itself. There is no place where it can go; it follows itself. Indeed, someone with a guilty conscience cannot retreat from himself, for the sin he commits is interior. He commits sin so that he might enjoy some bodily pleasure. The pleasure passes and the sin remains. That which was delightful has passed away, but that which stings remains. O wretched **slave**ry! . . .

Therefore, since **every one who commits sin is a slave to sin**, listen to where our hope of freedom lies. **The slave**, Christ says, **does not continue in the house for ever** (8:35). The **house** is the church, and the **slave** is the sinner. Many sinners enter into the church. Thus he did not say, "The slave is not in the house," but rather, **does not continue in the house for ever**. So if no **slave** will be there, who will be there? Indeed, *when a king sits on the throne of judgment,* as Scripture says, *who can say "I have made my heart clean" or "I am pure from my sin"?* (Prov 20:8-9). He greatly frightened us, my brothers and sisters, by saying **The slave does not continue in the house for ever**. Yet this is joined with what he also said, **The son continues for ever** (8:35). So the only one in his **house** will be Christ? Nobody will be joined with him? How will he be the head if there will be no body? Perhaps this refers to the whole Son, head and body? He neither frightens us nor gives us hope without a reason. He frightens us, lest we love sin; he gives us hope, lest we mistrust his solution to **sin**. **Everyone**, he says, **who commits sin is a slave to sin. The slave does not continue in the house for ever**. What then is our hope, we who are not without **sin**? Hear your hope: **The son continues for ever. So if the Son makes you free, you will be free indeed** (8:35-36). This is our hope, brothers and sisters: that we be made **free** by one already **free**, and by **free**ing us, he makes us **slaves**. For we were **slaves** of desire, but were made free **slaves** of love. This is what the apostle says: *For you were called to freedom, brethren; only do not use your freedom as an opportunity for the flesh, but through love be servants of one another* (Gal 5:13). Therefore, let the Christian not say, "I am **free**; I have been called into freedom; I was a **slave**, but now I have been redeemed, and I have been made **free** in that very redemption. Let me do what I will; no one can prevent me from doing my will if I am **free**." If by that will you commit **sin**, you are a **slave to sin**. Therefore, freedom is not to be used for sinning freely, but rather for not sinning. Your will is **free** if it has become holy. You will be **free** if you will be a **slave**: **free** from **sin**, but a **slave** of righteousness, as the apostle says: *When you were slaves of sin, you were free in regard to righteousness. . . . But now that you have been set free from sin and have become slaves to God, the return you get is sanctification and its end, eternal life* (Rom 6:20, 22). Let us strive for this; let us practice it.

John 8:39–47

[39]They answered him, "Abraham is our father." Jesus said to them, "If you were Abraham's children, you would do what Abraham did, [40]but now you seek to kill me, a man who has told you the truth which I heard from God; this is not what Abraham did. [41]You do what your father did." They said to him, "We were not born of fornication; we have one Father, even God." [42]Jesus said to them, "If God were your Father, you would love me, for I proceeded and came forth from God; I came not of my own accord, but he sent me. [43]Why do you not understand what I say? It is because you cannot bear to hear my word. [44]You are of your father the devil, and your will is to do your father's desires. He was a murderer from the beginning, and has nothing to do with the truth, because there is no truth in him. When he lies, he speaks according to his own nature, for he is a liar and the father of lies. [45]But, because I tell the truth, you do not believe me. [46]Which of you convicts me of sin? If I tell the truth, why do you not believe me? [47]He who is of God hears the words of God; the reason why you do not hear them is that you are not of God."

8:39 "If you were Abraham's children, you would do what Abraham did."

---

(20) Origen of Alexandria

There are some who pick out only one of the **works of Abraham** (8:39),[7] such as *Abraham believed God, and it was reckoned to him as righteousness* (Rom 4:3), and think that this is what Jesus means when he says, **Do the works of Abraham**. Even though they do this in hopes that we might agree with them that faith is a **work**, it would not be agreed upon by those who accept the words: *Faith without works is dead* (Jas 2:20), nor by those who understand that there is a distinction between being justified *by faith* and being justified by *works of the law* (Rom 3:28). Let them explain why Jesus said, **If you were Abraham's children, you would do the works of Abraham**, not in the singular ("work") but in the plural (**works**). I think that to **do the works of Abraham** is the same as doing all **the works of Abraham**. . . .

Clearly we learn here that it is necessary to understand the entire narrative of **Abraham** allegorically, and to see each of his **works** as being done spiritually. We can begin with: *Go from your country and your kindred and your father's house to the land that I will show you* (Gen 12:1). This is said not only to **Abraham** but to all who will be his **children**.

Before the divine message arrives, each of us has a certain *country* and *kindred* that is not good. Before the word of God comes to us, each of us belongs to our *father's house*. It is because of all these things, according to God's word, that we must *go* when we hear the Savior telling us, **If you were Abraham's children, you would do the works of Abraham**.

---

7. RSV: **What Abraham did**, but the Greek is literally "the works of Abraham." Origen is interested in knowing exactly what the "works" are which **Abraham did**.

So, as those who abandon their own *country*, we come to the *country* that God will show us, a *country* which is truly *good and broad* (Exod 3:8), a *country* which the Lord God fittingly gives to those who do what has been commanded in the words: *Go from your country.* . . . If **Abraham's children do the works of Abraham**, the first of their **works** is to *go from his country and his kindred and his father's house*, and come *to the land that* God *shows* him (Gen 12:1).

(21) Augustine of Hippo

Let us hear how the Lord responded to them: he praised **Abraham** while condemning them. Jesus said to them, **If you were Abraham's children, you would do what Abraham did, but now you seek to kill me, a man who has told you the truth which I heard from God; this is not what Abraham did** (8:39–40). See, Abraham was praised, but they were condemned. Abraham was not a murderer. . . . He doesn't deny their family roots, but condemns their actions; they shared Abraham's lineage, but not his lifestyle.

However, my brothers and sisters, have we come from the lineage of Abraham? Was Abraham in any way our father according to the flesh? The bloodline of the Jews traces back to him—not so for Christians. We have come from other races; and yet, by imitating him, we are made **Abraham's children**. Listen to the apostle: *Now the promises were made to Abraham and to his offspring. It does not say, "And to offsprings," referring to many; but, referring to one, "And to your offspring," which is Christ. And if you are Christ's, then you are Abraham's offspring, heirs according to promise* (Gal 3:16, 29). So we are made the *offspring* of **Abraham** by the grace of God. . . .

8:42 "I proceeded and came forth from God."

---

(22) Origen of Alexandria

Let us consider the text **I proceeded and came forth from God** (8:42). It seems good to me to put this together with the text from Micah, *Hear words, you peoples, and let the earth pay attention and all those in it, and the Lord shall be a witness against you, the Lord from his holy house. For behold, the Lord is coming out of his place and will come down and tread upon the high places of the earth. And the mountains will quake under him, and the valleys will melt like wax from before the fire and like water being carried in a descent* (Mic 1:2–4 LXX). Consider whether the phrase **I proceeded from God** has the equivalent force as *the Lord is coming out of his place* (Mic 1:3). When the Son is in the Father, being in the *form of God* before he *emptied himself* (Phil 2:6–7), it is as if God was his *place*. If you consider him who was in the true *form of God* before he *emptied himself*, you will see the Son who has not yet **proceeded from God** himself, and the *Lord* who has not yet *come out of his place*.

When you compare what he is when he *emptied himself* and assumed the *form of a servant* (Phil 2:7) on the one hand, with the situation of the Son on the other, you will understand how the Son of God **proceeded and came forth** to us. He has **come forth**, so to speak, from the one who sent him. This is true even if in another sense, the Father did not leave him alone, but is with him (cf. John 8:29), and is in the Son just as the Son is in the Father (cf. John 17:21). But unless you understand that the Son is in the Father in a different sense than he was before he **proceeded from God**, there will seem to be a disagreement between his having **proceeded from God** and then, having **proceeded from God**, to say he is still in God.

(23) Novatian

If Christ is only human, why does he say, **I proceeded and came forth from God** (8:42)? It is obvious that humans are made by God, but do not **proceed from God**. Just as humans do not **proceed from God**, the Word of God does **proceed**, about whom it was said: *My heart overflows with a good word* (Ps 45:1). Since he is **from God**, we rightly say that he is **with God** (1:1). Since this Word was not spoken idly, he rightly made all things. For **all things were made through him, and without him was not anything made** (1:3). This Word, through whom **all things were made**, is God. As it says, **And the Word was God** (1:1). So God **proceeded** from God; that is, the Word which **proceeded** is the God who **proceeded** from God.

(24) Hilary of Poitiers

All who have God as Father have him as Father by the same faith which confesses that Jesus Christ is the Son of God. But if we confess that he is a son in a general sense, as a title belonging to all the saints, what kind of faith is that? We would simply be saying, "He is one of many sons." Are then all the rest of us, with our frail bodies, also sons in the same sense? In what way, then, is our faith notable which confesses that Jesus Christ is the Son of God, if he is like one of many sons, having the title but not the very nature of "Son"? Such unbelief does not **love** Christ, nor does such impious profession correctly presume to have God as Father. If they had God as Father, then they would love Christ, because he **proceeded from God**.

I ask: what does it mean that he **proceeded from God**? It cannot be that **proceeded** is the same thing as **came forth from God**, for he mentions both: **I proceeded** *and* **came forth from God**. Having indicated that he both **proceeded** and **came forth from God**, he immediately adds: **I came not of my own accord, but he sent me.** When he says, **I came not of my own accord**, he taught us that he was not the source of his existence. He testifies that he **proceeded from God** but then was also **sent forth** from him a second time. When Christ tells those who claim God as their Father to love himself because he **proceeded from God**, he taught us that the reason we should love him was his begetting. The word **proceeded**, then, evokes his incorporeal birth, since we earn the right of calling God our Father by our love for Christ who was begotten from the Father.

When he says, *He who hates me hates my Father also* (15:23), his use of the word **my** indicates his unique relationship with the Father. Moreover, he condemns as a usurpation of the paternal name anyone who professes that God is his Father but does not love the Son, since **he who hates** the Son **hates the Father**, and anyone who does not **love** the Son does not rightly call God, Father. The only reason for loving the Son is because he **proceeded from God**. Thus, the Son **proceeded** from God not at the incarnation, but at his eternal generation. And complete love for the Father comes only from believing that the Son is from him.

8:44 "You are of your father the devil, and your will is to do your father's desires. He was a murderer from the beginning, and has nothing to do with the truth, because there is no truth in him. When he lies, he speaks according to his own nature, for he is a liar and the father of lies."

---

(25) Origen of Alexandria

It is not absurd to say that the **desires** of the **devil** are **murders**, acts of injustice, and greed, since he practically gave birth to these desires in his children. It is not difficult to believe that the **desires** of the **devil** are, in general, impurities which are naturally opposed to purity. From these, the **desires** for impurity are produced in the children of the **devil**. . . .

In regards to these things, we should clarify: the **devil desires**, let us say, this boy to be corrupted, or this woman to commit adultery, or these men to commit fornication. From these **desires**, he produces in those who are able to serve him, the **desire** to do what he wants done. In this way, we could say that the one who caused the fornication or adultery actually committed fornication and adultery before the human being did. The same can be said about all sins. That is, the **devil** does not **desire** money, but he does **desire** to make people lovers of money who are passionately attached to worldly things. Those who love money, even if they only wish for it, **desire** to do his **desires**.

Therefore everything we want to do needs to be considered and carefully examined, lest what we want to do comes from the **desires** of the **devil**. When we have contemplated those things that come from the **desires** of the **devil**, we can stop willing to do them. We certainly know that the one who **wills** to do the **desires** of the **devil** is in no way a child of God the Father, but has become a child of the **devil**. Such people are shaped by **will**ing to do the **desires** of the inferior one. . . .

If we forget, as it were, the better part of ourselves and submit ourselves to the form which comes from the dust, even the better part will take on that earthly image. But if we understand what has been made in his image and what has been received from the dust of the earth, and then completely incline ourselves toward him in whose image we have been made, we will be in the *likeness of God* (Gen 1:26). We will have abandoned every passionate attachment to material and bodily things, even toward certain things which are in his *likeness*.

The Greeks distinguish the meaning of words precisely. For example, they call "willing" a good thing, defining it as a rational longing, but consider **desire** to be a bad thing, calling it an irrational or excessive longing. But since the divine Scriptures did not know about these lexical distinctions, **desire** can be a morally neutral term, and we ought to say that every created nature wants to do the **desires** of its own **father**, just as all things do the works of their own **father**. One is from a holy and unbegotten **Father**, that is, God; the other is from the wicked **father**, who is actually a **father** from nothing. There was no father who caused wickedness to exist in him, but his rejection of God gave birth to wickedness. . . . Therefore, let us consider not only the things we do, but the things we **will** to do.

8:45 "But, because I tell the truth, you do not believe me."

---

(26) Origen of Alexandria

If we remember that the word here is addressed to those Jews who had believed in Jesus and had received the promise that if *they continue in the word* of Jesus, they will *truly be* his disciples and will *know the truth* which *makes* them **free** (8:31–32), we might be puzzled that Jesus says to them, **Because I tell the truth, you do not believe me** (8:45). Understand then that it is possible for someone to **believe** him in one sense but **not** to **believe** in another sense. For example, those who **believe** that Jesus was crucified in Judea by Pontius Pilate may **not believe** that he was born of the Virgin Mary. They **believe** and yet **do not believe** the same one. Likewise, those who **believe** that Jesus performed signs and wonders in Judea, as it is written, may **not believe** that he is the Son of the one who made heaven and earth. They both **believe** and **do not believe** in the same one. Again, those who **believe** in the Father of Jesus may **not believe** in the creator and maker of all things. They **believe** and **do not believe** the same one. . . . You can see this now among many people. They marvel at Jesus whenever they observe the narrative about him, but no longer **believe** whenever the word is unfolded to them which is deeper and greater than their capacity to understand. They think he is a liar. So let us never hear it spoken to us: **Because I tell the truth, you do not believe me**. . . .

However, when we consider what it is to **believe** in the proper sense, according to the text, *Every one who believes that Jesus is the Christ is a child of God* (1 John 5:1), we see that our weakness prevents us from **believ**ing in the proper sense. Let us respond to this situation by exhorting the physician of the eyes of the soul, by his wisdom and goodness, to uncover our eyes which are still covered by the dishonor of our sin, as it is said, *Our dishonor has covered us* (Jer 3:25). He will hear us when we confess the reasons we do not yet **believe**. He will help us who are sick and need a physician, and he will work to bring us to the gift of **believ**ing. After the *utterance of wisdom* and the *utterance of knowledge* (1 Cor 12:8), Paul adds "faith" as the third in his list of gifts: *to another faith by the same Spirit* (1 Cor 12:9).

8:47 "He who is of God hears the words of God."

---

(27) Gregory the Great

If **he who is of God hears the words of God** (8:47), and he who is not **of God** cannot hear his words, let each of us ask ourselves whether we perceive the **words of God** with the ears of our heart. Then we will understand where we are from. Truth commands us to desire our heavenly home, to trample underfoot our physical desires, to turn away from the world's praises, not to covet what belongs to another, to give of what is one's own. Let each one of us then consider within ourselves whether this voice of God prevails in the ears of our hearts. Then we will recognize whether we are now **of God**.

There are some who choose not to listen to God's precepts with the ears of their body; there are some who listen to them with their bodily ears but who do not embrace them with their heart's desire; and there are some who freely accept the **words of God** so that they feel compunction even to weeping, yet after the time of tears they turn back to wickedness. They do not **hear the words of God** who refuse to put them into practice in their deeds. Call your life before the eyes of your hearts, dearly beloved. After you seriously reflect on it, take alarm at what you hear from Truth himself: **The reason why you do not hear them is that you are not of God** (8:47).

John 8:48-59

[48]The Jews answered him, "Are we not right in saying that you are a Samaritan and have a demon?" [49]Jesus answered, "I have not a demon; but I honor my Father, and you dishonor me. [50]Yet I do not seek my own glory; there is One who seeks it and he will be the judge. [51]Truly, truly, I say to you, if any one keeps my word, he will never see death." [52]The Jews said to him, "Now we know that you have a demon. Abraham died, as did the prophets; and you say, 'If any one keeps my word, he will never taste death.' [53]Are you greater than our father Abraham, who died? And the prophets died! Who do you claim to be?" [54]Jesus answered, "If I glorify myself, my glory is nothing; it is my Father who glorifies me, of whom you say that he is your God. [55]But you have not known him; I know him. If I said, I do not know him, I should be a liar like you; but I do know him and I keep his word. [56]Your father Abraham rejoiced that he was to see my day; he saw it and was glad." [57]The Jews then said to him, "You are not yet fifty years old, and have you seen Abraham?" [58]Jesus said to them, "Truly, truly, I say to you, before Abraham was, I am." [59]So they took up stones to throw at him; but Jesus hid himself, and went out of the temple.

8:48 "Are we not right in saying that you are a Samaritan and have a demon?"

---

(28) Origen of Alexandria

When the Jews responded to Jesus, they laid two accusations against him: **You are a Samaritan and you have a demon** (8:48). (These were not the Jews who had believed in Jesus.) But someone might wonder why Jesus does not respond to both of these accusations, but only to the latter, saying, **I have not a demon** (8:49). Consider whether it is possible to compare this to the parable which is told by Luke the Evangelist. That parable tells about a man who was *going down from Jerusalem to Jericho and fell among robbers* (Luke 10:30). The priest and the Levite passed him by, but *the Samaritan, as he journeyed, came to where he was; and when he saw him, he had compassion, and went to him and bound up his wounds, pouring on oil and wine* (Luke 10:33–34). If someone who considers this parable should be able to prove that what is written about the Samaritan who healed the half-dead man who fell among robbers is actually about none other than the Savior, he will also explain why the Savior did not deny that he was a **Samaritan**.

(29) Gregory the Great

The Jews answered him, "Are we not right in saying that you are a Samaritan and have a demon?" (8:48). Let us listen to what the Lord replied after receiving such abuse: **I have not a demon; but I honor my Father, and you dishonor me** (8:49). **Samaritan** means "watchman,"[8] and he truly is the "watchman" about whom the psalmist says, *Unless the Lord watches over the city, in vain do they keep watch who guard it* (Ps 126:1 Vulgate). It is he to whom Isaiah says, *Watchman, what of the night? Watchman, what of the night?* (Isa 21:11). The Lord would not answer, "I am not a **Samaritan**," but said, **I have not a demon**. Two charges were brought against him. He denied one and gave assent to the other by being silent. He had come as a "watchman" of the human race, and if he had said that he was not a **Samaritan** he would have been denying that he was a "watchman." He was silent about what he knew was true, and he patiently rejected the false accusation by saying, **I have not a demon**.

8:51 "Truly, truly, I say to you, if any one keeps my word, he will never see death."

---

(30) Didymus the Blind

When the Savior said that the one who **keeps** his **word will never see death** (8:51), the Jews who were present gave a reply which mistook **seeing death** to be the same as **tasting** it

---

8. A definition taken from Saint Jerome.

(8:52). Their words indicate that it seemed to them that the one who does not **taste death** (8:52) does not experience earthly death. But this seems to contradict the Lord's promise about those who have died and those who have **kept** his **word**. Their mistake was in wanting to seem wise and clever, understanding **seeing** and **tasting** as equivalent terms. The one who **keeps** Jesus's **word will never** *see* the **death** which follows sin, even if he *tastes* that bodily death which is common to all.

(31) Cyril of Alexandria

The divine **word** is **kept** when one does not transgress the divine commandment, but takes possession of what has been commanded and performs it without delay. This person is in no way accused of laziness in the divine laws. Observe again how much precision his word contains: he is not content to say, "If anyone hears my word," but, **If anyone keeps my word** (8:51). Not only sinful people, but even the unholy masses of demons themselves receive unto themselves the word of God. Satan, the leader of them all, when he dares to tempt our Lord Jesus Christ in the desert, kicking against the goads through his great and fierce dispositions, quoted to Christ the divine word, saying, *It is written that he will give his angels charge of you, to guard you in all your ways* (Luke 4:10; Ps 91:11). Therefore the word of salvation is not in hearing alone, nor is life found only in learning, but in **keeping** what is heard. Christ placed before them the divine word as some rule and guide of life. He says that the one who firmly **keeps** his **words will never see death** (8:51), not by entirely removing death in the flesh, but by God not counting **death** to be **death**. The dead is nothing to him, since he produces and brings into existence that which did not exist, and easily makes alive that which, having been brought forth, is being destroyed. He says that the saints **will never see death** in the age to come—an age which is understood properly and more truly as not having an end like ours. But he says that those who **keep** the divine **word, will never see death** during that age. It is not that some will die after the resurrection, for the **death** of all has been demolished in the **death** of Christ, and the power of decay has been destroyed, so that by **death** he likely means eternal punishment.

(32) Peter Chrysologus

Abraham and the prophets were steadfast in hearing and keeping the **word**; nevertheless, they died, but not forever. Therefore when he says: **He will not taste death**, and he adds **never**, he is promising the resurrection, but not denying that they will die for a time. . . . Hear him speaking more openly: Everyone who believes, *shall never die* (11:26), but will *pass from death to life* (5:24). How does he not die since he **passes from death to life**? He does die, for everyone who is born in this mortal state dies. He also lives, for everyone who is born of the life-giving generation lives, and lives forever.

But I say: why did the one who was able to take away **death** want humans to pass through **death**? The physician who prevents sickness is better than one who painfully applies medicine too late. O Jew, Christ the physician would have done this too, if the sick person had not been ungrateful to the physician. He both gave life and warned humankind that **death** was coming. But humankind, who had not experienced adversity, did not know how to preserve their good fortune. We are unable to know how good the good is, except by a knowledge of evil. Therefore Christ, who both gave life which no one previously possessed, and who now restores that life once destroyed, will be greatly praised. Those who are more aware of their life will be more cautious with it and more grateful to the creator.

8:56–58 "Your father Abraham rejoiced that he was to see my day. . . . Before Abraham was, I am."

---

(33) Novatian

If Christ is only human, why does he say, **Before Abraham was, I am** (8:58)? No human can exist **before** the one who gives him existence, nor is it possible for anyone to exist prior to the one from whom he received his birth. Christ, although he is from **Abraham**'s seed, says that he was **before Abraham**. Or, if the one who was from **Abraham**'s seed was not **before Abraham**, does he then lie and deceive? No. He does not deceive if he was God when he was **before Abraham**. So although he was from **Abraham**'s seed, he could not be **before Abraham** unless he was God.

(34) John Chrysostom

Why did he not say, "Before Abraham was, I was," but rather, **I am** (8:58)? Just as his Father had proclaimed this expression, *I am* (Exod 3:14), so also did he. It signifies continuous existence, separated from all time. For this reason, his speech seemed blasphemous to them. If they could not bear the comparison to **Abraham**, although it was small, if he had continually made himself equal to the Father, would they ever have ceased throwing stones at him?

(35) Theodore of Mopsuestia

Your father Abraham longed[9] to see my day; he saw it and was glad (8:56). What he means is this: "Since there was a testimony about me from my Father, listen now to the things that conform to that testimony about me. **I am** greater than **Abraham** because he also yearned for and longed to see the time when I would reform the world through my passion. What he desired to see, insofar as he was able, **he saw and was glad**. He says that after the slaughter of his son (Gen 22) his spirit rejoiced and he received a revelation from God that enabled him to know future events. Just as he received a revelation to offer his son as a sacrifice to God, so too God gave his only-begotten Son for the salvation of the world."

---

9. Theodore's text has "longed for" (not rejoiced), a point that Theodore will press in his exposition.

(36) Augustine of Hippo

Your father Abraham rejoiced that he was to see my day; he saw it and was glad (8:56). The descendant of **Abraham**, the creator of **Abraham**, gives great testimony to **Abraham**. **Abraham rejoiced**, he says, **that he was to see my day**. He did not fear, but rather **rejoiced that he was to see**. He had that love which *casts out fear* (1 John 4:18). Christ does not say, "He rejoiced because he saw," but he **rejoiced that he was to see**. Believing, of course, he **rejoiced** by hoping that he might **see** by understanding. And **he saw it**. What more could the Lord Jesus Christ have said? What more ought he to have said? **He saw it**, he says, **and was glad**. Who will explain this gladness, my brothers and sisters? If those were **glad** whose eyes of the flesh the Lord opened, what gladness would there be for those who with the eyes of the heart see that ineffable light, the enduring Word, the brilliance which shines upon godly minds, that unfailing wisdom, God who remains with the Father, but one day comes in the flesh without ever leaving the **bosom of the Father** (1:18)?

All of this, Abraham **saw**. When he says **my day** it's not clear whether he's speaking about the temporal **day** of the Lord when he came in the flesh, or the **day** of the Lord which knows no beginning or end. But I have no doubt that **father Abraham** knew it all. . . .

The Jews were angry and responded: **You are not yet fifty years old, and have you seen Abraham?** (8:57). The Lord replied: **Truly, truly, I say to you, before Abraham was, I am** (8:58). Understand the word **was** as indicating Abraham's creation as a human; but understand the phrase **I am** as indicating Christ's divinity. He said **was** because Abraham was a creature. He did not say, "**Before Abraham was**, I *was*," but **before Abraham was**—who couldn't exist apart from me—**I am**. Neither did he say, "**Before Abraham was**, I came into existence." For *in the beginning God created the heavens and the earth* (Gen 1:1), and *in the beginning was the Word* (1:1). **Before Abraham was, I am.** Recognize the creator here! Distinguish him from the creature! The one who was speaking became the seed of Abraham. But so that Abraham might come into existence, he himself existed **before Abraham**.

(37) Cyril of Alexandria

Therefore (he says) **your father Abraham rejoiced that he was to see my day; he saw it and was glad** (8:56). How or when should we think that the blessed **Abraham** had seen the day of Christ our Savior, that is, the time of his coming in the flesh? The meaning is not clear, for one cannot take the controversial text and simply declare its plain sense. Yet, considering it well as one of the difficulties encountered so far, we will say that God revealed his own mystery to **Abraham** just as he did to one of the holy prophets. That is to say, we will grant that he truly saw the day of the sacrifice of the Lord itself, through which all things have come down to us auspiciously, just as it came down from heaven when **Abraham** was commanded to offer as a sacrifice his only-begotten and firstborn son, that is Isaac, as a type of Christ (Gen 22). It was like he was acting as a priest and clearly establishing the exact meaning of the mystery typologically. Therefore (he says) the blessed **Abraham saw**, and seeing, **he was glad for my day**. . . .

Again Christ proceeds in his usual and beloved habit, for at times he speaks very enigmatically, obscuring his meaning in diverse ways. He conceals it and does not allow it to be clear to all ears. But when he sees that his hearers understand nothing, he strips away the obscurity of meaning and presents the word naked and clear, which in fact he hastens to do in this present situation. He finds no one who understands, even though they had just experienced a lengthy discourse. He finds no one able to comprehend that he is eternal as from the eternal Father, and that, as God, he is incomparably greater than **Abraham**. Therefore, he now speaks openly, in the manner of an oath, adding the word **truly** as a confirmation of the things said, **Before Abraham was, I am** (8:58). . . . It is exceedingly fitting and proper that he uses **was** for Abraham, but **I am** for himself. He shows that corruption necessarily follows for the one who was born from non-existence, while for the one who has always existed, falling into non-existence could never occur. He is greater, therefore, and superior to **Abraham**; greater as the eternal one, superior in not facing corruption as **Abraham** does.

(38) Gregory the Great

We must note that the Lord sees them opposing him with an open attack, but does not cease preaching insistently to them. **Your father Abraham rejoiced that he was to see my day; he saw it and was glad** (8:56). Abraham **saw the day** of the Lord when he hospitably received three angels as a prefiguration of the most Holy Trinity (cf. Gen 18:1–3). After he had received them, he spoke to the three as to one, since although there are three persons in the Trinity, the nature of the divinity is one. But the unspiritual minds of his hearers did not raise their eyes from his body. Although he was God they took account only of his age in the flesh: **You are not yet fifty years old, and have you seen Abraham?** (8:57).

Our Redeemer graciously turns their gaze away from his body and draws it to contemplation of his divinity. He says, **Truly, truly, I say to you, before Abraham was, I am** (8:58). **Before** indicates past time; **I am** indicates present time. Because divinity does not have past and future time, but always is, he did not say, "I *was* before Abraham," but **before Abraham was, I *am*.** Hence it was said to Moses: *I am who I am,* and: *Say to the people of Israel, "I am has sent me to you"* (Exod 3:14). Therefore he who could draw near by manifesting his presence, and depart after completing his life, existed both **before Abraham** and after **Abraham**. Truth always exists, because nothing begins for it in time, nor comes to an end after it.

John 9

In this chapter, nearly all of the early church fathers address Jesus's response to the disciples when they asked him why this man was born blind: Jesus answered, "It was not that this man sinned, or his parents, but that the works of God might be made manifest in him" *(9:3).* *Augustine, John Chrysostom, Cyril of Alexandria, Theodore of Mopsuestia, and Caesarius of Arles each stress that Jesus did not mean that the blind man and his parents were without sin. In fact, the fathers painstakingly explain that they were indeed sinners—as are all humans— and that Jesus was merely making it clear that the man's blindness was not caused by a specific sin. John Chrysostom goes further and states emphatically that no one is punished for the sins of another. Cyril concludes that we are not to scrutinize the mysteries of God and that some things are "hidden in the divine and ineffable plan alone." John Chrysostom asserts that he did not suffer any injustice, for he gained not only physical but also spiritual sight from Christ.*

Each commentator finds deep theological meaning in the physical details of this miracle: As he said this, he spat on the ground and made clay of the spittle and anointed the man's eyes with the clay *(9:6). While they acknowledge that Christ often healed with only a word, here he mixed his spittle with the dust. This recalls creation when God creates humans from the dust of the earth, providing clear evidence that Christ was the creator of all. For Augustine, this sign takes on a sacramental character. He notices the use of the word* anointed *(9:6) and the subsequent command of Jesus that the blind man should* wash in the pool of Siloam *(9:7). He connects this miracle to the ritual in which a catechumen is anointed and then approaches the baptismal font. Ambrose, Augustine, Caesarius, among others, highlight the etymology of the name* Siloam *(which means Sent). They connect this with Christ, who was* sent *from the Father. The blind man was* washed *(i.e., baptized) in the one who was* sent *from above. Augustine and Caesarius explicitly connect the spittle with the incarnate Christ: Jesus was truly a human in every way. John Chrysostom notes that the spittle shows that the miracle derived from Christ and not from ordinary earth or water.*

Other elements in this chapter elicit unexpected comments from the fathers. When examining the Jews' interrogation of the parents, Augustine, Cyril, and Theodore offer a sympathetic tone regarding the blind man's parents. Cyril acknowledges that fear hinders people from doing what is in their best interest. Augustine states that if they would have been put out of the synagogue *(9:22), they would have been met by Christ.*

When commenting on the second meeting between the blind man and the Jews, John

Chrysostom, Cyril, and Theodore each notice the radical change in the blind man's demeanor. While he had previously called Jesus a prophet *(9:17), he now counts himself among the disciples:* Do you too want to become his disciples? *(9:27). When the Jews vehemently respond that they are* disciples of Moses *(9:28), Augustine, Cyril, and Theodore each state that this is not possible, since Moses spoke about Christ. John Chrysostom goes further and states that they have "heard" that* God has spoken to Moses *(9:29), but they fail to "see" what has taken place before their very eyes. Augustine and John Chrysostom both state that after he was thrown out of the synagogue, he was received by Christ. He in turn says,* "Lord, I believe!" And he worshiped him *(9:38). For Cyril and John Chrysostom, his obeisance declares the reality of Christ's identity: he is the incarnate Word of God who enlightens the world.*

(1) Augustine of Hippo

The long story about the man born blind whom the Lord Jesus enlightened was just read aloud. However, if we should attempt to treat the whole story by considering each part carefully, an entire day would not be sufficient. So I request your patience and ask you not to demand explanations for those passages which are clear, for it will take too long to dwell on each verse. Accordingly, I will set forth the mystery of the enlightenment of this blind man briefly. The things which our Lord Jesus did, both his words and deeds, are wonderful and astonishing: the deeds because they are facts; the words because they are signs. If we consider what is signified by the deed which is done, this blind man signifies the human race. For this blindness through sin affected the first human, from whom we inherited not only sin but even death. If blindness signifies unfaithfulness and seeing faith, whom did Christ find faithful when he came?

Accordingly, the apostle Paul, a son of the nation of prophets, said, *And so we were by nature children of wrath, like the rest of mankind* (Eph 2:3). If *children of wrath*, then children of vengeance, children of punishment, and children of hell. How *by nature* unless it is due to the sin of that first man? . . . So if sin grew in us according to our nature and according to the mind, every human is born mentally blind. If he sees, he does not need a guide. But if he is blind from birth, he needs a guide and illuminator.

John 9:1-12

[1]As he passed by, he saw a man blind from his birth. [2]And his disciples asked him, "Rabbi, who sinned, this man or his parents, that he was born blind?" [3]Jesus answered, "It was not that this man sinned, or his parents, but that the works of God might be made manifest in him. [4]We must work the works of him who sent me, while it is day; night comes, when no one can work. [5]As long as I am in the world, I am the light of the world." [6]As he said this, he spat on the ground and made clay of the spittle and anointed the man's eyes with the clay, [7]saying to him, "Go, wash in the pool of Siloam" (which means Sent). So he went and washed and came back seeing. [8]The neighbors and those who had seen him before as a beggar, said, "Is not this the man who used

to sit and beg?" ⁹Some said, "It is he"; others said, "No, but he is like him." He said, "I am the man." ¹⁰They said to him, "Then how were your eyes opened?" ¹¹He answered, "The man called Jesus made clay and anointed my eyes and said to me, 'Go to Siloam and wash'; so I went and washed and received my sight." ¹²They said to him, "Where is he?" He said, "I do not know."

9:1–3 He saw a man blind from his birth. And his disciples asked him, "Rabbi, who sinned, this man or his parents, that he was born blind?"

---

(2) Ambrose of Milan

Brothers and sisters, you have heard the lesson of the gospel where it is said, **As he passed by, he saw a man blind from his birth** (9:1). Since the Lord saw him and did not pass him by, we should not pass by the one whom the Lord did not overlook. This is especially true since he was **blind from his birth**. This is not mentioned without reason. There is a type of blindness where the vision of the eyes is obscured by illness. This type is alleviated with the help of time. There is another type of blindness caused by disease. When it is removed by the aid of medicine, the blindness is cured. However, I tell you that the man who was blind from birth was healed not by skill but by divine power. The Lord renewed health as a free gift not by any medicinal skills. Those whom the Lord Jesus healed were those whom no one else could cure!

How foolish was the question of the Jews.[1] **Who sinned, this man or his parents?** (9:2). They held that bodily diseases were a result of sin. The Lord said in response, **It was not that this man sinned, or his parents, but that the works of God might be made manifest in him** (9:3). Anything that nature created, the creator was able to correct since he was the author of nature itself. He then added, **As long as I am in the world, I am the light of the world** (9:5). In other words, all who are blind may see if they need me, for *I am the Light: Come* and *be enlightened* so that you may see (Ps 34:5 [33:6 LXX]).

(3) John Chrysostom

When the Jews did not believe the loftiness of the words but instead called him a demon and attempted to kill him, he left the temple and healed the blind man.[2] Through doing this sign, he appeased their rage, pacified their stubbornness and harshness, and fulfilled the things that he had said. . . . It was not a common sign, for it happened for the very first time ever: *Never since the world began has it been heard that anyone opened the eyes of a man born blind* (9:32). Perhaps someone opened the eyes of a blind man, but of one blind from birth? *Never!*

---

1. Since the Johannine text clearly indicates that the disciples asked this question, Ambrose's statement that the Jews asked this seems odd.

2. John Chrysostom is referencing the event that took place immediately before John 9, when Jesus is charged with having a demon (8:48–59).

When Jesus left the temple, he intended to do this deed. This is clear from what follows: **He saw the blind man** (9:1). The blind man did not come to him. In fact, Jesus looked at him with such earnestness that even his disciples noticed. For this reason, **his disciples asked him, "Rabbi, who sinned, this man or his parents, that he was born blind?"** (9:2). This is a mistaken question. How could he possibly sin before he was born? How, if his parents had sinned, could he be punished? From where did this question arise? Earlier he had healed a paralytic and said, **See, you are well! Sin no more, that nothing worse befall you** (5:14). The disciples, therefore, surmised that this man was paralyzed on account of his sin. They asked themselves, "Since that one was paralyzed on account of sin, should we say the same about this one?" The paralyzed man sinned, but it is not possible to say the same about this one, for **he is blind from his birth** (9:1). Was it his parents who sinned? This is not possible either, for a child is not punished on account of his parents. When we see a child suffering evil, we ask, "What should we say about this? What has the child done?" We ask this not as if truly asking, but as if perplexed. In this same way, the disciples asked these questions, for they were puzzled. What did Christ say? Jesus answered, **It was not that this man sinned, or his parents** (9:3). . . . But he added, **that the Son of God might be made manifest** (9:3).[3] Both this man and his parents sinned, but his blindness was not the result of their sin.

In saying this, he in no way implied that some other people were born blind on account of the sins of their parents. For no one is punished on account of the sins of another. Nor did he imply that the blind man sinned before his birth. When he said, **It was not that this man sinned** (9:3), he did not state that it was possible for one to sin from birth and be punished for it. When he added **or his parents** (9:3), he did not say that one is punished on account of his parents. He removes this supposition in accordance with the prophet Ezekiel: *As I live, says the Lord GOD, this proverb shall no more be used by you in Israel: "The fathers have eaten sour grapes, and the children's teeth are set on edge"* (Ezek 18:2–3). And Moses said, *The fathers shall not be put to death for the children, nor shall the children be put to death for the fathers; every man shall be put to death for his own sin* (Deut 24:16). . . . But if someone asks, "why does Scripture say elsewhere, *for I the LORD your God am a jealous God, visiting the iniquity of the fathers upon the children to the third and fourth generation of those who hate me*? (Deut 5:9)," we should answer that this statement did not apply to everyone but was said about the people who came out of Egypt. They came out of Egypt after witnessing many signs and wonders and became worse than their forefathers who saw none of these things. They will suffer these same things as those, since they have dared to do the very same deeds. Anyone who examines this passage of Scripture will become more certain that it was spoken only about those men.

(4) Augustine of Hippo

On account of certain questions raised in this section, let us run through the words of the Lord and the whole lesson itself rather than discussing each part in depth. **As he passed by, he saw a man blind from his birth** (9:1). He was blind not just in any way but **from birth**. **And his disciples asked him, "Rabbi, who sinned, this man or his parents, that he was**

---

3. The RSV reads **works of God,** not "glory of God."

born blind?" (9:2). You know that he was called **Rabbi**, because he was a teacher. They called him teacher, because they desired to learn. They asked the Lord questions as if he were a teacher: **Who sinned, this man or his parents, that he was born blind? Jesus answered, "It was not that this man sinned, or his parents that he was born blind"** (9:2–3). Why did he say this? If no human is without sin, the parents of the blind man are not without sin, are they? Was he himself born without original sin? Or had he committed no sin during his life? Because his eyes were closed, did his desires lack alertness? Blind people also commit much evil. Even if the eyes are closed, from what evil does an evil mind abstain? He was not able to see, but he knew how to think and perhaps how to desire something which, as a blind man, he was not able to satiate. But his heart could be judged by the one who searches through hearts. If his parents had sin and this one had sin, why did the Lord say, **It was not that this man sinned, or his parents that he was born blind** (9:3), except to indicate this point about which he was questioned: **that he was born blind** (9:2)? His parents had sin, but it was not due to their sin that he was born blind. If it were not on account of this, why was he born blind? Hear the master teaching. He seeks one who believes so that he might . . . explain the reason why this man was born blind: **It was not that this man sinned, or his parents, but that the works of God might be made manifest in him** (9:3).

(5) Cyril of Alexandria

But that the works of God might be made manifest in him (9:3). This text is hard to explain and can be confusing. Perhaps it would be wise to ignore it, for it is nearly incomprehensible. . . . However, I think it is beneficial to offer a few words about this in that we can ward off any harm it might bring and leave no opening for deceitful arguments. Earlier we showed that God does not punish the children for the sins of parents unless they engaged in the same evil deeds. Moreover, we showed that corporeality is not due to the sins previously committed by the soul. . . .[4] Do we agree that these things have been stated correctly? It is not easy to see what explanation someone can give to those who suffer such horrors from infancy or their first few years of life or even to those who are affected by disease from the womb. We do not believe that the soul existed previously or that it sinned prior to being in the body. For how could the soul sin prior to being called into birth? Since there was no sin or error before the suffering, what is the reason for this suffering? We are not able to comprehend such inscrutable things with our human minds. Indeed, I suggest that it is prudent to refrain from wishing to examine these issues too closely. It is necessary to remind ourselves what we have been commanded. We are not to scrutinize things which are too deep, nor inquire into things too hard, nor attempt to uncover the things which are hidden in the divine and ineffable plan alone (cf. Sir 3:21). Rather, we should turn piously to God who knows things that are suitable and distinctive of him alone. Moreover, we should uphold and trust completely that since he is the well[5] of all righteousness, he will

---

4. In an earlier section of his commentary, which is not reproduced here, Cyril had exposited Ezek 18:1–4 (see John Chrysostom's commentary above, which echoes many of the same themes).

5. Cyril has in mind the discussion of the *well* between Jesus and the Samaritan woman in John 4.

do nothing either in the affairs of humans or in the rest of creation unless it is suitable to his very nature and does not depart from the true rectitude of his law.

9:4–5 "We must work the works of him who sent me, while it is day. . . . I am the light of the world."

---

(6) John Chrysostom

I must work while it is day.[6] What do these words mean? What sort of consequence do they have? A great deal! What he says is of this sort: While it is day, while it is still possible for people to believe in me, while this life remains, **I must work. Night comes**—this is the future—**when no one can work** (9:4). He did not say, **When I cannot work** but **when no one can work.** This is when there is no longer faith, nor work, nor repentance. Because he calls faith **work,** they ask him, *What must we do, to be doing the works of God?* (6:28). Jesus answered them, *This is the work of God, that you believe in him whom he has sent* (6:29). How then is no one able to **work** this **work** at that time (in the future)? Because there is no faith, all will submit either willingly or unwillingly. . . . They had the power to believe only **while it is day** but no longer were able to gain something good **when night comes.** For this reason, Jesus did these works although the blind man did not approach him. That he was worthy to be healed is clear from what follows, and from his courage, and from his faith.

Certainly if he had been able to see, he would have believed and would have come to Jesus; and if he had heard from someone that Jesus was nearby, he would not have hesitated in coming to him. It is possible that he thought to himself and said: "What is this? **He spat on the ground, made clay, and anointed my eyes and said to me 'Go, wash'** (cf. 9:6–7). Could he have not just healed me and then sent me to **Siloam**? I have washed there many times with many people, and I have never received any benefit. If he possessed any power, he could have healed me while he was present." Naaman said this very thing to Elisha. For when he was commanded to go and wash in the Jordan, he did not believe, although Elisha was famous at that time (2 Kgs 5:10–11). But the blind man did not disbelieve or disagree or think to himself: "What is this? Did he need to apply clay? Doesn't this just blind me more? Who has recovered his sight in this way?" But he thought none of these thoughts! Do you see his strong faith and zeal?

(7) Augustine of Hippo

We must work the works of him who sent me (9:4). Pay attention! He is the one who has been **sent.**[7] In him, the blind man washed his face. Do you see what he says? **We**

---

6. This differs from the RSV, which has the pronoun **we,** not "I."

7. Augustine is connecting the etymology of *Siloam,* which means "sent," with Christ who was "sent" by the Father.

must work the works of him who sent me, while it is day. Bear in mind how Christ gives universal **glory** (9:3) to this one from whom he receives his being. . . . But why, O Lord, do you say, **While it is day**? Hear why! **Night comes, when no one can work** (9:4). Not even you Lord? Will that night be so powerful that not even you are able to work during the night? . . . I believe and confirm that you were there when God said: *"Let there be light"; and there was light* (Gen 1:3). If he made all things by means of the Word, then he created through you. And for that reason, it is written: *All things were made through him, and without him was not anything made that was made* (1:3), and *God separated the light from the darkness. God called the light "Day" and the darkness "Night"* (Gen 1:4–5). What is this **night** which when it comes no one will be able to work? Hear what the **day** is, and then you will understand what the **night** is. Where do we hear what that **day** is? Let Christ himself tell us: **As long as I am in the world, I am the light of the world** (9:5). He himself is the **day**. Let the blind man wash his eyes in the **day** so that he might see the **day**. Christ says, **As long as I am in the world, I am the light of the world** (9:5). I am ignorant regarding what sort of **night** it is when Christ will not be here and when no one will be able to work.

My brothers and sisters, be patient as I examine this. Together we seek, and together we will find whom we seek. It is certain that the Lord stated definitively in this passage that he is the **day**, that is, **the light of the world**. He said, **As long as I am in *this* world, I am the light of the world**. Indeed, he is working. But how long is he **in this world**? Brothers and sisters, are we to think that he was present then and is not here now in some way? If we think this, then after the ascension of the Lord, this fearful night descended **when no one can work**. If that **night** came after his ascension, how did the apostles **work** so much? Was it that **night** when the Holy Spirit came and filled all who were in that place giving them the ability to speak the languages of every nation (Acts 2:1–6)? Or was it on that **night** when the lame man was healed by Peter's word, or rather, by the Word of the Lord dwelling in Peter (Acts 3:6–8)? Or was it on the **night** when the sick were placed on cots so that they might be touched by the shadows of the disciples who passed by (Acts 5:15)? When the Lord was here, his passing shadow healed no one. But he said to his disciples: *You will do greater things than these* (14:12), but flesh and blood should not exalt itself. Hear what he also said: *Without me, you can do nothing* (15:5). . . .

What then shall we say about that **night**? . . . When will no one be able to **work**? That **night** will be the night of the wicked. It is the **night** which belongs to those to whom it will be said, *Depart from me, you cursed, into the eternal fire prepared for the devil and his angels* (Matt 25:41). But it is called **night**, not flame or fire. Hear why it is also called **night**. He says about a certain servant: *Bind him hand and foot, and cast him into the outer darkness* (Matt 22:13). Let humans work while they live so that they will not hindered by that **night when no one can work**. At the present time, faith works through love. If we **work** now, the **day** is here, which is Christ. Hear his promise, and do not think that he is absent. . . . *And lo*, he says, *I am with you always, to the close of the age* (Matt 28:20). An ordinary day which is marked by the revolution of the sun has only a few hours. In contrast the day of Christ's presence extends even *to the close of the age*. After the resurrection of the living and the dead, he will say to those at his right hand: *Come, O blessed of my Father, inherit the* *kingdom prepared for you from the foundation of the world* (Matt 25:34). But he will say to those at his left: *Depart from me, you cursed, into the eternal fire prepared for the devil and his angels* (Matt 25:41). In that place there will be only **night** where **no one can work**. There one will receive only what has been **worked** before. It is now the time for working. Then, it will be the time for receiving, for the Lord will repay each one according to his **works** (cf. Matt 16:27). When you are alive, **work**! For that terrible **night** will certainly come, when the wicked will be swept away. But even now every unbeliever, when he dies, is received into that **night**. No **work** can be done there. In that **night** the rich man was burning. He begged the poor man for a drop of water from his finger. He suffered, was tormented, and confessed, but no aid was given to him. He even tried to do some good. He said to Abraham: *Then I beg you, father, to send Lazarus to my father's house, for I have five brothers, so that he may warn them, lest they also come into this place of torment* (Luke 16:27–28). O miserable man! The time for **work** was when you were living, but now you are in the **night**, **when no one can work** (9:4).

9:6–7 As he said this, he spat on the ground and made clay of the spittle and anointed the man's eyes with the clay, saying to him, "Go, wash in the pool of Siloam" (which means Sent). So he went and washed and came back seeing.

---

(8) Irenaeus of Lyons

He gave sight to that man who had been **blind from his birth**. He did not do this with a word but with a visible action. He did not do this haphazardly or without intention but in order to demonstrate the hand of God which had formed man at the beginning. . . . As Scripture says, he made humans by a type of process: *And God formed man, dust from the earth* . . . (Gen 2:7 LXX). Here the Lord **spat on the ground and made clay of the spittle and anointed the man's eyes with the clay** (9:6). This highlights how humanity was fashioned originally and shows the hand of God to those who can understand how humans were *formed* out of the *dust*. The creator—the Word—supplied publicly the things (i.e., functioning eyes) omitted when he formed him in the womb so **the works of God might be made manifest in him** (9:3) and so we might not look for another hand—nor another Father—by which humans were *formed*. We know that this hand of God which formed us at the beginning and forms us in the womb has in these last times sought us out who were lost and takes back his own. He places the lost sheep upon his shoulders and restores it joyfully to the fold of life!

The Word of God forms us in the womb. He says to Jeremiah, *Before I formed you in the womb I knew you, and before you were born I consecrated you; I appointed you a prophet to the nations* (Jer 1:5). Similarly, Paul says, *But when he who had set me apart before I was born, and had called me through his grace, was pleased to reveal his Son to me, in order that I might preach him among the Gentiles* . . . (Gal 1:15–16). Just was we are formed in the womb by the Word, this very same Word formed the power of sight in the one who had been **blind from his birth** (9:1). When the Word himself had appeared to humans, he revealed clearly who it is who fashions us in secret. He declares the original formation of Adam, the manner in which he was created, and by whose hand he was formed, demonstrating the whole from a part. The Lord, carrying out the will of the Father and forming the power of sight, is the one who made the whole man. Since humans needed the washing of regeneration because the formation had fallen into sin after Adam, the Lord, after anointing his **eyes with clay** (9:6), said to him: **Go, wash in the pool of Siloam** (9:7). In this way, he restored him to perfect acceptance by the regeneration which takes place in the fount. For this reason, after he washed, he came back able to see so that he might know the Lord who had formed him and so that all humanity might learn that the Lord is the one who gives life to all. . . .

The very same being, who formed Adam at the beginning and with whom the Father spoke, said, *Let us make man in our image, after our likeness* (Gen 1:26). He is the one who reveals himself to humanity in these last times. He is also the one who formed the organs of sight for the man who had been **blind from his birth** (9:1) in the body inherited from Adam. For this reason Scripture shows what would happen when it says that Adam had hidden himself because of his disobedience. The Lord came in the evening and *called to the man, and said to him, "Where are you?"* (Gen 3:9). This means that in these last times, the very same Word of God came to call humanity. He reminds them of their actions and how they live in such a way as to be hidden from the Lord. Just as God at that time spoke to Adam in the evening trying to find him, so also in these last times, the Lord has visited them and seeks out Adam's descendants with the very same voice.

(9) Ambrose of Milan

You must come to the altar. You must see things which you have not seen before. This is the mystery which you have read about in the gospel. Even if you have not actually read it, you certainly have heard it! A blind man came to the Savior who had restored others only by a word and restored the light of the eyes by a command to be healed. Yet in the gospel according to John, the evangelist who saw, described, and declared the great mysteries more deliberately than the others wished to prefigure the mystery of baptism in the account of this miracle. Certainly all the evangelists were holy. Every one of the apostles, except the traitor, was also holy. Yet Saint John who was sought out and chosen to be in a sense his brother (cf. John 19:26–27) wrote his gospel last and proclaimed eternal mysteries with a louder trumpet. Everything he uttered is a mystery! Other evangelists reported the healing of a blind man. Matthew did. Luke did. And Mark did. What does John alone report? [**He**] **anointed the man's eyes with the clay, saying to him, "Go, wash in the pool of Siloam." . . . So he went and washed and came back seeing** (9:6–7).

Consider the eyes of your heart. Earlier you saw only fleshly things with fleshly eyes. However, you were not able to behold the spiritual things with the eyes of your heart. When you declared your name, **he anointed** your **eyes with the clay** (9:6). This means that you should confess your sin, recognize your guilt, and repent of your transgressions. In other words, you should acknowledge the consequences of human birth.

Although the one who comes to the baptismal font does not confess his sin, in fact he makes a complete confession of his sins when he requests to be baptized so that he might be justified. Indeed, he passes from guilt into grace. Do not think baptism is unnecessary! There are some who think this. I certainly know of one who said this![8] When we told him, "At your stage of life you should be baptized," he objected and said, "Why should I be baptized? I do not have any sin. Am I afflicted with sin?" He lacked **clay** (9:6), because Christ had not washed him. Christ had not opened his eyes, for no human is free of sin.

Anyone who seeks safety in the baptism of Christ acknowledges that he is a human. He has put **clay** on you, which is modesty, prudence, and awareness of your weakness. He has said to you, **"Go** to the **pool of Siloam."** What is **Siloam**? It means **Sent** (9:7). In other words, **go** to that font where the cross of Christ is proclaimed. **Go** to that font where Christ redeemed the sins of all humans. You did go! You did wash! You went to the altar! You began to see what you had not been able to see before. Through the font of the Lord and the proclamation of his passion, your eyes have been opened. You who were formerly blind in your heart began to see the light of the sacraments!

(10) Ambrose of Milan

Why did the one who restored people to life with a command—for he said to the dead, *Come out!* (11:43), and Lazarus came out from the grave—and why did the one who restored people to health with a word—for he said to the paralyzed man, *Rise, take up your pallet* (5:8), and this man rose and began to carry his pallet himself although he was not able to carry it when his limbs were paralyzed—why, I ask, did **he spit on the ground and make clay of the spittle and anoint the man's eyes with the clay, saying to him, "Go, wash in the pool of Siloam" (which means Sent). So he went and washed and came back seeing** (9:6–7)? What is the reason for this? If I am not mistaken, the reason is certainly wonderful; when Jesus teaches, one sees more clearly. Notice simultaneously both his divinity and his holiness. Since he was himself the **Light** (8:12), he touched and in this way gave light to others. As a priest, he fulfilled the mysteries of spiritual grace in the figure of baptism. Certainly anyone who is cleansed by baptism is able to see. His **spittle** (9:6) cleanses as does his word. As it is written, *You are already made clean by the word which I have spoken to you* (15:3). When he made **clay** and **anointed** (9:6) the eyes of the blind man, he intended to show us that the very one who made humans from **clay** restored him back to health by **anointing** him with **clay**. He also intended to signify that our flesh of **clay** must receive the light of eternal life by the sacrament of baptism. Do you also go near to **Siloam** (9:7), that is, to the one who was sent from the Father? As it is written, **My teaching is not mine, but his who sent me** (7:16). Let Christ wash you so that you might see. Come to baptism. The time is now. Make haste and come so that you may say: **I went and washed and received my sight** (9:11); so that you may also say, *Though I was blind, now I see* (9:25); and so that you may say as that

---

8. It is uncertain whom Ambrose has in mind.

man on whom light was poured, *The night is far gone, the day is at hand* (Rom 13:12). The **night** (9:4) was blindness. When Judas received the *morsel* and *Satan entered into him* (13:26–27), it was **night** (9:4). To Judas, in whom the devil resided, it was **night**; to John, who was *lying close to the breast of Jesus* (13:23), it was **day** (9:4). To Peter, when he saw the *light* of Christ on the *mountain* (Matt 17:1), it was **day**. To others, it was **night**, but to Peter, it was **day**. However, to Peter, when he denied Christ, it was **night**. But when the cock crowed, he began to weep so that he might correct his error, for at that time the **day** was at hand.

(11) John Chrysostom

As he said this, he spat on the ground and made clay of the spittle and anointed the man's eyes with the clay, saying to him, "Go, wash in the pool of Siloam" (9:6–7). For those who wish to reap a harvest from what they read, they must not pass over even a small part of the words. We are urged to search the Scriptures, for many of the words, although they seem to be easy in themselves, have much of their meaning hidden deep within. Notice that the present passage is just that sort: **As he said this, he spat on the ground** (9:6). Why did he do this? **So that the glory of God might be made manifest in him** (9:3), and because **I must work the works of him who sent me** (9:4). The evangelist has not simply reminded us of his words but added them to make clear that he guarantees his word through his deeds. Why did he not use water instead of **spittle** to make the **clay**? He intended to send the man to **Siloam**. To make certain that nothing might be attributed to the fount itself and in order that you might learn that the power proceeds from his mouth which both formed the man's eyes and opened them, **he spat on the ground** (9:6). Indeed the evangelist signaled this very thing when he said that Christ **made clay of the spittle** (9:6). Then, he commanded him to wash so that the healing did not seem to stem from the earth itself.

Why did he not heal him immediately instead of sending him to the **pool of Siloam** (9:7)? He did this so that you might learn about the faith of the blind man and so that the arrogance of the Jews might be silenced. Indeed, it is likely that they all saw him as he left with the **clay** spread upon his **eyes**. He would certainly attract to himself all those who knew him and even those who did not due to the strangeness of his appearance. Moreover, they would pay very close attention. Since it is not easy to recognize a **blind man** who has already recovered his sight, he created many witnesses as he walked the long road to **Siloam** and he caused many to pay close attention due to his unusual appearance. In fact, they were so attentive that they were no longer able to argue over whether or not it was him. In addition, by sending the **blind man** to the **pool of Siloam** (9:7), he wanted to prove also by that action that he is not hostile toward the law and the Old Testament. Nor was it surmised that **Siloam** would receive the glory since many washed their eyes often in that place but received no such benefit. It was the power of Christ which effected the healing. Accordingly, the evangelist provided for us the interpretation of the name **Siloam**. For after saying, **in the pool of Siloam**, he added, **which means Sent** (9:7), in order that you might learn that it was Christ who healed him in that place.

Similarly, Paul said, *For they drank from the supernatural Rock which followed them, and the Rock was Christ* (1 Cor 10:4). Just as Christ was the spiritual rock, so also he was the spiritual **Siloam** (9:7).

It also seems to me that the sudden appearance of this water hints at a sacred mystery. What is that? The unexpected nature of his appearance was beyond all expectation. Notice the mind of the blind man, obedient in every way. For he did not say, "If it is the clay or this spittle which gives me eyes, what is the necessity of going to **Siloam**? Or if going to **Siloam** is necessary, what is the purpose of the clay? Why did he anoint me? Why did he command me to wash?" But he considered none of these things. Rather, he prepared to do only one thing: to obey the one who commanded him to do all these things, and he took no offense at any of it. If anyone asks, "How did he recover his sight after he had removed the clay?," he will hear no answer from us other than we do not know how it happened. Is it a marvel that we do not know? Neither the evangelist nor the very man who was healed knew. He knew what had been done but was not able to comprehend how it was accomplished. So when he was asked this, **he answered, "The man called Jesus made clay and anointed my eyes and said to me, 'Go to Siloam and wash'; so I went and washed and received my sight"** (9:11). But how this happened he is not able to explain although they may ask him ten thousand times.

(12) Augustine of Hippo

When the Lord passed by, what did he do? He set forth a great mystery. **He spat on the ground** (9:6). **He made clay** from his **spittle**, because the Lord was made flesh. He **anointed the blind man's eyes** (9:6). He was **anointed**, but he did not yet see. Christ then sent him to the pool called **Siloam** (9:7). It is the tendency of John the Evangelist to explain for us the name of this pool: the **pool of Siloam means, "He who was Sent"** (9:7). You now understand who was **Sent** (9:7). Unless this one had been **sent**, none of us would have been set free from sin. Therefore, he washed his eyes in this **pool** which is interpreted as **He who was Sent** (9:7). In other words, he was baptized in Christ. When he baptized him in himself as it were, Christ enlightened him. When Christ anointed him, he was perhaps made a catechumen. Certainly, it is possible to expound and treat the profound nature of such a sacramental act in many different ways, but let this be sufficient for you, brothers and sisters: You have heard a great mystery! Ask a man: Are you a Christian? If he is either a Jew or a pagan, he will respond to you, "I am not." If, however, he responds, "I am," then inquire of him if he is a catechumen or a believer. If he responds, "a catechumen," he has been **anointed** (9:6) but not yet baptized. How was he **anointed** (9:6)? Ask, and he will respond. Ask, in whom he believes? For the very reason that he is a catechumen, he will answer: "In Christ." In this way, I am speaking to both believers and catechumens. Why am I speaking about **spittle** and **clay** (9:6)? Because *the Word was made flesh* (1:14). This text is heard even by catechumens, but it is not sufficient for them to be only **anointed** (9:6). Let them hasten to the font if they seek enlightenment.

9:8–12 They said to him, "Then how were your eyes opened?" He answered, "The man called Jesus made clay and anointed my eyes and said to me, 'Go to Siloam and wash.'"

(13) Augustine of Hippo

The neighbors and those who had seen him before as a beggar, said, "Is not this the man who used to sit and beg?" Some said, "It is he"; others said, "No, but he is like him" (9:8–9). The opening of his eyes changed his face. **He said, "I am the man"** (9:8–9). His voice is grateful; he is not condemned as ungrateful. **They said to him, "Then how were your eyes opened?"** (9:10). **He answered, "The man called Jesus made clay and anointed my eyes and said to me, 'Go to Siloam and wash'; so I went and washed and received my sight"** (9:11). See how he has become the spokesman of grace; see how he preaches the gospel. Able to see, he now confesses. The blind man confesses and the heart of the ungodly is troubled, because they did not have in their hearts what he now had in his face. **They said to him, "Where is he?" He said, "I do not know"** (9:12). By responding in this way, this man's mind was similar to one who is still only **anointed**, for he does not yet see. Let us consider it this way, brothers and sisters, as if his mind had been **anointed**. He preaches, but he does not yet know whom he preaches.

John 9:13–17

[13]They brought to the Pharisees the man who had formerly been blind. [14]Now it was a Sabbath day when Jesus made the clay and opened his eyes. [15]The Pharisees again asked him how he had received his sight. And he said to them, "He put clay on my eyes, and I washed, and I see." [16]Some of the Pharisees said, "This man is not from God, for he does not keep the sabbath." But others said, "How can a man who is a sinner do such signs?" There was a division among them. [17]So they again said to the blind man, "What do you say about him, since he has opened your eyes?" He said, "He is a prophet."

(14) John Chrysostom

Some of the Pharisees—not all, but the more impetuous ones—**said, "This man is not from God, for he does not keep the sabbath." But others said, "How can a man who is a sinner do such signs?"** (9:16). Do you see how they were taught by this miracle? Listen to what they say now. Although they sent for him, he ended up teaching **some** of them. They were leaders who loved honor and thus fell into unbelief, but it happened that many of them came to believe in Christ even though they would not confess it publicly. While the masses were easily dismissed since they had no important role in the synagogues, the leaders in contrast had a greater difficulty speaking boldly since they were quite visible. **Others** were restrained due to their love of power, cowardice, or the fear of the masses.

Because of this, he said: *How can you believe, who receive glory from one another and do not seek the glory that comes from the only God?* (5:44). Those who were seeking to kill him unjustly insisted that they were of God. They also claimed that the one who healed the blind could not be of God since he did not keep the **sabbath** (9:16). Others, however, responded that a **sinner** could not do **such signs** (9:16). The former group maliciously remained silent regarding what happened and brought forward supposed transgression. They did not charge that "he heals on the sabbath day," but rather that "**he does not keep the sabbath**" (9:16). The other group again responded weakly. They should have demonstrated that the **sabbath** was not broken, but they only argued by referencing the miracle. This was reasonable, however, since they still believed that he was a **man**. If, however, this had not been the case, they could have adduced the defense that he was Lord of the **sabbath**. Christ himself made this argument, but they did not yet hold this opinion. Regardless, none of them dared to say openly what they desired to proclaim in terms of speaking on his behalf. **Some** remained silent since they lacked boldness; **others** because of their love of power. Only those who wished to express doubts spoke up. And **there was a division among them** (9:16). . . .

So they again said to the blind man, "**What do you say about him, since he has opened your eyes?" He said, "He is a prophet**" (9:17). The Jews did not believe. We must not examine the Scriptures in a careless or perfunctory way but with all exactness so as not to become entangled. It is quite probable that someone might be puzzled over this passage. First, they assert, **This man is not from God, for he does not keep the sabbath** (9:16), but then ask him, **What do you say about him, since he has opened your eyes?** (9:17). Why did they not ask him, **What do you say about him, for he has not kept the Sabbath?** They are presenting the man's defense, not the accusation put forth against Christ. What can be concluded? Those who are questioning the man are not the same as those who said, **This man is not from God** (9:16). They are the men who **divided** themselves from the others, who also asked, **How can a man who is a sinner do such signs?** (9:16). Although they wished to silence their opponents even more, they brought in the man who had experienced his miraculous power and questioned him in order that they may not seem to be advocates for Christ. Pay attention to the wisdom of the poor man, for he speaks more wisely than any of them. First he says, **He is a prophet** (9:17). Moreover, he did not cower at the judgment of the perverse Jews who spoke against him and proclaimed, **This man is not from God, for he does not keep the sabbath** (9:16). Instead, he proclaimed to them, **He is a prophet** (9:17). . . . First they attempted to attack him regarding the manner of the cure. **They said to him, "What did he do to you? How did he open your eyes?"** (9:26). What they were really asking is, "Was it not by some sort of sorcery?" At another time, when they had no charge against Jesus, they attempted to demean the manner of his cure by claiming, *It is only by Beelzebul, the prince of demons, that this man casts out demons* (Matt 12:24). Here again, since they have nothing to say, they fall back to attacking the time of the cure, claiming that **he does not keep the sabbath** (9:16) and that **he is a sinner** (9:16).

(15) Cyril of Alexandria

And he said to them, "He put clay on my eyes, and I washed, and I see" (9:15). It is marvelous how the man rightly added to his account of these events a most useful flourish: the words: **And I see** (9:15). It is as if he said all but the following: "I will prove that the power of the healer was not trivial. I will not deny this gift, for I now possess what I desired for a long time." He says, "I was blind from birth and diseased from my mother's womb, but after he anointed me with clay, I was healed, **and I see** (9:15). . . . I really can **see**! For the rest of my life I will be able to look clearly upon things which before I could only hear about. Look, the bright light of the sun shines around me. Look, the beauty of strange sights surrounds my eyes. Recently I hardly knew Jerusalem, but now **I see** (9:15) the divine temple enlightening the city and I can see the holy altar in its midst." . . . **Some of the Pharisees said, "This man is not from God, for he does not keep the sabbath"** (9:16). Foolishly they say that he who is able to do the works of God is **not from God** (9:16). Although they see that the Son has been crowned with an equal measure of glory with the Almighty Father, they are not ashamed to cast upon him unfounded charges of impiety. They disregard the account of this miracle and jealously attack the wonder-worker. They even rashly accused the one who knew no sin of being a **sinner** (9:16). They ignorantly assume that he broke the entire law by moving just one finger on the **sabbath** (9:16), although they themselves would *untie his ox or his ass from the manger, and lead it away to water it on the sabbath* (Luke 13:15). Moreover, *if a sheep fell into a pit,* they would *lift it out* as soon as possible (Matt 12:11). Accordingly, *they strain out a gnat and swallow a camel* (Matt 23:24), according to the Savior! This was their common custom. Foolishly and ignorantly they do not acknowledge the miracle performed by Christ or recognize who he is from this good work. Rather, they discuss the **sabbath** frivolously. Since in their opinion all virtue is achieved by remaining idle on the **sabbath**, they dismiss out of hand his relationship with God, saying that he was **not from God** (9:16). They should have concluded that the one who was among them had authority over his own laws and that it was pleasing and acceptable to God to do good even on the **sabbath**. Moreover, it was not right to leave one who needed mercy devoid of hope. . . . So they were unexpectedly baffled when they heard his reply: **He is a prophet** (9:17). For the man who had been healed rightly concurred with the group who decided based on the evidence that a **sinner** could not perform such deeds. Following the same logic, the man who had been miraculously healed, declares that Jesus **is a prophet**, although he had not yet learned fully who he is truly. He adopted the opinion held commonly by the Jews, that men who do such things were to be called wonder-working prophets, for the holiness of their deeds testify to God.

John 9:18-23

[18]The Jews did not believe that he had been blind and had received his sight, until they called the parents of the man who had received his sight, [19]and asked them, "Is this your son, who you say was born blind? How then does he now see?" [20]His parents answered, "We know that this is our son, and that he was born blind; [21]but how he now sees we do not know, nor do we know who opened his eyes. Ask him; he is of age, he will speak for

himself." ²²His parents said this because they feared the Jews, for the Jews had already agreed that if anyone should confess him to be Christ, he was to be put out of the synagogue. ²³Therefore his parents said, "He is of age, ask him."

(16) Theodore of Mopsuestia

Having exhausted every alternative, the Pharisees came to the point of doubting whether he had been **born blind** (9:19), which is why they came to speak with his **parents**, asking them if this blind man was **born** to them. Additionally, they were also asking: **How then does he now see?** (9:19). Even though they knew that they would not be able to say how he was healed, in their ignorance the Jews were hoping that the parents might deny that he was their own son. . . . The **parents** replied with great shrewdness that he was their own son and did not deny that he was **born blind** (9:20). However, they stated that they did **not know** how he was healed or who healed him, saying that the Jews ought to ask him who was an adult and could reasonably **speak for himself** (9:21). . . . It seems, therefore, that the **parents** knew neither the healer nor the manner of the healing, but because of their fear they were recusing themselves so as not to say anything that was displeasing to the Jews. . . . They said the two things that were most essential and reproached the unbelief of those who were ungrateful, namely that he was indeed their **son** and that **he was born blind** (9:20). But they also left it to them to consider how he gained his sight so that, by searching insistently, they would be brought to shame by the truth itself. Because they were afraid of the authorities, they were pretending that they did not know the physician; for they knew that the Jews had agreed to **put out of the synagogue** (9:22) anyone who would **confess him to be the Christ** (9:22). That is why they deflected the question back to their son who was formerly **blind**.

(17) Cyril of Alexandria

His parents answered, "We know that this is our son, and that he was born blind; but how he now sees we do not know, nor do we know who opened his eyes. Ask him; he is of age, he will speak for himself" (9:20–21). They affirm that which could not be doubted and what would most likely not cause them any ill consequences. They state directly that they recognize their own son. They do not deny the true nature of his birth but affirm that he was **born blind** (9:20). Nevertheless, they are reluctant to speak about the miracle but allow the nature of the deed to testify for itself. They argued strongly that it would be more fitting to ask their son how he had been healed. Fear which is caused by potential danger is a powerful tool for hindering people from doing what is in their best interest. Since they were greatly worried due to the harshness of the Pharisees, they do not observe what is said well in the Scriptures: *Exert yourself to the death for the truth* (Sir 4:28 LXX). However, they probably suffered in some other way. A poor man is always timid. On account of his poverty, he loses his will to put up a fight. He finds safety in begrudged silence and habitual resignation. It is as if his spirit has been crushed by his poverty so that he is unwilling to take on other abuse. We surmise that the **parents** of the blind man had suffered similarly even though on the surface their reply seems reasonable. Certainly, everyone would acknowledge that it was more reasonable to ask the **parents** if the man was their **son** than to ask the man himself. However, the question regarding the physician should not have been directed to the **parents** but to the man who had benefited from the miraculous deed.

John 9:24–27

[24]So for the second time they called the man who had been blind, and said to him, "Give God the praise; we know that this man is a sinner." [25]He answered, "Whether he is a sinner, I do not know; one thing I know, that though I was blind, now I see." [26]They said to him, "What did he do to you? How did he open your eyes?" [27]He answered them, "I have told you already, and you would not listen. Why do you want to hear it again? Do you too want to become his disciples?"

(18) John Chrysostom

They said to him, "What did he do to you? How did he open your eyes?" He answered them, "I have told you already, and you would not listen. Why do you want to hear it again? Do you too want to become his disciples?" (9:26–27). What did he say? Having defeated and overthrown them, he no longer speaks reservedly to them. While the matter needed to be reviewed and discussed, he spoke reservedly while he presented his arguments. However, after he scored a brilliant victory, he insults them with a newfound boldness. What did he say? **I have told you already, and you would not listen. Why do you want to hear it again?** Do you notice the boldness of this beggar toward the scribes and the Pharisees? So strong is truth; so weak is falsehood! When the truth takes hold of ordinary men, it makes them appear brilliant. But when falsehood is with the strong, it reveals them as weak. In other words, he says, "You do not pay attention to my words; therefore, I will not continue to speak to you or answer your questions. You question me not to learn what I have to say but because you desire to attack my answers." He asks, **Do you too want to become his disciples?** (9:27). Now he ranks himself as one of the disciples. The phrase **do you too** indicates that he is declaring himself to be a disciple. He seeks to ridicule and attack them vehemently. He said this for he knew that it would strike them hard, and he wished to accost them still further. It was an act of a courageous soul, for he lifted himself up and despised their madness. He proved the greatness of this dignity with utter confidence and showed that they insulted him although he should be admired. Instead of being harmed by their insults, he took what they intended as a reproach as a great honor.

(19) Augustine of Hippo

So for the second time they called the man who had been blind, and said to him, "Give God the praise" (9:24). What do they mean when they say, **Give God the praise** (9:24)?

To deny what one has received? Surely this is not praising God. It is blaspheming God! They said, **Give God the praise; we know that this man is a sinner** (9:24). **He answered, "Whether he is a sinner, I do not know; one thing I know, that though I was blind, now I see"** (9:25). They said to him, "What did he do to you? How did he open your eyes?" (9:26). Then he became irritated at the hardness of the Jews. Although formerly blind, he now is able to see and can no longer tolerate those who are now blind! **He answered them, "I have told you already, and you would not listen. Why do you want to hear it again? Do you too want to become his disciples?"** (9:27). What does he mean by the phrase **Do you too want to become his disciples** (9:27)? Except to assert, "I am one already! **Do you too want to?** I now see, but I do not see obliquely."[9]

(20) Cyril of Alexandria

He answered, "Whether he is a sinner, I do not know; one thing I know, that though I was blind, now I see" (9:25). It seems that the blind man received two gifts from Christ. His mind was somehow enlightened along with his physical eyes. He has the light of the sun shining in his physical eyes just as he possesses the illumination of his mind. The latter I call the enlightenment of the Spirit which dwells in him and which he receives into his heart. Hear how he stands up to the horrible conduct of the religious leaders out of his great love toward Christ. . . . "I will not slander my patron. I will not aid those who desire to dishonor the one who is worthy of all honor. I will not call such a wonder-worker a sinner. I will not cast an unjust vote against the one who has the strength to do the works of God. The miracle of sight given to me does not allow me to condone your words. **Although I was blind, now I see** (9:25). I have not trusted in the account of another man concerning Christ's deeds. I am not swayed by the reports of strangers. I do not marvel at the healing of others." For he says, "I myself am evidence of his power. I, who was born blind, stand here able to see. I am a kind of image who displays the beauty of his love for men and shows forth the greatness of his divine power." . . . To say **Whether he is a sinner, I do not know** and then to add immediately **one thing I know, that though I was blind, now I see** is not simple reflection but sets forth a hidden meaning that is the result of very wise contemplation.

Do you too want to become his disciples? (9:27). . . . It is possible that in his reply there is hidden a deep and secret meaning. I will briefly summarize this. Some of the leaders of the Jews recognized that the miracle-worker was indeed Christ. However, they kept this knowledge hidden within so that they were not discovered by the rest of their companions. The wise evangelist himself testifies that some of the leaders knew that he was the Christ *but for fear of the Pharisees they did not confess it, lest they should be put out of the synagogue* (12:42). This claim is strengthened also by Nicodemus, who boldly says to our Lord Jesus Christ, *Rabbi, we know that you are a teacher come from God; for no one can do these signs that you do, unless God is with him* (3:2). Some of the leaders of the Jews certainly knew who he was. The account of this fact spread throughout all of Jerusalem.

---

9. Literally a play on words: *Iam video, sed non invideo.*

The majority of the Jews suspected that their leaders knew who he was but were not willing to acknowledge him because of their hatred and envy. We will show through the church's writings that this is true.

The blessed John himself says that Jesus stood teaching in the temple and proclaimed teachings which seemed to his audience to violate the law (7:10–30). When the leaders of the Jews did not confront him or even say, "Stop teaching those things which conflict with our ancient laws," they raised suspicion about themselves among the crowds as we have just seen. For example, it is written: *Some of the people of Jerusalem therefore said, "Is not this the man whom they seek to kill? And here he is, speaking openly, and they say nothing to him! Can it be that the authorities really know that this is the Christ?"* (7:25–26). He all but declares the following: "Those who are chosen as leaders know that he is the Christ. Look! Although they definitely would like to kill him, he speaks with great directness, and they do not rebuke him even with words. For this reason, this suspicion spread throughout Jerusalem." At some point the blind man had heard this and had the report about these men in his mind. We might even suppose that he reproved them graciously: "Certainly there is no reason for you to ask me to repeat again the very same works or to praise once more the miraculous event. Or perhaps you like hearing the story? Do you thirst even now for his teaching? Do you allow your fear of others to hinder such exceptional knowledge?"

John 9:28–34

[28]And they reviled him, saying, "You are his disciple, but we are disciples of Moses. [29]We know that God has spoken to Moses, but as for this man, we do not know where he comes from." [30]The man answered, "Why, this is a marvel! You do not know where he comes from, and yet he opened my eyes. [31]We know that God does not listen to sinners, but if anyone is a worshiper of God and does his will, God listens to him. [32]Never since the world began has it been heard that anyone opened the eyes of a man born blind. [33]If this man were not from God, he could do nothing." [34]They answered him, "You were born in utter sin, and you are trying to teach us?" And they cast him out.

(21) Augustine of Hippo

They cursed him and said, **You are his disciple, but we are disciples of Moses** (9:28). If only such a curse would be upon us and our children (cf. Matt 27:25)! For this is a curse, if you examine their heart but not if you pay close attention to their words. **We are disciples of Moses. We know that God has spoken to Moses, but as for this man, we do not know where he comes from** (9:28–29). If only you had truly known that **God spoke to Moses**. If only you had truly known that Moses preached about God. The Lord said, *If you believed Moses, you would believe me, for he wrote of me* (5:46). In this way do you follow the servant, but turn your back to God? But in reality you do not follow the servant, for through him you would have been led to the Lord. **The man answered,**

"**Why, this is a marvel! You do not know where he comes from, and yet he opened my eyes. We know that God does not listen to sinners, but if anyone is a worshiper of God and does his will, God listens to him** (9:30–31). Just now he speaks as one who is only anointed (i.e., a catechumen), for **God *does* listen to sinners** (9:31). If **God does not listen to sinners**, the tax collector who looked toward the ground and beat on his chest would have said in vain: *God, be merciful to me a sinner!* (Luke 18:13). That confession merited justification just as this blind man won enlightenment. **Never since the world began has it been heard that any one opened the eyes of a man born blind. If this man were not from God, he could do nothing** (9:32–33). He spoke freely, firmly, truthfully, for these things were done by God. When would such things be done by the disciples? Only when the Lord dwelled within them. **They answered him, "You were born in utter sin."** What does the phrase **born in utter sin** mean? It means when his eyes were closed. But he who opened his eyes, healed him completely. The one who enlightened his face will raise him to his right hand (cf. Matt 25:34). "**You were born in utter sin, and would you teach us?" And they cast him out** (9:34). They made him their teacher. In fact, they asked him many questions in order that they might learn. Yet ungratefully, **they cast out** their teacher.

(22) Cyril of Alexandria

And they reviled him, saying, "You are his disciple, but we are disciples of Moses" (9:28). We can almost see the evangelist smile as he recounts this. He observes that the ones who were chosen to hold the sacred offices were so debased by their mental confusion that they tried to make an object of such excellence, namely discipleship under Christ, into one of scorn. In contrast, some of the saints, enamored with a commendable love of Christ, say, *How sweet are your sayings to my throat, beyond honey and honeycomb to my mouth* (Ps 119:103 [118:103 LXX])! Another says, as if speaking to our Lord Jesus Christ about those who disobey him, *Thy words were found, and I ate them, and thy words became to me a joy and the delight of my heart; for I am called by thy name, O Lord, God of hosts* (Jer 15:16). In contrast, they give no value to his sacred words and think that one who is being taught by him is worthy of ridicule just because of that fact. They think that they alone are without blame, for they speak of Christ as the blind man's teacher and of Moses as their own. Truly, the gentiles were illuminated by Christ through the teaching of the evangelists, and Israel died in the types given by Moses and was buried in the shadow of the letter. Therefore, Paul says regarding them: *Yes, to this day whenever Moses is read a veil lies over their minds* (2 Cor 3:15). . . .

    We know that God has spoken to Moses, but as for this man, we do not know where he comes from (9:29). They say that the Lord is a transgressor of the sacred Scriptures for he holds opinions contrary to those stated by Moses and that he has visibly broken the law concerning the Sabbath, for he healed on the Sabbath. . . . Therefore, he has not observed the divine law. When they say, **We do not know where he comes from**, they certainly do not say this out of ignorance regarding who he is or where he is from. In another place they are found publicly confessing that they know all about him. They ask, *Is not this* *the carpenter's son* (Matt 13:55) *whose father and mother we know?* (6:42). How does he now say, *I have come down from heaven* (6:42)? For this reason, we cannot accept the statement, **We do not know where he comes from**, as proof of their ignorance: Rather, we should consider it as an expression of their arrogance.

They say this about him after they disparaged and rendered useless their previous judgment. Indeed, their words, which we should certainly scrutinize more carefully, indicate that they made the following sort of argument. They say, "**We know that God has spoken to Moses** (9:29); therefore, **we** must believe without doubt what was spoken by him and observe the commandments that God gave to him. **But as for this man, we do not know** (9:29), for God has not spoken to him. We do not see any evidence of this regarding him." However, the Pharisees, who arrogantly hold that they are wise and boast of their knowledge of the divine word, should have considered that God the Father proclaims the future coming of Jesus when he speaks through the very wise Moses: *I will raise up for them a prophet like you from among their brethren; and I will put my words in his mouth, and he shall speak to them all that I command him. And whoever will not give heed to my words which he shall speak in my name, I myself will require it of him* (Deut 18:18–19). Certainly, someone could have rebuked the Jews reasonably: If you, who only know how to disbelieve, are so ready to trust the words of Moses because **God has spoken to Moses**, should you not similarly believe Christ when you hear him publicly say: **The words that I say to you are not my own, but the Father's who sent me** (cf. 14:10)? Again, he says, *For I have not spoken on my own authority; the Father who sent me has himself given me commandment what to say and what to speak* (12:49). The words of the Pharisees are a mere excuse and a figment of their arrogant imaginations. For if they say that they would rather follow Moses because **God has spoken** to him, why do they not also think the same thing regarding Christ when he clearly says what we have just quoted? Although they honor the law partially and pretend to hold the will of God in high esteem, they violate and dishonor it greatly by rejecting its proclamation about their own time. Namely, it announced concerning Christ that he should appear by his incarnation in the guise of a prophet.

The man answered, "Why, this is a marvel! You do not know where he comes from, and yet he opened my eyes" (9:30). . . . By saying that he is astonished that they are completely ignorant regarding the wonderful and strange miracle which had happened to him, the former blind man slyly and implicitly rebukes them. He hints that they are far removed from holiness and piety for they shamelessly admitted that they were completely ignorant regarding the one who is truly holy, that is, Christ. You should not wonder whether there were such hopes and thoughts among the Jews. Even among the other nations, the same thoughts were circulating. For example, the Samaritan woman said, *I know that Messiah is coming (he who is called Christ); when he comes, he will show us all things* (4:25). Clearly, the Jews knew that Christ would come, for this is what the word "Messiah" means, and proclaim the higher will of God to them. In addition, he would also open the eyes of the blind. Isaiah says this clearly: *Then the eyes of the blind shall be opened* (Isa 35:5). However, there was another opinion common in Jerusalem. The prophet Isaiah speaks of the ineffable Son of God the Father as unrecognizable, when he asks: *Who will describe his generation?* (Isa 53:8 LXX). The Jews, distorting here once again the intention of the words to bring them into accord with their own notions, imagined that the Christ would be completely unrecognizable and no one would know where he was from. This is despite the fact that the divine Scriptures state very clearly for us his birth in the flesh: *Look, the virgin shall be with child and bear a son* (Isa 7:14 LXX). The mind of the Jews was again unable to comprehend the essential truths since they supposed that the Christ would not be recognizable. This is easily seen from the clear declaration of the blessed evangelist John concerning Christ when he spoke to the people of Jerusalem. Some of the people of that city asked: *Is not this the man whom they seek to kill? And here he is, speaking openly, and they say nothing to him! Can it be that the authorities really know that this is the Christ? Yet we know where this man comes from; and when the Christ appears, no one will know where he comes from* (7:25–26).

If this man were not from God, he could do nothing (9:33). The man, who had just received his sight and had been miraculously released from his old blindness, more quickly perceived the truth than those who had been instructed in the law. Notice how he unveils the utter depravity of the Pharisee's opinions by his many and wise arguments. When they foolishly said of Christ, **As for this man, we do not know where he comes from** (9:29), he severely rebukes them for their outrageous claim to deny all knowledge of the one who worked such miraculous deeds. For it was evident to all that anyone who was **not from God** would be unable to do any of those deeds which are accomplished only by divine power.

John 9:35–41

[35]Jesus heard that they had cast him out, and having found him he said, "Do you believe in the Son of man?" [36]He answered, "And who is he, sir, that I may believe in him?" [37]Jesus said to him, "You have seen him, and it is he who speaks to you." [38]He said, "Lord, I believe"; and he worshiped him. [39]Jesus said, "For judgment I came into this world, that those who do not see may see, and that those who see may become blind." [40]Some of the Pharisees near him heard this, and they said to him, "Are we also blind?" [41]Jesus said to them, "If you were blind, you would have no guilt; but now that you say, 'We see,' your guilt remains."

9:35–38 "Do you believe in the Son of man?" He answered, "And who is he, sir, that I may believe in him?"

---

(23) John Chrysostom

And they cast him out. Jesus heard that they had cast him out, and having found him he said, "Do you believe in the Son of man?" He answered, "And who is he, sir, that I may believe in him?" (9:34–36). The Jews **cast him out** of the temple, and the Lord of the temple found him. He was separated from that fatal group and met with the fountain of salvation. He was dishonored by those who dishonored Christ and was honored by the

Lord of angels. These are the prizes of truth. Similarly, if we abandon our possessions in this world, we will find certainty in the next. If we give to the afflicted here, we will find rest in heaven. If we are abused for God's sake, we will be honored both here and there. . . . What did Christ ask him? **Do you believe in the Son of God?** (9:35). What is this? After he argued so much with the Jews and after so many words, Christ asks him, **Do you believe?** He did not ask this out of ignorance. Rather, he wanted to reveal himself and demonstrate that he valued the man's faith. It is as if he said, "This great crowd has insulted me, but I do not pay any attention to them. I only care for one thing, that you **believe**. One who does the will of God is better than ten thousand who break it." **Do you believe in the Son of God?** (9:35). Since he is present and approves what the blind man had said, Christ asks this question. He brings the blind man into a state of longing for him. He does not say emphatically, **Believe!** But he puts it as a question. What did the man then say? **And who is he, sir, that I may believe in him?** This expression is that of a longing and enquiring soul. He does not know the one whom he had defended so much. This is so that you might learn of his love for the truth. He had not even seen him yet. . . . **Jesus said to him, "You have seen him, and it is he who speaks to you." He said, "Lord, I believe!" And he worshiped him** (9:37-38). Jesus did not say directly, "I am he," but he used a neutral and reserved manner, **You have seen him** (9:37). This was still too indefinite. He then added for clarity, **It is he who speaks to you** (9:37). The blind man said, **Lord, I believe! And he worshiped him** (9:38). Jesus did not say, "I am the one who healed you and commanded you, **Go, wash in the pool of Siloam**" (9:7). Holding his silence regarding these details, he asked him, **Do you believe in the Son of God?** (9:35). The man, showing his great passion, **worshiped him** (9:38) immediately. Very few of those who were healed by him—for example, the lepers and others—did this. By this act of worship, he declared Christ's divine power. And in order that no one would think that what he said was only words, he added also the act of worship.

(24) Augustine of Hippo

As I already mentioned, they cast him out and the Lord received him. Indeed, he became a Christian because he was expelled! Jesus heard that they had cast him out and after he found him, he asked, **Do you believe in the Son of God?** (9:35).[10] He now begins to wash the face of his heart. **He answered**—as if he just was anointed—**"And who is he, sir, that I may believe in him?" Jesus said to him, "You have seen him, and it is he who speaks to you"** (9:36-37). He was **sent**, and he washed his face in **Siloam**, which means **Sent**. Finally, with the face of his heart washed and his conscience cleansed, he acknowledges him not only as a *Son of man* (9:11, 17), which he had confessed before, but now he believes that he is the **Son of God** who has taken on flesh. **He says, "Lord, I believe!"** (9:38). But it is not enough to say, **I believe**. Do you wish to see how he **believes? And he fell down and worshiped him** (9:38).

---

10. Augustine's Latin text read "Son of God," not **Son of Man**.

(25) Cyril of Alexandria

Having found him he said, "Do you believe in the Son of God?"[11] The man who was formerly blind had been **cast out** by the Pharisees. After a while, Christ searches and finds him. He then initiates him into the mysteries. This is a sign for us that God remembers those who are willing to speak on his behalf and who through faith in him do not shrink from dangers. For you hear how Christ, after making himself present so that he can dispense his good rewards, seeks to implant in him the highest perfection of the doctrines of the faith. He asks this question in order that he might receive his assent. This is the way to demonstrate one's faith. Therefore, as a mode of preparation, those who are going to divine baptism are asked questions beforehand concerning their belief. When they have assented and confessed, then at once we admit them as ready for the grace. The significance of this event is demonstrated in his way. We have learned from our Savior Christ himself how important it is that this confession of faith should be made. For this reason, the inspired Paul asserted that Timothy *confessed the confession* of these things *in the presence of many witnesses* (1 Tim 6:12), which means the holy angels. If it is a horrible thing to lie before angels, how much more so is this true before Christ himself? . . .

    Jesus said to him, "You have seen him, and it is he who speaks to you" (9:37). . . . Even now some of those who consider themselves Christians, although they do not accurately understand the significance of the incarnation, have dared to separate the Word from God. They have divided the Word into two sons because he was made man. . . . Since they hold to their strange opinions, they find fault with his divine and philanthropic design. In their minds they separate as far as possible the temple taken from woman from the true sonship. They do not accept his humiliation. They hold an opinion which is far from the truth: they say that the only-begotten Son of God the Father (the Word begotten of his essence) is one and that the son born of woman is a distinct being.[12] When the inspired Scripture proclaims the Son and Christ to be one, are they not completely impious when they divide him who is truly and certainly one Son into two beings? As God the Word, he is considered distinct from the flesh; as fleshly man, he is thought of as distinct from the Word. However, God the Father made the Word of God flesh (that is, the incarnate Word), therefore, the two natures cease to be distinct through their ineffable union and conjoining. The Son is one and only one, both before his conjoining with flesh and when he came with flesh. By flesh we mean a fully integral human, consisting of soul and body. Therefore, because of this mistaken interpretation, the Lord with very great foresight did not say, "It is I," when the man asked, **And who is the Son of God?** (9:36). Perhaps it then would have been possible for someone to suppose ignorantly that the Word alone who shone forth from God the Father was signified. Rather, he showed himself in the very manner which

---

11. Cyril of Alexandria is using a text of the Gospel of John that reads "Son of God," not **Son of Man.**

12. Cyril of Alexandria is attacking a common heresy in the fourth and fifth centuries of early Christianity: Nestorianism. This heretical theology, named for Nestorius, divided Jesus Christ into God the Word and Jesus the man. He held that these two hypostases (persons) were united in purpose and will but fundamentally remain two individuals. Cyril disagreed vehemently and argued that there was a "hypostatic union" between the Word and his human flesh: he is the incarnate Word of God.

to some seems so implausible, saying, **You have seen him** (9:37). He showed that the Word himself was dwelling in the flesh when he spoke once again and added, **it is he who speaks to you** (9:37). Do you see how the Word possesses a unity? He makes no distinction. He says that he is both that which shows itself to physical eyes and that which is known by speech. Therefore, it is completely ignorant and impious to say thoughtlessly as some do: "O man of Christ." As God, he was made man without being cut off from his divinity, and as God, he is the Son with flesh. In these statements are found the most perfect confession and knowledge of faith in him.

He said, "Lord, I believe"; and he worshiped him (9:38). The man who had been blind makes his confession regarding his faith quickly and shows his piety warmly. Although he saw Christ in the flesh without the divine glory which is rightly his, **he worshiped him** as God when he believed since he then recognized that the one who was before him and visible to his eyes was truly the only-begotten Son. Since his heart had been illumined by Christ's indwelling power and authority, he progressed by reason to wise and noble thoughts and beheld the beauty of his divine and ineffable nature. He would not have **worshiped him** as God unless he believed that he was God. He had been prepared and led to think this by the miraculous deed that had happened to him.

Since we have connected all the events concerning the blind man to the history of the gentiles, let us now speak once again about this. I urge you to see how he fulfills the ancient promise by which the gentiles were led through their faith to worship in spirit. For it was the custom for Israel to serve the Lord of all in accordance with the commands of the law. They sacrificed oxen and incense and offered other animals. But the faithful among the gentiles did not follow this manner of service. They turned to the other way of service, that is, the spiritual, which God says is truly and especially precious and sweet to him. For he says, *Surely, I shall not eat the flesh of bulls or drink the blood of he-goats* (Ps 50:13 [49:13 LXX]). He commands us rather to *offer to God a sacrifice of praise* (Ps 50:14 [49:14 LXX]). The psalmist through faith in the Holy Spirit foresees that all the gentiles would go up to worship with song and to celebrate. As if to our Lord and Savior, the psalmist says: *Let all the earth do obeisance to you and make music to you; let them make music to your name* (Ps 65:4 [66:4 LXX]). Our Lord Jesus Christ himself also demonstrates that spiritual worship is better than legal service. When he speaks to the Samaritan woman, *Jesus said to her, "Woman, believe me, the hour is coming when neither on this mountain nor in Jerusalem will you worship the Father. But the hour is coming, and now is, when the true worshipers will worship the Father in spirit and truth, for such the Father seeks to worship him. God is spirit, and those who worship him must worship in spirit and truth"* (4:21, 23–24). If we reason correctly, we will conclude that the holy angels also are distinguished by this kind of service. They present their worship as a sort of spiritual offering to God. For example, when the Spirit commanded those above to offer God-befitting honor to the firstborn and only-begotten, he says: *Let all the angels of God worship him* (Deut 32:43). Additionally, the divine psalmist summons us to do the same: *Come, let us worship and bow down, let us kneel before the Lord, our Maker!* (Ps 95:6).

(26) Caesarius of Arles

Dearest brothers and sisters, in the section of the gospel just read we heard that Jesus acted out a sign for the *man who was blind from birth* (9:1). Why do you marvel at that? Jesus is the Savior. Since Jesus is the Savior, he did something that was appropriate to his name: through his mercy he restored that which he had given to a lesser degree in the womb. When he made his eyes less powerful, certainly he did not make a mistake. Rather, he deferred it for this miracle. Perhaps you might say to me, "How do you know this?" We heard it from the Lord. When the disciples asked Jesus Christ, *Lord, who sinned, this man or his parents, that he was born blind?* (9:2).[13] *He replied to them, It was not that this man sinned, or his parents, but that the works of God might be made manifest in him* (9:3). Pay attention to why Christ made the eyes less powerful in the womb. Do not think that the parents of that blind man were without sin. Do not think that the blind man himself failed to contract original sin when he was born. On account of original sin, even the smallest children are baptized! However, this blindness was not due to his parents' sin nor his own, *but that the works of God might be made manifest in him* (9:3). When we are born, all of us contract original sin; yet we are not born physically blind. That blind man, brothers and sisters, was prepared as a medicinal balm for the human race: he was restored to light physically so that we might be enlightened in our hearts by contemplating this miracle.

Although the blind man was enlightened, he still erred. You might perhaps ask, "In what way did he err?" First of all, he erred because he thought Christ was a *prophet* (9:17). We hear his reply which is undoubtedly false. He said, *We know that God does not listen to sinners* (9:31). However, if **God does not listen to sinners,** what hope do we have? Why do we pray? Do not be afraid, brothers and sisters! The man who said **that God does not listen to sinners** was still blind in his heart, and he failed to tell the truth. Although he was enlightened physically, he was still blind spiritually. If **God does not listen to sinners**, where does the tax collector stand who went up into the temple with the Pharisee? When that Pharisee was boastfully proclaiming his own virtues, the tax collector stood to the side and cast his eyes to the ground. He struck his chest in sorrow and confessed his sins. This man departed from the temple justified rather than that Pharisee (cf. Luke 18:9–14). Brothers and sisters, God certainly listens to sinners! However, the man who said this had not yet washed the face of his heart in **Siloam** (9:7). The mystery had benefited his **eyes**, but the fruits of grace had not yet affected his heart. Although he had received physical sight, he had not yet recovered the eyes of his heart. When did the blind man recover the eyes of his heart? When he was **cast out** by the Jews (9:35). He found the Lord who received him. He found him, because he looked for him. Jesus asked him, "**Do you believe in the Son of man?**"[14] **The blind man asked, "Who is he, sir, that I may believe in him?" Jesus said to him, "You have seen him, and it is he who speaks to you"** (9:35–37). The blind man did not delay. Immediately, he washed the face of his heart, and he saw! In order to recover his physical sight, he washed his face in **Siloam** (9:7). In order to see with the eyes of his heart, he believed in Christ the Lord. The **pool of Siloam** signified our Lord and Savior because

---

13. Caesarius changes the text from the Gospel of John to read "Lord," not **Rabbi**.
14. Caesarius's text reads "Son of God," not **Son of Man.**

Siloam means, "He who has been *sent*" (9:7). Who is the one who has been sent, except Christ? He said, *I was sent only to the lost sheep of the house of Israel* (Matt 15:24). Again, he said, *I do the will of the father who* sent *me* (cf. 5:30; 6:39). For this reason Christ was the **pool of Siloam**. That blind man listened. He **worshiped and believed** (9:38). After he washed his face, he saw Christ the Lord with bodily eyes. . . .

And so the *spittle* (9:6) of Christ sank into the ground and mixed with the earth. Let the very one who made the earth, remake it. Let the very one who created it, reform and recreate it. Similarly, the *spittle* signifies the word of God, his real human body on earth. For this reason, let the *spittle* of Christ come down in order that the earth may be gathered up. Let the grace of Christ come in order that the law may be fulfilled. *He made clay of the spittle* (9:6). What is *spittle* mixed with *clay*, except the incarnate Word? That blind man represents an image of the whole human race. For this reason, the *spittle* was mixed with *clay*, and the blind man was given sight. The Word became incarnate, and the world was illuminated.

Dearest brothers and sisters, since we who are in Christ have recovered the eyes of the heart which we had lost in Adam, let us give great thanks to the one who condescended to enlighten us, who were not worthy in any way to be able to see him. With as much strength as we can muster and with his assistance, let us strive to open our **eyes** to the good and close them to evil in accordance with what the prophet requests of the Lord when he cries out, *Turn my eyes from looking at vanity* (Ps 119:37 [118:37 LXX]). The Lord lives and reigns forever and ever. Amen.

9:39-41 "For judgment I came into this world."

---

(27) Theodore of Mopsuestia

Jesus said, "For judgment I came into this world, that those who do not see may see, and that those who see may become blind" (9:39). In another passage, he said, *God did not send his Son into the world to judge[15] the world, but that the world might be saved through him* (3:17). This is not contrary to the statement, **For judgment I came into this world** (9:39). While he spoke previously about the purpose of his coming—namely, that every human being **might be saved**—here he speaks about the fulfillment of his actions. . . . What he means is this: "You see, I have come to the trial of human beings so that those who are **blind** and those who can **see** might be exposed. After all, the one who seemed **blind** twice received eyes in order to **see** with them: he acquired both **eyes** of the body and he received the instruction of reverence for God in the enlightenment of his soul. But those who think that they **see** with bodily **eyes** (and we have entrusted them to explain the other commandments of the law!) seem **blind** in two ways: they neither accept the truth nor do they believe the works that they have seen with their own **eyes**.

15. This is a change from the RSV, which has **condemn** instead of "judge." However, Theodore's argument relies on the presence of the word "judge" in both passages.

(28) Augustine of Hippo

Jesus said to him that it is now the day of **judgment** between light and darkness: **For judgment I came into this world, that those who do not see may see, and that those who see may become blind** (9:39). What do you mean, Lord? Certainly, you have introduced a great problem for those who are already weary. Therefore, revive our strength in order that we might be able to understand what you said. You came **that those who do not see may see** (9:39). This is correct, because you are the *light* (9:5)! This is right, because you free us from darkness! Every soul accepts and understands this idea. But what does, **and that those who see may become blind**, mean? Because you have come, those who see will become **blind**. Listen to what comes next, and perhaps you will understand. **Some of these Pharisees** were troubled on account of his words and asked: **Are we also blind?** (9:40). Now I hear what it is that so disturbed them: **and that those who see may become blind. Jesus said to them, "If you were blind, you would have no guilt,"** although blindness itself is a sin. **If you were blind**—that is, if you noticed that you were **blind** or if you said that you were **blind**—you would go to a physician. **If you were blind, you would have no guilt,** because I can take away sin. Now you speak truly: **but now that you say, "We see," your guilt remains.** Why is this? Because you say, **We see**, you do not seek a physician, and you remain in your blindness. This then is what we did not understand above when he said, **I came into this world, that those who do not see may see** (9:39). What does the phrase **that those who do not see may see** mean? This is the one who confesses that he is not able to **see** and who seeks out a physician so that he might be able to **see**. What does the phrase **that those who see may become blind** mean? The one who thinks that he **sees** and who believes that he does not need a physician remains in his blindness. Therefore, he calls this **judgment**. When he says, **For judgment I came into this world**, he is distinguishing between those who believe and confess from the haughty who think that they are able to **see**. On this account, they are in fact more seriously blinded. It is as if the sinner who confesses and seeks the physician says to him, *Judge me, O God, and defend my cause against an ungodly people* (Ps 42:1). Certainly he speaks of those *ungodly people* who say, **We see**, for their sin remains. It is clear that in this place he was not speaking of the final judgment. In the end of this age, he will judge between the living and the dead, but here he said, *I judge no one* (8:15). He came into the flesh *not to condemn the world, but that the world might be saved through him* (3:17).

John 10

Early Christian interpreters understand Jesus's shepherd metaphors in a variety of ways. John Chrysostom likens those who climb in by another way *(10:1) to the scribes who elevate their own teachings above God's law. Augustine of Hippo takes those who* climb in by another way *to represent those who may lead a good life but do not have eternal life in Christ. Cyril of Alexandria offers a contemporary application regarding anyone "who ascends to take leadership of the people without divine guidance or will."*

The shepherd *(10:2) is interpreted by John Chrysostom as Christ, and the* gatekeeper *(10:3) as Moses. Theodore of Mopsuestia also sees the* gatekeeper *as Moses, but interprets the* shepherd *as faithful ministers in the church who lead Christ's sheep. Augustine of Hippo, on the other hand, identifies Christ with the* door, *the* shepherd, *and the* gatekeeper *(while allowing that the Holy Spirit may also be the* gatekeeper*).*

Clement of Alexandria, Cyril of Jerusalem, and Cyril of Alexandria all see the door *(10:7) as Christ, connecting this passage with John 14:6 ("I am the way . . ."). Theodore of Mopsuestia explains how Christ can both enter through the* door, *and be the* door *at the same time.*

Augustine puzzles over the passage that all who came before me are thieves and robbers *(10:8), wondering whether that included the prophets who came before Christ. He denies that notion, explaining that when the prophets spoke the "word of God," they in fact came with Christ, the "Word of God" (John 1:1). Augustine also tackles the question about how those who lived before Christ could possibly enter salvation through Christ, noting that faith in the Messiah to come and faith in Christ who has come already are the same, even if held in different time periods. Augustine explains the meaning of the words* he will go in and out *(10:9) by understanding* to go in *as thinking internally according to faith in Christ, while to* go out *is to act according to that same faith.*

Both Tertullian and the clergy in third-century Rome warn that Christian ministers who flee during persecution are the equivalent of a bad shepherd who sees the wolf coming and leaves the sheep and flees *(10:12). Aphrahat the Persian and John Chrysostom connect Christian leadership of the* flock *with the prophetic warnings of Ezek 34. Augustine of Hippo offers a thoughtful, extended application about the* hirelings, *drawing on Phil 2:21 and those who "look after their own interests, not those of Jesus Christ." True leaders, says Augustine, must rebuke sinners, even at the risk of losing public honor. Finally, the Apostolic Constitutions commend the bishop who acts like a good shepherd, drawing back his wayward flock.*

*In considering verses 14–15 (*I am the good shepherd . . . I lay down my life for the sheep*), Cyril of Alexandria expounds on the effect Christ's death had for the sheep: "He delivered us from the darkness of death so that he might prepare to gather us together into the heavenly choirs." Peter Chrysologus offers a moving sermon about the benefit received by the death of the shepherd. Rather than leaving his sheep abandoned to the wolves, Christ's death defeats the devil and death, and promises resurrection even for those Christians who have died already.*

Cyril of Alexandria ponders how Christ can say that he knows us and we know him as the Father knows me and I know the Father *(10:15). Recognizing that finite humans can never comprehend the full essence of God, Cyril interprets our knowledge of God in terms of relationship: "I will enter into an intimate relationship with my sheep, and my sheep will be in an intimate relationship with me, in the same way in which the Father is intimate with me and I am intimate with the Father."*

Regarding Christ's words about one flock, one shepherd *(10:16), Cyprian warns that those who claim leadership in a church without a proper line of succession are enemies "to the peace of the Lord and the divine unity." Theodore of Mopsuestia, on the other hand, sees Christ's words fulfilled in the existence of Jews and gentiles gathered together into one church.*

*Hilary of Poitiers wrestles with the tension between Christ's words in verses 17–18 (*I lay down my life, that I may take it again*) with Scripture elsewhere which claims that it was God who raised Jesus from the dead (cf. Acts 2:24; Rom 10:9). Hilary sees no contradiction here, but instead an affirmation that "Christ himself is God." John Chrysostom notes the uniqueness of Christ's claims. Unlike any of us, who can have our lives taken against our will, Christ alone has full authority to decide when his life will be taken. Likewise, our confidence in the resurrection should be secure, for if Christ had the power to lay down his life, then he also had the power to take it up again. Cyril of Alexandria agrees, but focuses on that second aspect—the taking up his life again—as the most important. If Christ died, even willingly, but never rose again, there is no benefit to us.*

On Jesus's confrontation with the Jews in verses 22–39, Novatian offers a richly Trinitarian reading of Christ's divine claim to give eternal life (10:28) and his unity with the Father. John Chrysostom and Theodore of Mopsuestia similarly see Christ's claims that no one can snatch them out of my hand *(10:28), and his affirmation of unity with the Father, as assertions of a shared essence between Father and Son. Hilary of Poitiers agrees, noting that "the Son's hand is the Father's hand" because they share the same divine essence. Likewise, Augustine affirms the shared power between the Father and the Son.*

*Verse 30 (*I and the Father are one*) receives considerable attention by early interpreters. Tertullian offers an incisive, and rather technical, linguistic argument that in the phrase* I and the Father are one, *the subjects of the sentence (*I *and* Father*) are masculine nouns, indicating two persons, but the predicate nominative (*one*) is neuter, indicating its reference to a "unity of being," not persons. Thus, "those whom Christ has equated and joined together are two separate entities," rather than "one person" as Tertullian's Modalist opponents would have it. Hippolytus likewise uses this verse to affirm the orthodox position about the unity and plurality of God: Jesus did not say "I and the Father* am *one, but* are *one. The word* are *is not used in reference to one thing, but two. It indicates two persons, but one power." Likewise, Hilary of Poitiers, Gregory of Nyssa, and Cyril of Alexandria all aver that this simple statement* *affirms both the unity of divine nature between Father and Son, but also their distinction as two separate persons of the Godhead.*

Near the end of John 10, Jesus uses Ps 82 in defense of his title as "Son of God." Both Hilary of Poitiers and Augustine of Hippo explain the logic of Jesus's argument: if Scripture used the title "gods" for holy men of old, how much more should Jesus, the one sanctified and sent by the Father, claim the title "Son of God."

Finally, the brief comment that many believed *(10:42) leads John Chrysostom to observe the faith of the crowd once they are removed from the negative influence of the Jewish leaders and given time to reflect. Chrysostom offers a profound application by calling us all to remove ourselves from busyness and enter into silence: "For the ship that is free from tumult sails with a fair wind, and the soul that is free from activity remains at rest in harbor."*

John 10:1–10

[1]"Truly, truly, I say to you, he who does not enter the sheepfold by the door but climbs in by another way, that man is a thief and a robber; [2]but he who enters by the door is the shepherd of the sheep. [3]To him the gatekeeper opens; the sheep hear his voice, and he calls his own sheep by name and leads them out. [4]When he has brought out all his own, he goes before them, and the sheep follow him, for they know his voice. [5]A stranger they will not follow, but they will flee from him, for they do not know the voice of strangers." [6]This figure Jesus used with them, but they did not understand what he was saying to them.

[7]So Jesus again said to them, "Truly, truly, I say to you, I am the door of the sheep. [8]All who came before me are thieves and robbers; but the sheep did not heed them. [9]I am the door; if any one enters by me, he will be saved, and will go in and out and find pasture. [10]The thief comes only to steal and kill and destroy; I came that they may have life, and have it abundantly.

10:1–3 "He who does not enter the sheepfold by the door but climbs in by another way is a thief and a robber; but he who enters by the door is the shepherd of the sheep. To him the gatekeeper opens."

---

(1) John Chrysostom

Truly, truly, I say to you, he who does not enter the sheepfold by the door but climbs in by another way, that man is a thief and a robber (10:1). Observe the marks of a **thief**. First, he does not come openly. Second, he does not come by way of the Scriptures, for this is what is meant by, **does not enter by the door**. Christ also refers to those who came before him and to those who will come after him, that is, the antichrist and the false christs, such as Judas and Theudas and any others like them (cf. Acts 5:36–37). He calls the Scriptures a **door** for a good reason, because they lead us to God and open to us the knowledge of

God. They create the **sheep**; they guard them; and they do not allow the **wolves** to enter in. Scripture, like some steadfast **door**, closes the entrance to the heretics, placing us in safety with respect to everything we may desire, and not allowing us to wander off. If we do not separate from it, we will not easily be overcome by our enemies. Through Scripture we will recognize everyone, both the shepherds and those who are not shepherds.

What does **the sheepfold** mean? It refers to the **sheep** and to their protection. The one who does not use the Scriptures, but **climbs in by another way**, that is, who forges for himself another, unlawful, way—this one is a **robber**. Do you see here how Christ agrees with the Father and introduces the Scriptures into our midst? This is why he also says to the Jews, *Search the scriptures* (5:39), and brings in Moses and all the prophets as witnesses. "For all who hear the prophets," he says, "shall come to me." Again, *If you believed Moses, you would believe me* (5:46). Our passage presents the same thing metaphorically. By saying, **he climbs in by another way**, Christ refers to the scribes, because they taught *as doctrines the precepts of men* and transgressed the law (Matt 15:9). With these words he reproached them and said, *None of you keeps the law* (7:19). There is a good reason he says **climbs up** and not "enters in," since the act of climbing is what the risk-taking **thief** desires to do when he leaps over the wall.

You have now seen how he outlined the features of a **robber**. Observe now the distinctive features of the **shepherd: He who enters by the door is the shepherd of the sheep. To him the gatekeeper opens; the sheep hear his voice, and he calls his own sheep by name and leads them out. When he has brought out all his own, he goes before them** (10:2–4). Here he set forth the marks of the shepherd and of the spoiler. Let us see how he uses what follows to accommodate to their level. **To him**, he says, **the gatekeeper opens** (10:3). Christ is continuing with a metaphor so he can make his point more emphatic. But if you want to examine the parable word for word, nothing prevents us here from understanding the **gatekeeper** as Moses, for the words of God were entrusted to him.

The sheep hear his voice, and he calls his own sheep by name (10:3). Since they were everywhere saying that he was a cheat, they confirmed this by their own unbelief, saying, *Who of the authorities believed in him?* (7:48). . . . Consequently, by not receiving him, they were excluded from being among the **sheep**. If it's the responsibility of the **shepherd** to enter through the lawful **door**, and he did enter through it, then all who follow the **shepherd** would be counted as **sheep**. Those who have broken away have not slandered the **shepherd**, but have cast themselves out of the company of the **sheep**. If a little later he says that he is **the door** (10:7), there is no need to be troubled. He also says that he is the **shepherd**, and a sheep, and in various ways declares his dispensations. Whenever he leads us to the Father, he calls himself **the door**. Whenever he cares for us, a **shepherd**. And lest we think that his only task is to bring us to the Father, he also says that he is the **shepherd**.

(2) Theodore of Mopsuestia

The **sheepfold** is the teaching of the law, while the **sheep** are those who are under this teaching and have promised to conduct themselves according to the commandments. The **gatekeeper** of this **sheepfold** is the blessed Moses. He established this **sheepfold** through the commandments of the law so that those who live in the **sheepfold** according to his will, will be able to dwell in it securely. The **shepherd** of the **sheep** is the one who through his actions possesses the ministry of teaching and uses the lawful entrance. He is the one whose way of life is consistent with the law, and therefore enters into this **sheepfold** along with those who are suited for it. He then leads the others, like **sheep**, to the pasture of his teaching by showing them the nourishment of his words with which they should first feed themselves.

(3) Augustine of Hippo

Truly, truly, I say to you, he who does not enter the sheepfold by the door but climbs in by another way is a thief and a robber (10:1). The Pharisees had said they were not blind (cf. 9:39–41). But, then, they would have been able to see whether they were Christ's sheep. How did those who raged against the day get light for themselves? Because of their own empty, overbearing, incurable conceit, the Lord Jesus connects the words about blindness with these words here, in which he warns us for our own good—if we pay attention!

According to the customary way of speaking, there are many who are called good people, good men, good women, and virtuous—as if they obey the things taught in the law. They honor their parents, don't commit adultery, don't murder, don't steal, don't bear false witness against anyone, and behave as if they were observing the other things commanded in the law. Yet, they are not Christians. Frequently, they boast about themselves as the Pharisees did, **Are we also blind?** (9:40). However, they don't understand why they do what they do, and they act in vain. So, in today's reading, the Lord presents an analogy about his flock and the **door** by which the **sheepfold** is entered.

Let the pagans say, "We live good lives." If they don't **enter by the door**, what's the point of their boasting? Whoever wants to benefit from living a good life should do it for this purpose: to be granted eternal life. What good is it for the one who is not granted eternal life to live a good life? For those who either by their blindness are ignorant of the purpose of living a good life, or who despise that purpose because of their insolence, cannot be said to be living a good life. However, no one has a true and certain hope for eternal life unless they acknowledge the life—that is, Christ—and **enter the sheepfold by the door**.

(4) Augustine of Hippo

We understand the **door** as the Lord Christ, and the **shepherd** as well, for these two things he himself explained; but whom do we understand as the **gatekeeper** (10:3)? He has left the meaning of the **gatekeeper** to be sought by us. And what does he say about the **gatekeeper**? **To him**, he says, **the gatekeeper opens** (10:3). To whom does he open? To the **shepherd**. What does he open to the **shepherd**? The **door**. And who is this **door**? The **shepherd** himself. You see, if the Lord Christ had not explained it, if he himself had not said, **I am the shepherd** (10:11) and, **I am the door** (10:7), would any of us dare to say that Christ was himself both **shepherd** and **door**? For if he had said, **I am the shepherd**, and had not said,

I am the door, we would have set about investigating what the **door** was, and perhaps come to the wrong conclusion while standing right in front of it. His grace and compassion have revealed the **shepherd**, since he said that it was he himself; he has revealed the **door** in the same way; but he has left the **gatekeeper** to be sought by us.

Who are we going to say is the **gatekeeper**? Whomever we discover, we must be careful lest he be thought greater than the **door** itself, since in people's homes, the **gatekeeper** is greater than the **door**. For the **gatekeeper** is placed before the **door**, not the **door** before the **gatekeeper**. The **gatekeeper** watches over the **door**, not the **door** over the **gatekeeper**. I don't daresay that anyone is greater than the **door**, for I've heard already what the **door** is. . . .

We should, perhaps, understand the **gatekeeper** to be the Lord himself. For in human terms, there's a greater difference between a **shepherd** and a **door** than between a **gatekeeper** and a **door**. Why, then, may we not understand him as the **gatekeeper** also? For if we consider his personal identity, the Lord Christ is neither a **shepherd**, as we have been accustomed to know and see shepherds, nor is he a **door**, for no carpenter made him; if, however, we consider these things as a kind of metaphor, he is both **door** and **shepherd**, and, I daresay, a **sheep**. Certainly the **sheep** is beneath the **shepherd**, yet he is both **shepherd** and **sheep**. Where is he a **shepherd**? Behold, you have it here, read the gospel: **I am the good shepherd** (10:11). Where is he a **sheep**? Examine the prophet: *As a sheep he was led to the slaughter* (Isa 53:7). Ask the friend of the bridegroom: *Behold, the Lamb of God, who takes away the sin of the world!* (1:29).

Still I'm going to say something even more marvelous about these metaphors. The lamb, the **sheep**, and the **shepherd** are friendly with each other. However, **sheep** are usually guarded by their **shepherds** against lions; and yet although he is **sheep** and **shepherd**, we read this word about Christ: *The Lion of the tribe of Judah has conquered* (Rev 5:5). Understand these things, brothers and sisters, as metaphors, not as his personal identity. We are used to seeing **shepherds** sit on top of a rock, and from there, they watch over the herd entrusted to them. Certainly the **shepherd** is greater than the rock upon which he sits; and yet, Christ is both **shepherd** and rock (cf. 1 Cor 10:4). All of this is metaphorical.

If you seek from me his personal identity: *In the beginning was the Word, and the Word was with God, and the Word was God* (1:1). If you seek from me his personal identity, he is the only Son, begotten of the Father from eternity to eternity, equal to his begetter, through whom all things were made, unchangeable along with the Father, and unchanged by taking human form, a man by incarnation, the Son of Man and the Son of God. All this that I have said is not metaphor, but reality.

Therefore do not let it trouble us, brothers and sisters, to understand metaphorically that the same one who is the **door** is also the **gatekeeper**. What is a **door**? That by which we enter. What is a **gatekeeper**? The one who opens it. Who, therefore, opens himself, except the one who explains himself? Behold, the Lord had spoken of **the door** and we hadn't understood. When we didn't understand, it was closed. He who opened it is the **gatekeeper**. There is no need, therefore, to seek anything else; no need, but perhaps there is desire.

If there is desire, don't wander off, don't move away from the Trinity. If you seek another person as the **gatekeeper**, let the Holy Spirit come to mind, for the Holy Spirit will not disdain to be the **gatekeeper** since the Son deigned himself to be the **door**. See the Holy

Spirit, perhaps, as the **gatekeeper**; the Lord himself spoke to his disciples about the Holy Spirit: *He will guide you into all the truth* (16:13). What is the **door**? Christ. What is Christ? Truth. Who opens the **door**, except the one who guides into all the truth?

(5) Cyril of Alexandria

In his usual manner, Jesus molds the form of his speech to a spiritual meaning as though it springs from the narrative itself. He takes things that are all but obvious to the eyes and contain nothing difficult to understand and makes them into images of things perceived only dimly. The **thieves** and **robbers**, he says, who freely attack the **sheepfold** do not **enter** in through the **door** but **climb in by another way** (10:1). By leaping over the top of the **fold**, they put themselves in danger, for indeed it is very likely that someone who **robs** and heedlessly wreaks havoc like this will be detected and seized. But those who **enter by the door** (10:2) itself, make a risk-free entrance since they are obviously well known to the master of the **sheep**. When the guard opens the **doors** to them, they run in. These, he says, will be free to mingle with the **sheep**, since they enter as lawfully as those who are uncorrupted and beyond suspicion of being a **robber**.

Thus, the narrative has a typological meaning, turning us to what is spiritually edifying: those who ascend to leadership of the people without divine guidance or will, are like those who entirely avoid entering through the **door**. They will perhaps be destroyed. By the logic of their claims, they pervert the divine judgment. But those who obtain a God-given leadership by coming to it through Christ will take charge of the most sacred **fold** with great boldness and grace, and will surely avoid the wrath which comes on the others. They will even receive honor for their work and will obtain heavenly crowns beyond their expectations since their aim is not at all to treat their **sheep** shamefully. Rather, they aim to assist the **sheep** in doing things that are well pleasing to the master of the **fold**, and to love keeping those under him safe in every way possible.

10:7 "I am the door."

---

(6) Clement of Alexandria

If you yourself truly long to see God, participate then in a purification worthy of God. That is, not with laurel leaves and headbands of embroidered wool and purple,[1] but rather, when you have crowned yourself with righteousness and have put on the leaves of self-control, seek after Christ. Somewhere he says, **I am the door** (10:7), which we must search out if we desire to know God, so that he may throw the gates of heaven wide open for us. The gates of the Word are spiritual and are opened by the key of faith. *No one has known God, except the Son and those to whom the Son shall reveal him* (cf. Matt 11:27). I know well that he who

---

1. Common outward displays of wealth and achievement.

has opened the **door** (which has so far been shut), reveals what is within. He will show us the sorts of things which we did not know beforehand, unless we had been brought in by Christ, through whom alone God is beheld.

(7) Cyril of Jerusalem

Those who have been taught to believe in "one God, the Father Almighty," ought also to believe in "the only-begotten Son."[2] For *no one who denies the Son has the Father* (1 John 2:23). Jesus said, **I am the door** (10:7). *No one comes to the Father, except through me* (14:6). If you deny the **door**, then knowledge of the Father will be shut to you. *No one knows the Father, except the Son, and the one to whom the Son reveals him* (cf. Matt 11:27; Luke 10:22). If you deny the one who reveals the Father, you will remain in ignorance. There is a passage in the gospel that says, *The one who does not believe in the Son, will not see life, but rather the wrath of God remains upon him* (3:36), because the Father becomes angry when the only-begotten Son is rejected. For a king is angry even when a simple soldier is dishonored, but whenever someone dishonors a more distinguished officer or his friend, then an even greater anger arises in him. However if someone despises the only-begotten Son of the King, who then will appease the Father's anger on behalf of his only-begotten Son?

Therefore if you wish to be devout to the one God, worship the Son, since the Father will not receive worship in any other way. The Father spoke out in a voice from heaven saying, *This is my beloved Son, in whom I am well pleased* (Matt 3:17). The Father was *well pleased* with the Son, so unless you are also *well pleased* with him, you do not have life. Do not be carried away with those who cunningly say that "God is one" (cf. Deut 6:4). Instead, to know that God is one, know that the Son is the only-begotten of the Father. I am not the first to say this; the psalmist in the person of the Son said, *The Lord said to me, you are my Son* (Ps 2:7). . . .

Therefore believe "in one Lord Jesus Christ, the only-begotten Son of God."[3] We say "one Lord Jesus Christ" so that his sonship would be "only-begotten." We say "one" so that you might not conjecture about another. We say "one" so that you might not irreverently distribute the many names of his divine activity among many sons. For he is said to be a **door**, but do not think the term refers to anything wooden. Rather, it refers to a spiritual, living **door** which is able to discern those who enter in. He is called a *way* (14:6) but not one which is being walked on by feet. Rather, he is the *way* which leads to the Father in heaven.

He is called a *sheep* (1:29), not one incapable of reasoning, but the one who cleanses the world of sins through his precious blood: the sheep who is led before the shearers and knows when to keep silent (cf. Isa 53:7). This sheep is again called a *shepherd* who says: *I am the good shepherd* (10:11). He is a sheep because of his humanity and a *shepherd* because of his divine love toward humanity.

---

2. Taken from the Nicene Creed.
3. Taken from the Nicene Creed.

(8) Theodore of Mopsuestia

Truly, truly, I say to you, I am the door of the sheep (10:7). Notice: it seems that Christ is contradicting himself, for he knows (according to his words above) that because he entered through the **door** (10:2), he receives authority to tend the **sheep**. But here he says the opposite by calling himself the **door of the sheep** (10:7). Earlier, however, when he spoke with the Pharisees (the leaders of the people in matters of the law), he showed them that they had unjustly cast out the blind man (cf. John 9). He rightly compared his own conduct in the law with theirs because he consistently fulfilled its commandments. So he is the true **shepherd of the sheep**. For that reason, he speaks the truth about himself when he says that he entered by the **door** insofar as he was under the law and used the lawful entrance.

Here, however, he is not talking about the same issue; he is talking about himself. He is the **door of the sheep** because he is the primary entrance into truth for everyone. His instruction is unique because he has made it the way through which everyone is called. . . . Therefore, it was correct for him to call himself **the door of the sheep**, for there is no other possible way to enter the truth unless we first believe in our Lord and draw near to the entrance of truth through his commandments. Then we will take delight in the blessings we will obtain through his proximity to God the Father.

(9) Cyril of Alexandria

So Jesus said to them, "Truly, I say to you, I am the door of the sheep" (10:7). Jesus, being by nature God and seeing what lies in the depths (cf. Ps 139:8), knew all too well that the Pharisees understood nothing that he had said, even though they were accustomed to think of themselves as being great learners of the law, and were unmatched in their pride in thinking themselves wise. This is why Jesus gives them a very clear explanation and, as if summarizing a long argument, carefully points out in just a few words the aim of his **figure** (10:6). Being by nature good, he gently leads them toward understanding, even if they do not deserve it, so that perhaps some manner of assistance might illuminate their minds. He speaks plainly of himself as **the door of the sheep** (10:7), teaching a fact which is generally agreed upon. Only through faith in him do we enter into a relationship with God, as he himself is a witness to this, saying, *No one comes to the Father, but by me* (14:6).

10:8 "All who came before me are thieves and robbers."

---

(10) Augustine of Hippo

All who have come are thieves and robbers (10:8).[4] What does this mean, Lord, **all who have come**? Didn't you **come**? Understand what he meant: "**All who have come**, except me,

---

4. Augustine's Latin text has no **before me** as does the RSV.

of course." Therefore, let's consider this. Before the coming of Christ the prophets came. Were they **thieves and robbers**? Far from it. They didn't come in addition to him, for they came with him. When he was about to come, he sent heralds, but the hearts of those whom he had sent, he already possessed. Do you want to know that they came with him, the one who always exists? Indeed, he took on flesh in time, so what do I mean by "always"? *In the beginning was the Word* (1:1). Therefore, those who came with the "word of God,"[5] came with him. For he also said, *I am the way, and the truth, and the life* (14:6). If he himself is the truth, those who were truthful were with him. Therefore, **all**, except him, were **thieves and robbers**; that is, they came to steal and kill.

But the sheep did not heed them (10:8). This is the greater question. **The sheep did not heed them.** Before the coming of our Lord Jesus Christ, who humbly came in the flesh, righteous men preceded him, believing in the one who was going to come, just as we believe in the one who has come. The times have varied; the faith has not. Words themselves are varied according to their tense, when they are inflected in various ways. He **will come** has one sound; he **has come** has another. The sound changes according to the tense: he will come; he has come (*venturus est, venit*). Nevertheless, the same faith binds the two together, both those who believed that he was going to come, and those who believe that he has come. Indeed, although residing in different times, we see that both groups have entered through the one doorway of faith, that is, through Christ.

10:9–10 "He will be saved, and will go in and out and find pasture. The thief comes only to steal and kill."

---

(11) Augustine of Hippo

What does it mean: **He will go in and out and find pasture** (10:9)? Of course, to **go in** to the church through the **door** of Christ is all well and good; but to **go out** of the church is certainly not good, as John the Evangelist himself said in his letters: *They went **out** from us, but they were not of us* (1 John 2:19). So, this kind of **going out** could not be praised by the good shepherd when he says **he will go in and out and find pasture**. Therefore not only is there a good **going in**, but there is some sort of good **going out** as well, namely, through the good **door** of Christ.

What is this praiseworthy and blessed **going out**? We **go in** when we ponder something internally; and so, to **go out** is to perform tasks outwardly. Since, as the apostle says, *Christ dwells in our hearts through faith* (Eph 3:17), then to **go in** through Christ is to think according to that same faith; but to **go out** through Christ is to act according to that same faith, even outside—that is, in public. Hence, it says in the Psalms: *Man goes out to his work* (Ps 104:23), and the Lord says, *Let your light so shine before men, that they may see your good works* (Matt 5:16).

It pleases me even more that truth itself, like a good shepherd and therefore a good teacher, has in a way prompted us to understand what he means. When he says, **he will go**

---

5. Augustine means prophets who proclaimed God's word.

in and out and find pasture, he joins it with the following verse: **The thief comes only to steal and kill and destroy; I came that they may have life, and have it abundantly** (10:10). To me, this seems to say that those who **go in** have **life,** and those who **go out** have it more **abundantly.** However, no one is able truly to **go out** through the **door** of Christ to eternal life, unless he **goes in** by that very same **door** of Christ to his church (which is his fold) to a temporal life of faith. Therefore he said: **I came that they may have life** (10:10), that is, faith which works by love (cf. Gal 5:6). Through faith they **go in** to the fold in order to live, because *He who through faith is righteous shall live* (Rom 1:17). **And they shall have life abundantly**—they who, by enduring until the end, **go out** through that **door,** that is, the faith of Christ, because they die as true believers. They shall have **life abundantly** when they arrive at the place wherein the shepherd has preceded them, where they shall never die.

John 10:11–21

[11]I am the good shepherd. The good shepherd lays down his life for the sheep. [12]He who is a hireling and not a shepherd, whose own the sheep are not, sees the wolf coming and leaves the sheep and flees; and the wolf snatches them and scatters them. [13]He flees because he is a hireling and cares nothing for the sheep. [14]I am the good shepherd; I know my own and my own know me, [15]as the Father knows me and I know the Father; and I lay down my life for the sheep. [16]And I have other sheep, that are not of this fold; I must bring them also, and they will heed my voice. So there shall be one flock, one shepherd. [17]For this reason the Father loves me, because I lay down my life, that I may take it again. [18]No one takes it from me, but I lay it down of my own accord. I have power to lay it down, and I have power to take it again; this charge I have received from my Father." [19]There was again a division among the Jews because of these words. [20]Many of them said, "He has a demon, and he is mad; why listen to him?" [21]Others said, "These are not the sayings of one who has a demon. Can a demon open the eyes of the blind?"

10:11–12   "I am the good shepherd. . . . He who is a hireling and not a shepherd . . . sees the wolf coming and leaves the sheep and flees."

---

(12) Tertullian of Carthage

When those in authority **flee** (that is, deacons, priests, and bishops), how will the layperson be able to understand why Jesus said, *"flee from city to city"* (Matt 10:23)? When the leaders **flee,** who among the commoners will be able to persuade others to remain firm in battle? Certainly, a **good shepherd lays down his life for the sheep** (10:11). As Moses says, who already prefigured the yet-unrevealed Lord Christ: *If you destroy this people*, he says, *then also destroy me along with them* (cf. Exod 32:32). But Christ confirms these figural passages and he himself states that the bad **shepherd** is the one who **sees the wolf coming and flees, leaving the sheep to be snatched** (10:12).

A **shepherd** of this kind will be thrown off the farm; the wages which would have been given to him at his departure will be held back in compensation. Indeed, from his private savings a restitution of his master's losses will also be required, since *to him who has more will be given, and from him who has not, even what he thinks that he has will be taken away* (Luke 8:18). So Zechariah threatens: *Strike the shepherd, that the sheep may be scattered; I will turn my hand against the little ones* (Zech 13:7). In the same way, both Ezekiel and Jeremiah plead the very same threats, not only for their wicked eating of the **sheep** (feeding themselves rather than the **sheep**), but also for their scattering of the flock and making them shepherdless prey among all the beasts of the land.

This happens especially when the church is abandoned by the clergy in times of persecution. If anybody recognizes the Spirit, he will hear him identifying the deserters. When **wolves** rush in, it is both inappropriate and unlawful for those in charge of the flock to **flee**—for Christ, who proclaimed such a man a bad **shepherd**, certainly has condemned him. And what has been condemned has undoubtedly been made unlawful. This is why leaders of the church in persecution ought not to **flee**.

(13) Epistle from the Roman Clergy to the Carthaginian Clergy

There are those of us who seem to be placed in charge and have the responsibility to care for the flock in place of the **shepherd**. If we are found to be neglecting our duties, then what was said to our predecessors (who were just as neglectful when placed in charge) will also be said to us, namely, that we did not seek the lost, we did not correct those who went astray, we did not gather the lame, we consumed their milk, and we clothed ourselves in their wool (cf. Ezek 34:2–4).

In fact, the Lord himself who fulfills what was written in the law and the prophets taught this, saying, **I am the good shepherd** who **lays down his life for the sheep. He who is a hireling, whose own the sheep are not, sees the wolf coming and leaves the sheep and flees; and the wolf scatters them** (10:11–12). He also spoke to Simon this way: *"Do you love me?"* He answered, *"I love you."* The Lord said to him, *"Feed my sheep"* (21:15–17). We know that this exchange took place because Peter abandoned the Lord, and other disciples did similar things.

(14) Aphrahat the Persian

Those who are **shepherds** take their place at the head of the flock and give the **sheep** the food of life. Whoever keeps watch and works hard for his **sheep** cares for his flock, and is a disciple of the **good shepherd, who gave himself for his sheep** (10:11). Whoever does not lead his **flock** well, however, is like the **hireling** (10:12) who does not care for his **sheep**. . . .

These are the greedy and reprehensible **shepherds**, the **hirelings** who did not tend the sheep, lead them well (cf. Ezek 34:2–19), or rescue them from the **wolves**. When the great **shepherd** comes, this chief of the **shepherds** will call and inspect his **sheep** and review his **flock**. He will summon those **shepherds** and settle accounts with them, condemning them for their actions. But the chief of the **shepherds** will make those who have tended the **sheep** well rejoice and inherit life and rest. . . .

The good shepherd lays down his life for the sheep (10:11). He also said, **I have other sheep and I must bring them also. So there will be one flock, one shepherd. For this reason the Father loves me, because I lay down my life** for the sheep (10:16–17). Again, he said, *I am the door of the sheep; if anyone enters by me, he will live, and will go in and out and find pasture* (10:9). You **shepherds**! Imitate this diligent **shepherd**, the leader of the **flock**, who cared so much for his **sheep**! He brought near those that were far away, brought back the wanderers, cared for the sick, strengthened the weak, bound up those that were broken, and guarded those that were healthy (cf. Ezek 34:2–4). He delivered himself up on behalf of his **sheep**.

He chose and instructed brilliant leaders, delivered the **sheep** into their hands, and gave them authority over his whole *flock*. He said to Simon Peter, *Feed my sheep, my lambs and my ewes for me* (20:15–17). Simon tended his **sheep**, and when his time was fulfilled he delivered the **flock** to you and departed. You also ought to tend and lead them well. For the **shepherd** who cares for his **sheep** engages in no other work. He does not establish a vineyard, or plant gardens, or fall into the troubles of this world. We have never seen a **shepherd** who abandoned his **sheep** in the field to become a merchant, nor one who became a farmer and allowed his **sheep** to wander. If he abandons his **sheep** and does these things, he delivers his **flock** to **wolves**.

(15) John Chrysostom

It is a great matter, my beloved, a great matter to have authority over the church. This is a matter that requires much wisdom and as much courage as what Christ speaks about here: that a man should **lay down** his **life for the sheep** (10:11). He should never leave them alone and naked. He should nobly stand up against the **wolf** (10:12). In these ways the **shepherd** distinguishes himself from the **hireling** (10:12). The **hireling** is always on the lookout for his own safety and does not care for the **sheep**. The **shepherd** always seeks the safety of the **sheep**, even neglecting his own safety. . . .

For this reason, Ezekiel of old rebuked the leaders of Israel and said, *O you shepherds of Israel! Do the shepherds feed themselves? Do not shepherds feed the sheep?* (Ezek 34:2 LXX). They did the opposite, which is the worst sort of evil and the cause of all other evils. This is why he says that they have not *brought back the strayed*, or *sought the lost*, or *bound up the crippled*, or *healed the sick* (Ezek 34:4). They fed themselves and not the **sheep**.

In another passage, Paul clearly makes the same point, saying, *They all look after their own interests, not those of Jesus Christ* (Phil 2:21). Again, he says, *Let no one seek his own good, but the good of his neighbor* (1 Cor 10:24). But Christ distinguishes himself from both. From those who came to spoil, he distinguishes himself by saying, *I came that they may have life, and have it abundantly* (10:10). From those who overlooked the sheep being snatched away by the **wolves**, he distinguishes himself by not abandoning them, but by **laying down** his **life for** them so that the **sheep** do not die.

(16) Augustine of Hippo

Who is this **hireling** (10:12)? There are of course some in the church who have been placed in charge, of whom the apostle Paul says: *They all look after their own interests, not those of Jesus Christ* (Phil 2:21). What does this mean, *they all look after their own interests*? They are not freely devoted to Christ, and do not *look after* the *interests* of God for his own sake; they strive for temporary delights, they covet after money, they seek humanly bestowed honors. When leaders love these things and serve God for the sake of these things, whoever this person is, he is a **hireling**. Don't let him think that he's among the brethren. Of such people, the Lord said: *Truly, I say to you, they have received their reward* (Matt 6:5). Listen also to what the apostle Paul said of Saint Timothy: *I hope in the Lord Jesus to send Timothy to you soon, so that I may be cheered by news of you. I have no one like him, who will be genuinely anxious for your welfare. They all look after their own interests, not those of Jesus Christ* (Phil 2:19–21). The **shepherd** here groans about the **hirelings**; he sought someone who sincerely favored the flock of Christ, but from all those around him at that time, he found none. It wasn't as if there was no one in the church of Christ who was genuinely concerned for the flock except the apostle Paul and Timothy; rather, it happened that at the time he sent Timothy, he had none of his brethren around him, but only **hirelings**, *all looking after their own interests, not those of Jesus Christ*. Although he himself was genuinely concerned for the flock, he preferred to send his brother and stay among the **hirelings**.

We too may discover **hirelings**, but only the Lord examines them. The one who inspects their hearts examines them, but sometimes they become known to us as well. There's a good reason the Lord said of the wolves: *You will know them by their fruits* (Matt 6:16). Temptations test many, and then their thoughts are revealed; even so, many still lie hidden. Brothers and sisters, the Lord's flock has leaders, and it has **hirelings**. Those leaders of the church, who are also brethren, are **shepherds**. But if they are **shepherds**, how is there one **shepherd**, unless it's because all the other **shepherds** are members of a single **shepherd**, to whom each of the **sheep** belongs? They are also members of him, together as one **sheep**, because *as a sheep he was led to the slaughter* (Isa 53:7).

But listen: the **hirelings** are necessary! Of course, many in the church pursue earthly gain, but still proclaim Christ. Through them the voice of Christ is heard, and the sheep follow not the **hireling**, but the voice of the shepherd through the **hireling**. Listen to the **hirelings**, pointed out by the Lord himself: *The scribes and the Pharisees sit on Moses's seat; so practice and observe whatever they tell you, but not what they do* (Matt 23:2–3). What else was he saying except: "Listen to the voice of the shepherd through the **hirelings**"? They teach the law of God by sitting in Moses's chair; therefore God teaches through them. If they should wish to teach their own ideas, don't listen to them and don't do what they say. Surely they *look after their own interests, not those of Jesus Christ*; nevertheless, no **hireling** has dared to say to the people of Christ: "Look after your own interests, not those of Jesus Christ." He doesn't preach from Christ's seat the sins he commits; he does harm by the evil he does, not by the good things he speaks. Pluck grapes, but beware of thorns! . . .

Therefore the seat of Moses is the grapevine; the actions of the Pharisees are thorns. True teaching by wicked men are sprouts among hedges, clusters of grapes among thorns. Harvest carefully, lest while you seek fruit, you cut your hand; and when you hear someone saying good things, do not imitate them in doing bad things. Do as they say—harvest grapes—not as they do—watch out for thorns! Hear the voice of the shepherd even through the **hirelings**, but don't be a **hireling**, since you are members of the **shepherd**. . . .

Who is a **hireling**? Who **sees the wolf coming** and flees (10:11)? The one who *looks after his own interests, not those of Jesus Christ* (Phil 2:21); the one who does not dare to openly accuse a sinner. Behold, someone has sinned; he has sinned gravely. He should be rebuked and excommunicated. But if he is excommunicated, he will be an enemy, he will plot against you, he will harm you whenever he can. Now the one who *looks after his own interests, not those of Jesus Christ*, will remain silent so that he doesn't lose what he's after (the benefit of human friendship), or run up against the troubles of human hostility. He remains silent and doesn't rebuke him. Look, the **wolf** has the **sheep** by the throat; the devil has seduced a believer into adultery. You remain silent; you make no protest. O **hireling**! You have **seen the wolf coming** and you have **fled**!

(17) *Apostolic Constitutions*

Draw back the one who is excommunicated; that is, do not allow the one who is in sin and has been cast down in rebuke to remain outside. Rather, welcoming and drawing him back, restore him to the flock, that is, to the people of the spotless church (cf. Eph 5:27). Seek after the lost; that is, do not allow someone who despairs of their salvation because of the multitude of their transgressions to utterly perish. Seek after the one who has become sleepy, sluggish, and lazy, forgetful of his own life because of the weight of sleep, and standing at a great distance from his own flock, so as to become food for **wolves**. Seek for him! Draw him back with warnings! Exhort him to beware; implant hope! Do not agree with him in saying what others have said: *Our sins are upon us, and in them we waste away; how will we live?* (cf. Ezek 33:10).

So if it is possible, let the bishop make the transgression his own; let him say to the sinner: "If only you will return, I will take upon myself your death, just as Christ took upon himself my death and the death of all." For **the good shepherd lays down his life for the sheep. He who is a hireling and not a shepherd, whose own the sheep are not, sees the wolf coming**, that is the devil, **and leaves the sheep and flees; and the wolf snatches them** (10:11–12). We ought to understand that God is merciful to those who have sinned, and he promised repentance with an oath. The one who sins and is unaware of God's promise about repentance, who does not know about God's patience and slowness to anger, and who is ignorant of the holy Scriptures which proclaim this—which he has never learned from you!—this one will perish by his despair. But you, like a tender **shepherd** and a zealous herdsman, seek after the full number of your flock. Seek after the lost, just as the Lord God, our good Father, has sent his Son, the **good shepherd** and Savior, Jesus our teacher, and has commanded him to *leave the ninety-nine on the mountains, and go after the one which is lost, and when he has found it, to lay it on his shoulders*, and to carry it into the flock, *rejoicing* that he had found that which was lost (cf. Matt 18:12–13; Luke 15:4–6). In the same way, O bishop, be obedient and *seek the lost*, correct the *strayed*, and *bring back* the excommunicated (cf. Ezek 34:16).

10:15 "I lay down my life for the sheep."

---

(18) Cyril of Alexandria

Jesus sets forth the way in which one knows whether one is a good shepherd; while fighting for the salvation of the **sheep**, one ought not to shrink back from offering his own **life**. This, of course, is what Christ did. The one inclined toward sin has moved away from a love of God, and for this reason has been removed from the holy and divine fold (I am speaking of the regions of paradise). Having been distressed by this misfortune, he has been ensnared by the devil (who has deceived him to sin), by death which has arisen from his sin, and by truly bitter and clever **wolves**. But when Christ was received as the good shepherd over all, he fought with the band of savage beasts and **laid down his life** for us (10:15). He *endured the cross* (Heb 12:2) for us in order that by death he might destroy death. He was condemned for us in order that he might deliver us all from the condemnation we deserve for our sins. He abolished the tyranny of sin through faith, *nailing to* his *cross the bond which stood against us*, as it is written (Col 2:14). So while the father of sin placed us in *Sheol like sheep*, handing us over to *death* as our *shepherd*, according to what is said in the Psalms (Ps 49:14), the truly good shepherd died for us. He delivered us from the darkness of death so that he might prepare to gather us together into the heavenly choirs. Instead of the regions which lie in the bottomless depths and the far-reaching places of the sea, he will even give us rooms above with the Father (cf. John 14:2). This is why he says to you somewhere, *Fear not little flock, for it is your Father's good pleasure to give you the kingdom* (Luke 12:32).

(19) Peter Chrysologus

The good shepherd, he says, **lays down his life for the sheep** (10:11). The power of love makes a man courageous, because true love does not consider what is difficult, harsh, burdensome, or deadly. What sword, what wound, what punishment, what death is able to separate true love? Love is an impenetrable breastplate. It repels the spear, rebuffs the sword, scoffs at danger and ridicules death. If there is love, it conquers all.

Let us inquire whether that death of the **shepherd** is a benefit to the **sheep**. Such a death abandons the **sheep**! It hands over the defenseless flock to the **wolves** (10:12) and thus deserts the beloved herd to the jaws of wild animals. It surrenders them to plundering and exposes them to death. Even the death of Christ himself demonstrates this. In fact, when he **laid down his life for his sheep** (10:11), he allowed himself to be killed by the fury of the Jews. His **sheep** have been torn apart by the attacks of the gentiles, who act like **thieves** (10:8). They are slaughtered in prisons as if closed up in the caves of **robbers** (10:8). They are torn to pieces by ceaseless persecutors who act like raging **wolves**. They are seized upon by heretics who act like wild dogs with raging teeth.

The slain choir of the apostles demonstrates this; the blood of the martyr proclaims this throughout the whole world; the members of Christ given to the beasts, devoured by the flames, plunged into rivers—all openly demonstrate this. Certainly, just as the death of the **shepherd** brought all this in, so also would his life have been able to prevent it. Therefore, does the **shepherd** prove his love for you by his death? When he sees a crisis threatening the **sheep**, and is unable to defend the flock, does he prefer to die before seeing any evil come upon his **sheep**?

What should we make of this? Life himself cannot die unless he is willing. Who could take away life from the giver of life if he were unwilling? He himself said, **I have power to lay down** my life, **and I have power to take it again; no one takes it from me** (10:18). Therefore the one who permitted himself to be killed, even though he could not die, willed to die.

So, let us investigate what power and reasonableness there is in this love, what cause there is for this death, what benefit there is in this passion. Clearly there is a sure power, true reasonableness, an evident cause, a clear benefit with such bloodshed. By the death of this one **shepherd**, a unique power burst forth. By his death for the **sheep**, the **shepherd** ran to meet what was threatening the **sheep**, so that by the plan of letting himself be seized he might seize the devil, the author of death itself. Having been defeated, he might conquer; having been killed, he might make retribution; and by dying for his **sheep**, he might open the way for them to conquer death. . . .

With such a pattern the **shepherd** went before the **sheep**. He did not withdraw from the **sheep**, nor did he give them to the **wolves**. Rather, he delivered the **wolves** to them and enabled them to pick out the **robbers** for themselves so that, although they were killed, they would live, and although torn apart, they would rise again, and although stained with their own blood, they would gleam with royal purple and shine forth with snow-white fleece. So, when the **good shepherd laid down his life for the sheep** (10:11), he did not lose it. In this way, he held on to them rather than abandon them. Nor in this way did he desert them, but rather summoned them. By taking on human nature and walking the path of death he called them and led them to life-giving **pastures** (10:9).

But someone says, "When will this happen? Look at the **sheep** now, that is, the apostles, the prophets, the martyrs and confessors. They all lie in their tombs! Being torn to pieces, they are scattered throughout the world; covered in blood, they are closed in their foul sepulchers." But who doubts that the slain martyrs will rise again, that they will live and reign, since Christ, himself having been killed, has arisen and lives and reigns? Hear the voice of this *shepherd: My sheep hear my voice and they follow me* (10:27). It must be that those who **follow**ed him to death will **follow** him to life. Those who accompanied him to situations of cruelty will accompany him to honor. And those who stepped forth to share his passion share in his glory.

10:15 "as the Father knows me and I know the Father"

---

(20) Cyril of Alexandria

I do not think that any living person with a sound mind would say that they are able to obtain a **know**ledge of Christ as God the Father had of his Son. For the Father alone **knows** his own offspring and is **know**n only by his own offspring. As the Savior himself says, *No one knows the Son except the Father and no one knows* what *the Father* is *except the Son* (Matt 11:27). That the Father is God and the Son is also "truly God," we both know and have believed.[6] But understanding what the ineffable nature is in its very essence is utterly beyond comprehension, both to us and to other rational creatures. How then will we **know** the Son **as the Father knows** him (10:15)? We must consider how it is that he boldly affirms that he will **know** us and be **known** by us, just as he **knows** the **Father** and the **Father knows** him. . . .

I think that by these words Jesus speaks of **know**ledge not simply as familiarity with something, but rather as an intimacy of birth and nature, or through participation in grace and honor. It is the custom of the Greeks to say that they **know** not only their relatives, but also their actual brothers and sisters. The divine Scripture also understands **knowledge** as intimacy, as we will see. For Christ somewhere speaks about those who were in no way intimate with him, saying *On that day*, obviously meaning the day of judgment, *many will say to me, "Lord, Lord, did we not do many mighty works and cast out demons in your name?" Then will I declare to them, "I never knew you"* (Matt 7:22–23). If **know**ledge means for us only familiarity, how can the one who has *all things open and laid bare to his eyes*, as it is written (Heb 4:13), and *knowest all things before they be* (Sus 42), not **know** any living thing? Therefore it is entirely unreasonable, even impious, to think that the Lord does not **know** anyone in this sense. Rather, we think he means that they have in no way been brought into an intimate relationship with him. "For," he says, "I do not know you to have been lovers of virtue, or to have honored my word, or to have united yourselves to me through good deeds."

Similar to this idea is what God says to the all-wise Moses when he declares, *I know you above all men, and you have found favor in my sight* (Exod 33:12 LXX). Put another way: "You, above all others, have been placed in an intimate relationship with me and I have brought you great favor." When we say such things, we do not preclude the idea of **know**ledge entailing familiarity, but we understand it here in a way more fitting to our comprehension of these texts. Therefore he says, **I know my own and** am **known** by **my own, as the Father knows me and I know the Father** (10:14–15). Put another way, "I will enter into an intimate relationship with my sheep, and my sheep will be in an intimate relationship with me, in the same way in which the Father is intimate with me and I am intimate with the Father." Just as God the Father **knows** his own truly-begotten Son and the fruit of his essence, so also the Son, being God and begotten of the **Father**, truly **knows** the **Father**. In the same way, we are brought into an intimate relationship with him and consider ourselves his offspring and are called his children, as he says, *Behold, I and the children whom God has given me* (Isa 8:17). . . .

The Son is intimate with the Father, and because they share the same nature, the Father is intimate with the Son. So also, we are intimate with Christ and he with us, having been made man. Through him as our mediator, we are united to the Father. Christ is some sort of connecting link between the loftiest Godhead and humanity, having in himself both natures, and joining together in himself those separate things. As God by nature, he is united with God the Father; as a true man he is united to our humanity.

6. A reference to the Nicene Creed.

10:16 "one flock, one shepherd"

---

(21) Cyprian of Carthage

When the Lord describes unity for us, he states that it comes from divine authority, saying, *I and the Father are one* (10:30). He brings his church back to this unity and says again, **There will be one flock and one shepherd** (10:16). If the **flock** is one, how can someone be considered part of the **flock** who is not numbered among the **flock**? When the true **shepherd** remains and his ordained successor presides in the church of God, how can someone be considered a **shepherd** who is hostile and impious, succeeding no one and starting out all on his own? He is an enemy to the peace of the Lord and the divine unity, and does not reside in the house of God, that is, in the church of God, in which only the like-minded and united reside, as the Holy Spirit spoke in the Psalms: *God makes those who are united to dwell in a house* (Ps 67:6 Vulgate).

(22) Theodore of Mopsuestia

And I have other sheep, that are not of this fold; I must bring them also, and they will heed my voice. So there shall be one flock, one shepherd (10:16). Here Christ points to those among the gentiles who will believe, namely, those among the pagans and Jews who were ordained to gather together into one church and to recognize one shepherd and Lord, who is Christ. This has now happened!

10:17–18 "No one takes it from me. . . . I have power to take it again."

---

(23) Hilary of Poitiers

The apostle often says that God the Father raised Christ from the dead (cf. Acts 2:24; Rom 10:9). But this is not incompatible with what the apostle says elsewhere, or with the faith of the gospel where the great Lord himself states, **For this reason the Father loves me, because I lay down my life, that I may take it again. No one takes it from me, but I lay it down of my own accord. I have power to lay it down, and I have power to take it again; this charge I have received from my Father** (10:17–18). Elsewhere, when he had been asked by another to reveal a sign about himself in order to bring them to faith, the Lord speaks about the temple of his body: *Destroy this temple, and in three days I will raise it up* (2:19). Indeed, by the **power** of **taking up** his life and by the power of raising the temple, the Lord teaches that he himself is God, and that the resurrection is his own; yet, he refers this entirely to the authority of the Father's **charge**.

The apostle does not contradict this by preaching Christ as *the power of God and the wisdom of God* (1 Cor 1:24), referring all the magnificence of his work to the glory of the Father. For whatever Christ does, God's power and wisdom does, and whatever God's power and wisdom does, without a doubt God does, of whom Christ is both wisdom and power. In short, by the work of God, Christ now has been raised from the dead, because he performed the works of God the Father himself with a nature indistinguishable from God's. Our faith is in the God of the resurrection, who raised Christ from the dead.

(24) John Chrysostom

No one takes it from me, but I lay it down of my own accord. I have power to lay it down, and I have power to take it again (10:18). Since they often wanted to kill him, Christ says, "Unless I am willing, your labor is in vain." From the first reality, death, he proves the second, the resurrection. This is the marvelous and unexpected thing: both occurred in a new and unusual way. Let us look closely at what he says: **I have power**, he says, **to lay down my life**. But who does not have **power to lay down** his own **life**? Anyone who wants to can kill himself; but this is not what he means. What does he mean then? **I have** such **power to lay it down** that no one can take it from me unwillingly. This kind of **power** does not belong to anyone. For the only **power** we have is the **power** to kill ourselves. If we fall among some who plot to kill us, we no longer have the **power** to lay it down or not. They can take it even if we are unwilling. This was not so with Christ, for even when others plotted against him, he had the **power** not to **lay it down**. So after he said, **No one takes it from me**, he then adds, **I have power to lay down my life**, that is, "I alone have the power to lay it down." Such **power** certainly does not belong to us, for there are many others who have the **power** to take it from us.

He did not say this from the beginning, for that claim would not have been believed. Previously, his actions provided a witness: they often plotted against him but were unable to seize him because he escaped from their hands many times. Only later did he say, **No one takes it from me**. If this is true, then the other claim follows, that he came to his death willingly. Likewise, if this is true, then the next claim also stands, that he can **take it again** whenever he wants to. If his dying was a greater thing than any other human could do, then do not have doubts about the resurrection. Since he alone had the **power** to let go of his life, he indicates that, from the same **power**, he is able to **take it again**. Do you see how he proves the second claim from the first, and demonstrates that his resurrection from death is indisputable?

(25) Cyril of Alexandria

Christ declares that he is loved by God the **Father**, not only because he **lays down his life**, but because he **lays it down, that** he **may take it again** (10:17). Of course this point, most of all, becomes the basis for the magnitude of Christ's blessings bestowed upon us. If he had only died, but not risen again, what would have been the advantage? How would he have appeared to benefit our nature if he remained dead with us, being tyrannized with all the others by the bonds of death and its imposing corruption? But since he **laid it down that** he **may take it again**, he thereby saved our entire nature. He destroyed the grip of death and will show us forth as a new creation. . . .

No one takes it from me, but I lay it down of my own accord. I have power to lay it down, and I have power to take it again; this charge I have received from my Father (10:18). In this passage, Jesus teaches that he was not only the good shepherd who faced danger for his sheep, but is also God by nature. He would only have undergone death willingly because he possessed the God-befitting **power** of this divine plan which was so very beneficial to us. The arrangement of his discourse teaches the Jews this as well, that they would never overcome him if he were unwilling. Not only did he say, **I have power** to **lay down my life**, but he said **I have power** with respect to both death *and* resurrection. In this way, this ability and activity might not seem to belong to someone else, as if it was granted to him like an assistant or servant in office. So he demonstrates that his ability to exercise **power** over the very bonds of death, and easily to change the nature of things however he wants, was a product of his own nature. This, of course, is truly a distinct attribute of one who is God by nature. This is what he wanted to demonstrate by saying, **I have power to lay it down, and I have power to take it again**. He was not given a command like a servant or an assistant, nor was he moved by necessity, nor was he compelled by someone else; rather, he did this willingly.

This charge I have received from my Father (10:18). He said this so that no one might say that the Father is unable to take away the Son's life without his will, and so introduce dissension and discord into the one Godhead of the Father and Son. By saying, **I have received a charge**, he demonstrates that the Father agrees and assents to this, and confesses that they come to it with one mind, although he is the will of the Father (cf. John 6:38–39). This is in harmony with his incarnation. By saying that he received, by way of a **charge**, an idea that seems right to the Father, he does not make himself inferior to the Father (since he is God by nature), but he retains what is fitting for his humanity. Clearly, he suggests that he is the prophet about whom the Father said, *He shall speak whatever I command him* (Deut 18:18 LXX), saying that his shared will with God the Father has been received as a **charge**. He said this to the Jews so that they would not think that he speaks contrary to the commands of the Father.

John 10:22–42

[22]It was the feast of the Dedication at Jerusalem; [23]it was winter, and Jesus was walking in the temple, in the portico of Solomon. [24]So the Jews gathered round him and said to him, "How long will you keep us in suspense? If you are the Christ, tell us plainly." [25]Jesus answered them, "I told you, and you do not believe. The works that I do in my Father's name, they bear witness to me; [26]but you do not believe, because you do not belong to my sheep. [27]My sheep hear my voice, and I know them, and they follow me; [28]and I give them eternal life, and they shall never perish, and no one shall snatch them out of my hand. [29]My Father, who has given them to me, is greater than all, and no one is able to snatch them out of the Father's hand. [30]I and the Father are one."

[31]The Jews took up stones again to stone him. [32]Jesus answered them, "I have

shown you many good works from the Father; for which of these do you stone me?" [33]The Jews answered him, "It is not for a good work that we stone you but for blasphemy; because you, being a man, make yourself God." [34]Jesus answered them, "Is it not written in your law, 'I said, you are gods'? [35]If he called them gods to whom the word of God came (and scripture cannot be broken), [36]do you say of him whom the Father consecrated and sent into the world, 'You are blaspheming,' because I said, 'I am the Son of God'? [37]If I am not doing the works of my Father, then do not believe me; [38]but if I do them, even though you do not believe me, believe the works, that you may know and understand that the Father is in me and I am in the Father." [39]Again they tried to arrest him, but he escaped from their hands.

[40]He went away again across the Jordan to the place where John at first baptized, and there he remained. [41]And many came to him; and they said, "John did no sign, but everything that John said about this man was true." [42]And many believed in him there.

10:27-28 "My sheep hear my voice. . . . I give them eternal life."

---

(26) Novatian

If Christ is just a man, how does he say, **I know them and they follow me; and I give them eternal life, and they shall never perish** (10:27–28)? In fact, since every man has been bound by the laws of death, and therefore cannot protect himself forever, to a much greater degree will he be unable to protect someone else forever. Yet Christ promises that he will **give eternal** salvation. If he does not **give** it, he is lying; if he does **give** it, he is God. But Christ does not deceive, for he **gives** what he promises. Therefore, he who extends **eternal** salvation is God; whereas man, who cannot protect himself, will be unable to grant salvation to another.

(27) Gregory of Nazianzus

Do you offer yourselves to God and to us as a well-shepherded flock, having been settled in a green pasture and nourished by the waters of rest? Do you know your **shepherd** well? Are you known by him? Do you freely follow when he calls you as a **shepherd** through the door, not following a stranger climbing into the fold like a robber and a traitor? Do you avoid listening to a strange *voice* (10:16) which would take you away by stealth and scatter you from the truth on mountains, deserts, precipices, and places which the Lord does not visit? Do you avoid the **voice** which would lead you away from sound faith in the Father, the Son, and the Holy Spirit, the one power and Godhead, whose **voice** is always heard by **my sheep**? May they always hear it! This other **voice**, with deceitful and corrupt words, seeks to tear them from their true shepherd. May we all, both shepherd and sheep, be kept from this, as from a poisonous and deadly pasture; may we guide and be guided far from it, that we may all be one in Christ Jesus our Lord, now and in the heavenly rest which is to come. To him be the glory and the might forever and ever. Amen.

(28) Cyril of Alexandria

Christ says: **My sheep follow me** (10:27). Those who are obedient and **follow** after the footsteps of Christ, by some God-given grace, no longer serve the shadows of the law, but follow Christ's commands. **Follow**ing his word, they will ascend, through grace, to the honor of Christ, being called *sons of God* (Matt 5:9). When Christ ascends to the heavens, they also will **follow** him. And he says that to those who **follow** him, the reward and gift of **eternal life** (10:28) will be given. They will avoid death, corruption, and the anguish which is brought by the judge upon the offenders. By giving **life**, he shows that he is **life** by nature. He supplies this himself and is not given it from someone else. And we think that **eternal life** is not that length of days which all will participate in after the resurrection, both good and evil, but rather a continuation in joy.

10:28–30 "No one is able to snatch them. . . . I and the Father are one."

---

(29) John Chrysostom

Is it because of the Father's power that **no one snatches them** away, while Christ is weak and powerless to guard them? Not at all! Rather, you must learn that when he says, **The Father, who has given them to me** (10:29), it is for their sake so that they might not say that he is opposed to God. By saying that **no one snatches them out of *my* hand** (10:29), he indicates that his **hand** and the Father's **hand** are one. . . . Then, so that you will not think that he is weak, or that the **sheep** are safe only because of the Father's power, he adds: **I and the Father are one** (10:30). It was as if he had said, "I did not say that **no one snatches them** because of the Father, as if I was too weak to retain them myself. **I and the Father are one.**" He is speaking here about power, for his entire discourse was about this. If they share the same power, they obviously share the same essence as well. . . .

If **no one snatches them** from Christ's hand, simply because the Father empowered him, then it would have been strange to say what followed: **I and the Father are one.** If the Son were inferior to the Father, then these words would be utterly audacious, for they declare nothing other than an equality of power.

(30) Theodore of Mopsuestia

No one shall snatch them out of my hand (10:28), that is, it is impossible for them to be separated from me. He meant to clarify these words to his listeners when he said, **My Father, who has given them to me, is greater than all, and no one is able to snatch them**

out of the Father's hand (10:29). He pointed to the Father as the cause of all this so as to absolutely confirm his statement to those who were not persuaded. His argument seemed very weak because he had said that no one snatches them from *his* hand; therefore, he publicly proclaimed the strength of the Father and his greatness over all by adding **no one is able to snatch them out of the *Father's* hand** (because everything is inferior to the Father).

Then, in order to show why his words, **no one is able to snatch them out of the Father's hand**, are necessary for the argument, he says, **I and the Father are one** (10:30). After saying that no one can snatch them from my hand, nor out of the Father's hand because he is greater than all, he added appropriately, **I and the Father are one.** What he means is this: "Since I am greater than all, like the Father is, and since I am the Maker of creation, like he is, and since I created with him, I am therefore equal to him in strength. We **are one** in greatness and in the power of strength. This is why **no one can snatch them out of my hand** (10:28) or **out of the Father's hand** (10:29)."

(31) Hilary of Poitiers

No one snatches them out of *his* hand (10:28) because he has received from the **Father** that which is **greater than all**. What does he mean by the opposite declaration that **no one shall snatch them** again **from *the Father's*** hand? The Son's hand received them from the Father, and the **Father's hand** gave them to the Son. So how is it that that which cannot be snatched from the Son's hand cannot be snatched from the **Father's hand**? If you want to know, pay attention: **I and the Father are one** (10:30). The Son's **hand** is the **Father's hand**, for the divine nature does not deteriorate or cease to be itself when it is begotten. Nor does such a nature prevent us from understanding his begetting, because his begetting allowed nothing foreign to enter into its nature. So he mentions the Son's **hand** and the **Father's hand** in order that we can understand the power of his nature through a bodily analogy: the holy nature and power of the Father is in the Son. Finally, so that through the sacred act of begetting you might know the truth of the indistinguishable nature of God, he says: **I and the Father are one** (10:30). He said that they **are one** so that we might know that they are neither separated nor isolated; no second nature came into being through that unique begetting and generation.

(32) Augustine of Hippo

What does this mean, **No one shall snatch them out of *my* hand**, and **no one shall snatch them out of *my Father's* hand** (10:28–29)? Are we to think that there is one **hand** of the Father and one of the Son, or perhaps that the Son himself is the **hand** of his Father? If we understand **hand** to mean power, the power of the Father and the Son is one, for their divinity is one. If, however, we understand **hand** in the way the prophet says, *To whom has the arm of the Lord been revealed?* (Isa 53:1), then the very **hand** of the Father is the Son. This is not to say that God has a human form, or that he has bodily members, but rather that all things have been made by him. For people are accustomed to say that other people are their **hands**, through whom they accomplish their desires. Sometimes the same is said of a person's work; what is made by one's **hand** is called one's **hand**, just as it's also said that we recognize our **hand**, when we recognize what we have written.

Therefore, since there are certainly many ways in which we can speak of a human **hand**, where indeed a **hand** is counted among the members of the body, how much more must it be understood when the "**hand** of God" is read, for whom there is no bodily form.

For this reason, it is better that we understand the **hand** of the Father and the Son here, to mean the power of the Father and Son. Otherwise, if we understand the **hand** of the Father to mean the Son himself, a carnal thought might begin to look for a son of the Son himself, who would likewise be thought to be the **hand** of Christ. Therefore, **no one shall snatch them out of my Father's hand** means "no one shall snatch them from me."

10:30 "I and the Father are one."

---

(33) Tertullian of Carthage

We must still take care to refute our opponents' arguments when they select certain texts from the Scriptures to support their opinions. They refuse to consider other texts that support the rule of faith and even confirm the unity of the Godhead and the nature of the "one rule" (monarchy).[7] While they cling to nothing from the Old Testament other than *I am God, and there is no other besides me* (Isa 45:5), so now in the gospel they uphold the response of the Lord to Philip: **I and the Father are one** (10:30), and *He who has seen me has seen the Father* (14:9), and *I am in the Father and the Father in me* (14:10). They want the entirety of both testaments to yield to these three verses, when instead we ought to understand these few verses in light of the more numerous. This is typical of all heretics. Since they are able to find only a few verses in an abundance of passages, they defend these very few against the many and support the later texts against the earlier. However, the rule of interpretation established from the beginning for every situation prescribes what to do with earlier and later texts, and certainly what to do with fewer texts. . . .

Concerning his sheep and the claim that no one would **snatch them out of his hand** (10:28), Jesus says: **My Father, who has given them to me, is greater than all** (10:29), and then, **I and the Father are one** (10:30). Here, then, is where the fools—no, the blind!—wish to take a stand: first, they fail to see that **I and the Father** indicates two persons; second, they fail to see that the plural **are** is not used about just one person; and last, they fail to see that he says **are one** "thing," not **are one** "person."[8] If it had said, **are one** "person," he would have been able to help out their case, for one "person" would seem to be an indication of a singular number. Here, though, he speaks of two persons using a masculine subject, but he

7. Tertullian is arguing against the false teaching of "Monarchianism" (or "modalism"), which affirms God's unity while denying any distinction within the Godhead. For them, the Father and the Son are not two distinct persons of the Trinity, but rather the same person, expressed in different, temporary "modes" or "faces."

8. Tertullian is making a distinction between a neuter noun and a masculine noun, as he makes clearer in the argument to follow.

uses the neuter word for **one**, which does not relate to singularity of number, but to a unity of being, to likeness, to intimacy, to the Father's love for the Son, and to the obedience of the Son who voluntarily follows the Father's will. In saying **I and the Father are one**, he makes it clear that those whom he has equated and joined together are two separate entities. . . . So all along, the Lord continued to lead them to the conclusion that while the Father and the Son were **one** in power, they should still be believed as two persons. Otherwise, it would be impossible to believe in the Son if they did not believe there were two persons.

(34) Hippolytus of Rome

But if Noetus[9] says: "Jesus himself said, **I and the Father are one**" (10:30), let him understand its meaning and learn that Jesus did not say: **I and the Father** *am* **one**, but **are one**. The word **are** is not used in reference to one thing, but two. It indicates two persons, but one power. Jesus himself made this clear when he spoke to the Father concerning his disciples: *The glory which thou hast given me I have given to them, that they may be one even as we are one, I in them and thou in me, that they may become perfectly one, so that the world may know that thou hast sent me and hast loved them even as thou hast loved me* (17:22–23).

(35) Hilary of Poitiers

In my judgment, there is no doubt that the phrase **I and the Father are one** (10:30) speaks about the nature of Christ's begetting. The Jews had been accusing him by saying that he, being a man, made himself God. His answer proves that when he said **I and the Father are one** (10:30), he declared himself the Son of God, first by name, then by nature, and finally by his begetting. The words **I** and **Father** are names of things that exist. **One** is certainly a profession of nature, because what is in **one** is no different from what is in the other; however, **are** does not allow a confusion of the two. Where the phrase **are one** does not allow a confusion, his begetting proves that they are one. This entire truth is what Christ, sanctified by the Father, professes by calling himself the Son of God. His saying **I and the Father are one** (10:30) confirms his profession as the Son of God, for the nature of the offspring can have no other nature than that from which it is born.

(36) Theodoret of Cyrus

We confess that God is one. We confess that the divinity of the Father and Son are one. No one ever denies that the Father is greater than the Son: not because of another essence, or because of their difference, but because the very name of Father is greater than that of the

---

9. Noetus was a third-century teacher who denied the distinction of the persons of the Godhead, at times using John 10:30 as proof.

Son.[10] Those who hold to a blasphemous and corrupt interpretation claim that Jesus said **I and the Father are one** (10:30) because of the unity of their sentiment and thought. We, as catholics, have all condemned their foolish and pathetic way of thinking. They think that discord and disagreement can exist between God the Father Almighty and his Son, like it does with mortal humans who disagree, quarrel and then make up. It is quite absurd even to consider such a thing. We believe and affirm the idea that the holy words **I and the Father are one** (10:30) indicate the unity of their essence, which is the same in both the Father and the Son.

(37) Cyril of Alexandria

We say that the Son and the **Father are one** (10:30), not confusing their uniqueness by that number, as some do who say that the Father and the Son are the same person. We believe that the Father and the Son each exist individually, and that they share a unity of essence. We also know that they have **one** power which is identical in both.

I and the Father are one. By the word **one**, the sameness of essence is signified. But by saying **we are**, he divides them into two, and yet ties them together into one Godhead. Clearly, in opposition to the Arians, we must understand that in saying **I and the Father are one**, he does not indicate merely the declaration of a common will, but a unity of essence. Even the Jews understood that he was calling himself God and equal to the Father. Even Christ did not deny that this is what he meant.

10:31–38 "Is it not written in your law, 'I said, you are gods'?"

---

(38) Novatian

Christ boldly refuted his adversaries by the example and witness of the Scriptures, saying, **If he called them gods to whom the word of God came (and scripture cannot be broken), do you say of him whom the Father consecrated and sent into the world, "You are blaspheming," because I said, "I am the Son of God"?** (10:35–36). In saying this, he did not deny that he is God. On the contrary, he confirms that he is God. Since those **to whom the word of God came** are, without a doubt, said to be **gods** (Ps 82:6), how much more is this man God, who is found to be better than all these. Nonetheless, he appropriately refuted their callous blasphemy with a proper argument. He wanted himself to be understood as God, as the **Son of God**, but he did not want to be understood as the **Father** himself. So he said that he had been **sent**, and taught that he had **shown many works from the Father** (10:32). By these he wanted himself to be understood not as the Father, but as the Son. This is what he refers to in the final part of his defense, when he mentions the Son rather than the Father: **Do you say "You are blaspheming," because I said, "I am the *Son* of God"?**

---

10. Theodoret understands the word **Father** to indicate a "source" for the **Son**.

(10:36). As for the charge of blasphemy, he says that he is the **Son**, not the **Father**. Yet regarding his divinity, he says, **I and the Father are one** (10:30), proving himself to be the Son and God. Therefore, he is God; but he is God as the **Son**, not the **Father**.

(39) Hilary of Poitiers

The reason for Christ's reply in these verses is found in the charge of blasphemy brought against him. It was regarded as a crime, that he, being a man, made himself God. However, he was accused of making himself God because of what he had said: **I and the Father are one** (10:30). Therefore, having indicated that he and the Father were one, and that he shared in the divine nature even at his begetting, he first refutes the absurd charge about why he, a man, would make himself God. The law had conferred this title upon holy men, and the indissoluble word of God had confirmed the bestowal of such a name (cf. Ps 82:6). Therefore, how did Jesus, whom the Father had sanctified and sent into this world, blaspheme by confessing himself to be the Son of God when the indissoluble word of God had established through the law the name "gods" for some? So he, being a man, is not guilty of making himself God, since the law has called other people "gods" as well. If others may use this name without blasphemy, so also may the one whom the Father sanctified. . . .

Therefore, the accusation of blasphemy—that he, being a man, makes himself God— fails. The word of God has bestowed this name upon many people, and the one who was sanctified and sent by the Father did nothing other than profess that he is the Son of God.

(40) John Chrysostom

The Jews understood this claim and they attempted to **stone him** (10:31); yet even here, he did nothing to remove their opinion and suspicion. If they had concluded wrongly, Christ should have corrected them and said, "Why are you doing these things? I was not claiming an equality of power between me and the Father." No, he does just the opposite. He reestablishes and reinforces their suspicion, even when they were furious about it. He does not make an excuse for what he said, as if it had been poorly spoken, but reproaches them for not having the appropriate opinion of him. When they said, **It is not for a good work that we stone you but for blasphemy, because you, being a man, make yourself God** (10:33), listen to his response: **If the** Scriptures **called them gods to whom the word of God came, how do you say that I blaspheme because I said, "I am God"?** (10:35–36).[11] What he said is something like this: "If those who have received this honor by grace are not blamed for calling themselves gods (cf. Ps 82:6), how could the one who has it by nature rightly be reproached?" . . . Later, he said, **If I am not doing the works of my Father, then do not believe me; but if I do them, even though you do not believe me, believe the works** (10:37–38). Do you see how this proves what I said, that there is nothing inferior in

11. Not an exact quotation from John 10.

him, but that he is equal with the Father in every way? When it was impossible to see his essence, he offers the proof that his power is equal to the Father's by both the equality and sameness of his **works**.

(41) Augustine of Hippo

They responded to Jesus saying, **I and the Father are one** (10:30). See, the Jews understood what the Arians don't! They were filled with wrath because they understood that he couldn't say, **I and the Father are one** (10:30) unless the Father and the Son were equal.

Look, though, at how the Lord responded to their slowness. He saw that they couldn't bear the splendor of truth, so he softened it with his words. **Is it not written in your law** (that is, the law which was given to you), **I said, you are gods?** (10:34). God spoke to humankind through the prophet in the psalm, *I said you are gods* (Ps 82:6). . . . **If he called them gods to whom the word of God came (and scripture cannot be broken), do you say of him whom the Father consecrated and sent into the world, "You are blaspheming," because I said, "I am the Son of God"?** (10:35–36). If the word of God came to men so that they might be called "gods," how is the **Word of God** himself (1:1), who is **with God** (1:1), not God? If by the word of God men were made "gods," and if by participation they were made "gods," how is he through whom they participate not God? If lights which are lit are called "gods," how is the light which illuminates not God? If by growing warm in a certain way by a health-giving fire they are made "gods," how is he through whom they grow warm not God? You approach the light and are illuminated, and you are numbered among the children of God; if you withdraw from the light, you are darkened, and you are counted among the shadows. Nevertheless, that light does not come near to itself, because it does not withdraw from itself. Therefore, if the word of God made you "gods," how is the **Word of God** not God?

10:42 And many believed in him.

---

(42) John Chrysostom

Many believed in him (10:42). There were many things that drew them along. They remembered the words which John the Baptist spoke, calling Jesus *mightier* than himself (Matt 4:11; Mark 1:7; Luke 3:15), and **light**, and **life**, and **truth** and all the rest (cf. John 8:12; 14:6). They remembered *the voice which came from heaven*, and the *Spirit* which appeared in the *form of a dove* and showed him to all (Matt 3:17; Mark 1:11; Luke 3:22). Along with this they remembered the proof from miracles, and by seeing them they were made secure. "For if it was fitting to believe John," someone says, "how much more should we believe Jesus? If we believed John without signs, how much more Jesus who, along with the testimony of John, also has the proof from his signs?"

Do you see how much their stay in this place and their removal from wicked company benefited them? This is why Jesus continually leads them and draws them away from the presence of such people. He also seems to have done this in the old covenant, forming and directing the Israelites in every way while in the desert, far from the Egyptians. He recommends us to do this as well, commanding us to flee marketplaces, crowded assemblies, and political tumults, and to *pray* quietly *in your room* (cf. Matt 6:6). The ship that is free from tumult sails with a fair wind, and the soul that is free from activity remains at rest in harbor.

John 11

The central issue in John 11 is resurrection. Ancient Christian thinkers typically see Lazarus's resurrection as unique among Jesus's resurrection miracles in the gospels. Extended attention is given to the Lazarus narrative as it relates to the general resurrection of believers and Christ's triumph over death. Excerpts from the church fathers begin with a poetic selection from Romanos the Melodist. Taking the narrative as a whole, Romanos personifies Death and Hades in a moving attempt to portray the destruction of death's grip in the face of Christ's powerful calling forth of Lazarus.

The description of Lazarus as the one whom you love *(11:3) leads some writers to consider why God allows those he loves to suffer. Peter Chrysologus and Cyril of Alexandria argue that Christ's ultimate purpose is not merely to remove suffering but to defeat death once and for all, and to raise people's faith, both of which happened in the Lazarus account. Augustine of Hippo and Cyril of Alexandria also acknowledge the faith of the sisters in sending for Jesus in the first place.*

Several thinkers explain the words of Jesus: Our friend Lazarus has fallen asleep, but I go to awake him out of sleep *(11:11). Augustine of Hippo, Cyril of Alexandria, and Theodore of Mopsuestia note that, for Jesus, raising the dead is as easy as waking someone from sleep. Mopsuestia makes the further observation that by waiting for Lazarus to die before beginning the journey, Jesus intensifies the miracle and strengthens the disciples' faith.*

Augustine of Hippo and Cyril of Alexandria comment on Lazarus being dead four days *(11:17). Augustine applies a figural interpretation, each day of death representing the progression of sin in a person's life. Cyril offers a more pragmatic approach. Four days meant that Lazarus was certainly dead; no one could accuse Jesus of merely healing a sick person.*

*Verse 21 (*If you had been here, my brother would not have died*) prompts Christian interpreters to consider the belief (or unbelief) of Martha. John Chrysostom, Peter Chrysologus, and Cyril of Alexandria all recognize some basic faith in Martha, even while admitting that she does not possess a full understanding of Christ's identity and nature. Chrysologus also employs this text for a playful comparison between Eve, who "carried death to man," and Martha, who "is now breathless in her attempt to restore life to a man."*

Jesus's declaration, I am the resurrection and the life *(11:25), produces both theological and practical commentary. Novatian points out that Jesus could not have made such lofty claims if he were a mere man. Cyprian of Carthage, John Chrysostom, and Cyril of Alexandria use this passage to grapple with the troubling experience of death in our world, and the proper response toward the death of a loved one. Augustine of Hippo sees in this verse a lesson about Christ raising us all from the grip of sin. And Cyril of Alexandria observes a parallel between Christ's question to Martha in verse 26 (Do you believe this?) and Christian baptism. Just as Christ elicited Martha's confession of faith before raising her brother Lazarus, so an infant's sponsor offers a confession of faith before the baptism of the child.*

Several thinkers comment on verses 33 and 35 (When Jesus saw her weeping . . . he was deeply moved in spirit and troubled . . . Jesus wept). For most, Jesus's weeping signifies not only Christ's human nature (Chrysostom, Augustine, Cyril of Alexandria), but also expresses his sorrow over all of humanity, which has come under the curse of sin and death (Augustine and Cyril of Alexandria). Theodore of Mopsuestia, however, understands Jesus's emotions as anger at the disbelief of those around him, and Peter Chrysologus interprets Jesus's weeping as tears of joy in anticipation of the coming resurrection of Lazarus.

Jesus's question in verse 34 (Where have you laid him?) leads commentators to puzzle over how it is that Jesus, being God, is ignorant of something. Cyril of Alexandria, like Romanos earlier, sees here a parallel with God's inquiry of Adam in Gen 3:9: "Where are you?" Jesus does not ask his question out of ignorance but as a way to show his equality with the Father and to draw a larger crowd to witness his miracle.

Early Christian thinkers explore the scene where Jesus commands, Take away the stone *(11:38), and Martha replies,* Lord, by this time there will be an odor *(11:39). Origen of Alexandria offers a moral application about the need to obey Christ's commands immediately rather than hesitating. Cyril of Jerusalem observes that the faith of Martha actually played a role in saving Lazarus from death. And several writers wonder why Jesus commanded the stone to be removed at all, rather than just perform the miracle without the aid of others. John Chrysostom argues that it was to provide proof that the man whom Jesus called forth was the same Lazarus who had died. Peter Chrysologus and Augustine of Hippo turn to other Scriptures with the word* stone *in them to demonstrate that raising of faith requires a change of heart. Augustine also compares the Lazarus raising with two other miracles of raising the dead—the synagogue ruler's daughter (Mark 5:35–42) and the widow's son (Luke 7:11–15). Each episode represents the raising of the soul burdened with sin. The raising of Lazarus represents the soul entangled in sin, whose habits have become like a foul* odor. *Finally, John of Damascus makes the brief but poignant point that resurrection must include the body as well as the soul—the Lazarus who was raised was the same one whose body had been dead for four days.*

In response to Jesus's prayer in 11:41–42 (Father, I thank thee that thou hast heard me), early Christian thinkers consider why Jesus would even need to ask for anything in prayer. Origen of Alexandria notes that the prayer is not a request, but a public acknowledgment that God had already responded to Christ's words. Likewise, Hilary of Poitiers suggests that Jesus's prayer was intended primarily to develop our own faith. John Chrysostom and Peter Chrysologus argue that Jesus's prayer demonstrates the unity of will, activity, and love between the Father and the Son. Chrysologus also offers a moving personification of Tartarus, the mythical place of the dead, as he protests Christ's claim upon Lazarus and the defeat of death.

The subsequent calling forth of Lazarus with hands and feet bound (11:43–44) is routinely understood by the church fathers both as a portrait of the general resurrection (Ambrose of Milan, Augustine of Hippo, and Cyril of Alexandria) and as a figure of Christ's calling the sinner from the entanglement of sin (Origen of Alexandria, Ambrose of Milan, and Augustine of Hippo).

John Chrysostom and Augustine of Hippo comment on the words of the Pharisees: What are we to do? For this man performs many signs. If we let him go on thus, everyone will believe in him, and the Romans will come and destroy both our holy place and our nation *(11:47–48). Both note the irony in misunderstanding the identity and purpose of Jesus.*

Caiaphas's words about the expiatory nature of Christ's death and the fear of losing the Temple and land (11:49–52) move ancient commentators to consider whether Caiaphas spoke by the guidance of the Holy Spirit or not. While Origen of Alexandria seems to conclude in the negative, John Chrysostom, Gregory of Nyssa, Augustine of Hippo, and Cyril of Alexandria take the opposite view, arguing that the Spirit was at work through Caiaphas, even if he did not understand what he was saying. This will lead some, like Augustine and Cyril of Alexandria, to explore the fulfillment of Caiaphas's words through the inclusion of gentiles into the church.

Finally, Augustine of Hippo offers a figural understanding of the words: the Passover of the Jews was at hand *(11:55), noting that while ancient doorposts were marked with the blood of a lamb, "our foreheads are marked with the blood of Christ."*

(1) Romanos the Melodist

Strophe 8: Now Jesus goes into Judea in his body;

       For in his divinity he cares for and occupies

       The whole world and even those from out of the earth like the miserable locusts.

     He who fills the universe arrived, then,

          in Bethany to accomplish his divine work.

     When Hades heard the sound of his footsteps,

HADES   He whispered to Death: "What are those feet, O Death,

       Which march over my head?

     Probably Jesus is coming; and again he has come to exact payment from us.

       Just as formerly the son of the widow escaped us (cf. Luke 7:11–16),

       So now it is Lazarus.

         He will be resurrected and he will rise up

         Saying, 'Thou art the **resurrection and the life**' (11:25).

Strophe 9: "Victorious Death, unconquerable, listen

HADES   To Hades, your friend, and be freed from your toil.

       Do not bring me nourishment for I cannot digest it.

     You bring me the bound dead, and when I swallow them, I vomit.

       When they are buried, I seize them and rejoice;

          but when they are spoiled I cannot hold them.

       Those who are within me, I exact for myself,

         And those whom I cause to be prepared I claim for myself;

       Why, then, are you disturbed?

Stop, make ready, and take possession of the friend of the Nazarene, O Death,
    Be obedient, bearing in mind
    That he after a short time of **four days** (11:17)
        Will be resurrected and he will rise up
        Saying, 'Thou art the **resurrection and the life**.'"

Strophe 10: When he heard these words, Death bellowed
Death   And, crying out with anger, said to Hades:
"You give me good advice as though you were free from evils;
Give advice to your stomach which you have never fed up until now,
    For indeed I grew weary of bringing food to you; yet you have
        never said, 'That is enough.'
    But you were as insatiable as the sea in receiving the rivers of the dead,
    Never reaching satiety.
Why, then, do you talk to me like this? First learn what you are teaching me,
    Be calm and make ready.
    For the one whom you have in you, after a brief critical moment
        Will be resurrected and he will rise up
        Saying, 'Thou art the **resurrection and the life**.'

Strophe 11: "The life of mortals has always seemed as water to you;
Death   That is why you open wide and never cease to swallow them.
    Then let this be enough and do not become more full;
For the feet which you hear, and I see they are threatening,
    Are footsteps of one who is raging, and who is angered at you.
    As he draws near the tomb, he kicks at your gates,
    And searches for the contents of your belly.
He has come, he who will purge you; and you have need of him,
        For you are all distended.
    You will then be lightened if Lazarus,
    Emptied from your entrails,
        Will be resurrected and will rise up
        Saying, 'Thou art the **resurrection and the life**.'"

Strophe 12: "These are foul and shameful remarks you address to me,
Hades   Hades, your friend. Seeing my misfortunes, you rejoice;
    But I, because of these things, weep over myself.
For I see the limbs of Lazarus, already disintegrating before putrefaction
    As though they seem to rise again, they work at reassembling,
    For they are crawling like ants when the worms withdraw,
    And the foul **odor** (11:39) has disappeared.
Alas, Jesus has really come; and he, sending His fragrance toward us,
    Has perfumed the ill-smelling corpse.
    And now the man who perished and was reduced to ashes

> Will be resurrected and will rise up
> Saying, 'Thou art the **resurrection and the life**.'"

Strophe 13: When he heard this, Death cried out;
> And then he ran and seized Hades by the hand.
> And they both beheld the terrifying and awesome sight.

The fragrance of the Son of God permeated his friend,
> And made ready his body for the call of the giver of life,
> It reordered his hair and reconstructed his skin,
> And put together his inner organs,

And stretched out his veins so that the blood could again flow through them,
> And repaired his arteries,
> So that Lazarus be made ready when called.
> > He will be resurrected and will rise up.
> > Saying, 'Thou art the **resurrection and the life**.'"

Strophe 14: Hades and Death had barely seen all the things
HADES
AND Which took place, when they spoke to one another with sorrow:
DEATH "Never will our empire be prominent and victorious.

The tomb has become like a dye which changes corruption into life.
> The funeral monument is considered as a thread,
> > and whoever wishes cuts it without any trouble,
> And it redeems whomever it wishes, brother, son, daughter,
> And those who dwell on earth laugh at us.

Whether a man be slave or free, if he wishes, he despoils us.
> And whether a heavenly or earthly being,
> One has only to say a word, and immediately the dead
> > Will be resurrected and will rise up
> > Saying, 'Thou art the **resurrection and the life**.'"

Strophe 17: All these things, then, they said as they groaned
> And as they lamented about the resurrection from the dead,
> Bemoaning themselves and all that was theirs.

But the Creator arrived at the tomb of the dead man for whom he had come
> After asking, it seems, where Lazarus was buried.
> He asked, through irony, he who made man with his own hand.
> As he says, "Where does Lazarus lie?"

He wishes to know what he already knew; just as he
> > formerly asked: "Where are you Adam?" (Gen 3:9)
> Just so, he said: "Where is Lazarus?"
> Just a short time ago, he said to Martha:
> > "He will be resurrected and will rise up
> > Saying, 'Thou art the **resurrection and the life**.'"

Strophe 18: Almighty Lord, merciful father of the humble,
         Thou who hast saved Lazarus
         Just now by the sound of thy voice,
     Just so, from thy throne, allow those who have gone before us
              to see thy joyous countenance.
         And grant that we may live out our present span of life in peace,
         And that we come to the end pleasing to thee, so that, living or dying,
         We may be governed by thy will.
    Give us a sign, an order, tell us thy purpose to save us,
         For thou shalt not destroy the one who loves thee,
         But thou dost control him in life and summon him in death
             And he will be resurrected and will rise up
             Saying, "Thou art the **resurrection and the life**."

John 11:1–6

[1]**Now a certain man was ill, Lazarus of Bethany, the village of Mary and her sister Martha.** [2]**It was Mary who anointed the Lord with ointment and wiped his feet with her hair, whose brother Lazarus was ill.** [3]**So the sisters sent to him, saying, "Lord, he whom you love is ill."** [4]**But when Jesus heard it he said, "This illness is not unto death; it is for the glory of God, so that the Son of God may be glorified by means of it."** [5]**Now Jesus loved Martha and her sister and Lazarus.** [6]**So when he heard that he was ill, he stayed two days longer in the place where he was.**

(2) John Chrysostom

Many people, whenever they see those who are pleasing to God suffer something terrible, such as becoming sick or impoverished or such things, they are offended, not knowing that those who are especially loved by God are called to suffer these things. **Lazarus** was a friend of Christ and he was **ill**. This is what those who sent word said: Look, **he whom you love is ill** (11:3). . . . What does the evangelist wish to teach to us by saying, **Jesus loved Martha, and her sister, and Lazarus** (11:5)? That we are never to be disconcerted or perplexed if those who are zealous or loved by God become **ill**. . . .

    After saying, **This illness is not unto death** (11:4), Jesus **stayed two days longer** (11:6). Why did he **stay**? So that Lazarus would breathe his last and be buried. So that no one would have a reason to say that Lazarus was not yet dead when Jesus raised him. So that no one could say that he was faint, or weary, or partially dead but not completely dead. This is why he **stayed** for a time, until decomposition began and they could say, *He has an odor* (11:39).

(3) Peter Chrysologus

If it is pleasing, before we enter upon the open seas of the reading, before we undertake the waves of questions, before we penetrate the depth of so great a deed, let us carefully consider the great image of this resurrection. In it we see the sign of signs, we perceive the power of powers, and we consider the wonder of wonders. The Lord had also raised the daughter of Jairus, the leader of the synagogue (Mark 5:21–43; Matt 9:18–26; Luke 8:40–56), but her body was still warm, she was still in the midst of death, her body was still present, she was still a human remaining among humans, her spirit was still journeying, and her soul did not yet know the bonds of Tartarus.[1] In short, he restored the life of the dead girl but let the strength of hell remain. He also raised a mother's only son (cf. Luke 7:11–15), but did so by holding back the funeral bier, obviating the need for a tomb, suspending the decay of the body, and preventing a stench. He returned life to the dead man before he had fully entered into the dominion of death.

Certainly, in the case of Lazarus, the whole thing is unique. His death and resurrection have nothing in common with the preceding cases. With Lazarus, the full power of death was in place, and a full picture of resurrection shines forth brightly. I daresay that if Lazarus had returned from hell after three days, he would have surpassed the mystery of the Lord's resurrection. For Christ returns after three days as Lord, whereas Lazarus is called forth after four days as a servant. Now, in order to prove the things we have said, let's take a taste of some of the reading.

So his sisters sent to him, saying, "Lord, he whom you love is ill" (11:3). Speaking this way, they appeal to his affection, stir up his love, evoke his charity, and desire to hint at the obligation he owes to his friend. Christ's aim is to conquer death rather than remove suffering. His idea of love is not to raise someone from the sickbed but lead them back from hell. So he soon prepared for the one he loved not the remedy for suffering, but the glory of resurrection. When **he heard that Lazarus was ill**, as the evangelist says, **He stayed two days longer in the place where he was** (11:6). You all see how he gives way to death and a license to the tomb. He permits the strength of corruption to persist and denies nothing to the power of decay and stench so that Tartarus might seize, drag, and possess him. Christ's actions are intended to extinguish all human hope and to allow the power of worldly despair to draw near, since what is about to happen is divine, not human. . . .

For that reason Christ extends the death of Lazarus all the way to the fourth day. He allows death to prevail to the point of stench so that the disciples would not doubt that the Lord himself is still able to rise after three days. Since they had seen a servant who already began to stink rise after four days, they might believe that the one who had called another back to life could easily restore life to himself. This is why he says: *For your sake I am glad . . . so that you may believe* (11:15). So the death of Lazarus was necessary for the faith of the disciples, buried along with Lazarus, to rise with him.

---

1. In this sermon Chrysologus personifies Tartarus, the place of the dead in classic mythology.

(4) Augustine of Hippo

They sent messengers to the Lord reporting that their brother was **ill**, so that if Jesus deemed it fitting he would come and free him from sickness. But Jesus delayed the healing so that he might be able to raise him up. What did his sisters report? **Lord, he whom you love is ill** (11:3). They didn't tell him to come; a report was all that was needed for the one who loved Lazarus. They didn't daresay: "Come and heal." Nor did they daresay: "Command from there, and it will happen here." Indeed, if the faith of that centurion is praised, why not them as well? The centurion had said: *I am not worthy to have you come under my roof; but only say the word and my servant will be healed* (Matt 8:8). The sisters say none of these things, only: "**Lord, he whom you love is ill.** It's enough for you to know, for you do not forsake those **whom you love**."

(5) Cyril of Alexandria

The women send to the Lord because they always want him to be near. They send for him eagerly this time because of the one who is **ill**. They knew that if only Christ would appear, the one who was **ill** would recover from his disease. They remind Christ of his **love** for the **ill** man when they summon him there especially for this purpose. They knew that he cared for this man and that, as God who cares for all things, he could indeed heal him. Still, they thought that if Christ would come near, he would stretch out his hands and raise up Lazarus.

These women had not yet reached perfection in faith, for it seems they are distressed because they think Lazarus would not have become **ill** unless Christ neglected him. They say, "Since those who are loved by God have every good thing, why is **he whom you love ill**?" They might also say, "The boldness of the disease is so great that it dares to attack those who are loved by God." It is the same as saying, "Since you love and heal your enemies, you owe it that much more to show such love and healing to those who love you. You are able to do all things simply by willing it." Yet their reasoning is full of faith and is a demonstration of their intimacy with Christ.

But when Jesus heard it he said, "This illness is not unto death; it is for the glory of God, so that the Son of God may be glorified by means of it" (11:4). . . . If he said that Lazarus was not sick **unto death**, but then death came anyway, there is nothing strange about this. When we look at the end of the matter, we see that he was about to raise him after a short time. We look not at what happens in the meantime but at the end result. The Lord decided to demonstrate death's weakness, showing that what happened was for the **glory of God**, that is, his own **glory**.

John 11:7–16

[7]Then after this he said to the disciples, "Let us go into Judea again." [8]The disciples said to him, "Rabbi, the Jews were but now seeking to stone you, and are you going there

again?" [9]Jesus answered, "Are there not twelve hours in the day? If any one walks in the day, he does not stumble, because he sees the light of this world. [10]But if any one walks in the night, he stumbles, because the light is not in him." [11]Thus he spoke, and then he said to them, "Our friend Lazarus has fallen asleep, but I go to awake him out of sleep." [12]The disciples said to him, "Lord, if he has fallen asleep, he will recover." [13]Now Jesus had spoken of his death, but they thought that he meant taking rest in sleep. [14]Then Jesus told them plainly, "Lazarus is dead; [15]and for your sake I am glad that I was not there, so that you may believe. But let us go to him." [16]Thomas, called the Twin, said to his fellow disciples, "Let us also go, that we may die with him."

11:11–14 "Our friend Lazarus has fallen asleep, but I go to awake him out of sleep." . . . Then Jesus told them plainly, "Lazarus is dead."

---

(6) Theodore of Mopsuestia

Our friend Lazarus has fallen asleep, but I go to awake him out of sleep (11:11). Given what Jesus was about to do, he called death sleep, indicating how easily he would raise him. This is why he said earlier, *This illness is not unto death* (11:4). Because the disciples did not understand, they were saying, "Our Lord, if he is asleep, he will get better." For if he really was asleep, he needed only to be woken; that is what human nature requires. Therefore, since they did not understand that Jesus called death sleep, Jesus said to them clearly, "**Lazarus is dead, and for your sake I am glad that I was not there, so that you may believe** (11:14–15). My absence is useful for strengthening your faith. If I had been there, I would have healed the sick man and the miracle would have been small in demonstrating my power. Because I was far away, death overcame him, and I am about to go and raise him. Therefore, you will be made especially strong in faith when you see that I am able to raise even the dead who are already decaying. Let us go! The time demands it."

(7) Augustine of Hippo

Our friend Lazarus has fallen asleep, but I go to awake him out of sleep (11:11). Christ spoke the truth. Lazarus was dead to his sisters, but to the Lord he was sleeping. To humankind, he had died and they were unable to wake him, but the Lord raised him so easily from the grave. You wouldn't be able to urge a sleeping person from their bed with such ease! So he called Lazarus **asleep** in reference to his own power because the Scriptures often call those who are dead **asleep**, just as when the apostle says: *But we would not have you ignorant, brethren, concerning those who are asleep, that you may not grieve as others do who have no hope* (1 Thess 4:13). Here, Paul called them **asleep** because he was foretelling their resurrection. So all the dead are **asleep**—the good and the bad. . . .

Responding insofar as they understood, **the disciples said to him, "Lord, if he has fallen asleep, he will recover"** (11:11–12), for the sleep of the sick is commonly thought to be a sign of health. **Now Jesus had spoken of his death, but they thought that he meant taking rest in sleep. Then Jesus told them plainly** (11:13–14). He had spoken obscurely when he said, **He has fallen asleep**; but now he says plainly: "**Lazarus is dead; and for your sake, I am glad I was not there, so that you may believe** (11:14–15). I know that he has died, and yet I was not there. News of a sick man, not a dead man, has been brought to us." What could remain hidden from the one who had created him, the one into whose hands the soul of the dying man had passed? This is why he said, **I am glad I was not there, so that you may believe** (11:15): so that now they might begin to be amazed that the Lord was able to declare Lazarus **dead**, although he had neither seen nor heard.

(8) Cyril of Alexandria

Showing his own God-befitting power, he calls the soul's departure from the body **sleep** (11:11), and rightly so. The one who created humans for immortality and, as it is written, proclaimed *the generative forces of the world as wholesome* (Wis 1:14), does not think it fitting to call it death. What is more, the description is true. The temporary death of our body is nothing other than **sleep** in the presence of God, which is then overcome by one simple sign from the one who is life by nature, that is, Christ. Notice that Christ did not say, "Lazarus has died, and I go to raise him from the dead," but rather: he **has fallen asleep**. For our instruction and edification, he avoids boasting. He would not have proclaimed something so enigmatic that even his disciples did not understand its meaning, unless he had a good reason. He did not say, "I go to give him life, or to raise him from the dead," but **to awake him out of sleep**, which for the moment is a comment free from suspicion.

John 11:17–27

[17]Now when Jesus came, he found that Lazarus had already been in the tomb four days. [18]Bethany was near Jerusalem, about two miles off, [19]and many of the Jews had come to Martha and Mary to console them concerning their brother. [20]When Martha heard that Jesus was coming, she went and met him, while Mary sat in the house. [21]Martha said to Jesus, "Lord, if you had been here, my brother would not have died. [22]And even now I know that whatever you ask from God, God will give you." [23]Jesus said to her, "Your brother will rise again." [24]Martha said to him, "I know that he will rise again in the resurrection at the last day." [25]Jesus said to her, "I am the resurrection and the life; he who believes in me, though he die, yet shall he live, [26]and whoever lives and believes in me shall never die. Do you believe this?" [27]She said to him, "Yes, Lord; I believe that you are the Christ, the Son of God, he who is coming into the world."

11:17 He found that Lazarus had already been in the tomb four days.

---

(9) Augustine of Hippo

Let us say what it signifies that a man was dead for **four days** (11:17). Just as that blind man (John 9), in a way, signifies the human race, so perhaps in the case of the dead man we ought to understand it to indicate many people as well. Something can be signified in different ways. When a man is born, he is born already with death because he contracts the sin of Adam. This is why the apostle says: *Therefore as sin came into the world through one man and death through sin, and so death spread to all men because all men sinned* (Rom 5:12). See, you have one day of death because a man contracts it from the seed of death. Then he grows older and enters upon the years of reason. He begins to understand the natural law which everyone has fixed in their hearts, that is, what you don't want done to you, don't do to another. . . . Behold the law in your heart: what you don't want to suffer, don't do to another. Yet we transgress this law; behold a second day of death.

The law has also been divinely given through the servant of God, Moses, who says: *You shall not kill; you shall not commit adultery; you shall not bear false witness; honor your father and mother; you shall not covet anything that is your neighbor's; you shall not covet your neighbor's wife* (Exod 20:13, 14, 16, 17). See! The law which has been written is the same law that is scorned. Behold a third day of death. What remains? The gospel comes, the kingdom of heaven is proclaimed, and everywhere Christ is slandered. He threatens gehenna and promises eternal life, yet this too is disregarded. People transgress the gospel; behold a fourth day of death. Now one deservedly stinks. Yet surely mercy must not be denied to such a person? God forbid! The Lord agreed to come in order to raise such people from death.

(10) Cyril of Alexandria

The evangelist speaks of an interval of **four days** (11:17) after the death of Lazarus so that the miracle might be truly marvelous. No one could say that Jesus came after just one day, and since Lazarus was not really dead, Jesus raised him from illness.

11:20-24 Martha said to Jesus, "Lord, if you had been here, my brother would not have died." . . . Jesus said to her, "Your brother will rise again."

---

(11) John Chrysostom

Lord, if you had been here, my brother would not have died (11:21). See how great the women's wisdom is, even though their understanding is weak. After they saw Christ, they did not immediately start into a lament or begin wailing and crying out. This is the very thing we tend to do whenever we see a close friend encounter us in our sorrow. Instead, the women immediately honor their teacher. Each of them believed in Christ, but not in the right way, for they did not yet accurately know either that he was God or that he did these things by his own power and authority.

He had taught them both of these things, but their ignorance was made evident when they said: **If you had been here**, our **brother would not have died** (11:21); and also when they added: **Whatever you ask from God, he will give you** (11:22). They speak as if Jesus was merely some virtuous and honorable man. Yet see what Christ says: **Your brother will rise again** (11:23). Meanwhile he refutes the phrase **whatever you ask** for he did not say: "I ask." What did he say? **Your brother will rise again.** He could have said, "O woman, are you still looking below? I do not need help from another, for I do all things from myself." This would have been very difficult to bear and would have given offense to the woman. So by saying: **He shall rise again,** he chose a fitting and mediating approach.

(12) Peter Chrysologus

Lord, if you had been here, my brother would not have died. And even now I know that whatever you ask from God, God will give you (11:21–22). This woman does not believe, but she makes an effort to believe. Disbelief confuses her belief. **Whatever you ask from God** (11:22)? God gives from himself; he does not seek from himself! Why do you delay your supplication, woman, when the one intending to grant it is already standing nearby? O woman, it is the judge himself whom you desire as a mere advocate. He himself has the power to give; there is no need for him to ask. She says, **I know that whatever you ask from God, God will give you** (11:22). O woman, to believe this means you don't believe! To know this means you remain ignorant! . . .

Now, let us hear how the Lord responded. **Your brother will rise again** (11:23). And the woman: **I know that he will rise again in the resurrection at the last day** (11:24). Martha, once again you know but you do not know. Again, Martha, do you really know, if you do not know that your brother is able to rise again even here? Or is it perhaps that God, who is one day able to raise all, is now unable to raise a single dead man? He is able! The God who will one day raise all the dead to perpetual life is able now to raise a single dead man, as a sign. **I know that whatever you ask from God, God will give you**, and **I know that he will rise again in the resurrection on the last day** (11:22, 24).

(13) Peter Chrysologus

When Martha heard that Jesus was coming, she went and met him (11:20) saying: **Lord, if you had been here, my brother would not have died** (11:21). Woman, do you confess that he is God and yet say: **If you had been here**? Neither places nor times cause God to be absent or present. Lazarus would not have died if the Lord had been there, which he was, but only if you, woman, had not been in paradise![2] Woman, you sought tears, you found sighs, you bought death for the price of your appetite, and yet you blame the absence of God when you do not object that the cause of death was your own presence. When you had introduced death, then there was an occasion for lamenting. Now, however, it has become an occasion for power. Previously death was given as a punishment for sinning, but now it is permitted for a glorious reawakening. Previously Tartarus[3] had obtained humanity, but now he loses it. O woman, seek now through faith what you ruined through faithlessness. . . .

When Martha heard that Jesus was coming, she went and met him (11:20). . . . The woman who ran toward death now runs because of death;[4] she who hastened toward her guilt now hastens toward forgiveness; she whom the worst seducer hindered now comes to the faithful Redeemer; she who sought ruin now seeks the resurrection; and the very one who carried death to man, is now breathless in her attempt to restore life to a man. This is why Christ paused in this place, why Christ waited, why he did not enter the crowd, why he did not strive for the house, why he did not turn away to the tomb, why he did not hasten to Lazarus, the one for whom he had come. Instead he stays back with this woman and detains her. He first receives the woman whom the tempter first corrupted. He puts to flight faithlessness from woman and calls her back to faith so that the one who was compliant in destruction might also aid in salvation, and she who had long since become the mother of the dead, because of the devil, might in the end become the mother of the living, through her faith. And because a woman had been the origin of evil and the cause of death, Christ acts in a way that washes off the guilt before he grants pardon, and removes the cause before he remits the sentence. He is careful that man not avoid sharing life with the woman, through whom he had once been deceived. In brief, the woman would have died if Christ the Lord had come to the man first. This is why, brothers and sisters, Christ was born of a woman; this is why the woman always raises a man from the tomb of her own womb, so that she may call back with her pains the one whom she drove out with her charms, and so that she may revive in her morning sickness the one whom she destroyed by eating.

Martha acknowledged Christ and, through her faithful confession, destroyed whatever was at fault in womanhood. Then she is sent to Mary because without Mary[5] death was unable to be put to flight, nor was life able to be restored. Let Mary come, let the one who bears his mother's name come, so that humanity may see that as Christ dwelt hidden in the virgin's womb, and just as the dead come forth from hell, the dead will come forth from their tombs.

(14) Cyril of Alexandria

What Martha says is this: "The reason my brother died was not because it is the nature of humans to die, but because you, who can conquer death with a command, were not

2. Here Chrysologus shifts back and forth between a discussion of the "woman" Martha and the "woman" Eve in Gen 3.
3. A name for the Greek deity of the underworld.
4. Chrysologus again shifts between Martha and Eve in this sermon.
5. Chrysologus is playing with the name **Mary**, shared by both Martha's sister and Jesus's mother.

here." Being led astray by an inappropriate grief, she thought that it was too late for the Lord to be able to do anything about it. She thought that he came not to raise Lazarus, but to console her. She subtly blames him for delaying rather than coming immediately when he was able to help, when they sent messengers saying, *Lord, he whom you love is ill* (11:3).

When she says, **Whatever you ask from God, he will give you** (11:22), she is clearly embarrassed to ask what she really wants. At the same time, she is confused about the truth, not thinking of Jesus as God, but as one of the saints. Because of his visible flesh, she thinks that whatever he asks as a saint, he receives from God. She fails to understand that he is God by nature and the power of the Father, and that he has an irresistible authority over all things. If she understood that he was God, she would not have said, **If you had been here** (11:21), for God is everywhere. I am sure that in order to avoid arrogance, the Lord did not say, "I will raise your brother," but **he will rise again** (11:23). He rebukes her gently, saying, "He will be raised in the way I want, not in the way you think. If you think that this is accomplished through prayer and supplication, make the prayer yourself; do not command me the wonder-worker to do it, who can raise the dead by my own power." When the woman hears these things, she is embarrassed, on the one hand, to tell him to raise her brother, while on the other hand, she urges him now to do some appropriate work. She seems somehow troubled by the delay of time, saying, "**I know that he will rise again at the last day** (11:24), but I desire to see my brother raised even before then."

11:25–27 Jesus said to her, "I am the resurrection and the life; he who believes in me, though he die, yet shall he live, and whoever lives and believes in me shall never die."

---

(15) Cyprian of Carthage

The apostle Paul rejected, rebuked, and blamed anyone who should grieve because of death. He says, *we would not have you ignorant, brethren, concerning those who are asleep, that you may not grieve as others do who have no hope. For since we believe that Jesus died and rose again, even so, through Jesus, God will bring with him those who have fallen asleep* (1 Thess 4:13–14). He says that those who grieve over the death of their friends have no hope. We, however, who live in hope, believe in God, and trust that Christ died and rose again on our behalf, remain in Christ. Through him and in him we rise again. Why then do we either refuse to depart from this life or we mourn and grieve over our deceased brothers and sisters as if they were lost forever? Christ himself, our Lord and God, advises us saying: **I am the resurrection and the life; he who believes in me, though he die, yet shall he live, and whoever lives and believes in me shall never die** (11:25–26). If we believe in Christ, let us have faith in his words and promises. Since we will not be bound to death forever, let us come joyfully and lightheartedly to Christ with whom we will conquer and reign forever.

(16) Novatian

If Christ was only a man, why did he say, **all who live and believe in me shall never die** (11:26)? Whoever believes in a man by himself alone is called *cursed* (Jer 17:5), but whoever believes in Christ is not *cursed*, but is said to **never die**. Therefore, if he was only a man, as the heretics want to say, how does someone believe in him and **never die**, while the one *who trusts in man* is held to be *cursed* (Jer 17:5)? If he is not *cursed*, but is rather destined to attain eternal life, as it is read, then Christ is not only a man, but also God. In Christ, the one who believes both eliminates the danger of a curse and approaches the fruit of righteousness.

(17) John Chrysostom

Whoever lives and believes in me shall never die (11:26). See how Christ raises Martha's mind upward! Raising Lazarus was not the only thing he sought to do. Both she and those present with her needed to learn of the resurrection. This is why he speaks his words of wisdom prior to raising Lazarus. . . . See how Martha's mind is still focused below, for when she heard, **I am the resurrection and the life** (11:25), she still did not respond by saying, "Resurrect him." Instead, she said, **I believe that you are the Christ, the Son of God** (11:27). . . . It seems to me that the woman didn't understand what he said but did understand that it was something great. She did not comprehend it entirely. So when she was asked one thing, she answered another. . . .

In our present day a certain disease, along with other evils, takes control of women: they show it through their lamentations and wailings, through exposing their arms, tearing out their hair and scratching their cheeks. Some do this out of grief, others do it to make a show and because they love attention, and still other do it because of their licentiousness. They expose their arms, and what's more, they do it in the eyes of men. What are you doing, O woman? Tell me, do you uncover yourself indecently in the middle of the marketplace while men are there, even though you are a part of Christ? Do you pull out your hair, tear your clothes, wail out loud, join the dance, and keep alive the image of the raving Bacchanalian women? Do you not consider that it displeases God? What madness! Will the Greeks not laugh? Will they not consider our beliefs to be myths? They will say, "There's no resurrection; the beliefs of the Christians are all trash, deceit, and trickery! Since there is nothing beyond this life, their women wail and abandon the teachings set down in their books. They themselves show that these words are all fictions. If they believed that the one who died is not dead but has passed to a better life, they wouldn't lament him as if he no longer existed; they wouldn't torment themselves this way; they wouldn't utter cries so full of disbelief: 'No longer will I see you! No longer will I hold you!' All their beliefs are myths. If the chief example of their good things is disbelieved, then much more should all the rest of the things held sacred by them be disbelieved as well." . . .

Weep, therefore, as one who is sending someone on a trip to a foreign country. I say this not as one laying down the law but as one showing sympathy. On the one hand, if those who have died are sinners and have committed numerous offenses against God, you should weep. Not just weep—for this does them no good—but do all that is in your power to provide them some relief through alms and offerings. You should also be happy because their acts of wickedness have stopped. On the other hand, if they are righteous, it is better to glory because their situation is now secure; they have been freed from the uncertainty of the future. If they are young, they have quickly escaped the common evils; if old, they have left life after having fully gained that which seems desirable.

Yet you dismiss this reasoning and urge your servant girls to mourn as if you were honoring one who has died—which is actually the utmost dishonor. Real honor does not come to the dead from cries and lamentations but rather from hymns, songs, and an excellent life. . . .

Nevertheless, some might say, "How can one who has lost a son, daughter, or wife not grieve?" I'm not saying to refrain from grief, but not to do it immoderately. If we keep in mind that God took them away himself and that we had a husband and son who were mortal, we will quickly gain comfort. Such complaints suit those who seek something beyond their own nature. You were born a mortal human being. Why then are you upset that nature took its course? Surely you don't get upset that you are nourished by eating? Surely you don't seek to live without this? Do the same also with death and don't seek immortality while being mortal. This has already been decided. Don't be upset then, and don't mourn; rather, embrace those laws commonly set down for all, and be upset about sins instead. This kind of grief is good; this is wisdom at its best. Therefore, we should continually grieve over sin so that we may receive joy in heaven by the grace and generosity of our Lord Jesus Christ, to whom be the glory forever and ever. Amen.

(18) Peter Chrysologus

Why does Christ say **I am the resurrection**, and not "I raise him up"? Why is this? Because he assumed humanity and death, and he who raised up one man by commanding him, will raise again all humanity by his own resurrection. The ones for whom Adam became the well of death, let Christ become for them the fount of life. Let that saying of the apostle be fulfilled: *For as in Adam all die, so also in Christ shall all be made alive* (1 Cor 15:22). **I am the resurrection and the life**, he says. **He who believes in me, though he die, yet shall he live, and whoever lives and believes in me shall never die.** He asks: **Do you believe this?** And the woman replies: **Yes, Lord;** I have believed it, **and I do believe that you are the Christ, the Son of** the living **God, who is coming into this world** (11:25–27). Why is the one who had come for Lazarus so preoccupied with Martha? Why? So that she might rise in faith before Lazarus is raised in the flesh. This is the way Jesus acts; he came to care for both the living and the dead. He is not afraid of making delays since he has both the power and the means to act.

(19) Augustine of Hippo

Jesus said to her, "I am the resurrection (11:25). You say, 'My brother will rise at the last day'; indeed, that's true! But the one who will raise him then is able to do so right now, for

I am the resurrection and the life" (11:25). Listen, brothers and sisters, listen to what he says. Surely the entire expectation of those gathered was that Lazarus, the one four days dead, would come back to life. Let us listen, and let us too rise again. How many are there in this crowd on whom a mass of sinful habits presses down! By chance there may be some hearing me to whom it ought be said: *Do not get drunk with wine, for that is debauchery* (Eph 5:18). Yet they cry out, "We cannot!" Perhaps there are others hearing me who are filthy, having been stained with wantonness and shame, to whom it ought to be said: "Do not do this, lest you die." Yet they reply, "We cannot do away with our habits!" O Lord, raise them again. Jesus says, **I am the resurrection and the life**. Because he is **the life**, therefore he is **the resurrection**.

(20) Cyril of Alexandria

Eternal life is indeed our reward and honor for faith in Christ, and this does not come to the human soul in any other way. If through Christ we are all raised up, this is surely true life, living without end in happiness. Coming back to life only for punishment is no different than death. So, if someone sees the saints dying, who have received the promises of life, this means nothing, for this is only what happens naturally. The manifestation of grace is preserved for the proper time and prevails not just in part but continuously in everyone, even among the saints who have already died and are in some measure tasting death until the general resurrection. At that time, all will enjoy good things together.

When the Savior said, **Though he die, yet shall he live** (11:25), he did not destroy death in this age. He allows it to prevail against the faithful up to a point, only insofar as this is the natural course of things. He has preserved the grace of resurrection for the proper time. In fact, he says that because of his human nature, **he who believes in me** will not be without a share in the death of the flesh. However, he will still experience nothing dreadful because of this since God is easily able to give life to whomever he pleases. In the age to come **he who believes** in him has unending life in happiness and perfect immortality.

Therefore let none of the unfaithful scoff. Christ did not say, "He will not see death from now on." Rather, when he said absolutely, you **shall never die**, he spoke of the time to come, reserving the completion of his promise until that time.

(21) Cyril of Alexandria

Do you believe this? (11:26). . . . One should notice that when Lazarus lay dead and buried, in a way the woman was asked about her assent to the faith on his behalf, so that this example might be useful for the churches. When a newborn child is brought forward to receive either the anointing of instruction or the anointing of perfection in holy baptism, the one bringing the child forward utters the "Amen" for the child. And for those who have been seized by their final illness and are about to be baptized, some individuals are set apart and appointed, out of love, to lend their own voice to the ones who are bound by illness. This is what we see in the case of Lazarus and his sister. Martha wisely and responsibly sows the confession of faith so that he might reap the fruit from it.

John 11:28–37

²⁸**When she had said this, she went and called her sister Mary, saying quietly, "The Teacher is here and is calling for you." ²⁹And when she heard it, she rose quickly and went to him. ³⁰Now Jesus had not yet come to the village, but was still in the place where Martha had met him. ³¹When the Jews who were with her in the house, consoling her, saw Mary rise quickly and go out, they followed her, supposing that she was going to the tomb to weep there. ³²Then Mary, when she came where Jesus was and saw him, fell at his feet, saying to him, "Lord, if you had been here, my brother would not have died." ³³When Jesus saw her weeping, and the Jews who came with her also weeping, he was deeply moved in spirit and troubled; ³⁴and he said, "Where have you laid him?" They said to him, "Lord, come and see." ³⁵Jesus wept. ³⁶So the Jews said, "See how he loved him!" ³⁷But some of them said, "Could not he who opened the eyes of the blind man have kept this man from dying?"**

11:33–35 When Jesus saw her weeping, and the Jews who came with her also weeping, he was deeply moved in spirit and troubled. . . . Jesus wept.

---

(22) John Chrysostom

Why does the evangelist carefully say several times that **he wept** (11:35) and was **deeply moved** (11:33)? So that you would learn that he truly took on our nature. Although this evangelist is more zealous than the others in speaking lofty things about Christ, here, when it comes to the body, he speaks more humbly than the other evangelists. For example, concerning Jesus's death, when the other evangelists say that Jesus was deeply grieved and in anguish, John says no such thing; on the contrary, he records that Jesus cast the soldiers backward (John 18:6). So to make up for what was lacking there, he mentions Jesus's grief here. When speaking about his death, Jesus says, *I have power to lay it down* (10:18); he says nothing humble at that time. For this reason, the other evangelists attribute many things to his humanity at the passion, demonstrating the truth of the incarnation. Matthew does this by showing his distress, his troubles, and his sweat (Matt 26:36–45),[6] but John by his grief. If he had not shared our nature, he would not have been agitated by sorrow again and again.

---

6. Matthew actually makes no mention of Jesus's "sweat." That can be found in Luke 22:44.

(23) Theodore of Mopsuestia

His being **deeply moved in spirit** (11:33) was a sign of his anger. Our Lord expressed his anger here because he knew beforehand that the Jews would not believe, even when they saw this miracle.

(24) Peter Chrysologus

Mary is **weeping**, the Jews are **weeping**, and even Christ is **weeping**. Do you think they all **weep** for the same reason? Let it be that the sister Mary **weeps** because she was able neither to hold on to her brother, nor to prevent his death. Although she was secure in her belief in the resurrection, nevertheless because she was without present comfort, because its delay would mean a long absence, and because she was grieved about his separation from God, she had to **weep**. At the same time, because death is so savage, so deadly, and so very cruel, it would disturb and unsettle any mind, whatever faith it had.

The Jews were **weeping**, both mindful of their own situation and seized by despair about the future life. Although death is bitter enough for those who are alive, and disturbing when someone dies, it is even more upsetting by the example it gives. Every time a person sees a corpse, he laments that he himself is destined for death. So a mortal cannot but grieve over death.

For which of these reasons did Christ **weep**? If none of them, why was he **weeping**? Indeed, it is he himself who had said: **Lazarus is dead; and I am glad** (11:14–15). The dead man about whom he was **glad** Christ now **weeps** over when he is about to raise him up. When he loses him, he does not **weep**, but when he lifts him up, then he **weeps**; he pours forth mortal tears at the very time when he pours in the spirit of life. Brothers and sisters, the nature of the human body is such that both the power of joy and the power of sorrow produce tears. As soon as our inward parts are tightened by an excessive impulse of happiness or sadness, our eyes erupt into tears. This is why Christ **wept**, not from the pain of death, but rather from the recollection of that joy when, by his own voice, and by his voice alone, he would raise all the dead to eternal life.

He was deeply moved in spirit and was very **troubled** (11:33) by the whole agitation of his inward parts. At this point he was going to raise Lazarus alone, but not all the dead. So who could think that Christ **wept** here out of human weakness when the heavenly Father **wept** over the prodigal son, not when he lost him but when he received him back (cf. Luke 15:11–32)? So Christ **wept** because he received Lazarus back, not because he lost him. Christ **weeps** not when he sees the **crowd weeping**, but when he inquires of them and sees no faith in those who answer him.

(25) Augustine of Hippo

I do not know what Christ has suggested to us by **deeply moving** his spirit and **troubling** himself. Who, except Jesus himself, is able to **trouble** him? So, my brothers and sisters, first attend to his power, and then inquire about its significance. You are **troubled** against your will; Christ is **troubled** because he wills it. Jesus hungers, it is true, but because he wills it. Jesus sleeps, indeed, but because he wills it. Jesus is saddened, truly, but because he wills to be so. Jesus dies, yes, but only because he wills it. It was in his power either to be affected or not to be affected. The Word received both soul and flesh by joining the nature of all humanity to himself in the unity of his person. . . .

So far, I've spoken of his power; attend now to its significance. It's a great sinner indeed who is signified by that four-day death and burial. Therefore, why does Christ **trouble** himself except to reveal how you ought to be **troubled** when so great a mass of sinful habits weighs you down and presses upon you? You have been examining yourself. You have seen your guilt. You have been thinking to yourself, "I did this and God spared me. I brought this about, and he was patient with me. I heard the gospel, and treated it with contempt. I have been baptized, and yet I have returned back to the same manner of life. What do I do? Where do I go? How do I escape?" When you say this, already Christ is **deeply moved**, because your faith is **deeply moved**. In the voice of one **deeply moved**, there appears the hope of rising again. If this faith is within you, there too is Christ **deeply moved**. If this faith is in us, Christ is in us. For this reason the apostle says: *That Christ may dwell in your hearts through faith* (Eph 3:17). Therefore, your faith in Christ is Christ himself dwelling in your heart.

(26) Cyril of Alexandria

Since Christ was not only God by nature but also human, his human nature suffers with the others. When grief is somehow **moved** in him and his holy flesh is already inclined toward tears, he does not allow himself to suffer this without restraint as is the custom for us. He was **moved in spirit**; that is, in the power of the Holy Spirit he rebukes his own flesh, in a way. The flesh will not endure the movement of divinity united to it. It trembles and takes the form of confusion. I think this is the meaning of the phrase, **he was troubled**. How could it submit to confusion otherwise? In fact, can the eternally untroubled and peaceful nature be **troubled** in any way? So the flesh is rebuked by the Spirit and taught to understand things beyond its own nature.

Notice then that the Word of God who conquers all exists in the flesh. Rather, he has become flesh in order to strengthen the weakness of the flesh by the activities of his own Spirit. He sets human nature free from more earthly thoughts and unifies those who please God. So, on the one hand, it is the disease of human nature to be under the sway of grief. On the other hand, this is first abolished in Christ, along with other things, so that he might also come to us.

(27) Cyril of Alexandria

Seeing the tearless nature weeping, the evangelist is amazed, even though his emotion was unique to the flesh and not befitting the Godhead. The Lord weeps when he beholds the man made in his own image having been corrupted, so that he might bring our tears to an end. For this is why he died: so that we too might be freed from death. He not only weeps, he also immediately holds back his tears, both so that someone may not think that he was cruel and inhuman, and to instruct us not to succumb to such grief for too long over those who have died. It is one thing to have sympathy for others, but another thing to become effeminate and unmanly. This is why Christ allows himself to weep a little in his own flesh, although in his own nature he was tearless and entirely unable to grieve. . . .

The Jews thought that Christ wept over Lazarus's death, but in reality he wept out of compassion for all human nature, bewailing not only Lazarus but understanding what happens to everyone, since all humanity has come under death, justly having fallen under such a penalty.

11:34 And he said, "Where have you laid him?"

---

(28) Cyril of Alexandria

It is not out of ignorance that he asks: **Where have you laid him?** (11:34). How could the one who knew of Lazarus's death even while in another part of the land not know where the tomb was? He speaks this way because he does not want to boast. He certainly does not say, "Let us go to the tomb, for I will raise him," although the way he answers most certainly means the same thing. Nevertheless, he answered the way he did and made many go ahead of him as if to show him what he sought. He wisely speaks this way in order to draw many to the place with those words. He feigns ignorance, not at all shrinking from the poverty of humanity even though he is God by nature and knows all things, not just the things that have been, but also the things that will be before they happen.

So his question does not indicate any ignorance in the one who for our sakes became like us. Rather, his question demonstrates his equality with the Father. For the Father also asks, *Adam, where are you?* (Gen 3:9). In the same way, Christ also feigns ignorance and inquires, **Where have you laid him?** (11:34). By this question the multitude gathers together for the demonstration, and many become witnesses against his enemies of the resurrection of one who had already died.

John 11:38-44

[38]Then Jesus, deeply moved again, came to the tomb; it was a cave, and a stone lay upon it. [39]Jesus said, "Take away the stone." Martha, the sister of the dead man, said to him, "Lord, by this time there will be an odor, for he has been dead four days." [40]Jesus said to her, "Did I not tell you that if you would believe you would see the glory of God?" [41]So they took away the stone. And Jesus lifted up his eyes and said, "Father, I thank thee that thou hast heard me. [42]I knew that thou hearest me always, but I have said this on account of the people standing by, that they may believe that thou didst send me."

⁴³**When he had said this, he cried with a loud voice, "Lazarus, come out." ⁴⁴The dead man came out, his hands and feet bound with bandages, and his face wrapped with a cloth. Jesus said to them, "Unbind him, and let him go."**

11:39–40 Jesus said, "Take away the stone." Martha . . . said to him, "Lord, by this time there will be an odor."

---

(29) Origen of Alexandria

Between the command **take away the stone** (11:39), and the response **so they took away the stone** (11:41), the words of the dead man's sister prevented the stone from being taken away. It would not have been taken away at all unless Jesus had responded to her unbelief by saying, **Did I not tell you that if you would believe you would see the glory of God?** (11:40). Therefore, it is a good thing when nothing comes between the command Jesus gives and the resulting action. I think, at any rate, that it is fitting to say that such a person has become an imitator of Christ.

Just as in one instance God *spoke, and it came to be; he commanded, and it stood forth* (Ps 33:9), so also Christ speaks to the believer and the believer does it. The Son of God commands, and the believer fulfills the commandment, neither exceedingly praising himself nor penalizing himself by the disobedience of delay between the command and its completion. . . . So let us remember this: *Do not delay to turn to the Lord, nor postpone it from day to day* (Sir 5:7); and this: *Do not say "Go, come back, and tomorrow I will give,"* *when you are able to do good* (Prov 3:28 LXX).

(30) Cyril of Jerusalem

Do you want to see more certain proof that some are saved by the faith of others? Lazarus died; one day had passed, and a second, and a third. His sinews were dissolved and corruption already fed upon his body. How could a man dead for four days believe and call for his own Redeemer? Yet what the dead man lacked, his true sisters fulfilled. When the Lord had come, the sister fell before him, and when he said, **Where have you laid him?** (11:34), she answered, **Lord by this time there will be an odor, for he has been dead four days** (11:39). The Lord said, **If you believe, you will see the glory of God** (11:40), as if he was saying, "You fulfill what is lacking in the dead man's faith." The faith of the sisters was so strong that it summoned the dead man from the gates of Hades. Some then, by believing on behalf of another, have been able to raise a man from the dead. Will you not, then, if you believe sincerely on your own behalf, benefit even more? Even if you are without faith or of little faith, the Lord is loving; he accommodates himself to the one who repents. Just say honestly: *I believe; help my unbelief!* (Mark 9:24).

(31) John Chrysostom

Christ says, **Take away the stone** (11:39). Why didn't he call out Lazarus from a distance and present him to them? Moreover, why didn't he raise him up while the **stone** was still laid in place? Surely, the one who is able to move the dead with his voice and show him living again is able to move the **stone** with his voice. The one who called Lazarus to walk, having been bound and entangled with burial clothes, could easily have moved the **stone**. Why then did he not do this? In order to make them witnesses of the miracle, so they would not say, like the blind man, *It is he*, or *It is not he* (9:9). They testified that it was Lazarus by coming to the tomb and touching it. If they had not come they would have thought it was a ghost or just a different man in his place. Instead, they came to the tomb and saw the removal of the stone. They were commanded to remove the bonds of the entombed man. The friends who brought him from the grave recognized him from his grave clothes. And his sisters, who were not left behind, said, **There will be an odor, for he has been dead four days** (11:39). All of these things were sufficient to silence the arrogant ones who were now witnesses of the miracle.

(32) Peter Chrysologus

Jesus said, "Take away the stone" (11:39). Does Christ seek humans to aid his divine powers? Is not the one who can drive off death able to remove the **stone**? Is not the one who can open the gates of Tartarus[7] strong enough to open the bars of the tomb? He had said through the prophet: *I will take the heart of stone out of them and give them a heart of flesh* (Ezek 11:19). Therefore, he instructed the Jews to remove the heart of **stone** from themselves, to roll away the boulder of faithlessness. He instructed them to expel the **stone** of hardened unbelief, so that their souls, dead through faithlessness, might leap from the tombs of their hearts and might rejoice, not so much because Lazarus had been raised, but because they had been raised with Lazarus. **Take away the stone** (11:39). **Take away** the bondage of wretched humanity so that the works of blessed divinity might now become manifest. **Take away the stone** that you all have put in place so that now I might restore the human being whom I have placed.

(33) Augustine of Hippo

Then Jesus came to the tomb; it was a cave, and a stone lay upon it (11:38). Dead under the **stone**, guilty under the law. You know that the Jewish law has been written on **stone** (cf. Exod 31:18). However, all the guilty are under the law while those who are well live with the law. The law is not placed on a just person (cf. 1 Tim 1:9). What then does Jesus mean: **Take away the stone** (11:39)? Proclaim grace! The apostle Paul calls himself a minister of the new covenant, not of the written code, but of the spirit: *For the written code*, he

7. The mythical place of the dead.

says, *kills, but the Spirit gives life* (2 Cor 3:6). The *written code* which *kills* is like the **stone** pressing down. **Take away the stone**, says Jesus. **Take away** the weight of the law; proclaim grace. *For if a law had been given which could make alive, then righteousness would indeed be by the law. But the scripture consigned all things to sin, that what was promised to faith in Jesus Christ might be given to those who believe* (Gal 3:21–22). Therefore, **take away the stone**.

(34) Augustine of Hippo

The Lord in his great grace and mercy raises our souls so that we do not suffer eternal death. Therefore, we understand well those three dead persons whom he raised bodily to signify figuratively the resurrection of souls which occurs through faith: he raised the synagogue ruler's daughter who was still lying in her house (Mark 5:35–42); he raised the widow's son who was carried outside of the city's gates (Luke 7:11–15); and he raised Lazarus who was buried for four days.

Consider the soul. If you sin, you die, for sin is the death of the soul. Sometimes we sin in thought. Perhaps you've taken delight in something evil; you've consented to it, and so you've sinned. That consent has killed you, but it's an internal death because the evil thought didn't yet become an action. By raising that girl (Mark 5:35–42) who had not yet been carried outside, who was lying dead in her house as if sin lay hidden, the Lord demonstrates that he raises such souls.

However, if you've not only delighted in evil, but also have done that evil thing itself, it's as if you have carried the dead outside the gate. Already you're outside the gate being carried away as dead. Yet the Lord has raised this one as well, restoring him to his widowed mother. If you have sinned, repent! The Lord raises you and restores you to your mother, the church.

The third dead one is Lazarus. He represents an extreme type of death, driven by a wicked habit. It's one thing to sin, another to make a habit of sinning. He who sins and immediately corrects his ways quickly grows strong, because he is not yet habitually entangled in sin; he is not yet buried. However, he who consents to sin is buried, and it's rightly said of him: **there will be an odor** (11:39); for he begins to have the worst kind of reputation, like a terrible **odor**. . . .

Yet the power of Christ was able to raise this one as well. We know and have seen— indeed we see every day—people who have exchanged the worst kinds of habits for better ones, living even better lives than those who were blaming them. You loathed such a person. Consider the sister of Lazarus herself (if indeed she was the one who anointed the Lord's feet with oil and wiped with her hair what she washed with her tears [cf. Luke 7:36–50]). She has been raised better than her brother; she has been freed from a great burden of wicked habits. She was an infamous sinner, and it has been said of her: *Her sins, which are many, are forgiven, for she loved much* (Luke 7:47). We see and know many like this. Let no one despair, but let no one presume too highly upon himself. It's evil to despair, and evil to presume upon yourself. Refuse to despair, so that you might choose to hope upon the one you ought to hope upon.

(35) Cyril of Alexandria

Jesus said to her, "Did I not tell you that if you would believe you would see the glory of God?" (11:40). . . . Because of a poverty of reason Martha lost her faith. The Lord, however, did not allow this to last, and he quickly gave her the appropriate remedy. He says that it is necessary to believe in order to behold the things beyond hope. Double-mindedness is a great illness and it deprives us of God's gifts. By admonishing her for this, he corrected the whole human race in order that it would not be defeated by the evil of double-mindedness.

(36) John of Damascus

Not only in word, but also in deed, did the Lord reveal the resurrection of the body. In the first place, he raised Lazarus who had been **dead four days** and there was an **odor** (11:39). He did not raise his soul deprived of the body, but the body with the soul—and not a different body, but the same one that had died. How would the resurrection of the dead man have been known or believed without confirming the very characteristics of his own personage? Therefore, the Lord raised Lazarus, who would one day die again, in order to demonstrate his own divinity and our belief in the resurrection—both his and ours.

> **11:41-42** "Father, I thank you that you have heard me. I knew that thou hearest me always, but I have said this on account of the people standing by, that they may believe that thou didst send me."

(37) Origen of Alexandria

The Savior was about to pray for the resurrection of Lazarus, but the only good God and Father received his prayer ahead of time; he heard the request about to be made in his prayer. So instead of a prayer, the Savior offers up thanksgiving over these things in the hearing of the crowd standing around him. Here he was doing two things at once, both giving thanks for the things which had happened concerning Lazarus, and establishing faith in the crowd standing around him. Indeed, he wanted to receive them, for this was why he was sent by God and dwelt in this life.

He knew that he had been heard, for in the spirit he saw the soul of Lazarus, which had been sent up from the place of souls, restored to his body. It must not be thought that Lazarus's soul was still present in the body after his death, and that because present, it immediately heard Jesus when he cried out and said: **Lazarus come out** (11:43). Perhaps someone does think this about Lazarus's soul and believes the ludicrous idea that the soul, once it has been released from the body, just sits there beside the dead person. Well then, explain to us how it was that Jesus was heard by the Father, if Lazarus's body remained there dead while his soul, separated from his body (as someone saying this would believe), is just sitting there next to it. . . .

Perhaps, as great as Jesus was, he saw the soul of Lazarus itself either being brought forth by those who are appointed for this task, or being brought by the Father's own will after he heard Jesus. After he saw it going in through the place from where the stone was removed, he said: **Father, I thank thee that thou hast heard me** (11:41).

(38) Hilary of Poitiers

Jesus prayed to the Father to raise Lazarus. Was his prayer somehow lacking when he said, **Father, I thank thee that thou hast heard me. I knew that thou hearest me always, but I have said this on account of the people standing by, that they may believe that thou didst send me** (11:41–42)? He prayed this way on our behalf, so that we would know he was the Son. He would not have gone further in his spoken prayer to the Father, but he was speaking so as to further develop our faith. So, he is not deficient in needing assistance, we are deficient in our learning.

(39) John Chrysostom

From this prayer, did Jesus receive divine help and raise the dead? How was it then that he did other miracles without praying, when he says: *I say to you demon, come out of him* (Mark 9:25); and *I will; be clean* (Mark 1:41); and *Rise, take up your pallet* (Mark 2:11); and *Your sins are forgiven you* (Luke 5:20); and to the sea, *Peace! Be still!* (Mark 4:39)? What greater power, if any, does he have than the apostles, if he himself must do things by prayer? Moreover, it would be better to say that they didn't do all things by prayer, but rather frequently called upon the name of Jesus. If his name has such great strength, how did Jesus stand in need of prayer? If he needed prayer, then his name would not have been strong. . . .

Let's look at what the prayer was: **Father, I thank thee that thou hast heard me** (11:41). Well then, who has ever prayed like this? Before he offers any prayer, he says **I thank thee**, which shows that he was not in need of prayer. **I knew that thou hearest me always** (11:42). This he says not as one powerless in himself, but as someone who is of one mind with the Father. Why did he even take up the form of a prayer? Don't listen to me; Jesus himself says: **On account of the people standing by, that they may believe that thou didst send me** (11:42).

He did not say: "That they may believe that I am lesser, that I have need of divine help from above, that without prayer I am not able to act," but **that thou didst send me**. Prayer indicates all of these ideas if we take it too simplistically. He did not say: "You have sent me—the weak one, the one who was a servant, the one who can do nothing of himself." Rather, putting aside all of these sentiments, so you won't hold him in suspicion, he sets forth the true essence of the prayer. "So that they may not consider me hostile to God," "so that they may not say—he is not from God," "so that I may show that the works have been done according to your judgment," as much as to say "that if I were hostile to God, then the things done would not have succeeded."

(40) Peter Chrysologus

Jesus lifted up his eyes (11:41) in order to show us how to make supplication, not to prepare a means of obtaining it for himself. In fact, the one who looks **up** is always **up** with the Father; the Father is in him, and he himself is always in the Father. As he says elsewhere: **I am in the Father and the Father in me** (14:10). Here he says: **Father, I thank thee that thou hast heard me** (11:41). Does Scripture say that he gives thanks for what has been fulfilled, and that the Father heard him, yet remains silent about what the Son asked for?

Brothers and sisters, between the Father and the Son there is a disposition for listening; there is no need for making supplication. There is an agreement of love, not the harshness of commands. There, all things are borne in love, where there is no need for subservience, as is clear from the following: **Father, I thank thee that thou hast heard me. I knew that thou hearest me always** (11:41–42). There is no concern about making a request where there is a certainty about being heard. What is the point of making a request when the means of accomplishing it is shared in common? Therefore no one should think less of the Son because of his prayer to the Father, nor think less of the Father's role in human salvation.

Yet why the Son speaks this way, he himself openly declares, saying: **Father, I thank thee that thou hast heard me. I knew that thou hearest me always, but I have said this on account of the people standing by** (11:41–42). You see that by speaking in this way he reveals the affection between him and the Father. He manifests gratitude and speaks about their unity. Elsewhere he said: *All that the Father has is mine* (16:15). If all things are his, why then does he make a request? He who asks for what is already his, asks not out of necessity, but out of love. **Father, I thank thee that thou hast heard me. I knew that thou hearest me always, but I have said this on account of the people standing by, that they may believe that thou didst send me** (11:41–42). He said that he was sent, so that the people might know that Christ had come from heaven, but had not withdrawn from heaven. So, as he is sent, so also he receives what he already has, just as he does not withdraw from whence he came. Therefore, the Son receives what he already has, and the Father does not lose what he has given. . . .

What does it mean when he says: **Father, I thank thee that thou hast heard me** (11:41)? What is this? Christ began to knock at the entrance of hell, to break the gates of Tartarus,[8] to open death's doors, to loosen the old law of gehenna, to overthrow the most ancient law of punishment, to demand back the soul of Lazarus, and to create a pathway out of hell. So the whole raging power of Tartarus met him, presented the edict of the heavenly ruler, carried the decree of the high king, and bore the sentence God spoke so many ages ago.[9] Upon seeing the man Jesus, he inquired who he was, what he dared to do, what his intentions were, and why, all alone and without fear, he attacked the fearful entrance to death.

To the one asking who he was, the angels, servants of the resurrection, responded with the words of the prophet: *He is the King of glory*, he is *strong and mighty in battle* (Ps 24:8, 10). Tartarus responded: "I know that the *King of glory* guards the celestial powers in all the heavens, and nothing in creation can endure his command. Yet this one that I see is from the earth, made out of mud and enveloped in a mortal body. His human condition is

---

8. The mythical place of the dead.
9. That is, the punishment of death for sin.

more worthless than other men. In short, he will quickly be surrendered to the grave and immediately put under my authority."

But the angels persisted and kept repeating: He is *the LORD of hosts, he is the King of glory* (Ps 24:10); he is the ruler of heaven, the Creator of the earth, the Savior of the world, and the Redeemer of all. He is the one who issued the sentence of death about which you are raging. He is going to trample on your head (cf. Gen 3:15), crush your authority, and destroy you with his own judgment, you who had been commanded to seize the innocent defendants you drag together, who tears apart the saints, and now threatens the very Son of God. So give back one before you are compelled to set all free.

Tartarus, still not believing the reports he received from his usual messengers, responded with this odious appeal to heaven: "O Lord, even though I am the lowest of your creation, even though I am subjected to sorrowful slavery, I am unfailing in preserving your commands. I remain watchful, lest any new violator alter the age-old authority of your sentence. But a man has appeared, who is called Christ, boasting that he is your Son. He censures your priests, accuses your scribes, violates your Sabbaths, abolishes your law, and compels souls who are released from their flesh and already assigned to my custody and punishment, to return to the bodies in which they had lived sinfully. His daring actions grow stronger every day so that now he has broken open the bars of hell and is trying to pluck out Lazarus—who has already been locked in our prison, already subject to our law, already remains in our custody. Either quickly come to help me, lest if he opens the doors once, you will lose all those whom I have guarded for so many ages."

To this the Son, from the bosom of the Father, responds: "Father, it is right that prison should hold the guilty, not the innocent; that punishment should torment the unjust, not the just. But how long, because of the fault of one man, on account of the guilt of Adam alone, has this executioner continued, with cruel violence, to drag to himself patriarchs, prophets, martyrs, confessors, virgins, widows, spouses remaining in chastity, people of all ages and of both sexes, and even little children who are ignorant of good or evil? Father, I will die, so that all may not die. Father, I will pay back Adam's debt, so that those who through Adam are dead in hell, may live for you through me. Father, on account of your sentence I will pour out my own blood, so important it is that your creation should return to you. May the price of my beloved blood be the redemption of all the dead."

To these words the whole Trinity agreed and commanded Lazarus to exit and Tartarus to obey Christ in returning all the dead. This is why the Son cries out: **Father, I thank thee that thou hast heard me** (11:41).

11:43–44 He cried with a loud voice, "Lazarus, come out." The dead man came out, his hands and feet bound with bandages.

---

(41) Origen of Alexandria

You should know that even today there are many Lazaruses who were friends of Jesus but became ill, passed away, and resided entombed in the land of the dead. They came back to life through Jesus's prayer and were called by him with a **loud voice** (11:43) to come out of the tomb. The one who trusts Jesus comes out tightly **bound**—by his previous sins—with bonds worthy of death and with his **face** still **wrapped** (11:44). He is unable to see or walk, or do anything because of the bonds of death, until Jesus gives the order to those who can release him and let him go. . . .

Christ **cries out with a loud voice** (11:43), calling his friend from the pagan way of life, the tomb, the cave. Then a disciple of Jesus can see how this kind of man can **come out** because of Jesus's voice. **Bound** and tied with the **bandages** of his own sins, he lives because he has repented and heard the voice of Jesus. Yet he still has his feet and hands **bound** with the bonds of death. He has still not been set free from the chains of sin. He still does not have even one foot free with which to walk or lead the good life. Because of this state of death which is in him, such a man is **bound** hand and foot, and his **face** is hidden in ignorance.

Jesus did not want him simply to come alive and then remain in the tomb. . . . So Jesus said to those who could help him: **Unbind him, and let him go** (11:44). I think that this is in agreement with the teaching about the possibility of repentance after sin. Lazarus came forth from the tomb still very weak in his ability to live by himself and to manage the active and contemplative powers of his soul. His **hands and feet** are still **bound**, and his **face** was **bound** with a cloth.

Christ's command is like that of a master, and he told those who could release him, **Unbind him, and let him go.** Then Lazarus's **feet and hands** were released, and the veil covering his **face** was removed and discarded. In fact, he advances so far that he thinks that he might become one of those who sit at the table with Jesus (cf. John 12:2).

(42) Ambrose of Milan

Seeing the heavy burden of sinners, the Lord Jesus weeps. He does not allow the church to weep alone, but has compassion for his loved one and says to the dead man: **Come out** (11:43), that is: "You who lie in the darkness of conscience and in the filth of your transgressions, in that prison of sinners, **come out**, declare your own sin that you may be justified." For *he confesses with his lips and so is saved* (Rom 10:10).

If upon Christ's call you will make confession, the bars will be destroyed and every bond will be untied, even if the odor of bodily corruption should be oppressive. Lazarus, whose flesh was reeking, spent four days in the tomb (John 11:39). However, Christ whose *flesh did not see corruption* (Acts 2:31) was in the tomb three days; he has not known the sins of the flesh, which consist of the four natural elements. So, no matter to what degree one may be dead, all is dispelled where the holy ointment will have emitted a scent. The dead man rises, and they who till now have been in sin are commanded to **unbind him** (11:44), to lift from his **face** the veil that was concealing the truth of grace which he had received. Since pardon has been given, he commands them to uncover his **face** to reveal his beauty; for the one whose sin is forgiven has nothing to be ashamed of. . . .

Therefore, what we read about Lazarus, we should believe the same about each converted sinner. Although he may have a foul stench, nevertheless, he is cleansed with the ointment of precious faith. Faith possesses so much grace that where the dead one previously lay stinking, now the whole house is filled with a fragrant aroma.

(43) Ambrose of Milan

Even now the Lord offers you an example in the gospel of how you will rise again. He has caused not just the one man Lazarus to rise, but the faith of all! If you believe what you read, your mind (which was also dead) comes to life again in that man Lazarus. What does the Lord desire when he approaches the tomb, **crying out with a loud voice, "Lazarus, come out"** (11:43)? He supplies a picture of the future resurrection by way of example. Why did he **cry out with a loud voice**, as though he was not accustomed to work with the Spirit or used to commanding silently? He did so in order to reveal what is written, since *in a moment, in the twinkling of an eye, at the last trumpet, the dead will be raised imperishable* (1 Cor 15:52). The **cry** of a **voice** imitates the blast of trumpets.

(44) Augustine of Hippo

Christ was deeply troubled; he wept and **cried with a loud voice** (11:43). With what great difficulty does someone rise who is crushed down by the weight of sinful habits![10] He rises nonetheless; he is brought back to life by grace hidden within; he rises after a **loud voice**.

What happened? **He cried with a loud voice, "Lazarus, come out." The dead man came out, his hands and feet bound with bandages, and his face wrapped with a cloth** (11:43–44). Are you astonished that he **came out** with **bound feet**, but not amazed that he rose after being dead four days? Both of these display the power of the Lord rather than the strength of death.

He **came out**, and still is **bound**; still **wrapped with a cloth**, he now **came out**. What does this signify? When you disdain Christ, you lie dead; and if you disdain him to such a degree as I have said, you lie buried. When you confess, you **come out**. For what is it to **come out**, except to make known your **coming out** as if from hiding? God makes it possible for you to confess by **crying out with a loud voice**, that is, **crying out** with great grace. The dead man came forth still **bound**. He came confessing but was still guilty. Yet, in order for him to be loosed from his sins, the Lord said to the servants: **Unbind him, and let him go** (11:44). What does he mean by saying, **Unbind him, and let him go**? *Whatever you loose on earth shall be loosed in heaven* (Matt 16:19).

(45) Augustine of Hippo

Among all the miracles which our Lord Jesus Christ performed, the resurrection of Lazarus is foremost in our preaching. If we pay close attention to who did it, we ought to delight

---

10. Augustine is referring to Lazarus, who represents someone who is crushed under sin.

rather than marvel. . . . For you heard that the Lord Jesus raised a dead man; this suffices for you to know that if he wanted to, he could raise all the dead. This indeed he has reserved for himself until the end of the world. While you have heard that by a great miracle he raised from the tomb one who was dead for four days, *the hour is coming*, as he himself says, *when all who are in the tombs will hear his voice and come forth* (5:28–29). He raised one who was rotting, yet the form of limbs was still in that rotten body. On the last day, he will restore ashes into flesh with a single word. Yet, it was appropriate for him to perform only a few such miracles, so that we, taking it as evidence of his power, might believe in him and be prepared for that resurrection to life, not to judgment.

(46) Cyril of Alexandria

Oh what a miracle! He managed to bring forth from the tomb a dead man reeking of a noxious odor because four days had passed since his burial. Moreover, he commanded him to walk, he whose **hands and feet** were **bound**. Immediately the dead man was no longer dead; he threw off his burial shrouds, lost his odious smell, and escaped from the gates of death. Even though his face covering prevented him from seeing, he ran without any difficulty toward him who had been calling him, recognizing his authoritative voice. . . .

What can we say when we see him **crying** out so unusually? Surely no one would be so foolish as to say that Christ ever acted in an unfitting way or strayed from absolute perfection.[11] How, then, can we explain it? Certainly the **cry** has a reason and a purpose, and it is something that we have to mention. It was for the benefit of those listening. Christ performed the miracle on Lazarus as a type of the general resurrection of the dead. That which was fulfilled for an individual he set forth as a beautiful image of what will be universal and common to the whole race. It is part of our faith that the Lord will come, and we believe that there will be a **cry** from the *sound of a trumpet*, in Paul's words (1 Thess 4:16), proclaiming the resurrection to those who lie in the earth. . . .

Jesus said to them, "Unbind him, and let him go" (11:44). Here we have a demonstration of the general resurrection when sin and the corruption of death are unbound and one is truly set free. Shame falls as a veil over the **face** of those who have fallen into sin, and they are bound to death. Therefore, at the time of the resurrection, Christ will bring us out of our tombs in the earth, **unbind** us from our former evils, and remove, so to speak, the veil of shame. He will command that we be **let go** freely from that time forward—no longer under the dominion of sin, nor subject to corruption or indeed any of the other evils that cause us to suffer. In this way, it will be fulfilled in us what was said by one of the holy prophets: *You shall go out and leap like calves let loose from their tethers* (Mal 4:2 LXX).

---

11. Cyril is thinking of the passage in Isa 42:2 that speaks of the coming Messiah: *He will not cry or lift up his voice.*

John 11:45–53

[45]Many of the Jews therefore, who had come with Mary and had seen what he did, believed in him; [46]but some of them went to the Pharisees and told them what Jesus had done. [47]So the chief priests and the Pharisees gathered the council, and said, "What are we to do? For this man performs many signs. [48]If we let him go on thus, every one will believe in him, and the Romans will come and destroy both our holy place and our nation." [49]But one of them, Caiaphas, who was high priest that year, said to them, "You know nothing at all; [50]you do not understand that it is expedient for you that one man should die for the people, and that the whole nation should not perish." [51]He did not say this of his own accord, but being high priest that year he prophesied that Jesus should die for the nation, [52]and not for the nation only, but to gather into one the children of God who are scattered abroad. [53]So from that day on they took counsel how to put him to death.

11:47–48 "What are we to do? For this man performs many signs. If we let him go on thus, every one will believe in him, and the Romans will come and destroy both our holy place and our nation."

---

(47) John Chrysostom

When the **sign** occurred, some of the people were amazed. Others went and reported to the Pharisees. Why do they do this? When they ought to be dumbstricken and amazed, they're planning to do away with the one who had raised a dead man to life. O what stupidity! They thought they should hand over to death the very one who had overcome death in the bodies of others. They say, **What are we to do? For this man performs many signs?** (11:47). They still call him a man, even though they have received proof of his divinity.

　　What are we to do? they say (11:47). Believe and worship! Bow down before him! Consider him a man no longer! **If we let him go on thus, the Romans will come and will destroy our nation** and our city, they say (11:48). What are they planning to do? They want to persuade the people that they're in danger of coming under suspicion for setting up a new kingdom. One of them says, "For if the Romans learn that he is gathering crowds, they will suspect us and come and demolish our city." Why? Here's the reason. He wasn't teaching you to revolt, was he? He was instructing you to give tribute to Caesar, was he not (Matt 22:15–22)? Didn't you want to make him king, and didn't he reject this (John 6:14–15)? Didn't he display a frugal and modest way of life without possessing either a home or anything else of that sort? Well they said all this, not expecting it to happen, but rather intending evil for him. And it did come about, even though they did not expect it; since they killed him, the Romans took both their **nation** and their city.

(48) Augustine of Hippo

So they said, "What are we to do? For this man performs many signs. If we let him go on thus, every one will believe in him, and the Romans will come and destroy both our holy place and our nation" (11:47–48). They feared that they might lose temporary things, but they didn't realize that they might lose eternal life. So they lost both; for after the passion and glorification of the Lord, the Romans took both their **holy place and their nation**—one by destruction, and the other by transformation.

11:49–52 Caiaphas [said]: "It is expedient for you that one man should die for the people, and that the whole nation should not perish." . . . Being high priest that year he prophesied.

---

(49) Origen of Alexandria

A person is not a prophet simply because he recites prophecies. Indeed **Caiaphas**, who was high priest that year, **prophesied** that Jesus should **die** for the **nation**, and not only for the **nation** but also to **gather into one the children of God who are scattered abroad** (11:52). Yet he is not a prophet. Balaam prophesied those things which have been recorded in the book of Numbers, saying, *The word that God puts in my mouth, that must I speak* (Num 22:38) and his discourse which he begins by saying, *From Mesopotamia, Balak has sent for me* (Num 23:7). Even so, it is clear that he was not a prophet, for it has been written that he was a soothsayer (cf. Josh 13:22). Therefore, if someone is a prophet, he always prophesies, but just because he recites prophesies does not necessarily make him a prophet. . . .

Even if **Caiaphas prophesied**, the Holy Spirit was not in him, for it was said, *For as yet the Spirit had not been given, because Jesus was not yet glorified* (7:38). Indeed, if the Spirit was not even in the apostles before Jesus was glorified, how much less in **Caiaphas**? After the Savior's resurrection, Jesus *breathed on* his disciples and *said to them, "Receive the Holy Spirit,"* and so on (20:22). Someone will then take what we have said and boldly make the case that **Caiaphas** did not prophesy by the Holy Spirit. At the same time, though, he will say that it is possible even for wicked spirits to give witness to Jesus, that is, to prophesy about him or to give witness to him, as the spirit who said, *I know who you are, the Holy One of God* (Mark 1:24), and those spirits who beseeched him so that he would not order them to return to the abyss saying, *Did you come to destroy us?* (Mark 1:24). . . .

Moreover, if one wants **Caiaphas** to have **prophesied** through the instigation of some lesser power, he will say that it is not contradictory for an evil power to have said these things. Even the devil is not altogether ignorant; even he recognizes that Jesus is the Son of God, as the writings of the evangelists record that the devil spoke to the Lord (cf. Luke 4:41; Mark 3:11). One can also say that the power that here initiates the prophecy about the Savior possesses a certain wickedness. Its goal is not to make the listeners believe but rather to stir up the chief priests and Pharisees of the Sanhedrin against Jesus so that they will kill him—which was clearly not in accord with the Holy Spirit's activity.

Consider the statement: **You know nothing at all; you do not understand that it is expedient for us that one man should die for the people, and that the whole nation should not perish** (11:49–50). Do either **Caiaphas** or the one giving him power to prophesy want to incite the listeners to kill Jesus? Indeed, he says **it is expedient for us**—and as for this part of the prophecy, is he telling the truth or is he lying? If he is telling the truth, then, when Jesus dies on behalf of the people, **Caiaphas** is saved along with the rest of those in the Sanhedrin who were accusing Jesus, and they all gain that which is **expedient**. Yet, if it is absurd to say that **Caiaphas** and the others who accused Jesus in the Sanhedrin are saved and that they have gained what is **expedient** after Jesus's death, then clearly the Holy Spirit was not the one who inspired him to say these things. For the Holy Spirit does not lie.

(50) John Chrysostom

What did Caiaphas say? **You know nothing at all, nor do you understand that it is expedient that one man should die, and that the whole nation should not perish. He did not say this of his own accord, but being high priest that year he prophesied** (11:49–51). Do you see how great the power of the high priest's authority is? Since he was considered wholly worthy of the high priesthood, **he prophesied**, not understanding what he was saying. Grace was declared by his mouth alone but didn't touch his impure heart. Indeed, many others have spoken of things to come, and yet were unworthy, such as Nebuchadnezzar (Dan 2 and 4), Pharaoh, and Balaam (cf. Num 22–24). The cause of all this is obvious. . . . See how great the power of the Spirit is! From a wicked thought, it was able to bring forth words full of marvelous prophecy.

(51) Gregory of Nyssa

The truth seems to be made apparent even by those who fight against it, since falsity cannot utterly prevail over truth, even by words of the enemy. For this reason, the orthodox faith is preached by the mouth of those who oppose it, even when they do not know what they are saying, just as the Lord's saving passion for us was foretold by **Caiaphas**, even when he did not know what he was saying (11:51).

(52) Augustine of Hippo

Here we learn that the Spirit of prophecy foretells the future even through wicked men, although the evangelist attributes this to divine mystery, because he was the pontifex (that is to say, the high priest). . . . So then, what is it that **Caiaphas prophesied? That Jesus should die for the nation, and not for the nation only, but to gather into one the children of God who are scattered abroad** (11:51–52). The evangelist has added this last bit, for Caiaphas prophesied only for the Jewish nation which contained the sheep that the Lord himself spoke of: *I was sent only to the lost sheep of the house of Israel* (10:16). The evangelist knew that there were other sheep which were not of this flock, which also needed to be drawn in so that they might be **one flock with one shepherd** (10:16). These things were said by predestination, for those who did not yet believe were neither his sheep nor the children of God.

(53) Cyril of Alexandria

They were conspiring to do just what we were saying earlier, and the high priest openly counsels them to do that: to kill Christ. That was why he said that it would be good **for the nation**, although **the nation** was unjust. Although what he said was true, he did not realize that his words were proven right not by the moral perversity of the people, but by the power and wisdom of God. To their own detriment they killed him, but he, *being put to death in the flesh* (1 Pet 3:18), became the source of all good things for us.

When **Caiaphas** spoke about the destruction of the **nation** (11:48), he was referring to what would happen at the hands of the Romans which would cause the loss of the shadow of the law. In the end they suffered the very thing they were trying to avoid. Therefore **Caiaphas** spoke what he did from an unlawful intention, but his explanatory speech was as true as if he occupied the office of a prophet. He proclaimed beforehand the good things which the death of the Christ would bring about, saying something which he did not understand. He glorified God, just like Balaam did, under compulsion because he was holding the office of the priesthood. It was as if the prophecy was given not to him personally, but to the position of the priesthood.

So, of all the things that **Caiaphas** said, the last one happened and he passed away without receiving the prophetic gift. For it is likely that what some people say will actually happen, although they may say it without knowing for certain that it will come to pass. **Caiaphas** said that the death of Christ would be for the Jews only, but the evangelist says that it was for all humanity, so that we all might be the offspring and children of God. He is the Father of all, having created all things and brought into existence that which did not exist. We had from the beginning the honor of being made in his image. We had supremacy over the earth and were accounted worthy of the divine covenant, enjoying life and the bliss of paradise. But unwilling to allow us to remain in that state, Satan **scattered** us, and in a variety of ways led humanity away from their nearness to God. Christ **gathered** us all together again and brought us through faith into **one** fold, the church. He united us under one yoke, making us all one—Jews, Greeks, Barbarians, Scythians. We are fashioned again into *one new man* (Eph 2:15) and worship one God.

John 11:54-57

[54]Jesus therefore no longer went about openly among the Jews, but went from there to the country near the wilderness, to a town called Ephraim; and there he stayed with the disciples. [55]Now the Passover of the Jews was at hand, and many went up from the country to Jerusalem before the Passover, to purify themselves. [56]They were looking

for Jesus and saying to one another as they stood in the temple, "What do you think? That he will not come to the feast?" [57] Now the chief priests and the Pharisees had given orders that if any one knew where he was, he should let them know, so that they might arrest him.

11:55 Now the Passover of the Jews was at hand.

---

(54) Augustine of Hippo

Now the Passover of the Jews was at hand (11:55). They wanted to have the feast day stained with the blood of the Lord. On that feast day, the lamb was slaughtered, and he consecrated the day for us with his own blood. There was a plan among them to kill Jesus, the one who had come from heaven to suffer; and he wished to hasten on to the place of his suffering because the hour of his passion was drawing near. **And many went up from the country to Jerusalem before the Passover, to purify themselves** (11:55). They did this according to the word of the Lord given through holy Moses in his law. On the feast day (which was the **Passover**) everyone gathered together from all places and was sanctified in celebrating that day.

That celebration was a shadow of the future. What is this shadow? It's the prophecy of the coming of Christ, the prophecy that he should suffer that day on our behalf; that he might pass through the shadows and arrive in light; that symbols might pass away, and only the truth remain. They held their **Passover** in shadow, but we celebrate in light. For why would the Lord instruct them to sacrifice a lamb on the feast day unless it was because of the prophecy that he is *like a lamb that is led to the slaughter* (Isa 53:7)? Their doorposts were marked with the blood of the slaughtered animal (Exod 12:7); our foreheads are marked with the blood of Christ. That seal, which was only a symbol itself, is said to have chased death away from the houses that bore it; likewise the sign of Christ repels death if our heart welcomes the Savior.

Why have I said this? Because many doorposts bear seals, but no inhabitant remains inside. Many people easily bear the seal of Christ on their foreheads, but their hearts do not welcome the words of Christ. Therefore I have said this, brothers and sisters, and I will say it again: the seal of Christ repels death from us only if our heart welcomes Christ as an inhabitant. I have said these things in case someone should wonder what the feast of the Jews has to do with them. The Lord came as though to a sacrifice, so that we might know the true meaning of the **Passover** when we celebrate his passion as the true sacrificial lamb.

John 12

The church fathers are intrigued by the inclusion of Judas Iscariot in the group of disciples and the unique responsibility he holds as the bursar (12:6). John Chrysostom shows that he was a thief and that his love of money corrupted his heart. Augustine states that he was not a true disciple; he symbolically stands for the evil people who abound in the world and also in the church. The contrast between Judas's selfish act and Mary's anointing of Jesus with the costly ointment (12:5) is highlighted by Cyril of Alexandria and Theodore. In response to Jesus's rebuke to Judas, The poor you always have with you, but you do not always have me *(12:8), Cyril states that after the ascension of the Savior, the disciples were able to focus entirely on the needs of the poor since they were no longer following their teacher.*

When Lazarus was raised from the dead by Jesus, great crowds of Jews came to see. The evangelist states that the chief priests plotted Lazarus's death (12:9–10). John Chrysostom says that they sought to kill him because he was a well-known man from Bethany, a town near Jerusalem. Augustine ridicules their foolish plan: "Could Christ the Lord who raised the dead not also raise a person who is murdered?" Cyril notes that the disciples failed to understand the meaning of Christ's triumphal entry into Jerusalem (12:12–15); however, when Jesus was glorified—that is, resurrected—the disciples were enlightened by his Spirit and understood.

The attention of Augustine, John Chrysostom, and Cyril is drawn to the inclusion of Greeks at the Jewish Feast of Passover (12:20). Finding this at odds with general Jewish custom, they discover the hermeneutical key to this puzzle in John 12:23: The hour has come for the Son of man to be glorified. *Why this* hour? *Many of the Jews had turned against Jesus, but some Greeks had come to see Jesus. This foreshadows that his crucifixion and resurrection would be for the whole world. John Chrysostom uses the metaphor of the dying seed that* bears much fruit *to explain the doctrine of the bodily resurrection. John Cassian, commenting on 12:26, unfolds the meaning of the resurrection for those who* serve *Christ.*

When Christ says, Now is my soul troubled *(12:27), Tertullian, Ambrose, and Augustine use this as an occasion to explore his two natures. They identify his* troubled *soul as part of his assumed human nature and seek to dispel the notion that the divine person suffered emotional turmoil. Athanasius states that John 12:32 does not just indicate that Jesus was crucified but that his crucifixion accomplished symbolically the embrace of humanity. Jesus said,* I, when I am lifted up from the earth, will draw all men to myself *(12:32). Athanasius states that only a person who is crucified dies with his arms outstretched and thus* draws *all people to himself in that act.*

Augustine wrestles with the tension between divine determination and human free will, indicated by John's conclusion that they could not believe. *For Isaiah again said, "He has blinded their eyes and hardened their heart, lest they should see with their eyes and perceive with their heart, and turn for me to heal them" (12:39-40). Augustine maintains that God foresees human disobedience and impiety but does not cause it; rather, each person is permitted freely to choose or reject God. He states that the phrase* could not believe *is better rendered "would not believe," for the fault rests solely with the human will. Augustine and Jerome both analyze verse 41 to identify the enthroned figure of the Godhead beheld by Isaiah.*

The concluding verses of this chapter provide an occasion for Ambrose, John Chrysostom, and Augustine to parse the relationship of the Father and the Son. The evangelist records the following: And Jesus cried out and said, "He who believes in me, believes not in me but in him who sent me. And he who sees me sees him who sent me" *(12:44-45). Both Ambrose and John painstakingly show that sometimes Christ speaks in a self-deprecating manner vis-à-vis the Father in respect to his humanness (cf. 12:44); at other times he speaks as one wholly equal to the Father (cf. 12:45). Augustine offers a similar analysis but highlights the fact that Christ is the Word of God and thus communicates the truth of God in a mode that can be heard by humans, for he is the incarnate Son who speaks audibly. For Augustine, this condescension of the divine Word is an accommodation to our weakness; he proclaims that the truth ultimately does not "teach with sounds but floods our minds with the light of understanding."*

John 12:1-8

[1]Six days before the Passover, Jesus came to Bethany, where Lazarus was, whom Jesus had raised from the dead. [2]There they made him a supper; Martha served, and Lazarus was one of those at table with him. [3]Mary took a pound of costly ointment of pure nard and anointed the feet of Jesus and wiped his feet with her hair; and the house was filled with the fragrance of the ointment. [4]But Judas Iscariot, one of his disciples (he who was to betray him), said, [5]"Why was this ointment not sold for three hundred denarii and given to the poor?" [6]This he said, not that he cared for the poor but because he was a thief, and as he had the money box he used to take what was put into it. [7]Jesus said, "Let her alone, let her keep it for the day of my burial. [8]The poor you always have with you, but you do not always have me."

12:6-8 This [Judas] said, not that he cared for the poor but because he was a thief. . . . Jesus said, "Let her alone, let her keep it for the day of my burial. The poor you always have with you, but you do not always have me."

---

(1) Ambrose of Milan

Perhaps it may be asked of the **thief** (12:6): "You were rich, so why did you take someone else's things? Necessity did not force you; poverty did not compel you. Did I not make you rich for that very reason so that you would have no excuse?" It might also be asked of those in power: "Why did you not help the widows and the orphans when they were suffering from injustices? Is it possible that you were powerless? Were you not able to come to their aid? For this reason I made you powerful so that you might not do wrong but instead resist it. Is it not written for you: *Deliver him who is wronged* (Sir 4:9)? Is it not also written: *Rescue the weak and the needy; deliver them from the hand of the wicked* (Ps 82:4 [81:4 LXX])? It may be said to the prosperous man: "I have blessed you with children and honors and have given you physical health. Why did you not follow my commandments? My servant, *what have I done to you? In what have I wearied you?* (Mic 6:3). Did I not give you children, confer honors, and grant you good health? Why did you reject me? Why did you think that your conduct would not come to my attention? Why did you accept my gifts but despise my commands?"

It is possible to consider the same lesson concerning **Judas** (12:4) the traitor. He was chosen as an apostle among the Twelve. He was also placed in charge of the **money box** (12:6) which he disbursed to the poor so that it would not seem that he betrayed the Lord because he was dishonored or in need. Accordingly, the Lord granted this responsibility to **Judas** in order that he may be justified in him. Since he was not provoked by a wrong against him, **Judas** was guilty of a greater offense. Instead he sinned against grace.

(2) John Chrysostom

Judas then rebuked Mary under the pretense of discretion. What does Christ say? "She has done a good deed for my burial" (cf. Mark 14:8). Why did he not expose the disciple by using the example of this woman? Why did he not declare what the evangelist said, namely that Judas rebuked her **because he was a thief** (12:6)? With his abundant patience, Christ wished to reform him. From the beginning, he reproached Judas often because he knew that he was a traitor. He said, *Not all believe* (6:64), and *One of you is a devil* (6:70). He showed that he knew Judas was a traitor; yet he did not expose him openly but persisted with the hope of calling him back. How then does Matthew say that all the disciples said this same thing?[1] They made the same statement as Judas but did not share his motive.

If someone asks why Christ put the collection bag for the poor into the hands of a **thief** (12:6) and made a money-grubber the bursar, we should reply that only God knows the real reason. But we might surmise that he did it to destroy every possible excuse. Judas could not say that he did this from a love of money, because he had enough from the collection bag to satisfy his desire. Instead, Christ wished to restrain his excessive wickedness by meeting him where he was. Even though he knew about his stealing, he did not expose him as a **thief** (12:6). Instead he hindered his wicked desires and removed every excuse from him.

---

1. John Chrysostom has in mind Matthew's account of Mary's devotion at Bethany: *But when the disciples saw it, they were indignant, saying, "Why this waste? For this ointment might have been sold for a large sum, and given to the poor"* (Matt 26:8–9).

(3) John Chrysostom

Jesus said, "Let her alone, let her keep it for the day of my burial" (12:7). Again he mentions the traitor when he speaks about his burial. But Christ's reproach does not touch him. Nor do his words mollify him although they are sufficient to instill him with grief. It is as if Christ had said, "I am tired and grieved, but will only remain a little longer, and then I will depart." He intended this also when he said, **But you do not always have me** (12:8). However, none of these utterances redirected that madman. Jesus said and did much more even than this. He washed Judas's feet that night and shared his table and salt with him. These actions are known to constrain even the souls of thieves. He spoke other words which were capable even of softening a stone. He uttered these not many days before but on that very day in order that the passage of time would not cause it to be forgotten. But Judas withstood all of these things.

The love of money is horrible! It maims both the eyes and the ears and makes humans more dangerous than a wild beast. It incapacitates a person from considering his conscience, friendship, community, or even the salvation of his soul. After separating a man from all these things, the love of money makes those whom it ensnares slaves, just as a harsh tyrant. The terrible part of such a bitter enslavement is that it persuades them to be thankful for it. The more they become enslaved to the love of money, the more their pleasure increases. In this way the sickness becomes incurable; the beast becomes nearly unstoppable. The love of money made Gehazi a leper instead of a disciple and a prophet (2 Kgs 5:20–27). It also destroyed Ananias and his wife (Acts 5:1–10). The love of money made Judas a traitor. It corrupted rulers of the Jews, who received gifts and became *companions of thieves* (Isa 1:23). Moreover, it has caused ten thousand wars, filling roads with blood and cities with dirges and funeral songs. The love of money has rendered meals impure, tables unclean, and filled meat with pollution. For these reasons, Paul called the love of money *idolatry* (Col 3:5).

(4) Theodore of Mopsuestia

Jesus defended Mary so that he did not leave Judas's accusation hanging over her head. He also spoke gently, so that it would not appear as if he put himself before the poor. For this reason he speaks in an obscure manner. He does not rebuke Judas who reproached her without reason, nor does he charge him with being a liar. He knew that there was nothing to be gained from that rebuke. What Jesus means is something like this: "Why blame the woman, who ought to be praised because of her love for me? However, because I am rushing toward my suffering, you should show sympathy instead of assuming that I, who will die soon, received a great benefit. Do you not think that I am even worthy of a burial? She will not be able to do this when I will die. It will not be possible, for two days later she will no longer find me dead." That is what the saying **Let her alone, let her keep it for the day of my burial** (12:7) means. If you truly care about the poor, you have many opportunities to do the right thing for **the poor you always have with you, but you do not always have me** (12:8).

(5) Augustine of Hippo

Many suppose that **Judas** only perished at the time when he accepted the money from the Jews to betray the Lord. He did not perish at that point, for he was already a **thief** (12:6). He was already lost when he accompanied the Lord, for he followed with his body and not with his heart. He was the twelfth apostle in number, but he did not possess the apostolic blessing. He was the twelfth in likeness only. When he fell and another replaced him, the true and the complete apostolic number was established (cf. Acts 1:21–26). What was our Lord Jesus Christ trying to teach his church when he included a lost soul among the Twelve unless it was that we should put up with the wicked and resist dividing the body of Christ? Here among the saints is **Judas** the **thief** (12:6)! Do not disregard this! He is not just a common thief, but one who steals sacred objects! A robber of the Lord's **money box** (12:6)! A robber of the sacred satchel! If public courts distinguish between ordinary theft and embezzlement of public property and render different sentences on private and public theft, how much more severe should the sentence be on the **thief** who steals not from an ordinary place but from the church? The one who steals from the church is regarded as equal to the immoral **Judas**. He was such a person, and yet he went in and out with the eleven holy disciples. He ate at the table of the Lord with them. He lived with them, but he did not defile them. Peter and Judas both took pieces of bread from the same loaf, yet what portion did the believer share with the unbeliever? Peter took it, and it led to life; Judas took it, and it led to death. . . . This good bread with its sweet odor gave life to the good, yet brought death to the wicked. *For anyone who eats and drinks without discerning the body eats and drinks judgment upon himself* (1 Cor 11:29), but not upon you. Since the judgment is delivered against him and not against you, the good should tolerate the wicked so that you might attain the rewards of the good and not be thrown into the punishment of the wicked. . . .

 The poor you always have with you, but you do not always have me (12:8). We can certainly understand **The poor you always have**. What he has said is true. When has the church been without the poor? However, what does he mean when he says, **But you do not always have me**? How should we understand **but you do not always have me**? Don't be frightened! This was said to Judas. But why did he not say **you will not have** instead of *all of* **you will not always have**? Because Judas is not alone. One bad man stands for the whole body of the wicked. In a similar way Peter stands for the whole body of the good and particularly the good ones within the body of the church. If Peter is not the symbol of the church, the Lord would not have said, *I will give you the keys of the kingdom of heaven, and whatever you bind on earth shall be bound in heaven, and whatever you loose on earth shall be loosed in heaven* (Matt 16:19). If this was said to Peter only, the church is not able to carry out this charge. If it is given to the church, then what is bound on earth is bound in heaven and what is loosed on earth is loosed in heaven. When the church excommunicates someone, that person is bound in heaven. Conversely, when one is reconciled by the church, this person is loosed in heaven. Since this is the case with the church, Peter symbolized the holy church when he received the keys. If Peter signified the good in the church and Judas represented the bad, then the statement **but you do not always have me** was addressed to the latter group. What does **not always** mean? If you are good and if you belong to the body of the church which is symbolized by Peter, you will have Christ both now and in the future. You have him now by faith, by a sign, by the sacrament of baptism, by the bread and wine of the altar. You have Christ now, and you will have him **always**. When you depart this world, you will come to the one who said to the thief, *Today you will be with me in Paradise* (Luke 23:43). If however you live wickedly, you may seem to have Christ now because you enter the church, cross yourself with sign of Christ, are baptized with the baptism of Christ, surround yourself with the members of Christ and kneel before his altar. You have Christ now, but you will **not always** have him, because you live wickedly.

The poor you always have with you, but you do not always have me may be also understood in the following way. If he were speaking of his bodily presence, the good may understand this as addressed to them without being troubled. According to his majesty, his providence, his ineffable and invisible grace, his words were fulfilled: *And lo, I am with you always, to the close of the age* (Matt 28:20). However, in respect to his fleshly body which he assumed as the Word—which was born from a virgin, seized by the Jews, nailed to the tree, taken down from the cross, wrapped in a burial sheet, laid in the tomb, manifested in his resurrection, he said, **You do not always have me.** Why? Because he spent forty days with his disciples leading them away so that they could see him, yet not follow. Then he ascended into heaven and is no longer here (cf. Acts 1:1–11). He is seated at the right hand of the Father. Yet he is here, because he did not withdraw his divine presence. We always have Christ in respect to his divine presence. He was referring to his presence in the flesh when he said to his disciples, **You do not always have me.** The church had him in his bodily presence for only a few days. Now it possesses him by faith, because it does not see him with eyes. So it should be said that the saying **you do not always have me** could be understood in either of these two ways.

(6) Cyril of Alexandria

Six days before the Passover, Jesus came to Bethany, where Lazarus was, whom Jesus had raised from the dead. There they made him a supper; Martha served, and Lazarus was one of those at table with him (12:1). Jesus ate with Lazarus and his friends **six days before the Passover** since it was necessary that the lamb be purchased and kept until the fourteenth day (cf. Exod 12:6). It was a long-held custom, albeit not derived from the law, for the Jews to celebrate on the day before the lamb was acquired. From the time that the lamb was procured up until the feast, they devoted themselves to fasting and to purification rituals. In this way the Lord is shown to have honored the customs of the festival. Amazingly, the evangelist says that Lazarus, who had been dead for four days, was eating with Christ. This serves to remind us of Christ's divine power. He adds that **Martha**, due to her love for Christ, **served** and waited on those at the table. . . .

But Judas Iscariot, one of his disciples (he who was to betray him), said, "Why was this ointment not sold for three hundred denarii and given to the poor?" This he said, not that he cared for the poor but because he was a thief, and as he had the money box he used to take what was put into it. Jesus said, "Let her alone, let her

keep it for the day of my burial. The poor you always have with you, but you do not always have me" (12:4–8). . . . Jesus defended his anointing with the **ointment**, for it was not done on account of extravagance but as a sort of mystery for his **burial**, even if the woman who did it was ignorant of the divine plan behind the mystery. Some people have said or done things that appear to be a mystical type, although they are ignorant of that fact. The Lord again rebukes Judas, because he said this not on account of his piety but shameful greed! Indeed, he intended to betray his Master for a little coin. The word **burial** and the allusion to his death reveal this plainly. The Savior also adduces an argument that shows us that nothing is better than reverence of him. He says that love for the poor is very commendable but that it should be subordinated to the worship of God. What he says is similar to this: "The time that has been established for honoring me does not demand that the poor be honored before me." He said this about the time of his incarnation on earth.

Certainly, he does not hinder the sympathetic person in any way from loving the poor. But when it is the time for worship or song, it is necessary that these be done prior to loving the poor. It is possible to do this very well after the spiritual worship is completed. He says that it is not necessary to devote ourselves continually to honoring him or to spend everything on the divine worship but to spend a great deal on the poor. And so it happened. He instructs his disciples to fast after he ascends to the Father. He also says that they may devote more attention to the care of the poor and carry out their love of the poor with less distractions and more spare time.[2] After the ascension of the Savior, they had more time since they were no longer following their teacher. At that time they eagerly used all the offerings for the poor.

John 12:9–16

[9]**When the great crowd of the Jews learned that he was there, they came, not only on account of Jesus but also to see Lazarus, whom he had raised from the dead. [10]So the chief priests planned to put Lazarus also to death, [11]because on account of him many of the Jews were going away and believing in Jesus. [12]The next day a great crowd who had come to the feast heard that Jesus was coming to Jerusalem. [13]So they took branches of palm trees and went out to meet him, crying, "Hosanna! Blessed is he who comes in the name of the Lord, even the King of Israel!" [14]And Jesus found a young ass and sat upon it; as it is written, [15]"Fear not, daughter of Zion; behold, your king is coming, sitting on an ass's colt!" [16]His disciples did not understand this at first; but when Jesus was glorified, then they remembered that this had been written of him and had been done to him.**

---

2. Cyril is alluding to the early church tradition of the Fast of the Apostles, which was observed for seven days after Pentecost. This practice is drawn partly from the account in Matt 9:15 (cf. Mark 2:19–20; Luke 5:34–35).

12:9–11 So the chief priests planned to put Lazarus also to death, because on account of him many of the Jews were going away and believing in Jesus.

(7) John Chrysostom

When the great crowd of the Jews learned that he was there, they came, not only on account of Jesus but also to see Lazarus, whom he had raised from the dead (12:9)....
After seeing this miracle, many in Bethany believed. The leaders however were not satisfied with their evil deeds, but they also set out to kill **Lazarus**. It may be supposed that they desired to kill Christ because he broke the Sabbath or because he made himself equal to the Father (cf. John 5:18) or even because of the Romans, as you imagine. But what charge did they have against Lazarus that they should attempt to kill him? Is it a crime to benefit from a good deed? Do you see how murderous their plan is? Christ had done many signs, but none of them had infuriated them as much as this one. Not the healing of the paralytic. Not the healing of the blind man. This sign, performed after so many others, was more marvelous by its very nature. Certainly it was strange to see a person who had been dead for four days walking about and speaking. It is surely not a virtuous action to combine murder with a solemn festival! In the previous case they tried in vain to charge him with regard to the Sabbath and in this way to draw the crowds away from him. This time they make the attempt against the one who was healed since they could find no fault with Christ. They could not say that he was acting contrary to the Father in this instance, for his prayer shut them up. Since the accusation which they always brought against him was not available and the sign was so visible, they rushed to murder Lazarus. They would have done the same thing in the case of the blind man had they not been able to accuse Christ regarding the Sabbath (cf. John 9:13–17). Besides, that man was a nobody. They threw him out of the temple. But **Lazarus** was a man of stature. This is clear from the fact that men came to comfort his sisters. This miracle was done in front of all of them in a most spectacular manner. Because of this everyone ran to see what had happened. This vexed them! While the feast was taking place, all left and went to Bethany. Therefore, they attempted to kill him. They did not even think that they were doing a bad thing, so murderous were they! For this reason the very start of the law begins with this decree: *You shall not kill* (Exod 20:13). The prophet Isaiah also accuses them of this: *Your hands are full of blood* (Isa 1:15).

(8) Augustine of Hippo

When the great crowd of the Jews learned that he was there, they came, not only on account of Jesus but also to see Lazarus, whom he had raised from the dead (12:9). **They came** and saw, but they were drawn by curiosity, not by love. Listen to their strange and deceitful plan! They saw plainly that Lazarus was raised from the dead, for this miracle was accompanied by such evidence and done so openly that they could not conceal or deny what had been done. But consider the plan that they contrived. **So the chief priests planned to put Lazarus also to death, because on account of him many of the Jews were going**

away and believing in Jesus (12:10–11). What a foolish plan! What blind rage! Could Christ the Lord who raised the dead not also raise one who is murdered? When you were planning the death of Lazarus, were you also taking away the power of the Lord? If you think that a dead man is one thing and a murdered man another, notice that the Lord made both. He raised Lazarus who had died to life, and he raised himself who had been murdered!

12:13 So they took branches of palm trees and went out to meet him, crying, "Hosanna! Blessed is he who comes in the name of the Lord, even the King of Israel!"

---

(9) Augustine of Hippo

The gospel text which you have just been hearing says, **The next day a great crowd who had come to the feast heard that Jesus was coming to Jerusalem. So they took branches of palm trees and went out to meet him, crying, "Hosanna! Blessed is he who comes in the name of the Lord, even the King of Israel!"** (12:12–13). The branches of **palm trees** are symbols of praise which signify victory. Since the Lord was about to conquer death by dying and triumph over the devil, the prince of death, by the trophy of the cross . . . the crowd praised him saying, **Hosanna! Blessed is he who comes in the name of the Lord, even the King of Israel!** (12:13). What a cross of envy must the Jewish leaders have suffered when the great crowd proclaimed Christ as their **King**. What benefit did the Lord accrue from being proclaimed the **King of Israel**? What greatness did the **King** of eternity gain from becoming the **King** of men? Christ as the **King of Israel** did not demand tribute, arm his soldiers with swords, or subdue his enemies. Rather, he was the **King of Israel**, because he ruled their hearts. He was mindful of their eternal needs, and he brought those who believed, hoped, and loved him into the heavenly kingdom. The Son of God, being equal to the Father, was the Word by whom *all things* were *made* (1:3). Through an act of condescension, not of promotion, he desired to become the **King of Israel**. This was a mark of compassion; it was not an augmentation to his power. He who was called King of the Jews on earth is called the Lord of the angels in heaven.

12:16 His disciples did not understand this at first; but when Jesus was glorified, then they remembered that this had been written of him and had been done to him.

---

(10) John Chrysostom

His disciples did not understand this at first; but when Jesus was glorified, then they remembered that this had been written of him and had been done to him (12:16). Do you see that they were ignorant regarding almost everything since he did not unveil it for them?

When he said, *Destroy this temple, and in three days I will raise it up* (2:19), the disciples did not **understand** it at that time. Another evangelist says that *this saying was hidden from them* (Luke 18:34). They did not know that he would rise from the dead. This was however concealed from them reasonably. Why? Because this evangelist recounts that although they heard this saying periodically, they were sad and upset because they did not **understand** the words concerning the resurrection. For this reason, *it was hidden from them*. It was too lofty for them to **understand**. Why then was the meaning of the **ass** not revealed to them? This was an important event as well. Pay attention to the wisdom of John the Evangelist, for he is not ashamed to show their former ignorance. They knew that this prophecy was written; however, they did not know that it was written about Jesus. It would have certainly offended them greatly if they knew that he, being a king, was about suffer such things and be betrayed in such a way. Besides, they could not have immediately absorbed the idea about the kingdom of which he spoke, for another evangelist says that they thought that the words were about a kingdom of this world (cf. Matt 20:21).

(11) Cyril of Alexandria

His disciples did not understand this at first; but when Jesus was glorified, then they remembered that this had been written of him and had been done to him (12:16). At first they were ignorant **that this had been written of him**. But after his resurrection, they did not continue to suffer from the blindness of the Jews. The Spirit revealed the knowledge of the divine words to them. When he came to life again after being crucified, it was then that Christ **was glorified**. The evangelist does not hesitate to mention the ignorance of the disciples nor their knowledge. His purpose was not to highlight his opinions about men but to argue for the glory of the Spirit and to show what kind of men the disciples were before his resurrection and what they became after the resurrection. If his disciples were ignorant, how much more were the other Jews? After he was crucified, *the curtain of the temple was torn in two* (Matt 27:51), so that we might know that nothing remains hidden or concealed anymore from the faithful and the godly. They were enlightened with knowledge after the resurrection. Christ breathed into their faces (cf. John 20:22), and they became different from other men. To an even greater degree they were enlightened on the *day of Pentecost*, when they were transformed by the power of the *Holy Spirit* who came upon them (cf. Acts 2:1–4).

John 12:17–26

[17]The crowd that had been with him when he called Lazarus out of the tomb and raised him from the dead bore witness. [18]The reason why the crowd went to meet him was that they heard he had done this sign. [19]The Pharisees then said to one another, "You see that you can do nothing; look, the world has gone after him." [20]Now among those who went up to worship at the feast were some Greeks. [21]So these came to Philip, who was from Bethsaida in Galilee, and said to him, "Sir, we wish to see Jesus." [22]Philip went

and told Andrew; Andrew went with Philip and they told Jesus. [23]And Jesus answered them, "The hour has come for the Son of man to be glorified. [24]Truly, truly, I say to you, unless a grain of wheat falls into the earth and dies, it remains alone; but if it dies, it bears much fruit. [25]He who loves his life loses it, and he who hates his life in this world will keep it for eternal life. [26]If any one serves me, he must follow me; and where I am, there shall my servant be also; if any one serves me, the Father will honor him."

12:20–23 Now among those who went up to worship at the feast were some Greeks [who] wish to see Jesus. . . . And Jesus answered them, "The hour has come for the Son of man to be glorified."

---

(12) Augustine of Hippo

Now among those who went up to worship at the feast were some Greeks. So these came to Philip, who was from Bethsaida in Galilee, and said to him, "Sir, we wish to see Jesus." Philip went and told Andrew; Andrew went with Philip and they told Jesus (12:20–22). Let us listen to the Lord's reply. Notice how the Jews wish to kill him, but the gentiles desire to see him. Yet, there were Jews among those who cried out, *Hosanna! Blessed is he who comes in the name of the Lord, even the King of Israel!* (12:13). Notice that those of the circumcision (Jews) and those of the uncircumcision (gentiles) join together in the one faith of Christ with the kiss of peace, just as two walls coming together from two different directions. Let us listen then to the voice of the *cornerstone* (Eph 2:20). **And Jesus answered them, "The hour has come for the Son of man to be glorified"** (12:23). Perhaps someone thinks the gentiles wished to see him because he was speaking of himself as **glorified**. This is not the case. Rather, he foresaw that the gentiles in every nation would believe after his passion and resurrection. The apostle Paul says, *A hardening has come upon part of Israel, until the full number of the Gentiles come in* (Rom 11:25). When the gentiles wished to see him, Jesus uses this occasion to announce the future fullness of the gentiles and promises the coming **hour** when he would be glorified in heaven and the gentiles would become believers. For this reason, it was foretold, *Be exalted, O God, above the heavens, and let your glory be over all the earth* (Ps 108:5 [107:6 LXX]). This is the *fullness of the Gentiles*. Accordingly, the apostle Paul says, *A hardening has come upon part of Israel, until the full number of the Gentiles come in.*

(13) Cyril of Alexandria

Now among those who went up to worship at the feast were some Greeks (12:20). Someone might be puzzled at these words and wonder why **some Greeks** would be going **up** to Jerusalem to **worship**, especially when **the feast** was being celebrated in accordance with the law. Certainly, no one will say that they went up as spectators; rather, they journeyed to Jerusalem in the company of Jews with the intention of participating in **the feast** which was lawful only for Jews. What was their goal and their reason for worshiping? Was the motive of the Greeks and Jews the same? Surely we shall discover that the two groups diverged very widely with respect to both their actions and their reasoning. The Jews honored the truth, but the Greeks honored what was false. What should we say then about this verse?

Since the land of the Jews was located near the territory of the Galileans and since they and the Greeks had cities and villages which were located next to each other, both peoples were always intermingling. They visited one another, and they were invited together to various events. Since it is usual that the disposition of idol worshipers almost always seeks a change for the better and because nothing is easier than to prove that their false worship is completely futile, some of the Greeks simply were persuaded to change. They did not reach full perfection in their worship of the one who alone is truly God, but they remained divided regarding the arguments in favor of abandoning idolatry. They tended to follow the ideas of their own teachers—I mean, Plato and those wise men of his school—who say that one God is the Creator of all things and that the other gods are connected with the created world and have been appointed by him to serve as administrators over human affairs. There was a general trend among certain inhabitants of Palestine, especially the Greeks who shared a border with the territory of the Jews, to be impressed somewhat by the Jewish way of thinking. They also honored the name of the one sovereign God. This was the current approach of those Greeks whom we just mentioned (i.e., the Platonists) although they did not say it in the same way that we do. They did not hold to Judaism fully nor did they separate themselves from the customs which were important to the Greeks. Rather, they held to an intermediate position which did not privilege either way. They were called "worshipers of God" (cf. Acts 10:1–2). These people perceived that their own way of thinking was not sharply distinguished from that of the Jews in respect to the sacrificial rites and the conception of a sovereign ruler. Even the Israelites did not previously hold to the doctrine of the holy and consubstantial Trinity or the importance of spiritual worship. Accordingly, the Greeks were accustomed to going up to worship with the Jews especially during the national festivals. They did not intend to slight their own religion but sought to honor the one, supreme God.

Now among those who went up to worship at the feast were some Greeks. So these came to Philip, who was from Bethsaida in Galilee, and said to him, "Sir, we wish to see Jesus." Philip went and told Andrew; Andrew went with Philip and they told Jesus (12:20–22). Even though they were ignorant of it, the Pharisees were proclaiming the truth when they said: **Look, the world has gone after him** (12:19). The Jews and the gentiles were destined to accept the faith. At that time, the request of the Greeks happened as a kind of "firstfruits." The Galilean Greeks came to Philip since he was also a Galilean. Since they continually heard everyone speak well of him, they asked him to bring them to Jesus whom they wished to see. They desired to see him and worship him. However, Philip remembered that the Lord had said to them, *Go nowhere among the Gentiles, and enter no town of the Samaritans* (Matt 10:5). He was afraid that he might somehow offend Christ by bringing those who did not believe. Philip was unaware of why the Lord had forbidden the disciples from approaching the gentiles. First the Jews had to reject the grace offered to them. So **Philip went and told Andrew**. Andrew was more acquainted with and knowledgeable about such matters. With his approval, they both took the message to the Lord. . . .

And Jesus answered them, "The hour has come for the Son of man to be glorified" (12:23). Seeing that the gentiles earnestly desire to see him and to turn toward him, he says: **The hour has come**. The time of his passion was drawing near. The calling of the gentiles would follow immediately. He calls the present time **the hour**. By this he intends to show that no other time, except this one which he set forth, was able to bring about this necessary period of suffering. After finishing all the things which led humans to faith and after preaching the word of the kingdom of heaven, he now wants to move on to the crowning achievement of his desire: the destruction of death. In no other way could this be accomplished unless life itself underwent death for the sake of all in order that all might live in him. For this reason, he speaks of himself as **glorified** in his death and in the suffering of so many terrible things at the hands of sinners who dishonor him. Although he had been **glorified** eternally by the angels of heaven, his cross initiated his glorification as God on earth by the gentiles. After he had left the Jews who had despised him openly, he turns to the gentiles and is **glorified** as God by them. Certainly he is expected to come again *in the glory of the Father* (Matt 16:27). He declares that the Word will be **glorified** at that time, and he shows that he is the only Son who is understood mysteriously to share in humanity and divinity equally. For this reason, he uses the title **Son of man**. He is one Son and one Christ. Due to his incarnation, the separation of the two natures is impossible. He remains—and is fully understood to be—God, although he is clothed in flesh.

12:24 "Truly, truly, I say to you, unless a grain of wheat falls into the earth and dies, it remains alone; but if it dies, it bears much fruit."

---

(14) John Chrysostom

What does the phrase **unless a grain of wheat falls into the earth and dies** (12:24) mean? He is speaking of the cross. In order that they might not be confused when they discovered he was killed just when the Greeks came to him, he says, "It is this very event that makes the Greeks come, and it will increase the proclamation about me!" Since he was not able to persuade them easily with words, afterward he shows this from practical experience. It is as if he said, "This happens with seeds. They bring forth more fruit when they die. If this is the case with seeds, it is even more so with respect to me." But the disciples did not understand what he had said. The evangelist constantly references this fact as if defending why they fled after the crucifixion. Paul made a similar argument when he spoke of the resurrection. What sort of defense will those who do not believe in the resurrection put forth when this process is carried out daily in seeds, plants, and in our own birth? . . . Someone says, "But there is no resurrection of the body." They do not listen to Paul who says, *This perishable nature must put on the imperishable* (1 Cor 15:53). He is not speaking of the soul, for the soul is not *perishable*. Additionally, resurrection concerns that which fell. The body is what fell! Why do you think that there is no resurrection of the body? Is that not possible for God? (To say this is utter nonsense!) Is it not right? Why would it be unseemly for the *perishable*, which shared the toil and death, to share also the crown? If the body were undignified, it would not have been created at the beginning. Christ would not have taken up the flesh after his resurrection. To prove that he took on flesh and raised it up, hear what he says: *Put your finger here* (20:27), and *Handle me, and see; for a spirit has not flesh and bones as you see that I have* (Luke 24:39). Why did he raise Lazarus from the dead, if it would have been better to rise without a body (cf. John 11:21–40)? Why does he do this? Why is this event classified as a miracle and a blessing? Why did he give nourishment for the body at all? Brothers and sisters, do not be deceived by the heretics! There is a resurrection, and there is a judgment. They deny these things, because they do not want to give an account of their actions!

12:25 "He who loves his life loses it, and he who hates his life in this world will keep it for eternal life."

---

(15) Augustine of Hippo

It was absolutely necessary that the depth of his passion precede the height of his glorification. Following this thought, he adds, **Truly, truly, I say to you, unless a grain of wheat falls into the earth and dies, it remains alone; but if it dies, it bears much fruit** (12:24). He was speaking of himself. He was the grain that had to die and be multiplied; die by the faithlessness of the Jews and be multiplied by the faith of many others. Next he exhorts them to follow the path of his own passion. He says, **He who loves his life loses it** (12:25). This can be understood in two ways: **He, who *loves*, shall lose.** In other words, "If you love, be ready to lose." If you desire to have life in Christ, do not be afraid to die for him. It can also be understood in this way: **He, who loves *his life*, shall lose it.** Do not love your life, for you might lose it. In other words, do not love your life in this world, for you might lose it in eternity. This second meaning seems to correspond better to the meaning of the gospel, for the verse continues, **And he who hates his life in this world will keep it for eternal life** (12:25). This clarifies the former clause. **He who loves** is understood as referring to **life in this world**, for he will certainly **lose it**. **He who hates his life**, at least in this world, **will keep it for eternal life**. What a magnificent, yet astonishing, idea! In some way a person who **loves** his **life** will **lose** it, but conversely she who **hates** her **life** will gain it. If you **love** your body in a sinful manner, then you actually **hate** it. If, however, you **hate** your body in a holy manner, then you really **love** it. Happy are those who have hated their **life** so they might **keep** it. By loving their **life**, they might well **lose** it. But be on guard against the insidious notion that you should destroy yourself, because you understand that you are to **hate** your **life** in this world. This misunderstanding has led certain wrongheaded and perverted people to kill themselves in very cruel and profane ways: to throw themselves into the fire, to drown in water, to hurl themselves from a cliff and perish. Christ did not teach this! He responded instead to the devil's suggestion that he hurl himself down, saying, *Get behind me, Satan; for it is written, "You shall not tempt the Lord your God"* (Matt 4:7).[3]

---

3. Only the last clause of this quote is from Matthew's account of the confrontation between Jesus and Satan. Augustine is likely quoting from memory.

He said to Peter, signifying by what death he would glorify God, *When you were young, you girded yourself and walked where you would; but when you are old, you will stretch out your hands, and another will gird you and carry you where you do not wish to go* (21:18). In these places Christ clearly indicates that the one who follows in his footsteps must be killed not by one's own hand but by the hand of another. When the time of trial comes and he is confronted with either acting against the divine commandment or giving up this life, a man is compelled by the one threatening him with death to choose one of these paths. At that time, let him choose to die in the love of God rather than live with the hatred of God. In this way, let him **hate his life in this world** in order to **keep it for eternal life** (12:25).

12:26 "If any one serves me, he must follow me; and where I am, there shall my servant be also; if any one serves me, the Father will honor him."

---

(16) Augustine of Hippo

If any one serves me, he must follow me (12:26). . . . We must inquire further what it means to **serve** Christ since such a great reward is connected to it. Perhaps we have the idea that serving Christ is preparing the things needed by his body, the cooking and serving of food or the mixing and serving of drinks. This kind of service was done for him by those who were in his bodily presence. Martha and Mary served when Lazarus was at the table (cf. 12:2). In the same way the immoral Judas served Christ, for he held the *money bag* (12:6). Although he stole its contents in a most impious manner, he nonetheless did what was necessary for the meal. When our Lord said to him, *What you are going to do, do quickly* (13:27), some thought that he had commanded Judas to make the necessary preparations for the feast or to give something to the poor. In no way however did the Lord say to servants like Judas, **And where I am, there shall my servant be also**, and **If any one serves me, the Father will honor him** (12:26). We see that Judas who served in this way received condemnation more than honor. Why should we seek other places in Scripture to discover what it means to serve Christ? Do we not know what it means from these very words? He said, **If any one serves me, he must follow me** (12:26). He wanted it to be understood as if he had said, **If any one does *not* follow me, he does *not* serve me**. The apostle Paul reminds us that Christ's servants are those who seek not their own interests, but those of Jesus Christ (cf. Phil 2:21). The phrase **he must follow me** (12:26) means this: Let him walk in my way and not his own. As it is written elsewhere, *He who says he abides in him ought to walk in the same way in which he walked* (1 John 2:6). If he is giving food to the hungry, he should do it out of mercy, not to offer a public display. He should seek nothing but the act of doing a good deed. *Do not let your left hand know what your right hand is doing* (Matt 6:3) so that any intention of being self-serving is removed from an act of charity. The one who serves in this way serves Christ, and it will be said to him rightly, *Truly, I say to you, as you did it to one of the least of these my brethren, you did it to me* (Matt 25:40). The one who not only does acts of mercy that pertain to the physical body but every good work on account of Christ is his servant. For then all things will be good, because *Christ is the end* *of the law so that there may be righteousness for everyone who believes* (Rom 10:4). The one who does that very special work of love by laying down his life for his brother is Christ's servant. This action is truly laying down his life for Christ. He said to his followers, *When you did it for these, you did it for me* (cf. Matt 25:40, 45). Surely, he had in mind such an act of sacrifice when he called himself a servant and said, *The Son of man came not to be served but to serve, and to give his life as a ransom for many* (Matt 20:28). Therefore, everyone who is a servant of Christ is a servant in the very same way as Christ. The one who serves Christ like this will be honored by his Father with this great honor: he will stand in the presence of the Son and will never again lack happiness.

Brothers and sisters, when you hear the Lord saying, **And where I am, there shall my servant be also** (12:26), do not think this only refers to faithful bishops and priests. You also in your own way serve Christ though good lives, giving charitable gifts, proclaiming his name and doctrines as you are able. Every father who has a household should declare in Christ's name that he owes his fatherly love to his family. Let him admonish, teach, exhort, and correct his whole family on account of Christ and his eternal life. Let him also show kindness and instill discipline. In this way he will fulfill an ecclesiastical role, similar to a bishop, over his own household and serve Christ that he might be with him forever. Many who are not bishops or priests but adolescents and virgins, young and old, male and female, married, fathers and mothers of families, have served Christ with the supreme act of suffering. They have laid down their lives in martyrdom for Christ's sake and have been honored by the Father, for they received their crowns of highest glory.

(17) John Cassian

If anyone serves me, he must follow me; and where I am, there shall my servant be also (12:26). Just as the kingdom of the devil is attained by succumbing to sin, the kingdom of God is gained by the practice of virtue with a pure heart and spiritual knowledge. Where the kingdom of God is, there eternal life is certainly enjoyed, and where the kingdom of the devil is, death and the grave surely are. The man who is in this predicament cannot praise the Lord. For this reason the saying of the prophet tells us accordingly: *The dead will not praise you, O Lord, nor will all who go down to Hades* in ignorance of their sin. *But we,* he says, *who live*—certainly not for sin or for this world, but for God!—*will bless the Lord from now on and forevermore* (Ps 115:17–18). *In death there is no one who makes mention of you, and in Hades who will acknowledge you?* (Ps 6:5). For no man confesses God when he is sinning, even if he calls himself a Christian—or a monk!—a thousand times. No one who does things that the Lord hates remembers God. Nor can anyone truly call himself a servant of the Lord, whose commands he disregards obstinately. The blessed apostle states that the widow who gives herself to pleasure is already experiencing a similar sort of death: *She who is self-indulgent is dead even while she lives* (1 Tim 5:6).

In this way many are *dead* while still living in this body. They are lying in the grave and cannot *praise God.* Conversely, there are many who bless God in the spirit and praise him although they are physically dead: *Bless the Lord, spirits and righteous souls!* (Dan 3:86 LXX), and *Let everything that has breath praise the LORD!* (Ps 150:6). In the Apocalypse of

John the souls of those who are slain are said not only to praise God but to cry out to him also (cf. Rev 6:9–10). In the Gospel of Matthew, the Lord says to the Sadducees even more directly: *And as for the resurrection of the dead, have you not read what was said to you by God, "I am the God of Abraham, and the God of Isaac, and the God of Jacob"? He is not God of the dead, but of the living* (Matt 22:31–32). About these, the apostle says: *Therefore God is not ashamed to be called their God, for he has prepared for them a city* (Heb 11:16). The parable in the Gospel of Luke reports to us the story of the beggar Lazarus and the rich man. It demonstrates that the dead are not motionless after the separation from this body but are capable of feeling. One of them secured a position of heavenly blessing; the other was consumed by the dreadful flames of eternal fire (Luke 16:19–26). If you want to understand the words spoken to the thief, *Today you will be with me in Paradise* (Luke 23:43), they show that the former intellect remains in their souls and that they receive some status which is commensurate with their actions and merits in their transformed state. The Lord would certainly never have promised this to him if he had known that the thief's soul would be either stripped of intelligence or unraveled into nothingness after it was separated from the flesh. It was not his flesh but his soul which was about to enter *Paradise* with Christ. At a minimum we must reject with vehemence that wicked interpretation of the heretics. They do not believe that Christ could enter *Paradise* on the very same day on which he descended into hell.[4] For this reason, they accentuate, *Today, I truly say to you.* After adding a period, they then add: *You will be with me in Paradise.* In this way they imagine that this promise was not fulfilled immediately after he departed from this life. Rather, they fancy that it will be fulfilled after the resurrection. They do not understand what he said to the Jews before his resurrection. They assumed that he was hindered as they were by human difficulties and limitations of the flesh: *No one has ascended into heaven but he who descended from heaven, the Son of man who is in heaven* (3:13 Vulgate). He clearly indicates that the souls of the dead not only retain their intellect but also their feelings such as hope and sorrow, joy and fear. They already experience a foretaste of what has been prepared for them at the last judgment. They are not dissolved into nothingness after their departure from this life as some unbelievers hold.[5] Instead, they live a life which is more real and more desirous of the praises of God.

Let us put aside for a moment proofs from Scripture and discuss as far as we are able the nature of the soul itself. Is it completely and utterly irrational to hold the notion that the nobler part of man, in which the blessed apostle Paul shows that *the image and likeness of God* resides (1 Cor 11:7; Col 3:10; cf. Gen 1:26–27), will become insensible when the oppressive burden of the body in this world is cast aside? Indeed, the intellect contains every power of reason. It elevates by participation the ignorant and senseless material flesh to sensibility. Certainly it is logical—and reason itself demands—that when the mind has cast away the materiality of the flesh by which it is weighed down, the intellectual powers will be restored to a better state than ever and receive them in a purer and finer state. The

---

4. The difficulty is how to reconcile the word *today* with the statement in Matt 12:40, that the Son of Man will spend three days and nights in the "heart of the earth." Some interpreters thought the apparent contradiction put into question the reliability of the Scriptures.

5. Augustine may have in mind the Epicureans.

blessed apostle recognized the truth of what we say to such a degree that he actually wanted to depart from the flesh so that he would be joined more completely to the Lord in this separation. He said: *My desire is to depart and be with Christ, for that is far better* (Phil 1:23) *. . . for while we are at home in the body we are away from the Lord* (2 Cor 5:6); and therefore, *We are of good courage, and we would rather be away from the body and at home with the Lord. So whether we are at home or away, we make it our aim to please him* (2 Cor 5:8–9).

John 12:27–33

27"Now is my soul troubled. And what shall I say? 'Father, save me from this hour'? No, for this purpose I have come to this hour. 28Father, glorify thy name." Then a voice came from heaven, "I have glorified it, and I will glorify it again." 29The crowd standing by heard it and said that it had thundered. Others said, "An angel has spoken to him." 30Jesus answered, "This voice has come for your sake, not for mine. 31Now is the judgment of this world, now shall the ruler of this world be cast out; 32and I, when I am lifted up from the earth, will draw all men to myself." 33He said this to show by what death he was to die.

12:27–28 "Now is my soul troubled. . . . Father, glorify thy name." Then a voice came from heaven, "I have glorified it, and I will glorify it again."

---

(18) Tertullian of Carthage

When Martha acknowledged Jesus to be the Son of God (cf. John 11:27), she was no more mistaken than Peter (cf. Matt 16:16) or Nathanael were (cf. John 1:49). Even if she were mistaken, she would nonetheless have learned the truth immediately. When the Lord was about to raise her brother from the dead, he looked up to heaven and addressed the Father as the Son. He said: *Father, I thank thee that thou hast heard me. I knew that thou hearest me always, but I have said this on account of the people standing by, that they may believe that thou didst send me* (11:41–42). However, later while he was troubled in his soul, he said: **And what shall I say? "Father, save me from this hour"? No, for this purpose I have come to this hour. Father, glorify thy name** (12:27–28). Here again he spoke as the Son. Again, he said, **I have come in my Father's name** (5:43). It follows then that while the Son's discourse with the Father was alone sufficient, the Father replies from heaven to testify to the Son: *This is my beloved Son, with whom I am well pleased; listen to him* (Matt 17:5); so also in the following statement, **I have glorified it, and I will glorify it again** (12:28). . . . How many persons do you detect? Are there not as many persons as there are voices? You have the Son on earth, and you have the Father in heaven. Now this is not a separation; it is the divine dispensation. We certainly know that God exists everywhere with power and authority, even in the *bottomless pit* (Rev 9:1). We also know that the Son, who is indivisible from him, is with him everywhere. In the divine economy however the Father desired that the Son should reside on earth and he in heaven. The Son looked up, prayed, and made supplication of the Father in heaven. He also taught us to stand and pray, *Our Father who art in heaven . . .* (Matt 6:9), although he is truly present everywhere. The Father willed the Son's *throne* to be in heaven (cf. Isa 66:1). Although he made the Son a little lower than the angels by sending him down to the earth, he intended to crown him with glory and honor by restoring him to heaven (cf. Ps 8:5). He shows this definitively when he now says, **I have glorified it, and I will glorify it again** (12:28). The Son utters his request from earth, and the Father proclaims his promise from heaven. . . . Accordingly, the Lord declared to those who were present, **This voice has come for your sake, not for mine** (12:30), so that they may believe both in the Father and the Son and individually in their own names, persons, and locations. Jesus then proclaims, *He who believes in me, believes not in me but in him who sent me* (12:44). It is through the Son that humans believe in the Father, but the power to believe in the Son comes from the Father.

(19) Ambrose of Milan

Christ suffered and did not suffer, died and did not die, was buried and was not buried, rose again and did not rise again. His very body was awakened, because that which fell rose again. But that which did not fall, did not rise again. He rose according to the flesh. Since the flesh died, it rose again. However, he did not rise again in respect to the Word. The Word was not destroyed on earth but remained always with God. In other words, he died in respect to the assumption of our fleshly nature, yet he did not die in respect to the essence of his eternal life. He suffered in accordance with the passion of his body so that the truth of his assumption of the flesh might be believed. However, he did not suffer in respect to the impassible divinity of the Word which is entirely devoid of pain. The very same one said, *My God, My God attend to me; why did you forsake me?* (Ps 22:1 [21:1 LXX]). According to the flesh, he was *forsaken*; but according to his divinity, he was not able to be either deserted or forsaken. This one also says, *Far away from my deliverance are the words of my transgressions* (Ps 22:1 [21:1 LXX]). In other words, let no one be confused when they hear the phrase: *Why did you forsake me?* Let him understand that these words are said about his flesh. They are *far away* from the fullness of God. *The words of my transgressions* are foreign to God because sins themselves are alien to him. However, Christ says, "Because I have assumed the sins of others, I have assumed the *words of the transgressions* of others. In this way I declare that I—who am always *with God* (1:1) truly—have been *forsaken* by God the Father." He was immortal in death and impassible in his passion. Just as the affliction of death did not seize him as God, hell saw him as a man. Then, *he yielded up his spirit* (Matt 27:50). *He yielded up his spirit*, as the one who had the power both to remove and assume a body. But he did not lose *his spirit*. He hung upon the cross and disturbed everything. He trembled on the cross, and this whole world shuddered before him. In the middle of being tortured to death, he received the blows and handed over the heavenly kingdom. When he took on the sins of all, he washed away the sins of the human race. Finally, he died—and I say again and again with exultation and joy *he died*!—in order that his death might become the life of the dead.

Even his tomb features a miracle. After he had been anointed by Joseph and while he was buried in his tomb (cf. Luke 23:53), he miraculously opened the tombs of the dead although he was also dead (cf. Matt 27:52–53). While his body lay in the tomb, he was *free among the corpses* (Ps 88:5 [87:5 LXX]), offering forgiveness to those in hell by unbinding the law of death. His body was in the tomb, but his power operated from heaven. It was revealed to all through the truth of his body that his flesh was not the Word but that his flesh was assumed by the Word. His flesh *tasted death* (Heb 2:9), but the *power of God* (1 Cor 1:18) was impassible. If he casts off the body, there was no harm to God in respect to his body. Why do you connect the afflictions of the body to his divinity and conversely the sickness of human suffering to his divine nature? He says, **Now my soul is troubled** (12:27). His **soul**, not his wisdom, is **troubled**. His divine wisdom remained immutable even though it was encircled by a fleshly garment. The fullness of **true light** (1:9) was in that *form of a servant* (Phil 2:7), and when he *emptied himself* (Phil 2:7), there was the light. He said, *Walk while you have the light* (12:35). When he was dead, he was not in the *dark* (Matt 4:16). Even then he poured out the light of eternal life on those in hell. The **true light** of wisdom shone forth even there. It illuminated hell, but it was not contained there. . . .

Do not confuse the darkness of our nature with the brightness of his glory. Do not cover over his **light** with the umbrage of human flesh. If you do not discern clearly what aspects of Christ are possible when proclaiming his passion, you deny the love of God and your own salvation. For this reason, we should consider all those to be insane who, when they hear the Son of God say, *Why do you strike me?* (18:23), think that he was suffering an injury according to his divine nature. Although he said, *Why do you strike me?*, his divine nature did not feel the blows. He said, *I have given my back to scourges and my cheeks to blows, but I did not turn away my face from the shame of spittle* (Isa 50:6). He mentions his *back*, *cheeks*, and *face*, which are all parts of the human body. The things that the flesh of the Word suffered while incarnate, the Word of God also suffered by the flesh, since it is written, *Christ suffered in the flesh* . . . (1 Pet 4:1). He certainly was referring to his assumption of a body. He took upon himself what is ours and encircled the human with what is his. Certainly, his flesh suffered according to its nature; however, the nature of the Word was not changed by the suffering of his body. We proclaim that our resurrection is true and Christ's passion is also true.

(20) Augustine of Hippo

Let the person who wishes to follow, learn how he should go about it. Perhaps a terrible time has come, and the choice is placed before you either to sin or endure suffering. Your weak **soul is troubled** (12:27). For this very reason, the unconquerable soul of Christ was willingly **troubled**. Place the will of God before your own. Pay attention to what was accomplished by your Creator and Master who made you. He became the very thing that he made in order to teach you. He who made humanity became a human. Yet, he remained also the unchangeable God and transformed humanity into a superior state. Listen to what he adds to the words, **Now is my soul troubled.** He says: **And what shall I say? "Father, save me from this hour"? No, for this purpose I have come to this hour. Father, glorify**

thy name (12:27–28). Here he has taught you what to think, what to say, on whom to call, in whom to hope. He has also taught you to prefer his certain and divine will before your own weak, human will. Do not imagine that he lost anything from his own exalted position when he desired to lift you out of the depths of your ruin. He also considered it proper to be tempted by the devil. Had he not been willing, he would never have been tempted by the devil nor would he have suffered! The replies he made to the devil are the very ones that you should use when you are tempted (cf. Matt 4:1–10). Certainly he was tempted, but he was not in peril. He desired to show you how to answer the tempter when you are endangered through desires so you are not carried away by temptation but can escape it. Similarly, he says, **Now is my soul troubled** (12:27). In another place he says, *My soul is very sorrowful, even to death. . . My Father, if it be possible, let this cup pass from me* (Matt 26:38–39). He assumed the infirmity of humanity to teach us that when we are saddened and troubled, he should say, *Nevertheless, not as I will, but as you will* (Matt 26:39). In this way, a person is turned from the human to the divine when he prefers God's will to his own. To what else do the words **glorify thy name** (12:28) refer except to his passion and resurrection? What else can they mean except that the Father should **glorify** the Son? Similarly, he **glorifies** his own **name** in the sufferings of his own servants. For this reason, it is reported about Peter that the Lord said to him: *Another will gird you and carry you where you do not wish to go. This he said to show by what death he was to glorify God* (21:18–19). Therefore, God glorified his name on account of Peter, for he glorifies Christ on account of his members.

Then a voice came from heaven, "I have glorified it, and I will glorify it again" (12:28). **I have glorified it** before I created the world, **and I will glorify it again** when Christ will rise from the dead and ascend into heaven. This may be understood in other ways. **I have glorified it** when he was born of the virgin, when he applied miraculous powers, when the Magi led by a star in the heavens prostrated themselves before him, when he was acknowledged by the saints who were filled with the Holy Spirit, when he was proclaimed by the Spirit descending in the form of a dove and identified by the voice calling out from heaven, when he was transfigured on the mountain, when he worked many miracles, when he healed and cleansed the crowds, when he fed such a great crowd with only a few loaves of bread, when he commanded the winds and the waves, and when he raised the dead. **And I will glorify it again** when he rises from the dead, when death no longer has power over him, and when he is exalted above the heavens as God and his glory is over all the earth.

12:31–32   "Now is the judgment of this world, now shall the ruler of this world be cast out; and I, when I am lifted up from the earth, will draw all men to myself."

---

(21) Athanasius of Alexandria

If any Christian wants to know why the Lord suffered death on the cross instead of some other way, we respond that it was the most appropriate way for us. Certainly the Lord offered the one death that was especially good for us. He had come to bear the curse that lay upon us. How could he *become a curse* (Gal 3:13) apart from accepting the cursed death? That sort of death is the cross, for it is written, *Cursed be everyone who hangs on a tree* (Gal 3:13). The death of the Lord ransoms everyone. By his death, *the dividing wall of hostility* (Eph 2:14) is broken down and the call of the gentiles goes forth. How could he have called us if he had not been crucified? It is only on the cross that a man dies with his arms outstretched. Here we witness the propriety of his death and of those outstretched arms; he would **draw** his ancient people with the one and the gentiles with the other, and join both peoples together in himself. For this reason, he foretold the manner of his redeeming death: *I, when I am lifted up from the earth, will draw all men to myself* (12:32).

The air is the realm of the devil, the enemy of our race, who fell from heaven. With the other evil spirits who participated in his disobedience, he strives to keep souls from the truth and to slow the progress of those who are trying to follow it. The apostle Paul refers to this when he says, *Following the prince of the power of the air, the spirit that is now at work in the sons of disobedience* (Eph 2:2). The Lord came to overthrow the devil, to purify the air, and to make **a way** (14:6) for us up to heaven. The apostle says accordingly, *through the curtain, that is, through his flesh* (Heb 10:20). This had to be accomplished through death. By what other sort of death could it be done, except by a death in the *air*, which is death on the cross? You see once again how appropriate and natural it was that the Lord should suffer in this way. When he was **lifted up**, he cleansed the air from all the evil influences of the enemy. He says, *I saw Satan fall like lightning from heaven* (Luke 10:18). In this way he reopened the way to heaven, saying, *Lift up your heads, O gates! And be lifted up, O ancient doors!* (Ps 24:9). It was not the Word who needed the gates opened. None of the created works are closed to their Maker. Instead, it is we who need this. He **lifted** us **up** in his own body which he offered to death and through which he opened the way to heaven for everyone.

The death on the cross for us was utterly fitting and wholly appropriate. We see how reasonable it was and why the salvation of the world could be accomplished in no other way. Even on the cross he did not hide himself from sight. Instead, he made all creation bear witness to the presence of its Creator. Then, after it was clearly seen that his body truly suffered death, he did not allow the temple of his body to tarry. Instead, on the third day he raised up his impassible and incorruptible body as a pledge and token of his victory. Certainly it was in his power to have raised his body and shown it as alive directly after death, but the Savior displaying complete wisdom did not do this. Some might have denied that his body had really or completely died. Moreover, if the period between his death and resurrection had been only two days, the glory of his incorruption might not have been so apparent. He waited one whole day to show that his body was really dead, and then on the third day, he showed everyone that it was incorruptible. The interval was also not longer than three days so that no one would forget about it or doubt that it was truly the same body. While the events were still resounding in their ears, their eyes were still straining, and their minds still spinning and while those who put him to death were still nearby and testifying to their deed, the Son of God showed his previously dead body as both immortal and incorruptible after three days. It was evident to all that the body in which the Word dwelt had died not from some natural weakness but to show that the Savior's power had destroyed death.

(22) Theodore of Mopsuestia

Now is the judgment of this world (12:31). The first man, who was condemned to death on account of disobedience, became subject to the devil. In the same way all who came after him, when they became evil, brought the devil upon themselves. He became an exceedingly burdensome tyrant over them. And so they became even more impious. They made the kingdom of death worse for themselves. Because no one was able to wage war against it, Christ, being God and able to do everything, gave himself up on behalf of everyone, both the ones who existed before and those who exist now.

Christ said, "The **world** is judged in me and through me. Since I have not committed any sin but instead have done every kind of virtue, I am in no way worthy of death. Nevertheless, I accept death unjustly so that I may make my case against the one who killed me. Therefore, the devil is condemned. Since I have been freed from the bonds of death, I will rise. By my action, I will also raise humanity with me. All will be acquitted by the verdict. In contrast the devil, who controlled the people through evil in this life, will be deposed from power. The bonds of death, which he used to ensnare the people and control them easily, will be taken away. Those bonds caused them to sin even more and allowed the devil to attain a greater mastery over them. Yet, when they are released from being enslaved to him, they all will be attached to me. After the cross and the resurrection, **I will draw all men to myself** (12:32).

He said, **I will draw** (12:32). This shows that he will rip them away with force from the one who controls them. He **draws** everyone by his resurrection and bestows the hope of the resurrection upon all, for they will participate in the resurrection themselves. He will gather everyone together in himself and release them from death. He will give them perfect knowledge of himself. It follows then that when the evangelist said **lifted up** (12:32), he was referring to Christ's crucifixion.

(23) Augustine of Hippo

Pay attention to what follows! He says, **Now is the judgment of this world** (12:31). What then should we expect at the end of time? The final judgment will be the judging of the living and the dead and the allotting of eternal rewards and punishments. What does **now is the judgment** mean? Dear brothers and sisters, I have previously emphasized as much as I could that the **judgment** spoken of here is not the **judgment** of damnation but of separation. As it is written, *Vindicate me, O God, and defend my cause against an ungodly people* (Ps 43:1). God's judgments are many! As it is said in the Psalms, *Thy judgments are like the great deep* (Ps 36:6). The apostle Paul also says, *O the depth of the riches and wisdom and knowledge of God! How unsearchable are his judgments and how inscrutable his ways!* (Rom 11:33). It is regarding these sorts of judgments to which this statement of the Lord belongs: **Now is the judgment of this world** (12:31). In contrast, the **judgment** at the end of time, when the living and the dead must finally be judged, is held in abeyance. The devil possessed the human race and held them as accused criminals subject to punishment by the written confessions of their sins. He ruled in the hearts of unbelievers and enticed those whom he deceived and held captive to forsake the Creator and worship the creature. However, thousands of believers are delivered from the dominion of the devil by faith in Christ. They are strengthened by his death and resurrection and by his blood, which was shed for the remission of sins. They are united to the body of Christ and are made alive as faithful members under his great head by his Spirit. This is what he calls **the judgment**: the separation and expulsion of the devil from the ones he has redeemed. . . .

Someone however might ask the following: Since the devil has been cast out of the hearts of believers, does he not tempt any of the faithful now? In no way does he stop tempting them! It is one thing to reign inside and a very different thing to attack from outside. Similarly, a heavily fortified city is sometimes attacked by an enemy but not captured. If some of the devil's arrows are fired and hit us, the apostle Paul commands us how to avoid being injured by them. He reminds us of the *breastplate* and the shield of *faith* (1 Thess 5:8). If the devil wounds us at times, the one who heals is with us. It was said, as if addressed to fighters, *I am writing this to you so that you may not sin.* Those who are wounded should hear what follows: *But if any one does sin, we have an advocate with the Father, Jesus Christ the righteous; and he is the expiation for our sins, and not for ours only but also for the sins of the whole world* (1 John 2:1–2). When we say, *Forgive us our debts, as we also have forgiven our debtors; lead us not into temptation, but deliver us from evil* (Matt 6:12–13), what are we praying for except that the one who lies in ambush or attacks us from outside may fail to secure an entrance from any side and fail to conquer us either by deception or by direct assault? As long as he no longer has a foothold in our hearts where faith resides, he is pushed back regardless how huge the siege engines are that he arrays against us. *Unless the Lord watches over the city, the watchman stays awake in vain* (Ps 127:1). Do not rely only on yourselves, if you do not want to recall the devil back inside after he has been already **cast out** (12:31). Let us not think in any way that the devil is called the **ruler of this world** (12:31), as if we suppose that he has the power to rule over the heavens and the earth. **World** refers to the wicked men who have spread over the whole earth. Similarly, the word "house" refers to those who live in it. For this reason, we say, "It is a good house, or it is a bad one." But in this way we are not casting aspersions or praise on the construction of the walls or the roof but upon the character of either the good or the bad men who are within. The phrase **the ruler of this world** is used similarly: **the ruler of** all the wicked who live in **this world**. The **world** is also used in reference to the good men who are scattered over the whole earth. Accordingly, the apostle Paul says, *In Christ God was reconciling the* world *to himself* (2 Cor 5:19). These are the ones from whose hearts **the ruler of this world** has been **cast out**.

John 12:34–36

[34]The crowd answered him, "We have heard from the law that the Christ remains forever. How can you say that the Son of man must be lifted up? Who is this Son of man?" [35]Jesus said to them, "The light is with you for a little longer. Walk while you have the light, lest the darkness overtake you; he who walks in the darkness does not know where he goes. [36]While you have the light, believe in the light, that you may become sons of light." When Jesus had said this, he departed and hid himself from them.

(24) Theodore of Mopsuestia

The crowd answered him, "We have heard from the law that the Christ remains forever. How can you say that the Son of man must be lifted up? Who is this Son of man?" (12:34). It becomes evident from this verse that the Jews had a very high expectation of the coming of the Messiah. The phrase **the Christ remains forever** means that he will not die. You see, they were expecting him to **remain** in the fashion of Elijah. It is no wonder that the Jews were divided about the predictions and ignorant about the exact meaning of the words before the events took place.

Jesus said to them, "The light is with you for a little longer. Walk while you have the light, lest the darkness overtake you; he who walks in the darkness does not know where he goes" (12:35). Through an analogy he showed both that he had to be tested by death and that he would not remain dead. He calls himself **light**. It is as if he says, "Because this light is like the light from the sun, when it departs, it seems to those who no longer see it as if it no longer exists. But it is not quenched forever and lost. It retains its own nature and form of being and reappears at the proper time. In this way, you should think about me. I do not die in such a way as to remain dead, for my body will not be corrupted. Even though my soul will be separated from my body for a short time, the former will receive its own incorruptibility, while the latter will be raised again."

Notice that by adding the term **with you** he meant that he would not completely cease to be but would be removed from them. It is as if he said, "In this way you will neither be unaffected in ignorance, if you listen to my advice, nor will you have the experience of those who are in darkness. You will attain the status of children when you believe in me and do what I teach, for my teaching will shine like a light in your souls forever."

"While you have the light, believe in the light, that you may become sons of light." When Jesus had said this, he departed and hid himself from them (12:36). He **hid himself from them** so that he would suffer at the appropriate day: Easter. At that time he created a new *Pascha*. He offered himself as a rational lamb instead of as the sheep of the Jews on behalf of the sin of the world.

(25) Augustine of Hippo

The crowd answered him, "We have heard from the law that the Christ remains forever. How can you say that the Son of man must be lifted up? Who is this Son of man?" (12:34). It had stuck in their minds that the Lord constantly called himself the Son of Man. Although in the passage before us—*when I am lifted up from the earth* (12:32)—he does not call himself Son of Man. However, he certainly had called himself this before . . . as he did when those gentiles who desired to see him were introduced (cf. 12:20–21). He then said, *The hour has come for the Son of man to be glorified* (12:23). Holding this in their minds and understanding what he said here, they remarked: **We have heard from the law that the Christ remains forever. How can you say that the**

Son of man must be lifted up? Who is this Son of man? If he is **the Christ**, they say, he **remains forever**. Yet, if he **remains forever**, how will he be *lifted up from the earth* (12:32)? In other words, how will **the Christ** die by suffering on the cross? They understood that he had spoken of the very thing that they were plotting to do. He did not make clear the obscurity of these words by an infusion of wisdom but by poking their conscience.

Then Jesus said to them, **A little light is in you** (12:35 Vulgate). In this way you understand that **the Christ remains forever** (12:34). **Walk while you have the light, lest the darkness overtake you** (12:35). **Walk**, draw near, come to the full understanding that Christ shall both die and shall live forever. He will shed his blood to redeem us and will ascend to heaven to carry his redeemed along with him. If however your belief in Christ's eternity forces you to deny the fact of the humiliation of death, **darkness** will descend upon you. **He who walks in the darkness does not know where he goes** (12:35). He might stumble on that *stone* of stumbling and *rock* of offense which the Lord was to the Jews who were blind (cf. 1 Pet 2:8). However, to those who believed, *The very stone which the builders rejected has become the head of the corner* (1 Pet 2:7). They did not believe that Christ was worthy because they held his death in contempt due to their impiety. They ridiculed the idea that Christ was slain even though it is the death of the grain that leads to its own multiplication. It was the **lifting up** that permitted him to draw all things to himself. He adds, **"While you have the light, believe in the light, that you may become sons of light." When Jesus had said this, he departed and hid himself from them** (12:36). He did not hide from those who had begun to believe and to love him. Nor did he hide from those who had come to meet him with **branches of palm trees** and songs of praise (12:13). He hid himself from those who saw him yet nonetheless hated him. They did not really see him but only stumbled on that *stone* in their blindness (cf. 1 Pet 2:8). When Jesus **hid himself** from those who desired to kill him (as you need to be often reminded because of your forgetfulness), he acted in accordance with our human weakness, yet lost none of his power.

John 12:37–43

[37]**Though he had done so many signs before them, yet they did not believe in him;** [38]**it was that the word spoken by the prophet Isaiah might be fulfilled: "Lord, who has believed our report, and to whom has the arm of the Lord been revealed?"** [39]**Therefore they could not believe. For Isaiah again said,** [40]**"He has blinded their eyes and hardened their heart, lest they should see with their eyes and perceive with their heart, and turn for me to heal them."** [41]**Isaiah said this because he saw his glory and spoke of him.** [42]**Nevertheless many even of the authorities believed in him, but for fear of the Pharisees they did not confess it, lest they should be put out of the synagogue:** [43]**for they loved the praise of men more than the praise of God.**

12:39-40 "He has blinded their eyes and hardened their heart, lest they should see with their eyes and perceive with their heart, and turn for me to heal them."

(26) Augustine of Hippo

The words of the gospel which follow are very important and raise a profound question. He continues, **Therefore they could not believe. For Isaiah again said, "He has blinded their eyes and hardened their heart, lest they should see with their eyes and perceive with their heart, and turn for me to heal them"** (12:39-40). It might be said to us as an objection: If they **could not believe**, how is it sin if humans do not do what they are not able to do? They sinned by not believing. Therefore, they **could believe** but did not. If they **could**, how then does the gospel say, **Therefore they could not believe. For Isaiah again said, "He has blinded their eyes and hardened their heart"** (12:39-40)? This is very serious! Is God himself the cause of their unbelief since **he has blinded their eyes and hardened their heart**? . . . Brothers and sisters, as you have just heard, this is the question before us. Certainly you understand how serious it is. However, we will try to give you an answer. **They could not believe** (12:39), because Isaiah the prophet foretold it in accordance with what God foreknew to be the case. If however I am asked why they **could not believe**, I reply immediately that they *would* not. Their depraved will was surely foreseen by God from whom nothing that is to come can be hidden. He foretold this through the prophet. Do you think that the prophet assigns a cause other than their will? What cause? Paul says, *God gave them a spirit of stupor, eyes that should not see and ears that should not hear* (Rom 11:8), and John says, he **has blinded their eyes and hardened their heart** (12:40). I reply that their depraved will deserved this. God **blinds** and **hardens** simply by letting them alone to their own devices and by withdrawing his aid. This is a doctrine that must be preserved fully with integrity by the pious. The apostle says the same thing when dealing with the same intricate question: *What shall we say then? Is there injustice on God's part? By no means!* (Rom 9:14). We must not hold in any way that God is evil. Therefore, the only answer to this question is the following: When he gives his aid, he acts mercifully; when he withholds it, he acts righteously. In everything that he does, he acts with judgment and not in a rash way. Moreover, if the judgments of the saints are righteous, how much more so are the judgments of the sanctifying and justifying God? The judgments of God are just even though they are hidden. When questions are raised and asked of us—Why is one treated in such a way, and another treated in some other way? Why is one blinded when abandoned by God, and why is another enlightened when helped by him?—let us not attempt to offer a verdict on the judgment of such a mighty judge, but with fear and trembling, let us exclaim with the apostle, *O the depth of the riches and wisdom and knowledge of God! How unsearchable are his judgments and how inscrutable his ways!* (Rom 11:33). Similarly it is said in the Psalms, *Thy judgments are like the great deep* (Ps 36:6).

Brothers and sisters, do not force me to attempt the task of penetrating into such depths, probing such an abyss, and searching the inscrutable. I hold that my ability is feeble, and I perceive that yours is equally weak. This task is higher than my height and stronger than my strength. I think that it is the same for you. Let us listen together to the admonition and to the words of Scripture: *Seek not what is too difficult for you, nor investigate what is beyond your power* (Sir 3:21). These things are not forbidden. The divine Master says, *There is nothing covered that will not be revealed* (Matt 10:26). However, if we should conduct ourselves according to what we have received, then as the apostle Paul tells us, not only what we do not know and ought to know, but also, *If in anything you are otherwise minded, God will reveal that also to you* (Phil 3:15–16). Since we have already attained the path of faith, let us keep to it with all persistence. It will lead us to the chamber of the king *in whom are hid all the treasures of wisdom and knowledge* (Col 2:3). The Lord Jesus Christ did not begrudgingly act toward his great and carefully chosen disciples when he said, *I have yet many things to say to you, but you cannot bear them now* (16:12). We must walk, make progress, and grow so that our hearts may become ready to hold the things which we cannot yet receive. If we have progressed enough by that last day, we shall then learn there what we were unable to know here.

If anyone thinks that he is able to give a clearer and better exposition of the question before us, God forbid that I should be more ready to teach than to learn. Only let no one dare to defend free will in such way that deprives us of the prayer, *Lead us not into temptation* (Matt 6:13). Conversely, let him not deny free will and thus find an excuse for sin. Let us listen to the Lord who instructs and offers his aid and who tells us what we should do and helps us do it. He has allowed some to be elevated by pride, trusting too much in their own will. On the other hand, he has permitted others to fall into carelessness due to an excessive distrust of their will. The former ask: Why do we ask God not to allow temptation to overcome us when it is all in our own power? The latter retort: Why should we try to live well when that is in God's power? O Lord, O Father, *who art in heaven . . . lead us not into* any of these *temptations; but deliver us from evil* (Matt 6:9, 13)! Let us listen to the Lord when he says to Peter, *I have prayed for you that your faith may not fail* (Luke 22:32). May we never think that our faith is so beholden to our free will that it has no need of divine assistance. Let us also listen to the evangelist who says, *He gave them power to become children of God* (1:12). May we not imagine that what we believe is completely our own **power**. Let us instead acknowledge his help in both instances. We must give him thanks that he gives us this **power** and must pray that our small measure of strength may not fail us completely. This is *faith working through love* (Gal 5:6) *according to the measure of faith which God has assigned him* (Rom 12:3) in order that *the one who boasts, let him boast in the Lord* (1 Cor 1:31).

It is not surprising that **they could not believe** (12:39) when their will was so prideful. As the apostle says of them, *For, being ignorant of the righteousness of God, and seeking to establish their own, they did not submit to God's righteousness* (Rom 10:3). They were puffed up not by faith but by works as it were. Since they were **blinded** by this self-inflation, they stumbled against the *stone* of stumbling (1 Pet 2:8). For this reason, it is said, **they could not believe** (12:39). From this we are to conclude that they *would* **not believe**; similarly it was said about the Lord our God, *If we are faithless, he remains faithful—for he cannot deny himself* (2 Tim 2:13). Regarding the omnipotent God, it is said: *He cannot!* It is in praise of the divine will that the Lord *cannot deny himself.* That **they could not believe** (12:39) is a fault of the human will.

Pay attention! I say that those who hold themselves in such high regard to think that whatever they do is done in accordance with their own will and therefore deny that they need God's help to lead a righteous life and cannot believe in Christ. When faith in Christ is resisted, there is no benefit given by the mere syllables of Christ's name and the Christian sacraments. Faith in Christ is to *trust him who justifies the ungodly* (Rom 4:5), to believe in the mediator without whose interposition we cannot be reconciled to God, to believe in the Savior *who came to seek and to save the lost* (Luke 19:10), to believe in him who said, *Apart from me you can do nothing* (15:5). A human who ignores the righteousness of God that justifies the ungodly person and sets up his own justice due to his pride cannot believe in Christ. Accordingly, they **could not believe** (12:39). It is not that humans cannot be changed for the better, but they cannot **believe** as long as they hold such ideas. They are **blinded** and **hardened** (12:40) by this because they deny the need of divine assistance and therefore are not helped. God foreknew this about them. They were **blinded** and **hardened**, and the prophet foretold it by his Spirit.

12:41 Isaiah said this because he saw his glory and spoke of him.

---

(27) Jerome

I saw the Lord sitting upon a throne, high and lifted up; and his train filled the temple (Isa 6:1). Certain Greeks and Romans have interpreted this passage before me and declared that the Lord sitting *upon the throne* is God the Father and the two seraphim which stand at each side are our Lord Jesus Christ and the Holy Spirit.[6] Although they are very learned men, I do not agree with their opinion. It certainly is better to set forth the truth in a simple manner than to declare falsehood in a learned style. I disagree particularly because John the Evangelist wrote that it was not God the Father but Christ who was seen in this vision. When he was speaking of the unbelief of the Jews, he set forth clearly the reasons for their unbelief: **Therefore they could not believe. For Isaiah again said, "He has blinded their eyes and hardened their heart, lest they should see with their eyes and perceive with their heart, and turn for me to heal them." Isaiah said this because he saw his glory** of the only-begotten **and spoke of him** (12:39–41). In the book of Isaiah, the prophet is instructed by the one who sits on the throne to say: *Hear and hear, but do not understand* (Isa 6:9). As the evangelist understands it, the one who gives this command is Christ. Since Christ is the one who is seated, we understand that the seraph cannot be interpreted as Christ.

(28) Augustine of Hippo

Isaiah said this because he saw his glory and spoke of him (12:41). What Isaiah saw and how it refers to Christ the Lord must be read and learned in his book. He did not see him

---

6. Jerome is referring to Origen of Alexandria, Eusebius of Caesarea, and Rufinus of Aquileia.

exactly as he is but in some symbolic way in accordance with what the prophet's vision required. Moses saw him as well. Yet he says to the one he saw, *If I have found favor in your sight, disclose yourself to me. Let me see you recognizably in order that I might find favor in your sight* (Exod 33:13 LXX). Moses did not see him as he actually is. Saint John the Evangelist reports in his letter when this will happen for us: *Beloved, we are God's children now; it does not yet appear what we shall be, but we know that when he appears we shall be like him, for we shall see him as he is* (1 John 3:2). He could have said *for we shall see him* without adding *as he is*. However, John knew that he was seen by some of the fathers and prophets, but not *as he is*. So after saying *we shall see him*, he added *as he is*. Brothers and sisters, do not be deceived by any of those who assert that the Father is invisible and the Son visible. This assertion is made by those who think that the latter is a creature. Their understanding runs contrary to the words *I and the Father are one* (10:30). The Son is also invisible in the form in which he is equal to the Father. However, in order to be seen by men, he took *the form of a servant* and was *born in the likeness of men* (Phil 2:7) and became visible to humans. Before his incarnation, he revealed himself willingly to human eyes in the form of a creature under his command but not actually *as he is*. Let us cleanse our hearts by faith so that we may be prepared for that ineffable and "invisible" vision, as it says: *Blessed are the pure in heart, for they shall see God* (Matt 5:8).

John 12:44–50

[44]And Jesus cried out and said, "He who believes in me, believes not in me but in him who sent me. [45]And he who sees me sees him who sent me. [46]I have come as light into the world, that whoever believes in me may not remain in darkness. [47]If any one hears my sayings and does not keep them, I do not judge him; for I did not come to judge the world but to save the world. [48]He who rejects me and does not receive my sayings has a judge; the word that I have spoken will be his judge on the last day. [49]For I have not spoken on my own authority; the Father who sent me has himself given me commandment what to say and what to speak. [50]And I know that his commandment is eternal life. What I say, therefore, I say as the Father has bidden me."

12:44–45 And Jesus cried out and said, "He who believes in me, believes not in me but in him who sent me."

---

(29) Ambrose of Milan

They say that it is written, **He who believes in me, believes not in me but in him who sent me** (12:44). Examine what follows and discover how the Son of God desires to be seen. For it continues, **And he who sees me, sees him who sent me** (12:44). The Father is seen in the Son. In this way he has explained what he said earlier: the one who confesses the Father believes in the Son. The one who does not know the Son, does not know the Father: *No* *one who denies the Son, has the Father. He who confesses the Son, has the Father also* (1 John 2:23). What then is the meaning of the phrase **believes not in me**? This means that you do not believe merely in that body, which you can perceive nor in the man whom you see. He has said that we are not to believe only in a man. You are to believe that Jesus Christ himself is both God and man. For both of these reasons, he says, *I have not come of my own accord* (7:28), and *I am the beginning, concerning which also I speak to you* (8:25). As man, he did not *come* of his *own accord* (7:28). As Son of God, he does not derive his beginning from his humanity, but he says, *I am the beginning, concerning which also I speak to you* (8:25). These words which I speak to you are not human but divine.

It is wrong to think that he said we were not to believe in him since he himself said, **That whoever believes in me may not remain in darkness** (12:46). In another place he says, *For this is the will of my Father, that everyone who sees the Son and believes in him should have eternal life* (6:40). Again, he says, *Believe in God; believe also in me* (14:1). Although we read about the Son, no one should receive the Son without the Father. Christ is not the Son of the Father in a temporal sense, nor due to his passion, nor owing to his conception, nor by grace. I have read of his generation, but I have not read about his conception. The Father says, *I have begotten you* (Ps 2:7). He does not say, "I have created you." The Son does not call God his Creator, but Father in respect to his eternal, divine generation. He shows himself sometimes in the guise of a man and at other times in the majesty of God. Now he claims for himself oneness with the Father in respect to the Godhead, and then he takes upon himself all the frailty of human flesh. He says at one point that he does have his own teaching, and then he says that he does not seek his own will. He points out that his testimony is not true, and then later that it is true. For he said, *If I bear witness to myself, my testimony is not true* (5:31). Later he says, *Even if I do bear witness to myself, my testimony is true* (8:14). Lord Jesus, how is your testimony not true? Did the one who was hung upon the cross and paid the penalty for his crime not jettison the traits of a robber and gain the reward of the innocent when he believed your testimony (cf. Luke 23:39–43)? Was Paul, who was blinded before he believed, deceived when he received his sight once again because he believed (cf. Acts 9:2)? Did Joshua, the son of Nun, err in recognizing the *commander of the army of the Lord* (Josh 5:14)? After he believed the words of that *commander*, he was immediately victorious in the battle of faith. He did not lead his armed soldiers into the fight nor did he destroy the enemy's walls with battering rams or other siege engines, but he conquered with the sound of the priests' seven trumpets. Indeed, the blast of the trumpet and the badge of the priest brought a cruel war to an end (cf. Josh 6:1–17). The harlot Rahab witnessed this. Although she lost all hope for her safety when her city was destroyed, her faith then conquered her and she bound a *scarlet cord in the window* (Josh 2:18). This was lifted up both as a sign of her faith and as the banner of the Lord's passion. The *scarlet cord* symbolized and called to memory the mystical blood which would redeem the world. Outside the city, the name of Joshua was a sign of victory to those who fought; inside, the semblance of the Lord's passion was a sign of salvation to those in danger. Because Rahab understood the heavenly mystery, the Lord says accordingly in the psalm, *I mention Rahab and Babylon among those who know me* (Ps 87:4). How then is your **testimony not true** (5:31) unless it is due to the frailty of humanity? For *every man is a liar* (Rom 3:4).

In order to prove that he spoke as man, he says, *The Father who sent me bears witness to me* (8:18). But when speaking as God, his testimony is true, for he says: *My testimony is true, for I know whence I have come and whither I am going, but you do not know whence I come or whither I am going. You judge according to the flesh* (8:14–15). Those who do not think that Christ had the ability to testify truthfully, they decide this according to his humanity. So when you hear, **He who believes in me, believes not in me** (12:44), or **The Father who sent me has himself given me commandment what to say and what to speak** (12:49), you have now learned how you ought to interpret those words. He shows what this **commandment** is, for he says: *I lay down my life, that I may take it again. No one takes it from me, but I lay it down of my own accord* (10:17–18). You see then that he said this to prove that he had the power fully to *lay down* or *take up his life*. He also said, *I have power to lay it down, and I have power to take it again; this charge I have received from my Father* (10:18). This *charge* . . . was certainly not given to him as God, but as incarnate man, in accord with the victory he would gain in undergoing his passion.

(30) John Chrysostom

Jesus said, **He who believes in me, believes not in me but in him who sent me** (12:44). It is as if he had said, "Why are you afraid to **believe in me**? Faith and unbelief both pass to the Father through me." Notice how he displays the immutability of his divine essence in every way. He did not say, **He who believes in me**, so that someone might assert that he was speaking about his words. This could be said in respect to mere humans. For example, the one who believes in the apostles does not believe in them, but in God. However, in order that you might learn that he speaks here of the belief in his divine essence, he did not say, **He who believes** *in my words*, but, **He who believes in me**. Someone might ask why has he not somewhere said the opposite: "He who believes in the Father, believes not in the Father but in me." He did not say this because they would have replied: "We believe in the Father, but we do not believe in you." Their disposition was still too weak. When conversing with the disciples, he did say the following: *Believe in God, believe also in me* (14:1). However, when he saw that they were still too weak to understand such words properly, he led them in another way. He shows that it is not possible to believe in the Father without believing in him. In order that you might not assume that these words are spoken in respect to his humanness, he adds, **And he who sees me sees him who sent me** (12:45). How can this be? Does God have a bodily form? In no way! When he says, **He who sees me**, he is speaking of seeing with the mind. By this, he is showing his consubstantiality with the Father. What then does **he who believes in me** mean? It is as if he said, "The one who takes water from the river does not get it from the river but from the well." Actually, this image is too insufficient when compared to the matter before us.

12:46–48 "I have come as light into the world, that whoever believes in me may not remain in darkness. If any one hears my sayings and does not keep them, I do not judge him; for I did not come to judge the world but to save the world. He who rejects me and does not receive my sayings has a judge; the word that I have spoken will be his judge on the last day."

---

(31) Ambrose of Milan

Let us consider another passage: *He who believes in the Son has eternal life; he who does not obey the Son shall not see life, but the wrath of God rests upon him* (3:36). The **wrath of God** that **rests upon him** certainly came about from some offense. Namely, that he did not believe. When someone believes, the **wrath of God** departs and **life** comes. To believe in Christ is to gain **life**, for *he who believes in him is not condemned* (3:18). Referencing this passage, they allege that the one who believes in Christ should keep his sayings. They also say that it is written in the Lord's own words: **I have come as light into the world, that whoever believes in me may not remain in darkness. If any one hears my sayings and does keep them, I do not judge him; for I did not come to judge the world but to save the world** (12:46–47).[7] He does **not judge**. Do you? He says that **whoever believes in me may not remain in darkness**. In other words, if he is in **darkness**, he will not **remain** there. He should amend his errors, correct his faults, and keep my commandments. Christ says, *I do not will the death of the impious but that he should turn [and live]* (Ezek 33:11 LXX). Christ continues, "I said above that the one who **believes in me** (12:44) is not judged, and I hold firmly to this. I came *not to condemn the world, but that the world might be saved through me* (3:17). I pardon willingly; I forgive quickly; *I desire mercy and not sacrifice* (Hos 6:6). By *sacrifice* the righteous person is rendered more acceptable, but by *mercy* the sinner is redeemed. *I came not to call the righteous, but sinners* (Matt 9:13). *Sacrifice* was under the law, but *mercy* is in the gospel." *For the law was given through Moses; grace and truth came through Jesus Christ* (1:17).

Next he says, **he who rejects me and does not receive my sayings has a judge** (12:48). Does the one who has not corrected himself strike you as one who has received Christ's words? Certainly not. The one who corrects himself receives his word. This is his word: that everyone should turn away from sin. So then you must either reject his saying, or if you cannot deny it, you must accept it. It is also necessary that the one who turns away from sin must keep the commandments of God and renounce his sins. We should not interpret this saying as if he is speaking to someone who has always kept the commandments. If this had been his meaning, he would have added the word "always." By leaving out this word, he shows that he was speaking to the one who has held to what he heard and accordingly has corrected his faults. He has kept what he has heard. It is very difficult to condemn someone to a lifetime of penance who begins keeping the commandments of the Lord. Let the one who has not held back forgiveness teach us himself. As you read in the psalm, he has not restricted forgiveness even to those who do not keep his commandments: *If they violate my statutes and do not keep my commandments, then I will punish their transgression with the rod and their iniquity with scourges; but I will not remove from him my steadfast love* (Ps 89:31–33). He promises mercy to all.

---

7. Ambrose removes the negating adverb in John 12:47. Originally, it read: *If anyone hears my sayings and does* not *keep them, I do not judge him.*

(32) John Chrysostom

I have come as light into the world (12:46). Since the Father is called **light** everywhere both in the Old Testament and in the New, Christ also uses the same name. For this reason, Paul also calls him the *radiance* (Heb 1:3). Paul learned this from this very passage. Here Christ shows his close relationship with the Father. There is no separation between them, for he says that faith in him is not actually in him, but it passes through him to the Father. He called himself **light**, because he delivers humans from error and destroys the darkness of the mind.

(33) Augustine of Hippo

Pay attention to what follows: **I have come as light into the world, that whoever believes in me may not remain in darkness** (12:46). In another place he said to his disciples: *You are the light of the world. A city built on a hill cannot be hid. No one after lighting a lamp puts it under the bushel basket, but on the lampstand, and it gives light to all in the house. In the same way, let your light shine before others, so that they may see your good works and give glory to your Father in heaven* (Matt 5:14–16). He did not say to them, *You* **have come as light into the world, that whoever believes in** *you* **may not remain in darkness** (12:46). I hold that such a statement can be found nowhere! All the saints, therefore, are **lights**. But they are illuminated by him through faith; however, everyone who becomes separated from him will be enveloped in **darkness**. The **light**, which enlightens them, cannot become separated from itself, for it is entirely immutable. We believe that the **light** that has been lit illumines the prophet or the apostle. We believe them for this reason. We do not **believe in** the person who is enlightened. Rather, we **believe in** that **light** which has given them illumination so that we too may be enlightened along with them by the same **light**. When Christ says **that whoever believes in me may not remain in darkness** (12:46), he makes it very clear that he has found everyone in a state of **darkness**. They should believe in that **light** which has come into the world so that they **may not remain in darkness** in which they have been found. By this **light**, the world was made (cf. Gen 1:3; John 1:5, 9).

John 13

The night when Jesus gathered with his disciples to eat his final meal and wash their feet is celebrated during Holy Week as Maundy Thursday by Christians throughout the world. Although it was connected to the Jewish Festival of Passover, the Venerable Bede contrasts the sacrifice of the Passover lambs with the ultimate sacrifice of the Lamb of God who takes away the sin of the world *(John 1:29). Through his passion and resurrection, Christ is about to pass-over from this world to his Father.*

The Fathers are puzzled by the footwashing scene. The Lord of the universe, who healed the sick, fed the poor, and gave sight to the blind, began to wash the disciples' feet *(13:5) with those same hands. Origen, Ambrose, John Chrysostom, Theophilus, and Bede all draw lessons from the humility shown in his act and call on their fellow Christians to serve each other fully by meeting all daily needs. This act of washing also calls to mind the sacrament of baptism and the forgiveness of sins. For Ambrose, the footwashing implies the daily need for forgiveness, for* he who has bathed does not need to wash, except for his feet, but he is clean all over *(13:10). Bede concurs that this act is done to remind us to forgive the sins of others and to pray for them continually.*

John Chrysostom and Augustine are intrigued by Judas's presence at this meal. John Chrysostom states that Christ offers his merciful forbearance even at the table. He gives Judas a final chance to repent when he says, He who ate my bread has lifted his heel against me *(13:17). However, Judas carries out the* plot that was placed in his *heart (13:2). John then states that Christians should not bear hatred toward those who injure them if the Lord shows such mercy to his betrayer. Augustine grapples with the fact that Judas remains with the* chosen *(13:18) disciples even to this last moment, but he concludes that Judas was never truly one of the faithful.*

Augustine pauses to consider the statement: He was troubled in spirit *(13:21). He asks why Christ is* troubled. *Was it because one of his disciples was about to betray him? Or that his passion was approaching swiftly? Augustine concludes that this text regards his human nature. He voluntarily assumed our weaknesses, including our weak affections, in his body. He felt the full array of human emotions, but by his strength of spirit and his divine power, he overcame these human limitations.*

Then after the morsel, Satan entered into him. Jesus said to him, "What you are going to do, do quickly" *(13:27). Origen and Augustine both state that this* morsel *must be contrasted with the Eucharistic bread that brings life. According to Origen, Jesus is speaking not to Judas but to Satan, for it is the Evil One who propels Judas after the morsel. Augustine states that Judas hands him over, but Christ willingly gives himself up. Cyril is interested in why Jesus hastens this deed. He concludes that Christ knew the final purpose of his suffering and foresaw all that would happen from this event. Satan, death, and decay would all be abolished, the gates of paradise would be opened, and the things below would be united with the things above. He was eager to see the fulfillment of what he longed for and thus moved forward with confidence.*

Origen notes that the phrase it was night *(13:30) is not added by the evangelist super-fluously. It indicates not simply the time of day but that Judas went out into darkness when he left the Light of the world (John 8:12).*

Cyril of Alexandria puts the accent on time: Jesus said, "Now is the Son of man glori-fied" *(13:31). Cyril asks: Was he not glorified earlier when he worked the mighty deeds, raised Lazarus, fed the five thousand, and healed the blind? How is it that he is* now *glorified? While he was "glorified" in those instances, the Son of Man is* glorified *completely in his suffering, death, and resurrection which opened the way to life for all. Origen concludes that Christ was glorified from his human nature being united to the divine Word.*

Jesus said, Yet a little while I am with you *and* where I am going you cannot come *(13:33). Augustine concludes that these statements foreshadow the post-resurrection fellowship that Jesus will enjoy with his disciples; yet he will eat and drink with them only for a limited period before he returns to the Father. Cyril concurs with Augustine and adds that the disciples cannot come* with him yet because they have not received the Spirit. Without the Spirit, they are not able to endure death; afterward, they will confidently face death, for it was about to be conquered by Christ's resurrection.*

Augustine is intrigued by Christ's new mandate: A new commandment I give to you, that you love one another; even as I have loved you *(13:34). He asks: What is new about this? Is this not already stated in the law of God as the dual commandment: To love God and love neighbor? Augustine concludes that it is the same law as that found in the Old Testament, but it is enhanced by the clause* even as I have loved you. *Christ showed the fullness of his love through his passion and through this has made us a new people who are united in love.*

John 13:1–11

[1]Now before the feast of the Passover, when Jesus knew that his hour had come to depart out of this world to the Father, having loved his own who were in the world, he loved them to the end. [2]And during supper, when the devil had already put it into the heart of Judas Iscariot, Simon's son, to betray him, [3]Jesus, knowing that the Father had given all things into his hands, and that he had come from God and was going to God, [4]rose from supper, laid aside his garments, and girded himself with a towel. [5]Then he poured water into a basin, and began to wash the disciples' feet, and to wipe them with the towel with which he was girded. [6]He came to Simon Peter; and Peter said to him, "Lord, do you wash my feet?" [7]Jesus answered him, "What I am doing you do not know now, but

afterward you will understand." ⁸Peter said to him, "You shall never wash my feet." Jesus answered him, "If I do not wash you, you have no part in me." ⁹Simon Peter said to him, "Lord, not my feet only but also my hands and my head!" ¹⁰Jesus said to him, "He who has bathed does not need to wash, except for his feet, but he is clean all over; and you are clean, but not every one of you." ¹¹For he knew who was to betray him; that was why he said, "You are not all clean."

13:1 Now before the feast of the Passover, when Jesus knew that his hour had come to depart out of this world to the Father, having loved his own who were in the world, he loved them to the end.

---

(1) Venerable Bede

When John the Evangelist was about to narrate that memorable act of the Lord—when he deigned to wash the disciples' feet on Passover before he went to his passion—he first explained what the name **Passover** signifies spiritually. He began, **Now before the feast of the Passover, when Jesus knew that his hour had come to depart out of this world to the Father, having loved his own who were in the world, he loved them to the end** (13:1). The word **Passover** means "crossing over." It receives its ancient name from that day when the Lord passed throughout Egypt, striking down the firstborn of the Egyptians and freeing the children of Israel (Exod 12:11–12, 23–27). The name also comes from that night when the children of Israel crossed over from their slavery in Egypt so that they might come into the land which was promised as an inheritance. It also signifies mystically that our Lord was about to cross from **this world to the Father** (13:1). Moreover it means the faithful, after casting aside their worldly desires and slavery to vices by the continual practice of virtues, might pass over to the promised land of their heavenly Father by his example. The evangelist indicates in a beautiful statement how Jesus crossed over from **this world to the Father**, when he says, **Having loved his own who were in the world, he loved them to the end** (13:1). In other words he loved them so much that he would end his bodily life temporally on account of that very love itself. Soon he would pass from death to life, from **this world to the Father** (13:1). *Greater love has no man than this, that a man lay down his life for his friends* (15:13). Therefore, one passed under the law and the other passed under the gospel, but each was consecrated by blood. The former by the blood of the paschal lamb and the latter by the blood of the one about whom the apostle says, *For Christ, our paschal lamb, has been sacrificed* (1 Cor 5:7). The former by its blood slathered on the lintel and the door posts in the manner of a cross (cf. Exod 12:21–23); the latter with Christ's blood poured out on the cross.

13:2–5 [He] rose from supper, laid aside his garments, and girded himself with a towel. Then he poured water into a basin, and began to wash the disciples' feet.

---

(2) Origen of Alexandria

Let us consider what is said after the words **he rose from supper**. It says, **He laid aside his garments, and girded himself with a towel** (13:4). We would ask those who are not willing to ascend from the literal meanings and to understand the nourishments for the soul which are presented in this text in a spiritual manner, to consider the following question: What prevented him from **washing the disciples' feet** (13:5) while clothed? This does not present any problem if we consider what sort of **garments** Jesus wore while eating and rejoicing with the disciples. We should reflect on what attire the **Word** who **became flesh** wears (cf. 1:14). He lays aside this **garment** which is a sort of fabric of phrases woven with phrases and sounds mixed with sounds. He unveils himself more in the form of a servant. This is made clear through the words: he **girded himself with a towel** (13:4). He did this so that he would not be completely naked and so he might dry them with a more intimate fabric after washing the **disciples' feet**. See how the great and glorified **Word** who **became flesh** humbles himself to wash the **disciples' feet**. The text says, **He poured water into a basin** (13:4). When Abraham *lifted up his eyes, he saw three men standing over him. When he saw them, he ran forward from his tent door to meet them and he prostrated himself on ground and said, "Lord, if I have somehow found favor before you, do not pass by your servant"* (Gen 18:2–3). Abraham himself did not fetch water nor did he offer to wash their feet as guests who had come to visit him. Instead, he says, *Let them draw out water and wash your feet* (Gen 18:4 LXX). Similarly, Joseph did not bring water to wash the feet of his eleven brothers. The man who was over Joseph's house *led Symeon out to them, and he brought water to wash their feet* (Gen 43:23–24 LXX). In contrast, the one who says, *I did not come as one who sits at the table, but as one who serves* (Luke 22:27) and correctly adds, *Learn from me, for I am gentle and lowly in heart* (Matt 11:29) himself **poured water into a basin** (13:4). He knew that no one was capable of washing the **disciples' feet** in such a way that they would have a **part** in him (13:8). In my opinion the **water** was the Word. When they came to the **basin** that Jesus set before them, the Word cleansed the **disciples' feet**.

(3) Theophilus of Alexandria

Listen to the account in the divine gospels regarding these matters: *Now as they were eating, Jesus took bread, and blessed, and broke it, and gave it to the disciples and said, "Take, eat; this is my body." And he took a cup, and when he had given thanks he gave it to them, saying, "Drink of it, all of you; for this is my blood of the covenant, which is poured out for many for the forgiveness of sins"* (Matt 26:26–28). What a marvel! What a holy act! What a mysterious, divine ritual! He led us through the letter, and he perfected us through the spirit. He taught us using symbols; he blessed us with grace through his deeds. In Zion he fulfilled the law of the letter; from Zion he proclaimed the law of grace.

Let us now examine the holy acts conducted during the course of the supper and consider their nature and significance. The text says: **He rose from supper, laid aside his garments, and girded himself with a towel. Then he poured water into a basin, and began to wash the disciples' feet, and to wipe them with the towel with which he was girded** (13:4–5). What is more amazing than this? What is more laudable? The one who wraps himself in *light as with a garment* (Ps 104:2) **girds himself with a towel**. The one who binds *up the waters in his thick clouds and covers the darkness* (cf. Job 26:5, 8) binds a **towel** to his waist. The one who *gathers the waters of the sea as in a bottle* (Ps 33:7) **pours water into a basin**. The one who held back the **water** with his firmament (Gen 1:7) **washes the disciples' feet** with **water**. *The one who measured the water with his hand and heaven with a span and all the earth by a handful* (Isa 40:12 LXX) cleanses the feet of his servants with his spotless hands. The one to whom *every knee should bow in heaven and on earth and under the earth* (Phil 2:10) bows his neck to his servants. Angels saw it and were astonished! Heaven observed it and shuddered! The created world witnessed it and was terrified!

(4) Venerable Bede

John continues: **And during supper, when the devil had already put it into the heart of Judas Iscariot, Simon's son, to betray him, Jesus, knowing that the Father had given all things into his hands, and that he had come from God and was going to God, rose from supper, laid aside his garments** (13:2–4). When John is about to report that greatest act of servitude of the one who took on human nature, he first reminds us of the eternal nature of Jesus's divine power. This showed that Jesus is both true God and true man and also reminds us of the teaching that the greater we are the more we should humble ourselves in every way (cf. Sir 3:18 [3:20 LXX]). Certainly, he was true man since he was able to touch and wash the feet of men, was betrayed by another man, and was crucified by other humans. Yet he was indeed true God since **the Father had given all things into his hands**, and **he had come from God and was going to God** (13:3). Our Lord knew that **the devil had already put into the heart of Judas to betray him** (13:2). He knew that **the Father had given all things into his hands** (13:3). The phrase **all things** included the traitor himself, those to whom he would be handed over, and even the death which he was about to suffer. He was given **all things** so that he might do with them what he willed and by his power might turn their evil into good. He knew that through the humility of his incarnation **he had come from God**, and he knew that through the victory of the resurrection he **was going to God** (13:3). Christ did not abandon God when he came forth from him nor did he abandon us when he returned to him. He knew **all** these **things**. Yet as a sign of his great benevolence toward us and as an example of his great humility, he **rose from supper, laid aside his garments** (13:4), and washed his disciples' feet. By this he fulfilled the duty not of the Lord God but that of a servant of humanity. He even humbly washed the feet of the one whose hands he knew were shamefully defiled by his betrayal.

If anyone desires to examine this most humble act of our Savior more deeply—this sacred **supper** at which the Lord reclined with the disciples—he will find that it represents the entire time when he remained bodily with the church. . . . When he **rose from supper** and **laid aside his garments** (13:4), he drew to a close the time when he would live among humans. He **laid aside** on the cross the bodily limbs which he had taken up. He **girded himself with a towel** (13:4) when he took up the requirement of suffering on our behalf from the Father. He wrapped his body with the torment of his passion, for it is customary that suffering is symbolized by a **towel**, for it is woven through the unending exertions of twisting the fibers together. When the Lord **laid aside his garments**, he **girded himself with a towel** (13:4) to signify that he was putting aside the garment of body which he had put on. He was not able to do this without the trial of suffering, without the prolonged anguish of the cross. **He poured water into a basin, and began to wash the disciples' feet, and to wipe them with the towel with which he was girded** (13:5). When he was dead on the cross, he **poured water** together with blood upon the earth from his side (cf. John 19:34). With these he cleansed the works of the faithful. He humbly sanctified all these works by the sacrament of his passion but also strengthened them by the example of his passion.

13:6–10   Peter said to him, "Lord, do you wash my feet?" . . . Simon Peter said to him, "Lord, not my feet only but also my hands and my head!"

---

(5) Ambrose of Milan

We read that the Lord **laid aside his garments, girded himself with a towel, poured water into a basin, and began to wash the disciples' feet** (13:4–5). This water was the dew of heaven. It was prophesied that the Lord Jesus would **wash the disciples' feet** (13:5) with that heavenly dew. Let us now stretch forth the feet of our souls. The Lord Jesus also wants to wash our *feet*. He says not only to Peter but to all of the faithful: **If I do not wash you, you have no part in me** (13:8). O Lord Jesus, come! Lay aside your **garments** which you have put on for my sake. Strip yourself so that you may clothe us with your mercy. For our sake gird yourself with a **towel** so that you may wrap us with your gift of immortality. Pour **water into the basin** and wash **not my feet only but also my head** (13:9). Wash not only the soles of our bodies but also of our minds. I wish to lay aside all of the filth of my frailty in order that I might also say: *I had put off my garment, how could I put it on again? I had bathed my feet, how could I soil them?* (Song 5:3). How magnificent this is! As a servant, you wash the **feet** of your disciples. As God, you pour dew from heaven. . . . This water is the dew of the heavenly message. Lord Jesus, allow this **water** to flow into my body and soul so that the valley of my mind and the field of my heart may grow green from the moisture of this rain (cf. Ps 72:6). Let your dew fall upon me, sprinkling grace and immortality. Wash the footsteps of my mind so that I may not sin again. Cleanse the *heel* of my spirit (cf. Gen 3:15) so that I may be able to nullify the curse and not feel the bite from the snake in my inner sole.[1] Just as you commanded your disciples, may I too have the *authority to tread*

---

1. While Ambrose speaks of the snake's bite on the inner sole/foot with a mind toward Gen 3, the use of the word "inner" suggests he also is thinking of the inner soul.

upon serpents and scorpions with an uninjured foot (cf. Luke 10:19)? You have redeemed the world; redeem also the soul of one sinner.

(6) Ambrose of Milan

Yesterday we discussed the font whose form is a sort of sepulcher into which we are received and immersed and rise,[2] if we believe in the Father, the Son, and the Holy Spirit. In other words, we are resuscitated. You also receive myrrh upon your head as an anointment. Why upon the head? Because Solomon says, *The wise man has his eyes in his head* (Eccl 2:14). Wisdom without grace grows cold, but when wisdom has received grace, then it begins to be perfected. This is called regeneration. But what exactly is regeneration? You find it described in the Acts of the Apostles (cf. Acts 13:33). The verse from the second psalm seems to refer to the resurrection: *You are my son, today I have begotten you* (Ps 2:7). The holy apostle Paul in the Acts of the Apostles likewise explained that the voice of the Father resounded when the Son rose from the dead: *You are my Son, today I have begotten you* (Acts 13:32–34).[3] Accordingly, Christ is called *the first-born from the dead* (Col 1:18). What then is resurrection except when we rise from death to life? Baptism, similarly, is a likeness of death. When you are immersed and when you rise again, it becomes an image of resurrection. According to the interpretation of the apostle Paul, the resurrection of Jesus was a regeneration. In the same way the resurrection from the font is a regeneration (cf. Rom 6:3–11). . . .

You came out of the font. What followed? You then heard the reading. Next, the girded priest (or perhaps a presbyter did this under the auspices of the priest) washed your feet. What is the meaning of this mystery? Certainly, you have heard that the Lord, after he had washed the feet of the other disciples, **came to Simon Peter; and Peter said to him, "Lord, do you wash my feet?"** (13:6). He actually meant the following: "**Lord, do you wash** the feet of a servant? Do you, the spotless one, wash my feet? Do you, the Maker of the heavens, wash my feet?" You find this same response elsewhere. He went to John the Baptist, and John said to him, *"I need to be baptized by you, and do you come to me?"* (Matt 3:14). "I am a sinner; have you come to a sinner so that you who have not sinned might be rid of your sins?" Behold *all righteousness* (Matt 3:15)! Behold humility! Behold grace! Behold sanctification! Christ said, **If I do not wash you, you have no part in me** (13:8). . . .

He who has bathed does not need to wash, except for his feet (13:10). Why is this the case? Because in baptism all sin is washed away. Sin retreats. But the devil overthrew Adam and poured venom on his feet (Gen 3:1–6, 15). For this reason, you wash the **feet**. It is in this place where the serpent lay in wait. The greater protection of sanctification is added here so that he cannot overthrow you later. Therefore, you wash the **feet** in order to wash away the poisons of the serpent. Additionally, the washing of **feet** is done to increase humility. This is to prevent us from disdaining this mystery as if it was an act of submission.

2. In the early church, baptism included a full immersion in a small pool with steps on either end for descending and ascending. The baptized person was fully immersed three times as the triune name of God is pronounced over the catechumen.

3. Ambrose seems mistakenly to have named Peter instead of Paul (cf. Acts 13:15–41; 2:14–36).

(7) John Chrysostom

He began to wash the disciples' feet (13:5). It then says, **he came to Simon Peter; and Peter said to him, "Lord, do you wash my feet?"** (13:6). This question is so direct. It is as if he asked, "Do you wash my feet with those hands which you used to open eyes of the blind, cleanse lepers, and raise the dead?" Of course, he did not need to ask anything more than, **You**? This word alone would have conveyed his meaning. Someone might reasonably ask why none of the other disciples besides Peter tried to stop him, for this was a sign of his great love and reverence. What then is the reason? It seems to me that Jesus washed the traitor first. Then he came to Peter. The others learned from Peter's experience. That Jesus washed someone before Peter is clear from the text: When **he came to Simon Peter** (13:6). The evangelist is not one who aggressively casts blame; the word **began** implies this order. Yet even if Peter were the first, it is likely that the traitor, being impetuous, had reclined prior to him. His boldness is shown also when he dipped his hand into the dish with his Master (cf. Matt 26:23). Although Judas was guilty, he felt no remorse. Peter, in contrast, was rebuked once before even though he spoke out of love (Matt 16:22–23). Nonetheless he was so ashamed, even to the point of physical distress, that he begged another to ask a question (cf. 13:24). Conversely, Judas did not feel anything although he was continually convicted. Therefore, when Jesus came to Peter, he asked, **Lord, do you wash my feet? Jesus answered him, "What I am doing you do not know now, but afterward you will understand"** (13:6–7). In other words, Jesus says, "You will know later how great and important this lesson is and how it can guide us into full humility."

What does Peter do next? He still tries to hinder Jesus: **You shall never wash my feet** (13:8). Peter, what are you doing? Do you not remember what was said to you before? Did you not say, *This shall never happen to you!* (Matt 16:22)? Did you not hear in response, *Get behind me, Satan!* (Matt 16:23)? Are you still not chastened? Are you still impetuous? "Yes," Peter says, "for this act is exceedingly wonderful and amazing!" Since he does this out of his abundance of love, Christ in turn tempers him in the same way. Formerly, he chastened him by rebuking him sharply: *You are a hindrance to me* (Matt 16:23). But here he says, **If I do not wash you, you have no part in me** (13:8). What does that hothead say next? **Lord, not my feet only but also my hands and my head!** (13:9). Impassioned in his demands, he becomes even more heated in his acquiescence, but both flow from his love. Why did Christ not say this without also adding a threat? Certainly, Peter would not have been persuaded. If Christ had said, "Allow me to do this so that I might show you how to be humble," Peter would have promised ten thousand times that he would do this in order to prevent his master from washing his feet.

So what does Christ say? He speaks about the thing that Peter feared and dreaded the most: to be separated from his Lord. Peter is the one who continually asks, *Where are you going?* (13:36). He also said, *I will lay down my life for you* (13:37). If Peter still resisted him even after hearing Jesus say, **What I am doing you do not know now, but afterward you will understand** (13:7), how much more would he have done this had he understood the meaning of this action? Since Christ knew that Peter would continue to resist him if he learned the meaning immediately, he said, **but afterward you will understand.** Peter does not say, "Tell me, so I may permit you to do this." He does not even try to understand what he means but ardently resists him: **You shall never wash my feet** (13:8). But as soon as Christ issued this threat, Peter immediately relaxed his tone. But what does the phrase **but afterward you will understand** mean? **Afterward**? When? When you have cast out demons in my name, when you have seen me taken up into the heavens, and when you have learned from the Spirit that I sit on the right hand of the Father, then you will **understand** what is being done to you now.

(8) Theophilus of Alexandria

He came to Simon Peter; and Peter said to him, "Lord, do you wash my feet?" (13:6). It is as if he said, "Did I not state my own unworthiness earlier when I said, *Depart from me, for I am a sinful man, O Lord* (Luke 5:8). How could I now be so presumptuous? Certainly, if I permit this, my sinful nature will be paralyzed and perish from fear. If I dare permit this, all of creation will undoubtedly condemn my arrogance. Master, do not weigh your servant down in this way. Do not let the sun witness my impetuousness and take its light away from me. Lord, please spare me, your servant, for I am not worthy to be called your slave (cf. John 1:27). **You shall never wash my feet** (13:8). I bear witness to this and tremble. I perceive and am astounded. God ministers to humans; the king serves the subject; the master submits to the slave. I pray that you will not permit the world to learn of my impiety."

How did the wise dispenser of these rites respond to these objections? "Peter, **what I am doing you do not know now, but afterward you will understand** (13:7). Let me perform this sacred act for you, too. **If I do not wash you, you have no part in me** (13:8). When the apostle heard this, he changed his attitude to one of obedience. He was at a loss for words. He said, "O Lord, I am afflicted in every way. My stubbornness against you weighs me down. My opposition is harmful. My denial is damaging. Yet consenting to your plan is completely burdensome. But let God's decree overcome your servant's resistance. Let God's wisdom conquer your servant's self-justification. I withdraw my objections. Will you permit me to stay and receive this sacred enactment? Master, do what you will. Lord, do what you think is right. Wash **not my feet only but also my hands and my head** so that I may have a **part** in you (13:9). I now beseech you; I beg you! May I be able to fulfill the imitation of the divine so that I may receive the divine grace. May I be able to live in accordance with your lovely will so that I will secure your joy. I will extend my **feet** and hold out my **hands** and bow my **head**. Above all, may I not be separated from a **part** of my Lord. May I not lose that blessedness which passes all understanding (cf. Phil 4:7). May I not undermine my own interests by resisting God. Let all of creation know that today I have purchased the kingdom of heaven for a **basin**" (13:5).

(9) Venerable Bede

After he had begun washing the disciples' feet, it is reported that **he came to Simon Peter** (13:6). This should not be understood as if Jesus came to Peter after the other disciples; rather, he started with the one who was the first among the apostles. Not surprisingly, Peter recoiled at this act of service, for he did not understand the meaning of the mystery. We should not doubt that the other disciples would have reacted in the same way had they not heard the statement spoken to Peter: **If I do not wash you, you have no part in me** (13:8). Here it is clearly revealed that this washing of feet implies the spiritual purification of body and soul. Without this, one cannot arrive at fellowship with Christ. When Peter heard these things, he was quickly carried away with his customary fervor of divine love and responded: **Lord, not my feet only but also my hands and my head!** (13:9). It is as if he were clearly saying, "I now understand, since you have pointed it out to me, that you are cleansing my missteps by washing my feet. Therefore, I offer you not only my **feet** but also my **hands** and my **head** for washing. I know that I do many things not only when I walk about but also by my actions—with my vision, my hearing, tasting, smelling, and touching—that need to be forgiven by you." Let us hear how the Lord responds to Peter's earnest love and how he gradually leads him to a mystical understanding of the washing.

Jesus says, **He who has bathed does not need to wash, except for his feet, but he is clean all over** (13:10). He declares plainly that this washing of feet indicates the remission of sins. It reveals not only the cleansing which was given once in baptism but also the washing away of the daily sins of the faithful. No one lives in this life without accruing these, but they are cleansed daily by his grace. We are unable to keep our feet free from contact with the ground as we can the rest of our body, for our feet touch the ground when we walk about. They signify the necessity of our earthly existence by which we who are lazy and negligent are afflicted daily. Even outstanding men and women who live sublime lives are distracted from heavenly contemplation which they love exceedingly. It follows then that *if we say we have no sin, we deceive ourselves, and the truth is not in us* (1 John 1:8). Therefore, **he who has bathed does not need to wash, except for his feet, but he is clean all over.** The person who has been washed in the baptismal font and has received the remission of every sin does not need to be cleansed again. Indeed, he cannot be washed again in the same way. He only needs to have the daily defilements of this world wiped away by the daily forgiveness of his redeemer. His whole body, including its actions, is cleansed. The only exceptions are those temporal cares which necessarily cling to the mind. For their ongoing defiling and subsequent cleansing, we pray each day, *And forgive us our debts, As we also have forgiven our debtors* (Matt 6:12).

John 13:12–20

¹²**When he had washed their feet, and taken his garments, and resumed his place, he said to them, "Do you know what I have done to you? ¹³You call me Teacher and Lord; and you are right, for so I am. ¹⁴If I then, your Lord and Teacher, have washed your feet, you also ought to wash one another's feet. ¹⁵For I have given you an example, that you also should do as I have done to you. ¹⁶Truly, truly, I say to you, a servant is not greater than his master; nor is he who is sent greater than he who sent him. ¹⁷If you know these things, blessed are you if you do them. ¹⁸I am not speaking of you all; I know whom I have chosen; it is that the scripture may be fulfilled, 'He who ate my bread has lifted his heel against me.' ¹⁹I tell you this now, before it takes place, that when it does take place**

you may believe that I am he. [20]Truly, truly, I say to you, he who receives any one whom I send receives me; and he who receives me receives him who sent me."

13:14–15 "If I then, your Lord and Teacher, have washed your feet, you also ought to wash one another's feet."

---

(10) John Chrysostom

The Lord says, **If I then, your Lord and Teacher, have washed your feet, you also ought to wash one another's feet. For I have given you an example, that you also should do as I have done to you** (13:14–15). However, it is not the same thing! He is the **Lord and Teacher**, but you are all fellow servants of each other. What does the phrase *as* **I have done to you** mean? It means "with the same eagerness." In this way he provides an example from his greater action so that we may be able to carry out a lesser one. Similarly, teachers write out the letters of the alphabet for their students in a very elegant way so that they can imitate them, although in an inferior manner. In light of this statement, where are those who utterly despise their fellow servants? Where are those who demand honors? Christ washed the feet of the traitor, the blasphemer, the thief! And this happened on the eve of his betrayal! As incurable as he was, Christ allowed him to share his table. Do you hold yourself in high regard? Do you wrinkle your nose in scorn? Someone says, "If we are to **wash one another's feet,** then we must wash the **feet** of our servants. If we do wash their **feet,** is that not a great act?" In our case "slave" and "free" are a difference in word only. In his case there is an actual difference! By nature Christ is the Lord, yet we are servants. However, he did not refuse even to do this act. If we do not treat the free person as one who has been sold into slavery, we do this because we are content with the current situation. What should we then say about that night? Should we not imitate those events at all after receiving proofs of such forbearance? Instead we act contrarily, as if we are diametrically opposed. Do we hold ourselves aloof, refusing to forgive the debt? God put us under an obligation to each other. But the Lord himself did this first and made us debtors of each other in a lesser way. He was our Lord. But when we do this—if we do it at all—we serve our fellow servants. He implied this when he said, **If I then, your Lord and Teacher, have washed your feet, you also ought to wash one another's feet. For I have given you an example, that you also should do as I have done to you** (13:14–15). Certainly, it would have followed logically if he had said how *much more* should you do as I have done to you. But he left this up to the conscience of those who listened to him.

(11) Theophilus of Alexandria

If I then, your Lord and Teacher, have washed your feet, you also ought to wash one another's feet. For I have given you an example, that you also should do as I have done to you (13:14–15). Imitate me, your Lord, so that through my work of love you may *become* *partakers of the divine nature* (2 Pet 1:4). I lay out for you in advance this sublime way of exaltation. Long ago I knelt to the ground when I provided both the beginning of your existence and the well-being of your human race. After taking clay from the earth, I formed man and gave him the spirit (cf. Gen 2:7). Once again I have willingly stooped down to strengthen the foundations and footings of my ruined creation. I set *enmity* and a *curse* between the deceiver and the deceived, a boundary between the heel and head (cf. Gen 3:14–15). Now I am arming the bruised heel against the serpent so that it should no longer limp along the straight path. *Behold, I have given you authority to tread upon serpents and scorpions, and over all the power of the enemy; and nothing shall hurt you* (Luke 10:19). The whisperer took the authority which was held by the earth-born ancestor of the human race on account of Adam's pride. Lessen this impudence through humility toward one another. Strive to attain this with all your strength. I am the Lord who gives grace to the humble, and the one who despises arrogance. *Everyone who exalts himself will be humbled, but he who humbles himself will be exalted* (Luke 18:14). This is why I command you to love one another: *By this all men will know that you are my disciples, if you have love for one another* (13:35).

13:16–18 "I am not speaking of you all; I know whom I have chosen; it is that the scripture may be fulfilled, 'He who ate my bread has lifted his heel against me.'"

---

(12) John Chrysostom

He says, **I am not speaking of you all**. What amazing forbearance! He does not convict the traitor yet. He cloaks the matter, giving him a chance for repentance. But when he says, **He who ate my bread has lifted his heel against me** (13:18; cf. Ps 41:9), he issues an accusation. Yet he does not convict him. It also seems to me that the phrase **a servant is not greater than his master** was stated purposefully as well. If anyone is harmed either by their servants or by a person who is of lower status, they should not be offended. Rather they should look to the example of Judas. Although he enjoyed myriad blessings, he repaid the good with evil. Accordingly the Lord said, **He who ate my bread** without itemizing all the other things. He stated that which was most suitable to restrain and shame him: "**He who ate bread** (13:18; cf. Ps 41:9), and he who shared my *table*" (Luke 22:21). He said these things to teach them to do good to those who do evil to them, even though they might remain incorrigible.

(13) Augustine of Hippo

We have just heard the Lord say in the holy gospel, **Truly, truly, I say to you, a servant is not greater than his master; nor is he who is sent greater than he who sent him. If you know these things, blessed are you if you do them** (13:16–17). The **master** of humility in both word and deed said this because he had washed *the disciples' feet* (13:5). With his help we should be able to explain what must be examined more carefully, if we do not exhaust ourselves with what is clear. When the Lord had said this, he added appropriately: **I am not speaking of you all; I know whom I have chosen; it is that the scripture may be fulfilled, "He who ate my bread has lifted his heel against me"** (13:18). What does the phrase **lifted his heel against me** mean except that he will "trample upon me"? We know that he is referring to Judas, the one who betrayed him. It follows then that he had not **chosen** him from among his chosen ones when he said this. Rather, I say it was when he said, **Blessed are you if you do them. I am not speaking of you all** (13:17–18). There is one among you who will not be **blessed**, for he will not **do them. I know whom I have chosen** (13:18). **Whom?** Whom except all those who will be **blessed** by the one who can truly bless them when they do what has been commanded and what has been shown as necessary? He says that the traitor Judas is not one of those who has been **chosen**. What then is meant when he says elsewhere, *Did I not choose you, the twelve, and one of you is a devil?* (6:70). Was it because he was **chosen** for another purpose, one for which he was absolutely necessary? He was certainly chosen not for the blessedness of which he had just been speaking: **Blessed are you if you do them** (13:17). He does not say this about all of them. He knows **whom** he has **chosen** to be connected to his blessedness. The one who **ate** his **bread** in order to **lift his heel against** him is not one of these **whom he has chosen** (13:18). They **ate** the **bread** which was the Lord himself; in contrast, Judas **ate** the Lord's **bread** in hostility toward the Lord. They **ate** life; he **ate** judgment. The apostle Paul says, *For anyone who eats unworthily, eats judgment unto himself* (cf. 1 Cor 11:29).

13:20 "He who receives any one whom I send receives me; and he who receives me receives him who sent me."

---

(14) Augustine of Hippo

Truly, truly, I say to you, he who receives any one whom I send receives me; and he who receives me receives him who sent me (13:20). If we want to understand the words **he who receives me receives him who sent me** as expressing that the Father and the Son are one in respect to their nature, consequently it would seem that the pattern of the words in the other clause **he who receives any one whom I send receives me** would be indicating that the Son and his apostle (whom he sends) are one in respect to their nature. Indeed it would not be inappropriate to understand it in this way because that one, who has delighted in running the *race* (cf. 1 Cor 9:24; 2 Tim 4:7), has a dual substance, for *the Word became flesh* (1:14). God became man. Following this, it might seem that he said, **he who receives any one whom I send receives me** in accordance with his human nature **and he who receives me** in accordance with my divine nature **receives him who sent me** (13:20). However, in speaking in this way, he was speaking of the authority of the sender. He was not drawing attention to the unity of their nature. So let everyone receive anyone whom he sends so that they may direct their attention to the one who sends him. If you look for Christ in Peter, you will find the disciple's teacher. If you look for the Father in the Son, you will find the one who begets the only-begotten. Thus you receive the sender in truth when you receive the one whom he sends.

John 13:21–30

²¹**When Jesus had thus spoken, he was troubled in spirit, and testified, "Truly, truly, I say to you, one of you will betray me."** ²²The disciples looked at one another, uncertain of whom he spoke. ²³One of his disciples, whom Jesus loved, was lying close to the breast of Jesus; ²⁴so Simon Peter beckoned to him and said, "Tell us who it is of whom he speaks." ²⁵So lying thus, close to the breast of Jesus, he said to him, "Lord, who is it?" ²⁶Jesus answered, "It is he to whom I shall give this morsel when I have dipped it." So when he had dipped the morsel, he gave it to Judas, the son of Simon Iscariot. ²⁷Then after the morsel, Satan entered into him. Jesus said to him, "What you are going to do, do quickly." ²⁸Now no one at the table knew why he said this to him. ²⁹Some thought that, because Judas had the money box, Jesus was telling him, "Buy what we need for the feast"; or, that he should give something to the poor. ³⁰So, after receiving the morsel, he immediately went out; and it was night.

13:21 When Jesus had thus spoken, he was troubled in spirit, and testified, "Truly, truly, I say to you, one of you will betray me."

---

(15) Augustine of Hippo

Brothers and sisters, it is no trivial question that confronts us in the gospel of the blessed John: **When Jesus had thus spoken, he was troubled in spirit, and testified, "Truly, truly, I say to you, one of you will betray me"** (13:21). Was it because he was about to say, **One of you will betray me**, that was the reason why Jesus **was troubled** not in flesh but **in spirit**? Did this notion occur to him just then for the first time? Was it suddenly revealed to him at that moment? Was he **troubled** by such a surprising and unexpected calamity? Did he not just a moment before use the words, *He who ate my bread has lifted his heel against me* (13:18)? Had he not also said previously, *You are not all clean* (13:11)? This phrase the evangelist added, *For he knew who was to betray him* (13:11). He had pointed this out on still an earlier occasion when he asked, *Did I not choose you, the twelve, and one of you is a devil?* (6:70). Why is it now that **he was troubled in spirit**, when **he testified, "Truly, truly, I say to you, one of you will betray me"** (13:21)? Was **he troubled in spirit** because he now had to identify him so that he could no longer remain concealed among the others but be separated fully? Or was it because the traitor himself was just about to depart to bring those to whom he betrayed the Lord? Was he **troubled** by the nearness of his passion, the imminence of the danger, and the impending hand of the traitor whose treacherous heart was already known? Certainly it was for one of these reasons that Jesus **was troubled in spirit**. Similarly, he said, *Now is my soul troubled. And what shall I say? "Father, save me* *from this hour"? No, for this purpose I have come to this hour* (12:27). It follows then that his **spirit was troubled** as the hour of his passion approached. So here also, since Judas was on the point of going and coming and his heinous act was about to be completed, **he was troubled in spirit** (13:21).

The one who had the power to **lay down** his life and the **power to take it again** was **troubled** (cf. John 10:18). His extraordinary power is **troubled**; the solidity of the rock is shaken. Or is it rather our weakness that is **troubled** in him? Certainly this is true! Let the servants believe nothing that is unworthy of their Lord, but let them recognize their own members joined with their head (cf. 1 Cor 12:12). He died for us, but he was also **troubled** for us. Therefore, the one who died with power and authority was also **troubled** in the midst of this power. The one who transformed our lowly body into conformity with his glorious body also transferred into himself the passions of our weaknesses, for he sympathizes with us according to the affections in his own soul. Let us not fear for the one who is great, mighty, sure, and invincible when he is **troubled** as if he were able to fail. He is not lost; rather, he is seeking us. Us! He is seeking only us so that we might learn about ourselves in his **trouble** and so we might not fall into despair when troubles befall us. He, who willingly **was troubled** for us, comforts those who are unwillingly besieged by troubles.

Let the arguments of the philosophers who posit that a wise man is not affected by passions fade away.[4] *Has not God made foolish the wisdom of the world?* (1 Cor 1:20). The Lord knows that the thoughts of humans are vain. Certainly, the mind of a Christian may be **troubled** by compassion but not by despair. The Christian may fear that people might be lost to Christ. He may fall into sorrow when one is lost. He may ardently desire to bring others to Christ. He may rejoice when he brings them to the Lord. He may be afraid that he himself might fall away from Christ. He may be sad that he has wandered away from his Lord. He may desire to reign with Christ. He may rejoice in the hope that he will wear the crown with Christ. These are the four so-called passions: fear and sorrow, love and joy. It is proper for Christians to feel these passions and to assert that the Stoic philosophers and others like them are in error. They hold that truth comes from falsehood and regard insensibility as soundness of mind. They do not perceive that a human mind, like the appendages of one's body, is even more perilously diseased when it has lost the sensation of pain.

Someone might ask the following: "Should the mind of the Christian be **troubled** when facing the prospect of death?" What do we do with the words of the apostle Paul who said, *My desire is to depart and be with Christ* (Phil 1:23), if the object of his desire would **trouble** him when it comes? Our answer to this question is easy if we follow those who call the emotion of joy itself as a "troubling" of the mind. What if the **trouble** that he feels comes from the joy he experiences at the prospect of death? . . . Let us direct our attention to the sacred Scriptures and seek a solution with the Lord's help to this question that is in harmony with them. Since it is written, **When Jesus had thus spoken, he was troubled in spirit** (13:21), we will not say that he was **troubled** by joy. His own words should prove this, *My soul is very sorrowful, even to death* (Matt 26:38). We should understand that it is a similar feeling that is being expressed here when his betrayer was just about to depart alone and then return at once with his coconspirators: **Jesus was troubled in spirit** (13:21).

---

4. Augustine is referring to the Stoic quest for a life without passion (*apatheia*).

Christians who are not **troubled** at the prospect of death are certainly very steadfast. But are they stronger-minded than Christ? Who would be crazy enough to say this? What else then does his being **troubled** mean except that he assumed voluntarily their weakness in his body? In this way he relieved those who were weak in his body, that is, in his church. If any of them are **troubled in their spirit** at the prospect of death, they may turn their attention to the Lord and be prevented both from thinking that they are cast aside for this reason and from being swallowed up by the more dreadful death of despair. How magnificent will it be when we participate fully in his divine nature for which we hope if his experience of being **troubled** calms us and his assumption of our weakness strengthens us? Whether he was **troubled** on account of his sorrow for Judas who was about to perish or by his own impending death, it is not possible to think that it was due to a weakness of his spirit but instead it was on account of his divine power. So when we are **troubled**, not due to our possession of power but on account of our weakness, no despair regarding our salvation should creep into our minds. He took on the infirmity of our flesh, a disease that was swallowed up in his resurrection. The one who was both man and God outstripped by an incalculable distance the whole human race in respect to the strength of his spirit. He was not **troubled** as if this affection were external to his nature, but he was **troubled** in his very self. This is stated very clearly about him when he raised Lazarus from the dead. It is written that *he was deeply moved in spirit and troubled* (11:33). Even though the text does not express this idea plainly, it may be understood this way since it declares that he was **troubled**. He assumed our full humanity by his divine power. By that very power, he roused all our human passions in himself whenever he decided that it was necessary to do so.

13:22 The disciples looked at one another, uncertain of whom he spoke.

---

(16) Origen of Alexandria

When the Savior said, *Behold the hand of him who betrays me is with me on the table. For the Son of man goes as it has been determined; but woe to that man by whom he is betrayed!* (Luke 22:21–22), Luke recorded that the disciples *began to question one another, which of them it was that would do this* (Luke 22:23). They then discussed it, **uncertain of whom he spoke** (13:22). In the Lucan account it does not seem that each disciple suspected himself. According to Matthew and Mark, even this is suggested. Matthew says, *And they were very sorrowful, and began to say to him one after another, "Is it I, Lord?"* (Matt 26:22). Mark says, *They began to be sorrowful, and to say to him one after another, "Is it I?"* (Mark 14:19). I think they remembered that they were humans and that the plans of those who are still progressing are subject to change, for they are susceptible to desiring the opposite of what they originally preferred. Perhaps they had learned about those *powers against which we are contending* (cf. Eph 6:12) and were therefore cautious due to the unpredictability of humans. They did not want to be overcome and then to betray their teacher. Certainly Peter did not intend to deny Jesus. He firmly declared, *Though they all fall away because of you, I will never fall away* (Matt 26:33). But he was overcome by a spirit of cowardice and *denied him three times* before *the cock crowed* (cf. Matt 26:75; John 18:27). We learn this from the following words: *Let anyone who thinks that he stands take heed lest he fall* (1 Cor 10:12), and *Do not boast about tomorrow, for you do not know what a day may bring forth* (Prov 27:1). The statement **the disciples looked at one another** (13:22) may provide clarity to someone who has a more simple understanding in the following way: each one, as far as human understanding allowed, scrutinized the plans of the others because Jesus proclaimed, **Truly, truly, I say to you, one of you will betray me** (13:21). For this reason, they considered whether their souls had done these things and whether they were capable of turning away from and forgetting the lessons of their teacher, even to the point of betraying him. The statement about the disciples—that they were **uncertain of whom he spoke** (13:22)—is striking. They were not able to discern **of whom he spoke**. They were confused about this and were not able to think or say anything with clarity.

13:26-28 So when he had dipped the morsel, he gave it to Judas. . . . Jesus said to him, "What you are going to do, do quickly."

---

(17) Origen of Alexandria

Let us contemplate what the Lord meant when he said, **It is he to whom I shall give this morsel when I have dipped it** (13:26). Next it says, **So when he had dipped the morsel, he gave it to Judas, the son of Simon Iscariot** (13:26). After Jesus gave him the **morsel**, then Satan entered him. Satan had not been able to enter him earlier. He was not even able to do this at the moment when *the devil put it into his heart that Judas Iscariot, Simon's son, should betray him* (13:2). I think that it was necessary to take back the better gift by means of the gift of the **morsel** from that unworthy man who had it, for *even what he has will be taken from him who does not have* (cf. Matt 25:29; Luke 8:18). When Judas had been separated from the greater gift of the one who addressed him on account of his unworthiness, then he allowed Satan to enter into him. Let us make this into an example. To understand how the Lord **gave a morsel to Judas** and how Judas then cast aside something in him that was better, we shall quote the words from the Second Epistle to the Corinthians: *Let your abundance at the present time supply their want, so that their abundance may also supply your want* (2 Cor 8:14). Perhaps, it was peace that he cast aside, for the one who hears this and does not accept it sends it back to the speaker according to the words, *And if a son of peace is there, your peace shall rest upon him; but if not, it shall return to you* (Luke 10:6). When you understand that earthly things have been exchanged for spiritual ones in these words, you will be able to see how Jesus gave a **morsel** to the one who was unworthy of bread. By means of the **morsel**, peace was stripped from that man since he was unworthy to continue to hear the words, *For even the man of my peace, in whom I trusted, who ate my bread, lifted up his heel against me* (Ps 41:9 LXX), and *Let the evildoer continue to do evil, and the filthy one remain filthy* (Rev 22:11). Once the peace of the Lord was removed, the one who was looking for an *opportunity* to enter Judas's soul did so, for Judas give him a way in (Eph 4:27). Notice also that Satan did not enter Judas earlier. He only *put it into* *the heart of Judas Iscariot, Simon's son, to betray* the teacher (13:2). According to what we have just examined, it is clear that Satan entered him after Judas received the **morsel**. . . .

When Satan had entered Judas, the text reports that **Jesus said to him, "What you are going to do, do quickly"** (13:27). It is uncertain to whom the expression **to him** refers. The Lord could be speaking either to Judas or to Satan. **What you are going to do, do quickly** could be understood as a summoning his opponent to battle or as calling on the betrayer to carry out his role in the divine plan that was about to bring salvation to the world. Jesus no longer wished this plan to be about to happen or to be slowed down but to happen as soon as possible. He was not afraid. Some have thought this, for they have misunderstood what he meant when he said, *My Father, if it be possible, let this cup pass from me* (Matt 26:39). But he stripped down—if I may say it in this way with the utmost confidence—for this contest. I think that the twenty-sixth psalm also prophesies accurately about the passion of the Savior as he struggles against the evil one and all his henchmen. Christ sees these forces equipped and drawn up for battle against him: *The kings of the earth stood side by side, and the rulers gathered together, against the Lord and against his Anointed* (Ps 2:2 LXX). The psalmist also says, *The Lord is my light, and the Lord is my Savior; whom shall I fear? The Lord is my life's protector; of whom shall I be afraid? When the wicked would approach me to devour my flesh—those who afflict me and my enemies—they became weak and fell. Though a company of soldiers be arrayed against me, my heart will not fear; though war may rise up against me, in this I hope* (Ps 27:1–3 [26:1–3 LXX]). But none of the disciples who were reclining at the table knew why he uttered the statement, **What you are going to do, do quickly** (13:27)—which was said either to Satan or to Judas.

(18) Augustine of Hippo

Satan entered into the Lord's betrayer **after the morsel** (13:27). Satan took full possession of the one whom he had previously entered to lead him only into error. Certainly, we should presume that Satan was in him when he went to the Jews and bargained with them regarding the price for betraying the Lord. The evangelist Luke states this very plainly: *Then Satan entered into Judas called Iscariot, who was of the number of the twelve; he went away and conferred with the chief priests* (Luke 22:3–4). Notice that it is shown in this passage that **Satan** had already **entered into Judas**. Satan first entered him when he **put** the idea of betraying Christ *into the heart of Judas* (13:2), for he had come to the supper already with this in mind. But now **Satan entered into him after the morsel**. He no longer sought to tempt one who belonged to another but to take possession of him as his own.

It was not at that point, as some careless readers think, that Judas received the body of Christ. We must understand that the Lord had already distributed the sacrament of his body and blood to all of them when Judas himself was there. This is stated clearly by Saint Luke: *But behold the hand of him who betrays me is with me on the table* (Luke 22:21). Following this, we come to the account in John when the Lord exposed his traitor openly by dipping and holding out to him the **morsel** of bread (cf. John 13:26). . . .

At this point, Judas was possessed not by the Lord but by the devil, for when the bread entered his belly, the enemy entered the mind of this ungrateful man. Nonetheless, I think that there was a great deal of wickedness already contained in his heart which was waiting to issue forth its full, damnable effect. For this reason, when the Lord, the **living bread** (6:51), had given this morsel to the one who was dead and by this act revealed this traitor, he said, **What you are going to do, do quickly** (13:27). He did not order him to carry out this wickedness. Rather, he proclaimed evil for Judas and good for us. What could be worse for Judas, or what could be better for us, than the betrayal of Christ? It was a deed done by him which led to his destruction but done, despite him, for our benefit. **What you are going to do, do quickly.** What a wondrous utterance of one who desires to be prepared instead of angry! What an amazing statement which proclaims the reward awaiting the redeemer instead of the punishment of the traitor! He said, **What you are going to do, do quickly**, not as if he was ferociously desiring the destruction of the traitor, but desperately wanting to accomplish the salvation of the faithful. Christ was delivered *for our trespasses* (Rom 4:25), and he *loved the church and gave himself up for her* (Eph 5:25). As the apostle Paul also says, he is the one *who loved me and gave himself for me* (Gal 2:20). Therefore, had Christ not handed himself over, no one could have. But what does Judas possess except sin? He was not thinking about our salvation when he handed Christ over; rather, he thought only about the money. He delivered up Christ for this reason, but he found only the loss of his soul. He received the payment he desired, but he also received that which he did not want, the payment he deserved. Judas handed Christ over, but Christ gave himself up. The former conducted the transaction of selling his master, but the latter transacted our redemption. **What you are going to do, do quickly.** Not because you are able to do this, but because the one who desires that this be done is able to accomplish it fully!

(19) Cyril of Alexandria

Then after the morsel, Satan entered into him. Jesus said to him, "What you are going to do, do quickly" (13:27–28). . . . The wise evangelist, with careful foresight, told us in the preceding verses that Satan had forced his way and **entered** the heart of the traitor. This resulted in the fact that our Lord Jesus Christ now actually addresses Satan himself rather than the disciple who fell under his power by his inattentive impetuousness. Jesus said to Satan, **What you are going to do, do quickly** (13:27). It is as if he said plainly: "O Satan, see to it that you quickly carry out that plan which you alone know and which is always on your mind. You killed the prophets; you always led the Jews to impiety; you secured the death of those who were sent as ambassadors bearing the word of salvation to Israel; you did not even spare one of those sent by God; and you displayed your incredible brutality and your unending madness toward them. Following in their footsteps, I have now come. To those who are still wandering in error, I bring the power to prevent them from ever straying again. To those who are in darkness, I secure a life within God's light. To those who have fallen into your net and have become ensnared by your cruelty, I give the power to escape from all your traps. I have come to destroy the reign of sin which you have established. I have come to reveal to everyone the one who is by nature the true God. But I know fully your unrelenting anger. I know that you are already working against me. You are trying to harm all those who desire to do the things that I have come to do. But you will not cause me any more distress although you strike quickly and attack with the utmost vehemence. You will cause me no more grief, despite how great the suffering will be when it pierces me at first."

I assume that these words of the Savior hint at the ideas I have just laid out. But let us now try to uncover the reason why he urges this reckless deed to be hastened. The impudence of these wicked men, who in madness planned this outrageous plot, is terrible. He understood what lay before him: the torture and unbearable blasphemies, the blows and the spitting, the nails and the cross, vinegar and gall, the wounds from the spear, and the final misery of death on the tree. Given this, one might ask, why he hastens it and desires that the devil's plans for his passion be brought to a speedy conclusion. . . .

He knew the final purpose of his suffering and foresaw all that would happen from that event. The tyranny of the devil was about to fall into utter ruin on account of the precious cross; death was to be abolished, the power of decay was to be destroyed, humanity was to be freed from that ancient curse and was to hope that the statement, *You are dust, and to dust you shall return* (Gen 3:19), would be annulled by the love and grace of our Savior Jesus Christ. According to the words of the prophet, *all wickedness* was about to *stop up its mouth* (Ps 107:42). Those in the world who did not know the one who alone is truly God by nature were about to be wiped away entirely. They were no longer allowed to condemn those who had been previously held under this power but were now justified by faith in Christ. The gates of paradise were about to be opened. The things below were about to be united with the things above. According to the words of the Savior, the *heavens* were to be *opened* and the assembly of holy *angels* were *ascending and descending upon the Son of man* (1:51). Seeing that such wonderful blessings awaited humanity and such a brilliant hope was created in us by the cross of salvation, does it not follow naturally that the one who thirsted for our salvation and for this reason was *made like us except for sin* (cf. Heb 4:15) would be eager to see the fulfillment of what he longed for so earnestly? Was it not natural for the one who did not know evil to despise the evil deeds of the devil and to hasten eagerly to the joyous completion of these events? The Savior addressed the words **What you are going to do, do quickly** (13:27) to Satan himself who was entirely unaware that he was fighting against his very existence and was driving headlong to ruin in his attempt to bring about Christ's death upon the cross. This saying is a threat rather than a request! It is as if some handsome, young warrior, being full of vigor and power, saw an opponent running to attack him at full speed. Taking up a sharp battle-ax in his right hand and knowing with complete confidence that his enemy will die as soon as he reaches him, he might then cry out, **What you are going to do, do quickly**, for you will feel the force of my right arm! Certainly this would not be the exclamation of one who desires to die but rather of one who knows with certainty that he will be victorious and will conquer the one who desires to harm him. In this way our Lord Jesus, the Christ, urges Satan to hasten more quickly to carry out his bold assault against him. Then he will show that the wicked one has fallen into ridicule and reveal that the world has been liberated from the tyrant who held it arrogantly for ages and conquered it by his cunning deceit so as to turn it away from faith in God. The disciples did not even understand the meaning of this saying. This was likely in accordance with the divine plan, for Christ did not disclose its meaning to them (cf. Matt 17:22–23), although in other places we find him teaching them that he would be *betrayed into the hands of sinners* (Mark 14:41), he would be *crucified*, put to death, and rise on the third day (Matt 20:19).

However, he commanded them not to tell anyone these things (cf. Luke 9:21). He desired to prevent the prince of this world from knowing who he was in respect to his very nature so that he might actually be crucified. He desired to destroy death itself by his crucifixion so that he would bring about the salvation of those who believe in him. Therefore, he concealed the deeper meaning of his words in accordance with his divine plan, because as God he always knows what is best for humanity.

13:30 So, after receiving the morsel, he immediately went out; and it was night.

---

(20) Origen of Alexandria

If we must prove that the phrase **and it was night** (13:30) was not added superfluously by the evangelist, we must state that **night** was both actual and symbolic. It is an image of the **night** that was in Judas's soul when Satan, the *darkness over the abyss* (Gen 1:2), entered him. *And the darkness God called night* (Gen 1:5). Regarding this, Paul says that we are not children of the **night** or the darkness: *Brothers and sisters, we are not of the night or of the darkness* (1 Thess 5:4–5). He also says, *Since we belong to the day, let us be sober* (1 Thess 5:8). For those whose *feet* (13:3) were washed by Jesus, there was no **night**, only the brightest day. They were cleansed, and the filth on the feet of their souls was cast aside. There was no **night** whatsoever in the one who was **lying close to the breast of Jesus, for Jesus loved him** (13:23) and destroyed all darkness with his love. Similarly, there was no **night** in Peter when the heavenly Father revealed it to him and he confessed, *"You are the Christ, the Son of the living God"* (Matt 16:16). In contrast, there was **night** in Peter at the moment of his denial (cf. Matt 26:69–70).

Here, however, **after receiving the morsel, he immediately went out** (13:30). At that moment when he left, he had **night** in him, for the man whose name is *Morning Dawn* (Zech 6:12 LXX) was not present in Judas because he abandoned the *sun of justice* (Mal 4:2 [3:20 LXX]) when he **went out**. Then Judas, who was filled with darkness, pursued Jesus; but *the darkness* itself and the one who assumed the *darkness* did not *apprehend the light* which they pursued (1:5). For this reason, after he said, *I have sinned in betraying innocent blood* as a word of justification, *he went and hanged himself* (Matt 27:4–5). Satan, who was in him, led him by the hand to the noose and hung him upon it. At that time the devil also touched his soul, for Judas was not the sort that the Lord could say to the devil on his behalf what he said on Job's, *But do not touch . . . his soul* (Job 1:12; 2:6 LXX).

John 13:31–35

[31]**When he had gone out, Jesus said, "Now is the Son of man glorified, and in him God is glorified; **[32]**if God is glorified in him, God will also glorify him in himself, and glorify him at once. **[33]**Little children, yet a little while I am with you. You will seek me; and**

as I said to the Jews so now I say to you, 'Where I am going you cannot come.' ³⁴A new commandment I give to you, that you love one another; even as I have loved you, that you also love one another. ³⁵By this all men will know that you are my disciples, if you have love for one another."

13:31-32 "Now is the Son of man glorified, and in him God is glorified; if God is glorified in him, God will also glorify him in himself, and glorify him at once."

---

(21) Origen of Alexandria

The departure of Judas—and Satan who had entered him—from the place where Jesus was begins the glorification of the **Son of man** (13:31). This brings to culmination the glories revealed in his signs, wonders, and transfiguration. This is why the Lord said, *Now is the Son of man glorified* (13:31). The Savior also said, *When I am lifted up from the earth, I will draw all men to myself* (12:32) in order to *show by what death he was to glorify God* (21:19). In his death, he also glorified God. When Judas had gone out **after the morsel** (13:27) to execute the plot against Jesus, the divine plan regarding the death of Jesus was put into full motion. For this reason, Jesus said, **Now is the Son of man glorified** (13:31). Since it is not possible for Christ to be **glorified** if the Father is not glorified in him, the phrase **and in him God is glorified** is then attached to the words **Now is the Son of man glorified** (13:31). But the glory that comes from his death for humanity does not belong to the only-begotten Word, who according to his nature cannot die, nor to wisdom, truth, or whatever else is said of the divine nature of Jesus. The glory instead belongs to the man who was also called the **Son of man** and *who was descended from David according to the flesh* (Rom 1:3). Because of this he said earlier, *Now you seek to kill me*, a man *who has told you the truth* (8:40). But he says in the words we are examining, **Now is the Son of man glorified**. Now I think that God *highly exalted* this man when he *became obedient unto death, even death on a cross* (Phil 2:8-9). *The Word was in the beginning with God,* but *God as the Word* (cf. 1:1) was not capable of being **highly exalted.** The exaltation of the **Son of man** which happened to him when he **glorified** God in his death was due to the fact that he was no longer different from the Word but was the same in him. If *he who is united to the Lord becomes one spirit with him* (1 Cor 6:17) so that this one and his spirit are no longer said to be two, how much more should we say that the humanity of Jesus became one with the Word when the one who *did not count equality with God a thing to be grasped* was *highly exalted* (Phil 2:6-9)? The Word remained exalted, or was restored to it, when he again was **with God**, for **God, the Word,** became man (cf. 1:1). When Jesus **glorified** God by his death, *He disarmed the principalities and powers and made a public example of them, triumphing over them* in the cross (Col 2:15), and he made *peace by the blood of his cross, whether in respect to the things on earth or the things in heaven* (Col 1:20). In all these ways, **Now is the Son of man glorified, and in him God is glorified** (13:31).

(22) Cyril of Alexandria

When he had gone out, Jesus said, "Now is the Son of man glorified, and in him God is glorified; if God is glorified in him, God will also glorify him in himself, and glorify him at once" (13:31–32). . . . After the departure of the traitor and his quick exit from the house, Christ now at the proper time reveals the mysteries to his true disciples. **Jesus said, "Now is the Son of man glorified"** (13:31). In this way he points to his suffering as the Savior as if the enemies were already at the door and about to come upon him. However, he says that **the Son of man** is **glorified**. He means himself. He is not implying a separation from himself as some have thought. For Christ, the Son, is one both before and after his incarnation and both before he had become man and after he had come like one of us. But now we must examine in what way he states that he is **glorified**. Some might ask: Was he not **glorified** before this when he did such mighty deeds? Certainly, he was **glorified** when he rebuked the angry sea with a word and drove back the rushing of the violent winds, for *those in the boat worshiped him, saying, "Truly you are the Son of God"* (Matt 14:33). And again, when he commanded Lazarus to come back to life at Bethany (cf. John 11:43–44), the story of this wondrous deed spread so rapidly that when he went up to Jerusalem at the time of the feast, all the people with their children came out to meet him. They joined their voices in the highest praise of him, saying: *Blessed is he who comes in the name of the Lord* (12:13). Then there was the time when he broke five loaves and two small fish and with these satisfied the hunger of the crowds that had come to him. The crowd numbered five thousand men, not including women and children (cf. Matt 14:17–21; John 6:9–11). The evangelist himself testified that the miracle which he did seemed so wonderful that some of them, being so amazed at the greatness of this deed, sought to proclaim **him king** (6:15).

It would not be difficult to extend this argument more by listing many other deeds that he did. Christ's glory was not manifested in an inferior way in these deeds that we have just mentioned. How then does the one who had been glorified long before say that he is **now glorified**? He had been glorified in other ways and had a reputation for holding divine authority. The perfect fulfillment of his glory and the fullness of his fame clearly lie in this, in his suffering for the life of the world and opening a new way through himself for the resurrection of all. If we examine as far as possible the true reality of the mystery of his work, we will see that he died not for himself nor for his own sake but on behalf of humanity. He suffered and brought to completion the suffering itself and the resurrection that followed. He died according to the flesh and offered his own life in exchange for the life of all. In this substitution for all, he satisfied in himself the demands of that ancient curse. He was raised again from death to an imperishable and unceasing life and thus raised all nature in himself. Accordingly, it is written that since he died once for all, *he will never die again; death no longer has dominion over him. The death he died he died to sin, once for all, but the life he lives he lives to God* (Rom 6:9–10). On account of Christ, this will also be true for us. We will be raised. We are no more subject to death but are given never-ending life. Despite this, there will be a great difference among those who are raised. I speak about their glory and the repayment of debts to each according to his character. According to the words of Paul, after Christ *became obedient unto death, even death on a cross*, he was once again *highly exalted* and received *the name which is above every name* (Phil 2:8–9). The one who was believed to be a mere man was glorified very much beyond that when he was shown to be in truth God and the Son of God. He was not elevated to a new rank by possessing the divine nature; rather, he returned in the flesh to the very status which he held completely before he took on human flesh. For this reason we acknowledge that he was **now glorified**, although truly there was never a time when he was not the Lord of Glory.

None of Christ's divine attributes appear as new; he possessed all of these naturally as God before it is said that he *emptied himself* (Phil 2:7). When he had *taken the form of a servant* and raised himself to that status once again after he had become man, he is considered to have been **glorified** and to have *received the name which is above every name* (Phil 2:7-9). When Christ is **glorified**, **God** the Father also is **glorified**. He is **glorified in** the Son. He does not receive any additional glory from his begotten, for the divine and ineffable nature does not need any augmentation, but he is **glorified** because it is disclosed that he is the Father of such a Son. For just as the Son receives honor and glory for having such a being for his Father, I also think that the Father experiences pride and glory to have begotten such a Son from **himself**. Accordingly, Christ says, **God is glorified in him, and God will also glorify him in himself, and glorify him at once** (13:32), for the Father is **glorified** on account of the Son and he immediately **glorifies** the Son in return. The designation of glory extends to both for the sake of both. However, so that we might bring the application of this passage down to our level and thus make it a source of edification to our audience, we will add the following to what has already been said. If we ourselves glorify God, then we may expect that we will be **glorified** by him. As I live, *says the Lord, those who honor me I will honor*, and they will not be *lightly esteemed* (1 Sam 2:30). When we cast away the defilement of sin and when we adorn our lives wholly in the beauty of good works, God is **glorified** by us and in us. In this way, we live to his glory.

13:33-34 "Little children, yet a little while I am with you. . . . A new commandment I give to you, that you love one another; even as I have loved you, that you also love one another."

---

(23) Augustine of Hippo

Dear brothers and sisters, it is necessary for us to pay attention to the arrangement of our Lord's words. Earlier when Judas had departed and separated himself from the assembly of the saints, the Lord said, **Now is the Son of man glorified, and in him God is glorified** (13:31). Whether he said this as if pointing to his future kingdom when the evil will be separated from the good or that he said this to indicate that his resurrection was to take place at that time instead of being delayed until the end of the world like ours, he added without any ambiguity, **If God is glorified in him, God will also glorify him in himself, and glorify him at once** (13:32). Here he testifies to the immediacy of his own resurrection. He then adds, **Little children, yet a little while I am with you** (13:33), to prevent them from thinking that God was going to **glorify** him in such a way that he would not associate anymore with them on earth. He said, **Yet a little while I am with you** (13:33). This is as if he said directly, "Certainly, I will be glorified in my resurrection, but I am not ascending to heaven immediately, but **yet a little while I am with you**." Just as it is written in the Acts of the Apostles, he spent *forty days* with them after his resurrection (Acts 1:3). He associated with them, both eating and drinking. However, he did not really experience hunger or thirst. By these actions he indicated the true nature of his flesh. He had the power to eat and drink although he no longer needed to. Was he drawing attention to these *forty days* when he said, **Yet a little while I am with you**, or did he have something else in mind? This saying is also able to be understood as follows: "Naturally, until I die and rise again, I am just like you, for I am still in this state of physical infirmity." However, after he rose from the dead, he remained with them, as was said, for *forty days* manifesting his bodily presence. But he no longer shared their human infirmity.

There is another form of his divine presence which is unknown to the mortal senses. Regarding this, he says, *And lo, I am with you always, to the close of the age* (Matt 28:20). This is certainly not the same as **yet a little while I am with you**. It is not a **little while** until the end of the world. On the contrary, even if it is a **little while** (for instance, "time flies," or *a thousand years are in God's sight as one day* [2 Pet 3:8], or as *a watch in the night* [cf. Matt 25:1–13]), you should not think that he intended this meaning on this occasion since he went on to say, **You will seek me; and as I said to the Jews so now I say to you, "Where I am going you cannot come"** (13:33). In other words, after the **little while** when I am with you, **You will seek me**, and **Where I am going you cannot come.** Where is he going that they will not be able to come? Is it after the end of the world? Where then is that place which he references a little later on in this same discourse: *Father, I desire that they may be with me where I am* (cf. 17:24)? In this passage he speaks of his presence with those who are with him until the end of the world. But when he said, **Yet a little while I am with you**, he was referring either to that state of mortal infirmity which he shared with them until his passion or to that bodily presence which he continued to have alongside them until his ascension. One can choose either of these interpretations without violating the faith. . . .

You will seek me; and as I said to the Jews so now I say to you, "Where I am going you cannot come" (13:33). . . . At that time they were not able to **come** to **where** he was **going**, but *afterward* (13:36) they would be able to. Just a little while later he tells the apostle Peter this in the simplest terms possible. Peter asked: **Lord, where are you going?** (13:36). Jesus replied to him, **Where I am going you cannot follow me now; but you shall follow afterward** (13:36). What this means should not be skipped over carelessly. To where could the disciples not follow the Lord at first but then were able to follow **afterward?** To death? If we say this, we must ask when any human finds it impossible to die. Death is the fate of humans in this perishable body, for life is not more easily retained than death. At that time they were more able to follow the Lord to death; certainly, they were less able to follow him to the life which does not experience death. Obviously, that is where the Lord was going: *Christ being raised from the dead will never die again, and death no longer has dominion over him* (Rom 6:9). Since the Lord was about to die for righteousness, how could they, who were not yet ready for martyrdom, have followed him **now** (13:33)? Or since the Lord was about to enter the state of fleshly immortality, how could they, who although being ready to die and who would not be resurrected until the end of the world, have followed him **now** (13:33)? Or since the Lord was about to go to the bosom of the Father without abandoning them—just as he never separated himself from that bosom when he came to them (cf. John 1:18)—how could they follow him now? No one can enter that state of happiness except the one who has been perfected in love. To teach them how they could proceed properly to the place where he was going prior to them, he says, **A new commandment I give to you, that you love one another** (13:34).

The Lord Jesus declares that he is giving his disciples a new commandment: **A new commandment I give to you, that you love one another** (13:34). However, was this not already commanded in the ancient law of God, where it is written, *You shall love your neighbor as yourself* (Lev 19:18)? Why does the Lord then call this a **new commandment** when it is old? Is it called a **new commandment** because he has stripped us of the old man and clothed us with the new? It is not every kind of **love** that renews the person who hears it, or better the one who gives himself wholly to it; rather, it is that sort of **love** which the Lord augmented when he said, **even as I have loved you** (13:34). He added this to distinguish it from other kinds of human love. Husbands and wives love each other. Parents and children share this love. It binds together all other human relationships. Of course, this **new** kind of **love** is also quite different from the unchaste and damnable love which is felt mutually by adulterous men and women, by philanderers and prostitutes, and all others who join themselves together not because of human relationships but due to the shameful depravity of human life. For this reason, Christ has given us a **new commandment**, that we should **love one another, even as he also has loved us** (13:34). This is the **love** that makes us **new**. From this **love** we become **new** people, heirs of the New Testament, and singers of a new song. Dearest brothers and sisters, it was this **love** that renewed those long ago, the righteous, the patriarchs, the prophets. Later it renewed the blessed apostles. And now it is renewing the nations and is gathering and making a new people from the whole human race spread around the world. This new people is the body of the newly married spouse of the only-begotten Son of God. . . .

Brothers and sisters, do not think that when the Lord says, **A new commandment I give to you, that you love one another** (13:34), that the greater commandment, which requires us to *love the Lord our God with all our heart, and with all our soul, and with all our mind* (cf. Matt 22:37), is to be neglected. Similarly, these words—**that you love one another**—do not seem to eschew any reference to that second command which says, *You shall love your neighbor as yourself* (Lev 19:18). Jesus says, *On these two commandments hang all the law and the prophets* (Matt 22:40). For those with a good understanding, both commandments may be found in the other. On the one hand, the one who loves God is not able to despise the divine commandment to love his neighbor; and on the other, the one who loves his neighbor does so in a holy and spiritual way, for what does he love in his neighbor but God himself? This is the love that the Lord distinguished clearly from all other ordinary modes of love when he added, **As I have loved you** (13:34). What did he love in us except God? Not because we already possessed God, but he loved us so that we might possess God. He desired to lead us, as I said before, to where *God is all in all* (cf. 1 Cor 15:28). Similarly, we might say that a physician loves the sick. What is it in them that he loves other than their health which he wants to recover? Certainly, he does not love their sickness which he seeks to remove. Let us then also love one another as much as possible and draw together everyone through love to possess God within us. This **love** is given to us by the one who said, **As I have loved you, that you also love one another** (13:34). He loved us for this very purpose: that we should **also love one another**. He bestowed this on us by his own **love** for us so that we would be bound to each other in mutual **love**.

John 13:36–38

[36]Simon Peter said to him, "Lord, where are you going?" Jesus answered, "Where I am going you cannot follow me now; but you shall follow afterward." [37]Peter said to him, "Lord, why cannot I follow you now? I will lay down my life for you." [38]Jesus answered, "Will you lay down your life for me? Truly, truly, I say to you, the cock will not crow, till you have denied me three times."

(24) John Chrysostom

Peter said to him, "Lord, why cannot I follow you now? I will lay down my life for you." (13:37). When he had shaken off the fear that he might be the traitor and was shown to be one of the true disciples, he then asked this question boldly while the others remained silent. Peter, what did you ask? Jesus said, **you cannot follow me** (13:36). Do you reply, "I can!"? From this experience you will know that your love is nothing without the impetus given from above. It is clear in this instance that Jesus allowed this fall because he cared for Peter. He wanted to teach him by his first words, but when he persisted in his stubbornness, he did not pour it on or force him into denial but left him alone so that he might learn about his own weakness. Christ had declared that he must be betrayed, but *Peter began to rebuke him, saying, "God forbid, Lord! This shall never happen to you"* (Matt 16:22). Peter in turn was rebuked, but he did not learn. When Christ wanted to wash his feet, Peter said, *You shall never wash my feet* (13:8). Here, when Peter hears, **You cannot follow me now** (13:37), he replies, "Although all will deny you, I will not!" (cf. Matt 26:35). Since it was likely that Peter would be given over to his madness of habitual contradiction, Jesus then teaches him not to oppose what he says. Luke also implies this when he reports that Christ said to Peter, *I have prayed for you that your faith may not fail* (Luke 22:32), which means "that you will not be lost forever." In all these ways, Jesus teaches him humility and proves that human nature is nothing by itself. Since Peter's great love made him naturally contradictory, Jesus chastens him so that he might not suffer from this tendency afterward when he would receive the management of the world. He did this so that Peter would remember what he had suffered and be more mindful of himself. Look at the abruptness of his fall. It did not happen to him once or twice, but he was so upset that in a short period of time he spoke the words of denial three times. He learned that he did not love as much as he was loved. Yet, Christ speaks once again to the one who had fallen in this way: *Simon, son of John, do you love me more than these?* (21:15). His denial was not caused by the coldness of his heart but from being stripped of help from above. Then the Lord accepts Peter's love, but he removes his spirit of contradiction which flowed from it. "If you love, you should obey the one you love. I said to you and those with you that **you cannot follow me** (13:36).

Why are you so obstinate? Do you know how serious it is to contradict God? But since you would not learn that everything I say will happen in this very way, you will learn it from your denial. This outcome however seemed to you to be impossible. But you did not understand this. However, you did know in your heart that everything I say will happen. Yet, what actually happened was not expected at all by you: **I will lay down my life for you**" (13:37). Since Peter had heard Christ say, *Greater love has no man than this* (15:13), he leapt forward immediately because he was desirous to attain the highest virtue.

(25) Augustine of Hippo

When the Lord Jesus was commending to his disciples that holy love with which they should love one another, **Simon Peter said to him, "Lord, where are you going?"** (13:36). The disciple spoke to his master, the servant to his Lord, in this way as if he were prepared to follow him. For that reason the Lord, who saw his heart and knew why he asked this, replied in this way: **Where I am going you cannot follow me now** (13:36). It is as if he said, "Because of the reason you asked me this, **you cannot follow me now**." He does not say, **You cannot follow me**, but adds the word **now**. He introduced the idea of delay, but he did not take away hope. Rather, he gave hope and confirmed it with his next words when he added, **But you shall follow afterward** (13:36). Peter, why are you in such a hurry? The Rock, which is Christ, has not yet solidified you with his Spirit.[5] Do not be lifted up by presumption, for **you cannot follow me now**. But do not fall into despair either, for **you shall follow afterward** (13:36). How does he reply to this? **Peter said to him, "Lord, why cannot I follow you now? I will lay down my life for you"** (13:37). Peter took note only of what the desire was in his heart, but he was not aware of his lack of power. The weak man was boasting of his willingness, but the Physician was examining the state of his health. The one promised, but the other already knew. The one who was ignorant was daring, but the one who knew all was teaching. How much had Peter taken upon himself? He was looking only at what he wanted without being aware of what he was capable. How much had he taken upon himself? Although the Lord had come to lay down his life for his friends (cf. 15:13) and for Peter as well, he boldly offers to do the same for the Lord! Although Christ had not yet laid down his life for Peter, he guaranteed to lay down his own life for Christ! **Jesus answered, "Will you lay down your life for me?"** (13:38). Will you do for me what I have not yet done for you? **Will you lay down your life for me?** Are you, who are not able to follow, able to go before me? Why are you so presumptuous? What do you think about yourself? Who do you think you are? Listen to what you are! **Truly, truly, I say to you, the cock will not crow, till you have denied me three times** (13:38). Pay attention! That is how you will quickly reveal your true nature. You who are speaking so magnificently do not know that you are like a child. You promise me your death, but you will deny me your life. You who think that you are able to die for me now, should learn to live for yourself first. Since you fear the death of your flesh, you will bring death to your soul. Just as there is much life when one confesses Christ, there is death when one denies him.

---

5. Augustine is making a play on the meaning of Peter's name, which means "rock."

(26) Cyril of Alexandria

Simon Peter said to him, "Lord, where are you going?" Jesus answered, "Where I am going you cannot follow me now; but you shall follow afterward" (13:36). Jesus uses a style of speech which he wisely selected in light of their present feelings, and he tenderly refrains from disclosing fully what was in his mind. He knew very well that if he declared plainly that he was about to enter into heaven and to leave them on earth without his presence—despite the fact that he would always be with them as God—the grief inflicted on his disciples would be heavy and hard to bear. For this reason, he allows them to continue in their ignorance, for those who are wise sometimes will cloak the things that seem likely to cause pain with weightier words. Even though he was returning to the heavens above to present himself exquisitely to God the Father as the firstfruits of humanity and even though he was doing this to secure the advantage for all humankind—for he opened up a path for us that the human race had not known before—nevertheless, it seemed unbearable to the holy disciples, who were anxious to be with him, to be separated from Christ, despite the fact that he would always be with them through the power and cooperation of the Spirit.

Christ therefore leaves the blessed Peter and the other disciples in the condition of their ignorance about the seriousness of what was being said. He did not fully expound what he had said at that time. Due to his kindness, he waited to do this until he finished teaching the things that would give them the strength to bear it. Certainly, we perceive that he is doing just that in the words that follow a little while later. He says to them at that time, *It is to your advantage that I go away, for if I do not go away, the Counselor will not come to you* (16:7). However, as God, he promises that the disciple who desires eagerly to follow him and to be always with him will not be hindered. He says, **Where I am going you cannot follow me now; but you shall follow afterward** (13:36). This saying is pregnant with two meanings. The first is very easy and obvious; the other is more obscure and enigmatic. He says that Peter **cannot follow** him **now** on his way to the world above and his return to heaven, but **he shall follow afterward**. This will happen fully when Christ gives the saints the honor and glory for which they hoped: to reign with him forever after they arrive in the heavenly city. But these words also contain another meaning which I will explain. The disciples had not yet been *clothed with* the *power from on high* (Luke 24:49) nor had they received the strength that was to restore and remold the human race with courage. By this, I mean the gift of the Holy Spirit. For this reason they were not able to grapple with death and battle the terrors that were hard to confront. There is another meaning that is also probable. Since it was both appropriate and fitting for Christ the Savior alone to break the power of death into pieces, it was not possible that others should be seen doing this before him. What could being free from the fear of death mean other than to despise death as if it is powerless to harm us? In our view at least, this is why the blessed prophets themselves used to tremble at the approach of death: it had not yet been conquered by the resurrection of Christ. Understanding this properly, the apostle Paul said that the Word, who was from God the Father and in God, took hold of *the same nature* of *the descendants of Abraham* in order that *through* the *death* of his holy flesh, *he might destroy . . . death . . . and deliver all those who through fear of death were subject to lifelong bondage* (Heb 2:14–16).

The saving passion of Christ was the first release from death; the resurrection of Christ became for the saints the beginning of their boldness when standing against it. Certainly, our human nature was incapable of destroying death. Our nature had not even been able to shatter the fear that it casts over our souls. Yet the disciples were still somewhat weak when confronting these dangers. For this reason the Lord carefully intimates that Peter would be crucified at the proper time and follow the path of his Lord.[6] When he says, **Where I am going you cannot follow me now; but you shall follow afterward** (13:36), the Lord shows in a veiled way that Peter was not yet prepared sufficiently for such a severe struggle. If Christ in these words is not hinting carefully at the death of Peter, why is it that he is applying the force of these words to Peter alone? Certainly, all the other holy apostles admittedly have received the promise that they will be with Christ and follow him at the time of the resurrection. They will receive a spotless life along with all the other blessings for which they hope. But it is certainly clear that in these words the Lord intimates in a veiled way what will happen especially to Peter at a later time. In another passage he shows this more clearly. He says, *When you were young, you girded yourself and walked where you would; but when you are old, you will stretch out your hands, and another will gird you and carry you where you do not wish to go. This he said, adds the evangelist, to show by what death he was to glorify God* (21:18–19). Even though suffering for the sake of Christ is pleasing to the saints, this danger is not to be sought. But it must be endured nevertheless if it is brought upon them forcefully. Therefore, he commands us to *pray that you may not fall into temptation* (cf. Matt 26:41).

6. Cyril is referencing the ecclesiastical tradition that Peter was martyred by crucifixion.

John 14

Irenaeus, Tertullian, and Augustine each explain that the Lord promises eternal life to those who love him: In my Father's house are many rooms; if it were not so, would I have told you that I go to prepare a place for you? *(14:2). For Irenaeus and Augustine,* my Father's house *refers to the heavenly home in which all will dwell, yet the phrase* many rooms *indicates a distinction of the reward commensurate with one's merit. Eternal life is enjoyed by all, for all see God (Matt 5:8), yet it is experienced distinctly. Tertullian emphasized that the reward of eternal life outweighs all sufferings in this life and that the fleshly house in which we dwell now will be replaced by an eternal one.*

Jesus said, I am the way, and the truth, and the life; no one comes to the Father, but by me *(14:6). Cyril of Alexandria states that Christ is the guide to the Father and the mediator through whom all come to the Father. Through the incarnation, "he has become the figure who straddles the divine and human border and in whom perfect unity and friendship flow together." Leo the Great states that* the way *is the path to Calvary and to the cross. Cyprian of Carthage says that only the name of Christ can forgive sins and restore someone to the knowledge of the Father, for* no one comes to the Father, but by me *(14:6).*

Hilary of Poitiers is intrigued by the dialogue between Philip and Jesus: Philip said to him, "Lord, show us the Father, and we shall be satisfied." Jesus said to him, "Have I been with you so long, and yet you do not know me, Philip? He who has seen me has seen the Father" *(14:8–9). Hilary states that the Son alone has revealed the Father through his incarnation and through his divine miracles, yet Philip seeks a higher, spiritual vision. Hilary quickly points out that what Philip seeks is laudable, yet he has the very image of the invisible God standing in front of him (Col 1:15). Contemplating the Godhead is dark, difficult, and shrouded in mystery; therefore, the Father is seen only through the Son.*

Augustine is troubled by an apparent contradiction in the text that arises when Jesus says, If you love me, you will keep my commandments. And I will ask the Father, and he will give you another Counselor, to be with you forever *(14:15–16). He notes that receiving the Spirit seems contingent on whether or not we* love *Christ and* keep *his commandments. But throughout the Scriptures, it is clearly and often stated that we cannot love without the Spirit indwelling and enabling us. Augustine writes: "How can we love so that we can receive the Spirit if we cannot love without him? Or how can we keep his commandments so that we can receive the Spirit if we have no ability to* keep *these without him?" Augustine*

434

concludes that there are two bestowals of the Spirit: the first is given by Christ to allow us to begin to love, and the second is given to bring that love to perfection. On what does he base this interpretation? Augustine finds the answer to this riddle in the phrase another Counselor *(14:16). How? The word* Counselor *can also be translated "advocate," and Jesus Christ is our advocate with the Father (1 John 2:1); he is* another Counselor. *The Venerable Bede emphasizes that it is necessary for us to demonstrate the sincerity of our love through keeping the commandments so that we may receive* another Counselor. *Finally, John Chrysostom and Augustine both address the phrase* and I will ask the Father *to dispel any interpretation that might undermine the proper Trinitarian distinction between the operations of the three persons of the Godhead. The phrase indicates temporally that the Spirit would come after Christ's resurrection. It does not suggest that the Spirit is in any way subordinated to the Son.*

Although the Lord says, Yet a little while, and the world will see me no more, but you will see me *(14:19), Basil and Augustine state clearly that we see him and know him only with eyes of faith. Certainly, Jesus was seen physically during his earthly sojourn, but he was not seen (i.e., known) fully without spiritual eyes. While many saw the man, not all saw the Word of God in the man. Gregory the Great is intrigued by the notion that God would come to dwell in our hearts (14:23). But he notes that this will happen only if we are truly repentant, love God with our whole being, and keep his commandments fully.*

A few verses later, Jesus promises to send his peace into our hearts: Peace I leave with you; my peace I give to you; not as the world gives do I give to you. Let not your hearts be troubled, neither let them be afraid *(14:27). Cyril states that this* peace *is his very Spirit which is sent to dwell in us. Just as we are commanded to keep his commandments, the Lord does as he is commanded by the Father,* so that the world may know that I love the Father *(14:31). John Chrysostom and Theodore of Mopsuestia both state that he tastes death, although he was not culpable or deserving of this fate. He was led to death because of his love of the Father and his love for us.*

Cyril's attention is drawn to the final words of chapter 14: Rise, let us go hence *(14:31). He states that one can interpret these words literally and physically, for Christ was about to go to his betrayal in the garden of Gethsemane. But Cyril suggests there is another hidden, spiritual meaning: to go on a spiritual journey with our Lord, for he is "our leader, our protector, and our guide on the path toward incorruption and a life in holiness and love of God."*

John 14:1-4

[1]"Let not your hearts be troubled; believe in God, believe also in me. [2]In my Father's house are many rooms; if it were not so, would I have told you that I go to prepare a place for you? [3]And when I go and prepare a place for you, I will come again and will take you to myself, that where I am you may be also. [4]And you know the way where I am going."

(1) Irenaeus of Lyons

Since humans are real, there must be a real transformation. They will not vanish away into non-existence but will progress into a fuller existence. Neither the substance nor the essence of creation will be annihilated, because the one who established it is faithful and trustworthy. But *the form of this world is passing away* (1 Cor 7:31). That is, those things that were the occasion for sin, for humans have grown old in them. This is why *the form of this world* was created temporally. . . . When *the form of this world* passes away and humans have been transformed into an incorruptible state so that they can no longer grow old, then there will be *a new heaven and a new earth* (Isa 66:22) where the new human will dwell continually and will always engage in a new conversation with God. Isaiah declares that these things will continue forever without end: *For as the new heavens and the new earth which I will make shall remain before me, says the LORD; so shall your descendants and your name remain* (Isa 66:22). As the presbyters say, those who are judged worthy to dwell in heaven will go there. Some will enjoy the delights of paradise, and still others will behold the splendor of the city. For everywhere God will be seen insofar as each is able to behold him.[1]

This is the difference in the dwellings between those who have produced a *hundred-fold*, and those who produce *sixty*, and those *thirty* (Matt 13:8). The first will be raised to heaven, the second to paradise, and the third will dwell in the city. This is why the Lord declared, **In my Father's house are many rooms** (14:2). All things belong to God. He grants to each one a **room** which is fitting. His Word also says that the Father awards a share as each is worthy. This is the room in which the guests who have been invited to the wedding recline (cf. Matt 22:1–14). The elders, who are the disciples of the apostles, state that this is the order and pattern of those who are saved and how they progress through various degrees. Through the Spirit, they ascend to the Son, and through the Son, to the Father. Finally, the Son hands over his work to the Father, as the apostle Paul said, *For he must reign until he has put all his enemies under his feet. The last enemy to be destroyed is death* (1 Cor 15:25–26). In the time of the kingdom, the righteous humans who live upon the [new] earth will no longer die. Accordingly, the apostle also states, *But when it says, "All things are put in subjection under him," it is plain that he who put all things under him is not included. When all things are subjected to him, then the Son himself will also be subjected to him who put all things under him, that God may be everything to everyone* (1 Cor 15:27–28).

(2) Tertullian of Carthage

The apostle Paul says that the rewards are greater than the sufferings. He says, *For we know that if the earthly house we live in is destroyed, we have a building from God, a house not made with hands, eternal in the heavens* (2 Cor 5:1). In other words, we will receive a *house*

---

1. It is unclear what reference Irenaeus has in mind. The beatific vision of the new heaven and the new earth in Rev 21–22 does not suggest a tripartite division of the heavenly city of Jerusalem. His indication that the "presbyters" say this suggests that he has in mind a tradition promulgated during the period of the Apostolic Fathers (late first and early second centuries).

in heaven as compensation for our flesh being *destroyed* by its sufferings. He remembered what the Lord said in the gospel: *Blessed are those who are persecuted for righteousness' sake, for theirs is the kingdom of heaven* (Matt 5:10). He however did not deny the restoration of the flesh when he contrasted it with this compensatory reward. Certainly, amends are due to the very substance which suffers destruction, namely the flesh. Because he had called the flesh a *house* (2 Cor 5:1), he desired to use the same word when making the comparison with the ultimate reward. He promises to that very *house* which undergoes destruction through suffering a better *house* by means of the resurrection. The Lord also promises that **in my Father's house are many rooms** (14:2).

While **house** might be understood as referring to the earthly home of this world (i.e., the flesh) which after it is destroyed an eternal home is promised in heaven, the following statement makes clear by referring directly to the flesh that the verse from the gospel does not refer to this sort of fleshly **house**. The apostle makes a distinction when he adds, *Here indeed we groan, and long to put on our heavenly dwelling, so that by putting it on we may not be found naked* (2 Cor 5:2–3). By this he means that we desire to be clothed with the heavenly virtue of immortality before we put off the flesh. The privilege of this special gift awaits those who will be found in the flesh when the Lord comes and who will be found worthy of an instantaneous death on account of the sufferings endured during the time of the antichrist. They will experience a death by a sudden transformation along with those who will rise, as the apostle says to the Thessalonians: *For this we declare to you by the word of the Lord, that we who are alive, who are left until the coming of the Lord, shall not precede those who have fallen asleep. For the Lord himself will descend from heaven with a cry of command, with the archangel's call, and with the sound of the trumpet of God. And the dead in Christ will rise first; then we who are alive, who are left, shall be caught up together with them in the clouds to meet the Lord in the air; and so we shall always be with the Lord* (1 Thess 4:15–17).

(3) Theodore of Mopsuestia

What does the phrase **I will come again and will take you to myself, that where I am you may be also** (14:3) mean? He says, "By my ascension to heaven, I will give you the ability to enjoy all good things in order that it might be revealed to you who the originator of all these things was." When he says, **I will come again**, he is speaking of his second coming. **I will come again and will take you to myself, that where I am you may be also** so that you may take delight in those same good things. Paul says accordingly, *If we endure, we shall also reign with him* (2 Tim 2:12). In another place, he adds, *Provided we suffer with him in order that we may also be glorified with him* (Rom 8:17). It is not that we will reign or be glorified like him, but that we will delight as much as possible in fellowship with him. But the phrase **and you know the way where I am going** (14:4) means something like this: "You will always be with me as those who are used to traveling along a common path; the way is consequently known to them since it is their mutual habit." He spoke to them in parables because these things were too sublime for their understanding.

(4) Augustine of Hippo

In my Father's house are many rooms (14:2). What is the meaning of this verse except that the disciples were afraid? They should have heard that verse, **Let not your hearts be troubled** (14:1), with this one in mind. But who among them could be free from fear when even Peter, who was boldest and most confident of them, was told *the cock will not crow, till you have denied me three times* (13:38)? From this statement, they thought that they were about to perish, and naturally they were **troubled**. But when they hear, **In my Father's house are many rooms; if it were not so, would I have told you that I go to prepare a place for you?** (14:2), they are restored from their **trouble**. They also are made certain and confident that after they pass through the dangers of temptations, they will then dwell with Christ in the presence of God. Even though one person is stronger than another, one wiser than another, and one more righteous, **in my Father's house there are many rooms**. None of them will remain outside that house. Each one will receive a **room** according to his merit.

The master of the house commands that everyone who has worked in the *vineyard* receive a *denarius*, making no distinction between those who have labored more or less (cf. Matt 20:1–15). Undoubtedly, the *denarius* signifies eternal life where no one lives a longer life than another. In eternity there is no difference in the measure of the length of life. But the phrase **many rooms** signifies the degrees of merit within that shared eternal life. Just as there is one glory of the *sun*, another glory of the *moon*, and another of the *stars*, and just as one *star* differs from another in respect to glory, *so it is with the resurrection of the dead* (cf. 1 Cor 14:41–42). The saints, just like the stars, receive different rooms of varying degrees of brightness in the kingdom. However, just as in the case of the awarding of that one *denarius*, no one is separated from the kingdom. In this way, *God* will be *everything to everyone* (1 Cor 14:28). Because *God is love* (1 John 4:8), love will cause whatever is possessed by one to be common to all. Everyone in this way will possess in himself what he does not personally have when he lovingly beholds it in another. Therefore, there will not be any envy among this diversity of glory, because all will reign in the unity of love. . . .

Why did he go away to **prepare a place for us** (14:2) when it is we ourselves who need the preparation which he cannot do if he leaves? Lord, I will try to explain this as I am able. By the preparation of these **rooms**, you were evidently signifying that *the righteous ought to live by faith* (Rom 1:17). Truly it is necessary for the one who is living *away from the Lord* to live *by faith*, because this person is preparing to behold his glory through *faith* (cf. 2 Cor 5:6–8). Consider the following verses: *Blessed are the pure in heart, for they shall see God* (Matt 5:8), and he *cleansed their hearts by faith* (Acts 15:9). The former verse is found in the gospel, the latter in the Acts of the Apostles. This *faith cleanses the hearts* of those living apart from God who will eventually *see God*. Moreover, this *faith* believes what it does not see, for if there is sight, there is no longer belief. Merit accrues to the one who believes; the reward is given to the one who sees. Let the Lord therefore go and **prepare a place** (14:3). Let him go so that he might not be seen. Let him be hidden so that faith might appear. Truly the **place is prepared** if we live by *faith*. Let belief be desired so that we might come to possess what we desire. The desire of love is the preparation of the **rooms**. Lord, bring to completion what you are preparing. You are **preparing a place** for you in us and for us in you, as you have said, *Abide in me, and I in you* (15:4). The degree to which each person more or less has been a participant in you will determine the diversity of rewards in proportion to the diversity of merits. Likewise, the number of **rooms** (14:2) will be apportioned according to the different inhabitants. Yet all of them will be living eternally and blessed forever. Why is it that you **go** away? Why is it that you **come again** (14:3)? If I understand you well, you do not withdraw either from the place you **go** to or the place you **come** from; instead, you **go** away by concealing yourself, and you **come again** by appearing visible to us. But unless you remain to direct us how to advance in living well, how will the **place** be **prepared** (14:2) where we will be able to live in complete joy?

John 14:5–11

⁵Thomas said to him, "Lord, we do not know where you are going; how can we know the way?" ⁶Jesus said to him, "I am the way, and the truth, and the life; no one comes to the Father, but by me. ⁷If you had known me, you would have known my Father also; henceforth you know him and have seen him." ⁸Philip said to him, "Lord, show us the Father, and we shall be satisfied." ⁹Jesus said to him, "Have I been with you so long, and yet you do not know me, Philip? He who has seen me has seen the Father; how can you say, 'Show us the Father'? ¹⁰Do you not believe that I am in the Father and the Father in me? The words that I say to you I do not speak on my own authority; but the Father who dwells in me does his works. ¹¹Believe me that I am in the Father and the Father in me; or else believe me for the sake of the works themselves.

14:5–6 "I am the way, and the truth, and the life; no one comes to the Father, but by me."

---

(5) Cyprian of Carthage

In the gospels and in the letters of the apostles, the name of Christ is uttered for the forgiveness of sins. The name of the Son alone apart from the Father, or in opposition to him, cannot offer an advantage to anyone. However, the use of Christ's name in this way showed the Jews, who haughtily claimed to possess the Father, that this would not benefit them in any way unless they believed in the Son whom he had sent. For those who know God the Father and Creator, should also know Christ the Son. Otherwise, they extol and applaud themselves regarding the Father alone without acknowledging his Son who said, **No one comes to the Father, but by me** (14:6). The Lord himself established that it is the knowledge of both of them which saves, when he says, *And this is eternal life, that they might know you, the only true God, and Jesus Christ whom you have sent* (17:3). From the preaching and testimony of Christ himself, it is clear that the Father who sent the Son must be known first and then afterward Christ who was sent would be known. There cannot be any hope of salvation apart from knowing the two together.

(6) Cyril of Alexandria

Christ did not tell his disciples directly that he was going to the world above and returning to his Father, even though he had referred to this event with both enigmatic hints and outward signs. But now his disciple, Thomas, questions him directly. By devising a sort of argument, Thomas nearly forces the Lord against his will to tell them where he is going and where the **way** of his journey runs. Thomas asked, **Lord, we do not know where you are going; how can we know the way?** (14:5). In his answer Christ eludes the excessive curiosity of his disciple. He does not give the answer that Thomas desired; rather, he tucked it away in the recesses of his mind and held it for a more appropriate moment. Instead he unveils the very thing which was more useful and necessary for them to learn at that moment.

He says, **I am the way, and the truth, and the life** (14:6). No reasonable person can doubt in any way the truth of the Lord's words about himself. Nonetheless, I propose that it is useful to examine this matter carefully. In the inspired Scriptures he is called light, wisdom, power, and many other names. Why is it that in this instance he selects only a few as particularly significant when he calls himself **the way, and the truth, and the life** (14:6)? It seems to me that the power of these words is deep and not easily discovered; nonetheless, we must try. I will say what comes to my own mind, and I will urge those who are in the habit of deep contemplation to set forth the higher meaning of these words.

Certainly, we will arrive at the divine courts above and enter the church of the first-born by three actions: by the practice of virtue in every way, by faith in righteousness, and by hope in the life to come. Is there anyone other than our Lord Jesus Christ who could be our leader, assistant, or agent in accomplishing these things? Certainly not! Do not even consider that! For he has taught us things that are higher than the law, and has shown us **the way** that anyone can safely follow, the path that leads to a life of virtue and zealous pursuit of those things patterned after Christ. Therefore, he is **the truth** and **the way**. In other words, he is the true measure of faith and the exact rule and standard for the perfect conception of God. We will embrace the true faith with utter confidence when we believe that the Son was truly begotten of the very being of God the Father and in no sense was created or made. The one who has received the Son as truly a Son has also surely confessed a belief in the one from whom the Son receives his being. In this way he knows and receives God the Father also, for he is **the truth** and **the life**. No one else can restore the **life** for which we hope, that **life** which is incorruptible, blessed, and holy. He is the one who delivers us who were dead from the ancient curse and is the one who raises us again to the state we had at the beginning. . . .

Since he has added the phrase **no one comes to the Father, but by me** (14:6), let us say something about this. First let us examine how one might go to the **Father**. We are able to come to him in two ways. After becoming holy to the extent possible for human beings, we unite with the holy God: *You shall be holy; for I am holy* (Lev 19:2). Or we slowly come to the knowledge of the Father through faith and contemplation, as it is written: *In a mirror dimly* (1 Cor 13:12). However, no one would ever be holy and reach a virtuous way of life, unless Christ guides him in every way. And no one would be united to God the Father except through the mediation of Christ. He is the *one mediator between God and men* (1 Tim 2:5), uniting humanity to God through himself and in himself. Since he was born of the very essence of God the Father, he is the Word, the Reflection, and his exact Image. He is one with the Father, since he is entirely in the Father and the Father is in him. He has become human just like us and has united with all those upon the earth in every way except in sin. He has become a figure who straddles the border between the divine and human and in whom perfect unity and friendship flow together.

No one comes to the Father (14:6). In other words, no one will partake of this divine nature, except through Christ alone. If he had not become a *mediator* by becoming human, our condition could not have been elevated to the highest level of blessedness. But if **anyone comes to the Father** by means of a mindful faith and pious knowledge, he does so through our Savior Jesus Christ. I will restate this very argument again, since it does not deviate in any way. Anyone who receives the Son truly as a son, also comes to know God the Father. It is not possible that one could know the Son without accepting fully the one who brought him into existence. The knowledge of the Father flows together with knowledge of the Son and vice versa. Therefore, the Lord speaks truthfully when he says, **No one comes to the Father, but by me** (14:6). The Son is the image of God the Father both in his nature and his essence.

(7) Leo the Great

Brothers and sisters, the complete Easter mystery has been laid before us in the gospel narrative. All of you should have a clear picture of the events, as these have just reached the ears of your minds through your physical ears. The divinely inspired account has clearly reported the treacherous betrayal of the Lord Jesus Christ, the trial by which he was condemned, the barbarity of his crucifixion, and the glory of his resurrection. Nonetheless, a sermon is still required of us so that our priestly exhortation might augment the solemn reading of holy Scripture. I am certain that you are demanding from us with pious expectation what is due. Since there is no room for ignorance in the ears of the faithful, the seed of the Word, delivered by the preaching of the gospel, should grow in the soil of your hearts. When the choking thorns and thistles are uprooted (cf. Matt 13:7), the plants of pious thoughts and the buds of righteous passions are able to blossom freely into full fruit. The cross of Christ, which was erected for the salvation of mortal humans, is both a mystery and an example. It is a sacrament by which divine power accomplishes its effect; it is also an example which excites human devotion. Redemption enlivens the desire of those who are rescued from the prisoner's yoke to follow **the way** of the cross through imitation. If the world's wisdom prides itself in its errors in such a way that everyone follows the opinions, customs, and entire way of life of the one chosen to be the leader, how can we share in the name of Christ except by uniting ourselves inseparably to him entirely who asserted that he is **the way, the truth, and the life** (14:6)? That is, **the way** of holy living, **the truth** of divine doctrine, and **the life** of eternal happiness.

14:7–10 Philip said to him, "Lord, show us the Father, and we shall be satisfied." Jesus said to him . . . "He who has seen me has seen the Father."

---

(8) Hilary of Poitiers

If you had known me, you would have known my Father also (14:7). The man, Jesus Christ, is the one who was seen. How is it possible that knowledge of him is knowledge of the **Father**? The apostles see the physical form of his human nature, but God does not have a carnal body and cannot be seen by those who possess a weak and carnal body. The Lord confirms that the divine nature of the **Father** remained within him when he had assumed human flesh in the mystery of his incarnation. He establishes this arrangement: **If you had known me, you would have known my Father also** (14:7); and **henceforth you know him and have seen him** (14:7). He distinguishes the time of sight from the time of knowledge. He says that they will now **know him** whom they had previously **seen** and heard. From the time of this revelation, they will possess the knowledge of his very nature which they had previously just seen.

This new way of speaking troubled the apostle Philip. They see a man before them. He asserts that he is the Son of God and declares that when they have **known** him, they will **know the Father** (14:7). . . . Due to human weakness, they cannot grasp this idea; the acknowledgment of such paradoxes overwhelms their faith. Christ says when **the Father** has been **seen**, then he will be **known**, since he is **known** by being **seen**. He then says that if the Son has been **known**, then **the Father** has been **known also** (14:7), because the Son has provided knowledge about him through his visible and tangible incarnation. It follows then that the essence of the Father cannot be known, as it is different from human nature which is seen. For this reason, the Son often stated that **no one has seen the Father** (cf. 1:18; 5:37; 6:46). Philip then rushes headlong with the confidence of a close apostle and says, **Lord, show us the Father, and we shall be satisfied** (14:8). He was not endangering the faith. This was an error born of ignorance. . . . Indeed, he did not desire a vision that could be seen physically but requested one that could enable him to understand the Father who had been **seen**. Certainly he had seen the Son in the form of a human, but he did not understand how he could see the **Father** through the Son. He added **and we shall be satisfied** to the phrase **Lord, show us the Father** (14:8). This shows that he desired a vision that was more intellectual than physical. He did not reject the Lord's words but asked for a spiritual manifestation that would allow him to believe. . . .

The Lord then answered Philip: **Have I been with you so long, and yet you do not know me, Philip?** (14:9). He rebukes the apostle for his ignorance. Previously, he had said that when he was **known**, the Father was also **known** (14:7). What is the meaning of his question: after **so long, you do not know me** (14:9)? It means that if they had known him, they should have perceived the divine nature of the **Father** dwelling in him. His special deeds belonged to God. He walked upon the water, commanded the winds, miraculously changed the water into wine, multiplied the loaves, cast out demons, drove away diseases, repaired injured bodies, corrected birth defects, forgave sins, and returned the dead to life. He did all these things in the flesh and proclaimed while he did them that he was the Son of God. For this reason he complains that they did not recognize his divine nature in his mysterious human birth and in the deeds which he did through the human body which he had assumed.

The Lord rebuked them because they did **not know** him, although he had been doing these works for **so long** (14:9). He responds to their request that he should show them the **Father** by saying, **He who has seen me has seen the Father** (14:9). He did not mean it was a bodily manifestation or a vision beheld with physical eyes but that they had seen with the . . . eyes of their mind.

It is the same with his present words, **He who has seen me has seen the Father** (14:9). It was not his physical body, which he had received by birth from the virgin, that could reveal the image and likeness of God to them. His human form which he wore could not assist the mental vision of the incorporeal God. But God was recognized in Christ by those who were able to recognize from the evidence of the powers of his divine nature that Christ was the God the Son. . . . In this way, the Son is the image, for he is one with the **Father** in essence, yet he is originated from the **Father**. Other images, such as those made of metals, colors, or other materials used in different sorts of art, reproduce the appearance of the objects which they represent. But can lifeless copies be compared equally with their living originals? Can painted, carved, or molten models share the nature of the one they imitate? The Son is not the image of the **Father** in this way. He is the living image of the living God. The Son who is begotten of the **Father** has a nature that does not differ in any way from the Father's. Since his nature is the same, he possesses the very same power of his nature. The fact that he is the image proves that God the Father is the originator of the birth of the only-begotten who is shown to be the likeness and *image of the invisible God* (Col 1:15). Since he is joined in union with the divine nature, his likeness is indelible, for the powers of that nature are innately his own. This is the meaning of following passage: **Have I been with you so long, and yet you do not know me, Philip? He who has seen me has seen the Father; how can you say, "Show us the Father"? Do you not believe that I am in the Father and the Father in me?** (14:9–10).

In our discussion about divine things, we are only able to contemplate the Word of God. All other aspects of the Godhead are dark and difficult, obscure and dangerous. If anyone tries to express what is known in words that are different from those provided by God, he will undoubtedly reveal his own ignorance or will leave his readers in complete confusion. When he was asked to **show the Father**, the Lord said, **he who has seen me has seen the Father** (14:9). . . . If we find ourselves perplexed, let us blame our own reason. If God's statements seem obscure, let us assume the cause is our lack of faith. These words state clearly that God is not solitary; however, there are no differences within the divine nature. The **Father** is seen in the Son. This could not be true if the Father was an isolated being or if he were unlike the Son. Through the Son, the **Father is seen**. This is the mystery that the Son reveals: They are one God, but not one person. What other meaning can be attached to this statement of the Lord: **He who has seen me has seen the Father** (14:9)?

John 14:12-17

[12]"Truly, truly, I say to you, he who believes in me will also do the works that I do; and greater works than these will he do, because I go to the Father. [13]Whatever you ask in my name, I will do it, that the Father may be glorified in the Son; [14]if you ask anything in my name, I will do it. [15]If you love me, you will keep my commandments. [16]And I will ask the Father, and he will give you another Counselor, to be with you forever, [17]even the Spirit of truth, whom the world cannot receive, because it neither sees him nor knows him; you know him, for he dwells with you, and will be in you."

14:15-17 "If you love me, you will keep my commandments. And I will ask the Father, and he will give you another Counselor."

---

(9) Basil of Caesarea

The greatness of the nature of the Spirit is seen not only in that he has the same name as the Father and the Son and shares in their divine operations but is likewise incomprehensible to the human mind due to his nature. The Lord says that the Father and the Son are far beyond human conception. He says the same about the Holy Spirit: *O righteous Father, the world has not known thee* (17:25). In this passage, *the world* does not refer to heaven and earth as a collective but to our human life which is subjected to constant turmoil and even death. The Lord says about himself, *Yet a little while, and the world will see me no more, but you will see me* (14:19). Here he uses the phrase *the world* to refer to those who are imprisoned by this material and corporeal life and who are able only to see the truth with physical eyes due to their disbelief in the resurrection. They were not able to see our Lord with the eyes of their hearts. He said the same thing about the Spirit: **The Spirit of truth, whom the world cannot receive, because it neither sees him nor knows him; you know him, for he dwells with you** (14:17). The carnal human who has never trained his mind for contemplation is unable to behold the spiritual light, for he has kept it buried in the affections of the flesh as if covered in mud. Similarly, **the world**, since it is enslaved by the passions of the flesh, is no more able to receive the gift of the Spirit than a diseased eye can behold the light of the sun. But the Lord proclaimed the purity of life through his teachings and from that already gave them the ability to see and to contemplate the Spirit. For he says, **You are** already **made clean by the word which I have spoken to you** (15:3). In contrast, **the world cannot receive, because it neither sees him nor knows him; you know him, for he dwells with you** (14:17). Isaiah said something similar, *He who established the earth and all which comes from him; he who gives breath to the people upon it and the Spirit to those who trample upon it* (Isa 42:5 LXX). Those who *trample upon* earthly things and rise above them are shown to be worthy of the gift of the Holy Spirit. What should we think about the Spirit whom **the world cannot receive** (14:17)? What should we think about the Spirit whom only the saints can contemplate through the purity of their hearts (cf. Matt 5:8)? What sorts of honors are suitable for him?

(10) John Chrysostom

We always need deeds and actions not just a show of words. To make statements and promises is easy for everyone, but to act on those is not so easy. Why have I said this? Because there are many who say that they fear and love God but show the opposite in their deeds. But God requires love which is shown by works. For this reason he said to the disciples, **If you love me, you will keep my commandments** (14:15). After he said to them, **Whatever you ask in my name, I will do it** (14:14), he added the phrase **if you love me** (14:15) so that they would not think that it would happen just because they asked. Only then does he say, **I will do it** (14:14). Since it was likely that they would be troubled when they heard him say, **I go to the Father** (14:12), he tells them that to be troubled is not to love; rather, to love is to obey his words: "I have given you **a commandment that you love one another** and that you should love each other **as I have loved you** (13:34). This is love: to obey these words and to submit to the one who is the object of your love.

    And I will ask the Father, and he will give you another Counselor (14:16). He once again lowers his speech to our level. Since they did not fully understand him, it was very likely that they would desire his company, his words, and his physical presence, and would not be consoled in any way when he left. How does he respond? **And I will ask the Father, and he will give you another Counselor** (14:16), that is, **another** like me. Let those who do not hold the right opinion about the Spirit but hold to the heresy of Sabellius be ashamed.[2] The amazing thing about this dialogue is that it strikes down contradictory heresies with one blow. When he says **another**, he indicates the difference in person; when **Counselor**, the similarity in substance. But why did he say, **I will ask the Father**? If he said, "I will send him," they would not likely have believed him. And the goal is that he is believed. Later, the Lord says that he sends the Spirit: *Receive the Holy Spirit* (20:22). Here he says, **I will ask the Father,** in order to make his words credible to them. How did he receive from another what he already possessed? Had not John already said about him, *From his fullness have we all received* (1:16)? Again it was said, *He will baptize you with the Holy Spirit and with fire* (Luke 3:16). If he had to ask the Father to send the Spirit to others, what did he possess that the apostles did not, for they appear to have done this very thing even without prayer? How does the Spirit descend by its own will if it is sent because of a request from the Father? How is that which is present everywhere and *who apportions to each one individually as he wills* (1 Cor 12:11) and who says authoritatively, *Set apart for me Barnabas and Saul* (Acts 13:2), sent by another? Those ministers were serving God. Yet the Spirit called them authoritatively to his own work to demonstrate clearly his power, not to suggest that the Spirit was called to a different sort of work. What then does the phrase **I will ask the Father** (14:16) mean? The Lord says this to reveal the time of the Spirit's coming. When he had cleansed them through his sacrifice, then the Holy Spirit came upon them. Why did the Spirit not come while the Lord was still with them? Because the sacrifice had not yet

2. The heresy of Sabellianism was named after a third-century theologian who held to a modalist understanding of the Trinity. Followers of this heresy posited that God the Father was a unified, singular, divine essence who manifested himself in the modes of the Father, Son, or Holy Spirit. Thus, the three persons of the Trinity were not understood to be separate persons (*hypostases*) that shared one substance (*ousia*) as was confessed by the orthodox community.

been offered. But after sin had been destroyed and they were about to be sent forth into various dangers and were preparing themselves for the contest, it was necessary that the anointer should come. Why did the Spirit not come immediately after his resurrection? It was delayed so that they might desire the Spirit greatly and thus receive him with great joy. As long as Christ was with them, they were not distressed. After he departed, they were left defenseless and found themselves mired in fear. At that point, they received the Spirit with eagerness. **He will give you another Counselor, to be with you forever** (14:16). This verse shows that the Spirit will not depart, even after death! And in order that they would not imagine a second incarnation or expect to see the Spirit with their eyes when they heard about this **Counselor**, he declares plainly that **the world cannot receive, because it neither sees him** (14:17): "He will not be with you as I have been, but he will make his home in your very souls." This is what he means when he says, **He will be in you** (14:17).

(11) Augustine of Hippo

Christ promised the Spirit, the **Comforter**, to his apostles, but let us examine how he gave this promise. Christ says, **If you love me, you will keep my commandments. And I will ask the Father, and he will give you another Counselor, to be with you forever, even the Spirit of truth** (14:15–17). Certainly, the Holy Spirit is included in the Trinity, for the catholic faith confesses that the Holy Spirit is consubstantial and co-eternal with the Father and the Son. About this one, the apostle says, *God's love has been poured into our hearts through the Holy Spirit which has been given to us* (Rom 5:5). How then does the Lord say, **If you love me, you will keep my commandments. And I will ask the Father, and he will give you another Counselor** (14:15–16), when he also says that without the Holy Spirit we cannot **love** God or keep his **commandments**? How can we love so that we can receive the Spirit if we cannot love without him? Or how can we keep his **commandments** so that we can receive the Spirit if we have no ability to **keep** these without him? Or perhaps the love by which we love Christ came into us previously. By this, we **love** Christ and **keep his commandments** and become worthy of receiving the Holy Spirit in order that the love of God the Father—not the love of Christ which came previously—might be *poured into our hearts through the Holy Spirit which has been given to us* (Rom 5:5). This opinion is completely wrong. The one who believes that he loves the Son but does not love the Father, in reality does not love the Son but something he dreamed up. Finally, this is an apostolic dictum: *No one can say "Jesus is Lord" except by the Holy Spirit* (1 Cor 12:3). If we understand this statement in the way the apostle intended, who can call Jesus Lord except someone who loves him? Many say this with their mouths but deny him in their hearts and with their actions (cf. Matt 15:8). It is said about these that *they profess to know God, but they deny him by their deeds* (Tit 1:16). If he is denied *by their deeds*, undoubtedly he is also proclaimed by deeds. Therefore, *no one can say "Jesus is Lord"* with their mind, with words, with deeds, with the heart, with the mouth, or with actions *except by the Holy Spirit* (1 Cor 12:3). No one says this unless he loves the Lord. For this reason the apostles were already saying, *"Jesus is Lord."* If they called him this, they did not do so in a false way. They did not confess him with their mouths and deny him in their hearts and with their actions. Certainly, if they said this truly, undoubtedly they loved him. How then did they love *except by the Holy Spirit* (1 Cor 12:3)? Nevertheless, they are commanded first to **love** him and **keep** his **commandments** (14:15) in order to receive the Holy Spirit, and yet they are not able to **love** him and **keep** his **commandments** (14:15) unless they have the Spirit.

It follows then that the one who loves already possesses the Holy Spirit. Since he has the Spirit, he is worthy of possessing even more; by possessing more, he is able to love even more. The disciples already possessed the Holy Spirit whom the Lord promised, for they could not call him *Lord except by the Holy Spirit* (1 Cor 12:3). But they did not possess him in the way that the Lord had promised. Therefore, they both possessed and did not possess the Spirit since they did not yet possess him to the same extent that they would. They held the Spirit in a more limited way. Yet he was to be given to them in a fuller sense; what they possessed secretly, they would possess openly. Their current possession of the Spirit was connected to that more abundant gift insofar as it revealed to them what they had. Concerning this, the apostle says, *Now we have received not the spirit of the world, but the Spirit which is from God, that we might understand the gifts bestowed on us by God* (1 Cor 2:12). The Lord bestowed the Holy Spirit upon them not only once, but twice. Soon after his resurrection from the dead, *he breathed on them, and said to them, "Receive the Holy Spirit"* (20:22). Surely he did not fail to send the Spirit which he promised at a later time because he gave it to them now, did he? Was it not the very same Holy Spirit who was *breathed on them* here and sent from heaven later (Acts 2:1–4)? It is still another question why he bestowed this same gift publicly twice. Perhaps this double-bestowal was revealed publicly on account of the two commandments of love—the love of God and the love of neighbor—so that love might be shown to belong to the Holy Spirit. If another reason must be sought, we cannot allow this discussion to be lengthened improperly now by such an inquiry as long as we agree that we can neither **love** Christ nor **keep** his **commandments** (14:15) without the Holy Spirit. The less we know him, the less we are able to do; however, the more we experience him, the more complete we become. It is not promised in vain either to the one who possesses the Holy Spirit or to the one who does not, for it is a promise made to the one who does not have the Spirit in order that he might come to have him and to the one who already possesses him, that he may possess him more abundantly. If the Spirit was not possessed in a smaller portion by some, Saint Elisha would not have said to Saint Elijah, *Let the spirit which is in you be a double portion in me* (2 Kgs 2:9 LXX).

When John the Baptist said, *For it is not by measure that God gives the Spirit* (3:34), he was speaking about the Son of God, who did not receive *the Spirit by measure* (3:34), because the entire *fullness of divinity dwells* in him (cf. Col 2:9). The *Mediator between God and men, the man Christ Jesus* (1 Tim 2:5), is not independent of the grace of the Holy Spirit. He tells us himself that the word of the prophet had been fulfilled in him: *The Spirit of the Lord is upon me, because he has anointed me to preach the gospel to the poor* (Luke 4:18–21). That he is the only-begotten, equal to the Father, is not due to grace but to his nature; but the assumption of human nature into the unity of the person of the only-begotten is not due to nature, but to grace. The gospel acknowledges this when it says, *And the child grew and became strong, filled with wisdom; and the grace of God was upon him* (Luke 2:40). But *the Spirit* is given *by measure* to all others. This measure is increased until each has received the full amount in accordance with the limitations of his own perfection. About this, the apostle Paul advises: *Not to think of himself more highly than he ought to think, but to think with sober judgment, each according to the measure of faith which God has assigned him* (Rom 12:3). It is not the Spirit that is divided but the gifts of the Spirit, *for there are varieties of gifts, but the same Spirit* (1 Cor 12:4).

When he says, **And I will ask the Father, and he will give you another Counselor** (14:16), he shows that he was also a **Counselor**. In Latin the word **counselor** means "advocate." It is said of Christ that *we have an advocate with the Father, Jesus Christ the righteous* (1 John 2:1). Just as he said that **the world cannot receive the Spirit** (14:17), so also it was said, *The mind that is set on the flesh is hostile to God; it does not submit to God's law, indeed it cannot* (Rom 8:7). Similarly, we might say, "The unrighteousness cannot be righteous." When he says, **the world**, he is referring to those who love this world. Such a love is *not from the Father* (1 John 2:16). The love of this world, which we struggle to weaken and vanquish within us, stands in direct opposition to *God's love which has been poured into our hearts through the Holy Spirit which has been given to us* (Rom 5:5). Therefore, **the world cannot receive** him, **because it neither sees him nor knows him** (14:17), for worldly love does not possess those invisible eyes. Without those eyes, the Holy Spirit cannot be seen.

He says, **You know him, for he will dwell with you and will be in you** (14:17). . . . To prevent us from thinking that his words **he will dwell with you** were spoken in the same sense as when a guest dwells visibly with someone, he explains this phrase. When he says, **He will dwell with you**, he adds, **And will be in you** (14:17). The Spirit is seen in an invisible way. We cannot have any knowledge of him unless he is in us. Similarly, we see our own conscience within ourselves. We can see the face of another person, but we cannot see our own; conversely, we can see our own conscience, but not another's. But our conscience only exists within us, but the Holy Spirit can exist apart from us. He is given so that he might dwell in us too, but unless he is in us, we cannot see and know him as he ought to be seen and known.

(12) Venerable Bede

Dearest brothers, since we are celebrating the arrival of the Holy Spirit today, we ought to conduct ourselves in accordance with the solemnity of the occasion we are honoring.[3] Indeed we celebrate the joys of this feast in a worthy manner only if we conform ourselves with God's help to those to whom the Holy Spirit comes and in whom he dwells. We are ready for the coming and illumination of the Holy Spirit only if our hearts have been filled with divine love and our bodies have been dedicated to the Lord's teachings. For this reason, the Truth says to his disciples at the beginning of this section of the gospel, **If you love me, you will keep my commandments. And I will ask the Father, and he will give you another Counselor** (14:15–16). **Counselor** means the one who consoles. The Holy Spirit is rightly called **Counselor**, because he lifts up and restores the hearts of the faithful with desires for the heavenly life so that they do not grow weak among the evils of this age. Accordingly, as

---

3. The Venerable Bede delivered this homily to his monastic community on the occasion of the Feast of Pentecost.

the church was growing, it was said in the Acts of the Apostles that *the church . . . was built up; and walking in the fear of the Lord and in the comfort of the Holy Spirit it was multiplied* (Acts 9:31). The Lord's promise, **If you love me, you will keep my commandments. And I will ask the Father, and he will give you another Counselor** (14:15–16), was brought to completion in the disciples themselves. They were revealed to have loved him and to have obeyed his **commandments** truly on that very day when the Holy Spirit appeared to them as tongues of fire when they were praying in the upper room. The Spirit taught them how to speak a diversity of languages and strengthened their hearts through the comfort of his love (Acts 2:2–4). Earlier however they had possessed the **Counselor** himself, namely the Lord remained with them in the flesh. By the sweetness of his miracles and the power of his preaching, they were accustomed to being lifted up and comforted so that they would not be tripped up by the persecution of unbelievers. But since Christ truly departed from them in respect to his bodily presence when he ascended into heaven after the resurrection, he was never absent from them in respect to his divine majesty. He rightly added that the **Counselor**, that is the Holy Spirit, would **be with you forever** (14:16). The Spirit remains **forever** with the saints. He always enlightens them internally in this life and leads them to the everlasting contemplation of the splendor of his majesty in the future.

Dearest brothers, if we love Christ perfectly in such a way that we demonstrate the sincerity of our **love** by keeping his **commandments**, he **will ask the Father, and he will give** us **another Counselor** (14:15–16). Through his humanity, he will ask the Father; through his divinity, he will join the Father in giving the Spirit to us. We must not think that he prayed for the church only prior to his passion and that he does not continue to pray after his ascension. The apostle Paul says that he is the one *who is at the right hand of God, who indeed intercedes for us* (Rom 8:34). We also have the Lord Jesus Christ as our **Counselor**. Although we cannot see him bodily, nevertheless, we have the memoirs of what he did and taught in the body written for us in the gospels. If we devote our full attention to hearing, reading, discussing these things with one another and if we preserve them in our hearts and our bodies as though the Lord was dwelling with us and comforting us forever, then without a doubt we will very easily conquer the troubles of this age. If we **love** this **Counselor**, and we **keep his commandments**, he **will ask the Father**, and **he will give** us **another Counselor** (14:15–16). In other words, he will pour the grace of his spirit into our hearts. It will cheer our hearts with the expectation of our heavenly home even while we experience troubles during our present exile so that we can join the prophet in saying, *When the cares of my heart are many*, your **Counselor**, which is *your consolations, O Lord, cheer my soul* (Ps 94:19). In this way, Christ says, **he will give you another Counselor to be with you forever** (14:16), and he adds, **the Spirit of truth, whom the world cannot receive** (14:17).

John 14:18–26

[18]"I will not leave you desolate; I will come to you. [19]Yet a little while, and the world will see me no more, but you will see me; because I live, you will live also. [20]In that day you will know that I am in my Father, and you in me, and I in you. [21]He who has

my commandments and keeps them, he it is who loves me; and he who loves me will be loved by my Father, and I will love him and manifest myself to him." ²²Judas (not Iscariot) said to him, "Lord, how is it that you will manifest yourself to us, and not to the world?" ²³Jesus answered him, "If a man loves me, he will keep my word, and my Father will love him, and we will come to him and make our home with him. ²⁴He who does not love me does not keep my words; and the word which you hear is not mine but the Father's who sent me. ²⁵These things I have spoken to you, while I am still with you. ²⁶But the Counselor, the Holy Spirit, whom the Father will send in my name, he will teach you all things, and bring to your remembrance all that I have said to you."

14:19-20 "Yet a little while, and the world will see me no more, but you will see me; because I live, you will live also. In that day you will know that I am in my Father, and you in me, and I in you."

---

(13) Augustine of Hippo

Christ goes on to say, **Yet a little while, and the world will see me no more** (14:19). What does this mean? Did the **world** see him at that time? Those who are labeled **the world** should be understood as those whom he had spoken of previously when he said about the Holy Spirit, **Whom the world cannot receive, because it neither sees him nor knows him** (14:17). Christ, while visible in the flesh, was clearly seen with the fleshly eyes of **the world**. But it did not see the Word that was hidden in the flesh. It saw the man, but it did not see God. It saw the clothing but not the one hidden within. Since he refused to show his flesh after his resurrection to those who were not his own—even though he showed it and allowed himself to be touched by his own disciples—perhaps we ought to understand the meaning of the following words accordingly: **Yet a little while, and the world will see me no more, but you will see me; because I live, you will live also** (14:19).

What is the meaning of the words **because I live, you will live also** (14:19)? Why did he speak about his own life in the present tense and of theirs in the future? Clearly it was meant as a promise that the body would also live after being resurrected. This was happening in his case first and then would certainly happen later in theirs. Since his own resurrection was about to happen, he used the present tense to signify its immediacy. However, because their resurrection would be delayed until the end of the world, he did not say, "you live," but **you will live also** (14:19). Using only two verbs, one in the present and the other in the future, he elegantly and briefly promised two resurrections: namely, his own, which was to happen immediately, and ours, which would come at the end of the world. **Because I live, you will live also** (14:19). Because he lives, therefore we will also live: *For as by a man came death, by a man has come also the resurrection of the dead. For as in Adam all die, so also in Christ shall all be made alive* (1 Cor 15:21-22). Since no one comes to death except by that man, no one comes to life unless it is through Christ. Because we have lived, we are dead; however, because he lives, we will live. We are dead to him when we live for ourselves alone, but because he died for our sake, he lives both for himself and for us. Because he lives, we will live also. Although we were able to secure death by ourselves, we are not able to take hold of life by ourselves.

On that day, he says, **you will know that I am in my Father, and you in me, and I in you** (14:20). What does **on that day** mean unless it is that day about which he said, **You will live also** (14:19)? At that time we will be able to see what we now believe. Now he is in us, and we are in him; we believe this now, but then we will know it. We will then know by direct vision what we can now only know by faith. As long as we are in the body as it now exists, namely a corruptible thing that weighs down the soul, we wander far away from the Lord, *for we walk by faith, not by sight* (2 Cor 5:7). Then, however, we will walk by sight, *for we shall see him as he is* (1 John 3:2). If Christ were not already in us now, the apostle would not say, *But if Christ is in you, although your bodies are dead because of sin, your spirits are alive because of righteousness* (Rom 8:10). He shows us clearly that we are also truly in him now when he says, *I am the vine, you are the branches* (15:5). It follows then that **on that day** when we live in that life by which death is swallowed up (cf. Isa 25:8), we will know that he is **in the Father**, and we are **in him**, and he is in us (14:20). At that time, the very state which has already begun now through him will be brought to completion, namely, that he is in us and we are in him.

14:23–24 "My Father will love him, and we will come to him and make our home with him. He who does not love me does not keep my words."

---

(14) Gregory the Great

And my Father will love him, and we will come to him and make our home with him (14:23). Dearest brothers and sisters, ponder how great this mystery is: that God would **come** as a guest into our hearts. Certainly, if a rich and very powerful friend were coming to your home, you would quickly clean it so that nothing there would offend the eyes of your friend. Accordingly, let everyone wipe away the detritus of his wicked deeds to prepare the abode of his mind for God. Pay attention to what the truth says: **We will come to him and make our home with him** (14:23). He enters the hearts of some and yet does not **make a home** there because they have acquired a respect for God only through remorse. But in a time of temptation they forget the very thing that caused them to feel regret, and then they return to committing sins, as if they had not lamented these things at all. However, the Lord **comes** and **makes a home** in the heart of the one who truly loves God and keeps his commandments since the love of God penetrates him in such a way that he does not abandon this love in time of temptation. It follows then that such a person, who does not allow corrupt habits to overwhelm his mind, truly loves God. The more one rejoices in base things the more he is cut off from heavenly love. For this reason, the following words are added: **He who does not love me does not keep my words** (14:24). Dearest brothers and sisters, examine yourselves and discover if you truly love God. Regardless how your soul responds, do not trust yourselves without the testimony of deeds. Let him examine his words, his mind, and his entire life concerning his love of the Creator, for the love of God is never idle. Indeed, love does great things if it is present, but if it refuses to work, it is not truly love.

14:26 "But the Counselor, the Holy Spirit, whom the Father will send in my name, he will teach you all things."

---

(15) Augustine of Hippo

He said, **But the Counselor, the Holy Spirit, whom the Father will send in my name, he will teach you all things, and bring to your remembrance all that I have said to you** (14:26). Is it possible that the Son speaks and the **Holy Spirit** teaches so that we only take hold of the words spoken by the Son and then understand them only by the teaching of the **Spirit**? Is it possible that the Son can speak without the **Holy Spirit** or that the **Holy Spirit** can teach without the Son? Instead, is it not the case that the Son also teaches and the **Spirit** also speaks? Whenever God speaks and teaches anything, the Trinity itself speaks and teaches! Since it is a Trinity, it is necessary that the individual persons are introduced separately so that we might hear the persons distinctly and know the Trinity as a unity. Listen to the Father speaking when you read, *The Lord said to me, "You are my son"* (Ps 2:7). Hear the Father teaching when you read, *Everyone who has heard and learned from the Father comes to me* (6:45). On the other hand, you have just heard the Son speaking, when he says about himself: **all that I have said to you** (14:26). If you want to know him as a teacher, recall what the Master said: *You have one teacher, the Christ* (Matt 23:10). In addition, the **Holy Spirit** also teaches, as you just heard in the words, **He will teach you all things** (14:26). Listen to the **Spirit** when he speaks; in the Acts of the Apostles we read that the **Holy Spirit** said to the blessed Peter: *Accompany them without hesitation; for I have sent them* (Acts 10:20). The whole Trinity, therefore, both speaks and teaches, but unless it were revealed to us in its individual persons, in our human weakness we would not be able to understand it. Since the Trinity is completely inseparable, it would never be known as the Trinity if it were always spoken of as a unity. When we speak about the Father, Son, and **Holy Spirit**, we do not speak of them together as a unity, although they cannot exist apart from a unified whole. But when Christ added, **He will bring to your remembrance all that I have said to you** (14:26), we should understand that we are commanded not to forget that these restorative reminders are connected to the grace which the Holy Spirit **brings to our remembrance**.

John 14:27–31

[27]"Peace I leave with you; my peace I give to you; not as the world gives do I give to you. Let not your hearts be troubled, neither let them be afraid. [28]You heard me say to you, 'I go away, and I will come to you.' If you loved me, you would have rejoiced, because

I go to the Father; for the Father is greater than I. [29]And now I have told you before it takes place, so that when it does take place, you may believe. [30]I will no longer talk much with you, for the ruler of this world is coming. He has no power over me; [31]but I do as the Father has commanded me, so that the world may know that I love the Father. Rise, let us go hence."

14:27 "Peace I leave with you. . . . Let not your hearts be troubled, neither let them be afraid."

---

(16) Cyril of Alexandria

I do not think that it is necessary to make a long argument to demonstrate fully that the **peace** of Christ is his Spirit. . . . Certainly, the apostle Paul said, *And the peace of God, which passes all understanding, will keep your hearts and your minds in Christ Jesus* (Phil 4:7). It is certainly correct to think that he is not speaking about some sort of ordinary **peace** in respect to thoughts and actions. Anyone who has a temperament that loathes conflict and strife already possesses **peace** and acts as he is naturally inclined. We should not think that this sort of **peace** has actual substance and exists independently. But we should suppose that such **peace** flows out of the temperament of the one who loves it. How can someone think that this sort of peace surpasses *all understanding*? How could this kind of **peace**, which does not have any independent existence, be considered better and more excellent than humans, angels, or even loftier, noetic beings? It follows then that the **peace** that is *far above all rule and authority and power and dominion* (Eph 1:21) and all noetic beings is the Spirit of Christ, through whom the Son *reconciles all things* to God the Father (Col 1:20). . . . In the same way that the Son is life by his very nature, wisdom, and power, the Spirit is both called and, in reality, is his spirit. He is the spirit of life, of wisdom, and of power. Since the Son himself is the only true and authoritative **peace**, his Spirit might be properly called **peace** according to his true nature. For this reason, after he ascribes **peace**—that is, the Spirit—to his very nature, he says concerning the Spirit, **Peace I leave with you** (14:27). You will easily perceive that the Spirit of Christ has been named this way in the holy prophets when you hear the following from the mouth of Isaiah: *O Lord our God, give us peace: for you have given us all things* (Isa 26:12 LXX). Since the law has brought nothing to completion, and righteousness which is secured through the law is not sufficient to bring humans to perfect piety, Isaiah asks that the Holy Spirit be given. Through the Spirit, we, who have been revealed as fugitives enslaved to the sin within us, have been reconciled to God the Father and called back into fellowship with him. He says, *O Lord, give us peace: for you have given us all things* (Isa 26:12 LXX). What he wishes to explain, I think, is something like the following: "Lord, give us **peace**, for then we will confess that we have everything! The one who has finally reached the fullness of Christ lacks no blessing, for the culmination of all goodness occurs when God dwells in us through the Spirit." Since the Spirit is wholly sufficient in every way to dispel every fear from our minds and to remove all cowardice in us, Christ promises to give us what is necessary for the journey, as if assigning a companion to maintain our courage and tranquility, when he says, **Peace I leave with you. . . . Let not your hearts be troubled, neither let them be afraid** (14:27).

14:28 "The Father is greater than I."

---

(17) Tertullian of Carthage

This is the rule of faith that I proclaim: the Father, the Son, and the Spirit are indivisible from each other. Pay attention, and you will understand how I can say this. Indeed, I assert that the Father is one, the Son is one, and the Spirit is one. Only an ignorant and degenerate person would take these words to mean that this distinctiveness implies a separation between the Father, Son, and Spirit. When they assert that the Father, Son, and Spirit are identical—favoring the monarchy over the economy—it is necessary for me to say that their distinctiveness is not a matter of division. The Son differs from the Father, but only in respect to the distribution [of operations] and by the distinction [of person]. The Father is not identical with the Son, because they differ from one another in their mode of being. Truly the Father is the entire essence [of the Godhead]; the Son is drawn from the whole and shares in it, as he acknowledges, **The Father is greater than I** (14:28). In the Psalms, his inferior status is described as being *a little lower than the angels* (Ps 8:5 LXX). Therefore, the Father is distinct from the Son in that he is greater. The one who generates is one being and the one who is generated is another. The one who sends is distinct from the one who is sent, and the one who makes something is different from the one through whom it is made.

Of course when the Lord speaks this way he surely does not imply a distinction [in substance] but a difference [in operations] when referencing the person of the Counselor. The Lord says, *And I will ask the Father, and he will give you another Counselor, the Spirit of truth* (14:16–17). In this way, he shows that the Counselor is different from himself just as we say that the Son is different from the Father. He reveals that the Counselor is the third rank just as we believe that the Son is the second according to the order we observe in the divine economy. Does not the fact that they are called Father and Son suggest that they differ from one another?

14:30–31 "But I do as the Father has commanded me, so that the world may know that I love the Father."

---

(18) John Chrysostom

So that the world may know that I love the Father (14:31). He says, "I am not liable to death nor am I under any obligation to it, but I submit myself to it because **I love the Father**." He says this to raise the disciples' spirits that they might learn that he willingly undergoes death to heap scorn on the devil. It was not sufficient for him to say, *I shall be with you a little longer*

(7:33). Instead, he continually and reasonably returns to this painful subject until he could make it acceptable to them by connecting it with better things. For this reason, he says at one point, **I go away, and I will come to you** (14:28), and in another place, says, *That where I am you may be also* (14:3). He says, **Where I am going you cannot follow me now; but you shall follow afterward** (13:36), and **I go to the Father** (14:28), and **the Father is greater than I** (14:28), and **I have told you before it takes place** (14:29). Here he says also, "I do not suffer these things due to coercion, but because **I love the Father**" (14:31). He said all these things so they would know that this deed could not be ultimately destructive or harmful, for it was willed by the one who loved him who in turn was loved. This was why he continually mixed in the pleasant with the painful: he was training their thoughts. He encouraged them by saying, *He dwells with you* (14:17), and *It is to your advantage that I go away* (16:7). He said many things about the Spirit: *He dwells with you* (14:17), and *The world cannot receive him* (14:17), and *He will bring to your remembrance all that I have said to you* (14:26). He called him the *Spirit of truth* (14:17), *Holy Spirit* (14:26), *Counselor* (14:26). He also said that *it is to your advantage that I go away* (16:7). He said all these things beforehand so that they might not lose heart thinking there was no one to stand before them to assist them.

(19) Theodore of Mopsuestia

When he was drawing near to his suffering and wishing to comfort the disciples, he said, **For the ruler of this world is coming. He has no power over me; but I do as the Father has commanded me, so that the world may know that I love the Father** (14:30–31). Since sin was the reason for our death, and Satan enticed everyone toward transgressions as to increase their culpability, the Lord said, "Pay attention! . . . Satan wants to bring death upon me even though he is not able to find a pretext for why I deserve this. For this reason, if I wanted, it would be fully permissible for me to avoid tasting death. However, I will take on death. Great and astonishing things will be done through my suffering and great and astonishing things will be done after my suffering for those who believe. And their word will drive out demons, heal the sick, and perform all sorts of signs. My power will remove all human suffering and the various punishments meted out against sinners, and it will be known that it was not for justice that I was led to death but because of the **love** for **my Father**. For the sake of the salvation of everyone, I fulfilled his will. The Lord of all by grace will abolish death from me and afterward will abolish death for the whole human race."

14:31 "Rise, let us go hence."

---

(20) Cyril of Alexandria

Rise, let us go hence (14:31). The way these words are commonly heard suggests the following interpretation. When the period of the senselessness of the Jews had come and the precious cross of our Savior had already been constructed, he was ready to depart with his holy disciples to the place where the mob and officials found and apprehended him. This interpretation is persuasive. But there is another reasonable interpretation which is hidden; namely, a spiritual and mysterious one. When he says the words, **Rise, let us go hence** (14:31), he wants to show all of us that through him and with him there is a change from one state to another and a pathway that leads from a worse state to a better one. He wants us to understand something like this: the passing from death to life and from corruption to incorruption—through him and with him, as I have just said—is similar to going from one place to another. Therefore, the phrase **rise, let us go hence** (14:31) communicates this well.

Certainly, you may choose to interpret this in some other way. From this point we are destined to be changed from wanting to think about only earthly things into someone who chooses willingly what God wishes him to do. Additionally, we should pass from slavery into the honorable state of an adopted son, from the earth to the city above, from sinfulness into righteousness (which is through faith in Christ), from the impurity of human nature into holiness (which is through the Spirit), from dishonor into honor, from ignorance into knowledge, from cowardice and unmanliness into courage in virtue. . . .

We certainly do not have an elder or an angel but the Lord of all to guide us on the path of every virtue and turn us from our old passions to better things, because he was not subject to our infirmities. We have been ransomed, not by our own doing or by some other created being, but by Christ our Savior. Therefore, when he was escaping along with us from the wickedness of this world, he says, **Rise, let us go hence** (14:31). He speaks these words not as if he is accountable or bound to human sickness as we are, but as our leader, our protector, and our guide on the path toward incorruption and a life in holiness and love of God.

John 15

For many church fathers, the vineyard imagery calls to mind the Eucharistic celebration of the church. Cyril of Alexandria and Augustine of Hippo both interpret the relationship of the vine and the branches *as a metaphor of the relationship that believers have with the incarnate Christ (15:1). He shares our nature and in turn nourishes us just as a* vine *gives living sustenance to its* branches. *Hilary of Poitiers joins Augustine in saying that Christ is called the* vine *in respect to his human nature, which he shares with us, and the* vinedresser *in respect to his divinity, since he prunes away our sins so that we may* bear more *virtuous* fruit *(15:2).*

Augustine is careful to expound the verse, if you keep my commandments, you will abide in my love, just as I have kept my Father's commandments and abide in his love *(15:10), so that it is not read to suggest that we secure Christ's love through keeping the commandments. It is only through that love that one is able to keep the commandments. Cyril says that Christ keeps his* Father's commandment *when he obediently and lovingly takes on human flesh to fulfill the divine plan of our salvation.*

The sentence This is my commandment, that you love one another as I have loved you *(15:12) intrigues Augustine. He says that loving friends and family is commendable, but the phrase* as I have loved you *suggests something deeper and more profound. What would it mean to love like this? The following verse identifies this sort of love:* Greater love has no man than this, that a man lay down his life for his friends *(15:13). For Augustine, this calls to mind the martyrs who died for the Church, their friends, and for Christ. He is quick to point out, however, that martyrs are not equal with Christ. Martyrs die for Christ's sake, but Christ died for all and destroyed death itself. Never has the blood of a martyr been shed for the remission of sins of another. Gregory the Great expands Augustine's interpretation. He states that Christ did not die just for his friends but for his enemies. In fact, from the cross, Christ said, "Father, forgive them; for they know not what they do" (Luke 23:34). Gregory then asks a poignant question: "Since the teacher at the very moment when he was being killed loved his enemies, is it really surprising that the disciples should also love theirs?" True love is expressed in love of one's enemy.*

Cyprian of Carthage finds a reference to martyrdom in Christ's declaration, If the world hates you, know that it has hated me before it hated you *(15:18). After reciting the history of martyrs from Abel through the infants slaughtered by Herod at Jesus's nativity, Cyprian warns that all should be willing to lay down their lives for Christ since* a servant is not greater than his master *(15:20). Even if we suffer from the hatred of the world, Christ endured this hatred first. Augustine puzzles over the meaning of* world. *We are prohibited from loving the world (1 John 2:15), yet we are commanded to love our enemies (Luke 6:27). These are the very people who constitute* the world that hates us *(15:19). Augustine concludes that we are not to love the sin in the world but to love the things in the world created by God and connected to his goodness.*

Origen, Ambrose, and Augustine are drawn to Jesus's proclamation that he would send the Counselor *(15:26) to them. For Origen, the Holy Spirit comes to those who are living the divine life. Ambrose defends the Trinitarian confession of the Church. The Counselor is fully God since he* proceeds from the Father *and* bears witness to the Son *(15:26). Augustine shows that the Counselor both bears witness and "makes invincible witnesses" when he transforms Peter from the one who denied Christ to the one who proclaimed the resurrection of his Lord with boldness to all those* who hated Christ without cause *(15:25). But the Spirit shone in him and flowed through him so that the hatred of his enemies was turned into love.*

John 15:1–7

[1]"I am the true vine, and my Father is the vinedresser. [2]Every branch of mine that bears no fruit, he takes away, and every branch that does bear fruit he prunes, that it may bear more fruit. [3]You are already made clean by the word which I have spoken to you. [4]Abide in me, and I in you. As the branch cannot bear fruit by itself, unless it abides in the vine, neither can you, unless you abide in me. [5]I am the vine, you are the branches. He who abides in me, and I in him, he it is that bears much fruit, for apart from me you can do nothing. [6]If a man does not abide in me, he is cast forth as a branch and withers; and the branches are gathered, thrown into the fire and burned. [7]If you abide in me, and my words abide in you, ask whatever you will, and it shall be done for you."

15:1–6 "I am the true vine, and my Father is the vinedresser. . . . I am the vine, you are the branches . . . for apart from me you can do nothing."

---

(1) Origen of Alexandria

We must add how the Son is the **true vine** (15:1) to what we have already said. Those who understand the phrase *wine makes glad the heart of man* (Ps 104:15 LXX) in a way that is worthy of the prophetic sentiment will have no difficulty in comprehending what is meant. If the *heart* is the intellect and what *makes* it *glad* is the exceptionally sweet Word which removes human anxieties from us, makes us feel inspired, and intoxicates us in a way that is divine instead of irrational, then it is the most pleasant of all drinks. I think this is the drink by which Joseph made his brothers *merry* (Gen 43:34). It is very evident that the one who brings *wine* that *makes glad the heart of man* is the **true vine**. He is the **true vine**, because the grapes he bears are the truth and the disciples are his **branches** (15:5). They also produce truth as their *fruit*. It is somewhat difficult to differentiate between the **vine** and *bread*, for he says that not only is he the **vine** but also the *bread of life* (6:35). Bread both nourishes and makes one strong. It is said that *bread strengthens the heart of man* (Ps 104:15 LXX), but wine, in contrast, pleases, delights, and softens him. It follows then that the moral virtues, which bring life to the one who learns them and puts them into practice, are the **bread of life**. But these cannot be called the **fruit** (15:2) of the **vine**. Rather, they are the secret and mystical speculations, which *make glad the heart* and create a feeling of inspiration in those who adopt them. They in turn take delight in the Lord and desire not only to be nourished but to be made happy. They are called the juice of the **true vine** (15:1), because they flow from it.

(2) Hilary of Poitiers

In his desire to **do as the Father has commanded** (14:31), Christ rises and hastens to complete the mystery of his bodily passion.[1] But in the next moment, he unfolds the mystery of the assumption of flesh. We are in him, as **branches** (15:5) are in the **vine** (15:5), through this assumption (15:5). Unless he had become the **vine**, we could not have borne good **fruit** (15:5). He urges us to **abide** (15:5) in him through faith in his assumed body. In this way, since *the Word became flesh* (1:14), we may participate in the nature of his flesh, just as **branches** are in the **vine**.

He distinguishes the form of the Father's glory from the lowliness of the assumed flesh by calling himself the **vine**—the source of unity for all the **branches**—and by calling the Father the careful **vinedresser** (15:1), who prunes away the useless and barren **branches** (15:5) to burn them in the fire (cf. 15:6). In the words *he who has seen me has seen the Father* (14:9), and *the words that I say to you I do not speak on my own authority; but the Father who dwells in me does his works* (14:10), and *believe me that I am in the Father and the Father in me* (14:11), he reveals the truth of his birth and the mystery of his incarnation. He continues this line of thinking until he comes to the saying, *The Father is greater than I* (14:28). Afterward, he seeks to complete the meaning of these words by adding the imagery of the **vinedresser** (15:1), the **vine**, and the **branches**, which directs our thoughts to his submission to take on human flesh. He says that *he is going to the Father; for the Father is greater than himself* and that *if you loved me, you would have rejoiced, because I go to the Father* (14:28). In other words, he will receive once again his glory from the Father.

(3) Augustine of Hippo

Brothers and sisters, this passage of the gospel, where the Lord calls himself the **vine** and his disciples the **branches** (15:5), proclaims that the *mediator between God and men, the man Christ Jesus* (1 Tim 2:5), is the head of the church and that we are his members. Since

---

1. Hilary notices that the statement found at the end of chapter 14, **Rise, let us go hence** (14:31), does not fit seamlessly with John 15:1.

the **vine** and the **branches** share one nature, he became human since his actual nature as God was different from our own. In this way, the human nature which was in him became the **vine**, and we who are also human become the **branches** of that very **vine**. What do the words **I am the true vine** (15:1) mean? Did he intend to point to an actual vine, from which the metaphor was drawn, by adding the word **true**? He is called a vine metaphorically, not literally. He is also called a sheep, a lamb, a lion, a rock, a cornerstone, etc. which refer to actual things. However, these names are applied to him analogously, not actually! When he says, **I am the true vine** (15:1), he is certainly distinguishing himself from that vine to which the following words are spoken: *How then have you turned to bitterness, O wild vine?* (Jer 2:21 LXX). How could a vine that was expected to *yield grapes*, but produced *wild grapes* (Isa 5:4) instead, be the **true vine**?

He says, **I am the true vine, and my Father is the vinedresser. Every branch of mine that bears no fruit, he takes away, and every branch that does bear fruit he prunes, that it may bear more fruit** (15:1–2). Are the **vinedresser** and the **vine** one? Christ is the vine in the same sense as when he said, *The Father is greater than I* (14:28). But he is also the **vinedresser** in that sense when he said, *I and the Father are one* (10:30). However, he is not like those whose work is merely external, for he supplies the *growth* from within himself. He is not like the one who merely plants and waters, but *God* who *gives the growth* (1 Cor 3:6), because Christ is certainly God, for *the Word was God* (1:1), and he and *the Father are one* (10:30). Even if *the Word was made flesh* (1:14), and so becomes that which he was not previously, he nevertheless still remains what he was.

But there is more to consider. After he says that the Father, as the **vinedresser** (15:1), removes the **branches** (15:5) that do not bear **fruit** and prunes those **branches** that do so that they **may bear more fruit** (15:2), he immediately identifies himself also as one who purifies the **branches**. He says, **You are already made clean by the word which I have spoken to you** (15:3). Notice that he also prunes the **branches** (15:5). This is the task that belongs to the **vinedresser**, not the **vine**. Additionally, he makes the **branches** carry out his work. Although they do not *give the growth*, they assist. But even this assistance does not come from them, for he says, **apart from me you can do nothing** (15:5). Listen to their own statement: *What then is Apollos? What is Paul?* They are the *servants through whom you believed, as the Lord assigned to each. I planted, Apollos watered.* The Lord also gave this task to all humans; it does not come from themselves. But *God gave the growth* (1 Cor 3:5–6). This phrase indicates clearly that this task belongs to the Lord himself. He does not accomplish this through them, for this sort of task exceeds the limited ability of humans and transcends the extraordinary powers of the angels. Rather, this task belongs completely to the triune **vinedresser**.

You are already made clean (15:3), but you still need to be cleansed further. Why? Had they not already been made clean, they could not have borne **fruit**. But **every branch that does bear fruit is pruned** by the **vinedresser, that it may bear more fruit** (15:2). Because he is **clean**, he **bears fruit**. But when he is cleansed further, then he will **bear more fruit**. Who in this life is so **clean** that he does not need to be cleansed even more? *If we say we have no sin, we deceive ourselves, and the truth is not in us; but if we confess our sins, he is faithful and just, and will forgive our sins and cleanse us from all unrighteousness* (1 John 1:8–9). Considering this, it is necessary to cleanse those who are clean, that is, the fruitful, in every way so that they might be even more fruitful, just as they have been made cleaner.

You are already made clean by the word which I have spoken to you (15:3). Why does he not say, "You are clean through the baptism by which you were washed"? Instead, he says, **By the word which I have spoken to you.** This is because in the water of baptism, it is the **word** which also cleanses. Take away the **word**, and the water is only water. The **word** is added to this element; the result is the sacrament, as if it is a type of visible **word**. He said something similar when washing the disciples' feet: *He who has bathed does not need to wash, except for his feet, but he is clean all over* (13:10). How can water have such great power that it touches the body and cleanses the soul except by the operation of the **word**? It is not because it is uttered but because it is believed! The ephemeral sound of the **word** is one thing, its lasting efficacy something else. The apostle Paul says that this is the **word** of faith that we preach: *If you confess with your lips that Jesus is Lord and believe in your heart that God raised him from the dead, you will be saved. For man believes with his heart and so is justified, and he confesses with his lips and so is saved* (Rom 10:9–10). We also read in the Acts of the Apostles: He *cleansed their hearts by faith* (Acts 15:9). The blessed Peter writes in his epistle: *Baptism now saves* us, *not as a removal of dirt from the body but as an appeal to God for a clear conscience* (1 Pet 3:21). This is the word of faith that we preach and by which baptism certainly is consecrated and gains the power to cleanse: *Christ*, who is with us as the **vine** and with the Father as the **vinedresser**, *loved the church and gave himself for her* (Eph 5:25). The apostle Paul adds: *That he might sanctify her, having cleansed her by the washing of water with the word* (Eph 5:26). The ephemeral and perishable element of water is not capable of such cleansing apart from the power of the **word**. This **word** of faith possesses so much power in the church of God that the word, through the one[2] who believes, presents, blesses, and immerses, cleanses even a tiny infant who is not yet able *to believe with its heart and be justified or to confess with its lips and be saved* (Rom 10:10). All this is done through the word, concerning which the Lord said, **You are already made clean by the word which I have spoken to you** (15:3).

(4) Cyril of Alexandria

Now the Savior appropriately calls the **Father** a **vinedresser** (15:1), and it is not very difficult to find the reason. His intention was to prevent someone from thinking that by himself the only-begotten took care of us. Rather, he shows that God the Father operates together with him. He calls himself the **vine** which gives life and productive power to the **branches** (15:5) and the Father a **vinedresser** (15:1–2). In this way he teaches that providential care over us is a distinctive action of his divine nature. We need to know that God not only made us to share in his nature, which is understood to belong to the holy and consubstantial Trinity,

---

2. Two different variants are presented in Augustine's commentary. The primary reading states that baptism is conducted by the priest (i.e., *ipsum*) who believes, presents, blesses, and immerses the infant. The alternative reading indicates that it is the church herself (i.e., *ipsam*) who baptizes the infant. Both fit well with Augustine's sacramental and ecclesiastical theology.

but also that he watches over us with the utmost care. This is illustrated very well by the image of vine dressing. Since he has already spoken of the **vine** and its **branches** (15:5), the image of the **vinedresser** (15:1) is certainly appropriate since it introduces the one who takes care of the whole, namely God. . . .

As **branches** (15:5) in this analogy, we receive life proceeding out of him into ourselves, as Paul says, *Because there is one bread, we who are many are one body, for we all partake of the one bread* (1 Cor 10:17). Can anyone make sense of this and offer an interpretation that fails to mention the power of the blessed mystery? Why do we receive it into ourselves? Isn't it so that Christ may dwell in us bodily through participation in and communion with his holy flesh? I suspect he would agree with this, for Paul writes *that the Gentiles are fellow heirs, members of the same body, and partakers of the promise in Christ Jesus through the gospel* (Eph 3:6). How are they shown to be *members of the same body*? By their admission to share the holy Eucharist, they become one body with him, just as each of the holy apostles does. Why did Paul call all of them the *members* of Christ? He writes accordingly: *Do you not know that your bodies are members of Christ? Shall I therefore take the members of Christ and make them members of a prostitute? Never!* (1 Cor 6:15). Additionally, the Savior himself says: *He who eats my flesh and drinks my blood abides in me, and I in him* (6:56). It is important to notice here that Christ says that he will be in us, not only in a relational way experienced through the emotions but also by a physical participation. Just as when one interlaces one piece of wax with another and melts them together with fire, the result is that both become one. So also are we co-united with Christ through the participation of the body of Christ and his precious blood, when he is in us and we are in him. In no other way could that which is corruptible by nature be made alive unless it were bodily entwined with the body of the one who is by nature life itself, the only-begotten!

If anyone is not convinced by my words, pay attention to Christ when he cries out: *Truly, truly, I say to you, unless you eat the flesh of the Son of man and drink his blood, you have no life in you; he who eats my flesh and drinks my blood has eternal life, and I will raise him up at the last day* (6:53–54). You hear him saying plainly that **unless** we **eat his flesh and drink his blood**, we have **no life** in ourselves, that is, in our flesh. From this, we might rightly consider eternal life to be the flesh of the only-begotten who is life itself. Listen now to how and in what way this flesh will **raise** us **up at the last day**, for I will not hesitate to tell you. Since life itself, which is the Word which came forth from God the Father, took upon himself flesh, this flesh in turn became transformed into a living substance. It is unthinkable that life itself could be conquered by death; therefore, since this very life exists in us by participation, it will not be held captive by the bonds of death. Instead, life will conquer corruption completely since it cannot tolerate such an outcome. As Paul says, *the perishable* does not *inherit the imperishable* (1 Cor 15:50). Since Christ himself stated emphatically, **I will raise him up** (6:54), he not only imbued his own flesh with the power to raise those who are asleep, but the divine and incarnate Word, which is united to his own flesh, says, **I will raise him up**. This is stated correctly, because Christ is not divided into two Sons. No one can think that his body is distinctly different from the only-begotten, just as no one can posit that his body in which the soul dwells is different from it. From this it should be clear that Christ is the **vine** and we the **branches** (15:5) in the sense that we participate with him in a fellowship that is not merely spiritual but also corporeal. . . . Should we not agree that

Christ is the **vine** in a way that is in fitting with his fellowship of the flesh and that we are **branches** through the similarity of our nature? It follows that what proceeds from the **vine** shares its same nature. We say this . . . with a desire to show clearly that Christ is the vine and we are the branches both in a spiritual and corporeal sense.

15:7 "If you abide in me, and my words abide in you, ask whatever you will, and it shall be done for you."

---

(5) Augustine of Hippo

If you abide in me, and my words abide in you, ask whatever you will, and it shall be done for you (15:7). If someone **abides** in Christ in this very way, are they able to wish for anything that is incompatible with Christ? Or if they **abide** in the Savior, can they desire anything that is at odds with salvation? Certainly, we wish for some things because we are in Christ and desire other things because we are still in this world. Because of our ties to this present age, we are continually prompted from within to ask for those things which we know would not be helpful to receive. May such a thing never be given to us if we **abide** in Christ. When we ask, he only gives us what will be helpful. When we **abide** in him and his **words abide** in us, we will **ask whatever** we **will** and **it shall be done** for us (15:7). It follows then that if we ask and it does not happen, whatever we asked for is incompatible with **abiding** in him or with his **words** which also **abide** in us. Rather, it flows from the cupidity and infirmity of the flesh which are not in him and in which his **words** do not **abide**. The prayer that he taught us is connected in every way to these **words**. When we say, *Our Father, who art in heaven* (Matt 6:9), let us hold to the words and meaning of this prayer in our petitions and **whatever** we **ask shall be done** for us (15:7). Only when we do what he has commanded and love what he has promised can his **words** then be said to **abide in us**.

John 15:8–10

[8]"**By this my Father is glorified, that you bear much fruit, and so prove to be my disciples.** [9]**As the Father has loved me, so have I loved you; abide in my love.** [10]**If you keep my commandments, you will abide in my love, just as I have kept my Father's commandments and abide in his love.**"

(6) Augustine of Hippo

The Lord says, **As the Father has loved me, so have I loved you; abide in my love** (15:9). Notice that this is the source of all our good works. From where else do they come except that *faith works through love* (Gal 5:6)? How could we love unless we were first loved? In his epistle, John the Evangelist stated this with amazing clarity: *We love God, because he* *first loved us* (1 John 4:19). When he says, **As the Father has loved me, so have I loved you** (15:9), he is not stating that there is equality between our nature and his, as there is between the Father and him. Rather, he is indicating the grace by which *the man Christ Jesus* is the *mediator between God and men* (1 Tim 2:5). When he says, **The Father has loved me** and **I have loved you**, he is shown to be the *mediator*. Certainly, the **Father** also **loves** us, but he does so through the Son: **By this my Father is glorified, that** we **bear much fruit** in the **vine**, that is in the Son, **and so prove to be** his **disciples** (15:8).

The Lord says, **abide in my love** (15:9). How can we **abide**? Listen to what follows: **If you keep my commandments, you will abide in my love** (15:10). Does love lead to the keeping of his **commandments**, or does the keeping of his **commandments** bring about **love**? Who will doubt that **love** comes first? The one who is devoid of **love** is not able to **keep the commandments**. Accordingly he does not identify the source from which **love** flows but the way it is shown when he says, **If you keep my commandments, you will abide in my love** (15:10). It is as if he said, "Do not think that you can abide in my love if you fail to keep my commandments; you will abide in my love, only if you have kept them." . . . We **love** him in the same proportion that we **keep his commandments**: the less we **keep** them, the less we love him. Despite the fact that the saying **abide in my love** does not indicate clearly what love he is speaking about—is it the love that we have for him, or the love he has for us?—it is understood at once from the former verse. There he said, **So have I loved you** (15:9). Then he adds immediately, **Abide in my love** (15:9). Thus, it is the **love** that he has for us. What then do the words **abide in my love** (15:9) mean except, **abide** in my grace? And what do the words **if you keep my commandments, you will abide in my love** (15:10) mean except, you will know that you **abide in the love** I have for you if you keep my **commandments**? We do not keep his **commandments** to awaken his **love** for us. Rather, we cannot keep his **commandments** unless he first **loves** us. This is the grace that is disclosed to the humble but is hidden from the proud.

How are we to understand the following: **Just as I have kept my Father's commandments and abide in his love** (15:10)? Certainly from this he wanted us to understand the sort of love with which the Father loved him. He had just said, **As the Father has loved me, so have I loved you** (15:9). Then he added the words **abide in my love** (15:9), with which I have certainly loved you. It follows then that we are to understand the phrase **I abide in his love** (15:10) as referring to the love the Father has for him. Is it the case then that the love that the Father has for the Son is analogous to the grace by which we are loved by the Son, since we ourselves are sons, not by nature but by grace, while the only-begotten is a Son by nature and not by grace? Or is this phrase referencing also his condition as a man? Yes, indeed! When he says, **As the Father has loved me, so have I loved you** (15:9), he indicates the grace of the mediator, not in respect to his divinity but to his humanity: *Christ Jesus* is *the mediator between God and men* (1 Tim 2:5). Without a doubt when we read, *And Jesus increased in wisdom and in stature, and in favor with God and man* (Luke 2:52), his human nature is being referenced. In light of this we can rightly say that although human nature does not belong to God's nature, human nature does indeed belong to the person of the only-begotten Son of God by grace. This grace is so great that there is none greater. In fact, nothing even comes close to equaling it! There were no benefits that preceded his assumption of humanity, but from that assumption all benefits began. Therefore, the Son

abides in the love with which the **Father has loved** him, and for this reason he **kept his commandments** (15:9–10). What is he, who assumed human nature, except the one whom *God lifts up* (Ps 3:3 Vulgate)? The *Word was God*, the only-begotten, co-eternal with his begetter (1:1–2), but through divine grace, *the Word became flesh and dwelt among us* (1:14) so that he might be given to us as our *mediator* (1 Tim 2:5).

(7) Cyril of Alexandria

As the Father has loved me, so have I loved you; abide in my love. If you keep my commandments, you will abide in my love, just as I have kept my Father's commandments and abide in his love (15:9–10). We must contemplate the mysteries set forth in this text with a sharper eye. This saying has a deep meaning and points out for us the significance of the incarnation in its entirety. . . . Our Lord Jesus Christ reveals himself as an example and an outline of the holy state of life. For this reason, he was placed under the law and did not refuse to take a measure of our poverty. By deliberately conforming himself with our nature by becoming human, he became a guide and example to those who are his. In this way, he guided us to recover the state and life which was strange and utterly alien to us. We must now ask what **commandment** of the Father he has kept and in what way or in what manner the **Father has loved** him. Let Paul, who is very wise, come near and guide us in this mystery by his words about *Christ Jesus who, though he was in the form of God, did not count equality with God a thing to be grasped, but emptied himself, taking the form of a servant, being born in the likeness of men. And being found in human form he humbled himself and became obedient unto death, even death on a cross. Therefore God has highly exalted him and bestowed on him the name which is above every name* (Phil 2:5–9). You have heard that, even though he was the true God because he shared the same form with his Father, he *humbled himself* and *became obedient to death*. When God the Father decided to save the corrupted race that was upon the earth, it was not possible that any created being could fulfill the requirement of justice. The only-begotten, who knows the will of the Father, took upon himself the divine plan as if its success required all the power there was in the created world. For this reason, he freely entered into subjugation, even descending into that most shameful *death*. How could it be honorable to be nailed to a cross? How would it not surpass every other disgrace? Since he endured these things, the text says, *Therefore God has highly exalted him*. In his willing obedience, you find the fulfillment of the plans of the Father. The Son says that these plans were listed as **commandments**. For as the Word of God, he understands the plans of the Father and uncovers the hidden thoughts of the one from whom he was begotten. It might be better to say that since he is the Wisdom and Power of the Father, he understands his plan and counts it as a command. In this way, he names it in accordance with a human analogy. In the following, you see the full measure of his love: *God has highly exalted him*. . . .

He says, **Abide in my love** (15:9). In other words, devote yourself wholeheartedly and seek with every ounce of eagerness and desire to be worthy of my love as I have from God the Father. I carried out the will of my Father wholly, and for this reason, **Abide in his love** (15:10). **If you keep my commandments**, in a similar way **you will abide in my love** completely (15:10). He says, then you will have no excuse for indifference in this way, for you will not toil in these ways without reward. I will give you as much love as I have from the Father in a visible way and will crown those who keep my words with honors nearly equal to my own, for the Father *has highly exalted* me and has given me *the name which is above every name* (Phil 2:9). I have been publicly named the God of all, but I will not be jealous or withhold good things from you. Although you are humans and on account of this were given the nature of slaves, I have made you holy and sons of God. I have purified you through my grace with honors far beyond your nature. I admitted you into the fellowship of my kingdom and *changed* your form *to be like my glorious body* (Phil 3:21). I have honored you with incorruptibility and life. But these things are still hoped for and will be seen in the age to come.

John 15:11–17

[11]"These things I have spoken to you, that my joy may be in you, and that your joy may be full. [12]This is my commandment, that you love one another as I have loved you. [13]Greater love has no man than this, that a man lay down his life for his friends. [14]You are my friends if you do what I command you. [15]No longer do I call you servants, for the servant does not know what his master is doing; but I have called you friends, for all that I have heard from my Father I have made known to you. [16]You did not choose me, but I chose you and appointed you that you should go and bear fruit and that your fruit should abide; so that whatever you ask the Father in my name, he may give it to you. [17]This I command you, to love one another."

15:11–14 "This is my commandment, that you love one another as I have loved you. Greater love has no man than this, that a man lay down his life for his friends."

---

(8) John Chrysostom

All good things secure their reward when they arrive at their proper end. If they are cut off in the middle, a shipwreck befalls them, just as a large transport ship gains nothing from the length of the voyage if it sinks in the middle of the sea and does not reach its harbor. Indeed, the disaster is greater since that ship has endured more hardships. This is the same for those souls who stumble when they are near the end of their toil and fall exhausted during the contest. For this reason, Paul said that those who ran the race with *patience in well-doing* should receive *glory and honor* and peace (Rom 2:7).

In this passage Christ readies his disciples for this process. When he had called them, they rejoiced in him. But then his gloomy words and his impending passion were about to cut short their joy. After he had spoken with them and calmed them sufficiently, he added, **These things I have spoken to you, that my joy may be in you, and that your joy may**

be full (15:11). It is as if he said, "These things I have spoken to you so that you might not be separated from me or that you might not cut short your race. You were rejoicing in me greatly, but now a deep sadness has settled upon you. I will therefore remove this so that your joy may reach the finish line and that you might see that the events occurring now are not a cause for grief but for joy. I saw that you were offended, but I did not hold you in contempt . . . but in order **that your joy may be full**, **these things I have spoken to you. This is my commandment, that you love one another as I have loved you**" (15:11–12). Do you see that God's love is intertwined with our own? That it is connected like a chain? For this reason, Scripture sometimes says that there are two commandments. At other times, only one. Why? It is not possible for a human who has grasped the first to not also hold the second. One time Christ said, *On these two commandments depend all the law and the prophets* (Matt 22:40). Another time, he said, *So whatever you wish that men would do to you, do so to them; for this is the law and the prophets* (Matt 7:12). And again, *Love is the fulfilling of the law* (Rom 13:10). He also says the same here. If abiding in him proceeds from love and love in turn proceeds from the keeping of the commandments and the commandment is that we love one another, then it follows that abiding in God proceeds from **loving one other** (15:10–12). He does not just speak of love but indicates the manner of this love: **As I have loved you** (15:12). Again, he shows that his departure was also due to love, not to hatred. It is as if he said, "I should be honored greatly for this reason: I **lay down** my **life** for you" (15:13). But nowhere does he utter these very words. However, he intimates this earlier when he was sketching out the image of the **good shepherd** (10:1–18), and here again, when he is exhorting them, showing them the depth of his love, and revealing who he actually is. But why does he lift up **love** everywhere? Because this is the mark of the disciples and the cord of virtue which binds them together.

(9) Augustine of Hippo

When the Lord said, **Greater love has no man than this, that a man lay down his life for his friends** (15:13), brothers and sisters, he characterized the sort of love with which we should love one another. Although he had stated previously, **This is my commandment, that you love one another as I have loved you** (15:12), he added the words which you just heard: **Greater love has no man than this, that a man lay down his life for his friends** (15:13). What the evangelist John says in his epistle follows logically from this: *Christ laid down his life for us; and we ought to lay down our lives for the brethren* (1 John 3:16). Just as he has loved us and **laid down his life for us**, we should truly **love one another** (15:12). Certainly, this is the meaning of what we read in the Proverbs of Solomon: *If you sit down to eat at the table of rulers, observe carefully what has been set for you, extend your hand, since you know that you will have to prepare such things* (Prov 23:1–2 LXX). What is the *table of rulers*, except that table from which we receive the body and blood of the one who *laid down his life for us* (1 John 3:16)? What does it mean to *sit down* there, apart from the idea to approach the table humbly? What does the phrase *observe carefully what has been set for you* mean unless it encourages one to reflect carefully on the sublimity of this gift? What does *extend your hand, since you know that you will have to prepare such things* mean except what

I have already said? Just as *Christ laid down his life for us,* so *we ought to lay down our lives for the brethren* (1 John 3:16). The apostle Peter says, *Christ also suffered for* us, *leaving* us *an example, that* we *should follow in his steps* (1 Pet 2:21). To follow is to prepare similarly. The blessed martyrs accomplished this with their fervent love. If we celebrate their memories with an intentional devotion and approach the table of the Lord and partake of the banquet where they themselves were filled to the fullest, we also must make similar preparations as they did. For this reason we do not commemorate them at that table in the same way as we do for those who rest in peace. We pray for the latter ones, but the former should pray for us so that we may follow in their *steps.* Why? Because they have already attained that full measure of love of which the Lord spoke when he said, **Greater love has no man than this, that a man lay down his life for his friends** (15:13). They showed this very love to their brothers and sisters which they had received in equal measure at the table of the Lord.

Do not suppose, however, that we have claimed we can attain equality with Christ the Lord, even if we should be martyred for his sake. He had the *power to lay down his life, and to take it again* (10:18). In contrast, we do not have the power to live as long as we want. In fact, we must die regardless of whether we are willing. By dying, he destroyed death in himself; by his death, we are delivered from death. *His flesh did not see corruption* (Acts 2:31); our flesh after it is subject to corruption, will be clothed by him with incorruption at the end of the world. In order to accomplish our salvation, he did not need us. But without him, we can do nothing. He gave himself as the **vine** to us, the **branches** (15:5); apart from him, we are not able to live. Finally, although brothers die for brothers, never has the blood of a martyr been shed for the remission of the sins of another. Rather, he did this for us, and in this way, gave us something not to be imitated but to be lauded. Whenever martyrs have shed their blood for their brothers, in this act they show the proof of the **love** that they themselves experienced at the table of the Lord. Although I am not able to mention everything, I have tried in every way to declare that the martyr of Christ is far inferior to the Lord himself. . . . Let us therefore love one another as *Christ loved* us, and *gave himself* for us (Gal 2:20). **Greater love has no man than this, that a man lay down his life for his friends** (15:13). Let us imitate him with a spirit of solemn obedience that reminds us to never arrogantly compare ourselves with him.

(10) Gregory the Great

Since all the Lord's holy utterances are filled with his teachings, why does the Lord speak about love, as if it were a single commandment? **This is my commandment, that you love one another** (15:12). Perhaps it is because every commandment is ultimately about **love**. All commandments are in essence just one commandment because whatever is commanded is confirmed in love alone. For just as many *branches* of a tree come forth from one root, in the same way the different virtues spring from love alone. The *branch* of good works does not maintain its verdant appearance unless it remains rooted in love. Therefore, the Lord's commandments are both many and one: many by the diversity of their work; one by being rooted in love. He instructs us how we should **love** throughout the Scriptures. He commands us to love our friends in him and enemies for his sake. The human who loves a friend in God and loves an enemy for God's sake truly possesses the love of God. There are some who love their neighbors due to natural or physical connections. The holy Scriptures certainly do not speak against this sort of love. What we give willingly is one thing, but the obedience we owe to the commandments of the Lord due to love is another. These undoubtedly love their neighbor, but they do not attain love's sublime rewards because their love flows from their natural motives instead of spiritual ones. Therefore, when the Lord says, **This is my commandment, that you love one another**, he immediately adds, **As I have loved you** (15:12). If he were to speak more directly, he would say, "**Love** to this extent: **love as I have loved you**."

Brothers and sisters, we must consider this carefully. When the ancient enemy drags our minds toward the love of temporal things or incites another to rise up against us and seize what we love, he does not do so to destroy our earthly possessions but to destroy the divine love within us. At once, we are seized by hateful rage. While we desire to be invincible outwardly, we are gravely wounded within. When we defend a few, external things, we lose the greater things inside. By loving something temporal, we lose the love which is true. Certainly, our enemy is anyone who destroys our love. If we begin to hate our enemy, we lose the love that is within. But when we suffer outwardly on account of our neighbor, we must be on guard against the hidden, inward marauder who is conquered in no better way than when we love that neighbor. It follows then that the most convincing evidence of true love is to love the person who is opposed to us. This is why Truth himself endured the suffering of the cross and yet poured out his love on his persecutors, saying: *Father, forgive them; for they know not what they do* (Luke 23:34). Since the teacher at the very moment when he was being killed loved his enemies, is it really surprising that the disciples should also love theirs? Jesus declares the highest form of love, when he adds, **Greater love has no man than this, that a man lay down his life for his friends** (15:13). The Lord had come to die for his enemies, yet he said that he would **lay down his life for his friends.** Certainly, he wanted to reveal that although we benefit from loving our enemies, even those who persecute us are our friends.

Since no one persecutes us to the point of death now, how are we to prove that we love our friends? During this time of peace for the church, there is still something that can be done to show we would be strong enough to die for love in the time of persecution. John certainly indicates the very same thing: *But if anyone has the world's goods and sees his brother in need, yet closes his heart against him, how does God's love abide in him?* (1 John 3:17). In the same way John the Baptist says, *He who has two coats, let him share with him who has none* (Luke 3:11). Will the one who won't share his coat for the sake of God now give up his life during the time of persecution? Let us nourish the virtue of charity in peaceful times by giving up worldly goods, so that in a period of persecution we may be strong enough to lay down our lives for God.

Jesus continues: **You are my friends** (15:14). How great is the mercy of our Creator! Although we were not worthy to be servants, we are called **friends**! What a tremendous honor to be called the **friends** of God! But now that you have heard the loftiness of this honor, listen to what we must do: **You are my friends if you do what I command you** (15:14). If he were to speak more candidly, he'd say, "You rejoice from the very heights, but consider how one reaches the summit." Certainly, when the sons of Zebedee, through their mother, asked that they should sit at the right and left hands of God, they heard him ask, *Are you able to drink the cup that I am to drink?* (Matt 20:22). They were already seeking a place of honor. But truth calls them back to the path by which they might reach this pinnacle. It is as if he said, "The place of height delights you, but the way of suffering should train you first (cf. Isa 58:14). By this *cup*, one can reach the heights. If your soul longs for what delights, first drink what causes it pain. Only through the bitter cup which is prepared for it does the soul arrive at the joy of salvation."

15:15 "No longer do I call you servants . . . but I have called you friends."

---

(11) Irenaeus of Lyons

For those in bondage, the law was established to instruct the soul by external, carnal means. The law dragged the soul, as if with a chain, to obey its commandments so that it might learn to serve God. But the Word set the soul free and taught it that the flesh should be purified willingly. When this was accomplished, it followed in due course that the bonds of slavery, to which humanity had grown accustomed, should be removed and that they should follow God without chains. It followed also that the laws of freedom should be extended, and subjection to the king be increased, so that no one who was summoned would appear unworthy to the king who set him free. Instead, both servants and children should equally offer the piety and obedience owed to the master of the household. The children however possess greater courage than the servants, for deeds done freely are greater and more glorious than servile obedience.

For this reason, instead of the commandment, *You shall not commit adultery* (Exod 20:14), the Lord forbade lust (cf. Matt 5:27–28); instead of the law, *You shall not kill* (Exod 20:13), he prohibited anger (cf. Matt 5:21–22); and instead of commanding us to give tithes, he said that we must share all our possessions with the poor (cf. Matt 19:21). He commanded us not only *to love our neighbors*, but even *our enemies* (cf. Matt 5:43–44), and not only to give freely, but that we should offer an additional gift to those who steal our possessions. He says, *From him who takes away your coat, do not withhold even your shirt; . . . of him who takes away your goods, do not ask them again; And as you wish that men would do to you, do so to them* (Luke 6:29–31), so that we may not be sullen as those who are swindled unwillingly but may rejoice as those who have given willingly and as those who have offered a gift to our neighbors instead of acquiescing to force. He says, *If anyone forces you to go one mile, go with him two miles* (Matt 5:41) so that you do not follow him as a slave but walk ahead of him as a free man. In every way, present yourself as kind, useful, and helpful to your neighbor, not in response to their evil intentions but to become like your Father *who makes his sun rise on the evil and on the good, and sends rain on the just and on the unjust* (Matt 5:45). All of these commandments, as I have already noted, did not cancel the existing law but rather fulfilled, extended, and expanded it among us. Accordingly, one might say that these more expansive requirements of liberty imply that a more complete subjection and affection toward the one who freed us has been implanted within us. He did not set us free that we should withdraw from him (certainly, no one is able to secure the means of salvation for himself while he is located far away from the blessings of God), but that as we received more grace from him, the more we should love him. And the more that we love him, the more glory we receive from him since we are continually in the presence of the Father.

The commandments are common both to us and to the Jews. Certainly the commandments were given anew to them, but they have been expanded and brought to completion among us. To give oneself over to God and to follow his Word, to love him above all else and to love one's neighbor as oneself, and to eschew every evil deed, and to do every other similar thing which is found in both covenants, reveals the same God. But our Lord, the Word of God, who in the first instance drew slaves to God, afterward set those who were subjected to him free. He himself declares to his disciples: **No longer do I call you servants, for the servant does not know what his master is doing; but I have called you friends, for all that I have heard from my Father I have made known to you** (15:15). When he says, **No longer do I call you servants**, he indicates very clearly that he originally established that humans through the law would be **servants** of God, but afterward, he gave them freedom. When he says, **For the servant does not know what his master is doing**, he demonstrates, through his own advent, the ignorance of people who are considered **servants**. But when he calls his disciples the **friends** of God, he plainly states that he is the Word of God, whom Abraham followed willingly and not in a slavish way due to the noble character of his faith. He then became *the friend of God* (Jas 2:23). The Word of God did not accept the friendship of Abraham, as if he had need of it, for the Word was perfect from the beginning. For this reason, he says, *Before Abraham was, I am* (8:58). But in accordance with his goodness he bestowed eternal life upon Abraham, since friendship of God offers immortality to those who accept it.

15:16 "You did not choose me, but I chose you."

---

(12) Augustine of Hippo

You did not choose me, but I chose you (15:16). Such grace is beyond words! What were we when Christ had not yet chosen us and we did not know love? . . . What were we except sinful and lost? We did not believe in him so that he would **choose** us; for if he **chose** only those who already believed, then Christ **chose** only after he himself had been chosen. How could he say, **You did not choose me**, except that his mercy preceded us? Certainly, the empty theorizing of those who defend the foreknowledge of God against his grace and who declare accordingly that we were chosen *before the foundation of the world* (Eph 1:4) because God knew beforehand that we would be good—and not that he himself would make us good—is proven from this verse to be vacuous.[3] Christ does not say this! Instead,

---

3. Augustine is arguing against the Pelagians, who denied the idea of original sin and posited that humans, through the exercise of free will, could obey the laws of God and achieve salvation without divine assistance.

he declares: **You did not choose me** (15:16). Had he chosen us based on the idea that he knew beforehand that we would be good, then he also would have known beforehand that we would not have chosen him first. For we could not possibly be good in any other way unless perhaps one can be called good who has never chosen that which is good. What then did he **choose** in those who were not good? They were not chosen because they were good, for they could not be good, unless they were chosen. If we hold to the idea that merits precede grace, *then grace is no longer grace* (Rom 11:6). This is what Paul means when he speaks of being selected by grace: *So too at the present time there is a remnant, chosen by grace.* To this, he adds: *But if it is by grace, it is no longer on the basis of works; otherwise grace would no longer be grace* (Rom 11:5–6). Listen, you ungrateful one, listen: **You did not choose me, but I chose you** (15:16).

You may not say that "I am **chosen**, because I already believed." If you believed in him, then you had already chosen him. But listen: **You did not choose me** (15:16). You may not say, "Before I believed, I was already doing good works and that is why I was chosen." What good work can exist before faith? The apostle Paul says, *For whatever does not proceed from faith is sin* (Rom 14:23). What should we say when we hear the words **you did not choose me** except that we were evil and were chosen in order that we might be good through the grace of him who chose us? If merits come first, it is not grace. But it is grace! Therefore, this grace did not discover the merits but generated them.

Brothers and sisters, notice how he does not choose the good but makes those whom he has chosen good. He says, **I chose you and appointed you that you should go and bear fruit and that your fruit should abide** (15:16). Is this not the fruit about which he had already said, **For apart from me you can do nothing** (15:5)? Therefore, he has **chosen and appointed that** we **should go and bear fruit** (15:16). Therefore, it follows that we had no **fruit** which caused him to choose us. He said, **That you should go and bear fruit** (15:16). We go for the purpose of *bearing fruit*, and he himself is the *way* by which we should go (14:6). In every way, then, his mercy precedes us. He says, **And that your fruit should abide; so that whatever you ask the Father in my name, he may give it to you** (15:16). In this way, let love endure, for this is our **fruit**. This love is present now as a desired hope and not yet in fullness. But through this ardent longing, whatever we ask in the name of the only-begotten Son, the Father gives to us. Let us not ask for anything in the Savior's name that is not useful for us to receive in order to be saved. We ask only in his **name** for that which truly belongs to the way of salvation.

John 15:18–27

[18]"If the world hates you, know that it has hated me before it hated you. [19]If you were of the world, the world would love its own; but because you are not of the world, but I chose you out of the world, therefore the world hates you. [20]Remember the word that

---

Augustine was one of the primary opponents of their theology and was instrumental in securing its condemnation at the Council of Carthage in AD 418. The ecumenical Council of Ephesus (AD 431) sustained this earlier condemnation reached by the North African church.

I said to you, 'A servant is not greater than his master.' If they persecuted me, they will persecute you; if they kept my word, they will keep yours also. [21]But all this they will do to you on my account, because they do not know him who sent me. [22]If I had not come and spoken to them, they would not have sin; but now they have no excuse for their sin. [23]He who hates me hates my Father also. [24]If I had not done among them the works which no one else did, they would not have sin; but now they have seen and hated both me and my Father. [25]It is to fulfill the word that is written in their law, 'They hated me without a cause.' [26]But when the Counselor comes, whom I shall send to you from the Father, even the Spirit of truth, who proceeds from the Father, he will bear witness to me; [27]and you also are witnesses, because you have been with me from the beginning."

15:18-20 "If the world hates you, know that it has hated me before it hated you. . . . If they persecuted me, they will persecute you."

---

(13) Cyprian of Carthage

Brothers and sisters, let us imitate Abel who was the first slain for righteousness' sake (Gen 4:8). The practice of martyrdom started with him. Let us imitate Abraham, the friend of God, who did not hesitate to offer his son with his own hands as an offering to God, obeying him faithfully (Gen 22:9-12). Let us also emulate the three children: Hananiah, Mishael, and Azaria (Dan 2:17).[4] Though young, they were not afraid nor were they worn down by captivity after Judea was defeated and Jerusalem was seized. By the power of faith, they overcame the king in his own kingdom. When they were commanded to worship the image which King Nebuchadnezzar had made, they withstood the king's threats and the flames. They proclaimed and professed their faith with these words: *O Nebuchadnezzar, we have no need to answer you in this matter. If it be so, our God whom we serve is able to deliver us from the burning fiery furnace; and he will deliver us out of your hand, O king. But if not, be it known to you, O king, that we will not serve your gods or worship the golden image which you have set up* (Dan 3:16-18). They believed that they might escape by their faith. But they added that if they did not escape, the king would know that they were willing to die for the God they worshiped. This is the power of courage and faith: to believe and to know that God can deliver us from impending death and yet not to fear death nor yield in any way so that faith might be shown in its full might. The pure and victorious power of the Holy Spirit came forth from their mouths and confirmed the truth of the words that the Lord spoke in his gospel: *When they deliver you up, do not be anxious how you are to speak or what you are to say; for what you are to say will be given to you in that hour; for it is not you who speak, but the Spirit of your Father speaking through you* (Matt 10:19-20). He said *what you are to say* and to answer *will be given* to us *in that hour* from heaven. But it is not we

---

4. These three companions of Daniel are also known by their Chaldean names: Shadrach, Meshach, and Abednego (Dan 2:49).

who speak, but the Spirit of your Father speaking through us and is glorified in us since he never leaves nor is separated from those who confess him. When Daniel was ordered to venerate the idol Bel, which the people and the king worshiped, he also spoke boldly with complete faith and freedom to confess his God, saying: *I do not revere man-made idols, but the living God who created heaven and earth* (Bel 1:5).

What should we say about blessed martyrs in Maccabees who were tortured so cruelly? The seven brothers suffered many agonies. Their mother, who comforted them during their sufferings, then died along with her children (2 Macc 7:1–22, 41). Are they not examples of great courage and faith? Do they not urge us by their own sufferings to gain the crown of martyrdom? What should we say about the prophets to whom the Holy Spirit gave the knowledge of future events? What about the apostles whom the Lord chose? Since these men were killed for righteousness' sake, have they not also taught us how to die? The account of the birth of Christ testifies to the martyrdom of infants. Those who were two years old and younger were slain for his name (Matt 2:16–18). An age not yet suitable for the battle was deemed suitable for the crown. Innocent babies were put to death on account of his name so that it might be shown that those who are slain for Christ's sake are innocent. Since even these were martyred, it is clear that none are free of the dangers of persecution. How serious is it if a Christian man, **a servant**, is unwilling to suffer, even though **his master** suffered first (15:18–20)! How terrible is it if we are unwilling to suffer for our own sins when he who had no sin of his own suffered for us! How horrible is it that the Son of God suffered to make us sons of God, but the Son of Man will not suffer so that he can remain a Son of God! If we suffer from the hatred of the **world**, Christ endured this hatred first. If we suffer rejection, exile, or torture in this **world**, the Maker and Lord of the **world** suffered worse things than these. He warns us: **If the world hates you, know that it has hated me before it hated you. If you were of the world, the world would love its own; but because you are not of the world, but I chose you out of the world, therefore the world hates you. Remember the word that I said to you, "A servant is not greater than his master." If they persecuted me, they will persecute you** (15:18–20). Our Lord and God did the very things that he taught so that his disciples might not be excused if they learned them but did not do them.

Beloved brothers and sisters, do not be so afraid of future persecution or the coming of the menacing antichrist that you fail to prepare yourself for these things with the exhortations and teachings of the evangelists or with the warnings from heaven. *Antichrist is coming* (1 John 2:18). But Christ, who surpasses him, is also coming! The enemy sweeps in and wreaks havoc, but the Lord pursues him at once to avenge our sufferings and our wounds. The enemy rages and threatens, but there is one who can *deliver us* from his hands (cf. Matt 6:13). Rather, as Christ himself warns, fear the one whose anger you cannot escape: *Do not fear those who kill the body but cannot kill the soul; rather fear him who can destroy both soul and body in hell* (Matt 10:28). And again: *He who loves his life loses it, and he who hates his life in this world will keep it for eternal life* (12:25).

(14) Augustine of Hippo

This **world**, which God is reconciling to himself in Christ (cf. 2 Cor 5:19), which is saved through Christ, and which has all its sins forgiven through Christ, has been chosen out of that **world** which is hostile, condemned, and defiled. For out of that *lump*, which completely perished in Adam, were formed *the vessels of mercy* (Rom 9:23) from which the **world** of redemption is created. These are **hated** by the **world** which belongs to *the vessels of wrath* that are made from the same *lump* and are destined *for destruction* (Rom 9:22). After saying, **If you were of the world, the world would love its own**, he then adds, **But because you are not of the world, but I chose you out of the world, therefore the world hates you** (15:19). These men too were **of that world**. But in order that they would no longer be **of the world**, they were **chosen** out of it, not due to their own merit (for none of their good works preceded this) nor due to their nature (for free will became totally corrupted at its source), but freely, that is, by pure grace. For the one who **chose** the world **out of the world** created by himself, instead of finding, what he would choose: *There is a remnant, chosen by grace. But if it is by grace, he adds, it is no longer on the basis of works; otherwise grace would no longer be grace* (Rom 11:5–6).

If we are asked about how the **world** of destruction, which hates the **world** of redemption, loves itself, we reply that it loves itself with a false love and not with true love. It follows then that it loves itself falsely and hates itself truly: for *he who loves injustice, hates his own soul* (Ps 11:5 [10:5 LXX]). But the **world** is said to love itself, because it loves the wickedness which makes it wicked. Conversely, it is said to hate itself, because it loves that which causes it harm. It hates its true nature which is in it and loves its vices. In other words, it hates what it was made to be by the goodness of God and loves what it has become through the exercise of free will. It follows then, if we understand correctly, that we are both prohibited from loving that **world** and are commanded to love it. We are prohibited, of course, when it is said, *Do not love the world* (1 John 2:15). But we are commanded, when it is said, *Love your enemies* (Luke 6:27). These make up **the world that hates** us. We are forbidden to love that which it loves in itself, and we are commanded to love that which it hates in itself, the craftsmanship of God and the various gifts of his goodness.

15:22 "If I had not come and spoken to them, they would not have sin; but now they have no excuse for their sin."

---

(15) Origen of Alexandria

It seems right to inquire as to why the one who is *born anew* (1 Pet 1:3) through God to salvation needs the Father, Son, and Holy Spirit and is not saved without the cooperation of the entire Trinity, and why it is impossible to participate in the Father and the Son without the Holy Spirit? In discussing these points, it will be absolutely necessary to describe the activity which is peculiar to the Holy Spirit and that which is special to the Father and the Son. I think that the activity of the Father and Son is found in both saints and sinners, in rational beings and in irrational animals, even in lifeless things, and in everything that exists. But the activity of the Holy Spirit does not operate in lifeless things or in irrational, living animals. Indeed, it is not even found in those who are rational but who are engaged in evil and have not turned completely to a better life. I think the activity of the Holy Spirit occurs only in those who are already pursuing a better life and are *walking* in the ways of Jesus Christ (cf. Eph 2:10). Those are the people who do good deeds and who *abide in God* (1 John 4:13).

That the activity of the Father and the Son is found in both saints and sinners is made clear in the fact that all rational beings participate in the word of God, which is reason.[5] Thus, they have implanted within them some seeds, so to speak, of wisdom and righteousness which is Christ. All things which exist participate in him who truly exists. He said through Moses, *I AM WHO I AM* (Exod 3:14). Participation in God the Father is shared by all: both the righteous and sinners, the rational and the irrational, and indeed everything which exists. Certainly, the apostle Paul also demonstrates that all participate in Christ when he says, *Do not say in your heart, "Who will ascend into heaven?" (that is, to bring Christ down) or "Who will descend into the abyss?" (that is, to bring Christ up from the dead). But what does scripture say? The word is near you, on your lips and in your heart* (Rom 10:6–8). By this he shows that Christ is in the *heart* of all humans. Because Christ is the Word or Reason, those who participate in him are rational beings. The passage in the gospel, **If I had not come and spoken to them, they would not have sin; but now they have no excuse for their sin** (15:22), clearly refers to all of those who have reached the period of rational knowledge. Prior to this time, humans do **not have sin**, but once they possess rationality, from that time onward, **they have no excuse for their sin.** From the time when they are able to understand and have knowledge and when reason, implanted within them, has taught them the difference between good and evil, then they are responsible for the sins that they commit, for they have begun to know what evil is. This is the meaning of the verse: **but now they have no excuse for their sin** (15:22).

15:24–25 "If I had not done among them the works which no one else did, they would not have sin; but now they have seen and hated both me and my Father."

---

(16) Augustine of Hippo

The Lord said, **He who hates me hates my Father also** (15:23). It is absolutely certain that he who hates the truth must also hate the one from whom truth is born. . . . Then, he added the words which we will now explain: **If I had not done among them the works which no one else did, they would not have sin** (15:24). Of this sin, he said previously, **If I had not come and spoken to them, they would not have sin** (15:22). Their sin was not believing the one who

---

5. Origen is drawing on the multiple meanings of the Greek word *Logos.* This word, often translated in the Gospel of John as "Word," also means logic, rationality, reason, intellect, etc.

spoke and did these things. Certainly, they were not sinless before he **had spoken to them** (15:22) or before he **had done these works among them** (15:22). But the sin of not believing him is mentioned specifically because it contains within itself all other sins. If they had been innocent of this one and believed in him, all their others sins would have been forgiven.

After he said, **If I had not done among them the works**, he immediately added, **Which no one else did** (15:24). What is meant by this latter phrase? Among all the **works** of Christ, certainly none seem greater than when he raised the dead. Yet we know that the ancient prophets did the same thing. Elijah did (cf. 1 Kgs 17:21–22). Elisha also did this when he was alive in the flesh (2 Kgs 4:35). He also did this when he lay buried in his tomb. When some men who were carrying a dead man fled to that spot to hide from their enemies, they laid him down upon Elisha's tomb. Immediately, the dead man came back to life (2 Kgs 13:21).

There were some **works** of Christ that no one else did. He fed five thousand men with five loaves (John 6:1–14) and four thousand with seven (Matt 15:32–39). He walked on water and gave Peter the power to do the same thing (Matt 14:25–29). He changed water into wine (John 2:9). He opened the eyes of a man who was born blind (John 9:7). He did many others things like this which would take too long to delineate.

Someone might respond that others have done **works** that no other human has done, not even the Lord. Only Moses struck down the Egyptians with so many, mighty plagues (Exod 7–12). He led the people through the sea which had been parted (Exod 14:21–29). He secured manna for them from heaven when they were hungry (Exod 16:4–17) and water from the rock when they were thirsty (Exod 17:6). Joshua, the son of Nun, alone divided the Jordan for the people to pass through (Josh 3:7). Through his prayer to God, he tamed and stopped the revolving sun (Josh 10:12–14). . . . I will skip over other examples since I think that these are sufficient to show that some of the saints have done miraculous works that no one else has. But in all of the ancient books we read about no one who cured so many with bodily defects, bad health, and physical ailments with such power. This is to say nothing about those specific cases as they happened when he healed with an authoritative word. The evangelist Mark says: *That evening, at sundown, they brought to him all who were sick or possessed with demons. And the whole city was gathered together about the door. And he healed many who were sick with various diseases, and cast out many demons* (Mark 1:32–34).[6] Matthew, when recording this same story, added the testimony of the prophet: *This was to fulfill what was spoken by the prophet Isaiah, "He took our infirmities and bore our diseases"* (Matt 8:17). Mark says elsewhere: *And wherever he came, in villages, cities, or country, they laid the sick in the market places, and besought him that they might touch even the fringe of his garment; and as many as touched it were made well* (Mark 6:56). No other man did such things **in them** (15:24). We must understand the words **in them**—not "among them" or "in their presence" but specifically **in them**—because he healed them.[7] He desired that

---

6. Augustine seems to have in mind the account in Matthew, not Mark, where Jesus heals the sick "with a word": *That evening they brought to him many who were possessed with demons; and he cast out the spirits with a word, and healed all who were sick* (Matt 8:16).

7. The Latin text reads: *If I had not done in them the works which no one else did, they would not have sin* (15:24). For Augustine, the prepositional phrase "in them" is significant, for it references his healing act, not his location.

they would understand these **works** not only as actions that generated awe but conferred actual healing. The benefits of these **works** certainly should have produced a response of love, not **hatred**. . . .

The **works** (15:24) are certainly his miraculous healings of their bodily ailments which no one else had ever done among them in this way. They saw these **works**. For this reason, he reproaches them when he says: **But now they have seen and hated both me and my Father. It is to fulfill the word that is written in their law, "They hated me without a cause"** (15:24–25). He calls it **their law**. He does not mean that they created it but that it was given to them. Similarly, we say, *Our daily bread*. But certainly we ask this of God by adding the words, *Give us* (Matt 6:11). But the one who **hates without cause** does not seek an advantage from the hatred nor seek to avoid misfortune. Just as the wicked **hate** the Lord so also the righteous love him. They love him freely—**without cause**—since they do not expect rewards beyond loving him, for he will be *all in all* (1 Cor 15:28).

15:26 "But when the Counselor comes . . . he will bear witness to me."

---

(17) Ambrose of Milan

The Lord said in the gospel: **But when the Counselor comes, whom I shall send to you from the Father, even the Spirit of truth, who proceeds from the Father, he will bear witness to me** (15:26). It follows then that the Holy Spirit proceeds **from the Father** and **bears witness** to the Son. This **witness** is both faithful and true and also **bears witness** to the Father. There is no fuller expression of the divine majesty and no clearer expression regarding the unity of divine power than this fact: The Spirit possesses the same knowledge of the Son and is himself the witness and the one who shares the Father's secrets.

The Lord excludes created beings from being able to possess the knowledge of God. By including the Holy Spirit, he shows clearly that the Spirit is not a created being. It follows that the Holy Spirit is not included in the ones referenced in this gospel: **No one has ever seen God; the only Son, who is in the bosom of the Father, he has made him known** (1:18). How could the Spirit *not have seen God* who *searches everything, even the depths of God* (1 Cor 2:10)? How could he *not have seen God* who *knows the thoughts of God* (1 Cor 2:11)? How could he *not have seen God* who *is from God* (1 Cor 2:12)? Since it is established that **no one has ever seen God** yet it is also evident that the Holy Spirit has seen him, the Holy Spirit certainly is exempted from this statement.

(18) Augustine of Hippo

And you also are witnesses, because you have been with me from the beginning (15:27). The Holy Spirit will **bear witness** (15:26), and so will you. Although **you have been with me from the beginning**, you cannot preach what you know now, because the fullness of the Spirit is not yet present within you. The Spirit **will bear witness to me**, and you will also be

witnesses, for *God's love has been poured into our hearts through the Holy Spirit which has been given to us* (Rom 5:5). God's love will give you the confidence to be **witnesses**. Peter certainly lacked that confidence, for he was seized by fear at the question of the maid. He was unable to offer true testimony but was overcome by his strongest fear to deny the Lord three times, contrary to his own promise (Matt 26:69–70). But *there is no fear in love*, for *perfect love casts out fear* (1 John 4:18). Before the passion of the Lord, Peter's servile fear was interrogated by a female servant; after the resurrection, his free love was examined by the very Lord of freedom (John 21:15–17). In the first instance, he was troubled; on the second, he was soothed. At first, he denied the one he had loved; then, he loved the one he had denied. But even at that point his love was weak and limited until it was strengthened and expanded by the Holy Spirit. At that point, the Spirit infused him with such an abundance of grace that it ignited his previously frigid heart into one that bore witness for Christ and unlocked his lips which earlier had suppressed the truth due to fear. When the Holy Spirit had descended on all of them and they were speaking in various languages to the crowds of Jews who had gathered, Peter outstripped the others in testifying about Christ and confounded those who killed him with the account of his resurrection. If anyone would enjoy looking upon a spectacle like this which is so delectably holy, let him read the Acts of the Apostles (Acts 2:1–47). Let him be amazed at the preaching of the blessed Peter, who had just been grieving his own denial of his Lord. Let him see that tongue which was transformed from diffidence to confidence and from slavery to freedom. Let him witness that tongue which turned the tongues of so many of his enemies into ones who confessed Christ. This is the same Peter who could not withstand one of these tongues when he fell into denial.

What more can I say? Such a radiance of grace and such a fullness of the Holy Spirit shone in him and such an abundance of the most precious truth flowed from his lips as he preached that he changed that large crowd of Jews. He changed those who were the adversaries and killers of Christ and at whose hands he himself was previously terrified to die with his Lord, into people who were willing to die for Christ's name. The Holy Spirit, who had previously only been promised, did all of this when he was sent. The Lord had foreseen these great and marvelous gifts when he said: **They have seen and hated both me and my Father. It is to fulfill the word that is written in their law, "They hated me without a cause." But when the Counselor comes, whom I shall send to you from the Father, even the Spirit of truth, who proceeds from the Father, he will bear witness to me; and you also are witnesses, because you have been with me from the beginning** (15:24–27). The Spirit, **bearing witness** and making invincible witnesses, removed fear from the friends of Christ and transformed the hatred of his enemies into love.

John 16

Augustine of Hippo interpreted Jesus's warning of what would befall the disciples (16:2) to mean that as Jesus was rejected, arrested, and killed, so his followers should expect the same fate. Yet, they should rejoice! John Chrysostom states that sorrow *fills their* hearts (16:6) when they hear that they would be killed at the hands of the gentiles and the Jews (16:2) and that *Christ is* going away (16:7). *He notes however that their grief was lessened because Christ was aware of their despair. Cyril concludes that the coming of the Spirit after Christ's departure assuages their sorrow.*

Jesus's statement about the arrival of the Spirit—When the Spirit of truth comes, he will guide you into all the truth (16:13)—*illustrates the moment when the disciples moved from a literal understanding of the truth to a spiritual understanding, learned from Spirit. Peter is transformed in this way when he sees the vision of unclean animals (Acts 10:9–16). Although Christ previously had declared all things clean (cf. Mark 7:19; Acts 10:28), the coming of the Spirit guides him into all the truth. Didymus the Blind concurs that the Spirit teaches the disciples the spiritual meaning of Christ's words. The Spirit who is not subordinated to the Father and the Son reveals the Trinitarian God fully. He is not subordinate to the Father and Son. The statement* for he will not speak on his own authority, but whatever he hears he will speak, and he will declare to you the things that are to come (16:13) *does not tell us anything about the nature of the three persons of the Godhead, for they do not hear and speak with each other as humans do; this statement is an accommodation to guide us to* the truth.

John Chrysostom is intrigued as to why the Spirit did not come until Christ departed. He concludes that sin and death first had to be removed through the salvific work of Christ before the Spirit could dwell within us. However, he is quick to point out that the Spirit also participates in salvation, for the Spirit is equal and shares the same purpose with the Father and Son. Leo the Great concurs with John and shows that the Trinity is seen in the mysteries. Leo, following the tradition of the early church, argues that the rite of baptism must be celebrated either during the paschal feast (Easter) or on Pentecost. If the rite is celebrated on Pascha, the rebirth in the font recalls the death and resurrection. The threefold immersion of the candidate matches the three days in the tomb. Rising from the water emulates Christ's rising from the dead. A baptism on Pentecost commemorates the descent and working of the Spirit and is a completion of the paschal celebration.

Cyril's attention is drawn to Christ's enigmatic statement: A little while, and you will see me no more; again a little while, and you will see me *(16:16)*. *According to Cyril, the first clause refers to the period of time before the onset of his passion:* A little while, and you will see me no more *means that he would be hidden from them by death for a brief time. Then he says,* Again a little while, and you will see me. *This refers to his resurrection. Augustine disagrees, for he states that this verse cannot be interpreted without reference to the following:* I will see you again and your hearts will rejoice *(16:22). Augustine says these words do not refer to his resurrection but to the life to come.* A little while, and you will see me no more; again a little while, and you will see me *(16:16). The first clause refers to his death and resurrection; the second to his ascension and his eventual return in glory. The span of this present age is a* little while, *although to those waiting for his return, it seems an eternity. On that day,* I will see you again and your hearts will rejoice *(16:22).*

John Chrysostom *finds an odd curiosity in Christ's analogy of the sorrow and joy of birth:* When a woman is in travail she has sorrow, because her hour has come; but when she is delivered of the child, she no longer remembers the anguish, for joy that a man is born into the world *(16:20–21). Certainly, the new mother forgets the* travail *of birth as she experiences the joy of her newborn child. But the odd shift in the text from* child *to* a man *piques his interest. John concludes that Christ is "hinting here at his own resurrection and that he is about to be brought into the world, not of death, but of the kingdom." Resurrection is a rebirth into a new life.*

John Chrysostom *and* Cyprian *state that material possessions and physical beauty can bring temporary joy, but they eventually fade away, for they are ephemeral. Christ promises a* joy *that* no one will take *(16:22). True joy, which is found in piety and the cultivation of the virtues of the soul, in charity and good deeds, is stored in the heavenly vaults and cannot be lost once it is deposited there. Gregory the Great follows their logic to answer another puzzle found in the text:* Hitherto you have asked nothing in my name; ask, and you will receive, that your joy may be full *(16:24). He adduces the example of Paul who asks that the messenger of Satan (2 Cor 12:7) be removed from him. But this request is refused. What then does Christ mean when he says,* you have asked nothing in my name; ask, and you will receive? *Gregory concludes that the answer is found in the meaning of the word* joy. *True joy is found in salvation; therefore, one must ask for that which is connected to salvation in the name of Jesus who is the Savior.*

Augustine's *attention is drawn to Jesus's final words at the end of chapter 16:* The hour is coming, indeed it has come, when you will be scattered, every man to his home, and will leave me alone *(16:32). Indeed, they abandoned him when he was arrested, tried, and crucified. But after his resurrection, they would not abandon him again. During their own persecutions—their trials, beatings, and deaths—which they suffered for his name, they would witness to their love for him with their very lives. For this reason, he said:* In the world you have tribulation; but be of good cheer, I have overcome the world *(16:33).*

John 16:1–11

[1]"I have said all this to you to keep you from stumbling. [2]They will put you out of the synagogues; but, the hour is coming when whoever kills you will think he is offering

service to God. ³And they will do this because they have not known the Father, nor me. ⁴But I have said these things to you, that when their hour comes you may remember that I told you of them. I did not say these things to you from the beginning, because I was with you. ⁵But now I am going to him who sent me; yet none of you asks me, 'Where are you going?' ⁶But because I have said these things to you, sorrow has filled your hearts. ⁷Nevertheless I tell you the truth: it is to your advantage that I go away, for if I do not go away, the Counselor will not come to you; but if I go, I will send him to you. ⁸And when he comes, he will convince the world concerning sin and righteousness and judgment: ⁹concerning sin, because they do not believe in me; ¹⁰concerning righteousness, because I go to the Father, and you will see me no more; ¹¹concerning judgment, because the ruler of this world is judged."

16:1–6 "I have said all this to you to keep you from stumbling. They will put you out of the synagogues; but, the hour is coming when whoever kills you will think he is offering service to God. . . . But because I have said these things to you, sorrow has filled your hearts."

---

(1) Cyprian of Carthage

You should know and believe without a doubt that the day of affliction has begun and the end of the world and the time of the antichrist has drawn near. All of us must stand ready for the battle and think of nothing other than the glory of *eternal life* and the crown of the confession of the Lord (cf. 1 Tim 6:12). Nor should we consider the events that are coming as similar to those which have come to pass. A more severe and harsh battle is threatening, and the soldiers of Christ must ready themselves for it with an uncorrupted faith and ample courage. They drink the cup of Christ's blood daily so that they may be able to shed their blood for Christ. This desire to stand united with Christ is found in the emulation of what he taught and did. Accordingly, the apostle John said, *He who says he abides in him ought to walk in the same way in which he walked* (1 John 2:6). The blessed apostle Paul persuasively teaches the same when he says, *We are children of God, and if children, then heirs, heirs of God and fellow heirs with Christ, provided we suffer with him in order that we may also be glorified with him* (Rom 8:16–17).

Now we must ponder these things so that no one will set his heart on anything from this world which is currently dying. Instead, let us follow Christ who lives forever and gives life to his servants who stand firm in the Christian faith. Dear friends, the hour is coming which our Lord foretold was approaching when he said: **But, the hour is coming when whoever kills you will think he is offering service to God. And they will do this because they have not known the Father, nor me. But I have said these things to you, that when their hour comes you may remember that I told you of them** (16:2–4). Let no one be puzzled as to why we are harassed continually by persecutions and constantly tested with afflictions that grow more severe. The Lord predicted that these things would happen at the end of the age and has prepared us for these battles by his teaching and exhortations.

His apostle, Peter, also taught us in his epistle that persecutions occur to test us and that we should be joined to the love of God by our own sufferings and death just as the righteous ones who preceded us have: *Beloved, do not be surprised at the fiery ordeal which comes upon you to prove you, as though something strange were happening to you. But rejoice in so far as you share Christ's sufferings, that you may also rejoice and be glad when his glory is revealed. If you are reproached for the name of Christ, you are blessed, because the spirit of glory and of God rests upon you* (1 Pet 4:12–14). The apostles taught us the things that they learned from the Lord's heavenly commands. The Lord himself strengthens us when he says, *There is no man who has left house or wife or brothers or parents or children, for the sake of the kingdom of God, who will not receive manifold more in this time, and in the age to come eternal life* (Luke 18:29–30). Similarly, he said, *Blessed are you when men hate you, and when they exclude you and revile you, and cast out your name as evil, on account of the Son of man! Rejoice in that day, and leap for joy, for behold, your reward is great in heaven* (Luke 6:22–23).

(2) John Chrysostom

The tyranny of despair is great! We must have a large amount of courage to stand up to this feeling. After we have taken from it what is useful, we need to dispense with the rest. It can prove somewhat useful. When we or others sin, it is good to feel sorrowful. But if we fall into a state of uncertainty, then the despair that arises proves useless. When despair had cast down the disciples who were not yet perfected, notice how Christ lifts them up once again with his rebuke. Those who had asked him previously ten thousand questions (e.g., Peter asked, *Lord, where are you going?* [13:36]; Thomas said, *Lord, we do not know where you are going; how can we know the way?* [14:5]; and Philip said, *Show us the Father* [14:5]), now upon hearing his declaration that **they will put you out of the synagogues** (16:2), and will *hate you* (15:18), and **whoever kills you will think he is offering service to God** (16:2), were themselves so despondent that they said nothing to him as if they had become speechless. He then rebukes them. **I did not say these things to you from the beginning, because I was with you. But now I am going to him who sent me; yet none of you asks me, "Where are you going?" But because I have said these things to you, sorrow has filled your hearts** (16:4–6). Uncontrolled sorrow, such as this, is terrible and leads to death. For this reason, Paul said that one should not be *overwhelmed by excessive sorrow* (2 Cor 2:7).

Christ says, **I did not say these things to you from the beginning** (16:4). Why did he not tell them these things **from the beginning**? So that no one would say that he was surmising that these would occur from the way things ordinarily happened. Why did he now bring up such an unpleasant topic? He says that he knew these things **from the beginning** but did not speak about them. This was not because he was ignorant, but **because I was with you** (16:4). He said these things in a human way, as if he had said, "Because you were safe, you were able to question me when you wanted. I received the brunt of all the storms at that time, so it was not necessary to tell you all these things **from the beginning**." But did he really not speak to them about any of this? Did he not call the Twelve together and say, *You will be dragged before governors and kings for my sake, to bear testimony before them and the Gentiles*, and *they will flog you in their synagogues* (Matt 10:17–18)? How does he now say, **I did not say these things to you from the beginning** (16:4)? Certainly he told them previously that they would be flogged and dragged before rulers, but he did not tell them that their deaths would be so desired that the very deed would be considered as **offering service to God** (16:2). Of all things, this caused them to be stricken with abject fear: that they would be judged to be agitators and blasphemers. It may also be said that in this passage he was saying that they would suffer at the hands of the gentiles, but he emphasized the actions of the Jews and told them that their suffering was close at hand.

But now I am going to him who sent me; yet none of you asks me, "Where are you going?" But because I have said these things to you, sorrow has filled your hearts (16:5–6). It was a great comfort for them to learn that he was aware of their great despair, for they were beside themselves with the agony of being left by him and the anticipation of the terrible events that were about to befall them. They did not know if they would be able to endure all of this with courage. Why then did he not tell them after this that the Spirit would be bestowed upon them? So that you might learn that they were extremely virtuous. If they had not retreated, even though they were overwhelmed with **sorrow** and even though they had not yet been granted the Spirit, consider what sort of men they would be after they had received this gift. If they had heard at this time that they would receive the Spirit and then endure all these things, we would consider that it was due to this fact, but now it is entirely attributable to their own minds. This then clearly shows their love for Christ.

(3) Augustine of Hippo

I have said all this to you to keep you from stumbling (16:1). As it is sung in the psalm, *Great peace have those who love your law; nothing can make them stumble* (Ps 119:165). Rightly the Lord added this statement—**I have said all this to you to keep you from stumbling** (16:1)—to the promise of the Holy Spirit who would work in their hearts so that they would become his witnesses. They have *great peace who love God's law; nothing can make them stumble* (Ps 119:165), because *God's love has been poured into our hearts through the Holy Spirit which has been given to us* (Rom 5:5).

Then Jesus stated directly what they would suffer: **They will put you out of the synagogues** (16:2). What harm did the apostles suffer by being expelled from the **synagogues** of the Jews? Were they not already intending to separate themselves even if no one threw them out? Undoubtedly he was announcing that the Jews would reject Christ whom the disciples could never abandon. It was certain that since they could not exist apart from him, they would also be cast out along with their Lord by the very ones who did not wish to be in him.

Since there was not another people of God except those of the seed of Abraham, they certainly would have remained the natural *branches of the olive tree* (Rom 11:17) if they would have acknowledged and received Christ. If they had desired to abide in him, the churches of Christ would not have been distinct from the synagogues of the Jews, for they would have been unified. After they refused and cast themselves away from Christ, they

put out of the synagogues (16:2) those who would not abandon Christ. After receiving the Holy Spirit and becoming his witnesses, they certainly were not counted among those of whom it is said: *Many even of the authorities believed in him, but for fear of the Pharisees they did not confess it, lest they should be put out of the synagogue: for they loved the praise of men more than the praise of God* (12:42–43). They **believed in him** but not in the way he wanted them to believe, for he said: *How can you believe, who receive glory from one another and do not seek the glory that comes from the only God?* (5:44). Therefore, those disciples who *believe in him* and are filled with the Holy Spirit, or in other words with the gift of divine grace, no longer are connected to those who are *ignorant of the righteousness of God that comes from God and seek to establish their own, for they did not submit to God's righteousness* (Rom 10:3). . . . So they expelled those who were lifted up by the *righteousness of God*, not *their own*. They should not be ashamed that they were cast out by humans, for Christ is **the glory** of their strength (5:44).

To what he had just told them, he added the following: **Indeed, the hour is coming when whoever kills you will think he is offering service to God. And they will do this because they have not known the Father, nor me** (16:2–3). In other words, **they have not known the Father** or his Son to whom they think they are **offering service** when they **kill you**. The Lord added these words to console his followers who would be **put out of the synagogues** (16:2). By saying, **They will put you out of the synagogues** (16:2), he announces in advance what evils they would have to endure for their witness on his behalf. He does not say, *And* **the hour is coming when whoever kills you will think he is offering service to God** (16:2). What does he say? ***But, the hour is coming***. This is the way he would have spoken if he were foreshadowing that something good would happen after these evils. . . . What then do these words mean: **They will put you out of the synagogues; but, the hour is coming** (16:2)? Shouldn't he have said: And **the hour is coming when whoever kills you will think he is offering service to God** (16:2)? He did not say, **But, the hour is coming** when they will **kill you**, as if he implied that their reward for being expelled would be found in their deaths. Instead, he says, **But, the hour is coming when whoever kills you will think he is offering service to God** (16:2). So I do not think that he wished to convey any other meaning than that they should both understand and rejoice that they would win so many over to Christ by being **put out of the synagogues** of the Jews. In fact, the Jews would discover that it was not enough just to expel them. They could not allow them to continue to live since they feared that the disciples would turn everyone away from the observance of Judaism—as if such observances were the very truth of God!—through their preaching in the name of Christ. This is how we should understand his words about the Jews: **They will put you out of the synagogues** (16:2).

The witnesses—the martyrs of Christ—were also killed by the gentiles. However, they thought that they were **offering service** to their own false gods—not to the true God—when they did this. Every Jew who killed a person who was proclaiming Christ **thinks he is offering service to God** (16:2). Why? He believed that all who converted to Christ were abandoning the God of Israel. By this same reasoning, they were incited to murder Christ himself as their own words regarding this have been recorded. They thought that *the world has gone after him* (12:19) and that *if we let him live . . . the Romans will come and destroy both our holy place and our nation* (11:48). The words of Caiaphas suggest the same: *It is* *expedient for us that one man should die for the people, and that the whole nation should not perish* (11:50). With these words, Christ wanted to lift up his disciples by his own example, for he had just told them, *If they have persecuted me, they will also persecute you* (15:20). By killing Christ, they thought that they had **offered service to God** (16:2). It would be the same in respect to the disciples.

This then is the meaning of the words: **They will put you out of the synagogues** (16:2). Do not fear being alone when you are **put out** of their congregation. You will gather so many people in my name that they will **kill you** on account of their great fear that their temple and all the sacraments of the old law will be abandoned. When they shed your blood, they will believe fully that they are **offering service to God** (16:2). This is certainly an example of the apostle's words: *They have a zeal for God, but it is not enlightened* (Rom 10:2). . . . Indeed, it is a horrible mistake! Would you please God by striking down the very ones who please God? Do you please God by razing the living temple of God to the ground with blows so that the temple made with stone may not be abandoned? What wicked blindness! *But this blindness has partly come upon Israel, until the full number of the Gentiles come in* (Rom 11:25). I say this has happened *partly*, not entirely. Only *some of the branches were broken off*—not all of them!—so that *a wild olive shoot was grafted into the olive tree* (Rom 11:17). At that very time the disciples of Christ, after being filled with the Holy Spirit, spoke in the languages of all nations, performed many divine miracles, and proclaimed divine prophecies everywhere. Although Christ was killed, he was so loved that his disciples, after being expelled from the congregations of the Jews, gathered a great number of those very Jews into their own congregation. In this way, they had no fear of being left alone (cf. Acts 2–4).

16:7 "If I do not go away, the Counselor will not come to you."

---

(4) Cyril of Alexandria

When Christ's mission on earth was accomplished, it was necessary that he should finish what was still left: his ascension to the Father. For this reason, he says: **It is to your advantage that I go away, for if I do not go away, the Counselor will not come to you; but if I go, I will send him to you** (16:7). . . . He finally completed all his work on earth, as we have already shown. However, it was absolutely necessary that we should become sharers and participants in the divine nature of the Word and that we should relinquish the life that originally belonged to us and be transformed into another sort of human. The very essence of our being should be changed into a new kind of life that is pleasing to God. But we were not able to attain this new life in any way other than by having fellowship with and by participating in the Holy Spirit. The most suitable and appropriate time for both the sending of the Spirit and his descent to us happened at the right moment—I am of course speaking of the time of our Savior Christ's departure from earth. When he was still in the flesh with those who believed in him, I think he revealed himself as the giver of every blessing. But when the time came for his restoration to his Father in heaven, it was imperative that he would connect himself to his worshipers by the Spirit and *dwell in our hearts by faith* (cf. Eph 3:7). When we have his presence in us and possess the omnipotent Spirit, we are able to shout boldly, *Abba! Father!* (Gal 4:6), make steady progress in every virtue, and be strengthened and made invincible against the craftiness of the devil and the attacks of other men.

From the Old and New Scriptures, it is easily proved that the Holy Spirit changes the character of those in whom he dwells. He fashions them into a new life. When the holy Samuel was speaking with Saul, he said, *Then the spirit of the Lord will come mightily upon you . . . and you will be turned into another man* (1 Sam 10:6). The blessed Paul writes similarly, *And we all, with unveiled face, beholding the glory of the Lord, are being changed into his likeness from one degree of glory to another; for this comes from the Lord who is the Spirit* (2 Cor 3:18). *The Lord is the Spirit* (2 Cor 3:17). Notice how the Spirit fashions those in whom he visibly dwells into another *likeness*. They change willingly from a tendency of wanting to contemplate only earthly things to heavenly ones and from a cowardly disposition to one of courage. We find that the disciples are changed in this way and are strengthened by the Holy Spirit against the assaults of their persecutors. That they tenaciously take hold of the love for Christ cannot be doubted. Therefore, the Savior's words are true: **It is to your advantage that I go away** (16:7), for this was the occasion for the Spirit's descent.

16:8-11 "**And when he comes, he will convince the world concerning sin and righteousness and judgment.**"

---

(5) Cyril of Alexandria

After he had demonstrated that his ascension to the Father is the proper moment for the descent and mission of the Spirit and through this had assuaged the sorrow of his holy disciples, he then moved on to reveal what the Holy Spirit will do. Christ says, **And when he comes, he will convince the world concerning sin and righteousness and judgment** (16:8). He has clearly pointed out how each rebuke will take place. However, since some will not likely understand these ideas fully, I think that it is necessary to interpret each section and to indicate more clearly what is intended.

The refutation of **sin** comes first. How will the Spirit **convince the world**? When those who love Christ become worthy of him and believe in him, then he will condemn the **world**. In other words, those who are ignorant and maintain their unbelief and who are held captive by their love for the things of this world—these will see by their own deeds that they are guilty of their transgressions and bound to die for their sins. God will not receive everyone. He will not bestow the Spirit upon humans without reason nor upon those who deny him; however, he will send the Comforter to abide only in those who are worthy, who have honored him through faith as God, and who have confessed that he is the Creator and Lord of all. After the Comforter has come, he will prove that what the Lord said to the Jews beforehand is true: *You will die in your sins unless you believe that I am he* (8:24).

Additionally, Christ says, **He will convince the world . . . concerning righteousness, because I go to the Father, and you will see me no more** (16:8, 10). After his ascension into heaven, he will rightly support those who believe and are justly justified in Christ. They accepted the one whom they had not seen as the true God. They still believe that he sits on his Father's throne. By calling to mind what Thomas said and did, one can easily learn that Christ calls those who believe without seeing **blessed**. When Thomas doubted that the Son had been restored to life, he said, *Unless I see in his hands the print of the nails, and place my finger in the mark of the nails, and place my hand in his side, I will not believe* (20:25). What did Thomas hear Christ say after he was permitted to do what he desired and then subsequently believed? *Have you believed because you have seen me? Blessed are those who have not seen and yet believe* (20:29). Those who have believed without seeing have been correctly declared **righteous**. But the **world** has missed out on gaining the same sort of blessedness. They preferred to wallow in the world's wickedness instead of trying to secure the **righteousness** that comes from faith.

One must understand that the two reproofs mentioned already apply not only to the Jews but to every human who is stubborn and disobedient. The phrase **the world** (16:8) does not pertain only to the human who is constantly wallowing in pleasure and who is obsessed with the devil's wickedness but applies equally to those who are scattered about and inhabit the entire **world**. Therefore, these two reproofs apply to everyone. Christ gathered up, not only Judea, as was the case in ancient times, nor the seed of Israel exclusively, but the entire race that was descended from Adam. The gift of faith was given to the whole world, for his grace is not limited.

The Savior says that the Comforter's third refutation will be the righteous judgment of **the ruler of this world** (16:11). I will explain how this will happen. The Comforter will testify to the glory of Christ. By proving that Christ is truly the Lord of all, he will convict **the world** of having gone astray and abandoning the one who is truly God by nature to fall down and worship Satan who is not by nature God. The judgment against him, in my opinion, is sufficient to prove that this statement is true. Certainly he could not have been condemned and stripped of his power nor could he have paid the penalty of his fight with God by being bound by the chains of the underworld, if he were by nature God. In contrast, Satan would prove himself to be resolute in strength and power. But now we see that he is powerless to save his honor. He is placed under the feet of those filled with the Spirit, the faithful who confess that Christ is God. . . .

God has called him **the ruler of this world** (16:11). This however is not actually true. It is not as if his power to rule was innately part of his essence, but it was an honor seized by guile and greed. Yet he still has power and rules over those who are wandering in error due to their innate, purposeful desire for utter wickedness. Their minds are held captive by error, and they are inescapably bound by the chains of captivity, although they could have escaped by turning through faith to Christ whom they could have acknowledged as the one true God. Satan therefore holds the title of **ruler** fraudulently. He does not hold it legitimately against God but only through the wickedness of those who have gone astray.

John 16:12–15

[12] "I have yet many things to say to you, but you cannot bear them now. [13]When the Spirit of truth comes, he will guide you into all the truth; for he will not speak on his own authority, but whatever he hears he will speak, and he will declare to you the things that are to come. [14]He will glorify me, for he will take what is mine and declare it to you. [15]All that the Father has is mine; therefore I said that he will take what is mine and declare it to you."

16:12–13 "When the Spirit of truth comes, he will guide you into all the truth."

---

(6) Origen of Alexandria

Since we are now discussing Peter and those who taught Christianity to those who were circumcised (i.e., the Jews), I think it is fitting to quote a statement of Jesus found in the Gospel of John and then offer an interpretation of it. It is recorded there that Jesus said, **I have yet many things to say to you, but you cannot bear them now** (16:12). However, **when the Spirit of truth comes, he will guide you into all the truth; for he will not speak on his own authority, but whatever he hears he will speak** (16:13). When we investigate what the **many things** are which Jesus had **to say** to his disciples which they **cannot bear now** (16:12), I have to point out that he could not declare these to them because the apostles were Jews who were trained according to the letter of the Mosaic law. What are the **many things**? What the true law was, how Jewish worship was *a copy and shadow of the heavenly* things (Heb 8:5), and how future blessings were foreshadowed by the laws regarding *food and drink, festivals, new moons,* and *sabbaths* (cf. Col 2:16–17). . . . There are many aspects of the law which need to be explained and clarified by the spiritual sense. The disciples were not able to **bear** these things since they were born and raised as Jews. I think that since these were such common customs and since the Holy Spirit would teach them the **truth**, the following words were added: **When the Spirit of truth comes, he will guide you into all the truth** (16:13). It is as if he had said, "**He will guide you into all the truth** about those things which are merely types which you currently believe constitute the true worship of God." It follows then according to the promise of Jesus that **the Spirit of truth came** to Peter and said regarding the *animals and reptiles and birds of the air: "Rise, Peter; kill and eat."* **The Spirit came** *while Peter was inwardly perplexed,* for he responded to this divine command by saying, *"No, Lord; for I have never eaten anything that is common or unclean."* However, the **Spirit** taught him the true and spiritual meaning about this food: *"What God has cleansed, you must not call common"* (cf. Acts 10:12–17). After this vision, **the Spirit of truth guided** Peter **into all the truth** (16:13) and told him the **many things** which he could not **bear** (16:12) while Jesus was still physically present with him.

(7) Didymus the Blind

These words of mystery teach us that, after Jesus had taught his disciples many things, he said, **I have yet many things to say to you** (16:12). The phrase **I have yet many things to say to you** is not directed to novices or those totally ignorant of the wisdom of God but to hearers of his words who have not yet attained all **things**. For he handed on to them whatever they could **bear** (16:12) and deferred for a future time the rest which they would not be able to understand without the teaching of the Holy Spirit. Now the Spirit was not given to humanity before the Lord's passion took place, as the evangelist says, *For as yet the Spirit had not been given, because Jesus was not yet glorified* (7:39). Being **glorified** here means that Jesus *tastes death for everyone* (Heb 2:9). And so, after the resurrection he appeared to his disciples, breathed on their faces, and said: *Receive the Holy Spirit* (20:22). And again: *You shall receive power when the Holy Spirit has come upon you* (Acts 1:8). When the Holy Spirit comes into the hearts of believers, they are filled with words of wisdom and knowledge. When they are made spiritual in this way, they receive the teaching of the Holy Spirit which can guide them toward the whole truth.

Therefore, since it was still not appropriate for them to be filled with the Holy Spirit at the time when he said to them, **I have yet many things to say to you**, accordingly he added, **but you cannot bear them now** (16:12). Because they were still *serving a copy and shadow* (Heb 8:5) and a type of the law, they were not able to look upon the truth *since the law conveyed but a shadow* (Heb 10:1). It is for this reason that they were unable to **bear** the weight of spiritual things. **When the Spirit of truth**—that is, the Paraclete (i.e., Counselor)—**comes, he will guide you into all the truth** (16:13), through his own teaching and instruction, conveying you from the death of the letter to the Spirit that gives life (cf. 2 Cor 3:6). In him alone resides the truth of all Scripture. And so, when the **Spirit of truth** himself enters into a pure and simple mind, he will impress upon you the knowledge of truth; since he always joins the new to the old, **he will guide you into all the truth** (16:13). Moreover, someone praying to God the Father said, *Guide me in your truth* (Ps 25:5), meaning "in your only-begotten." He bears witness to this with his own voice: **I am the truth** (14:6). God grants this perfection by sending the **Spirit of truth** who guides believers into the whole truth. . . .

In what follows, the Savior, who is also the truth, speaks about the **Spirit of truth** who is sent by the Father and is the Paraclete: **He will not speak on his own authority** (16:13). By this he means "not without me and not without my and the Father's authority, seeing that he is inseparable from my and the Father's will because he is not from himself but from the Father and me. For his very being and speaking belongs to him from the Father and from me. As for me, I speak the truth, by which I mean that I inspire what he speaks, for he is the **Spirit**, after all, **of truth**" (16:13). Now when we say that there is "saying and speaking" within the Trinity, we should not understand this as taking place in the manner to which we are accustomed when we converse and speak among ourselves, but in the way that conforms with incorporeal natures and especially with the Trinity, who instills his will in the hearts of believers and those worthy of hearing it. This is what "saying and speaking" means. . . . But God, who is simple and of a nature that is incomposite and unique, possesses neither ears nor organs with which he emits a voice. Rather, his solitary and incomprehensible substance is not composed of any members or parts. The very same point should be understood likewise with regard to the Son and the Holy Spirit. Therefore, when we read in Scriptures: *The Lord says to my Lord* (Ps 110:2), and elsewhere: *God said: "Let there be light"* (Gen 1:3), and things similar to these, we ought to understand them in a way worthy of God. The Father does not announce his will to the Son, who is wisdom and truth, as if he does not already know it. For the Son, who is wise and true, has in wisdom and substance everything that the Father speaks. Therefore, when the Father speaks and the Son hears, or vice versa, when the Son speaks and the Father hears, it indicates that in the Father and the Son there is the same nature and agreements. Nor is it possible for the Holy Spirit, who is the **Spirit of truth** (16:13) and the Spirit of wisdom, to hear what he does not know when the Son speaks, since he is the very thing expressed by the Son. . . .

Therefore, just as we understand the natures of incorporeal beings in our discussion above, so too we now ought to acknowledge that the Holy Spirit receives from the Son that which belongs to his own nature. This does not signify that there is a giver and a receiver, but one substance. The Son is said to receive the same things from the Father which belong to his very being (i.e., wisdom, truth, etc.). For the Son is nothing other than those things which are given to him by the Father, and the substance of the Holy Spirit is nothing other than that which is given to him by the Son. These statements are made for this reason: so that we may believe that in the Trinity the Holy Spirit's nature is the same as that of the Father and the Son. . . . And so, the Holy Spirit glorifies the Son by showing and manifesting him to *the pure in heart* (cf. Matt 5:8) who are worthy of understanding him, seeing him, and knowing the splendor of his *nature* (cf. Heb 1:3) and *the image of the invisible God* (Col 1:15). The *image* himself glorifies the Father in turn, by showing himself to pure minds, thereby introducing him to those who do not know him: *He who has seen me has seen the Father* (14:9). In addition, the Father glorifies his only-begotten by revealing the Son to those who have become worthy to attain the summit of knowledge, showing his magnificence and power. Furthermore, the Son himself glorifies the Holy Spirit by bestowing him on those who have prepared themselves to be worthy of his gift and by distributing to them the sublimity of his glory and greatness.

(8) John Chrysostom

Why did the Spirit not come before Christ departed? Since all were still liable to punishment, the Spirit could not come until the curse had been removed and sin had been destroyed. He says that this hostility had to be abolished and we had to be reconciled to God. Then we received the gift of the Spirit (cf. Eph 2:15). Why then does he say, **I will send him to you** (16:7)? He means, "I will prepare you to receive him." But how can the Spirit which exists everywhere be sent? In this way, he makes the distinction of the persons of the Godhead clear. For these two reasons, he speaks in this way. Even though they were cleaving to him, Christ urges them to adhere to the Spirit in order that they might also honor him. Christ was able to do the very same things as the Spirit, but he acquiesces to the Spirit to work miracles so that the disciples might learn of his importance. Although the Father could have brought all things that exist into being, the Son did this so that we might understand his power. It is the same here. He also took on human flesh and yielded the inner workings to the Spirit. In this way, he also stopped up the mouths of those who take the plan of his unspeakable love as a starting point to spread impiety. When they say that the Son took on flesh because he was inferior to the Father, we ask them what they say about the Spirit. The Spirit did not take on flesh. But certainly you would not call him greater than the Son, nor the Son inferior to the Spirit, on account of this, would you? For this reason the Trinity presides over baptism. The Father is able to accomplish this completely, as is the Son and the Holy Spirit. However, since no one held doubts about the Father but there were doubts about the Son and the Spirit, they were included in this sacred rite in order that we might learn about their communion of honor from their common participation in these mysteries. Since the Son is able in baptism to do by himself that which he is able to accomplish with the Father, and the Holy Spirit likewise, hear these things clearly. To the Jews, he said, *That you may know that the Son of man has authority on earth to forgive sins* (Mark 2:10); and again, *That you may become children of light* (12:36); and, *I give to them eternal life* (10:28). Then, after these, he said, *that they may have life, and have it abundantly* (10:10).

Let us also see the Spirit doing this same thing. Where can we see it? He says, *The manifestation of the Spirit is given to each for the common good* (1 Cor 12:7). After supplying these things, he then forgives sins even more. And it is said again, *It is the spirit that gives life* (6:63); and, *The Spirit will give life to your mortal bodies through his Spirit which dwells in you* (Rom 8:11); and, the *Spirit is life because of righteousness* (Rom 8:10); and, *If you are led by the Spirit, you are not under the law* (Gal 5:18). Indeed, *you did not receive the spirit of slavery to fall back into fear, but you have received the Spirit of adoption* (Rom 8:15). All the miracles that they did, they did after the Spirit came. When writing to the Corinthians, Paul also said, *But you were washed, you were sanctified, you were justified in the name of the Lord Jesus Christ and in the Spirit of our God* (1 Cor 6:11). Although they had heard many things about the Father and had seen the Son do various deeds, they did not yet know anything with certainty about the Spirit. Yet the Spirit does miracles and reveals perfect knowledge. But the Spirit should not on account of this be considered greater than the Son; for this reason, Christ says, **Whatever he hears he will speak, and he will declare to you the things that are to come** (16:13).

(9) Leo the Great

Those things connected with Christ's humiliation and those connected to his exaltation come together in the one and same person, and all aspects of his divine power and human weakness join together to bring about our restoration. Therefore, it is fitting that the power of baptism should change the old creature into a new being on the very day when the one who was crucified died and the very day when the dead are resurrected. This rebirth is accomplished through Christ's death and his resurrection, as the blessed apostle Paul says: *Do you not know that all of us who have been baptized into Christ Jesus were baptized into his death? We were buried therefore with him by baptism into death, so that as Christ was raised from the dead by the glory of the Father, we too might walk in newness of life. For if we have been united with him in a death like his, we shall certainly be united with him in a resurrection like his* (Rom 6:3–5). The teacher of the gentiles explains this matter further and recommends the sacrament of baptism.

From the spirit of his teaching, it is understood that this particular day (i.e., Pascha/Easter), in accordance with its mystical symbolism and pattern, is the proper time for the regeneration of humans and their adoption as the sons and daughters of God. What is done in their body corresponds with what was done in respect to the head of the body (cf. 1 Cor 12:12–14). In the baptismal rite, sin is killed and death ensues. The threefold immersion imitates that Christ lay in the tomb for three days, and the rising out of the water simulates that he rose again from that tomb. The very nature of the act of baptism teaches us that the day on which the power of this gift and these particular actions happened is the sanctioned day for receiving this grace. This is certainly validated when we reflect upon the actions of our Lord Jesus Christ. After he rose from the dead, he handed on to his disciples both the pattern and the power of baptism. He instructed all the leaders of the churches with these words: *Go therefore and make disciples of all nations, baptizing them in the name of the Father and of the Son and of the Holy Spirit* (Matt 28:19). Of course, he could have taught them these things before his passion, but he wanted them to understand very well that the grace of regeneration began with his resurrection.

Certainly, it should be noted that baptism is permitted during the solemn season of Pentecost which was sanctified by the coming of the Holy Spirit. It is, so to speak, the continuation and completion of the paschal feast. While other festivals are held on different days of the week, the Festival of Pentecost always occurs on Sunday, which marks the Lord's resurrection. It is as if this day extends an inviting and helping hand of grace to those who have been deprived of the Easter feast due to debilitating illness, length of a journey, or hardships of sailing.[1] Through the gift of the Holy Spirit, they gain that which they long for. In respect to the faith of believers and the efficacy of his work, the only-begotten of God did not want any difference to be experienced between himself and the Holy Spirit, for there is no difference in their nature. Accordingly, he says, *I will ask the Father, and he will give you another Counselor, to be with you forever, even the Spirit of truth* (14:16–17); and again: *But the Counselor, the Holy Spirit, whom the Father will send in my name, he will teach you all things, and bring to your remembrance all that I have said to you* (14:26), and again: **When the Spirit of truth comes, he will guide you into all the truth** (16:13). Since Christ is the **truth** and the Holy Spirit is the **Spirit of truth** and the appellation **Counselor** applies to both, these two festivals are not dissimilar, for the sacrament is the same.

John 16:16–24

[16]"A little while, and you will see me no more; again a little while, and you will see me." [17]Some of his disciples said to one another, "What is this that he says to us, 'A little while, and you will not see me, and again a little while, and you will see me'; and, 'because I go to the Father'?" [18]They said, "What does he mean by 'a little while'? We do not know

---

1. Leo the Great indicates here that baptism during Pascha is preferred. Celebrating this rite during the Festival of Pentecost is reserved for those who were not able to participate during the Easter celebration.

what he means." [19]Jesus knew that they wanted to ask him; so he said to them, "Is this what you are asking yourselves, what I meant by saying, 'A little while, and you will not see me, and again a little while, and you will see me'? [20]Truly, truly, I say to you, you will weep and lament, but the world will rejoice; you will be sorrowful, but your sorrow will turn into joy. [21]When a woman is in travail she has sorrow, because her hour has come; but when she is delivered of the child, she no longer remembers the anguish, for joy that a child is born into the world. [22]So you have sorrow now, but I will see you again and your hearts will rejoice, and no one will take your joy from you. [23]In that day you will ask nothing of me. Truly, truly, I say to you, if you ask anything of the Father, he will give it to you in my name. [24]Hitherto you have asked nothing in my name; ask, and you will receive, that your joy may be full."

16:16 "A little while, and you will see me no more; again a little while, and you will see me."

---

(10) Cyril of Alexandria

After he had said that he would reveal through his Spirit everything that they must know, he speaks to them about his passion. Since his ascension into heaven would happen immediately afterward, it was very necessary for the Spirit to come because it would not be possible for him to speak with his holy apostles after he had gone to the Father. He speaks with them cautiously to remove the sharp sting from their sorrow. . . . In his great affection for them, he softens his words and shows them that their suffering would be followed closely by the joy of his resurrection (cf. 16:20). He says, **A little while, and you will see me no more; again a little while, and you will see me** (16:16). The time of his death was drawing near. For this reason, the Lord would not be seen by his disciples for a very short period of time until he raised his bodily temple after he disarmed Hades and threw open the gates of darkness for those inside (cf. Col 2:15; 1 Pet 3:19). After these things, he revealed himself once again to his disciples and promised them in the words of the gospel, *I am with you always* (Matt 28:20).

Although he is absent bodily because he is seated at the right hand of the Father for our sake, he still dwells in those who are worthy by the Spirit and is united continually with those who are holy. Indeed, he has promised us that **he will not leave us desolate** (14:18). Since there was very small period of time before the onset of his passion, he says, **A little while, and you will see me no more** (16:16). He would be hidden from them by death for a brief time, but then he says, **Again a little while, and you will see me** (16:16). After he *preached to the spirits in prison* (1 Pet 3:19), he came back to life again. The demonstration of his love toward humanity was fully revealed in this way: he saved not only those who were still living, but he also announced the forgiveness of sins to those who were sitting in the depths of the abyss in *darkness* (Isa 42:7).

Notice how he speaks about his passion and resurrection when he says, **A little while, and you will see me no more; again a little while, and you will see me** (16:16). After adding, **because I go to the Father** (16:17), he is silent about everything else. He did not tell them how long he would remain there or when he would come again. What is the reason? According to the words of our Savior himself, it is not for us *to know times or seasons which the Father has fixed by his own authority* (Acts 1:7).

16:20–24 "You will weep and lament, but the world will rejoice; you will be sorrowful, but your sorrow will turn into joy. . . . And no one will take your joy from you."

---

(11) Cyprian of Carthage

Our souls suffer many attacks each day and our hearts are burdened by many dangers. Yet we are willing to stay here among the devil's weapons even though we should desire to go to Christ through a quick death. He teaches us this very thing when he says, **Truly, truly, I say to you, you will weep and lament, but the world will rejoice; you will be sorrowful, but your sorrow will turn into joy** (16:20). Who does not want to rid himself of **sorrow**? Who does not want to secure **joy**? The Lord himself tells us when our **sorrow will turn into joy** (16:20). He says, **I will see you again and your hearts will rejoice, and no one will take your joy from you** (16:22). Since we will **rejoice** when we **see** Christ and since we cannot experience **joy** unless we **see** Christ, it is mental blindness and absolute madness to love the afflictions, punishments, and tears of the world. Rather, we should secure the **joy** that can never be taken away!

Dearest brothers and sisters, we act this way since our faith is weak and because no one believes that God's promises are true. But God is truth, and his word is eternal and immutable for believers! If a serious and honorable man were to promise you something, you would certainly trust him and not think that you'd be cheated or deceived by the man whom you knew would stand by his word and actions. But here God is speaking with you. Does your unbelieving mind dither from a lack of faith? God promises you eternity and immortality when you depart from this world. Do you doubt this? You do not know God at all. You offend Christ, who is the teacher of those who believe, with the sin of unbelief. You, who belong to the church, do not possess faith in the very house of faith.

Christ himself shows us what benefit it is to leave this world. The teacher of salvation and good works said to the disciples when they were **sorrowful** that he was about to leave: *If you loved me, you would have rejoiced, because I go to the Father* (14:28). From this, he taught and demonstrated that we should rejoice, not grieve, when those whom we love leave this world. We should remember the truth that the blessed apostle Paul established in his epistle: *For to me to live is Christ, and to die is gain* (Phil 1:21). He says that the greatest *gain* is to be freed from the snares of this world, liable no longer for the sins and vices of the flesh, removed from afflictions that sting, released from the venomous fangs of the devil, and to go to the joy of eternal salvation when Christ calls.

(12) John Chrysostom

Truly, truly, I say to you, you will weep and lament (16:20)—these are connected to his death and his cross—**but the world will rejoice; you will be sorrowful, but your sorrow will turn into joy** (16:21). Because the disciples did not want him to die, they clung to the belief that he would not die. But when they heard that he would die, they fumbled about not knowing what **a little while** (16:16) meant. He says, **you will weep and lament . . . but your sorrow will turn into joy** (16:21). Then after he showed them that **joy** comes after **sorrow**, that **sorrow** creates **joy**, and that **sorrow** is short lived but the pleasure is unending, he arrives at a common example. What does he say? **When a woman is in travail, she has sorrow** (16:21). He has used a parable that the prophets also use continually when they compare grief to the pains of childbirth. What he means is this: **travails** will seize you, but the pains of childbirth produce **joy**. In this way he validates his works about the resurrection and shows that leaving from here is similar to being born and coming into the radiant light. It is as if he had said, "Do not be surprised that I lead you through such sorrow to what is advantageous for you. Even a mother to become a mother passes similarly through sorrow. In this he hints at a mystery. He has destroyed the pangs of death and has caused a new **man** to be born (16:21).[2] He did not say that the **anguish** alone will pass away, but that **she no longer remembers** it (16:21). The **joy** that comes next is that great. So also it will be for those who are holy. However the woman does not rejoice because **a man** has come **into the world**, but because a child has been born to her. If she rejoiced because **a man** was born **into the world**, nothing would have prevented even barren women from rejoicing over another woman who bears a child. Why does he speak in this way? He puts this example forward for this reason only: to show that **sorrow** is for a brief time but **joy** is everlasting, and to show that death is changed into life, and to show the great reward for their travails. He did not say "a child has been born," but **a man**. It seems to me that he is hinting here at his own resurrection and that he is about to be brought **into the world**, not of death, but of the kingdom. Therefore, he did not say, "a child has been born to her," but **a man is born into the world** (16:21).

(13) John Chrysostom

Christ says, **I will see you again and your hearts will rejoice, and no one will take your joy from you** (16:22). There is much comfort in this brief saying, but what does the phrase **joy that no one will take from you** (16:22) mean? If you have money, many are able to **take** away **your joy** that comes from your wealth. For example, a thief can burrow through your wall, a servant can carry off what was entrusted to him, and an emperor can confiscate it, and the envious man can take your **joy** by insolence. . . . If you have physical strength,

---

2. John Chrysostom notices that the noun shifts in verse 21 from *child* (Greek = paidion) to *man* (Greek = anthropos). While this shift is not usually captured in English translations, such as the RSV used above, it must be noted to make sense of what John Chrysostom is arguing, namely, that true **joy** is found only in the fact that **a man**—Jesus Christ—**is born into the world** (16:21).

the onslaught of disease can destroy any **joy** from your body. If you are beautiful and attractive, old age causes it to fade and takes away that **joy**. If you enjoy an extravagant table, the **joy** of the meal comes to an end when evening arrives. Everything connected to this life is subject to destruction and is not able to give us lasting pleasure; however, piety and the virtue of the soul are the opposite of this. If you have done a charitable act, no one is able to **take** away that good work. Even if an army, kings, or thousands of enemies or traitors were to attack you from every side, they could not take away this possession once it has been deposited in heaven. The **joy** from that lasts forever, as it is written, *He scatters abroad, he gives to the poor; his righteousness endures forever* (2 Cor 9:9; cf. Ps 112:9). This is certainly right, for it is deposited in the storehouses of *heaven, where neither moth consumes and where thieves do not break in and steal* (Matt 6:20). If you offer heartfelt prayers continually, no one will be able to deprive you of the fruits of them, for their produce is stored in the heavens. It is secured from all injury and remains beyond the reach of those who are mortal. If you have done a benevolent action when you were treated poorly, if you have patiently endured listening to others slander you, if you have given blessings in exchange for contempt, these are the good works that last forever: **no one will take their joy from them** (16:22).

(14) Augustine of Hippo

Up to this point it seems easy to understand everything we have been discussing in this section of the gospel; now, however, we will need to pay much closer attention to the words that follow. What does Christ mean by the words: **In that day you will ask nothing of me** (16:23)? The verb **ask** means both "to request" and "to question." . . . We read that after the Lord Christ rose again, he was both questioned and petitioned. On the night before he ascended into heaven, his disciples **asked** when he would reveal himself and when the *kingdom of Israel* would come (Acts 1:6). Then, after he was already in heaven, Saint Stephen **asked** him to *receive his spirit* (Acts 7:59). Who would dare to say or even think that Christ should not be **asked** while he is sitting in heaven since he certainly was while living on earth? Or that as an immortal, he should not be asked, but while mortal, he should be? Dear friends, let us **ask** him to untie the knot of this puzzle by shining in our hearts so that we might understand what he means.

I do not think that the words **but I will see you again and your hearts will rejoice, and no one will take your joy from you** (16:22) refer to the time of his resurrection and to the time when he allowed his flesh to be examined and touched (cf. John 20:19–29). These words are connected to what he had already said: *He who loves me will be loved by my Father, and I will love him and manifest myself to him* (14:21). When the apostle John, who wrote this gospel, said in his epistle, *Beloved, we are God's children now; it does not yet appear what we shall be, but we know that when he appears we shall be like him, for we shall see him as he is* (1 John 3:2), Christ had already risen, had already revealed himself to them in the flesh, and had already taken his seat at the right hand of the Father. It follows then that this vision refers to the life to come, not to this life; it is not a temporal vision but an eternal one. Life himself says clearly: *And this is eternal life, that they know* *you, the only true God, and Jesus Christ whom you have sent* (17:3). Regarding this vision and knowledge, the apostle Paul says: *For now we see in a mirror dimly, but then face to face. Now I know in part; then I shall understand fully, even as I have been fully understood* (1 Cor 13:12). . . . In this way I think the following words are better understood: **A little while, and you will see me no more; again a little while, and you will see me** (16:16). The whole span of this present age extends for **a little while.** For this reason, John the Evangelist says in his epistle, *It is the last hour* (1 John 2:18). In the same way, he also added, *Because I go to the Father* (16:9). This statement is connected to the preceding clause where he says, **A little while, and you will see me no more** (16:16). It is not connected to the clause that follows, where he says, **Again a little while, and you will see me** (16:16). Because he *goes to the Father* (16:9), they would not see him anymore. In this way, these words do not mean that he was about to die and be hidden from their sight until his resurrection. Instead, it means that he was about to *go to the Father* (16:9) which he did after his resurrection. Indeed, after he had spoken with them for forty days, he ascended into heaven (Acts 1:10–11). Therefore, he spoke the words **a little while, and you will see me no more** (16:16) to those who saw him at that time in his bodily form. Since he was about to *go to the Father* (16:9), they would not see him again in his mortal form that they beheld when he was speaking with them. Thus, he promised to the entire church that **again a little while, and you will see me** (16:16). Likewise, he promised: *Lo, I am with you always, to the close of the age* (Matt 28:20). *The Lord is not slow* in fulfilling his promise (cf. 2 Pet 3:9): **a little while,** and we will see him. Then, we will no longer have to **ask** for anything (16:23). We will not have to ask anything, because nothing will be left to desire and nothing will remain hidden. This **little while** seems to us to be long because it is still unfolding. When it reaches its end, we will then understand what **a little while** it actually was. Do not let our **joy** be like the world's, about which it is said, **the world will rejoice** (16:20). And do not let our **sorrow** that comes from the **travails** (16:21) of these desires be removed from the **joy** (cf. 16:21), but as the apostle Paul says, *Rejoice in your hope, be patient in tribulation* (Rom 12:12). For even the **woman** who is in **travail** (16:21), to whom we are compared, experiences more **joy** over the **child** who is to come than **sorrow** over her present **anguish** (16:21).

(15) Gregory the Great

The evangelist says, **If you ask anything of the Father, he will give it to you in my name. Hitherto you have asked nothing in my name** (16:23–24). If the Father gives us all that we ask in the Son's name, why is it that Paul petitioned the Lord *three times* and was not found worthy to be heard (cf. 2 Cor 12:8)? Instead, he was told, *My grace is sufficient for you, for my power is made perfect in weakness* (2 Cor 12:9). Is it possible that Paul—so exceptional a preacher—did not ask in the Son's **name**? Why did he not receive what he asked for? How is it then true that whatever we ask in the Son's **name** the Father gives us, if the apostle asked in the Son's **name** that *a messenger of Satan* (2 Cor 12:7) be taken from him, and yet he did not receive what he asked for? Because the Son's name is Jesus, and Jesus means "Savior" or "salvation." Anyone who asks therefore in the Savior's name asks him for what is connected to true salvation. If what he asks for is not related to obtaining salvation, then the Father is not asked in Jesus's name. Therefore, the Lord says to his apostles who were still weak: **Hitherto you have asked nothing in my name** (16:24). If he would have spoken directly, he would have said, "You, who do not know how to seek eternal salvation, do not ask in the name of 'Salvation.'" This is why even Paul is not heard. If he had been set free from this temptation, it would not help him obtain salvation.

Dear friends, notice how many have gathered for the martyr's feast.[3] You bend your knees, beat your chests, raise your voices in prayer and confession, and you wet your faces with tears, but I beg you to consider your petitions carefully. Make certain that you ask in Jesus's name; that is, that you pray for the joys of eternal salvation. If you pray for temporal things in the eternal temple, you do not appropriately seek Jesus in Jesus's house. Pay attention! One man seeks a wife in his prayers, another asks for a villa, still another asks for clothes, and yet another asks that food be given to him. Certainly when these things are lacking, we should request them from the Almighty God. But we should always remember what we learn from the commandment of our redeemer: *Seek first his kingdom and his righteousness, and all these things shall be yours as well* (Matt 6:33). To ask for these things from Jesus is not wrong unless they are sought in excess. What is much more serious is that one demands the death of his enemy and pursues with prayer the one he cannot chase with his sword. But the one who is cursed with this evil petition lives, and the one who curses him is found guilty of desiring his death, for God commands that we should *love our enemies* (cf. Matt 5:44), and yet God is asked to kill this enemy. Whoever prays in this way fights against the Creator in his very prayers! Therefore, it is said—as pertaining to Judas—*let his prayer be counted as sin!* (Ps 109:7). Obviously the sinful prayer is the one that asks for the very thing which the one being asked has prohibited.

John 16:25–33

[25]"I have said this to you in figures; the hour is coming when I shall no longer speak to you in figures but tell you plainly of the Father. [26]In that day you will ask in my name; and I do not say to you that I shall pray the Father for you; [27]for the Father himself loves you, because you have loved me and have believed that I came from the Father. [28]I came from the Father and have come into the world; again, I am leaving the world and going to the Father." [29]His disciples said, "Ah, now you are speaking plainly, not in any figure! [30]Now we know that you know all things, and need none to question you; by this we believe that you came from God." [31]Jesus answered them, "Do you now believe? [32]The hour is coming, indeed it has come, when you will be scattered, every man to his home, and will leave me alone; yet I am not alone, for the Father is with me. [33]I have said this to you, that in me you may have peace. In the world you have tribulation; but be of good cheer, I have overcome the world."

---

3. Gregory the Great is very likely referencing the feast day of May 12, which was held in honor of Saint Pancras (also known as Saint Pancratius). Pancras was a fourteen-year-old boy who was martyred near Rome in AD 304 during the Great Persecution ordered by the Emperor Diocletian.

16:25 "The hour is coming when I shall no longer speak to you in figures but tell you plainly of the Father."

---

(16) Cyril of Alexandria

I have said this to you in figures; the hour is coming when I shall no longer speak to you in figures but tell you plainly of the Father (16:25). He says that **figures** are words that are both opaque and hidden and that those who hear them cannot easily understand them, for they are shrouded by very subtle obscurities. Indeed, this is the outline of what is said in **figures**. He says, "What I have said to you then, I have uttered only in **figures** and in riddles. I have kept the unveiling of these for the proper time which has not yet come. But he says, **the hour is coming**. That is the time when I will describe the Father's glory in plain language and implant in you a knowledge that is above human understanding" (cf. Phil 4:7). He did not tell them precisely when this would be. We should suppose that he will reveal that time either when we have been enriched with the knowledge given through the Spirit which Christ supplies to us after his resurrection from the dead or when we will see the glory of God clearly and distinctly after the end of the world when he gives us the purest knowledge about himself. Accordingly, Paul says that *prophecies will pass away and knowledge will cease* (1 Cor 13:8). He means nothing more than what we have already learned presently: *For now we see in a mirror dimly*, and *we know in part* (1 Cor 13:12), as we just said. *But when the perfect comes, the imperfect will pass away* (1 Cor 13:10). I will explain how and in what way this will happen.

At night, the beautiful light of the stars shines brightly, for each casts forth its own light. But when the sun rises with its full radiance, then the light which is *in part* disappears and the brightness of the stars grows weak and ineffective. In the same way, I think that the knowledge we possess now will cease and that which is *in part* will drop away at that moment when the perfect light will enter into us and shine forth and fill us completely with the knowledge of God. Then we are able to approach God, for Christ will speak to us **plainly of the Father** (16:25). Now with difficulty we stumble along the path of dim knowledge due to the weakness of our minds, following only shadows, patterns, images, and **figures** drawn from our experiences here. However, at that time there will be no need for any type, riddle, or parable, but we will see the vision of the divine nature of God the Father *face to face* (1 Cor 13:12) and with a mind that is set free, since we have already seen the glory of the one who proceeded from the Father. According to John, *We shall see him as he is* (1 John 3:2). Now we know his divine glory in human flesh. But when the time of his incarnation is complete and the mystery of our redemption is wholly finished, then we will see his own glory and the glory of God the Father. Since he is God by nature and is of the same substance with his Father, he will certainly have equal honors with him and will shine in his full divine glory.

16:31–33 "The hour is coming, indeed it has come, when you will be scattered. . . . I have said this to you, that in me you may have peace."

---

(17) Augustine of Hippo

I have said this to you, that in me you may have peace. In the world you have tribulation; but be of good cheer, I have overcome the world (16:33). The beginning of their **tribulation** is found in what he had said to them earlier. To prove that they were children who still lacked intelligence and who mistakenly took one thing for another and that to them all the wondrous and divine things that he had said were little more than figures, he said: **Do you now believe? The hour is coming, indeed it has come, when you will be scattered, every man to his home** (16:31–32). Pay attention! This was the beginning of their **tribulation** but not the sort that would last. By adding the words, **and will leave me alone** (16:32), he shows that they would not have the same character in the **tribulation** to follow. They would not abandon him while enduring the **tribulation in the world** after his ascension. Instead, by abiding in him, they had peace. When he was arrested, they abandoned his body physically and their faith mentally. It is in reference to this that he says: **Do you now believe? The hour is coming, indeed it has come, when you will be scattered, every man to his home and will leave me alone** (16:31–32). It is as if he had said: "You will be so shaken that you will abandon even what you now believe." They experienced such despair and such a death, so to speak, of their earlier faith that Cleopas, for example, did not know that he was speaking with Christ after his resurrection. Instead he narrated what had happened to Christ when he said, *But we had hoped that he was the one to redeem Israel* (Luke 24:21).

This was how they had abandoned him. They had left behind even the faith by which they had previously believed in him. But in the **tribulation** which they experienced after his glorification and after they themselves had received the Holy Spirit, they did not abandon him. Although they ran from city to city, they did not run away from him. While experiencing **tribulation in the world** (16:33), they had **peace** in him. Instead of fleeing from him, they found refuge in him. After receiving the Holy Spirit, the very thing that was said to them was actually realized: **Be of good cheer, I have overcome the world** (16:33). They had **good cheer**, and they **overcame**. In whom, except in Christ? He would not have **overcome the world**, if it were still able to **overcome** his followers. For this reason, the apostle says, *Thanks be to God, who gives us the victory*. Then, he adds immediately, *through our Lord Jesus Christ* (1 Cor 15:57) who himself had said to those who belonged to him: **Be of good cheer, I have overcome the world** (16:33).

(18) Cyril of Alexandria

I have said this to you, that in me you may have peace. In the world you have tribulation; but be of good cheer, I have overcome the world (16:33). In this statement Christ usefully sums up his discourses with them. He compresses the meaning of what he had said into a few words and reveals his plan to them concisely. He says, "I have spoken these words to you to urge you to **have peace in me** and so that you will know for certain that troubles will befall you **in the world** and you will encounter many **tribulations** on account of me. But you will not be conquered by these dangers that surround you, for **I have overcome the world** (16:33).

In order to make what I say as clear as possible for you, let me first explain what it means to **have peace** in Christ (16:33). **The world** and those who love the things of this world are at peace with each other, but they do not **have peace** in Christ. For example, degenerate lovers of bodily pleasures are most dear and pleasing to those who share the same character. The one who desires wealth that does not belong to him becomes greedy and rapacious for this reason and will be acceptable to those who practice similar vices. As it is written, *Every creature loves its own kind; a man clings to one like himself* (Sir 13:15–16). But in each of these cases, the solemn name of **peace** is corrupted. This proverb is certainly true, but it is true in a different way for those who are holy. Sin is not the bond of **peace**! *Faith, hope, love* (cf. 1 Cor 13:13) and the power of piety toward God are! This is **peace** in Christ! It has been revealed that **peace** in Christ is the very highest good for us. **Peace** is connected intimately with brotherly love for each other. Paul says that love is the fulfillment of every divine law (cf. Gal 5:14). The highest love of God will come to those who love one another, just as John says: "If someone loves his brother, undoubtedly he will love God" (cf. 1 John 4:20–21).

I think he points out something else when he says, **In the world you have tribulation; but be of good cheer, I have overcome the world** (16:33). If anyone prefers to understand these words in a simple way, he will say that Christ revealed himself to be stronger and more powerful than every sin and worldly obstacle and that since Christ has conquered, he will give the power to conquer to those who attempt such things for his sake. But if anyone wishes to contemplate a more mysterious meaning of these words, he might reflect in the following way: Since the incarnate Christ came back to life again for us and on our behalf, we have overcome corruption and death in this way. His own resurrection was the beginning of the victory over death. The power of this act will extend also to us because the one that overcame death was one of us. As we overcome sin which completely died in Christ first, he gives us every good thing as his children. For this reason, we should **be of good cheer** because we shall overcome **the world** (16:33). Christ, as a human, **overcame** it for our sake. In this way he became the *Beginning* (Col 1:18), the **Gate** (10:9), and the **Way** (14:6) for the human race. We who previously had fallen and were conquered have now overcome and conquered through him who conquered as one of us and for our sake. If he conquered as God, to us it is nothing; but if he conquered as a human, we conquered in him. To us he is the second Adam who has come from heaven according to the Scriptures. Therefore, *just as we have borne the image of the man of dust* and according to this likeness have fallen under the yoke of sin, similarly we also *bear the image of the man of heaven* (1 Cor 15:49), which is Christ. He conquered the tyranny of sin and triumphed over every **tribulation** of this **world**; indeed, Christ **has overcome the world** (16:33).

John 17

Augustine of Hippo and Hilary of Poitiers recognize that the term "glorify" resonates with various tones in the Gospel of John. Simultaneously it can refer to the Son's essence that he shares with the Father and to the proclamation of God's splendor in the world. Yet the word "glorify" receives its deepest and loveliest expressions of timbre Christ's passion draws near. This chapter opens with the following declaration: Father, the hour has come; glorify thy Son that the Son may glorify thee *(17:1). Augustine and Hilary state that the phrase* glorify thy Son *refers to the Father's glorification of Christ in his passion and resurrection. Augustine notes that since the Son was glorified by the Father through his exaltation, he glorifies the* Father *through the proclamation of his resurrection and the dissemination of his holy name among the gentiles.*

John Chrysostom and Hilary offer an interpretation that highlights yet another nuance of the term "glorification" in this gospel. I glorified thee on earth, having accomplished the work which thou gavest me to do; and now, Father, glorify thou me in thy own presence with the glory which I had with thee before the world was made *(17:4–5). Certainly the Son glorifies the Father by fulfilling all* the work *of the divine economy, from his incarnation to his death to his resurrection. However, the attention of the church fathers is drawn by Christ's request:* Glorify thou me in thy own presence with the glory which I had with thee before the world was made *(17:5). Here* glory *refers to the fullness of divinity which he shared with the Father and the Holy Spirit before he humbled himself and took on human flesh. John Chrysostom and Hilary conclude that he is not requesting to be restored to that original state, for his hypostatic union with the flesh and its subsequent glorification at his resurrection bound him intimately with humanity. Instead, he prays that his human nature—and therefore ours—may be elevated and glorified to that divine state which he shared with the Godhead* before the world was made *(17:5).*

Origen of Alexandria concludes from the words All mine are thine, and thine are mine, and I am glorified in them *(17:10) that the Father and Son share one essence. It follows then that what belongs to the one belongs to the others. Cyril of Alexandria offers a slightly different interpretation. He argues that this verse emphasizes Christ's oneness with the Father in respect to his divinity and Christ's oneness with us in his humanity. Next, Cyril expands this idea by examining the subsequent verse:* And now I am no more in the world, but they are in the world, and I am coming to thee. Holy Father, keep them in thy name, which thou hast given me, that they may be one, even as we are one *(17:11)*. *Since Christ willingly underwent his descent into the flesh and ultimately death for us, he shares a union with us forged in love. So intimate is his union with us that we are said to be "members of one body" according to the apostle Paul. Christ prays that we may be bound to one another and to himself in love and that we may share the same will. Hilary's attention is not drawn to our unity with one another and with Christ; rather, he notes that Christ asks the Father to* keep *(17:11) and guard those who belong to him. Why? He is about to undergo his passion, death, and resurrection and worries about those whom the Father has* given *him.*

Leo the Great is incredulous that Judas, the son of perdition *(17:12), would exchange the riches he had as a follower of Christ for thirty pieces of silver (Matt 26:13). In fact, he sold the redeemer who was about to purchase back everyone from death—even Judas himself!— with his precious blood. Cyril of Alexandria is quick to point out that Judas was doomed by his own choice. If interpreted wrongly, the clause* that the scripture might be fulfilled *(17:12) might suggest that Judas's betrayal of the Son of Man was foreordained and determined by the will of God. Cyril emphatically states that scripture is the Word of God. While it announces beforehand what it knows because God is omniscient, Cyril concludes: "The foreknowledge and the proclamation of the future does not indicate either the will or decree of God. Rather, the prophecy was uttered to avert this. When Judas received this knowledge, he could have rejected and avoided this evil if he had wished, for he was free to choose a different outcome." For this reason, Judas was fully culpable for his betrayal of the Lord.*

I consecrate myself, that they also may be consecrated in truth *(17:19). Ambrose of Milan states that when Christ says,* I consecrate myself, *he is speaking of his assumption of human flesh. Certainly it could not refer to his divine nature, for that was already consecrated by its essence and subject to no enhancement. John Chrysostom says that Christ consecrated himself in his sacrificial death. Through the death of his flesh and its subsequent resurrection, he reconciles the flesh and the spirit and sanctifies all those who are in Christ.*

Augustine of Hippo examines the words of one of Christ's prayers: I do not pray for these only, but also for those who believe in me through their word *(17:20). This request includes the disciples and those who would come to believe in Christ through* their word. *Augustine states that this includes himself and all those in his congregation, and it extends logically to the present day, for all Christians have come to believe in Christ* through their word. *Augustine, however, recognizes that this prayer seemingly excludes many who were said to have believed in Christ. This is an illustrious list: Nathanael, Joseph of Arimathea, his mother Mary, and others who were not with him in the garden of Gethsemane. It includes still others who previously confessed their faith in him: Simeon, Anna, Zechariah, Elizabeth, and John the Baptist. Augustine concludes that Christ did not pray for them at this time because they did not believe through the word of the disciples but through the Word himself. For what does* through their word *mean except that they believed through the gospel of the Lord?*

Augustine's attention is drawn to yet another petition from the Lord's prayer in Gethsemane: Father, I desire that they also, whom thou hast given me, may be with me where I am, to behold my glory which thou hast given me in thy love for me before the foundation of the world *(17:24). He asks what the phrase* may be with me where I am *could mean. What does the present tense convey? Augustine posits that Christ is speaking here of his eternity, not his humanity. He speaks from a heavenly perspective, since as God he never ceased being there. In fact, as God, he is omnipresent. To demonstrate this principle, Augustine cites the Lord's gracious interaction with the thief on the cross in the Gospel of Luke. Upon hearing his confession, the Lord said to him: "Today you will be with me in Paradise" (Luke 23:43). On that very day Christ's own soul was to harrow hell and his body was to be in the tomb. But in respect to his divine nature, he was also in paradise. So here the Lord prayed,* I desire that they also, whom thou hast given me, may be with me where I am, to behold my glory *(17:24).*

John 17:1-8

[1]When Jesus had spoken these words, he lifted up his eyes to heaven and said, "Father, the hour has come; glorify thy Son that the Son may glorify thee, [2]since thou hast given him power over all flesh, to give eternal life to all whom thou hast given him. [3]And this is eternal life, that they know thee the only true God, and Jesus Christ whom thou hast sent: [4]I glorified thee on earth, having accomplished the work which thou gavest me to do; [5]and now, Father, glorify thou me in thy own presence with the glory which I had with thee before the world was made. [6]I have manifested thy name to the men whom thou gavest me out of the world; thine they were, and thou gavest them to me, and they have kept thy word. [7]Now they know that everything that thou hast given me is from thee; [8]for I have given them the words which thou gavest me, and they have received them and know in truth that I came from thee; and they have believed that thou didst send me."

17:1 "Father, the hour has come; glorify thy Son that the Son may glorify thee."

---

(1) Hilary of Poitiers

The Lord said, **Father, the hour has come** (17:1). He revealed **the hour** of his passion, for he spoke these words at that very moment. Next he added, **Glorify thy Son** (17:1). But how was the **Son glorified**? He was born of a virgin. From infancy through childhood, he grew into a man. He lived a human life of sleep, hunger, thirst, weariness, and tears. Even now he was spat upon, scourged, and crucified. Why? All these things happened to prove the humanity of Christ. But the disgrace of the cross is not shared by us. We are not sentenced to be scourged. We are not defiled by spit. The **Father glorifies the Son**. How? He is nailed to the cross. What happened next? The sun, instead of setting, hid! How did this happen? It did not withdraw behind a cloud but abandoned its ordinary course. Every part of the world experienced the same shock of the death of Christ. In order to avoid being complicit in this crime, the stars extinguished themselves so that they would not witness this event. What did the earth do? It trembled beneath the weight of the Lord hanging on the tree, proclaiming that it was powerless to hold the one who was dying. . . .

What happened next? The centurion of the cohort, the guardian of the cross, cries out, *Truly, this was the Son of God!* (Matt 27:54). Creation itself is set free by the reconciliation of this sin offering. Even the rocks lose their solidity and strength. Those who nailed him to the cross confess that this is *truly the Son of God.* The result confirms this proclamation. The Lord had said, **Glorify thy Son** (17:1). By the insertion of the word **thy**, he had proclaimed that he was God's **Son** not only in name but also in nature. Many of us are sons of God, but he is the **Son** in another sense. He is God's true and only Son, by generation not by adoption, in truth not only in name, born not created. After he was **glorified**, that confession of his true nature followed. The centurion confessed that he was the true *Son of God* (Matt 27:54) so that no believer could doubt what even a servant of his persecutors was unable to deny.

(2) John Chrysostom

Father, the hour has come; glorify thy Son that the Son may glorify thee (17:1). He shows us once again that he goes to the cross willingly. How could the one who prayed that this should occur and who called this deed glorification for himself, the crucified, and also for his Father, be unwilling? Since this was the case, not only the Son but also the Father was **glorified**. Before the crucifixion, the Jews did not even know him. Scripture says, *Israel has not known me* (Isa 1:3 LXX). But after the crucifixion, the entire world ran to him.

(3) Augustine of Hippo

The glorification of the Son by the Father is understood in this way: that the Father did not *spare his own Son but gave him up for us all* (Rom 8:32). But if we say that he was **glorified** by his passion, how much more was he **glorified** by his resurrection! In his passion his humility is emphasized more than his **glory.** The apostle Paul testifies to this when he says, Christ *humbled himself and became obedient unto death, even death on a cross* (Phil 2:8). But then he speaks about his glorification: *Therefore God has highly exalted him and bestowed on him the name which is above every name, that at the name of Jesus every knee should bow, in heaven and on earth and under the earth, and every tongue confess that Jesus Christ is Lord, to the glory of God the Father* (Phil 2:9–11). The glorification of our Lord Jesus Christ begins with his resurrection. . . .

He was first humbled by his passion in order that the *mediator between God and men, the man Christ Jesus* (1 Tim 2:5) might be made lustrous or glorious by his resurrection. If he had not died, he would not have risen from the dead. Humility secures **glory,** and **glory** is the reward of humility. However, he accomplished this in *the form of a servant* (Phil 2:8). But his glory will be forever, for he was always in the form of God. . . . He not only said, **Father, glorify thy Son,** but also added, **that the Son may glorify thee** (17:1). It is worth asking how the **Son glorified the Father,** for the eternal **glory** of the **Father** did not experience any lessening in human form nor was he able to experience any increase in his divine perfection. The **glory** of the **Father** itself is not able to decrease or increase;

however, among humans undoubtedly it was diminished when God was only *known in Judah* (Ps 76:1). Children did not yet *praise the name of the Lord from the sun's rising to its setting* (Ps 113:3 [112:3 LXX]). This indeed was accomplished through the gospel of Christ. The **Father** became known to the gentiles through the **Son**, and in this way the **Son glorified the Father**. If the **Son** had only died and not risen again, undoubtedly he would not have been **glorified** by the **Father** or have **glorified** him. But since he was **glorified** by the **Father** through his resurrection, he **glorifies** the **Father** through the proclamation of his resurrection. This is made clear in the very order of the words. He says, **Glorify thy Son that the Son may glorify thee** (17:1); this is just as if he had said, "Raise me up in order that through me you might be known by the whole world."

17:4–6 "I glorified thee on earth, having accomplished the work which thou gavest me to do; and now, Father, glorify thou me in thy own presence with the glory which I had with thee before the world was made. "I have manifested thy name to the men whom thou gavest me out of the world; thine they were, and thou gavest them to me, and they have kept thy word."

---

(4) Tertullian of Carthage

Previously, the name of God the Father had not been revealed to anyone. Even Moses, who asked him directly about this very matter, heard a different name (cf. Exod 3:13–16). But it has been revealed to us in the Son. When the Son came into existence, the new name of Father did as well. He says, *I have come in my Father's name* (5:43). Again, he says, *Father, glorify your name* (12:28). He declares more directly, **I have manifested thy name to men** (17:6). We also pray that this **name** may *be hallowed* (Matt 6:9). This does not mean that humans wish God well as if he were blessing another person or that he might suffer harm unless we do so. Clearly, it is wholly appropriate for God to be blessed in every place and time by humans whenever they remember his blessings. Indeed, this petition also brings us a blessing in turn. How can it be otherwise? Is the **name** of God not holy and *hallowed* in itself? He alone sanctifies all others. To him alone the retinue of angels unceasingly say, *Holy, holy, holy* (Isa 6:3; Rev 4:8). Similarly, we are also candidates for angelhood if we earn this reward.[1] On earth we begin to learn that heavenly proclamation and the devotion of our future glory.

This is true in respect to the glory of God. But in reference to our petition, *Hallowed be your name* (Matt 6:9), we ask the following: that his **name** may be *hallowed* in us who are in him and in all others for whom the grace of God is still waiting (cf. Isa 30:18), and that we may obey this precept which requires us to pray for all humans (cf. 1 Tim 2:1), even

---

1. Tertullian likely has in mind Ps 8:4–5: *What is man that thou art mindful of him, and the son of man that thou dost care for him? Yet thou hast made him little less than God, and dost crown him with glory and honor.* How are we crowned with such glory and honor? Through our union with Christ, we are sanctified and elevated to such a place (cf. Heb 2:7–11). Following this line of thinking, the apostle Paul says that in heaven we will be still higher than the angels: *Do you not know that we are to judge angels?* (1 Cor 6:3).

for our *enemies* (Matt 5:44). Therefore we do not say, "Hallowed be your name among us," but say confidently, "among all humans."

(5) Hilary of Poitiers

The Son **glorifies** the Father wholly and completely in the following words: **I glorified thee on earth, having accomplished the work which thou gavest me to do** (17:4). Praise of the Father comes completely from the Son. All the praise bestowed on the Son is actually praise of the Father, for he **accomplished** everything that the Father willed. The Son of God is born as a man, but the power of God is found in the virgin birth. The Son of God is seen as man, but God is present in his human actions. The Son of God is nailed to the cross, but God conquers human death on that cross. Christ, the Son of God, dies, but flesh itself is made alive in Christ. The Son of God is in hell, but humanity is restored to heaven. The praise Christ receives from us for these **works** is bestowed proportionally on the one with whom Christ's Godhead exists. These are the ways in which the Father **glorifies** the Son **on earth**. Through his works of power in the sight of the impious and the foolish world, the Son reciprocally reveals the one from whom he receives his being. . . . The Father is **glorified on earth**, because **the work** which he commanded had been **accomplished**.

Let us next examine what sort of **glory** the Son expects to receive from the Father and then our exposition will be complete. The text continues: **I glorified thee on earth, having accomplished the work which thou gavest me to do; and now, Father, glorify thou me in thy own presence with the glory which I had with thee before the world was made. I have manifested thy name to the men** (17:4–6). The Father is **glorified** by the Son's **works**. The **Father** of the only-begotten is recognized as God. He willed that his Son should be born as a man from a virgin. From that beginning, everything was **accomplished** fully in his passion. The Son of God, who was completely perfect and born from the eternal fullness of the Godhead and who had become incarnate as a man and was ready for his death, prays now that he may be **glorified** with God even as he was **glorifying his Father** on the earth. At that very moment the divine powers were **glorified** in the flesh before the eyes of *the world which knew him not* (1:10). What is the **glory** which he requests from the Father? Of course, it is the **glory** which he had with the Father **before the world was made** (17:5). He possessed the fullness of the Godhead; he still possessed it because he is the Son of God. But the one who was the Son of God had also become the Son of Man, for *the Word became flesh* (1:14). He had not lost his former essence, but he had become what he was not before. He had not relinquished his former position, but he had taken ours. He prays that the nature which he had assumed may be elevated to the **glory** which he had not renounced. It follows then that since the Son is *the Word* (1:1), and *the Word became flesh* (1:14), and *the Word was God* (1:1), and he *was in the beginning with God* (1:2), and **the Word** was the Son *before the foundation of the world* (17:24), this Son, who is now incarnate, prayed that the flesh might be to the Father what the Word was. He prayed that the flesh, although born in time, might receive the splendor of the everlasting **glory** and that the corruption of the flesh might be swallowed up (cf. 1 Cor 15:54) and be transformed by the power of God and the purity of the Spirit. This is his prayer to God: the Son's acknowledgment of the Father and his appeal on behalf of the flesh. This is the very flesh in which all will see him on that day of judgment: flesh which is pierced and bears the marks of the cross. It is also that flesh in which he ascended into heaven and is seated at the right hand of God, the very flesh which Paul saw (cf. Acts 16:13–16) and Stephen worshiped (cf. Acts 7:55–56).

(6) John Chrysostom

I glorified thee on earth (17:4). Rightly, he said, **on earth**. In heaven, he had already been **glorified** since he possessed glory naturally and was worshiped by the angels. Therefore, here Christ does not speak of that glory which is connected to his essence—for he possesses that glory completely, even if none **glorify** him—but instead he speaks of that glory which comes from the worship of humans. . . . In order that you may understand in what way he speaks about that glory, listen to what follows: **I have accomplished the work which thou gavest me to do** (17:4). But the deed was still just beginning or had not yet begun, so how then did he say, **I have accomplished [the work]** (17:4)? Either he means that he has finished all his deeds; or he is speaking about what is to come as if it had already happened; or, as is most likely, it is said that everything had already been **accomplished** because the foundation of blessings from which the benefits would necessarily follow and his participation in the very events that were about to take place had been established.[2] For this reason, he says, **which thou gavest me to do** (17:4). He is referencing his condescension. If he had waited to hear and learn [what he was to do], it would have fallen far short of his divine glory. That he arrived at this of his own accord is clear from many passages. For example, Paul says, *Christ loved us and gave himself up for us* (Eph 5:2); and, *He emptied himself, taking the form of a servant* (Phil 2:7); and also, *As the Father has loved me, so have I loved you* (15:9).

And now, Father, **glorify thou me in thy own presence with the glory which I had with thee before the world was made** (17:5). Where is that **glory**? Understandably, he was not honored because of the fleshly garment which enveloped him, so how does he seek to be **glorified** with the Father? What is he saying here? Since his fleshly nature had not yet been **glorified**, not yet experienced incorruption, and not yet shared the kingly throne, his statement refers to his divine economy. Therefore, he did not say, "on earth," but **with thee**.

John 17:9–13

[9]**"I am praying for them; I am not praying for the world but for those whom thou hast given me, for they are thine;** [10]**all mine are thine, and thine are mine, and I am glorified in them.** [11]**And now I am no more in the world, but they are in the world, and I am coming to thee. Holy Father, keep them in thy name, which thou hast given**

---

2. John Chrysostom is connecting **work** with Christ's crucifixion, death, and resurrection, which temporally speaking was yet to come, although Christ's glorification had in a sense begun as they embarked on his final night and entered the garden of Gethsemane.

me, that they may be one, even as we are one. [12]While I was with them, I kept them in thy name, which thou hast given me; I have guarded them, and none of them is lost but the son of perdition, that the scripture might be fulfilled. [13]But now I am coming to thee; and these things I speak in the world, that they may have my joy fulfilled in themselves."

17:10 "All mine are thine, and thine are mine, and I am glorified in them."

---

(7) Origen of Alexandria

In order that you might understand that the omnipotence of Father and Son is one and the same, just as God and Lord[3] are one and the same with the Father, listen to John speaking similarly in the Apocalypse: *Thus says the Lord God, who is and who was and who is to come, the Almighty* (Rev 1:8). Who other than Christ is the one *who is to come*? Just as no one should be offended that the Savior is also called *God*, so also no one should be offended that the Son of God is called *Almighty* when the Father is also called *Almighty*. For in this way, what he says to the Father is true: **All mine are thine, and thine are mine, and I am glorified in them** (17:10). If everything which is the Father's is also Christ's, it is certain that the Father's omnipotence is counted among those things. Certainly, the only-begotten Son should also be called *Almighty* in order that the Son may possess all the things which the Father has. He says, **I am glorified in them.** Truly, *at the name of Jesus every knee should bow, in heaven and on earth and under the earth, and every tongue confess that Jesus Christ is Lord, to the glory of God the Father* (Phil 2:10–11). Therefore, it follows that he is *pure emanation of the glory* of God, because he is *Almighty* and the pure and illustrious Wisdom of God, the *emanation* of omnipotence or glory.

So that you may understand even more clearly what the glory of his omnipotence is, we will add the following: God the Father is *Almighty*, because he has power over **all**, that is over the heaven and earth, sun, moon, stars, and all things in them. He rules over them through his Word, because *at the name of Jesus every knee* of those *in heaven, on earth, and under the earth should bow* (cf. Phil 2:10). If *every knee should bow* to Jesus, then, undoubtedly **all** things are subjected to Jesus. He exercises power over **all**, and it is through him that **all** things are subjected to the Father. They are subjected not by force or by necessity but through wisdom, which is through both Word and reason. His glory therefore is found in this—that he possesses **all** things. This is the purest and brightest glory of his omnipotence: **all** things are subject to him not by force or necessity but by reason and wisdom.

---

3. Origen is treating the phrase "God and Lord" as referring explicitly to the Son (cf. John 20:28), not to the Father and the Son.

17:11-12 "And now I am no more in the world, but they are in the world, and I am coming to thee. Holy Father, keep them in thy name, which thou hast given me, that they may be one, even as we are one. While I was with them, I kept them in thy name, which thou hast given me; I have guarded them, and none of them is lost but the son of perdition, that the scripture might be fulfilled."

(8) Hilary of Poitiers

Each of the gospels completes what is lacking in the others. We learn some things from one, other things from another, and so on, because all are the proclamation of one Spirit. Therefore, John, who teaches about the Spirit in his gospel, preserves this prayer of the Lord on behalf of the apostles that the other gospels overlooked. Accordingly, Christ prayed: **Holy Father, keep them in thy name. . . . While I was with them, I kept them in thy name, which thou hast given me** (17:11-12). That prayer was for the benefit of his apostles, not for himself. He was not sorrowful for himself, but he urges them to pray so that they might not be tempted (cf. Matt 26:41). No angel is sent to him, although he could have called down twelve thousand angels from heaven if he desired (cf. Matt 26:53).[4] He was not afraid of death even when he was troubled to death. Certainly, he does not pray that *the cup* may pass over him, but that it *may pass away from* him (Matt 26:39). However, before it could *pass away from him*, it was necessary that he *drink* it (cf. Matt 26:42). The phrase *pass away* does not only mean to leave its place but also not to exist anymore at all. This definition is indicated in the language of the gospels and the epistles. For example, *Heaven and earth will pass away, but my words will not pass away* (Matt 24:35). The apostle Paul also says, *The old has passed away, behold, the new has come* (2 Cor 5:17); and also, *for the form of this world is passing away* (1 Cor 7:31). Therefore, *the cup*, about which he prays to the Father, cannot *pass away* unless it is drunk (cf. Matt 26:42). When he prays, he does so for those whom he **guarded, while** he **was with them** (17:12). He now entrusts them to the Father so that he may **keep them** (17:11). Since Christ was about to complete the mystery of his death, he asks the Father to **keep them** (17:11). If this incident about the appearance of *the angel* who was sent to him is true, it is certainly significant, for it clearly shows that his prayer was answered.[5] Accordingly, when Jesus finished his prayer, he urged the disciples to continue to sleep (cf. Matt 26:43-44).[6] John the Evangelist in the course of the passion recognizes that Jesus's command to sleep on was a result of his prayer. . . . Just previously he said that the apostles had escaped from the hands of the pursuers: *This was to fulfill the word which he had spoken, "Of those whom you gave me, I lost not one"* (18:9). He himself fulfills the petition of his prayer; all of them are saved. But he asks the Father to **keep them**, whom

4. The reference to the angels occurs at Matt 26:53, where the phrase is *twelve legions of angels*, not "twelve thousand angels." It is unclear from where Hilary derives this number.

5. The tradition of a visiting angel (Luke 22:43-44) does not occur in the earliest manuscripts, but is found in the Latin version used by Hilary.

6. It is unclear what Hilary is referring to. None of the canonical gospels record that Jesus commanded them to continue to sleep. If anything, Jesus seems exasperated that they cannot remain awake and watchful.

he has **guarded** in his own **name**. They are kept safe. Peter's faith does not fail. It shrunk back, but repentance followed immediately.

(9) Cyril of Alexandria

Holy Father, keep them in thy name, which thou hast given me, that they may be one, even as we are one (17:11). In every respect he upholds the blending of the two elements into a single entity. I am referring both to the human nature, which in our case possesses a humble status, and the divine element, which brings forth the highest of all glories. For this text represents a mingling of both. . . . The divine element neither soars wholly to the heights nor indeed does it attach itself completely with our level. He who became man is God; accordingly, he occupies, as it were, a middle position by an ineffable and indescribable union, since he has neither left the truly divine realm nor has he entirely abandoned the human one. His ineffable generation from God the Father raises him up to the divine nature and to the glory that naturally accompanies him since he is Word and only-begotten. His self-emptying lowers him down somewhat to our world, but this humiliation is not powerful enough to overwhelm by force, so to speak, the one who is the king of the universe together with the Father. The only-begotten could never be compelled to do anything that is against his will. Rather, he humbled himself and carried out this task according to his own will and his love for us . . . so he did all of this for us willingly. We would never have been called *sons* and *gods* (cf. Ps 82:6) by grace if the only-begotten had not undergone humiliation for us and on our behalf. When we are formed through participation in the Spirit to be like Christ, we are called *children of God* and *gods*. Therefore, when he says something that combines in some way the human with the divine, do not take offense at that and foolishly stop admiring the incomparably skillful way in which he has chosen his words, elegantly preserving for us in every way his dual character. We see the one who is truly God by nature speaking at the same time as a man. He brilliantly combines the humble nature of humanity with the glory of the divine nature, and he maintains an equality pertaining to both, in a way that is entirely blameless and free from any reproach. . . .

He says, **Holy Father, keep them in thy name, which thou hast given me, that they may be one, even as we are one** (17:11). He wants the disciples to be preserved by the power and authority of the ineffable nature. . . . In this way he glorifies his very nature in the person of the Father by whom he was begotten as God. That is why he says, **Keep them in thy name, which thou hast given me**, i.e., in the divine name. He says, moreover, that the **name** of divinity was given to him. This does not imply that he was not previously by nature God or that he was given the distinct honor of divinity. If so, he would then be adopted as we are and would possess false glory and fraudulent nature. We should not ever entertain this thought, for this idea would undermine that he is the Son by nature. But since, as the divine Scriptures proclaim, **the Word became flesh** (1:14), i.e., a human being, he says that he received what he already had as God. The **name** and reality of the divine glory could not belong to human nature. You should also consider and understand exactly how he showed himself to be the living and hypostatic power of God, through which the Father accomplishes all things. When addressing the Father, he says, **Keep them**. He was not content with these words but skillfully included himself as well . . . he says, **Keep them in thy name, which thou hast given me.** Do you see how carefully expressed this is? By assigning and attributing the supervision and providential care of us to the nature of the divinity—something wholly appropriate to divinity alone—he immediately asserts that divine glory was given to him because of the form of his human nature. He says that *the name which is above every name* (Phil 2:9) was something granted to him. Consequently, we say that those things which he receives as a human are in one sense the natural attributes of the Son since he is from the Father, but in another sense they are received in the form of a gift since he is human. For a human is not by nature God, but Christ is God by nature, even though we think about him in terms of our own makeup.

Nevertheless he wants the disciples to be kept in a state of unity by maintaining a like-mindedness and an identity of their will. He wants them to be mingled together, as it were, in soul and spirit and in the bond of peace and love for one another. He wishes them to be bound together tightly with an unbreakable chain of love so that they may advance to such a degree of unity that their freely chosen association might become an image of the natural unity that is known to exist between the Father and the Son. That is to say, he wishes them to enjoy a unity which is inseparable and indestructible and which cannot not be enticed away into a dissimilarity of wills by anything that exists in the world or any pursuit of pleasure, but rather preserves the power of love in the unity of devotion and holiness. And this is what actually happened. As we read in the Acts of the Apostles, *The company of those who believed were of one heart and soul* (Acts 4:32), that is, in the unity of the Spirit. This is also what Paul himself meant when he said, *one body and one spirit* (Eph 4:4), *We who are many are one body, for we all partake of the one bread* (1 Cor 10:17; cf. Rom 12:5), and we have all been anointed in the one Spirit of Christ (cf. 1 Cor 12:1f.). Therefore since they were members of the same body and fellow participants in one and the same Spirit, he wishes his disciples to be kept in a unity of spirit that can never be pried apart and in a oneness of mind that cannot be broken. If anyone should suppose that the disciples were united in the same way as the Father and the Son are one, not only according to essence but also in will—there is a single will in the divine nature and an identical purpose in every respect—let them think this. They will not stray outside the bounds of orthodoxy since an identity of will may be observed among those who are true Christians, even if our substance is not of the same kind as that which exists in the case of the Father and of God the Word, who is from him and in him.

(10) Cyril of Alexandria

He says that he **kept** his disciples and cared for them in such a way that **none of them is lost**, except the one whom he called **the son of perdition** (17:12). Judas was called this to indicate that he was doomed to destruction by his own choice or rather by his own wickedness and impiety. We should never think that the betrayer was caught as if in a net of a hunter or in the snare of the devil by a divine and unbreakable decree. Indeed, then he would have been blameless when he yielded to the judgment from above. Who can resist the judgment of God? But certainly he is guilty and cursed: *It would have been better for that man if he had not* *been born* (Matt 26:24). What is the reason? This wretched man was convicted and suffered this on account of his own choice and not from necessity. The one who was so in love with destruction is aptly named a **son of perdition** (17:12), because he was indebted to ruin and corruption and awaits the day of **perdition** which is filled with sorrow and lamentation.

Since Christ added the phrase **that the scripture might be fulfilled** (17:12) to his words about this traitor, we give the following interpretation which may prove useful to those who read it. The traitor was not lost because of anything said in **scripture**. It was because of his own vicious wickedness that he traded the precious blood of Christ for a few coins and betrayed his Lord. He was destined to destruction for this reason. The **scripture** announced in advance that this would happen because it does not lie. **Scripture** is the Word of God who knows all things and holds in his own mind the character and life of each of us from our beginning to the end. Likewise, the psalmist attributes to him omniscience of the past and the future when he speaks to him: *O Lord, you examined me and knew me. It was you who knew my sitting down and my rising up; it was you who discerned by thoughts from far away. My path and my miles you tracked and all my ways foresaw* (Ps 139:1–3 [138:1–3 LXX]). The divine Word, which possessed complete foreknowledge and saw the future as if it were already happening in addition to all the others things which it said about Christ, revealed to us that one of the disciples would perish as a traitor. The foreknowledge and the proclamation of the future does not indicate either the will or decree of God. Certainly, the prophecy did not necessitate the completion of this evil deed that was foretold or the conspiracy against the Savior. Rather, the prophecy was uttered to avert this. When Judas received this knowledge, he could have rejected and avoided this evil if he had wished, for he was free to choose a different outcome.

(11) Leo the Great

O most wicked man! You, who are a *seed of Canaan and not Judah* (Sus 56 [Dan 13:56]), are no longer a *chosen instrument* (Acts 9:15) but a **son of perdition** (17:12) and death! Did you think that the devil's enticements would be more profitable for you since you were inflamed with the fire of greed? Were you burning to gain *thirty pieces of silver* (Matt 26:13)? Did you not see what riches you would lose? Even if you did not trust the Lord's promises, why did you choose such a small amount of money compared to what you had already received? You were able to command the demons, you healed the sick, and you received honor along with the other apostles. And so that you might quench your avaricious thirst for profit, you were easily able to steal from the satchel. But your mind, which desired things that were forbidden, was more strongly enticed by those which were less lawful. The amount of money did not please you nearly as much as the enormity of the sin! Your heinous deal is not detestable only because you valued the Lord so cheaply but because you sold the redeemer! Yes, even your own! You did not even show pity to yourself. Rightly, your punishment was conducted by your own hands.[7] Certainly, no one was more cruelly inclined toward destroying you than yourself.

---

7. According to the Gospel of Matthew, Judas committed suicide by hanging himself (Matt 27:3–10).

John 17:14–19

[14]"I have given them thy word; and the world has hated them because they are not of the world, even as I am not of the world. [15]I do not pray that thou shouldst take them out of the world, but that thou shouldst keep them from the evil one. [16]They are not of the world, even as I am not of the world. [17]Sanctify them in the truth; thy word is truth. [18]As thou didst send me into the world, so I have sent them into the world. [19]And for their sake I consecrate myself, that they also may be consecrated in truth."

(12) Ambrose of Milan

Note the difference between the Godhead and the flesh. One and the same Son of God speaks in each nature, for both are present in him. However, while it is the same person who speaks, he does not always speak in the same way. Pay attention! Now the glory of God speaks; then the human. As God, he utters divine things, because he is the Word; as man, he declares human things, because he speaks in accordance with my own nature.

This is *the living bread which came down from heaven* (6:51). This bread is his flesh. He said, *The bread which I shall give for the life of the world is my flesh* (6:51). This is the one who **came down from heaven**. This is the one whom the Father has sanctified and sent to the world. Scripture itself teaches us that it was not the nature of the Godhead but that of the flesh that needed to be sanctified. The Lord himself said, **And for their sake I sanctify myself** (17:19), in order that you may know that he is sanctified in the flesh for us and sanctifies us by virtue of his divine nature.

(13) John Chrysostom

He says, **As thou didst send me into the world, so I have sent them into the world** (17:18). Paul says the same thing: *He entrusted the word of reconciliation to us* (2 Cor 5:19). They took possession of the **world** for the very same reason that Christ came to the **world**. In this verse the word **as** is not used to indicate a similarity between himself and the apostles but to show that they were **sent**. It was his general tendency to speak of the future as if it had already happened: **And for their sake I consecrate myself, that they also may be consecrated in truth** (17:19). What does the phrase **consecrate myself** mean? It means, "I offer you a sacrifice." All sacrifices are called holy (i.e., sanctified). Those things dedicated to God are rightly called holy. Formerly, a person was **consecrated** in sheep as a type, but now he is **consecrated** not in a type but **in truth** itself. Therefore, he says, **That they also may be consecrated in truth** (17:19). In other words, "Indeed, I dedicate them to you and present them as an offering." He was being made an offering as their head or because they were also sacrificed. Indeed, Scripture says, *Present your bodies as a living sacrifice, holy* (Rom 12:1), and *We are accounted as sheep for the slaughter* (Ps 44:22). He makes them, without actually dying, both a sacrifice and offering. It is clear that he was alluding to his own death when he said, **I consecrate myself**. . . . After he has spoken in this way about their salvation and how they were sanctified by faith and his own sacrifice, then he speaks of reconciliation. Finally, he ends his discourse the way he began it. For when he started this dialogue, he said, *A new commandment I give you* (13:34).

(14) Augustine of Hippo

When the Lord was speaking to the Father and praying for his disciples, he says, **I have given them thy word; and the world has hated them** (17:14). They had not yet experienced that sort of hatred in their own sufferings which would follow later. He speaks about this in his customary way: speaking of the future with words in the past tense. Then he adds the reason why they are hated by the world; he says, **Because they are not of the world, even as I am not of the world** (17:14). By rebirth this was given to them, for by birth they were **of the world**. . . . However, the Lord was never of the world even in respect to *his form of a servant* (Phil 2:7). He was born of the Holy Spirit from whom they also were reborn. If they were no longer **of the world** because they were reborn of the Holy Spirit, it follows that he was never **of the world**, because he was born of the Holy Spirit.

I do not pray, he adds, **that thou shouldst take them out of the world, but that thou shouldst keep them from the evil one** (17:15). They considered it necessary to be in the world although they were no longer **of the world**. He then repeats the same idea: **They are not of the world, even as I am not of the world. Sanctify them in the truth** (17:16–17). . . . However, it is possible to ask how they were no longer **of the world** if they were not yet **sanctified in the truth**. If they already were, why does he ask that they should be? Is it not because those who are already sanctified advance in sanctification and become holy? This is not done without the help of the grace of God; rather, it is carried out by the one who sanctified them from the beginning. For this reason, the apostle says, *He who began a good work in you will bring it to completion at the day of Jesus Christ* (Phil 1:6). The heirs of the New Testament are **sanctified in the truth** which was foreshadowed by the sanctifying rituals of the Old Testament. When they are **sanctified in the truth**, they are **sanctified** in Christ who declared truthfully: *I am the way, and the truth, and the life* (14:6). Similarly, he said: *The truth will make you free* (8:32). After explaining what he said, he added, *So if the Son makes you free, you will be free indeed* (8:36), in order to demonstrate that what he had previously called **the truth** is later called the Son. What else does he mean by the phrase **sanctify them in the truth** (17:17) except **sanctify them** in me?

Next he does not hesitate to hint at this more clearly: **Thy word is truth** (17:17). What else does he mean than "I am the **truth**"? The Gospel of John in Greek has the word *logos*.[8] This is the word that is found in the passage which says, *In the beginning was the Word, and the Word was with God, and the Word was God* (1:1). . . . After he had said, **And for their sake I consecrate myself** (17:19), he then added, **That they also may be consecrated in truth** (17:19) so we might understand that he said this because he would **consecrate** them in himself. What does this mean other than "in me"? It follows then that **truth** is that *Word*

---

8. The word *Logos* in Greek is translated as *Verbum* in Latin. Both are rendered into English by the term *Word* (e.g., *In the beginning was the* Word [1:1]).

which was *in the beginning God* (cf. 1:1) in whom the Son of Man himself was **consecrated** from the beginning of his creation, when *the Word became flesh* (1:14). The Word and the human became one person. At that time he **consecrated** himself in himself, i.e. himself the man in himself the Word. The Word and the man is one Christ who sanctifies human nature in the Word.

John 17:20–23

[20]"I do not pray for these only, but also for those who believe in me through their word, [21]that they may all be one; even as thou, Father, art in me, and I in thee, that they also may be in us, so that the world may believe that thou hast sent me. [22]The glory which thou hast given me I have given to them, that they may be one even as we are one, [23]I in them and thou in me, that they may become perfectly one, so that the world may know that thou hast sent me and hast loved them even as thou hast loved me."

17:20 "I do not pray for these only, but also for those who believe in me through their word."

---

(15) Augustine of Hippo

As his passion was drawing near, the Lord Jesus when he was praying for his disciples . . . added all the other people who were about to believe in him. He said to the Father, **I do not pray for these only** (17:20)—that is, for the disciples who were with him then—**but also for those who believe in me through their word** (17:20). In this way he desired that it would be understood that he prayed for all, not only those who were there in the flesh but also for those who were to come. All who have believed in him since that time certainly have believed through the **word** of the apostles, as will all who believe until he returns. Accordingly, he said to them, *And you also are witnesses, because you have been with me from the beginning* (15:27). The gospel was ministered by them even before it was written. Everyone who believes in Christ believes in the gospel. It follows then that those who will believe in him **through their word** are not only those who heard the apostles themselves when they were alive but others also after they died. Although we were born much later, we also have believed in Christ **through their word**. Those who were with him proclaimed to others what they had heard; thus, **their word** has come to us in order that we also might believe. Wherever his church is, this word will also reach successive generations who will believe in him, whomever and wherever they are.

In this prayer it may not seem that Jesus prayed for all those who belong to him. But we must carefully examine his words in the prayer itself. If he prayed first for those who were with him at that time, as we have already shown, and then for those who would believe in him **through their word**, it might be supposed that he did not pray for those . . . who believed at a time before the disciples or in some other way. Surely, Nathanael was not with him at that time, was he?[9] Was Joseph of Arimathea, who requested his body from Pilate and who John the Evangelist states was already *a disciple* (19:38) there? Were his mother, Mary, and the other women who, according to the gospel, were his disciples there also? Were those about whom the evangelist often says, *Many believed in him* (10:42; cf. 12:42), with him at that time? . . . At this particular time, the Savior did not pray for these people. Instead, he was praying for those who were with him . . . and for those who would believe in him **through their word**. None of these were with him on that particular occasion, but they had believed in him previously.

I have neglected to mention the elder Simeon, who believed in him when he was an infant (cf. Luke 2:25–35); Anna the prophetess (cf. Luke 2:36–38); Zechariah and Elizabeth, who prophesied about him even before he was born of the virgin (cf. Luke 1:5–25); and their son John, his forerunner, friend of the bridegroom, who acknowledged him in the Holy Spirit, proclaimed him when he was away, and pointed him out when he was present so that others might recognize him (cf. John 1:19–36). I have neglected these individuals since one might respond that he should not have prayed for such a distinguished group of people who have already died. They have already departed with their great merits and have been welcomed and are now resting. A similar answer is given about the righteous ones from ancient times. Which of them would have been saved from the condemnation of every evil caused by the one man (i.e., Adam), unless through the revelation of the Spirit he or she believed in the *one mediator between God and men* (1 Tim 2:5) who would come in the flesh? . . . So when he said, **I do not pray for these only, but also for those who believe in me through their word** (17:20), he prayed for all those who had already believed in him. . . .

Therefore, if we believe that the Lord Jesus prayed in this prayer for all those who in this life . . . belong to him—either those who were with him at that particular time or those who would be in the future—then we understand the phrase **through their word** as referring to the word of faith which they preached in the world. It was called **their word** because it was first and foremost preached by them. They were already preaching this on earth when Paul received that very same **word** *through a revelation of Jesus Christ* (Gal 1:12). After this, he conferred with them regarding this gospel, *lest somehow* he *should be running or had run in vain* (Gal 2:2). They gave him *their right hand of fellowship* (Gal 2:9), because they found in him the very **word** that they were preaching and in which they were confirmed, although they had not given it to him. . . . Properly it was called **their word**. This is the **word** of faith through which all, wherever they heard it, believed in Christ. Or they will hear it, and they will believe. In this prayer, our redeemer prayed for all those whom he redeemed, both those who were alive at that time and those who would come in the future. When he prayed for the apostles who were with him then, he also added those who would believe in him **through their word**.

---

9. Augustine notes that Nathanael was not with Jesus and the disciples in the garden of Gethsemane. In fact, Nathanael is mentioned only two times in the Gospel of John. In chapter 1 Philip invites Nathanael to meet Jesus. From their brief encounter, Nathanael ostensibly confesses that Jesus is the Christ, for he says, **Rabbi, you are the Son of God! You are the King of Israel!** (1:49). Although some have identified Nathanael in the Gospel of John with the disciple Bartholomew named in the Synoptic Gospels, Augustine infers that Nathanael is not a disciple but is a believer. Indeed, Nathanael is there when Jesus reveals himself to the disciples at the Sea of Tiberias (cf. John 21:2).

17:21 "That they may all be one; even as thou, Father, art in me, and I in thee, that they also may be in us, so that the world may believe that thou hast sent me."

(16) Cyril of Alexandria

We must carefully consider how we should explain the following statement: **That they may all be one; even as thou, Father, art in me, and I in thee, that they also may be in us** (17:21). Previously, we affirmed that the harmonious unity of the hearts and souls of believers should be similar to the divine unity and character of the Holy Trinity and the intimate relationship between them. But now we desire to show a type of natural unity which joins us to each other and all of us to God. This is similar to a sort of physical unity that we share even though we are separated because each of us has a different body and can withdraw, so to speak, into one's private, individual nature. Certainly Peter cannot be Paul or be referred to in this way, nor Paul as Peter, despite the fact that they are both one according to their union through Christ. Assuming then the natural unity that exists between the Father and Son, and also the Holy Spirit—for we believe and glorify one Godhead in the Holy Trinity—let us examine how we are shown to be **one** (17:21) with each other and with God, both in a corporeal and spiritual sense.

The only-begotten, who proceeds from the very essence of God the Father and shares completely in himself the nature of the one who has begotten him, became incarnate according to Scripture (cf. John 1:14). In this way, he joined himself with our nature in an ineffable mixture and union with his earthly body. So that the one who is God by nature truly became a man from heaven. He was not merely an inspired human, as some of those think who do not correctly understand the depth of this mystery. Instead, he is at the same time both God and man. He united in himself natures which are completely opposed and resist fusion with each other in order that he might enable humans to share in and partake of God's nature. The fellowship and indwelling presence of the Spirit, which originated first through Christ and in Christ, has come even to us, because he has truly become human as we are and has received anointing and sanctification although he is by nature God. Because he proceeded from the Father, he sanctified the temple of his body and all of creation which owes its existence to him . . . by his own Spirit. The mystery then is that Christ is both the beginning and the very way by which we partake of the Holy Spirit and union with God. We are all sanctified in him in the way I have just explained.

Although each of us is different from one another because we possess distinct individuality of soul and body, the only-begotten has created a way . . . that we may be joined together and fused with God and each other. He makes us members of the same body with himself and with each other through his own body. He blesses those who believe in him through a mysterious participation. Who could rip apart or divide the natural union one shares with another by being connected through his holy body, which is one in Christ? If *we all partake of the one bread* (1 Cor 10:17), then we are all made *one body* (1 Cor 10:17) since Christ cannot be divided. Therefore, the church also becomes *the body of Christ* (1 Cor 12:27). We are individually its members, according to Paul's wisdom. Since all of us are united to Christ through his holy body insofar as we have received him who is united indivisibly in our own bodies, we are obligated, as members, to serve him rather than ourselves. Christ is called the head, and the church is called the body since it is constituted by individual members. . . . Paul also testifies that those who partake of his holy flesh are actually united in a physical way with Christ. Referring to this holy mystery, Paul says: *It was not made known to the sons of men in other generations as it has now been revealed to his holy apostles and prophets by the Spirit; that is, how the Gentiles are fellow heirs, members of the same body, and partakers of the promise in Christ Jesus* (Eph 3:5-6). If we are all members of the same body in Christ together—not just with one another but with the one who is in us through his very flesh—are we not then unified with one another and with Christ? Christ, who is both God and man, is the unifying bond.

When we speak about the unity that comes by the Spirit, we may follow the same path of inquiry. We say once again that all of us are joined together with one another and with God since we receive one and the same Holy Spirit. If Christ, who is the Spirit of the Father and his own Spirit, dwells in each of us as individuals, nonetheless the Spirit is both one and indivisible. The Spirit binds the distinctive, individual spirits of all of us—for we are separate beings—together into a unity in accordance with his nature. Through this Spirit, he shows that we are unified in him. Just as the power of his holy flesh makes those in whom it dwells one body, so also the indivisible Spirit of God who abides in all binds everyone together in spiritual unity (cf. John 14:17). So the inspired Paul says: *Forbearing one another in love, eager to maintain the unity of the Spirit in the bond of peace. There is one body and one Spirit, just as you were called to the one hope that belongs to your call, one Lord, one faith, one baptism, one God and Father of us all, who is above all and through all and in all* (Eph 4:2-6).

17:23 "I in them and thou in me, that they may become perfectly one, so that the world may know that thou hast sent me and hast loved them even as thou hast loved me."

---

(17) Augustine of Hippo

I in them and thou in me, that they may become perfectly one (17:23). Here he briefly describes himself as *the mediator between God and men* (1 Tim 2:5). This was not said to suggest that the Father is not in us or that we are not in the Father, for he had said elsewhere, **We will come to him and make our home with him** (14:23). Just before this current passage, he did not say as he says here, **Even as thou art in me, and I in thee** (17:23) or "They in me, and I in You," but **thou art in me, and I in thee**, and **they . . . in us** (17:21). Since he now says, **I in them and thou in me**, these words are stated from the perspective of the *mediator*. The apostle Paul says the same thing: *You are Christ's; and Christ is God's* (1 Cor 3:23). Because Christ added the words **that they may become perfectly one** (17:23), he showed that reconciliation through the *mediator* leads us in such a way that we can thoroughly enjoy that perfect happiness which cannot be enhanced. . . .

What is said next follows closely: **Thou . . . hast loved them even as thou hast loved me** (17:23). Certainly, the Father loves us in the Son, because *he chose us in him before the foundation of the world* (Eph 1:4). Truly the one who loves the only-begotten also loves his members whom he adopted into himself through his own actions. But we are not in this way equal to the only-begotten Son through whom we have been created and re-created, for it is said, **Thou . . . hast loved them even as thou hast loved me** (17:23). . . .

The love by which God loves us is both incomprehensible and immutable. He did not begin to love us from that point when we were reconciled to him through the blood of his Son. He loved us *before the foundation of the world* (Eph 1:4) in order that we might be his sons along with his only-begotten Son, even before we existed in any way. . . . But we were reconciled with the one who already loved us even though we were at enmity with him because of our sin. Let the apostle testify whether or not I speak the truth; he says, *God shows his love for us in that while we were yet sinners Christ died for us* (Rom 5:8). He possessed love for us even when we were practicing enmity against him and working iniquity. To him it is said truthfully: *You hate, O Lord, all those who work iniquity* (Ps 5:5 LXX). Accordingly, it is said in a wonderful and divine manner: even when he hated us, he loved us. He hated us in accordance with that which he had not made. Because our iniquity had not fully consumed his workmanship, he knew simultaneously how, in each of us, to hate what we had done and to love what he had made.

John 17:24–26

[24]"Father, I desire that they also, whom thou hast given me, may be with me where I am, to behold my glory which thou hast given me in thy love for me before the foundation of the world. [25]O righteous Father, the world has not known thee, but I have known thee; and these know that thou hast sent me. [26]I made known to them thy name, and I will make it known, that the love with which thou hast loved me may be in them, and I in them."

17:24 "Father, I desire that they also, whom thou hast given me, may be with me where I am, to behold my glory which thou hast given me in thy love for me before the foundation of the world."

---

(18) Cyprian of Carthage

When we die, we pass over to immortality through death. Unless we depart from this life, eternal life cannot follow. Death is not an end but a journey. On this journey we pass from time into eternity. Who would not rush toward better things? Who would not desire to be changed and renewed into the likeness of Christ and arrive more quickly to the honor of heavenly glory? The apostle Paul proclaims, *But our commonwealth is in heaven, and from it we await a Savior, the Lord Jesus Christ, who will change our lowly body to be like his glorious body, by the power which enables him even to subject all things to himself* (Phil 3:20–21). Christ the Lord also promises that we may be with him, live with him in eternal mansions (cf. John 14:2), and rejoice in the heavenly kingdoms. He asks the Father on our behalf: **Father, I desire that they also, whom thou hast given me, may be with me where I am, to behold my glory which thou hast given me . . . before the foundation of the world** (17:24). The one who will reach the throne of Christ and the glory of the heavenly kingdom should not mourn or lament, but rather should rejoice in his departure and transformation in accordance with the promise of the Lord and his faith in the truth.

(19) Augustine of Hippo

Let us examine, as far as we are able, what he was promising when he said, **I desire that they also, whom thou hast given me, may be with me where I am** (17:24). Regarding his created nature by which he *was descended from David according to the flesh* (Rom 1:3), he was not where he would be in the future. But he said, **Where I am**, in such a way that we would understand that he would soon ascend into heaven. He spoke of himself as already being where he would be soon. He was able to speak in the same mode which he formerly used when speaking to Nicodemus: *No one has ascended into heaven but he who descended from heaven, the Son of man who is in heaven* (3:13). In this passage he did not say, *will be*, but **is**, because of the unity of the person in which God is man and man is God. He promised that we would be in heaven where his servant-form, which he assumed from the virgin, was lifted up and placed at the right hand of the Father. On account of this same noble hope, the apostle also says, *But God, who is rich in mercy, out of the great love with which he loved us, even when we were dead through our trespasses, made us alive together with Christ—by grace you have been saved—and raised us up with him, and made us sit with him in the heavenly places in Christ Jesus* (Eph 2:4–6). In this same way, we can understand what the Lord said earlier: *That where I am you may be also* (14:3). Certainly, he said that he was already there. But in our case, he only stated that he wished that we were there with him. He did not state that we were already there. However, what the Lord said he wished would happen, the apostle spoke of as already finished. He did not say, "He will raise us up and will make us sit in the heavenly places," but *He raised us up with him, and made us sit with him in the heavenly places* (Eph 2:6). He counts it as already done what he is certain will be done. He does not do this foolishly, but faithfully. If we wish to understand his words, **I desire that they also . . . may be with me where I am** (17:24), as if they refer to the form of God which is equal to the Father, let us purge our minds of every corporeal image . . . let us turn, as much as it is able, from all such lines of contemplation or efforts. Let us not ask where the Son, who is equal to the Father, is, since no one has yet discovered where he is not. But if anyone would desire to inquire, let him seek to discover how he might be with him: not everywhere as he is, but with him, wherever he may be. To the man who was hanging on the cross for his crimes and confessing them for his salvation, Christ said in respect to his own human nature, *Today you will be with me in Paradise* (Luke 23:43). On that very day Christ's own soul was about to be in hell and his body in the tomb. But in respect to his divine nature, he was also in paradise. Therefore, the soul of the thief, which was absolved from its previous crimes . . . was already with him on that very day in paradise from which he, who is always everywhere, had not withdrawn. For this reason, it was certainly not sufficient for him to say, **I desire that they . . . may be . . . where I am**, but he added **with me** (17:24). To be **with** him is a great blessing. Although the wicked can be where he is . . . only the blessed are **with** him, because they are able to be blessed only from him. Was it not said truthfully to God, *If I ascend to heaven, thou art there! If I make my bed in Sheol, thou art there!* (Ps 139:8)? Is Christ not the wisdom of God who *pervades and penetrates all things because of its pureness* (Wis 7:24 LXX)? But *the light shines in the darkness, and the darkness has not comprehended it* (1:5). Accordingly, let us use an illustration from something that can be seen, although it is certainly dissimilar. Just as a blind man, even though he happens to be where the light is, is not actually **with** the light, for he is actually deprived of that which is present; similarly, the unbeliever and the impious—and even the believer and the pious—are not able to contemplate the light of wisdom. Although he is not able to be anywhere where Christ is not, yet he is not **with** Christ, at least in terms of sight. Of course, we must not doubt that the true believer is **with** Christ through faith. For this reason, Christ said, *He who is not with me is against me* (Matt 12:30). However, when he said to God the Father, **I desire that they also, whom thou hast given me, may be with me where I am** (17:24), he was speaking particularly about that sight by which *we shall see him as he is* (1 John 3:2).

Let no one disturb the absolutely clear meaning of this passage with cloudy contradictions. Instead, let what follows provide evidence for what was already said. After Christ said, **I desire that they also . . . may be with me**, he immediately added, **To behold my glory which thou hast given me in thy love for me before the foundation of the world** (17:24). He said, **To behold my glory**. He did not say, "That they may believe." This is the reward of faith, not faith itself. If faith has been defined correctly in the Epistle to the Hebrews as *the conviction of things not seen* (Heb 11:1), why is the reward of faith not defined as seeing the things which were hoped for through faith? Although we will behold the **glory** which the Father has given the Son—certainly we understand what is said here is not referring to that **glory** which the Father gave his co-equal Son while begetting him, but to that which he gave to the Son of Man after his death on the cross—when we see the **glory** of the Son, certainly the judgment of the living and the dead will happen. At that time the wicked will be removed so that such a one *does not see the glory of the Lord* (Isa 26:10). What **glory** is this, except the **glory** of his divine nature? For *blessed are the pure in heart, for they shall see God* (Matt 5:8).

(20) Cyril of Alexandria

In short, Christ wanted his friends to be granted the gift of being with him and beholding his **glory** (17:24). When he states that he was loved **before the foundation of the world** (17:24), he reveals clearly how ancient this powerful mystery of redemption is and that the mode of our salvation which had been accomplished by the mediation of Christ was foreknown by God the Father. This knowledge was not given to those upon the earth in the beginning, but the law came which served as our *custodian* (Gal 3:24) in the divine life and formed in us a faint knowledge of it through types. But God the Father held back the grace of the Savior until the proper time. This knowledge is very useful to show us how to dispel the scorn and unholy insolence of the Jews who continually advocate the law. When the truth came, the types were no longer necessary. It also seems very useful to fight against those who think that the Father's plan of this powerful mystery of our redemption was a new idea. That is why Paul also spoke against those who hold this opinion when he said that Christ was known *before the foundation of the world* (1 Pet 1:20; cf. John 17:24) and was made known at these last times.[10]

10. Certainly Cyril meant Peter, not Paul, for he quotes 1 Peter.

John 18

John 18 marks the betrayal, arrest, and trial of Jesus. Theodore of Mopsuestia, Cyril of Alexandria, and Leo the Great all use the opening verses of this chapter to demonstrate not only Christ's willingness to suffer death, but the crowd's inability to arrest Jesus without his full consent. Cyril points out that Jesus went to the garden precisely so that Judas, with the band of soldiers, could find him. Both Cyril and Leo note the irony of the crowd's use of lanterns and torches in order to see Jesus, all the while failing to recognize the true identity of Christ.

Jesus's identification of himself to the crowd in verse 5 (I am he) is evidence that he is in control of the situation. Origen of Alexandria recognizes that some critics doubt the veracity of some accounts in the gospels, but counters that the disciples' willingness to die for such "stories" certainly undermines any motivation for "inventing falsities." Athanasius of Alexandria, John Chrysostom, Augustine of Hippo, and Cyril of Alexandria all observe Christ's willingness to suffer death in his words I am he, while both Chrysostom and Augustine perceive Christ's divine power in the crowd's response: They drew back and fell to the ground (18:6). Cyril sees the crowd's response as a picture of what will happen in the end: "All who practice evil against Christ are altogether destined to fall."

Peter's use of the sword against Malchus, and Jesus's quick rebuke (18:10–11), elicit several comments about the appropriate Christian use of force. Tertullian, John Chrysostom, and Cyril of Alexandria all see Christ's actions as preventing the Christian from taking up the sword or striking one's enemies. Augustine of Hippo, however, employs a figural reading where the slave Malchus is interpreted as "one going to reign." Like Malchus, those who are freed from slavery in Christ are destined to "reign" with him.

Peter's denial of Christ (verses 15–18 and 25–27) leads John Chrysostom and Augustine of Hippo to marvel that the disciple, so confident earlier, would now deny Christ because of a simple question from a maid. Chrysostom and Romanos the Melodist observe that, in part, Peter's denial demonstrates the truthfulness of Christ's prediction, while Chrysostom goes further, seeing here a warning about "trusting ourselves rather than entrusting all things to God." Augustine points out that Peter's denial of being a follower of Christ was equivalent to denying Christ himself. Only Cyril of Alexandria offers a sympathetic reading. While not condoning Peter's denial, Cyril argues that "his mistake comes from love," and that before the grace of the Holy Spirit was given, Christ's disciples were "not yet fully freed from human *weakness." After Pentecost, Peter and the other disciples would demonstrate a boldness beyond their human nature.*

Augustine of Hippo and Cyril of Alexandria each attempt to explain Christ's words: I have spoken openly (18:20). Augustine observes that throughout Christ's earthly ministry the opposite appears true—Christ speaks in obscure riddles and oftentimes discloses truth only to his close-knit disciples. In a less-than-satisfactory solution, Augustine suggests that Christ's words in verse 20 mean that the ultimate intention was not to keep his teaching a secret, but to proclaim it to the world. Cyril, on the other hand, contrasts the figural, obscure teaching of the old law to one nation, Israel, with the clear and direct teaching of Christ to the whole world.

Several writers comment on Christ's examination before Caiaphas. John Chrysostom examines the details of the proceedings and concludes: "These proceedings weren't a court of justice, but a conspiracy and a tyranny." Augustine of Hippo and Cyril of Alexandria focus rather on the character of Jesus, who shows patience, gentleness, and willingness to suffer. Cyril offers an appropriate challenge to all who "become embittered like dragons" at the smallest offense.

Christ's words to Pilate, My kingship is not of this world (18:36), gain the attention of several interpreters. John Chrysostom, Theodore of Mopsuestia, and Cyril of Alexandria all make the point that Christ was indeed a king, just not the earthly king Pilate was asking about. Augustine of Hippo also recognizes that Christ was a king, but presses the importance of the preposition of. Christ and his kingship "is not of the world, but he wanders as a stranger in the world."

Finally, this chapter ends with John Chrysostom's reflection upon the whole of John 18, and a sharp challenge to all. In contrast to Christ's willing endurance of insult and mockery, many live only for the praise and honor of others. Chrysostom ends his homily with a call to imitate Christ's humility in the face of ill treatment.

John 18:1–11

[1]When Jesus had spoken these words, he went forth with his disciples across the Kidron valley, where there was a garden, which he and his disciples entered. [2]Now Judas, who betrayed him, also knew the place; for Jesus often met there with his disciples. [3]So Judas, procuring a band of soldiers and some officers from the chief priests and the Pharisees, went there with lanterns and torches and weapons. [4]Then Jesus, knowing all that was to befall him, came forward and said to them, "Whom do you seek?" [5]They answered him, "Jesus of Nazareth." Jesus said to them, "I am he." Judas, who betrayed him, was standing with them. [6]When he said to them, "I am he," they drew back and fell to the ground.

[7]Again he asked them, "Whom do you seek?" And they said, "Jesus of Nazareth." [8]Jesus answered, "I told you that I am he; so, if you seek me, let these men go." [9]This was to fulfil the word which he had spoken, "Of those whom thou gavest me I lost not one." [10]Then Simon Peter, having a sword, drew it and struck the high priest's slave and cut off his right ear. The slave's name was Malchus. [11]Jesus said to Peter, "Put your sword into its sheath; shall I not drink the cup which the Father has given me?"

18:1–3 Now Judas, who betrayed him, also knew the place.

---

(1) Theodore of Mopsuestia

Here too the evangelist shows that it was Jesus's own will not to escape his passion. Instead, he went out to meet those who were about to seize him, although he knew very well that his passion was approaching. When he asked them what they wanted and they said, **Jesus of Nazareth** and he replied to them, **I am he**, they **fell back** (18:6). Our Lord did not do this randomly, but with a purpose: to make it known to everyone that if he wanted to destroy them, he could very easily have done so. Instead he accepted his passion willingly, for the benefit of all humanity. He who simply cast everyone of them **to the ground** with his words, could have even more easily destroyed them all if he had made use of his strength.

(2) Cyril of Alexandria

When the Jews chose to do offensive things to Jesus, and in their madness attempted to stone him, he used his divine power to escape, made himself invisible, and easily withdrew from those who sought him (cf. John 10:39). He was not yet willing to suffer; the appropriate time was not yet calling him to that end. But now the time had arrived, so he departed from the home in which he had instructed his disciples in the mysteries. Christ, the Savior of all, came to **the place** (18:2) where he often dwelled with his holy disciples. He did this in order to make it easier for the betrayer to find him. The place was a **garden** (18:1), depicting a figure of the ancient paradise (cf. Gen 2:8–9). This **garden** was a kind of summation of all places, a return to that ancient **garden**. The beginning of our sad estate occurred in paradise, while Christ's suffering also began in the **garden**, a suffering which brought the restoration of all that happened to us long ago. . . .

    When they pressed their attack against Christ, the crowd which was joined with the traitor carried **lanterns and torches** (18:3). It seems likely that they were prepared against stumbling in the dark and involuntarily falling into ditches, for such things so often happen in the dark. But O how foolish they are! In their great ignorance those unhappy men failed to see that they were stumbling on the *stone* about which God the Father said, *Behold, I am laying in Zion a stone that will make men stumble, a rock that will make them fall* (Rom 9:33; cf. Isa 8:14–15). Those who for a while were afraid of a ditch, did not realize that they were rushing into the fount of the abyss and into the depths of the earth. Those who were avoiding the darkness of evening displayed no recognition of that perpetual and eternal night. Those who impiously plotted against the light of God, that is Christ, were about to *walk in* darkness at *midnight*, as the prophet says (Isa 59:9).

(3) Leo the Great

Dear brothers and sisters, in our last sermon we made our way through the events which occurred before the Lord's arrest. It now remains for us, with the assistance of God's grace, to examine the account of the passion itself, as we promised. When the Lord had revealed, through the words of his holy prayer, that he truly and fully had both a human and a divine nature, he demonstrated that from his humanity came his unwillingness to suffer. Yet from his divinity came his willingness to suffer by expelling his fear of weakness and strengthening the greatness of his power. He had returned his thought to that eternal purpose, and with the devil raging against him through the help of the Jews, Christ opposed him in the *form* of a sinless *servant* (cf. Phil 2:7). He, who contained all our nature without sin, did this so that he might remove the cause of all sin.

So the children of darkness rushed in upon the true light. Using **lanterns and torches** (18:3), but not recognizing the source of true light, they failed to escape their own night of unfaithfulness. They seized one who was ready to be seized; they dragged off one who was willing to be dragged off. If he had wanted to resist, their wicked hands could not have caused him any harm. Yet the redemption of the world would have been hindered and the one who was to die for the salvation of all would not have saved a single one.

18:4-6 "Whom do you seek? . . . I am he."

---

(4) Origen of Alexandria

When the text says that Jesus was taken prisoner (18:12), I would say that if being taken prisoner means being taken unwillingly, then Jesus was not really taken prisoner. At the appointed time, he did not resist being taken into the hands of men so that, as *Lamb of God*, he might *take away the sin of the world* (1:29). For **knowing all that was to befall him, he came forward and said to them, "Whom do you seek?" They answered, "Jesus of Nazareth." Jesus said to them, "I am he." Judas, who betrayed him, was standing with them. When he said to them, "I am he," they drew back and fell to the ground. Again he asked them, "Whom do you seek?" And they said again, "Jesus of Nazareth." Jesus answered them, "I told you that I am he; so, if you seek me, let these men go"** (18:4-8). . . .

Someone may think that these accounts are mere inventions of the gospel writers. Should you not rather consider the hateful and hostile things said against Christ and Christians to be the real inventions, and these accounts the truth? These accounts come from those who demonstrated a true affection for Christ by enduring everything, whatever it might be, for the sake of his words! The disciples of Jesus bore such endurance and resolution to death itself. Given their state of mind, they would not have invented falsities about their teacher. Their endurance of such great trials, out of their belief that Jesus was the Son of God, should make it quite clear to those who are fair and balanced that the disciples truly believed what they wrote.

(5) Athanasius of Alexandria

Because he was God and the Word of the Father, the Lord knew the appointed time for all things measured out by him, and when he was supposed to suffer. He himself had designated that time for his own body. Since, however, he became man for our sakes, he hid himself from those seeking him (just as we do) because the appointed time had not yet arrived (cf. John 8:59). When he was persecuted, he fled; avoiding their plots and *passing through the midst of them, he went away* (Luke 4:30). But when he himself brought forth that time appointed by him in which to suffer bodily for all, he announced it to the Father saying, *Father, the hour has come; glorify thy Son* (17:1). He no longer hid himself from those who sought him; instead, he stood willing to be seized by them. The evangelist tells us that Christ spoke to the approaching crowd: **"Whom do you seek?" They answered him, "Jesus of Nazareth." Jesus said to them, "I am he** whom you seek" (18:4–5). He does this not just once, but twice (18:7–8). So they led him to Pilate. Christ did not allow himself to be seized before the appointed time had come, nor did he hide when the time arrived. He gave himself up to those who plotted against him so that he might demonstrate to us all that human life and death depend upon the decision from above and that without our Father in heaven no one can *make one hair white or black* (Matt 5:36) nor can a sparrow fall into a trap (cf. Matt 10:29).

(6) John Chrysostom

Then Jesus, knowing all that was to befall him, came forward and said to them, "Whom do you seek?" (18:4). That is, he did not wait to learn these things when they happened, but speaks and acts calmly as one **knowing all** things. But why did they come to arrest him with weapons? They feared his followers and so came upon him in the dead of night. Then Jesus **came forward and said to them, "Whom do you seek?" They answered him, "Jesus of Nazareth"** (18:4–5). Do you see his irresistible power, how standing in their midst he afflicts their eyes? The evangelist makes it clear that the darkness was not the problem, noting that they had torches (18:3). Even if there were no torches, they should have known him by his voice. Even if they did not know his voice, how could Judas not know it? He had been with Jesus continually. Yet he too stood with them and did not recognize Jesus any more than they did. He too **fell** backward with them (18:5–6). Obviously Jesus was doing this. Not only were they unable to arrest him, but unless he allowed it they were unable to see him standing right in front of them!

 Again he asked them, "Whom do you seek?" (18:7). O what madness! His word threw them backward, yet even after learning how powerful he was they did not turn away but instead set themselves to the same task again. Thus when Jesus had fulfilled all things, only then did he surrender himself.

(7) Augustine of Hippo

Where now were the cohorts of soldiers, the servants of the chief priests and Pharisees? Where was the fear and defense of weapons? Clearly, a voice saying **I am he** (18:5), without any spear, pierced, drove back, and knocked down so great a mob, cruel with hatred and terrible with weapons. For God was hidden in flesh, and everlasting day, hidden by human limbs, was being sought with lanterns and torches in order to be struck down by darkness. **I am he**, he says, flinging aside the unbelievers. What will he do when he comes to judge, the one who did this when he was about to be judged? What power will he have when he comes to rule, the one who had this power when he was about to die? . . .

They **drew back and fell to the ground** (18:6); they deserted heavenly things and desired earthly things. Certainly the persecutors came with the traitor to seize Jesus; they found the one whom they were seeking, but when they heard, **I am he**, why didn't they seize him? Why did they **draw back and fall down** except for one reason: unless Jesus wills it, who could accomplish what one wanted to do? Truly, if he hadn't allowed himself to be apprehended by them, they would not have accomplished their purpose for coming, but neither would Christ have accomplished the purpose for his coming. To be sure, in their rage they were seeking to kill him; but the very same one was seeking us by dying.

(8) Cyril of Alexandria

By anticipating the beginning of their plan and quite intentionally going out to meet them, Christ rebukes **Judas** for considering him a mere man and holding such worthless ideas. By his actions, Christ shows that he was well aware of what **Judas** was trying to do. He also demonstrates that even though his foreknowledge would have made it easy for him to run away and escape, he comes to his passion without being called, and was not involved in an unwanted danger by some sort of superiority of the mob. He also does this so that the wise among the Greeks, who make the cross a *stumbling block* and an accusation against him (cf. 1 Cor 1:18–25), might not sneer at him. He also does this so that **Judas**, the murderer of the Lord, might not become exceedingly arrogant toward Christ, thinking he had overcome the Lord against his will. He questions those who came to arrest him, asking them for whom they **seek** (18:4), not because he does not know (how can that be?), but so that he might prove that those who had come to arrest him, and had beheld him, were unable even to recognize the one whom they sought. In acting this way, he confirms that it is right to think that he would not have been arrested unless he had not gone willingly to those who sought him. . . .

How could the traitor not recognize the Lord? You might suggest that it was dark at night and not easy to see the one whom they sought. Is not the author of the book worthy of admiration for not omitting such insignificant or small details? He has said that when they entered the garden, they were carrying lanterns and torches. A subtle point is made in these words and the divine dignity of Christ is revealed. Even though they could not recognize Christ, he gave himself over to those who sought him. In order to prove that they suffer from an inability to recognize him, he said clearly, **I am he** (18:5). In order to show the uselessness of a multitude of hands and the utter powerlessness of humanity against the ineffable power of God, he answers with a gentle and kind word which casts **to the ground** (18:6) the crowd which had sought him. From this we might learn that the nature of created beings is incapable of bearing threats, even one word of God spoken in kindness, as it says in the Psalms: *But thou, terrible art thou! Who can stand before thy wrath?* (Ps 76:7). This is symbolic: what happened to a small portion who came to arrest Christ represents the humbling of all nations. As the prophet Jeremiah laments, *The house of Israel is fallen with none to raise her up* (Amos 5:1–2).[1] What happened here is an image of what inevitably will happen. It teaches us that all who commit evil against Christ are altogether destined to fall.

18:10–11 Simon Peter, having a sword, drew it and struck the high priest's slave.

---

(9) Tertullian of Carthage

The question is this: can one of the faithful be enlisted in the military, or can one in the military be accepted into the faith, even a common soldier of an inferior rank for whom it is not necessary to engage in sacrifices or capital punishments? Human and divine oaths of loyalty cannot be harmonized, nor the battle standards of Christ and the devil, nor the armies of light and darkness; one soul cannot serve two masters—both God and Caesar (cf. Matt 6:24). Moses held a staff, Aaron wore a buckle, John the Baptist was girded in leather, and Joshua the son of Nun led the army and the people fought. . . . But how will a Christian fight? Moreover, how will one serve in the army even during peace time, without his sword, which the Lord has taken away (cf. John 18:36)? Even though soldiers had come to John the Baptist and received guidelines on how to perform their duty (cf. Luke 3:14), and a centurion had come to faith (cf. Matt 8:5), nevertheless the Lord afterward disarmed every soldier by disarming Peter (18:10–11). No state of life is permissible among us if it has been designated as forbidden.

(10) John Chrysostom

Peter, being emboldened by Jesus's voice and the events taking place, arms himself against those coming at him (John 18:10). Someone may say, "Why does Peter, who was commanded to have neither *a bag nor two tunics* (Matt 10:10), have a sword?" I think he prepared it beforehand, fearing this very thing. If you say, "Why does the one who was commanded to strike no one (Matt 5:39) now become murderous?" I reply: Indeed, he had been commanded not to defend himself, but here he did not defend himself but his teacher. Anyway, the disciples were not yet perfect and complete. If you want to see Peter endowed with wisdom, you will see him later on wounded and bearing it humbly, suffering ten

---

1. Cyril incorrectly identifies the passage as belonging to Jeremiah.

thousand horrible things yet not provoked to anger. Jesus here works a miracle, in a single instance both showing us to do good to those who do us evil, and revealing his own power. He restores the slave's ear and says to Peter, *All who take the sword will perish by the sword* (Matt 26:52). Just as he did when he used the **basin** earlier, calming Peter's anxiety with a threat (cf. John 13:3–8), so he does here.

(11) Augustine of Hippo

The slave's name was Malchus (18:10). The **slave's name** is given by this evangelist alone, just as Luke alone records that the Lord touches his ear and heals him (Luke 22:51). Moreover, the name **Malchus** means "one going to reign." What does it mean that the **ear** was **cut off** for the Lord and healed by the Lord? It signifies hearing restored, that is, **cut off** from old ways so that it may exist in the new life of the Spirit, not in the old ways of the letter (cf. 2 Cor 3:6). Who doubts that he, to whom this was done by Christ, will also "reign" with Christ? Moreover, he has been found a **slave**, relating to those old ways which produce slavery, that is Hagar (cf. Gal 4). And when health came, freedom was also depicted.

Nevertheless, Peter's action was condemned by the Lord, and Christ restrained him from advancing further, saying: **Put your sword into its sheath; shall I not drink the cup which the Father has given me?** (18:11). In acting this way, the disciple wished to defend his master, not realizing what was being signified. So the disciple was commanded to exercise patience, while this episode was recorded to encourage understanding.

(12) Cyril of Alexandria

Then Simon Peter, having a sword, drew it and struck the high priest's slave and cut off his right ear. The slave's name was Malchus (18:10). Someone may ask why it was necessary for the inspired evangelist to mention these things. Why does he show the disciple acting against his custom by using a **sword** against those who had come to arrest Christ? Why show the disciple responding in a way that was harsher and more eager than necessary, and then Christ rebuking him for it? The narration of these events may seem superfluous but it is not; has he not introduced to us a model of what happened for our benefit? Through this incident, we will know how far our pious zeal toward Christ may go and still remain blameless, and what we may decide to do in such trials without stumbling on something by which God is grieved. The example of what happened here forbids us from stretching out our sword, lifting up stones against anyone, or striking our enemies with a stick even when our piety toward Christ puts us at odds with them. As Paul says, *Our weapons are not worldly* (2 Cor 10:4). Rather, we ought to behave with kindness even to our murderers, whenever the opportunity for escape has been cut off. . . .

Jesus said to Peter, "Put your sword into its sheath; shall I not drink the cup which the Father has given me?" (18:11). Christ's command produces a law of evangelical citizenship, and the power of the commandment does not come from the law Moses gave to men of old. This one is established through Christ; it prevents us from using the sword or defending ourselves. If someone should desire to strike us on one cheek, Christ requires us to turn the other cheek as well (cf. Matt 5:39). It is as if he cuts out by the roots the human faintheartedness from each soul. "But," says Christ, "even if I had not laid down a law to exercise patience, your mind, O Peter, has failed to reason properly and you have attempted to do something entirely inappropriate to the situation. It was decreed and desired by God the Father for me to drink this cup, that is, to be willing to endure the deep sleep, as it were, of death, in order to destroy death and corruption. Therefore, how can I go on to avoid it when so much goodness is believed to result for the human race through drinking it?"

John 18:15-18, 25-27

[15]**Simon Peter followed Jesus, and so did another disciple. As this disciple was known to the high priest, he entered the court of the high priest along with Jesus,** [16]**while Peter stood outside at the door. So the other disciple, who was known to the high priest, went out and spoke to the maid who kept the door, and brought Peter in.** [17]**The maid who kept the door said to Peter, "Are not you also one of this man's disciples?" He said, "I am not."** [18]**Now the servants and officers had made a charcoal fire, because it was cold, and they were standing and warming themselves; Peter also was with them, standing and warming himself. . . .** [25]**Now Simon Peter was standing and warming himself. They said to him, "Are not you also one of his disciples?" He denied it and said, "I am not."** [26]**One of the servants of the high priest, a kinsman of the man whose ear Peter had cut off, asked, "Did I not see you in the garden with him?"** [27]**Peter again denied it; and at once the cock crowed.**

(13) John Chrysostom

What does the woman say? **"Are not you also one of this man's disciples?" He said, "I am not"** (18:17). What are you saying Peter? Didn't you just a little earlier say, "If I need to lay down my life for you, I will do it!" (cf. John 13:37)? What has happened now that you can't even bear questioning from a doorkeeper? It's not a soldier who questions you, is it? It's not one of those who arrested Jesus, is it? No, it's a poor, downtrodden doorkeeper, and she's not even questioning you roughly! She doesn't say, "Are you a disciple of that deceiver and corrupter?" She says: **Of this man**. Her inquiry expressed compassion and empathy, but Peter couldn't bear any of these words. . . . The woman converses gently, but Peter understood none of this. He didn't pay attention the first, second, or third time, only when the **cock crowed** (18:27). Even this didn't bring him to his senses, it was only when Jesus looked at him piercingly. **Peter stood warming himself** with the servants of the high priest (18:18) while Christ remained bound inside. We say these things not to accuse Peter but to demonstrate the truthfulness of what Christ said (cf. John 13:38). . . .

    Now Simon Peter was standing and warming himself (18:25). Amazing! That rash, hotheaded Peter was possessed by such lethargy while Jesus was being led away. Even after these things take place, Peter doesn't move, but continues to **warm himself**, so that we might learn just how weak our nature is if God abandons us.

Being questioned again, he denies Jesus. **One of the servants of the high priest, a kinsman of the man whose ear Peter had cut off, asked, "Did I not see you in the garden with him?"** (18:26). Neither the garden nor Jesus's great love which he had shown Peter by his words jog Peter's memory about what had happened. The distress drives everything from his mind. Why then have the evangelists written with such agreement about Peter? Not to accuse the disciple; they wanted to teach us the seriousness of trusting ourselves rather than entrusting all things to God.

(14) Augustine of Hippo

The maid who kept the door said to Peter, "Are not you also one of this man's disciples?" He said, "I am not" (18:15–17). Behold, the firmest pillar has trembled completely at the impact of one breath. Where is that boldness of the one who made promises? Where is the great confidence he had in himself previously (cf. Matt 26:33, 35)? Where are those words when he said, *Why cannot I follow you now? I will lay down my life for you* (13:37)? Is this how to follow the teacher, by denying being his disciple? Is this the way one's life is laid down for the Lord, that lest this be done, the voice of a **maid** is feared?

What surprise is it if God truly foretold, and man falsely presumed? Certainly in what we have here (the denial of the apostle Peter), we ought to direct our attention to this fact: Christ is denied not only by one who says that Jesus is not the Christ, but also by one who is a Christian but denies that he is. For the Lord did not say to Peter, "My disciple, you will deny me," but simply, *You will deny me* (Matt 26:34). Therefore, Peter denied Christ when he denied that he was Christ's disciple. What else do his words imply except that he denied he was a Christian? For although Christ's disciples had not yet been given this name—as you see, after the ascension, his disciples first began to be called Christians in Antioch (Acts 11:26)—nevertheless there already existed the thing itself, afterward called by this name. There were already disciples who afterward are named Christians. This common name, just like the common faith, they transmitted to future generations. So, he who denied being Christ's disciple denied the reality itself, of which the name "Christian" is given.

(15) Cyril of Alexandria

Peter's threefold denial was already foretold by our Savior Christ—that his faith would fail before the rooster crowed. The inspired evangelist now describes in detail where and how the matter was fulfilled. The **maid who kept the door** (18:17) inquires whether Peter was one of the disciples of the one now undergoing the unjust trial. Peter denies it and rejects it as if it were some kind of accusation, saying **I am not** (18:17). In no way does he do this out of fear of being captured or from an aversion to proclaiming the truth, but simply because he considers being in the presence of Christ something far better than enduring misfortune against his will. His mistake, then, comes from love, and his denial has its root in a love for God. Admittedly, it does not proceed from accurate thinking, but nevertheless it does show the eagerness of his desire to be with Christ. . . .

Perhaps some of our opponents will present a terrible accusation against Peter, depicting this genuine disciple as a matchless coward. They will say that he quite easily erred in his words, and already fell three times into denial when he had not even experienced any terrible trials nor had been led to the very beginnings of danger. It may be appropriate to say such things for the uninitiated, but I abandon such ideas as much as possible. I advise us to be strong against their trickery. I will attempt to defend what Peter did, presenting my argument for those who are well-established in the knowledge of the mystery of the divine economy.

It was necessary for the most-wise evangelist to mention such things so that those who heard them might understand what the teachers of the divine economy were before the resurrection of Christ, before the Holy Spirit descended upon them, and what they were after they had received the grace of the Spirit which Christ called *power from on high* (Luke 24:49). Anyone can see that the disciples were most eager to acquire virtue. They were exceedingly active in their desire to follow Christ and to overcome every danger which they quite often encountered.

When Christ our Savior had not yet abolished the power of death, the fear of death was still firm and unapproachable. Those that had not yet received the Spirit, nor had been joined with that heavenly grace, had minds not yet fully freed from human weak-mindedness nor moved toward manly nature. They showed that they were not entirely unshaken in the face of the fears of suffering. Iron is hard by nature, but can be damaged when struck by harder stones if it has not been strengthened by being made into steel. In the same way, the human soul can act in great haste out of an unrelenting desire for all that is good, but it never surpasses the extreme perfection of good things unless it is first brought to maturity by the grace of the Spirit of God. So the disciples themselves were perhaps weaker at first, but when they were joined by the Spirit of the Almighty God (Acts 2), they cast down their weakness and were transformed into a spiritual fortitude. By fellowship with the Spirit they advanced toward a boldness which was beyond their human nature.

There was a good reason for recording the weakness of these saints: it brought praise and glory to God who changed their weakness into power, and raised them up like some irresistible tower, even though they were easily upset by slight fears and there were times when they broke down by the mere hint of suffering. What happened to one or a few of these saints might become an example and consolation for us. For we are taught here not to focus on our weaknesses and grow lazy in our service to God, but rather to trust in the one who can strengthen us all, and to boast in the right actions we perform beyond our nature, and in having received grace beyond hope.

(16) Romanos the Melodist

Strophe 10: In the great confusion, Peter was carried along with the crowd
        And entered eagerly. Coming within the house he sees there

The fire burning, and the judge seated in the courtyard,
    And Christ standing before the high priest,
    And not enduring the evil sight, he wept
    And beat his breast and said to himself:

PETER   "Thou art bound, O Christ, and thou dost endure it manfully and remain steadfast.
    They spit upon his face at whose sight the seraphim hide their eyes,
    As they shudder in awe and fear and cry out,
       'Hasten, Holy One, save thy sheep.'"

Strophe 12: After saying this, Peter became silent, and, overwhelmed by panic fear, he said nothing;
    But suddenly, having done well to keep silent, he spoke with bad effect,
In order that Christ, the truth, might be fulfilled,
    And every mortal become a liar.
    What, then, shall we say, brothers and sisters? That Peter
    Denied him that truth might be revealed?
Let it not be true that I should speak thus about Christ;
    But this I know that he foresees all things
    And reveals all, and he establishes in advance security for all who cry:
       "Hasten, Holy One, save thy sheep."

Strophe 13: For a short time, then, as we have said, Peter was quiet.
    Soon he ceased from his anguish and sat down in the courtyard,
       Thoughtful and gloomy.
    One **maid**servant walked around the disciple
    And looked him up and down with a keen glance
    And, taking in the situation, she said to him:

MAID   "Clearly you, too, were with the Galilaean" (cf. Luke 22:59).
PETER   But Peter answered: "I do not know what you are talking about (cf. Luke 22:60);
    I do not know the one whom people invoke as they cry:
       'Hasten, Holy One, save thy sheep.'"

Strophe 14: Quickly, O apostle, you let go your support, and the **maid**en threw you down.
    But rise up, spring up, and regain your first strength as an athlete.
You did not have a contest against someone stronger than you,
    Then how were you brought down by a kindly word?
    A young girl came up to you, and probably
    In a faltering voice said what she did to you;
And you, terrified at her stammer, as though it were a gnashing of teeth,
    Spoke out clearly to her: "I do not know what you are talking about."
    Why did the maiden terrify you and why did you not cry out:
       "Hasten, Holy One, save thy sheep"?

Strophe 15: The apostle, noticing that the maiden was looking at the people within,
Left the courtyard, and, stumbling against the gate, fell down there.
And another **maid**servant, coming up, as the gospel reports,
Said to those who were warming themselves:

MAID "It is clear that this man also was
With the Nazarene every day" (cf. Luke 22:56).
But Cephas, thoroughly terrified, answered her:

PETER "I do not know the man; I do not know him well.
I am ignorant of the man whom they greet as they cry out:
'Hasten, Holy One, save thy sheep.'"

Strophe 17: O Master, we sing hymns to thee, since it is good to sing; we praise thee, O Lord,
That thou hast suffered all things; and yet Peter, who suffered nothing,
denies thee.
Thou wast lashed, and Peter denied thee.
Though he endured nothing, the disciple
Now that he was twice overthrown by women,
Is worsted a third time by some other men.
For after a short time, some other men came up
And accosted Peter, and he denied with oaths.
And straightway the cock convicted him and he cried out:
"Hasten, Holy One, save thy sheep."

Strophe 18: When Peter heard the cock crow, immediately he cried out

PETER With shrieks and lamentations: "Woe is me, woe is me,
Where am I to go, where am I to stay, where am I to appear?
What shall I say, what word can I utter, what shall I offer as an excuse,
what have I left?
What shall I do? What shall I suffer? What can I undergo as expiation?
How shall I lament my calamity? A first time, a second time,
a third time this disaster has come upon me.
Three times the treacherous one has overthrown me, naïve me.
Invisibly was the arrow cast, visibly was I overpowered.
Where did I lose my bearings and not cry out:
'Hasten, Holy One, save thy sheep'?"

Strophe 20: The Merciful One is touched by the tears of Peter and grants him forgiveness.
For, speaking to the robber on the cross, he makes a covert allusion to
Peter:

CHRIST "Robber, beloved of me, come with me,
Since Peter has deserted me.
Nevertheless, to him and to you and to all mortals
I disclose my mercy, as lover of humanity.

Weeping, robber, you say, 'Remember me.'
And Peter, lamenting, cries out: 'Do not desert me.'
Hence to him and to you, I speak with all those who cry out:
'Hasten, Holy One, save thy sheep.'"

John 18:19-24

[19]The high priest then questioned Jesus about his disciples and his teaching. [20]Jesus answered him, "I have spoken openly to the world; I have always taught in synagogues and in the temple, where all Jews come together; I have said nothing secretly. [21]Why do you ask me? Ask those who have heard me, what I said to them; they know what I said." [22]When he had said this, one of the officers standing by struck Jesus with his hand, saying, "Is that how you answer the high priest?" [23]Jesus answered him, "If I have spoken wrongly, bear witness to the wrong; but if I have spoken rightly, why do you strike me?" [24]Annas then sent him bound to Caiaphas the high priest.

18:20 "I have spoken openly to the world . . . I have said nothing secretly."

---

(17) Augustine of Hippo

A question arises that should not be disregarded: why did the Lord Jesus say, **I have spoken openly to the world,** and especially why did he say, **I have said nothing secretly** (18:20)? In that recent conversation with his disciples after dinner, did he not say to them, *I have said this to you in figures; the hour is coming when I shall no longer speak to you in figures, but tell you plainly of my Father* (16:25)? So, if he did not speak **openly** to his own intimate disciples, but promised a time when he would speak **openly,** how can he claim to have **spoken openly to the world?** The authority of the other evangelists also testifies that to his own disciples he certainly spoke much more clearly when he was alone with them, apart from a crowd, than he did with those who were not his disciples. To his disciples, he opened the meaning of the parables he had spoken, which remained closed to others (cf. Mark 4:10-11). So what does he mean by saying, **I have said nothing secretly?** When he said, **I have spoken openly to the world,** what he meant was, "Many have heard me." However, his speaking **openly** was at one time **open,** at another time it was not. Indeed he spoke **openly** because many heard him; on the other hand, he did not speak **openly** because they did not understand him. When he spoke to the disciples privately, he certainly said **nothing in secret.** Who speaks in **secret** when speaking in the presence of so many men, since it is written, on the evidence of two, or of three witnesses, shall a charge be sustained (Deut 19:15)? This is especially true if he spoke to a few men and intended his message to be made known through them to many, just as the Lord himself said to the few he had with him: *What I tell you in the dark, utter in the light; and what you hear whispered, proclaim upon housetops* (Matt 10:27). So this very thing that seems to be spoken by him in **secret**, in a certain way was not said in **secret**, because it was not said with the intention of being kept **secret** by those to whom it was spoken. Rather, it was intended to be preached to the whole world.

(18) Cyril of Alexandria

When Christ says, **I have spoken openly to the world** (18:20) he means that the oracles mediated through Moses come through types and shadows; they do not teach the will of God **openly** but instead form a conception of the truth beyond itself. Enfolded in the dullness of the letter, it does not produce the knowledge of things which ought to be done. On the other hand, **I have spoken openly to the world.** Without riddles and shadowy forms of good things, I presented what the virtuous life is like and indicated the straight path of piety toward God, removing all obscurity. **I have spoken to the world**, he says, not to the single race of Israel. For if my teachings are not yet known throughout the entire **world**, they will be in due time.

18:21-23 "Why do you ask me? . . ." When he had said this, one of the officers standing by struck Jesus with his hand.

---

(19) John Chrysostom

Why do you ask me? Ask those who have heard me (18:21). These are not the words of someone speaking arrogantly, but of one who is confident in the truth of what he said. What he said in the beginning, *If I bear witness to myself, my testimony is not true* (5:31), he now hints at, desiring to establish the absolute trustworthiness of his testimony. When Annas mentioned the disciples, what does Jesus say? "Do you ask me about my own? Ask my enemies, those who plotted against me and bound me. Let them speak to you." When someone calls his enemies as witness to what he said, it's indisputable proof of the truth. What does the **high priest** do? When it would have been appropriate to make investigations into the matter, he does not do so.

 When he had said this, one of the officers standing by struck Jesus with his hand (18:22). What could be more audacious than this? Tremble O heavens; be astonished O earth at the patience of the Lord and the arrogance of the servants! Yet what did he say? He didn't say, **Why do you ask me?** as if refusing to speak; rather, he wanted to remove all grounds for arrogance. When he was **struck** for this, even though he was able to shake, destroy, and remove all things, he does none of these things. Instead, he speaks words able to dissolve all savagery.

 Jesus says, **If I have spoken wrongly, bear witness to the wrong** (18:23), that is, "If you can counter what I am saying, prove it, but if not, then why do you strike me?" Do you see how the judgment hall is full of tumult, disorder, rage, and confusion? The **high priest** questioned Jesus with secret hostility and deceit; Jesus answered honestly and with appropriate words. What then could follow? Either to argue against what Jesus said or to prove it. This didn't happen; instead, the servant **struck** him. These proceedings weren't a court of justice, but a conspiracy and a tyranny.

(20) Augustine of Hippo

Here someone will say, "Why didn't Jesus do what he himself taught? He should not have responded this way to the one who struck him, but should have offered his cheek" (cf. Matt 5:39). Well, insofar as he answered him truthfully, gently, and justly, didn't he not only offer his other cheek to the one who struck it, but also prepared his whole body to be fixed to the cross? In this way he demonstrated what needed to be demonstrated, namely, that his great teachings about patience are not accomplished outwardly with the body, but by a preparation of the heart. It's possible that even a visibly enraged man can offer his other cheek. How much better was Christ who peacefully gave a truthful answer, and with a calm mind was prepared for more serious suffering?

(21) Cyril of Alexandria

It is obvious that in these events the Savior sketches out for us an example of his incomparable and marvelous patience toward us. Through his manner of life, like the arrangement of a clear image, he demonstrates the form of his surpassing kindness. The one who can utterly and entirely destroy the Jews by a single command is now **struck** as a servant. He does nothing. He does not retaliate against these wrongdoers with immediate punishment. He is not like us in our weakness, dictated by rage or pain. He is not conquered by the influence of an overbearing temper; rather, he quietly shames his opponent by telling him it was wrong to strike someone who spoke with reserve. Even when he has been confined by what seem to be terrible men, Christ does not disregard his usual manner of life. Through an appropriate argument, he attempts to persuade the servant to turn away from such rash arrogance. Christ himself received *evil for good*, as the Scripture says (Ps 35:12), but gave to those who were dishonoring him good instead of evil.

Our Lord Jesus Christ, although truly God and Lord of heaven and earth, bears it patiently when **struck**. What about us wretched creatures, *dust and ashes* (Gen 18:27), the smallest and weakest of all, like young green plants as the Scripture says: *As for man, his days are like grass; he flourishes like a flower of the field* (Ps 103:15)? If one of our brothers or sisters should drop some slight word of offense, we think it is righteous to become embittered like dragons over it, and we unceasingly hurl a barrage of words against them. We do not grant forgiveness for this human littleness of soul; we do not consider the weak nature we share in common; we do not bury our earthly passions with appropriate love; and we do not *look to Jesus the pioneer and perfecter of our faith* (Heb 12:2). We are eager to avenge ourselves vehemently even though the divine Scriptures say that *he who pursues evil will die* (Prov 11:19), and again, *Let none of you devise evil against his brother in your heart* (Zech 7:10). So let Christ himself, the Lord of all, be for us an example of gentleness and abundant patience toward one another. It was for this very reason that he said to us: *A disciple is not above his teacher, nor a servant above his master* (Matt 10:24).

John 18:28-40

²⁸Then they led Jesus from the house of Caiaphas to the praetorium. It was early. They themselves did not enter the praetorium, so that they might not be defiled, but might eat the passover. ²⁹So Pilate went out to them and said, "What accusation do you bring against this man?" ³⁰They answered him, "If this man were not an evildoer, we would not have handed him over." ³¹Pilate said to them, "Take him yourselves and judge him by your own law." The Jews said to him, "It is not lawful for us to put any man to death." ³²This was to fulfil the word which Jesus had spoken to show by what death he was to die.

³³Pilate entered the praetorium again and called Jesus, and said to him, "Are you the King of the Jews?" ³⁴Jesus answered, "Do you say this of your own accord, or did others say it to you about me?" ³⁵Pilate answered, "Am I a Jew? Your own nation and the chief priests have handed you over to me; what have you done?" ³⁶Jesus answered, "My kingship is not of this world; if my kingship were of this world, my servants would fight, that I might not be handed over to the Jews; but my kingship is not from the world." ³⁷Pilate said to him, "So you are a king?" Jesus answered, "You say that I am a king. For this I was born, and for this I have come into the world, to bear witness to the truth. Every one who is of the truth hears my voice." ³⁸Pilate said to him, "What is truth?"

After he had said this, he went out to the Jews again, and told them, "I find no crime in him. ³⁹But you have a custom that I should release one man for you at the Passover; will you have me release for you the King of the Jews?" ⁴⁰They cried out again, "Not this man, but Barabbas!" Now Barabbas was a robber.

18:28 They themselves did not enter the praetorium, so that they might not be defiled.

---

(22) Augustine of Hippo

It was early. They themselves, that is, the ones who were leading Jesus, did not enter the praetorium (18:28). . . . Explaining the reason why they **did not enter the praetorium**, the evangelist says: **So that they might not be defiled, but might eat the passover** (18:28). They were starting the celebration of unleavened bread, and they considered it a contamination to enter a foreigner's house during these days. O impious blindness! Would they really be contaminated by a foreigner's house, and yet not contaminated by their own wickedness? They feared contamination by the **praetorium** of a foreign judge, but did not fear contamination by the blood of an innocent brother!

18:36 "My kingship is not of this world."

---

(23) John Chrysostom

My kingship is not of this world (18:36). Pilate was neither an excessively wicked man, nor like the Jewish leaders, but Christ leads him upward and desires to show him that he is not merely a man, but God and the Son of God. What does he say? **If my kingship were of this world, my servants would fight, that I might not be handed over to the Jews** (18:36). For a moment Pilate had fears about Jesus, a suspicion that he was interested in **king**ly power; Jesus destroys that suspicion. Is then Jesus's **kingship not of this world**? It very much is. Why then does Jesus say that it is not? Not because he doesn't rule here on earth, but because he has his authority from above, one that is not of a human sort but much greater than this and more splendid. If it is greater, then how was he taken prisoner by Pilate? He **handed** himself **over** willingly. For the time, though, he does not reveal this. What does he say? **If my kingship were of this world, my servants would fight, that I might not be handed over** (18:36). He demonstrates the weakness of human **king**ship: its strength lies in having **servants**. **King**ship from above is sufficient in itself; it needs nothing else.

(24) Theodore of Mopsuestia

My kingship is not of this world (18:36). . . What he means is this: "If you ask me whether I want to take **kingship** of the Jews by force, then you already know that I am a **king**. However, I do not possess an earthly **kingship**, otherwise my soldiers would have fought for me so that I would not have been defeated by my enemies. Since I am now naked and I have been handed over without a fight to those who want to seize me, it is obvious that my **kingship** is different—when I am in it, I will be victorious.

(25) Augustine of Hippo

My kingship, he said, **is not of this world** (18:36). What more do you want? Come to the **kingship** that **is not of this world**; come through believing, and do not rage in anger because of your fear. He even says in prophecy about God the Father: *I was established king by him on Zion, his holy mountain* (Ps 2:6). But that *Zion* and that *mountain* are **not of this world**. For what is his **kingship** other than those believing in him, to whom he says: *You are not of the world, even as I am not of the world* (17:16). However, he wants those believers to be *in* the world; that is why he speaks of them to the Father: *I do not pray that thou shouldst take them out of the world, but that thou shouldst keep them from the evil one* (17:15). So here he does not say: **My kingship is not *in* this world**, but it **is not *of* this world**. He proved this when he said: **if my kingship were of this world, my servants would fight, that I might not be handed over to the Jews** (18:36). He didn't say, "My kingship is not *here*," but rather it **is not *from* here**. This world is his **kingship**

until the end of the age, and it has weeds mixed in it until the harvest; for the harvest is the end of the age, when the harvesters will come (that is, the angels) and gather out of his **kingship** all causes of sin (cf. Matt 13:38–41). That certainly would not happen if this were not his **kingship**. It is not *of* **the world**, but it wanders as a stranger *in* **the world**. He says of his *kingship: You are not of the world, but I chose you out of the world* (15:19). Therefore they were **of the world** when they were not his **kingship**, but belonged to the prince of the **world**. Therefore humanity is something **of the world**, created indeed by a true God, but born from the spoiled and condemned root of Adam. His **kingship** is no longer **of the world** because it has been regenerated in Christ. God snatched us away from the powers of darkness and transferred us into the **kingship** of the Son of his love. About this **kingship** he says: **My kingship is not of this world**, or "My kingship is not from here."

(26) Cyril of Alexandria

Jesus answered, "My kingship is not of this world; if my kingship were of this world, my servants would fight, that I might not be handed over to the Jews; but my kingship is not from the world" (18:36). Christ dispels Pilate's fear. Appointed as the guardian of Caesar's kingdom, Pilate thought that Christ was attempting to stir up a revolt against earthly law, as the Jews had foolishly suggested. They hinted at this when they said: **If this man were not an evildoer, we would not have handed him over** (18:30). They meant "revolt" when they spoke of **evil**. They pretended to desire the Romans' good will and would not even bring their lips to mention the word "revolt." This is why they said that they had brought Christ to endure just punishment. In giving his reply, Christ did not deny that he was a **king** (he had to speak the truth!), but he clearly proved that he was not an enemy of Caesar's **king**dom. He only indicated that his own authority was not of an earthly kind, but that it was a God-befitting authority over heaven and earth and of even greater things than these.

(27) John Chrysostom

So, hearing these things, and seeing your Lord being bound and led about, consider the present state of things as nothing. How odd it is that Christ endured such things for you, but you often can't even bear his words. He was spat upon while you beautify yourself with robes and rings, and if you don't gain the praise of everyone, you think that life's not worth living. Christ is insulted; he endures mockeries and disrespectful blows upon his face. You, on the other hand, always want to be honored, and you don't endure the insults of Christ. You don't hear Paul saying, *Be imitators of me, as I am of Christ* (1 Cor 11:1).

So when someone mocks you, remember your Lord, that they bowed before him in mockery, abused him with words and deeds, and exhibited great irony toward him. Not only did Christ refrain from self-defense, he also repaid them with opposite things: gentleness and mercy. Let us also imitate this, and in this way we shall be able to be delivered from all ill treatment.

John 19

John chapter 19 continues the passion of Christ. John Chrysostom uses the extreme suffering of Christ as an example of how to endure abuse with patience and humility, and Augustine of Hippo sees Christ's suffering as a model for future martyrs who also endured unjust persecution. Cyril of Alexandria reflects on the theological fruit of Christ's suffering on our behalf. Employing Paul's Adam-Christ typology in Rom 5, Cyril sees Christ's righteousness extended to all humanity through his obedient suffering. The silence of Christ before his accusers (But Jesus gave no answer [19:9]) leads both Augustine and Cyril to see a fulfillment of Isa 53: "Like a lamb that before its shearers is dumb, so he opened not his mouth."

Christ's bearing his own cross to the place of the skull (19:17) prompts several writers to notice the theological irony here. John Chrysostom regards the place of cruel crucifixion as a "monument of victory over the tyranny of death." Augustine of Hippo recognizes the contrary perspectives: for the impious spectator, Christ's death is a "grand example of dishonor," but for the pious observer, a "grand bulwark of faith." Cyril of Alexandria, likewise, notes the "unexpected reversal of events." The cross that we deserved because of our transgressions is instead borne by Christ. Theodore of Mopsuestia is more concerned to harmonize John's account of Jesus bearing his own cross with Luke's claim that Simon of Cyrene was forced to carry Christ's cross for him (Luke 23:26).

Augustine of Hippo and Cyril of Alexandria both find meaning in the title placed above Jesus's head (I am the king of the Jews [19:19]). Augustine points out that although the title mentions the Jews, the gentiles are meant to be understood as well. Cyril notes that the threefold language in which the title was written indicates a fulfillment that all nations and languages will one day bow before Christ as lord and king.

Christ's garments, especially the division of his clothes into four parts, and the soldiers' casting lots for his seamless tunic (19:23–24), capture the attention of several commentators. Cyprian of Carthage sees the undivided tunic as a symbol of Christ's undivided church. Rufinus understands Christ's scarlet garment as a fulfillment of Isa 63:1–2 and a picture of Christ's death, which takes away the sin of the world. John Chrysostom proclaims the fulfillment of Ps 22 in the soldiers' treatment of Christ's clothes. And both Augustine of Hippo and Cyril of Alexandria see the division of Christ's garments into four parts, and the preservation of the tunic undivided, as a picture of the church spread throughout the four corners of the world, yet united as one church.

As the chapter comes to the scene before the cross, Romanos the Melodist imagines a moving exchange between mother and son. Mary questions whether death is really necessary in order to redeem the world; Christ insists that death alone can conquer death and restore fallen Adam and Eve. John Chrysostom, Augustine of Hippo, and Cyril of Alexandria take Jesus's words to the disciple (Behold, your mother! [19:27]) as a contemporary exhortation to care for our parents, whatever the circumstances.

Verse 34, there came out water and blood, *became a classic reference to the birth of the church. Cyril of Jerusalem and Augustine of Hippo see a parallel between the birth of Eve from Adam's side and the birth of the church through Christ's side. Cyril of Jerusalem also sees the* water *as referring to Baptism and the* blood *to martyrdom—both of which confirm our faith in Christ. On the other hand, John Chrysostom, Theodore of Mopsuestia, Cyril of Alexandria, and John of Damascus identify* water *with Baptism, but the* blood *with the sacrament of the Eucharist.*

*The burial of Christ in verses 38–42 yielded details of theological significance for several of the church fathers. Origen of Alexandria, for example, sees a fitting parallel between Christ's birth from the pure womb of the virgin and Christ's burial in "*a new and pure tomb.*" John Chrysostom finds it important that Christ's burial was a public event witnessed by believers and unbelievers alike. If his death and burial had been a secret, "it would have undermined the account of his resurrection." Finally, Cyril of Alexandria notes that the* new tomb is in a garden, *symbolizing our entry into a new paradise with Christ. As a result, the death we experience because of Adam has been turned into "a kind of sleep . . . filled with a beautiful hope."*

John 19:1–16

¹Then Pilate took Jesus and scourged him. ²And the soldiers plaited a crown of thorns, and put it on his head, and arrayed him in a purple robe; ³they came up to him, saying, "Hail, King of the Jews!" and struck him with their hands. ⁴Pilate went out again, and said to them, "See, I am bringing him out to you, that you may know that I find no crime in him." ⁵So Jesus came out, wearing the crown of thorns and the purple robe. Pilate said to them, "Behold the man!" ⁶When the chief priests and the officers saw him, they cried out, "Crucify him, crucify him!" Pilate said to them, "Take him yourselves and crucify him, for I find no crime in him." ⁷The Jews answered him, "We have a law, and by that law he ought to die, because he has made himself the Son of God." ⁸When Pilate heard these words, he was the more afraid; ⁹he entered the praetorium again and said to Jesus, "Where are you from?" But Jesus gave no answer. ¹⁰Pilate therefore said to him, "You will not speak to me? Do you not know that I have power to release you, and power to crucify you?" ¹¹Jesus answered him, "You would have no power over me unless it had been given you from above; therefore he who delivered me to you has the greater sin."

¹²Upon this Pilate sought to release him, but the Jews cried out, "If you release this man, you are not Caesar's friend; every one who makes himself a king sets himself against Caesar." ¹³When Pilate heard these words, he brought Jesus out and sat down on the judgment seat at a place called The Pavement, and in Hebrew, Gabbatha. ¹⁴Now it was the day of Preparation of the Passover; it was about the sixth hour. He said to the

Jews, "Behold your King!" ¹⁵They cried out, "Away with him, away with him, crucify him!" Pilate said to them, "Shall I crucify your King?" The chief priests answered, "We have no king but Caesar." ¹⁶Then he handed him over to them to be crucified.

19:2–3 And the soldiers plaited a crown of thorns, and put it on his head . . . and struck him with their hands.

---

(1) John Chrysostom

Let us not only read about these things, but keep them in our minds: the crown of thorns, the robe, the reed, the blows, the strikes on the cheek, the spittings, the irony of it all. Keeping such images continually in our minds is sufficient to destroy all anger. Even if we are mocked or suffer unjustly, let us continually say, *A servant is not greater than his master* (13:16). . . . This is why Christ endured all these things, so that we might walk in his footsteps and endure the scoffings which work more than other abuses to drive us mad. Not only did Christ bear these abuses, but he also did everything he could to save and deliver them from punishment reserved for those who did these things. He sent the apostles out to them for their salvation. You hear them saying, *We know that you acted in ignorance* (Acts 3:17), attempting to draw them to repentance through their words. Let us imitate these things as well, for nothing pleases God more than loving our enemies and doing good to those who insult us. So when someone insults you, don't look at the person, look at the spirit stirring the person. Relent from all your anger against him and have mercy on the one who is stirred up this way.

(2) Augustine of Hippo

And the soldiers plaited a crown of thorns, and put it on his head, and arrayed him in a purple robe; they came up to him, saying, "Hail, King of the Jews!" and struck him with their hands (19:2–3). In this way, the things that Christ had said about himself were fulfilled and the martyrs were given a pattern for enduring everything that persecutors were pleased to do. By briefly concealing his tremendous power, we are encouraged to imitate his patience. The *kingship which was not of this world* (18:36) conquered the proud world, not by the fury of battle, but by the humility of suffering. The seed which was to be multiplied was sown by a terrible abuse so that it might spring forth in astonishing glory.

(3) Cyril of Alexandria

Christ was beaten unjustly so that he might deliver us from just punishment. He was mocked and struck so that we might mock Satan who has mocked us, and so that we might escape the sin which was inflicted upon us through Adam's transgression. If we are thinking correctly, we will understand that Christ suffered everything for us and on our behalf. His sufferings had the power to liberate us from everything that justly happened to us because of our rebellion against God. Just as he was able to abolish the death of all, the one who knew no death offered his own flesh on behalf of our life. One died on behalf of all. So it is correct to understand that the Lord's suffering on our behalf was sufficient to release us all from beatings and dishonor. How is it that *by his stripes we are healed*, as it is written (Isa 53:5)? For all *have gone astray, every one to his own way*, as the blessed prophet Isaiah says (Isa 53:6). The Lord gave himself up for our sins, and *suffers pain for us* (Isa 53:4 LXX). He was bruised for our transgressions and has given his own *back to scourges and his cheeks to blows*, as it also says (Isa 50:6 LXX). . . .

Just as in Adam the whole of humanity was conquered in one man, demonstrating that humanity was weighed down in sins, so also here Christ is conquered by humanity. The one who had no sin, who was God by nature, was also human. Just as condemnation for transgression was brought to fruition for all humanity through one man, the first Adam, in the same way the blessing of Christ's righteousness was extended to all humanity through one man, the second Adam. Paul also testifies to this, saying, *As one man's trespass led to condemnation for all men, so one man's act of righteousness leads to acquittal and life for all men* (Rom 5:18). We are diseased through the disobedience and curse of the first man, Adam, and we are made rich through the obedience and blessing of the second man, Christ.

19:8–9 "Where are you from?" But Jesus gave no answer.

---

(4) Augustine of Hippo

Pilate entered the praetorium again and said to Jesus, "Where are you from?" But Jesus gave no answer (19:8–9). This silence of our Lord Jesus Christ did not occur this one time only; when we compare all the gospel accounts, we see it repeated with the chief priest, with Herod where Pilate sent him for a hearing (according to Luke), as well as with Pilate himself. So it was not in vain that the prophet foretold: *Like a lamb that before its shearers is dumb, so he opened not his mouth* (Isa 53:7). Indeed, Christ likewise did not respond when interrogated. Although he often responded when questioned, the comparison to the *lamb* is supplied to account for those times when he did not wish to respond, so that in his silence he is not guilty but innocent. Therefore when he was tried and did not open his mouth, he is like the *lamb* that *did not open its mouth*; that is, he acts not as a wicked person who is guilty and knows the sins for which he is convicted, but as a gentle person who is sacrificed for the sins of others.

(5) Cyril of Alexandria

Pilate thinks that Christ's silence is the action of an insane man. For this reason, he extends his power and authority over him like a rod and thinks that he can use fear to make Christ unwillingly give some useless response. He says clearly that whatever he wanted to do, either to punish or to show mercy, he would have the power to do it, that no one could push him toward a judgment against his will, and that to him alone lies the decision for the one accused.

So he accuses him, like one insulted by inappropriate silence, and as much as it came to this, he is incited to rage against him. He does not understand the mysterious meaning of Christ's silence. In this silence you will see that which was announced through the voice of the prophet being beautifully fulfilled: *Like a sheep he was led to the slaughter, and as a lamb is silent before the one shearing it, so he does not open his mouth. In his humiliation, his judgment was taken away* (Isa 53:7–8 LXX). While the blessed Isaiah tells us this, the psalmist, taking up the person of Christ, says in the Spirit: *I set watch to my mouth when the sinner organized against me. I became dumb and was humbled, and I was silent from good things* (Ps 39:1–2 [38:2–3 LXX]).

John 19:17–30

¹⁷So they took Jesus, and he went out, bearing his own cross, to the place called the place of a skull, which is called in Hebrew Golgotha. ¹⁸There they crucified him, and with him two others, one on either side, and Jesus between them. ¹⁹Pilate also wrote a title and put it on the cross; it read, "Jesus of Nazareth, the King of the Jews." ²⁰Many of the Jews read this title, for the place where Jesus was crucified was near the city; and it was written in Hebrew, in Latin, and in Greek. ²¹The chief priests of the Jews then said to Pilate, "Do not write, 'The King of the Jews,' but, 'This man said, I am King of the Jews.'" ²²Pilate answered, "What I have written I have written."

²³When the soldiers had crucified Jesus they took his garments and made four parts, one for each soldier; also his tunic. But the tunic was without seam, woven from top to bottom; ²⁴so they said to one another, "Let us not tear it, but cast lots for it to see whose it shall be." This was to fulfil the scripture, "They parted my garments among them, and for my clothing they cast lots."

²⁵So the soldiers did this. But standing by the cross of Jesus were his mother, and his mother's sister, Mary the wife of Clopas, and Mary Magdalene. ²⁶When Jesus saw his mother, and the disciple whom he loved standing near, he said to his mother, "Woman, behold, your son!" ²⁷Then he said to the disciple, "Behold, your mother!" And from that hour the disciple took her to his own home.

²⁸After this Jesus, knowing that all was now finished, said (to fulfil the scripture), "I thirst." ²⁹A bowl full of vinegar stood there; so they put a sponge full of the vinegar on hyssop and held it to his mouth. ³⁰When Jesus had received the vinegar, he said, "It is finished"; and he bowed his head and gave up his spirit.

19:17–18   So they took Jesus, and he went out . . . to the place called the place of a skull. . . . There they crucified him.

---

(6) John Chrysostom

And he went out to the place of a skull (19:17). Some say Adam died and was buried there, and that in this place where death had reigned, Jesus erected his monument of victory.

He **went out bearing the cross** (19:17) as that monument of victory over the tyranny of death. Just as victors do, Jesus bore upon his shoulders the symbol of victory. . . . They also crucified him with robbers, unknowingly fulfilling prophecy. What they did as an insult to Christ actually added to the truth so that you might learn how powerful that prophecy was. The prophet had foretold this from the beginning: *He was numbered with the transgressors* (Isa 53:12). The devil wanted to conceal what had happened, but he was unable to do so.

(7) Theodore of Mopsuestia

Some think that the words of the evangelists do not agree with one another because while John said **he went out, bearing his own cross** (19:17), the other evangelist mentioned that they seized Simon of Cyrene to carry his cross (cf. Luke 23:26). Rather, both happened. After Pilate made his decree and handed him over to them to be crucified, they laid on him the cross and then led him out from the judgment seat. While they were going to the **place of Golgotha** (19:17) to crucify him, they came across *Simon* and laid the cross on him. The other evangelists wanted to mention this, but John was focused on his own purpose here, mentioning only what was omitted by the others. . . . Here is what Luke says: *And as they led him away, they seized one Simon of Cyrene, who was coming in from the country, and laid on him the cross, to carry it behind Jesus* (Luke 23:26). John said this: **He went out, bearing his own cross**, while Luke said: *And as they led him away, they seized one Simon of Cyrene, who was coming in from the country*. It is obvious that this event in Luke happened toward the end of their journey to Golgotha, but the event in John happened immediately after he was condemned to die, when he left the judgment seat.

(8) Augustine of Hippo

Jesus went to **the place** where he was about to be crucified, **bearing his own cross** (19:17). A grand spectacle! To an impious observer, a grand mockery; to a pious observer, a grand mystery. To an impious spectator, a grand example of dishonor, but to a pious spectator, a grand bulwark of faith. An impious viewer laughs at the king **bearing the cross** of his own punishment instead of a rod of royal power; a pious viewer sees the king **bearing the cross** for his own crucifixion, a sign which he would fix on the brows of kings. That which is scorned by the eyes of the impious, the hearts of the saints will glory in.

(9) Cyril of Alexandria

They led away to his death the author of life, and this was done on our behalf. According to the purpose of his divine power and skill, his suffering accomplished his plan to bring about an unexpected reversal of events. The suffering of Christ was prepared as a trap for the power of death, and the death of the Lord was the source of restoration for an incorruptible and new life. **Bearing** on his shoulders **the cross** (19:17) upon which he was about to be crucified, he went forth, his condemnation already secured. On our behalf, he completely submitted to the sentence of death, even though he committed no evil. He bore in himself the judgment rightly hanging over sinners by the law. He became *a curse for us—for it is written, "Cursed be everyone who hangs on a tree"* (Gal 3:13, citing Deut 21:23). We are all accursed for we are unable to satisfy the law of God, for *we all make many mistakes* (Jas 3:2,) and human nature has an extreme tendency in this direction. Again, since the divine law says somewhere, *Cursed be everyone who does not abide by all things written in this book of the law, and do them* (Gal 3:10, citing Deut 27:26), the curse belongs to us, not to someone else. It would be appropriate to hold those accountable who can be charged with transgression of the law, who are inclined to drift away from the commandments. Therefore, the one *who knew no sin* (2 Cor 5:21) was accursed for us so that he might deliver us from that ancient curse. The God of all, who suffered on behalf of all, was sufficient for this task, securing the redemption of all through the death of his own flesh.

So Christ did not **bear the cross** he deserved, but **the cross** which hung over us, as we deserved, by the condemnation of the law. He was numbered among the dead, not for himself, but for us, so that the author of eternal life might be found in us, destroying the power of death through his death. So he took upon himself **the cross** that we deserved, taking on himself the condemnation of the law so that every lawless *mouth* might be *stopped*, according to what is sung in the Psalms (Ps 107:42). The one without sin has been condemned on behalf of the sin of all. What Christ has accomplished will be of great benefit to our souls (I mean here that he is a pattern of true courage). For I think that it is possible to lay hold of the perfection of good things and complete union with God in no other way than to form our love for him above our earthly life, and eagerly to desire to wage battle for the truth when the time calls us to it. Therefore, our Lord Jesus Christ says that everyone who *does not take his cross and follow me is not worthy of me* (Matt 10:38). I think taking up **the cross** means nothing other than to abandon the world for God's sake and (if it should happen) to consider our very life in the body of second importance compared to the virtuous life of hope. Our Lord Jesus Christ was not ashamed to **bear the cross** we deserved, but suffered out of love for us. We miserable creatures, however, who have the insensible earth beneath our feet as our mother, who were called into being from nothing, do not even dare to break a sweat in our devotion to God. If it should happen that we have to suffer because of our devotion to Christ, we immediately consider the shame unbearable.

19:19–20 Pilate also wrote a title and put it on the cross; it read, "Jesus of Nazareth, the King of the Jews." . . . It was written in Hebrew, in Latin, and in Greek.

---

(10) Augustine of Hippo

Is Christ **king of the Jews (19:19)** only, or also of the gentiles? Surely he is king of the gentiles as well. It was said in the prophets, I have set my **king** on Zion, my holy hill, I will tell of the decree of the Lord (Ps 2:6–7). So that no one would think that the reference to *Zion* means that he was established as **king of the Jews** alone, it immediately adds, The Lord said to me, "You are my son, today I have begotten you. Ask of me and I will make the gentiles your heritage, and the ends of the earth your possession" (Ps 2:7–8). So also that same voice, now speaking through his own mouth with the Jews, said *I have other sheep, that are not of this fold; I must bring them also, and they will heed my voice. So there shall be one flock, one Shepherd* (10:16). So, how is the mystery of this inscription to be understood, that **King of the Jews** had been written, if Christ is king of the gentiles as well? . . .

If what was written on that inscription is true, that Christ is the **King of the Jews**, then who should we understand the **Jews** to be except the seed of Abraham, his promised children, who are also children of God? The apostle says, *It is not the children of the flesh who are the children of God, but the children of the promise are reckoned as descendants* (Rom 9:8). And the gentiles were those about whom it was said, *If you are Christ's, then you are Abraham's offspring, heirs according to the promise* (Gal 3:29). Therefore, Christ is **King of the Jews**, but **Jews** by the circumcision of the heart (Rom 2:29), **Jews** by the spirit, not the letter (2 Cor 3:6), whose praise is not from men, but from God, **Jews** who belong to our eternal *free mother, Jerusalem above*, the spiritual Sarah, who cast the slave woman and her children out of the house of liberty (cf. Gal 4:26–31). Indeed, for that reason Pilate wrote what he wrote because the Lord had said what he said.

(11) Cyril of Alexandria

Some would say that it was by the skillful and ineffable divine plan that the **title** was erected with three inscriptions, **Hebrew, Latin, and Greek** (19:20). It was placed before all, clearly proclaiming the kingdom of our Savior in three of the most well-known languages of all. It brought the firstfruits to the Crucified One, just as the prophecy had said about him through the most-wise Daniel: *To him was given glory and kingdom, that nations and languages should serve him* (Dan 7:14). Saint Paul also announces to us the same thing, crying out: *Every knee should bow, in heaven and on earth and under the earth, and every tongue confess that Jesus Christ is Lord, to the glory of God the Father* (Phil 2:10–11). So the **title** that proclaimed Jesus as king was a kind of true firstfruits of the confession of tongues.

19:23–24 When the soldiers had crucified Jesus they took his garments and made four parts. . . . But the tunic was without seam, woven from top to bottom.

---

(12) Cyprian of Carthage

This sacrament of unity, this inseparable and shared bond of concord,[1] is shown in the gospel when the **tunic** of the Lord Jesus Christ is not at all divided or torn. Rather, those

---

1. Cyprian is speaking of the unity of the church.

casting lots for Christ's garment (who should have instead *put on Christ* [cf. Rom 13:14]), received the whole garment and possessed the **tunic** uncorrupted and undivided. Divine Scripture speaks and says: **But the tunic was without seam, woven from top to bottom, so they said to one another, "Let us not tear it but cast lots for it to see whose it shall be"** (19:23–24). That **tunic** bore a unity which came down from a higher part, that is, from heaven and from the Father. It was unable to be torn at all by him who received and took possession of it, but at once inseparably maintained a complete and entire stability. No one is able to possess Christ's **garment** who tears and divides Christ's church.

(13) Rufinus of Aquileia

The preaching of the gospel teaches that the soldiers divided Jesus's **garments**, and over his **tunic** they cast lots. The Holy Spirit took care that this was also proclaimed by the voices of the prophets, when it says: *They divide my **garments** among them, and for my raiment they cast lots* (Ps 22:18). Even concerning that **garment** which the mocking soldiers are said to have put on him, that is a scarlet **garment** (cf. John 19:5; Mark 15:17), the prophets were not silent. Listen to what Isaiah says: *Who is this that comes from Edom, in crimsoned **garments** from Bozrah? Why is thy apparel red and thy **garments** like his that treads in the wine press?* (Isa 63:1–2). Again, the same prophet responds: *I have trodden the wine press alone*, O daughters of Zion (Isa 63:3). For he alone is without sin and has taken away the sin of the world (cf. John 1:29). If through one man death was able to enter the world, how much more through one man, who also was God, was life able to be restored?

(14) John Chrysostom

The soldiers divided up the **garments**, but not the **tunic** (19:23). Observe how by their wicked actions the prophecies are entirely fulfilled, for this had been foretold from the beginning (cf. Ps 22:18). While there were three men crucified, the details of the prophecies were fulfilled in Christ. Why else did the soldiers do such things only to Christ but not to the others? Consider also the precision of the prophecies: the prophet not only said something would be divided, but also that something would not be divided. In fact, the soldiers divided up the **garments** but not the **tunic**; instead they committed the matter to **lots**. The phrase **woven from the top** (19:23) is mentioned for a good reason. Some say that an allegory is intended here, that the Crucified One was not just a human but also possessed divinity from above.

(15) Augustine of Hippo

Perhaps someone may ask what the dividing of the **garments** and the **casting of lots** for the **tunic** could mean (19:23–24). The **four parts** of the Lord Jesus Christ's **garments** represent the **four parts** of his church which fit together, even while scattered across the world. That church is distributed among all **four parts** equally, that is, harmoniously. This is why he says elsewhere that he will send his angels to *gather his elect from the four winds* (Matt 24:31). What is this, if not the **four parts** of the world—the east, west, north, and south? The **tunic** over which **lots** were **cast** signifies the unity of all the parts, held together by the bond of love. . . .

His clothes, however, were not sewn together so they would never be ripped at the seams; they belonged to one person because he gathers everything together into one. Just as the apostles themselves numbered twelve, that is **four parts** of three, and all were questioned, only Peter responded: *You are the Christ, the Son of the living God.* To him it was said: *I will give you the keys of the kingdom of heaven* (Matt 16:15, 19), as if he alone received the powers of binding and loosing. Yet one had spoken for all and had received those powers with all, as if personifying unity itself. Therefore one stands for all, because there is unity among all. When the evangelist said here that the **tunic** was **woven from the top**, he added: **throughout** (19:23 Vulgate). If we understand what this signifies, it means that whoever has a part of the church is found to belong to the whole church **throughout** the world, and as the Greek language indicates, the church being called "catholic" refers to this whole church **throughout** the world.

(16) Cyril of Alexandria

Their division of the Savior's **garments** into **four parts**, and their keeping the one **tunic** undivided, represents the administration of the only-begotten's marvelous wisdom. It symbolizes the mysterious economy through which the **four** corners of the world would be saved. The **four** corners of the world divided, as it were, the holy **tunic** of the Word, that is his body, which was still undivided. The only-begotten is divided individually among many and through his own flesh sanctifies the soul and body of each partaker; yet he is altogether whole and undivided, being everywhere one. For as Paul says, *Christ* can never be *divided* (cf. 1 Cor 1:13).

19:25 Standing at the cross of Jesus were his mother, and his mother's sister, Mary the wife of Clopas, and Mary Magdalene.

---

(17) Romanos the Melodist

Strophe 4:   "Why dost thou weep, **Mother**, why dost thou advance with these other women?
CHRIST   Is it that I should not suffer, that I should not die? How, then,
           shall I save Adam?
      Is it that I should not inhabit the tomb? How then shall I restore to life
      those in Hades?
And surely thou dost know that I am to be crucified unjustly.
      Why, then, O **Mother**, dost thou weep? Rather, cry aloud
      'It is gladly and willingly He suffered,
           My son and my God.'"

Strophe 7: "See, my child," she says, "I rub the tears from my eyes,
MARY   And I rub my heart still more,
      But my thinking cannot be silenced.
Why dost thou say to me, merciful one, 'If I do not die, Adam is not healed'?
      For indeed thou hast cured many without suffering.
      Thou hast cleansed the leper and thou didst suffer no pain but thou didst
      will it.
Having given strength to the paralytic, thou wast not harmed;
      Again, thou didst give sight to the blind by a word, O righteous one,
      And thou didst remain without harm,
         My son and my God.

Strophe 8: "Raising up the dead, thou didst not become dead
MARY   Nor rest in a tomb, O my son and my life. Why, then, dost thou say,
      'If I do not suffer, Adam is not redeemed'?
Command, O Savior, and straightway the cripple picking up his bed walks.
      Indeed, even if Adam has been buried deep in a tomb,
      As thou hast raised up Lazarus from the tomb with thy voice,
         do even so with him.
All things serve thee as Creator of all.
      Why, then, dost thou hasten, my child? Do not hurt to slaughter;
      Do not court death,
         My son and my God."

Strophe 9: "Thou dost not know, O **Mother**, thou dost not know what I am saying,
CHRIST   Why I revealed my purpose and established the word which thou hearest,
      Yet in thy heart thou knowest the truth of what I am saying.
This poor Adam, whom I mentioned, was sickened,
      Not only in body but also in soul.
      Willfully he suffered; for he had not heard of me and he is in danger.
Thou knowest what I say. Then do not weep, **Mother**;
      But rather say this: 'Free Adam
      And pity Eve,
         My son and my God.'

Strophe 10: "By profligacy and by gluttony
CHRIST   Did Adam become ill and was cast into lowest Hades,
      Where he weeps in the sorrow of his spirit.
But Eve, since she taught him the lawless deed,
      Mourns with him; for she became ill with him
      So that they might learn together to keep watch for the message of the
      physician.
Dost thou now understand? Art thou fully aware of what I say?
      Again, O **Mother**, cry: 'If thou dost pardon Adam,

Also pardon Eve,
My son and my God.'

Strophe 14: "Lay aside thy grief, **Mother**,
CHRIST   And advance with joy; for I now hasten to that for which I came,
To *do the will of him who sent me* (6:38);
For, from the first this was ordained for me by my Father,
And it was not displeasing to my spirit
That I should assume human form and suffer for the fallen.
Then, O **Mother**, hastening, tell all people
That by suffering he strikes down the one who hates Adam
And, having conquered, he comes,
My son and my God."

Strophe 15: "I shall conquer, child, I shall conquer my suffering;
MARY   And truly I shall not mourn when I am in my chamber
And thou art on the cross—
I in my house and thou in the tomb.
Grant that I come with thee for it helps me to look upon thee.
I know the boldness of those who honored Moses;
For, as then, the blind were taking vengeance on him, so now they
Have come to slay thee.
Moses said to Israel
That the time would come that they would see life upon the tree (Num 21:8).
Who is the life? It is
My son and my God."

Strophe 17: Son of the virgin, God of the virgin,
And Maker of the world, thine is the suffering, thine, the depths of wisdom.
Thou knowest what thou art and what thou art to become.
Willing to suffer, thou hast deemed it of worth to save man.
As *Lamb of God*, thou hast *taken away our sins* (1:29);
Thou hast destroyed them through thy death; as Savior thou hast saved all.
Thou art, as a human, able to suffer, and as God, thou knowest no suffering.
Dying, thou art saving. Thou dost grant to the holy virgin
Fearless confidence to cry to thee,
"My son and my God."

19:26–27 Then he said to the disciple, "Behold your mother!"

---

(18) John Chrysostom

While being crucified, Christ entrusts his **mother** to his **disciple**, teaching us to make every care for our **mothers**, even to our last breath. When Mary pestered him inappropriately, he said, *What have you to do with me?* (2:4). Later he asked, *Who is my mother?* (Matt 12:48). But here he displays great tenderness and affection for her and entrusts her to the **disciple whom he loved.** . . .

(19) Augustine of Hippo

The good teacher does now what he urged others to do, and by his own example he instructs his disciples so that pious children would devote their care to their parents. It was as if that cross, on which the dying man's body was fixed, had also become the seat by which the master taught them. From this sound doctrine the apostle Paul had learned what Christ taught: *If anyone does not provide for his relatives, and especially for his own family, he has disowned the faith and is worse than an unbeliever* (1 Tim 5:8). Who is as familiar as parents to their children, or children to their parents? So from himself the very teacher of the saints established an example of this most healthy precept. Acting not as God to the handmaid whom he had created and ruled, but as a human to the **mother** from whom he had been created and whom he was leaving behind, he was in a way providing another son in place of himself. The reason why he does this is indicated in what follows; indeed, the evangelist, speaking of himself, goes on to say, **And from that hour the disciple took her to his home** (19:27).

(20) Cyril of Alexandria

What was Christ's purpose in these words to his disciple? First he wanted to confirm the teaching which is emphasized in the law. What does the Mosaic law say? *Honor your father and your mother, that it may be well with you* (Exod 20:12 LXX). His word not only requires us to show such *honor*, but also threatens us with an extreme penalty if we choose not to follow it. Sin against God and sin against our parents have been laid out as equal. The law commanded the blasphemer to be put to death: *He who blasphemes the name of the LORD shall be put to death* (Lev 24:16). But the law applies the same penalty for those who attack their parents with intemperate and unbridled tongues: *Whoever curses his father or his mother shall be put to death* (Exod 21:17). Since the lawgiver has obligated us to assign such *honor* to our *parents*, how could the well-known commandment not be confirmed by the Savior's judgment? Since the principle of every good and virtuous thing has proceeded through him first, why should this virtue not be taken together with the others? Surely honoring our parents is a precious kind of virtue. Showing our love for them is not a trivial thing, even if some of us are overwhelmed by unbearable circumstances. But tell me, how would we learn this except in and through Christ first? Best of all are those who truly keep in mind the holy commandments and are not distracted from their appropriate duty, not only in peaceful circumstances, but in stormy and turbulent times as well.

19:30 When Jesus had received the vinegar, he said, "It is finished," and he bowed his head and gave up his spirit.

---

(21) Augustine of Hippo

Matthew says: *Jesus cried again with a loud voice and yielded up his spirit* (Matt 27:50). Mark similarly notes: *Jesus uttered a loud cry, and breathed his last* (Mark 15:37). Luke, moreover, declared what was said with the same loud voice, for he said: *Then Jesus, crying with a loud voice, said, "Father, into thy hands I commit my spirit!" And having said this he breathed his last* (Luke 23:46). John was truly silent about that first cry—*Eli, Eli*—which Matthew and Mark repeated (cf. Matt 27:46; Mark 15:34). He also remained silent about what Luke alone proclaimed (which Matthew and Mark signified by the phrase *loud voice*), that is, *Father, into thy hands I commit my spirit* (Luke 23:46). Luke himself similarly attested that he had spoken with a loud voice, so that we might understand that this was the loud cry that Matthew and Mark related. But John said what none of those three had said, namely that Jesus had said, **It is finished**, when he **had received the vinegar** (19:30).

In my understanding, Jesus said this before that *loud cry*. For these are the words of John: **When Jesus had received the vinegar, he said, "It is finished," and he bowed his head and gave up his spirit** (19:30). Between **It is finished** and **he bowed his head and gave up his spirit**, that *loud cry* was uttered, about which John himself was silent, but the other three related. This appears to be the order of events: first when the prophecy about him had been completed in him, he said, **It is finished.** Then, as if he was waiting for this, indeed as one who died when he willed it, he commended his **spirit** and **gave** it **up**. But whatever the order of events anyone should think these words were said, one must surely avoid the notion that any one of the evangelists opposes another, either when one of them is silent about what another said, or when one of them says what another is silent about.

John 19:31-37

[31]Since it was the day of Preparation, in order to prevent the bodies from remaining on the cross on the sabbath (for that sabbath was a high day), the Jews asked Pilate that their legs might be broken, and that they might be taken away. [32]So the soldiers came and broke the legs of the first, and of the other who had been crucified with him; [33]but when they came to Jesus and saw that he was already dead, they did not break his legs. [34]But one of the soldiers pierced his side with a spear, and at once there came out blood and water. [35]He who saw it has borne witness—his testimony is true, and he knows that

he tells the truth—that you also may believe. [36]For these things took place that the scripture might be fulfilled, "Not a bone of him shall be broken." [37]And again another scripture says, "They shall look on him whom they have pierced."

19:34 One of the soldiers pierced his side with a spear, and at once there came out blood and water.

---

(22) Cyril of Jerusalem

The power of baptismal salvation in the gospels is twofold: one is given to the enlightened through **water**, and one which is given in persecution to the holy martyrs through their own **blood**. For this reason, **there came out** of his saving **side blood and water** (19:34). This confirms the grace common to our confession of Christ, both for those who are baptized and those who are martyred.[2]

There is another reason for mentioning his **side**. The woman who became the first cause of sin was formed from the **side** of Adam, while Jesus comes to grant forgiveness to men and women alike. He was **pierced** in the **side** on behalf of women in order to destroy the sin.

(23) John Chrysostom

There came out water and blood (19:34). These springs didn't come forth without reason: the church was created by both of these elements. Those initiated in the mysteries know this—they are regenerated by **water** and are fed by flesh and **blood**. Here those mysteries take their beginning so that when you approach the awe-inspiring cup, you may approach as if you are drinking from his very **side**.

(24) Augustine of Hippo

The evangelist's word choice here wakes us up, because he does not say: "pierced his side" or "wounded his side," or something else; but **he opened** it.[3] The door of life is spread **open**, from which the sacraments of the church pour forth, and without which we would not enter into the life that is the true life. That **blood** was shed for the forgiveness of sins; that **water** mixes into the cup of salvation and provides both a bath and a drink. This was foretold when Noah was ordered to make a door in **the side** of the ark, through which the animals entered who did not perish in the flood (Gen 6:16–20); the animals together prefigured the church. Because of this the first woman was made from **the side** of a sleeping man, and is

---

2. Martyrdom was considered a form of baptism in the early church.

3. Augustine's Latin text differs from the RSV and reads: "**One of the soldiers opened his side with a spear.**"

called "life"[4] and *mother of the living* (Gen 2:21–22; 3:20). This of course signified a great good, before the great wickedness of transgression. The second Adam bowed his head and fell asleep on the cross in order to form his bride, who flowed out of **the side** of his sleeping body. O death made alive again out of death! What is purer than that **blood**? What is more health-giving than that wound?

(25) Cyril of Alexandria

They **pierced his side with a spear** and **there came out blood and water** mingled together (19:34). This was God's way of giving us a kind of image and firstfruits of the mystery of the Eucharist and holy baptism. Holy baptism comes from Christ, and the power of the mystery of the Eucharist sprang forth to us from his holy flesh.

(26) John of Damascus

God made us for incorruption, but when we transgressed his saving command, he sentenced us to the corruption of death so that that which is evil might not be immortal. When in his compassion he condescended to his servants and became like us, he redeemed us from corruption through his own suffering. He caused the fount of forgiveness to **come forth** for us out of his pure and holy **side**: **water** for rebirth and the cleansing of sin and corruption, and **blood** to drink as the host of eternal life.

John 19:38–42

[38]**After this Joseph of Arimathea, who was a disciple of Jesus, but secretly, for fear of the Jews, asked Pilate that he might take away the body of Jesus, and Pilate gave him leave. So he came and took away his body.** [39]**Nicodemus also, who had at first come to him by night, came bringing a mixture of myrrh and aloes, about a hundred pounds' weight.** [40]**They took the body of Jesus, and bound it in linen cloths with the spices, as is the burial custom of the Jews.** [41]**Now in the place where he was crucified there was a garden, and in the garden a new tomb where no one had ever been laid.** [42]**So because of the Jewish day of Preparation, as the tomb was close at hand, they laid Jesus there.**

(27) Origen of Alexandria

It is sufficient to notice the clean garment in which the pure body of Jesus was to be wrapped, and the **new tomb** (19:41), which Joseph *had hewn in the rock* (Matt 27:60), *where no one was yet lying* (Luke 23:53), or as John says, **where no one had ever been laid** (19:41). Observe

---

4. The meaning of the word "Eve."

whether we might understand some harmony among these three evangelists. They wrote that the **tomb** was carved or *hewn in the rock* so that the one who examines the words of the texts might perceive something worthy of meaning. There is also meaning in the **new**ness of the **tomb**, as Matthew and John recount, and in the point that no dead body had yet been **laid** there, as Luke and John report. It was fitting that Christ, who was not like other dead men (although he demonstrated in his death signs of life in *water and blood* [19:34]), was a **new** dead man, so to speak, buried in a **new** and pure **tomb**. Just as his birth from a virgin, without sexual union, was purer than all other births, so also his burial was the purest of all, symbolized by his body being placed in a **new tomb**, not built from gathered stones or having a natural unity, but carved and *hewn* in one *rock*, united throughout.

(28) John Chrysostom

It was providential that Christ was placed in a **new tomb where no one had ever been laid** (19:41). This way the resurrection might not be thought to be someone else who was lying there in the tomb with him. Also the disciples might easily come to see what had happened, since the place was nearby. The disciples weren't the only witnesses of his **burial**; his enemies were also. The soldiers who placed the seal on the tomb and sat by to guard it (Matt 27:65–66) were also witnesses to the **burial**. Christ deeply desired that his burial should be witnessed no less than the resurrection, and the disciples are quite anxious, as well, to show that he did in fact die. For all subsequent time would testify to the resurrection, but if his death had been hidden, or not made exceedingly obvious, it would have undermined the account of his resurrection. These weren't the only reasons he was placed in a nearby **tomb**, but so that story about the stealing of his body might be shown to be false as well.

(29) Cyril of Alexandria

Christ was counted among the dead, who became dead in the flesh for us. In reality he is understood to be, and is in fact, life on account of himself and his Father. So that he might fulfill all righteousness, that is, what was fitting for the human form, he willingly subjected the temple of his body not only to death, but also to the experiences after death, that is, to **burial** and being **laid** in the **tomb**. The writer says that this **tomb** in the **garden** was a **new** one, signifying to us a kind of figure and model that the death of Christ was for us the introduction and beginning of our entry into paradise. *He has gone as a forerunner on our behalf* (Heb 6:20). What else can it mean that the dead Jesus was carried over into a **garden**? The **new**ness of the **tomb** signifies the unworn and somewhat strange return from death to life, and our re**new**al from corruption which was intended through Christ. In Christ's death, our death has now been changed into a kind of sleep with regard to its power and purpose. We are *alive to God* and shall live on, according to the Scriptures (Rom 6:11). Paul also says in another place that those who have died in Christ are *asleep* (cf. 1 Thess 4:13). In ancient times, the horror of death acted defiantly against our human nature, and *death reigned from Adam to Moses, even over those whose sins were not like the transgression of*

Adam (Rom 5:14). *We have borne the image of the man of dust* (1 Cor 15:49), in his likeness, and have endured the death which came from the divine curse. However, when the second Adam came among us, the divine one from heaven who fought for the life of all, he purchased for us, by the death of his own flesh, the life of all. He destroyed the power of corruption and rose again to life. We were transformed into his image, and underwent a kind of **new** death which does not destroy with corruption. Instead, it lays sleep upon us filled with a beautiful hope, namely, of being made in the likeness of the one who has re**new**ed this path for us, that is, Christ.

John 20

As the Gospel of John nears its close, the evangelist presents a series of resurrection appearances of Jesus to his followers. In examining this chapter, early Christian thinkers insightfully (and oftentimes beautifully) explore questions related to faith in the resurrection, the state of Jesus's resurrection body, and the commissioning of his disciples with authority to forgive and retain sins.

John 20 opens with Mary Magdalene finding an empty tomb and reporting the news to the disciples. Theodore of Mopsuestia discusses the significance of the placement of the linen cloths and napkin in the tomb (20:6–7) as "signs of the resurrection." John Chrysostom uses the text as a pastoral occasion to exhort his congregation gently toward a more proper theology of death, dying, and funeral practices.

Some commentators discuss the state of Mary's recognition of the events she is witnessing. While John Chrysostom finds in Mary a limited understanding that needs to be elevated to faith in the resurrection, Gregory the Great commends Mary for her zealous love and "holy desire" for the Lord, demonstrated in her weeping and repeated stooping to look in the empty tomb (20:11). Cyril of Alexandria puzzles over why the angels would proclaim the resurrection to Mary but not to the disciples, and offers the playful conclusion that the Savior's act of restoration in turning Mary's sorrow to joy has now ended the original woman's curse of sorrow in the garden of Eden.

Jesus's words in 20:17 (Do not hold me, for I have not yet ascended to the Father) lead to much commentary. John Chrysostom, Augustine of Hippo, Leo the Great, and Gregory the Great all see in Mary a lack of understanding about Jesus's full divinity. Both Augustine and Gregory the Great observe that other disciples (including other women) did in fact touch Jesus after his resurrection. Jesus's words about ascending to the Father, then, are the clue. They point to Jesus's relationship with the Father and serve to "raise her mind so that she might regard him in a more venerable manner" (Chrysostom). Cyril of Alexandria, on the other hand, suggests that Christ "established the event as a type for the holy churches"; just as Mary was prevented from handling Jesus prior to her receiving the Spirit, so also the catechumens in the church should not partake of the holy flesh of Christ in the Eucharist prior to their receiving the Spirit in baptism.

The second half of 20:17 (I am ascending to my Father and your Father, to my God and your God) also receives considerable attention. Of special importance is Jesus's seeming distinction between "my" and "your" Father and God. Why not simply say "our Father," or "our God"? The early fathers are nearly unanimous in their view that these words bear Christological significance. Cyril of Jerusalem, Ambrose of Milan, Augustine of Hippo, and John of Damascus all similarly explain that God is Jesus's Father by his very nature, but our Father by grace and adoption. Jesus's relationship to God is as one of equal substance, while we relate to God as creatures to our Creator. Augustine makes the further point that Jesus, being not only God but man, speaks of "God" by virtue of his having taken on our human nature: "He calls his own Father his God, not wanting to dishonor his likeness with us because of his inherent kindness and love toward humanity."

Later the evangelist reports that Jesus entered the room where the disciples were staying, despite the doors being shut *(20:19). This prompts several thinkers to explore the nature of Jesus's resurrected body. While Peter Chrysologus sees in this text a demonstration of Christ's divinity, Cyril of Alexandria argues that while certainly divine, Jesus also manifests his humanity by exposing the marks of crucifixion in his hands and side. He, along with Jerome and Gregory the Great, affirms that the body that had undergone crucifixion was the same body that now stood before the disciples, albeit in a transformed and glorious state. Cyril will continue that line of reasoning while commenting on the later verse:* Unless I see in his hands the print of the nails, and place my finger in the mark of the nails, and place my hand in his side, I will not believe *(20:25).*

There were two central issues of discussion around Jesus's imposition of the Spirit in 20:21–23: And when he had said this, he breathed on them, and said to them, "Receive the Holy Spirit. If you forgive the sins of any, they are forgiven; if you retain the sins of any, they are retained." *First, some thinkers puzzle over how this inbreathing of the Spirit should relate to the events of Pentecost in Acts 2. When, exactly, did the apostles receive the Spirit? Cyril of Jerusalem suggests that the disciples received the Spirit here only in part, but at Pentecost they received the Spirit in full. John Chrysostom argues that the disciples received different spiritual graces at different times. In the Johannine text, the apostles received not the power to perform miracles but the authority to forgive sins. Cyril of Alexandria, after confessing some uncertainty about the issue, concludes that the disciples did receive the gift of the Spirit from Jesus but that in the more open manifestation of the Spirit at Pentecost they received the special gift of speaking in tongues.*

The other issue in this text is that of the authority to forgive *and* retain *sins. Cyprian of Carthage, Ambrose of Milan, Cyril of Alexandria, and Gregory the Great all, in various ways, affirm the right of ecclesiastical leadership to exercise this authority. Peter Chrysologus celebrates it as Christ's gracious declaration that our sins can, through repentance, be forgiven. Yet several commentators recognize the possibility for abuse in this office. Ambrose of Milan, for example, underscores the point that no religious leader forgives sin of his own authority. Likewise, Gregory the Great takes special pains to instruct bishops in the correct administration of their office, noting that "there is true absolution on the part of the one presiding only when it is in accord with the decision of the internal judge."*

The words of Thomas, My Lord and my God! *(20:28), attract the focused attention of the early fathers. Hilary of Poitiers, for example, notices the boldness of Thomas's language. How could a faithful Jew confess Jesus with the same words as the Shema: "Hear, O Israel, the Lord our God is one" (Deut 6:4)? Hilary concludes, along with Cyril of Alexandria, Gregory the Great, Romanos the Melodist, and others, that Thomas's words confess his belief that Christ is in fact true God. Moreover, many thinkers recognize Thomas's doubt-turned-to-belief as an appropriate lesson on the blessedness of faith in Christ, even if we have not had the privilege of seeing him in the flesh. John Chrysostom and Gregory the Great each make a point of reminding their hearers that Jesus's words in 20:29 (Blessed are those who have not seen and yet believe) are speaking of us. Thomas's doubt and belief should serve as an example and catalyst for our own faith.*

John 20:1–10

[1]Now on the first day of the week Mary Magdalene came to the tomb early, while it was still dark, and saw that the stone had been taken away from the tomb. [2]So she ran, and went to Simon Peter and the other disciple, the one whom Jesus loved, and said to them, "They have taken the Lord out of the tomb, and we do not know where they have laid him." [3]Peter then came out with the other disciple, and they went toward the tomb. [4]They both ran, but the other disciple outran Peter and reached the tomb first; [5]and stooping to look in, he saw the linen cloths lying there, but he did not go in. [6]Then Simon Peter came, following him, and went into the tomb; he saw the linen cloths lying, [7]and the napkin, which had been on his head, not lying with the linen cloths but rolled up in a place by itself. [8]Then the other disciple, who reached the tomb first, also went in, and he saw and believed; [9]for as yet they did not know the scripture, that he must rise from the dead. [10]Then the disciples went back to their homes.

(1) Theodore of Mopsuestia

When the disciples heard Mary's report, they ran with purpose because they desired to know what happened. While both of them were running together, John went ahead of Peter, but he did not go into the tomb. After he had looked around, he saw the **linens lying** there (20:5). Then Simon came after him and when he went into the tomb, he saw that the rest of the **linens** were **lying** in one place while the **napkin** (20:7) that had only been on his head was in another place. Our Lord did this for a reason so that the disciples would not think that some robbery had occurred. No one would have stolen just the body and leave the **linen cloths** in the tomb. Even though the idea of a resurrection was beyond human thought at that time, the **cloths** forced them to think about the possibility of a resurrection, and they **believed** (20:8). In order that they might not think that the **cloths** were left by thieves who hastily tried to rob the tomb, Christ arranged the **linens** in an orderly fashion. He made it so that the **napkin** that had been on his head was laid alone in one place and the rest of the **linens** were laid in another place. All of this would help them understand that the one who was crucified, who also died from the weakness of his nature, astonishingly rose again through an incomprehensible divine power beyond human expectations. It showed that he possessed a better life where he had received immortality in his body and immutability in his soul. So he laid his clothes in an orderly fashion and left them as a sign of his resurrection.

(2) John Chrysostom

When you hear that the Lord arose naked, cease from your fervor about funerals. What does that excessive and useless expense mean? It only brings great loss to the mourners and provides no benefit for the deceased. If it brings anything at all, we'd have to say it brings harm. The lavish expense of the burial has often encouraged grave-robbing, exposing the one so carefully buried, now naked and unburied. Woe to such vanity! What great tyranny is exhibited in sorrow, what great foolishness! . . .

I don't say these things in any way to abolish burial practices, only to minimize its unwholesome exercise and inappropriate flamboyancy. Yet someone might say, "Feeling and sorrow and sympathy for the deceased moves us to act this way." Well, these actions do not express sympathy for the deceased, but vanity. If you want to sympathize with the dead, I'll show you another way to mourn. I'll teach you to put garments on the deceased which will rise up with him and shine forth brilliantly. These garments will neither be consumed by moths, nor wasted by time, nor stolen by grave robbers. What kind of garments are these? The clothing of mercy! This robe will rise again with him because the seal of mercy is with him. These garments shine forth on those who hear, *I was hungry and you gave me food* (Matt 25:35). These are the garments which make us distinguished, these make us illustrious, these establish our safety. The garments we wear now are nothing other than food for moths and a table for worms. Again, I don't say these things so as to forbid you from having funerals, but to observe them with simplicity. Simply cover the body so that it is not placed in the earth naked. . . .

When someone is about to die, let the friend of the dying person prepare the appropriate burial garments by persuading the dying one to leave something behind for those who are in need. Send him to the grave with these kind of garments, convinced that he has left his inheritance with Christ.

(3) Gregory the Great

My friends, what does the running of the disciple signify? Can we believe that the evangelist's very profound narrative lacks a mystical meaning? Surely not! John would not have said that he arrived first but did not enter unless he believed that there was a mystical significance to his hesitation. What does John signify, then, if not the synagogue, and Peter, if not the church? We should not be surprised to find the synagogue signified by the younger apostle, and the church by the elder. Although the synagogue was earlier than the church of the gentiles in worshiping God, still by the world's reckoning the multitude of gentiles existed prior to the synagogue, as Paul testifies when he says that *it is not the spiritual which is first but the physical* (1 Cor 15:46). So the church of the gentiles is designated by the older of the two, Peter, and the synagogue of the Jews by the younger, John. They both ran together, because from the time of their beginning right up to the end, the gentiles ran forward with the synagogue at the same pace and by a shared route, though not with the same shared understanding. The synagogue came first to the **tomb**, but **did not go in** (20:5), because although it received the commandments of the law and listened to prophecies of the incarnation and passion, it was unwilling to believe in the one who had died. John **saw the linen cloths lying there**, but even so **he did not go in** (20:5). The synagogue knew the mysteries of the holy Scriptures, yet delayed entering by putting its faith in the Lord's passion. It had prophesied long and extensively about him, it saw him when he was present, but it denied him and rejected him, refusing to believe that God had become an embodied human being. . . .

Then follows: **Then the other disciple, who reached the tomb first, also went in** (20:8). After Peter entered, John also **went in**. He who had come first entered second. We know, my friends, that at the end of the world even Judea will be brought to faith in the Redeemer. Paul testifies to this by saying: *Until the full number of the Gentiles come in, and so all Israel will be saved* (Rom 11:25-26).

John 20:11-18

[11]**But Mary stood weeping outside the tomb, and as she wept she stooped to look into the tomb;** [12]**and she saw two angels in white, sitting where the body of Jesus had lain, one at the head and one at the feet.** [13]**They said to her, "Woman, why are you weeping?" She said to them, "Because they have taken away my Lord, and I do not know where they have laid him."** [14]**Saying this, she turned round and saw Jesus standing, but she did not know that it was Jesus.** [15]**Jesus said to her, "Woman, why are you weeping? Whom do you seek?" Supposing him to be the gardener, she said to him, "Sir, if you have carried him away, tell me where you have laid him, and I will take him away."** [16]**Jesus said to her, "Mary." She turned and said to him in Hebrew, "Rabboni!" (which means Teacher).** [17]**Jesus said to her, "Do not hold me, for I have not yet ascended to the Father; but go to my brethren and say to them, I am ascending to my Father and your Father, to my God and your God."** [18]**Mary Magdalene went and said to the disciples, "I have seen the Lord"; and she told them that he had said these things to her.**

(4) John Chrysostom

The others left, but Mary stood near the place, for as I have said, even seeing the tomb brought her great comfort. Now, do you see her **stoop** down (20:11)—so she can more readily see the place where the body lay? This is why she received a great reward for such great earnestness. What not even the disciples got to see, this woman observed first: **Angels sitting in white, one at the feet and one at the head** (20:12) whose appearance was filled with great brightness and joy. Since the woman's mind was not elevated enough to entertain the resurrection from observing the *napkins* (20:7), something more happens: she beholds **angels sitting** in bright appearance so as to raise her temporarily from her misery and to comfort her. They do not speak anything to her about the resurrection, and yet she is gently raised to this doctrine. She saw a bright vision and something rather unusual. She saw a shining appearance and heard a sympathetic voice. What does he say? **Woman, why are you weeping?** (20:13). Through all of this, as if a door was being opened, she was led step by step to grasp the reality of his resurrection.

(5) Cyril of Alexandria

Someone may appropriately wonder why the angels said nothing to the holy disciples, and in fact did not appear to them at all, but instead appeared and spoke to the woman. My answer is that it was the plan of Christ the Savior to plant in the minds of those who loved him the full certainty of the mystery concerning himself. However, the manner by which he accomplished this certainty varied according to what was fitting for the one before him. For the holy disciples, the process of the events themselves, agreeing with the expectation found in holy Scripture, was enough to give them certainty and to implant in them an undoubting faith.

They withdrew already believing in the holy Scriptures; how strange it would be for those who already had firm faith to be taught by the mouth of holy angels. For the woman, however, such a method was necessary, for she did not know the holy and divine Scriptures, nor was there any other means by which she could understand the deep mystery of the resurrection.

(6) Gregory the Great

We must consider the great force of love which inflamed Mary's state of mind. When even the disciples departed from the **tomb**, she did not depart. She sought the one she had not found, **weeping** as she searched (20:11). Being inflamed with the fire of her love, she burned with desire for the one she believed had been taken away. And so it happened that the one who stayed behind to seek him was the only one who saw him. . . .

But **as she wept she stooped to look into the tomb** (20:11). It is true that she has already seen that the tomb was empty, and had already reported that the Lord had been taken away. Why did she **stoop** down again, why did she again long to **look**? It is not enough for a lover to have **look**ed once, because the force of love intensifies the effort of the search. She sought a first time and found nothing; she persevered in seeking, and so it happened that she found him. It came about that her unfulfilled desires increased, and as they increased they took possession of what they had found.

Holy desires, as I have told you before, increase by delay in their fulfillment; if delay causes them to fail, they were not desires. Anyone who has been able to reach out for the truth has been on fire with this love. . . . So Mary loved, and turned a second time to the **tomb** she had already **look**ed into. Let us see the result of her search, which had been redoubled by the power of love: **She saw two angels in white, sitting where the body of Jesus had lain** (20:12). . . . The angels asked Mary, saying, **"Woman, why are you weeping?"**

She said to them, "Because they have taken away my Lord, and I do not know where they have laid him" (20:13). The sacred message which stirs up tears of love in us provides consolation for these tears when it promises us the sight of our Redeemer. . . .

Jesus said to her, "Mary" (20:16). After he had called her by the common name of "woman," he called her by her own name, as if to say, "Recognize him who recognizes you." . . . And so because Mary was called by name, she acknowledged her Creator, and called him at once **Rabboni (which means Teacher)** (20:16). He was both the one she was outwardly seeking and the one who was teaching her inwardly to seek him.

(7) John Chrysostom

Mary said, **If you have carried him away, tell me where you have laid him, and I will take him away** (20:15). She speaks of laying down, taking away and carrying, as if speaking about a corpse. What she means is this: "If you have carried him away out of fear for the Jews, tell me and I will take him." How great is this woman's kindness and tender love, but there isn't anything elevated about her understanding yet. So now Christ presents the matter before her not through his appearance but through his voice. Just as he was known to the Jews at one time and then at another time he was unknown, even though present, so now when speaking to Mary he chooses to make himself known. When he said to the Jews, **Whom do you seek?** (18:4), they did not know his face or his voice until he was willing to be known. The same thing happened here.

(8) Cyril of Alexandria

Christ's question is meant to restrain the woman's sorrow, for it was necessary for the Lord to restore this part of humanity as well. Because of Adam's transgression, God said to all humanity, as if to the firstfruits of the race: *You are dust, and to dust you shall return* (Gen 3:19), but to the woman in particular it was said, *In pain you shall bring forth children* (Gen 3:16). Now an abundance of sorrow overshadowed the woman as her due penalty. So it was fitting for the voice of the one who had passed the original sentence of judgment to end the misery of that ancient curse. Our Savior Christ removed the tears of the woman, or rather all womankind, Mary being a kind of firstfruits.

20:17 "Do not hold me . . . I am ascending to my Father."

---

(9) John Chrysostom

Why did Jesus say, **Do not hold me** (20:17)? It seems to me that Mary wanted to engage with him as she had before, and that because of her joy she did not perceive anything great in him, even though he had become far greater in the flesh. Therefore, leading her from this understanding, and so that she might speak to him with great freedom, he raises her mind so that she might regard him in a more venerable manner (for not even with the disciples does he appear in his customary way). It would have been empty prattling to have said, "Do not approach me as you did before, because things are not the same as they were and I cannot be with you in the same way." Instead, by saying, **I have not yet ascended to the Father** (20:17), although not painful to hear, it clearly held the same meaning. By saying, **I have not yet ascended**, he makes it clear that he is hastening on to that place, and that it was inappropriate to look with the same feelings upon the one who was about to depart and no longer engage himself with humankind.

(10) Augustine of Hippo

Jesus said to her, "Do not hold me, for I have not yet ascended to the Father; but go to my brethren and say to them, I am ascending to my Father and your Father, to my God and your God" (20:17). These are words which we should investigate carefully, albeit briefly. Indeed, when Jesus answered her this way, he was inculcating faith in the woman who recognized and called him **Teacher;** that gardener was sowing faith in her heart like sowing a mustard seed in his garden. So what does he mean, **Do not hold me** (20:17)? Likewise, as if the reason for his prohibition were sought, he added: **For I have not yet ascended to the Father** (20:17). What does that mean? If he is not touched while standing on earth, how can he be touched by humans while sitting in heaven? Certainly, before he **ascended** he offered himself to his disciples to be touched, saying (as the evangelist Luke testifies): *Handle me, and see; for a spirit has not flesh and bones as you see that I have* (Luke 24:39). Or consider when he speaks to his disciple Thomas: *Put your finger here, and see my hands; and put out your hand, and place it in my side* (20:27). Who would be so absurd as to say that Jesus wished to be touched by his disciples before he **ascended to the Father**, but did not wish to be touched by women until he had **ascended to the Father**?

It would be foolish to think that is what he meant, for we read that after the resurrection and before Jesus **ascended to the Father**, women did touch him. Among them was Mary Magdalene; as Matthew recounts, Jesus ran to meet them, saying, *"Hail!" And they came up*, it says, *and took hold of his feet and worshiped him* (Matt 28:9). This was passed over by John, but recounted as true by Matthew.

So, it remains that some mystical meaning lies hidden in these words. Whether we discover it or whether we are unable to discover it at all, we should never doubt that it is there. The words **do not hold me, for I have not yet ascended to the Father** (20:17) were said in one of two ways. Either the woman represents the church of the gentiles who did not believe in Christ until he had **ascended to the Father**, or Jesus wanted people to believe in him by **hold**ing him spiritually, understanding that he and the Father were one (cf. John 10:30). Indeed, in a certain way, Christ has **ascended to the Father** in the innermost mind of anyone who has come to understand that Christ is equal with the Father. Otherwise, Jesus is not **held** correctly; that is, he is not correctly believed in.

Mary was able to believe in a way that Jesus was somehow inferior to the Father, and certainly Jesus prevents this when says to her: **Do not hold me** (20:17), that is, "Do not believe in the way in which you understand things so far. Do not persist in understanding me as someone made for you without going on to understanding me as the one by whom you were made." Was she not believing in him carnally when she was weeping for him as a man? **For I have not yet ascended**, he says, **to the Father** (20:17). You will **hold me** when you believe that I am not inferior to God the Father.

(11) Cyril of Alexandria

Why then does Jesus speak to Mary this way, preventing her from approaching him or attempting to touch his holy flesh? What would the Lord wish to signify by saying, **I have not yet ascended to the Father?** . . . When he had completed the plan of our salvation and endured the cross, *even death on the cross* (Phil 2:8), and rose again, and demonstrated that his own nature was stronger than death, instead of readily granting favor, he prevents those who are near him from touching his own holy flesh. He thereby established the event as a figure for the holy churches and his own sacrament. The law itself gave us this through the all-wise Moses when it presented the sacrifice of the lamb as a type of Christ. For the law says, *No uncircumcised person shall eat of it* (Exod 12:48), indicating that the uncircumcised are impure. Likewise humanity may fittingly be thought of as unclean in its own nature, for what is the nature of humanity compared with God's essential purity? It is necessary, therefore, that those who are uncircumcised, that is impure, should touch his holy body only when we have been made pure through the circumcision understood *in the Spirit*. As Paul says, *Circumcision is a matter of the heart, in the Spirit* (Rom 2:29). We would not have the *circumcision in the Spirit* if the Holy Spirit was not dwelling in us through faith and holy baptism.

Is it not fitting, then, that for a while Mary should be prevented from touching his body, which is clearly holy, before she has received the Spirit? Even though Christ was raised from the dead, the Spirit had not yet been given to humanity from the Father through him. . . . So this is a figure which relates to the churches. Indeed, we exclude from the holy table those who understand the divinity of Christ and already confess the faith, but who have not yet been enriched with the Holy Spirit, that is, those who are catechumens. The Spirit does not indwell those who are not yet baptized. However, when they become partakers of the Holy Spirit, then they are not prevented from touching our Savior Christ. Indeed, for those who desire to participate in the blessed mysteries, the ministers of the divine mysteries call out, "Holy things for the holy,"[1] teaching us that participation in holy things is most fitting for those who have been made holy by the Spirit.

(12) Leo the Great

Consider what the Lord said after his resurrection, when Mary Magdalene, bearing in herself the figure of the church, hurried to approach and **hold** him: **Do not hold me, for I**

---

1. The words spoken by the priest while elevating the Eucharistic elements.

have not yet ascended to my Father (20:17). That is, "I do not want you to come to me as a human, nor to recognize me by the bodily senses. I am putting you off for more exalted ideas; I am preparing you for greater things. When I have **ascended to my Father**, then you shall **hold** me more truly and perfectly. Then you will embrace what you cannot touch, and you will believe what you cannot see.

(13) Gregory the Great

Mary's teacher told her, **Do not hold me** (20:17), but not because the Lord refused the touch of women after his resurrection. It is said of the two women at his tomb: *They came up and took hold of his feet* (Matt 28:9).

The reason he was not to be **held** was added in the following words: **For I have not yet ascended to the Father** (20:17). In our hearts, Jesus **ascends to the Father** when he is understood to be the Father's equal. In the heart of one who does not believe that he is equal to the Father, the Lord has still not **ascended to his Father**. The one who believes that Jesus is co-eternal with the Father is the one who truly **holds** Jesus.

(14) Romanos the Melodist

Strophe 10: He who searches the hearts and reigns, and watches over them,
    Knowing that Mary would recognize his voice,
    Like a shepherd, called his crying lamb,
   Saying, **Mary** (20:16). She at once recognized him and spoke:
    "Surely my wonderful shepherd calls me,
    In order that henceforth he may number me among the nine and ninety lambs;
   For I see behind him who calls me
    The bodies of the saints, the ranks of the just,
   And so, I do not say, 'Who art thou who callest me?'
    For I know clearly who he is who calls me.
   It is my teacher and my Lord,
     He who offers resurrection to the fallen."

Strophe 11: Carried away by the warmth of her affection, and by her fervent love,
    The maiden hastened and wished to seize him,
    The one who fills all creation without being confined by boundaries;
   But the Creator did not find fault with her eagerness;
    He lifted her to the divine when he said,
    "**Do not hold me** (20:17); or do you consider me merely human?
     I am God, **Do not hold me** (20:17).
   O holy woman, lift up your eyes
    And consider the heavenly spheres;

Seek me there, for **I ascend**
>> **To my Father** (20:17), whom I have not left;
> For I share his throne, and with him I am without time and beginning,
>> I who offer resurrection to the fallen.

Strophe 12: "Let your tongue, O woman, declare these things for the rest of time
>> And let it explain them to the sons of the kingdom
>> And to those who eagerly await the resurrection of me, the living.
> Hasten, Mary, and gather together my disciples
>> I use you as a trumpet with a powerful voice;
>> Sound forth peace to the fearful ears of my concealed friends;
> Arouse them all as from a sleep,
>> In order that they may come to greet me and light torches.
> Say, 'The bridegroom has arisen from the tomb,
>> And nothing has been left in the tomb;
> O apostles, banish deadness, since he is arisen,
>> He who offers resurrection to the fallen.'"

20:17b "I am ascending to my Father and your Father, to my God and your God."

---

(15) Cyril of Jerusalem

So that you do not think that God is the Father of the Son and the Father of creatures in the same way, Christ makes a distinction in what comes next. He did not say: "I ascend to our Father"; in this way there would be confusion between what is created and what is the only-begotten Son. Instead he said: **My Father and your Father** (20:17); that is, in reference to me, Father by nature, and in reference to you, Father by adoption. Likewise he says: **To my God and your God** (20:17); that is, in reference to me as the genuine and only-begotten Son and in reference to you as to what is created.

(16) Ambrose of Milan

The Son of God demonstrates the distinction between generation and grace when he says, **I am ascending to my Father and your Father, to my God and your God** (20:17). He did not say, **I am ascending to our Father,** but **I am ascending to my Father and your Father** (20:17). This division demonstrates a distinction, that his **Father** is our Creator.

He then added: **To my God and your God** (20:17). He and *the Father are one* (10:30), and he is his **Father** by possession of the same nature God. Yet, he came to be **our Father** through the Son, not by virtue of our own nature, but by grace. Nevertheless, he seems to indicate here two natures in Christ, both divinity and humanity, divinity from his Father and humanity from his mother. He is divine before all ages; he is human from the virgin. Indeed, as the Son, he called God his **Father**, and as a man he called him **God**.

(17) Augustine of Hippo

But go to my brethren and say to them, I am ascending to my Father and your Father (20:17). He does not say "our father"; therefore he is **my** father in one way and **your** father in another: mine by nature, yours by grace. **To my God and your God** (20:17): nor does he say "our God"; so again, he is **my** God in one way and **your** God in another: **My God** under whom I also am human, but **your God** because between you and him I am the mediator.

(18) Cyril of Alexandria

Although we are slaves both by rank and by nature (for that which is created is subject to the Creator), he does call us his own **brethren**, and calls God the shared Father of us both on account of his human likeness with us. Taking on human nature by becoming like us, he called our God his God, even though he is a Son by nature. We **ascend** to the dignity which is above our nature through our becoming like him. It is not by being sons by nature that we are called sons of God, for he cries in us through his own Spirit, *Abba, Father* (Rom 8:15). Even so, since he received our form when he became human (according to the Scriptures), he might have God as his God, even though he is truly "God from God" by nature.[2]

Do not be scandalized then, even if you hear him calling our God his God; rather, make a careful and wise consideration of the exact meaning of the words, as one who is eager to learn. When he says that his own Father is his God and our God, he speaks truthfully with respect to each subject. The God of all is the Father of Christ by nature and truth. For us he is not our Father by nature, but rather our God as Creator and Lord.

It seems, however, that the Son has joined himself to us and granted to our nature the honor which is properly and uniquely his own, calling the one who begot him our common Father. Yet by becoming like us, he also takes upon himself that which belongs to our nature. He calls his own Father his God, not wanting to dishonor his likeness with us because of his inherent kindness and love toward humanity. . . .

Therefore, he is both God and man. He is exalted because of his divine generation, for he is "God from God" and truly Son from the Father. But he is humbled because of us, for he became human like us, for our sakes. So do not let your mind be disturbed when you hear his saying, **I am ascending to my Father and your Father, to my God and your God** (20:17). It is most fitting and proper for the one who is God and the Son of God by nature, to call the one who begot him Father, and for the one who is human like us, to call our God his God.

---

2. Cyril is alluding to the Nicene Creed: "God from God, light from light, true God from true God."

(19) John of Damascus

He who is by nature the son of God became firstborn among us who were made sons of God, and his brethren, by adoption and grace. This is why he said, **I am ascending to my Father and your Father** (20:17). He did not say, "our Father," but **my Father**, obviously meaning **my Father** by nature and **your Father** by grace. Likewise: **my God and your God** (20:17). He did not say "our God," but **my God**. If you make a careful distinction between what is seen and what is thought, he also refers to **your God** as our Creator and Lord.

John 20:19-23

[19]**On the evening of that day, the first day of the week, the doors being shut where the disciples were, for fear of the Jews, Jesus came and stood among them and said to them, "Peace be with you."** [20]**When he had said this, he showed them his hands and his side. Then the disciples were glad when they saw the Lord.** [21]**Jesus said to them again, "Peace be with you. As the Father has sent me, even so I send you."** [22]**And when he had said this, he breathed on them, and said to them, "Receive the Holy Spirit.** [23]**If you forgive the sins of any, they are forgiven; if you retain the sins of any, they are retained."**

20:19-20 On the evening of that day, the first day of the week, the doors being shut where the disciples were, . . . he showed them his hands and his side.

---

(20) Jerome

Tell me, how do you explain Thomas touching the **hands** of the risen Lord and seeing his **side** wounded by the spear (20:25)? How do you explain Peter perceiving the Lord standing on the shore eating a honeycomb and part of a *roasted fish* (21:9)? Surely the one who was standing had feet! Certainly the one who pointed out his wounded **side** had both a stomach and a chest, without which he could have no **sides** which attach to the stomach and chest. The one who spoke did so with a tongue, a palate, and teeth—for like a bow and strings, the tongue is struck against the teeth and gives back a vocal sound. In the same way, it follows that the one whose **hands** have been touched also had arms. Since he had all the bodily parts, he therefore had a whole body which consisted of those parts. Moreover, it was not a female body, but a male body, that is, a body of the same sex in which he died.

(21) Cyril of Alexandria

Let no one say, "How does the Lord, having a real body, enter in unhindered even though the **doors were shut** (20:19)?" Rather, let him understand that the divine evangelist does not speak about someone who is like us, but rather about one who is seated with God the

Father and who easily does whatever he wants. It is quite necessary that, being truly God by nature, he should not be subjected to the normal principles of cause and effect, as someone who simply lets things happen to him. Rather, he exercises authority over necessity itself and over what typically occurs in the normal course of events. How did he subject the sea to his own feet, and run as if on a solid wave, given that our bodies are not intended to use water as a footpath? How did he perform his other wondrous works with God-befitting authority? You will say that all these things are beyond our understanding.

Yet you should not think as some do who, out of the narrowness of their own minds, are seized with the worst kind of ideas. Would you think that the Lord was raised without his own body, without flesh and entirely free from the temple which he had taken on? . . . Consider: through the surprise of entering through the **shut doors**, he demonstrated again that he is God by nature and the very one who dwells together with him from eternity. Yet by exposing the very side of his body and revealing the *mark of the nails* (20:25), he openly offers certainty that he had raised the temple of the very body which had hung on the cross itself. This very body he resurrected, clearly abolishing the death which is fitting for the flesh, since by nature he is life, and God. What is the point of revealing his **hands** and **side** (20:20) if, according to the stupidity of some, he was not raised with his own flesh? . . .

It is appropriate then that our Lord Jesus Christ appeared in the form of his original body. The temple of his body had not yet been transformed into the glory which was appropriately owed to him, and he did not want to instill faith in the resurrection to some person or body other than the one which he received from the holy virgin and in which he was crucified and died according to the Scriptures. The power of death rules over the very flesh from which he came, but if his body which had died was not raised, how is death conquered and how is the power of corruption weakened?

(22) Peter Chrysologus

The doors being shut, for fear of the Jews, Jesus came and stood among them (20:19). I ask you, why is it doubted that perfect divinity could penetrate the secret, enclosed womb of the virginal body while maintaining her full chastity? After the resurrection, that same divinity which had taken on the solidity of our body in the mystery of the incarnation was able to enter and exit through **doors** which were **shut**! By such proof he reveals that he is the Maker of all creation, that no creation withstands him, and all creation serves him. If virginity is unable to resist conception and giving birth to its own Creator, and **doors** that are **shut** are unable to deny entrance and exit to its own Creator, how could the stone of the tomb, however large, . . . withstand the Savior's resurrection? Just as virginity and the **door**, both being **shut**, bring about faith in his divinity, so too the stone rolled back affirms faith in the resurrection. Having been rolled back, the stone did not make a way for the Lord's exit, but supplied an entrance for our faith.

(23) Gregory the Great

The first question this reading of the gospel brings to mind is how the Lord's body, which came in to the disciples through **shut doors** (20:19) after the resurrection, could be a real one. We must be certain that if a divine work is rationally comprehended, it is not wonderful. Our faith does not have any merit when human reason provides a proof. These works, which can in no way be understood by themselves, must be considered in light of his other works, so that his more miraculous deeds may provoke faith in the miraculous.

The Lord's body which made its entrance to the disciples through **shut doors** (20:19) was the same as that which issued before the eyes of men from the virgin's closed womb at his birth. Is this surprising? The one who came to die made his appearance from the unopened womb of the virgin. Now the one who was now going to live forever made his entrance through **shut doors** (20:19) after his resurrection! Yet, because the faith of those who beheld it wavered concerning the body they could see, he immediately showed them his **hands** and **his side** (20:20), offering to their touch the body which he brought in through the **shut doors**. By this action he revealed two wonderful things (and according to human reason quite contradictory). He showed them that after his resurrection his body was both incorruptible and yet could be touched. We cannot deny that what is touched is corruptible, and what is not corruptible cannot be touched. But in a wonderful and incomprehensible way our Redeemer, after his resurrection, manifested a body that was incorruptible and touchable. By showing us that it is incorruptible he would urge us on toward our reward. By offering it as touchable he would dispose us toward faith. He manifested himself as both incorruptible and touchable to truly show us that his body after his resurrection was of the same nature as ours but of a different sort of glory.

20:22–23 "Receive the Holy Spirit. If you forgive the sins of any, they are forgiven; if you retain the sins of any, they are retained."

---

(24) Cyprian of Carthage

After the resurrection, Christ speaks to the apostles again, saying: **"As the Father has sent me, even so I send you." And when he had said this, he breathed on them, and said to them, "Receive the Holy Spirit. If you forgive the sins of any, they are forgiven; if you retain the sins of any, they are retained"** (20:21–23). From this we understand that unless someone has been given authority in the church and has been established by the law of the gospel and the Lord's institution, they are not permitted to baptize and **forgive sins**. Outside of the church there can be no *binding or loosing* (cf. Matt 18:18), for there is no one who has the power to *bind* or *loose*.

(25) Cyril of Jerusalem

Christ granted the fellowship of the Holy Spirit to the apostles. For it is written: **And when he had said this, he breathed on them, and said to them, "Receive the Holy Spirit. If you forgive the sins of any, they are forgiven; if you retain the sins of any, they are retained"** (20:22–23). This was the second inbreathing, for the first was weakened because of voluntary sin.[3] . . .

He gives grace now but will lavish on even more. He says to them: "I am ready to give it even now, but the container does not yet have room. So for now, receive the grace which you are able, but also look forward to more. *Stay in the city*, Jerusalem, *until you are clothed with power from on high* (Luke 24:49). Receive it partly now, though later you shall bear it completely." The one who receives something often, only has what is given in part, but the one *clothed* by his robe is covered completely.

(26) Ambrose of Milan

Let us now see whether the Spirit **forgives sins**. On this issue there can be no doubt, for the Lord himself said: **Receive the Holy Spirit. If you forgive the sins of any, they are forgiven** (20:22–23). See that **sins** are **forgiven** through the **Holy Spirit**. However, when men offer their ministry of the **forgiveness of sins**, they do not exercise the right of any authority of their own. They do not **forgive sins** in their own name, but in the name of the Father and the Son and the Holy Spirit. They ask, but God grants. The ceremony is human, but the generosity belongs to the heavenly power.

(27) John Chrysostom

He breathed on them, and said to them, "Receive the Holy Spirit. If you forgive the sins of any, they are forgiven; if you retain the sins of any, they are retained" (20:22–23). Just as a king sends out rulers and gives them authority to put people into prison, and to release them, so also he sends out his disciples and invests them with his authority. Yet, how can he give them the Spirit if earlier he said, *If I do not go away, the Counselor will not come to you* (16:7)? Some say that he did not give the Spirit here, but rather made them ready to receive it by **breathing** on them. . . .

For this reason, he did not say, "You have received the Holy Spirit," but rather, **Receive the Holy Spirit** (20:22). Nevertheless, one would not be wrong in saying that they also did **receive** some spiritual authority and grace—not in order to raise the dead and perform miracles, but in order to **forgive sins**. There are different gifts of the Spirit (cf. 1 Cor 12:4). That is why Christ added the words, **If you forgive the sins of any, they are forgiven** (20:23), revealing what kind of power he was giving them. After forty days in that place, then they

---

3. For Cyril, the first inbreathing was Gen 2:7 (*then the LORD God formed man of dust from the ground, and breathed into his nostrils the breath of life*).

received the power of miracles. This is why he said, *You shall receive power when the Holy Spirit has come upon you; and you shall be my witnesses in Jerusalem and in all Judea* (Acts 1:8); in fact, they became witnesses through their miracles. Indeed, the grace of the Spirit is indescribable and his gifts are diverse. This took place so that you might learn that the gifts and authority of the Father, Son, and Holy Spirit are one. Whatever seems to be specially attributed to the Father is also attributed to the Son and the Holy Spirit.

(28) Cyril of Alexandria

Christ appointed these illustrious men to the great honor of apostleship and declared them ministers and priests of the divine altar (as I just said earlier). He immediately set them apart by giving them his own **Spirit** through the sign of his **breath**, in order that we also might firmly believe that the **Holy Spirit** is not foreign to the Son, but is the same essence with him, and through him proceeding from the Father. He was demonstrating that the gift of the **Spirit** necessarily follows upon those who are chosen by him for divine apostleship. Why? Because they would not have done anything pleasing to God, and would not have conquered the entanglements of sin, if they had not been *clothed with power from on high* (Luke 24:49) and been transformed into something other than what they were. . . .

Where and when were the disciples of our Savior provided with the gift of the **Spirit**? Immediately, when the Savior appeared to them in his own flesh after the resurrection, when **he breathed on them, and said to them, "Receive the Holy Spirit"** (20:22)? Or was it in the days of Pentecost, when they were gathered together in one place and *a sound came from heaven like the rush of a mighty wind. And there appeared to them tongues as of fire, distributed and resting on each one of them. And they began to speak in other tongues, as the Spirit gave them utterance* (Acts 2:2–4)? Either we must think that the gift was given to them twice, or we must remain ignorant of the time when they became partakers of the **Holy Spirit**. Both the word of our Savior and what is written in the Acts of the holy disciples should be held as true. Indeed the matter deserves our uncertainty, especially since the Savior himself said: *It is to your advantage that I go away, for if I do not go away, the Counselor will not come to you; but if I go, I will send him to you* (16:7). . . .

He promised to send us the **Counselor** from heaven when he was with God the Father above. He did this when he departed to the Father and gave a most abundant outpouring of the **Spirit** to those who were willing to receive it. Anyone could receive this very gift through faith in him and through holy baptism. That which was spoken through the prophet was then fulfilled, *I will pour out my Spirit upon all flesh* (Joel 2:28; cf. Acts 2:17).

It was necessary for the Son to appear with the Father as a joint supplier of the Spirit. It was also necessary that those who believe in him should understand that he is the power of the Father, the very Creator of the universe, and that he brought forth humanity into existence from nothing. . . . Moses, writing about our ancient creation, says that God **breathed** into Adam's face the *breath of life* (Gen 2:7). Just as humanity was formed and came into existence in the beginning, so also now humanity is renewed. Just as humanity was then formed in the image of its Creator, so also now, by participation in the **Spirit**, humanity is transformed into the likeness of its own Maker. . . .

In the same way, I suppose, by saying that he will send the **Counselor** to us when he departs to the Father, and by determining this as the time of grace for all, he accomplished in his disciples something like the firstfruits of his promise. . . . Therefore, they received the participation of the Holy Spirit when **he breathed on them, and said to them, "Receive the Holy Spirit"** (20:22). It was impossible for Christ to be mistaken in his speaking, nor would he say, **Receive the Spirit**, if he did not give it. However, in the days of Pentecost, when God established a more open proclamation and manifestation of grace, and the **Holy Spirit** had been implanted in them, there appeared tongues of fire. This did not signify the beginning of the gift in them, but rather the beginning of their ability to speak in tongues. . . .

When Christ had given the **Holy Spirit**, he said, **If you forgive the sins of any, they are forgiven; if you retain the sins of any, they are retained** (20:23), even though only one who is God by nature has the ability and authority to **forgive** those who have sinned. Who has the authority to extend grace to those who are convicted of having transgressed the divine law, except the one who appointed the law? Let us consider the meaning of this saying, if you will, by comparing their situation with our own. Who has the authority to supplement the oracles of earthly kings, who tries to dismiss what has been commanded by the decree and decision of rulers, except someone who has been invested with royal honor and glory? Indeed, on this occasion he would not be accused of wrongdoing. . . .

Christ thought it was fitting that those who had already received the divine and sovereign **Spirit** in them should have authority to **forgive** and **retain the sins** of whomever they wanted. The **Holy Spirit** who lives in them does the **forgiving** and **retaining sins** according to his own will, even though the work is completed through men.

(29) Peter Chrysologus

Christ gave the power to **forgive sins** (20:23), the one who poured out the **Spirit** into their hearts with his **breath** and generously bestowed remission. **And . . . he breathed on them, and said to them, "Receive the Holy Spirit. If you forgive the sins of any, they are forgiven"** (20:22–23). Where are those who declare that sins cannot be forgiven by humans? Where are those who suppress others who have once fallen through the devil's pressure, so that they will never rise? Where are those who with a cruel spirit remove the cure for the faint and deny medicine for the wounded? Where are those who sound forth with a wicked hopelessness about **forgive**ness and **retention of sins**? Peter **forgives sins** and receives penitents with complete joy. He fully understands that this power has been granted by God to all priests. For after Peter's denial, he would have lost the glory of his apostleship and life itself, if he had not been restored through penitence. If Peter returned through penitence, who could stand without it?

(30) Gregory the Great

If you forgive the sins of any, they are forgiven; if you retain the sins of any, they are retained (20:23). It is pleasant to observe the disciples lifted up to a height of glory equal to the burden of humility to which they were called. You see how they not only acquire peace of mind concerning themselves, but even receive the power of releasing others from their bonds. They share in the right of divine judgment so that as God's vicars they may withhold **forgiveness of sins** from some and grant it to others. So it was fitting that only those who had consented to be humbled for the sake of God may be raised up by him. Those who feared God's strict judgment were made judges of hearts; those who were themselves fearful of being condemned, condemn some and set others free. Their place in the church is now held by the bishops. Those who obtain the position of governing receive authority to **forgive** and to **retain**.

It is a great honor, but the burden is heavy. In truth it is difficult for one who does not know how to exercise control over his own life to become the judge of someone else's life. It often happens that someone whose life is hardly in accord with his position holds this place of judgment. It frequently comes about that either he condemns those who do not deserve to be condemned, or he **forgives** others who should be **retained**. Often in **forgiving** and **retaining** those who are subject to him he follows the inclination of his own will and not the merits of the case. So the one who exercises this authority according to his own inclination, rather than the character of those subject to him, deprives himself of this very authority of **retaining** and **forgiving**. It frequently happens that a pastor is moved by hatred or favor toward some neighbor. Those who allow hatred or favor to influence them are unable to make worthy judgments in the case of those under their authority.

The prophet has rightly said that they were *putting to death persons who should not die and keeping alive persons who should not live* (Ezek 13:19). Anyone who condemns a righteous person is *putting to death persons who should not die*; and anyone who tries to absolve a guilty person from his punishment is *keeping alive persons who should not live*. All cases must be carefully considered, and only then the power of **retaining** and **forgiving** used. The pastor must look at the sin, and the repentance following after the sin, so that his sentence absolves those to whom Almighty God grants the grace of sorrow. There is true absolution on the part of the one presiding only when it is in accord with the decision of the internal judge.

John 20:24–31

²⁴**Now Thomas, one of the twelve, called the Twin, was not with them when Jesus came.** ²⁵**So the other disciples told him, "We have seen the Lord." But he said to them, "Unless I see in his hands the print of the nails, and place my finger in the mark of the nails, and place my hand in his side, I will not believe."**

²⁶**Eight days later, his disciples were again in the house, and Thomas was with them. The doors were shut, but Jesus came and stood among them, and said, "Peace be with you." **²⁷**Then he said to Thomas, "Put your finger here, and see my hands; and put out your hand, and place it in my side; do not be faithless, but believing." **²⁸**Thomas answered him, "My Lord and my God!" **²⁹**Jesus said to him, "Have you believed because you have seen me? Blessed are those who have not seen and yet believe."**

³⁰**Now Jesus did many other signs in the presence of the disciples, which are not written in this book; **³¹**but these are written that you may believe that Jesus is the Christ, the Son of God, and that believing you may have life in his name.**

20:25 "Unless I see in his hands the print of the nails, and place my finger in the mark of the nails, and place my hand in his side, I will not believe."

---

(31) John Chrysostom

When you look at the disbelieving disciple, consider the kindness of the Lord. He shows himself with his wounds for the sake of a single person. He appears so that he might also save this one person, even though Thomas is duller than the other disciples. This was why Thomas wanted proof for his dull sense-perception, and yet he would not **believe** with his eyes. Indeed, he did not just say, **Unless I see** (20:25), but "Unless I touch," so that what he sees might not prove to be his imagination. . . .

Why does Jesus not appear to Thomas immediately, but rather after eight days? So that, while being informed by the disciples and hearing the same things over and over again, Thomas might be incited to a greater desire and disposition to **believe** what was about to happen.

(32) Cyril of Alexandria

Christ reveals to us the reason for our assemblies and gathering together on his account. Surely he visits and, in a way, dwells with those who have assembled on his behalf, especially on the **eighth day** (20:26), that is, the Lord's day. . . .

There is good reason, then, that we hold sacred assemblies in our churches on the **eighth day**. As we have need, we *shut the doors* (20:19), spiritually speaking, but Christ visits and appears to us all, both invisibly and visibly—invisibly, as God, but visibly, in the body. He even allows us to hold his holy flesh and gives it to us.[4] By the grace of God we approach to partake of the blessed mystery, receiving Christ into our hands, so that we may strongly believe that he truly raised the temple of his own body. Sharing in the blessed mystery is a confession of participation in the resurrection of Christ. By his own words he makes this clear when he performed the image of the mystery. After he broke the bread, as it is written, he gave it to them, saying, *This is my body which is given for you for the forgiveness of sins. Do this in remembrance of me* (Luke 22:19; Matt 26:28).

For this reason, then, participation in the divine mysteries both fills us with divine blessing, and is a true confession and remembrance of the Lord's dying and returning to life for us and on our behalf. So then, having touched Christ, let us avoid unbelief as something deadly; instead let us be found faithful, having a steadfast mind. . . .

Given these events, I think it is necessary to investigate the following question. Thomas touched the **side** of the Savior, examined the wounds made by the soldier's spear, and saw the **mark of the nails** (20:25). How then, someone will say, is it possible that the **mark** of corruption was visible in Christ's incorruptible body? . . . Indeed, will anyone who is lame possibly return to life again having the same disability in his foot or leg? If anyone

---

4. Cyril refers to the Eucharist.

has lost his eyes in this life, will he be raised again unable to see? How then, someone might say, can we have shaken off corruption if its results are preserved and even prevail over our bodies? There is great benefit in asking these questions; we are addressing the difficulties present in the passage.

Insofar as it is possible, we are diligently attempting to affirm that at the time of the resurrection no remnant of foreign corruption will remain in us. Rather, as the wise Paul said concerning this body, what is sown *in weakness is raised in power*, and what is sown *in dishonor is raised in glory* (1 Cor 15:43). What should we expect to be different about the resurrection of this body in *power* and *glory*, if not that every weakness and dishonor from corruption and sickness has been removed, returning to its created state? The body has not been made for death and corruption. Since Thomas sought proof in order to gain full assurance and certainty, our Lord Jesus Christ necessarily appeared as Thomas sought him, allowing no excuse for a lack of faith.

(33) Peter Chrysologus

Unless I see the print of the nails, and place my hand in his side, I will not believe (20:25). Why does Thomas seek this proof for faith? Why does he inquire so harshly into the resurrection of one who suffered so piously? Why does a devoted hand reopen, in this way, those wounds that a wicked hand inflicted? Why does the hand of a faithful follower strive to pierce again the **side** which the lance of a wicked soldier laid open? Why does the harsh curiosity of a servant renew the sorrows inflicted by the raging persecutors? Why does a disciple seek to prove that he is Lord by his tortures, that he is God by his punishments, that he is the heavenly physician by his wounds? . . .

Brothers and sisters, his piety asked these things, his devotion examined them, so that future impiety itself might not doubt that the Lord had risen. Thomas cured not only his own uncertain heart, but the uncertain hearts of all; and because he was about to proclaim these things to the gentiles, this vigorous seeker made a thorough investigation about how he might add to the mystery of such great faith.

20:27-29 "Do not be faithless, but believing." Thomas answered him, "My Lord and my God!" Jesus said to him, "Have you believed because you have seen me? Blessed are those who have not seen and yet believe."

---

(34) Origen of Alexandria

Some say that **those who have not seen and yet believe** (20:29) are more blessed than those who have seen and **believed**. They misunderstand what the Lord says to Thomas at the end of the Gospel of John: **Blessed are those who have not seen and yet believe** (20:29). It does not say that **those who have not seen and yet believe** are *more* blessed than those who have **seen** and **believed**. According to their interpretation, this would mean that those who come after the apostles are more blessed than the apostles themselves, which is even more foolish.

In order to see with the mind the things being **believed**, it is necessary for those about to be blessed like the apostles, to be able to hear the saying: *But blessed are your eyes, for they see, and your ears, for they hear* (Matt 13:16), and *Many prophets and righteous men longed to see what you see, and did not see it, and to hear what you hear, and did not hear it* (Matt 13:17). Even so, it is still of value to receive the lesser blessing which says: **Blessed are those who have not seen and yet have believed** (20:29). For how could it be that the eyes which Jesus called **blessed** for what they have **seen**, not be more **blessed** than those who have never had a vision of such things?

(35) Hilary of Poitiers

Let us see whether the confession of the apostle Thomas, when he says, **My Lord and my God!** (20:28), agrees with the proclamation of the evangelist. The one whom Thomas confesses as **God**, he even calls **my God**. Surely Thomas was not ignorant of the Lord's command: *Hear O Israel, the Lord our God is one* (Deut 6:4). How then could the faith of an apostle become so forgetful of that primary command that in order to have life one must confess the divine unity? How could he confess Christ as **God**? Because: the apostle understood the whole mystery of faith through the power of the resurrection. He had frequently heard Jesus say, **I and the Father are one** (10:30), and **All that the Father has is mine** (16:15), and **I am in the Father and the Father in me** (14:11), but now he confessed Christ's name without jeopardizing the faith.

From the profession of one **God** the Father, our worship would not be jeopardized by confessing the Son of God as **God**, because he believed that the nature of the Son was truly the same as the nature of the Father. Nor would he endanger our belief in the unity of the divine nature by an impious confession of another **God**, because God's perfect begetting had not brought forth the existence of another **God**.

In the end Thomas understood the truth of the evangelical mystery and confessed Christ as both his **Lord** and his **God**. This was not a name of honor, but a confession of Christ's very nature. He believed that Christ was **God** in his very substance and power. The Lord, likewise, showed that Thomas's worship was not merely a profession of honor, but a declaration of faith, when he said: **Have you believed because you have seen me? Blessed are those who have not seen and yet believe** (20:29). When he saw, Thomas **believed**. But, you ask, what did Thomas **believe**? What else did he **believe** except what he professed: **My Lord and my God!**

(36) John Chrysostom

Jesus appears to them again and does not wait to be honored by Thomas, nor to hear anything of the sort. Instead, without Thomas saying anything, Christ anticipates it himself and fulfills what Thomas was longing for. He demonstrates that, in fact, he was present when

Thomas was speaking these things to the disciples. Indeed, he used the same words as a sharp criticism of Thomas, and as instruction about what was to come. After he said, **Put your finger here, and see my hands; and put out your hand, and place it in my side**, he added, **do not be faithless, but believing** (20:27).

Do you see that his doubt was due to unbelief? Yet this was before he received the Spirit (John 20:22); afterward, that was no longer the case, and the disciples were finally perfected. Moreover this was not the only way in which Jesus rebuked Thomas; he also did so by what came next. After Thomas took a deep breath, became convinced, and cried out, **My Lord and my God!** (20:28), Jesus says, **Have you believed because you have seen me? Blessed are those who have not seen and yet believe** (20:29). This is the essence of faith, to accept things that are not seen. Indeed, *faith is the assurance of things hoped for, the conviction of things not seen* (Heb 11:1). Jesus here blesses not only the disciples, but also those who **believe** after them.

Yet someone might say, "The disciples saw, and then believed." But they were not seeking such assurance. Instead, they accepted the testimony concerning the resurrection because of the linen cloths (John 20:6–7), and showed complete faith prior to seeing his body. So when someone says in our present day, "I wish I had been living in those times and had seen Christ performing miracles," let him be mindful that **blessed are those who have not seen and yet believe** (20:29).

It's also appropriate to wonder how an incorruptible body showed the **print of the nails** (20:25), and how it could be touched by mortal hands. However, do not worry, for what took place was an act of condescension. What was light and airy so as to enter through **shut doors** (20:19), was free from all mass. He shows himself in this way so that they would **believe** in his resurrection and learn that he was the same one who was crucified, that another man did not rise in his place. This is why he arose with the marks of the cross; this is why he eats. Yes indeed, the apostles everywhere made this a sign of his resurrection, saying, *We who ate and drank with him* (Acts 10:41). So when we see him walking on water prior to the cross, we do not say that his body was of a different nature as ours; it was the same nature. Likewise, even though we see him bearing the marks of the cross after the resurrection, we must not say that he is now corruptible. He showed these things for the sake of the disciple Thomas.

(37) Augustine of Hippo

Thomas saw and touched the man and confessed as **God** the one whom he had not seen and had not touched. Yet through what he saw and touched, his doubt was removed and he believed it. **Jesus said to him, "Have you believed because you have seen me?"** (20:29). He did not say, "You have touched me," but **you have seen me**, because in a way, sight is the generic sense. . . . However, it's possible for someone to say that the disciple did not dare to touch Jesus, even when Jesus offered himself to be touched, for the text does not say explicitly, "Thomas touched him." Nevertheless, whether by seeing him only, or by also touching him, Thomas saw and believed. What follows predicts and commends even more the faith of the gentiles: **Blessed are those who have not seen and yet believe** (20:29).

(38) Cyril of Alexandria

The blessed Thomas confidently confessed his faith in Christ, saying, **My Lord and my God** (20:28). It necessarily follows that the one who is **Lord** by nature and has power over all things is indeed **God**, since it is obvious that the ability to rule completely over all things belongs to **God** by nature, who is clothed with the glory of **lord**ship.

We should also take note that Thomas uses the definite article when he says, **My Lord and my God** (20:28) to show that he speaks of *the* Lord and *the* God.[5] He does not simply say, **My lord and my god** in a general sense, because he does not want anyone to think that he called Christ "lord" or "god" in the same way that he might speak to us or the holy angels. *There are many "lords" and "gods" in heaven and on earth*, as the wise Paul taught us (1 Cor 8:5). But Thomas confesses Christ as the one, unique **Lord and God**, begotten of the Father, both **Lord and God** by nature. This is what he means when he says, **My Lord and my God** (20:28).

(39) Peter Chrysologus

Thomas answered him, "My Lord and my God!" (20:28). Let the heretics come and listen, and as the Lord said, let them **not be faithless, but believing** (20:27). Behold! Not only his human body, but the punishments and sufferings of that body made known that Christ is both **Lord and God**, as Thomas proclaimed. Truly he is **God**, who comes to life from the dead, who rises up from his wounds, and who, since undertaking such great sufferings, lives and reigns, **God** forever and ever. Amen.

(40) Gregory the Great

One disciple was absent. When he returned and heard what had happened, he refused to believe what he heard. The Lord came again and offered his **side** to the unbelieving disciple to be touched. He showed his **hands**, and by showing the scars of his wounds he cured the wound of Thomas's unbelief. Dearly beloved, what do you notice in all this? Do you believe that it was by chance that this chosen disciple was absent then? That on coming later he heard, that on hearing he doubted, after doubting he touched Jesus, and after touching him he **believed**? This did not happen by chance, but by divine providence. Divine compassion brought it about in a wonderful way that when the doubting disciple touched the wounds in his master's body, he cured the wounds of *our* unbelief. Thomas's unbelief was of more advantage to our faith than the faith of the believing disciples, because when he was led back to faith by touching Jesus, our minds were relieved of all doubt and made firm in faith. So after his resurrection Jesus allowed his disciple to doubt, but he did not desert him in his doubt. . . .

---

5. Cyril's point is that in the original Greek, Thomas does not speak of "lord" and "god" in a generic sense, but uses the definite article to show that he speaks of *the* Lord and *the* God.

Why then, when Thomas saw Jesus and touched him, was it said to him: **Have you believed because you have seen me** (20:29)? He saw one thing, and he believed another. Divinity could not be seen by a mortal person. He saw a human being, and he confessed him as God, saying: **My Lord and my God!** (20:28). Seeing, he believed. He perceived a mere man, and testified that this was the invisible God.

We rejoice greatly at what follows: **Blessed are those who have not seen and yet believe** (20:29). Certainly this saying refers to us who keep in our minds one whom we do not see in his body. It refers to us, but only if we follow up our faith with our works. That person truly believes who expresses his belief in his works.

(41) Romanos the Melodist

Strophe 1: Who protected the hand of the disciple which was not melted
At the time when he approached the fiery **side** of the Lord?
Who gave it daring and strength to probe
The flaming bone? Certainly the **side** was examined.
If the **side** had not furnished abundant power,
How could a right hand of clay have touched
Suffering which had shaken heaven and earth?
It was grace itself which was given to Thomas
To touch and to cry out,
"Thou art our **Lord and God**" (20:28).

Strophe 3: For truly the boundary line of faith was subscribed for me
By the hand of Thomas; for when he touched Christ
He became like a pen of a fast-writing scribe
Which writes for the faithful. From it gushes forth faith.
From it, the robber drank and became sober again;
From it the disciples watered their hearts;
From it Thomas drained the knowledge which he sought,
For he drank first and then offered drink
To many who had a little doubt. He persuaded them to say,
"Thou art our **Lord and God**."

Strophe 7: But when Thomas saw him, he lowered his head;
And he said to himself: "What am I going to do?
How now can I defend myself to those whom I formerly distrusted?
What shall I say to Peter and the others?
Those whom I reproached a while back—How shall I appease them and cry,
'Thou art our **Lord and God**'?

Strophe 8: "Would that I had exercised control and kept quiet when there was the discussion about Jesus.

    But the sight of those who were rejoicing roused me to speak;
I was irritated by the words of those who cried with joy,
    'We have clearly seen alive the one who died voluntarily.'
When I saw Peter who had denied him rejoicing,
    And again when I saw those who fled with Peter rejoicing,
    I was jealous, for I wanted to join the rejoicing with them.
In my zeal, I said what I openly proclaimed.
    Do not blame me, my Jesus; may I be received favorably as I cry:
    'Thou art my **Lord and my God.**'"

Strophe 10: So Didymus,[6] speaking to himself, spoke also to our God.
    Christ, testing his nerves, when he beheld Thomas,
Who was brokenhearted, took pity on him, as once he pitied
    The tax-collector, and he said: "**Put out your hand** (20:27);
Why do you hesitate? Tell me, man of little faith,
    What is there of my experiences which seemed incredible?
    Was it the crucifixion, the death, or the resurrection itself?
At what point do you raise a question with me?
    As you see me whom you longed to see, lo, cry out,
    'Thou art our **Lord and God.**'

Strophe 11: "Sleeping a short sleep in the tomb, after three days I arose.
    I lay in the tomb for you and those like you;
And you, in place of gratitude, gave me lack of faith.
    For I heard what you said to your brothers."
Thomas was terrified at this and answered:
    "Do not blame me, Savior, for I always trust thee;
    But I find it hard to trust Peter and the others,
For I know that, though they were not deceived,
    Still in a time of trouble they were afraid to say to thee,
    'Thou art our **Lord and God.**'"

Strophe 12: When the one who sees all things, saw that Thomas wished
    To cast aside the accusation of lack of faith, he answered him:
"You too were with them in that time to which you referred;
    For everyone left me to suffer alone.
It was a hard time, Didymus, do not utter reproaches.
    About it, it was written: *Strike the shepherd,*
That the sheep may be scattered (Zech 13:7).
Understand what I say; do what you say.

---

6. Didymus was Thomas's Greek name.

Do you wish to touch me? Touch and say,
 'Thou art **Lord and God**.'"

Strophe 13: O the marvel! The forbearance! The immeasurable meekness!
  The untouched is felt; the master is held by a servant,
And he reveals his wounds to one of his inner circle.
  Seeing these wounds, the whole creation was shaken at the time.
Thomas, when he was considered worthy of such gifts,
  Lifted up a prayer to the one who deemed him worthy,
  Saying, "Bear my rashness with patience,
Have pity on my unworthiness and lighten the burden
  Of my lack of faith, so that I may sing and cry,
   'Thou art our **Lord and God**.'"

Strophe 17: "Hear, then, and understand clearly: you have become the ally of the wise;
  I was recognized by men as the wisdom of the Father.
Blessed are you in your faith. Still more do I bless
  Those who come to me merely on hearing of me.
You yourself in touching me just now recognized my glory;
  But they worship me from the sound of words.
  Great is the insight of **those who believe** (20:29) on me in this way.
I am beheld by you, my disciple,
  And by those holy servants who cry:
   'Thou art our **Lord and God**.'"

John 21

The last chapter of John records the final appearance of Jesus to his disciples. The shoreline meal Jesus shared with seven disciples signified to Gregory the Great the eschatological banquet of Revelation 19:9 and the grace of the sevenfold Spirit in Isa 11:2–3. Several commentators wonder why Peter would return to fishing, especially in light of Jesus's words that "No one who puts his hand to the plow and looks back is fit for the kingdom of God" (Luke 9:62). John Chrysostom suggests that because the Spirit had not yet been given, the disciples had not yet been charged with a mission. Augustine of Hippo defends the disciples, noting that they still had to make a living. Gregory the Great argues that any vocation held prior to conversion is acceptable, so long as it is not entangled with sin.

Jesus's command to cast the net on the right side of the boat (21:6) received a figurative interpretation from Augustine of Hippo, who sees this catch of fish representing the church at the end of the age. Likewise, Cyril of Alexandria understands casting the net to mean proclaiming the gospel. While it was night (21:3) their work is ineffective, but after Christ's resurrection, apostolic preaching will reap a worldwide harvest, much like the large quantity of fish obtained by the disciples. The specific number of fish recorded in verse 11 (full of large fish, a hundred and fifty-three of them) leads both Augustine of Hippo and Cyril of Alexandria to seek the meaning of the number. Augustine suggests that the law (valued at ten), combined with the sevenfold Spirit, produces seventeen. Added sequentially, he arrives at 153. Cyril, on the other hand, sees 100 as the fullness of the gentiles, 50 as the remnant of Israel, and 3 as representing the Trinity.

Christ's threefold interrogation of Peter in verses 15–17 produced much commentary from the church fathers. Theodore of Mopsuestia, Augustine of Hippo, Cyril of Alexandria, and the Venerable Bede all see Christ's threefold question of Peter as a counterbalance to his threefold denial. Theodore suggests that Christ was calling Peter to "repay me with the same love that I have shown to you," while Augustine likens Christ's painful questioning to a skilled doctor who applies the needed treatment to a sick patient. Other thinkers, however, used this text as an occasion to reflect on the importance of Peter in the church. Cyprian of Carthage notes that Christ's threefold command to feed my sheep (21:15) indicates the primacy of Peter for the unity of the church. Popes Leo the Great and Gregory the Great point to this and other passages as demonstrating the supremacy of the chief apostle who, in the words of Leo, "even now carries out and accomplishes the Lord's command by . . . never ceasing to pray for us."

Finally, the Venerable Bede takes Christ's words to Peter and John at the end of the gospel (21:20–23) as "designating the two ways of life in the church . . . the active and the contemplative." Peter represents the active way of life with its attending trials and temptations. John represents the sublime path of contemplation and its intimacy with Christ "which is not to be ended through death."

John 21:1–14

[1]After this Jesus revealed himself again to the disciples by the Sea of Tiberias; and he revealed himself in this way. [2]Simon Peter, Thomas called the Twin, Nathanael of Cana in Galilee, the sons of Zebedee, and two others of his disciples were together. [3]Simon Peter said to them, "I am going fishing." They said to him, "We will go with you." They went out and got into the boat; but that night they caught nothing.

[4]Just as day was breaking, Jesus stood on the beach; yet the disciples did not know that it was Jesus. [5]Jesus said to them, "Children, have you any fish?" They answered him, "No." [6]He said to them, "Cast the net on the right side of the boat, and you will find some." So they cast it, and now they were not able to haul it in, for the quantity of fish. [7]That disciple whom Jesus loved said to Peter, "It is the Lord!" When Simon Peter heard that it was the Lord, he put on his clothes, for he was stripped for work, and sprang into the sea. [8]But the other disciples came in the boat, dragging the net full of fish, for they were not far from the land, but about a hundred yards off.

[9]When they got out on land, they saw a charcoal fire there, with fish lying on it, and bread. [10]Jesus said to them, "Bring some of the fish that you have just caught." [11]So Simon Peter went aboard and hauled the net ashore, full of large fish, a hundred and fifty-three of them; and although there were so many, the net was not torn. [12]Jesus said to them, "Come and have breakfast." Now none of the disciples dared ask him, "Who are you?" They knew it was the Lord. [13]Jesus came and took the bread and gave it to them, and so with the fish. [14]This was now the third time that Jesus was revealed to the disciples after he was raised from the dead.

21:1 After this Jesus revealed himself again to the disciples by the Sea of Tiberias.

---

(1) John Chrysostom

Do you see that Jesus does not remain with his disciples continuously, nor does he stay with them as he had done before? For example, he appeared to them in the evening, then vanished. After eight days he again appeared once, then vanished again. Then, after this, **by the Sea** (21:1) he appeared filling them with great terror.

What does it mean that he **revealed himself** (21:1)? It is obvious that he was not seen unless he condescended himself, because his body was pure and incorruptible. But why does the evangelist mention the place? To show that Christ had removed most of their fear, as they now emerged from their homes and went about everywhere. They were no longer shut up in their homes, but went to Galilee, avoiding the danger of the Jews. So Simon comes to fish. Since Christ was not with his disciples continuously, the Spirit had not been given. The disciples had not been given any task; they had nothing to do, so they returned to their trade.

21:2 Simon Peter, Thomas called the Twin, Nathanael of Cana in Galilee, the sons of Zebedee, and two others of his disciples were together.

---

(2) Gregory the Great

We ought to notice that the Lord is described as having had his final banquet with seven disciples. **Peter and Thomas, Nathanael, the sons of Zebedee**, and **two other of his disciples** (21:2) are remembered to have been there. Why does he celebrate this last banquet with seven disciples if not to announce that only those who are filled with the sevenfold grace of the Holy Spirit (cf. Isa 11:2–3) would be with him at that eternal meal? All time unfolds in seven days, and the number seven often designates perfection. Therefore, those who feast at the final banquet in the presence of truth are those who now ascend beyond earthly things in their zeal for perfection. Their love is not tied to this world; when they are tempted in every way, they do not lessen the divine longings which have begun in them. About this last banquet, John says elsewhere: *Blessed are those who are invited to the marriage supper of the Lamb* (Rev 19:9). He does not record that they were called to a lunch, but to a *supper* since a *supper* is obviously a banquet at the end of the day. Those who come to the refreshment of celestial contemplation at the final days of this present life are not called to a lunch *of the lamb*, but to a *supper.* . . .

Conduct yourselves in this way, my brothers and sisters. Desire to be filled with the presence of the Spirit. Consider carefully what can come to you in the future because of the present. Examine whether you are filled with this Spirit, and you will know whether you are able to come to that banquet. For whoever is not now renewed by that Spirit will be made to abstain from the refreshment of that eternal banquet. Remember what Paul says about that same Spirit: *Any one who does not have the Spirit of Christ does not belong to him* (Rom 8:9).

21:3 Simon Peter said to them, "I am going fishing." They said to him, "We will go with you."

---

(3) Augustine of Hippo

With regard to the disciples' fishing, it is usually asked why Peter and the sons of Zebedee returned to the task they had been engaged in prior to the Lord calling them. They were fishermen when he said, *Follow me, and I will make you fishers of men* (Matt 4:19). Indeed, they clung to him as their master, abandoned everything, and followed him. So much so that when the rich man went away saddened because Jesus said, *Go, sell what you possess and give to the poor, and you will have treasure in heaven; and come, follow me* (Matt 19:21), Peter said to him, *Lo, we have left everything and followed you* (Matt 19:27). Why have they now seemingly abandoned their apostleship, become what they once were, and returned to what they had previously abandoned? It's as if they have forgotten what they had heard from Jesus: *No one who puts his hand to the plow and looks back is fit for the kingdom of God* (Luke 9:62). . . .

We need to provide a response to those who are disturbed by this matter. Certainly the disciples were not prohibited from using their own trade to obtain necessary provisions, especially if it was lawful. So long as they guarded their apostleship intact and had no other means by which to make a living, it was permissible. That is, unless someone has the audacity to think and say that the apostle Paul did not reach the perfection of those who had abandoned everything to follow Christ, since Paul obtained his own provisions with his own hands so as not to become a burden to those to whom he preached the gospel.

(4) Gregory the Great

The reading from the holy gospel which was just read in your hearing, my brothers and sisters, presses a question to our minds, and that pressing question indicates the power of discretion. You may ask why Peter, a fisherman before his conversion, returned to his fishing after his conversion. Since Truth said: *No one who puts his hand to the plow and looks back is fit for the kingdom of God* (Luke 9:62), why did Peter return to a vocation he had abandoned? Yet, if we consider the virtue of discretion, we quickly and undoubtedly see that there was no fault in returning to a vocation after his conversion which he did without sin before his conversion. Indeed, we know that Peter was a fisherman and Matthew a tax collector. After their conversions, however, Peter returned to fishing while Matthew certainly did not sit down again to the business of tax collecting, because it is one thing to seek a living through fishing, but another to enlarge one's income through the profit of tax collecting. There are many vocations which produce sin to some degree. Therefore, after our conversion we must not return to those vocations which entangle us with sin.

21:3–6 That night they caught nothing. . . . He said to them, "Cast the net on the right side of the boat, and you will find some."

---

(5) Augustine of Hippo

There is a great mystery in the great Gospel of John! By placing it at the end of the gospel, the mystery is highlighted more clearly. Seven disciples were fishing (Peter, Thomas, Nathanael, two sons of Zebedee, and two others whose names are not mentioned), and this sevenfold number signifies the end of time. Indeed, there is a full sequence of time in seven days. Related to this: when morning came, Jesus **stood on the beach** (21:4). The beach is the end of the sea and therefore signifies the end of the world. That same end of the world is shown when Peter **hauled the net ashore** (21:11), that is, to **the beach**. The Lord himself explained this when in another place he provided a simile, casting a net into the sea. *Men drew it ashore*, the author says, and then Jesus explains what the shore was by saying, *So it will be at the close of the age* (Matt 13:48, 49).

That, however, was a parable in word, not one enacted in reality. Just as here the Lord indicated the end of the world by his action, so there, by another instance of fishing, he signified what the church is now. By his actions at the beginning of his preaching he showed that the catching of fish signifies the good and the bad which are now in the church. Here after his resurrection he signifies only the good whom the church will contain in eternity, when the resurrection of the dead is completed at the end of this age. . . .

In that other parable, the nets are not lowered on the right side, lest they signify only the good, nor on the left, lest they signify only the bad; rather, they are lowered without distinction. *Let down your nets for a catch*, he says (Luke 5:4), so that we might understand a mixture of good and bad. Here, however, he says, **Cast the net on the right side of the boat** (21:6), indicating those who stood on the right, the good alone. In the previous instance the net was broken (Luke 5:6) to signify schisms; here, since there will be no more schisms in that great peace of the saints, the evangelist would be permitted to say, **Although there were so many**, that is so great, **the net was not torn** (21:11). . . .

(6) Cyril of Alexandria

Let us present some meager instruction inviting a spiritual contemplation of the text. *Give instruction to a wise man, and he will be still wiser; teach a righteous man and he will increase in learning* (Prov 9:9). I think that the mention of the disciples fishing through the whole **night**, laboring in vain but catching **nothing** (21:3), has significance. We will find that no one, or at least very few, had been swept up and entirely persuaded by the preaching of the original teachers to please God in all things. An exceedingly small amount is essentially **nothing**, especially when taken from a great multitude; certainly the population of the whole world is exceedingly great. What was it that hindered the work of the original disciples and made it worthless? Why did their preaching fail to bear fruit? Because it was **night** and it was still dark; there was some kind of intellectual mist and demonic deceit prevailing upon the mind's eye which did not allow people to see the true light of God. . . .

Therefore, they labored, so to speak, through the whole **night** and their spiritual net was empty of fish before Christ arrived. Then **day broke** (21:4), that is, the diabolical mist was driven off and the light of truth had risen, namely Christ. He inquired of those men who were growing weary, "Do you have anything in your nets which might be food for God who thirsts, as it were, for the salvation of us all?" (for the Scriptures called the conversion of the Samaritans his *food* [4:31–35]). When they responded to his inquiry by admitting that they had absolutely **nothing**, Christ commanded them to **cast** their **nets** again **on the right side of the boat** (21:6). The blessed Moses also cast out a net of instruction through the letter of the law, but this was fishing on the left side while Christ's commandment to us was on the **right side**. For the teaching of Christ is incomparably greater and far more superior in honor and glory than the commandments of the law since the truth completely surpasses the types, the Lord surpasses his servants, and the gift of the Spirit which justifies surpasses the letter which condemns (cf. 2 Cor 3:6). The teaching of Christ, then, is placed on the **right side**, signifying to us its superiority over the law and the prophets. . . .

The great **quantity of fish** in the nets was so large that the disciples were no longer able to **haul it in** easily (21:6). Those who have been caught in the **net**, and believed, are beyond counting, and the wonder of this greatly surpasses the strength of the holy apostles. This is the strength of Christ who has in his own power gathered the multitude of those being saved into the church on earth, as if into the apostolic **net**.

(7) Peter Chrysologus

Just as day was breaking, Jesus stood on the beach (21:4), so that while the disciples were now being thrown about by the waves of the sea, he might return the church to a place of faith in him. Because he discovered them devoid of the power of faith and completely decimated in any mature strength, he accused them by calling them **children**, such as they were, when he spoke to them: **Children, have you any food?**[1] (21:5). There stood Peter who denied, Thomas who doubted, and John who fled.[2] So he speaks to them not as to the bravest of soldiers, but as to scared **children**. Since he discovers them not yet suited for battle, he invites them to the table as tender children, saying, **Children, have you any food?** (21:5). He intends kindness to call them back to grace, bread to call them back to confidence, and food to call them back to faith. They would not believe that his body had been resurrected unless they discerned that he was eating in a completely human manner. This is why the one who completely fills all things asks them for food. Bread himself eats, not because he hungers for food, but because he always hungers for the love of his own.

21:11 So Simon Peter went aboard and hauled the net ashore, full of large fish, a hundred and fifty-three of them.

---

(8) Augustine of Hippo

Here the fish are not described with some generally large number, but with a definite number: **a hundred and fifty-three** (21:11). We must now give an explanation for this number, with the Lord's help. If we were to pick a number which signifies the law, what else would it be but ten? Indeed, we most certainly believe that the Decalogue of the law, that is those

---

1. Chrysologus's Latin text has "food" here rather than **fish**.
2. Chrysologus, like other church fathers, believed that John was the unnamed naked young man who fled the garden in Mark 14:51–52.

well-known Ten Commandments, were first written on two tablets of stone by the finger of God. The law, however, when not assisted by grace, makes us transgressors and exists only in the letter. Because of this the apostle says, *The letter kills, but the Spirit gives life* (2 Cor 3:6) . . . so that we may perform the commandments of the law not by our strength but by the gift of the Savior. When, however, grace is added to the law, that is the Spirit to the letter, the number seven is added to the number ten. By that number, that is the number seven, the Holy Spirit is signified, as the examples of the holy law attest. . . . For Isaiah the prophet says, *The Spirit of the LORD shall rest upon him* (Isa 11:2), and then designates him in his sevenfold work or office: *The spirit of wisdom and understanding, the spirit of counsel and might, the spirit of knowledge and godliness, and the spirit the fear of the LORD will fill him* (Isa 11:2 Vulgate). . . . So when the Holy Spirit, seven in number, is added to the law, ten in number, they become seventeen. When we add all these numbers together from one to seventeen, we arrive at a **hundred and fifty-three** (21:11).[3]

Therefore, not only are a **hundred and fifty-three** (21:11) saints signified as resurrecting again to eternal life, but thousands of saints who belong to the grace of the Spirit. By this grace harmony is established with the law of God as with an adversary, so that as the Spirit gives life the letter may not kill. Rather, what is commanded by the letter may be fulfilled by the help of the Spirit, and if anything is left undone, it may be forgiven. Therefore all who belong to that grace are represented in this number, that is, they are figuratively signified.

(9) Cyril of Alexandria

The amount of fish is indicated by the number **a hundred and fifty-three** (21:11). The number one **hundred**, as it seems best to me, signifies the fullness of the gentiles, for the number one **hundred** is a perfect number, being ten times ten. Indeed the Lord Jesus Christ himself said, in one place, that there are a **hundred** sheep which belong to him (cf. Matt 18:12), signifying by this number the sum of all rational creatures. In another place, Jesus affirmed that the ground *brought forth a hundredfold* (cf. Matt 13:8), thereby signifying the perfect fecundity of devout souls. On the other hand, the number **fifty** seems to indicate the remnant of Israel elected by grace, for **fifty** is half of a **hundred** and lacks the perfection of a **hundred**. The number **three** likewise implies the holy and consubstantial Trinity, as the number itself makes clear.

John 21:15–19

[15]**When they had finished breakfast, Jesus said to Simon Peter, "Simon, son of John, do you love me more than these?" He said to him, "Yes, Lord; you know that I love you." He said to him, "Feed my lambs." [16]A second time he said to him, "Simon, son of John, do you love me?" He said to him, "Yes, Lord; you know that I love you." He said to him, "Tend my sheep." [17]He said to him the third time, "Simon, son of John, do you love me?"**

---

3. That is, 1 + 2 + 3 + 4 . . . + 16 + 17 = 153.

Peter was grieved because he said to him the third time, "Do you love me?" And he said to him, "Lord, you know everything; you know that I love you." Jesus said to him, "Feed my sheep. ¹⁸Truly, truly, I say to you, when you were young, you girded yourself and walked where you would; but when you are old, you will stretch out your hands, and another will gird you and carry you where you do not wish to go." ¹⁹(This he said to show by what death he was to glorify God.) And after this he said to him, "Follow me."

(10) Cyprian of Carthage

The Lord said to Peter: *I tell you*, he says, *you are Peter, and on this rock I will build my church, and the powers of death shall not prevail against it. I will give you the keys of the kingdom of heaven, and whatever you bind on earth shall be bound in heaven, and whatever you loose on earth shall be loosed in heaven* (Matt 16:18–19). In a similar way, after his resurrection he says to Peter: **Feed my sheep** (21:17). On Peter he *builds the church* and to him he entrusts the sheep to be fed. Although he allots equal power to all the apostles, he nevertheless established one chair, and by his own authority arranged the origin and plan of the church's unity. Indeed the other apostles were everything that Peter was, but the primacy is given to Peter and through this it is demonstrated that there is one church and one chair. The apostles are all shepherds, but one flock is demonstrated, fed by all the apostles in harmonious agreement.

(11) John Chrysostom

Why does Jesus pass over the others and speak with Peter this way? He was the chosen one of the apostles, the mouth of the disciples, and the head of the dance. This was why even Paul once went up to inquire of him rather than the others (cf. Gal 1:18). In order to show Peter that he ought to take heart now that his denial was in the past, Jesus entrusts him with authority among the brethren. Indeed, Jesus does not mention Peter's denial or rebuke him for what happened. Instead, he says, "If you love me, lead the brethren. Exhibit that warm love which you always demonstrated, in which I now rejoice. The life which you said you would lay down for me (cf. John 13:37), give now for my sheep" (21:16, 17).

(12) Theodore of Mopsuestia

When they had eaten, Jesus said to Simon, "Simon, son of John, do you love me more than these?" He said to him, "Yes, my Lord; you know that I love you" (21:15 Syriac). Simon does not dare simply to affirm his own word, but submits his affirmation to the Lord's knowledge. He thought about earlier events—when he said that he would lay down his life for Jesus (John 13:37)—and remembered that the Messiah had rebuked his prideful words, saying, "You will deny me three times." All of this to say that since Peter remembered this, he rightly said **you know** (21:15), that is, "**you know** most of all. Beforehand, I used to think differently about myself, but then your words were shown to be true, and so I am careful now."

Jesus said to him, **Feed my lambs** (21:15). Since **Peter** responded with a simple, quiet voice to the one who is all-knowing, who *searches the depths of the heart* and the considerations of the soul (cf. Jer 17:10), Jesus made him chief pastor. Giving him charge over the **lambs** of his flock, he said, "**Feed my lambs**, that is, all those who believe in me by their words and who are weaker on account of their childish instruction. This is why you need to carry their burden, **tend** to them, comfort their faintheartedness, and raise them up with the grace that was given to you."

A second time he said to him, "Simon, son of John, do you love me?" He said to him, "Yes, my Lord; you know that I love you." Jesus said to him, "Feed my sheep" (21:16 Syriac), that is, those consummate men perfected in wisdom, who follow after you in the hierarchical orders of the church, the apostolate, the priesthood, and pastoral care.

He said to him the third time, "Simon, son of John, do you love me?" Peter was grieved because he said to him the third time, "Do you love me?" And he said to him, "My Lord, you know everything; you know that I love you." Jesus said to him, "Feed my ewes"[4] (21:17 Syriac); that is, the rational ones amidst them all, the holy virgins, the daughters of the righteous covenant, the pure and modest wives, and the pure and worthy women who are elected in the spirit, together with all the men who are members of the lay orders.[5]

The Savior does not say to him, "fast" or "keep watch for me." Instead, since it is more valuable and beneficial to those within the community, Jesus entrusts Peter with the pastoral care of souls. What he means is this: "I do not need anything. Just **feed my sheep** and repay me with the same love that I have shown you. You can repay the grace that you owe me in this way. I will receive your care for them as if it were for me."

(13) Augustine of Hippo

Jesus says to Peter, in whom alone he forms the church: **Peter, do you love me?** (21:15). He responds, **Lord, I love you.** Then: **Feed my sheep** (21:15). A third time he says: **Peter, do you love me?** (21:17). Peter is discouraged because Christ asked him three times, as if Christ saw only the conscience of one who denies, but not the faith of one who confesses. He had always known Peter; he had known him even when Peter had not known himself. Peter had not known himself even at that time when he said: *I will be with you until death* (Luke 22:33); of his own weakness he was not aware.

It often happens this way with the infirm. A sick person does not know what needs to be treated, but the doctor knows. The patient suffers the illness, not the doctor. A doctor is better able to offer a plan of treatment for the patient than the one who is sick. So, at

---

4. This selection is a Syriac translation of Theodore of Mopsuestia's original Greek commentary. Unlike the Greek text (and RSV), the Syriac uses a new word in verse 17 so that there are three different words for sheep in each of the three verses. These three different words are used as a linguistic cue for three different types of people whom Jesus tells Peter to feed.

5. Theodore of Mopsuestia means lay monks who are not priests.

that time Peter was sick and the Lord a doctor. He who had no strength was claiming that he did. Yet Christ, touching the vein of his heart, said that he was going to deny him three times. Thus it happened just how the doctor predicted, not how the sick man assumed. So after his resurrection, the Lord inquired of Peter, not out of ignorance for whether Peter would confess his love for Christ, but so that the threefold confession of love might destroy the threefold denial of fear.

(14) Augustine of Hippo

So comes the end for that denier and lover, elevated by his presumption but humbled by his denial; cleansed by his weeping, accepted by his confession, and crowned by his suffering. So comes the end, to die with a perfect love for the name of him for whom, with a perverse haste, he had promised to die. Now strengthened by Christ's resurrection, Peter would do what he had promised to do when weakened by his immaturity. It was fitting that Christ should die first for Peter's salvation, and then Peter should die for preaching Christ. That human rashness should initiate such boldness was an inversion of the order which the truth had arranged. Peter, the one to be redeemed by the Redeemer, thought he would lay down his life for Christ. In reality Christ had come to lay down his life for all, including Peter, which you see was now accomplished. From now on, a heart strengthened by the gift of truth itself would be obtained in facing death for the name of the Lord rather than a false heart presumed upon by our own misjudgment. We should no longer fear our death in this life because in the Lord's resurrection we have an example of a surpassing life of another sort.

(15) Cyril of Alexandria

Could not someone reasonably ask why Christ interrogates Simon alone, even though the other disciples were there? What is the meaning of the words **feed my lambs** (21:15) and the related commands? We say that the inspired Peter had already been chosen, along with the other disciples, to be an apostle for God. Our Lord Jesus Christ himself called them apostles, as it is written (Mark 3:14). But when the plot of the Jews occurred, Peter's fall intervened. The inspired Peter was seized with extreme fear and denied the Lord three times. Christ now heals his suffering disciple by using various means to draw out a threefold confession, offering a counterbalance, as it were, to his failures by providing a correlating correction. For a failure in word has the ability to bring an accusation in mere words, and could certainly be forgiven in the same way. So Christ demands Peter to say whether he loves him **more than these** (21:15). . . .

Therefore, the blessed Peter's threefold denial was removed by his threefold confession. We must understand the Lord's saying, **Feed my lambs** (21:15), as a renewal of Peter's apostleship which was already bestowed upon him. It was a washing away of the intervening reproach of Peter's failure, and a destruction of the littleness of spirit that comes from human weakness.

(16) Leo the Great

In **Peter** the strength of the whole church is built up and the assistance of divine grace established, so that the stability found in Christ is attributed to **Peter**, and through him to the apostles. So, most beloved, since we see the protection established for us by divine assistance, most reasonably, justly, and fittingly we delight in the merits of our leader **Peter**. We give thanks to the eternal King and Redeemer, our Lord Jesus Christ, because he gave such great power to **Peter** whom he made the leader of the whole church. Even in our time anything that is conducted and appointed correctly through us,[6] should be assigned to his guidance and works. To him it was said: *And when you have turned again, strengthen your brethren* (Luke 22:32). To him the Lord, after his resurrection, responded three times to Peter's threefold profession of eternal love with this mystical speech: **Feed my sheep** (21:17). That the pious shepherd even now carries out and accomplishes the Lord's command is without doubt, strengthening us by his exhortations and never ceasing to pray for us, so that we might not be overcome by temptation.

(17) Gregory the Great

Who does not know that the holy church is made firm in the solidity of the chief apostle, who derived a firm mind in agreement with his name; that is, he was called "Peter" from the word *petra* (rock). To him it was said by the voice of truth: *I will give you the keys of the kingdom of heaven* (Matt 16:19); to him it was also said: *And when you have turned again, strengthen your brethren* (Luke 22:32); and again: **Simon, son of John, do you love me? . . . Feed my sheep** (21:17). Although there are many apostles, nevertheless because of his supremacy, the seat of this chief apostle alone grew strong in authority.

(18) Venerable Bede

It was with benevolent foresight that our Lord inquired three times of Peter as to whether he loved him, so that by this triple confession Christ might free him from the chains which bound him as a result of his threefold denial. As often as he had denied that he knew Christ, when he was terrified during his passion, so often was he to bear witness that he loved him with his whole heart when he had been renewed by his resurrection. By his provident divinely arranged plan, Christ three times commended to Peter his sheep for feeding, as Peter was confessing his love three times. It was fitting that as often as he had wavered in his shepherd's trust, so often should he be ordered to take care of the shepherd's members when his shepherd's trust had been restored.

---

6. Leo means himself, as bishop of Rome and successor of Peter.

John 21:20–25

²⁰Peter turned and saw following them the disciple whom Jesus loved, who had lain close to his breast at the supper and had said, "Lord, who is it that is going to betray you?" ²¹When Peter saw him, he said to Jesus, "Lord, what about this man?" ²²Jesus said to him, "If it is my will that he remain until I come, what is that to you? Follow me!" ²³The saying spread abroad among the brethren that this disciple was not to die; yet Jesus did not say to him that he was not to die, but, "If it is my will that he remain until I come, what is that to you?"

²⁴This is the disciple who is bearing witness to these things, and who has written these things; and we know that his testimony is true. ²⁵But there are also many other things which Jesus did; were every one of them to be written, I suppose that the world itself could not contain the books that would be written.

(19) Venerable Bede

Mystically speaking we can take these things which were predicted by the Lord to Peter and John, and which later took place, as designating the two ways of life in the church. They are carried out in the present, namely the active and the contemplative. Of these, the active is the way of living common to all the people of God. Very few ascend to the contemplative, and these more sublime ones do so after achieving perfection in good deeds. The active life is Christ's zealous servant devoting himself to righteous labors. First one remains unspotted by this world, keeping the mind, hand, tongue, and other members of the body from every stain of tempting fault, and perpetually subjugating oneself to divine servitude. One should assist a neighbor in need, as much as possible, by ministering with food to the hungry, drink to the thirsty, and clothing to those who feel the cold. One should receive the needy and the wandering into one's house, visit the sick, bury the dead, snatch the destitute from the hand of those who are stronger, and the poor and needy from those laying hold of them. One should also show the way of truth to the erring, serve others in love, and struggle for justice even to the point of death.

The contemplative life, however, is lived when one who has been taught by the long practice of good actions, instructed by the sweetness of prolonged prayer, and habituated by the frequent sting of tears, learns to be free of all affairs of the world and directs the eye of the mind toward love alone. Even in the present life, one begins to gain a foretaste of the joy of perpetual blessedness which will be attained in the future. This is done by ardently desiring it, and even sometimes, insofar as is permitted to mortals, by contemplating it sublimely in mental ecstasy. This life of divine contemplation takes in those especially who, after long practice in the rudiments of monastic virtue, spend their lives cut off from human beings, knowing that they will have a mind which is freer for meditating on heavenly things because it has been separated from earthly tumults. . . .

That which the Lord said to Peter, *You will stretch out your hands, and another will gird you and carry you where you do not wish to go* (21:18), represented the perfection of the active way of life, which is normally proven by the fire of temptations. Hence elsewhere he says more clearly about this, *Blessed are those who are persecuted for righteousness' sake* (Matt 5:10). To these words to Peter he properly adds, Follow **me** (21:19), because undoubtedly, according to the words of the same Peter, *Christ also suffered for you, leaving you an example, that you should follow in his steps* (1 Pet 2:21).

Christ's saying about John, **it is my will that he remain until I come** (21:22, 23), suggests the state of contemplative virtue. This state is not ended in death, as the active life is, but after death it is to be more perfectly completed with the coming of the Lord.

Appendix 1: Authors of Works Excerpted

Ambrose of Milan (ca. 339–397), bishop of Milan, the capital of the western Roman Empire in the late fourth century, one of the four "doctors" (teachers) of the Latin church (along with Augustine, Jerome, and Gregory the Great). As bishop, he exerted much influence on the Roman emperors of his time and was partly responsible for the conversion of Augustine. He is the author of many works, including a treatise on Christian ethics, exegetical homilies, several writings on virginity, two series of homilies on baptism and the Eucharist for the newly baptized, and hymns. He also wrote several theological treatises, including *The Faith*, *The Holy Spirit*, *Repentance*, and *The Death of a Brother*.

Ammonius of Alexandria (fifth or sixth century), presbyter of Alexandria, wrote commentaries on Luke, John, Acts, 1 Corinthians, 1 Peter, and Psalms. Today, these are extant solely in fragmentary form.

Aphrahat (early fourth century), Syriac Christian writer, sometimes called the "Persian Sage." He lived in the Sassanid Empire (in present-day Iran) and is the author of twenty-three "Demonstrations," that is, orations, on doctrinal and ascetical topics.

Apostolic Constitutions, a collection of liturgical and legal sources dating from the late fourth century, probably from Syria. It includes such works as the *Didache* and the *Apostolic Tradition*.

Athanasius of Alexandria (ca. 296–373), bishop of Alexandria, was a strong supporter of the creed adopted at the Council of Nicea (325), which he attended as a deacon and secretary. In his writings against Arius he defended the full divinity of the Son, often employing the Gospel of John as the basis of his argument. As a consequence of his ardent defense of Nicean orthodoxy, he ran afoul with the imperial powers of his day and was exiled from Alexandria five times. His most famous and influential work is entitled *On the Incarnation*. He also wrote a life of the ascetic hermit Anthony, which became a model for Christian hagiography.

Augustine of Hippo (354–430), bishop of Hippo in North Africa, was the preeminent theologian of the patristic period. Trained as a teacher of rhetoric, he spent many years as a Manichean before being baptized by Ambrose in Milan in 387. A church leader with wide influence, he sought to build up the one, universal catholic church, opposing Manicheans, Donatists, and Pelagians. A brilliant theologian and exegete, Augustine is known, among other things, for his emphasis on human beings' radical dependence on divine grace, his teaching about original sin, and his articulation of the soul's burning desire for and delight in God. The immense corpus of his writings includes the autobiographical *Confessions*; the *Trinity*, his most important dogmatic work; and *The City of God*, in which he answers pagan critics of Christianity through a synthesis of philosophical, theological, and political ideas that was to become a foundational text for Western civilization. Devoted to Scripture, Augustine wrote many commentaries, for example, on Genesis (the *Literal Commentary on Genesis*), the Psalms, Galatians, and part of a commentary on Romans. Most important for this volume, he wrote an expansive and very influential commentary on the Gospel of John.

Basil of Caesarea (ca. 330–379), known also as Basil the Great, was bishop of Caesarea in Cappadocia (modern Turkey) and founder of a monastery and of charitable institutions. One of the three Cappadocian fathers, he was the brother of Gregory of Nyssa and the friend of Gregory of Nazianzus. His rules for monks, published in several different forms, are still influential in Eastern churches. Basil defended the Christology of Nicea against the neo-Arians, who denied the full divinity of Christ. His treatise *On the Holy Spirit* defends the divinity of the Holy Spirit and draws consistently from the Gospel of John.

Bede (ca. 673–735), the "Venerable," monk at the abbey in Jarrow, England, Anglo-Saxon historian, biblical commentator, chronographer, and educator. He is the author of the *Ecclesiastical History of the English People*, works on Latin grammar, a work on the date of Easter, and various biblical commentaries that reveal his indebtedness to his ecclesiastical predecessors, specifically, Ambrose, Augustine, and Jerome. He also wrote a series of homilies on the gospels.

Caesarius of Arles (ca. 470–542), bishop of Arles, was notable as a homilist, and more than two hundred of his sermons are extant. They were widely read throughout the Middle Ages. He was heavily influenced by his own monastic devotion and was instrumental in creating a sustainable Christian community in southern Gaul (modern France), which included the establishment of a women's monastery in Arles.

Clement of Alexandria (ca. 150–ca. 215), a philosopher, polymath, and Christian apologist, was the first Christian to attempt a thoroughgoing synthesis of the Bible and Greek philosophy. He is known primarily for a trilogy that consists of the *Exhortation to the Greeks*, an invitation to the Christian faith directed at educated Greeks; the *Pedagogue*, a moral treatise that focuses on the elementary stages of the Christian life; and the *Stromateis* or *Miscellanies*, an enigmatic, diffuse work in seven books that discusses various theological and moral topics.

Cyprian of Carthage (ca. 200–258), a rhetorician by profession, converted to Christianity in his forties and was elected bishop of Carthage shortly afterward. He guided the church of Carthage during the dark days of the Decian persecution (ca. 249–251) and proved a decisive leader in the churches of North Africa at a time of disagreements and schisms occasioned by differences over the treatment of Christians who had fallen away during the persecution. He is the author of theological, moral, and devotional works and a large number of letters.

Cyril of Alexandria (ca. 375–444) was the patriarch of Alexandria and an influential theologian who played an important role in the formulation of the classic doctrine of the person of Christ. He led opposition to the teaching of the Antiochene Nestorius, bishop of Constantinople. His writings include theological treatises, letters, and commentaries, including complete commentaries on the Pentateuch, the Minor Prophets, and the Gospel of John.

Cyril of Jerusalem (ca. 315–387), bishop of Jerusalem, was the author of the *Catechetical Lectures*, more accurately called "homilies," addressed to candidates for baptism and five "mystagogic catecheses" delivered in Easter week after baptism.

Didymus the Blind (ca. 313–398), head of the Catechetical School in Alexandria, was much influenced by Origen, especially in his biblical interpretation. Although blind from childhood, he wrote many commentaries on Scripture, most of which are no longer extant. His most important extant writing is a treatise on the Holy Spirit that argued for the full divinity of the third person of the Trinity.

Ephrem the Syrian (ca. 306–373) was a Syriac writer and poet, and a native of Nisibis in southeastern Turkey. He is the author of many hymns and verse homilies dealing with biblical persons and events, ascetical topics, and theological themes, as well as biblical commentaries. The only Syriac writer recognized by the Catholic Church as a "Doctor of the Universal Church," he is celebrated in the Eastern church as the "Lyre of the Holy Spirit."

Gregory the Great (ca. 540–604) was a bishop of Rome, monk, writer, and an energetic, practical, and thoughtful administrator of the papacy at a difficult time. He wrote an important text for ecclesiastical leaders entitled *The Book of Pastoral Rule*. He also authored many letters, a popular spiritual commentary on the book of Job, known as the *Moralia*, and a collection of forty exegetical sermons on the gospels, including several dedicated to expositing the Gospel of John.

Gregory of Nazianzus (ca. 329–389), known as "the Theologian," was bishop of Sasima and a prominent preacher in Constantinople. Along with the other two Cappadocian fathers (Basil of Caesarea and Gregory of Nyssa), he defended the orthodox teaching formulated at Nicea in 325. Well educated in Greek culture and rhetoric, he was known for his eloquence and theological acumen, evident, for example, in his *Five Theological Orations*. These writings, which were occasioned by theological challenges proposed by neo-Arians, became pivotal doctrinal treatises that logically and systematically defended the Trinitarian formula articulated at the Council of Nicea.

Gregory of Nyssa (ca. 330–395), bishop of Nyssa, a leading theologian and mystical writer, was the brother of Basil of Caesarea and one of the three Cappadocian fathers (along with Gregory of Nazianzus). He championed the creed of Nicea (325) against Arians who denied the full divinity of Christ, as is evident from his polemic work *Against Eunomius*. Among his many works are his *Great Catechesis*, an introduction to the Christian faith and sacraments; *On Virginity*, which recommends the ascetic life; his *Life of Moses*; and homilies on the Beatitudes, the Lord's Prayer, and the Song of Songs, which he understands as an allegory of the love between God and the soul. His exegesis, which emphasizes the mystical sense of Scripture, was influenced by Origen.

Hilary of Poitiers (ca. 317–367) was bishop of Poitiers (modern France), a Latin theologian, biblical commentator, and hymn writer. His most important work, *The Trinity*, is a defense of the teaching of the Council of Nicea and was likely occasioned by his need to educate the faithful in Poitiers. This work in particular draws heavily on the sayings of Jesus in the Gospel of John. He is also the author of a commentary on the Gospel of Matthew as well as on the Psalms.

Hippolytus of Rome (ca. 170–236) was a Greek Christian writer, the most important theologian of the Roman Church in the third century, and author of polemical and theological works, commentaries on Daniel and the Song of Songs, and an early church order, *The Apostolic Tradition*. He was martyred on the island of Sardinia.

Irenaeus of Lyons (ca. 130–200), bishop of Lyons in southern Gaul (modern France), wrote *Against the Heresies* to oppose gnostic teachers such as Valentinus and Ptolemy. He defends Christian use of the Old Testament and argues that it forms a unity with the New Testament, which he is one of the first to cite as Scripture. His theology emphasizes God's action in the world and encapsulates the main themes of the biblical narratives: creation, redemption, and eschatological fulfillment.

Jerome (ca. 347–420), biblical scholar and ascetic, was educated in Rome and then devoted himself to the ascetic life, spending several years as a hermit in the Syrian desert, and then serving as head of a monastery in Bethlehem. Jerome's extreme asceticism is evident in his *Against Jovinian*. However, he is best known for the Vulgate, his translation of the Bible from Hebrew and Greek into Latin; his translation of the Bible became the standard text in Western Christianity. He produced many biblical commentaries (including commentaries on Paul's letters, the Gospel of Matthew, and the Prophets), and an extensive collection of letters. He was much influenced by Origen, some of whose works he translated into Latin, but he engaged in strong polemic against Origenism, and also against Arianism and Pelagianism.

John Cassian (ca. 360–433) was a monk who spent more than a decade devoting himself to Eastern Christian monastic practices. In Constantinople, he befriended John Chrysostom. Eventually, he founded a monastery for men and women in southern France. He wrote several works on the monastic life, including the *Conferences*, a series of conversations with outstanding leaders of Eastern monasticism.

John Chrysostom (ca. 347–407) studied rhetoric under the pagan orator Libanius and theology under Diodore of Tarsus, head of the Christian school of Antioch. As a priest at Antioch and later bishop in Constantinople (from 398), he was known especially for his high moral tone, his courage in difficult political circumstances, and his eloquence. His honorific title "Chrysostom" means "golden tongued," and it reflects his great reputation as a preacher. He preached extended series of sermons on many biblical books. His homilies on the Gospel of John resemble a commentary in that they go through the book chapter-by-chapter and deal with historical and theological questions. Their setting in preaching is evident especially in the moral exhortation addressed to his congregants; frequent subjects are the danger of wealth and the need to care for the poor.

John of Damascus (ca. 655–750) was an important Greek monk and theologian who lived under the Muslims and defended the use of images during the Iconoclastic Controversy (726–773). His major work, *The Fount of Wisdom,* is a compendium that offers a comprehensive synthesis of the teaching of the Greek fathers, especially Gregory of Nazianzus. Embedded within is a treatise entitled *An Exposition of the Orthodox Faith* that systematically summarizes the central points of Christian doctrine.

John Scotus Eriugena (ca. 810–877), theologian and philosopher from Ireland (hence, Scotus=Ireland and Eriugena=of Ireland), produced several original treatises that combined Christian theology and neo-Platonist philosophy. He translated many works from Greek into Latin, including those of Maximus the Confessor, Gregory of Nyssa, and Dionysius the Pseudo-Areopagite. He also wrote a number of exegetical works, including a commentary on the Gospel of John.

Justin Martyr (d. ca. 165) authored two apologies in defense of Christianity, first to Emperor Antoninus Pius and the second to the Roman Senate. He is also the author of the *Dialogue with Trypho*, a debate with a Jewish teacher on the meaning of passages from the Old Testament. His combined works offer an important testimony to second-century Christianity, especially in Rome. During the reign of Marcus Aurelius, he was martyred (beheaded) with a group of his disciples for refusing to sacrifice to the Roman gods.

Leo the Great (d. 461), pope from 440, greatly enhanced the authority of the see of Rome over all the Western provinces during an unstable time. When Attila the Hun invaded Italy, Leo persuaded him to withdraw. Later he saved Rome from utter destruction by the Vandals. In these two instances, he demonstrated the power of the bishop of Rome beyond just the ecclesiastical realm. He opposed all forms of heresy, and in his *Tome* he forcefully denounced monophysite Christology promoted by Eutyches. He wrote dozens of letters and sermons (called treatises) that address every facet of fifth-century Christianity.

Maximus of Turin (d. 408/423), bishop and author of more than a hundred sermons, some of which were widely read in the Middle Ages.

Novatian (third century), counter-bishop (anti-pope) of Rome, held an absolutist position against the readmission of apostates to the church who fell way during Decian persecutions; they could return to the church only by being rebaptized. Cyprian of Carthage and Cornelius, bishop of Rome, opposed this strict interpretation and argued that the lapsed could be reinstated through contrite repentance. By 251, this schism was resolved in part when he was excommunicated and Cornelius was elected pope. Despite the schismatic drama, Novatian's *On the Trinity* demonstrates his orthodox confession of Christ's divinity.

Origen of Alexandria (ca. 185–254), the true godfather of Christian biblical scholarship and interpretation. Despite posthumous condemnations occasioned by some of his bolder theological speculations, Origen exerted an unrivaled influence on early Christian biblical interpretation not only in the Eastern Christian tradition but in the West as well, through the medium of Latin translations. He wrote many commentaries and series of homilies on Old and New Testament books (e.g., on Genesis, Exodus, Leviticus, Jeremiah, Luke, John), and apparently commented on all the Pauline epistles. His other works include *Against Celsus*, a defense of Christianity against its pagan critics, and *On First Principles*, a compendium of Christian theology. Known especially for his allegorical or symbolic exegesis, Origen also concerns himself with historical and philological questions. His philological training is evident in his careful attention to the definitions of words, to shades of meaning expressed by similar phrases, and to textual variants. Unfortunately, only nine of thirty-two books of his expansive *Commentary of the Gospel of John* are extant.

Peter Chrysologus (ca. 400–454), bishop of Ravenna, authored dozens of sermons, primarily scriptural expositions that convey orthodox Christian doctrines and practices over and against Arianism and Eutychianism.

Romanos the Melodist (ca. 485–560) was a Greek Christian poet and author of metrical hymns to be sung in liturgy (hence, the honorific Melodist). These hymns, of which approximately eighty are extant, are noteworthy due to their thorough exposition of the biblical text. The best known are *The Nativity*, *The Presentation in the Temple*, and *The Resurrection*.

Rufinus of Aquileia (ca. 345–410) devoted himself to the monastic life, including time spent with the desert fathers in Egypt. His attraction to the ascetic life was shared by Jerome, whom he had met and befriended in Rome in his youth. They had a severe falling out over the Origenist controversy. When Rufinus translated Origen's *On First Principles* into Latin and noted that Jerome was an admirer of Origen, Jerome severed all ties to his former friend. Rufinus, like Jerome, translated many Greek Christian works for the Latin West, including many of Origen's homilies and scriptural commentaries and Eusebius of Caesarea's *Ecclesiastical History*. He wrote his own *Commentary on the Apostles' Creed*.

Severian of Gabala (d. ca. 408), bishop of Gabala in Syria, was an exegete of the Antiochene school who became well known for his preaching in Constantinople, where he was especially popular with the imperial court. Appointed by John Chrysostom as his vicar, Severian later opposed John and became one of his accusers at the Synod of the Oak (403). His surviving works include more than fifty homilies.

Sophronius of Jerusalem (ca. 560–639), known also as Sophronius the Wise, devoted himself to the monastic life both in Palestine and Egypt for more than two decades and fought against monothelitism, a heterodox theology that posited Christ had only one will, the divine. In 634 he was elevated as the patriarch of Jerusalem. After the city had endured a prolonged siege by Arab forces, Sophronius negotiated the surrender of Jerusalem to Caliph Umar I in 637. Although many of his theological writings have been lost, a few poems of lament mourning the fall of Jerusalem are extant. His *Life of the Evangelist John* was embedded in the liturgical texts of the Eastern Church and preserved in the gospel commentaries of Theophylact of Ohrid.

Tertullian of Carthage (ca. 160–225), from North Africa, was the first to write theological treatises in Latin. He also wrote apologetic, anti-heretical, and moral works, all of which display great skill in rhetoric. In his *On the Resurrection of the Dead*, which is directed against gnostics, he argues vigorously for the physical reality of the resurrection body. He also wrote two influential treatises: *On Baptism* and *On Prayer*. For a time, it seems that Tertullian was a Montanist, attracted in part by the rigorous moralism of this movement. In the early third century, he wrote his treatise *Against Praxeas* in which he proposed the formula for the doctrine of the Trinity.

Theodore of Mopsuestia (ca. 350–428) was a bishop of Mopsuestia in Cilicia in southeastern Asia Minor, theologian, and author of a series of catechetical homilies dealing with the Nicene Creed, the Lord's Prayer, the liturgy of baptism, and the Eucharist. As a biblical commentator, he produced a *Commentary on John*, originally written in Greek, but fully extant only in a Syriac translation.

Theodoret of Cyrus (ca. 393–460), bishop of Cyrus in Syria (near Antioch), was educated in Antioch and defended Nestorius and Antiochene Christology against the criticisms of Cyril of Alexandria. His works include an apology that compares Christian and pagan teaching, a church history, biographies of monks, a refutation of heresies, and commentaries on many Old Testament books (including Isaiah) and on the letters of Paul.

Theophilus of Alexandria (d. 412), bishop of Alexandria and uncle to Cyril who succeeded him as bishop. He is known for his vehement attacks against paganism in Egypt and the Origenist theology of Egyptian monks. He struggled against the see of Constantinople and especially its bishop, John Chrysostom. His extant homilies reveal the spiritual meaning of biblical texts and the church's rituals, as is witnessed in his *Homily on the Institution of the Eucharist* (preserved erroneously under Cyril of Alexandria's name).

Appendix 2: Sources of Texts Translated

1. Abbreviations of Sources Titles

CCSL   Corpus Christianorum: Series Latina. Turnhout (Belgium): Brepols, 1953ff.

CSCO   Corpus scriptorium ecclesiasticorum orientalium. Paris, 1903–.

CSEL   Corpus scriptorium ecclesiasticorum latinorum. Vienna, 1866ff.

GCS   Die grieschischen christlichen Schriftsteller der ersten drei Jahrhunderte. Berlin: Akademie Verlag, 1901ff.

GNO   Werner Jaeger et al., eds. Gregorii Nysseni opera. Leiden: Brill, 1960–72.

PG   J.-P. Migne, ed. Patrologiae cursus completes: Series Graeca. 161 vols. Paris, 1857–66.

PL   J.-P. Migne, ed. Patrologiae cursus completes: Series Latina. 221 vols. Paris, 1844–64.

Pusey   P. E. Pusey, Sancti patri nostril Cyrilli archiepiscopi Alexandrini in D. Joannis evangelium. 3 vols. Oxford: Clarendon, 1872.

SC   Sources chrétiennes. Paris: Éditions du Cerf, 1948ff.

WSA   Works of Saint Augustine. Brooklyn, NY: New City Press, 1990ff.

2. Sources of Individual Excerpts

Preface: The Gospel of John in the Early Church

(1)   Muratorian Fragment, 9–33; ed. Hans Lietzmann, *Das Muratorische Fragment und die Monarchianischen Prologue zu den Evangelien*, 2nd ed. (Berlin: de Gruyter 1933), 5–7.

(2)   Irenaeus of Lyons, *Against Heresies* 3.11.8, SC 211: 160–68.

(3)   Origen of Alexandria, *Commentary on the Gospel of John* 10.14–20, 21, 27, SC 157: 390–94, 396, 400.

(4)   Origen of Alexandria, *Commentary on the Gospel of John* 1.21–23, SC 120: 68–72.

(5)   John Chrysostom, *Homily* 1.1–2 *on John*, PG 59: 23–24.

(6)   John Chrysostom, *Homily* 2.1–3 *on John*, PG 59: 29–32.

(7)   Augustine of Hippo, *Tractate* 36.1 *on John*, CCSL 36: 323.

(8)   Augustine of Hippo, *Harmony of the Gospels* 4.10, 20, *CSEL* 43: 406–7, 418.

(9)   Anonymous, in Augustine of Hippo, *Tractates on John*, "Preface (by unknown author)," *CCSL* 36: xiv–xv.

(10)   Cyril of Alexandria, *Commentary on John* I. Introduction, in Pusey I: 14–15.

(11)   Cyril of Alexandria, *Commentary on John* I. Introduction, in Pusey I: 12–13.

(12)   Theodore of Mopsuestia, *Commentary on John,* Book 1, *CSCO* 4,3: 5–9.

(13)   Sophronius of Jerusalem, *The Life of the Evangelist John*; trans. Fr. Christopher Stade, *Theophylact*: *The Explanation of the Holy Gospel according to John*, Blessed Theophylact's Explanation of the New Testament, vol. 4 (House Springs, MO: Chrysostom Press, 2007), 2.

(14)   John Scotus Eriugena, *On the Prologue to the Gospel of John*, PL 122: 283–85.

John 1

(1)   Tertullian of Carthage, *Against Praxeas* 21.1–3, *CCSL* 2: 1186–87.

(2)   Origen of Alexandria, *Commentary on John* 1.90, 109–11, 116–18, 289, *SC* 120: 106, 118, 122, 204–6.

(3)   Origen of Alexandria, *Commentary on John* 2.1–2, 8–12, *SC* 120: 208–10, 212–14.

(4)   Hilary of Poitiers, *On the Trinity* 2.13, 15–17, *CCSL* 62: 50–54.

(5)   Gregory of Nyssa, *To Simplicius on the Faith*, *GNO* 3.1: 64–65.

(6)   John Chrysostom, *Homily* 4.1 *on John*, PG 59: 46–47.

(7)   John Chrysostom, *Homily* 2.4; 3.2–4; 4.1–2 *on John*, PG 59: 34–35, 39–41, 47–48.

(8)   Theodore of Mopsuestia, *Commentary on John*, Book 1, *CSCO* 4,3: 11, 13–17.

(9)   Theodore of Mopsuestia, *Commentary on John*, Book 1, *CSCO* 4,3: 19–24.

(10)   Augustine of Hippo, *Tractate* 1.1–2, 5–6 *on John*, WSA III/12: 39–40, 42–43, slightly revised.

(11)   Cyril of Alexandria, *Commentary on John* I.1, 2–3, in Pusey I: 18–19, 24, 31–32.

(12)   Venerable Bede, *Homily* I.8, *CCSL* 122: 53–54.

(13)   Theodore of Mopsuestia, *Commentary on John*, Book 1, *CSCO* 4,3: 25.

(14)   Augustine of Hippo, *On the Trinity* 1.9, WSA I/5: 70–71, slightly revised.

(15)   Augustine of Hippo, *Tractate* 1.9 *on John*, WSA III/12: 46–47, slightly revised.

(16)   John Chrysostom, *Homily* 5.3–4 *on John*, PG 59: 57–58.

(17)   Augustine of Hippo, *On the Trinity* 4.3–4, WSA I/5: 154–55.

(18)   Origen of Alexandria, *Commentary on John* 2.199, 202–3, 207–8, *SC* 120: 344–48.

(19)   John Chrysostom, *Homily* 8.1 *on John*, PG 59: 65.

(20)   Theodore of Mopsuestia, *Commentary on John*, Book 1, *CSCO* 4,3: 31.

(21)   Augustine of Hippo, *Tractate* 2.6 *on John*, WSA III/12: 59–60, slightly revised.

(22)   Augustine of Hippo, *Tractate* 2.11–13 *on John*, WSA III/12: 64–65, slightly revised.

(23)   Cyril of Alexandria, *On the Unity of Christ*, *SC* 97: 724–25.

(24)   Leo the Great, *Sermon* 27.2, *CCSL* 138: 133–34.

(25)   Novatian, *On the Trinity* 13, PL 3: 907–8.

(26)   Hilary of Poitiers, *On the Trinity* 1.11, *CCSL* 62: 11–12.

(27)   Jerome, *Against Jovinian* II.29, PL 23: 340C–341A.

(28)   John Chrysostom, *Homily* 11.1–2 *on John*, PG 59: 79, 80.

(29)   John Chrysostom, *Homily* 12.1 *on John*, PG 59: 81.

(30)   Theodore of Mopsuestia, *Commentary on John*, Book 1, *CSCO* 4,3: 33–34.

(31)   Augustine of Hippo, *On Christian Teaching* 1.13, WSA I/11: 111, slight revised.

(32) Augustine of Hippo, *Tractate* 2.15 *on John*, WSA III/12: 66–67, slightly revised.

(33) Augustine of Hippo, *On the Trinity* 13.12, WSA I/5: 353, slightly revised.

(34) Leo the Great, *Letter* 28.4, *PL* 54: 767B–C.

(35) Venerable Bede, *Homily* I.8, CCSL 122: 59.

(36) John Chrysostom, *Homily* 14.2–3 *on John*, PG 59: 94–95.

(37) Augustine of Hippo, *Tractate* 3.8–9 *on John*, WSA III/12: 74–75, slightly revised.

(38) Augustine of Hippo, *Tractate* 3.2, 14, 16–18 *on John*, WSA III/12: 69, 78–81, slightly revised.

(39) Cyril of Alexandria, *Commentary on John* I.9, in Pusey I: 151–53.

(40) Venerable Bede, *Homily* I.2, CCSL 122: 10.

(41) Origen of Alexandria, *Commentary on John* 6.88–91, SC 157: 194–96.

(42) Augustine of Hippo, *Tractate* 4.5–6 *on John*, WSA III/12: 89–91, slightly revised.

(43) Gregory the Great, *Homily* 7.3–4, CCSL 141: 48–49, 50–51.

(44) Origen of Alexandria, *Commentary on John* 6.264–75, SC 157: 330–38.

(45) John Chrysostom, *Homily* 17.1 *on John*, PG 59: 109.

(46) Augustine of Hippo, *Tractate* 4.10 *on John*, WSA III/12: 93–94, slightly revised.

(47) Augustine of Hippo, *Tractate* 7.5 *on John*, WSA III/12: 148.

(48) Theodore of Mopsuestia, *Commentary on John*, Book 1, CSCO 4,3: 41, 43.

(49) Leo the Great, *Sermon* 59.7, CCSL 138A: 358–59.

(50) Cyril of Alexandria, *Commentary on John* II, in Pusey I: 169–171.

(51) Venerable Bede, *Homily* I.15, CCSL 122: 106.

(52) Augustine of Hippo, *Tractate* 4.12 *on John*, WSA III/12: 95.

(53) Theodore of Mopsuestia, *Commentary on John*, Book 1, CSCO 4,3: 45–46.

(54) John Chrysostom, *Homily* 18.3 *on John*, PG 59: 117–18.

(55) Augustine of Hippo, *Tractate* 7.14 *on John*, WSA III/12: 157–58, slightly revised.

(56) Augustine of Hippo, *Tractate* 7.20–21, 22 *on John*, WSA III/12: 164–65.

John 2

(1) Romanos the Melodist, *Kontakion* 77, "On the Marriage at Cana," SC 110: 300–320; trans. Marjorie Carpenter, *Kontakia of Romanos, Byzantine Melodist*, vol. 1 (Columbia: University of Missouri Press, 1970), 68–74, slightly revised.

(2) Ammonius of Alexandria, *Fragment* 56 *on John*, ed. Joseph Reuss, *Johannes-Kommentare aus der griechischen Kirche* (Berlin: Akademie-Verlag, 1966), 211.

(3) Augustine of Hippo, *Tractate* 9.2–3, 5 *on John*, CCSL 36: 91–92.

(4) Cyril of Alexandria, *Commentary on John* II.1, in Pusey I: 200–201; 203–4.

(5) Venerable Bede, *Homily* I.14, CCSL 122: 95–97, 98–99; trans. Lawrence T. Martin and David Hurst, *Homilies on the Gospels*, vol. 1 (Kalamazoo, MI: Cistercian, 1991), 134–37; 139; 144.

(6) Irenaeus of Lyons, *Against Heresies* 3.16.7, SC 211: 314–18.

(7) John Chrysostom, *Homily* 21.2–3 *on John*, PG 59: 130–31; 134.

(8) Theodore of Mopsuestia, *Commentary on John*, CSCO 4,3: 56.

(9) Augustine of Hippo, *On True Religion* 31, CCSL 32: 206.

(10) Augustine of Hippo, *Faith and the Creed* 9, CSEL 41: 12–13.

(11) Cyril of Alexandria, *Commentary on John* II.1, in Pusey I: 204–5.

(12) Venerable Bede, *Homily* I.14, CCSL 122: 97; trans. Lawrence T. Martin and David Hurst, *Homilies on the Gospels*, vol. 1 (Kalamazoo, MI: Cistercian, 1991), 137.

(13) Irenaeus of Lyons, *Against Heresies* 3.11.5, *SC* 211: 152–54.

(14) John Chrysostom, *Homily* 22.2 *on John*, *PG* 59: 135–36.

(15) Augustine of Hippo, *Tractate* 9.2–3, 5 *on John*, *CCSL* 36: 92–93.

(16) Augustine of Hippo, *Tractate* 9.6, 10–16 *on John*, *CCSL* 36: 93–94, 96–99.

(17) Origen of Alexandria, *Commentary on John* 10.88–91, 99, 102–5, 108–10, *SC* 157: 436–38, 440–48.

(18) Origen of Alexandria, *Commentary on John* 10.138, 141–42, 145–49, *SC* 157: 470–76.

(19) Cyril of Jerusalem, *Catechetical Lecture* 7.6, *PG* 33: 612B–C.

(20) John Chrysostom, *Homily* 23.1–2 *on John*, *PG* 59: 139–40.

(21) Augustine of Hippo, *Tractate* 10.4–7 *on John*, *CCSL* 36: 102–4.

(22) Cyril of Alexandria, *Commentary on John* II.1, in Pusey I: 206–7.

(23) Venerable Bede, *Homily* II.1, *CCSL* 122: 185, 186–87, 188, trans. Lawrence T. Martin and David Hurst, *Homilies on the Gospels*, vol. 2 (Kalamazoo, MI: Cistercian, 1991), 2–7, revised slightly.

(24) Irenaeus of Lyons, *Against Heresies* 5.6.2, *SC* 153: 80–84.

(25) Tertullian of Carthage, *On the Resurrection of the Flesh* 18, *CCSL* 2: 942–44.

(26) Origen of Alexandria, *Commentary on John* 10.228–29, *SC* 157: 520.

(27) Theodore of Mopsuestia, *Commentary on John*, *CSCO* 4,3: 61–62.

(28) Augustine of Hippo, *Exposition of Psalm* 40:12, *CCSL* 38: 457–58; *WSA* III/16: 236–37, slightly revised.

(29) Augustine of Hippo, *Exposition of Psalm* 65:7, *CCSL* 39: 845–46; *WSA* III/16: 293, slightly revised.

(30) Augustine of Hippo, *Exposition of Psalm* 56:8, *CCSL* 39: 699; *WSA* III/16: 109, slightly revised.

(31) John Cassian, *First Conference of Abbot Isaac*, "On Prayer" 34, *SC* 54: 69–71.

(32) Theodoret of Cyrus, *Letter* 151, *PG* 83: 1420.

(33) Leo the Great, *Letter* 15.18, *PL* 54: 690A–C.

(34) John of Damascus, *Exposition of the Faith* 100.67–91, ed. P. B. Kotter, *Die Schriften des Johannes von Damaskos*, vol. 2, Patristische Texte und Studien 12 (Berlin: de Gruyter, 1973), 236–37; also in *PG* 94: 1224.

(35) John Chrysostom, *Homily* 24.1 *on John*, *PG* 59: 143.

(36) Cyril of Alexandria, *Commentary on John* II.1, in Pusey I: 213–16.

John 3

(1) Justin Martyr, *1 Apology* 61, ed. Miroslav Marcovich, *Iustini Martyris, Apologiae Pro Christianis* (Berlin: de Gruyter, 1994), 118–19.

(2) Theodore of Mopsuestia, *Commentary on John*, Book 2, *CSCO* 4,3: 65–66.

(3) Venerable Bede, *Homily* II.18, *CCSL* 122: 311–12, trans. Lawrence T. Martin and David Hurst, *Homilies on the Gospels*, vol. 2 (Kalamazoo, MI: Cistercian, 1991), 179, slightly revised.

(4) John Scotus Eriugena, *Commentary Fragments on John* 3, *PL* 122: 315A; 316A–316B.

(5) John Chrysostom, *Homily* 25.1–2 *on John*, *PG* 59: 149–51.

(6) Theodore of Mopsuestia, *Commentary on John*, Book 2, *CSCO* 4,3: 67–68.

(7) Augustine of Hippo, *Tractates* 11.6 and 12.5–6 *on John*, *CCSL* 36: 113–14, 122–23.

(8) John Scotus Eriugena, *Commentary Fragments on John* 3, *PL* 122: 316B–316D.

(9)   Venerable Bede, *Homily* II.18, *CCSL* 122: 312–13, trans. Lawrence T. Martin and David Hurst, *Homilies on the Gospels*, vol. 2 (Kalamazoo, MI: Cistercian, 1991), 180–81, slightly revised.

(10) Augustine of Hippo, *Tractate* 22.8–9 *on John*, *CCSL* 36: 125.

(11) John Scotus Eriugena, *Commentary Fragments on John 3*, *PL* 122: 319D.

(12) John Chrysostom, *Homily* 27.1–2 *on John*, *PG* 59: 158–60.

(13) Theodore of Mopsuestia, *Commentary on John*, Book 2, *CSCO* 4,3: 72.

(14) Augustine of Hippo, *Tractate* 12.11.1–5 *on John*, *CCSL* 36: 126–27.

(15) Severian of Gabala, in John of Damascus, *On Divine Images* I.58, ed. P. B. Kotter, *Die Schriften des Johannes von Damaskos*, vol. 3, Patristiche Texte und Studien 17 (Berlin: De Gruyter, 1975), 160.5–27; also *PG* 94: 1276–77.

(16) Cyril of Alexandria, *Commentary on John* II.1, in Pusey I: 225–26.

(17) Venerable Bede, *Homily* II.18, *CCSL* 122: 315–17, trans. Lawrence T. Martin and David Hurst, *Homilies on the Gospels*, vol. 2 (Kalamazoo, MI: Cistercian, 1991), 184–86, slightly revised.

(18) Irenaeus of Lyons, *Against Heresies* 5.27.2, *SC* 153: 342–46.

(19) John Chrysostom, *Homily* 28.1 *on John*, *PG* 59: 162–63.

(20) Theodore of Mopsuestia, *Commentary on John*, Book 2, *CSCO* 4,3: 73–74.

(21) Augustine of Hippo, *Tractate* 12.13 *on John*, *CCSL* 36: 128–29.

(22) John Scotus Eriugena, *Commentary Fragments on John 3*, *PL* 122: 323B–324B.

(23) John Chrysostom, *Homily* 29.1–2 *on John*, *PG* 59: 168–69.

(24) Ammonius of Alexandria, *Fragment* 95–96 on John, ed. Joseph Reuss, *Johannes-Kommentare aus der griechischen Kirche* (Berlin: Akademie-Verlag, 1966), 221.

(25) Augustine of Hippo, *Tractate* 14.4.1–5.2, 4–5 *on John*, *CCSL* 36: 143–44, 150.

(26) John Scotus Eriugena, *Commentary Fragments on John 3*, *PL* 122: 327B–327C.

(27) Cyril of Alexandria, *Commentary on John* II.2, in Pusey I: 240–44; 247.

(28) John Scotus Eriugena, *Commentary Fragments on John 3*, *PL* 122: 328B–329A.

(29) John Scotus Eriugena, *Commentary Fragments on John 3*, *PL* 122: 329C–329D.

(30) John Chrysostom, *Homily* 31.1 *on John*, *PG* 59: 175–76.

(31) Augustine of Hippo, *Tractate* 14.13 *on John*, *CCSL* 36: 150.

(32) John Scotus Eriugena, *Commentary Fragments on John 3*, *PL* 122: 330B–330C.

John 4

(1)   Romanos the Melodist, *Kontakion* 80, "On the Woman of Samaria," *SC* 110: 328–52; trans. Marjorie Carpenter, *Kontakia of Romanos, Byzantine Melodist*, vol. 1 (Columbia: University of Missouri Press, 1970), 87–89, 91–92, 95–96.

(2)   Ephrem the Syrian, *Hymn* 22; trans. Kathleen McVey, *Ephrem the Syrian: Hymns* (New York: Paulist Press, 1989), 355, slightly revised.

(3)   Ephrem the Syrian, *Hymn* 23, trans. Kathleen McVey, *Ephrem the Syrian: Hymns* (New York: Paulist Press, 1989), 361–63, slightly revised.

(4)   John Chrysostom, *Homily* 31.4–5 *on John*, *PG* 59: 181–82.

(5)   John Chrysostom, *Homily* 32.1–3 *on John*, *PG* 59: 184–87.

(6)   Augustine of Hippo, *Tractate* 15.10–15 *on John*, *CCSL* 36: 154–55.

(7)   Maximus of Turin, *Sermon* 22.2–22A.2, *CCSL* 23: 83–88.

(8)   Ambrose of Milan, *On the Holy Spirit* I.16.165, *CSEL* 79: 85.

(9)   John Chrysostom, *On the Samaritan*, PG 59: 535.

(10)   John Chrysostom, *Homily* 31.3 *on John*, PG 59: 179.

(11)   Augustine of Hippo, *Tractate* 15.6 *on John*, CCSL 36: 152.

(12)   Cyril of Alexandria, *Commentary on John* II.4, in Pusey I: 265–66.

(13)   John Scotus Eriugena, *Commentary Fragments on John 4*, PL 122: 332D–333A.

(14)   John Chrysostom, *Homily* 32.1 *on John*, PG 59: 183.

(15)   Theodore of Mopsuestia, *Commentary on John*, Book 2, CSCO 4,3: 88–89.

(16)   Augustine of Hippo, *Tractate* 15.16–17 *on John*, CCSL 36: 156.

(17)   Cyril of Alexandria, *Commentary on John* II.4, in Pusey I: 268–69.

(18)   John Scotus Eriugena, *Commentary Fragments on John 4*, PL 122: 334C–D; 335B–C.

(19)   Augustine of Hippo, *Tractate* 15.18–19 *on John*, CCSL 36: 156–57.

(20)   John Scotus Eriugena, *Commentary Fragments on John 4*, PL 122: 335D–336C.

(21)   Origen of Alexandria, *Commentary on John* 13.98–100, 105–10, SC 222: 82–84, 86–90.

(22)   Hilary of Poitiers, *On the Trinity* II.31, CCSL 62: 65–68.

(23)   Didymus the Blind, *Commentary on John*, Fragment 3, ed. Joseph Reuss, *Johannes-Kommentare aus der griechischen Kirche* (Berlin: Akademie-Verlag, 1966), 178.

(24)   Gregory of Nazianzus, *Fifth Theological Oration* 12, SC 250: 296–98.

(25)   Basil of Caesarea, *On the Holy Spirit* 26.63–64, SC 17bis: 476.

(26)   Ambrose of Milan, *On Faith* 5.4.49–54, ed. Christoph Markschies, *Fontes Christiani* 47 part 3 (Turnhout: Brepols, 2005), 626–30.

(27)   John Chrysostom, *Homily* 33.1–2 *on John*, PG 59: 188–90.

(28)   Theodore of Mopsuestia, *Commentary on John*, Book 2, CSCO 4,3: 90–91.

(29)   Cyril of Alexandria, *Commentary on John* II.5, in Pusey I: 276–77; 283–84.

(30)   John Scotus Eriugena, *Commentary Fragments on John 4*, PL 122: 338D–339A.

(31)   Cyril of Alexandria, *Commentary on John* II.5, in Pusey I: 285–87.

(32)   Origen of Alexandria, *Commentary on John* 13.167–70, 173–76, SC 222: 124–30.

(33)   John Chrysostom, *Homily* 34.1 *on John*, PG 59: 193.

(34)   Cyril of Alexandria, *Commentary on John* II.5, in Pusey I: 287.

(35)   Origen of Alexandria, *Commentary on John* 13.228, 235–42, 245–46, SC 222: 154, 158–62.

(36)   Cyril of Alexandria, *Commentary on John* II.5, in Pusey I: 291–93.

(37)   Origen of Alexandria, *Commentary on John* 13.305–9, SC 222: 198–202.

(38)   John Chrysostom, *Homily* 34.2 *on John*, PG 59: 194–95.

(39)   Cyril of Alexandria, *Commentary on John* II.5, in Pusey I: 295–96.

(40)   John Chrysostom, *Homily* 35.2–3 *on John*, PG 59: 201.

(41)   Augustine of Hippo, *Tractate* 16.3 *on John*, CCSL 36: 166.

(42)   John Cassian, *Thirteenth Conference: On God's Protection* 16.1–2, SC 54: 176.

(43)   Cyril of Alexandria, *Commentary on John* II.5, in Pusey I: 301–3.

(44)   Gregory the Great, *Homily* 28.1, CCSL 141: 239–20.

John 5

(1)   Irenaeus of Lyons, *Against Heresies* 2.22.3, SC 294: 218–20.

(2)   Tertullian of Carthage, *On Baptism* 5.5–7, CCSL 1: 281–82.

(3)   Ambrose of Milan, *On the Mysteries* 4:19–22, CSEL 73: 96–98.

(4)   John Chrysostom, *Homily* 36.1–2 *on John*, PG 59: 203–5.

(5)   Augustine of Hippo, *Tractate* 17.2–3 *on John*, CCSL 36: 170–71.

(6) John Chrysostom, *Homily* 36.2 *on John*, PG 59: 205.

(7) Venerable Bede, *Homily* I.23, CCSL 122: 162–63.

(8) Cyril of Jerusalem, *Homily on the Paralytic by the Pool* 6–9; 13, PG 33: 1137–45; trans. Edward Yarnold, S.J., *Cyril of Jerusalem*, The Early Church Fathers (London: Routledge, 2000), 72–76, slightly revised.

(9) Augustine of Hippo, *Tractate* 17.7–9 *on John*, CCSL 36: 174–76.

(10) Cyril of Jerusalem, *Homily on the Paralytic by the Pool* 14–15, PG 33: 1148–49; trans. Edward Yarnold, S.J., *Cyril of Jerusalem*, The Early Church Fathers (London: Routledge, 2000), 76, slightly revised.

(11) John Chrysostom, *Homily* 37.2 *on John*, PG 59: 209.

(12) Cyril of Alexandria, *Commentary on John* II.5, in Pusey I: 308–9.

(13) Cyril of Jerusalem, *Homily on the Paralytic by the Pool* 16, PG 33: 1149; trans. Edward Yarnold, S.J., *Cyril of Jerusalem*, The Early Church Fathers (London: Routledge, 2000), 76–77, slightly revised.

(14) Cyril of Jerusalem, *Homily on the Paralytic by the Pool* 16–17, PG 33: 1149–52; trans. Edward Yarnold, S.J., *Cyril of Jerusalem*, The Early Church Fathers (London: Routledge, 2000), 77–78, slightly revised.

(15) John Chrysostom, *Homily* 38.1 *on John*, PG 59: 211–12.

(16) Gregory of Nazianzus, *Oration* 40.33, PG 36: 405–8.

(17) Hilary of Poitiers, *On the Trinity* 7.15, SC 448: 306–8.

(18) Theodore of Mopsuestia, *Commentary on John*, Book 2, CSCO 4,3: 103–6.

(19) Augustine of Hippo, *The Literal Meaning of Genesis* 4:12, CSEL 28: 108–10.

(20) Augustine of Hippo, *Tractates* 17.16 and 18.2 *on John*, CCSL 36: 178–79; 180–81.

(21) Ambrose of Milan, *On the Holy Spirit* II.12, CSEL 79: 139.

(22) Theodore of Mopsuestia, *Commentary on John*, Book 2, CSCO 4,3: 109–11; 121.

(23) John Chrysostom, *Homily* 38.3–4 *on John*, PG 59: 216–17.

(24) Cyril of Alexandria, *Commentary on John* II.6, in Pusey I: 317–20.

(25) Hilary of Poitiers, *On the Trinity* 7.19–20, SC 448: 314–20.

(26) Augustine of Hippo, *Tractate* 21.6, 10–11, 13–15 *on John*, CCSL 36: 215; 217–21.

(27) Cyril of Alexandria, *Commentary on John* II.7–8, in Pusey I: 331–32; 335–37.

(28) Augustine of Hippo, *Tractate* 19.8–10, 16–17 *on John*, CCSL 36: 192–94, 199–200.

(29) Cyril of Alexandria, *Commentary on John* II.8, in Pusey I: 347–48.

(30) John Chrysostom, *Homily* 39.4 *on John*, PG 59: 225–26.

(31) Cyril of Alexandria, *Commentary on John* II.9, in Pusey I: 352.

(32) Gregory the Great, *The Book of Pastoral Rule* 3.18, SC 382: 370.

(33) John Chrysostom, *Homily* 40.1 *on John*, PG 59: 228–30.

(34) Augustine of Hippo, *Tractate* 23.3–4 *on John*, CCSL 36: 232–33.

(35) Cyril of Alexandria, *Commentary on John* III.1, in Pusey I: 366–68.

(36) John Chrysostom, *Homily* 40.3 *on John*, PG 59: 232–33.

(37) John Chrysostom, *Homily* 41.1–2 *on John*, PG 59: 235–37.

(38) Cyril of Alexandria, *Commentary on John* III.2–3, in Pusey I: 387–89.

John 6

(1) Theodore of Mopsuestia, *Commentary on John*, Book 2, CSCO 4,3: 132–34.

(2) John Chrysostom, *Homily* 42.2–3 *on John*, PG 59: 242–43.

(3) Augustine of Hippo, *Tractate* 24.2, 5–6 *on John*, *CCSL* 36: 244; 246–47.

(4) Cyril of Alexandria, *Commentary on John* III.4, in Pusey I: 410–12.

(5) John Chrysostom, *Homily* 42.3–4 *on John*, *PG* 59: 243–44.

(6) Augustine of Hippo, *Tractate* 25.1–2 *on John*, *CCSL* 36: 248–49.

(7) John Scotus Eriugena, *Commentary on the Gospel of John* 6.5–6, *SC* 180: 348–60.

(8) Augustine of Hippo, *Tractate* 25.5–7 *on John*, *CCSL* 36: 250–52.

(9) Cyril of Alexandria, *Commentary on John* III.4, in Pusey I: 426–32.

(10) Augustine of Hippo, *Tractate* 25.10 *on John*, *CCSL* 36: 252–53.

(11) Cyril of Alexandria, *Commentary on John* III.5, in Pusey I: 441–44.

(12) John Chrysostom, *Homily* 45.1 *on John*, *PG* 59: 251–52.

(13) Theodore of Mopsuestia, *Commentary on John*, Book 2, *CSCO* 4,3: 140–43.

(14) Augustine of Hippo, *Tractate* 25.12–13 *on John*, *CCSL* 36: 254–55.

(15) John Chrysostom, *Homily* 45.2 *on John*, *PG* 59: 253.

(16) Cyril of Alexandria, *Commentary on John* III.6, in Pusey I: 473–76.

(17) Augustine of Hippo, *Tractate* 25.16 *on John*, *CCSL* 36: 256–57.

(18) Cyril of Alexandria, *Commentary on John* IV.1, in Pusey I: 485–88.

(19) John Chrysostom, *Homily* 45.3–4 *on John*, *PG* 59: 255–56.

(20) Theodore of Mopsuestia, *Commentary on John*, Book 2, *CSCO* 4,3: 145–46.

(21) Theodore of Mopsuestia, *Commentary on John*, Book 2, *CSCO* 4,3: 147–48.

(22) Augustine of Hippo, *Tractate* 26.11–12 *on John*, *CCSL* 36: 264–66.

(23) Cyril of Alexandria, *Commentary on John* IV.2, in Pusey I: 518–20.

(24) Ambrose of Milan, *On the Christian Faith* 4.10.123–24, *CSEL* 78: 201.

(25) Augustine of Hippo, *Tractates* 26.14–15 and 26.17–18 *on John*, *CCSL* 36: 267, 268.

(26) Cyril of Alexandria, *Commentary on John* IV.2, in Pusey I: 528–36.

(27) Basil of Caesarea, *Letter 8*, *PG* 32: 252–53.

(28) John Chrysostom, *Homily* 46.1–2 *on John*, *PG* 59: 258–60.

(29) John Chrysostom, *Homily* 47.2 *on John*, *PG* 59: 265–66.

(30) Theodore of Mopsuestia, *Commentary on John*, Book 2, *CSCO* 4,3: 152–53.

(31) Augustine of Hippo, *Tractate* 27.5 *on John*, *CCSL* 36: 271–72.

(32) Augustine of Hippo, *Tractate* 27.11 *on John*, *CCSL* 36: 275–76.

John 7

(1) Augustine of Hippo, *Tractate* 28.5, 28.7(3) *on John*, *CCSL* 36: 279, 281.

(2) Theodore of Mopsuestia, *Commentary on John*, Book 3, *CSCO* 4,3: 155.

(3) John Chrysostom, *Homily* 48.2–3 *on John*, *PG* 59: 271–72, 274.

(4) Theodore of Mopsuestia, *Commentary on John*, Book 3, *CSCO* 4,3: 155.

(5) Cyril of Alexandria, *Commentary on John* IV.5, in Pusey I: 587–90.

(6) Augustine of Hippo, *Tractate* 28.8–9 *on John*, *CCSL* 36: 281–83.

(7) Cyril of Alexandria, *Commentary on John* IV.5, in Pusey I: 591–92.

(8) Cyril of Alexandria, *Commentary on John* IV.5, in Pusey I: 598–600.

(9) Augustine of Hippo, *Tractate* 29.3, 5 *on John*, *CCSL* 36: 285–86.

(10) Cyril of Alexandria, *Commentary on John* IV.5, in Pusey I: 604–5.

(11) John Chrysostom, *Homily* 49.3 *on John*, *PG* 59: 277, 278.

(12) Augustine of Hippo, *Tractate* 30.5 *on John*, *CCSL* 36: 291–92.

(13) Theodore of Mopsuestia, *Commentary on John*, Book 3, *CSCO* 4,3: 158–59.

(14) Hilary of Poitiers, *On the Trinity* 6.28, *CCSL* 62: 229–30.

(15) John Chrysostom, *Homily* 50.1 *on John*, *PG* 59: 279.18–52.

(16) John Chrysostom, *Homily* 50.2–3 *on John*, *PG* 59: 280–81, 282.

(17) Augustine of Hippo, *Tractate* 31.9–10 *on John*, *CCSL* 36: 298–29.

(18) Cyril of Jerusalem, *Catechetical Lecture* 16.11–12, *PG* 33: 932C–933C.

(19) Ambrose of Milan, *On the Holy Spirit* I.16.156–60, *CCSL* 79: 81–83.

(20) Augustine of Hippo, *Tractate* 32.9 *on John*, *CCSL* 36: 305–6.

(21) Cyril of Alexandria, *Commentary on John* V.2, in Pusey I: 690, 691–92, 693–94, 695–96.

(22) Augustine of Hippo, *Tractate* 32.6–8 *on John*, *CCSL* 36: 302–4.

John 8

(1) Augustine of Hippo, *Tractate* 33.4–6, 8 *on John*, *CCSL* 36: 307–9, 310–11.

(2) *Apostolic Constitutions* II.24, *SC* 320: 222–26.

(3) Venerable Bede, *Homily on the Gospels* I.25, *CCSL* 122: 178–82; trans. Lawrence Martin and David Hurst, *Homilies on the Gospels*, vol. 1 (Kalamazoo, MI: Cistercian, 1991), 245–50, slightly revised.

(4) Theodore of Mopsuestia, *Commentary on John*, *CSCO* 4,3: 164–65.

(5) Augustine of Hippo, *Tractate* 34.5 *on John*, *CCSL* 36: 313.

(6) Novatian, *On the Trinity* 15, *PL* 3: 911B–911C.

(7) Augustine of Hippo, *Tractate* 35.4 *on John*, *CCSL* 36: 319–20.

(8) Augustine of Hippo, *Tractate* 36.4 *on John*, *CCSL* 36: 325.

(9) Tertullian of Carthage, *Against Praxeas* 22.1–6, *CCSL* 2: 1189.

(10) Ambrose of Milan, *On the Faith* 5.3.44–45, *CSEL* 78: 233–34.

(11) Augustine of Hippo, *Tractate* 37.1–2, 7 *on John*, *CCSL* 36: 332–33, 335.

(12) Novatian, *On the Trinity* 15, *PL* 3: 911C–912B.

(13) Augustine of Hippo, *Tractate* 38.8, 10 *on John*, *CCSL* 36: 341–42, 344.

(14) Cyril of Alexandria, *Commentary* 5.4 *on John*, in Pusey II: 19–21.

(15) Augustine of Hippo, *Tractate* 40.5 *on John*, *CCSL* 36: 352–53.

(16) Cyril of Alexandria, *Commentary* 5.4 *on John*, in Pusey II: 34–35.

(17) John Chrysostom, Homily 54.1 on John, *PG* 59: 295–97.

(18) Theodore of Mopsuestia, *Commentary on John*, *CSCO* 4,3: 173–74.

(19) Augustine of Hippo, *Tractate* 41.4, 8 *on John*, *CCSL* 36: 359, 361–62.

(20) Origen of Alexandria, *Commentary on John* 20.66–68, 126, *SC* 290: 188–92; 218–20.

(21) Augustine of Hippo, *Tractate* 42.4–5 *on John*, *CCSL* 36: 367.

(22) Origen of Alexandria, *Commentary on John* 20.152–56, *SC* 290: 230–32.

(23) Novatian, *On the Trinity* 15, *PL* 3: 912B–912C.

(24) Hilary of Poitiers, *On the Trinity* 6.30, *CCSL* 62: 231–33.

(25) Origen of Alexandria, *Commentary on John* 20.177–81, 183–84, 194, *SC* 290: 244–46; 248–50; 254.

(26) Origen of Alexandria, *Commentary on John* 20.269–71, 275, 285, *SC* 290: 288, 290, 294–96.

(27) Gregory the Great, *Homily* 18.1, *CCSL* 141: 136; trans. Dom David Hurst, *Forty Gospel Homilies* (Kalamazoo, MI: Cistercian, 1990), 113–14, slightly revised.

(28) Origen of Alexandria, *Commentary on John* 20.316–18, *SC* 290: 312.

(29) Gregory the Great, *Homily* 18.2, *CCSL* 141: 137; trans. Dom David Hurst, *Forty Gospel Homilies* (Kalamazoo, MI: Cistercian, 1990), 114–15, slightly revised.

(30) Didymus the Blind, *Fragment* 12 *on John*, ed. J. Reuss, *Johannes-Kommentare aus der griechischen Kirche*, Texts und Untersuchungen 89 (Berlin: Akademie Verlag, 1966), 182.

(31) Cyril of Alexandria, *Commentary on John* VI. Preface, in Pusey II: 114–15.

(32) Peter Chrysologus, *Sermon* 131.8–9, in *CCSL* 24B: 807–8.

(33) Novatian, *On the Trinity* 15, PL 3: 912C–913B.

(34) John Chrysostom, *Homily* 55.2 *on John*, PG 59: 304.

(35) Theodore of Mopsuestia, *Commentary on John*, CSCO 4,3: 180.

(36) Augustine of Hippo, *Tractate* 43.16–17 *on John*, CCSL 36: 379–81.

(37) Cyril of Alexandria, *Commentary* 6 *on John*, in Pusey II: 129–30; 132–33.

(38) Gregory the Great, *Forty Gospel Homilies* 18.3, CCSL 141: 139; trans. Dom David Hurst (Kalamazoo, MI: Cistercian, 1990), 116–17.

John 9

(1) Augustine of Hippo, *Tractate* 44.1 *on John*, CCSL 36: 381–82.

(2) Ambrose of Milan, *Letter* 67 [80].1–3, CSEL 82.2: 165–66.

(3) John Chrysostom, *Homily* 56.1 *on John*, PG 59: 305–7.

(4) Augustine of Hippo, *Tractate* 44.3 *on John*, CCSL 36: 382–83.

(5) Cyril of Alexandria, *Commentary on John* VI.1, in Pusey II: 148–51.

(6) John Chrysostom, *Homily* 56 *on John*, PG 59: 308–9.

(7) Augustine of Hippo, *Tractate* 44.4–6 *on John*, CCSL 36: 383–84.

(8) Irenaeus of Lyons, *Against Heresies* 5.15.2–5, SC 153: 204–12.

(9) Ambrose of Milan, *On the Sacraments* 3.11–14, SC 25: 98–100.

(10) Ambrose of Milan, *Letter* 67 [80].4–7, CSEL 82.2: 166–68.

(11) John Chrysostom, *Homily* 57.1 *on John*, PG 59: 311–12.

(12) Augustine of Hippo, *Tractate* 44.2 *on John*, CCSL 36: 382.

(13) Augustine of Hippo, *Tractate* 44.8 *on John*, CCSL 36: 385.

(14) John Chrysostom, *Homilies* 57.2 and 58.1 *on John*, PG 59: 313, 315.

(15) Cyril of Alexandria, *Commentary on John* VI.1, in Pusey II: 165–67, 171.

(16) Theodore of Mopsuestia, *Commentary on John* 9.18–22; trans. George Kalantzis, *Commentary on John* (Strathfield, Australia: St. Paul's, 2004), 72–73, slightly revised.

(17) Cyril of Alexandria, *Commentary on John* VI.1, in Pusey II: 174.

(18) John Chrysostom, *Homily* 58.2 *on John*, PG 59: 318.

(19) Augustine of Hippo, *Tractate* 44.11 *on John*, CCSL 36: 386.

(20) Cyril of Alexandria, *Commentary on John* VI.1, in Pusey II: 179–80; 183–84.

(21) Augustine of Hippo, *Tractate* 44.12–14 *on John*, CCSL 36: 386–37.

(22) Cyril of Alexandria, *Commentary on John* VI.1, in Pusey II: 185; 186–90; 193–94.

(23) John Chrysostom, *Homily* 59.1 *on John*, PG 59: 321–22.

(24) Augustine of Hippo, *Tractate* 44.15 *on John*, CCSL 36: 387.

(25) Cyril of Alexandria, *Commentary on John* VI.1, in Pusey II: 198; 200–203.

(26) Caesarius of Arles, *Sermon* 172.1–4, CCSL 104.2: 701–4.

(27) Theodore of Mopsuestia, *Commentary on John*, Book 2, CSCO 4,3: 194–95.

(28) Augustine of Hippo, *Tractate* 44.16–17 *on John*, CCSL 36: 387–88.

John 10

(1)   John Chrysostom, *Homily 59.2–3 on John, PG* 59: 323.65–324.67.

(2)   Theodore of Mopsuestia, *Commentary on John, CSCO* 4,3: 197.

(3)   Augustine of Hippo, *Tractate 45.2 on John, CCSL* 36: 389.

(4)   Augustine of Hippo, *Tractate 46.2–4 on John, CCSL* 36: 398–400.

(5)   Cyril of Alexandria, *Commentary on John VI.1*, in Pusey II: 216–17.

(6)   Clement of Alexandria, *Exhortation to the Greeks I.10.2–3, GCS* 1: 10.

(7)   Cyril of Jerusalem, *Catechetical Lecture* 10.1–3, *PG* 33: 660A–664B.

(8)   Theodore of Mopsuestia, *Commentary on John, CSCO* 4,3: 199–200.

(9)   Cyril of Alexandria, *Commentary on John VI.1*, in Pusey II: 211–12.

(10) Augustine of Hippo, *Tractate 45.8–10 on John, CCSL* 36: 391–93.

(11) Augustine of Hippo, *Tractate 45.15 on John, CCSL* 36: 396–97.

(12) Tertullian of Carthage, *On the Flight from Persecution* 11, *CCSL* 2: 1148–49.

(13) *Epistle from the Roman Clergy to the Carthaginian Clergy* (in Cyprian of Carthage, *Epistle* 8, I.1–2), *CCSL* 3B: 40–41.

(14) Aphrahat the Persian, *Demonstration* 10.1, 3–4 (On Shepherds); trans. Adam Lehto, *The Demonstrations of Aphrahat, the Persian Sage*, Gorgias Eastern Christian Studies 27 (Piscataway, NJ: Gorgias, 2010), 251–52, 254–55, slightly revised.

(15) John Chrysostom, *Homily 60.1 on John, PG* 59: 327.39–52, 59–61; 328.1–329.8.

(16) Augustine of Hippo, *Tractate 46.5–6, 8 on John, CCSL* 36: 400–403.

(17) *Apostolic Constitutions* II.20, *SC* 320: 198–202.

(18) Cyril of Alexandria, *Commentary on John VI.1*, in Pusey II: 223–24.

(19) Peter Chrysologus, *Sermon 40, PL* 52: 313A–314B.

(20) Cyril of Alexandria, *Commentary on John VI.1*, in Pusey II: 230–33.

(21) Cyprian of Carthage, *Epistle* 69.5, *CCSL* 3C: 475–76.

(22) Theodore of Mopsuestia, *Commentary on John, CSCO* 4,3: 204–5.

(23) Hilary of Poitiers, *On the Trinity* 9.12, *CCSL* 62A: 383–84.

(24) John Chrysostom, *Homily 60.2 on John, PG* 59: 330–31.

(25) Cyril of Alexandria, *Commentary on John 6.1–7.0*, in Pusey II: 239; 243–45.

(26) Novatian, *On the Trinity* 15, *PL* 3: 913B.

(27) Gregory of Nazianzus, *Oration* 1.6–7, *SC* 247: 78–82.

(28) Cyril of Alexandria, *Commentary on John VII*, in Pusey II: 252.

(29) John Chrysostom, *Homily 61.1 on John, PG* 59: 338.

(30) Theodore of Mopsuestia, *Commentary on John, CSCO* 4,3: 213–14.

(31) Hilary of Poitiers, *On the Trinity* 7.22, *CCSL* 62: 285–86.

(32) Augustine of Hippo, *Tractate 48.7 on John, CCSL* 36: 416–17.

(33) Tertullian of Carthage, *Against Praxeas* 20, 22, *CCSL* 2: 1186, 1190–91.

(34) Hippolytus of Rome, *Contra Noetum* 7.1–2, ed. R. Butterworth, *Hippolytus of Rome. Contra Noetum* (London: University of London, 1977), 53.

(35) Hilary of Poitiers, *On the Trinity* 7.25, *CCSL* 62: 290–91.

(36) Theodoret of Cyrus, *Church History* 2.8.45–47, *SC* 501: 370–72.

(37) Cyril of Alexandria, *Commentary 7 on John*, in Pusey II: 254–55.

(38) Novatian, *On the Trinity* 15, *PL* 3: 913C–914B.

(39) Hilary of Poitiers, *On the Trinity* 7.24, *CCSL* 62: 289–90.

(40) John Chrysostom, *Homily 61.3 on John, PG* 59: 338–39.

(41) Augustine of Hippo, *Tractate 48.8–9 on John, CCSL* 36: 417–18.

(42) John Chrysostom, *Homily* 61.3 *on John*, PG 59: 340.

John 11

(1) Romanos the Melodist, *Kontakion* 70, "On the Raising of Lazarus I," *SC* 114: 164–76; trans. Marjorie Carpenter, *Kontakia of Romanos, Byzantine Melodist*, vol. 1 (Columbia: University of Missouri Press, 1970), 143–48, slightly revised.

(2) John Chrysostom, *Homily* 62.1 *on John*, PG 59: 341–43.

(3) Peter Chrysologus, *Sermon* 63.1–2, CCSL 24A: 373–76.

(4) Augustine of Hippo, *Tractate* 49.5 *on John*, CCSL 36: 422.

(5) Cyril of Alexandria, *Commentary on John*, Fragments on Book 7, in Pusey II: 264–65.

(6) Theodore of Mopsuestia, *Commentary on John*, Book 5, CSCO 4,3: 222–23.

(7) Augustine of Hippo, *Tractate* 49.9, 11–12 *on John*, CCSL 36: 424, 425–26.

(8) Cyril of Alexandria, *Commentary on John* VII, in Pusey II: 268–69.

(9) Augustine of Hippo, *Tractate* 49.12 *on John*, CCSL 36: 426.

(10) Cyril of Alexandria, *Commentary on John*, Fragments on Book 7, in Pusey II: 271.

(11) John Chrysostom, *Homily* 62.3 *on John*, PG 59: 345.

(12) Peter Chrysologus, *Sermon* 63.3–4, CCSL 24A: 376–77.

(13) Peter Chrysologus, *Sermon* 63.3; 64.2, CCSL 24A: 376, 379–81.

(14) Cyril of Alexandria, *Commentary on John*, Fragments on Book 7, in Pusey II: 272–73.

(15) Cyprian of Carthage, *On Mortality* 21, CCSL 3A: 28.

(16) Novatian, *On the Trinity* 16, PL 3: 914B–914C.

(17) John Chrysostom, *Homily* 62.3–5 *on John*, PG 59: 345–48.

(18) Peter Chrysologus, *Sermon* 63.3–4, CCSL 24A: 377–78.

(19) Augustine of Hippo, *Tractate* 49.14 *on John*, CCSL 36: 427.

(20) Cyril of Alexandria, *Commentary on John* VII, in Pusey II: 274–75.

(21) Cyril of Alexandria, *Commentary on John* VII, in Pusey II: 276–77.

(22) John Chrysostom, *Homily* 63.2 *on John*, PG 59: 350.

(23) Theodore of Mopsuestia, *Commentary on John*, Book 5, CSCO 4,3: 227–28.

(24) Peter Chrysologus, *Sermon* 64.3, CCSL 24A: 381–82.

(25) Augustine of Hippo, *Tractate* 49.18–19 *on John*, CCSL 36: 428–29.

(26) Cyril of Alexandria, *Commentary on John* VII, in Pusey II: 279–80.

(27) Cyril of Alexandria, *Commentary on John* VII, in Pusey II: 281–82.

(28) Cyril of Alexandria, *Commentary on John* VII, in Pusey II: 280–81.

(29) Origen of Alexandria, *Commentary on John* 28.14–22, SC 385: 66–68.

(30) Cyril of Jerusalem, *Catechetical Lecture* 5.9, PG 33: 516B–516C.

(31) John Chrysostom, *Homily* 63.2 *on John*, PG 59: 350–51.

(32) Peter Chrysologus, *Sermon* 65.3, CCSL 24A: 385–86.

(33) Augustine of Hippo, *Tractate* 49.22 *on John*, CCSL 36: 430–31.

(34) Augustine of Hippo, *Tractate* 49.3 *on John*, CCSL 36: 420–21.

(35) Cyril of Alexandria, *Commentary on John* VII, in Pusey II: 284, 285.

(36) John of Damascus, *Exposition of the Faith* 100 (4.27), *Die Schriften des Johannes von Damaskos*, vol. 12, Patristische Texte und Studien (New York: de Gruyter, 1973), 236.

(37) Origen of Alexandria, *Commentary on John* 28.42–44, 47, SC 385: 80–82.

(38) Hilary of Poitiers, *On the Trinity* 10.71, CCSL 62A: 526–27.

(39) John Chrysostom, *Homily* 64.2 *on John*, PG 59: 356–57.

(40) Peter Chrysologus, *Sermon* 65.5–8, CCSL 24A: 387–91.

(41) Origen of Alexandria, *Commentary on John* 28.54, 56–60, SC 385: 86–88, 90–92.

(42) Ambrose of Milan, *On Repentance* II.7.57–58, 63, CSEL 73: 186–89.

(43) Ambrose of Milan, *On the Death of a Brother* II.77, CSEL 73: 291–92.

(44) Augustine of Hippo, *Tractate* 49.24 *on John*, CCSL 36: 431.

(45) Augustine of Hippo, *Tractate* 49.1 *on John*, CCSL 36: 419–20.

(46) Cyril of Alexandria, *Commentary on John* VII, in Pusey II: 289–90, 292.

(47) John Chrysostom, *Homily* 64.3 *on John*, PG 59: 358.

(48) Augustine of Hippo, *Tractate* 49.26–27 *on John*, CCSL 36: 432.

(49) Origen of Alexandria, *Commentary on John* 28.98–100, 127, 150–53, SC 385: 112–14, 124–26, 134–36.

(50) John Chrysostom, *Homily* 65.1 *on John*, PG 59: 361.

(51) Gregory of Nyssa, *Against Eunomius* 3.2.86, GNO 2: 81.

(52) Augustine of Hippo, *Tractate* 49.26–27 *on John*, CCSL 36: 432–33.

(53) Cyril of Alexandria, *Commentary on John* VII, in Pusey II: 294–95.

(54) Augustine of Hippo, *Tractate* 50.2 *on John*, CCSL 36: 433–34.

John 12

(1) Ambrose of Milan, *On the Duties of the Clergy* 1.16.63–64, PL 13: 42.

(2) John Chrysostom, *Homily* 65.2–3 *on John*, PG 59: 362–63.

(3) John Chrysostom, *Homily* 65.2–3 *on John*, PG 59: 363–64.

(4) Theodore of Mopsuestia, *Commentary on John* 12.1; trans. George Kalantzis, *Commentary on John* (Strathfield, Australia: St. Paul's, 2004), slightly revised.

(5) Augustine of Hippo, *Tractate* 50.10–13 *on John*, CCSL 36: 437–39.

(6) Cyril of Alexandria, *Commentary on John* VII and VIII, in Pusey II: 298–99; 303.

(7) John Chrysostom, *Homily* 66.1–2 *on John*, PG 59: 365–66.

(8) Augustine of Hippo, *Tractate* 50.14 *on John*, CCSL 36: 439.

(9) Augustine of Hippo, *Tractate* 51.2, 4 *on John*, CCSL 36: 440–41.

(10) John Chrysostom, *Homily* 66.1–2 *on John*, PG 59: 366–67.

(11) Cyril of Alexandria, *Commentary on John* VIII, in Pusey II: 306–7.

(12) Augustine of Hippo, *Tractate* 51.8 *on John*, CCSL 36: 442.

(13) Cyril of Alexandria, *Commentary on John* VIII, in Pusey II: 308–11.

(14) John Chrysostom, *Homily* 66.2–3 *on John*, PG 59: 368.

(15) Augustine of Hippo, *Tractate* 51.9–10 *on John*, CCSL 36: 442–43.

(16) Augustine of Hippo, *Tractate* 51.12–13 *on John*, CCSL 36: 444–45.

(17) John Cassian, *Conferences* 1.14.1–2, CSEL 13: 21–24.

(18) Tertullian of Carthage, *Against Praxeas* 23, CCSL 2: 1191–93.

(19) Ambrose of Milan, *On the Sacraments* 5:36–41, 44–45, CSEL 79: 241–47.

(20) Augustine of Hippo, *Tractate* 52.3–5 *on John*, CCSL 36: 446–48.

(21) Athanasius of Alexandria, *On the Incarnation* 25–26, SC 199: 354–62.

(22) Theodore of Mopsuestia, *Commentary on John* 12.31; trans. George Kalantzis, *Commentary on John* (Strathfield, Australia: St. Paul's, 2004), 102, slightly revised.

(23) Augustine of Hippo, *Tractate* 52.6, 9–10 *on John*, CCSL 36: 448–50.

(24) Theodore of Mopsuestia, *Commentary on John* 12.34–36; trans. George Kalantzis, *Commentary on John* (Strathfield, Australia: St. Paul's, 2004), 102–3, slightly revised.

(25) Augustine of Hippo, *Tractate* 52.12–14 *on John*, CCSL 36: 450–51.
(26) Augustine of Hippo, *Tractate* 53.5–10 *on John*, CCSL 36: 454–56.
(27) Jerome, *Letter* 18A.4, CSEL 54: 78.
(28) Augustine of Hippo, *Tractate* 53.12 *on John*, CCSL 36: 457–58.
(29) Ambrose of Milan, *On the Christian Faith* 5.9.120–5.10.131, CSEL 78: 261–65.
(30) John Chrysostom, *Homily* 69.1 *on John*, PG 59: 377–78.
(31) Ambrose of Milan, *On Repentance* 1.12.53–57, CSEL 73: 145–46.
(32) John Chrysostom, *Homily* 69.1 *on John*, PG 59: 378.
(33) Augustine of Hippo, *Tractate* 54.4 *on John*, CCSL 36: 460–61.

John 13

(1) Venerable Bede, *Homily* II.5, CCSL 122: 214–15.
(2) Origen of Alexandria, *Commentary on John* 5.32, SC 385: 204–8.
(3) Theophilus of Alexandria, *Homily on the Institution of the Eucharist* (i.e., Cyril of Alexandria's *Homily* 10), PG 77: 1024.
(4) Venerable Bede, *Homily* II.5, CCSL 122: 215–16.
(5) Ambrose of Milan, *On the Holy Spirit* 1, Prol., 12–16, CSEL 79: 20–22.
(6) Ambrose of Milan, *On the Sacraments* 3.1.1–2, 4, 7, CSEL 73: 37–41.
(7) John Chrysostom, *Homily* 70.2 *on John*, PG 59: 383–84.
(8) Theophilus of Alexandria, *Homily on the Institution of the Eucharist* (i.e., Cyril of Alexandria's *Homily* 10), PG 77: 1024–25.
(9) Venerable Bede, *Homily* II.5, CCSL 122: 216–17.
(10) John Chrysostom, *Homily* 71.1 *on John*, PG 59: 385–86.
(11) Theophilus of Alexandria, *Homily on the Institution of the Eucharist* (i.e., Cyril of Alexandria's *Homily* 10), PG 77: 1025–28.
(12) John Chrysostom, *Homily* 71.2 *on John*, PG 59: 387.
(13) Augustine of Hippo, *Tractate* 59.1 *on John*, CCSL 36: 475–76.
(14) Augustine of Hippo, *Tractate* 59.3 *on John*, CCSL 36: 477.
(15) Augustine of Hippo, *Tractate* 60.1–5 *on John*, CCSL 36: 478–80.
(16) Origen of Alexandria, *Commentary on John* 5.32, SC 385: 292–94.
(17) Origen of Alexandria, *Commentary on John* 5.32, SC 385: 306–8; 312–14.
(18) Augustine of Hippo, *Tractate* 62.2–4 *on John*, CCSL 36: 478–80.
(19) Cyril of Alexandria, *Commentary on John* IX, in Pusey II: 370–73.
(20) Origen of Alexandria, *Commentary on John* 5.32, SC 385: 320–24.
(21) Origen of Alexandria, *Commentary on John* 5.32, SC 385: 318–27.
(22) Cyril of Alexandria, *Commentary on John* IX, in Pusey II: 377–79.
(23) Augustine of Hippo, *Tractates* 64.1–2, 4 and 65.1–3 *on John*, CCSL 36: 488–92.
(24) John Chrysostom, *Homily* 73.1 *on John*, PG 59: 395–96.
(25) Augustine of Hippo, *Tractate* 66.1 *on John*, CCSL 36: 493.
(26) Cyril of Alexandria, *Commentary on John* IX, in Pusey II: 392–94.

John 14

(1) Irenaeus of Lyons, *Against Heresies* 5.36.1–2, SC 153: 452–60.

(2)   Tertullian of Carthage, *On the Resurrection of the Flesh* 41, CCSL 2: 975–76.

(3)   Theodore of Mopsuestia, *Commentary on John*, Book 6, CSCO 4,3: 266–67.

(4)   Augustine of Hippo, *Tractates* 67.2 and 68.3 *on John*, CCSL 36: 495–96, 498–99.

(5)   Cyprian of Carthage, *Letter* 73.17, CCSL 62: 300–301.

(6)   Cyril of Alexandria, *Commentary on John* IX, in Pusey II: 408–11.

(7)   Leo the Great, *Sermon* 72.1, CCSL 3C: 548–49.

(8)   Hilary of Poitiers, *On the Trinity* 7.34–38, CCSL 62: 301–6.

(9)   Basil of Caesarea, *On the Holy Spirit* 22, SC 17: 440–42.

(10) John Chrysostom, *Homily* 75.1 *on John*, PG 59: 403–4.

(11) Augustine of Hippo, *Tractate* 74.1–5 *on John*, CCSL 36: 512–15.

(12) Venerable Bede, *Homily* II.17, CCSL 122: 301–2.

(13) Augustine of Hippo, *Tractate* 75.2–4 *on John*, CCSL 36: 515–17.

(14) Gregory the Great, *Homily 30.2 on the Gospels*, SC 522: 224–26.

(15) Augustine of Hippo, *Tractate* 77.2 *on John*, CCSL 36: 520–21.

(16) Cyril of Alexandria, *Commentary on John* IX, in Pusey II: 509–11.

(17) Tertullian of Carthage, *Adversus Praxean* 9.1–4, CCSL 2: 1168–69.

(18) John Chrysostom, *Homily* 75.4 *on John*, PG 59: 408–9.

(19) Theodore of Mopsuestia, *Commentary on John*, Book 6, CSCO 4,3: 280.

(20) Cyril of Alexandria, *Commentary on John* IX, in Pusey II: 531–33.

John 15

(1)   Origen of Alexandria, *Commentary on John* 1.30.205–8, SC 120: 160–62.

(2)   Hilary of Poitiers, *On the Trinity* 9.55, SC 462: 130–32.

(3)   Augustine of Hippo, *Tractate* 80.1–3 *on John*, CCSL 36: 527–29.

(4)   Cyril of Alexandria, *Commentary on John* X.2, in Pusey II: 537; 542–44.

(5)   Augustine of Hippo, *Tractate* 81.4 *on John*, CCSL 36: 531.

(6)   Augustine of Hippo, *Tractate* 82.1–4 *on John*, CCSL 36: 532–34.

(7)   Cyril of Alexandria, *Commentary on John* X.2, in Pusey II: 568–71.

(8)   John Chrysostom, *Homily* 77.1 *on John*, PG 59: 413–15.

(9)   Augustine of Hippo, *Tractate* 84.1–2 *on John*, CCSL 36: 536–38.

(10) Gregory the Great, *Homily 27 on the Gospels*, SC 522: 164–70.

(11) Irenaeus of Lyons, *Against Heresies* 4.13.2–4, SC 100: 528–38.

(12) Augustine of Hippo, *Tractate* 86.2–3 *on John*, CCSL 36: 542–43.

(13) Cyprian of Carthage, *Letter* 58.5–7, CCSL 3C: 325–30.

(14) Augustine of Hippo, *Tractate* 87.1–4 *on John*, CCSL 36: 544–45.

(15) Origen of Alexandria, *On First Principles* 1.3.5–6, GCS 22(5): 56–57.

(16) Augustine of Hippo, *Tractate* 91.1–4 *on John*, CCSL 36: 553–55.

(17) Ambrose of Milan, *On the Holy Spirit* 1.1.25–26, CSEL 79: 26–27.

(18) Augustine of Hippo, *Tractate* 92.2 *on John*, CCSL 36: 556–57.

John 16

(1)   Cyprian of Carthage, *Letter* 58.1–2, CCSL 3C: 321–22.

(2)   John Chrysostom, *Homily* 78.1 *on John*, PG 59: 419–21.

(3) Augustine of Hippo, *Tractate* 93.1–4 *on John*, CCSL 36: 558–61.

(4) Cyril of Alexandria, *Commentary on John* X.2, in Pusey II: 619–21.

(5) Cyril of Alexandria, *Commentary on John* X.2, in Pusey II: 621–25.

(6) Origen of Alexandria, *Against Celsus*, 2.2, GCS 2: 128–29.

(7) Didymus the Blind, *On the Holy Spirit* 33–38, PL 23: 132–35; trans. Mark DelCogliano, Andrew Radde-Gallwitz, and Lewis Ayers, *Works on the Spirit: Athanasius and Didymus*, Popular Patristic Series 43 (Yonkers, NY: St. Vladimir's Seminary Press, 2011), 190–92, 194–95, slightly revised.

(8) John Chrysostom, *Homily* 78.3 *on John*, PG 59: 423–24.

(9) Leo the Great, *Letter* 16.3, PL 54: 698–700.

(10) Cyril of Alexandria, *Commentary on John* XI.2, in Pusey II: 639–41.

(11) Cyprian of Carthage, *On Mortality* 5–7, CSEL 3.1: 299–301.

(12) John Chrysostom, *Homily* 79.1 *on John*, PG 59: 427.

(13) John Chrysostom, *Homily* 16.6 *on the Statues*, PG 49: 170.

(14) Augustine of Hippo, *Tractate* 101.4–6 *on John*, CCSL 36: 592–94.

(15) Gregory the Great, *Homily* 27 *on the Gospels*, SC 522: 174–78.

(16) Cyril of Alexandria, *Commentary on John* XI.2, in Pusey II: 642–43.

(17) Augustine of Hippo, *Tractate* 103.3 *on John*, CCSL 36: 600.

(18) Cyril of Alexandria, *Commentary on John* XI.2, in Pusey II: 655–57.

John 17

(1) Hilary of Poitiers, *On the Trinity* 3.10–11, CCSL 62: 80–83.

(2) John Chrysostom, *Homily* 80.1 *on John*, PG 59: 433.

(3) Augustine of Hippo, *Tractates* 104.3 and 105.1 *on John*, CCSL 36: 602–4.

(4) Tertullian of Carthage, *On Prayer* 3.1–4, CCSL 1: 258–59.

(5) Hilary of Poitiers, *On the Trinity* 3.15–16, CCSL 62: 86–88.

(6) John Chrysostom, *Homily* 80.2 *on John*, PG 59: 435.

(7) Origen of Alexandria, *On First Principles* 1.2.10, GCS 22(5): 43–44.

(8) Hilary of Poitiers, *On the Trinity* 10.42, CCSL 62A: 495–96.

(9) Cyril of Alexandria, *Commentary on John* XI.9, in Pusey II: 694–95; 696–98; trans. Norman Russell, *Cyril of Alexandria*, The Early Church Fathers (London: Routledge, 2000), 125–29, slightly revised.

(10) Cyril of Alexandria, *Commentary on John* XI.9, in Pusey II: 701–3.

(11) Leo the Great, *Sermon* 67.4, CCSL 138A: 410–11.

(12) Ambrose of Milan, *On the Christian Faith* 2.9.77–78, CSEL 78: 84–85.

(13) John Chrysostom, *Homily* 82.1–2 *on John*, PG 59: 443.

(14) Augustine of Hippo, *Tractate* 108.1–3, 5 *on John*, CCSL 36: 616–18.

(15) Augustine of Hippo, *Tractate* 109.1–3,5 *on John*, CCSL 36: 618–21.

(16) Cyril of Alexandria, *Commentary on John* XI.11, in Pusey II: 734–37.

(17) Augustine of Hippo, *Tractate* 110.4–6 *on John*, CCSL 36: 624–26.

(18) Cyprian of Carthage, *On Mortality* 22, CCSL 3A: 28–29.

(19) Augustine of Hippo, *Tractate* 111.2–3 *on John*, CCSL 36: 629–30.

(20) Cyril of Alexandria, *Commentary on John* XI.12, in Pusey III: 7–8.

John 18

(1) Theodore of Mopsuestia, *Commentary on John*, CSCO 4,3: 324.
(2) Cyril of Alexandria, *Commentary on John* XI.12, in Pusey III: 15, 17.
(3) Leo the Great, *Sermon* 59.1, CCSL 138A: 349–50.
(4) Origen of Alexandria, *Against Celsus* 2.10, SC 132: 308–10.
(5) Athanasius of Alexandria, *In Defense of His Flight* 15, SC 56: 150–51.
(6) John Chrysostom, *Homily* 83.1 *on John*, PG 59: 448.
(7) Augustine of Hippo, *Tractate* 112.3 *on John*, CCSL 36: 634–35.
(8) Cyril of Alexandria, *Commentary on John* XI.12, in Pusey III: 18–19.
(9) Tertullian of Carthage, *On Idolatry* 19, CCSL 2: 1120.
(10) John Chrysostom, *Homily* 83.2 *on John*, PG 59: 449.
(11) Augustine of Hippo, *Tractate* 112.5 *on John*, CCSL 36: 635.
(12) Cyril of Alexandria, *Commentary on John* XI.12, in Pusey III: 22, 25–26.
(13) John Chrysostom, *Homily* 83.2, 3 *on John*, PG 59: 450, 451.
(14) Augustine of Hippo, *Tractate* 113.2 *on John*, CCSL 36: 636–37.
(15) Cyril of Alexandria, *Commentary on John* XI.12 and 12, in Pusey III: 31, 44–46.
(16) Romanos the Melodist, *Kontakion* 18, "On Peter's Denial," SC 128: 122–40; trans. Marjorie Carpenter, *Kontakia of Romanos, Byzantine Melodist*, vol. 1 (Columbia: University of Missouri Press, 1970), 185–89.
(17) Augustine of Hippo, *Tractate* 113.3 *on John*, CCSL 36: 638.
(18) Cyril of Alexandria, *Commentary on John* XI.12, in Pusey III: 33–34.
(19) John Chrysostom, *Homily* 83.3 *on John*, PG 59: 450–51.
(20) Augustine of Hippo, *Tractate* 113.4 on *John*, CCSL 36: 638–39.
(21) Cyril of Alexandria, *Commentary on John* XI.12, in Pusey III: 38–40.
(22) Augustine of Hippo, *Tractate* 114.2 *on John*, CCSL 36: 641.
(23) John Chrysostom, *Homily* 83.4 *on John*, PG 59: 453.
(24) Theodore of Mopsuestia, *Commentary on John*, CSCO 4,3: 330–31.
(25) Augustine of Hippo, *Tractate* 115.2, 5 *on John*, CCSL 36: 644–45.
(26) Cyril of Alexandria, *Commentary on John* XII, in Pusey III: 53–54.
(27) John Chrysostom, *Homily* 83.5 *on John*, PG 59: 453.

John 19

(1) John Chrysostom, *Homily* 84.3 *on John*, PG 59: 458.
(2) Augustine of Hippo, *Tractate* 116.1 *on John*, CCSL 36: 647.
(3) Cyril of Alexandria, *Commentary on John* XII, in Pusey III: 61, 63.
(4) Augustine of Hippo, *Tractate* 116.4–5 *on John*, CCSL 36: 648.
(5) Cyril of Alexandria, *Commentary on John* XII, in Pusey III: 70–71.
(6) John Chrysostom, *Homily* 85.1 *on John*, PG 59: 459–60.
(7) Theodore of Mopsuestia, *Commentary on John*, CSCO 4,3: 335–36.
(8) Augustine of Hippo, *Tractate* 117.3 *on John*, CCSL 36: 652.
(9) Cyril of Alexandria, *Commentary on John* XII, in Pusey III: 79–81.
(10) Augustine of Hippo, *Tractate* 117.5 *on John*, CCSL 36: 653–54.
(11) Cyril of Alexandria, *Commentary on John* XII, in Pusey III: 85.
(12) Cyprian of Carthage, *On the Unity of the Church* 7, CCSL 3: 254.

(13) Rufinus of Aquileia, *Commentary on the Apostles' Creed* 23, *CCSL* 20: 159.

(14) John Chrysostom, *Homily* 85.1 *on John*, *PG* 59: 461.

(15) Augustine of Hippo, *Tractate* 118.4 *on John*, *CCSL* 36: 656–57.

(16) Cyril of Alexandria, *Commentary on John* XII, in Pusey III: 88.

(17) Romanos the Melodist, *Kontakion* 37, "On Mary at the Cross," *SC* 128: 164, 168–74, 180–84; trans. Marjorie Carpenter, *Kontakia of Romanos, Byzantine Melodist*, vol. 1 (Columbia: University of Missouri Press, 1970), 197, 199–200, 202–3.

(18) John Chrysostom, *Homily* 85.2 *on John*, *PG* 59: 461.

(19) Augustine of Hippo, *Tractate* 119. 2 *on John*, *CCSL* 36: 658.

(20) Cyril of Alexandria, *Commentary on John* XII, in Pusey III: 91–92.

(21) Augustine of Hippo, *Harmony of the Gospels* III.18.55, *PL* 34: 1192.

(22) Cyril of Jerusalem, *Catechetical Lecture* 13.21, *PG* 33: 797C–800A.

(23) John Chrysostom, *Homily* 85.3 on *John*, *PG* 59: 463.

(24) Augustine of Hippo, *Tractate* 120.2 *on John*, *CCSL* 36: 661.

(25) Cyril of Alexandria, *Commentary on John* XII, in Pusey III: 103.

(26) John of Damascus, *Exposition on the Faith* 82 (4.9), ed. P. B. Kotter, *Die Schriften des Johannes von Damaskos*, vol. 2, Patristische Texte und Studien 12 (Berlin: de Gruyter, 1973), 182–83.

(27) Origen of Alexandria, *Against Celsus* II.69, *SC* 132: 448–50.

(28) John Chrysostom, *Homily* 85.4 *on John*, *PG* 59: 464.

(29) Cyril of Alexandria, *Commentary on John* XII, in Pusey III: 105–6.

John 20

(1) Theodore of Mopsuestia, *Commentary on John*, Book 7, *CSCO* 4,3: 346–47.

(2) John Chrysostom, *Homily* 85.5–6 *on John*, *PG* 59: 465–68.

(3) Gregory the Great, *Homily* 22.2, 5, *CCSL* 141: 181–82, 184; trans. Dom David Hurst, *Forty Gospel Homilies* (Kalamazoo, MI: Cistercian, 1990), 165–67, revised slightly.

(4) John Chrysostom, *Homily* 86.1 *on John*, *PG* 59: 467–68.

(5) Cyril of Alexandria, *Commentary on the Gospel of John* XII, in Pusey III: 113.

(6) Gregory the Great, *Homily* 25.1–5, *CCSL* 141: 205–10; trans. Dom David Hurst, *Forty Gospel Homilies* (Kalamazoo, MI: Cistercian, 1990), 188–93, revised slightly.

(7) John Chrysostom, *Homily* 86.1 *on John*, *PG* 59: 469.

(8) Cyril of Alexandria, *Commentary on John* XII, in Pusey III: 115.

(9) John Chrysostom, *Homily* 86.2 *on John*, *PG* 59: 469–70.

(10) Augustine of Hippo, *Tractate* 121.3 *on John*, *CCSL* 36: 665–67.

(11) Cyril of Alexandria, *Commentary on John* XII, in Pusey III: 116–19.

(12) Leo the Great, *Sermon* 74.4, *CCSL* 138A: 458–59.

(13) Gregory the Great, *Homily* 25.5–6, *CCSL* 141: 210–11; trans. Dom David Hurst, *Forty Gospel Homilies* (Kalamazoo, MI: Cistercian, 1990), 193, revised slightly.

(14) Romanos the Melodist, *Kontakion* 20, "On the Resurrection VI," *SC* 128: 396–400; trans. Marjorie Carpenter, *Kontakia of Romanos, Byzantine Melodist*, vol. 1 (Columbia: University of Missouri Press, 1970), 318–19.

(15) Cyril of Jerusalem, *Catechetical Lecture* 11.19, *PG* 33: 713C.

(16) Ambrose of Milan, *On Christian Faith* I.14,90–91, *CSEL* 78: 39–40.

(17) Augustine of Hippo, *Tractate* 121.3 *on John*, *CCSL* 36: 667.

(18) Cyril of Alexandria, *Commentary on John* XII.1, in Pusey III: 122–23, 134.

(19) John of Damascus, *Exposition of the Faith* 81.15–21, ed. P. B. Kotter, *Die Schriften des Johannes von Damaskos*, vol. 2, Patristische Texte und Studien 12 (Berlin: de Gruyter, 1973), 180; also in *PG* 94: 1117.

(20) Jerome, *Epistle* 108.24, *CSEL* 55: 341–42.

(21) Cyril of Alexandria, *Commentary on John* XII.1, in Pusey III: 125–28.

(22) Peter Chrysologus, *Sermon* 84.3, *CCSL* 24A: 518.

(23) Gregory the Great, *Homily* 26.1, *CCSL* 141: 218–19; trans. Dom David Hurst, *Forty Gospel Homilies* (Kalamazoo, MI: Cistercian, 1990), 200–201, revised slightly.

(24) Cyprian of Carthage, *Epistle* 73.2, *CCSL* 3C: 537.

(25) Cyril of Jerusalem, *Catechetical Lecture* 17.12, *PG* 33: 984C–985A.

(26) Ambrose of Milan, *On the Holy Spirit* III.18.137, *CSEL* 79: 208.

(27) John Chrysostom, *Homily* 86.3 *on John*, *PG* 59: 471.

(28) Cyril of Alexandria, *Commentary on John* XII.1, in Pusey III: 131–32, 133–34, 135, 137.

(29) Peter Chrysologus, *Sermon* 84.7, *CCSL* 24A: 520–21.

(30) Gregory the Great, *Homily* 26.4–6, *CCSL* 141: 221–22; trans. Dom David Hurst, *Forty Gospel Homilies* (Kalamazoo, MI: Cistercian, 1990), 204–5, revised slightly.

(31) John Chrysostom, *Homily* 87.1 *on John*, *PG* 59: 473.

(32) Cyril of Alexandria, *Commentary on John* XII.1, in Pusey III: 144–45, 146–47.

(33) Peter Chrysologus, *Sermon* 84.8, *CCSL* 24A: 521–22.

(34) Origen of Alexandria, *Commentary on the Gospel of John* 10.301–4, *SC* 157: 568.

(35) Hilary of Poitiers, On the Trinity 7.12, *CCSL* 62: 271–22.

(36) John Chrysostom, *Homily* 87.1 *on John*, *PG* 59: 474.

(37) Augustine of Hippo, *Tractate* 121.5 *on John*, *CCSL* 36: 667–68.

(38) Cyril of Alexandria, *Commentary on John* XII.1, in Pusey III: 151.

(39) Peter Chrysologus, *Sermon* 84.10, *CCSL* 24A: 523.

(40) Gregory the Great, *Homily* 26.7–9, *CCSL* 141: 224–25; trans. Dom David Hurst, *Forty Gospel Homilies* (Kalamazoo, MI: Cistercian, 1990), 204–5, revised slightly.

(41) Romanos the Melodist, *Kontakion* 21, "On Doubting Thomas," *Sancti Romani Melodi Cantica*, ed. Paul Maas and C. A. Trypanis (Oxford: Clarendon), 235–36, 238–39, 241; trans. Marjorie Carpenter, *Kontakia of Romanos, Byzantine Melodist*, vol. 1 (Columbia: University of Missouri Press, 1970), 329–35.

John 21

(1) John Chrysostom, *Homily* 87.2 *on John*, *PG* 59: 475.

(2) Gregory the Great, *Homily* 24.6, *CCSL* 141: 202–3.

(3) Augustine of Hippo, *Tractate* 122.1–3 *on John*, *CCSL* 36: 668–69.

(4) Gregory the Great, *Homily* 24.1, *CCSL* 141: 197.

(5) Augustine of Hippo, *Tractate* 122.6–7 *on John*, *CCSL* 36: 671–72.

(6) Cyril of Alexandria, *Commentary on John* XII.1, in Pusey III: 157–58; 159–60.

(7) Peter Chrysologus, *Sermon* 78.4, *CCSL* 24A: 478–79.

(8) Augustine of Hippo, *Tractate* 122.7–9 *on John*, *CCSL* 36: 672–74.

(9) Cyril of Alexandria, *Commentary on John* XII.1, in Pusey III: 162.

(10) Cyprian of Carthage, *On the Unity of the Church* 4, *CCSL* 3: 251.

(11) John Chrysostom, *Homily* 88.1 *on John*, *PG* 59: 477–79.

(12) Theodore of Mopsuestia, *Commentary on John*, CSCO 4,3: 359–60.

(13) Augustine of Hippo, *Sermon* 137.3, *PL* 38: 754–63.

(14) Augustine of Hippo, *Tractate* 123.4 *on John*, CCSL 36: 677.

(15) Cyril of Alexandria, *Commentary on John* XII.1, in Pusey III: 164–66.

(16) Leo the Great, *Sermon* 4.3–4, CCSL 138: 20–21.

(17) Gregory the Great, *Epistle* 7.37, CCSL 140: 500–501.

(18) Venerable Bede, *Homily* II.22, CCSL 122: 345; trans. Lawrence T. Martin and David Hurst, *Homilies on the Gospels*, vol. 2 (Kalamazoo, MI: Cistercian, 1991), 223–24.

(19) Venerable Bede, *Homily* I.9, CCSL 122: 64–65; trans. Lawrence T. Martin and David Hurst, *Homilies on the Gospels*, vol. 1 (Kalamazoo, MI: Cistercian, 1991), 90–91, 92.

Index of Names

Index of Subjects

Index of Scripture References

Malachi

3:6	111
3:20 LXX	424
4:2	253, 364, 424

APOCRYPHA

Judith

9:11	139

Wisdom of Solomon

1:14	343
5:4–5	95
7:24	164, 523
8:1	164

Sirach (Ecclessiasticus)

1:22	230
3:18 (3:20 LXX)	8, 408
3:21	280, 397
4:9	372
4:28	291
5:7	355
5:8–9	252
10:9	230
13:15–16	502

Susanna

42	86, 321
56 [Dan 13:56]	514

Bel and the Dragon

1:15	474

2 Maccabees

7:1–22	474
7:41	474

NEW TESTAMENT

Matthew

1:1	3, 4, 21
1:1–17	10
1:18	3
2:1–12	65
2:16–18	474
3:3	51
3:7–8	72
3:11	44, 128, 129
3:14	410
3:15	410
3:17	184, 311, 332
4:1–10	390
4:2	125
4:7	383
4:11	332

4:16	33, 389
4:19	592
4:21	7
5:6	233
5:6, 10	xvi
5:8	xvii, 173, 217, 399, 434, 438, 444, 491, 523
5:9	326
5:10	437, 601
5:14	50, 182, 183
5:14–16	403
5:15	183
5:16	183, 313
5:21–22	470
5:27–28	470
5:36	529
5:39	xix, 531, 533, 540
5:41	176, 470
5:43–44	470
5:44	499, 507
5:45	470
6:3	384
6:5	78, 317
6:6	333
6:9	78, 165, 388, 397, 463, 507
6:10	83
6:11	478
6:12	213, 413
6:12–13	393
6:13	397, 474
6:16	317
6:20	497
6:24	531
6:33	499
7:7	126
7:12	467
7:21	113
7:22–23	321
7:24	183
7:24–27	54
8:5	531
8:8	341
8:11	143
8:16	477
8:17	477
8:22	193
9:15	64, 376
9:18–26	340
9:20	161
10:5	120, 381
10:8	78–79
10:10	531
10:16	50
10:17–18	484
10:19–20	473
10:20	10
10:23	314

10:24	541
10:26	397
10:27	538
10:28	474
10:29	529
10:32–33	186
10:38	550
11:9	45, 72, 109
11:11	46, 72
11:13	45
11:14	16, 46, 47
11:14–15	32
11:15	160
11:27	310, 311, 321
11:28	130, 232
11:29	230, 407
12:1	126
12:11	290
12:24	289
12:30	523
12:31–32	113
12:40	82, 386
12:48	66, 556
13:7	441
13:8	436, 595
13:16	583
13:17	583
13:33	220
13:38–41	543
13:48, 49	593
13:55	296
14:17–21	426
14:20	194
14:21	11
14:25–29	477
14:27	155
14:28–29	155
14:33	426
15:8	446
15:9	307
15:22–28	161
15:24	302
15:32–39	477
15:37	190
16:6	12
16:9	190
16:16	387, 424
16:18–19	596
16:19	363, 374, 599
16:22	411, 430
16:22–23	411
16:23	411
16:27	200, 283, 382
16:28	213
17:1	286
17:5	239, 387
17:10–12	46

John

*For John passages, an asterisk indicates a pericope used as a lemma under interpretation within the volume; page numbers with an asterisk are the corresponding pages for that lemma.